COMPUTER GRAPHICS

Annual Conference Series 1993

SIGGRAPH 93
Conference Proceedings
August 1–6, 1993
Papers Chair James T. Kajiya
Panels Chair Donna Cox

A publication of ACM SIGGRAPH
Production Editor Steve Cunningham

Sponsored by the Association for Computing Machinery's Special Interest Group on Computer Graphics

The Association for Computing Machinery, Inc.
1515 Broadway, 17th Floor
New York, NY 10036

Sample Citation Information:
...Proceedings of SIGGRAPH 93 (Anaheim, California, August 1-6, 1993). In *Computer Graphics* Proceedings, Annual Conference Series, 1993, ACM SIGGRAPH, New York, 1993, pp. xx–yy.

ORDERING INFORMATION

Orders from nonmembers of ACM placed within the United States should be directed to:

Addison-Wesley Publishing Company
Order Department
Jacob Way
Reading, MA 01867
Tel: 1-800-447-2226

Addison-Wesley will pay postage and handling on orders accompanied by check. Credit card orders may be placed by mail or by calling the Addison-Wesley Order Department at the number above. Follow-up inquiries should be directed to the Customer Service Department at the same number. Please include the Addison-Wesley ISBN number with your order:

A-W Softcover ISBN 0-201-58889-7
A-W CD-ROM ISBN 0-201-56997-3

Orders from nonmembers of ACM placed from outside the United States should be addressed as noted below.

Europe/Middle East:
Addison-Wesley Publishing Group
Concertgebouwplein 25
1071 LM Amsterdam
The Netherlands
Tel: +31 20 6717296
Fax: _31 20 6645334

Germany/Austria/Switzerland:
Addison-Wesley Verlag Deutschland GmbH
Wachsbleiche 7-12
W-5300 Bonn 1
Germany
Tel: +49 228 98 515 0
Fax: +49 228 98 515 99

United Kingdom/Africa:
Addison-Wesley Publishers Ltd.
Finchampstead Road
Wokingham, Berkshire RG11 2NZ
United Kingdom
Tel: +44 734 794000
Fax: +44 734 794035

Asia:
Addison-Wesley Singapore Pte. Ltd.
15 Beach Road
#05-02/09/10 Beach Centre
Singapore 0718
Tel: +65 339 7503
Fax: +65 339 9709

Japan:
Addison-Wesley Publishers Japan Ltd.
Nichibo Building
1-2-2 Sarugakucho
Chiyoda-ku, Tokyo 101
Japan
Tel: +81 33 2914581
Fax: +81 33 2914592

Australia/New Zealand:
Addison-Wesley Publishers Pty. Ltd.
6 Byfield Street
North Ryde, N.S.W. 2113
Australia
Tel: +61 2 878 5411
Fax: +61 2 878 5830

Latin America:
Addison Wesley Iberoamericana S.A.
Boulevard de las Cataratas #3
Colonia Jardines del Pedregal
Delegacion Alvaro Obregon
01900 Mexico D.F.
Tel: +52 5 660 2695
Fax: +52 5 660 4930

Canada:
Addison-Wesley Publishing (Canada) Ltd.
26 Prince Andrew Place
Don Mills, Ontario M3C 2T8 Canada
Tel: 416-447-5101
Fax: 416-443-0948

Orders from ACM Members:

A limited number of copies are available at the ACM member discount. Send order with payment in U.S. dollars to:

ACM Order Department
P.O. Box 64145
Baltimore, MD 21264

OR, for informatio on accepted European currencies and exchange rates, contact:

ACM European Service Center
Avenue Marcel Thiry 204
1200 Brussells
Belgium
Tel: +32 2 774 9602
Fax: +32 2 774 9690
Email: acm_europe@acm.org

ACM will pay postage and handling on orders accompanied by check.

Credit card orders only: 1-800-342-6626
Credit card orders may also be placed by mail.

Customer service, or credit card orders from Alaska, Maryland, and outside the U.S.:
+1 410 528 4261

Single-copy orders placed by fax:
+1 410 528 8596

Electronic mail inquiries may be directed to acmpubs@acm.org.

Please include your ACM member number and the ACM order number with your order.

ACM Order Number: 428930

ACM ISBN: 0-89791-601-8

ISSN: 1069-529X

Contents

Papers Sessions, Wednesday, 4 August 1993

Papers Sessions, Thursday, 5 August 1993

Paper Sessions, Friday, 6 August 1993

Panel Sessions, Tuesday, 3 August 1993

Panel Sessions, Wednesday, 4 August 1993

Panel Sessions, Thursday, 5 August 1993

Panel Sessions, Friday, 6 August 1993

Preface

You hold in your hands a distillation of the work of hundreds of people representing over a hundred thousand hours of collective brain work: the technical program of the 20th annual SIGGRAPH conference held in Anaheim, California.

Each year the technical program is modified in many small and hopefully better ways. This year you will notice that there are more papers than SIGGRAPH has accepted in many years, that we have expanded the number of sessions, and that the number of days during which papers are presented has grown.

But some things we've modified do not show up in the papers themselves. This year the composition of the selection committee is considerably different than in previous years. The SIGGRAPH conference planning committee mandated "term limits" for members of the selection committee. This year, no one was a senior reviewer if they served on the committee for the previous two years.

Also new this year is the establishment of reviewer ethics guidelines which sought to achieve a uniform level of protection for the information contained within SIGGRAPH submissions. The prospective author's kit also contained a look into how papers were processed, judged, and accepted or rejected. This information was intended to give people an insight into the paper review and selection mechanism. Since so much of this process deals with specific papers and people's opinions of the significance of someone's ideas, the record and discussion that occurs during this process is of necessity secret. However, everyone should know what happens in general.

We received 225 submissions this year, a new record, and accepted 46 papers, the most since 1978. Andrew Glassner and I read and discussed every submission and—within the constraints of load balancing—attempted to assign each submission with the best senior reviewer for that submission. The review process and the selection meeting were very much as in previous years. Everyone on the committee strove to include quality papers over as wide a range of topics as was feasible. The individual merits of papers were extensively discussed and judged by those members of the committee allowed to attend. As in previous years, those who had a connection with the institutions or authors represented in a particular paper were asked to leave the discussion. We tried to be as fair and objective as could be possible.

I wish to congratulate the committee on their display of wisdom and insight during the selection meeting. The discussion that occurred in March impressed me with its high professional level and sensitive consideration given to every possible conflict of interest.

Of course, as many well know, the SIGGRAPH review process is far from perfect: I may have sent a submission to the wrong person, reviewers may misunderstand the ideas in a paper, or some critical piece of information may not have reached the author. If you had a paper rejected unfairly by SIGGRAPH 93, I apologize for our mistakes. If you have ideas on how we may improve future cycles of reviewing, SIGGRAPH is eager to hear them. I urge you please to contact me or Andrew Glassner, the program chair for SIGGRAPH 94.

Even though we accepted more papers than ever before, the publication budget for this proceedings was fixed by the severe financial constraints that SIGGRAPH has been forced to adopt. We have thus had to be very careful on issues that impact the ultimate cost of this proceedings. Most of the authors of the papers in this document have struggled valiantly to accomplish the difficult task of meeting the hard page limits given to them. The committee considered the content of each paper and carefully set length and color restrictions. Steve Cunningham and I were given the unhappy task of enforcing these restrictions and denying many authors' desperate pleas for more space.

Those who know me personally know that I am, to put it delicately, organizationally challenged. Without the crucial support and help of of a number of people, SIGGRAPH 93 would probably not have had a technical program this year. These people have my deep thanks and gratitude: Debbie Buuck, Steve Cunningham, Mary Kate Haley, Kevin Luster, and Pey Jen Wu. I also wish to thank the SIGGRAPH 93 cochairs, Bob Judd and Mark Resch, for establishing an exciting and creative atmosphere that allowed us to take part in shaping the conference, its content, and its future.

James T. Kajiya
SIGGRAPH 93 Papers Chair

1993 ACM SIGGRAPH Awards

Steven A. Coons Award for Outstanding Creative Contributions to Computer Graphics

Ed Catmull

This year ACM SIGGRAPH has selected Dr. Edwin E. Catmull to receive the Steven A. Coons Award for Outstanding Creative Contributions to Computer Graphics. Over the past twenty years, Ed Catmull has made many and noteworthy advances in computer graphics as an individual researcher, as an inspiring leader in the field, as a director of organizations, and as a mentor for many.

Ed has made important direct contributions to the field of computer graphics. With his doctoral dissertation at the University of Utah, he introduced the notion of subdivision to pixel level as a display method, added a fast adaptive subdivision method for bicubic surface patches, and provided the first published description of the ubiquitous z-buffer visibility algorithm. He also developed the Catmull-Rom interpolating spline and an early system for generating animated articulated figures. At the New York Institute of Technology, he wrote the first spline inbetweening animation program. At Lucasfilm, with Alvy Ray Smith, he invented a two-pass image warping algorithm.

In addition to his own research contributions, Ed has founded and led three important and influential centers of computer graphics research and development: the Computer Graphics Laboratory at New York Institute of Technology (NYIT), the Lucasfilm Computer Division, and Pixar. In each of these organizations, he attracted and developed some of the best talent in the computer graphics business. These organizations rose quickly to become leading centers of research in our field. The common ingredient in these three organizations is Catmull and the talented people he attracts and develops; wherever Catmull goes, exciting things seem to happen.

Engineers at NYIT developed the first RGB painting program, were pioneers in the use of computer-controlled video equipment, invented mip-maps, and wrote the Tween and Bop animation programs. People working for Ed at Lucasfilm/Pixar made many contributions to image rendering, including particle systems, the first shading language, distributed ray tracing, stochastic sampling, and the Reyes/RenderMan software. They also developed volume rendering software, digital compositing, the Computer Animation Production System (CAPS) developed with Walt Disney Pictures, the Pixar Image Computer, laser input/output scanning, and video and audio editing systems. The group produced a number of special effects such as the "Genesis" effect in "Star Trek II: The Wrath of Khan" and the stained glass man in "The Young Sherlock Holmes," short animated films as exemplified by "Andre and Wally B.," "Red's Dream," "Luxo Jr.," and "Tin Toy," and numerous commercials.

Four of SIGGRAPH's first five Achievement Award winners (and six of eleven overall) have worked for Ed at one time or another. "Luxo Jr." was one of the earliest computer animated films to be nominated for an Academy Award and "Tin Toy" was the first to win one. The Academy of Motion Picture Arts and Sciences last year awarded a Scientific and Technical Academy Award for the development of CAPS to Disney employees and Pixar employees who reported to Catmull. This year the Academy gave a Scientific and Technical Academy Award for the RenderMan software to Catmull and his collaborators[1].

Ed Catmull earned the BS in Physics and the BS in Computer Science (1969) and then the Ph.D. in Computer Science (1974), all from the University of Utah. We note that his doctoral dissertation committee included Steve Coons and Ivan Sutherland, the first recipient of the Coons Award. As noted above, his career spans three positions as Director of the Computer Graphics Laboratory at the New York Institute of Technology (1974-79), Vice President and Managing Director of the Computer Division of Lucasfilm, Ltd. (1979-1986), and now as President of Pixar.

It is impossible to know how many of us have aimed higher and worked harder because Ed encouraged us by collaboration or by being an important figure in the field. It is impossible to know how many of us have taken our research a little further out on the fringe because we thought it was something that Ed might do. His influence at the person-to-person level is magical, and though difficult to describe in words, it continues to affect the practice of computer graphics in subtle and important ways.

References

Catmull, Edwin E., "A System for Computer Generated Movies," Proceedings of ACM Annual Conference, August 1972.

Catmull, Edwin E., "Computer Display of Curved Surfaces," Proceedings of the IEEE Conference on Computer Graphics, Pattern Recognition and Data Structures, May 1975.

Catmull, Edwin E. and Raphael Rom, "A Class of Local Interpolating Splines," *Computer Aided Design*, Academic Press, 1974.

Catmull, Edwin E., "The Use of the Computer in Animation Production," *Digital Video*, Vol.. 2, 1979.

Catmull, Edwin E., "Computer Aided Animation: A system in Full Production," *American Cinematographer*, October 1979.

Catmull, Edwin E., "The Problems of Computer Assisted Animation," SIGGRAPH Conference Proceedings, 1978.

Catmull, Edwin E., "A Hidden-Surface Algorithm with Anti-Aliasing," SIGGRAPH Conference Proceedings, 1978.

Catmull, Edwin E. and James Clark, "Recursively Generated B-spline Surfaces on Arbitrary Topological Meshes," *Computer Aided Design*, November 1978.

Catmull, Edwin E., "A Tutorial on Compensating Tables," SIGGRAPH Conference Proceedings, 1979.

Catmull, Edwin E. and Alvy Ray Smith, "3-D Transformations of Images in Scanline Order," SIGGRAPH Conference Proceedings, 1980.

Catmull, Edwin E., "An Analytic Visible Surface Algorithm for Independent Pixel Processing," SIGGRAPH Conference Proceedings, 1984.

[1]The colleagues from Pixar sharing the Scientific and Technical Academy Award are Patrick Hanrahan, Rob Cook, Loren Carpenter, Tony Apodaca, Darwyn Peachey, and Tom Porter. (This list includes three SIGGRAPH Achievement Award recipients!)

Previous award winners

1991	Andries van Dam
1989	David C. Evans
1987	Donald P. Greenberg
1985	Pierre Bézier
1983	Ivan E. Sutherland

1993 ACM SIGGRAPH Awards

Computer Graphics Achievement Award

Pat Hanrahan

The SIGGRAPH Computer Graphics Achievement Award is presented to Dr. Patrick M. Hanrahan for his contributions to rendering systems and algorithms. We recognize his research and publications on volume rendering, ray tracing, and radiosity algorithms as well as his role as the architect of the RenderMan™ interface.

Hanrahan started his career in physics and biology at the University of Wisconsin. He received a BS. Degree in Nuclear Engineering, graduating first in class of 1977. While at Wisconsin he worked in the Department of Zoology developing computer models of the motornervous system of the nematode *Ascaris*. During this period he became interested in models of shape and the potential of the computer for visualizing the results of simulations. He quickly recognized the importance of modeling and did some work on creating models from edge-vertex graphs (SIGGRAPH '82).

Realizing that he needed to know more, he inquired by letter about a summer position at the New York Institute of Technology (NYIT) Computer Graphics Laboratory. His letter was persuasive enough to land him a spot for the summer that quickly turned into a full-time staff position. There he was initially responsible for modeling and animation software and eventually was the Director of the 3D Animation Systems Group. While at NYIT, Hanrahan published papers on ray tracing algebraic surfaces ('83) and 'beam tracing' polygonal surfaces ('84).

Hanrahan returned to the University of Wisconsin to finish his dissertation, which ended up having much more to do with graphics than biology, and received the Ph.D. in Biophysics in 1985. After a short stint at Digital's Systems Research Lab in Palo Alto, he accepted a position at Pixar in 1986 shortly after Pixar separated from Lucasfilm. He collaborated with Bob Drebin and Loren Carpenter in developing the first volume rendering algorithms for the Pixar image computer ('88). These algorithms were quite different from earlier approaches in that they created images directly from three-dimensional arrays without the intermediate steps of converting to standard surface representations such as polygons. Volume rendering is now a major component of scientific and medical visualization systems.

He later joined the REYES machine group and was responsible for the rendering software and the graphics architecture. The rendering interface of the system evolved into the RenderMan standard that now is widely used in the movie industry[1]. In particular Hanrahan was the principal architect of the RenderMan Interface (Pixar '88). His paper with Jim Lawson describes one of the more interesting aspects of the system, the shading language, which allows users to extend the capabilities of the re ndering system by defining new procedurally defined appearances.

Since 1989 Hanrahan has been on the Faculty of the Computer Science Department at Princeton University, where he became tenured as Associate Professor in 1991. His goal since returning to academia is to put computer graphics on a sound mathematical and scientific foundation. Placed in an environment where publication is more than encouraged, Hanrahan's publications have blossomed. He has been arguably the most prolific single contributor to SIGGRAPH in the last few years. His name appears on no fewer than five papers in this year's proceedings. He is also extremely interested in computer graphics education and has won three university teaching awards since joining Princeton.

Recently Hanrahan made important contributions to accelerating radiosity computations through hierarchical methods (91a, 93c). He has continued his work in volume rendering (91b, 93b). He has contributed pioneering work for rendering caustics (92), for investigating wavelets for radiosity (93d), and determining global visibility (93e). He has discovered a fundamental closed form result for the radiosity form factor between two polygons (93a). In addition to these efforts he has also found time to contribute to texturing through direct manipulation (90a), to develop a shading language (90b), and to keep up with rendering architectures for parallel machines.

This extraordinarily high level of productivity is due in part to Hanrahan's ability to find and to cooperate with a wide variety of collaborators as well as his own creativity. In addition to the students at Princeton, he has managed to work with colleagues around the world in both academia and industry. Furthermore, the work just described has an element of scholarship to it that has often been elusive in computer graphics. The fast-moving nature of the field often makes work more than a few years old seem out of date. Hanrahan has been one of those who goes back to the basics both inside computer graphics and in the many fields that can contribute.

Hanrahan's work has a significant ongoing effect on computer graphics in a wide variety of rendering applications, in the high quality of his scholarship, and especially in the force of his ideas. His influence on computer graphics is still accelerating, leaving us eagerly anticipating his future achievements as well as honoring those of the past.

References
All references except one are to SIGGRAPH conference proceedings in the year indicated.
[82] "Creating Volume Models from Edge-Vertex Graphs," pp. 77-84.
[83] "Ray Tracing Algebraic Surfaces," PP 83-90.
[84] with P. Heckbert, "Beam Tracing Polygonal Objects," pp. 119-127.
[Pixar 88] The RenderMan Interface.
[88] with R. Drebin and L. Carpenter, "Volume Rendering," pp. 65-74.
[90a] with P. Haeberli, "Direct WYSIWYG Painting and Texturing on 3D Shapes," pp. 215-224.
[90b] with J. Lawson, "A Language for Shading and Lighting," pp. 289-298.
[91a] with D. Salzman and L. Aupperle, "A Rapid Hierarchical Radiosity Algorithm," pp. 197-206.
[91b] with D. Laur, "Hierarchical Splatting: A Progressive Refinement Algorithm for Volume Rendering," pp. 285-288.
[92] with D. Mitchell, "Illumination from Curved Reflectors," pp. 283-292.
[93a] with P. Schroeder, "On the Form Factor between Two Polygons."
[93b] with W. Krueger, "Reflection from Layered Surfaces due to Subsurface Scattering."
[93c] with L. Aupperle, "A Hierarchical Illumination Algorithm for Surfaces with Glossy Reflection."
[93d] with S. Gortler, P. Schroeder, and M. Cohen, "Wavelet Radiosity."
[93e] with S. Teller, "Global Visibility Algorithms for Illumination Computations."

[1]Earlier this year Hanrahan and his colleagues from Pixar, Ed Catmull, Rob Cook, Loren Carpenter, Tony Apodaca, Darwyn Peachey, and Tom Porter, were awarded a Scientific and Technical Academy Award by the Academy of Motion Picture Arts and Sciences for the development of software t hat produces images used in motion pictures from 3D computer descriptions of shape and appearance.

Previous award winners

1992	Henry Fuchs
1991	James T. Kajiya
1990	Richard Shoup and Alvy Ray Smith
1989	John Warnock
1988	Alan H. Barr
1987	Robert Cook
1986	Turner Whitted
1985	Loren Carpenter
1984	James H. Clark
1983	James F. Blinn

2–D Shape Blending: An Intrinsic Solution to the Vertex Path Problem

Thomas W. Sederberg[1], Peisheng Gao[1], Guojin Wang[2], and Hong Mu[1]

Abstract

This paper presents an algorithm for determining the paths along which corresponding vertices travel in a 2–D shape blending. Rather than considering the vertex paths explicitly, the algorithm defines the intermediate *shapes* by interpolating the intrinsic definitions of the initial and final shapes. The algorithm produces shape blends which generally are more satisfactory than those produced using linear or cubic curve paths. Particularly, the algorithm can avoid the shrinkage that normally occurs when rotating rigid bodies are linearly blended, and avoids kinks in the blend when there were none in the key polygons.

Categories and Subject Descriptors: I.3.3 [**Computer Graphics**]: Picture/Image Generation; I.3.5 [**Computer Graphics**]: Computational Geometry and Object Modeling.

General Terms: Algorithms

Additional Key Words and Phrases: Shape blending, character animation, numerical algorithms.

1 Introduction

This paper deals with shape blending of 2–D polygons. As illustrated in Figures 1 and 2, a shape blend algorithm determines the in-between polygons which provide a smooth transformation between two given 2–D polygons, referred to as the *key polygons*.

Shape blending requires the solution of two main subproblems: the vertex correspondence problem (that is, determining which vertex on one key polygon will travel to which vertex on the other key polygon), and the vertex path problem (that is, determining along what path each vertex will travel).

For 2–D polygonal shapes, a solution to the vertex correspondence problem is presented in [12]. Shape blending of 2–D Bézier curve shapes is addressed in [11]. Various solutions to the shape interpolation of 3–D polyhedra are presented in [3, 5, 7, 8].

This paper addresses the vertex path problem and is motivated by two figures from [12]. Figure 1.a provides an example of a shape blend in which the middle shapes is derived from its neighboring key polygons. This is basically a good shape blend, except that the dancer's arm in the middle frame is only half as long as it is in the key frames.

The shape blend in Figure 2.a looks fine except that the chicken's neck gets shorter. These shortenings occur because of the linear path followed by vertices during the shape blend, as shown by the path travelled by the chicken's beak.

a. Withered Arm b. Normal Arm

Figure 1: Dancer

a. Compressed Neck b. More Natural Neck

Figure 2: Chicken

These problems seriously weaken the practical use of 2–D shape blending using linear vertex motion, for applications such as character animation. The contribution of this paper is an improved method for computing in-between frames, once the correspondence between key polygons has been determined as in [12]. Sample results of the new vertex path algorithm are shown in Figures 1.b and 2.b.

A referee of paper [12] remarked: "I am unhappy with the phrase, 'physically based,' in this context. The 'physics' here has nothing to do with the physics of chickens, . . . , or any of the other nominal subjects of interpolation." That observation formulates precisely the problem we confront in trying to infer the correct motion between two changing shapes. While [12] demonstrates that an algorithm which knows nothing about the "physics of a chicken" is able to correlate the prominent features of two chicken outlines, the accurate computation of *motion* as a chicken lowers his head really calls for a model of the chicken's skeleton, musculature, etc.. What we seek is a tool that might assist a traditional animator to create convincing computer-assisted in-betweens, when the only information available is contained in the two key frames. The solution presented here is a heuristic whose justification lies

[1]Engineering Computer Graphics Laboratory
368 Clyde Building
Brigham Young University
Provo, UT 84602
tom@byu.edu
[2]Zhejiang University, China

in the fact that it generally seems to work rather well.

1.1 Proposed solution

A polygon definition which lists the Cartesian coordinates of its vertices might be called an *explicit* description. An alternate means of defining a polygon is in terms of the lengths of its edges and the angles at its vertices. Such a polygon description forms the basis of an approach to geometry, popular in elementary education, known as *Turtle Graphics* [2] wherein a polygon is defined by instructions such as: walk 10 paces to the east, turn 45° to the left and proceed 6 paces, turn 30° to the right and go 5 more paces, ...

This paper postulates that the heuristic of blending intrinsic definitions (edge lengths and vertex angles) of two key polygons will generally produce a more satisfactory in-between motion than will linear vertex paths. Evidence that this is so is provided in the figures.

1.2 Related work

One alternative to linear vertex paths is to define vertex paths of higher degree. For 3–D polyhedral shape transformations, [8] proposes using an Hermite cubic path with end tangents set equal to the vertex normals. While this idea evidently is effective for the transformations between highly dissimilar shapes addressed in [8], it would not generally work too well for character animation since motion does not uniformly occur normal to a curve outline.

[14] develops an approach to character animation using quadratic Bézier vertex paths. By default, vertices travel along a parabolic arc such that the distance from each vertex to the center of mass of all vertices changes monotonically. Also, it allows the user to signify a pivot point for appendages. The current algorithm works with less user interaction.

In other approaches to shape blending, such as Minkowski sums [7], the vertex path and vertex correspondence problems are coupled and solved simultaneously. Minkowski sums, however, blur even gross details such as arms and legs when blending non-convex objects, and hence are not suitable for character animation. Shape blends that operate on an *implicit* definition of the curve or surface, $f(x,y)=0$ or $f(x,y,z)=0$, [6] likewise don't currently support the detail required for character animation.

Of course, the substantial literature on physically based modelling and synthetic actors is also highly relevant, though such methods rely on more information than is available to us.

Ideas for modeling with intrinsically defined curves are proposed in [1], and [13] looks at curve and surface kinematics based on differential equations.

2 Intrinsic shape interpolation

Denote the vertices of the two key polygons by $\mathbf{P}_{A_i}, \mathbf{P}_{B_i}, (i = 0, 1, \ldots, n-1)$. We assume that both key polygons have the same number of edges, as will be the case after vertex correspondence is established [12]. In this discussion, we use the convention that counter-clockwise angles are positive. For convenience, we adopt the notation $m = n - 1$ where n is the number of polygon edges.

Our goal is to compute the vertices $\mathbf{P}_i (i = 1, 2, \ldots, m)$ for the polygon which is "t" of the way between $\mathbf{P}_A$ and $\mathbf{P}_B$, $0 \le t \le 1$. $\mathbf{P}_0$ will be taken as the *anchor point*, and its position determines the rigid body translation of the shape. This, along with the directed angles α_{A_0} and α_{B_0} formed by the x-axis and the vectors $\mathbf{P}_{A_0}\mathbf{P}_{A_1}$ and $\mathbf{P}_{B_0}\mathbf{P}_{B_1}$, is discussed further in section 3.

Begin by obtaining the intrinsic definitions of $\mathbf{P}_A$ and $\mathbf{P}_B$ by computing the polygon angles and edge lengths shown in Figure 3:

$$\theta_{A_i}, \theta_{B_i}, (i = 1, 2, \ldots, m). \quad (1)$$

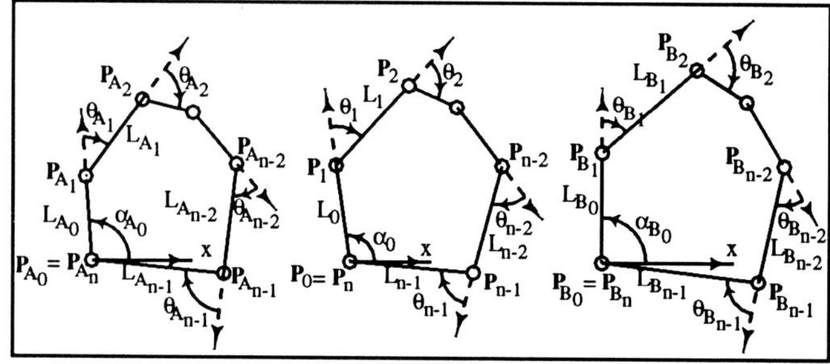

Figure 3: Intrinsic variables

$$L_{A_i} = |\mathbf{P}_{A_{i+1}} - \mathbf{P}_{A_i}| \text{ and } L_{B_i} = |\mathbf{P}_{B_{i+1}} - \mathbf{P}_{B_i}|. \quad (2)$$

The intermediate polygons in the shape blend are then computed by interpolating the respective vertex angles and edge lengths:

$$\alpha_0 = (1-t)\alpha_{A_0} + t\alpha_{B_0}, \quad (3)$$

$$\theta_i = (1-t)\theta_{A_i} + t\theta_{B_i}, \quad (i = 1, 2, \ldots, m). \quad (4)$$

$$L_i = (1-t)L_{A_i} + tL_{B_i}, \quad (i = 0, 1, 2, \ldots, m). \quad (5)$$

Unfortunately, the problem is not completely solved at this point, since the resulting polygon will not generally close. Figure 4 shows what the chicken and dancer polygons look like at this stage of the algorithm. It is somewhat surprising that

Figure 4: Unclosed polygons

these polygons, each with over 200 vertices, come so close to ending where they started (and this happens typically, in our experience). But the problem remains, how do we best adjust the lengths and angles so that the polygon *does* close.

There are two solutions to this problem. The first is to leave the angles unchanged and tweak the lengths (section 2.1). This turns out to have a straightforward, closed-form solution. The other approach is to treat the open polygon as a piece of wire for which we define the physical rules for stretching and vertex bending. Adjustments to angles and/or edges can then be computed iteratively by determining the equilibrium shape when the two open polygon vertices are forced to coincide.

2.1 Edge Tweaking

To close the polygons by adjusting the edge lengths only, rewrite equation 5 as

$$L_i = (1-t)L_{A_i} + tL_{B_i} + S_i, \quad (i = 0, 1, 2, \ldots, m). \quad (6)$$

It seems smart that the magnitudes of S_i should roughly be proportional to $|L_{A_i} - L_{B_i}|$, since if an edge has the same length on both key polygons, it ought to have about that same length throughout the shape blend. One can dream up simple examples for which this is not desirable, but for most reasonable cases, experience has verified this to be wise. Therefore, define

$$L_{AB_i} = \max\{|L_{A_i} - L_{B_i}|, L_{tol}\}, \quad (i = 0, 1, 2, \ldots, m). \quad (7)$$

where $L_{tol} = 0.0001 \times \left(\max_{i\in[0,m]} |L_{A_i} - L_{B_i}|\right)$ is needed to avoid division by zero.

Our goal is to find $S_0, S_1, \ldots, S_m$, so that the objective function

$$f(S_0, S_1, \ldots, S_m) = \sum_{i=0}^{m} \frac{S_i^2}{L_{AB_i}^2}$$

is minimized subject to the two equality constraints (which force closure of the polygon):

$$\varphi_1(S_0, S_1, \ldots, S_m) = \sum_{i=0}^{m} [(1-t)L_{A_i} + tL_{B_i} + S_i] \cos\alpha_i = 0,$$

$$\varphi_2(S_0, S_1, \ldots, S_m) = \sum_{i=0}^{m} [(1-t)L_{A_i} + tL_{B_i} + S_i] \sin\alpha_i = 0,$$

where α_i are the directed angles from the x-axis to the vectors $\mathbf{P}_i\mathbf{P}_{i+1}$,

$$\alpha_i = \alpha_{i-1} + \theta_i, \quad (i = 1, 2, \ldots, m). \quad (8)$$

The method of Lagrange multipliers [9] can now solve for the desired tweak values S_i as follows. Set

$$\Phi(\lambda_1, \lambda_2, S_0, S_1, \ldots, S_m) = f + \lambda_1\varphi_1 + \lambda_2\varphi_2,$$

where λ_1 and λ_2 are the multipliers.

From

$$\begin{cases} \frac{\partial\Phi}{\partial S_i} = \frac{2S_i}{L_{AB_i}^2} + \lambda_1\cos\alpha_i + \lambda_2\sin\alpha_i = 0 (i = 0, 1, \ldots, m) \\ \sum_{i=0}^{m}[(1-t)L_{A_i} + tL_{B_i} + S_i]\cos\alpha_i = 0 \\ \sum_{i=0}^{m}[(1-t)L_{A_i} + tL_{B_i} + S_i]\sin\alpha_i = 0, \end{cases}$$

we obtain

$$\begin{cases} E\lambda_1 + F\lambda_2 = U \\ F\lambda_1 + G\lambda_2 = V, \end{cases} \quad (9)$$

where

$$E = \sum_{i=0}^{m} L_{AB_i}^2 \cos^2\alpha_i, \quad (10)$$

$$F = \sum_{i=0}^{m} L_{AB_i}^2 \sin\alpha_i cos\alpha_i, \quad (11)$$

$$G = \sum_{i=0}^{m} L_{AB_i}^2 \sin^2\alpha_i, \quad (12)$$

$$U = 2\left\{\sum_{i=0}^{m}[(1-t)L_{A_i} + tL_{B_i}]\cos\alpha_i\right\}, \quad (13)$$

$$V = 2\left\{\sum_{i=0}^{m}[(1-t)L_{A_i} + tL_{B_i}]\sin\alpha_i\right\}. \quad (14)$$

Thus under the condition $EG - F^2 \neq 0$ we can get

$$\lambda_1 = \begin{vmatrix} U & F \\ V & G \end{vmatrix} / \begin{vmatrix} E & F \\ F & G \end{vmatrix}, \quad (15)$$

$$\lambda_2 = \begin{vmatrix} E & U \\ F & V \end{vmatrix} / \begin{vmatrix} E & F \\ F & G \end{vmatrix}, \quad (16)$$

and

$$S_i = -\frac{1}{2}L_{AB_i}^2(\lambda_1\cos\alpha_i + \lambda_2\sin\alpha_i), \quad (i = 0, 1, \ldots, m). \quad (17)$$

Using equations 4, 6, and 8, we can now calculate the coordinates (x_i, y_i) of the vertices $\mathbf{P}_i (i = 1, 2, \ldots, m)$:

$$x_i = x_{i-1} + L_{i-1}\cos\alpha_{i-1}, \quad y_i = y_{i-1} + L_{i-1}\sin\alpha_{i-1}. \quad (18)$$

2.2 Tweaking Lengths and/or Angles

The edge-tweaking-only method generally gives good results and is relatively fast. Also, as suggested from Figure 4, often very little edge length adjustment is needed.

However, some simple examples can be found where the edge lengths may change more than is desirable using the edge-tweaking-only method. This can be detected by checking the values of S_i. In such a case, the required edge length adjustments can be diminished by also allowing the angles to change.

A good solution to this problem is to treat the unclosed polygon as a piece of wire which can possibly stretch, but which can only bend at polygon vertices. The stretching stiffness for each polygon edge is inversely proportional to the change in length experienced by that edge between the two key frames. Likewise, the bending stiffness of each angle is inversely proportional to the change between key frames of the respective angle. These stiffness values tend to enforce rigidity for identical portions of the two key polygons.

The shape of the closed intermediate polygon is then computed by forcing the two unclosed joints to coincide, and determining the unique equilibrium shape of the wire. Further details can be found in [4].

3 Anchor points and angle lines

Since an intrinsic definition of a polygon is invariant to rigid body motion, a shape blend must specify translations and rotations for the intermediate shapes. Translation is specified using an anchor point path, and rotation is constrained by designating the rotation function of an angle line. The anchor point can be a polygon vertex, or any other point that is well defined for each step in the shape blend. For example, center of area is a good anchor point for objects in free fall. For bodies in free fall, such as a diver, a parabolic anchor path simulates the effects of gravity.

The angle line can be any line whose association with each shape in the blend can be determined, such as a non-degenerate polygon edge, the line between any two points on the polygon, or a principle axis of a shape (if the major and minor axes are well defined, ie., the product of inertia is non-zero). In Figure 3, the anchor point is $\mathbf{P}_0$ and the angle line is L_0.

4 Discussion

Figure 1 shows that the main advantage of using turtle graphics in shape blending is that it helps solve the withering arm problem. Another benefit is that it can provide more nearly monotonic angle changes than does linear-vertex-path shape blending. Figure 5 shows a shape blend, taken from [12], in which a shape which should undergo a simple rigid body motion experiences shrinking *and* kinking. The kinking occurs in this case because of a poor choice of vertices, a common occurrence in linear-vertex-path shape blending. Clearly, turtle graphics shape blending would have no problem in this case.

A more impelling example is the dancer's arm which withers under linear vertex path motion. The magnification in Figure 6 illustrates that the intrinsic method produces inherently smoother blends than the linear vertex paths. [12] goes

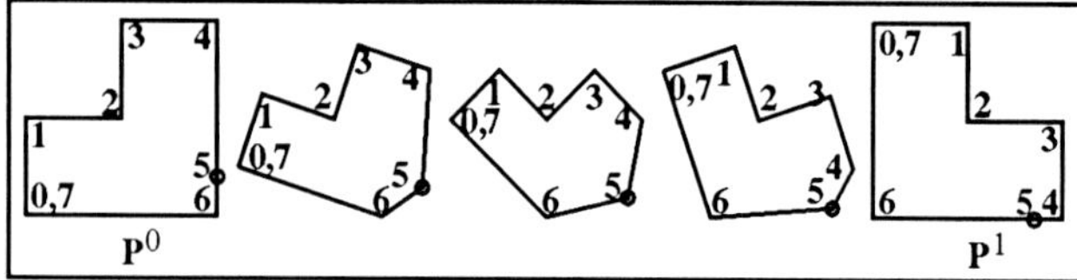

Figure 5: Shrinking plus kinking

to great lengths investigating how to minimize this angle non-monotonicity which can occur with linear vertex paths. As an added benefit of the intrinsic algorithm, this detailed search for non-monotonic angle changes is rendered unnecessary.

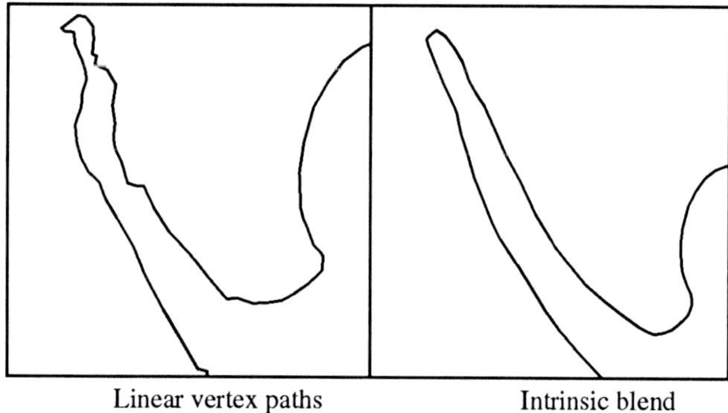

Figure 6: Closeup of dancer's arm

Although slower than the linear patch method, the intrinsic algorithm can compute a shape blend for the chicken in Figure 2.b (which has 230 vertices) in 0.02 seconds using the method in Section 2.1 and in 0.05 seconds using the method in Section 2.2, on an HP 730 workstation.

It is easy to contrive examples for which this algorithm performs poorly, although most of the realistic cases we have tried produced good results. In cases where some adjustment is called for, additional constraints can be imposed, such as specifying that the distance between specified pairs of non-adjacent polygon vertices should change monotonically from one key frame to the next. See [4] for more details.

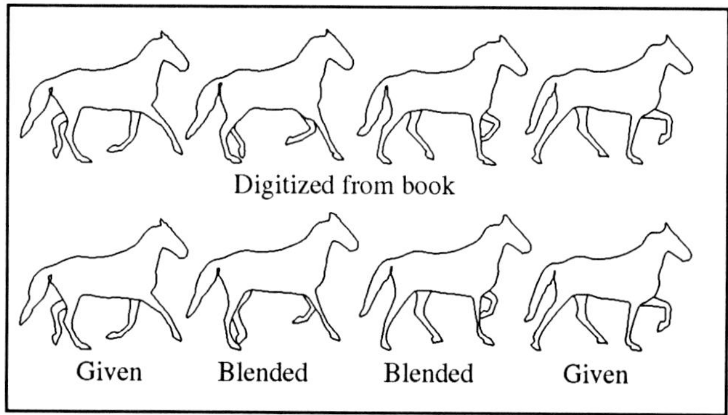

Figure 7: Cantering Horse

Experience suggests that this algorithm may work well enough for many applications to character animation. The sequence of a cantering horse in Figure 7 was taken from the classic photographic study, *Animals in Motion* [10], first published in 1887. The top four figures are digitizations of actual photographs from the book. In the bottom row, the middle two figures are shape blends interpolating the first and last figures. The vertex correspondence was determined using the algorithm in [12], and the vertex paths were computed using the algorithm in this paper. The horse's two left legs were treated as independent shape blends.

Acknowledgements

Geoffrey Slinker, Hank Christiansen, Alan Zundel, and Kris Klimaszewski provided much helpful discussion. This work was supported under NSF grant DMC-8657057.

References

[1] J. Alan Adams. The intrinsic method for curve definition. *Computer-Aided Design*, 7(4):243–249, 1975.

[2] Harold J. Bailey, Kathleen M. Brautigam, and Trudy H. Doran. *Apple Logo*. Brady Communications Company, Inc., Bowie, MD, 1984.

[3] Shenchang Eric Chen and Richard Parent. Shape averaging and its applications to industrial design. *IEEE CG&A*, 9(1):47–54, 1989.

[4] Peisheng Gao. 2–d shape blending: an intrinsic solution to the vertex path problem. Master's thesis, Brigham Young University, Department of Civil Engineering, 1993.

[5] Andrew Glassner. Metamorphosis. *preprint*, 1991.

[6] John F. Hughes. Scheduled fourier volume morphing. *Computer Graphics (Proc. SIGGRAPH)*, 26(2):43–46, 1992.

[7] Anil Kaul and Jarek Rossignac. Solid-interpolating deformations: Construction and animation of PIPs. In F.H. Post and W. Barth, editors, *Proc. Eurographics '91*, pages 493—505. Elsevier Science Publishers B.V, 1991.

[8] James R. Kent, Wayne E. Carlson, and Richard E. Parent. Shape transformation for polyhedral objects. *Computer Graphics (Proc. SIGGRAPH)*, 26(2):47–54, 1992.

[9] S. C. Malik. *Mathematical Analysis*. John Wiley & Sons, Inc., New York, 1984.

[10] Eadweard Muybridge. *Animals in Motion*. Dover Publications, Inc., New York, 1957.

[11] Thomas W. Sederberg and Eugene Greenwood. Shape blending of 2–d piecewise curves. *Submitted*.

[12] Thomas W. Sederberg and Eugene Greenwood. A physically based approach to 2–d shape blending. *Computer Graphics (Proc. SIGGRAPH)*, 26(2):25–34, 1992.

[13] Yoshihisa Shinagawa and Tosiyasu L. Kunii. The differential model: A model for animating transformation of objects using differntial information. In Tosiyasu L. Kunii, editor, *Modeling in Computer Graphics*, pages 5–15, Tokyo, 1991. Springer-Verlag.

[14] Geoffrey Slinker. Inbetweening using a physically based model and nonlinear path interpolation. Master's thesis, Brigham Young University, Department of Computer Science, 1992.

Mesh Optimization

Hugues Hoppe* Tony DeRose* Tom Duchamp† John McDonald‡ Werner Stuetzle‡

University of Washington
Seattle, WA 98195

Abstract

We present a method for solving the following problem: Given a set of data points scattered in three dimensions and an initial triangular mesh M_0, produce a mesh M, of the same topological type as M_0, that fits the data well and has a small number of vertices. Our approach is to minimize an energy function that explicitly models the competing desires of conciseness of representation and fidelity to the data. We show that mesh optimization can be effectively used in at least two applications: surface reconstruction from unorganized points, and mesh simplification (the reduction of the number of vertices in an initially dense mesh of triangles).

CR Categories and Subject Descriptors: I.3.5 [Computer Graphics]: Computational Geometry and Object Modeling.

Additional Keywords: Geometric Modeling, Surface Fitting, Three-Dimensional Shape Recovery, Range Data Analysis, Model Simplification.

1 Introduction

The *mesh optimization* problem considered in this paper can be roughly stated as follows: Given a collection of data points X in $\mathbf{R}^3$ and an initial triangular mesh M_0 near the data, find a mesh M of the same topological type as M_0 that fits the data well and has a small number of vertices.

As an example, Figure 7b shows a set of 4102 data points sampled from the object shown in Figure 7a. The input to the mesh optimization algorithm consists of the points together with the initial mesh shown in Figure 7c. The optimized mesh is shown in Figure 7h. Notice that the sharp edges and corners indicated by the data have been faithfully recovered and that the number of vertices has been significantly reduced (from 1572 to 163).

To solve the mesh optimization problem we minimize an *energy function* that captures the competing desires of tight geometric fit and compact representation. The tradeoff between geometric fit and compact representation is controlled via a user-selectable parameter c_{rep}. A large value of c_{rep} indicates that a sparse representation is to be strongly preferred over a dense one, usually at the expense of degrading the fit.

We use the input mesh M_0 as a starting point for a non-linear optimization process. During the optimization we vary the number of vertices, their positions, and their connectivity. Although we can give no guarantee of finding a global minimum, we have run the method on a wide variety of data sets; the method has produced good results in all cases (see Figure 1).

We see at least two applications of mesh optimization: surface reconstruction and mesh simplification.

The problem of surface reconstruction from sampled data occurs in many scientific and engineering applications. In [2], we outlined a two phase procedure for reconstructing a surface from a set of unorganized data points. The goal of phase one is to determine the topological type of the unknown surface and to obtain a crude estimate of its geometry. An algorithm for phase one was described in [5]. The goal of phase two is to improve the fit and reduce the number of faces. Mesh optimization can be used for this purpose.

Although we were originally led to consider the mesh optimization problem by our research on surface reconstruction, the algorithm we have developed can also be applied to the problem of mesh simplification. Mesh simplification, as considered by Turk [15] and Schroeder et al. [10], refers to the problem of reducing the number of faces in a dense mesh while minimally perturbing the shape. Mesh optimization can be used to solve this problem as follows: sample data points X from the initial mesh and use the initial mesh as the starting point M_0 of the optimization procedure. For instance, Figure 7q shows a triangular approximation of a minimal surface with 2032 vertices. Application of our mesh optimization algorithm to a sample of 6752 points (Figure 7r) from this mesh produces the meshes shown in Figures 7s (487 vertices) and 7t (239 vertices). The mesh of Figure 7s corresponds to a relatively small value of c_{rep}, and therefore has more vertices than the mesh of Figure 7t which corresponds to a somewhat larger value of c_{rep}.

The principal contributions of this paper are:

- It presents an algorithm for fitting a mesh of arbitrary topological type to a set of data points (as opposed to volume data, etc.). During the fitting process, the number and connectivity of the vertices, as well as their positions, are allowed to vary.
- It casts mesh simplification as an optimization problem with an energy function that directly measures deviation of the final mesh from the original. As a consequence, the final mesh

*Department of Computer Science and Engineering, FR-35
†Department of Mathematics, GN-50
‡Department of Statistics, GN-22

This work was supported in part by Bellcore, the Xerox Corporation, IBM, Hewlett-Packard, AT&T Bell Labs, the Digital Equipment Corporation, the Department of Energy under grant DE-FG06-85-ER25006, the National Library of Medicine under grant NIH LM-04174, and the National Science Foundation under grants CCR-8957323 and DMS-9103002.

© 1993 ACM-0-89791-601-8/93/008/0019 $01.50

Figure 1: Examples of mesh optimization. The meshes in the top row are the initial meshes M_0; the meshes in the bottom row are the corresponding optimized meshes. The first 3 columns are reconstructions; the last 2 columns are simplifications.

Simplicial complex K
vertices:{1}, {2}, {3}
edges: {1, 2}, {2, 3}, {1, 3}
faces: {1, 2, 3}

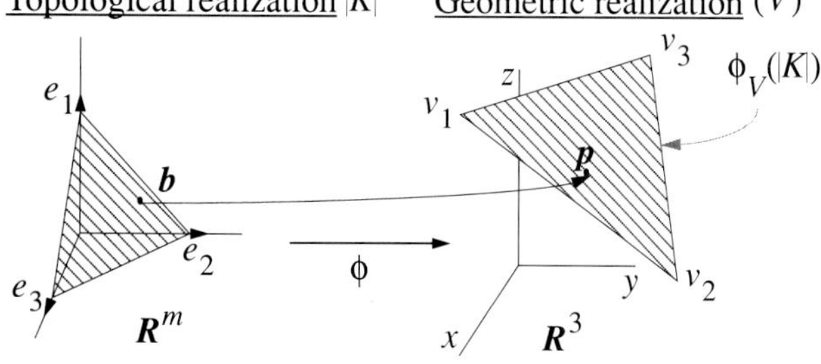

Figure 2: Example of mesh representation: a mesh consisting of a single face.

naturally adapts to curvature variations in the original mesh.

- It demonstrates how the algorithm's ability to recover sharp edges and corners can be exploited to automatically segment the final mesh into smooth connected components (see Figure 7i).

2 Mesh Representation

Intuitively, a *mesh* is a piecewise linear surface, consisting of triangular faces pasted together along their edges. For our purposes it is important to maintain the distinction between the connectivity of the vertices and their geometric positions. Formally, a mesh M is a pair (K, V), where: K is a *simplicial complex* representing the connectivity of the vertices, edges, and faces, thus determining the topological type of the mesh; $V = \{\mathbf{v}_1, \ldots, \mathbf{v}_m\}$, $\mathbf{v}_i \in \mathbf{R}^3$ is a set of vertex positions defining the shape of the mesh in $\mathbf{R}^3$ (its geometric realization).

A simplicial complex K consists of a set of vertices $\{1, \ldots, m\}$, together with a set of non-empty subsets of the vertices, called the simplices of K, such that any set consisting of exactly one vertex is a simplex in K, and every non-empty subset of a simplex in K is again a simplex in K (cf. Spanier [14]). The 0-simplices $\{i\} \in K$ are called vertices, the 1-simplices $\{i, j\} \in K$ are called edges, and the 2-simplices $\{i, j, k\} \in K$ are called faces.

A geometric realization of a mesh as a surface in $\mathbf{R}^3$ can be obtained as follows. For a given simplicial complex K, form its *topological realization* $|K|$ in $\mathbf{R}^m$ by identifying the vertices $\{1, \ldots, m\}$ with the standard basis vectors $\{\mathbf{e}_1, \ldots, \mathbf{e}_m\}$ of $\mathbf{R}^m$. For each simplex $s \in K$ let $|s|$ denote the convex hull of its vertices in $\mathbf{R}^m$, and let $|K| = \cup_{s \in K} |s|$. Let $\phi : \mathbf{R}^m \rightarrow \mathbf{R}^3$ be the linear map that sends the i-th standard basis vector $\mathbf{e}_i \in \mathbf{R}^m$ to $\mathbf{v}_i \in \mathbf{R}^3$ (see Figure 2).

The *geometric realization* of M is the image $\phi_V(|K|)$, where we write the map as ϕ_V to emphasize that it is fully specified by the set of vertex positions $V = \{\mathbf{v}_1, \ldots, \mathbf{v}_m\}$. The map ϕ_V is called an *embedding* if it is 1-1, that is if $\phi_V(|K|)$ is not self-intersecting. Only a restricted set of vertex positions V result in ϕ_V being an embedding.

If ϕ_V is an embedding, any point $\mathbf{p} \in \phi_V(|K|)$ can be parameterized by finding its unique pre-image on $|K|$. The vector $\mathbf{b} \in |K|$ with $\mathbf{p} = \phi_V(\mathbf{b})$ is called the *barycentric coordinate vector* of $\mathbf{p}$ (with respect to the simplicial complex K). Note that barycentric coordinate vectors are convex combinations of standard basis vectors $\mathbf{e}_i \in \mathbf{R}^m$ corresponding to the vertices of a face of K. Any barycentric coordinate vector has at most three non-zero entries; it has only two non-zero entries if it lies on an edge of $|K|$, and only one if it is a vertex.

3 Definition of the Energy Function

Recall that the goal of mesh optimization is to obtain a mesh that provides a good fit to the point set X and has a small number of vertices. We find a simplicial complex K and a set of vertex positions V defining a mesh $M = (K, V)$ that minimizes the energy function

$$E(K, V) = E_{dist}(K, V) + E_{rep}(K) + E_{spring}(K, V).$$

The first two terms correspond to the two stated goals; the third term is motivated below.

The distance energy E_{dist} is equal to the sum of squared distances from the points $X = \{\mathbf{x}_1, \ldots, \mathbf{x}_n\}$ to the mesh,

$$E_{dist}(K, V) = \sum_{i=1}^{n} d^2(\mathbf{x}_i, \phi_V(|K|)).$$

The representation energy E_{rep} penalizes meshes with a large number of vertices. It is set to be proportional to the number of vertices m of K:

$$E_{rep}(K) = c_{rep}m.$$

The optimization allows vertices to be both added to and removed from the mesh. When a vertex is added, the distance energy E_{dist} is likely to be reduced; the term E_{rep} makes this operation incur a penalty so that vertices are not added indefinitely. Similarly, one wants to remove vertices from a dense mesh even if E_{dist} increases slightly; in this case E_{rep} acts to encourage the vertex removal. The user-specified parameter c_{rep} provides a controllable trade-off between fidelity of geometric fit and parsimony of representation.

We discovered, as others have before us [8], that minimizing $E_{dist} + E_{rep}$ does not produce the desired results. As an illustration of what can go wrong, Figure 7d shows the result of minimizing E_{dist} alone. The estimated surface has several spikes in regions where there is no data. These spikes are a manifestation of the fundamental problem that a minimum of $E_{dist} + E_{rep}$ may not exist.

To guarantee the existence of a minimum [6], we add the third term, the spring energy E_{spring}. It places on each edge of the mesh a spring of rest length zero and spring constant κ:

$$E_{spring}(K, V) = \sum_{\{j,k\} \in K} \kappa \|\mathbf{v}_j - \mathbf{v}_k\|^2$$

It is worthwhile emphasizing that the spring energy is not a smoothness penalty. Our intent is not to penalize sharp dihedral angles in the mesh, since such features may be present in the underlying surface and should be recovered. We view E_{spring} as a regularizing term that helps guide the optimization to a desirable local minimum. As the optimization converges to the solution, the magnitude of E_{spring} can be gradually reduced. We return to this issue in Section 4.4.

For some applications we want the procedure to be scale-invariant, which is equivalent to defining a unitless energy function E. To achieve invariance under Euclidean motion and uniform scaling, the points X and the initial mesh M_0 are pre-scaled uniformly to fit in a unit cube. After optimization, a post-processing step can undo this initial transformation.

4 Minimization of the Energy Function

Our goal is to minimize the energy function

$$E(K, V) = E_{dist}(K, V) + E_{rep}(K) + E_{spring}(K, V)$$

over the set $\mathcal{K}$ of simplicial complexes K homeomorphic to the initial simplicial complex K_0, and the vertex positions V defining the embedding. We now present an outline of our optimization algorithm, a pseudo-code version of which appears in Figure 3. The details are deferred to the next two subsections.

To minimize $E(K, V)$ over both K and V, we partition the problem into two nested subproblems: an inner minimization over V for fixed simplicial complex K, and a outer minimization over K.

In Section 4.1 we describe an algorithm that solves the inner minimization problem. It finds $E(K) = \min_V E(K, V)$, the energy

```
OptimizeMesh(K0,V0) {
    K := K0
    V := OptimizeVertexPositions(K0,V0)
    – Solve the outer minimization problem.
    repeat {
        (K',V') := GenerateLegalMove(K,V)
        V' = OptimizeVertexPositions(K',V')
        if E(K',V') < E(K,V) then
            (K,V) := (K',V')
        endif
    } until convergence
    return (K,V)
}

– Solve the inner optimization problem
–    E(K) = min_V E(K,V)
– for fixed simplicial complex K.
OptimizeVertexPositions(K,V) {
    repeat {
        – Compute barycentric coordinates by projection.
        B := ProjectPoints(K,V)
        – Minimize E(K,V,B) over V using conjugate gradients.
        V := ImproveVertexPositions(K,B)
    } until convergence
    return V
}

GenerateLegalMove(K,V) {
    Select a legal move K ⇒ K'.
    Locally modify V to obtain V' appropriate for K'.
    return (K',V')
}
```

Figure 3: An idealized pseudo-code version of the minimization algorithm.

of the best possible embedding of the fixed simplicial complex K, and the corresponding vertex positions V, given an initial guess for V. This corresponds to the procedure OptimizeVertexPositions in Figure 3.

Whereas the inner minimization is a continuous optimization problem, the outer minimization of $E(K)$ over the simplicial complexes $K \in \mathcal{K}$ (procedure OptimizeMesh) is a discrete optimization problem. An algorithm for its solution is presented in Section 4.2.

The energy function $E(K, V)$ depends on two parameters c_{rep} and κ. The parameter c_{rep} controls the tradeoff between conciseness and fidelity to the data and should be set by the user. The parameter κ, on the other hand, is a regularizing parameter that, ideally, would be chosen automatically. Our method of setting κ is described in Section 4.4.

4.1 Optimization for Fixed Simplicial Complex

(Procedure OptimizeVertexPositions)

In this section, we consider the problem of finding a set of vertex positions V that minimizes the energy function $E(K, V)$ for a given simplicial complex K. As $E_{rep}(K)$ does not depend on V, this amounts to minimizing $E_{dist}(K, V) + E_{spring}(K, V)$.

To evaluate the distance energy $E_{dist}(K, V)$, it is necessary to compute the distance of each data point $\mathbf{x}_i$ to $M = \phi_V(|K|)$. Each of these distances is itself the solution to the minimization problem

$$d^2(\mathbf{x}_i, \phi_V(|K|)) = \min_{\mathbf{b}_i \in |K|} \|\mathbf{x}_i - \phi_V(\mathbf{b}_i)\|^2,$$

in which the unknown is the barycentric coordinate vector $\mathbf{b}_i \in$

$|K| \subset \mathbf{R}^m$ of the projection of $\mathbf{x}_i$ onto M. Thus, minimizing $E(K, V)$ for fixed K is equivalent to minimizing the new objective function

$$E(K, V, B) = \sum_{i=1}^{n} \|\mathbf{x}_i - \phi_V(\mathbf{b}_i)\|^2 + E_{spring}(K, V)$$
$$= \sum_{i=1}^{n} \|\mathbf{x}_i - \phi_V(\mathbf{b}_i)\|^2 + \sum_{\{j,k\} \in K} \kappa \|\mathbf{v}_j - \mathbf{v}_k\|^2$$

over the vertex positions $V = \{\mathbf{v}_1, \ldots, \mathbf{v}_m\}, \mathbf{v}_i \in \mathbf{R}^3$ and the barycentric coordinates $B = \{\mathbf{b}_1, \ldots, \mathbf{b}_n\}, \mathbf{b}_i \in |K| \subset \mathbf{R}^m$.

To solve this optimization problem (procedure OptimizeVertexPositions), our method alternates between two subproblems:

1. For fixed vertex positions V, find optimal barycentric coordinate vectors B by *projection* (procedure ProjectPoints).
2. For fixed barycentric coordinate vectors B, find optimal vertex positions V by solving a *linear* least squares problem (procedure ImproveVertexPositions).

Because we find optimal solutions to both of these subproblems, $E(K, V, B)$ can never increase, and since it is bounded from below, it must converge. In principle, one could iterate until some formal convergence criterion is met. Instead, as is common, we perform a fixed number of iterations. As an example, Figure 7e shows the result of optimizing the mesh of Figure 7c over the vertex positions while holding the simplicial complex fixed.

It is conceivable that procedure OptimizeVertexPositions returns a set V of vertices for which the mesh is self-intersecting, i.e. ϕ_V is not an embedding. While it is possible to check *a posteriori* whether ϕ_V is an embedding, constraining the optimization to always produce an embedding appears to be difficult. This has not presented a problem in the examples we have run.

4.1.1 Projection Subproblem
(Procedure ProjectPoints)

The problem of optimizing $E(K, V, B)$ over the barycentric coordinate vectors $B = \{\mathbf{b}_1, \ldots, \mathbf{b}_n\}$, while holding the vertex positions $V = \{\mathbf{v}_1, \ldots, \mathbf{v}_m\}$ and the simplicial complex K constant, decomposes into n separate optimization problems:

$$\mathbf{b}_i = \underset{\mathbf{b} \in |K|}{\operatorname{argmin}} \|\mathbf{x}_i - \phi_V(\mathbf{b})\|$$

In other words, $\mathbf{b}_i$ is the barycentric coordinate vector corresponding to the point $\mathbf{p} \in \phi_V(|K|)$ closest to $\mathbf{x}_i$.

A naive approach to computing $\mathbf{b}_i$ is to project $\mathbf{x}_i$ onto all of the faces of M, and then find the projection with minimal distance. To speed up the projection, we first enter the faces of the mesh into a spatial partitioning data structure (similar to the one used in [16]). Then for each point $\mathbf{x}_i$ only a nearby subset of the faces needs to be considered, and the projection step takes expected time $O(n)$. For additional speedup we exploit coherence between iterations. Instead of projecting each point globally onto the mesh, we assume that a point's projection lies in a neighborhood of its projection in the previous iteration. Specifically, we project the point onto all faces that share a vertex with the previous face. Although this is a heuristic that can fail, it has performed well in practice.

4.1.2 Linear Least Squares Subproblem
(Procedure ImproveVertexPositions)

Minimizing $E(K, V, B)$ over the vertex positions V while holding B and K fixed is a linear least squares problem. It decomposes into three independent subproblems, one for each of the three coordinates of the vertex positions. We will write down the problem for the first coordinate.

Let e be the number of edges (1-simplices) in K; note that e is $O(m)$. Let $\mathbf{v}^1$ be the m-vector whose i-th element is the first coordinate of $\mathbf{v}_i$. Let $\mathbf{d}^1$ be the $(n+e)$-vector whose first n elements are the first coordinates of the data points $\mathbf{x}_i$, and whose last e elements are zero. With these definitions we can express the least squares problem for the first coordinate as minimizing $\|A\mathbf{v}^1 - \mathbf{d}^1\|^2$ over $\mathbf{v}^1$. The design matrix A is an $(n + e) \times m$ matrix of scalars. The first n rows of A are the barycentric coordinate vectors $\mathbf{b}_i$. Each of the trailing e rows contains 2 non-zero entries with values $\sqrt{\kappa}$ and $-\sqrt{\kappa}$ in the columns corresponding to the indices of the edge's endpoints. The first n rows of the least squares problem correspond to $E_{dist}(K, V)$, while the last e rows correspond to $E_{spring}(K, V)$. An important feature of the matrix A is that it contains at most 3 non-zero entries in each row, for a total of $O(n + m)$ non-zero entries.

To solve the least squares problem, we use the conjugate gradient method (cf. [3]). This is an iterative method guaranteed to find the exact solution in as many iterations as there are distinct singular values of A, i.e. in at most m iterations. Usually far fewer iterations are required to get a result with acceptable precision. For example, we find that for m as large as 10^4, as few as 200 iterations are sufficient.

The two time-consuming operations in each iteration of the conjugate gradient algorithm are the multiplication of A by an $(n + e)$-vector and the multiplication of A^T by an m-vector. Because A is sparse, these two operations can be executed in $O(n + m)$ time. We store A in a sparse form that requires only $O(n + m)$ space. Thus, an acceptable solution to the least squares problem is obtained in $O(n + m)$ time. In contrast, a typical noniterative method for solving dense least squares problems, such as QR decomposition, would require $O((n + m)m^2)$ time to find an exact solution.

4.2 Optimization over Simplicial Complexes
(Procedure OptimizeMesh)

To solve the outer minimization problem, minimizing $E(K)$ over K, we define a set of three elementary transformations, *edge collapse*, *edge split*, and *edge swap*, taking a simplicial complex K to another simplicial complex K' (see Figure 4).

We define a *legal move* to be the application of one of these elementary transformations to an edge of K that leaves the topological type of K unchanged. The set of elementary transformations is complete in the sense that *any* simplicial complex in $\mathcal{K}$ can be obtained from K_0 through a sequence of legal moves[1].

Our goal then is to find such a sequence taking us from K_0 to a minimum of $E(K)$. We do this using a variant of random descent: we randomly select a legal move, $K \Rightarrow K'$. If $E(K') < E(K)$, we accept the move, otherwise we try again. If a large number of trials fails to produce an acceptable move, we terminate the search.

More elaborate selection strategies, such as steepest descent or simulated annealing, are possible. As we have obtained good results with the simple strategy of random descent, we have not yet implemented the other strategies.

Identifying Legal Moves An edge split transformation is always a legal move, as it can never change the topological type of K. The other two transformations, on the other hand, can cause a change of

[1]In fact, we prove in [6] that edge collapse and edge split are sufficient; we include edge swap to allow the optimization procedure to "tunnel" through small hills in the energy function.

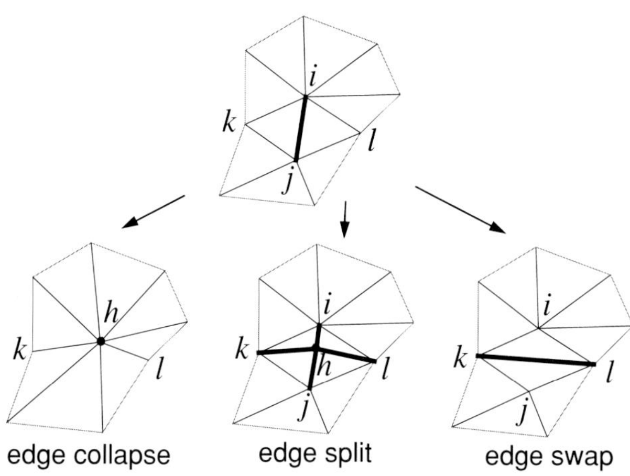

Figure 4: Local simplicial complex transformations

topological type, so tests must be performed to determine if they are legal moves.

We define an edge $\{i, j\} \in K$ to be a *boundary edge* if it is a subset of only one face $\{i, j, k\} \in K$, and a vertex $\{i\}$ to be a *boundary vertex* if there exists a boundary edge $\{i, j\} \in K$.

An edge collapse transformation $K \Rightarrow K'$ that collapses the edge $\{i, j\} \in K$ is a legal move if and only if the following conditions are satisfied (proof in [6]):

- For all vertices $\{k\}$ adjacent to both $\{i\}$ and $\{j\}$ ($\{i, k\} \in K$ and $\{j, k\} \in K$), $\{i, j, k\}$ is a face of K.
- If $\{i\}$ and $\{j\}$ are both boundary vertices, $\{i, j\}$ is a boundary edge.
- K has more than 4 vertices if neither $\{i\}$ nor $\{j\}$ are boundary vertices, or K has more than 3 vertices if either $\{i\}$ or $\{j\}$ are boundary vertices.

An edge swap transformation $K \Rightarrow K'$ that replaces the edge $\{i, j\} \in K$ with $\{k, l\} \in K'$ is a legal move if and only if $\{k, l\} \notin K$.

4.3 Exploiting Locality

The idealized algorithm described so far is too inefficient to be of practical use. In this section, we describe some heuristics which dramatically reduce the running time. These heuristics capitalize on the fact that a local change in the structure of the mesh leaves the optimal positions of distant vertices essentially unchanged.

4.3.1 Heuristics for Evaluating the Effect of Legal Moves

Our strategy for selecting legal moves requires evaluation of $E(K') = \min_V E(K', V)$ for a simplicial complex K' obtained from K through a legal move. Ideally, we would use procedure OptimizeVertexPositions of Section 4.1 for this purpose, as indicated in Figure 3. In practice, however, this is too slow. Instead, we use fast local heuristics to estimate the effect of a legal move on the energy function.

Each of the heuristics is based on extracting a submesh in the neighborhood of the transformation, along with the subset of the data points projecting onto the submesh. The change in overall energy is estimated by only considering the contribution of the submesh and the corresponding point set. This estimate is always pessimistic, as full optimization would only further reduce the energy.

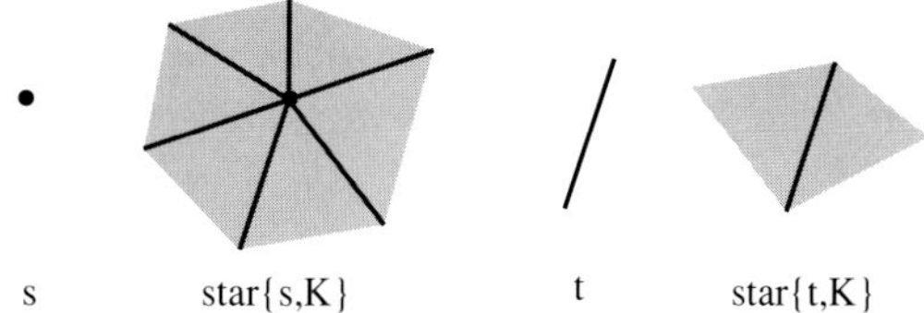

Figure 5: Neighborhood subsets of K.

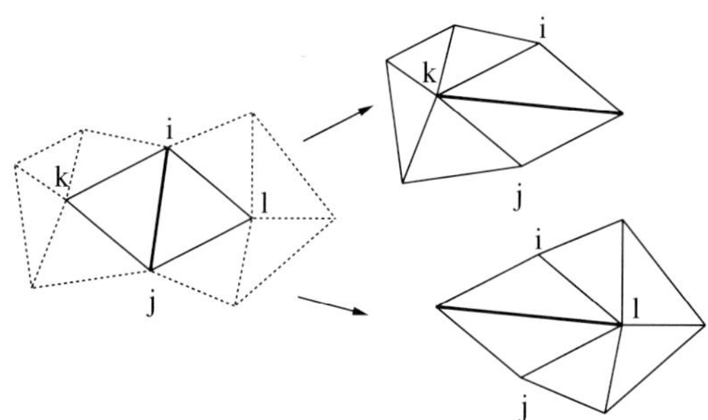

Figure 6: Two local optimizations to evaluate edge swap

Therefore, the heuristics never suggest changes that will increase the true energy of the mesh.

Definition of neighborhoods in a simplicial complex To refer to neighborhoods in a simplicial complex, we need to introduce some further notation. We write $s' \leq s$ to denote that simplex s' is a non-empty subset of simplex s. For simplex $s \in K$, $\text{star}(s; K) = \{s' \in K : s \leq s'\}$ (Figure 5).

Evaluation of Edge Collapse To evaluate a transformation $K \Rightarrow K'$ collapsing an edge $\{i, j\}$ into a single vertex $\{h\}$ (Figure 4), we take the submesh to be $\text{star}(\{i\}; K) \cup \text{star}(\{j\}; K)$, and optimize over the single vertex position $\mathbf{v}_h$ while holding all other vertex positions constant.

Because we perform only a small number of iterations (for reasons of efficiency), the initial choice of $\mathbf{v}_h$ greatly influences the accuracy of the result. Therefore, we attempt three optimizations, with $\mathbf{v}_h$ starting at $\mathbf{v}_i$, $\mathbf{v}_j$, and $\frac{1}{2}(\mathbf{v}_i + \mathbf{v}_j)$, and accept the best one.

The edge collapse should be allowed only if the new mesh does not intersect itself. Checking for this would be costly; instead we settle for a less expensive heuristic check. If, after the local optimization, the maximum dihedral angle of the edges in $\text{star}(\{h\}; K')$ is greater than some threshold, the edge collapse is rejected.

Evaluation of Edge Split The procedure is the same as for edge collapse, except that the submesh is defined to be $\text{star}(\{i, j\}; K)$, and the initial value of the new vertex $\mathbf{v}_h$ is chosen to be $\frac{1}{2}(\mathbf{v}_i + \mathbf{v}_j)$.

Evaluation of Edge Swap To evaluate an edge swap transformation $K \Rightarrow K'$ that replaces an edge $\{i, j\} \in K$ with $\{k, l\} \in K'$, we consider two local optimizations, one with submesh $\text{star}(\{k\}; K')$, varying vertex $\mathbf{v}_k$, and one with submesh $\text{star}(\{l\}; K')$, varying vertex $\mathbf{v}_l$ (Figure 6). The change in energy is taken to best of these. As is the case in evaluating an edge collapse, we reject the transformation if the maximum dihedral angle after the local optimization exceeds a threshold.

4.3.2 Legal Move Selection Strategy
(Procedure GenerateLegalMove)

The simple strategy for selecting legal moves described in Section 4.2 can be improved by exploiting locality. Instead of selecting edges completely at random, edges are selected from a candidate set. This candidate set consists of all edges that may lead to beneficial moves, and initially contains all edges.

To generate a legal move, we randomly remove an edge from the candidate set. We first consider collapsing the edge, accepting the move if it is legal and reduces the total energy. If the edge collapse is not accepted, we then consider edge swap and edge split in that order. If one of the transformations is accepted, we update the candidate set by adding all neighboring edges. The candidate set becomes very useful toward the end of optimization, when the fraction of beneficial moves diminishes.

4.4 Setting of the Spring Constant

We view the spring energy E_{spring} as a regularizing term that helps guide the optimization process to a good minimum. The spring constant κ determines the contribution of this term to the total energy. We have obtained good results by making successive calls to procedure OptimizeMesh, each with a different value of κ, according to a schedule that gradually decreases κ.

As an example, to obtain the final mesh in Figure 7h starting from the mesh in Figure 7c, we successively set κ to $10^{-2}, 10^{-3}, 10^{-4}$, and 10^{-8} (see Figures 7f–7h). This same schedule was used in all the examples.

5 Results

5.1 Surface Reconstruction

From the set of points shown in Figure 7b, phase one of our reconstruction algorithm [5] produces the mesh shown in Figure 7c; this mesh has the correct topological type, but it is rather dense, is far away from the data, and lacks the sharp features of the original model (Figure 7a). Using this mesh as a starting point, mesh optimization produces the mesh in Figure 7h.

Figures 7i–7k,7m–7o show two examples of surface reconstruction from actual laser range data (courtesy of Technical Arts, Redmond, WA). Figures 7j and 7n show sets of points obtained by sampling two physical objects (a distributor cap and a golf club head) with a laser range finder. The outputs of phase one are shown in Figures 7k and 7o. The holes present in the surface of Figure 7k are artifacts of the data, as self-shadowing prevented some regions of the surface from being scanned. Adaptive selection of scanning paths preventing such shadowing is an interesting area of future research. In this case, we manually filled the holes, leaving a single boundary at the bottom. Figures 7l and 7p show the optimized meshes obtained with our algorithm.

5.2 Mesh Simplification

For mesh simplification, we first sample a set of points randomly from the original mesh using uniform random sampling over area. Next, we add the vertices of the mesh to this point set. Finally, to more faithfully preserve the boundaries of the mesh, we sample additional points from boundary edges.

As an example of mesh simplification, we start with the mesh containing 2032 vertices shown in Figure 7q. From it, we obtain a sample of 6752 points shown in Figure 7r (4000 random points, 2032 vertex points, and 720 boundary points). Mesh optimization, with $c_{rep} = 10^{-5}$, reduces the mesh down to 487 vertices (Figure 7s). By setting $c_{rep} = 10^{-4}$, we obtain a coarser mesh of 239 vertices (Figure 7t).

Fig.	#vert. m	#faces	#data n	Parameters c_{rep}	κ	Resulting energies E_{dist}	E	time (min.)
7c	1572	3152	4102	-	-	8.57×10^{-2}	-	-
7e	1572	3152	4102	10^{-5}	10^{-2}	8.04×10^{-4}	4.84×10^{-2}	1.5
7f	508	1024	4102	10^{-5}	10^{-2}	6.84×10^{-4}	3.62×10^{-2}	(+3.0)
7g	270	548	4102	10^{-5}	10^{-3}	6.08×10^{-4}	6.94×10^{-3}	(+2.2)
7h	163	334	4102	10^{-5}	*varied*	4.86×10^{-4}	2.12×10^{-3}	17.0
7k	9220	18272	12745	-	-	6.41×10^{-2}	-	-
7l	690	1348	12745	10^{-5}	*varied*	4.23×10^{-3}	1.18×10^{-2}	47.0
7o	4059	8073	16864	-	-	2.20×10^{-2}	-	-
7p	262	515	16864	10^{-5}	*varied*	2.19×10^{-3}	4.95×10^{-3}	44.5
7q	2032	3832	-	-	-	-	-	-
7s	487	916	6752	10^{-5}	*varied*	1.86×10^{-3}	8.05×10^{-3}	9.9
7t	239	432	6752	10^{-4}	*varied*	9.19×10^{-3}	4.39×10^{-2}	10.2

Table 1: Performance statistics for meshes shown in Figure 7.

As these examples illustrate, basing mesh simplification on a measure of distance between the simplified mesh and the original has a number of benefits:

- Vertices are dense in regions of high Gaussian curvature, whereas a few large faces span the flat regions.
- Long edges are aligned in directions of low curvature, and the aspect ratios of the triangles adjust to local curvature.
- Edges and vertices of the simplified mesh are placed near sharp features of the original mesh.

5.3 Segmentation

Mesh optimization enables us to detect sharp features in the underlying surface. Using a simple thresholding method, the optimized mesh can be segmented into smooth components. To this end, we build a graph in which the nodes are the faces of mesh. Two nodes of this graph are connected if the two corresponding faces are adjacent and their dihedral angle is smaller than a given threshold. The connected components of this graph identify the desired smooth segments. As an example, Figure 7i shows the segmentation of the optimized mesh into 11 components. After segmentation, vertex normals can be estimated from neighboring faces within each component, and a smoothly shaded surface can be created (Figure 7m).

5.4 Parameter Settings and Performance Statistics

Table 1 lists the specific parameter values of c_{rep} and κ used to generate the meshes in the examples, along with other performance statistics. In all these examples, the table entry *"varied"* refers to a spring constant schedule of $\{10^{-2}, 10^{-3}, 10^{-4}, 10^{-8}\}$. In fact, all meshes in Figure 1 are also created using the same parameters (except that c_{rep} was changed in two cases). Execution times were obtained on a DEC uniprocessor Alpha workstation.

6 Related Work

Surface Fitting There is a large body of literature on fitting embeddings of a rectangular domain; see Bolle and Vemuri [1] for a review. Schudy and Ballard [11, 12] fit embeddings of a sphere to point data. Goshtasby [4] works with embeddings of cylinders and tori. Sclaroff and Pentland [13] consider embeddings of a deformed superquadric. Miller et al. [9] approximate an isosurface of volume data by fitting a mesh homeomorphic to a sphere. While it appears that their method could be extended to finding isosurfaces of arbitrary topological type, it it less obvious how it could be modified to handle point instead of volume data. Mallet [7] discusses interpolation of functions over simplicial complexes of arbitrary topological type.

Our method allows fitting of a parametric surface of arbitrary topological type to a set of three-dimensional points. In [2], we sketched an algorithm for fitting a mesh of *fixed* vertex connectivity to the data. The algorithm presented here is an extension of this idea in which we also allow the number of vertices and their connectivity to vary. To the best of our knowledge, this has not been done before.

Mesh Simplification Two notable papers discussing the mesh simplification problem are Schroeder et al. [10] and Turk [15].

The motivation of Schroeder et al. is to simplify meshes generated by "marching cubes" that may consist of more than a million triangles. In their iterative approach, the basic operation is removal of a vertex and re-triangulation of the hole thus created. The criterion for vertex removal in the simplest case (interior vertex not on edge or corner) is the distance from the vertex to the plane approximating its surrounding vertices. It is worthwhile noting that this criterion only considers deviation of the new mesh from the mesh created in the previous iteration; deviation from the original mesh does not figure in the strategy.

Turk's goal is to reduce the amount of detail in a mesh while remaining faithful to the original topology and geometry. His basic idea is to distribute points on the existing mesh that are to become the new vertices. He then creates a triangulation containing both old and new vertices, and finally removes the old vertices. The density of the new vertices is chosen to be higher in areas of high curvature.

The principal advantage of our mesh simplification method compared to the techniques mentioned above is that we cast mesh simplification as an optimization problem: we find a new mesh of lower complexity that is as close as possible to the original mesh. This is recognized as a desirable property by Turk (Section 8, p. 63): "Another topic is finding measures of how closely matched a given re-tiling is to the original model. Can such a quality measure be used to guide the re-tiling process?". Optimization automatically retains more vertices in areas of high curvature, and leads to faces that are elongated along directions of low curvature, another property recognized as desirable by Turk.

7 Summary and Future Work

We have described an energy minimization approach to solving the mesh optimization problem. The energy function we use consists of three terms: a distance energy that measures the closeness of fit, a representation energy that penalizes meshes with a large number of vertices, and a regularizing term that conceptually places springs of rest length zero on the edges of the mesh. Our minimization algorithm partitions the problem into two nested subproblems: an inner continuous minimization and an outer discrete minimization. The search space consists of all meshes homeomorphic to the starting mesh.

Mesh optimization has proven effective as the second phase of our method for surface reconstruction from unorganized points, as discussed in [5]. (Phase two is responsible for improving the geometric fit and reducing the number of vertices of the mesh produced in phase one.)

Our method has also performed well for mesh simplification, that is, the reduction of the number of vertices in a dense triangular mesh. It produces meshes whose edges align themselves along directions of low curvature, and whose vertices concentrate in areas of high Gaussian curvature. Because the energy does not penalize surfaces with sharp dihedral angles, the method can recover sharp edges and corners.

A number of areas of future research still remain, including:

- Investigate the use of more sophisticated optimization methods, such as simulated annealing for discrete optimization and quadratic methods for non-linear least squares optimization, in order to avoid undesirable local minima in the energy and to accelerate convergence.
- Gain more insight into the use of the spring energy as a regularizing term, especially in the presence of appreciable noise.
- Improve the speed of the algorithm and investigate implementations on parallel architectures.
- Develop methods for fitting higher order splines to more accurately and concisely model curved surfaces.
- Experiment with sparse, non-uniform, and noisy data.
- Extend the current algorithm to other distance measures such as maximum error (L^∞ norm) or average error (L^1 norm), instead of the current L^2 norm.

References

[1] Ruud M. Bolle and Baba C. Vemuri. On three-dimensional surface reconstruction methods. *IEEE PAMI*, 13(1):1–13, January 1991.

[2] T. DeRose, H. Hoppe, T. Duchamp, J. McDonald, and W. Stuetzle. Fitting of surfaces to scattered data. *SPIE*, 1830:212–220, 1992.

[3] Gene Golub and Charles Van Loan. *Matrix Computations*. John Hopkins University Press, 2nd edition, 1989.

[4] Ardeshir Goshtasby. Surface reconstruction from scattered measurements. *SPIE*, 1830:247–256, 1992.

[5] H. Hoppe, T. DeRose, T. Duchamp, J. McDonald, and W. Stuetzle. Surface reconstruction from unorganized points. *Computer Graphics (SIGGRAPH '92 Proceedings)*, 26(2):71–78, July 1992.

[6] H. Hoppe, T. DeRose, T. Duchamp, J. McDonald, and W. Stuetzle. Mesh optimization. TR 93-01-01, Dept. of Computer Science and Engineering, University of Washington, January 1993.

[7] J.L. Mallet. Discrete smooth interpolation in geometric modeling. *CAD*, 24(4):178–191, April 1992.

[8] Samuel Marin and Philip Smith. Parametric approximation of data using ODR splines. GMR 7057, General Motors Research Laboratories, May 1990.

[9] J.V. Miller, D.E. Breen, W.E. Lorensen, R.M. O'Bara, and M.J. Wozny. Geometrically deformed models: A method for extracting closed geometric models from volume data. *Computer Graphics (SIGGRAPH '91 Proceedings)*, 25(4):217–226, July 1991.

[10] William Schroeder, Jonathan Zarge, and William Lorensen. Decimation of triangle meshes. *Computer Graphics (SIGGRAPH '92 Proceedings)*, 26(2):65–70, July 1992.

[11] R. B. Schudy and D. H. Ballard. Model detection of cardiac chambers in ultrasound images. Technical Report 12, Computer Science Department, University of Rochester, 1978.

[12] R. B. Schudy and D. H. Ballard. Towards an anatomical model of heart motion as seen in 4-d cardiac ultrasound data. In *Proceedings of the 6th Conference on Computer Applications in Radiology and Computer-Aided Analysis of Radiological Images*, 1979.

[13] Stan Sclaroff and Alex Pentland. Generalized implicit functions for computer graphics. *Computer Graphics (SIGGRAPH '91 Proceedings)*, 25(4):247–250, July 1991.

[14] E. H. Spanier. *Algebraic Topology*. McGraw-Hill, New York, 1966.

[15] Greg Turk. Re-tiling polygonal surfaces. *Computer Graphics (SIGGRAPH '92 Proceedings)*, 26(2):55–64, July 1992.

[16] G. Wyvill, C. McPheeters, and B. Wyvill. Data structures for soft objects. *The Visual Computer*, 2(4):227–234, August 1986.

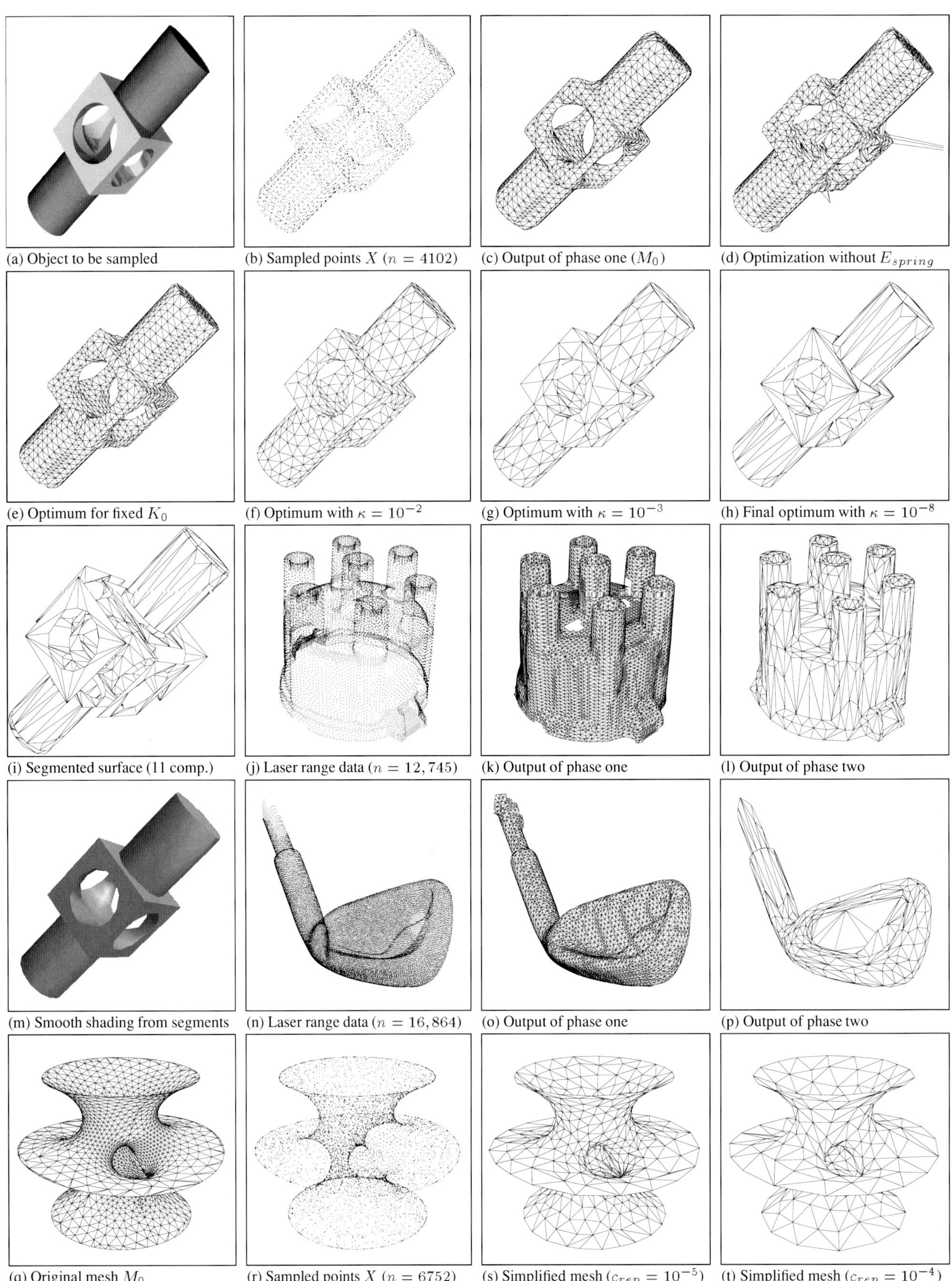

(a) Object to be sampled (b) Sampled points X ($n = 4102$) (c) Output of phase one (M_0) (d) Optimization without E_{spring}

(e) Optimum for fixed K_0 (f) Optimum with $\kappa = 10^{-2}$ (g) Optimum with $\kappa = 10^{-3}$ (h) Final optimum with $\kappa = 10^{-8}$

(i) Segmented surface (11 comp.) (j) Laser range data ($n = 12,745$) (k) Output of phase one (l) Output of phase two

(m) Smooth shading from segments (n) Laser range data ($n = 16,864$) (o) Output of phase one (p) Output of phase two

(q) Original mesh M_0 (r) Sampled points X ($n = 6752$) (s) Simplified mesh ($c_{rep} = 10^{-5}$) (t) Simplified mesh ($c_{rep} = 10^{-4}$)

Figure 7: Examples of surface reconstruction and mesh simplification.

Interactive Texture Mapping

Jérôme Maillot* , **Hussein Yahia‡**, **Anne Verroust‡**
* Thomson Digital Image
‡ INRIA-Rocquencourt

Abstract

This paper describes a new approach to texture mapping. A global method to lower the distortion of the mapped image is presented; by considering a general optimization function we view the mapping as an energy-minimization process. We have constructed an interactive texture tool, which is fast and easy to use, to manipulate atlases in texture space. We present the tool's large set of interactive operations on mapping functions. We also introduce an algorithm which automatically generates an atlas for any type of object. These techniques allow the mapping of different textures onto the same object and handle non-continuous mapping functions, needed for complicated mapped objects.

CR Categories and subject descriptors: I.3.3 [Computer Graphics] Picture/Image Generation. I.3.7 [Computer Graphics] Graphics and Realism - Color, Shading and Texture.

Additional Keywords: Texture Mapping, Texture Map Distortion, Realistic Rendering, Interaction.

1 Introduction.

Texture mapping is a method in Computer Graphics to enhance the richness of computer-generated images [3, 13]. A texture is a 2D image to be mapped onto a synthetic 3D object. The 2D space of the texture image is often called texture space. Each point on the object has to be associated with an element in texture space. One of the first algorithms used the parametric representation of patches to find texture addresses [3]. With this method, some problems may occur at the junction of two patches [4]. Another method is to project the texture onto the object using an intermediate 3D shape like a box or a cylinder [2]. Also, some applications have been developed to provide direct drawing onto the object, in which the user interactively modifies the texture via the mapping function [12].

* Thomson Digital Image, 20-22, rue Hégésippe Moreau, 75018 Paris, France.

‡ INRIA-Rocquencourt B.P. 105, 78153 Le Chesnay, France.

In addition, the rendering of an object mapped with a pre-existing image, such as a digitized one, has been improved using dedicated techniques [3, 8, 2, 1]. We are interested in the case of 2D textures. In general, there is no natural mapping from the texture to the object: the image is necessarily distorted (see [13]). Also, there is a need for interactive tools to help the user define how to map a pre-defined image onto a surface, or to improve a mapping function. We present new methods for solving these problems.

We first propose, in section two, a mathematical formulation for the distortion of the mapped image. After deriving a general formula for the deformation energy, we describe simplified formulae, fast enough to be used inside an interactive loop to improve the mapping function.

Section three is devoted to the notion of an *atlas*, derived from a mathematical notion and adapted to the special case of textures. In the first subsection curvature is used to build an ultrametric for automatically creating atlases on any object. In the second subsection a set of interactive functions is presented for manipulating atlases.

We address only the case of polygonized surfaces. This simplifies the definition of the mapping function to one that depends only on the position in the texture plane of the points associated to all vertices. Our texture mapping tool is designed for a naive user who is not necessarily a specialist in image synthesis. The interface is very intuitive for the basic functions, and also provides some control structures which free the user from repetitive tasks. This program could be used, for example, by fashion designers to map woven or leather textures onto polygonal surfaces describing shoes, clothes or seats.

2 Deformation measures.

The first problem one has to solve when mapping textures is to define the quality of the final rendered object. We propose to measure the distortion introduced by the mapping as the deformation energy E. In the first subsection, we derive a general formula for E. We then propose, in the following subsections, a simplified formula for E, whose minimization can be done in real-time, and which gives very good visual results.

2.1 General formula.

Suppose that the surface on which we want to map textures is defined by a parametric function:

$$\phi : U \longrightarrow \mathcal{E}$$

U being an open set of $\mathbb{R}^2$ and $\mathcal{E}$ Euclidean ordinary 3-space: to each point (u, v) of U, ϕ associates a point $\phi(u, v)$ on the surface; ϕ thus defines a trivial mapping function onto the surface (for example, in [5], the surface is a bicubic patch, and the mapping function is exactly given by the parameterization). It should be noticed that any regular surface can be defined in this way, at least locally.

If the texture is to be mapped onto an elastic surface, one can measure the deformation of the texture through ϕ by computing the elastic deformation of the planar section when one applies ϕ to it. We use the first fundamental form I_ϕ [9, chap 2.5, 4.2] to measure at each point $(u, v) \in U$ the differences of lengths and angles between the initial plane and the tangent plane of the surface. Denoting by $\nabla\phi$ the Jacobian Matrix of ϕ, we let

$$I_\phi(u, v) = \nabla\phi \cdot {}^t\nabla\phi \qquad (1)$$

In particular, I_ϕ is the identity matrix of $\mathbb{R}^2$ if and only if ϕ is an (infinitesimal) isometry, which means that the mapping function does not distort the image. Let Id be the identity matrix of $\mathbb{R}^2$, and $|| \ ||$ be any norm defined on the set of 2×2 matrices. We can take as a measure of deformation energy at a point (u, v) of parameter space the quantity $||I_\phi(u, v) - \mathrm{Id}||^2$, known by mechanical engineers as the Green-Lagrange deformation tensor. The deformation energy E can then be defined over the whole underlying set U since

$$E(U) = \int\!\!\int_U ||I_\phi - \mathrm{Id}||^2 \, du dv = \int\!\!\int_U ||e||^2 \, du dv \qquad (2)$$

This equation can be written as (see Appendix A):

$$E(U) = \int\!\!\int_U (\frac{\partial\phi}{\partial u}^2 - 1)^2 + 2(\frac{\partial\phi}{\partial u} \cdot \frac{\partial\phi}{\partial v})^2 + (\frac{\partial\phi}{\partial v}^2 - 1)^2 du dv \quad (3)$$

If the surface is defined locally by non-overlapping regions, then the total energy is obtained by summing all the energies of each region U_i: $E = \sum_i E(U_i)$.

2.2 Interpretation in the Linear Theory of Elasticity.

We may imagine that our surface is made of rubber, and that we want to deform it in such a way that it can be equated with the texture image. If the material is isotropic, the elastic energy depends only on two parameters λ and μ (see [17, 6]). Writing tr(e) for the trace of matrix e (the sum of its diagonal terms), then:

$$E = \int\!\!\int_U \frac{\lambda}{2} (\mathrm{tr}(e))^2 + \mu \, \mathrm{tr}(e^2) \qquad (4)$$

assuming that $\lambda + \mu > 0$ and $\mu > 0$, which express that E is positive definite. Since only the ratio $\frac{\lambda}{\mu}$ is significant for comparing mapping distortions, we can take $\mu = 1$. The

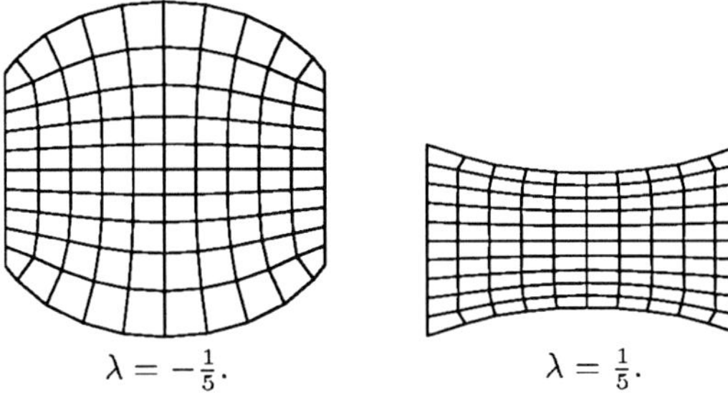

Fig. 1: Two squares of elastic material with different values of λ were stretched in u direction.

coefficient λ characterizes how the material is deformed orthogonally to the direction of a tensile stress. All existing materials have a positive λ, referring the fact that any object shrinks in direction v when one stretches it along u. With $\lambda = 0$ the deformation in u and v are independent. Figure 1 shows the influence of the sign of λ on the shape of a deformed object. Equation 3 correspond to the case $\lambda = 0$, $\mu = 1$. For texture mapping, except in very special cases, the best results are obtained with by setting $\lambda = 0$. It is important to note that two symmetrical surfaces have the same deformation energy. This implies that it is not possible to determine whether the mapping function inverts the image or not. We will show in section 2.4 that this may lead to problems.

2.3 Triangulated surfaces.

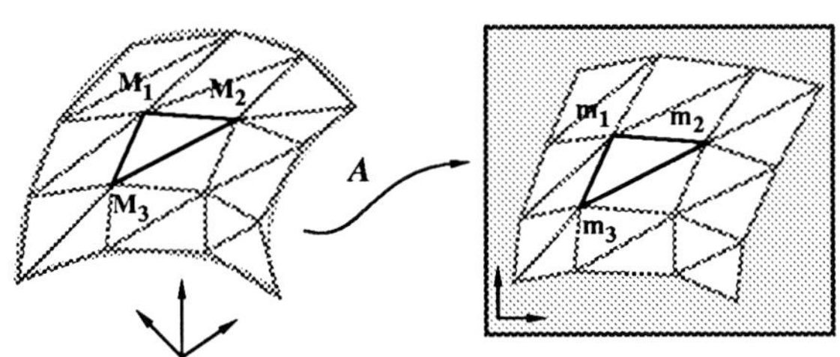

Fig. 2: Locally, the mapping function is an affine application A which associates triangle $M_1M_2M_3$ with triangle $m_1m_2m_3$. It is the inverse function of ϕ.

The deformation of the mapped image can be computed by evaluating the deformation of each triangle. As a result, the parametric function ϕ is affine (see figure 2), and its gradient is the associated linear map. Write M_i and m_i, $i \in \{1, 2, 3\}$, for the vertices in $\mathbb{R}^3$ and their associated positions in texture plane. Then ϕ is defined by nine numbers. If the previous formula is expanded, the total energy can be expressed as the sum of rational fractions of m_i, with numerator of degree 8 and denominator of degree 6. To find the best mapping function, one has to find the coordinates of all m_i's that minimize this energy. The solution can only be computed numerically, using an optimization method. The efficient algorithms need to know the gradient of the energy. Even in the simplest case of triangulated surfaces, the expression is complex and long to process. One can remark that most of the existing finite element programs are built to treat linear elasticity*. They are highly optimized, but cannot be used to solve texture mapping problems. Thus, to be fast enough for interactive applications, the optimization process requires a simplified form of the energy equation that we present below.

In [1] a flattening algorithm is proposed for parametric patches. It is based on a relaxation procedure and runs incrementally. We want to find a global minimum for any type of polyhedral surface, using energy-minimization techniques. The method to be presented here will tackle the problem from a different point of view.

2.4 A simple, distance based energy.

If the surface is triangulated, its first fundamental form is completely characterized by the length of its edges. Furthermore, the lengths measured in $\mathbb{R}^3$ and in the texture plane are all the same if and only if the mapping function is an isometry. This is a consequence of the fact that two triangles are isometric as soon as their three edges have same lengths. Let's introduce the length energy E_l. The simplest form of energy that preserves length is the following:

$$E_l = \sum_{(i,j)\in \text{Edges}} \frac{\left(||m_i - m_j||^2 - ||M_i - M_j||^2\right)^2}{||M_i - M_j||^2} \tag{5}$$

Using the squared norm gives us a simple form for the gradient. E_l represents the energy of a spring net initially lying on the surface, and for which each spring induces a force proportional to the square of the distance (instead of the distance, as for classical springs). This give a higher energy for the most elongated springs than is given by the classical spring response, and thus increases the mean elongation, but lowers the maximum elongation. The final state is not very different from what would be obtained with standard springs, but using this formula we obtain a faster optimization algorithm. Normalization (that is, dividing by the term $||M_i - M_j||^2$) is chosen so that the energy does not change when the surface is subdivided by splitting each triangle into four similar parts. Without such a normalization, an object with very different face sizes would not be processed correctly. This would be the case, for example, if the surface is constructed from hierarchical splines.

Taking the symmetry of formula 5 into account, the part of the energy depending on point i is:

$$E_l = 2 \sum_{m_k \text{ adjacent to } m_i} \frac{\left(||m_i - m_k||^2 - ||M_i - M_k||^2\right)^2}{||M_i - M_k||^2} \tag{6}$$

The energy gradient is a degree three polynomial:

$$\frac{\partial E_l}{\partial x_i} = 8\sum_k \frac{\left(||m_i - m_k||^2 - ||M_i - M_k||^2\right)}{||M_i - M_k||^2}(x_i - x_k)$$

$$\frac{\partial E_l}{\partial y_i} = 8\sum_k \frac{\left(||m_i - m_k||^2 - ||M_i - M_k||^2\right)}{||M_i - M_k||^2}(y_i - y_k)$$

This form of energy is easy to compute and gives good results as long as the surface is simple. But when the surface is difficult to map (when the total curvature is too large), some triangles reverse their orientations. One can notice this effect in figure 3. In figure 3a we show two objects: object 1 on the left and object 2 on the right. Object 2 is just object 1 with a little band added near the equator. In figure 3b we see the results of minimization, orthogonally mapped into texture space: the contraction becomes too high at the center and the best solution to preserve the lengths is to "fold" the map. This is a direct consequence of the fact that the energies of two symmetrical triangles are the same. The same problem occurs with linear springs. If one compresses a spring along its axis, it bends and its projection onto its axis may overlap. This phenomenon is named *buckling* (see [7]) in elasticity. The final result is chaotic, in the sense that compressing two almost identical springs may produce two very different results.

*Although in linear elasticity theory, the displacement of any point is supposed to remain small compared to the object, this is not the case in a rotation, for example. Such an approximation gives very bad results when applied to texture mapping.

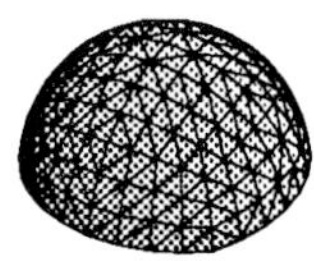
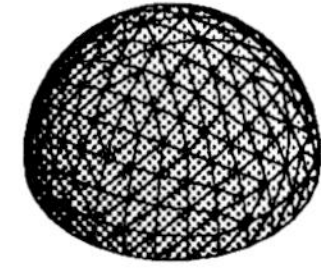

Fig. 3.a: Object 1 and object 2

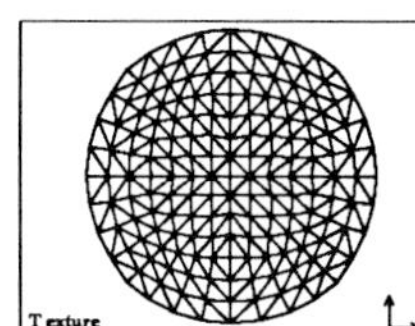

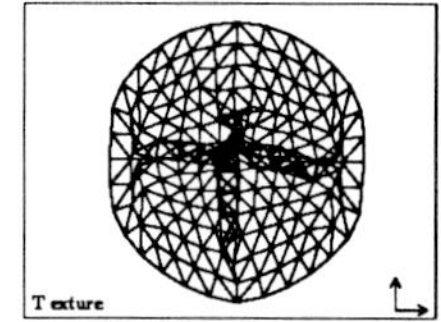

Fig. 3.b: The two maps.

Fig. 3.c: Rendered objects.

Fig. 3: Problems with length based energy.

The two main problems with energy measure E_l are that, firstly, the final state of the map becomes unstable when the object is complex. We can see for example in figure 3 that the symmetry along the X and Y axes is broken in the map. The result may depend strongly on small numerical errors. Secondly, the rendering is poor when some triangles have reversed their orientations. The patterns are multiplied, and grouped by triples, with opposite orientations. Such a final state is not acceptable.

2.5 A surface and length based energy.

To solve the problem of overlapping regions in the texture map, a second term can be added in the energy formula. It is chosen so that wrongly-oriented triangles will have a high energy. Energy E_s is defined using the difference of signed areas for each triangle. It can be computed with cross products in $\mathbb{R}^3$ and determinants in the texture plane. The final energy is a linear combination of E_l and E_s. By default we take the arithmetic mean.

$$E_s = \sum_{M_iM_jM_k \text{triangle}} \frac{\left[\det(\overrightarrow{m_im_j}, \overrightarrow{m_im_k}) - \left\|\overrightarrow{M_iM_j} \wedge \overrightarrow{M_iM_k}\right\|\right]^2}{\left\|\overrightarrow{M_iM_j} \wedge \overrightarrow{M_iM_k}\right\|}$$

For this definition, the surface is implicitly supposed to be orientable, and with all triangles $M_iM_jM_k$ described in a direct sense, according to the normal. Again we normalize E_s. The dimensions of E_l and E_s are identical, which justifies the final form:

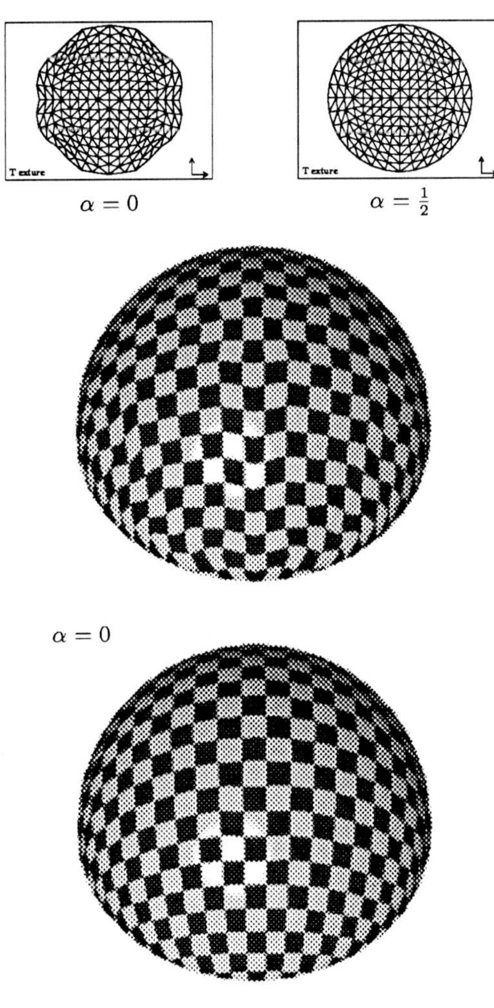

Fig. 4: Object 2 from figure 3 optimized with $E = \alpha E_l + (1 - \alpha)E_s$.

$$E = \alpha E_l + (1 - \alpha)E_s$$

where α is a real coefficient to be taken between 0 and 1.

Gradient ∇E is a degree three polynomial in x_i and y_i which can be quickly computed. Thus, a conjugate gradient method can be used to find the best mapping function [18].

Case $\alpha = 1$ correspond to E_l and is not satisfactory. Figure 4 shows that $\alpha = 0$ is not good either. The problem is that there are an infinite number of triangles with the same surface. In particular, when a vertex is translated in a parallel direction with the opposite edge, the surface does not change. This explains why triangles appear so stretched close to the border of the object. However, we have measured the surface differences surface, and our experience is that the differences between planar and 3-D triangles was less than 0.1%. A good result is obtained in figure 4 by combining both terms of the energy. Depending on the geometry, the optimal visual effect is obtained by tuning α between 0 and 1. In many cases, $\alpha = \frac{1}{2}$ is satisfactory.

There are still some objects for which optimization with any value of α would give bad results. In these cases, the problem results from the fact that the object is too complicated to be mapped with a single image. The solution is then to use atlases, as we will show in the next section.

3 Use of atlases.

As we have noticed in the previous section, a global continuous mapping function may excessively distort the image of a complex or a highly curved object. The natural way to solve this problem is to split the object into several independent regions. The practice has been to do so implicitly using the construction of the object. For example in [16], a textured teapot is split into three parts whose shape comes from the patch description. To be as general as possible, we disconnect the texturing regions from the 3-D representation of the surface: the user may want to represent a surface mapped only partially (for example, an object with a logo stuck on), with different textures, such as a patchwork, or with local discontinuities (as on some clothes). Thus we introduce a data structure called an "atlas" which is derived from the notion of atlas used in differential geometry [14, 21]. In our case, an *atlas* is composed of a set of *charts* $\{\phi_1, ..., \phi_n\}$, where each ϕ_i is an application from a subset U_i of the surface to the Euclidean plane, such that:

- $\{U_1, ..., U_n\}$ is a cover of the surface,
- each ϕ_i is continuous inside the faces, and discontinuities are allowed along edges
- for $i \neq j$, ϕ_i and ϕ_j do not overlap except on the edges.

Each chart is associated to its own image. The words *atlas* and *chart* have here slightly different meanings than the ones mathematicians give them, due to differences in the regularity and boundary conditions, but the main idea of atlases is kept: the covering of a surface.

Good atlases are closely linked to the geometry of the object and can be difficult to build. Hence in the first subsection we present an algorithm to automatically build an atlas from scratch. Then we describe in the second subsection an interactive tool which makes easy the manipulation of atlases and of texture mappings for a given polyhedral surface.

3.1 A creation tool.

To automatically define an atlas, it seems natural to use the curvature information: a surface is developable (isometric to a plane) if and only if the curvature matrix has a zero determinant [9, pp. 194-197]. In fact, a first rough subdivision of the surface in buckets is made using only the normal vectors of the surface and then the curvature information is used to control the merging of adjacent buckets and obtain the atlas. Then the regions are flattened on the texture plane (a more detailed description of the whole process can be found in [15]). The curvature information is essential in our computation. Let us describe first how we proceed to get this information.

3.1.1 Computing the curvature.

There exist precise but costly algorithms to compute the curvature of a polyhedral surface [19]. Since interactive visual feedback is one of our main goals, we designed a very fast algorithm, whose results are accurate enough for our needs. Let u be a tangent vector to the surface and $\underline{\mathsf{N}}$ the Gauss map [21] which associates to each point of the surface the unit normal vector at that point. The unit normal vector is represented as a point on the unit sphere $\mathcal{S}^2$. Curvature in direction u is defined by the formula [9, pp. 135-151]:

$$C(u) = u \cdot \mathrm{d}\underline{\mathsf{N}}(u) \qquad (7)$$

We use finite differences to approximate derivatives. Normals must be evaluated at three close, non-aligned locations to evaluate the three coefficients of the curvature matrix*. We use smoothed normals coming from the rendering procedure. We put normal N at the center of gravity of the face, G. We get the point G, normal N, and a set of vertices S_i associated to normals N_i. With this data we seek to evaluate $\mathrm{d}\underline{\mathsf{N}}$: we must find a symmetrical linear map $\mathcal{L}$ in the tangent plane $\mathcal{P} = (G, \{N\}^{\perp})$ such that, for all i, $\mathcal{L}(\overrightarrow{GS_i})$ draws nearer to $N_i - N$. Formula 7 shows that the matrix of the linear map $\mathcal{L}$ is also a curvature matrix. To eliminate the case of non-planar facets, all differences $N_i - N$ are projected in plane $\mathcal{P}$. Coefficients of curvature are then computed using a least-squares method. The reader is referred to Appendix B for the details.

3.1.2 Subdividing the surface.

The Gauss map defines for each surface a partition of $\mathcal{S}^2$ into areas of various densities. To efficiently define an atlas of connected regions related to curvature information, we introduce the buckets induced by a homogeneous cover $\mathcal{C}$ of $\mathcal{S}^2$ as shown in figure 5: the *buckets* are the maximal connected regions of the surface, composed of faces which normal vectors belong to the same element of $\mathcal{C}$.

A connectivity graph $\mathcal{G}_B$ is built from the sets of buckets, adding an edge between two buckets when they have a common boundary (see figure 6).

3.1.3 Merging of buckets.

To keep control of the distortion when merging two adjacent regions of the subdivision, we define a notion of similarity on the set of buckets. To each bucket β we compute

*Three coefficients because the curvature matrix is symmetric.

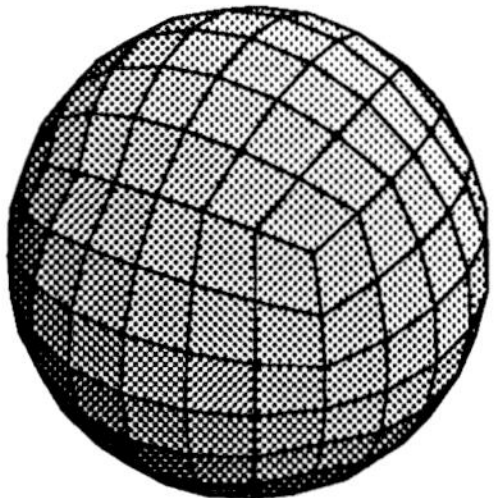

Squaring of the unit cube. Its projection on $\mathcal{S}^2$.

Fig. 5: Uniform cover of the sphere $\mathcal{S}^2$.

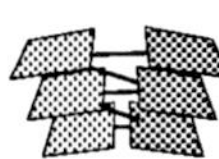

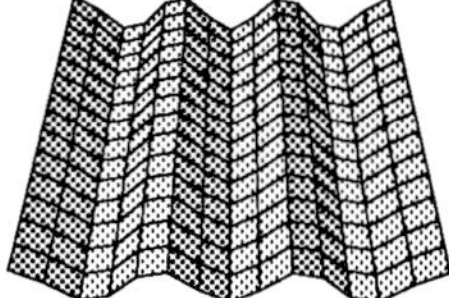

Fig. 6: The battered surface is represented by the buckets whose connectivity graph is on the right of the figure. One can see how this surface is simplified: only 6 average directions are kept from the initial surface.

the following information which will be used in defining the similarity:

- N_β: average of normal to faces in bucket β.
- Δ_β: average of directions of maximal curvature.

Besides these geometric attributes, we use the connectivity graph $\mathcal{G}_\beta$ defined in the last subsection. Between two neighboring buckets β_1 and β_2 we introduce the similarity $\mathrm{d}(\beta_1, \beta_2)$:

$$\delta N = \frac{N_{\beta_1} - N_{\beta_2}}{||N_{\beta_1} - N_{\beta_2}||}$$

$$\mathrm{d}(\beta_1, \beta_2) = (1 - |\delta N \cdot \Delta_{\beta_1}|)^2 + (1 - |\delta N \cdot \Delta_{\beta_2}|)^2$$

An ultrametric (see [10]) on the set of regions is then defined by:

$$\mathrm{d}(\mathcal{R}_1, \mathcal{R}_2) = \min_{\beta_1 \in \mathcal{R}_1, \beta_2 \in \mathcal{R}_2} \mathrm{d}(\beta_1, \beta_2)$$

Given a threshold value d, we build a segmentation of the object by merging all region whose distances are below d. The edges of the connectivity graph are sorted with respect to their corresponding similarity values in a preprocessing phase in which we sort the edges of graph $\mathcal{G}_\beta$ according to d. The selection of the n first edges on the connectivity graph will trigger n successive unions of the adjacent regions associated with the edges. The user can then choose the number of charts in the atlas by selecting a number corresponding to the number of edges in $\mathcal{G}_\beta$.

3.1.4 Flattening the regions.

Once the segmentation is computed, the last step is to flatten the regions in order to define the charts. We use a region growing algorithm in which new faces are added in such a way that the surface's geometry is not distorted too much and so that the final energy of flattened pieces not too high. We first pick up one face of each region, orthogonally flatten it with respect to its normal, and then depth-first traverse the faces graph from the initial facet. For each new vertex M_i adjacent to two already fixed points, the location m_i of M_i in texture space is computed taking the average of the $A_{jk}(M_i)$ over all the triangles $M_iM_jM_k$ such that

1. M_j and M_k have the corresponding points m_j and m_k in texture plane and

2. $A_{jk}(M_i)$ is such that the following two triangles are similar:

- the triangle defined by the projection of M_i M_j and M_k orthogonally w.r.t. the face M_i M_j M_k and
- the triangle $(A_{jk}(M_i), m_j, m_k)$.

This atlas creation algorithm is useful if the surface is complex, but it may not be entirely satisfying. For this reason we provide the set of interactive functions to manipulate atlases described below.

3.2 An interactive tool.

As emphasized in [12], interactivity is important when texturing 3D shapes.

3.2.1 Drawing an atlas.

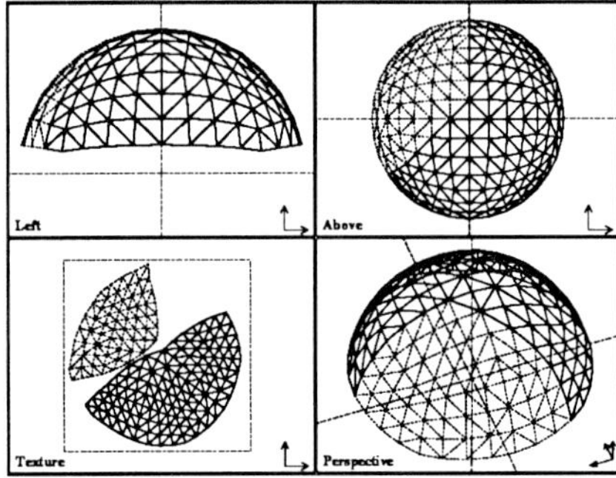

Fig. 7: Sphere portion associated with a two-charts atlas.

To visualize an atlas on the screen, we use two displays, one showing a wire frame projection of the polyhedral surface and the other showing the chart represented by the same network of polygons after the mapping transformation (see Figure 7). The chart is put in a special *Texture* view. The current chart and the selected points are highlighted in all the views.

3.2.2 Data structures.

To compute the texture mapping inside a face, the positions in the texture plane of all of its vertices are needed. Then, the rendering is computed using an algorithm similar to color calculation for Gouraud shading [11, 20]. Since local discontinuities are allowed along edges, a vertex may have as many 2-D positions as there are faces adjacent to it. Thus, an atlas depends on the location in the texture plane of the *angles* (v_i, f_j) where v_i is a vertex belonging to face f_j (see Figure 8.a). To avoid redundancies, angles are regrouped in *sectors*: sets of connected angles for which the mapping function is continuous (see Figure 8.b). The mapping function is then defined by a position in the texture plane for each sector. All sectors belonging to the same vertex are stored in a linked list. Pointers to the list heads are stored in an array associated with the 3-D vertices of the surface. Access to a sector and data structure modifications can be computed in almost constant time.

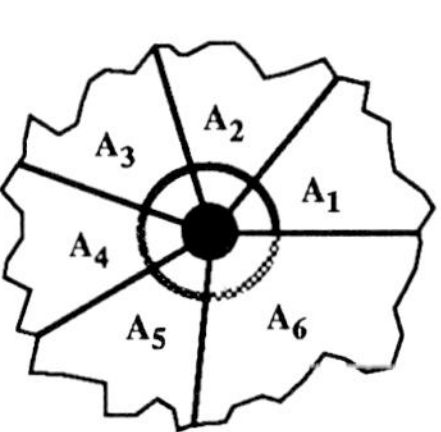

Fig. 8.a: A vertex on the 3-D polyhedron.

Fig. 8.b: The charts, involving three *sectors*.

Fig. 8: Case of a vertex corresponding to three *sectors* and six *angles*.

3.2.3 Interactive functions.

To modify an existing atlas, the user is provided with several types of interactive functions which operate in the texture plane.

Positioning functions let the user adjust the scale, stretch, angle and position of the whole atlas or of each chart using linear transformations. Finer-grained operations are obtained by selecting only a group of sectors. A function to align a set of sectors in the x or y direction is also provided. This simple function is very useful when one wants the edges of the charts to exactly match the border of a texture.

The constraint function marks sectors for the optimization procedure. Sectors can be fixed in x, y, or along both axes. With this function, one can adjust sectors in the mapped image so that a specific pattern lies precisely on a given place of the surface, and let all the rest of the texture be optimized.

The cut function defines discontinuities in the charts. Cuts can be seen as the snips of a tailor's scissors inside the piece of material that may stretch or shrink during the optimization procedure. The user gives a path along the edges which must not self-intersect. The chart is then possibly separated into several charts, or may be only internally cut.

The merge function reconnects charts along a given path. Faces connected do not necessarily belong to different charts. The user can either select the connection path, or pick two charts and let the program find the common edges and the best displacement to attach the first chart to the second.

The optimization function improves the charts, taking

into account the user specified constraints. Parameter α of the energy can be adjusted for special cases.

Note the difference between the constraint and the merge function: using the constraint function, one may fix sectors together corresponding to the adjacent path of two charts, producing the same visual result in a texture space as a merge between these two charts. But a call to the optimization function will lead to different results:

• when the charts have been merged, the optimization is performed on the resulting charts and globally reduces the distortion. The sectors belonging to the common path may have moved during this process.

• on the other hand, when the sectors of the common path have been fixed together, two optimization processes are performed independently, one for each chart, keeping the fixed sector in the same position in the texture space.

4 Applications in the field of animation.

The tool we have described has been built principally for static objects. Nevertheless, it appears that special effects in animation could be obtained very easily.

One example consists in moving and distorting some charts of the object. The result is a sliding texture onto a fixed shape. For example, one can draw a scrolling text onto any shape by simply translating down the chart of the object.

Another example involves interpolated objects. In this case, it is generally difficult to obtain a deformation that mimics an elastic deformation. Optimizing the mapping function with the criterion described previously can replace the 3-d elasticity system by a 2-d optimization which is simpler and faster. To obtain a realistic deformation of a textured object, one has to optimize the chart of the undeformed object, then apply any geometric transformation to it, and optimize again constraining the edge points not to move. This constraint corresponds to the fact that the piece of texture used for the object does not change with time. We made a short test animation in which the deformation was obtained by interpolating between key-objects, and it appeared that the mapping function could also be interpolated, thus requiring only a few optimizations, one for each key.

5 Remarks on Figures.

Let us add some comments on the figures appearing at the end of the paper:

• Figure 9 shows the different effects obtained using cylindrical and spherical projections of a checkerboard as a texture mapping onto the Utah teapot. We also display the same teapot textured with our tool, thus demonstrating automatic creation of an atlas and the use of interactive functions. Here the atlas is composed of four charts: the spout, the handle, the cap and the body of the teapot. The common boundaries of the cap and the body of the teapot are fixed in the texture plane to ensure visual continuity between the two charts. We see in this figure that the distortion is very low.

• The last two pictures illustrate the capabilities of atlases. Each shows geometrical objects whose atlases have been split into several charts (4 charts per object).

6 Conclusion.

We have presented a method for measuring the deformation energy of the mapping of an image onto a surface. The measure proposed here is an approximation of the integral of the Green-Lagrange deformation tensor. It can be minimized in real time and gives accurate results.

We have also addressed the problem of segmenting a 3D object in regions on which the mapping is not too distorted. We solved the problem by introducing the concept of an atlas together with interactive functions to edit and manipulate atlases and data structures which are efficient for these operations. We described a method which for any object automatically generates atlases, and we showed how to efficiently merge charts on an existing atlas. Efficient merging uses segmentation techniques based on curvature and ultrametrics. Specific data structures are proposed to handle atlases efficiently.

Acknowledgements: We wish to thank Alain Chesnais for revising an early version of this paper, Lars W. Ericson for carefully proof-reading the manuscript, Francis Lazarus, Arghyro Paouri, Marie-Luce Viaud and Jean-Luc De Antoni for their help during modeling, and the audiovisual department of INRIA for the photos and videos.

References

[1] **C. Bennis, J.M. Vezien, G. Iglesias,** *Piecewise flattening for non-distorted texture mapping.* SIGGRAPH 91, Proc. of Computer Graphics, 25(4):237-246. July 1991.

[2] **E.Bier, K.Sloan,** *Two-part texture mapping.* IEEE Computer Graphics and applications, 40-53. September 1986.

[3] **J. F. Blinn and M. E. Newell,** *Texture and Reflection in Computer Generated Images.* Communications of the ACM, 19(10):542-547. October 1976.

[4] **J. Bloomenthal,** *Modeling the mighty maple.* SIGGRAPH 85, Proc. of Computer Graphics, 19(3):305-311. July 1985.

[5] **E. Catmull,** *A subdivision algorithm for computer display of curved surfaces.* Phd dissertation, University of Utah. December 1974.

[6] **P. Ciarlet,** *Mathematical Elasticity, Vol. I, 3-Dimensionnal Elasticity.* North Holland, 1988

[7] **R. M. Christensen,** *Mechanics of Composite Materials.* McGraw-Hill, 1967

[8] **F. Crow,** *Summed-area tables for texture mapping.* SIGGRAPH 84, Proc. of Computer Graphics, 18(3):207-212. July 1984.

[9] **M.P. Do Carmo,** *Differential Geometry of curves and surfaces.* Prentice-Hall, Inc. 1976.

[10] **E. Diday, J.C. Simon,** *Clustering Analysis.* Communication and Cybernetics, 10, Digital pattern recognition, 47-94. 1976.

[11] **J.D. Foley, A. van Dam, S.K. Feiner and J.F. Hughes,** *Computer Graphics, Principles and Practice, 2nd edition.* Addison-Wesley, 1990

[12] **P. Hanrahan, P. Haeberly,** *Direct WYSIWYG painting and texturing on 3D shapes.* SIGGRAPH 90, Proc. of Computer Graphics, 24(4):215-223. August 1990.

[13] **P. S. Heckbert,** *Survey of Texture Mapping.* IEEE Computer Graphics and Applications 6(11):56-67. November 1986.

[14] **M. Hirsch,** *Differential topology.* Graduate texts in mathematics 33, Springer-Verlag. 1976.

[15] **J. Maillot,** *Trois approches du plaquage de texture sur un objet tridimensionnel.* Thèse de doctorat en sciences, Université de Paris-Sud, Centre d'Orsay, may 1992.

[16] **S.D. Ma, H. Lin,** *Optimal texture mapping.* EUROGRAPHICS 88, 421-428. September 1988.

[17] **J. E. Marsden, T. J. R. Hughes,** *Mathematical Fundations of Elasticity.* Prentice Hall, 1983

[18] **W. H. Press, B. P. Flannery, S. A. Teukolsky and W. T. Vetterling,** *Numerical Recipes.* Cambridge University Press, Cambridge, 1986

[19] **P. Sander, S. Zucker,** *Inferring surface trace and differential structure from 3-D images.* Rapport de recherche No 1117, INRIA. 1989.

[20] *Graphic library, programming guide.* Silicon Graphics manual, IRIS 4D VGX series.

[21] **M. Spivak,** *A comprehensive introduction to differential geometry, Vol I.* Publish or perish, Inc., Berkeley. 1979.

A Derivation of equation 5.

All norms on the vector space of 2 × 2 matrices being equivalent, we take the Euclidean norm. It is basis independent because an easy calculation shows that $||M|| = \mathrm{tr}(M\,^tM)^{\frac{1}{2}}$, tr being the trace i.e. the sum of diagonal coefficients. Now

$$E = \iint_U \left|\left| \begin{pmatrix} \frac{\partial\phi}{\partial u}^2 - 1 & \frac{\partial\phi}{\partial u}\cdot\frac{\partial\phi}{\partial v} \\ \frac{\partial\phi}{\partial u}\cdot\frac{\partial\phi}{\partial v} & \frac{\partial\phi}{\partial v}^2 - 1 \end{pmatrix} \right|\right|^2 \mathrm{d}u\mathrm{d}v$$

$$= \iint_U \mathrm{tr}((I_\phi - \mathrm{Id})\,^t(I_\phi - \mathrm{Id}))\mathrm{d}u\mathrm{d}v$$

$$= \iint_U (\frac{\partial\phi}{\partial u}^2 - 1)^2 + 2(\frac{\partial\phi}{\partial u}\cdot\frac{\partial\phi}{\partial v})^2 + (\frac{\partial\phi}{\partial v}^2 - 1)^2\mathrm{d}u\mathrm{d}v$$

B Computation of the curvature matrix.

Let n_i and s_i be the projected normals and vertices on $\mathcal{P}$, written in the same basis, G being the origin. By the definition of $\mathcal{P}$, the projection of N is the zero-vector. In a basis of the tangent plane, the curvature matrix is written as $C = \begin{pmatrix} a & b \\ b & c \end{pmatrix}$. We have to minimize:

$$A = \sum_i ||Cs_i - n_i||^2$$

We set $\sigma_x = \sum s_i^{x\,2}$, $\sigma_y = \sum s_i^{y\,2}$, $\sigma_{xy} = \sum s_i^x s_i^y$, and we get:

$$d = (\sigma_x + \sigma_y)\left(-\sigma_{xy}^2 + \sigma_x\sigma_y\right)$$

$$\begin{pmatrix} a \\ b \\ c \end{pmatrix} = \frac{1}{d} M_1 \cdot M_2$$

with

$$M_1 = \begin{pmatrix} -\sigma_{xy}^2 + \sigma_x\sigma_y + \sigma_y^2 & -\sigma_{xy}\sigma_y & \sigma_{xy}^2 \\ -\sigma_{xy}\sigma_y & \sigma_x\sigma_y & -\sigma_x\sigma_{xy} \\ \sigma_{xy}^2 & -\sigma_x\sigma_{xy} & \sigma_x^2 - \sigma_{xy}^2 + \sigma_x\sigma_y \end{pmatrix}$$

$$\text{and } M_2 = \begin{pmatrix} \sum s_i^x n_i^x \\ \sum s_i^x n_i^y + s_i^y n_i^x \\ \sum s_i^y n_i^y \end{pmatrix}$$

Eigenvectors v and eigenvalues α are given by:

$$v_\pm = \begin{pmatrix} 2b \\ c - a + \Delta \end{pmatrix}, \quad \alpha_\pm = \frac{1}{2}(\mathrm{tr}(C) + \Delta)$$

$$\text{with:} \quad \Delta = \pm\sqrt{\mathrm{tr}(C)^2 - 4\det(C)}$$

Fig. 9: Classical projections and optimized atlas.

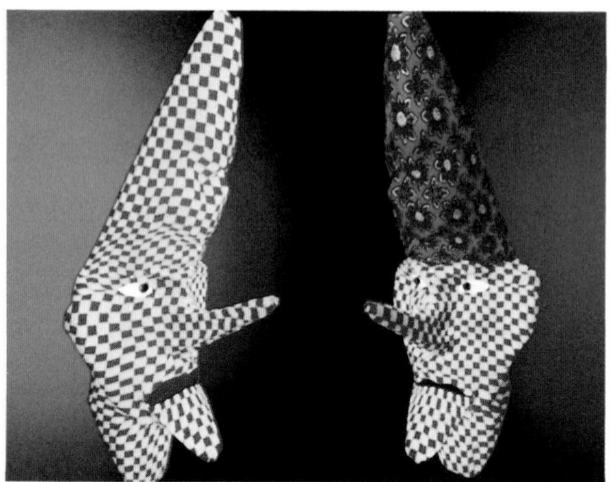

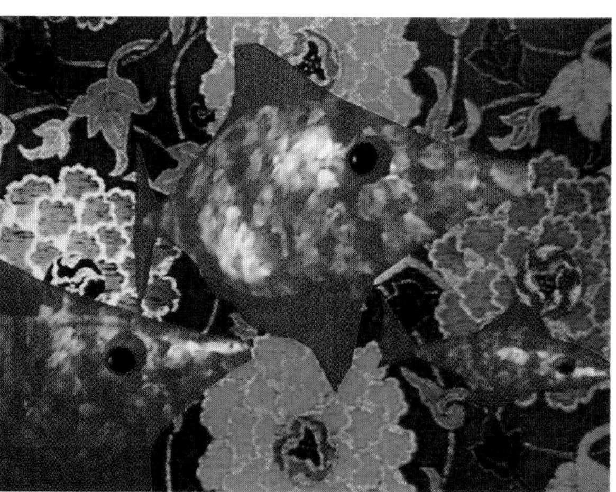

Efficient, Fair Interpolation using Catmull-Clark Surfaces

Mark Halstead* Michael Kass Tony DeRose†
Apple Computer, Inc.

Abstract

We describe an efficient method for constructing a smooth surface that interpolates the vertices of a mesh of arbitrary topological type. Normal vectors can also be interpolated at an arbitrary subset of the vertices. The method improves on existing interpolation techniques in that it is fast, robust and general.

Our approach is to compute a control mesh whose Catmull-Clark subdivision surface interpolates the given data and minimizes a smoothness or "fairness" measure of the surface. Following Celniker and Gossard, the norm we use is based on a linear combination of thin-plate and membrane energies. Even though Catmull-Clark surfaces do not possess closed-form parametrizations, we show that the relevant properties of the surfaces can be computed efficiently and without approximation. In particular, we show that (1) simple, exact interpolation conditions can be derived, and (2) the fairness norm and its derivatives can be computed exactly, without resort to numerical integration.

CR Categories and Subject Descriptors: I.3.5 [Computer Graphics]: Computational Geometry and Object Modeling - curve, surface, solid, and object representations; J.6 [Computer-Aided Engineering]: Computer-Aided Design (CAD); G.1.2 [Approximation]: Spline Approximation.

Additional Key Words and Phrases: Computer-aided geometric design, B-spline surfaces, subdivision surfaces, thin-plate splines.

1 Introduction

The construction of smooth interpolating surfaces is becoming increasingly important in a number of applications including statistical data modeling, interactive design, and scientific visualization. Typical input to an interpolating method is a collection of points to be interpolated, and a "mesh" that describes the connectivity of the points. Normal vectors are sometimes also specified at some or all of the data points.

If the shape to be modeled is a deformed plane, techniques from function approximation, such as Clough-Tocher interpolation [5], can be used. An advantage of the Clough-Tocher interpolant is that the construction is local, meaning that modification of a data point affects only a local portion of the surface. However, a drawback of Clough-Tocher interpolation is that there are typically remaining degrees of freedom not directly constrained by the data. These extra degrees of freedom are often set using local heuristics and typically result in surfaces that are not "fair", that is, surfaces having extraneous bumps and wiggles. Another serious drawback to Clough-Tocher interpolation, and indeed to any method that requires continuity of parametric derivatives (so-called parametric continuity), is the inability to model surfaces of arbitrary topological type (cf. Herron [8]). It is not possible, for instance, to model a sphere or a deformed sphere using a Clough-Tocher interpolant.

Celniker and Gossard [3] recently presented an interpolation method that extends Clough-Tocher interpolation by setting the remaining degrees of freedom so as to minimize a fairness norm. The fairness norm they use is quadratic, so it can be minimized by solving a (sparse) linear system. As a result, their method is fast enough for interactive design. However, being based on Clough-Tocher interpolants, their technique is not capable of describing surfaces of arbitrary genus.

A number of interpolation methods appropriate for surfaces of arbitrary genus have been developed in recent years. A survey of these can be found in Lounsbery et al. [10]. The method developed by Shirman and Séquin [14] is a generalization of Clough-Tocher interpolation to surfaces of arbitrary topology. The generalization is achieved by replacing parametric continuity with first order geometric continuity (continuity of tangent planes). Like Clough-Tocher interpolation, Shirman-Séquin interpolants have degrees of freedom not directly constrained by the data, and local heuristics for setting these degrees of freedom have fallen well short of producing fair surfaces (see Figure 4).

Last year Moreton and Séquin [11] presented a method capable of producing fair interpolating surfaces of arbitrary genus. They achieved this in much the same way as Celniker and Gossard by solving a minimization problem using finite elements. However, rather than using Clough-Tocher elements and a quadratic fairness norm, Moreton and Séquin used biquintic Bézier patches and a fairness norm based on

*Work done while a summer intern from the University of California, Berkeley.

†Work done while on sabbatical leave from the University of Washington.

intrinsic measures of curvature variation. The surfaces produced are the most impressive to date, but improved shape and arbitrary genus are obtained at the expense of dramatically increased running time. It appears that Moreton and Séquin's method is far too expensive for use in an interactive environment today (computation time is on the order of hours). Another shortcoming of their method is that it constructs surfaces that are only approximately tangent plane smooth since inter-patch continuity is modeled using a penalty function added to the fairness norm. Finally, their surfaces are only curvature continuous within each biquintic patch.

Here we present a scheme that combines the speed of Celniker and Gossard's method with the ability to model tangent plane continuous surfaces of arbitrary genus. We do this by using a quadratic fairness norm similar to the one used by Celniker and Gossard together with Catmull-Clark subdivision surfaces. We show that Catmull-Clark surfaces offer a number of advantages over previous methods based on piecewise polynomial elements; these include:

- They are curvature continuous everywhere except at a finite number of isolated "extraordinary" points.
- The high order of continuity is obtained with very few control points, meaning that the dimension of the space over which the optimizer must search is far lower for Catmull-Clark surfaces than for the method described by Moreton and Séquin.
- They reduce to traditional bicubic B-splines when the points to be interpolated form a regular rectangular grid. It should therefore be possible to more smoothly incorporate them into existing geometric modeling systems.

The use of Catmull-Clark surfaces presents some challenges, however. First, Catmull-Clark surfaces do not generally interpolate their control points, so to achieve interpolation, a system of interpolation constraints must be solved. The constraints relate the data points and normals to be interpolated with points and normals on the final surface. Formulating the interpolation constraints at first appears problematic for a Catmull-Clark surface because the surface is defined as the limit of an infinite number of subdivisions. We show that it is possible to derive *closed form* expressions for these constraints. A second challenge posed by Catmull-Clark surfaces is that efficient surface optimization depends on fast and reliable evaluation of the fairness norm and its derivatives. We show that it is possible to evaluate the fairness integral and its derivatives *exactly*, without resort to numerical integration, even though Catmull-Clark surfaces do not possess a closed form polynomial representation.

Figure 5 illustrates the basic idea of our approach. The original mesh is shown in the upper left. Subdividing it using Catmull-Clark subdivision results in the surface shown in the lower left. The surface approximates, but does not interpolate the vertices of the original mesh. By solving the system of interpolation constraints, we obtain a new mesh which is shown in the upper center. Subdividing the new mesh results in the surface in the lower center which does interpolate the vertices of the original mesh. Unfortunately, the direct application of the interpolation conditions to the mesh causes undesirable undulations in the surface. To combat this difficulty, we subdivide the mesh to add new degrees of freedom, and we set these new degrees of freedom to minimize a fairness measure subject to the interpolation constraints. The resulting mesh is shown in the upper right of

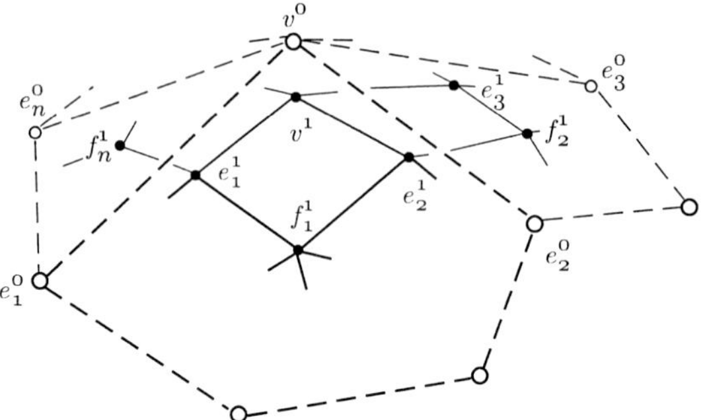

Figure 1: The situation around a vertex v^0 of order n.

Figure 5 and the corresponding subdivision surface is shown in the lower right. Note that minimizing the fairness measure removes the spurious undulations introduced by the direct application of the interpolation constraints.

The remainder of the paper is structured as follows. In Section 2 we provide some necessary background on subdivision surfaces in general, paying particular attention to Catmull-Clark surfaces. In Section 3, we derive the linear constraints on a Catmull-Clark mesh which guarantee that the surface interpolates given points and normals. We also show that applying these constraints directly to a mesh results in a surface which solves the interpolation conditions, but is unsatisfactory because of spurious wiggles. Then, in Section 4, we show how to reduce these artifacts by adding additional degrees of freedom through subdivision, and then setting them by optimizing a fairness norm based on the membrane/plate energy. Several implementation details along with performance statistics are provided in Section 5. In Section 6 we present a number of examples, and provide some comparisons to previous methods. Finally, in Section 7 we summarize our findings and describe several avenues of future research.

2 Subdivision Surfaces

In 1974 Chaikin [4] introduced the idea of generating a curve from a polygon by successively refining the polygon with the addition of new vertices and edges. In 1978, Catmull and Clark [2] and Doo and Sabin [6] generalized the idea to surfaces. In these schemes, an initial control mesh is refined by adding new vertices, faces and edges at each subdivision step. In the limit as the number of subdivision steps goes to infinity, the control mesh converges to a surface. With careful choice of the rules by which new vertices, edges and faces are introduced, it is possible to show that the limiting surface exists, is continuous, and possesses a continuous tangent plane. The Doo-Sabin subdivision rules generalize the subdivision rules for biquadratic B-splines, and the Catmull-Clark subdivision generalizes bicubic B-splines. An example of a Catmull-Clark surface of genus 3 is shown in Figure 3. A more recent method developed by Loop [9] generalizes quartic triangular B-splines. We focus on the Catmull-Clark scheme primarily because of the popularity of bicubic patches, however, much of the analysis we present is applicable to a wide class of subdivision schemes including those of Doo-Sabin and Loop.

When dealing with spline surfaces it is often helpful to maintain the distinction between global and local control meshes. By a local control mesh, we mean a subset of the global mesh that influences a local region of the surface. Toward this end we use carets to denote global quantities.

Let $\widehat{M}^0$ denote the initial mesh, and let $\widehat{M}^i$ denote the mesh produced after i applications of the Catmull-Clark subdivision step. To describe the $i+1$-st subdivision step, consider the neighborhood of a vertex v^i of $\widehat{M}^i$ surrounded by n edge points $e_1^i, ..., e_n^i$ and n faces, as shown in Figure 1 for $i = 0$. Such a vertex is said to be of order n. As indicated in Figure 1, a new face point $f_1^{i+1}, ..., f_n^{i+1}$ is placed at the centroid of each face of $\widehat{M}^i$. Each new edge point $e_1^{i+1}, ..., e_n^{i+1}$ is then computed by taking an average of surrounding points. Specifically,

$$e_j^{i+1} = \frac{v^i + e_j^i + f_{j-1}^{i+1} + f_j^{i+1}}{4},$$

where subscripts are to be taken modulo n. Finally, a new vertex point v^{i+1} is computed as

$$v^{i+1} = \frac{n-2}{n} v^i + \frac{1}{n^2} \sum_j e_j^i + \frac{1}{n^2} \sum_j f_j^{i+1}.$$

The Catmull-Clark subdivision process is such that:

- The surfaces can be of arbitrary genus since the subdivision rules can be carried out on a mesh of arbitrary topological type.
- After the first subdivision step all faces are quadrilaterals.
- Except at extraordinary vertices (vertices of order $n \neq 4$) the limiting surface can be shown to converge to a bicubic B-spline. The surface is therefore curvature continuous except at extraordinary vertices.
- The number of extraordinary vertices is fixed, and is equal to the number of extraordinary vertices in $\widehat{M}^1$, the mesh produced after the first subdivision step.
- Near an extraordinary vertex the surface does not possess a closed form parametrization; it consists of an infinite number of bicubic patches that converge to a limit point. The surface can be shown to have a well defined tangent plane at the limit point, but the curvature there is generally not well defined [1].

3 Interpolation using Subdivision Surfaces

Given a mesh $\widehat{I}$ of arbitrary topological type, the idea is to generate a control mesh $\widehat{M}^0$ such that the subdivision surface it defines interpolates some or all of the vertices of $\widehat{I}$. It is also possible to constrain the surface to have a specified normal at each interpolation point.

Nasri [12] generates interpolating surfaces using the biquadratic formulation of Doo and Sabin [6]. Like biquadratic B-splines, Doo-Sabin surfaces interpolate the centroid of each face in the control mesh. Thus a linear constraint on the control vertices can be generated for each interpolation point and the resultant system solved for the desired control mesh[1]. It appears that Nasri had no simple formulation for the surface normal at the centroid, and so was unable to specify normals at these points.

[1]Although Nasri does not mention it, it is possible for the coefficient matrix in the linear system to be singular.

To generate interpolating surfaces for other subdivision schemes we need a method of determining the position and normal at a set of points on the limit surface. Because the surface is the result of repeated application of a subdivision step, we can analyze the behavior of a small neighborhood of points as they converge to the limit surface in order to determine the surface properties at the point of convergence.

3.1 Interpolation Conditions

After one subdivision step there arises an arrangement of vertices that persists (i.e. the same topology will be observable) for any number of subsequent subdivisions. To analyze the limiting behavior of the surface near a vertex it is therefore convenient to introduce a matrix that describes the subdivision process locally, that is, in the neighborhood of the vertex [6]. It is not necessary to compute local subdivision matrices in practice; they are simply tools used to derive formulas describing the limiting behavior of the surface.

Let v^i be a vertex of order n of the mesh $\widehat{M}^i$, let $V_n^i = (v^i, e_1^i, ..., e_n^i, f_1^i, ..., f_n^i)^T$ be the column vector of vertices in the neighborhood of v^i, and let V_n^{i+1} be the corresponding column vector of points in the neighborhood after subdivision. Since the points in V_n^{i+1} are computed by linear combinations of the points in V_n^i, we can use a square matrix $\mathbf{S}_n$ to express the subdivision:

$$V_n^{i+1} = \mathbf{S}_n V_n^i.$$

For instance, for Catmull-Clark surfaces the matrix $\mathbf{S}_4$ is

$$\mathbf{S}_4 = \frac{1}{16} * \begin{pmatrix} 9 & \frac{3}{2} & \frac{3}{2} & \frac{3}{2} & \frac{3}{2} & \frac{1}{4} & \frac{1}{4} & \frac{1}{4} & \frac{1}{4} \\ 6 & 6 & 1 & 0 & 1 & 1 & 0 & 0 & 1 \\ 6 & 1 & 6 & 1 & 0 & 1 & 1 & 0 & 0 \\ 6 & 0 & 1 & 6 & 1 & 0 & 1 & 1 & 0 \\ 6 & 1 & 0 & 1 & 6 & 0 & 0 & 1 & 1 \\ 4 & 4 & 4 & 0 & 0 & 4 & 0 & 0 & 0 \\ 4 & 0 & 4 & 4 & 0 & 0 & 4 & 0 & 0 \\ 4 & 0 & 0 & 4 & 4 & 0 & 0 & 4 & 0 \\ 4 & 4 & 0 & 0 & 4 & 0 & 0 & 0 & 4 \end{pmatrix}.$$

Repeated subdivision is expressed by repeated multiplication and hence powers of $\mathbf{S}_n$, so

$$V_n^{i+1} = \mathbf{S}_n^i V_n^1.$$

The properties of the limit surface will be governed by the properties of V_n^{i+1} as i approaches infinity. Since V_n^{i+1} is the image of V_n^1 under $\mathbf{S}_n^i$, the eigenstructure of $\mathbf{S}_n$ naturally plays a key role.

In Appendix A we analyze the behavior of the limit surface in terms of the matrix $\mathbf{S}_n$ by building on the analytical techniques of Doo and Sabin [6] and Ball and Storry [1]. Like Loop [9], we find that the positions and normals of the limit surface can be expressed explicitly in terms of the vertices of the control mesh. However, whereas Loop's analysis was peculiar to his subdivision surfaces, our analysis applies to any subdivision scheme whose local matrix $\mathbf{S}_n$ satisfies the conditions listed in Appendix A. In particular, our analysis exposes the following simple dependence between the left eigenvectors of $\mathbf{S}_n$ and limit points and normals.

Let $\lambda_1 \geq \lambda_2 \geq \lambda_3$ be the three largest eigenvalues of $\mathbf{S}_n$ and let l_1, l_2, l_3 be the corresponding left eigenvectors. In Appendix A we show that a point v^1 having a neighborhood V_n^1 converges to the point

$$v^\infty = l_1 \cdot V_n^1 \tag{1}$$

and the normal vector to the surface at v^∞ is given by

$$N^\infty = c_2 \times c_3 \tag{2}$$

where $c_2 = l_2 \cdot V_n^1$ and $c_3 = l_3 \cdot V_n^1$, and where "$\times$" denotes vector cross product. Explicit formulas for l_1, l_2 and l_3 for Catmull-Clark surfaces can be found in Appendix A.

Equation 1 provides an interpolation condition that is linear in the control points of V_n^1, but Equation 2 at first appears to impose a quadratic constraint on V_n^1's control points. Fortunately, we can require a surface to have a given normal vector N, using the following two linear constraints:

$$N \cdot c_2 = 0 \qquad \text{and} \qquad N \cdot c_3 = 0 \tag{3}$$

In addition to providing interpolation constraints, the limit point and normal vector formulas can also be used to compute exact points and normal vectors on the surface for use during rendering [9]. The color images (Figures 3 through 7) have all been computed this way.

3.2 Solving the Interpolation Problem

Ignoring the interpolation of normals for the time being, we can use the interpolation condition in Equation 1 to compute a control mesh $\widehat{M}^0$ with the property that the subdivision surface it defines interpolates the vertices of a given mesh $\widehat{I}$. It is natural to do this by selecting $\widehat{M}^0$ to have the same mesh topology as $\widehat{I}$, that is, the same number and connectivity of vertices, faces, and edges. This approach leads to a square linear system of the form

$$\mathbf{A}x = b \tag{4}$$

where x is the column vector of the unknown vertex coordinates in $\widehat{M}^0$, and b is the corresponding column vector of vertex coordinates of $\widehat{I}$. The rows of the square matrix $\mathbf{A}$ are determined by the interpolation conditions and mesh topology. In some cases, the matrix $\mathbf{A}$ is singular, so we use a least-squares solution to Equation 4. An example is shown in Figure 5. The original mesh is shown in the upper left. Subdividing it according to the usual Catmull-Clark rules results in the lower-left surface which approximates, but does not interpolate the vertices of the original mesh. By solving Equation 4, we obtain a new mesh which is shown in the upper center. Subdividing the new mesh according to the usual Catmull-Clark rules gives the surface in the lower center which does interpolate the vertices of the original mesh.

4 Fairing

The surface in the lower center of Figure 5 is curvature continuous almost everywhere and interpolates the vertices of the original mesh. Nonetheless, for many purposes it is an unsatisfactory interpolating surface because of its excessive undulations. These undulations appear to be artifacts of the interpolation process since they are not indicated by the shape of the original mesh. For example, the surface has a number of concavities where the original mesh is convex. Note that some of the undulations are present in the ordinary approximating Catmull-Clark surface, but they have become more severe and objectionable in the interpolating surface. This difference is typical of interpolating and approximating surfaces.

Nothing in our formulation of the interpolation conditions in Section 3 prohibits or discourages undulations in the surface, so this type of behaviour should not be surprising. In order to improve the quality of the interpolant, we introduce additional degrees of freedom into the surface by subdivision, and then set the degrees of freedom by optimizing a fairness norm on the surface subject to a set of linear constraints given by the interpolation conditions.

4.1 Evaluating the Fairness Norm

Celniker and Gossard [3] were able to improve the quality of interpolating surfaces using a fairness norm based on a linear combination of the energy of a membrane and a thin plate. Without any fundamental changes, the norm can be given directional preferences and nonuniform weighting over the surface, but for clarity of presentation, we consider the isotropic uniform case:

$$E(W) = \alpha E_m(W) + \beta E_p(W) \tag{5}$$

where $E_m(W)$ and $E_p(W)$ denote the membrane and thin-plate energies respectively:

$$\begin{aligned} E_m(W) &= \int\!\!\int \|W_u\|^2 + \|W_v\|^2 \, du\, dv \\ E_p(W) &= \int\!\!\int \|W_{uu}\|^2 + 2\|W_{uv}\|^2 + \|W_{vv}\|^2 \, du\, dv, \end{aligned}$$

and where $W(u,v) = (x(u,v), y(u,v), z(u,v))$ is a parametric representation of the surface, where subscripts on W represent parametric derivatives, and where α and β are freely selectable weights.

Since the membrane/plate norm is defined in terms of a parametric representation of the surface, it cannot be directly applied to Catmull-Clark surfaces since in general they have no "natural" parametrization near extraordinary points. The remainder of this section describes how we extend the definition of the norm in a way that can be used with Catmull-Clark surfaces. As we show below, the extended norm will be constructed to be quadratic in the control points of the mesh. The optimization can consequently be performed quickly without iteration by solving a linear system. Moreover, there is a unique minimum since the Hessian of the norm is symmetric and positive definite.

The membrane/plate norm can be evaluated without modification on a bicubic patch W as follows. First, we note that the norm can be written as $E = E_x + E_y + E_z$, where E_x depends only on the x component of W, E_y only on the y component and E_z only on the z component of W. Let P_x be a 16-element column vector of positions of the x coordinates of the control points W. Figure 2(a) schematically depicts a 16 element control net and the bicubic patch it defines. The x component of the fairness norm for the patch can be expressed as

$$E_x = P_x^T \cdot \mathbf{K} \cdot P_x \tag{6}$$

where the entries of the 16×16 matrix $\mathbf{K}$ can be computed exactly from the integrals in Equation 5 for bicubic B-spline basis functions. Similar formulas hold for the y and z components.

Figure 2(b) depicts a mesh that includes an extraordinary point. The region of the limit surface corresponding to the central face in the mesh is shown at the center bottom, but the limit surface is not in general a parametric polynomial, so we cannot directly apply the membrane/plate norm used above for a bicubic mesh. However, we can subdivide the mesh in Figure 2(b) to obtain the mesh in (c). After subdivision, the limit surface is divided into four subpatches. Three of these subpatches (shown shaded in (c)) are bicubic B-splines, so on these patches we can in principle evaluate the fairness norm exactly. By repeating this procedure we can write an infinite series for the fairness norm of the original extraordinary patch of Figure 2(b). In order to fully define the series, we must choose a parametrization for each of the B-spline subpatches during subdivision. Unfortunately, the most straightforward way to assign the parametrizations causes the infinite series for the thin plate energy to diverge (see Appendix B).

There are several methods that could be applied to overcome the problem of the divergent series. For instance, we might try to find an alternate method of parametrizing the subpatches that leads to convergent sequences. We are currently investigating this possibility, but we have found that the following method gives good results. Intuitively, we intend to modify the thin plate energy so that it integrates to zero for surface patches defined by planar and "regular" control meshes. For a bicubic mesh it is relatively clear that a regular mesh is one that is an affine image of Figure 2(a) since such a mesh has vanishing second derivatives. As shown in Appendix B, it is possible to generalize the notion of regularity for meshes containing an extraordinary vertex. It is also possible to measure the deviation of an arbitrary mesh of control points P from it's regular component P'. We therefore define the modified thin plate energy of P to be the thin plate energy of $P - P'$. In symbols, the norm we use can be written as

$$E(P) = \alpha E_m(P) + \beta E_p(P - P'). \tag{7}$$

We have written this norm as a function of the control mesh P rather than the limit surface that P defines. This is to emphasize that the norm is not, strictly speaking, a property of the limit surface. It is more appropriate to think of Equation 7 as a norm on meshes, because it is not generally the case that $E(P^i) = E(P^{i+1})$ where P^i and P^{i+1} denote the mesh after i and $i+1$ subdivisions. Although this might be considered a theoretical deficiency, it has posed no difficulties in practice.

Using the modified norm, the infinite series is a convergent geometric series, so we can express its limiting value analytically. Appendix B contains the relevant details, but the result is that we can exactly compute the entries of a new quadratic form $\mathbf{K}_n$ that can be applied around an extraordinary vertex of order n.

Now that we have defined the local fairness norm for patches surrounding extraordinary patches, we define the global fairness norm as the sum of the fairness norms over each of the patches using the standard membrane/plate norm for bicubic patches and the modified norm of Equation 7 for extraordinary patches. We can write the global fairness norm as $\widehat{P}^T \widehat{\mathbf{K}} \widehat{P}$ where $\widehat{\mathbf{K}}$ is a sparse matrix obtained from the various $\mathbf{K}_n$ by iterating over the individual vertices and collecting the entries into a global system, and where $\widehat{P}$ is a column vector containing the x, y and z coordinates of the control vertices in the global mesh $\widehat{M}^0$.

4.2 Minimizing the Fairness Norm

Since we have a global expression for the fairness norm, we are now in a position to express and solve the minimization problem. Given a mesh $\widehat{I}$ with t vertices, r of which are

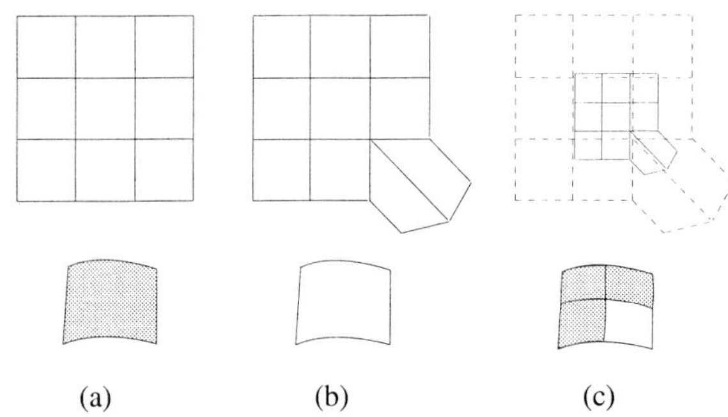

Figure 2: (a) A regular control mesh (above) which generates a bicubic B-spline patch on the limit surface (below). (b) A control mesh with an extraordinary point (above), and the extraordinary surface patch it defines (below). (c) The control mesh after one subdivision (above), and the four subpatches after subdivision (below). The three bicubic subpatches are shaded gray, and the remaining extraordinary subpatch is shaded white.

constrained to have a specified limit point and s of which are constrained to have specified normals, we seek the vector of $3t$ vertex coordinates $\widehat{P}$ such that the limit surface satisfies the $3r + 2s$ linear interpolation conditions and the fairness norm $\widehat{P}^T \widehat{\mathbf{K}} \widehat{P}$ is minimized over all possible $\widehat{P}$.[2] Because the constraints are linear and the norm is quadratic in the unknowns, this problem can be solved directly without iteration.

If we have only positional constraints, the x, y and z components of the mesh are independent, so the whole problem decouples into three completely independent optimizations, one for each component of the mesh. If normal vectors are to be interpolated, the x, y and z components of the mesh are no longer independent, so the problem must be solved as a single optimization. Even so, the x, y and z components of the mesh remain nearly decoupled (in the sense that the linear system is block diagonal except for a few off-diagonal terms) and sparse matrix methods exist that can exploit this fact[7].

The r position constraints and s normal constraints on the t mesh points can be represented by the equation $\mathbf{B}\widehat{P} = D$ where $\mathbf{B}$ is a $(3r+2s) \times 3t$ matrix and D is a vector of length $3r+2s$. Let $\mathbf{C}$ be the $3t$ by l matrix whose columns span the null space of $\mathbf{B}$ and let $\widehat{P}_0$ be any vector satisfying $\mathbf{B}\widehat{P}_0 = D$. Then all $\widehat{P}$ which satisfy the interpolation constraints can be written in the form $\widehat{P}_0 + \mathbf{C}R$ for some l-vector R. Therefore we wish to find the vector R that minimizes:

$$\begin{aligned}(\widehat{P}_0 + \mathbf{C}R)^T \, \widehat{\mathbf{K}} \, (\widehat{P}_0 + \mathbf{C}R) &= \\ R^T \mathbf{C}^T \widehat{\mathbf{K}} \mathbf{C} R + 2R^T \mathbf{C}^T \widehat{\mathbf{K}} \widehat{P}_0 &+ \widehat{P}_0^T \widehat{\mathbf{K}} \widehat{P}_0.\end{aligned}$$

$\widehat{\mathbf{K}}$ is symmetric and positive definite, so R is found by setting the gradient of this function to zero:

$$\mathbf{C}^T \widehat{\mathbf{K}} \mathbf{C} R + \mathbf{C}^T \widehat{\mathbf{K}} \widehat{P}_0 = 0. \tag{8}$$

[2] Each of the t vertices has three coordinates, so the total number of unknowns is $3t$. Each position interpolation constraint imposes three conditions, one per coordinate, and each normal vector constraint imposes the two conditions in Equation 3.

5 Implementation

For simplicity and speed, our current implementation of the fairing process uses only positional constraints and exploits the fact that the linear systems for x, y and z decouple in this case. As a result, the implementation is able to compute the minimum energy mesh by solving three linear systems, each involving one third as many variables as Equation 8. To further speed the computation, each of these systems is solved using sparse-matrix methods.

Given a mesh $\widehat{I}$ whose vertices are to be interpolated, we must first choose the structure of the mesh $\widehat{M}^0$ whose vertices we compute. Our current implementation chooses $\widehat{M}^0$ to have the structure that would result from subdividing $\widehat{I}$ twice. This choice has two benefits. First, it adds enough extra degrees of freedom for the fairing to be effective. Second, it places enough new vertices between the interpolation points to ensure that the interpolation conditions for all vertices of $\widehat{I}$ are independent, making the construction of a sparse representation of the required null space easy.

Since we are considering a single component x, y or z at a time and not allowing normal constraints, we can still write the interpolation conditions as $\mathbf{B}\widehat{P} = D$ but now $\mathbf{B}$ is an $r \times t$ matrix and D is a vector of length r. We compute a sparse set of null-space vectors for $\mathbf{B}$ as follows. Suppose the ith row of $\mathbf{B}$ has k non-zero entries in columns $(a_1, a_2, \ldots, a_k)$. Because of the way the positional constraints decouple after two subdivisions, all other entries of $\mathbf{B}$ in those k columns are zero. As a result, it is an easy matter to find $k-1$ independent null-space column vectors which are zero except in rows $(a_1, a_2, \ldots, a_k)$. Collecting these for each row of $\mathbf{B}$ yields a collection of sparse vectors that completely span the null space of $\mathbf{B}$ unless $\mathbf{B}$ contains zero columns. If $(b_1, b_2, \ldots, b_m)$ are the zero columns of $\mathbf{B}$, we complete the null space by adding the m vectors Q_s, $1 \leq s \leq m$ where Q_s is one in the b_sth entry and zero elsewhere.

In addition to the null space, we need a feasible mesh $\widehat{P}_0$ which satisfies the constraints. We construct this mesh as follows. For each row i in $\mathbf{B}$, with non-zero entries in columns $(a_1, a_2, \ldots, a_k)$, set the entries of $\widehat{P}_0$ at indices $(a_1, a_2, \ldots, a_k)$ to D_i and set any remaining entries of $\widehat{P}_0$ to zero. Then since all the rows of $\mathbf{B}$ sum to one, the resulting $\widehat{P}_0$ will solve the equation $\mathbf{B}\widehat{P}_0 = D$.

Finally, given the null space basis $\mathbf{C}$ and the feasible mesh $\widehat{P}_0$, we compute the minimum energy mesh by solving Equation 8 three times using sparse LU decomposition, once for each component of the mesh. If the mesh is a regular square grid, the bandwidth of the linear system will be $O(\sqrt{n})$, and the linear system will take $O(n^2)$ time to solve. The running time is more difficult to analyze for general meshes, but the times we have observed to date are consistent with $O(n^2)$ performance.

6 Results

Figure 5 shows the complete process of interpolation and fairing. The original mesh is shown in the top left. The interpolating mesh is shown at top center. The faired, interpolating mesh is shown at top right. Below each mesh is the corresponding Catmull-Clark limit surface. Note that the spurious undulations in the interpolating limit surface are greatly reduced in the faired interpolating surface. The additional subdivisions in the faired interpolating mesh provide the degrees of freedom necessary to do this. For the examples presented in this paper, we set $\alpha = 0$ and $\beta = 1$.

Often it is desirable to fair only a local region of the surface, either to have more control over the fairing or because the number of vertices in the control mesh is large. In this case we select a subset of control vertices that are free to move and compute the solution to the constrained minimization over the surface patches affected by this set. Figure 6 illustrates this process. The user has selected a subset of 52 vertices that are allowed to vary during the minimization process. These vertices are highlighted in red. Other nearby vertices which influence the minimization, but are not allowed to change, are shown in magenta. After fairing, the undulations in the faired region have been reduced, but they persist in the unfaired regions. In this case, the fairing took .18 seconds on an SGI Crimson workstation.

Lounsbery et al. [10] have done a survey of the previously published interpolation methods and found that existing local interpolation schemes do an unsatisfactory job of constructing fair surfaces, even for the simple cases such a data sampled from a torus. To facilitate comparison with these methods, we have run our algorithm and a representative local interpolant, that of Shirman and Séquin [14], on the same coarsely sampled toroidal data set. The results are shown in Figure 4. The upper left shows the original mesh used as input for the interpolants. The upper right shows the surface produced by the Shirman-Séquin algorithm. The odd looking specular highlights in the Shirman-Séquin interpolant point out some interpolation artifacts which are typical of local methods. Global methods tend to have a different appearance. The surface in the lower left of Figure 4 is a Catmull-Clark surface that interpolates the original mesh using the methods of Section 3. This surface has different (lower frequency) artifacts than the Shirman-Séquin interpolant, but they are nonetheless objectionable. The surface in the lower right is an interpolating faired surface computed using our method. The surface has no visible artifacts, an observation confirmed by examining the surface from other viewpoints. The implementation took 36.5 seconds to fair the entire 600 point mesh at once on an SGI Crimson workstation.

The result of applying the interpolation algorithm to a more complicated model is shown in Figure 7. The original mesh is shown at the far left. The left center shows the ordinary approximating Catmull-Clark surface. Note the artifacts throughout the stem and where the stem meets the base. These artifacts are accentuated in the interpolating Catmull-Clark surface shown in the right center. In addition, the interpolating surface shows severe overshoot at the bottom of the stem. This type of overshoot is typical of interpolation without fairing. The far right shows the faired interpolating Catmull-Clark surface computed using our method. The artifacts along the stem and where the stem joins the base have been removed. Fairing the 1273 point mesh took 127.8 seconds on an SGI Crimson workstation.

7 Conclusions

We have described an efficient method for constructing fair surfaces that interpolate the vertices of a mesh of arbitrary topological type; normal vectors can also be interpolated at an arbitrary subset of the vertices. Our approach is to compute a control mesh describing a Catmull-Clark surface that interpolates the given data and minimizes a quadratic norm that combines thin plate and membrane energies.

Our method improves on previous techniques by combining many of the strengths of the methods described by Celniker and Gossard and by Moreton and Séquin. Like Celniker and Gossard, we use a quadratic norm to achieve practical fairing at interactive rates. Like Moreton and Séquin, we use a representation capable of modeling arbitrary topological surfaces. In addition, the Catmull-Clark representation we use provides improved surface continuity with remarkably few degrees of freedom. More specifically, Celniker-Gossard surfaces meet with only tangent plane continuity along patch boundaries, and those of Moreton-Séquin meet with only approximate tangent plane continuity. Our surfaces, in contrast, are curvature continuous everywhere except at a finite number of isolated points.

Our work also provides two new analytical tools for analyzing and manipulating subdivision surfaces: limit point and normal vector analysis based on left eigenvectors of the local subdivision matrix, and a method for developing exact formulas for evaluating quadratic membrane/plate functionals and their derivatives.

As a topic for future research, we plan to investigate using the surfaces produced by our method as a starting point for minimizing the intrinsic "MVS" norm developed by Moreton and Séquin. We are also interested in developing subdivision schemes that are curvature continous everywhere.

References

[1] A. A. Ball and J. T. Storry. Conditions for tangent plane continuity over recursively defined B-spline surfaces. *ACM Transactions on Graphics*, 7(2):83–102, April 1988.

[2] E. Catmull and J. Clark. Recursively generated B-spline surfaces on arbitrary topological meshes. *Computer Aided Design*, 10(6):350–355, 1978.

[3] George Celniker and Dave Gossard. Deformable curve and surface finite elements for free-form shape design. In *Proceedings of SIGGRAPH '91*, pages 257–265, July 1991.

[4] G. Chaikin. An algorithm for high speed curve generation. *Computer Graphics and Image Processing*, 3:346–349, 1974.

[5] R. Clough and J. Tocher. Finite element stiffness matrices for analysis of plate bending. In *Matrix Methods in Structural Mechanics (Proceedings of the conference held at Wright-Patterson Air Force Base, Ohio, 26-28 October 1965)*, pages 515–545, 1966.

[6] D. Doo and M. Sabin. Behaviour of recursive division surfaces near extraordinary points. *Computer Aided Design*, 10(6):356–360, 1978.

[7] Gene H. Golub and Charles F. Van Loan. *Matrix Computations*. The Johns Hopkins University Press, Baltimore, 2nd edition, 1989.

[8] G. Herron. Techniques for visual continuity. In G. Farin, editor, *Geometric Modeling*, pages 163–174. SIAM, 1987.

[9] Charles T. Loop. Smooth subdivision surfaces based on triangles. M.S. Thesis, Department of Mathematics, University of Utah, August 1987.

[10] Michael Lounsbery, Stephen Mann, and Tony DeRose. Parametric surface interpolation. *IEEE Computer Graphics and Applications*, 12(5):45–52, September 1992.

[11] Henry P. Moreton and Carlo Séquin. Functional optimization for fair surface design. In *Proceedings of SIGGRAPH '92*, pages 167–176, July 1992.

[12] Ahmad H. Nasri. Polyhedral subdivision methods for free-form surfaces. *ACM Transactions on Graphics*, 6(1):29–73, January 1987.

[13] Malcolm Sabin. Recursive division singular points. Unpublished manuscript, June 1992.

[14] L. Shirman and C. Séquin. Local surface interpolation with Bézier patches. *Computer Aided Geometric Design*, 4(4):279–296, 1988.

Appendix

A Properties of the Limit Surface

To develop formulas for limit points and normals on subdivision surfaces, we examine the eigenstructure of the local subdivision matrix $\mathbf{S}_n$ associated with the subdivision scheme. (Some of the following analysis appears to have been developed independently by Sabin [13].)

Let $m = 2n + 1$ denote the size of $\mathbf{S}_n$, and let $\lambda_1 \geq \lambda_2 \geq \ldots \geq \lambda_m$ denote the eigenvalues of $\mathbf{S}_n$ with corresponding right eigenvectors $r_1, ..., r_m$ and left eigenvectors $l_1, ..., l_m$. If $\mathbf{S}_n$ is not defective, the right eigenvectors form a basis, and the left eigenvectors can be chosen so that (cf. Golub and Van Loan [7])

$$l_k \cdot r_j = \delta_{kj}. \tag{9}$$

Thus, assuming that $\mathbf{S}_n$ is not defective, the neighborhood V_n^1 can be expanded uniquely as

$$V_n^1 = c_1 r_1 + \cdots + c_m r_m \tag{10}$$

where the c's are geometric position vectors and where the r's are column vectors of scalars. The c_k, $k = 1, ..., m$ can be determined by dotting both sides of Equation 10 with l_k and using Equation 9:

$$l_k \cdot V_n^1 = c_1 l_k \cdot r_1 + \cdots + c_k l_k \cdot r_k + \cdots + c_m l_k \cdot r_m = c_k. \tag{11}$$

Using this expansion of V_n^1,

$$V_n^i = \mathbf{S}_n^i V_n^1 = \lambda_1^i c_1 r_1 + \cdots + \lambda_m^i c_m r_m.$$

For a non-trivial limit to exist as $i \to \infty$, it is necessary for the magnitude of the largest eigenvalue λ_1 to be 1. In this case,

$$V_n^\infty := \lim_{i \to \infty} V_n^i = c_1 r_1 = \left(l_1 \cdot V_n^1\right) r_1$$

For a subdvision scheme to be affine invariant (that is, independent of the coordinate system in which the calculation is performed), the points of $\widehat{M}^{i+1}$ must be affine combinations of the points in $\widehat{M}^i$, meaning that each of the rows of $\mathbf{S}_n$ must sum to one. In matrix form:

$$\mathbf{S}_n (1, ..., 1)^T = (1, ..., 1)^T.$$

In other words, the column vector of 1's is the eigenvector r_1 associated with eigenvalue 1. Since r_1 is a column vector of 1's, every point in the neighborhood converges to the point

$$c_1 = l_1 \cdot V_n^1 \tag{12}$$

on the limit surface. Stated more formally, we have proven that:

Proposition 1: A point v^1 of $\widehat{M}^1$ with neighborhood V_n^1 and local subdivision matrix $\mathbf{S}_n$, converges to the point

$$v^\infty = l_1 \cdot V_n^1$$

on the limit surface where l_1 is the left eigenvector of S_n associated with eigenvalue 1, assuming that S_n satisfies the following conditions:

i) $\mathbf{S}_n$ is not defective.
ii) $\mathbf{S}_n$ describes an affine invariant process.
iii) The magnitude of the largest eigenvalue is 1 and it has multiplicity 1.

Using a discrete Fourier analysis similar to the one described by Ball and Storry [1], one can show that for Catmull-Clark surfaces the above conditions on $\mathbf{S}_n$ hold and that

$$l_1 = \frac{1}{n(n+5)}(n^2, 4, ..., 4, 1, ..., 1),$$

meaning that

$$v^\infty = \frac{n^2 v^1 + 4\sum_j e_j^1 + \sum_j f_j^1}{n(n+5)}. \tag{13}$$

Equation 13 can be used as an interpolation condition on the points of $\widehat{M}^1$ by setting v^∞ to a point to be interpolated. Note that the interpolation conditions are on the vertices of $\widehat{M}^1$, not on the vertices of the initial control mesh $\widehat{M}^0$, since the analysis above requires that each face has exactly four edges. This apparent restriction poses no problem in practice since fairing requires the extra degrees of freedom present in $\widehat{M}^1$.

To develop an interpolation condition on normal vectors, we must determine the normal vector (if it exists) to the limit surface at v^∞. This normal vector can be simply computed from the eigenstructure of $\mathbf{S}_n$, as indicated by the following proposition.

Proposition 2: The normal vector to a subdivision surface at a limit point v^∞ corresponding to a vertex v^1 whose neighborhood is $\widehat{M}_n^1$ is the vector

$$N^\infty = c_2 \times c_3$$

where $c_2 = l_2 \cdot \widehat{M}_n^1$ and $c_3 = l_3 \cdot \widehat{M}_n^1$, assuming that the local subdivision matrix $\mathbf{S}_n$ satisfies the conditions of Proposition 1 in addition to:

iv) The eigenvalues $\lambda_1 = 1 \geq \lambda_2 ...$ are such that $\lambda_2 = \lambda_3 > \lambda_4$.

Proof sketch: The general idea behind the proof is to show that there is a common plane to which all points in the neighborhood are converging. The vector N^∞ will then be chosen to be perpendicular to this plane. Let u_j^i denote the vector from v^∞ to the j-th point p_j^i of the neighborhood $\widehat{M}^i$. Roughly speaking, if a common plane exists, then it should be possible to find an expression for a vector N^∞ that is perpendicular to each of the u_j^i's in the limit $i \to \infty$. Stated as an equation, we might seek a vector N^∞ such that

$$N^\infty \cdot u_j^i \to 0$$

for $j = 2, ..., m$ as $i \to \infty$. This does not quite work, however, because each u_j^i is approaching the zero vector, implying that the above condition would trivially hold for any vector N^∞. This problem is overcome by considering the unit vectors $\hat{u}_j^i$. Thus, we seek a vector N^∞ such that

$$N^\infty \cdot \hat{u}_j^i \to 0$$

for $j = 2, ..., m$ as $i \to \infty$.

If r_{jk} denotes the entry in the j-th row of r_k, then

$$\begin{aligned} \hat{u}_j^i &= \frac{p_j^i - v^\infty}{\|p_j^i - v^\infty\|} \\ &= \frac{\lambda^i(c_2 r_{j2} + c_3 r_{j3}) + \lambda_4^i c_4 r_{j4} + \cdots}{\|\lambda^i(c_2 r_{j2} + c_3 r_{j3}) + \lambda_4^i c_4 r_{j4} + \cdots\|} \\ &= \frac{(c_2 r_{j2} + c_3 r_{j3}) + \frac{\lambda_4^i}{\lambda^i} c_4 r_{j4} + \cdots}{\|(c_2 r_{j2} + c_3 r_{j3}) + \frac{\lambda_4^i}{\lambda^i} c_4 r_{j4} + \cdots\|} \end{aligned}$$

In the limit as $i \to \infty$,

$$\hat{u}_j^\infty = \lim_{i\to\infty} \hat{u}_j^i = \frac{c_2 r_{j2} + c_3 r_{j3}}{\|c_2 r_{j2} + c_3 r_{j3}\|}. \tag{14}$$

Equation 14 implies that each of the limiting unit vectors $\hat{u}_j^\infty$, $j = 2, ..., m$ is a linear combination of the vectors c_2 and c_3. All the vectors $\hat{u}_j^\infty$ must therefore lie in the plane spanned by c_2 and c_3. The normal vector N^∞ we seek is therefore $c_2 \times c_3$. □

Again using a discrete Fourier transform technique, one can show that for Catmull-Clark surfaces,

$$\lambda := \lambda_2 = \lambda_3 = \frac{4 + A_n}{16}$$

$$c_2 = \sum_j A_n \cos(\frac{2\pi j}{n}) e_j^1 + (\cos(\frac{2\pi j}{n}) + \cos(\frac{2\pi(j+1)}{n})) f_j^1$$

where

$$A_n = 1 + \cos(\frac{2\pi}{n}) + \cos(\frac{\pi}{n})\sqrt{2(9 + \cos(\frac{2\pi}{n}))}.$$

The vector c_3 is obtained from c_2 by replacing e_j^1 with e_{j+1}^1 and f_j^1 with f_{j+1}^1.

B Integrating the fairness functional

In this appendix, we consider the problem of evaluating the fairness norm of Equation 7 for a patch whose local control mesh P contains an extraordinary point, such as the one shown in Figure 2(b). As motivated in Section 4, we will ultimately evaluate only the non-divergent part of the thin plate energy corresponding to the deviation of P from its regular component P'. As we show below, it is not necessary to compute P' explicity, so we will for the time being evaluate the energy of P.

The quadratic form $\mathbf{K}$ referred to in Equation 6 can be written as a weighted sum of two quadratic forms $\mathbf{K}_m$ and $\mathbf{K}_p$, representing the membrane and plate energies, respectively for a bicubic patch:

$$\mathbf{K} = \alpha \mathbf{K}_m + \beta \mathbf{K}_p.$$

Let $E(n, P, j)$ denote the fairness norm of Equation 7 integrated over a patch containing at most one extraordinary point of order n whose local mesh is described by the column vector of control points P, and whose level of subdivision is j. As outlined in Section 4, when $n \neq 4$, we evaluate $E(n, P, j)$ by splitting the patch into four subpatches, three of which are ordinary (shown in gray in Figure 2), and one of the same form as the original. the This leads to the following recurrence relation for $E(n, P, j)$:

$$\begin{aligned} E(4, P, j) &= P^T \left(\alpha \mathbf{K}_m + 4^j \beta \mathbf{K}_p\right) P \\ E(n, P, j) &= \sum_{k=1}^{3} E(4, \mathbf{\Omega}_k P, j+1) + E(n, \mathbf{\Omega}_4 P, j+1) \end{aligned}$$

where $\mathbf{\Omega}_1, \mathbf{\Omega}_2, \mathbf{\Omega}_3$ are matrices that carry P into the local meshes for the ordinary (shaded) subpatches, and where $\mathbf{\Omega}_4$ is the matrix that carries P into the local mesh for the remaining (unshaded) extraordinary subpatch.

The factor of 4^j in front of $\mathbf{K}_p$ reflects the change of integration variables when a patch is subdivided j times. The choice of powers of 4 is somewhat arbitrary. It corresponds to the parametrization assigned to the bicubic subpatches created when the extraordinary patch is subdivided. We have chosen powers of 4 since it is the correct factor for bicubic patches. We are, however, currently experimenting with methods to select this factor based on n.

The above recurrence can be unrolled to produce an infinite series for $E(n, P, 0)$:

$$E(n, P, 0) = \sum_{j=1}^{\infty} \sum_{k=1}^{3} E(4, \mathbf{\Omega}_k \mathbf{\Omega}_4^{j-1} P, j)$$

which can be written as

$$E(n, P, 0) = P^T \mathbf{K}_n P$$

where

$$\mathbf{K}_n := \sum_{j=1}^{\infty} (\mathbf{\Omega}_4^{j-1})^T (\bar{\mathbf{K}}_m + 4^j \bar{\mathbf{K}}_p) \mathbf{\Omega}_4^{j-1},$$

and where

$$\bar{\mathbf{K}}_m := \sum_{k=1}^{3} \alpha \mathbf{\Omega}_k^T \mathbf{K}_m \mathbf{\Omega}_k,$$

$$\bar{\mathbf{K}}_p := \sum_{k=1}^{3} \beta \mathbf{\Omega}_k^T \mathbf{K}_p \mathbf{\Omega}_k.$$

The limiting value of the series can be found by expanding $\mathbf{\Omega}_4$ in its basis of eigenvectors:

$$\mathbf{\Omega}_4 = \mathbf{X} \mathbf{\Lambda} \mathbf{X}^{-1}$$

where $\mathbf{\Lambda}$ is a diagonal matrix containing the eigenvalues of $\mathbf{\Omega}_4$, and where the columns of $\mathbf{X}$ are the corresponding right eigenvectors. Without loss of generality we can assume that the eigenvalues appear in decreasing order down the diagonal. $\mathbf{K}_n$ can now be written as

$$\begin{aligned} \mathbf{K}_n &= \mathbf{X}^{-T} \underbrace{\left\{ \sum_{j=1}^{\infty} \mathbf{\Lambda}^{j-1} \mathbf{X}^T \bar{\mathbf{K}}_m \mathbf{X} \mathbf{\Lambda}^{j-1} \right\}}_{\tilde{\mathbf{K}}_m} \mathbf{X}^{-1} + \\ & \quad \mathbf{X}^{-T} \underbrace{\left\{ \sum_{j=1}^{\infty} 4^j \mathbf{\Lambda}^{j-1} \mathbf{X}^T \bar{\mathbf{K}}_p \mathbf{X} \mathbf{\Lambda}^{j-1} \right\}}_{\tilde{\mathbf{K}}_p} \mathbf{X}^{-1}. \end{aligned}$$

Since $\mathbf{\Lambda}$ is diagonal, the ab-th entry of $\tilde{\mathbf{K}}_m$ is

$$(\tilde{\mathbf{K}}_m)_{ab} = (\mathbf{X}^T \bar{\mathbf{K}}_m \mathbf{X})_{ab} \sum_{j=1}^{\infty} (\mathbf{\Lambda}_{aa})^{j-1} (\mathbf{\Lambda}_{bb})^{j-1}.$$

The above series is geometric, so if $\mathbf{\Lambda}_{aa}\mathbf{\Lambda}_{bb} < 1$, it converges to

$$(\tilde{\mathbf{K}}_m)_{ab} = \frac{(\mathbf{X}^T \bar{\mathbf{K}}_m \mathbf{X})_{ab}}{1 - \mathbf{\Lambda}_{aa}\mathbf{\Lambda}_{bb}}.$$

Using arguments as in appendix A, it can be shown that the largest eigenvalue of $\mathbf{\Omega}_4$ is one, meaning that the product $\mathbf{\Lambda}_{aa}\mathbf{\Lambda}_{bb}$ is at most one, and this occurs only when $a = b = 1$. The membrane energy is invariant under translation, which is reflected in the fact that $(\mathbf{X}^T \bar{\mathbf{K}}_m \mathbf{X})_{11}$ is zero; hence $(\tilde{\mathbf{K}}_m)_{11} = 0$.

A similar analysis for $\tilde{\mathbf{K}}_p$ shows that

$$(\tilde{\mathbf{K}}_p)_{ab} = 4(\mathbf{X}^T \bar{\mathbf{K}}_p \mathbf{X})_{ab} \sum_{j=1}^{\infty} 4^{j-1} (\mathbf{\Lambda}_{aa})^{j-1} (\mathbf{\Lambda}_{bb})^{j-1}.$$

Thus, $(\tilde{\mathbf{K}}_p)_{ab}$ is finite whenever $4\mathbf{\Lambda}_{aa}\mathbf{\Lambda}_{bb} < 1$. The factor $4\mathbf{\Lambda}_{aa}\mathbf{\Lambda}_{bb}$ can be shown to be one or larger when $1 \leq a, b \leq 3$. Just as for the membrane energy, the 11 entry poses no difficulty since $(\mathbf{X}^T \bar{\mathbf{K}}_p \mathbf{X})_{11} = 0$, indicating that the thin plate energy is invariant under translation.

The remaining 8 entries of $\tilde{\mathbf{K}}_p$ are unbounded for $n > 4$. When $n = 4$ (i.e., the ordinary case), $4\mathbf{\Lambda}_{aa}\mathbf{\Lambda}_{bb} = 1$, yet we know that the entries of $\tilde{\mathbf{K}}_p$ are finite since bicubic patches have finite thin plate energy. We therefore conclude that for $n = 4$, $(\tilde{\mathbf{K}}_p)_{ab} = 0$ for $1 \leq a, b \leq 3$. This reflects the fact that regular control meshes have zero thin plate energy. To generalize this idea to arbitrary n, we simply set the remaining 8 divergent terms to zero, which is equivalent to evaluating the norm on $P - P'$.

To summarize, the quadratic form related to the thin plate energy is taken to be

$$(\tilde{\mathbf{K}}_p)_{ab} = \begin{cases} \dfrac{4(\mathbf{X}^T \bar{\mathbf{K}}_p \mathbf{X})_{ab}}{1 - 4\mathbf{\Lambda}_{aa}\mathbf{\Lambda}_{bb}} & \text{if } 4\mathbf{\Lambda}_{aa}\mathbf{\Lambda}_{bb} < 1 \\ 0 & \text{otherwise} \end{cases}$$

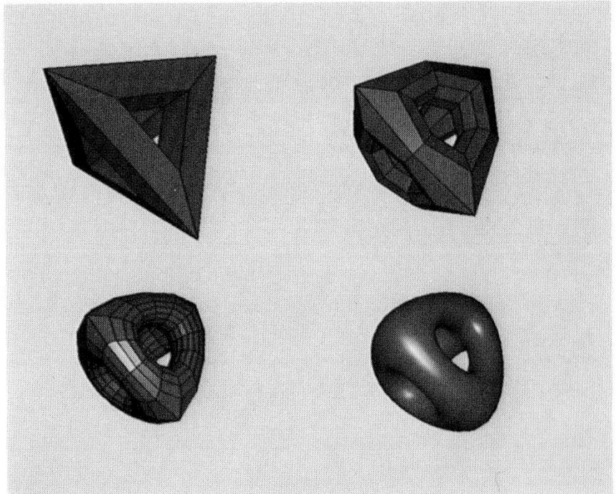

Figure 3: Upper Left: Tetrahedral mesh with holes. Upper Right: The mesh after one Catmull-Clark subdivision. Lower Left: The mesh after two subdivisions. Lower Right: The limit surface.

Figure 4: Interpolating a coarsely polygonized torus. Upper left: original mesh. Upper right: Shirman-Séquin interpolation[14]. Lower left: Interpolating Catmull-Clark surface. Lower right: Faired interpolating Catmull-Clark surface.

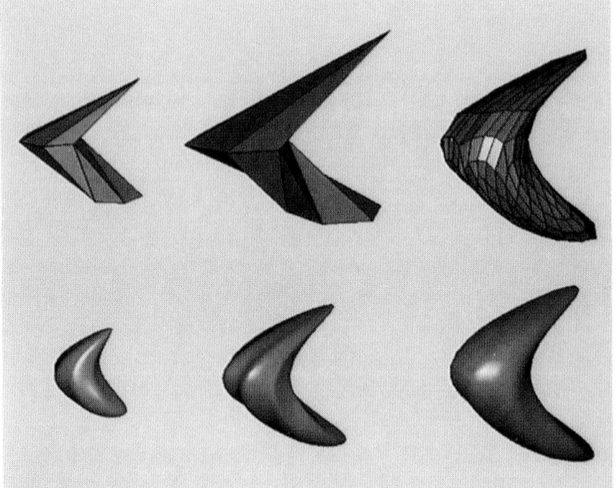

Figure 5: Top row: Original mesh, Interpolating mesh, Faired interpolating mesh. Bottom row: Corresponding Catmull-Clark surfaces. Interpolation introduces wiggles which are removed by fairing.

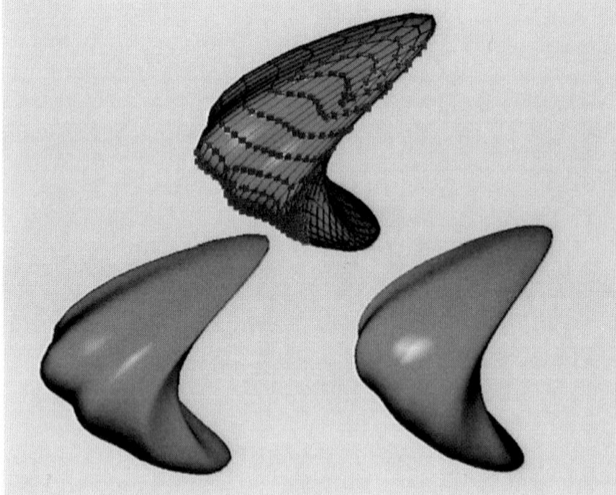

Figure 6: Lower left: unfaired interpolating surface. Upper center: Interactive fairing. Red vertices are allowed to move. Magenta vertices influence the minimization, but remain fixed. Lower right: Result after fairing.

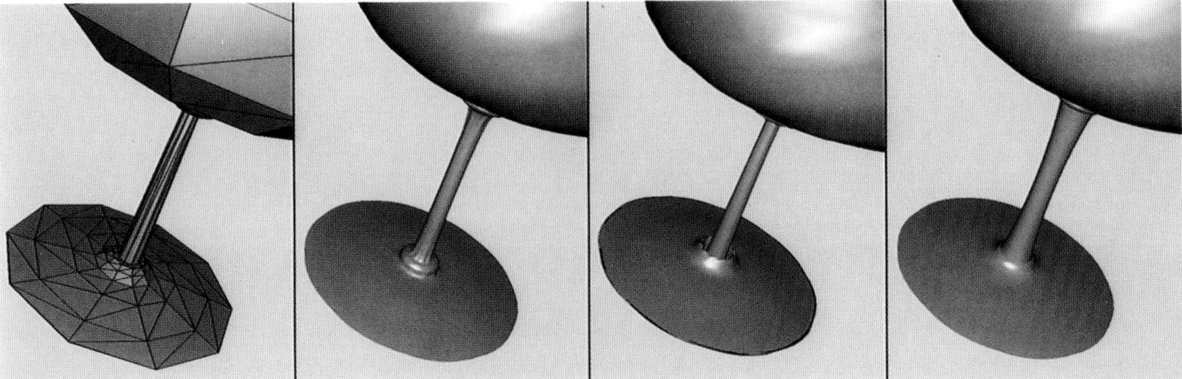

Figure 7: From left to right: Original goblet mesh containing 190 vertices. Ordinary Catmull-Clark surface (approximating). Interpolating Catmull-Clark surface. Faired interpolating Catmull-Clark surface. The far right surface interpolates the original mesh without the artifacts present in the middle two surfaces.

Implementing Rotation Matrix Constraints in Analog VLSI

David B. Kirk Alan H. Barr

California Institute of Technology
Computer Graphics 350-74
Pasadena, CA 91125
email: dk@egg.gg.caltech.edu

Abstract

We describe an algorithm for continuously producing a 3x3 rotation matrix from 9 changing input values that form an approximate rotation matrix, and we describe the implementation of that constraint in analog VLSI circuits. This constraint is useful when some source (e.g., sensors, a modeling system, other analog VLSI circuits), produces a potentially "imperfect" matrix, to be used as a rotation. The 9 values are continuously adjusted over time to find the "nearest" true rotation matrix, based on a least-squares metric. The constraint solution is implemented in analog VLSI circuitry; with appropriate design methodology [Kirk 93], adaptive analog VLSI is a fast, accurate, and low-power computational medium. The implementation is potentially interesting to the graphics community because there is an opportunity to apply adaptive analog VLSI to many other graphics problems.

CR Categories and Subject Descriptors: C.1.2—**[Processor Architectures]:** Multiprocessors - parallel processors; C.1.3—**[Processor Architectures]:** Other Architecture Styles; I.3.1—**[Computer Graphics]:** Hardware Architecture - raster display devices; I.3.3—**[Computer Graphics]:** Picture/Image Generation; I.3.5—**[Computer Graphics]:** Computational Geometry and Object Modeling; I.3.7—**[Computer Graphics]:** Three-Dimensional Graphics and Realism
General Terms: Algorithms, Graphics, Hardware
Additional Key Words and Phrases: Animation, rotation, robotics, simulation, constraint solution, interaction, adaptive, analog, CMOS, VLSI.

1 Introduction

This paper has two main purposes. First, we demonstrate the implementation of a nontrivial constraint technique in analog VLSI. Second, since some of the computer graphics community may not be familiar with recent developments in analog VLSI technology, we describe some of the potential benefits. We believe that analog VLSI has great potential as a computation medium for implementing rendering, modeling, and interactive operations.

1.1 Computation in Computer Graphics

There is a history of digital VLSI acceleration in computer graphics: geometry engines [Clark 82], hardware frame buffer assists [Rhoden 89], vector generators [Barkans 90], systems [Voorhies 88] [Fuchs 89], etc. Most high-performance graphics workstations have a substantial amount of special purpose digital chips to provide the kind of interactive performance that we have come to expect. Most of this silicon is dedicated to rendering tasks, although it can be argued that the geometric transformations performed in hardware constitute modeling hardware.

Any computational medium used for graphics needs to be able to perform mathematical operations accurately and precisely. The bulk of simulation and modeling calculations for computer graphics are performed in software. For instance, for *physically-based modeling*, the shapes and motions of graphical objects are computed according to the physics underlying the simulation. This process requires the solution of differential equations (for converting the relation $F = ma$ into position and velocity). As we consider collisions between objects, we may also be required to solve for roots of nonlinear equations. For modeling, we require the ability to accurately and precisely solve a variety of mathematical equations.

Applying real physical constraints to computer graphics models requires great computational resources. Even relatively simple simulations, involving only a few primitives, may consume many seconds of CPU time on a fast computer. The traditional arguments are that CPU price-performance doubles every year, and that massive parallelism will save us. We claim that current digital computation approaches are approximately a factor of 10,000 times too slow for real-time simulation of complex scenes.

In order to be effective in addressing this problem, a computational medium must be fast and accurate. If we can produce a technology which can accurately and precisely compute the solutions of equations, we can then use the technology to construct computer graphics hardware. We hope that adaptive analog VLSI can be used to realize the goal of performing graphics calculations thousands of times faster than is possible today.

1.2 Adaptive Analog VLSI

There has been increasing interest recently in using analog VLSI [Mead 89] for a variety of computational tasks. Mead and others have pursued the paradigm of using ana-

© 1993 ACM-0-89791-601-8/93/008/0045 $01.50

log transistors to model components of neural systems. Related research has focused on increasing the accuracy and precision of computation with analog VLSI [Kirk 93], and on developing a design methodology for creating analog VLSI circuits which can be adjusted to perform to the desired accuracy [Kirk 91]. These techniques make analog VLSI more tractable for quantitative computation.

This is not the first appearance of analog computation in computer graphics. Certainly, there is some amount of analog hardware in every graphics system, at least in the form of a D/A (digital-to-analog) converter in the path to the video monitor. There have also been more extensive uses of analog, however. For instance, Vector General implemented matrix multiplication for the purpose of performing coordinate transformations in analog circuitry, although not in analog VLSI.

It is important to note that in these discussions, we have chosen a *particular* constraint to demonstrate the general technique of implementing a constraint in analog VLSI. There are many other examples of useful constraint computation that could be formulated in a similar fashion [Platt 89] [Barzel 92], and also could be implemented in analog hardware. The particular constraint that we have chosen to implement is meant to be representative of a large set of possibilities. Our example raises the exciting prospect of implementation of extensive hardware *modeling* assists in analog VLSI. There are also many rendering tasks which are appropriate for analog VLSI hardware implementation, but we won't discuss them in this paper. We have chosen to describe a constraint technique that is appropriate for interactive input devices, and has application to modeling as well.

1.3 The Rotation Matrix Constraint

The constraint technique that we have chosen is the orthonormalization of a rotation matrix. We chose the 3x3 matrix formulation because it is easier to perform coordinate transformations with the same underlying computational modules that are used to implement the constraints. In Sec. 4, we describe several computational blocks that we can also use to construct coordinate transformation hardware. The matrix formulation is also complex enough to be interesting as an example problem for hardware.

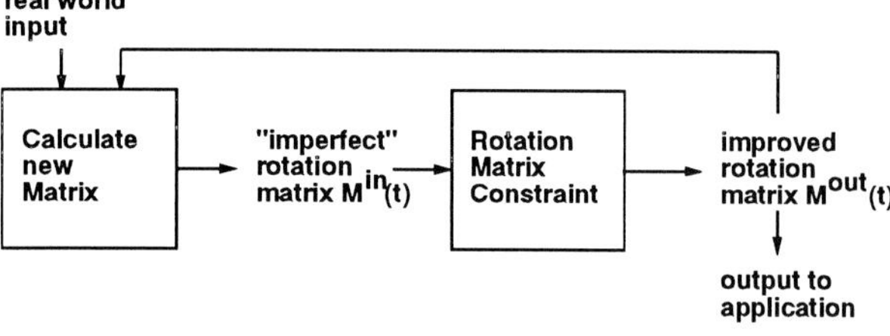

Figure 1: A system-level view of the rotation matrix constraint enforcement, and how the result of applying the constraint might be used.

The rotation matrix constraint is particularly useful as part of an interactive system, as shown in Fig. 1. For virtual reality applications, a sensor may be used to produce a 3D orientation, in the form of a 3x3 rotation matrix. Sensors are often flawed, noisy, or otherwise inaccurate and do not provide sufficient and reliable information for producing an accurate rotation matrix. In such cases, we then wish to continuously produce a "best estimate" rotation matrix, based on the sensor measurements. One example of such a system involves producing rotation matrices from approximate inputs from sensors or interactive devices. The system produces approximate rotation matrices over time from angular velocity $\omega(t)$, according to the following relation:

$$\underline{\underline{M}}'(t) = \underline{\omega} \times \underline{\underline{M}}(t) \tag{1}$$

Such a system would produce an approximate rotation matrix at each time step, and may accumulate errors over time. The errors could be corrected by the constraint technique described in this paper.

A similar task exists in robotics applications. We might have a sensor which can detect the position of an end effector of a robot arm, and also a measure of the control inputs. In practice, a robot arm is often controlled by providing joint angle control inputs. However, the control may be inaccurate, and there may be "slop" in the joints. We may want to then compute an estimate of the actual joint angles, which, if the arm segments are rigid, must be pure rotations.

There are also many applications to physically-based modeling. When solving constraint equations for motion of rigid bodies, we may produce values that are inaccurate due to accumulating arithmetic roundoff errors, integration step size, or approximations in our model. When combined to form a rotation matrix to describe the orientation of a body, the errors may cause the introduction of scaling or skewing into the matrix. The constraint technique described in this paper will allow us to automatically adjust for these errors.

In Sec. 2, we describe the constraint algorithm that we use to produce the rotation matrix. In Sec. 3, we introduce in more detail the technology used for the implementation (analog VLSI), and explain why we believe that it has great potential to be useful for computer graphics. In Sec. 4, we present a block diagram description of the constraint chip.

2 The Constraint Algorithm

Our goal is to produce a 3x3 rotation matrix containing no scale or skew components, given 9 numbers which are already nearly a rotation matrix.

For a mathematically perfect rotation matrix M,

$$MM^T = I \tag{2}$$

where I is the identity matrix.

We define the function $f()$:

$$f(M) = (MM^T - I) : (MM^T - I) \tag{3}$$

where the double-dot operator (:) denotes the sum of products of terms of the two matrices, producing a scalar result, analogous to the dot product of two vectors. When M is a rotation matrix (or reflection), $f(M)$ in Eqn. 3 is equal to zero, and when M is not purely a rotation matrix, $f(M) \neq 0$. Since $f(M)$ is always greater than or equal to zero, M is a rotation matrix when $f(M)$ is minimized.

We perform continuous gradient descent to minimize the function $f()$, as follows:

$$M'(t) = -\epsilon \, \nabla f(M(t)) \tag{4}$$

where epsilon is a parameter which determines the speed of the descent. Appendix 1 describes the derivation of our gradient calculation method in detail.

The analog VLSI implementation does not suffer from many of the problems of digital implementations, since analog circuits can operate in continuous time. For instance, in a digital implementation, Euler's method might be used to solve Eqn. 4. With large step sizes, Euler's method frequently becomes unstable. With small step sizes, Euler's method may converge slowly or not at all. Other techniques, such as the conjugate gradient method, may improve the performance in digital implementations. The continuous nature of an analog implementation, however, avoids this type of problem entirely.

As the computation proceeds, two kinds of changes are occurring. First, the imperfect input matrix may be changing over time. Second, based on our optimization process, the output matrix will be changing to fulfill our rotation matrix constraint. Since the analog VLSI circuit operates very quickly, and in continuous time, the optimization can occur at a much finer time scale than the changing of the input matrix.

3 Adaptive Analog VLSI

There has been increasing interest recently in using analog VLSI [Mead 89] for a variety of computational tasks. One of Mead's insights is that rather than developing an entirely new manufacturing technology for producing analog VLSI chips, we can produce analog CMOS VLSI chips using standard digital CMOS VLSI processes. The key element in this strategy is to produce designs that are tolerant to the device variations that are present in a digital production process. Another component of this design philosophy is the exploration of architectures and circuits that are tolerant of device variations.

Other research has focused on increasing the accuracy and precision of computation with analog VLSI [Kirk 93], and on developing a design methodology for creating analog VLSI circuits which can be adjusted to perform to the desired accuracy [Kirk 91]. This work can be characterized as using adaptation and optimization to harness analog VLSI for more "conventional computing" applications. This approach is attractive because analog transistors provide a rich computational gamut. Fig. 2 (upper) shows the current flowing through an analog transistor as its gate voltage is varied. Fig. 2 (lower) shows the current as the source-to-drain voltage is varied, while holding the gate voltage constant. These figures are meant as a qualitative demonstration of the variety of current-voltage responses available from a single transistor. Note the regions of roughly linear, exponential, and quadratic I-V relation.

It is possible make analog circuits more quantitatively useful, by designing *compensatable* circuit building blocks that can be adjusted to perform more closely to some performance metric. For example, let us assume that our goal is to build a "perfect" analog multiplier. In analog VLSI, we can easily build a circuit which computes an "imperfect" multiply-like operation, but the "perfect" multiply is more elusive. We can design a multiplier that is monotonic within some input range, and operates in four quadrants (the sign of the output is correct for all combinations of inputs' sign). Without extreme care in

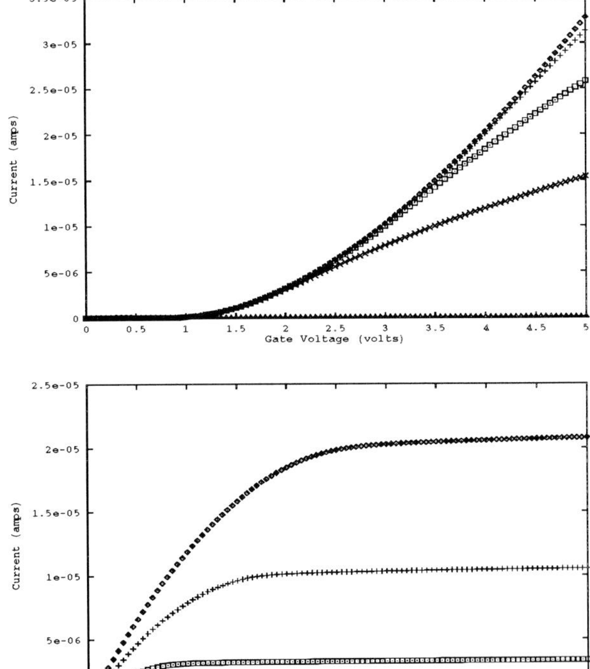

Figure 2: The upper graph shows the drain current of a single transistor, as the gate voltage is varied from 0 to 5 volts. The family of curves represents varying the difference between the source and drain voltage. The lower graph shows the drain current as the source-to-drain voltage difference is varied from 0 to 5 volts. The family of curves represents varying the gate voltage. The analog VLSI multipliers discussed in Sec. 3 operate in the nearly linear region to the right of the upper graph and to the left of the lower graph.

the design, however, the "multiplier" would have a number of drawbacks. The circuit's response might deviate significantly from the desired linear function of its inputs

$$f(x, y) = x * y \tag{5}$$

The "multiplier" would also, very likely, have nonzero input offsets[1].

A compensated multiplier has adjustable parameters which allow for the improvement of the linear range of behavior, as well as the cancellation of input offsets. A description of how to design, build, and optimize compensatable components is presented in detail in [Kirk 93]. Sec. 5 presents some measurements from chips implemented and compensated using these techniques.

4 Applying Analog VLSI to the Constraint Problem

Now that we have described the desired constraints (in Sec. 2) and the substrate technology of adaptive analog VLSI (Sec. 3), we will explain, at a block diagram level,

[1] Input offsets are present for an analog multiplier $f(x, y) \approx x * y$ when $f(x, 0) \neq 0$ or $f(0, y) \neq 0$.

how we use analog VLSI to solve the constraint problem. These block diagrams represent a hierarchical decomposition of the chip that we built.

As one might guess from the form of the equations of the derivation in Sec. 2, the circuit architecture is a nested, structured hierarchy of dot products, with some additional computation.

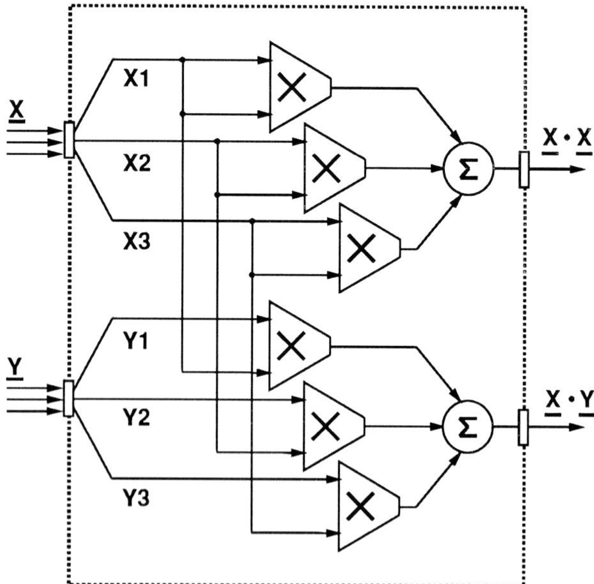

Figure 3: A functional block containing two dot products. The inputs are the matrix column vectors $\underline{X}$ and $\underline{Y}$, and the outputs are the scalars $X \cdot X$ and $X \cdot Y$.

We can think of the nine input values, the "imperfect" rotation matrix, as the three 3D basis vectors, $\underline{X}$, $\underline{Y}$, and $\underline{Z}$, (the three columns of the matrix). We can see by examining Eqn. 13 that the computation of the various components of the gradient, η_{pq}, requires dot products of the matrix basis vectors. Appendix 1 describes the calculation of η_{pq}. Fig. 3 shows a functional block which computes two of the six basis vector dot products that are required.

Fig. 4 shows a set of three functional blocks (from Fig. 3) which together compute the six 3D basis vector dot products that are required to form the gradient, η_{pq}, as shown in Eqn. 13. The details of the circuit, the device layout, and the compensation procedure for the multiplier and dot product blocks are presented in [Kirk 93].

Fig. 5 shows the use of the basis vector inputs and three of the dot product results to produce the gradient components for one of the basis vectors, in this case, $\underline{X}$.

Fig. 6 shows a set of three constraint blocks, from Fig. 5, which together compute all of the components of the gradient for the correction of the imperfect matrix. The combination of these three constraint blocks and the three dot product blocks from Fig. 4 forms the gradient calculation hardware. X_1', X_2', X_3', Y_1', Y_2', Y_3', Z_1', Z_2', and Z_3' are the nine derivative components. Together, they form the gradient, which we will use to optimize the components of the matrix $\underline{\underline{M}}$. Descending along the direction of the gradient will produce a matrix which fulfills our constraints.

We use the derivative terms from Fig. 6 to add or

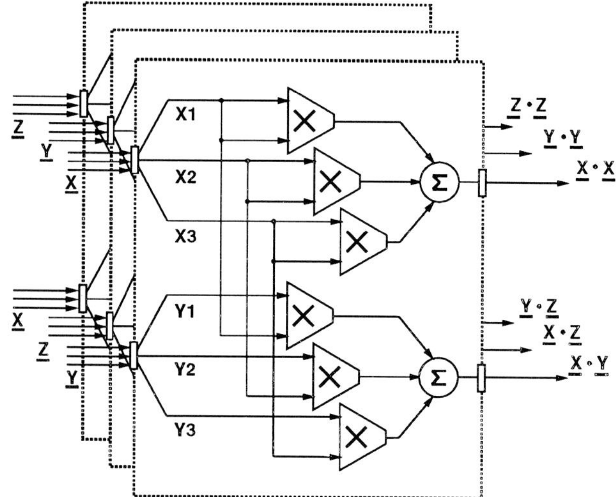

Figure 4: A collection of three dot product blocks, from Fig. 3. With the 3D basis vector inputs $\underline{X}$, $\underline{Y}$, and $\underline{Z}$, they compute the six dot products required to enforce the constraints.

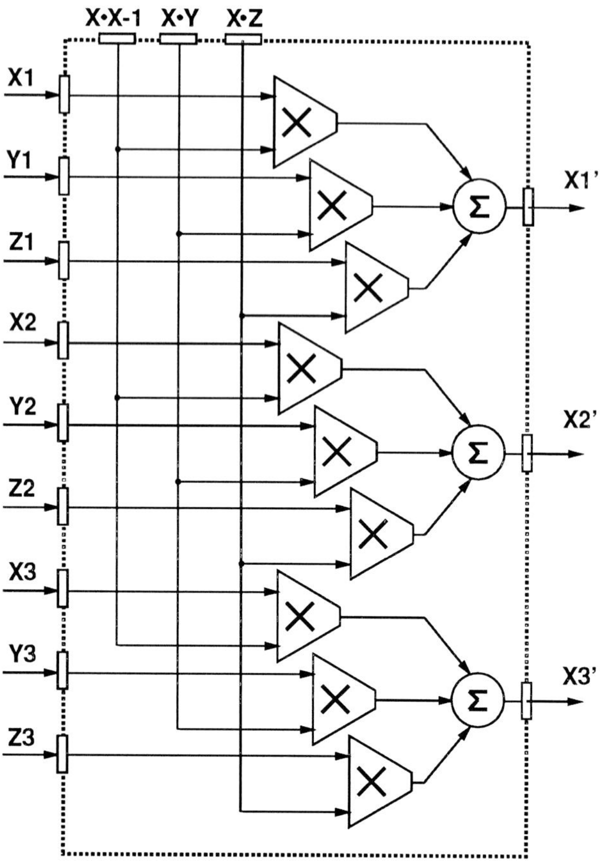

Figure 5: A basis vector constraint block, using the outputs from Fig. 4. This computational element implements the rotation matrix constraint for one of the three matrix column vectors.

subtract from the original input values of the matrix, $\underline{\underline{M}}$. Since the circuits are analog and operate in continuous

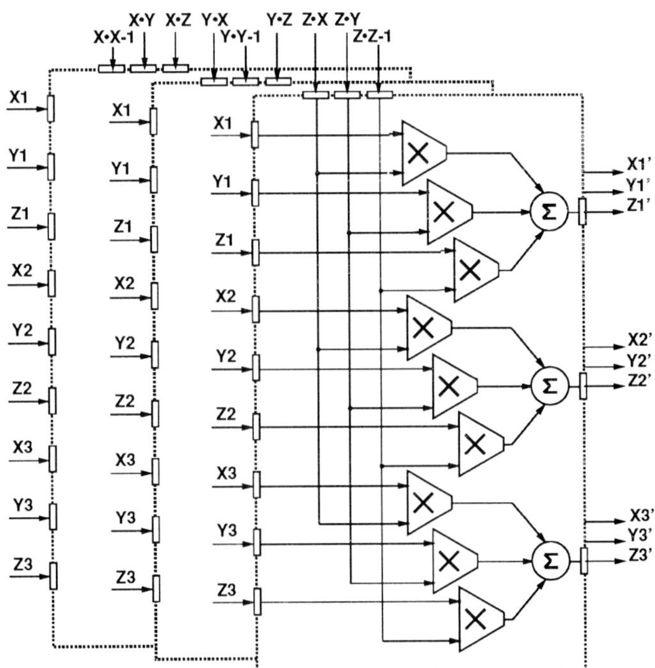

Figure 6: A collection of three constraint blocks, from Fig. 5. The combination of these three constraint blocks and the three dot product blocks from Fig. 3 forms the gradient calculation hardware.

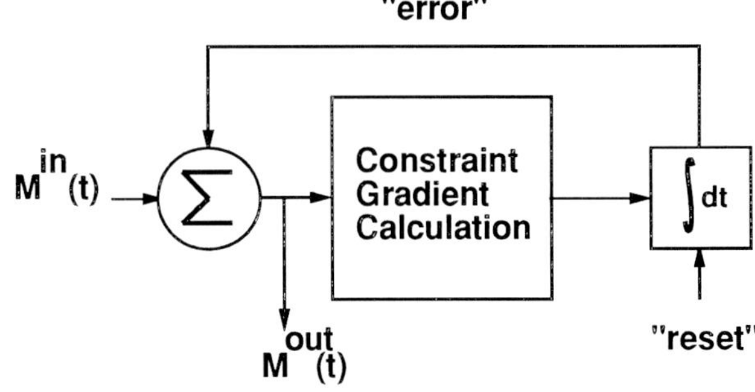

Figure 7: An example of a gradient descent process, as employed to enforce the rotation matrix constraint. The feedback from the gradient calculation modifies the effective inputs to the constraint gradient calculation box. As the constraint is satisfied, the output, $M^{out}(t)$ settles to a rotation matrix, if $M^{in}(t)$ is not changing, or is changing at a slower time scale. Note the "reset" input to the integrator box. If the input matrix $M^{in}(t)$ changes discontinuously, we want to restart the constraint optimization from the new matrix, and we can accomplish this using the integrator reset.

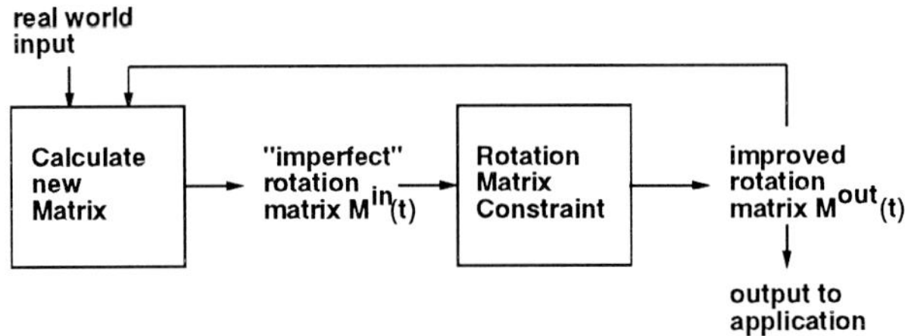

Figure 8: A system-level view of the rotation matrix constraint enforcement, and how the result of applying the constraint might be used.

time, we can integrate these corrections on capacitors, and use the gradient components to set the level of current to add/subtract. Thus, this circuit structure can be use to continuously track and correct a (potentially flawed) matrix that changes over time. Fig. 7 shows the connections required to provide the feedback from the calculated gradient components to modify the input matrix components. The gradient calculation occurs in continuous time, using the analog VLSI hardware. The input can change continuously, or discretely (using the "reset" input in Fig. 7), and the constraint solution will track the input.

Fig. 8 shows a schematic view of the the rotation matrix constraint solution box connected as part of a system. Given a source of approximate rotation matrices $M^{in}(t)$, the constraint enforcement produces rotation matrices $M^{out}(t)$, which can be used for modeling, rendering, or control applications.

5 Results

We have designed, implemented, fabricated, and tested chips which contain compensated multipliers, dot products, and constraint blocks, as described in Fig. 3 through Fig. 6. The design is modular (similar to the structure of the figures), so that we are confident that the system will work, given the partial test results. We have tested all of the components, and present the data in this paper. This section contains measured chip data for the compensated multiplier, (along with some raw data for the uncompensated version), and the dot product with hierarchical compensation. We also present a software simulation of the constraint process in action, using the constraint technique described herein.

Fig. 9 shows the results of the raw multiplier before compensation. Note the nonzero offsets, as evidenced by the nonzero slope line formed by the square symbols. That line represents the results of multiplying zero by a set of other quantities, so should be horizontal, at zero.

Fig. 10 shows the output of a compensated multiplier circuit. Note that the "zero" line (again delineated by the square symbols), is much closer to horizontal at zero, due to the effects of the compensation. It is appropriate to discuss accuracy and precision at this time. As a multiplier, the circuit is highly accurate: it computes a function that is very close to the desired $f(x, y) = kxy$. The precision is more difficult to quantify than the accuracy, however. The relative error quantity (0.1%) seems to indicate 10 bits of precision, although noise may reduce the repeatable precision to somewhat less than that. Although in this case we have only compensated for first-order effects of device variations, it is possible to design circuits which compensate for higher order nonlinearities as well. In order to use compensated components to produce an accurate and precise computational *system*, care must be taken to consider the quality and magnitude of errors that can be tolerated at each stage of the computation.

Fig. 11 shows the compensated voltage-in, voltage-out

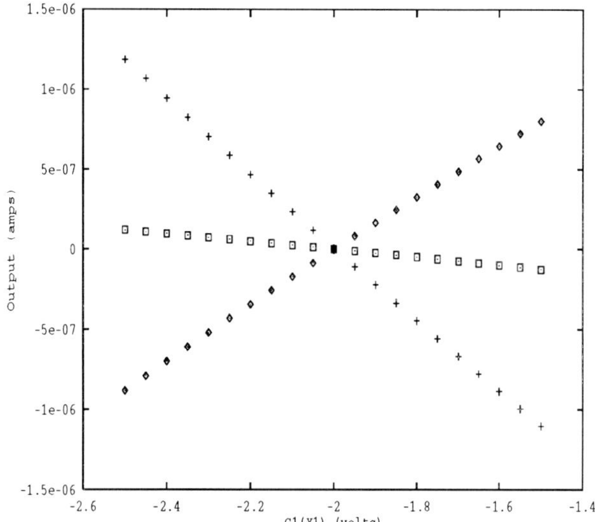

Figure 9: The output from an *uncompensated* multiplier circuit (actual measured chip data). The analog multiplier circuit has not been adapted to compensate for input offsets and other device variations. Note the nonzero offsets, as evidenced by the nonzero slope line formed by the square symbols. That line represents the results of multiplying zero by a set of other quantities, so should be horizontal, at zero.

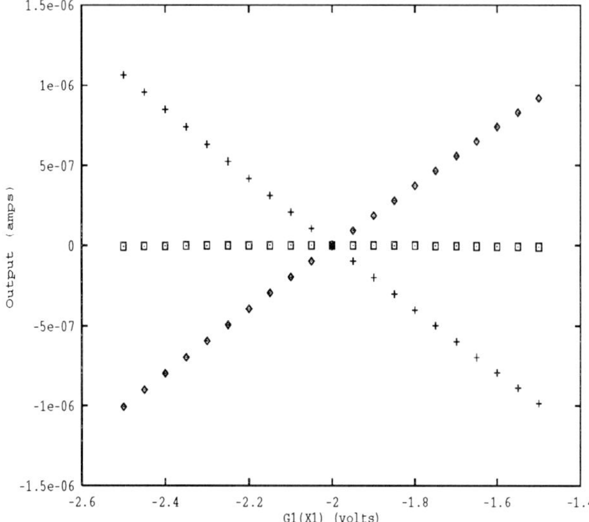

Figure 10: The output from a compensated multiplier circuit (actual measured chip data). The relative error (ourput error / input range) is less than 0.1% over most of the operating range. At extreme (large) inputs, the relative error may be as large as 2%. For this application, the precision is most important for small values.

multiplier performance. The signal presented in this figure is an intermediate value in the hierarchical constraint computation. Its nonlinearity and nonzero offset characteristics reflect the fact that this output contains biases to compensate for variations in the next stage of computation. These curves represent the sum of the multiplier output and the compensation input for a subsequent computational element. [Kirk 93] contains more detailed descriptions of hierarchical compensation techniques.

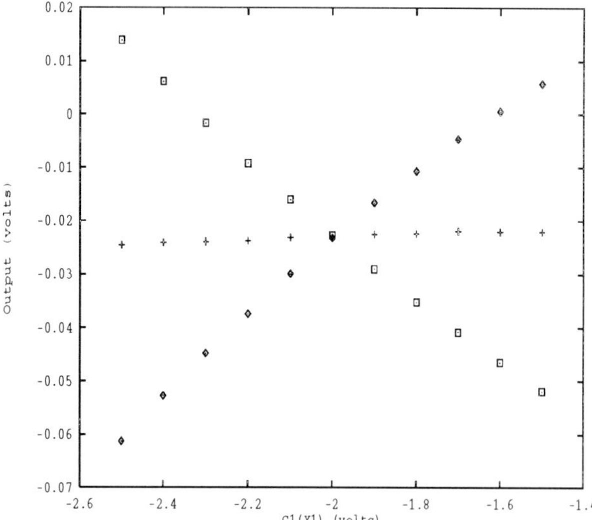

Figure 11: The output of a multiplier, after nearly linear current-to-voltage conversion (actual measured chip data).

Fig. 12 shows the three multiply components of a compensated dot product. Note that the offset correction is very accurate, but that the linearity is somewhat less accurate.

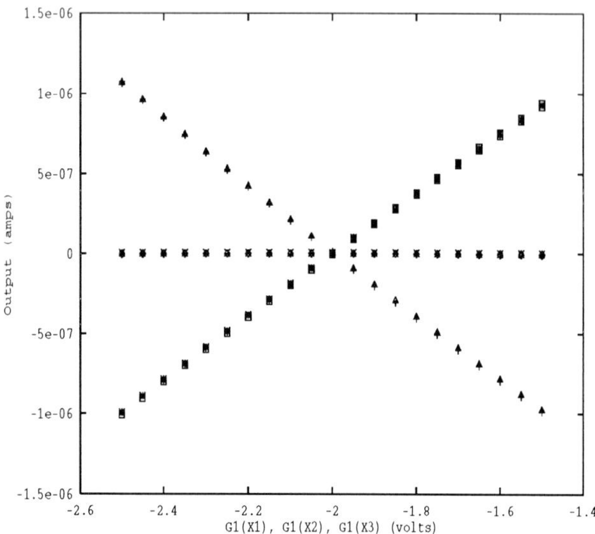

Figure 12: The 3 components of a dot product (actual measured chip data). The characteristics of the three multiply operations are similar, with respect to the input offset magnitudes and shape of nonlinearities.

Fig. 13 shows the results of a simulation of our constraint technique in action.

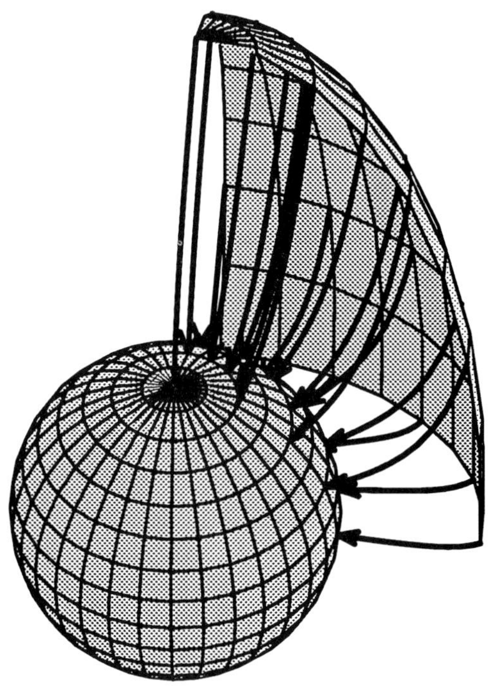

Figure 13: The results of a software simulation of our constraint technique in action. The outer curved octant represents the manifold of a set of points transformed using the input imperfect matrix. The inner, more spherical shape represents the same points (and more) transformed through the constrained rotation matrix. The lines drawn between the two shapes represent the constraint optimization path taken by our algorithm.

5.1 Expected Performance

We compare the expected performance of the continuous-time analog VLSI rotation constraint chip to a software implementation on a fast digital computer. Using the constraint algorithm described in this paper, and Euler's method to perform the optimization, we expect that the orthonormalized matrix can be produced in about 75 microseconds on a roughly 100 Mflop workstation.

The multiplier core used in the analog VLSI rotation constraint chip can easily be run at product rates in excess of 2 Mhz [Denyer 81]. Since the multipliers and constraint circuitry operate in continuous time, we expect convergence at a much greater rate than in the discrete digital case. The analog VLSI rotation constraint chip should produce an orthonormalized matrix in roughly 2-3 microseconds. So, the current implementation should outperform a general-purpose digital solution by about a factor of 25, and we believe that this is a conservative estimate. Furthermore, the analog VLSI solution is extremely low cost, and low power, and leaves the workstation processor free to pursue other tasks. The analog VLSI chips were fabricated in 2.0 micron CMOS using the MOSIS fabrication service, and dissipate power on the order of microwatts. The entire constraint solution circuit consumes roughly 2 square millimeters of chip area. Finally, faster multiplier circuits can be used to further increase the analog VLSI performance.

6 Conclusions

We describe a constraint technique for producing orthogonal, unit scale rotation matrices from "imperfect" inputs. The technique is potentially useful in a system which produces a sequence of approximate rotation matrices over time. Additional potential applications are covered briefly in Sec. 1.

We also describe the emerging and evolving technology of adaptive analog VLSI and speculate on its possible value to the field of computer graphics. In the example of the rotation system above, an analog VLSI rotation matrix constraint solver could enforce the rotation constraint *continuously* as the matrix is updated.

Interpreting this result with a broader view, we have demonstrated the implementation of a nontrivial constraint in analog VLSI. This is significant because it implies a future of implementing "hardware for modeling" in the form of hardware constraint solution. Current digital implementations of constraint systems cannot compute real time constraint solutions for models containing more than a few bodies.

Many of the tasks in computer graphics simulation and modeling involve the solution of various types of mathematical equations. The development of analog VLSI technology for accurate and precise computation [Kirk 93], makes it possible to build analog hardware to solve these equations. The use of CMOS VLSI fabrication makes analog implementations scalable and mass producible. Therefore, adaptive analog VLSI presents an exciting opportunity to consider building hardware to accelerate modeling to a level of performance commensurate with that of digital rendering hardware. We believe that Analog VLSI has the potential to be a significant tool for computer graphics.

7 Acknowledgements

This work was supported in part by an AT&T Bell Laboratories Ph.D. Fellowship, and by grants from Apple, DEC, Hewlett Packard, and IBM. Additional support was provided by NSF (ASC-89-20219), as part of the NSF/DARPA STC for Computer Graphics and Scientific Visualization. All opinions, findings, conclusions, or recommendations expressed in this document are those of the authors and do not necessarily reflect the views of the sponsoring agencies. Thanks also to the anonymous reviewers for their many helpful comments.

References

[Barkans 90] Barkans, Anthony C., "High Speed High Quality Antialiased Vector Generation," Computer Graphics, Vol. 24, No. 4, August, 1990, pp. 319-326.

[Barzel 92] Barzel, Ronen, "Structured Modeling for Computer Graphics," Academic Press, Cambridge, MA, 1992.

[Clark 82] Clark, James, "The Geometry Engine: A VLSI Geometry System for Graphics," Computer Graphics, Vol. 16, No. 3, July, 1982, pp. 127-133.

[Denyer 81] Denyer, Peter B., John Mavor, "MOST Transconductance Multipliers for Array Applications,"

IEEE Proceedings, Volume 128, Pt. I, Number 3, pp. 81-86, June 1981.

[Fuchs 89] Fuchs, Henry, J. Poulton, J. Eyles, T. Greer, J. Goldfeather, D. Ellsworth, S. Molnar, G. Turk, B. Tebbs, and L. Israel, "Pixel-Planes 5: A Heterogeneous Multiprocessor Graphics System Using Processor-Enhanced Memories," Computer Graphics, Vol. 23, No. 3, July, 1989, pp. 79-88.

[Kirk 93] Kirk, David B., "Accurate and Precise Computation using Analog VLSI, with Applications to Computer Graphics and Neural Networks," Ph.D. Thesis, California Institute of Technology, Caltech-CS-TR-93-08, June, 1993.

[Kirk 91] Kirk, David, Kurt Fleischer, and Alan Barr, "Constrained Optimization Applied to the Parameter Setting Problem for Analog Circuits," IEEE Neural Information Processing Systems 1991 (NIPS 91), Morgan Kaufman, San Diego, 1991.

[Mead 89] Mead, Carver, "Analog VLSI and Neural Systems," Addison-Wesley, 1989.

[Platt 89] Platt, John, "Constrained Optimization for Neural Networks and Computer Graphics," Ph.D. Thesis, California Institute of Technology, Caltech-CS-TR-89-07, June, 1989.

[Rhoden 89] Rhoden, Desi, and Chris Wilcox, "Hardware Acceleration for Window Systems," Computer Graphics, Vol. 23, No. 3, July, 1989, pp. 61-67.

[Voorhies 88] Voorhies, Douglas, D. Kirk, and O. Lathrop, "Virtual Graphics," Computer Graphics, Vol. 22, No. 4, August, 1988, pp. 247-253.

Appendix 1: Derivation of Constraint Equations

The expression $A : A$ can be written:

$$A : A = \sum_{jk} A_{jk} A_{jk} \tag{6}$$

So, we can rewrite Eqn. 3 as:

$$f(\underline{\underline{M}}) = \sum_{jk}((\sum_{i} M_{ij} M_{ik}) - \delta_{jk})((\sum_{\ell} M_{\ell j} M_{\ell k}) - \delta_{jk}) \tag{7}$$

where δ_{ij} indicates the identity matrix ($\delta_{ij} = 1$ when $i = j$ and 0 otherwise).

In order to use Eqn. 7 to enforce a constraint, we would like to pose it in a form which allows us to do some sort of optimization. More specifically, in order to perform a gradient descent operation, we require a gradient. So, we compute the gradient, using Einstein Summation Notation (ESN):

$$\begin{aligned} \nabla f &= \frac{\partial f}{\partial M_{pq}} && (8) \\ &= 2(M_{ij}M_{ik} - \delta_{jk})(\delta_{\ell p}\delta_{jq}M_{\ell k} + M_{\ell j}\delta_{\ell p}\delta_{qk}) && (9) \\ &= 4(M_{iq}M_{ik} - \delta_{qk})M_{pk} && (10) \end{aligned}$$

We wish to use Eqn. 8 to perform gradient descent to minimize the function $f()$, as follows:

$$M'(t) = -\epsilon \, \nabla f(M(t)) \tag{11}$$

where epsilon is a parameter which determines the speed of the descent.

We define η as the gradient of $f()$:

$$\eta_{pq} = 4(M_{iq}M_{ik} - \delta_{qk})M_{pk} \tag{12}$$

We can also simplify $M_{iq}M_{ik}$ by introducing $\underline{B}_1$, $\underline{B}_2$, and $\underline{B}_3$ as basis vectors of the matrix $\underline{\underline{M}}$, and D_{ij} as the dot product of $\underline{B}_i$ and $\underline{B}_j$:

$$\begin{aligned} \eta_{pq} &= 4(\underline{B}_q \cdot \underline{B}_k - \delta_{qk})M_{pk} && (13) \\ &= 4(D_{qk} - \delta_{qk})M_{pk} && (14) \end{aligned}$$

Since the dot products are symmetric, there are only 6 unique D_{qk} terms: the 3 diagonal terms, D_{11}, D_{22}, and D_{33}, and the three unique cross terms, D_{12} (or D_{21}), D_{23} (or D_{32}), and D_{13} (or D_{31}).

So, the following set of equations describe a form of the gradient descent process:

$$M_{pq}^{\text{new}} = M_{pq}^{\text{old}} - \epsilon \; \eta_{pq} \tag{15}$$

and we can absorb the 4 from Eqn. 13 into ϵ, since ϵ is an arbitrary constant.

We have the following set of 9 equations for the components of the gradient:

$$\begin{aligned}
\eta_{11} &= (D_{11} - 1)M_{11} + D_{12}M_{21} + D_{13}M_{31} && (16) \\
\eta_{12} &= D_{21}M_{11} + (D_{22} - 1)M_{21} + D_{23}M_{31} && (17) \\
\eta_{13} &= D_{31}M_{11} + D_{32}M_{21} + (D_{33} - 1)M_{31} && (18) \\
\eta_{21} &= (D_{11} - 1)M_{12} + D_{12}M_{22} + D_{13}M_{32} && (19) \\
\eta_{22} &= D_{21}M_{12} + (D_{22} - 1)M_{22} + D_{23}M_{32} && (20) \\
\eta_{23} &= D_{31}M_{12} + D_{32}M_{22} + (D_{33} - 1)M_{32} && (21) \\
\eta_{31} &= (D_{11} - 1)M_{13} + D_{12}M_{23} + D_{13}M_{33} && (22) \\
\eta_{32} &= D_{21}M_{13} + (D_{22} - 1)M_{23} + D_{23}M_{33} && (23) \\
\eta_{33} &= D_{31}M_{13} + D_{32}M_{23} + (D_{33} - 1)M_{33} && (24)
\end{aligned}$$

We can define $B_1 = \underline{X}$, $B_2 = \underline{Y}$, and $B_3 = \underline{Z}$, so we can now write the discrete time step gradient descent optimization as:

$$\begin{aligned}
\underline{X}^{\text{new}} &= \underline{X}^{\text{old}} - \epsilon \; \eta_{p1} && (25) \\
\underline{Y}^{\text{new}} &= \underline{Y}^{\text{old}} - \epsilon \; \eta_{p2} && (26) \\
\underline{Z}^{\text{new}} &= \underline{Z}^{\text{old}} - \epsilon \; \eta_{p3} && (27)
\end{aligned}$$

and, we can now write η in terms of $\underline{X}$, $\underline{Y}$, and $\underline{Z}$:

$$\begin{aligned}
\eta_{11} &= (D_{11} - 1)X_1 - D_{12}Y_1 - D_{13}Z_1 && (28) \\
\eta_{12} &= D_{21}X_1 - (D_{22} - 1)Y_1 - D_{23}Z_1 && (29) \\
\eta_{13} &= D_{31}X_1 - D_{32}Y_1 - (D_{33} - 1)Z_1 && (30) \\
\eta_{21} &= (D_{11} - 1)X_2 - D_{12}Y_2 - D_{13}Z_2 && (31) \\
\eta_{22} &= D_{21}X_2 - (D_{22} - 1)Y_2 - D_{23}Z_2 && (32) \\
\eta_{23} &= D_{31}X_2 - D_{32}Y_2 - (D_{33} - 1)Z_2 && (33) \\
\eta_{31} &= (D_{11} - 1)X_3 - D_{12}Y_3 - D_{13}Z_3 && (34) \\
\eta_{32} &= D_{21}X_3 - (D_{22} - 1)Y_3 - D_{23}Z_3 && (35) \\
\eta_{33} &= D_{31}X_3 - D_{32}Y_3 - (D_{33} - 1)Z_3 && (36)
\end{aligned}$$

Correcting for Short-Range Spatial Non-Linearities of CRT-based Output Devices

R. Victor Klassen
Xerox Webster Research Center

Krishna Bharat
Georgia Institute of Technology

ABSTRACT

Most graphical output devices exhibit what has been termed spatial non-linearity: the effect of setting two adjacent pixels to a given value is not the same as the sum of the effects of setting those two pixels to the same value in isolation: checkerboards of different frequencies do not have the same apparent luminance. We present a method applicable to bit-mapped devices for compensating for short-range spatial non-linearity in error-diffused images. The modification to error diffusion is such that it can be used with any error diffusion technique. In essence, it consists of finding the influence of the neighbouring (output) pixels when making the decision of whether to turn on a given pixel, and passing errors computed accordingly.

CR Descriptors: B.4.2 [**Input/Output and Data Communications**]: Input/Output Devices — *Image display;* I.3.1 [**Computer Graphics**]: Hardware Architecture — *Raster display devices* I.3.3 [**Computer Graphics**]: Picture/image generation — *Display algorithms;* I.3.6 [**Computer Graphics**]: Methodology and Techniques; I.4.3 [**Image Processing**]: enhancement.

1 Introduction

While the full-colour display is becoming more and more common, bit-mapped CRTs remain commonplace as well. These have advantages in terms of speed, resolution, and cost that cannot be matched by colour displays. Occasionally it is necessary to display an image on such a device. Moreover, certain colour-table animation techniques rely on the use of single bit-planes of a full-colour display. Here the full colour display is being used to simulate a bit-mapped display with a very fast frame update rate. A common method of converting from full-colour continuous tone to black and white binary is to error diffuse the luminance component. Various forms of error diffusion have been suggested[7, 14, 6, 8, 3, 15, 13]; the particular choice of error diffusion technique has relatively little effect on the appearance of an image when it is displayed on a sufficiently high-resolution monitor.

†Xerox Corporation, Webster Research Center, Building 128–27E, 800 Phillips Road, Webster, NY 14580.

‡College of Computing, Georgia Institute of Technology, 801 Atlantic Drive, Atlanta, GA 30332–0280

The value of gamma-correction of colour displays (or better still instrumented compensation)[2, 4], is well known. On a bit-mapped display the concept of gamma-correction is meaningless. As Naiman has noted, CRTs exhibit spatial non-linearities ([10], pp39–48), as can be easily seen by displaying a checkerboard of period two pixels adjacent to a checkerboard of twice that period. When viewed from a sufficient distance to cause the coarser checkerboard to appear smooth, these two images should in principle appear the same intensity. On most output devices they do not. (An LCD display may be an exception).

Much has been said about correcting for neighbourhood effects in prints. Commonly, it is based on a simple model of circular pixels with greater than unit area [12, 1, 11, 5]. For the SIGGRAPH audience, two more important display devices are the CRT and the film recorder. We begin with the simplest example: the bit-mapped CRT. Bit-mapped CRTs are so common that most readers of this paper are likely to have one. The improvement can be quite striking, as shown by figures 1 and 2. A linearity assumption (ie. that the phosphors are not saturated) allows the extension to greyscale and colour monitors, and to film recorders.

2 SIMPLE CRT CORRECTION

The general idea behind neighbourhood-based compensation is that the intensity generated at a pixel depends not only on the setting of that pixel but also on the intensity of the neighbouring pixels. The CRT is a special case. Here the non-linearities are primarily in the amplifiers driving the electron gun(s), so it is sufficient to consider only the left and right neighbours (whichever have been visited). An isolated pixel does not contribute as much intensity as it would with its neighbour on. (The amplifiers aren't fast enough to turn the electron beam on and off in one pixel). Neighbours in adjacent scanlines have no effect under this assumption.

To test the assumption of independent scanlines, display four images: with a) alternate scanlines b) alternate columns c) alternate pairs of scanlines, and d) alternate pairs of columns intensified. If scanlines are independent, a) and c) should have the same intensity. In the unlikely event that b) and d) appear the same, the monitor has excellent high frequency response, and no correction is necessary. If flicker causes a problem with interlaced displays when displaying single scanlines it can be alleviated by using a checkerboard and changing only the vertical frequency.

The second assumption is one of single neighbours contributing. This can be tested using a pattern of decreasing frequency vertical lines. For the (SONY) monitors we tested, the difference between single and double pixel lines was much greater than that between double and triple pixel width lines, so the assumption appears safe.

© 1993 ACM-0-89791-601-8/93/008/0053 $01.50

Figure 1 A radiosity-like scene, error diffused without correction. Note the dark band in the shadow.

To correct for the presence or absence of a neighbouring pixel, the algorithm in the CRT case is as follows:

for each pixel
  if no neighbouring output pixel is on (white)
    if value (including errors passed in) > threshold $- \delta$
      set the pixel
      quantization error = value $- (1 - \delta)$
    else *value* $\leq$ *threshold* $- \delta$
      quantization error = value
  else *a neighbouring output pixel is on*
    if value (including errors passed in) > threshold
      set the pixel
      quantization error = value $- 1$
    else *value* $\leq$ *threshold*
      quantization error = value
  Diffuse quantization error in the normal way

If there is no neighbouring pixel on, the effect of turning the current pixel on is reduced. This is reflected both in the turn-on decision, and in the calculation of the quantization error.

The specification deliberately leaves open the choice of error diffusion algorithm, including the order in which pixels are visited. Left and right neighbours are treated equally, although in reality pixels are only affected by the state of their left neighbours. The result of processing some pixels in right to left order, rather than left to right, results in the same average intensity overall, with a slight phase shift.

The value of δ must be determined experimentally: to do so, display a checkerboard containing 2×2 squares adjacent to a region of mid-grey that has been error diffused using the modified error diffusion algorithm. Vary δ across the error diffused region (Figure 3), and find the point where the two regions have the same luminance. We have found values in the 5–30% range apply to the monitors we tried. Figure 4 is a photograph of a screen with the pattern of Figure 3 displayed on the screen. The crossover point on the screen photographed is about midway across the figure (the process of photographing and printing the image may have changed the crossover point in the picture).

Figure 2 After correction the shadow fades smoothly through its penumbral region.

Figure 3 Finding the value of δ. The checkerboard has period two pixels. Below is an error diffused version of a 50% grey with δ varying from 0 (at the left) to 20%. Figure 4 shows the result of displaying this pattern on a CRT.

3 GREY SCALE MONITOR OR FILM RECORDER

The difference between a bit-mapped monitor and a greyscale one is the frame buffer behind it. Both employ an electron beam directed at phosphors; the spatial non-linearity effects are identical. As long as images displayed on greyscale monitors do not have high frequency information in them, their spatial non-linearities will be hidden. Where high contrast edges appear, the non-linearities can affect image quality. Fortunately, spatial non-linearities due to gun amplifier non-linearity are close enough to intensity invariant that the methods above can be safely generalized.

Before proceeding to correct for spatial non-linearities, it should be ascertained that the monitor is corrected for gun non-linearities. Given an otherwise corrected monitor, the value of δ can be determined as above, using patterns of full-on, full-off.

It is not normal to error diffuse images unless the display is operating from a low depth frame buffer (eg. 8 bits for all three components). If it is, the error diffusion algorithm can be adjusted in the same way as described above. In the typical

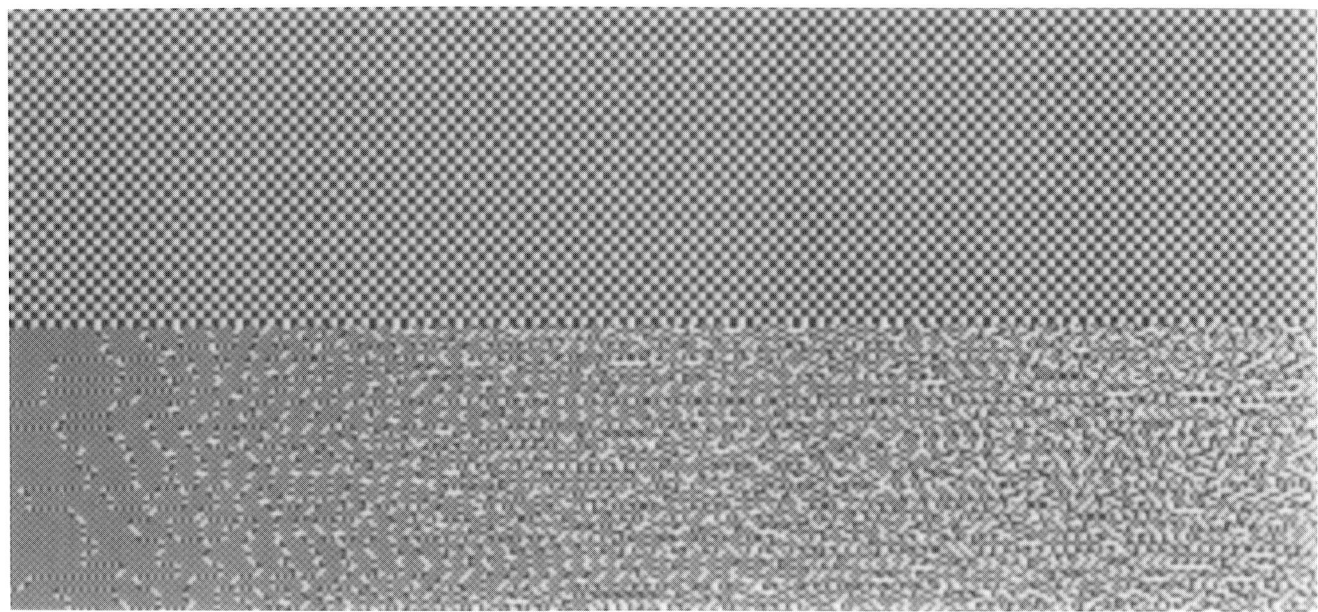

Figure 4 The result of displaying a pattern similar to that shown in Figure 3.

case of a 24 (or higher) bit frame buffer, error diffusion can still be applied, without the quantization step. Normally there would be no error generated, but the alteration to the input values can still be applied, possibly generating out-of-gamut values. For example, a white pixel immediately followed by a black pixel would lead to a request for a negative pixel value for the second one. A remapping of the input (reducing the contrast) can prevent such negative pixel values entirely. A partial contrast reduction can make such negative pixel values infrequent. This is similar to eliminating phosphor trails in temporally varying displays, as described in [9]

4 SUMMARY & CAVEAT

We have described a simple technique for improving the tonal reproduction accuracy of CRTs. For bit-mapped displays, it serves the usual function of gamma correction. For regular CRTs it performs in image regions of high spatial frequency what gamma correction or instrumented compensation does in image regions of low spatial frequency. The method involves very little extra computation over that required for conventional error diffusion, and is simple to implement and calibrate. It should be noted that the generalization to print is complicated by the larger neighbourhoods affecting pixels, two (spatial) dimensional interactions, and non-linear colour mixing in the case of coloured printing.

REFERENCES

[1] Allebach, J. Binary display of images when spot size exceeds step size. *Applied Optics 19*, 15 (August 1980), 2513–2519.

[2] Catmull, E. A tutorial on compensation tables. *Computer Graphics 13*, 2 (1979), 1–7.

[3] Cole, A. Naive halftoning. In *CG International '90* (1991), Springer-Verlag, pp. 203–222.

[4] Cowan, W. An inexpensive scheme for calibration of a colour monitor in terms of CIE standard coordinates. *Computer Graphics 17*, 3 (1983), 315–321.

[5] Dong, C.-K. Perceptial printing of gray scale images. Master's thesis, MIT, 1992.

[6] Fawcett, G., and Schrack, G. Halftoning techniques using error correction. In *Proceedings of the SID* (1986), vol. 27, no. 4, pp. 305–308.

[7] Floyd, R., and Steinberg, L. An adaptive algorithm for spatial gray scale. In *Society for Information Display 1975 Digest of Technical Papers* (1975), pp. 36–37.

[8] Griffiths, J., and Yang, C. Algorithms for generating improved images of curved surfaces by distributing errors along Hilbert's curve. *Computer-Aided Design 19*, 6 (July 1987), 299–304.

[9] Klassen, R. *Device Dependent Image Construction for Computer Graphics*. PhD thesis, University of Waterloo, 1989. Available as technical report #CS-91-19.

[10] Naiman, A. *The Use of Grayscale for Improved Character Presentation*. PhD thesis, University of Toronto, 1991.

[11] Pappas, T., and Neuhoff, D. Model-based halftoning. In *Proc. SPIE/IS&T Symposium on Electronic Imaging Science and Technology, Human Vision, Visual Processing, and Digital Display II* (1991).

[12] Roetling, P., and Holladay, T. Tone reproduction and screen design for pictorial electrographic printing. *Journal of Applied Phot. Eng. 15*, 4 (1979), 179–182.

[13] Velho, L., and Gomes, J. Digital halftoning with space filling curves. In *Proceedings SIGGRAPH '91* (1991), pp. 81–90.

[14] Whitten, I., and Neal, R. Using Peano curves for bilievel display of continuous tone images. *IEEE Computer Graphics and Applications 202* (May 1982), 47–52.

[15] Wyvill, G., and McNaughton, C. Three plus five makes eight: a simplified approach to halftoning. In *CG International '91* (1991), Springer-Verlag, pp. 397–392.

Pad
An Alternative Approach to the Computer Interface

Ken Perlin
David Fox

Courant Institute of Mathematical Sciences
New York University
719 Broadway 12th Floor
New York, NY 10003

Abstract

We believe that navigation in information spaces is best supported by tapping into our natural spatial and geographic ways of thinking. To this end, we are developing a new computer interface model called Pad.

The ongoing Pad project uses a spatial metaphor for computer interface design. It provides an intuitive base for the support of such applications as electronic marketplaces, information services, and on-line collaboration. Pad is an infinite two dimensional information plane that is shared among users, much as a network file system is shared. Objects are organized geographically; every object occupies a well defined region on the Pad surface.

For navigation, Pad uses "portals" - magnifying glasses that can peer into and roam over different parts of this single infinite shared desktop; links to specific items are established and broken continually as the portal's view changes. Portals can recursively look onto other portals. This paradigm enables the sort of peripheral activity generally found in real physical working environments. The apparent size of an object to any user determines the amount of detail it presents. Different users can share and view multiple applications while assigning each a desired degree of interaction. Documents can be visually nested and zoomed as they move back and forth between primary and secondary working attention. Things can be *peripherally* accessible.

In this paper we describe the Pad interface. We discuss how to efficiently implement its graphical aspects, and we illustrate some of our initial applications.

1 Introduction

Imagine that the computer screen is a section of wall about the size of a typical bulletin board or whiteboard. Any area of this surface can then be accessed comfortably without leaving one's chair. Imagine further that by applying extraordinarily good eyesight and eye-hand coordination, a user can both read and write as comfortably on any micron wide section of this surface as on any larger section. This would allow the full use of a surface which is several million pixels long and high, on which one can comfortably create, move, read and compare information at many different scales.

The above scenario would, if feasible, put vast quantities of information directly at the user's fingertips. For example, several million pages of text could be fit on the surface by reducing it sufficiently in scale, making any number of on-line information services, encyclopedias, etc., directly available. In practice one would arrange such a work surface hierarchically, to make things easier to find. In a collaborative environment, one could then see the layout (in miniature) of many other collaborators' surfaces at a glance.

The above scenario is impossible because we can't read or write at microscopic scale. Yet the concept is very natural since it mimics the way we continually manage to find things by giving everything a physical *place*. A good approximation to the ideal depicted would be to provide ourselves with some sort of system of 'magic magnifying glasses' through which we can read, write, or create cross-references on an indefinitely enlargeable ('zoomable') surface. This paper describes the Pad interface, which is designed using these principles.

1.1 Overview of the Paper

We begin section one with a brief summary of the basic ideas and components of the Pad Model. We then finish section one with a comparison of Pad to the window/icon paradigm and a summary of prior work. Section two is a description of a typical Pad application, and section three covers the principles of the Pad system. Section four covers several issues in our implementation of Pad, and section five lists some ongoing and future projects. Finally, section six presents our conclusions and acknowledgments.

1.2 Basic Pad Model

The **Pad Surface** is an infinite two dimensional information plane that is shared among users, much as a network file system is shared. It is populated by **Pad Objects**, where we define a Pad Object to be any entity that the user can interact with (examples are: a text file that can be viewed or edited, a clock program, a personal calendar). Pad Objects are organized geographically; every object occupies a well defined region on the Pad surface.

To make themselves visible, Pad Objects can create two types of "ink", **graphics** and **portals**, and place them on the Pad Surface. A graphic is simply any sort of mark such as a bitmap or a vector. Portals are used for navigation, they are like magnifying glasses that can peer into and roam over different parts of the Pad Surface. A portal may have a highly magnified view or a very broad, panoramic view, and this view can be easily changed. The screen itself is just a special "root" portal.

A portal is *not* like a window, which represents a dedicated link between a section of screen and a specific thing (e.g.: a Unix shell in X-Windows or a directory in the Macintosh Finder). A portal is, rather, a view into the single infinite shared desktop; links to specific items are established and broken continually as the portal's view changes. Also, unlike windows, portals can recursively look onto (and into) other portals.

Figure 1 shows a very large financial document on the Pad surface. The small portal at the top of the figure shows an overview of the entire report. The two other portals show successive closeups of portions of the report.

1.3 Object/Portal Interaction

A Pad object may look quite different when seen through different portals. There are two techniques that allow objects vary their appearance: *semantic zooming* and *portal filters*.

Every object visible on the screen has a magnification that depends upon the sequence of portals it is being seen through. As the magnification of an object changes, the user generally finds it useful to see different types of information about that object. For example, when a text document is small on the screen the user may only want to see its title. As the object is magnified, this may be augmented by a short summary or outline. At some point the entire text is revealed. We call this **semantic zooming.**

Semantic zooming works using the *expose event*, which says that a particular portion of the Pad Surface will be rendered at a particular magnification. When an object receives this event it generates the display items needed to give an appropriate appearance at that magnification.

Objects can also manage **portal filters** - portals that show non-literal views of cooperating objects. For example, a portal may show all objects that contain tabular data as a bar chart, but display other objects as would any other portal. This would enable an application to embed a bar chart within a document by placing in it a portal filter that looks onto an object that contains tabular data. Another application can then allow text or spreadsheet style editing of the tabular data itself by some user. These edits will be seen as changes in the bar chart by any user who is looking at the document.

The effect is that the bar chart filter portal will "see" any tabular data as a bar chart, but will see other objects in the usual way. Portal filters work by intercepting the expose event for objects which it knows how to render. It then asks the object or objects for any information it needs to create the display items to render them.

Another interesting portal filter would be a control modifier. Imagine for example that a paint program has several types of brush. Normally one would click on an image of a particular brush to select it. When seen through a control modifier portal filter, each brush image would appear as a panel of parameter controls with which the user can change that brush's internal state (width, spattering law, etc). The *same* portal filter could be used to modify the controls of any application on Pad that recognizes its message conventions.

1.4 Pad vs. the Window/Icon Paradigm

An important distinction between the Pad universe and the universe of other window systems is that in Pad every interaction object possesses a definite physical location. In this sense Pad is a two dimensional virtual reality. Yet a user's changing view can allow objects to *appear* larger or smaller.

This paradigm allows for the sort of peripheral activity found in real physical working environments. Each object on a user's screen commands a degree of attention commensurate with how big the object appears to that user. This allows each object to vary the amount of detail it presents to each user. Different users can share and view multiple applications while assigning to each one a desired degree of interaction. Documents can be visually nested and zoomed as they move back and forth between primary and secondary working attention. Things can be *peripherally* accessible.

For example, on the Macintosh desktop a user double clicks on a folder icon to see the contents of a directory in a window. But to see the contents of any folder within that folder, the user must double click to create a separate window.

In comparison, a user of Pad generally views a directory through a portal. The contents of any subdirectories are visible, in miniature, through sub-portals. This allows the user a peripheral awareness of a subdirectory's contents, without the user having to perform any explicit action. In this sense, Pad is better suited to non-command user interfaces[16].

1.5 Prior and related work

A number of researchers developed ways to visually structure interactive information that offer an alternative to windows/icons. One of the first such systems was the Spatial Data Management System [4] at MIT, which presented an information landscape on two screens: one screen for a panoramic overview and another (application) screen providing a closer view. The user could either pan locally around on the application screen or else could go directly to an area by pointing on the panoramic view.

On the other hand, Hypertext systems[15][10] allow the user to jump from one place to another in a conceptual information space. A notable problem with the current state of hypertext systems is the difficulty of knowing one's location in this space; unless the application is designed very carefully the user can easily get lost.

In other related work, many desktop publishing systems provide tiny "thumbnail sketches" of images that are stored on disk. To open an image file the user simply points to these miniature images instead of specifying a file name.

A unique approach to providing peripheral information has been developed by George Furnas at Bellcore Applied Research. His **Fisheye** user interface[8] shows information of current interest in great detail, while showing a progressively less detailed view of surrounding information.

Also, some of the components of fast image zooming have existed for a while. Williams[25] has used a pyramid of images for texture filtering, and Burt[2] for image processing, both based on the prior work of Tanimoto[22]. The **Bad Windows** interface[19] allows drawings to be accessed at multiple levels of detail.

Three dimensional interactive virtual offices that allow a user to change viewpoint are being developed by Mackinlay et. al. as well as Feiner [12][6]. Changes of scale have long been used in computer graphics for both entertainment and for scientific visualization.[3] One notable early example was the molecular simulation work of Nelson Max[13].

At Xerox PARC there has been a large body of interesting work on enabling groups to remotely share a common drawing surface for collaborative work.[11][14][21] This is part of their larger ongoing research effort in shared "Media Spaces"[1]. Similarly, the **Rendezvous** system at Bellcore is a general meta-system for building shared "conversational" interfaces for teleconferencing situations[9], as is the work of Smith et. al.[20]

2 An Example Application

The multiscale daily/monthly calendar is a study of "semantic zooming". Figures 2 through 4 show what the calendar looks

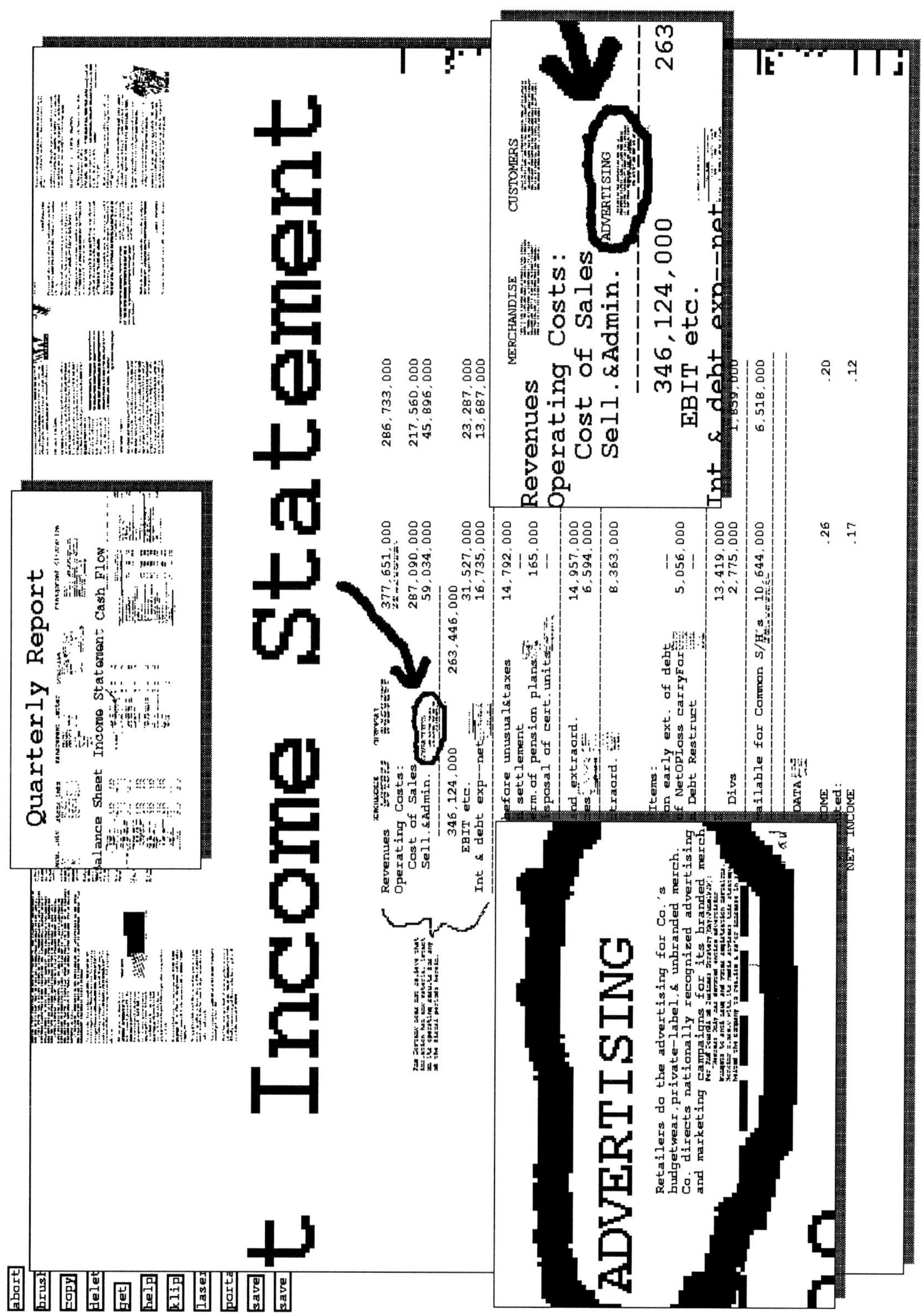

Figure 1: Quarterly report. Portals are views onto other parts of the Pad surface.

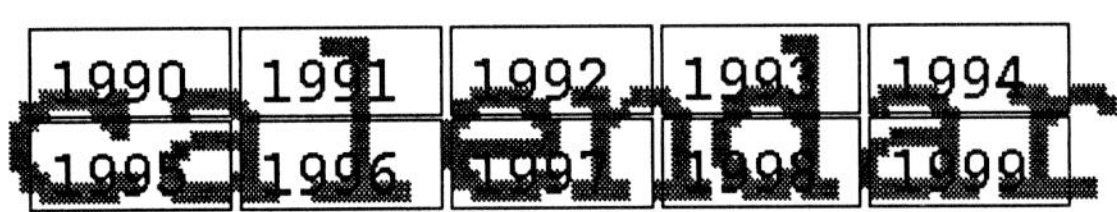

Figure 2: As you approach the calendar object the large scale display items fade out and disappear.

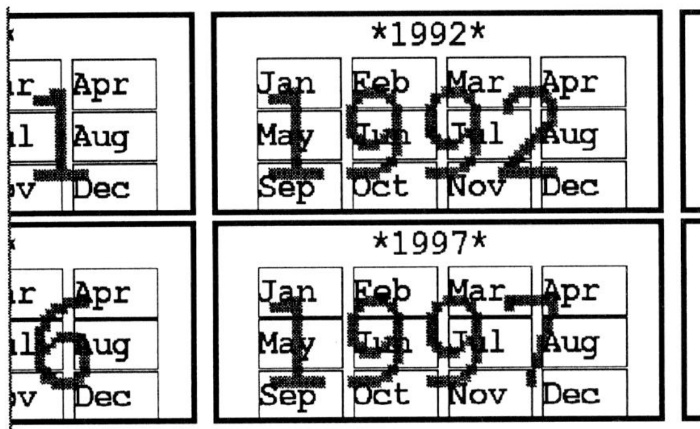

Figure 3: The calendar object generates smaller scale display items only for the area visible on the user's screen. Display items that are off the screen may be garbage collected and destroyed.

like at various successive magnifications. At any level, the user can type or draw on the calendar. As the user zooms away from the scale at which the annotations were drawn they become first translucent, then invisible. In this way, a user can overlay many levels of annotation on a calendar without confusion.

The major problem with an application of this type is that it can involve a large number of display items, since the spatial density of display items on the Pad grows geometrically as the user zooms into the calendar. Yet at any one time only a fairly small number of display items is visible, since as the user zooms in the screen occupies an ever smaller absolute area on the Pad.

We address this problem by designing the calendar object as an expandable semantic tree, and identifying display items with different nodes of this tree. Each time the calendar is displayed this semantic tree is traversed. As each node is reached, display items are generated as needed. Individual display items are ephemeral – if an item is off the screen for a while it is quietly removed by the calendar object. In this way the total number of display items always remains manageably small.

This general notion of a geographic database that will expand and self-prune as the user roams around the Pad has now been encapsulated in a Scheme library called an "ephemeral database manager". We plan to apply this library to other Pad applications that have an inherently tree structured semantics.

3 System Structure

In this section we introduce the abstract data types needed to implement Pad. First we will describe the concepts necessary for display, then those needed to support interaction.

3.1 Addresses and Regions

A Pad **address** $A = (x, y, z)$ has both a location and a scale, and defines the linear transformation $T_A : (u, v) \rightarrow (x+u2^z, y+v2^z)$. Here z represents the log_2 of scale.

A Pad **region** $R = [A, w, h]$ is a rectangle defined by an address together with a raster width and height (w, h). A region covers the portion of the Pad surface from $T_A(0,0)$ to $T_A(w,h)$, or from (x, y) to $(x + w2^z, y + h2^z)$.

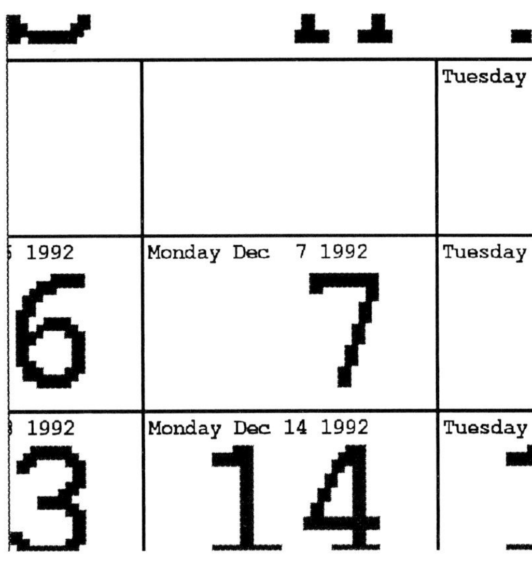

Figure 4: The user's annotations are created in ink that also fades out at greater magnifications.

3.2 Display Items

The lowest level entities in the Pad universe are the *display items*, which come in two basic types: **graphic** and *portal*. Display items are the only entities actually visible on the user's screen. A *graphic* consists of a raster image I and an address A. Every display item is said to have a region $[A, I_w, I_h]$, which is the portion of the pad surface which it occupies.

A *portal* is a graphic that has an additional address, called its *look-on* L. Using its raster image I as a mask, a portal have as its "look-on" the region $[L, I_w, I_h]$ on the Pad surface. The portion of the Pad surface which the look-on covers and which is not masked by the portal's graphic is visible at the location of the portal's region. This raster masking enables a portal to give a shaped view onto the Pad surface. Thus, a portal can be square, round, or even shaped like some well known corporate logo.

We refer to a display item's A_z as its "scale". In general, a display item becomes visible on the screen only after being viewed through a succession of portals, each of which may transform it. We refer to a display item's apparent z, as it is seen on the screen, as its "magnification".

The image on the user's screen is created from a set of display items. There is one portal associated with the user's screen called the "root portal"; the display process consists of rendering the root portal. This means rendering the region of the Pad surface which the root portal looks onto. Those display items that overlap the root portal's look-on are rendered. This procedure is then applied recursively to render any display item which is itself a portal.

As the display process recurses through each portal, the transformation $T(A)T^{-1}(L)$ is applied, where A is that portal's address and L is that portal's look-on. This recursion can be expanded to compute the location of any display item on the screen. Suppose item i is viewed through successively nested portals $p_1 \ldots p_n$. Then to determine where (and at what magnification) to display i on the screen, we apply the transformation:

$$T^{-1}(L_{root})T(A_{p_1})T^{-1}(L_{p_1})\dots T(A_{p_n})T^{-1}(L_{p_n})T(A_i)$$

Incrementing the z component of a display item's address will increase its magnification. Incrementing the z component of a portal's look-on will double the size of its looked on region – and will therefore decrease the magnification of every item seen through it. (Think of it as increasing the viewer's altitude.)

There are several other properties of primitive display items which are important to note:

Visibility Range: Each graphic object can have a range of magnification outside of which it is invisible. This is important since most display items are only useful within a certain range of magnification.

Transparency Range: Similarly, each graphic can have a range of magnification outside of which the graphic is transparent. This allows objects to fade away gracefully as they are magnified up or down. Transparency is achieved by masking with a patterned pixel mask at screen resolution.

Private Display Items: Display items may be attached to a portal, in which case they are only visible when viewed through that portal and their addresses are relative to that of the portal. This creates a hierarchy of display items and is used to implement the filters described below.

3.3 Pad Objects

Graphics and Portals suffice to make an interesting multi-scale drawing program. However to use Pad as a system for building general user interfaces requires a higher level structure called a *Pad Object* to interpret events and control these display items so they behave as a single application. In Pad an object consists of a region together with a package of code and data which respond to event messages. An object's behavior is specified by the application developer. In order to make itself seen, each object manages a collection of display items, creating, modifying, and deleting them.

Pad Objects receive events from the user's mouse and keyboard, plus timer events, channel events (events representing other types of input, e.g. the output of a process), and expose events which inform the object that some portion of itself will become visible on someone's screen. Events which would normally have an x-y location have instead an *address*, and this address is transformed if the event passes through a portal before being received by an object which is interested in it. Similarly, an expose event covers a *region* rather than just a rectangle, and this region is also transformed by portals so that each object can be informed which portion of its region will be rendered and at what magnification.

Objects are maintained in an order, just as display items have a drawing order, so that if two or more objects are at the mouse address the mouse events are sent to the one in front. The object may use this event for its own purposes, or it may pass the event on to the objects behind it, or it may transform the event's address and pass it on to some other part of the Pad. Events thus passed may go unused by the objects below, in which case the original object may then use the event for its own purposes.

3.4 Display

Display is complicated by the fact that objects may be continually creating and destroying display items. Before we can create the display we first need to give each object an opportunity to know at what magnification it will be called upon to appear, since this will probably influence what display items it chooses to show.

Therefore display is a two phase process. In the first phase, each object gathers all the necessary information about what portions of it will appear on the screen and at what magnifications. During this first phase display items may be spawned. In the second phase the screen image is actually drawn.

During phase one each portal is displayed by having the Pad object that controls it communicate with all objects that intersect the portal's look-on region. This process begins with a special root object, which controls the user's root portal. For a portal controlled by an object O_1 the procedure is as follows:

- O_1 sends an expose event for the portal's look-on region. This event will be received by all objects whose regions intersect the portal's look-on region.

- for each object O_2 that responds:
  - O_1 tells O_2 to produce display items for itself with the proper magnification and clip. If O_2 controls any portals, the procedure is invoked for them recursively.
  - any display items that O_1 receives back, it attaches to the portal.

This process continues recursively until all items large enough to see on the screen are accounted for.

In the second phase, each portal is painted from its accumulated list of display items. This process starts with the root portal, and continues on through all portals seen by the root portal, and then recursively through those portals. Note that if two portals on the screen have overlapping look-on regions, their lists may have display items in common.

3.5 Interacting Objects and Portals

Semantic zooming is implemented by having the object's display method depend upon its magnification. The object is always told its magnification during display phase one.

Portal filters are implemented as follows. Consider the case of the bar chart filter portal described earlier. Suppose this portal filter is managed by object O_1. During phase one of the portal display procedure, O_1 sends an expose event for this portal, and receives a number of acknowledgments. Suppose O_1 has just received such an acknowledgment from object O_2. O_1 queries O_2 to find out whether O_2 is a tabular object. If yes, then O_1 gets the tabular data from O_2, builds its *own* display items for the bar chart, and attaches these to the portal. If no, then O_1 asks O_2 to produce a list of display items as usual. The effect is that the filter portal will "see" any tabular data as a bar chart, but will see other objects in the usual way.

4 Implementation Details

The Pad system is written in three layers, a real-time display layer written in C++, a Scheme interpreter providing an interface to the C++ layer, and a collection of Scheme code implementing the Pad application interface. It currently runs under X Windows and MS-DOS. The X Windows version has been compiled and run on SunOS, AIX and Linux. The source code of the most recent released version is available via anonymous FTP from cs.nyu.edu in the directory pub/local/perlin.

4.1 Rendering Display Items

It is absolutely essential to our system that arbitrarily scaled bitmaps can be displayed in real time. Without an algorithm to achieve this, our desktop model would either require special purpose hardware, or else would lose real-time response. Either scenario would limit the model's general usefulness on typical currently available graphical workstations. The method we use to render the raster image of a graphic item depends upon the item's magnification. The following decisions are based on our trial and error experiences; they reflect our best results in "tuning" this process.

We use four different techniques for drawing the raster image of a graphic, depending on the range of magnification m.

- $m > 16$. At the largest magnifications it is quickest to simply draw individual filled squares for each pixel.
- $1 > m \geq 16$. At moderate magnifications we use look up tables indexed by the byte pattern, amount of magnification, and bits of shift to properly position the result within the destination word. Different tables are used depending on the depth of the image.
- $m = 1$. With no magnification we only need to worry about the amount of shift necessary to position the result.
- $\frac{1}{1024} \leq m < 1$. To demagnify images we index into a pre-computed pyramid of images.[25] This precomputation is done at the time a graphic is created; it creates about a 3/2 speed penalty to that process. Since graphic items are generally reused over many screen refreshes, this penalty is not usually a problem in practice.
- $m < \frac{1}{1024}$. Beyond some amount of demagnification the bitmap is not visible and need not be drawn at all.

These techniques yield a display time for each object approximately proportional to the size of the entire screen image. In practice this tends to keep refresh time dependent only upon screen resolution, not upon image complexity.

4.2 Address Space Limits

Addresses are implemented using floating point arithmetic, so we cannot claim an "infinite" address space for our current system. A true unbounded address space could be achieved by using extended integer arithmetic. Even in its current form, the space provided is astronomical. Suppose our numbers have a 48 bit mantissa and we have a 2^{12} by 2^{12} screen. To position an object on the screen uses 12 of those 48 bits, leaving a minimum of 36 bits of precision to position our look-on anywhere within the square $-1 \leq x, y \leq 1$. This means, for example, that you could lay out 2^{36} by 2^{36} pages of text in that area.

5 Ongoing and Future Work

5.1 Shared Object Space

Perhaps our most important goal is to create a truely distributed Pad system, where Pad objects can exist on remote machines and can migrate from machine to machine. When Pad objects are distributed over many computers the problem of updating the display of a region on one's screen becomes a combined distributed database and computational geometry problem. This is the subject of ongoing research,[7] and is beyond the scope of this paper. For in-depth discussions of the implementation problems we refer the readers to Preparata & Shamos[18] for an overview of computational geometry and to Edelsbrunner[5] for an optimal data structure for rendering.

5.2 Continuous Zoom

Early prototypes have used discreet zoom levels to achieve high performance. We have also implemented a continuous zoom algorithm (based on Bresenham's midpoint line drawing algorithm) that allows continuous scaling of raster images at approximately half the speed of discreet zooming on unenhanced bitmapped workstations. The algorithm uses table lookups to greatly speed up the calculation.

5.3 Hierarchical Text Editor

A number of generalizations of familiar applications to the hierarchical domain suggest themselves. A multiscale text editor is a generalization of a traditional text editor, with the added capabilities that text can appear at many different sizes, with recursively inserted text. Therefore the screen structure is no longer a two dimensional array - it is more like a set of nested boxes. This allows a more direct look-and-feel for hypertext - footnotes and references can be embedded in their entirety at the point of reference. Successive zooming by the user gradually expands the contents seen of the work referenced. Text is structured as hypertext – a text string may contain embedded links to other text strings. The structure of the document can be an arbitrary directed graph. Visually, text that is linked to appears to be at the location of the link, only smaller. Contents of a hyperlink can be accessed without a disruptive sudden change in the view of the text that references it.

Text can also be made semantically zoomable: When text is visibly small it appears only as a title. As the user zooms in, this expands to include an abstract. Further zooming reveals first an outline with short text descriptions, then finally the full text.

There are several options for where exactly to visually place linked-to text. The text can appear in miniature either beneath the lines of parent text or, alternatively, superimposed on the parent text. The latter option requires zoom-dependent translucency. As the user zooms in, text seen through hyperlinks "fades up" and the visually larger text that references it simultaneously "fades out".

Text can be visible simultaneously in any number of portals. Each view must maintain a certain amount of state information. For example, there needs to be a cursor for each view. This means that if the mouse is over a particular portal, and the user types, the insertion point is at the cursor of that view. Since portals can contain ownership attributes, they can be used to restrict access to parts of a document. Text visibility through any particular portal depends upon the text's ownership - public (shared by many users) or private (seen by only one user). Public text can contain links to private text. In general, the visibility attributes of text can vary, depending upon whether the text is being viewed by its owner or by someone else.

5.4 An Infinitely Scalable Painting Program

We have, together with Luis Velho, begun applying multiscale principles to an infinitely detailable painting program[17]. Organizing an infinite multiscale canvas is straightforward, requiring only a Quad-tree. Unfortunately, simulating the application of a paint brush requires a compositing operation - an *alpha* blending of the underlying image with the brush image.

Since this operation is non-commutative, it is easy to run into problems. For example, Let's say the user zooms way in to paint

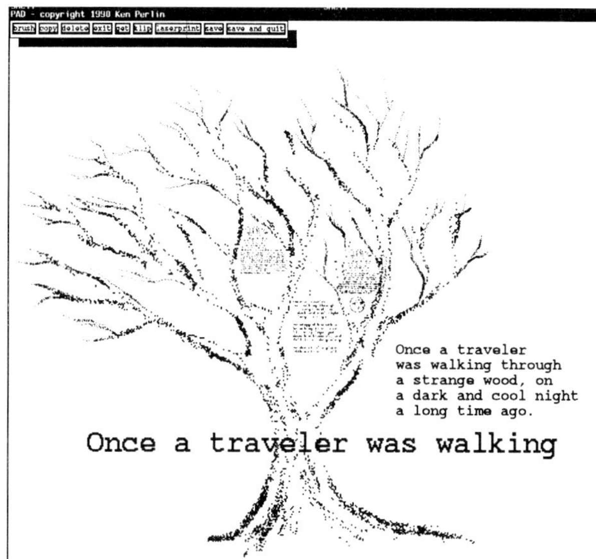

Figure 5: Overview of branching tree story. The story begins with a single sentence. The branches of the tree represent story paths - as the reader zooms into different branches, different stories unfold.

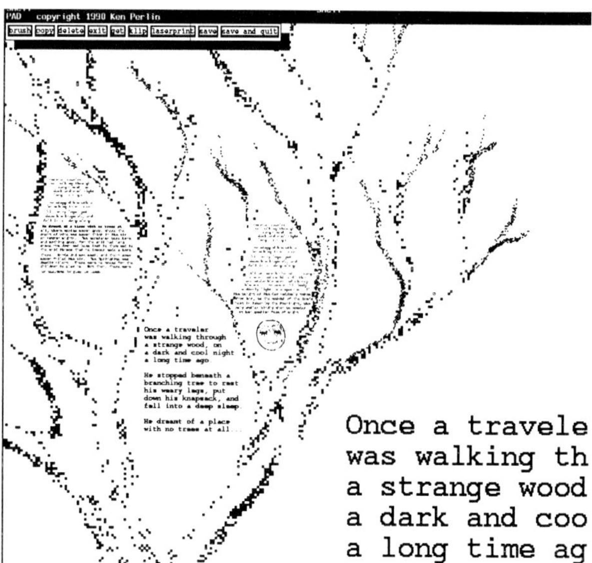

Figure 6: One level of zoom into branching tree story. At this scale the narrative contains one or two paragraphs of detail.

a scene at a fine scale, then pulls out to paint an atmospheric wash at a coarse scale, and finally zooms back in to touch up fine scale details. How should the system implement this? A straightforward approach, used by Williams[26], is to immediately apply the coarse scale operations to the finer level pixels. But this is computationally prohibitive for highly scaled scenes, since the number of fine scale pixels affected grows exponentially with the difference between coarse and fine scale.

Clearly a pyramid of some kind is called for. But because of non-commutativity, successive operations at different levels cannot be separated into a traditional Laplacian or similar multilevel pyramid (as they could be in, say, a strictly additive system). Our solution is to use B-spline wavelets. We break the brush image into its component wavelet basis, and apply independently at each level of a wavelet basis pyramid. Then the B-spline wavelet reconstruction will produce the correct result. We have implemented this to a one-dimensional canvas, and are now working on a two or more dimensional version.

5.5 Multiple Narrative Paths

Pad is a good way to store documents with hierarchy and multiple narrative pathways. Side discussions in a textbook can be embedded *in situ*. This allows for some interesting possibilities. For example, a novel may be written with bifurcations, allowing its reader to explore many interleaving stories - a sort of visual *Alexandria Quartet*. For example, we have been creating a user browseable novel literally shaped into a tree, as seen in figures 5, 6, 7.

5.6 Cooperative Pad Applications

With the onset of high bandwidth consumer information services, Pad provides a viable look-and-feel for information browsing. As the customer zooms in to an information service, the semantic zoom level (and hence the information content) increases. Zoomed-down browsing can be made freely available, and the customer can be billed at successively higher rates for more specific data.

For example, the title and a brief synopsis of a video may be accessible at low zoom levels. Higher zoom levels actually play the movie. At the browsing level, the customer might see geographically arranged clusters of films that may be of related interest (e.g. films by a particular director).

Similarly, our **Pad Map** project will provide a substantial user community with access to a shared map of Manhattan, annotated with information about cultural events. The users will be able to add their own annotations, such as restaurant or movie reviews, or just graffiti. As part of the Pad system, annotations could be at any scale, and contain links to other annotations: though it is desirable to keep all the reviews of a given film together, portals could make them visible at each theatre which is showing that film. The project will explore the mechanisms necessary manage user contributions without any one user monopolizing or degrading the system for others.

Our **Shared Spreadsheet** project re-casts the spreadsheet application in a more hierarchical and sharable form. For example, hierarchy can be imposed by placing spreadsheet A in a cell of spreadsheet B, and designating a particular cell of A to be the value that appears in B's cell when the magnification of A is low. The value of sharing such a spreadsheet among users comes from immediate access to the latest data, and the elimination of the need to merge copies of the spreadsheet which have been updated independently, etc.

Eventually, as display and communication technology improves, pieces of display surface scattered around a work environment will become more common – on walls, desks, electronic PostIt^{tm} notes[24]. Pad is well suited to such a distributed environment, since it places the user at a floating location in an information geography. The Windows/Icon/Menu/Pointer model is less well suited to this, since it is motivated by the desire to create a "desktop" metaphor on a single display screen.

6 Conclusions

We have described a new kind of graphical space that has a number of advantages over traditional window systems. Its key advantage is that it allows a user or a group of users to share and view multiple applications in a manner that assigns them vari-

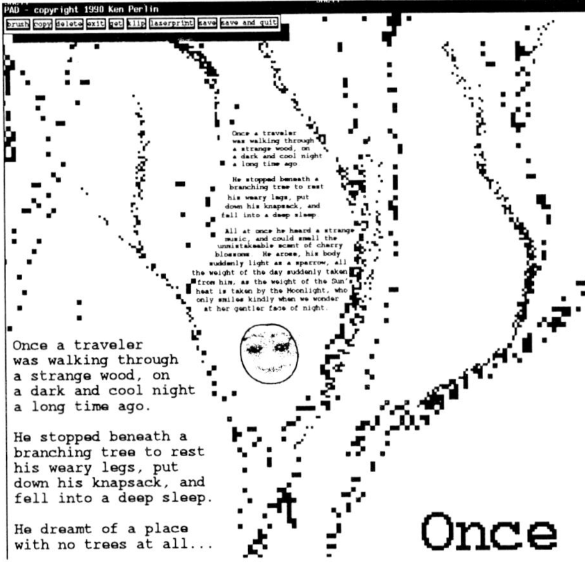

Figure 7: Two levels of zoom into branching tree story. Here we can see the story beginning to take a definite shape - in one possible narrative path.

ous levels of importance, with easy visual nesting and zooming of documents as they move from peripheral to primary working attention.

As compared to standard current window models, this system makes it easier for the user to exploit visual memory of places to organize informationally large workspaces.

We believe that this approach enriches the workstation/window paradigm in a fundamental way.

6.1 Acknowledgments

This research was funded by a grant from the NYNEX Corporation and by NSF grant number IRI-9015445. We would like to thank Nathan Felde at NYNEX for the initial discussions leading to this work, and Jack Schwartz, Lorie Loeb, Raj Raichoudhury, Allison Druin, and Gene Miller, all of whom contributed valuable ideas and time, as well as the Apple corporation for their generous equipment donation. Particular credit goes to Matthew Fuchs, who is developing the Distributed Pad/Scheme system DREME.

References

[1] Sara Bly et. al., *Media Spaces: Bringing People Together in a Video, Audio, and Computing Environment.*, CACM, Vol. 36, 1993, No. 1., pp. 28-47.

[2] Peter Burt, *A multiresolution spline with applications to image mosaics,* ACM Transactions on Graphics, Vol. 2, No. 4, Oct. 1983, pp. 217-236.

[3] James H. Clark. *Hierarichical geometric models for visible surface algorithms.* ACM Communications, Vol. 19, No. 10, Oct. 1976, pages 547-554.

[4] William C. Donelson, *Spatial Management of Information,* ACM SIGGRAPH 1978 Conference Proceedings.

[5] H. Edelsbrunner, *A new approach to rectangle intersections, Part II,* Int'l Journal of Computational Mathematics, No. 13, pp. 221-229, 1983.

[6] S. Feiner and C. Beshers, *Worlds within worlds: Metaphors for exploring n-dimensional virtual worlds.* Proc. UIST '90 (ACM Symp. on User Interface Software and Technology), Snowbird, UT, Oct. 3-5, 1990, pp. 76-83.

[7] Matthew Fuchs, unpublished Ph.D. dissertation in progress.

[8] George Furnas, *Generalized Fisheye Views, Human Factors & Computer Systems,* CHI 89 Conference proceedings, pp. 16-23.

[9] Ralph Hill, et. al., *The Rendezvous Language and Architecture,* CACM Vol. 36, 1993, No. 1., pp. 62-67.

[10] *Hypertext on Hypertext,* Macintosh Version: Disk #1 and #2. ACM Press, New York, 1988.

[11] I. Lu et. al., *Idea management in a shared drawing tool.* Proceedings of the Second European Conference on Computer-Supported Cooperative Work-ECSCW '91, Amsterdam, Holland, 1991.

[12] J. Mackinlay et. al., *Rapid Controlled Movement Through a Virtual 3D Workspace.* ACM SIGGRAPH 1990 Conference Proceedings.

[13] Nelson Max, ACM SIGGRAPH 1975 Film show.

[14] Minneman, S.. and Bly, S.a. *Managing a trois: A study of a multi-user drawing tool in distributed design work* Proceedings of the CHI'91 Conference on Human Factors in Computer Systems., New Orleans, La., 1991.

[15] Ted Nelson, *Literary Machines.* Swarthmore, PA, 1981.

[16] Jakob Nielsen, *Non-command User Interfaces,* CACM, Vol. 36 No. 4, (April 1993), pp. 83-99.

[17] Ken Perlin and Luis Velho, *A Wavelet Representation for Unbounded Resolution Painting,* NYU Technical Report.

[18] Franco P. Preparata, Michael Ian Shamos, *Computational Geometry: An Introduction,* Springer Verlag, New York, 1989.

[19] David Small, Masters Thesis, MIT Media Laboratory, 1989.

[20] Randall B. Smith, Tim O'Shea, Claire O'Malley, Eileen Scanlon, and Josie Taylor. *Preliminary Experiments with a distributed, multi-media, problem solving environment.* In Proceedings of the First European Conference on Computer Supported Cooperative Work (Gatwick, UK) 1989, pages 19-34.

[21] J.C. Tang and S.L. Minneman, *Videodraw: A video interface for collaborative drawing.* Proceedings of the CHI '90 Conference on Human Factors in Computing Systems, Seattle, Wash., 1990.

[22] S. L. Tanimoto, and T. Pavlidis, *A hierarchical data structure for picture processing.* Computer Graphics and Image Processing, Vol. 4, 1975, pp. 104-119.

[23] Edward Tufte, *The Visual Display of Quantitative Information,* Graphics Press, 1983.

[24] M. Weiser *The Computer for the 21st Century,* Sci. Am. 265,3 (September 1991), pp. 94-104.

[25] Lance Williams, *Pyramidal Parametrics.* ACM SIGGRAPH 1982 Conference Proceedings.

[26] Lance Williams, personal communication.

Autocalibration for Virtual Environments Tracking Hardware *

Stefan Gottschalk
Computer Science Department
University of North Carolina
Chapel Hill, NC
gottscha@cs.unc.edu

John F. Hughes
Computer Science Department
Brown University
Providence, RI
jfh@cs.brown.edu

Abstract

We describe two instances in which precise mechanical calibration of virtual environments equipment has been replaced by automated algorithmic calibration through software that encapsulates the hardware design and uses a goal-based approach to adjust calibration parameters. We describe a back-projection system for adjusting the assumed locations of beacons in a head-mounted display tracking system; the calculated errors in the navigation system are used to compute adjustments to the beacon positions to reduce such errors. In a second application, a piggyback head-tracking/hand-tracking system is calibrated by a similar reduction of computed errors.

CR Categories: I.3.m [Computer Graphics]: Miscellaneous; I.3.7 [Computer Graphics]: 3-dimensional Graphics and Realism — Virtual Reality; I.4.8 [Image Processing] Scene Analysis — Photometry

Additional Keywords: Virtual environments, tracking, autocalibration.

1 Introduction

A number of calibration issues for virtual environments (VE) hardware are approached with standard engineering techniques in which the accuracy of the calibration is directly dependent on the accuracy of the assemblies in the VE machinery. This approach is successful to a degree but has several drawbacks. First, it makes the machinery very sensitive to rough handling. Second, frequent realignment may be required, which may be time-consuming and may be necessary so frequently that extended use of the equipment becomes impossible. Third, modifications of the machinery become very difficult.

We therefore take a *goal-based* approach to these problems, applying methods learned in computer graphics to solve engineering problems. Instead of requiring precise calibration of parts, we ask the systems to autocalibrate, a notion that was inspired in part by the auto-assembling systems of Barzel and Barr [BB88] but which first appeared in Wang's dissertation [Wan90]. This allows us to write a program encoding the *design* of the system that uses the system's observations to adjust itself. Since realignment can sometimes actually be done while the machinery is in use, rather than in a separate calibration phase, the first and second problems above are reduced. And because the software that implements the autocalibration encodes the intent of the design, the mechanical design can be modified in parallel with software modification, helping to reduce the third problem. In this paper, we discuss two sample applications: calibration of a head-tracking system and of a piggyback hand tracker attached to the head-tracking unit.

We stress that the techniques here serve the general goal of head-tracking. The current interest in Virtual Reality, evidenced by the attention it has attracted in both the technical literature and the media, may well have led to unjustified expectations. There is a belief that "any day now" the technology will become available. But there are three substantial obstacles: (1) for comfort, the units need small, high-resolution displays; (2) graphics hardware must be capable of real-time, low-latency image generation; (3) a low-latency, high-accuracy system for head tracking in unprepared, possibly-noisy environments is necessary. We are addressing the third of these issues. There is as yet no tracking system that is lightweight and works in unprepared environments and in large spaces. As far as we know, no one has demonstrated a working head-tracking system for a room-sized environment (about 15' x 15'). The ceiling tracker described here is a start: the environment is large and expandable and the equipment, although heavy, is bearable. We envision an eventual system in which methods similar to those described here are used to calibrate the system's view of its environment. The algorithms may differ, but the principle — having the system model its sources of error and calibrate itself against them — will remain.

We wish to make one more point: the two examples presented in this paper give details of a general principle, and this general principle is applicable to cases other than the ones we describe. In short, as one designs a tracker (or other electro-mechanical assembly), one has the opportunity to leave some physical parameters fixed but unknown, and to then determine their exact values after construction. Doing this kind of post-construction calibration does, however, require that some aspects of the system be overdetermined. In the head-tracker example below, we could not have performed autocalibration if the tracker computed its position from just three LED beacons, since there would be no "error measure" as we computed the position–the equations would be exactly determined rather than overdetermined. Similarly, without multiple samples in the hand-tracking application, we could not determine the orientation matrix. So

*This work was supported in part by grants from NSF, DARPA, IBM, NCR, Sun Microsystems, DEC, and HP.

the principle is this: if one wishes to use autocalibration, the system must have a surplus of information and a way to measure whether this information is internally consistent. The cost of obtaining this surplus of information is a design tradeoff, and should be considered during the design rather than after.

2 Operation of the Ceiling Tracker

Most current head trackers achieve a large working volume at the expense of accuracy and precision. However, some virtual environments applications require a large working volume *and* some minimum tracking precision.

A team at UNC–CH has developed an optoelectronic tracking system capable of tracking head motion with precision of approximately 0.2 degrees orientation and 1 mm translation. (A description of this system and its design can be found in the references [WAB+92] [WAB+90].). System accuracy has not been measured precisely, but has been found to be very adequate for the purposes of head-mounted display (HMD) applications. At present, the working volume is a 10' by 12' area, but the tracking area can in principle be expanded arbitrarily by adding LED-studded ceiling panels.

The method used by the optoelectronic tracker is conceptually similar to celestial navigation. A mariner observes the angles between some number of stars and the horizon, and then, knowing the stars' locations in the heavens, determines the vessel's position. Similarly, we observe a number of ceiling-mounted infrared LEDs, and knowing their positions, we compute the location (and orientation) of the head-tracking unit.

To be more precise, we have a helmet with cameras mounted on it. Some of the ceiling LEDs are rapidly flashed in a known sequence, and each one is possibly sighted by a camera. The choice of subset and sequence is not preset, but is determined "on the fly" as it is learned which LEDs are visible to which cameras. The cameras are lateral-effect photodiodes with lenses, and each can report the centroid of a spot of light that strikes its surface. The centroid's location is reported in image plane coordinates, x and y. We call these *photocoordinates* (see Figure 1).

The placements of the cameras on the helmet are known, as are the locations of the principal points of the lens systems and the placements of the photodiodes' image planes within the camera casings. Thus, when the camera reports the photocoordinates of LED image on its image plane, we can compute the line, in head space, along which the LED must lie. We call this line a *back-projection*, because it is the result of projecting the ray from the photodiode back through the lens system and outward.

Now, given several back-projections in head space, and given the true locations of the LEDs in world space, where must the head be in world space so as to cause the back-projections to pass through their respective LEDs? With three (sufficiently general) back-projections, an unique solution can be found. With more than three, we have an overdetermined system and we compute a best fit according to a least-squares criterion, using a method called "space-resection by collinearity" (abbreviated "CA" for "collinearity algorithm"). We briefly describe CA in Section 3.1; full details can be found elsewhere [AW91]. Several questions about this tracker design that are often raised are discussed in an Appendix.

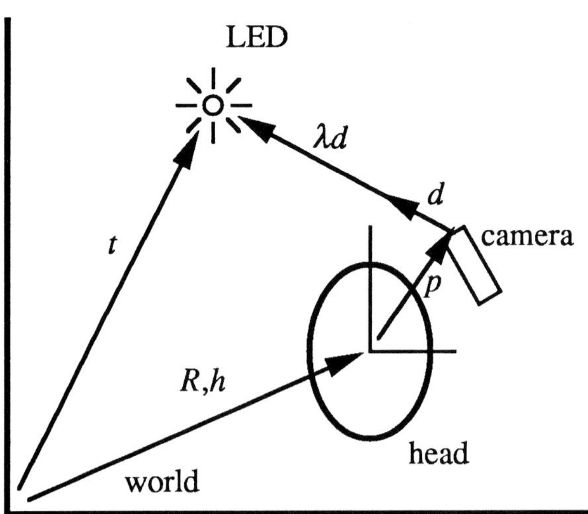

Figure 1: The geometry of the head-tracking system.

3 Explaining the Problem

The current design uses an adjustable superstructure to support the ceiling panels. The adjustments are needed because any conceivable support structure would bend under the loading of the panels, giving an undesirable curvature to the ceiling's surface.

With the current design of 10' by 12' (30 2' by 2' panels), the leveling process requires about 90 minutes of operator time, with specialized equipment.

We plan to build another, larger ceiling without this superstructure. The panels will be of the same size, but will drop directly into the standard ceiling grid, replacing the acoustic tiles found in many buildings. This ceiling will be 18' by 30'; the expense of a comparable-size superstructure is prohibitive, and leveling time would be several hours.

Standard ceiling grids are by no means flat, and we have therefore developed the autocalibration technique described here to determine the location of the LEDs after the panels are installed. Before describing that technique, however, we give more details of the collinearity algorithm.

3.1 The collinearity algorithm

The collinearity algorithm (CA) works by observing many (typically 10 to 20) LEDs and then computing a best estimate of headmount position and orientation. When an LED shines onto a photodiode, the photodiode reports the centroid of the LED's image on its face. Since the algorithm knows the headmount geometry, it is able to compute, in head space, where the back-projection emerges and in what direction it is pointed. Somewhere along this back-projection lies the LED (see Figure 2).

Thus

$$R(p + \lambda d) + h = t, \qquad \lambda > 0 \tag{1}$$

where t the is location of the LED in world space, R is the matrix that takes vectors in head coordinates to world coordinates (i.e., R defines the *orientation* of the head-mount), h is the world-space coordinates of the origin of the head-mount coordinate system; and p and d are the basepoint and direction (unit vector) of the back-projection ray in head-coordinates; λ is the distance from the camera to the LED.

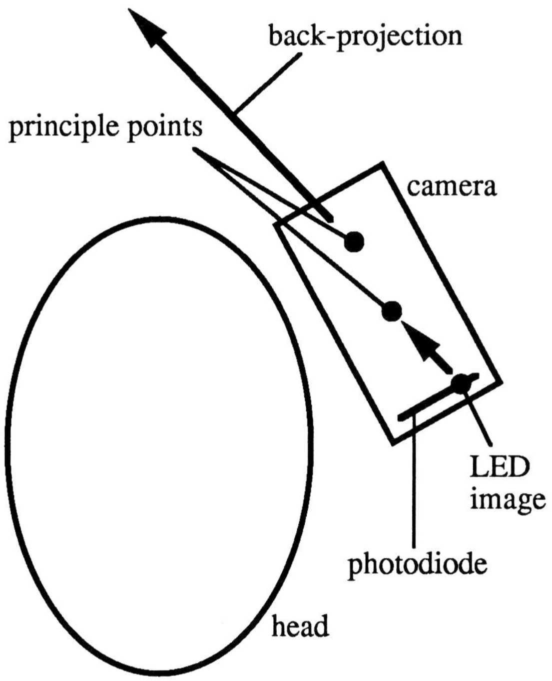

Figure 2: The back-projection ray from the camera towards the ceiling.

Equation 1 actually consists of three scalar equations, one for each of the x-, y-, and z-components. We can solve the z component for λ and substitute this into the x and y components. This eliminates λ and leaves us with two scalar equations in the unknowns R and h.

Many LEDs are seen at the same moment. Each of these generates two scalar equations. So each observation, which sights 12 to 20 LEDs, constructs a system of 24 to 40 equations in the unknowns R and h. CA seeks those values of R and h that minimize the residuals of these equations in the least-squares sense. These values are found by applying a multidimensional Newton's method.

The method is most successful when given an initial guess very close to the optimal solution. In practice, this is easy to supply. The optical tracker typically provides updates every 12 to 20 milliseconds, and a person does not move far in that interval. Thus, for the initial guess, the algorithm merely uses the value of the previous update, which is guaranteed to be close.

4 Autocalibration: Rationale and Description

We have pointed out that it is very desirable to be able to construct the ceiling with loose tolerances, and be able to determine the locations of the LEDs afterward. CA does not depend upon any particular configuration of LED beacons – all places are alike to it. It does, however, require an exact knowledge of the locations of the LEDs, wherever they may be.

An "engineering" approach to achieving agreement between the physical geometry of the beacons and their software representation is prohibitively expensive. Therefore, we sought a way to determine the locations of the LEDs using existing hardware and some numerical processing.

The collinearity algorithm was derived from photgrammetric methods. Our LED calibration method, which makes use of CA as one step, was based primarily on influences from mathematics and computer graphics rather than the photgrammetry literature. We have since learned, however, that our approach has parallels in that literature, although we have found no exact analog. Nonethless, we strongly recommend that others working on optical tracking systems consult the photogrammetry literature [Sla80] for many ideas which, with slight modifications, may prove valuable in tracking.

We begin with an estimate of the beacon locations. We then take several thousand headmount observations (collecting 25,000 observations takes about 45 minutes) from a variety of positions, and use CA to "fit" the position of each observation to its beacon data. Of course, we know only approximately where the LEDs are, but fitting the headmount position to the beacon data allows some of the error in the beacon location estimates to cancel. The CA solution for the location of the headmount at each of these thousands of observations is likely to be rather bad: the sum of squares value will be large. To return to the marine analogy, it is as though the several circles of positions on the earth, each determined by a single star, failed to intersect at a single point, and instead intersected pairwise at several different points that surrounded a large region. The mariner estimates the vessel's position as somewhere at the center of the region, and begins to doubt the accuracy of the almanac's star locations.

After this initial set of observations, we derive the back-projections from each of these computed headmount locations, to yield "sightings" of the LEDs from roughly known positions. An LED sighted from several positions should be located at the intersection of the back-projections extending from those positions, but in general, the back-projections do not come together at a point, but tend instead to cluster in a particular region. We therefore adjust our estimate of each LED to be closer to this back-projection cluster. (The mariner, after several sets of inconsistent observations, decides to correct the almanac). This is the second step of our autocalibration.

After we adjust all the LEDs, the old observation positions are no longer optimal solutions in CA. So, we apply CA again to the observation positions, using the same data as before, but with the new beacon location estimates. (The mariner re-computes the vessel's position on each of the previous days, and now has circles of position that come closer to intersecting at single points). Thus we repeat the first step. We now continue, alternating between the two steps in this fashion, adjusting first one set of parameters and then the other, until we have settled to some configuration.

It seems surprising at first that this process converges at all; it is even more surprising to see how fast and how accurately it converges. We tested this by perturbing three of the ceiling panels as shown in Figure 4, and then running the algorithm. The average error-vector magnitudes for the first five full iterations were 13.1 mm, 4.7 mm, 3.2 mm, 2.5 mm, 2.2 mm, and 1.9 mm. After 20 iterations, which takes about two hours for 25,000 observations, the average error vector is down to 1.1 mm. Figure 5 is a computer-generated picture of the tracker ceiling. The beacons on the tilted panels are clearly visible.

The adjustment made to an LED's location depends on its relationship to the back-projections associated with it. A back-projection, in general, passes nearby the LED's estimated location. The vector drawn from the LED's estimated position to the back-projection's closest approach to that position is the *error vector* for that back-projection. A given LED has many back-projections, for each of which there is an associated error vector. We average these error vectors, and use this average as the adjustment to the LED's estimated position.

In a sense, each observation of an LED "votes" in the adjustment. An observation typically sees many LEDs, and cannot find a position from which to spear all its LEDs with its back-projections. The smallest adjustment possible for each LED that would completely satisfy an observation's collinearity conditions, would be an adjustment along the error vector. However, such an adjustment might conflict with the adjustment required by another observation.

The averaging is thus done as a compromise among the needs of the various observations that sight a given LED. It *is* possible to determine a new position for the LED that actually minimizes the sum of the squared lengths of the error vectors, but it is computationally expensive, and the averaging method works well and fast in practice.

4.1 Concerns About Noise: the Method in Practice

The autocalibration method was originally tried with simulated data so that it could be evaluated in the absence of noise and other complicating factors. It was found to be quite effective, providing rapid convergence. Performance on real data was not nearly as good – for reasons we now discuss.

First, the photodiode readings are noisy. The photocoordinates have as much as 12 microns of uncertainty. If the LED is a meter away from the camera, which has a 50-mm lens, the back-projection will miss by more than .25 mm even if headmount's position and orientation are exactly correct.

Second, the system of equations produced by each observation assumes that the LEDs are sighted simultaneously, and this is not true in practice. The LEDs are sampled in sequence, and each sample may take as much as a millisecond. If the user's head is turning at the (reasonable) rate of 180 degrees per second, the LED is 1 m. away from the axis of rotation, and 20 LEDS are sampled for the observation, then in the 20 milliseconds of sampling, the back-projection to the first LED may have traveled 6 cm. This causes the system of equations given by the observation data to be inconsistent, so that it cannot be satisfied by any position and orientation. The fact that the equations cannot be satisfied implies that the back-projections are simply wrong, and hence will "pull on" the LEDs wherever the observation settles.

Third, acquiring the right spatial distribution of observations is surprisingly difficult. The LEDs in the corner of the ceiling are typically seen in many fewer observations than the ones in the center. And when the LEDs in the corner are seen, it tends to be from one direction. Naturally, an LED in the corner can be seen only from one octant: below ceiling height and beneath the ceiling. But diversity in the angles from which the LED is seen is helpful. If an LED is seen from within a narrow cone of positions, then the location of the back-projection cluster is more sensitive to the errors mentioned earlier: a slight distortion in the back-projections' placement tends to disperse the cluster, denying the LED a strong centering influence.

Three observations can be made about the first source of error. First, in addition to using superior photodiodes and electronics, the error can be reduced by using lenses of longer focal length. With longer focal lengths, the 12-micron error in the LED image location would translate to an even narrower error cone for the corresponding back-projection. The primary disadvantage of the resulting small fields of view is that they can slip between the LEDs and fail to see any at all. Second, one can allow the headmount to sit still, accumulating photocoordinates, and average them over time to distill a more accurate reading. Unfortunately, with thousands of observations required, data acquisition for calibration would be very time-consuming. Third and most important, however, sensor noise error is insignificant in comparison to the other two sources of error.

The second source of error comes from the motion of the headmount. Again, for calibration purposes, we could take data points only when the headmount is still. But this again would make data acquisition intolerably slow. In practice, we have found that moving the headmount slowly helps substantially in reducing this error. A better solution is to change the system of equations to take into account the headmount velocity, both linear and rotational. This would require a minimum of six LEDs per observation to obtain a fully-determined system, but typical counts are already 12 to 20 LEDs per observation. This is future work.

The third problem is being addressed by an graphics application that assists in data acquisition. A top view (map) of the ceiling is displayed on a nearby workstation, on which LEDs presently observed are marked. (This is needed because the LEDs emit infrared light, invisible to the naked eye.) The least-sampled LEDs are marked in a different color, allowing the operator to direct his efforts to sighting those LEDs. During the calibration process, in addition, certain LEDs are identified as having unusually large error vectors, meaning that their associated back-projections do not cluster tightly enough. A second run of data collection can be made, and special attention paid to these trouble spots.

In addition to the precautions and program assistance mentioned above, the calibration algorithm tests for high error vectors and culls out observations for which CA cannot find a satisfactory solution. (This is similar to computing robust statistics by eliminating outliers.) In this way, the algorithm is made somewhat more tolerant of operator mistakes or wild readings from the sensors (which are very rare).

Two features of the automated calibration method have not yet mentioned. First, the ceiling tracker is in frequent use. We can simply collect the observations *during use* and use these in an off-line calibration computation, so that we can keep the tracking system aligned without downtime. At present the system does not need frequent recalibration, and we do separate calibration runs, allowing us to collect only "good" data (i.e., data taken with slow head motion). Second, the entire algorithm is subject to a kind of systematic error: if we apply a rigid motion to our estimates of the beacon locations, CA converges exactly as well as before. This means that if one wishes to calibrate the system in absolute coordinates (relative to some frame of reference for the room in which the ceiling tracker sits), one may have to apply a rigid motion to the computed beacon positions so taht the estimated lcoations of a few key beacons are their actual positions as determined, for example, by measurements from the walls of the room.

5 Using a Headmounted Magnetic Tracker for Handtracking

Although the optical tracker gives satisfactory accuracy over a large working volume, its design does not lend itself to hand tracking for several reasons: the bulkiness of the cameras, the geometry of the situation (the user's body may obscure the hand's "view" of the ceiling, and the hand may not be held upright), and the dynamic range requirements on photodiode sensitivity (because of changing distances from the ceiling). We have found, however, that magnetic trackers [RBSJ79] usually provide satisfactory performance within a small tracking volume, although in our environment they report significantly distorted position and orientation outside of a range of about five feet. Since one's hands never get farther than a few feet from one's head, we decided to place a magnetic source on the headmount and track hand motion from there.

Ultimately, however, we want to know the hand's location in the ceiling coordinate system. The optical tracker reports the head location in ceiling space, the magnetic source lies at some fixed location in head space, and the Polhemus tracking system reports the hand's location in source space. We compose the change-of-coordinate transformations among these three systems to get the hand's location in ceiling space.

Of course, the fixed location of the magnetic source within head space must be known before we can compose the transforms. As before, we have two choices: engineering, i.e., careful placement of the source on a precise rigid mount attached to the headframe, and autocalibration, in which we place the source approximately and then infer its position precisely using autocalibration. We chose the latter approach.

5.1 The calibration problem and solution

We attach the magnetic source to the headmount with a rigid Plexiglas framework whose position is known within a few inches, and whose orientation is easy to measure within about 10 degrees. These are clearly not adequate measurements: if the hand is held 3' from the source, a 1 degree error in the measurement of the source's orientation would cause a 15 mm error in the computation of the hand's placement.

Our calibration approach is simple. We take simultaneous optical tracker and magnetic tracker readings, and use them to recover the placement of the source within head space. The algorithm starts with a very approximate estimate of the source's placement, such as might be obtained by inspection.

We start by fixing the Polhemus sensor at some location in ceiling space. The exact location is not important – it need only stay still.

Now consider what *should* happen (if the system were calibrated properly) as the headmount moves about in the proximity of the sensor. We receive readings from the optical and magnetic trackers. The optical tracker produces the *Ceiling-from-Head* transform, and the magnetic tracker provides the *Source-from-Sensor* transform. If the *Head-from-Source* is correct, then the composition of these transforms, *Ceiling-from-Head* × *Head-from-Source* × *Source-from-Sensor*, should remain constant and should be the *Ceiling-from-Sensor* transform, which is constant because the sensor is not moving) (see Figure 3.

If, for observation i, R_i is the reported *Ceiling-from-Head* transform, T_i is the reported *Source-from-Sensor* transform, S is the unknown but fixed *Head-from-Source* transform, and M is the unknown *Ceiling-from-Sensor* transform, then for any pair of reports from the trackers,

$$R_i S T_i = M,$$

provided the trackers are accurate. But if S is wrong, then as we walk around the room, the sensor's position and orientation (i.e., M), as computed by the transform composition,

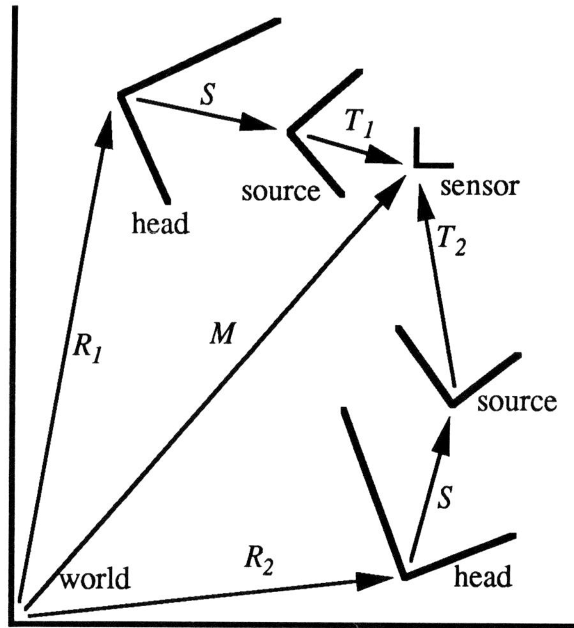

Figure 3: The geometry of the composite tracker during two different observations. The source is held fixed in the head-mounted-display coordinate system, and the sensor is fixed in the world coordinate system, but the relationship of the head to the world and of the sensor to the source change with each observation.

will drift, appearing to be in different places, depending on where we are standing.

After n readings from n different places, we have a system of n equations,

$$R_i S T_i = M_i, \qquad i = 0 \ldots n-1,$$

where S is our (incorrect) estimate of *Head-from-Source*, and each M_i is computed as $R_i S T_i$. We seek the value of S that will make the M_is equal (i.e., the value of S that keeps our reports of the sensor positions and orientation constant).

Our estimate of S and the readings R_i and T_i give rise to many estimates of the sensor location M_i. We might get closer to the true value of M by taking some compromise among the M_is, say, by estimating that it is the average of the M_is. We actually bias this average slightly by averaging the matrix entries, and then performing the Gram-Schmidt process on the rotational part of the matrix. This averaging and orthonormalization step is likely to prompt objections, which we address below. For now, we continue with our description of the algorithm.

Let's call this resulting average transform Q. If we imagine that this is the correct value for the sensor location, then we can write the system

$$R_i S T_i = Q, \qquad i = 0 \ldots n-1,$$

If Q really were the correct location, then we could take any one of the equations $R_i S T_i = Q$ and solve for S to recover that value, since the remaining transforms would be known. However, when we actually do this we find that we get different values for S. Why? Because Q is not correct – but it might be close. Solving for S gets us

$$S_i = R_i^{-1} Q T_i^{-1}, \qquad i = 0 \ldots n-1,$$

each of which suggests a different value for S. We average these in exactly the way we did the M_is to arrive at a new estimate for S.

This completes one iteration of the algorithm. With our new estimate of S we go back and acquire new M_is, which we average to get Q, which we substitute back into the system so we can solve for the S_i's, which we average to get our new S. We iterate until the value of S stabilizes.

5.2 Justification for averaging matrices

Averaging makes sense for points in a linear space like a plane, but we are trying to use it in a nonlinear space (the set of 3×3 rotation matrices). But in general, the average of a set of points on a non-linear space like a sphere is almost always a point that is not on the sphere. Even so, if all the points are very close together on the sphere, this averaging yields a point that is near to a point on the sphere that one might call the "average.". The reason is that the local geometry of the sphere is well approximated by any of the tangent planes within the local region, and so the sphere-based averaging is a close approximation to the tangent-plane averaging. Since the average of the sphere points does not lie on the sphere, however,to get a meaningful average we must project back onto the sphere. The critical properties of the projection map here are (1) it is continuous in a neighborhood of the sphere, and (2) for points already *on* the sphere, the projection is the identity. We now explain why the process we used in averaging matrices is analogous.

The set Q of 4×4 translation-and-rotation matrices is a subset of R^{16}; it is curved in much the same way that the sphere is a curved subset of R^3. We can average a collection of points on the object Q (i.e., several matrices), in much the same way as we averaged points on the sphere. Before this can make sense, though, we must honor the restriction that the points being averaged should be close to one another. And the same caveat applies: the R^{16}-average of a set of points in Q is not likely to lie in Q, and will need to be projected back to Q, which is what the Gram-Schmidt process does. Note, though, that the Gram-Schmidt process has the same properties as radial projection: it is a continuous function of the entries of the matrix (at least for matrices that are close to rotation matrices), and for a rotation matrix, the Gram-Schmidt process does nothing.

Still, there remains the question, "How small a region must the points be gathered in for averaging to make sense?" On the sphere, it certainly makes sense when all the points are contained in some hemisphere. For matrices, the averaging of the translational part is simply an average in a linear space, and needs no justification; for the rotational part, we *believe* (but have not proved formally) that the averaging process makes sense for any collection of (rotation) matrices $\{A_i\}$ for which all the inner products $z_{ij} = trace(A_i A_j^t)$ are greater than 1/2. In practice, however, our matrices are all quite close to one another, and these inner products are large. Furthermore, the algorithm in practice is far more robust than we had expected. In a 2D simulation of the problem, for example, it takes some effort to give an initial estimate of the matrix S that makes the algorithm diverge.

5.3 Noise in the data, and the algorithm in practice

The accuracy of this method depends on the accuracy of the trackers providing the data. The optical and magnetic trackers, providing the R_i's and T_i's are noisy. In general, no choice of S and M satisfies all the equations simultaneously. It is impossible to determine what the correct values are, and we can only hope to get an approximation to the correct S. Nonetheless, the error in the estimates of S and M, since they are based on multiple samples, should average out the random noise from the trackers. The *systematic* noise (e.g., one tracker always reports a slightly scaled x-coordinate) is not averaged out, but is also inherent in the system; if such systematic noise were too large, the system would be unusable in practice. Our experience is that the values of S and M converge quite rapidly to values that provide quite good hand-tracking.

There is one important observation about this instance of autocalibration: the sensor readings from which the calibration is done must be in fairly general position. In some cases, for example if the orientation of the headmount remains constant throughout the sampling process and the headmount is translated only along a single axis, then a little linear algebra shows that the estimates of S and M can all be identical but nonetheless be incorrect. But if the headmount is tilted and translated about all three axes during data gathering, and if multiple tilts and translations about each axis are included, then the equations will be sufficiently general to guarantee convergence (given a good enough initial estimate of S).

5.4 Remarks on the Method

One nice aspect of this method is that no exact measurements are needed. The location of the sensor somewhere in lab space may remain unknown. The position of the source in head space need only be estimated – and that is the only measurement necessary: the rest of the information is taken directly from the tracker sensors themselves.

The calibration procedure takes about 20 minutes in all: 5 minutes to put the sensor in place and gather data, and about 15 minutes (including graphical display of progress at each step) to settle on a value for S.

The number of equations and the "tightness" of the cluster of estimates can give a feel for the accuracy of the estimate. In averaging the S_is, we can compute a residual for each, that is the magnitude of the deviation from the average S_i (deviation, here, being the difference in the translation components of the transforms). The angular deviation could be treated in precisely the same manner: the angle of rotation required to get from one transform's orientation to the other's. The root mean square of these residuals can be used as a reasonable metric for the "tightness" of the estimates of S. In a typical calibration run of 25 measurements, the RMS value of the deviations from the mean S_i was about 4.6 millimeters.

These residuals are not the same as the error in the result, although they are related. The more equations we use, the more likely the resulting transform is to be close to the actual one. This is somewhat like averaging a random variable – the variance can be very high, but the longer we average, the closer we are likely to get to the expected value.

6 Conclusion

We have described two applications of a goal-based approach to alignment of mechanical systems in VE tracking. In both cases, the automated calibration simplifies the construction of the systems, and makes it easier to modify the systems without extensive redesign of hardware or software. Note that the autocalibration system is designed to calibrate against a particular source of error, LED position error in the first case and Polhemus source location error in the second. Other sources of error in the system will confound the autocalibration process, so that if they are persistent enough, the autocalibration model should be revised to incorporate them as well. As the number of variables to be calibrated is increased, the number of observations must increase as well, of course, but in the head-tracking system, we have calibrated about 3000 variables successfully.

7 Acknowledgments

We would like to thank Al Barr for his initial involvement in the discussion of autocalibration, which helped to lead us away from the engineering approach and into the mathematical one. We also thank J.-F. Wang for having the idea of autocalibration for headtracking systems in the first place. Henry Fuchs' persistent demands for greater accuracy and bigger tracking spaces have provided a constant impetus. And we both owe a debt to our colleagues who have supported us in this project, particularly Ron Azuma and Russell Taylor.

References

[AW91] Ronald Azuma and Mark Ward. Space Resection by Collinearity: Mathematics behind the Optical Ceiling Head-Tracker. Technical Report TR91-048, UNC-Chapel Hill Department of Computer Science, November 1991.

[BB88] Ronen Barzel and Alan H. Barr. A Modeling System Based on Dynamic Constraints. *Computer Graphics*, 22(4):179–188, August 1988.

[RBSJ79] F. H. Raab, E. B. Blood, T. O. Steiner, and H. R. Jones. Magnetic Position and Orientation Tracking System. *IEEE Transactions on Aerospace and Electronic Systems*, AES-15(5):709–718, September 1979.

[Sla80] C.C. Slama, editor. *Manual of Photogrammetry*. American Society of Photogrammetry, Falls Church, Va, fourth edition, 1980.

[WAB+90] J. F. Wang, R. Azuma, G. Bishop, V. Chi, J. Eyles, and H. Fuchs. Tracking a Head-Mounted Display in a Room-sized Environment with Head-Mounted Cameras. *Proc SPIE 1990 Technical Symposium on Optical Engineering and Photonics in Aerospace Sensing*, 1290, 1990.

[WAB+92] M. Ward, R. Azuma, R. Bennet, S. Gottschalk, and H. Fuchs. A Demonstrated Optical Tracker with Scalable Work Area for Head-Mounted Display Systems. In *Proceedings of 1992 Symposium on Interactive 3D Graphics, Cambridge, Mass.*, pages 43–52, March 1992.

[Wan90] Jih-Fang Wang. A Real-time Optical 6D Tracker for Head-mounted Display Systems. Technical Report TR90-011, UNC-Chapel Hill Department of Computer Science, March 1990.

8 Appendix: Head Tracker Design

Several issues concerning our current tracker design are often raised by those unfamiliar with it. First, why use exotic, expensive lateral-effect photodiodes instead of the highly developed, inexpensive CCD technologies?

The reason is timing. We want updates from the tracking system every 12 to 20 milliseconds. With CCDs, both the bandwidth required for data transfer and the image processing necessary per frame were prohibitive. We found it more feasible to digitize the voltages coming from the lateral-effect photodiodes (the only thing of interest after all in the image that a CCD camera would have seen) and transmit this comparatively low bandwidth signal.

Second, why use multiple cameras with narrow fields of view? Why not use a single camera with a wide-angle lens?

The problem here is the limited precision of the photocoordinates. We have observed that, in practice, the photocoordinates reported by the camera may be off by as much as 12 microns. A narrow field of view helps reduce this problem, but since CA requires disparate angles to operate effectively (otherwise the matrices involved tend to become ill-conditioned), this field-of-view requirement compels us to use multiple cameras.

Lastly, why put cameras on the head and LEDs on the ceiling, rather than vice versa, since the headmount would be much lighter with LEDs rather than cameras?

To explain our strategy, we call the cameras on the walls the "outside-looking-in" approach, and the cameras on the headmount the "inside-looking-out" approach. "Inside-looking-out" has three advantages over its counterpart: sensitivity to orientation, economical scalability, and energetics considerations.

Sensitivity to orientation is the ability to detect a head rotation. In the current system, a .5 degree turn of the head, for instance, causes a very significant change in the LEDs' coordinates on the photodiodes, regardless of their distances from the camera. By contrast, in the outside-looking-in approach this change in orientation would be almost imperceptible.

An *economically scalable system* is one in which the cost of increasing the working volume is low in terms of cost per unit tracking space. Because of the narrow field-of-view requirement on the cameras, the outside-looking-in approach (on a 30 ft^2 area) would need many cameras mounted on the walls. Covering the ceiling with LEDs is less expensive.

Energetics refers to how light energy is received from an LED. Quadrupling the distance between LED and camera, for instance, decreases the light energy received by a factor of 16. Furthermore, LEDs do not emit light uniformly in every direction: most of their power is emitted in the direction they face, and drops off with the angle away from their axis (depending on the packaging). If the cameras are wall-mounted, and the LEDs are head-mounted, then, as the user walks about, many LEDs may be oblique to the cameras, and the distances between user and cameras may vary a great deal. These two effects combine to make the range of signal strengths received by the cameras too wide.

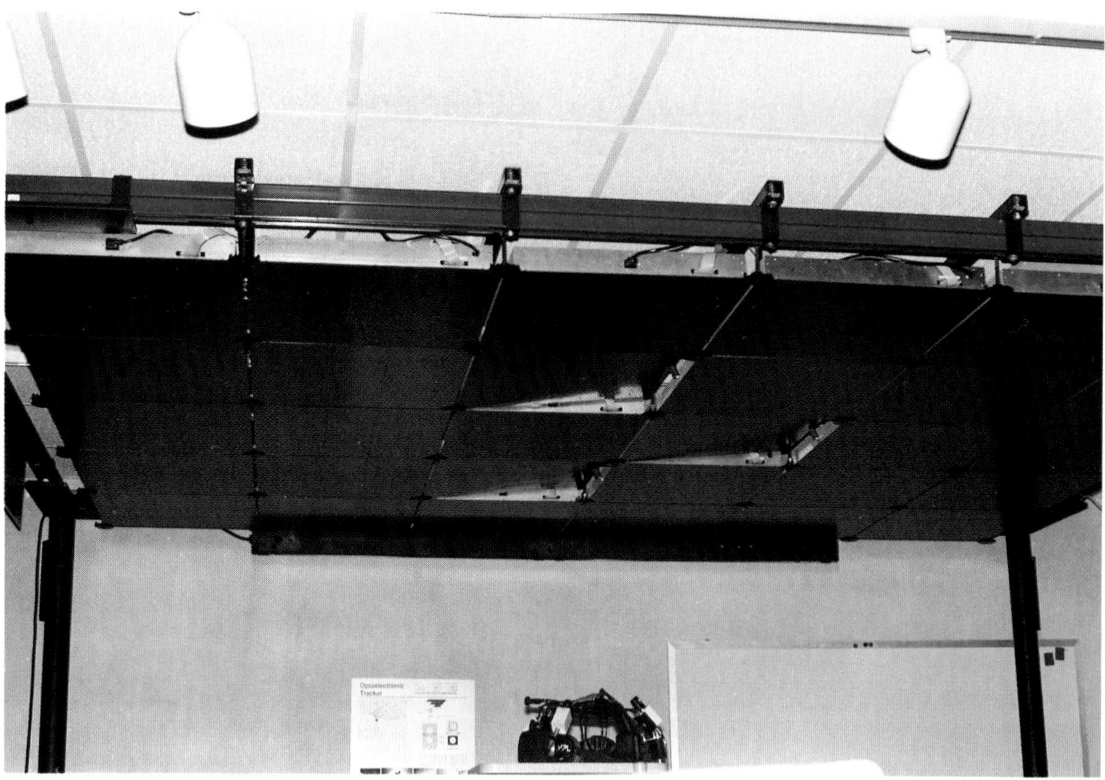

Figure 4: Tilting three panels in the ceiling to test autocalibration.

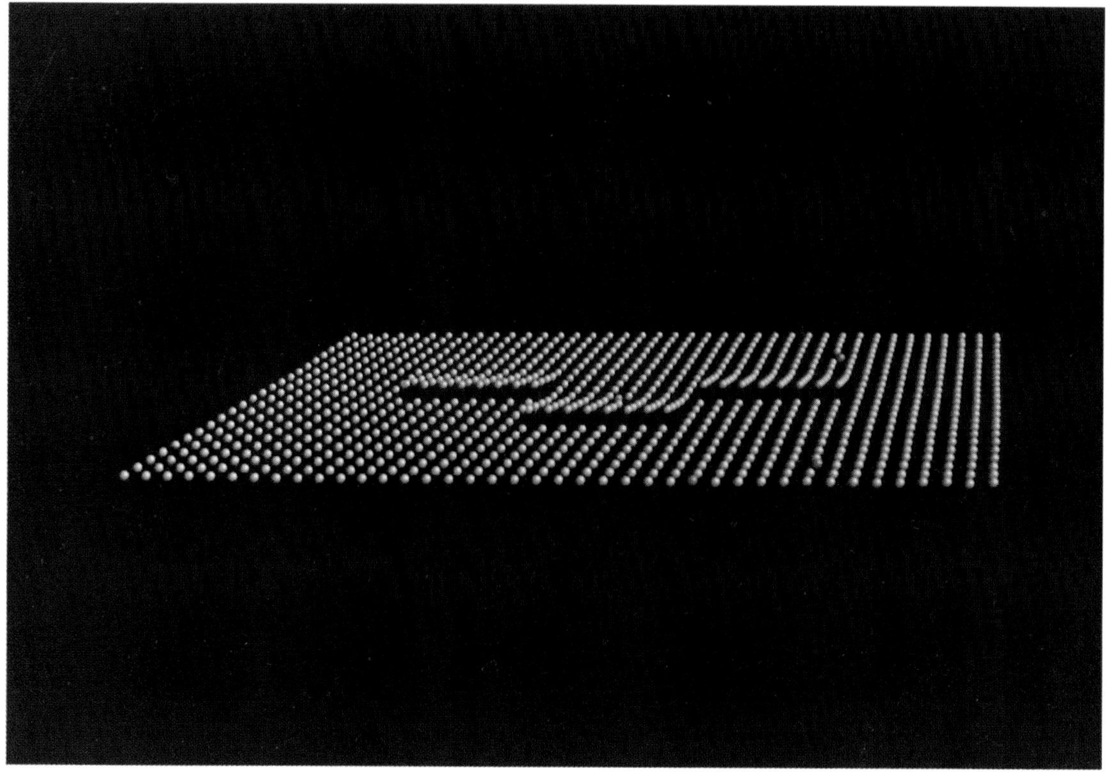

Figure 5: Computer display of calibrated beacon locations. The beacons shown in red were insufficiently sampled and could not be calibrated by the algorithm (see Section 4.1).

Toolglass and Magic Lenses: The See-Through Interface

Eric A. Bier, Maureen C. Stone, Ken Pier, William Buxton†, Tony D. DeRose‡
Xerox PARC, 3333 Coyote Hill Road, Palo Alto, CA 94304
†University of Toronto, ‡University of Washington

Abstract

Toolglass™ widgets are new user interface tools that can appear, as though on a transparent sheet of glass, between an application and a traditional cursor. They can be positioned with one hand while the other positions the cursor. The widgets provide a rich and concise vocabulary for operating on application objects. These widgets may incorporate visual filters, called *Magic Lens™ filters*, that modify the presentation of application objects to reveal hidden information, to enhance data of interest, or to suppress distracting information. Together, these tools form a *see-through interface* that offers many advantages over traditional controls. They provide a new style of interaction that better exploits the user's everyday skills. They can reduce steps, cursor motion, and errors. Many widgets can be provided in a user interface, by designers and by users, without requiring dedicated screen space. In addition, lenses provide rich context-dependent feedback and the ability to view details and context simultaneously. Our widgets and lenses can be combined to form operation and viewing macros, and can be used over multiple applications.

CR Categories and Subject Descriptors: I.3.6 [**Computer Graphics**]: Methodology and Techniques–interaction techniques; H.5.2 [**Information Interfaces and Presentation**]: User Interfaces–interaction styles; I.3.3 [**Computer Graphics**]: Picture/Image Generation–viewing algorithms; I.3.4 [**Computer Graphics**]: Graphics Utilities–graphics editors

Key Words: multi-hand, button, lens, viewing filter, control panel, menu, transparent, macro

1. Introduction

We introduce a new style of graphical user interface, called the *see-through interface*. The see-through interface includes semi-transparent interactive tools, called *Toolglass™ widgets*, that are used in an application work area. They appear on a virtual sheet of transparent glass, called a *Toolglass sheet*, between the application and a traditional cursor. These widgets may provide a customized view of the application underneath them, using viewing filters called *Magic Lens™* filters. Each lens is a screen region together with an operator, such as ''magnification'' or ''render in wireframe,'' performed on objects viewed in the region. The user positions a Toolglass sheet over desired objects and then points through the widgets and lenses. These tools create *spatial modes* that can replace temporal modes in user interface systems.

Two hands can be used to operate the see-through interface. The user can position the sheet with the non-dominant hand, using a device such as a trackball or touchpad, at the same time as the dominant hand positions a cursor (e.g., with a mouse or stylus). Thus, the user can line up a widget, a cursor, and an application object in a single two-handed gesture.

A set of simple widgets called *click-through buttons* is shown in figure 1. These buttons can be used to change the color of objects below them. The user positions the widget in the vicinity and indicates precisely which object to color by clicking through the button with the cursor over that object, as shown in figure 1(b). The buttons in figure 1(c) change the outline colors of objects. In addition, these buttons include a filter that shows only outlines, suppressing filled areas. This filter both reminds the user that these buttons do not affect filled areas and allows the user to change the color of outlines that were obscured.

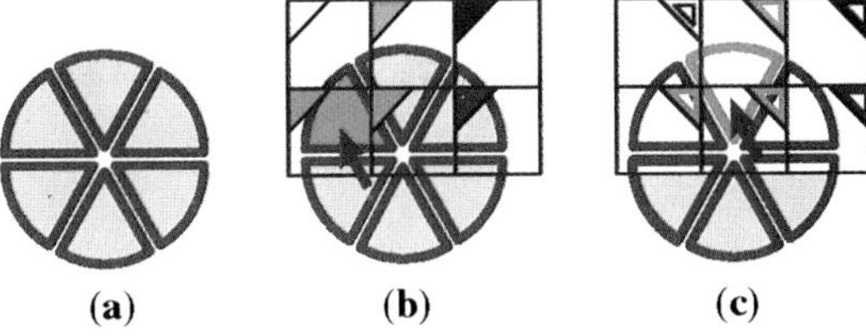

(a) (b) (c)

Figure 1. Click-through buttons. (a) Six wedge objects. (b) Clicking through a green fill-color button. (c) Clicking through a cyan outline-color button.

Many widgets can be placed on a single sheet, as shown in figure 2. The user can switch from one command or viewing mode to another simply by repositioning the sheet.

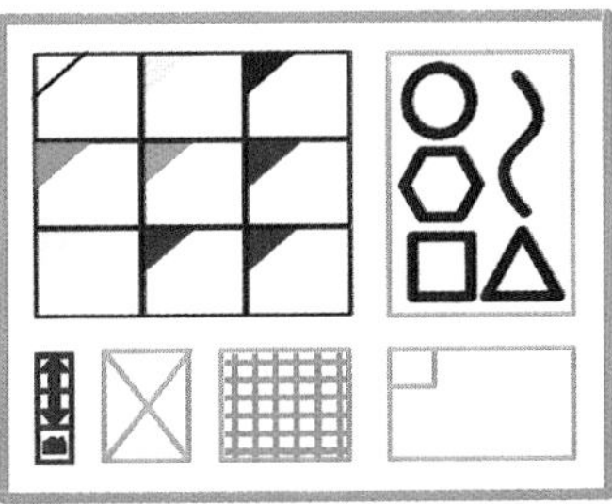

Figure 2. A sheet of widgets. Clockwise from upper left: color palette, shape palette, clipboard, grid, delete button, and buttons that navigate to additional widgets.

Widgets and lenses can be composed by overlapping them, allowing a large number of specialized tools to be created from a small basic set. Figure 3 shows an outline color palette over a magnifying lens, which makes it easy to point to individual edges.

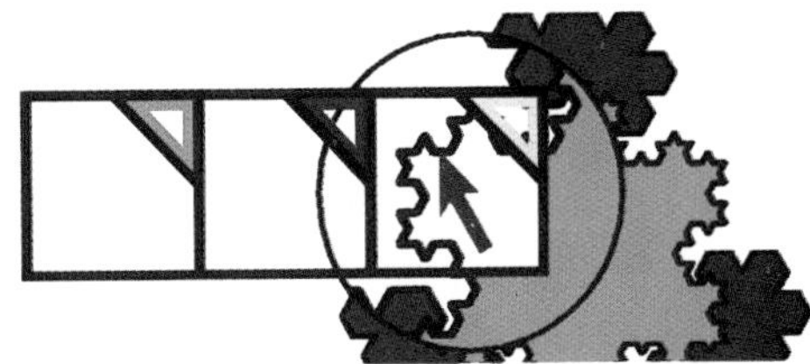

Figure 3. An outline color palette over a magnifying lens.

The see-through interface has been implemented in the Multi-Device Multi-User Multi-Editor (MMM) framework[5] in the Cedar programming language and environment,[24] running on the SunOS UNIX™-compatible operating system on Sun Microsystems SPARCstations and other computers. The Gargoyle graphics editor,[20] as integrated into MMM, serves as a complex application on which to test our interface. We use a standard mouse for the dominant hand and a MicroSpeed FastTRAP™ trackball for the non-dominant hand. The trackball includes three buttons and a thumbwheel, which can be used to supply additional parameters to the interface.

The remainder of this paper is organized as follows. The next section describes related work. Section 3 describes some examples of the tools we have developed. Section 4 discusses general techniques for using the see-through interface. Section 5 discusses some advantages of this approach. Section 6 describes our implementation. Sections 7 and 8 present our conclusions and plans for future work.

Except for figures 12 and 16, all of the figures in this paper reflect current capabilities of our software.

2. Related Work

The components of the see-through interface combine work in four areas: simultaneous use of two hands, movable tools, transparent tools, and viewing filters. In this section, we describe related work in these four areas.

Multi-Handed Interfaces

Several authors have studied interfaces that interpret continuous gestures of both hands. In Krueger's VIDEOPLACEs system,[15] the position and motion of both of a participant's hands, as seen by a video camera, determine the behavior of a variety of on-screen objects, including animated creatures and B-spline curves. Buxton and Myers discovered that users naturally overlap the use of both hands, when this is possible, and that, even when the two hands are used sequentially, there is still a performance advantage over single-hand use.[7,8]

Other work characterizes the situations under which people successfully perform two-handed tasks. Guiard presents evidence that people are well-adapted to tasks where the non-dominant hand coarsely positions a context and the dominant hand performs detailed work in that context.[4] Similarly, Kabbash presents evidence that a user's non-dominant hand performs as well or better than the dominant hand on coarse positioning tasks.[13]

Our system takes full advantage of a user's two-handed skills; the non-dominant hand sets up a context by coarsely positioning the sheet, and the dominant hand acts in that context, pointing precisely at objects through the sheet.

Movable Tools

Menus that pop up at the cursor position are movable tools in the work area. However, such a menu's position is determined by the cursor position before it appears, making it difficult to position it relative to application objects.

Several existing systems provide menus that can be positioned in the same work area as application objects. For example, MacDraw "tear-off menus" allow a pull-down menu to be positioned in the work area and repositioned by clicking and dragging its header.[17] Unfortunately, moving these menus takes the cursor hand away from its task, and they must be moved whenever the user needs to see or manipulate objects under them.

Toolglass sheets can be positioned relative to application objects and moved without tying up the cursor.

Transparent Tools

Some existing systems that allow menus to be positioned over the work area make these menus transparent. For example, the Alto Markup system[18] displays a menu of modes when a mouse button goes down. Each menu item is drawn as an icon, with the space between icons transparent. Bartlett's transparent controls for interactive graphics use stipple patterns to get the effect of transparency in X Windows.[2]

While these systems allow the user to continue to see the underlying application while a menu is in place, they don't allow the user to interact with the application through the menu and they don't use filters to modify the view of the application, as does our interface.

Viewing Filters

Many existing window systems provide a pixel magnifier. Our Magic Lens filters generalize the lens metaphor to many representations other than pixels and to many operations other than magnification. Because they can access application-specific data structures, our lenses are able to perform qualitatively different viewing operations, including showing hidden information and showing information in a completely different format. Even when the operation is magnification, our lenses can produce results of superior quality, since they are not limited to processing data at screen resolution.

The concept of using a filter to change the way information is visualized in a complex system has been introduced before.[25,10,14] Recent image processing systems support compostition of overlapping filters.[23] However, none of these systems combine the filtered views with the metaphor of a movable viewing lens.

Other systems provide special-purpose lenses that provide more detailed views of state in complex diagrams. For example, a fisheye lens can enhance the presentation of complicated graphs.[21] The bifocal display[22] provides similar functionallity for viewing a large space of documents. The MasPar Profiler[3] uses a tool based on the magnifying lens metaphor to generate more detail (including numerical data) from a graphical display of a program.

Magic Lens filters combine viewing filters with interaction and composition in a much broader way than do previous systems. They are useful both as a component of the see-through interface and as a general-purpose visualization paradigm, in which the lenses become an integral part of the model being viewed.

3. Examples

This section shows several tools that demonstrate features of the see-through interface. Because we have implemented primarily in the graphical editing domain, most of these tools are tailored to that application. However, the see-through interface can be used in a wide variety of other application domains.

Shape and Property Palettes

Palettes are collections of objects or properties that can be added to a scene. Figure 1 showed two widgets that apply color to shapes. Similar tools can be designed to apply other graphical properties, such as type and line styles to an illustration, shading parameters to a 3D model, or initial values to a simulation. Figure 4 illustrates a widget containing graphical shapes that can be "pushed through" from the tool into the illustration below. In figure 4(a), the user has positioned a shape palette widget (shown in cyan) over an illustration (shown in magenta). When the user clicks on a shape on the tool, a copy of that shape is added to the illustration. The widget attaches the copied shape to the cursor for interactive dragging until the final shape position is achieved (figure 4(b)).

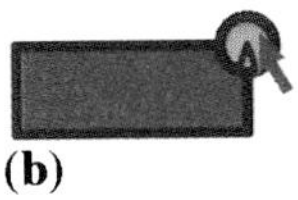

Figure 4. Shape palette. (a) Choosing a shape. (b) Placing the shape.

Figure 5 shows a design for a property palette for setting the face of text in a document. Each face (regular, bold, etc.) has an active region on the right side of the tool. Selecting the text displayed in this region changes its face.

temporal modes and modes created
regular | by holding down a keyboard key with
italic | *spatial modes.* Because these spatial
bold | modes can be changed **directly** in the
bold italic | application work area, the cursor and
the user's attention can remain on the

Figure 5. Font face palette. The word "directly" is being selected and changed to bold face.

Clipboards

Clipboard widgets pick up shapes and properties from underlying objects, acting as visible instantiations of the copy and paste keys common in many applications. Clipboards can pick up entire objects or specific properties such as color, dash pattern or font. They can hold single or multiple copies of an object. The objects or properties captured on the clipboard can be copied from the clipboard by clicking on them, as in the palette tools.

Figure 6 shows a symmetry clipboard that picks up the shape that the user clicks on (figure 6(a)) and produces all of the rotations of that shape by multiples of 90 degrees (figure 6(b)). Moving the clipboard and clicking on it again, the user drops a translated copy of the resulting symmetrical shape (figure 6(c)). Clicking the small square in the upper left corner of the widget clears the widget so that new shapes can be clipped.

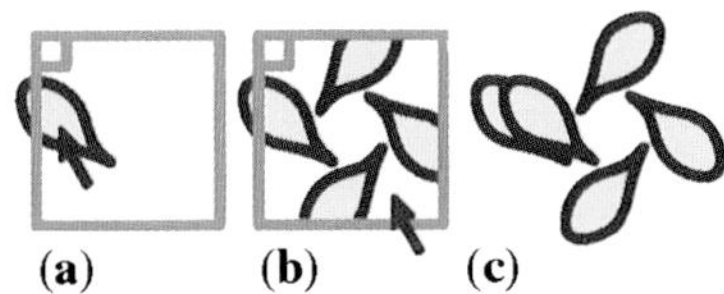

Figure 6. Symmetry clipboard. (a) Picking up an object. (b) Rotated copies appear. (c) The copies are moved and pasted.

Figure 7 shows an example of a type of clipboard that we call a *rubbing*. It picks up the fill color of an object when the user clicks on that object through the widget (figure 7(a)). The widget also picks up the shape of the object as a reminder of where the color came from (figure 7(b)). Many fill-color rubbings can be placed on a single sheet, allowing the user to store several colors and remember where they came from. The stored color is applied to new shapes when the user clicks on the applicator nib of the rubbing (figure 7(c)).

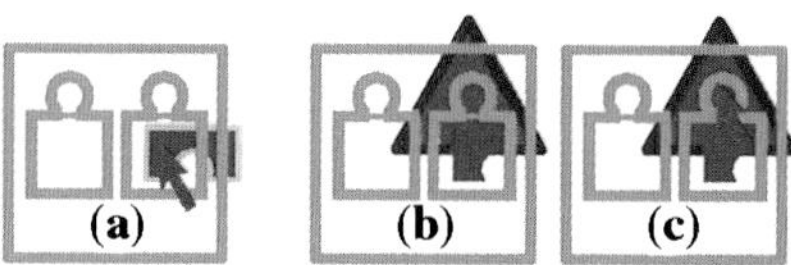

Figure 7. Fill-color rubbings. (a) Lifting a color. (b) Moving the clipboard. (c) Applying the color.

Besides implementing graphical cut and paste, clipboards provide a general mechanism for building customized libraries of shapes and properties.

Previewing Lenses

In graphical editing, a lens can be used to modify the visual properties of any graphical object, to provide a preview of what changing the property would look like. Properties include color, line thickness, dash patterns, typeface, arrowheads and drop shadows. A previewing lens can also be used to see what an illustration would look like under different circumstances; for example, showing a color illustration as it would be rendered on a black/white display or on a particular printer. Figure 8 shows a Celtic knotwork viewed through two lenses, one that adds drop shadows and one that shows the picture in black and white. The achromatic lens reveals that the drop shadows may be difficult to distinguish from the figure on a black/white display.

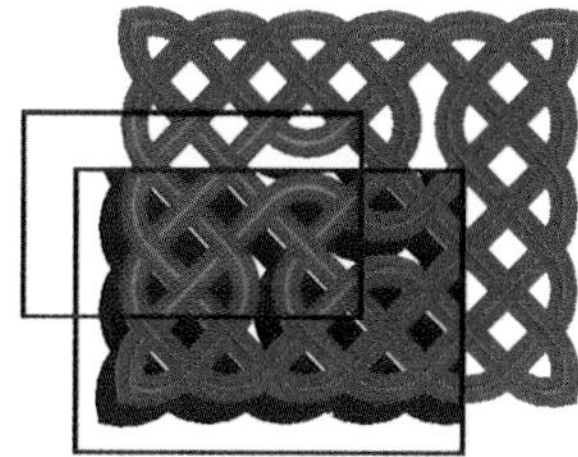

Figure 8. An achromatic lens over a drop shadow lens over a knotwork. (Knotwork by Andrew Glassner)

Previewing lenses can be parameterized. For example, the drop shadow lens has parameters to control the color and displacement of the shadow. These parameters can be included as graphical controls on the sheet near the lens, attached to input devices such as the thumbwheel, or set using other widgets.

Selection Tools

Selection is difficult in graphical editing when objects overlap or share a common edge. Our selection widgets address this problem by modifying the view and the interpretation of input actions. For example, figure 9 shows a widget that makes it easy to select a shape vertex even when it is obscured by other shapes. This tool contains a wire-frame lens that reveals all vertices by making shape interiors transparent. Mouse events are modified to snap to the nearest vertex.

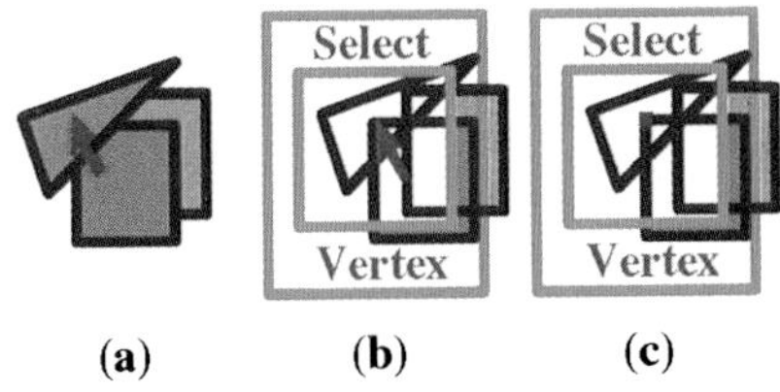

Figure 9. Vertex selection widget. (a) Shapes. (b) The widget is placed. (c) A selected vertex.

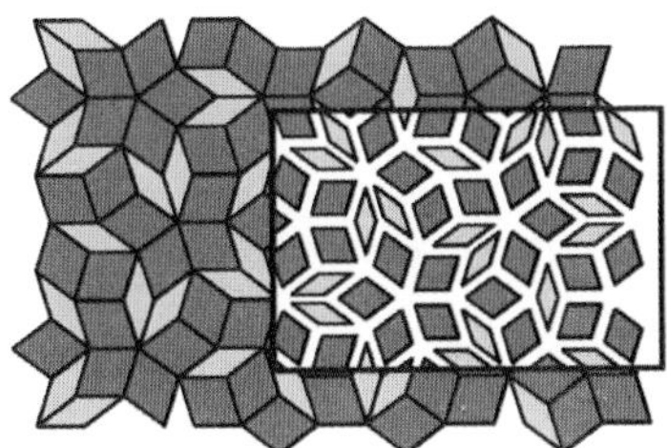

Figure 10. The local scaling lens. (Tiling by Doug Wyatt)

Figure 10 shows a lens that shrinks each object around its own centroid. This lens makes it easy to select an edge that is coincident with one or more other edges.

Grids

Figure 11 shows three widgets, each of which displays a different kind of grid. The leftmost two grids are rectangular with different spacings. The rightmost grid is hexagonal. Although each grid only appears when the lens is in place, the coordinates of the grid are bound to the scene, so that grid points do not move when the sheet moves. By clicking on the grid points and moving the widget, the user can draw precise shapes larger than the widget. If the sheet is moved by the non-dominant hand, the user can quickly switch between the grids during an editing motion.

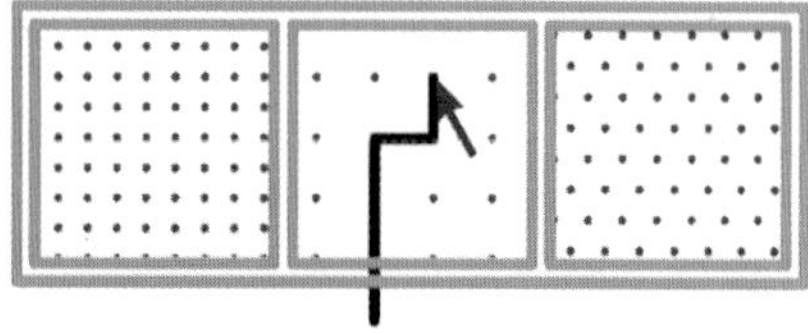

Figure 11. Three grid tools.

Visualization

Figure 12 illustrates the use of tools and lenses to measure Gaussian curvature in the context of a shaded rendering of a 3D model. The pseudo-color view indicates the sign and relative magnitude of the curvature,[9] and the evaluation tool displays the value at the point indicated.

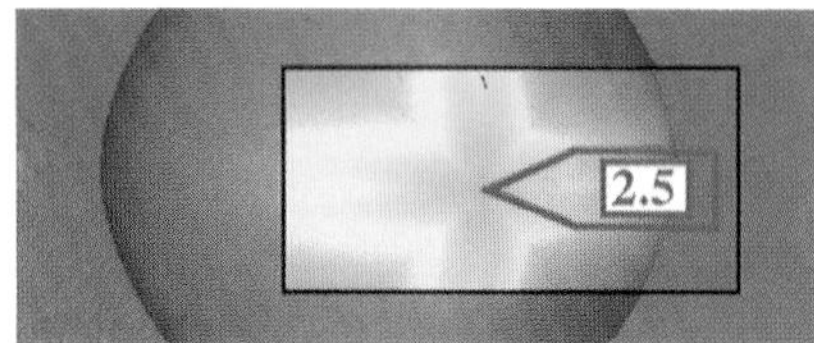

Figure 12. Gaussian curvature pseudo-color lens with overlaid tool to read the numeric value of the curvature. (Original images courtesy of Steve Mann)

4. Using the See-Through Interface

Widgets and lenses are most effective when supported by appropriate conventions specifying how to position, size, organize, and customize them. This section discusses a few of these issues.

Moving and Sizing the Sheet or the Application

A Toolglass sheet can be moved by clicking and dragging on its border with a mouse or by rolling the trackball. The sheet and all its widgets can stretch and shrink as a unit when the user works a a second controller such as a thumbwheel. With these moving and sizing controls, the user can center a widget on any application object and size the widget to cover any screen region. Large widgets can be used to minimize sheet motion when applying a widget to several objects. A widget that has been stretched to cover the entire work area effectively creates a command mode over the entire application.

By clicking a button on the trackball, the user can disconnect the trackball from the sheet and enable its use for scrolling and zooming a selected application area. If a sheet is over this application, the user can now move an application object to a widget instead of moving a widget to an object. This is a convenient way to use the see-through interface on illustrations that are too large to fit on the screen.

Managing Sheets

A typical application will have a large number of widgets in its interface. To avoid clutter, we need a way to organize these widgets and sheets. One approach is to put all of the widgets on a single sheet that can be navigated by scrolling and zooming. Perlin and Fox's paper in these proceedings[19] describes techniques for creating and navigating unlimited structures on a single sheet. A second approach is to have a master sheet that generates other sheets. Each of these sheets could generate more sheets, like hierarchical menus. A third technique, used in our prototype, is to allow a single sheet to show different sets of widgets at different times. The set to display can be selected in several ways: the user can click a special widget in the set, like the arrows in HyperCard,™[11] that jumps to another set. In addition, a master view provides a table of contents of the available sets allowing the user to jump to any one. To use different sets simultaneously, the user creates additional sheets.

Customizing Sheets

Because sheets can contain an unlimited number of widgets, they provide a valuable new substrate on which users can create their own customized widgets and widget sets. In effect, the sheets can provide a user interface *editor*, allowing users to move and copy existing widgets, compose macros by overlapping widgets, and snap widgets together in new configurations. Indeed, with the techniques described in this paper, one Toolglass sheet could even be used to edit another.

5. Advantages of See-Through Tools

In this section, we describe some advantages we see for using the see-through interface. Most of these advantages result from placing tools on overlapping layers and from the graphical nature of the interface.

In most applications, a control panel competes for screen space with the work area of the application. Toolglass sheets exist on a layer above the work area. With proper management of the sheets, they can provide an unlimited space for tools. The widgets in use can take up the entire work area. Then, they can be scrolled entirely off the screen to provide an unobstructed view of the application or space for a different set of widgets.

The see-through user interface can be used on tiny displays, such as notebook computers or personal digital assistants, that have little screen real estate for fixed-position control panels. It can also be used on wall-sized displays, where a fixed control panel might be physically out of reach from some screen positions. These tools can move with the user to stay close at hand.

A user interface layer over the desktop provides a natural place to locate application-independent tools, such as a clipboard that can copy material from one window to another.

These widgets can combine multiple task steps into a single step. For example, the vertex selection widget of figure 9 allows the user to turn on a viewing mode (wire-frame), turn on a command mode (selection), and point to an object in a single two-handed gesture.

Most user interfaces have temporal modes that can cause the same action to have different effects at different times. With our interface, modes are defined spatially by placing a widget and the cursor over the object to be operated on. Thus, the user can easily see what the current mode is (e.g., by the label on the widget) and how to get out of it (e.g., move the cursor out of the widget). In addition, each widget can provide customized feedback for its operation. For example, a widget that edits text in an illustration can include a lens that filters out all the objects except text. When several widgets are visible at once, the feedback in each one serves a dual role. It helps the user make proper use of the widget and it helps the user choose the correct widget.

The visual nature of the see-through interface also allows users to construct personalized collections of widgets as described above.

6. Implementation

This section provides an overview of our implementation of the see-through interface.

Toolglass Sheets

We describe three Toolglass subsystems: one that handles simultaneous input from two pointing devices and updates the screen after multiple simultaneous changes, one that modifies pointing events as they pass through widgets, and one that modifies graphical output as it passes up through each widget.

Multi-Device Input and Screen Refresh

Our Toolglass software uses the MMM framework.[5] The see-through interface relies on the following features of MMM.

MMM takes events from multiple input devices, such as the mouse and trackball, keeps track of which device produced which event, and places all events on a single queue. It dequeues each event in order and determines to which application that event should be delivered. MMM applications are arranged in a hierarchy that indicates how they are nested on the screen. Each event is passed to the root application, which may pass the event on to one of its child applications, which may in turn pass the event on down the tree. Mouse events are generally delivered to the most deeply nested application whose screen region contains the mouse coordinates. However, when the user is dragging or rubberbanding an object in a particular application, all mouse coordinates go to that application until the dragging or rubberbanding is completed. Keyboard events go to the currently selected application.

To support Toolglass sheets, MMM's rules for handling trackball input were modified. When a sheet is movable, trackball and thumbwheel events go to the top-level application, which interprets them as commands to move or resize the sheet, respectively. When the sheet is not movable, the trackball and thumbwheel events are delivered to the selected application, which interprets them as commands to scroll or zoom that application.

Filtering Input Through Lenses and Widgets

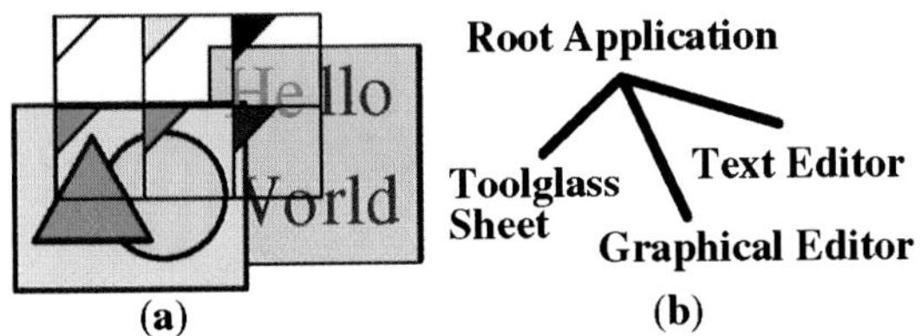

Figure 13. A simple hierarchy of applications

Ordinarily, MMM input events move strictly from the root application towards the leaf applications. However, to support the see-through interface, input events must be passed back up this tree. For example, figure 13(b) shows an application hierarchy. The left-to-right order at the lower level of this tree indicates the top-to-bottom order of applications on the screen. Input events are first delivered to the Toolglass sheet to determine if the user is interacting with a widget or lens. If so, the event is modified by the sheet. In any case, the event is returned to the root application, which either accepts the event itself or passes it on to the child applications that appear farther to the right in the tree.

The data structure that represents an MMM event is modified in three ways to support Toolglass sheets. First, an event is annotated with a representation of the parts of the application tree it has already visited. In figure 13, this prevents the root application from delivering the event to the sheet more than once. Second, an event is tagged with a command string to be interpreted when it reaches its final application. For example, a color palette click-through button annotates each mouse-click event with the command name "FillColor" followed by a color. Finally, if the widget contains a lens, the mouse coordinates of an event may be modified so the event will be correctly directed to the object that appears under the cursor through that lens.

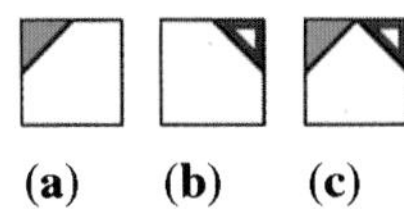

Figure 14. Composing color-changing widgets.

Widgets can be composed by overlapping them. When a stack of overlapped widgets receives input (e.g., a mouse click), the input event is passed top-to-bottom through the widgets. Each widget in turn modifies the command string that has been assembled so far. For example, a widget might concatenate an additional command onto the current command string. In figure 14, a widget that changes fill colors (figure 14(a)) is composed with a widget that changes line colors (figure 14(b)) to form a widget that changes both fill and line colors (figure 14(c)). If the line color widget is on top, then the command string would be "LineColor blue" after passing through this widget, and "LineColor blue; FillColor cyan" after both widgets.

Filtering Output Through Lenses and Widgets

Ordinarily, MMM output is composed from the leaf applications up. To support lenses, the normal screen refresh composition has been extended to allow information to flow down and across the tree as well as up. For example, if the widgets in figure 13 contain one or more lenses, and if any of those lenses is situated over the graphical editor, each lens must examine the contents of the graphical editor (which is the lens's sibling in the hierarchy) in order to draw itself.

In addition, to improve performance, MMM applications compute the rectangular bounding box of the regions that have recently changed, and propagate this box to the root application, which determines which screen pixels will need to be updated. Generally, this bounding box is passed up the tree, transformed along the way by the coordinate transformation between each application and the next one up the tree. However, lenses can modify the set of pixels that an operation affects. A magnifying lens, for example, generally increases the number of pixels affected. As a result, the bounding box must be passed to all lenses that affect it to determine the final bounding box.

Magic Lens Filters

A Magic Lens filter modifies the image displayed on a region of the screen, called the *viewing region*, by applying a *viewing filter* to objects in a model. The *input region* for the lens is defined by the viewing region and the viewing filter. It may be the same size as the viewing region, or different, as in the magnification lens. For a 3D model, the input region is a cone-shaped volume defined by the eye point and the viewing region. Input regions can be used to cull away all model objects except those needed to produce the lens image. Our current implementations do not perform this culling; as described below, there are advantages to lenses that operate on the entire model.

When several lenses are composed, the effect is as though the model were passed sequentially through the stack of lenses from bottom to top, with each lens operating on the model in turn. In addition, when one lens has other lenses below it, it may modify how the boundaries of these other lenses are mapped onto the screen within its own boundary. The input region of a group of lenses taken as a whole can be computed by applying the inverses of the viewing filters to the lens boundaries themselves.

Our lenses depend on the implementation of Toolglass sheets to manage the size, shape and motion of their viewing regions. This section describes two strategies we have tried for implementing viewing filters: a procedural method that we call *recursive ambush*, and a declarative method that we call *model-in model-out*. We also describe a third method that promises to be convenient when applicable, called *reparameterize-and-clip*. Finally, we discuss issues that arise in the presence of multiple model types.

Recursive Ambush

In the recursive ambush method, the original model is described procedurally as a set of calls in a graphics language such as Interpress™[12] or PostScript.®[1] The lens is a new interpreter for the graphics language, with a different implementation for each graphics primitive. In most cases, the implementation of a given graphics primitive first performs some actions that carry out the modifying effect of the lens and then calls the previous implementation of the primitive. For example, a lens that modifies a picture such that all of its lines are drawn in red would modify the "DrawLine" primitive to set the color to red and then call the original "DrawLine" primitive.

When lenses are composed, the previous implementation may not be the original graphics language primitive, but another lens primitive that performs yet another modification, making composition recursive.

Recursive ambush lenses appear to have important advantages. Because they work at the graphics language level, they work across many applications. Because they work procedurally, they need not allocate storage. However, the other methods can also work at the graphics language level. In addition, recursive ambush lenses have three major disadvantages. First, making a new lens usually requires modifying many graphics language primitives. Second, debugging several composed lenses is difficult because the effects of several cooperating interpreters are hard to understand. Finally, performance deteriorates rapidly as lenses are composed because the result of each lens is computed many times; the number of computations doubles with the addition of each lens that overlaps all of the others.

Model-In Model-Out

In the model-in model-out (MIMO) method, we make a copy of the original model as the first step. This model might be the data structure of an editor, a representation of graphics language calls, an array of pixels or some other picture representation. The implementation walks through this data structure and modifies it in accordance with the desired behavior of the lens. When composed with other lenses, a MIMO lens takes each model that is produced by each lens under it, produces a modified version of that model, and associates it with the clipping region formed by intersecting its clipping region with that of the lens underneath. The resulting models are passed on to lenses above.

Although MIMO lenses must allocate storage, this investment pays off in several ways. First, during the rendering of a single image, each lens computes its output models only once, and then saves them for use by any lenses that are over it. In addition, if the computed model is based on the entire original model, then redrawing the picture after a lens moves is just a matter of changing clipping regions; no new model filtering is needed. In this case, each lens maintains a table of the models it has produced. The table is indexed by the models it has received as input and when they were last modified. The action of such a lens often consists of a single table lookup.

MIMO lenses have many other advantages. Given routines to copy and visit parts of the model, the incremental effort to write a MIMO lens is small. Many of our lenses for graphical editor data structures were written in under 20 minutes and consist of under 20 lines of code. Debugging composed lenses is easy because the intermediate steps can easily be viewed. Finally, MIMO lenses can perform a large class of filtering functions because they can access the input model in any order. In particular, they can compute their output using graphical search and replace,[16] as shown in figure 15 where each line segment is replaced by multiple line segments to create a "snowflake" pattern.

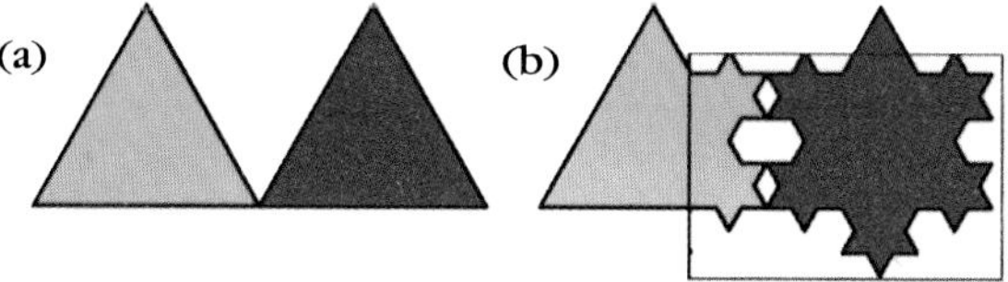

Figure 15. The snowflake lens. (a) Two triangles. (b) Snowflake lens over part of the scene.

An important variation of MIMO is to allow the output model to differ in type from the input model. For example, a lens might take a graphics language as input and produce pixels as output. In this case, the lens walks the original model, rather than copying it, and allocates data structures of the new model type.

Reparameterize and Clip

If the original image is being produced on the screen by a renderer with variable parameters, it is easy to implement lenses that show the effects of varying those parameters. To function, the lens modifies a renderer parameter and asks the renderer to redraw the model clipped to the boundary shape of the lens. For example, a lens showing the wireframe version of a 3D shaded model can be implemented this way.

Several reparameterize-and-clip lenses can be composed if the parameter changes made by these lenses are compatible. In the region of overlap, the renderer re-renders the original model after each of the overlapping lenses has made its changes to the renderer parameters. The flow of control and performance of a stack of these lenses is like that of MIMO lenses; a new output is computed for each input region received from lenses underneath. These lenses differ from MIMO in that each output is computed from the original model, and each output is always a rendering.

Multiple Model Types

In our discussion above, lenses are used to view a single type of model, such as a graphical editor data structure or a graphical language. In practice, multiple model types are often present, for two reasons. First, a lens can overlap multiple applications at the same time, where the applications have different model types, as shown above in figure 13. Second, a lens may overlap both an application and a lens, where the lens output and application model are of different types. For example, in figure 16, the wireframe lens converts from a 3D model to a 2D line drawing. The magnifier lens, which operates on 2D drawings, overlaps both the original image and the output of the wireframe lens. Rich illustrations can be produced by permitting lenses to overlap multiple model types in this way.

Supporting multiple model types requires *type conversion* and *type tolerance.* When a lens that expects one type of model as input is moved over a model of a different type, the system may automatically convert the model to be of the type required; this is type conversion. For example, all of our applications produce Interpress graphics language calls as part of drawing themselves on the screen. When a lens that takes Interpress as input is positioned over one of these applications, that application converts its model to Interpress on demand for that lens.

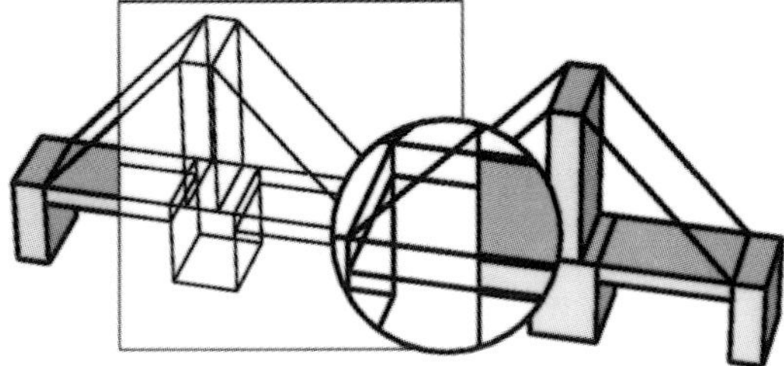

Figure 16. A bridge made of shaded, 3D blocks showing a 3D wireframe lens and a 2D magnifier.

Alternatively, when presented with a model it does not understand, a lens can simply pass that model through unchanged; this is type tolerance. For example, a lens that operates only on a graphics editor's data structures will only modify the image in the part of that lens's boundary that overlaps the graphics editor; other regions are unchanged.

Composing Widgets and Lenses

When a widget and a lens are composed, their functions combine. For example, consider a click-through button on top of a magnifying lens. Mouse events pass through the button, are annotated with a command, and then pass through the lens, which applies the inverse of its transformation to the mouse coordinates. During screen refresh, the widget adds its appearance to the output of the lens. If the lens is on top of the widget, input events are first transformed by the lens and then tested to see if they fall within the button or not; during refresh, the widget adds its appearance to the model, which is then acted on by the lens. A widget and lens can be very tightly coupled. For example, an editing tool could include a lens that displayed control points or editing handles implemented as widgets.

Performance

Our sheets and lenses are already fast enough to be useful on current hardware, but need to be faster for smooth motion. For example, using our prototype on a SPARCstation 10, we measured the time it takes to redraw the screen after moving a wireframe lens of size 70 by 70 pixels over the Penrose tiling of figure 10, containing 117 filled and outlined shapes. For the MIMO implementation of the lens, once it has cached its output scene, it takes an average of 300 milliseconds to repaint the scene, of which 120 milliseconds are spent drawing the lens interior. The same lens implemented using recursive ambush takes %15 longer to redraw the lens interior, which we attribute to the procedure call overhead of the recursive approach. Computing the filtered scene for the MIMO lens takes an average of 480 milliseconds for this example. This computation is performed whenever the illustration under the lens is changed or lens parameters are modified.

Figure 17. The Magic Lenses logo.

7. Conclusions

We have described a new style of user interface, the see-through interface, based on Toolglass widgets and Magic Lens filters. The see-through interface offers a new design space for user interfaces based on spatial rather than temporal modes and provides a natural medium for two-handed interaction. Because the interface is movable and overlays the application area, it takes no permanent screen space and can be conveniently adapted to a wide range of display sizes. Because the overlaid tools are selected and brought to the work area simply by moving the Toolglass sheet, the user's attention can remain focused on the work area. Because the operations and views are spatially defined, the user can work without changing the global context.

The see-through interface provides a new paradigm to support open software architecture. Because Toolglass sheets can be moved from one application to another, rather than being tied to a single application window, they provide an interface to the common functionality of several applications and may encourage more applications to provide common functionality. Similarly, Magic Lens filters that take standard graphics languages as input work over many applications.

In addition to their role in user interfaces, Magic Lens filters provide a new medium for computer graphics artists and a new tool for scientific visualization. When integrated into drawing tools, these filters will enable a new set of effects and will speed the production of traditional effects. Figure 17 shows a magnifying lens and a wireframe lens used to produce our Magic Lenses logo.

Integrated into scientific visualization tools, these filters can enhance understanding by providing filtered views of local regions of the data while leaving the rest of the view unchanged to provide context, as was shown in the visualization example in figure 12.

We hope the see-through interface will prove to be valuable in a wide variety of applications. While the examples in this paper stress applications in graphical editing, these tools can potentially be used in any screen-based application, including spreadsheets, text editors, multi-media editors, paint programs, solid modelers, circuit editors, scientific visualizers, or meeting support tools. Consider that most applications have some hidden state, such as the equations in a spreadsheet, the grouping of objects in a graphical editor, or the position of water pipes in an architectural model. A collection of widgets and lenses can be provided to view and edit this hidden state in a way that takes up no permanent screen space and requires no memorization of commands.

We believe that the see-through interface will increase productivity by reducing task steps and learning time, providing good graphical feedback, and allowing users to construct their own control panels and spatial modes.

8. Plans for Future Work

The see-through interface is a framework that can be used to create many new tools in many application domains. Exploring the current space of possibilities will take many people many years. Furthermore, this design space will be enlarged by future software and hardware. We will carry out some of this exploration ourselves, creating new widgets in different application domains, working out taxonomies for the tools we discover, designing new conventions for composing, editing, navigating, organizing and triggering these tools, combining them with existing user interface techniques, and testing them on users performing real work.

We are building two Toolglass widget toolkits. The first is a traditional toolkit in which widgets are created through object-oriented programming. The second toolkit is based on our EmbeddedButtons project;[6] here, users draw new widgets and collections of widgets using a graphical editor and then apply behavior to these graphical forms, where the behavior is expressed in a user customization language.

We are designing new algorithms to increase the speed of these tools. It is clear that Magic Lens filters and, to a lesser extent, Toolglass widgets provide a new way to consume the graphics power of modern computers.

Finally, we are working to better understand how to model and implement general composition of widgets and lenses, especially those that work with multiple model and applications types.

Acknowledgments

We thank Blair MacIntyre for implementing our first lenses for 2D graphics and Ken Fishkin for his demonstration of lenses for text editing. We thank many of our colleagues at PARC for fruitful discussions and enthusiasm, including Stu Card, Ken Fishkin, Andrew Glassner, David Goldberg, Christian Jacobi, Jock Mackinlay, David Marimont, George Robertson, Marvin Theimer, Annie Zaenen, and Polle Zellweger, plus our consultants Randy Pausch and John Tukey. Finally, we thank Xerox Corporation for supporting this work.

References

1. Adobe Systems Incorporated. *PostScript® Language Reference Manual, second edition.* Addison-Wesley, 1990.
2. Bartlett, Joel F. Transparent Controls for Interactive Graphics. WRL Technical Note TN-30, Digital Equipment Corp., Palo Alto, CA. July 1992.
3. Beck, Kent, Becher, Jon, and Zaide, Liu. Integrating Profiling into Debugging. *Proceedings of the 1991 International Conference on Parallel Processing, Vol. II, Software,* August 1991, pp. II-284-II-285.
4. Guiard, Yves. Asymmetric Division of Labor in Human Skilled Bimanual Action: The Kinematic Chain as a Model. *The Journal of Motor Behavior, 19,* 4, (1987), pp. 486-517.
5. Bier, Eric A. and Freeman, Steve. MMM: A User Interface Architecture for Shared Editors on a Single Screen. *Proceedings of the ACM SIGGRAPH Symposium on User Interface Software and Technology* (Hilton Head, SC, November 11-13), ACM, New York, (1991), pp. 79-86.
6. Bier, Eric A., EmbeddedButtons: Supporting Buttons in Documents. *ACM Transactions on Information Systems, 10,* 4, (1992), pp. 381-407.
7. Buxton, William and Myers, Brad A.. A Study in Two-Handed Input. *Proceedings of CHI '86* (Boston, MA, April 13-17), ACM, New York, (1986), pp. 321-326.
8. Buxton, William. There's More to Interaction Than Meets the Eye: Some Issues in Manual Input. *Readings in Human-Computer Interaction: A Multidisciplinary Approach.* (Ronald M. Baecker, William A.S. Buxton, editors). Morgan Kaufmann Publishers, Inc., San Mateo, CA. 1987.
9. Dill, John. An Application of Color Graphics to the Display of Surface Curvature. Proceedings of SIGGRAPH '81 (Dallas, Texas, August 3-7). *Computer Graphics, 15,* 3, (1981), pp. 153-161.
10. Goldberg, Adele and Robson, Dave, A Metaphor for User Interface Design, *Proceedings of the University of Hawaii Twelfth Annual Symposium on System Sciences,* Honolulu, January 4-6, (1979), pp.148-157.
11. Goodman, Danny. *The Complete HyperCard Handbook.* Bantam Books, 1987.
12. Harrington, Steven J. and Buckley, Robert R.. *Interpress, The Source Book.* Simon & Schuster, Inc. New York, NY. 1988.
13. Kabbash, Paul, MacKenzie, I. Scott, and Buxton, William. Human Performance Using Computer Input Devices in the Preferred and Non-preferred Hands. *Proceedings of InterCHI '93,* (Amsterdam, April 24-29), pp. 474-481.
14. Krasner, Glenn and Hope, Stephen, A Cookbook for Using the Model-View-Controller User Interface Paradigm in Smalltalk-80, *Journal of Object-Oriented Programming, 1,* 3, (1988), pp. 26-49.
15. Krueger, Myron W., Gionfriddo, Thomas, and Hinrichsen, Katrin. VIDEOPLACE – An Artificial Reality. *Proceedings of CHI '85* (San Francisco, April 14-18). ACM, New York, (1985), pp. 35-40.
16. Kurlander, David and Bier, Eric A.. Graphical Search and Replace. Proceedings of SIGGRAPH '88 (Atlanta, Georgia, August 1-5) *Computer Graphics, 22,* 4, (1988), pp. 113-120.
17. *MacDraw Manual.* Apple Computer Inc. Cupertino, CA 95014, 1984.
18. Newman, William. *Markup User's Manual.* Alto User's Handbook, Xerox PARC technical report, (1979), pp. 85-96.
19. Perlin, Ken and Fox, David. Pad: An Alternative Approach to the Computer Interface. this proceedings.
20. Pier, Ken, Bier, Eric, and Stone, Maureen. An Introduction to Gargoyle: An Interactive Illustration Tool. *Proceedings of the Intl. Conf. on Electronic Publishing, Document Manipulation and Typography* (Nice, France, April). Cambridge Univ. Press, (1988), pp. 223-238.
21. Sarkar, Manojit and Brown, Marc H.. Graphical Fisheye Views of Graphs. *Proceedings of CHI '92,* (Monterey, CA, May 3-5, 1992) ACM, New York, (1992), pp. 83-91.
22. Spence, Robert and Apperley, Mark. Data Base Navigation: An Office Environment of the Professional. *Behaviour and Invormation Technology, 1,* 1, (1982), 43-54.
23. *ImageVision,* Silicon Graphics Inc., Mountain View, CA.
24. Swinehart, Daniel C., Zellweger, Polle T., Beach, Richard J., Hagmann, Robert B.. A Structural View of the Cedar Programming Environment. *ACM Transactions on Programming Languages and Systems, 8,* 4, (1986), pp. 419-490.
25. Weyer, Stephen A. and Borning, Alan H., A Prototype Electronic Encyclopedia, *ACM Transactions on Office Systems, 3,* 1, (1985), pp. 63-88.

An Interactive 3D Toolkit for Constructing 3D Widgets

Robert C. Zeleznik, Kenneth P. Herndon, Daniel C. Robbins,
Nate Huang, Tom Meyer, Noah Parker and John F. Hughes

Brown University
Department of Computer Science
Providence, RI 02912
(401) 863-7693; {bcz,kph,dcr,nth,twm,nfp,jfh}@cs.brown.edu

CR Categories

I.3.6 [Computer Graphics]: Methodology and Techniques; Interaction Techniques D.1.7 [Programming Languages]: Programming Techniques; Visual Programming D.2.2 [Software Engineering]: Tools and Techniques; User Interfaces

1 Introduction

Today's user interfaces for most 3D graphics applications still depend heavily on 2D GUIs and keyboard input. There have been several recent attempts both to extend these user interfaces into 3D and to describe intermediary 3D widgets[1] that control application objects [3; 4; 5; 7; 13; 15]. Even though this style of interaction is a straightforward extension of interaction through intermediary 2D widgets such as dials or sliders, we know of no efforts to develop interactive 3D toolkits akin to UIMX or Garnet [11].

The Brown Graphics Group has had considerable experience using its Unified Graphics Architecture (UGA) system [16] to script 3D widgets such as deformation racks [14], interactive shadows [9], parameterized models, and other constrained 3D geometries. Using this experience, we have developed an interactive toolkit to facilitate the visual programming of the geometry and behavior of such interactive models. The toolkit provides both a core set of 3D widget primitives for constructing interactive behaviors based on constrained affine transformations, and an interactive 3D interface for combining these primitives into more complex widgets.

This video paper describes the fundamental concepts of the toolkit and its core set of primitives. In particular, we describe (i) the conceptual structure of the primitives, (ii) the criteria used to select a particular primitive widget set that would be expressive enough to let us construct a wide range of interactive 3D objects, and (iii) the constraint relationships among the primitives.

2 Overview of our 3D Toolkit

The traditional approach to designing user interface toolkits is to create a library of software objects and customize them through instantiation and specialization within standard programming languages [12; 15]. Although this approach is extremely powerful, exploring the full potential requires that programmers be able to visualize complex relationships among software objects (*e.g.*, constraint networks, data- and control-flow graphs). A second paradigm, based on graphically manipulating function networks [1; 8; 10], is more accessible to the non-programmer, but still suffers because inherently geometric relationships must be specified by wiring 2D boxes together.

Our toolkit uses direct manipulation of 3D widgets to model the construction of widgets and application objects whose geometric components are affinely constrained. This paradigm is more natural than scripting or dataflow programming because the process of constructing such objects is inherently geometric, and also enables non-programmers and designers to construct these objects visually. The scope of these constructions includes, for example, all of the widgets we have built in the last few years and standard joints such as slider, pin, and ball joints.

We introduce the notion of primitive 3D widgets that can be combined with other primitive 3D widgets, using a process called *linking*, to establish one or more constraint relations between them. In some cases, the resulting composite objects are still considered widgets; in others, they are thought of as the behavioral scaffolding to which the geometry of application objects can be attached. The fact that the interface and application objects exist in the same underlying system, UGA, allows us to blur the distinction between them. We feel that such blurring is natural for 3D applications in general, and especially for virtual reality applications.

Linking is related to snapping [3], but differs in requiring explicit interactive selection of source and destination objects, followed by explicit user confirmation. This protocol reduces clutter by eliminating alignment objects. In the interest of simplifying the user interface, all linking operations are unparameterized, although in future work, parameterized linking for more advanced users and more complicated widgets will be explored.

3 Conceptual Structure of Widget Primitives

A primitive widget combines the geometries and behaviors of its ports and other more simple primitives. A *port* is an encapsulation of one or more constraint values and a geometric representation. It can be loosely considered a data type with the additional requirement that its visual appearance suggest the meaning of the data. Ports are related to one another within a single widget via a network of bidirectional constraints. In addition, specific interaction techniques are associated with each port. Each interaction technique tells how to modify a port while maintaining constraints on other ports. For example, if a user manipulates a point that is constrained to be on a line, the constraint could be resolved by moving the line with the point, by restricting the user's interaction so that the point never leaves the line, or by a combination of the two. We must choose one of these as we implement the toolkit. These interaction techniques can be thought of as hints to a constraint solver when the constraint network is underdetermined so it can provide real-time, precise interactions.

[1] That is, encapsulations of geometry and behavior.

© 1993 ACM-0-89791-601-8/93/008/0081 $01.50

In addition to having an internal constraint network, a primitive widget can be related to another primitive widget by linking a port of the former to a port of the latter. This establishes a constraint (bi- or uni-directional) between the two ports. Ports are already constrained by the internal constraint network of a primitive, and the new constraints must be consistent with the existing constraints. Therefore, associated with each port is a function that determines how to attach new constraints to that port and how to modify its interaction techniques so as to facilitate constraint maintenance.

4 Description of the Toolkit Primitives

Having selected this framework to build our toolkit, we designed a general set of primitives to allow the interactive construction of not only the various 3D widgets previously scripted, but also application objects such as parameterized geometric models. These primitives are intended to be general enough to allow exploration of a wide set of object designs without having to resort to hand-coding.

We chose a "coordinate system" metaphor as a basis for our primitives. Each primitive visually represents a 0D, 1D, 2D, or 3D coordinate system and each can be constrained by affine transformations to the coordinate systems of other primitives. This metaphor can be used to express a wide variety of user interactions, including those of our previous 3D widgets [5; 14; 9]. However, the coordinate-system metaphor is only a framework for conceptualizing the primitives, not a strict definition of them. That is, the primitives were designed with regard to the sometimes antagonistic desires both to represent the coordinate system metaphor faithfully and to provide the semantics most useful for geometric and behavioral constructions.

The toolkit has primitives that correspond to position, orientation, measure (linear and angular), 2D and 3D Cartesian coordinate systems, a general extension mechanism for importing an arbitrary relationship, and the full set of UGA's geometric models.

The two most basic primitives, *Point* and *Ray*, encapsulate position and orientation respectively. Points and Rays represent 0D coordinate system entities; *i.e.*, there is only one element[2] of a Point or a Ray and therefore 0 coordinates are required to specify it. (Contrast this with a line, which has an infinite number of elements, each specified by one coordinate.) The Point primitive, represented by a small sphere, is an abstraction of a single 3D point. The Ray primitive, represented by an arrow, corresponds to a based vector, although we often treat it as just a vector (its position being a display convenience). Both primitives can be freely translated in space, but only the Ray can be rotated.

The notion of distance (linear measure) is represented through a 1D coordinate system primitive, the *Length*, represented by two Points, a port for the 1D coordinate system (represented by a thin cylinder connecting the Points), and a port for the Length's measure (represented by a small marker at the middle of the thin cylinder). While the Length appears as a bounded line segment, it actually encapsulates the notion of an infinite 1D coordinate system whose origin is at the line's start point (indicated by a small disc) and whose unit length is equal to the distance between the two points measured in the world coordinate system. We reuse the Point for the endpoints to help define the user interaction with the Length. Each of the Length's endpoints can be directly translated while the other remains fixed. Translating the cylinder joining the two Points translates both endpoints by the same amount. An alternate formulation of the Length would have both endpoints move whenever either was translated. Choosing either formulation is difficult in the absence of an application, so we chose the technique that seemed most useful.

Angular measure is represented by a two-handed clock-like primitive, the *Angle*. Each hand of the clock represents a vector and the outer ring of the clock represents the angle between the two vectors.

[2] In the sense of sets.

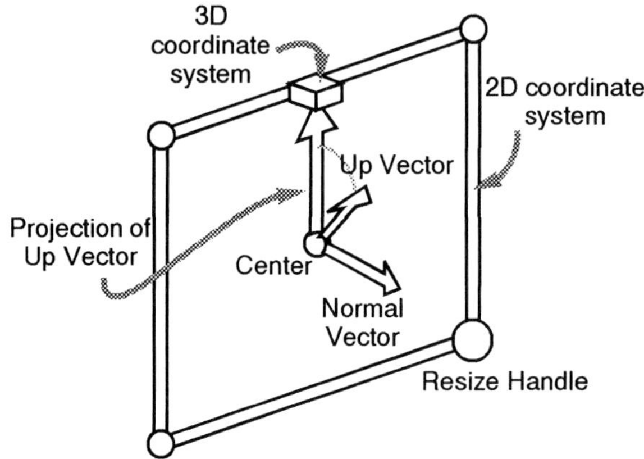

Figure 1: The ports of the Plane primitive.

The most complex primitive, the *Plane*, represents both a 2D Cartesian plane and a 3D Cartesian space. We opted to combine both concepts into a single primitive because users frequently use the two concepts in conjunction with one another and because the sets of ports are nearly identical, with a space being a superset of a plane. Visualizing an oriented plane requires ports for the plane's normal, center, and up-vector (similar to the PHIGS *VUP*), and for the size of a unit vector in each of the plane's axes. In addition, a port is required for the concept of the plane itself (as opposed to parameters that define the plane). A rectangle in the plane represents this port; its size determines the magnitude of each unit vector in the Plane's coordinate system. We also include a useful port for the projection of the plane's up-vector onto the plane, although this is not a required part of a Cartesian plane. To handle a 3D Cartesian space, the only additional port required is something to represent the concept of the space itself. The Plane reuses Points and Rays and introduces new geometry to represent the concept of the plane (a rectangle) and the space (a cube at the top of the up vector).

In order that the toolkit be extensible enough to handle new problem domains, there are also *Black-box* primitives, each representing a relationship with some number of ports that lacks a natural geometric representation. Ports on black-boxes are geometrically represented as labeled buttons. The accompanying video shows two Black-boxes: an interface to Barr's nonlinear deformation functions [2] and a PHIGS camera specification [6].

Finally, all the geometric objects in 3D modeling environments (cubes, spheres, CSGs, etc.) are considered collectively as a single primitive class called *Geometries*. In terms of the data it represents, each of the Geometries is essentially equivalent to a Cartesian space, although it is not annotated with additional geometry (as is the Plane primitive). In our system, each geometric object has an internal boundary representation relative to a local object coordinate system. This local coordinate system is used as a default coordinate system associated with a Geometry primitive to make it functionally equivalent to a Cartesian space. Since Geometries are not annotated with the ports of a Plane primitive, linking operations must infer from the context of the link operation which port of the implicit Cartesian space is intended. Linking operations usually apply to the origin of the Geometry's local coordinate system, though they can apply to the local coordinate system's normal and up-vector. When the default linking operation chooses the wrong port, the user can override the choice by making the object's local coordinate system explicit and choosing ports directly.

5 Linking the Toolkit Primitives

We now describe what occurs in the toolkit when a port of one primitive is linked to a port of another. Again, our choices for the semantics of inter-primitive linking are guided by the desire to stay close to the coordinate-system metaphor and the desire to have reasonable behaviors when there is no obvious answer in the underlying metaphor.

A linking operation generally asserts one of two types of relations: it either establishes a bi-directional equality relationship between two similarly typed ports or projects one port into the coordinate system of the other port, using their common 3D embedding as the medium of projection.

Consider linking a Point to another Point: here, the first Point is set to be positionally equivalent to the second Point. However, linking a Ray to a Ray is slightly different in that the orientation of the first Ray is made equivalent to that of the second Ray, but the positions of the two Rays remain distinct. Rotating either Ray causes the other to change, but translating either Ray has no effect on the other. This choice of how to link two Rays together is ambiguous, because a Ray actually represents two geometric values, a position and an orientation. Thus the action is chosen by considering the context of the linking operation. In linking a Ray to a Ray, the user typically wants them both to have the same orientation, so only the orientation values are linked. If a user wishes to equate the positions of the Rays, then the position port of the Ray must be made explicit by linking each Ray to a common Point.

A different form of linking occurs when a lower-dimensional primitive is linked to a higher-dimensional one. Such a link causes the lower-dimensional primitive to be geometrically projected onto the implied *span*[3] of the higher-dimensional primitive. After this projection, the lower-dimensional primitive is associated with a coordinate in the higher-dimensional primitive based on the location of the lower-dimensional primitive in the span of the higher-dimensional primitive. This association is then enforced during subsequent manipulation. Typically, higher-dimensional primitives are composed of a number of lower-dimensional primitives, each of which can still be linked to higher-level primitives (*e.g.*, the center point of a Plane primitive is a Point primitive and can be linked to other higher-dimensional primitives.)

To illustrate, consider linking a Point to a Plane. This link operation causes the Point's position to be projected onto the Plane. The Point is then constrained to be at the coordinate associated with that projection point, unless it is moved directly. Whenever the Plane is manipulated, the Point will remain at the same position relative to the origin and orientation of the Plane. Yet, if the Point is manipulated, it will move in the span of the Plane, and thereby change its associated coordinate in the Plane's span.

Some link operations do not fall directly into either category. When this occurs, we chose what we considered the most reasonable solution. For example, we defined the linking of a Geometry primitive to a Length's measure port as a scale operation on the Geometry primitive along the axis of the Length. If the Length's orientation is linked to a principal axis of the Geometry primitive (or vice versa), then the Length acts as a standard 1D scale operation along that axis; otherwise it is a shear.

Figure 2 displays the link behavior that applies to the toolkit primitives when neither primitive has been linked to anything else. In cases where one primitive has already been linked, very different behavior may result; space prevents us from defining all these possibilities. Consider a Point linked to a Plane. The Point becomes constrained to move only in the Plane. If the Point is subsequently linked to a second Point, a different table takes into account the pre-existing constraints on the first Point. In this case, the first Point is constrained to lie at the position of the projection of the second Point onto the Plane.

[3]In the linear algebra sense; a Length's span is the line defined by the endpoints, a Plane's span is the plane defined by the Plane's center point and normal vector.

6 Implementation details

The toolkit is implemented in UGA's scripting language, with geometry provided by UGA's interactive solids modeler. The linking constraints between primitives are established using UGA's object-dependency network.

User feedback is provided in the course of a linking operation to aid in link specification. When the user picks a primitive to be linked, it is highlighted and the cursor changes to indicate that the system is waiting for the user to pick the object to link to. After the user picks the object to link to, the system indicates its "ready" state through a cursor change that prompts for a mouse click to confirm the link.

Other highlighting methods indicate a primitive's degrees of freedom. For example, a Ray, like other primitive widgets, is green when it is created, indicating that it is unconstrained. If it is linked to another Ray, its orientation is linked but not its translation, and it turns yellow to indicate a partial constraint. When it is linked again to a Point, it turns red, indicating that all of its degrees of freedom are constrained. Another possibility would have been to change the primitive geometries after linking (*e.g.*, a spherical Point primitive could become a thin cylinder when it is linked to a Length, and could become a disc when linked to a Plane, although this strategy can result in a overly large collection of shapes).

7 Future Work

The toolkit as described lacks techniques for specifying range limits on a primitive's degrees of freedom. These would be especially useful when modeling the behavior of real-world objects, or when creating interface objects such as bounded sliders, joints, and dials. We intend to add this functionality (and perhaps other inequality constraints too), and also extend the range of our toolkit to deal with other graphics concerns, such as surface and volumetric modeling, scientific data exploration of scalar and vector fields, and behavior modeling including dynamic simulations.

When two primitives are linked together, a single constraint based on Figure 2 is installed. However, it would often be useful to have a set of possible link behaviors that the user can select from. Advanced users would be able directly select the desired behavior with only a single link operation.

Once a complex widget has been constructed from primitives, it is useful to interactively encapsulate it, along with appropriate parameters, for reuse in a tool library. For example, having constructed a shadow widget, the user should be able to easily apply the same process to any other object. This amounts to interactively defining a function and embodying it in a new, higher-level primitive.

Highly complex widgets linked together from dozens of primitives may present efficiency problems, especially for real-time interaction. It may be necessary to optimize the constraint network after the widget has been completed in order to maximize the toolkit's evaluation speed. It would also be useful to display graphically the constraint relations between primitives to provide feedback on the links established on any widget.

8 Conclusions

This toolkit provides a methodology for interactively constructing the geometric behavior of a variety of 3D widgets and parameterized 3D application objects, so that non-technical users can rapidly and interactively generate constrained 3D objects. Previously, such widget construction required programming in C or our scripting language. Even for experienced programmers, graphical construction is a more suitable and efficient environment to conceive, prototype, and implement many types of interactive 3D objects.

destination

source

Linking constrains	Point	Ray	Length Body	Length Measure	Angle Measure	Plane Frame	Plane Space	Geometry
Point	positions are equated	Point to lie on Ray	Point to lie on Length body	X	X	Point to lie in Plane	Point to be in Plane's 3D coordinate system	position of Point to position of Geometry
Ray	Ray to position of Point	orientations are equated	orientation of Ray to orientation of Length	orientation of Ray to be orientation of length measure	X	orientation and position of Ray to lie in Plane	Ray to be in Plane's 3D coordinate system	orientation of Ray to orientation of Geometry
Length Body	X	End Points of Length to lie on Ray	X	X	X	End Points of Length to lie in Plane	End Points of Length to be in Plane's 3D coordinate system	X
Length Measure	X	End Points of Length to lie on Ray	X	length of first Length to be length of second Length	length of Length to map to Angle's measure	X	X	X
Angle Measure	X	X	X	Angle's measure to map to length of Length	first Angle's measure to be second Angle's measure	X	X	X
Geometry	position of Geometry to position of second Point	orientation of Geometry to Ray's orientation	Geometry to lie on Length body	scale of Geometry to length of Length	X	Geometry to lie in Plane	Geometry to be in Plane's 3D coordinate system	positions are equated

Figure 2: Linking behaviors for unconstrained primitives.

Acknowledgments

This work was supported in part by the NSF/ARPA Science and Technology Center for Computer Graphics and Scientific Visualization and by ONR Contract N00014-91-J-4052, ARPA Order 8225. We also gratefully acknowledge the sponsorship of IBM, NCR, Sun Microsystems, Hewlett Packard, Digital Equipment Corporation, and NASA. We thank Andries van Dam and the members of the Brown University Graphics Group for their help and support. Please contact the authors for a copy of the accompanying videotape.

References

[1] AVS, Inc. *AVS Developer's Guide, v. 3.0*, 1991.

[2] A. H. Barr. Global and local deformations of solid primitives. *Computer Graphics (SIGGRAPH '84 Proceedings)*, 18(3):21–30, July 1984.

[3] Eric A. Bier. Snap-dragging in three dimensions. *Computer Graphics (1990 Symposium on Interactive 3D Graphics)*, 24(2):193-204, March 1990.

[4] Stuart K. Card, George G. Robertson, and Jock D. Mackinlay. The information visualizer, an information workspace. In *Proceedings of ACM CHI'91 Conference on Human Factors in Computing Systems*, pages 181–188, 1991.

[5] D. Brookshire Conner, Scott S. Snibbe, Kenneth P. Herndon, Daniel C. Robbins, Robert C. Zeleznik, and Andries van Dam. Three-dimensional widgets. *Computer Graphics (1992 Symposium on Interactive 3D Graphics)*, 25(2):183–188, March 1992.

[6] James D. Foley, Andries van Dam, Steven Feiner, and John F. Hughes. *Computer Graphics: Principles and Practice*. Addison-Wesley, 2nd edition, 1990.

[7] Michael Gleicher and Andrew Witkin. Through-the-lens camera control. *Computer Graphics (SIGGRAPH '92 Proceedings)*, 26(2):331–340, July 1992.

[8] Paul E. Haeberli. Conman: A visual programming language for interactive graphics. *Computer Graphics (SIGGRAPH '88 Proceedings)*, 22(4):103–111, August 1988.

[9] Kenneth P. Herndon, Robert C. Zeleznik, Daniel C. Robbins, D. Brookshire Conner, Scott S. Snibbe, and Andries van Dam. Interactive shadows. *1992 UIST Proceedings*, pages 1-6, November 1992.

[10] Michael Kass. CONDOR: Constraint-based dataflow. *Computer Graphics (SIGGRAPH '92 Proceedings)*, 26(2):321–330, July 1992.

[11] Brad A. Myers, Dario A. Guise, Roger B. Dannenberg, Brad Vander Zanden, David S. Kosbie, Edward Pervin, Andrew Mickish, and Philippe Marchal. GARNET comprehensive support for graphical, highly interactive user interfaces. *IEEE COMPUTER magazine*, pages 71–85, November 1990.

[12] Open Software Foundation. *OSF/Motif Reference Guide*.

[13] Steve Sistare. Graphical interaction techniques in constraint-based geometric modeling. In Steve MacKay and Evelyn M. Kidd, editors, *Graphics Interface '91 Proceedings*, pages 161–164. Canadian Man-Computer Communications Society, March 1991.

[14] Scott S. Snibbe, Kenneth P. Herndon, Daniel C. Robbins, D. Brookshire Conner, and Andries van Dam. Using deformations to explore 3d widget design. *Computer Graphics (SIGGRAPH '92 Proceedings)*, 26(2):351–352, July 1992.

[15] Paul S. Strauss and Rikk Carey. An object-oriented 3d graphics toolkit. *Computer Graphics (SIGGRAPH '92 Proceedings)*, 26(2):341-349, July 1992.

[16] Robert C. Zeleznik, D. Brookshire Conner, Matthias M. Wloka, Daniel G. Aliaga, Nathan T. Huang, Philip M. Hubbard, Brian Knep, Henry Kaufman, John F. Hughes, and Andries van Dam. An object-oriented framework for the integration of interactive animation techniques. *Computer Graphics (SIGGRAPH '91 Proceedings)*, 25(4):105–112, July 1991.

EXACT: Algorithm and Hardware Architecture for an Improved A-Buffer

Andreas Schilling, Wolfgang Straßer
Universität Tübingen
Bundesrepublik Deutschland *

Abstract

The EXACT (EXact Area Coverage calculaTion) algorithm presented in this paper solves the Hidden Surface Elimination (HSE) problem on the subpixel level.

The use of subpixel masks for anti-aliasing causes some problems with the HSE on the pixel level that are difficult to overcome. The approximations of the well known A-buffer algorithm are replaced by an exact solution that avoids erratic pixels along intersecting or touching surfaces.

With EXACT the HSE problem on the subpixel level is solved with the help of p-masks. P-masks (priority masks) are subpixel masks that indicate for each subpixel which one of two given planes is closer to the viewer. An algorithm to produce the p-masks in an efficient way and its hardware implementation are presented. The p-mask generator is used in a hardware implementation of an A-buffer algorithm in the form of a rendering pipeline. Of course the algorithm can also be used in software to enhance an existing A-buffer implementation.

The paper ends with the description of the list processing architecture for which the EXACT A-buffer has been built[1].

CR Categories and Subject Descriptors: I.3.1 **[Computer Graphics]:** Hardware Architecture - *raster display devices*; I.3.3 **[Computer Graphics]:** Picture/Image generation - *display algorithms*

Additional Key Words and Phrases: anti-aliasing, A-buffer, priority-masks, exact area coverage calculation.

*Wilhelm–Schickard–Institut für Informatik, Graphisch–Interaktive Systeme, Auf der Morgenstelle 10/C9, 7400 Tübingen, E-mail: andreas@gris.informatik.uni-tuebingen.de, strasser@gris.informatik.uni-tuebingen.de.

[1]The experiences described here were gained in a research project partly supported by the Commission of the European Communities through the ESPRIT II-Project SPIRIT-workstation, Project No. 2484.

1 The Problem: Exact anti-aliasing

Rasterizing produces aliasing artifacts. If a box filter is used to perform anti-aliasing the brightness and color of edge pixels are functions of the pixel area covered by the objects as well as of the object colors. The ideal intensity would be described by the formula $I = \frac{1}{A}\sum_i I_i A_i$, where A_i and I_i are the areas and intensities of the visible surfaces within the pixel and A is the total pixel area. Subpixel masks can be used to calculate the fraction of the pixel area covered by an object. However, if the sample point is outside the polygon, its z-value is more or less useless for a correct HSE. A complete hidden surface elimination for the pixel area is required [5].

2 Current Status

A traditional algorithm that approximately evaluates the box-filtered intensity is the A-buffer Algorithm described by Carpenter [1]. The contributions of surfaces that cover a pixel partially are arranged in a list that is sorted front-to-back. Two z-values are stored for each fragment, z_{min} and z_{max}. When all fragments have been added to the list, the intensity is calculated in a process called packing. Beginning with the frontmost object the contribution is determined using subpixel masks. For each fragment the exact covered pixel area is stored in addition to the subpixel mask. In certain cases the exact area can be used instead of the subpixel count to calculate the contribution. A subpixel already

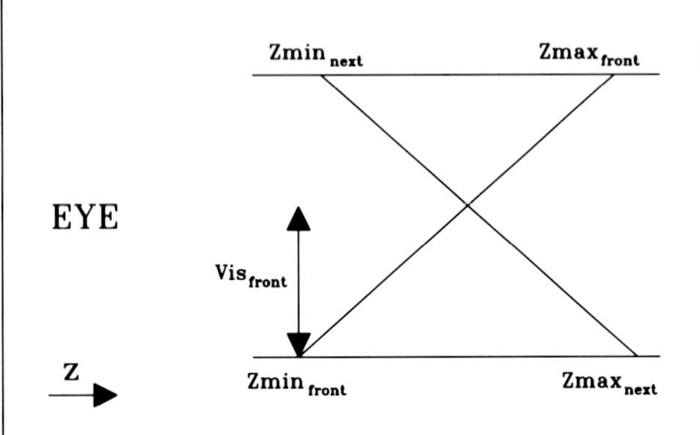

Figure 1: Visible fraction of front fragment ([1]).

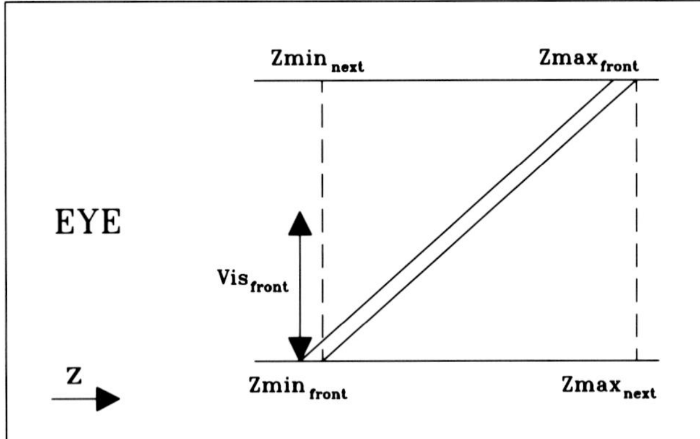

Figure 2: Front fragment should cover the whole pixel.

covered by an opaque object is excluded from further processing which results in a z-buffer-like behavior on the subpixel level. The difference to an actual z-buffer on the subpixel level is that for each fragment only two z values are stored per pixel. Intersecting surfaces are treated with an approximation. Intersection is assumed if the z ranges of two different objects overlap. It is further assumed that the two surfaces are oriented as indicated in Fig. 1.

The visible area of the front fragment is then calculated as:

$$Vis_{front} = \frac{Zmax_{next} - Zmin_{front}}{(Zmax - Zmin)_{front} + (Zmax - Zmin)_{next}}$$

The method will fail very often though, because it depends on assumptions that are hardly ever fulfilled. For example the surfaces in Fig. 2 are rendered exactly like the ones in Fig. 1 although one of the objects is not visible at all.

It should also be mentioned that other even more troublesome[2] problem cases exist that are very difficult

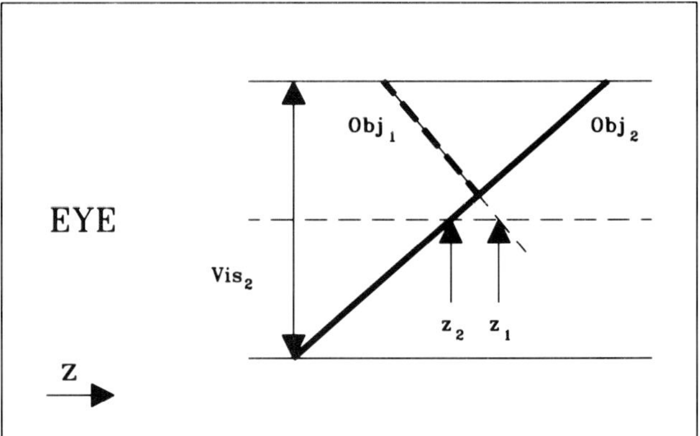

Figure 3: Object 1 disappears (z value sampled at pixel center seems further away).

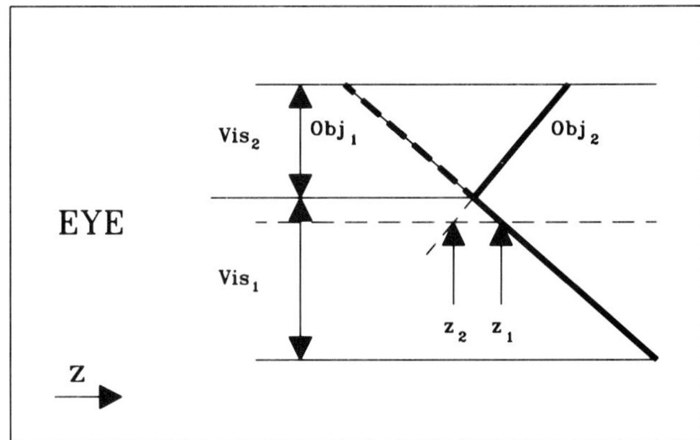

Figure 4: Object 2 shines through (z value sampled at pixel center seems closer).

to handle. If only one z-value is available as it is the case in the z-buffer things become especially difficult. If the center of the pixel where the z-values are sampled is outside of the object the z-values are nearly useless because they don't tell anything about the real location of the object if the slopes in z-direction are not known.

Some of the very common problem cases are shown in Fig. 3 - 5. The bold dashed objects are not drawn although they should be visible. These problems are not taken into account with most rendering algorithms. Fig. 13 shows some of the resulting artifacts; the correct image is produced with the EXACT method, described in the following section (Fig. 14).

3 Solution

If two objects (or the planes of the two objects resp.) intersect within a pixel a subpixel mask is generated which we call priority mask (p-mask). It indicates in

[2]More troublesome: Intersecting surfaces could be forbidden and don't exist in many implementations of rendering systems. But objects touching each other as e.g. in Fig. 3 appear in nearly every picture and cannot be avoided.

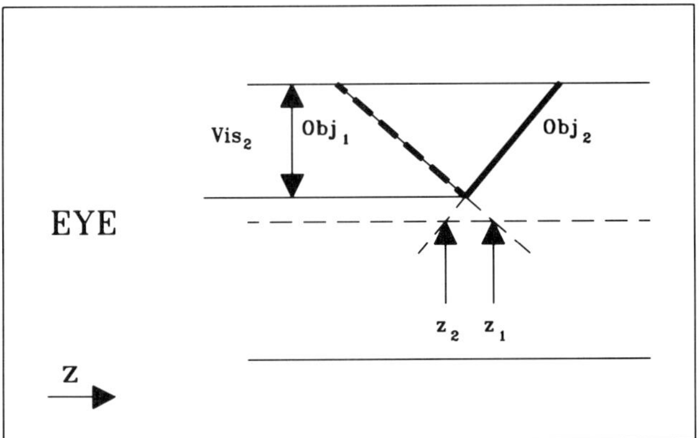

Figure 5: Object 1 disappears, but should be visible, object 2 is visible (situation similar to Fig. 3).

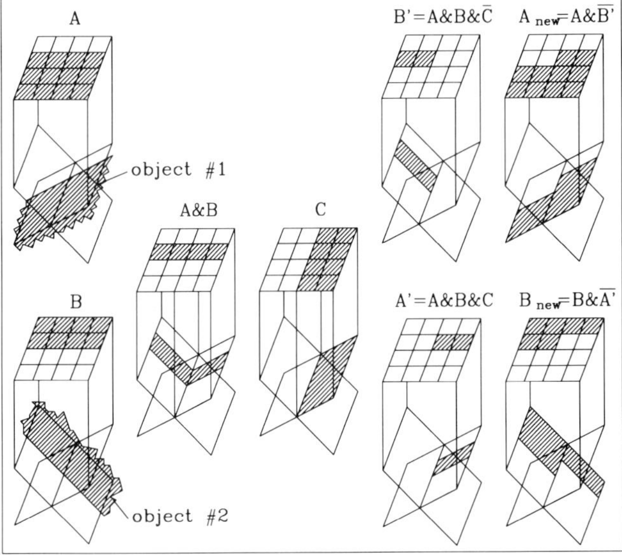

Figure 6: Generation of the modified edge subpixel masks A_{new} and B_{new} from the original edge subpixel masks A and B using the priority mask C. Shown is the subdivided pixel area, projected on the planes of two intersecting objects.

which part of the pixel object #1 is the front object and in which part of the pixel object #2 is the front object. This subpixel mask is used to modify the edge subpixel masks of the two objects in the following way (see Fig. 6):

$$A_{new} = A\&\overline{A\&B\&\overline{C}} \quad (1)$$

$$B_{new} = B\&\overline{A\&B\&C} \quad (2)$$

where
A: edge subpixel mask for object # 1
B: edge subpixel mask for object # 2
C: p-mask for objects #1 and #2,
plane #1 in front of plane #2 ⇒ subpixel = 1

Two tasks remain to be solved:

1. The priority mask has to be calculated in an efficient way.
2. The decision has to be made, when two object planes intersect within a pixel's area.

3.1 The calculation of the priority mask

Virtually any rasterization system uses a unit that interpolates colors and z-values by repeatedly adding increments to a starting value. The priority mask generator uses the increments for the z value in the x and y directions $dz_x = \frac{\partial z(x,y)}{\partial x}$ and $dz_y = \frac{\partial z(x,y)}{\partial y}$. (The values for the two objects are marked with indices, e.g. $dz_{1,x}$). The z-values at the pixel centers are known (z_1 and z_2). If we calculate the difference of the corresponding values for the two objects we get:

$$z = z_1 - z_2 \quad (3)$$

$$dz_x = dz_{1,x} - dz_{2,x} \quad (4)$$

$$dz_y = dz_{1,y} - dz_{2,y} \quad (5)$$

These parameters describe a plane that indicates, where plane #1 is in front of plane #2 by the sign of its z-value. The intersection with the plane z=0 denotes the border between the two areas where plane #1 or plane #2 resp. is in front of the other plane.

The representation of this plane with the above mentioned parameters resembles very much the representation of the polygon edges in some rendering systems, e.g. in the PIXEL PLANES system [6]. The mechanisms that exist to generate subpixel masks representing edges can therefore be used to generate the priority mask. A scheme producing subpixel masks that exactly represent the covered fraction of the pixel is described in [8].

The generation of the priority mask can be done by software of hardware. Our contribution aims for a hardware solution. If a software solution is considered, several criteria can be used to reduce significantly the number of cases where the priority mask has to be calculated:

$$A\&B \neq 0 \quad (6)$$

$$z_{1min} < z_{2max} \text{ and } z_{2min} < z_{1max} \quad (7)$$

or a much better criterion instead of (7):

$$z_2 - z_1 < (|dz_{2,x} - dz_{1,x}| + |dz_{2,y} - dz_{1,y}|)/2 \quad (8)$$

The first criterion (6) is obvious: if the subpixel masks of the two objects don't overlap, none of the objects can hide the other one.

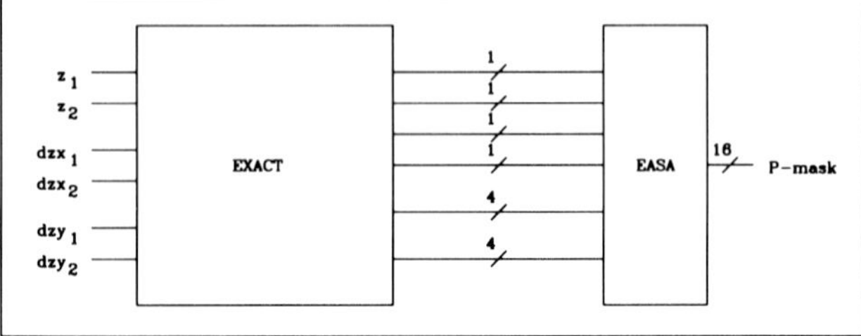

Figure 7: Block diagram of the p-mask generation on the EXACT-Chip

The second criterion is expressed by relations (7). It eliminates the trivial cases where the z-ranges of the two objects don't overlap. The priority mask thus consists of only 1s or only 0s, resp. This criterion is not very strong however, because objects with overlapping z-ranges do not necessarily have to intersect each other (see e.g. Fig. 2). Also the values of z_{min} and z_{max} might not be known, though they could easily be calculated. This leads us to the stronger criterion expressed in equation (8). Only if this relation is true, will an intersection of the two objects occur within the pixel area. Using this criterion, the case of Fig. 2 is a trivial case with only 0s or 1s in the priority mask.

4 Hardware Implementation of the P-Mask Generation

The block diagram of the p-mask generation in Fig. 7 shows, how the mask is calculated. The block labelled EXACT takes two z-values and the corresponding increments as input and calculates from these values the parameters of the intersection line. These parameters are used to lookup the final p-mask. The contents of the corresponding lookup table can simply represent the order of the planes at the subpixel locations. It should however, be consistent with the method used for the generation of the coverage masks. The EXACT chip, like the render chip in the SPIRIT workstation [4] uses the EASA concept[3], described in detail in [8].

The design of the EXACT block (Fig.8) is intended to exploit parallelism as much as possible. Three parallel subtractors calculate the z-difference and the differences of the z-increments. The absolute values of the results are calculated in the next stage.

The resulting three values (z, dz_x and dz_y) are the parameters of the equation (9) for a straight line, the line of intersection between the two planes (origin of the coordinate system is the pixel center).

[3]The EASA (Exact Area Subpixel Algorithm) is used to determine the subpixel mask. In contrast to the conventional approach, we do not sample at the subpixel centers. Instead, the covered portion of the pixel area is calculated exactly and converted into the corresponding subpixel count. The location of the subpixels is chosen in a way, that preserves the geometry best. For details see [8]

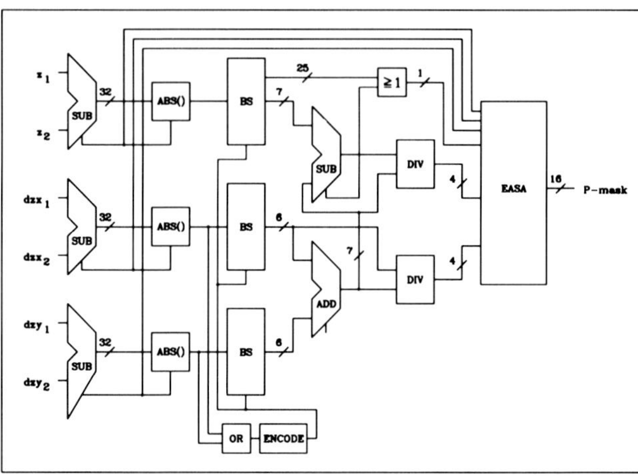

Figure 8: The p-mask generation on the EXACT-Chip (≈ 12000 Gates)

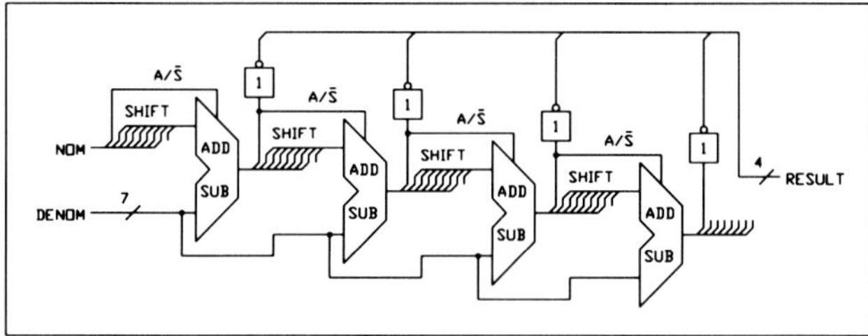

Figure 9: The Dividers on the EXACT-Chip

$$F(x, y) = z + x * dz_x + y * dz_y = 0 \qquad (9)$$

This equation has to be normalized so that the parameters can be used to look up the resulting p-mask. The normalization could be performed by dividing the equation by $\sqrt{dz_x^2 + dz_y^2}$. However the square root can be avoided if we divide by the L_1-norm instead of the L_2-norm[4]. This means that we divide by the sum of the absolute values of dz_x and dz_y.

The precision that is required so that the error introduced by the parameter calculation is smaller than one subpixel can be found if we apply the law of error propagation. For a 4×4 subpixel mask, only four bits are needed for each normalized parameter.

To keep the dividers simple (Fig. 9), barrel shifters are used to properly scale the input parameters.

[4]The L_1 norm is also known as Manhattan distance, because, rather than the shortest distance, it describes the distance between two points, one would have to walk in a city with a rectangular grid of streets.

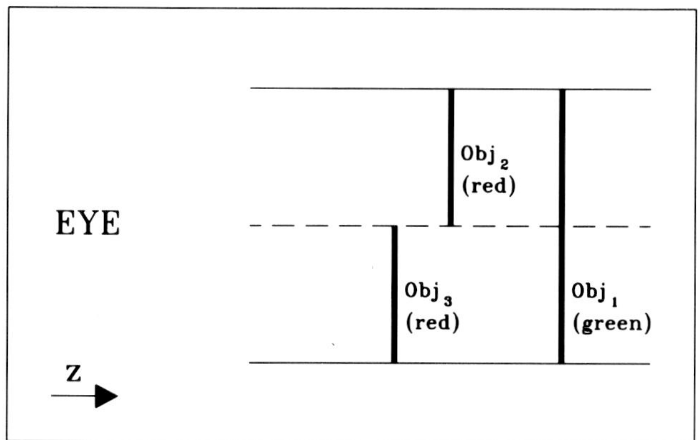

Figure 10: If the colors of object 1 and object 2 are blended (each of them contributing 50% to the final color), green will be part of the pixel color (25%). If the color of object 3 is then blended to the pixel color, green will erroneously still be part of the final pixel color.

5 System aspects

The EXACT-hardware is part of a new graphics system. The main concepts of its architecture are described in the following section.

5.1 Processing of lists — the concept of the A-buffer

A big difference between the A-buffer and a traditional z-buffer lies in the fact that in the A-buffer lists of contributions to each pixel are stored whereas in the z-buffer only one item per pixel has to be stored — the one currently closest to the viewer. Most rendering hardware today supports the z-buffer for obvious reasons: the list handling required by the A-buffer is much more difficult to implement in hardware.

The question that could be asked at this point is:

Why should we store more than one object per pixel?

There are several answers to this question. The first one: Anti-aliasing. The second one: Transparency.

Anti-aliasing of edges implies the blending of the colors of different objects. There are cases in which the colors can be blended using a normal z-buffer. For example, if one object appears in front of an other big object the colors can be blended with the weight factors A and $(1 - A)$, A being the pixel area covered by the second object. But what if three or more objects contribute to a pixel? A blending in the described way will lead to errors (see Fig. 10).

The second reason, transparency handling, is obvious. There may be several transparent objects covering a pixel. They have to be depth-sorted before their colors can be blended using the appropriate transparency factors and sorting requires that more than one object is stored.

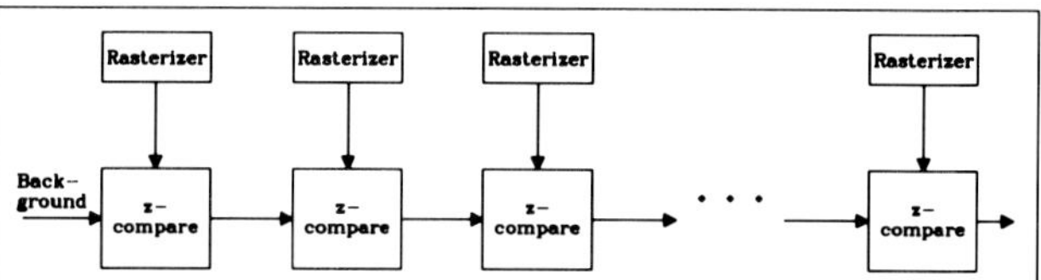

Figure 11: Pipeline of comparators performing n z-buffer operations simultaneously without problem of buffer access bottleneck. While e.g. the third comparator works on pixel #1, the second comparator works on pixel #2 and the first comparator is already working on Pixel #3.

5.2 The List Processing Pipeline

Which hardware architecture is capable of supporting an A-buffer like rendering scheme? It is an architecture that has been known quite a while but normally was only used as a functional replacement for the z-buffer: the pixel processing pipeline. Cohen and Demetrescu presented such a processor pipeline already in 1980 [2]. Systems like the Triangle Processor and Normal Vector Shader System [3] or PixelFlow [7] form such a pipeline and use it for what Molnar calls image composition. As multiple z-buffer operations take place at the same time (see Fig. 11), the traditional frame buffer access bottleneck problem is solved in an elegant way. This might be a reason for this type of system to be more widely used in the future. Simply by adding more stages to the pipeline the rendering speed of the system can be increased indefinitely. The only penalty is a slightly increased latency time that up to several hundred pipeline stages doesn't exceed the frame time.

But now this pipeline architecture can not only be used as a z-buffer replacement; it is an outstanding architecture to perform the list processing required by the A-buffer algorithm. Schneider proposed in 1988 the PROOF system [9] that uses a pipeline and transfers not only one object per pixel through the pipeline but a list of contributing objects for each pixel, similar to a proposal by Weinberg [10]. The hidden surface elimination was performed in a special post-processing stage. The architecture proposed in this paper performs the whole list processing in list processors that contain the EXACT hardware for the hidden surface elimination on the subpixel level[5].

[5]Other features of the list processing pipeline, like image processing capabilities (filtering with arbitrary kernel) are not subject of this paper but also are arguments for using such an architecture.

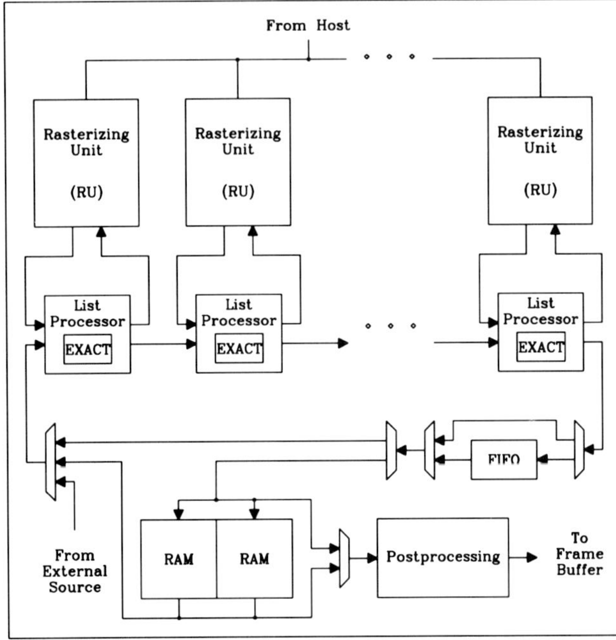

Figure 12: List Processor Pipeline Architecture

Fig. 12 shows the block diagram of a list processor pipeline. The polygon descriptions are distributed in a round robin fashion among the rasterizer units (RU), which ensures a good load distribution with minimum effort. The rasterizers interpolate the z- and color-values (or resp. normals or texture coordinates) and send the sorted pixel contributions down to the list processors. Each rasterization unit is capable of rendering several thousand objects per second (about 20 MPixel/sec.) and contains a standard RISC Processor and RAM as well as an ASIC for the pixel generation.

The list processors, realized as ASICs, contain the described hardware for the EXACT algorithm and perform the modification of the subpixel masks coming from the RUs as well as the depth-sorting of the pixel contributions. Visible fragments are inserted into the lists at their appropriate positions which is important for transparent objects. Mutually intersecting transparent objects can be handled by splitting the subpixel mask of one of the objects in two parts: one in front of, the other behind the second object. The output of the pipeline consists of a depth sorted list of object contributions for each pixel, with nonoverlapping subpixel masks for opaque objects and transparent objects appearing in the correct sequence.

As each list processor can only handle one additional object per pixel, list processors that receive several objects concerning one pixel flag all but the last of these objects as *not processed* and send them in front of the already processed list to the next stage. If this stage didn't receive an object from its RU for this pixel the last of the *not processed* objects is treated by this stage. If any objects remain unprocessed at the end of the pipeline the concerned pixels are cycled through the pipeline again to handle the unresolved objects. In order to keep the sequence of the pixels intact a FIFO is used to store the output of the pipeline during the recycling of the incompletely processed pixels. By adding several list processors without connected RUs to the end of the pipeline the probability for such cases can be significantly reduced.

The output of the pipeline can be directed to one of two RAM buffers. This allows the rendering of scenes with changing parts. The static parts are rendered once into the RAM buffer. Then the RAM serves as input for the pipeline where only the changing parts have to be added for each frame. The RAM buffer is also used in other applications like image processing or form factor calculations for a radiosity algorithm. In the post-processing stage the transparency calculations are performed and the subpixel contributions are summed up.

6 Conclusion

A principle of rasterization is, that it produces aliasing artifacts. The quest for increased realism by developing sophisticated illumination models can not be successful without properly dealing with anti-aliasing. This problem can be partially solved by increasing the screen resolution of color monitors, but this is very costly and limited by physical constraints. On the other hand anti-aliasing by means of the EXACT A-buffer solves the problem adequately and offers a better cost/performance ratio for future display systems.

References

[1] Carpenter, L. The a-buffer, an antialiased hidden surface method. *Computer Graphics 18*, 3 (July 1984), 103–108.

[2] Cohen, D. A vlsi approach to the cig problem. Presentation at SIGGRAPH 1980, 1980.

[3] Deering, M., Winner, S., Schediwy, B., Duffy, C., and Hunt, N. The triangle processor and normal vector shader: A vlsi system for high performance graphics. *Computer Graphics 22*, 4 (Aug. 1988), 21–30.

[4] Dunnett, G. J., White, M., Lister, P. F., Grimsdale, R. L., and Glemot, F. The image chip for high performance 3d rendering. *IEEE Computer Graphics & Applications 12*, 6 (Nov. 1992), 41–52.

[5] Fiume, E., Fournier, A., and Rudolph, L. A parallel scan conversion algorithm with anti-

Figure 13: Visible artifacts at edges are the result of using subpixel masks with the standard z-buffer.

Figure 14: Same scene with the EXACT algorithm.

aliasing for a general-purpose ultracomputer. *Computer Graphics 17*, 3 (July 1983), 141–150.

[6] Fuchs, H., Poulton, J., Eyles, J., Greer, T., Goldfeather, J., Ellsworth, D., Molnar, S., Turk, G., Tebbs, B., and Israel, L. Pixel-planes 5: A heterogeneous multiprocessor graphics system using processor-enhanced memories. *Computer Graphics 23*, 3 (July 1989), 79–88.

[7] Molnar, S. Pixelflow: High-speed rendering unsing image composition. *Computer Graphics 26*, 2 (July 1992), 231–240.

[8] Schilling, A. G. A new simple and efficient antialiasing with subpixel masks. *Computer Graphics 25*, 4 (July 1991), 133–141.

[9] Schneider, B.-O. A processor for an object-oriented rendering system. *Computer Graphics Forum 7* (1988), 301–310.

[10] Weinberg, R. Parallel processing image synthesis and anti-aliasing. *Computer Graphics 15*, 3 (Aug. 1981), 55–62.

Graphics Rendering Architecture for a High Performance Desktop Workstation

Chandlee B. Harrell
Farhad Fouladi

Silicon Graphics Computer Systems
2011 North Shoreline Blvd.
Mountain View, CA 94039-7311

Abstract

Hundreds of commercial applications used in mainstream design activities have demonstrated proven demand for 3D graphics rendering products. The demand is for faster and more powerful renderers, thus creating the system design problem of how to achieve maximum rendering performance from the technology available to implement the system. This paper describes a graphics rendering architecture that takes advantage of several novel architectural features: a custom floating point processing core with tailored data stores and bussing structures, the arrangement of these cores into a SIMD processor for low overhead multiprocessing, and the hyper-pipelining of the fixed point scan conversion units for low overhead, high bandwidth pixel generation into an interleaved frame buffer. These features combine to form a solution to the system design problem which distinguishes itself by its overall performance and its ability to maximize performance while minimizing system size. The resulting architecture is capable of over a half million gouraud shaded Z-buffered triangles per second, with a sustained fill rate for gouraud shaded and Z-buffered pixels of 80M pixels per second. The architecture fits in a desktop workstation.

Introduction

A graphics rendering architecture for a high performance desktop workstation is described.

3D graphics workstations are used by a broad range of applications [IRIS92]. Many of the applications fall into the categories traditionally called computer-aided design (CAD), where the designer makes progressive refinements on the shape and dimensioning of a product based on feedback from visual modeling, and computer-aided engineering (CAE), where the designer also wishes to analyze properties of the design such as thermal and stress gradients or structural strength, in addition to shape and appearance. 3D graphics workstations are used in the following applications, among others: car and airplane design, tool design, packaging design, industrial and product design, furniture design, clothing and shoe design, architectural and civil engineering, production floor and plant design, geothermal and atmospheric analysis, molecular modeling, pharmaceutical design, chemical analysis, and film animation and special effects.

Application packages today running on 3D workstations enable design efforts that are compute intensive, limited only by today's renderers. The complexity of models that renderers can effectively handle is far less than the model complexity with which users are attempting to work. This creates tremendous demand for faster and more powerful graphics rendering systems. How to achieve the highest performance rendering system from the technology available is the system design problem that this demand presents to the system designer.

Further clarification of the graphics rendering system design problem is necessary. Most graphics renderers today perform rapid, accelerated rendering of 3-sided polygons and straight line segments. The renderer receives these basic graphics primitives, each primitive with vertex descriptions defined by the application, and performs the calculations to render the primitive as pixel values into the frame buffer [FOLEY90,SEGAL92,VAND87]. The basic graphics primitives allow close approximation to any arbitrary curve or surface by sub-dividing the curve into line segments or the surface into polygons to the point where the rendered image is visually acceptable to the user. For the system designer, the primitives provide a simple and limited set of processing algorithms that must be accelerated, enabling the focus to achieve high performance systems.

A top level flow diagram is presented in Figure 1 illustrating the process for rendering the basic graphics primitives. The graphics renderer receives polygons or lines from the application process and performs the steps shown in the flow diagram to render each polygon or line as color and Z pixel values into the frame buffer. Details of each processing step are carefully discussed in [FOLEY90] and [NEWM79].

Implementation bottlenecks in a graphics rendering system typically appear: 1) in the floating point compute power available for the world coordinate to screen coordinate transformations and for vertex color computations; 2) in the floating or fixed point compute power available for triangle slope and line slope calculations; 3) in the rate of generation of pixel values from the fixed point iterators; 4) and in the achieved pixel bandwidth into the frame buffer.

Commercial architectures have approached these bottlenecks in a variety of ways. [KIRK90] presents an architecture where the per vertex and slope calculations are performed on the host CPU and multiple iteration engines drive an interleaved frame buffer. [APGAR88] also executes the per vertex calculations on the host, but off-loads most of the slope calculations to a fixed point engine, and uses a unique combination of multiple iteration units to drive pixel results into an interleaved system memory. [AKEL88,89] describe an approach utilizing a serial pipeline of floating point processors for the per vertex calculations, fixed point engines for the slope calculations, and multiple iteration units to drive an interleaved frame buffer. The architecture introduced in [TORB87] also uses multiple floating point processors but arranges them into a MIMD parallel processor, uses a fixed point slope engine, and multiple iterators to drive an interleaved frame buffer. [PERS88] uses a single floating point processor to perform both per vertex and slope calculations, and a single iterator to drive an interleaved frame buffer. Note that the interleaved frame buffer is the only feature common to all the approaches, and that most approaches use multiple iteration units.

The goal of the architecture described here is to provide a powerful graphics rendering system, maximizing performance while minimizing size. The architecture utilizes several novel approaches to overcoming rendering bottlenecks. Floating point performance is accomplished through the custom design of a highly efficient floating point processing core, and by employing multiple cores controlled in a low overhead SIMD parallel processor. The floating point core is tailored to accommodate both the per vertex calculations and the triangle and line slope calculations. Fixed point iteration performance is achieved through hyper-pipelining two identical iteration units, allowing each unit to sustain the pixel generation requirements of multiple pixel memory busses. Each iteration unit is pipelined until technology limits of integration are encountered. The multiple memory busses provide the necessary bandwidth into the frame buffer memory.

These features result in a graphics rendering system solution distinguished by overall performance, and by compactness of size. The architecture is implemented in a desktop workstation [INDIG93]. It is capable of over 1.3 million depth-cued lines per second, over half a million gouraud shaded Z-buffered polygons per second, with a sustained fill rate of 80M gouraud shaded Z-buffered pixels per second.

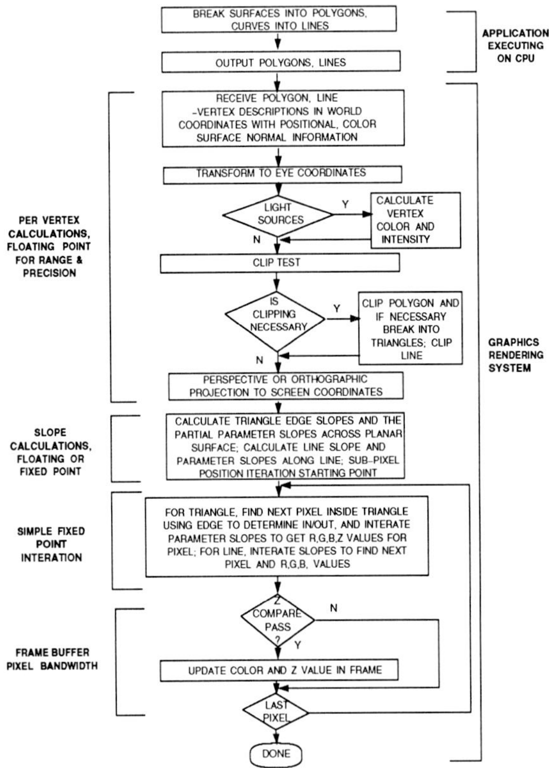

Figure 1. Process for rendering basic graphics primitives

TOP LEVEL SYSTEM VIEW

This section presents a block diagram of the architecture in Figure 2. The key components are briefly introduced, followed by a description of the overall control structure and the data flow through the system. The subsequent sections discuss each of these key components in detail, describing the critical decisions made to determine their structure, then detailing the internal operation of each component. The final section discusses the technology targeted for the architectural implementation and the implementation results.

The block diagram is shown in Figure 2. The key components are the FIFO interface to the system bus, the Command Processor (CP), the SIMD parallel processor, the dual Raster Engines (RE), and the frame buffer. The SIMD processor is made up of a sequencer, a microcode store, and multiple Geometry Engines (GE). Each GE is a custom floating point processing core. Each Raster Engine is a hyper-pipelined iteration unit.

The SIMD parallel processor executes all the per vertex calculations and the slope calculations shown in Figure 1, the REs perform the fixed point iteration, and the frame buffer pixel bandwidth is determined by the multiple busses into the frame buffer.

Operation is initiated by the CPU sending polygon and line rendering commands into the FIFO across the system bus. The FIFO allows the CPU to generate commands at a rate independent of how fast the rendering occurs. If the FIFO fills up, an interrupt is generated to the CPU for exception handling.

The SIMD parallel processor is fed data from the FIFO by the Command Parser. The CP moves data from the FIFO into the ping-pong input buffers of the Geometry Engines. The GEs read data from the ping-pong buffers, perform necessary floating point computations, and write results to their respective output FIFOs. GE execution is controlled by the common sequencer and control store.

A bus controller resident in the even Raster Engine reads data from the GE output FIFOs and transfers the data into the RE input ping-pong buffers. The REs perform necessary iterations to generate color and Z values and perform the correct pixel updates into the frame buffer. The odd RE generates pixels for the odd numbered scan lines of the frame buffer, and the even RE generates pixels for the even numbered scan lines.

The sections below first discuss the GE custom floating point core solution, followed by a discussion of the control structures required to arrange the GEs into the SIMD parallel processor. This is followed by a description of the hyper-pipelined RE iteration solution.

GEOMETRY ENGINE

The goal for the Geometry Engine design is to achieve the maximum *realized* floating point performance for graphics algorithms, in a single chip solution. The algorithms used for evaluating performance are the per vertex and slope calculations of Figure 1. The decision is made to combine the per vertex and slope calculations into a single floating point solution. Slope calculations are comprised of relatively complex algorithms, difficult to implement in a hard-wired fashion, and therefore most effectively implemented in a microcoded processor. Also, the compute cycles required for per vertex calculations is almost evenly balanced with the cycles required for slope calculations. Combining the per vertex and slope calculations into the GE relieves the need to design a second microcoded fixed point processor of similar complexity; and the replication of GEs in the SIMD parallel processor increases both the per vertex and slope processing power together.

The GE design goal is met with a custom floating point processing core. Analysis shows that a custom unit with tailored data stores,

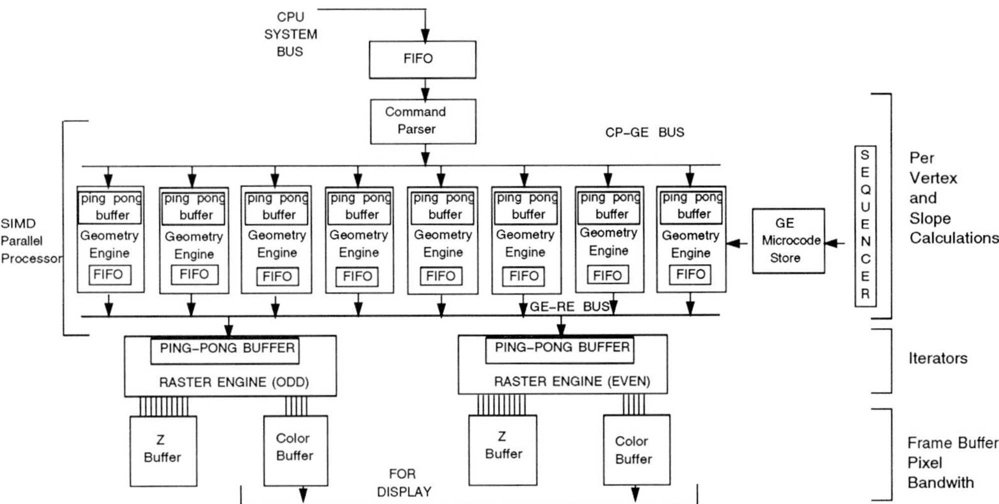

Figure 2. Block Diagram of the architecture

bussing structures, and sequencing control achieves higher realized performance and a more compact solution than available commercial alternatives. Therefore a custom approach is chosen.

Analysis of the per vertex calculations and the slope calculations shows an even balance between multiplies and adds, therefore one multiplier and one adder are chosen for the GE core. The GE design approach follows the fundamental principle of maximizing the utilization of the most expensive resource: the floating point multiplier (FMPY) and the floating point adder (FALU). The following observations for maximizing utilization are taken into account in the GE design: high data bandwidth to the correct operands is needed into the FMPY and FALU; multiple threads of the same algorithm must be active simultaneously. Enough bandwidth to appropriate data storage and data sources is needed to avoid lost cycles waiting on an operand that is slow to retrieve. A single thread of execution may have several additions followed by several multiply operations, thus wasting the FMPY or the FALU until a result is available from the other unit. Multiple threads of execution is the solution.

The Geometry Engine block diagram is shown in Figure 3. Six different busses and four ports from the register file drive the four inputs to the FMPY and the FALU. Two of the busses provide immediate wrap-around of FMPY and FALU results back to their inputs. One bus gives access to the ping-pong buffer loaded by the Command Parser, while two more busses give access to a pair of special data stores. The sixth bus accesses off-chip memory that is used for expansion, and typically holds the global variables for the GE.

A multi-port register file is included for scratch storage of intermediate results. The register file is critical to allowing multiple simultaneous threads of calculation. Feedback paths from FMPY and FALU result outputs are provided for single-threaded operation, but when two threads conflict by needing the same unit for their next computation, then one thread must be stalled by storing the intermediate result in the register file until the appropriate unit becomes free.

On the other hand, a multi-port register file is an expensive commodity and its size is limited. Reviewing the per vertex calculations concludes that the ping-pong buffer and the register file are sufficient to perform the per vertex calculations with maximum FMPY and FALU utilization. On reviewing the slope calculations, however, it is noted that frequently data from each vertex of a triangle, or both vertices of a line, are needed simultaneously during multi-threaded computation. The register file cannot be made big enough to hold the data structures for each vertex. The GE is designed to have three separate data stores, one for each vertex of a triangle or for the two vertices of a line, used during the slope calculation process. The ping-pong buffer is used to hold the data structure for one vertex, while the two special data stores hold the data structures for up to two more vertices.

This extensive memory and bussing structure is wasted without flexible independent addressing and flexible control of data movement. This is accomplished through a very wide instruction word which allows control of the breadth of resources.

The result of the described structure is that simultaneous access can be made to the ping-pong buffer, the two special data stores, the global variables memory, the result outputs, and the register file by any of the four FMPY and FALU inputs. Multiple threads of execution supported by this accessible bandwidth into the FMPY and FALU inputs maximizes FMPY and FALU utilization.

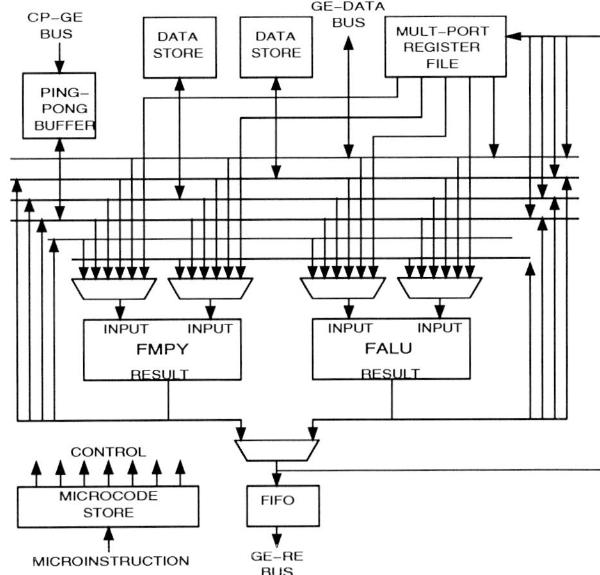

Figure 3. Geometry Engine block diagram

GE operation occurs as follows. The Command Parser loads data into the ping-pong buffer. The ping-pong buffer allows CP loading of data into one side of the buffer while the GE is executing and accessing the other side of the buffer. The CP initiates GE execution by informing the GE sequencer that data is fully loaded. The sequencer looks up instructions in the GE microcode store, and these instructions control the execution functions of the GE. For lines and triangles, the GE performs per vertex calculations, accessing data from the ping-pong buffer, then constructs vertex data structures based on screen space coordinates and puts one vertex data structure back in the ping-pong buffer and up to two more vertex data structures into each of the special data stores. Slope calculations are then performed, drawing operands from the ping-pong buffer and the two special data stores. Calculated iteration coefficients and initial values are passed to the Raster Engines by storing them to the output FIFO.

SIMD PARALLEL PROCESSOR

A single floating point processor cannot achieve the desired performance. Therefore multiple floating point processors are used in the design. The following goals for multiprocessing led to the SIMD parallel processor solution: 1) a linear performance increase must be achieved with the addition of Geometry Engines; 2) the multiprocessing solution must have the lowest possible impact over and above a uniprocessor solution.

Three approaches are considered for the multiprocessing solution. The first is a pipeline of floating point processors [AKEL88, 89]. Each pipeline stage performs a subset of the per vertex and slope computations, passing intermediate results to the next processor in the pipeline. Each pipeline processor is executing a different set of code to implement its separate subset of the algorithm. This approach has several disadvantages. The throughput of a pipeline is the speed of the slowest processing step. Overall performance is determined by the processor with the biggest subset of the algorithm to process. Since the algorithm cannot be divided into perfectly equal subsets, a less-than-linear performance gain is achieved. Also note, that to add processors, a new subdivision of the algorithm must take place and new code must be written and tuned. The final disadvantage of this approach is in the burden of overhead the approach requires. Although having the advantage of not requiring the distribution mechanism at the head of the pipe needed by the next two approaches considered, each processor does require its own sequencer, microcode store, globals data store, in addition to control logic to interface each of the pipeline stages.

The second approach considered is a parallel MIMD (Multiple Instruction Multiple Data) array of processors [TORB87]. Each processor performs independent execution of the per vertex and slope calculations for its own polygon or line primitive. Linear performance gains are attained when the same kind of primitive is distributed to each processor, thus satisfying the first multiprocessing goal. Processors may be added without requiring changes to processor code. The disadvantage of the MIMD parallel processor lies in the overhead required to implement such an approach. A parallel processor requires a distribution function that takes primitives in the FIFO (received from the CPU) and disburses a primitive to each of the processors present. A MIMD parallel processor also requires that each processor has its own sequencer, microcode store, and globals data store.

The third approach considered is a parallel SIMD (Single Instruction Multiple Data) array of processors. Each processor executes the same instruction in lockstep, but is computing results for its own polygon or line primitive. Like the MIMD processor already examined, the SIMD parallel processor achieves linear performance gains with the addition of processors when the same kind of primitive is distributed to each processor. The advantage of the SIMD approach is in the low overhead required to implement a multiprocessor. All processors share the same sequencer, the same microcode store, and the same globals data memory. The only implementation overhead required over a uniprocessing solution is the addition of the distribution function. It is worth noting that this is a simple function and therefore a small overhead to tolerate. The SIMD parallel processor is chosen as it optimally achieves the multiprocessing goals.

Note that a key assumption to accomplishing linear performance gain from a parallel processor (SIMD or MIMD) is that the same kind of primitive is distributed to each of the processors (all lines or all polygons). This requires that the primitives coming through the FIFO from the CPU arrive in significant groupings of lines together and polygons together, rather than a fully random distribution of lines and polygons. For a MIMD processor, if the FIFO holds alternating lines and polygons, the throughput slows down to the rate of the slower primitive - the polygon. For a SIMD processor, alternating lines and polygons is a worst case scenario. Performance will reduce to that of a uniprocessor. Extensive analysis of model data sets used on 3D workstations shows polygons typically clump in large bunches and lines do the same. This is particularly true of CAD/CAE applications. The result is linear performance gain for parallel processor arrangements.

The unique system features required for SIMD parallel processing will now be discussed. Please refer to Figure 2. The features included for SIMD processing are the distribution function performed by the CP, sequencing functions to allow SIMD branching, common bus for the microinstruction, common bus for the globals data store, and indirect addressing requirements into GE memories. The GE input ping-pong buffer and output FIFO are also crucial to performance.

COMMAND PARSER

To describe the operation of the Command Parser, we must first explain the needs of the distribution function. The purpose of the CP is to analyze the command and data stream coming through the FIFO, distribute data accordingly to the GEs, and subsequently initiate GE execution. To perform this function, the CP must detect boundaries between primitives, detect whether subsequent primitives are of the same or different kind, and maintain the correct order of primitive disbursement to the GEs.

Please refer to Figure 4 for a diagram of the Command Parser. The CP is microcoded for flexibility. This allows different routines for primitives comprised of vertices with different kinds of attributes, and the exception handling of polygons with greater than three sides.

CP operation begins with the arrival of a command token in the FIFO. The command token causes the CP sequencer to branch to a routine appropriate for the kind of primitive arriving in the FIFO. This branch mechanism inherently defines primitive boundaries. The command token is read from the FIFO and stored in the Current Command register. A compare function allows branching based on whether the current command token just arrived is identical or different from the last command token received. If the token is identical, then the arriving primitive can be distributed to the next GE in the parallel processor. If the token is different, then the GEs that have already been loaded with data must swap their input ping-pong buffer and begin executing before the arriving primitive can be distributed to the next GE. The token compare mechanism allows the CP to branch to different routines to handle these two cases.

The CP must determine to which GE the arriving primitive should be written. A round robin scheme of distribution is chosen,

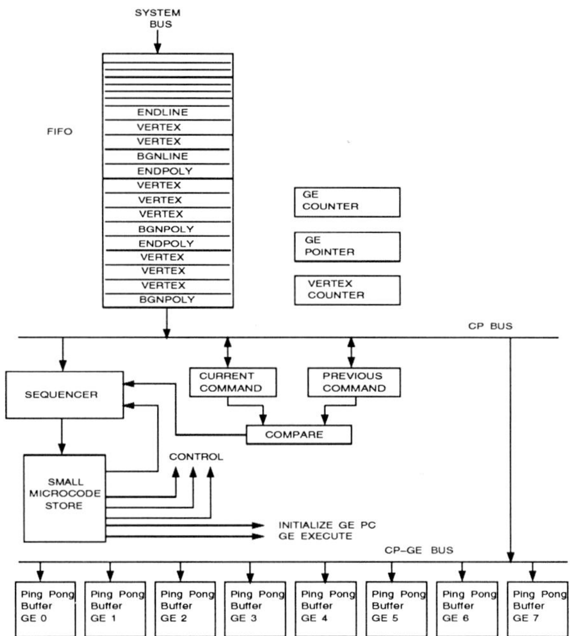

Figure 4. Command Parser block diagram

primitives being loaded in a continuous sequence from GE #0 through to GE #7, and back around. Referring back to Figure 2, primitive coefficients calculated by the GEs are pulled from the GE output FIFOs in the same round robin order. A pointer to the GE that is currently being loaded, and a counter which maintains the number of GEs that have been loaded since the last execute command provide the tools to determine for which GE the arriving primitive is destined. The incrementing and clearing of these counters is under microcode control. After choosing the appropriate GE, the CP pulls vertex data from the FIFO and writes it across the CP-GE Bus and into the GE's ping-pong buffer.

Once all 8 GEs have been loaded, or when the current primitive is different from the previous primitive, the CP must initiate GE execution. The CP first tells the GE sequencer which GEs are loaded, passes the GE sequencer the appropriate address to begin execution, and then issues the GE sequencer an execute command. An interlock mechanism will stall the CP if the GE is currently executing at the time of the CP execute command, and will initiate GE execution only when the previous execution is complete. Once the interlock mechanism clears, it is an indication that the GE ping-pong buffers have been swapped, and the CP resumes distribution of primitives from the FIFO.

GE SEQUENCER

The GE sequencer is shown in Figure 2. The sequencer is based on a standard uniprocessor design. Flexible branch functions are supported for jumps and subroutine calls. Branching is controlled within separate fields of the GE's wide instruction word. This allows concurrent branching with the GE datapath control, thus not affecting datapath performance thru branches.

To this uniprocessor design base are added functions which allow control of multiple SIMD processors. The GE sequencer has control to stall each of the GEs independently. This control is used in two different ways. The first is on receipt of an execute command from the CP once the GEs are idle. The GE sequencer will decode which GEs the CP has loaded from information passed by the CP. Those GEs not loaded will be stalled by the GE sequencer for the duration of the primitive execution. The second fashion the stall control is used is for implementing conditional subroutine calls across SIMD processors. If a subset of the processors does not pass the condition, that subset is stalled by the GE sequencer for the duration of the subroutine call, while the remaining processors execute the subroutine. As an example, conditional subroutine calls are used for implementing the lighting and clipping branches shown in Figure 1.

MICROCODE STORE AND GLOBALS MEMORY STORE

The GE sequencer accesses the next microinstruction from the GE microcode store (Figure 2). The microinstruction word controls all the GE internal functions, as well as the GE sequencer. The piece of the microinstruction word controlling the GEs is bussed to all the GEs for simultaneous execution.

Additional memory (not depicted) can be added external to the GEs as an expansion memory to store global variables required in execution. The GE Data Bus (Figure 3) of each GE is bussed together and connected to a globals memory store.

INDIRECT ADDRESSING

As explained in the section above on the Geometry Engine (Figure 3), data is read from the ping-pong buffer and the two special data stores to perform the slope calculations for a line or triangle. Depending upon orientation of the primitive on the screen, these data stores may need to be accessed differently by different processors. In order to do this effectively in a SIMD processing environment, indirect addressing is provided into these data stores. This minimizes cycles spent out of SIMD lockstep execution and is crucial to SIMD performance.

INPUT PING-PONG BUFFER AND OUTPUT FIFO

The GE input ping-pong buffer and the GE output FIFO are also crucial to SIMD performance. Without a ping-pong buffer at the input to the GE, the CP would have to load 8 GEs *after* GE execution of the previous primitive completes, eliminating significant parallelism. The FIFO at the GE output allows all GEs to write their results in lockstep execution. Without the FIFO, a SIMD implementation would not be feasible.

RASTER ENGINE

The goal for the Raster Engine is to obtain the fastest gouraud shaded Z-buffered fill rate in a single chip. It is also desired to be able to use multiple copies of the same chip to obtain further increases in rendering performance.

There are two major bottlenecks in rasterization: pixel generation, and memory bandwidth. Pixel generation, the first bottleneck, can be increased in two different ways. Contemporary architectures have traditionally increased the rate of pixel generation by replicating in parallel the number of fixed point iterators, utilizing enough iterators to achieve the desired pixel rate. Hyper-pipelining a single iteration unit is the approach taken in this architecture. Hyper-pipelining adds pipeline stages to a single iterator until the desired rate of pixel generation is achieved. The pipeline stages added to the iterator require significantly fewer gates than would be required to replicate iterators. Therefore, hyper-pipelining is chosen as the minimum solution for performance. Memory bandwidth, the second bottleneck, is increased by using an interleaved frame buffer across multiple memory banks.

Determining the total number of pipeline stages and the number of memory busses for the RE is a recursive process, and depends on the integration limits of technology. To achieve the maximum fill rates, the iteration pipeline must support a pixel generation rate of

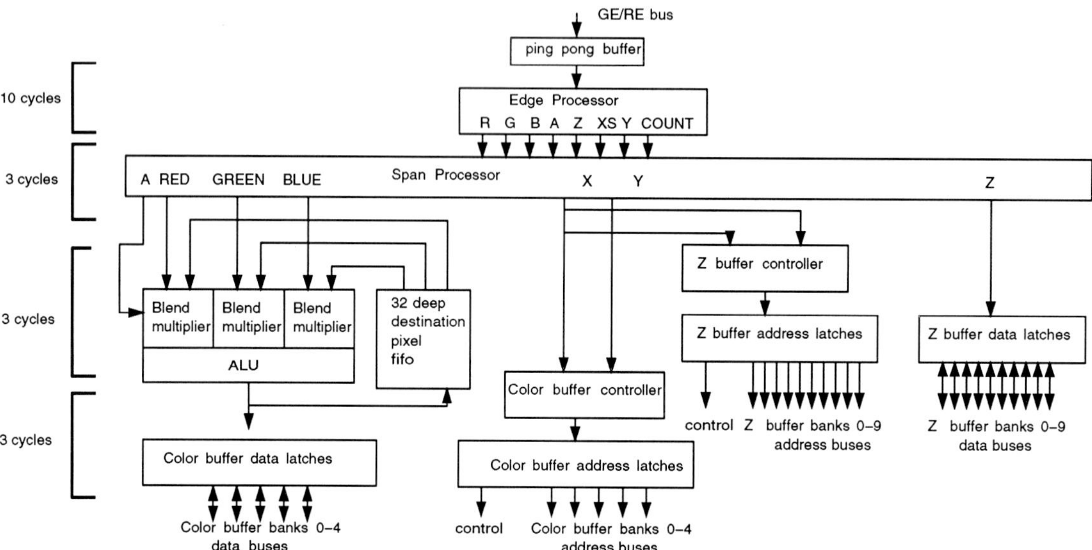

Figure 5. Raster Engine block diagram

N times the page mode bandwidth of a frame buffer DRAM, where N is the number of memory busses used. A sample pipeline depth is analyzed and the die size computed. The conclusion of this recursive process led to the resultant architecture with a single hyper-pipelined Raster Engine driving a five-way interleaved color buffer.

Given a five-way interleave on the color buffer, the pipeline clock rate is set at five times the DRAM page mode bandwidth, under the assumption a pixel is generated every clock. The slowest element of the RE pipeline is the key to ensuring the clock rate can be met, and is what was checked during the recursive analysis. This element is the DDA unit of the iterators. A DDA unit consists of a two input adder with a 2:1 multiplexer on one of its inputs. The output of the adder is fed into a register which is then fed back to the second input of the adder. The resultant clock rate for a five-way interleave color buffer drives the number of pipeline stages in the Raster Engine. The hyper-pipelined Raster Engine has 26 pipeline stages from the input ping-pong registers which hold the line and triangle iteration parameters to the point where pixels are written into the color buffer.

For the system architecture implemented, it is decided to incorporate two raster engines to obtain the desired performance on the desktop.

The RE implementation is now discussed in detail. A diagram of the Raster Engine is shown in Figure 5. The RE is capable of drawing rectangle, triangle and line primitives. Each primitive requires a set of iteration coefficients which are downloaded from the GE FIFOs into the RE ping-pong buffers. Once the ping-pong buffers are loaded, the RE initiates rendering of the primitive.

The execution units of the Raster Engine consist of four major sections:

- > edge processor;
- > span processor;
- > per-pixel operators;
- > memory controllers.

The edge processor combines with the span processor to perform the task of converting a primitive into pixels. The edge processor decomposes triangles into horizontal spans, and decomposes lines into pixels. It has two iterators for computing the beginning and end X location of the span, and six iterators to computer R,G,B,A,Z,Y for the first pixel on the span. Next some terms must be defined. The major edge of a triangle connects the vertex with maximum Y coordinate value to the vertex with minimum Y. The edge connecting the vertex with maximum Y to the vertex with the middle Y value is called the first minor edge. The edge that runs between the vertex with the middle Y and the vertex with the minimum Y value is termed the second minor edge. The edge processor begins by iterating down the major edge and the first minor edge. When the processor detects the middle Y has been crossed, it swaps the first minor edge with the second minor edge and continues down the triangle until the minimum Y coordinate is reached. For each span, the edge processor computes the initial R,G,B,A,X,Y,Z values for the first pixel on the span as well as the number of pixels that have to be rendered for that span. This information is passed to the span processor. When drawing lines, only one of the two edge iterators is used to generate the X coordinate. The edge processor has 10 pipe stages and can generate a new span every other clock.

The span processor has 6 iterators. These iterators walk through the pixels on a span and generate the R,G,B,A,X,Z parameters for each pixel on the span. The processor can generate one or four pixels per clock. When gouraud shading and/or Z-buffering, the span processor will generate one pixel per clock in the X direction. When a span is flat shaded and not Z-buffered, the span processor generates 4 pixels per clock. The block write feature of the VRAMs used in the color buffer is utilized to write all 4 pixels generated in one memory cycle, thus quadrupling the fill performance for screen clears and for rendering flat shaded 2D surfaces. For lines, parameters from the edge processor get passed through. The span processor has a pipeline latency of 3 clocks.

The Raster Engine supports a rich set of pixel operators required by commonly used graphics libraries [SEGAL92, VAND87]. Pixels operators fall into two categories. The first category of operators modify the color of the pixel, such as logicop and blend. Blend and logicop are operations performed between the generated source color and the destination color that is already stored in the color buffer. They require readback from the color buffer which is described below. There are three sets of multipliers to perform the blend function for the R,G,B components. These multipliers are followed by an ALU which performs the logic operations. These two sections together contain 10 pipeline stages.

The second category of pixel operators perform tests on pixel parameters to allow conditional updating of color pixel values. Examples in this category are the Z-compare test and stencil test. The Z-compare test is used to determine pixel visibility in the third dimension. The stencil test is used to provide more general conditional test operations. The Z-comparison is done in parallel with blend and logicop in the same number of pipeline stages.

There are memory controllers for two separate memory ports on the Raster Engine: the color buffer port and the Z-buffer port. The color buffer is a five-way interleaved memory port, and the Z-buffer is a 10-way interleaved memory port. The Z-buffer operation consists of reading back the old Z value stored in the Z-buffer, comparing that Z value with the newly generated Z value and, if the comparison passes indicating the new pixel is visible, the new Z value and color value are written into the Z-buffer and color buffer respectively. Since the Z-buffer requires two accesses (a read and a write) for every write access to the color buffer, the Z-buffer port is designed with twice the interleaving of the color buffer to accommodate Z-buffered fill at the color gouraud shaded update rates.

As we noted above, a write access to the color buffer takes 5 clocks. Similarly, the pipelined read-modify-write access to the Z-buffer takes 10 clocks. Adjacent pixels along a span are allocated to adjacent banks of the Z-buffer interleave. Since it takes 10 clocks to perform a read-modify-write, and we have a 10-way interleave, bank contention does not occur along a span and a one pixel per clock comparison rate is achieved.

The 10 banks of the Z-buffer interleave share the same page address to reduce memory controller complexity. There is a single block of logic for page fault detection. Each bank can access a different column address within the page. A score boarding technique is used to keep track of the state of each bank. When a pixel is dispatched to a bank, a bit in the score board is set to specify that the bank is busy. Thus, any pixel accesses to the same bank will be blocked and a bank contention stall generated to stop pixel flow until the bank is again idle.

The color buffer has a five-way interleave. As explained above, the pipeline depth is chosen such that five pixels are generated in a single VRAM page mode cycle time, allowing contentionless color fills along a span. Read-modify-write operations to the color frame buffer (for blend and logicop) are supported at half the fill performance of straight color write operations. Values in the color buffer are first read into a FIFO in the RE to await the "modify" step of the operation. When the FIFO fills, the contents of the FIFO are then merged with the newly generated incoming pixel stream and the result is written back into the color buffer. This two-pass operation is continued until rendering is complete. The color buffer memory controller has a 3 clock latency.

The operation of two REs together will be briefly discussed. The two Raster Engines work on the same primitive together. The rendering task is split based on span number. All even spans of a primitive (when the Y coordinate is even) are rendered by the "even" Raster Engine; all odd spans are rendered by the "odd" Raster Engine. This results in a doubling of fill performance. The edge processor in each RE iterates through all spans, but each RE rejects the spans that do not belong to it, and the edge processor continues iteration to the next span.

TECHNOLOGY

This section briefly discusses the technology used in the implementation. The technology targeted for the custom logic design is a 1.0 micron double metal CMOS gate array and standard cell process. The process can achieve the equivalent of 100K gates on a single die. The 1M-bit DRAM family is the targeted memory technology. The design consists primarily of custom parts and memory components. The design contains over a million gates of custom logic, and is implemented across three 5" x 13" PC boards.

CONCLUSION

A graphics rendering architecture has been described which is distinguished by its overall performance, and by its ability to maximize performance while minimizing system size. The architecture is shipping as a product in the IRIS Indigo Extreme. A scaled version of the architecture was introduced in IRIS Indigo^2 Elan. The architecture provides state-of-the-art rendering performance in a desktop 3D workstation.

ACKNOWLEDGEMENTS

Sincere thanks to Marc Hannah and Dave Galbi for their major efforts on the architecture. Thanks to Vimal Parikh for his advice on the floating point solution. Finally, overwhelming appreciation must go to the whole design team, every one of whom made significant contributions, and who made it possible.

REFERENCES

[AKEL88] K. Akeley, T. Jermoluk, "High-Performance Polygon Rendering", Computer Graphics (Proc. SIGGRAPH), Vol. 22, No. 4, August 1988, pp. 239-246.

[[AKEL89] K. Akeley, "The Silicon Graphics 4D/240GTX Superworkstation", IEEE Computer Graphics and Applications, Vol. 9, No. 4, July 1989, pp. 71-83.

[APGAR88] B. Apgar, B. Bersack, A. Mammen, "A display system for the Stellar Graphics Supercomputer Model GS1000", Computer Graphics (Proc. SIGGRAPH), Vol. 22, No. 4, August 1988, pp. 255-262.

[FOLEY90] J. Foley, A. van Dam, S. Feiner, J. Hughes, "Computer Graphics, Principles and Practice", 2nd edition,, Addison-Wesley Publishing, 1990.

[INDIG93] "The Indigo2 Technical Report", Silicon Graphics Computer Systems, 1993.

[IRIS92] "Iris Partner Catalogue", Silicon Graphics Computer Systems, 1992.

[KIRK90] D. Kirk, D. Voorhies, "The Rendering Architecture of the DN10000VS", Computer Graphics (Proc. SIGGRAPH), Vol. 24, No. 4, August 1990, pp. 299-308.

[NEWM79] W. Newman, R. Sproull, "Principles of Interactive Computer Graphics", McGraw-Hill Book Company, Second Edition, 1979.

[PERS88] "The Personnal Iris™: A Technical Report", Silicon Graphics Computer Systems, 1988.

[SEGAL92] M. Segal, K. Akeley, "The OpenGL™ Graphics System: A Specification (version 1.0)", Silicon Graphics Computer Systems, 30 June 1992.

[TORB87] J. Torborg, "A Parrallel Processor Architecture for Graphics Arithmetic Operations", Computer Graphics (Proc. SIGGRAPH), Vol. 21, No. 4, July 1987, pp 197-204.

[VAND87] A. van Dam, et. al., "PHIGS+ Functional Description Rev. 2", Jointly developed PHIGS+ specification, 1987.

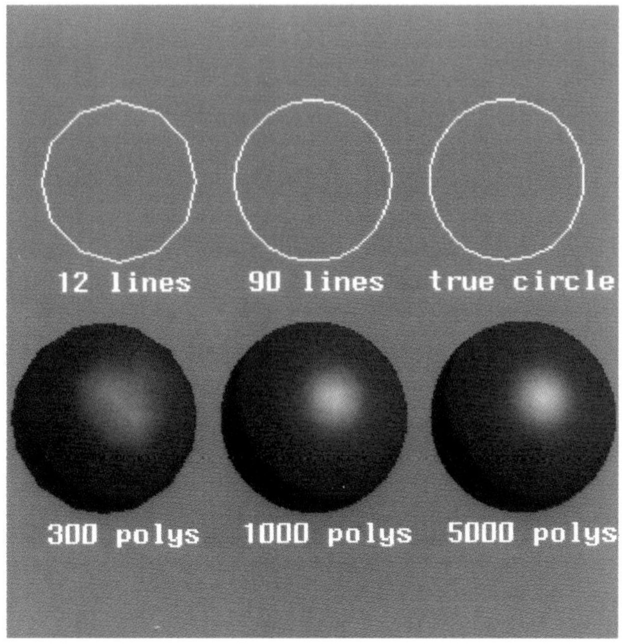

Figure 6. Demonstration of curve and surface approximation using graphics primitives. Note effect of increasing tessellation depth on image quality, and on the number of primitives to render.

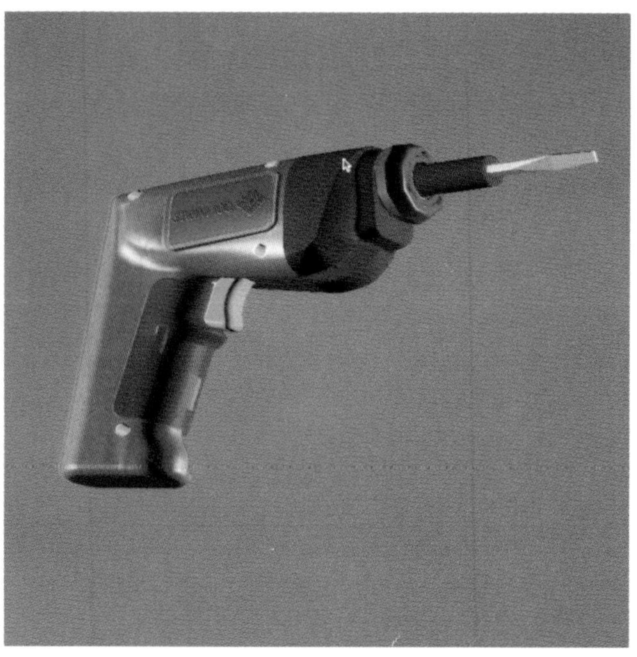

Figure 7. Shaded-lighted image (2 directional lights) (Data Courtesy of Cisigraph Corporation) has 31774 triangles, 827961 pixels and was rendered in 0.13 seconds.

Figure 8. Shaded-lighted image (2 directional lights) (data courtesy of Cisigraph Corporation) has 77420 triangles, 526235 pixels, and was rendered in 0.29 seconds.

Figure 9. Indigo^2 Extreme graphics render board set..

Leo: A System for Cost Effective 3D Shaded Graphics

Michael F Deering, Scott R Nelson
Sun Microsystems Computer Corporation†

ABSTRACT

A physically compact, low cost, high performance 3D graphics accelerator is presented. It supports shaded rendering of triangles and antialiased lines into a double-buffered 24-bit true color frame buffer with a 24-bit Z-buffer. Nearly the only chips used besides standard memory parts are 11 ASICs (of four types). Special geometry data reformatting hardware on one ASIC greatly speeds and simplifies the data input pipeline. Floating-point performance is enhanced by another ASIC: a custom graphics microprocessor, with specialized graphics instructions and features. Screen primitive rasterization is carried out in parallel by five drawing ASICs, employing a new partitioning of the back-end rendering task. For typical rendering cases, the only system performance bottleneck is that intrinsically imposed by VRAM.

CR Categories and Subject Descriptors: C.1.2 [Processor Architectures]: Multiprocessors; I.3.1 [Computer Graphics]: Hardware Architecture; I.3.3 [Computer Graphics]: Picture/Image Generation *Display algorithms*; I.3.7 [Computer Graphics]: Three Dimensional Graphics and Realism.

Additional Keywords and Phrases: 3D graphics hardware, rendering, parallel graphics algorithms, gouraud shading, antialiased lines, floating-point microprocessors.

1 INTRODUCTION

To expand the role of 3D graphics in the mainstream computer industry, cost effective, physically small, usable performance 3D shaded graphics architectures must be developed. For such systems, new features and sheer performance at any price can no longer be the driving force behind the architecture; instead, the focus must be on affordable desktop systems.

The historical approach to achieving low cost in 3D graphics systems has been to compromise both performance and image quality. But now, falling memory component prices are bringing nearly ideal frame buffers into the price range of the volume market: double buffered 24-bit color with a 24-bit Z-buffer. The challenge is to drive these memory chips at their maximum rate with a minimum of supporting rendering chips, keeping the total system cost and physical size to an absolute minimum. To achieve this, graphics architectures must be repartitioned to reduce chip count and internal bus sizes, while still supporting existing 2D and 3D functionality.

This paper describes a new 3D graphics system, Leo, designed to these philosophies. For typical cases, Leo's only performance limit is that intrinsically imposed by VRAM. This was achieved by a combination of new architectural techniques and advances in VLSI technology. The result is a system without performance or image quality compromises, at an affordable cost and small physical size. The Leo board set is about the size of one and a half paperback novels; the complete workstation is slightly larger than two copies of Foley and Van Dam [7]. Leo supports both the traditional requirements of the 2D X window system and the needs of 3D rendering: shaded triangles, antialiased vectors, etc.

2 ARCHITECTURAL ALTERNATIVES

A generic pipeline for 3D shaded graphics is shown in Figure 1. ([7] Chapter 18 is a good overview of 3D graphics hardware pipeline issues.) This pipeline is truly generic, as at the top level nearly every commercial 3D graphics accelerator fits this abstraction. Where individual systems differ is in the partitioning of this rendering pipeline, especially in how they employ parallelism. Two major areas have been subject to separate optimization: the floating-point intensive initial stages of processing up to, and many times including, primitive set-up; and the drawing-intensive operation of generating pixels within a primitive and Z-buffering them into the frame buffer.

For low end accelerators, only portions of the pixel drawing stages of the pipeline are in hardware; the floating-point intensive parts of the pipe are processed by the host in software. As general purpose processors increase in floating-point power, such systems are starting to support interesting rendering rates, while minimizing cost [8]. But, beyond some limit, support of higher performance requires dedicated hardware for the entire pipeline.

There are several choices available for partitioning the floating-point intensive stages. Historically, older systems performed these tasks in a serial fashion [2]. In time though, breaking the pipe into more pieces for more parallelism (and thus performance) meant that each section was devoting more and more of its time to I/O overhead rather than to real work. Also, computational variance meant that many portions of the pipe would commonly be idle while others were overloaded. This led to the data parallel designs of most recent 3D graphics architectures [12].

†2550 Garcia Avenue, MTV18-212
Mountain View, CA 94043-1100
michael.deering@Eng.Sun.COM (415)336-3017
scott.nelson@Eng.Sun.COM (415)336-3106

© 1993 ACM-0-89791-601-8/93/008/0101 $01.50

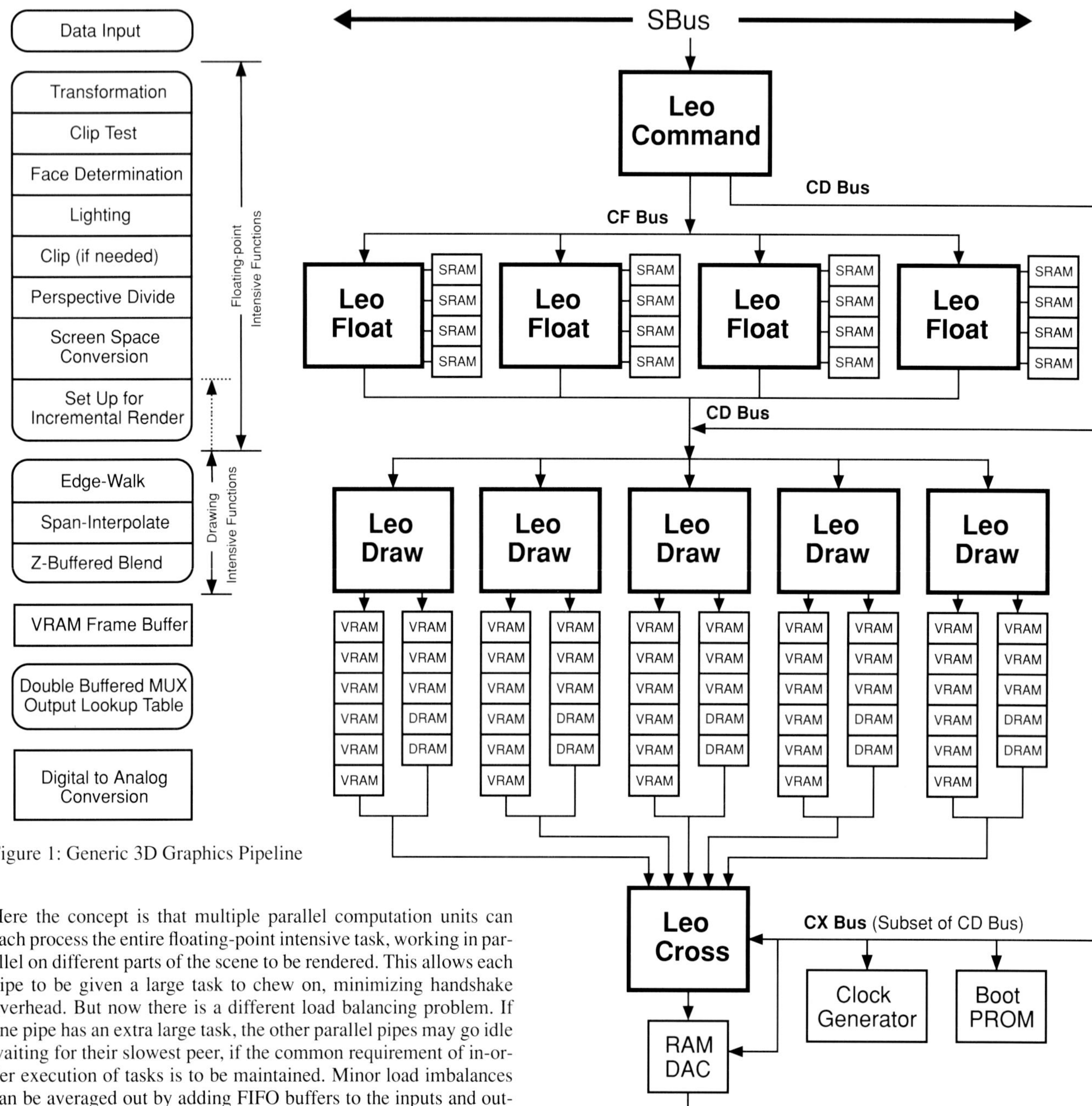

Figure 1: Generic 3D Graphics Pipeline

Figure 2: The Leo Block Diagram. Every chip in the system is represented in this diagram.

Here the concept is that multiple parallel computation units can each process the entire floating-point intensive task, working in parallel on different parts of the scene to be rendered. This allows each pipe to be given a large task to chew on, minimizing handshake overhead. But now there is a different load balancing problem. If one pipe has an extra large task, the other parallel pipes may go idle waiting for their slowest peer, if the common requirement of in-order execution of tasks is to be maintained. Minor load imbalances can be averaged out by adding FIFO buffers to the inputs and outputs of the parallel pipes. Limiting the maximum size of task given to any one pipe also limits the maximum imbalance, at the expense of further fragmenting the tasks and inducing additional overhead.

But the most severe performance bottleneck lies in the pixel drawing back-end. The most fundamental constraint on 3D computer graphics architecture over the last ten years has been the memory chips that comprise the frame buffer. Several research systems have attempted to avoid this bottleneck by various techniques [10][4][8], but all commercial workstation systems use conventional Z-buffer rendering algorithms into standard VRAMs or DRAMs. How this RAM is organized is an important defining feature of any high performance rendering system.

3 LEO OVERVIEW

Figure 2 is a diagram of the Leo system. This figure is *not* just a block diagram; it is also a *chip level* diagram, as every chip in the system is shown in this diagram. All input data and window system interactions enter through the LeoCommand chip. Geometry data is reformatted in this chip before being distributed to the array of LeoFloat chips below. The LeoFloat chips are microcoded specialized DSP-like processors that tackle the floating-point intensive stages of the rendering pipeline. The LeoDraw chips handle all screen space pixel rendering and are directly connected to the frame buffer RAM chips. LeoCross handles the back-end color look-up tables, double buffering, and video timing, passing the final digital pixel values to the RAMDAC.

The development of the Leo architecture started with the constraints imposed by contemporary VRAM technology. As will be derived in the LeoDraw section below, these constraints led to the partitioning of the VRAM controlling LeoDraw chips, and set a maximum back-end rendering rate. This rate in turn set the performance goal for LeoFloat, as well as the data input bandwidth and processing rate for LeoCommand. After the initial partitioning of the rendering pipeline into these chips, each chip was subjected to additional optimization. Throughput bottlenecks in input geometry format conversion, floating-point processing, and pixel rendering were identified and overcome by adding reinforcing hardware to the appropriate chips.

Leo's floating-point intensive section uses data parallel partitioning. LeoCommand helps minimize load balancing problems by breaking down rendering tasks to the smallest isolated primitives: individual triangles, vectors, dots, portions of pixel rasters, rendering attributes, etc., at the cost of precluding optimizations for shared data in triangle strips and polylines. This was considered acceptable due to the very low average strip length empirically observed in real applications. The overhead of splitting geometric data into isolated primitives is minimized by the use of dedicated hardware for this task. Another benefit of converting all rendering operations to isolated primitives is that down-stream processing of primitives is considerably simplified by only needing to focus on the isolated case.

4 INPUT PROCESSING: LEOCOMMAND

Feeding the pipe

Leo supports input of geometry data both as programmed I/O and through DMA. The host CPU can directly store up to 32 data words in an internal LeoCommand buffer without expensive read back testing of input status every few words. This is useful on hosts that do not support DMA, or when the host must perform format conversions beyond those supported in hardware. In DMA mode, LeoCommand employs efficient block transfer protocols on the system bus to transfer data from system memory to its input buffer, allowing much higher bandwidth than simple programmed I/O. Virtual memory pointers to application's geometry arrays are passed directly to LeoCommand, which converts them to physical memory addresses without operating system intervention (except when a page is marked as currently non-resident). This frees the host CPU to perform other computations during the data transfer. Thus the DMA can be efficient even for pure immediate-mode applications, where the geometry is being created on the fly.

Problem: Tower of Babel of input formats

One of the problems modern display systems face is the explosion of different input formats for similar drawing functions that need to be supported. Providing optimized microcode for each format rapidly becomes unwieldy. The host CPU could be used to pretranslate the primitive formats, but at high speeds this conversion operation can itself become a system bottleneck. Because DMA completely bypasses the host CPU, LeoCommand includes a programmable format conversion unit in the geometry data pipeline. This reformatter is considerably less complex than a general purpose CPU, but can handle the most commonly used input formats, and at very high speeds.

The geometry reformatting subsystem allows several orthogonal operations to be applied to input data. This geometric input data is abstracted as a stream of vertex packets. Each vertex packet may contain any combination of vertex position, vertex normal, vertex color, facet normal, facet color, texture map coordinates, pick IDs, headers, and other information. One conversion supports arbitrary re-ordering of data within a vertex, allowing a standardized element order after reformatting. Another operation supports the conversion of multiple numeric formats to 32-bit IEEE floating-point. The source data can be 8-bit or 16-bit fixed-point, or 32-bit or 64-bit IEEE floating-point. Additional miscellaneous reformatting allows the stripping of headers and other fields, the addition of an internally generated sequential pick ID, and insertion of constants. The final reformatting stage re-packages vertex packets into complete isolated geometry primitives (points, lines, triangles). Chaining bits in vertex headers delineate which vertices form primitives.

Like some other systems, Leo supports a generalized form of triangle strip (see Figure 3), where vertex header bits within a strip specify how the incoming vertex should be combined with previous vertices to form the next triangle. A stack of the last three vertices used to form a triangle is kept. The three vertices are labeled oldest, middle, and newest. An incoming vertex of type *replace_oldest* causes the oldest vertex to be replaced by the middle, the middle to be replaced by the newest, and the incoming vertex becomes the newest. This corresponds to a PHIGS PLUS triangle strip (sometimes called a "zig-zag" strip). The replacement type *replace_middle* leaves the oldest vertex unchanged, replaces the middle vertex by the newest, and the incoming vertex becomes the newest. This corresponds to a triangle star. The replacement type *restart* marks the oldest and middle vertices as invalid, and the incoming vertex becomes the newest. Generalized triangle strips must always start with this code. A triangle will be output only when a replacement operation results in three valid vertices. *Restart* corresponds to a "move" operation in polylines, and allows multiple unconnected variable-length triangle strips to be described by a single data structure passed in by the user,

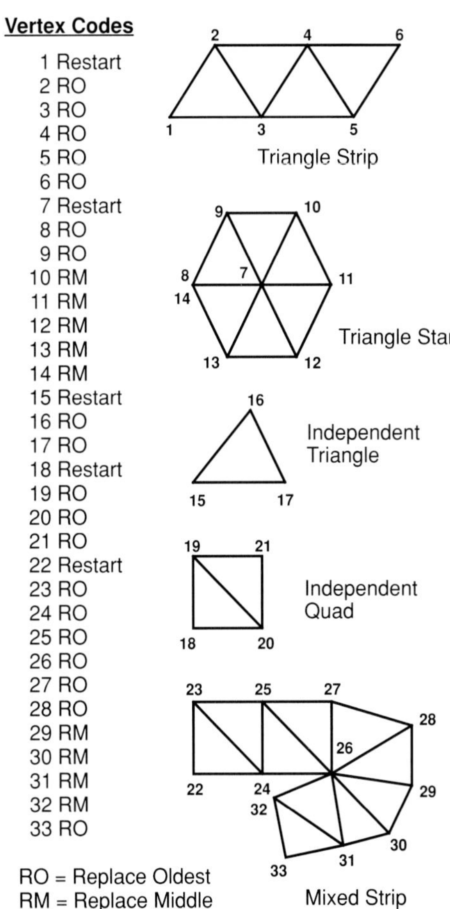

Figure 3: A Generalized Triangle Strip

reducing the overhead. The generalized triangle strip's ability to effectively change from "strip" to "star" mode in the middle of a strip allows more complex geometry to be represented compactly, and requires less input data bandwidth. The restart capability allows several pieces of disconnected geometry to be passed in one DMA operation. Figure 3 shows a *single* generalized triangle strip, and the associated replacement codes. LeoCommand also supports headerless strips of triangle vertices either as pure strips, pure stars, or pure independent triangles.

LeoCommand hardware automatically converts generalized triangle strips into isolated triangles. Triangles are normalized such that the front face is always defined by a clockwise vertex order after transformation. To support this, a header bit in each *restart* defines the initial face order of each sub-strip, and the vertex order is reversed after every *replace_oldest*. LeoCommand passes each completed triangle to the next available LeoFloat chip, as indicated by the input FIFO status that each LeoFloat sends back to LeoCommand. The order in which triangles have been sent to each LeoFloat is scoreboarded by LeoCommand, so that processed triangles are let out of the LeoFloat array in the same order as they entered. Non-sequential rendering order is also supported, but the automatic rendering task distribution hardware works so well that the performance difference is less than 3%. A similar, but less complex vertex repackaging is supported for polylines and multipolylines via a move/draw bit in the vertex packet header.

To save IC pins and PC board complexity, the internal Leo data busses connecting LeoCommand, LeoFloat, and LeoDraw are 16 bits in size. When colors, normals, and texture map coefficients are being transmitted on the CF-bus between LeoCommand and the LeoFloats, these components are (optionally) compressed from 32-bit IEEE floating-point into 16-bit fixed point fractions by LeoCommand, and then automatically reconverted back to 32-bit IEEE floating-point values by LeoFloat. This quantization does not effect quality. Color components will eventually end up as 8-bit values in the frame buffer. For normals, 16-bit (signed) accuracy represents a resolution of approximately plus or minus an inch at one mile. This optimization reduces the required data transfer bandwidth by 25%.

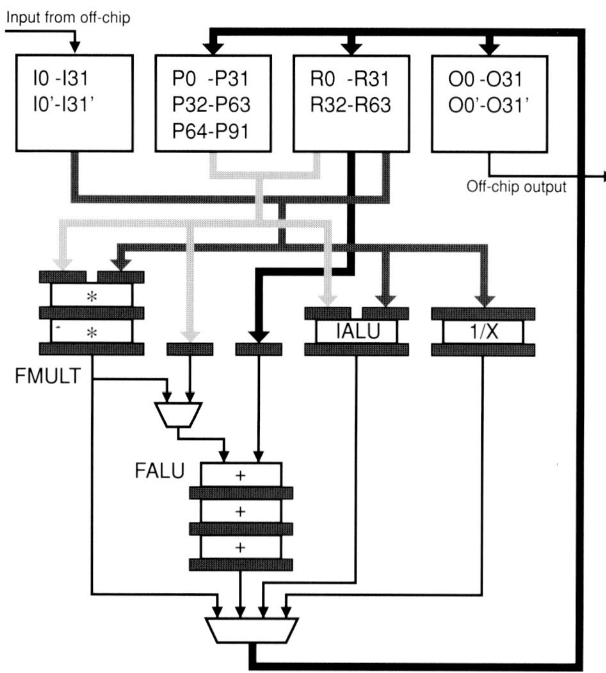

Figure 4: LeoFloat arithmetic function units, registers and data paths.

5 FLOATING-POINT PROCESSING: LEOFLOAT

After canonical format conversion, the next stages of processing triangles in a display pipeline are: transformation, clip test, face determination, lighting, clipping (if required), screen space conversion, and set-up. These operations are complex enough to require the use of a general purpose processor.

Use of commercially available DSP (Digital Signal Processing) chips for this work has two major drawbacks. First, most such processors require a considerable number of surrounding glue chips, especially when they are deployed as multi-processors. These glue chips can easily quadruple the board area dedicated to the DSP chip, as well as adversely affecting power, heat, cost, and reliability. Second, few of these chips have been optimized for 3D graphics.

A better solution might be to augment the DSP with a special ASIC that would replace all of these glue chips. Given the expense of developing an ASIC, we decided to merge that ASIC with a custom DSP core optimized for graphics.

The resulting chip was LeoFloat. LeoFloat combines a 32-bit microcodable floating-point core with concurrent input and output packet communication subsystems (see Figure 4.), similar to the approach of [3]. The only support chips required are four SRAM chips for external microcode store. A number of specialized graphics instructions and features make LeoFloat different from existing DSP processors. Each individual feature only makes a modest incremental contribution to performance, and indeed many have appeared in other designs. What is novel about LeoFloat is the combination of features, whose cumulative effect leads to impressive overall system performance. The following sections describe some of the more important special graphics instructions and features.

Double buffered asynchronous I/O register files. All input and output commands are packaged up by separate I/O packet hardware. Variable length packets of up to 32 32-bit words are automatically written into (or out of) on-chip double-buffered register files (the I and O registers). These are mapped directly into microcode register space. Special instructions allow complete packets to be requested, relinquished, or queued for transmission in one instruction cycle.

Enough internal registers. Most commercial DSP chips support a very small number of internal fast registers, certainly much smaller than the data needed by the inner loops of most 3D pipeline algorithms. They attempt to make up for this with on-chip SRAM or data caches, but typically SRAMs are not multi-ported and the caches not user-schedulable. We cheated with LeoFloat. We first wrote the code for the largest important inner loop (triangles), counted how many registers were needed (288), and built that many into the chip.

Parallel internal function units. The floating-point core functions (32-bit IEEE format) include multiply, ALU, reciprocal, and integer operations, all of which can often be executed in parallel. It is particularly important that the floating-point reciprocal operation not tie up the multiply and add units, so that perspective or slope calculations can proceed in parallel with the rest of geometric processing. Less frequently used reciprocal square root hardware is shared with the integer function unit.

Put all non-critical algorithms on the host. We avoided the necessity of building a high level language compiler (and support instructions) for LeoFloat by moving any code not worth hand coding in microcode to the host processor. The result is a small, clean kernel of graphics routines in microcode. (A fairly powerful macro-assembler with a 'C'-like syntax was built to support the hand coding.)

Software pipeline scheduling. One of the most complex parts of modern CPUs to design and debug is their scoreboard section, which schedules the execution of instructions across multiple steps in time and function units, presenting the programmer with the illusion that individual instructions are executed in one shot. LeoFloat avoided all this hardware by using more direct control fields, like horizontal microprogrammable machines, and leaving it to the assembler (and occasionally the programmer) to skew one logical instruction across several physical instructions.

Special clip condition codes & clip branch. For clip testing we employ a modified Sutherland-Hodgman algorithm, which first computes a vector of clip condition bits. LeoFloat has a clip test instruction that computes these bits two at a time, shifting them into a special clip-bits register. After the bits have been computed, special branch instructions decode these bits into the appropriate case: clip rejected, clip accepted, single edge clip (six cases), or needs general clipping. There are separate branch instructions for triangles and vectors. (A similar approach was taken in [9].) The branch instructions allow multiple other conditions to be checked at the same time, including backfacing and model clipping.

Register Y sort instruction. The first step of the algorithm we used for setting up triangles for scan conversion sorts the three triangle vertices in ascending Y order. On a conventional processor this requires either moving a lot of data, always referring to vertex data through indirect pointers, or replicating the set-up code for all six possible permutations of triangle vertex order. LeoFloat has a special instruction that takes the results of the last three comparisons and reorders part of the R register file to place vertices in sorted order.

Miscellaneous. LeoFloat contains many performance features traditionally found on DSP chips, including an internal subroutine stack, block load/store SRAM, and integer functions. Also there is a "kitchen sink" instruction that initiates multiple housekeeping functions in one instruction, such as "transmit current output packet (if not clip pending), request new input packet, extract op-code and dispatch to next task."

Code results: equivalent to 150 megaflop DSP. Each 25 MHz LeoFloat processes the benchmark isolated triangle (including clip-test and set-up) in 379 clocks. (With a few exceptions, microcode instructions issue at a rate of one per clock tick.) The same graphics algorithm was tightly coded on several RISC processors and DSP chips (SPARC, i860, C30, etc.), and typically took on the order of 1100 clocks. Thus the 379 LeoFloat instruction at 25 MHz do the equivalent work of a traditional DSP chip running at 75 MHz (even though there are only 54 megaflops of hardware). Of course these numbers only hold for triangles and vectors, but that's most of what LeoFloat does. Four LeoFloats assure that floating-point processing is not the bottleneck for 100-pixel isolated, lighted triangles.

6 SCREEN SPACE RENDERING: LEODRAW

VRAM limits

Commercial VRAM chips represent a fundamental constraint on the possible pixel rendering performance of Leo's class of graphics accelerator. The goal of the Leo architecture was to ensure to the greatest extent possible that this was the *only* performance limit for typical rendering operations.

The fundamental memory transaction for Z-buffered rendering algorithms is a conditional read-modify-write cycle. Given an XY address and a computed RGBZ value, the old Z value at the XY address is first read, and then if the computed Z is in front of the old Z, the computed RGBZ value is written into the memory. Such transactions can be mapped to allowable VRAM control signals in many different ways: reads and writes may be batched, Z may be read out through the video port, etc.

VRAM chips constrain system rendering performance in two ways. First, they impose a minimum cycle time per RAM bank for the Z-buffered read-modify-write cycle. Figure 5 is a plot of this cycle

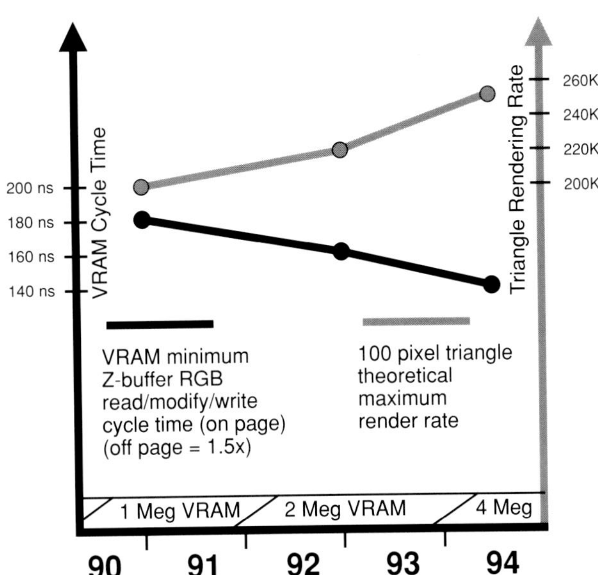

Figure 5: VRAM cycle time and theoretical maximum triangle rendering rate (for five-way interleaved frame buffers).

time (when in "page" mode) and its changes over a half-decade period. VRAMs also constrain the ways in which a frame buffer can be partitioned into independently addressable banks. Throughout the five year period in Figure 5, three generations of VRAM technology have been organized as 256K by 4, 8, and 16-bit memories. For contemporary display resolutions of 1280 × 1024, the chips comprising a minimum frame buffer can be organized into no more than five separately-addressed interleave banks. Combining this information, a theoretical maximum rendering speed for a primitive can be computed. The second line in Figure 5 is the corresponding performance for rendering 100-pixel Z-buffered triangles, including the overhead for entering page mode, content refresh, and video shift register transfers (video refresh). Higher rendering rates are only possible if additional redundant memory chips are added, allowing for higher interleaving factors, at the price of increased system cost.

Even supporting five parallel interleaves has a cost: at least 305 memory interface pins (five banks of (24 RGB + 24 Z + 13 address/control)) are required, more pins than it is currently possible to dedicate to a memory interface on one chip. Some systems have used external buffer chips, but on a minimum cost and board area system, this costs almost as much as additional custom chips. Thus, on the Leo system we opted for five separate VRAM control chips (LeoDraws).

Triangle scan conversion

Traditional shaded triangle scan conversion has typically been via a linear pipeline of edge-walking followed by scan interpolation [12]. There have been several approaches to achieving higher throughput in rasterization. [2] employed a single edge-walker, but parallel scan interpolation. [4][10] employed massively parallel rasterizers. [6] and other recent machines use moderately parallel rasterizers, with additional logic to merge the pixel rasterization streams back together.

In the Leo design we chose to broadcast the identical triangle specification to five parallel rendering chips, each tasked with rendering only those pixels visible in the local interleave. Each chip performs its own complete edge-walk and span interpolation of the triangle, biased by the chip's local interleave. By paying careful attention to proper mathematical sampling theory for rasterized pixels, the five chips can act in concert to produce the correct combined rasterized image. Mathematically, each chip thinks it is rasterizing the triangle into an image memory with valid pixel centers only every five original pixels horizontally, with each chip starting off biased one more pixel to the right.

To obtain the speed benefits of parallel chips, most high performance graphics systems have split the edge-walk and span-interpolate functions into separate chips. But an examination of the relative amounts of data flow between rendering pipeline stages shows that the overall peak data transfer bandwidth demand occurs between the edge-walk and span-interpolate sections, induced by long thin triangles, which commonly occur in tessellated geometry. To minimize pin counts and PC board bus complexity, Leo decided to replicate the edge-walking function into each of the five span-interpolation chips.

One potential drawback of this approach is that the edge-walking section of each LeoDraw chip will have to advance to the next scan line up to five times more often than a single rasterization chip would. Thus LeoDraw's edge-walking circuit was designed to operate in one single pixel cycle time (160 ns. read-modify-write VRAM cycle), so it would never hold back scan conversion. Other usual pipelining techniques were used, such as loading in and buffering the next triangle to be drawn in parallel with rasterizing the current triangle. Window clipping, blending, and other pixel post processing are handled in later pipelined stages.

Line scan conversion

As with triangles, the mathematics of the line rasterization algorithms were set up to allow distributed rendering of aliased and antialiased lines and dots, with each LeoDraw chip handling the 1/5 of the frame buffer pixels that it owns. While the Leo system uses the X11 semantics of Bresenham lines for window system operations, these produce unacceptable motion artifacts in 3D wireframe rendering. Therefore, when rendering 3D lines, Leo employs a high-accuracy DDA algorithm, using 32 bits internally for sufficient subpixel precision.

At present there is no agreement in the industry on the definition of a high quality antialiased line. We choose to use the image quality of vector strokers of years ago as our quality standard, and we tested different algorithms with end users, many of whom were still using calligraphic displays. We found users desired algorithms that displayed no roping, angle sensitivities, short vector artifacts, or end-point artifacts. We submitted the resulting antialiased line quality test patterns as a GPC [11] test image. In achieving the desired image quality level, we determined several properties that a successful line antialiasing algorithm must have. First, the lines must have at least three pixels of width across the minor axis. Two-pixel wide antialiased lines exhibit serious roping artifacts. Four-pixel wide lines offer no visible improvement except for lines near 45 degrees. Second, proper endpoint ramps spread over at least two pixels are necessary both for seamless line segment joins as well as for isolated line-ends. Third, proper care must be taken when sampling lines of subpixel length to maintain proper final intensity. Fourth, intensity or filter adjustments based on the slope are necessary to avoid artifacts when rotating wireframe images. To implement all this, we found that we needed at least four bits of subpixel positional accuracy *after* cumulative interpolation error is factored in. That is why we used 32 bits for XY coordinate accuracy: 12 for pixel location, 4 for subpixel location, and 16 for DDA interpolation error. (The actual error limit is imposed by the original, user-supplied 32-bit IEEE floating-point data.)

Because of the horizontal interleaving and preferred scan direction, the X-major and Y-major aliased and antialiased line rasterization algorithms are not symmetric, so separate optimized algorithms were employed for each.

Antialiased dots

Empirical testing showed that only three bits of subpixel precision are necessary for accurate rendering of antialiased dots. For ASIC implementation, this was most easily accomplished using a brute-force table lookup of one of 64 precomputed 3×3 pixel dot images. These images are stored in on-chip ROM, and were generated using a circular symmetric Gaussian filter.

Triangle, line, and dot hardware

Implementation of the triangle and antialiased vector rasterization algorithms require substantial hardware resources. Triangles need single pixel cycle edge-walking hardware in parallel with RGBZ span interpolation hardware. To obtain the desired quality of antialiased vectors, our algorithms require hardware to apply multiple waveform shaping functions to every generated pixel. As a result, the total VLSI area needed for antialiased vectors is nearly as large as for triangles. To keep the chip die size reasonable, we reformulated both the triangle and antialiased vector algorithms to combine and reuse the same function units. The only difference is how the separate sequencers set up the rasterization pipeline.

Per-pixel depth cue

Depth cueing has long been a heavily-used staple of wireframe applications, but in most modern rendering systems it is an extra time expense feature, performed on endpoints back in the floating-point section. We felt that we were architecting Leo not for benchmarks, but for users, and many wireframe users want to have depth cueing on all the time. Therefore, we built a parallel hardware depth cue function unit into each LeoDraw. Each triangle, vector, or dot rendered by Leo can be optionally depth cued at absolutely no cost in performance. Another benefit of per-pixel depth cueing is full compliance with the PHIGS PLUS depth cueing specification. For Leo, per-pixel depth cueing hardware also simplifies the LeoFloat microcode, by freeing the LeoFloats from ever having to deal with it.

Picking support

Interactive graphics requires not only the rapid display of geometric data, but also interaction with that data: the ability to pick a particular part or primitive within a part. Any pixels drawn within the bounds of a 3D pick aperture result in a pick hit, causing the current pick IDs to be automatically DMAed back to host memory.

Window system support

Many otherwise sophisticated 3D display systems become somewhat befuddled when having to deal simultaneously with 3D rendering applications and a 2D window system. Modern window systems on interactive workstations require frequent context switching of the rendering pipeline state. Some 3D architectures have tried to minimize the overhead associated with context switching by supporting multiple 3D contexts in hardware. Leo goes one step further, maintaining two completely separate pipelines in hardware: one for traditional 2D window operations; the other for full 3D rendering. Because the majority of context switch requests are for 2D window system operations, the need for more complex 3D pipeline context switching is significantly reduced. The 2D context is much lighter weight and correspondingly easier to context switch. The two separate graphics pipelines operate completely in parallel, allowing simultaneous access by two independent CPUs on a multiprocessor host.

2D functionality abstracts the frame buffer as a 1-bit, 8-bit, or 24-bit pixel array. Operations include random pixel access, optimized character cell writes, block clear, block copy, and the usual menagerie of boolean operations, write masks, etc. Vertical block moves are special cased, as they are typically used in vertical scrolling of text windows, and can be processed faster than the general block move because the pixel data does not have to move across LeoDraw chip interleaves. Rendering into non-rectangular shaped windows is supported by special clip hardware, resulting in no loss in performance. A special block clear function allows designated windows (and their Z-buffers) to be initialized to any given constant in under 200 microseconds. Without this last feature, 30 Hz or faster animation of non-trivial objects would have been impossible.

7 VIDEO OUTPUT: LEOCROSS

Leo's standard video output format is 1280×1024 at 76 Hz refresh rate, but it also supports other resolutions, including 1152×900, interlaced 640×480 RS-170 (NTSC), interlaced 768×576 PAL timing, and 960×680 113 Hz field sequential stereo. LeoCross contains several color look-up tables, supporting multiple pseudo color maps without color map flashing. The look-up table also supports two different true color abstractions: 24-bit linear color (needed by rendering applications), and REC-709 non-linear color (required by many imaging applications).

Virtual reality support

Stereo output is becoming increasingly important for use in Virtual Reality applications. Leo's design goals included support for the Virtual Holographic Workstation system configuration described in [5]. Leo's stereo resolution was chosen to support square pixels, so that lines and antialiased lines are displayed properly in stereo, and standard window system applications can co-exist with stereo. Stereo can be enabled on a per-window basis (when in stereo mode windows are effectively quad-buffered). Hooks were included in LeoCross to support display technologies other than CRT's, that may be needed for head-mounted virtual reality displays.

8 NURBS AND TEXTURE MAP SUPPORT

One of the advantages to using programmable elements within a graphics accelerator is that additional complex functionality, such as NURBS and texture mapping, can be accelerated. Texture mapping is supported through special LeoFloat microcode and features of LeoCommand. LeoFloat microcode also includes algorithms to accelerate dynamic tessellation of trimmed NURBS surfaces. The dynamic tessellation technique involves reducing trimmed NURBS surfaces into properly sized triangles according to a display/pixel space approximation criteria [1]; i.e. the fineness of tessellation is view dependent. In the past, dynamic tessellation tended to be mainly useful as a compression technique, to avoid storing all the flattened triangles from a NURBS surface in memory. Dynamic tessellation was not viewed as a performance enhancer, for while it might generate only a third as many triangles as a static tessellation, the triangles were generated at least an order of magnitude or more slower than brute force triangle rendering. In addition it had other problems, such as not handling general trimming. For many cases, Leo's dynamic tesselator can generate and render triangles only a small integer multiple slower than prestored triangle rendering, which for some views, can result in *faster* overall object rendering.

9 RESULTS

Leo is physically a-two board sandwich, measuring $5.7 \times 6.7 \times 0.6$ inches, that fits in a standard 2S SBus slot. Figure 6 is a photo of the two boards, separated, showing all the custom ASICs. Figure 7 is a photo of the complete Leo workstation, next to two of our units of scale and the board set.

Leo can render 210K 100-pixel isolated, lighted, Gouraud shaded, Z-buffered, depth cued triangles per second, with one infinite diffuse and one ambient light source enabled. At 100 pixels, Leo is still VRAM rendering speed limited; smaller triangles render faster. Isolated 10-pixel antialiased, constant color, Z-buffered, depth cued lines (which are actually 12 pixels long due to endpoint ramps, and three pixels wide) render at a 422K per second rate. Corresponding aliased lines render at 730K. Aliased and antialiased constant color, Z-buffered, depth cued dots are clocked at 1100K. 24-bit image rasters can be loaded onto the screen at a 10M pixel per second rate. Screen scrolls, block moves, and raster character draws all also have competitive performance. Figure 8 is a sample of shaded triangle rendering.

10 SIMULATION

A system as complex as Leo cannot be debugged after the fact. All the new rendering mathematics were extensively simulated before being committed to hardware design. As each chip was defined, high, medium, and low level simulators of its function were written and continuously used to verify functionality and performance. Complete images of simulated rendering were generated throughout the course of the project, from within weeks of its start. As a result, the window system and complex 3D rendering were up and running on a complete board set within a week of receiving the first set of chips.

11 CONCLUSIONS

By paying careful attention to the forces that drive both performance and cost, a physically compact complete 3D shaded graphics accelerator was created. The focus was not on new rendering features, but on cost reduction and performance enhancement of the most useful core of 3D graphics primitives. New parallel algorithms were developed to allow accurate screen space rendering of primitives. Judicious use of hardware to perform some key traditional software functions (such as format conversion and primitive vertex reassembly) greatly simplified the microcode task. A specialized floating-point core optimized for the primary task of processing lines and triangles also supports more general graphics processing, such as rasters and NURBS. The final system performance is limited by the *only* chips not custom designed for Leo: the standard RAM chips.

ACKNOWLEDGEMENTS

The authors would like to thank the entire Leo team for their efforts in producing the system, and Mike Lavelle for help with the paper.

REFERENCES

1. **Abi-Ezzi, Salim, and L. Shirman.** Tessellation of Curved Surfaces under Highly Varying Transformations. Proc. Eurographics '91 (Vienna, Austria, September 1991), 385-397.

2. **Akeley, Kurt and T. Jermoluk.** High-Performance Polygon Rendering, Proceedings of SIGGRAPH '88 (Atlanta, GA, Aug 1-5, 1988). In *Computer Graphics* 22, 4 (July 1988), 239-246.

3. **Anido, M., D. Allerton and E. Zaluska.** MIGS - A Multiprocessor Image Generation System using RISC-like Microprocessors. Proceedings of CGI '89 (Leeds, UK, June 1989), Springer Verlag 1990.

4. **Deering, Michael, S. Winner, B. Schediwy, C. Duffy and N. Hunt.** The Triangle Processor and Normal Vector Shader: A VLSI system for High Performance Graphics. Proceedings of SIGGRAPH '88 (Atlanta, GA, Aug 1-5, 1988). In *Computer Graphics* 22, 4 (July 1988), 21-30.

5. **Deering, Michael.** High Resolution Virtual Reality. Proceedings of SIGGRAPH '92 (Chicago, IL, July 26-31, 1992). In *Computer Graphics* 26, 2 (July 1992), 195-202.

6. **Dunnett, Graham, M. White, P. Lister and R. Grimsdale.** The Image Chip for High Performance 3D Rendering. *IEEE Computer Graphics and Applications* 12, 6 (November 1992), 41-52.

7. **Foley, James, A. van Dam, S. Feiner and J Hughes.** Computer Graphics: Principles and Practice, 2nd ed., Addison-Wesley, 1990.

8. **Kelley, Michael, S. Winner, K. Gould.** A Scalable Hardware Render Accelerator using a Modified Scanline Algorithm. Proceedings of SIGGRAPH '92 (Chicago, IL, July 26-31, 1992). In *Computer Graphics* 26, 2 (July 1992), 241-248.

9. **Kirk, David, and D. Voorhies.** The Rendering Architecture of the DN10000VS. Proceedings of SIGGRAPH '90 (Dallas, TX, August 6-10, 1990). In *Computer Graphics* 24, 4 (August 1990), 299-307.

10. **Molnar, Steven, J. Eyles, J. Poulton.** PixelFlow: High-Speed Rendering Using Image Composition. Proceedings of SIGGRAPH '92 (Chicago, IL, July 26-31, 1992). In *Computer Graphics* 26, 2 (July 1992), 231-240.

11. **Nelson, Scott.** GPC Line Quality Benchmark Test. GPC Test Suite, NCGA GPC committee 1991.

12. **Torborg, John.** A Parallel Processor Architecture for Graphics Arithmetic Operations. Proceedings of SIGGRAPH '87 (Anaheim, CA, July 27-31, 1987). In *Computer Graphics* 21, 4 (July 1987), 197-204.

Figure 6: The two boards, unfolded.

Figure 7: The complete SPARCstation ZX workstation, next to two of our units of scale and the Leo board set.

Figure 8: **Traffic Jam to Point Reyes**. A scene containing 2,322,000 triangles, rendered by Leo Hardware. Stochastically super-sampled 8 times. Models courtesy of Viewpoint Animation Engineering.

RealityEngine Graphics

Kurt Akeley
Silicon Graphics Computer Systems*

Abstract

The RealityEngine™ graphics system is the first of a new generation of systems designed primarily to render texture mapped, antialiased polygons. This paper describes the architecture of the RealityEngine graphics system, then justifies some of the decisions made during its design. The implementation is near-massively parallel, employing 353 independent processors in its fullest configuration, resulting in a measured fill rate of over 240 million antialiased, texture mapped pixels per second. Rendering performance exceeds 1 million antialiased, texture mapped triangles per second. In addition to supporting the functions required of a general purpose, high-end graphics workstation, the system enables realtime, "out-the-window" image generation and interactive image processing.

CR Categories and Subject Descriptors: I.3.1 **[Computer Graphics]:** Hardware Architecture; I.3.7 **[Computer Graphics]:** Three-Dimensional Graphics and Realism - *color, shading, shadowing, and texture*

1 Introduction

This paper describes and to a large extent justifies the architecture chosen for the RealityEngine graphics system. The designers think of this system as our first implementation of a third-generation graphics system. To us a generation is characterized not by the scope of capabilities of an architecture, but rather by the capabilities for which the architecture was primarily designed – the target capabilities with maximized performance. Because we designed our first machine in the early eighties, our notion of first generation corresponds to this period. Floating point hardware was just becoming available at reasonable prices, framebuffer memory was still quite expensive, and application-specific integrated circuits (ASICs) were not readily available. The resulting machines had workable transformation capabilities, but very limited framebuffer processing capabilities. In particular, smooth shading and depth buffering, which require substantial framebuffer hardware and memory, were not available. Thus the target capabilities of first-generation machines were the transformation and rendering of flat-shaded points, lines, and polygons. These primitives were not lighted, and hidden surface elimination, if required, was accomplished by algorithms implemented by the application. Examples of such systems are the Silicon Graphics Iris 3000 (1985) and the Apollo DN570 (1985). Toward the end of the first-generation period advances in technology allowed lighting, smooth shading, and depth buffering to be implemented, but only with an order of magnitude less performance than was available to render flat-shaded lines and polygons. Thus the target capability of these machines remained first-generation. The Silicon Graphics 4DG (1986) is an example of such an architecture.

*2011 N. Shoreline Blvd., Mountain View, CA 94043 USA, kurt@sgi.com

Because first-generation machines could not efficiently eliminate hidden surfaces, and could not efficiently shade surfaces even if the application was able to eliminate them, they were more effective at rendering wireframe images than at rendering solids. Beginning in 1988 a second-generation of graphics systems, primarily workstations rather than terminals, became available. These machines took advantage of reduced memory costs and the increased availability of ASICs to implement deep framebuffers with multiple rendering processors. These framebuffers had the numeric ability to interpolate colors and depths with little or no performance loss, and the memory capacity and bandwidth to support depth buffering with minimal performance loss. They were therefore able to render solids and full-frame scenes efficiently, as well as wireframe images. The Silicon Graphics GT (1988)[11] and the Apollo DN590 (1988) are early examples of second-generation machines. Later second-generation machines, such as the Silicon Graphics VGX[12] the Hewlett Packard VRX, and the Apollo DN10000[4] include texture mapping and antialiasing of points and lines, but not of polygons. Their performances are substantially reduced, however, when texture mapping is enabled, and the texture size (of the VGX) and filtering capabilities (of the VRX and the DN10000) are limited.

The RealityEngine system is our first third-generation design. Its target capability is the rendering of lighted, smooth shaded, depth buffered, texture mapped, antialiased triangles. The initial target performance was 1/2 million such triangles per second, assuming the triangles are in short strips, and 10 percent intersect the viewing frustum boundaries. Textures were to be well filtered (8-sample linear interpolation within and between two mipmap[13] levels) and large enough (1024 × 1024) to be usable as true images, rather than simply as repeated *textures*. Antialiasing was to result in high-quality images of solids, and was to work in conjunction with depth buffering, meaning that no application sorting was to be required. Pixels were to be filled at a rate sufficient to support 30Hz rendering of full-screen images. Finally, the performance on second-generation primitives (lighted, smooth shaded, depth buffered) was to be no lower than that of the VGX, which renders roughly 800,000 such mesh triangles per second. All of these goals were achieved.

The remainder of this paper is in four parts: a description of the architecture, some specifics of features supported by the architecture, alternatives considered during the design of the architecture, and finally some appendixes that describe performance and implementation details.

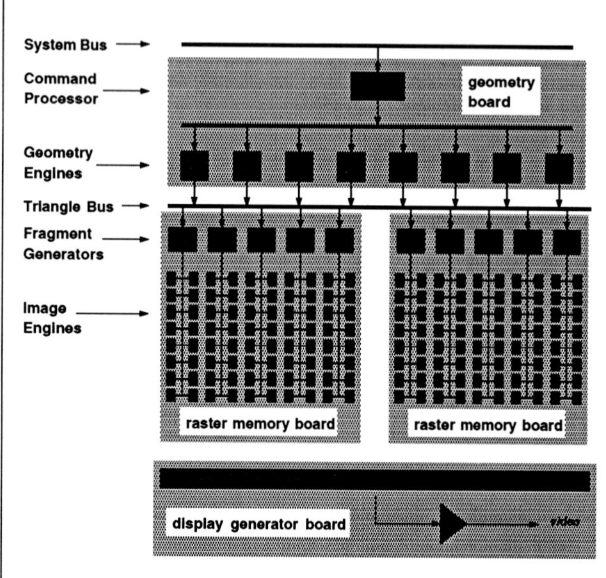

Figure 1. Board-level block diagram of an intermediate configuration with 8 Geometry Engines on the geometry board, 2 raster memory boards, and a display generator board.

2 Architecture

The RealityEngine system is a 3, 4, or 6 board graphics accelerator that is installed in a MIPS RISC workstation. The graphics system and one or more MIPS processors are connected by a single system bus. Figure 1 is a board-level block diagram of the RealityEngine graphics accelerator. The geometry board comprises an input FIFO, the Command Processor, and 6, 8, or 12 Geometry Engines. Each raster memory board comprises 5 Fragment Generators (each with its own complete copy of the texture memory), 80 Image Engines, and enough framebuffer memory to allocate 256 bits per pixel to a 1280×1024 framebuffer. The display generator board supports all video functions, including video timing, genlock, color mapping, and digital-to-analog conversion. Systems can be configured with 1, 2, or 4 raster memory boards, resulting in 5, 10, or 20 Fragment Generators and 80, 160, or 320 Image Engines.

To get an initial notion of how the system works, let's follow a single triangle as it is rendered. The position, color, normal, and texture coordinate commands that describe the vertexes of the triangle in object coordinates are queued by the input FIFO, then interpreted by the Command Processor. The Command Processor directs all of this data to one of the Geometry Engines, where the coordinates and normals are transformed to eye coordinates, lighted, transformed to clip coordinates, clipped, and projected to window coordinates. The associated texture coordinates are transformed by a third matrix and associated with the window coordinates and colors. Then window coordinate slope information regarding the red, green, blue, alpha, depth, and texture coordinates is computed.

The projected triangle, ready for rasterization, is then output from the Geometry Engine and broadcast on the Triangle Bus to the 5, 10, or 20 Fragment Generators. (We distinguish between pixels generated by rasterization and pixels in the framebuffer, referring to the former as fragments.) Each Fragment Generator is responsible for the rasterization of 1/5, 1/10, or 1/20 of the pixels in the framebuffer, with the pixel assignments finely interleaved to insure that even small triangles are partially rasterized by each of the Fragment Generators. Each Fragment Generator computes the intersection of the set of pixels that are fully or partially covered by the triangle and the set of pixels in the framebuffer that it is responsible for, generating a fragment for each of these pixels. Color, depth, and texture coordinates are assigned to each fragment based on the initial and slope values computed by the Geometry Engine. A subsample mask is assigned to the fragment based on the portion of each pixel that is covered by the triangle. The local copy of the texture memory is indexed by the texture coordinates, and the 8 resulting samples are reduced by linear interpolation to a single color value, which then modulates the fragment's color.

The resulting fragments, each comprising a pixel coordinate, a color, a depth, and a coverage mask, are then distributed to the Image Engines. Like the Fragment Generators, the Image Engines are each assigned a fixed subset of the pixels in the framebuffer. These subsets are themselves subsets of the Fragment Generator allocations, so that each Fragment Generator communicates only with the 16 Image Engines assigned to it. Each Image Engine manages its own dynamic RAM that implements its subset of the framebuffer. When a fragment is received by an Image Engine, its depth and color sample data are merged with the data already stored at that pixel, and a new aggregate pixel color is immediately computed. Thus the image is complete as soon as the last primitive has been rendered; there is no need for a final framebuffer operation to resolve the multiple color samples at each pixel location to a single displayable color.

Before describing each of the rendering operations in more detail, we make the following observations. First, after it is separated by the Command Processor, the stream of rendering commands merges only at the Triangle Bus. Second, triangles of sufficient size (a function of the number of raster memory boards) are processed by almost all the processors in the system, avoiding only 5, 7, or 11 Geometry Engines. Finally, small to moderate FIFO memories are included at the input and output of each Geometry Engine, at the input of each Fragment Generator, and at the input of each Image Engine. These memories smooth the flow of rendering commands, helping to insure that the processors are utilized efficiently.

2.1 Command Processor

That the Command Processor is required at all is primarily a function of the OpenGL™ [8][7] graphics language. OpenGL is modal, meaning that much of the state that controls rendering is included in the command stream only when it changes, rather than with each graphics primitive. The Command Processor distinguishes between two classes of this modal state. OpenGL commands that are expected infrequently, such as matrix manipulations and lighting model changes, are broadcast to all the Geometry Engines. OpenGL commands that are expected frequently, such as vertex colors, normals, and texture coordinates, are shadowed by the Command Processor, and the current values are bundled with each rendering command that is passed to an individual Geometry Engine. The Command Processor also breaks long connected sequences of line segments or triangles into smaller groups, each group passing to a single Geometry Engine. The size of these groups is a tradeoff between the increased vertex processing efficiency of larger groups (due to shared vertexes within a group) and the improved load balancing that results from smaller groups. Finally, because the Command Processor must interpret each graphics command, it is also able to detect invalid command sequences and protect the

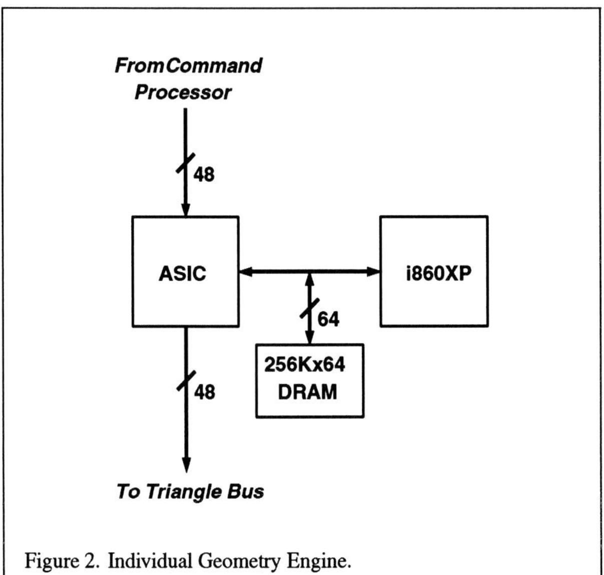

Figure 2. Individual Geometry Engine.

subsequent processors from their effects.

Non-broadcast rendering commands are distributed to the Geometry Engines in pure round-robin sequence, taking no account of Geometry Engine loading. This approach was chosen for its simplicity, and is efficient because the processing requirements of primitives are usually very similar, and because the input and output FIFOs of each Geometry Engine smooth the imbalances due to data-dependent processing such as clipping.

2.2 Geometry Engines

The core of each Geometry Engine is an Intel i860XP processor. Operating at 50MHz, the combined floating point multiplier and ALU can achieve a peak performance of 100 MFLOPS. Each Intel processor is provided 2 Mbytes of combined code/data dynamic memory, and is supported by a single ASIC that implements the input and output FIFOs, a small register space from which the i860XP accesses incoming commands, and specialized data conversion facilities that pack computed slope data into a format accepted by the Fragment Generators. (Figure 2.)

All Geometry Engine code is first developed in C, which is cross compiled for the i860XP on MIPS RISC development systems. Code that is executed frequently is then re-coded in i860XP assembly code, showing the greatest improvement in performance where scheduling of the vector floating point unit is hand optimized. The assembly code is written to conform to the compiler's link conventions, so that hand-coded and compiled modules are interchangeable for development and documentation purposes.

Most floating point arithmetic is done in single precision, but much of the texture arithmetic, and all depth arithmetic after projection transformation, must be done in double precision to maintain the required accuracy. After transformation, lighting, and clipping, the rasterization setup code treats each parameter as a plane equation, computing its signed slope in the positive X and Y screen directions. Because the parameters of polygons with more than 3 vertexes may be non-planar, the Geometry Engine decomposes all polygons to triangles.

2.3 Triangle Bus

The Triangle Bus acts as a crossbar, connecting the output of each Geometry Engine to the inputs of all the Fragment Generators. Because all Geometry Engine output converges at this bus, it is a potential bottleneck. To avoid performance loss, the Triangle Bus was designed with bandwidth to handle over one million shaded, depth buffered, texture mapped, antialiased triangles per second, more than twice the number of primitives per second that were anticipated from an 8 Geometry Engine system. This performance cushion allows the later-conceived 12 Geometry Engine system to render at full performance, in spite of the greater than expected performance of the individual engines.

In addition to broadcasting the rasterization data for triangles to the Fragment Generators, the Triangle Bus broadcasts point and line segment descriptions, texture images, and rasterization mode changes such as blending functions.

2.4 Fragment Generators

Although each Fragment Generator may be thought of as a single processor, the data path of each unit is actually a deep pipeline. This pipeline sequentially performs the initial generation of fragments, generation of the coverage mask, texture address generation, texture lookup, texture sample filtering, texture modulation of the fragment color, and fog computation and blending. These tasks are distributed among the four ASICs and eight dynamic RAMs that comprise each Fragment Generator. (Figure 3.)

Fragments are generated using Pineda arithmetic[9], with the algorithm modified to traverse only pixels that are in the domain of the Fragment Generator. A coverage mask is generated for 4, 8, or 16 sample locations, chosen on a regular 8×8 subsample grid within the square boundaries of the pixel. The hardware imposes no constraints on which subset of the 64 subsample locations is chosen, except that the same subset is chosen for each pixel. The subset may be changed by the application between frames.

Depth and texture coordinate sample values are always computed at the center-most sample location, regardless of the fragment coverage mask. The single depth sample is later used by the Image Engines to derive accurate depth samples at each subpixel location, using the X and Y depth slopes. Taking the texture sample at a consistent location insures that discontinuities are avoided at pixels that span multiple triangles. Color sample values are computed at the center-most sample location only if it is within the perimeter of the triangle. Otherwise the color sample is taken at a sample location within the triangle perimeter that is near the centroid of the covered region. Thus color samples are always taken within the triangle perimeter, and therefore never wrap to inappropriate values.

Based on a level-of-detail (LOD) calculation and the texture coordinate values at the fragment center, the addresses of the eight texels nearest the sample location in the mipmap of texture images are produced. Eight separate banks of texture memory are then accessed in parallel at these locations. The 8 16-bit values that result are merged with a trilinear blend, based on the subtexel coordinates and the LOD fraction, resulting in a single texture color that varies smoothly from frame to frame in an animation. The entire bandwidth of the 8-bank texture memory is consumed by a single Fragment Engine, so each Fragment Engine includes its own complete copy of all texture images in its texture memory, allowing all Fragment Generators to operate in parallel. Separate FIFO memories on the address and data ports of each texture memory bank

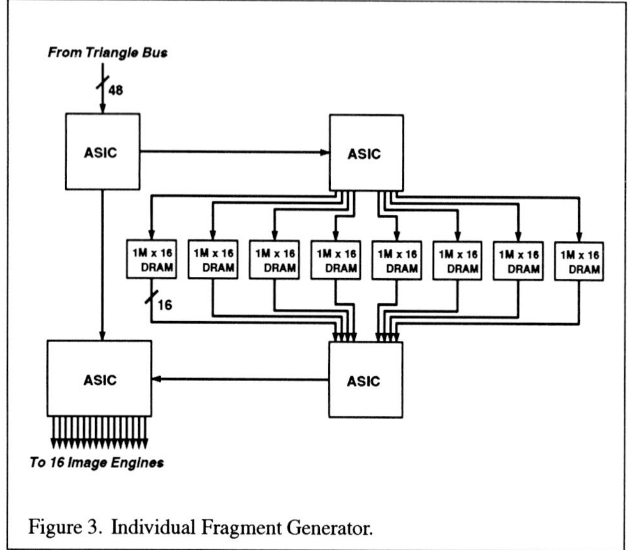

Figure 3. Individual Fragment Generator.

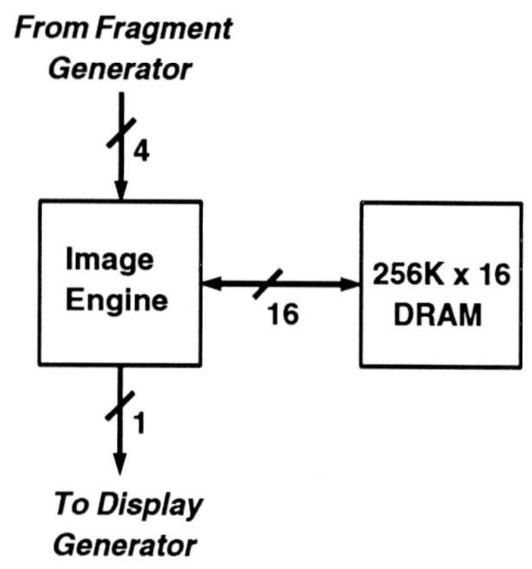

Figure 4. Individual Image Engine.

insure that random page boundary crossings do not significantly degrade the bandwidth available from the dynamic RAMs.

The last ASIC in the Fragment Generator applies the texture color to the fragment's smooth shaded color, typically by modulation. It then indexes its internal fog table with the fragment's depth value and uses the resulting fog blend factor (computed by linear interpolation between the two nearest table entries) to blend the fragment color with the application-defined fog color.

2.5 Image Engines

Fragments output by a single Fragment Generator are distributed equally among the 16 Image Engines connected to that generator. When the triangle was first accepted by the Fragment Generator for processing, its depth slopes in the X and Y screen directions were broadcast to each Image Engine, which stored them for later use. When an Image Engine accepts a fragment, it first uses these two slope values and the fragment's depth sample value to reconstruct the depth values at each subpixel sample location. The arithmetic required for this operation is simplified because the subpixel sample locations are fixed to a regular 8×8 grid. The calculations are linear because depth values have been projected to window coordinates just like the X and Y pixel coordinates. At each sample location corresponding to a '1' in the fragment's coverage mask, the computed depth value is compared to the depth value stored in the framebuffer. If the comparison succeeds, the framebuffer color at that subsample location is replaced by the fragment color, and the framebuffer depth is replaced by the derived fragment depth. If any change is made to the pixel's contents, the aggregate pixel color is recomputed by averaging the subpixel sample colors, and is immediately written to the displayable color buffer that will contain the final image.

Each Image Engine controls a single $256\text{K} \times 16$ dynamic RAM that comprises its portion of the framebuffer. (Figure 4.) When the framebuffer is initialized, this memory is partitioned equally among 4K, 8K, or 16K pixels, resulting in pixels with 1024, 512, or 256 bits. All subsample depth and color samples, as well as the one, two, or four displayable color buffers and other auxiliary buffers, are stored in this memory. By default, colors are stored with 12 bits per red, green, blue, and alpha component in both the displayable buffers and the subpixel samples. Depth values are 32 bits each, and are normally required only for each subpixel sample, not for the displayable color buffer or buffers. Color and depth sample resolutions can be reduced to 8,8,8 and 24 bits to allow more samples to be stored per pixel. The 4K partition stores 8 high-resolution samples per pixel, or 16 low-resolution samples per pixel, in addition to two displayable color buffers of the same resolution. The 8K partition stores 4 high-resolution samples per pixel, or 8 low-resolution samples per pixel, again with two displayable color buffers of the same resolution. The 16K partition cannot be used to support multisample antialiasing.

Because the number of raster memory boards (1, 2, or 4) and the number of pixels per Image Engine (4K, 8K, or 16K) are independent, the RealityEngine system supports a wide variety of framebuffer dimensions, color and depth resolutions, and subpixel samples. For example, a single raster board system supports 16-sample antialiasing at 640×512 resolution or aliased rendering at 1280×1024 resolution, and a 4-board system supports 8-sample antialiasing at true HDTV (1920×1035) resolution or 16-sample antialiasing at 1280×1024 resolution.

2.6 Display Hardware

Each of the 80 Image Engines on the raster memory board drives a single-bit, 50 MHz path to the display board, delivering video data at 500 MBytes per second. All 160 single-bit paths of a two raster memory board configuration are active, doubling the peak video data rate. The paths are time multiplexed by pairs of raster memory boards in the four board configuration. Ten crossbar ASICs on the display board assemble the 80 or 160 single-bit streams into individual color components or color indexes. Color components are then dithered from 12 bits to 10 bits and gamma corrected using 1024×8 lookup tables. The resulting 8-bit color components drive digital-to-analog converters and are output to the monitor. Color indexes are dereferenced in a 32K-location lookup table, supporting separate color lookup tables for each of up to 40 windows on the screen. Per-pixel display modes, such as the color index offset, are supported by a combination of Image Engine and display board hardware, driven by window ID bits stored in the framebuffer [1].

3 Features

This section provides additional information regarding the architecture's antialiasing, texture mapping, stereo, and clipping capabilities.

3.1 Antialiasing

The architecture supports two fundamentally different antialiasing techniques: alpha and multisample. Alpha antialiasing of points and lines is common to second generation architectures. Alpha antialiasing is implemented using subpixel and line-slope indexed tables to generate appropriate coverage values for points and lines, compensating for the subpixel position of line endpoints. Polygon coverage values are computed by counting the '1's in the full precision 8×8 coverage mask. The fragment alpha value is scaled by the fractional coverage value, which varies from 0.0, indicating no coverage, to 1.0, indicating complete coverage. If pixel blending is enabled, fragments are blended directly into the color buffer – no subpixel sample locations are accessed or required. Alpha antialiasing results in higher quality points and lines than does multisample antialiasing, because the resolution of the filter tables is greater than the 4 bit equivalent of the 16-sample mask. While alpha antialiased primitives should be rendered back-to-front or front-to-back (depending on the blend function being used) to generate a correct image, it is often possible to get an acceptable point or line image without such sorting. Alpha antialiased polygons, however, must be sorted near to far to get an acceptable image. Thus this technique is efficiently applied to polygons only in 2D scenes, such as instrument panels, where primitive ordering is fixed and a slight increase in quality is desired.

Multisample antialiasing has already been described. Its principal advantage over alpha antialiasing is its order invariance - points, lines, and polygons can be drawn into a multisample buffer in any order to produce the same final image. Two different mask generation techniques are supported in multisample mode, each with its own advantages and disadvantages. The default mask generation mode is called point sampled; the alternate mode is area sampled. A point sampled mask is geometrically accurate, meaning that each mask bit is set if and only if its subpixel location is within the perimeter of the point, line, or polygon outline. (Samples on the primitive's edge are included in exactly one of the two adjacent primitives.) Such masks insure the correctness of the final image, at the expense of its filtered quality. The final image is correct because all the samples that comprise it are geometrically valid - none having been taken outside their corresponding primitives. It is poorly sampled because the number of bits set in the mask may not closely correspond to the actual area of the pixel that is covered by the primitive, and the final filtering quality depends on this correspondence. Area sampling attempts to insure that the number of '1's in the sample mask is correct plus or minus 1/2 a sample, based on the actual coverage of pixel area by the primitive. (Figure 5.) In order to accomplish this, area sampled masks necessarily include samples that are outside the primitive outline, resulting in image artifacts such as polygon protrusions at silhouettes and T-junctions. Area sampled masks are implemented with a technique that is related to the one described by Andreas Schilling[10]. Point and area sampling can be selected by the application program on a per-primitive basis.

The desirable multisample property of order invariance is lost if alpha transparency and pixel blending are used. Alpha does sometimes carry significant information, usually as a result of the alpha channel in the texture application. For example, trees are often drawn as single polygons, using an alpha matte to express their shape. In order to handle alpha transparency without requiring pixel blending, the Image Engines have the ability to convert fragment alpha values to pseudo-random masks, which are then logically ANDed with the fragment's coverage mask. This method, while not geometrically accurate, provides usable antialiasing of texture mattes, and is order invariant.

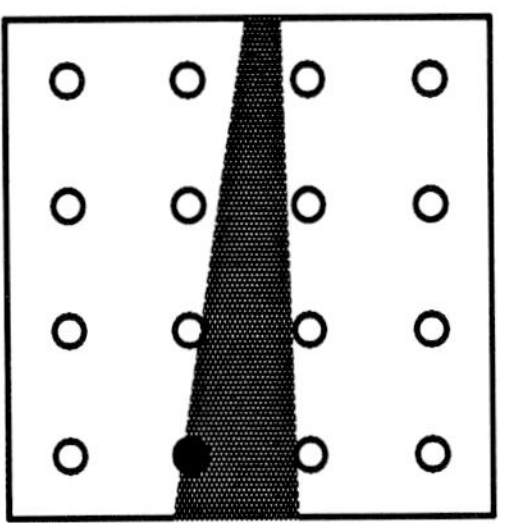

The single sample selected by the point sample method is darkened.

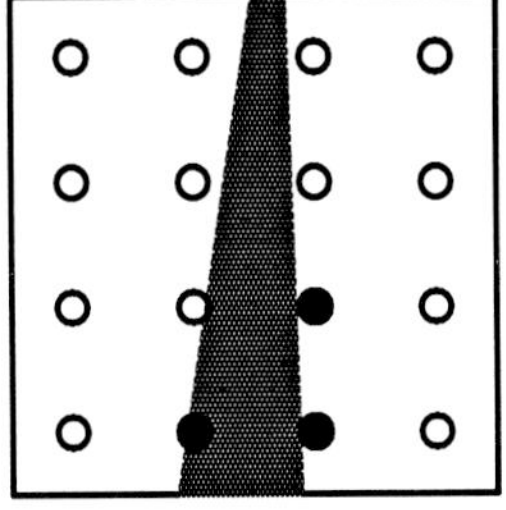

The three samples selected by the area sample method are darkened.

Figure 5. A narrow triangle intersected with a single, 16-sample pixel. The three samples selected by the area sample method accurately represent the fact that almost 20 percent of the pixel is covered by the triangle.

3.2 Texture Mapping

In addition to the 2-dimension texture maps described in the architecture section, 1- and 3-dimension maps are also supported. The eight million texel memory associated with each Fragment Generator stores 2D mipmapped images up to 1024×1024, and 3D non-mipmapped images up to $256 \times 256 \times 64$. Thus 3D textures can be used to render volumetric images of substantial resolution, at rates up to 30 frames per second. The S, T, and R texture coordinates of each fragment are computed by interpolating S/W, T/W, R/W, and 1/W, then doing the correct divisions at each pixel, resulting in perspective-corrected mapping. Level-of-detail is also computed for each pixel, based on the worst-case of the four pixel-to-texel X and Y ratios.

Linear filtering of the nearest texels and mipmap levels is supported for 1D, 2D, and 3D textures, blending a total of 16 texel colors in the 3D mode. In the 2D case such linear filtering is commonly known as trilinear. Bicubic interpolation is supported for 2D, nonmipmapped textures, again blending 16 texels. There is no support for cubic filtering of 1D or 3D textures, or of any mipmapped textures. The default 16-bit texel size supports RGBA texels at 4-bits per component, RGB texels at 5-bits per component (6 bits for green), intensity-alpha texels at 8-bits per component, and intensity texels at 12-bits per component. 32-bit and 48-bit texels can be specified by the application with proportional loss of performance. The maximum RBGA texel resolution is 12-bits per component, equal to the maximum framebuffer color resolution.

Texture magnification can be done by extrapolation of mipmap levels, resulting in a sharpening of the highest resolution mipmap image, or the highest resolution image can be blended with a replicated 256×256 detail image, greatly increasing the apparent resolution of the texture without requiring excessive texture storage. Filter functions for RGB and for alpha can be specified separately to improve the quality of texture mattes. Finally, texture memory can be loaded from the application processor's memory at the rate of 80 million 16-bit texels per second, allowing the application to treat texture memory as a managed cache of images.

3.3 Stereo in a Window

Image Engine memory can be configured with separate left and right color buffers for both the visible and nonvisible displayable color buffers, resulting in a total of four 48-bit color buffers per pixel. The display hardware alternately displays the left and right buffer contents of the visible buffers of all windows so configured, and drives a sync signal that can be used to control screen or head-mounted shutters. This stereo-in-a-window capability is both formally and practically compatible with the X protocol: formally because neither framebuffer dimensions nor pixel aspect ratio are changed when it is enabled or disabled, and practically because it allows monoscopic windows such as menus to be rendered and displayed correctly. To reduce eye fatigue, it is advisable to select a reduced-dimension framebuffer when the window system is initialized, allowing the frame display rate to be increased to 90+ Hz within the 140 MHz pixel limit of the display board.

3.4 Fast Clipping

RealityEngine polygon clipping is faster than that of our earlier designs for two fundamental reasons: it is implemented more efficiently, and it is required less often. Higher efficiency results from the MIMD Geometry Engine architecture. Because each of the engines executes an independent code sequence, and because each has significant input and output FIFOs, random clipping delays affect only a single engine and are averaged statistically across all the engines. Also, because each Geometry Engine comprises only a single processor, all of that engine's processing power can be devoted to the clipping process. SIMD architectures are less efficient because all processors are slowed when a single processor must clip a polygon. Pipelines of processors, and even MIMD arrangements of short pipelines, are less efficient because only a fraction of available processing power is available to the clipping process.

The requirement for clipping is reduced through a technique we call scissoring. Near and far plane clipping are done as usual, but the left, right, bottom, and top frustum edges are moved well away from the specified frustum, and all triangles that fall within the expanded frustum are projected to extended window coordinates. If culling is done by the application, almost no triangles will actually intersect the sides of the expanded frustum. Projected triangles that are not fully within the viewport are then scissored to match the edges of the viewport, eliminating the portions that are not within the viewport. The Pineda rasterization algorithm that is employed easily and efficiently handles the additional rectilinear edges that result, and no fragment generation performance is lost on scissored regions.

4 Design Alternatives

We think that the most interesting part of design is the alternatives considered, and the reasons for choices, rather than the details of the result. This section highlights some of these alternatives, in roughly decreasing order of significance.

4.1 Single-pass Antialiasing

Multi-pass accumulation buffer antialiasing using an accumulation buffer [3] is order invariant, and produces high-quality images in 10 to 20 passes. Further, a system that was fast enough to render 10 to 20 full scene images per frame would be a fantastic generator of aliased images. So why design a complex, multisample framebuffer to accomplish the same thing in one pass? The answer is that significantly more hardware would be required to implement a multi-pass machine with equivalent performance. This is true not only because the multi-pass machine must traverse and transform the object coordinates each pass, but in particular because texture mapping would also be performed for each pass. The component costs for traversal, transformation, parameter interpolation, and texture mapping constitute well over half of the multisample machine cost, and they are not replicated in the multisample architecture. A competing multi-pass architecture would have to replicate this hardware in some manner to achieve the required performance. Even the PixelFlow architecture[6], which avoids repeated traversal and transformation by buffering intermediate results, must still rasterize and texture map repeatedly.

4.2 Multisample Antialiasing

Multisample antialiasing is a rather brute-force technique for achieving order invariant single-pass antialiasing. We investigated alternative sorting buffer techniques derived from the A-buffer algorithm[2], hoping for higher filter quality and correct, single-pass transparency. These techniques were rejected for several reasons. First, sort buffers are inherently more complex than the multisample buffer and, with finite storage allocations per pixel, they may fail in undesirable ways. Second, any solution that is less exact than multisampling with point sampled mask generation will admit rendering errors such as polygon protrusions at silhouettes and T-junctions. Finally, the multisample algorithm matches the single-sample algorithm closely, allowing OpenGL pixel techniques such as stencil, alpha test, and depth test to work identically in single or multisample mode.

4.3 Immediate Resolution of Multisample Color

Our initial expectation was that rendering would update only the multisample color and depth values, requiring a subsequent resolution pass to reduce these values to the single color values for display. The computational expense of visiting all the pixels in the framebuffer is high, however, and the resolution pass damaged the software model, because OpenGL has no explicit scene demarcations. Immediate resolution became much more desirable when we realized that the single most common resolution case, where the fragment completely replaces the pixel's contents (i.e. the fragment mask is all ones and all depth comparisons pass) could be implemented by simply writing the fragment color to the color buffer, making no change to the 4, 8, or 16 subsample colors, and specially tagging the pixel. Only if the pixel is subsequently partially covered by a fragment is the color in the color buffer copied to the appropriate subsample color locations. This technique increases the performance in the typical rendering case and eliminates the need for a resolution pass.

4.4 Triangle Bus

All graphics architectures that implement parallel primitive processing and parallel fragment/pixel processing must also implement a crossbar somewhere between the geometry processors and the framebuffer[5]. While many of the issues concerning the placement of this crossbar are beyond the scope of this paper, we will mention some of the considerations that resulted in our Triangle Bus architecture. The RealityEngine Triangle Bus is a crossbar between the Geometry Engines and the Fragment Generators. Described in RealityEngine terms, architectures such as the Evans & Sutherland Freedom Series™ implement Geometry Engines and Fragment Generators in pairs, then switch the resulting fragments to the appropriate Image Engines using a fragment crossbar network. Such architectures have an advantage in fragment generation efficiency, due both to the improved locality of the fragments and to only one Fragment Generator being initialized per primitive. They suffer in comparison, however, for several reasons. First, transformation and fragment generation rates are linked, eliminating the possibility of tuning a machine for unbalanced rendering requirements by adding transformation or rasterization processors. Second, ultimate fill rate is limited by the fragment bandwidth, rather than the primitive bandwidth. For all but the smallest triangles the quantity of data generated by rasterization is much greater than that required for geometric specification, so this is a significant bottleneck. (See Appendix 2.) Finally, if primitives must be rendered in the order that they are specified, load balancing is almost impossible, because the number of fragments generated by a primitive varies by many orders of magnitude, and cannot be predicted prior to processor assignment. Both OpenGL and the core X renderer require such ordered rendering.

The PixelFlow[6] architecture also pairs Geometry Engines and Fragment Generators, but the equivalent of Image Engines and memory for a 128×128 pixel tile are also bundled with each Geometry/Fragment pair. The crossbar in this architecture is the compositing tree that funnels the contents of rasterized tiles to a final display buffer. Because the framebuffer associated with each processor is smaller than the final display buffer, the final image is assembled as a sequence of 128×128 logical tiles. Efficient operation is achieved only when each logical tile is rasterized once in its entirety, rather than being revisited when additional primitives are transformed. To insure that all primitives that correspond to a logical tile are known, all primitives must be transformed and sorted before rasterization can begin. This substantially increases the system's latency, and requires that the rendering software support the notion of frame demarcation. Neither the core X renderer nor OpenGL support this notion.

4.5 12-bit Color

Color component resolution was increased from the usual 8 bits to 12 bits for two reasons. First, the RealityEngine framebuffer stores color components in linear, rather than gamma-corrected, format. When 8-bit linear intensities are gamma corrected, single bit changes at low intensities are discernible, resulting in visible banding. The combination of 12-to-10 bit dithering and 10-bit gamma lookup tables used at display time eliminates visible banding. Second, it is intended that images be computed, rather than just stored, in the RealityEngine framebuffer. Volume rendering using 3D textures, for example, requires back-to-front composition of multiple slices through the data set. If the framebuffer resolution is just sufficient to display an acceptable image, repeated compositions will degrade the resolution visibly. The 12-bit components allow substantial framebuffer composition to take place before artifacts become visible.

Figure 6. A scene from a driving simulation running full-screen at 30 Hz.

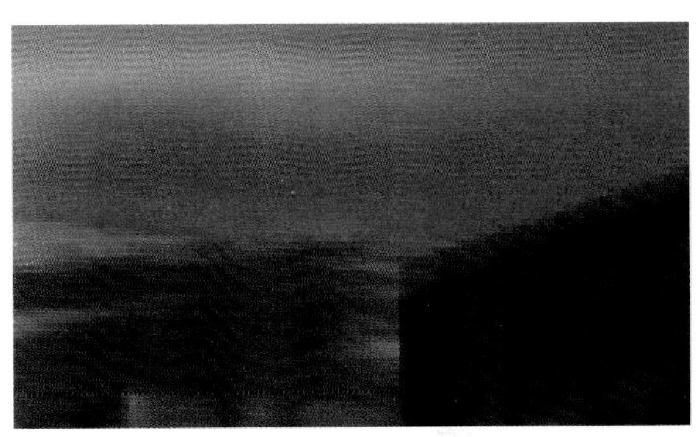

Figure 7. A 12x magnified subregion of the scene in figure 6. The sky texture is properly sampled and the silhouettes of the ground and buildings against the sky are antialiased.

Conclusion

The RealityEngine system was designed as a high-end workstation graphics accelerator with special abilities in image generation and image processing. This paper has described its architecture and capabilities in the realm of image generation: 20 to 60 Hz animations of full-screen, fully-textured, antialiased scenes. (Figures 6 and 7.) The image processing capabilities of the architecture have not been described at all; they include convolution, color space conversion, table lookup, histogramming, and a variety of warping and mapping operations using the texture mapping hardware. Future developments will investigate additional advanced rendering features, while continually reducing the cost of high-performance, high-quality graphics.

Acknowledgments

It was a privilege to be a part of the team that created RealityEngine. While many team members made important contributions to the design, I especially acknowledge Mark Leather for developing the multisample antialiasing technique that was eventually adopted, and for designing a remarkable integrated circuit (the Image Engine) that implemented his design. Also, special thanks to Doug Voorhies, who read and carefully marked up several drafts of this paper, Finally, thanks to John Montrym, Dan Baum, Rolf van Widenfelt, and the anonymous reviewers for their clarifications and insights.

Appendix 1: Measured Performance

The two most significant performance categories are transform rate: the number of primitives per second that can be processed by the Geometry Engines, and fill rate: the number of fragments per second that can be generated and merged into the framebuffer. Running in third-generation mode (lighting, smooth shading, depth buffering, texturing and multisample antialiasing) a 12 Geometry Engine system can process 1.5 million points, 0.7 million connected lines, and 1.0 million connected triangles per second. In second-generation mode (lighting, smooth shading, and depth buffering) the same system can process 2.0 million points, 1.3 million connected lines, and 1.2 million connected triangles per second. Measured third-generation fill rates for 2 and 4 raster board systems are 120 and 240 million fragments per second. Measured second-generation fill rates for 1, 2, and 4 raster board systems are 85, 180, and 360 million fragments per second. The third-generation fill rate numbers are somewhat dependent on rendering order, and are therefore chosen as averages over a range of actual performances.

Appendix 2: Bandwidth and other Statistics

Triangle Bus, fragment transfer path, and Image Engine to framebuffer memory bandwidths are in roughly the ratios of 1:10:20. Specific numbers for the typical two raster board configuration are 240 Mbyte/sec on the Triangle Bus, 3,200 Mbyte/sec aggregate on the 160 Fragment Generator to Image Engine busses, and 6,400 Mbyte/sec aggregate on the 160 Image Engine to framebuffer connections.

Because the 6,400 Mbyte/sec framebuffer bandwidth is so much larger than the bandwidth required to refresh a monitor (roughly 800 Mbyte/sec at $1280 \times 1024 \times 76$Hz) we implement the framebuffer memory with dynamic RAM rather than video RAM, accepting the 12 percent fill rate degradation in favor of the lower cost of commodity memory. Geometry Engine memory and texture memory are also implemented with commodity, 16-bit data path dynamic RAM. Total dynamic memory in the maximally configured system is just over 1/2 Gigabyte.

References

[1] AKELEY, KURT AND TOM JERMOLUK. High-Performance Polygon Rendering. In *Proceedings of SIGGRAPH '88* (August 1988), pp. 239–246.

[2] CARPENTER, LOREN. The A-buffer, An Antialiased Hidden Surface Method. In *Proceedings of SIGGRAPH '84* (July 1984), pp. 103–108.

[3] HAEBERLI, PAUL AND KURT AKELEY. The Accumulation Buffer: Hardware Support for High-Quality Rendering. In *Proceedings of SIGGRAPH '90* (August 1990), pp. 309–318.

[4] KIRK, DAVID AND DOUGLAS VOORHIES. The Rendering Architecture of the DN10000VS. In *Proceedings of SIGGRAPH '90* (August 1990), pp. 299–308.

[5] MOLNAR, STEVEN. *Image-Composition Architectures for Real-Time Image Generation.* University of North Carolina at Chapel Hill, Chapel Hill, NC, 1991.

[6] MOLNAR, STEVEN, JOHN EYLES AND JOHN POULTON. PixelFlow: High-Speed Rendering Using Image Composition. In *Proceedings of SIGGRAPH '92* (July 1992), pp. 231–240.

[7] NEIDER, JACQUELINE, MASON WOO AND TOM DAVIS. *OpenGL Programming Guide.* Addison Wesley, 1993.

[8] OPENGL ARCHITECTURE REVIEW BOARD. *OpenGL Reference Manual.* Addison Wesley, 1992.

[9] PINEDA, JUAN. A Parallel Algorithm for Polygon Rasterization. In *Proceedings of SIGGRAPH '88* (August 1988), pp. 17–20.

[10] SCHILLING, ANDREAS. A New Simple and Efficient Antialiasing with Subpixel Masks. In *Proceedings of SIGGRAPH '91* (July 1991), pp. 133–141.

[11] SILICON GRAPHICS, INC. *Iris 4DGT Technical Report.* Silicon Graphics, Inc., Mountain View, CA, 1988.

[12] SILICON GRAPHICS, INC. *Technical Report - Power Series.* Silicon Graphics, Inc., Mountain View, CA, 1990.

[13] WILLIAMS, LANCE. Pyramidal Parametrics. In *Proceedings of SIGGRAPH '83* (July 1983), pp. 1–11.

VIEW – An Exploratory Molecular Visualization System with User-Definable Interaction Sequences

Lawrence D. Bergman*, Jane S. Richardson†, David C. Richardson†, and Frederick P. Brooks, Jr.*

* GRIP Molecular Graphics Research Resource
Department of Computer Science
University of North Carolina at Chapel Hill

† Department of Biochemistry
Duke University

ABSTRACT

VIEW is an exploratory visualization system for studying the structures of molecules. The system supports a high degree of complex user interaction with the image. Visualizations are constructed by selecting drawing tools from a library. Each tool uses parameters obtained from interactive selection of on-screen geometry by the user, and from a molecular database.

The system is based on a tight coupling of on-screen geometry with the underlying database. Using these links, tools can create true-scale drawing elements that are constrained to database values.

VIEW is highly extensible by the user or a paraprogrammer associated with the user. Drawing tools are written in a C-like programming language with constructs for managing databases, constructs for creating and altering geometry, as well as standard statements such as If-Else and For loops.

An event-definition mechanism allows the user to describe actions to be performed when keys are depressed or dials turned. In addition, the user is able to specify conditional events – actions that are to be taken whenever a user-defined condition becomes true. These conditions are automatically evaluated by the system as part of event processing. Such conditional events allow simple simulations to be readily programmed. Applications of conditional events have included animations of protein binding activity, and an interactive "flashlight" which highlights structures as a cursor is steered through a molecule.

The system includes a development environment complete with a WYSIWYG editor, an interactive debugger, and a set of innovative graphical debugging features.

* CB 3175, UNC, Chapel Hill NC 27599-3175.
(919) 962-1932 bergman@cs.unc.edu
(919) 962-1931 brooks@cs.unc.edu

† Department of Biochemistry, Duke University 27710
(919) 684-6010 jsr@suna.biochem.duke.edu
dcr@suna.biochem.duke.edu

VIEW has been installed for over a year in a protein crystallography laboratory at Duke University. Graduate students and faculty have used the system both for exploring molecular structures and for producing presentation graphics. These users have developed their own set of tools and made extensive use of the tool library. In January 1993, a beta-version of the software was released to a small set of laboratories in the US and Europe. It is now generally available.

CR Categories and Subject Descriptors: D.2.2 [**Software Engineering**]: Tools and Techniques – *Programmer workbench, Software libraries, User interfaces*; D.2.6 [**Software Engineering**]: Programming Environments – *Interactive*; D.3.2 [**Software Engineering**]: Language Classifications – *Design languages, Extensible languages, Specialized application languages*; I.3.6 [**Computer Graphics**]: Methodology and Techniques – *Interaction techniques*; I.3.8 [**Computer Graphics**]: Applications; J.3 [**Computer Applications**]: Life and Medical Sciences – *Biology.*

Additional keywords: scientific visualization, graphical debugging, molecular graphics, data-constrained sketching.

MOTIVATION

Visualization is powerful. Over the past few years, scientific visualization has received a great deal of attention and is widely acknowledged as an important tool for the exploration of scientific data. Through visualization, a scientist assimilates large quantities of data, and may acquire new insights [1].

The visualization design space is large. Different representations of a dataset highlight and reveal different properties (see [2] for an excellent example). The number of possible exploratory visualizations of any dataset is limitless. Some of them will reveal or emphasize certain properties of the data; others will reveal or emphasize other properties; most will be uninformative. For this reason, a great deal of guidance by the scientist is usually required in constructing useful visualizations.

Creating new geometric representations is important but difficult. Graphical representations consist of a display of geometry with associated surface attributes such as color and texture. The shapes used to represent data entities and their relative position, size, and orientation tell us a great deal – they often contain most of the information in an image.

Designing new geometry is difficult. The user must specify the algorithm used to convert database information into geometric parameters. Using existing visualization systems, the user writes new code, usually in C, for each new geometric representation. Little support is provided for this code development. The user usually works outside the boundary of the visualization system, employing a cumbersome code-compile-link-test-recode cycle.

The problem. The problem addressed in this work is: "How can we facilitate the design of new visual representations of scientific data, particularly new forms of geometry?"

The design process. A system for visualization should be based on the process by which a scientist or programmer designs a new visualization:

— Design usually starts with some sketching, done outside the confines of any visualization system – what we call the "paper napkin stage."

— Design is an iterative process – the user repeatedly tries new approaches and gradually refines her notion of what is needed to understand or emphasize the data. Most of the tries are unsuccessful.

— When a satisfactory sketch is achieved, a scale drawing reflecting the actual data is made.

— Visual feedback is crucial in guiding the design process. The user usually determines what she wants based on what she sees; she rarely knows exactly what she wants when she begins.

— New designs usually start with an existing design. Simple and aggregate elements from one design are often reused in a series of designs.

Examination of the design process tells us that the user needs a sketching facility, and an easy way to get from sketch to scale drawing. The ability to interact with a partially complete image, to try and discard a number of alternatives, is critical. Users must also be able to customize the tools or craft their own.

Lack of design-process-based systems. Existing visualization systems fall into two categories, neither of which have heretofore tried to support the design process as described. Application-specific software systems (such as commercial molecular modeling packages, geographic information systems, or flow visualization systems) often provide for interactive design, but the toolkit is fixed and often small. General-purpose visualization systems (such as AVS or Explorer) provide for user-specification of a visualization in a highly interactive fashion, but do not allow the user to directly interact with the visualization itself.

THE VIEW SOLUTION

A design-process-based exploratory system. VIEW is a molecular visualization system designed to provide an exploratory environment. The goals of VIEW are to bring the "napkin" on-line, to support an iterative design process, to provide immediate visual feedback, to allow user-extension of the design tools, and to promote reuse of the design components.

The data-drawing model. Sketching for visualization is distinguished from that for most other forms of design in one important respect – the visualization represents an underlying database. We want geometric parameters of the visualization, primarily positions, to be specified using information from the database. Unlike a free-hand sketch, which can only portray the topology of a form, a database-driven sketch may be constrained to data values, providing a true-scale representation of the geometry.

The VIEW system supplies a method for interactive visualization design that we call *data-drawing*. With data-drawing, the user specifies database parameters by selecting geometric objects on-screen. These geometric objects serve as stand-ins for records in the database.

Design tools that incorporate the data-drawing method operate as follows:

1) The user picks a graphical element.

2) The tool retrieves data associated with that element and additional related data.

3) The tool creates new geometry based on the database information and associates that information with the geometry. This new geometry is in turn available as a visual template for future data-drawing.

With the language that specifies drawing tools, the user associates database records with on-screen geometry and retrieves this information from picks. This uniform philosophy of tool design and use incorporates two desirable features:

— As the user constructs geometries, the new forms are available for data-drawing.

— The tool-user may select any form of geometry that represents the desired database element. She is not restricted to a small set of special representations.

Use of VIEW. A user of the VIEW system starts a session with a simple representation of a molecule. An initial tool creates geometry from molecular data such as Brookhaven Protein Databank atomic coordinates. Often vectors are chosen to represent atomic bonds. Using a variety of drawing tools from a library provided, the user sketches in additional geometry. For example, a user may sketch: individual amino acids with the bonds represented as small cylinders, larger cylinders that represent the axes of helices within a protein, a spline-like representation of a portion of the backbone, or any of a number of other representations.

Interaction with the image is crucial. We recognize that each user has preferred interaction styles. For this reason, the user may customize interaction sequences. The drawing tool language provides a facility known as *interactive events-monitors* for defining actions that are to be performed based on mouse movement, dial movement, and key presses.

Interactive sequences that have been coded to date include: moving a small molecule with the mouse, changing sphere and cylinder radii using a dial, moving atoms using dials while maintaining bond connections, and triggering actions on key depressions.

Geometry and data closely linked. Central to the data-drawing model is a tight coupling of on-screen geometry with the underlying data. This allows on-screen picks to return database records directly to the drawing routines.

Design of new drawing tools. The VIEW user can code new drawing tools which become members of the library. This ability to design new tools is an important feature in an impromptu visualization system.

Tool development environment. VIEW supports the user in extending the toolkit by providing a development environment that includes a Macintosh-like text editor and a visual debugger that interacts with the on-screen image.

AN EXAMPLE

Most of the visualizations produced using VIEW have displayed protein molecules. Proteins consist of a linear chain of *amino acid residues* which fold into a few well-defined 3-D structures such as *beta sheets* and *alpha helices*. These in turn form larger motifs such as *beta barrels*. A protein has a *mainchain* consisting of carbon, oxygen, and nitrogen atoms. Extending from the mainchain are *sidechains*. Each amino acid type, of which there are approximately twenty, has a distinctive sidechain. Hydrogen bond connections between non-sequential amino acids define the *topology* of the protein.

Jane Richardson produced the visualization of the protein Concanavalin A shown in Figure 1 using VIEW drawing tools. A variation of this image appeared in *Biophysical Journal* [3]. The image shows the orientation of a phenylalanine amino acid and two possible but less favorable orientations.

The steps in constructing the visualization were:

1) Richardson selected a tool that creates initial geometry starting with atomic coordinates. The tool produces vectors connecting just the alpha carbons of adjacent amino acids (Figure 2a). This representation gives a clear global view of the structure.

2) Using a mainchain drawing tool, she sketched in atomic-level detail for three strands of the chain. She specified starting and ending points by picking atom positions in the original representation. On each pick, the tool drew a small red sphere to mark the selection. After both ends were selected, the tool drew the connecting main chain at the atomic level automatically, using atom coordinates fetched from the molecular data. After drawing the main chain, the tool removed the marker spheres. Figure 2b shows the drawing after specification of the second strand, just before the system removed the red markers. Only one tool selection and four datapoint selections were required to produce this detailed scale drawing.

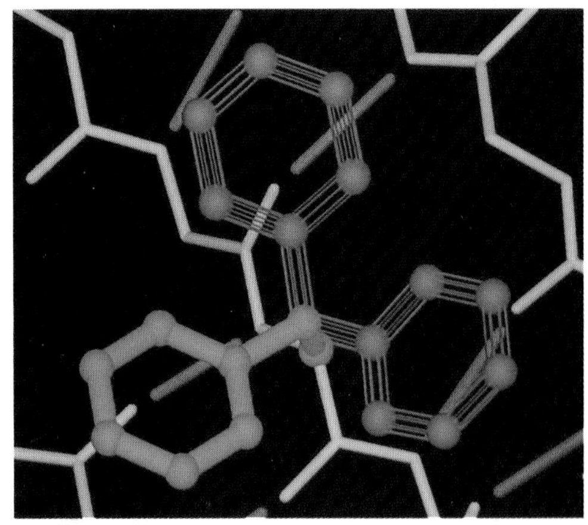

Figure 1: A VIEW visualization

3) Using a line drawing tool, she sketched in hydrogen bonds that couple the strands together. The particular tool employed knows nothing about hydrogen bonds; Richardson selected the termini of each bond. We could have written a new tool to automatically draw in all hydrogen bonds for the molecule. Since we wanted only a small, selected set, manual specification of each bond seemed reasonable.

The line drawing tool bases each drawing operation on two atom selections. This time, the selections were made using the geometry produced in step 2; display of the original representation was toggled off. VIEW users often turn off individual groups of geometry by pressing virtual buttons in the interface. Users frequently switch between sparse global views and detailed local views.

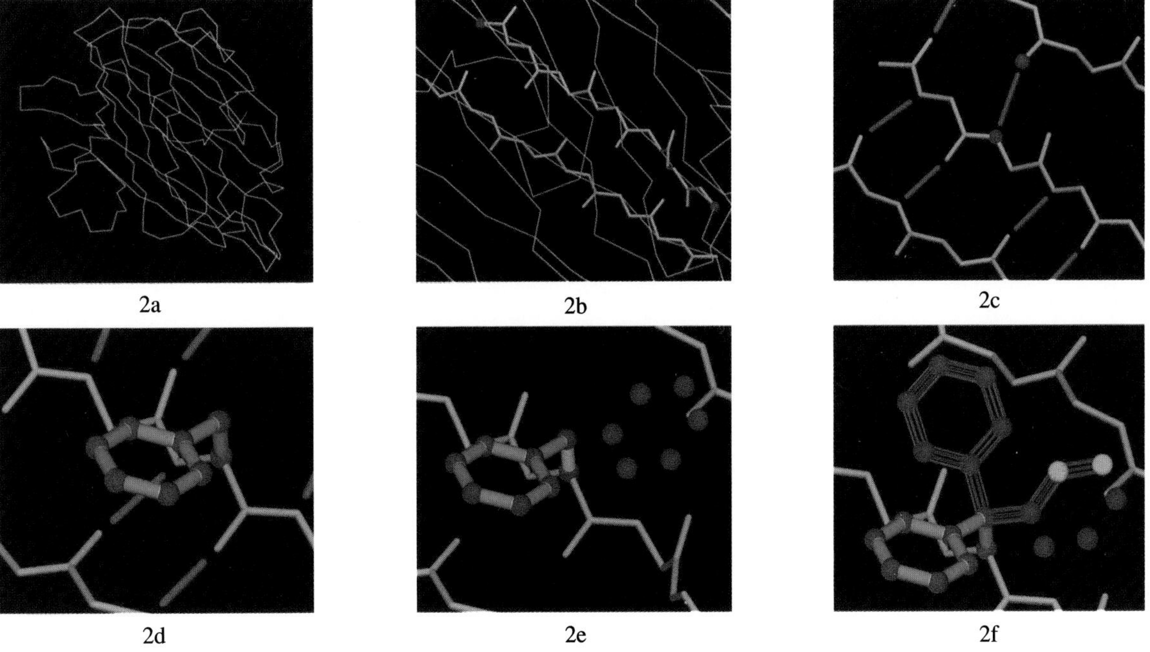

Figure 2. Construction of a visualization using VIEW drawing tools

With the line drawing tool, the user may lengthen or shorten lines that connect the centers of selected atoms. By pressing the "l" key, Richardson triggered an interactive event for defining the length scaling. The event popped up a query window requesting a scaling factor. She specified .65 before proceeding with the drawing shown in Figure 2c.

4) Next, she sketched a single sidechain using a tool which draws an entire sidechain based on one atom selection and information from the molecular database. Once the bonds of the sidechain were drawn, Richardson used a marker-sphere tool to mark the sidechain atoms. Figure 2d shows the result of a single selection with the sidechain tool and eight selections with the marker-sphere tool.

5) In order to produce the two rotated positions of the sidechain, Richardson created a duplicate of the marker spheres using a group duplication tool. VIEW places the geometry created by each drawing tool in a separate *geometry group* labeled with the name of the tool that produced it. These groups may be individually manipulated by other tools. The duplication tool requested that she select any element of geometry from the group to be duplicated, and then queried her for a name for the new group. This specification of group by identifying a member is a common theme in VIEW drawing tools.

6) Once the group had been duplicated, she used a rotation tool to rotate the duplicate into position. The rotation tool requests selection of a rotation axis, followed by requests for selection of one or more geometry groups to be rotated. Rotation may then be performed with a dial or by key presses. In this case, Richardson wanted to rotate the group by a precise amount. An event triggered by pressing the "d" key allowed her to type in the desired angle (120 degrees). She applied the rotation by pressing the "r" key. Figure 2e shows the rotated markers. The rotation axis is highlighted in white.

7) Steps 4 and 5 were repeated to produce a second duplicate rotated to 240 degrees.

8) In order to generate the open framework of lines connecting markers at the rotated positions, Bergman coded a new drawing tool that connects a sequence of selected positions with wireframe cylinders. The tool was created by merging and modifying two prior tools. The first of these tools connected a sequence of positions with solid cylinders using the system cylinder primitive. The other produced a tessellated cylinder not using the system cylinder primitive. The new tool was developed in under a half-hour, including testing. Figure 2f shows the open cylinders being drawn; the last two selected positions are highlighted white.

9) Richardson used a group recoloring tool to finalize colors in the image, shown in Figure 1. The sequence of operations described (excluding the tool development in step 8) can be carried out in about fifteen minutes. In actuality, Richardson spent a couple of hours producing the visualization. A large amount of trial-and-error is required to design a useful image. She tried a score of possibilities before settling on the above result, including: changing colors, radii, lengths, and number of facets for the wireframe cylinders.

SYSTEM DESCRIPTION

The VIEW system (Figure 3) is written in C++ and runs on SGI 4D, Indigo, and Crimson workstations. Three-dimensional manipulation of geometry is performed using a mouse-based virtual trackball or a dialbox.

Drawing tools. The toolkit supplied with the VIEW system contains

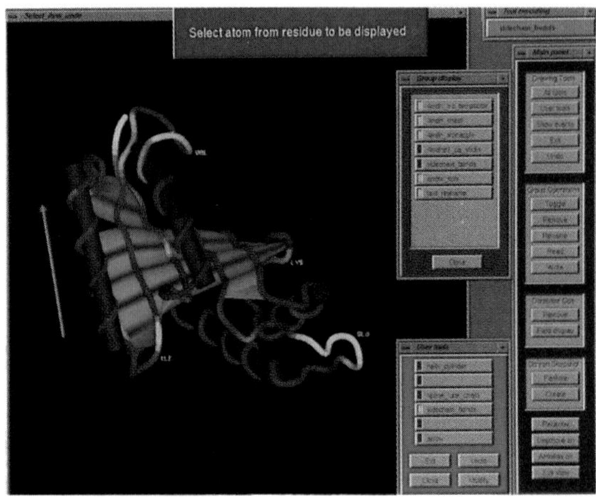

Figure 3: The VIEW system

about fifty interactive drawing tools. Several tools are provided to generate initial representations of a database; the majority of the tools are used for click-and-draw geometry generation or modification. Drawing operations are reversible using a multi-level undo feature.

Tool language. Drawing tools are specified in a C-like language with most of the standard C datatypes and control structures. Additionally, the language includes geometric and database datatypes, constructs for database access and modification, and constructs for selecting and manipulating individual geometric elements and groups of geometry. A key feature is the ability to associate database records with individual geometric primitives. Picking a geometric primitive will retrieve its associated data properties.

The drawing tool language was designed for ease of use. Ability to prototype quickly was given higher priority than runtime speed. For this reason the language is dynamically typed with no type declaration statements. Objects are sized dynamically – no size declarations are given for arrays, sets, geometry groups or databases. Scope rules are very simple. All variables are global within a routine, and they are also global to all event-monitors defined within the routine. Variables are only available outside a routine if passed as subroutine parameters.

The language is interpreted, allowing changes to a tool to be quickly retried. The tools in the library are all coded in the tool language, not in C++. The prompts, highlighting, and final geometry created are specified by tool language statements. The user can readily change the interaction sequence and any of the intermediate or final representations produced by these tools.

Several considerations led to development of a new, interpreted language:

1) We wanted a procedural language similar to C or FORTRAN. Scientists are understandably reluctant to invest in learning new programming styles. This consideration ruled out popular interpreted languages such as LISP and Smalltalk.

2) We wanted to supply special syntax to simplify expression of certain commonly used constructs, particularly database and geometry access. This could have been accomplished by supplying a subroutine library for a language such as C. However, code developed with such a library will be less concise and less readable than if special constructs are available.

3) To simplify coding, we wanted to avoid type statements and size declarations. We also wanted to avoid certain constructs such as pointers that provide flexibility at the expense of code comprehensibility.

4) We wanted to support interactive event definition.

5) We wanted interpretation of the language to be closely integrated with debugging functions, particularly graphical debugging facilities.

Close connection between geometry and databases. One of the characteristics that most distinguishes VIEW from existing general-purpose visualization systems, is the intimate connection between on-screen geometry and an underlying database that the geometry represents. This connection is fundamental to on-screen sketching in a representation of the database – the basic notion of the data-drawing model.

VIEW drawing tools typically associate atom or bond records with each element of geometry created. This association allows other tools to use these elements as visual stand-ins for database entries; the user may select atoms or bonds by clicking on geometry that represents them. Although this is a tried-and-true technique, VIEW is unique in allowing the user to specify the connections; she is not tied down to a system-defined schema. The following code fragment presents an example of establishing links between a geometric object and database records:

```
cyl = CYLINDER (pnt1, pnt2, radius);    (1)
cyl.DB_PTR = atom_rec;                  (2)
cyl.DB_PTR = bond_rec;                  (3)
```

Statement (1) creates a cylinder with the variable name *cyl*. Statement (2) establishes a connection between the cylinder and the atom record stored in *atom_rec*. Statement (3) assigns an additional database pointer to the cylinder, this time to a bond record.

Another tool can access the database information associated with this on-screen geometry as follows:

```
SELECT (item, "Select an object");      (1)
selected_atom_rec = item.atom;          (2)
```

Statement (1) is a pick. The user is told to select a geometric object on-screen using the mouse. The selected object will be returned in the variable *item*. Statement (2) specifies that the atom record pointed to by that object is to be assigned to the variable *selected_atom_rec*. If the geometric object selected happens to be the cylinder created in the previous example, the value of *selected_atom_rec* will be the record contained in *atom_rec*.

Databases. VIEW databases are stored in a non-application specific format. In fact, the only portion of the VIEW system that is specific to molecular visualization is certain drawing tools in the library. We convert molecular data from Brookhaven Protein Databank format to the more generic VIEW format using a filter run outside of VIEW.

Databases are stored in ASCII files, each consisting of one or more named *subsets*. Our molecular databases have two subsets – an atom subset, and a bond subset. A subset consists of a header which describes the record format, followed by a sequence of records. All records in a subset have the same number and ordering of fields. Record fields may be integers, floating point numbers, or strings. Each record contains a single integer- or string-valued key field used for key-access.

Record access from a database requires naming the subset to be accessed and the retrieval key. For example:

```
rec = dbase.atom(num);
```

will retrieve the record that has atom number *num* from the *atom* subset of the database *dbase*. Fields can be retrieved from a record by naming the field. For example:

```
type = rec.atom_type;
```

will retrieve the *atom_type* field from the record *rec*. These forms may be combined. For example:

```
type = dbase.atom(num).atom_type;
```

A special iterator, FOREACH, allows iteration through a subset's records in the order in which they are stored in the file (FOREACH is also used for iterating on arrays, sets, and geometry groups). The NEXT_RECORD statement retrieves the record following a given record, allowing manual control of record access. Similarly a PREV_RECORD statement allows backward movement through a subset.

The VIEW drawing tool language allows the user a great deal of flexibility in modifying databases including: 1) changing fields, 2) adding or deleting fields or records, and 3) writing and reading databases to and from files. Additionally, the user may define her own database formats.

Geometry groups. The drawing tool language provides constructors for geometric objects including spheres, triangles, lines, cylinders, and text. Geometric objects, created by drawing tools, or read from files are stored in *geometry groups*. Groups allow named access to related sets of geometric objects. The system provides a mechanism for controlling which groups are displayed on-screen. Other management functions are available including: 1) removing groups from the system, 2) writing groups to file, and 3) renaming groups.

Each geometric object is contained in one and only one geometry group. There is no nesting of groups. These properties were dictated by two simple design rules.

1) We wanted all geometric objects to be contained in a named geometry group. This ensures that display of any object may be turned on and off using a "group display" function in the interface.

2) We wanted to be able to access a group through a geometric object. This allows the user to specify a geometry group by selecting a member of that group. The "geometry group by example" model focuses the user's attention on on-screen geometry, not on interface buttons or menus. For this reason, we wanted a tool language construct that would query an object: "what group are you in?" To make this construct simple, both syntactically and semantically, we restricted objects to membership in a single group.

The contents of each geometry group is thus distinct. This property is highly desirable. The semantics of group display and group removal are thereby simple and intuitive. If groups are permitted to overlap, these semantics become more involved and may be counterintuitive.

By default, each drawing tool adds geometry to a group that has the name of the tool. If no such group exists, the system automatically creates it the first time the tool generates display geometry. In addition, the tool writer may define groups with other names in which geometry is to be placed. Tools for duplicating geometry groups and merging the contents of geometry groups are provided in the tool library.

Interface operations. Another design criterion for the language was that tools be able to specify any operation that can be performed from the user interface. Statements are available to provide tool control over user interface functions such as toggling the display of geometry groups, removing groups, reading and writing databases from and to files, etc.

Event-monitor definition. The tool language provides a mechanism which allows the tool creator to specify blocks of code that are to be executed when specified keyboard keys are pressed or when dials are rotated. These definitions, known as *interactive event-monitors*, consist of two portions – a *monitor*, which watches the specified device; and an *event body*, which is the code to be executed when the monitor is triggered. A tool may define a suite of event-monitors on different devices which communicate through a common symbol table; the tool builder can readily design a sophisticated interactive interface to her tools.

The following example specifies a dynamic radius-changing tool.

```
SELECT (obj, "Select a geometric object to be
                          changed");                (1)

EVENT ("change_radius"; ON DIAL 7)                  (2)
{
    obj.RADIUS = obj.RADIUS *
                          (1 + DIALRATE/50 );       (3)
    IF (obj.RADIUS < 0.01) obj.RADIUS = 0.01;       (4)
    REDRAW();                                       (5)
}
```

Line (1) is a pick specification. Line (2) defines an event named "change_radius" which will be executed whenever dial 7 is rotated. Line (3) modifies the selected object's radius, using a system-defined variable, DIALRATE, which contains the angular change in dial position, positive for clockwise movement, negative for counter-clockwise. Line (4) ensures that the radius remains positive, and line (5) redraws the screen. With this tool, the user selects an object and then rotates dial 7 to increase or decrease its radius. The radius will alter smoothly as the dial is rotated, because the system continually reexecutes the event body as long as the dial state is changing.

Although only one drawing tool may execute at a time, the event-monitors that it defines persist. Thus, a whole set of event-monitors defined by different tools can be active simultaneously, each monitoring a different device. For example, the rotation tool described above might be used in conjunction with a translation tool that translates geometry along a selected axis using a different dial. The two dials may be used to rotate and translate "concurrently." A panel in the interface gives a summary of all currently active event-monitors.

Conditional event-monitors. In addition to event-monitors that are bound to dials and keys, the system supports *conditional event-monitors*. The monitor is a conditional expression; the event is triggered when the monitor expression is True. The system event manager stores a parse tree for each of these expressions, and the interpreter evaluates them on each iteration of the inner event loop. When any of the conditionals is True, the event body is executed. Thus, the tool builder defines actions to be taken based on certain conditions without coding a polling loop. The conditional evaluation slows the system, but it still responds at interactive rates even when several event-monitors are defined. A simple conditional event-monitor is shown in the following example. This code segment will turn a predefined object red when a probe is within a specified distance.

```
EVENT ("highlight_dist"; DIST(probe.CENTER,
                         obj.CENTER) < 5.0)         (1)
{
    obj.COLOR = COLOR(255,0,0);                     (2)
    REDRAW();
    STOP_EVENT ("highlight_dist");                  (3)
}
```

Statement (1) is a conditional event-monitor definition. This statement creates an event, "highlight_dist", which will be triggered whenever the distance between the center of the object stored in *probe* and the object stored in *obj* is less than 5 units (*probe* and *obj* would be defined elsewhere in the tool, and additional event-monitors provided for moving *probe* through the scene). Line (2) sets the color of *obj* to red, and line (3) deactivates the monitor so that the color change is only applied once.

Spatial search. Frequently we wish a tool to simultaneously monitor a group of 3-D points. When any point is near a specified location, an event is to be triggered. This function occurs so often that it calls for its own underlying mechanism. Simultaneous monitoring is implemented by means of a spatial search function. The function takes as input an array of points to be checked, a probe location and a radius. Any points from the check list that fall within the search radius are placed in an output array. If the output array contains any points, the function returns True. This mechanism allows the tool to trigger events at any of a large number of positions.

Programmable undo. The language allows the developer to define the scope of the system **undo** function. The keyword UNDOABLE may be supplied as an argument to either the pick function or in an event-monitor header. This keyword indicates that a checkpoint is to be created prior to execution of the statement. Whenever **undo** is clicked, the system restores the state of the latest checkpoint. The undo stack stores up to twenty-five checkpoints, allowing the user to backup through a number of drawing operations.

Tool development environment. The VIEW development environment is modeled on that of Smalltalk-80. Code may be modified and executed from editors or pop-up debuggers, allowing a rapid code-test-recode cycle. The debugger supports many features of traditional interactive debuggers including setting breakpoints, step, next, and print.

Graphical debugging. Several *graphical debugging* features are provided that go beyond those provided in Smalltalk or interactive debuggers such as dbx. Using a *construction* facility, the developer automatically views graphical representations of intermediate construction points and lines as they are created by the code. This graphical auto-print makes it easy to follow the progress of algorithms that construct geometry. The *display* function within the debugger highlights the representation corresponding to any selected geometric variable.

Graphical breakpoints are also available. These are similar to the conditional breakpoints provided in interactive debuggers such as dbx. Rather than providing an expression that must be True for execution to pause, however, the user selects a graphical entity, whose display is the condition on which execution is to pause. With this facility, the user selects an object at which the algorithm is to stop. The system will pause on reexecution, allowing her to display variable values (graphically or textually) or manually control the execution.

SAMPLE APPLICATIONS

Interactive superposition. We have developed several interactive exploratory applications using VIEW. Kim Gernert, a biochemist at Duke University, has been studying the geometry of close atomic contacts within protein molecules. She wished to superimpose similar structures from a number of proteins, and then measure geometric parameters from each.

Bergman and Gernert prototyped the superpositioning procedure using a sequence of tools. We began by sketching an axis in each of two structures to be superimposed. We then selected a tool that computes a transformation to superimpose two selected axes. The tool applies the transformation to the geometry of the structure to be superimposed. Once the two structures were oriented on a common axis, the rotation tool described previously was used to rotate one of the structures around that axis. A dial controlled the rotation. Using a translation tool, we moved the structure along the common axis under control of a different dial. The rotation and translation tools allowed us to manually superimpose the structures. Figure 4 shows the completed superposition.

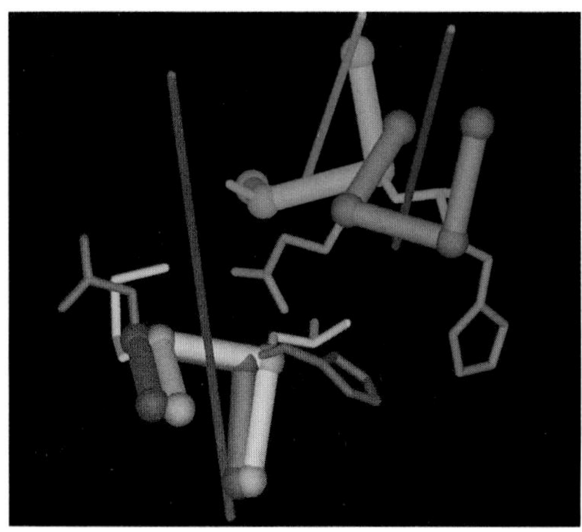

Figure 4: Superposition of alpha helix turns using interactive tools

Interactive structure highlighting. Using the conditional event mechanism with spatial search, we have constructed a "flashlight" tool for exploring proteins. Using the mouse, we steered a probe sphere through a skeletal representation of a protein. As the probe comes near portions of the molecule, more detailed representations are generated. The flashlight has several "lenses" selected by key toggles. With one lens, amino acid sidechains near the probe are dynamically drawn in. With another lens, the mainchain is highlighted. Yet another lens displays pinwheel icons representing close contacts between neighboring atoms. Figure 5 shows a protein with sections of the molecule traced by the flashlight.

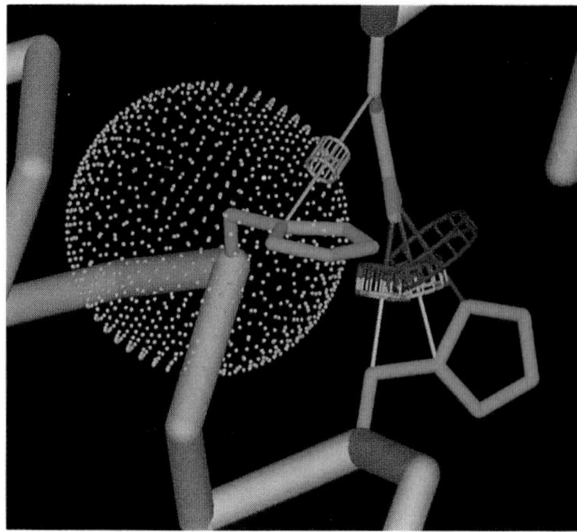

Figure 5: Flashlight tool for highlighting protein structure

Algorithm construction and visualization. VIEW has proven to be quite useful for visualizing geometric algorithms. We used a set of 3-D "ruler-and-compass" construction tools to develop a parameterization of the helix contact geometry discussed above. Using four tools: "project a point onto a line", "construct a plane normal to a line through a given point", "project a point onto a plane", and "connect two points", we were able to construct the geometry in Figure 6. The figure displays in a plane the angles that we decided to use for the study.

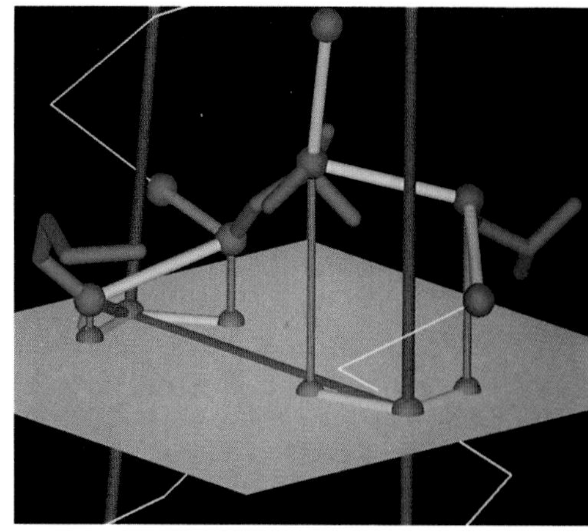

Figure 6: Ruler-and-compass construction of an algorithm

VIEW has also allowed us to visualize the workings of existing algorithms. Figure 7a shows the technique used for constructing axes of alpha helices in proteins (shown in Figure 7b). The red spheres mark user-selected atoms. The yellow spheres mark positions obtained from the database. The blue spheres mark positions computed by the tool. Display statements to generate the construction spheres and cylinders that illustrate the algorithm were added to the already working tool in about 15 minutes.

Interactive topology tracing. Several educational applications have been constructed using VIEW. Figure 8 shows a tool that is used to interactively outline the topology of protein backbone. With a sequence of events on keyboard keys, the user guides a cursor along the backbone, indicating where segments of interest begin and end (Figure 8a). As each segment is identified, a simplified representation replaces the backbone. Once all segments are identified, an event is available to specify ordering and orientation of the segments (Figure 8b). Finally, the tool flattens the connected segments into a map of the chain topology (Figure 8c).

Interactive simulation of binding activity. Another educational application is simulation of the binding activity of enzymes. Several interactive applications have been constructed that allow a student to steer a small molecule into a protein's active site, triggering an animated conformational change.

Binding of a dipeptide in the active site of the protein carboxypepsidase (Figure 9) requires that the dipeptide be close to the ideal position, and oriented properly. The simulation is implemented using a conditional event-monitor that checks the distance between the dipeptide and the binding site and also evaluates orientation by checking two dot products. When the distance and both dot products are within specified limits, the event is triggered. The dipeptide is rotated and translated into the exact binding alignment, while the

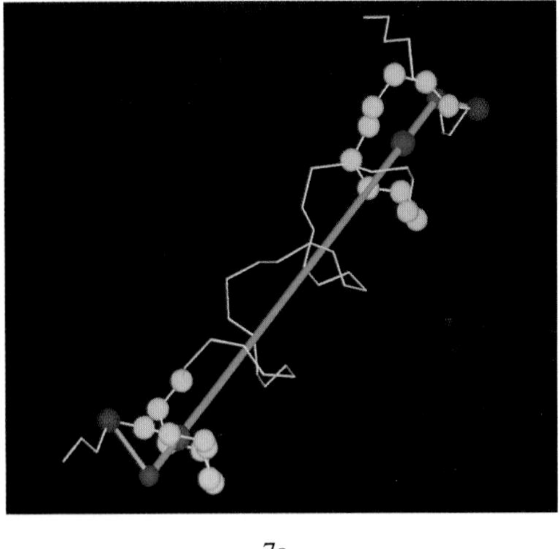

7a

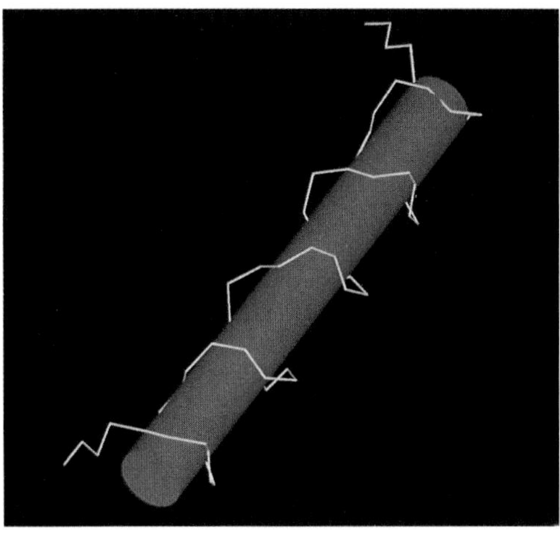

7b

Figure 7: Display of helix axis tool algorithm

conformational change is animated by displaying a series of precomputed frames. The dipeptide may be driven in and out of the binding sites with alternate conformational changes.

RELATED WORK

The vision driving development of the VIEW system was first described by Brooks [4].

General purpose visualization systems (such as AVS [5], ApE [6], Explorer [7], Data explorer [8]) allow the user to configure their own applications using a data-flow programming model. These systems tend towards a batch visualization pipeline – the user's ability to interact with the image (beyond viewing manipulations) is limited. VIEW extends the capability of these systems by adding a high degree of interaction with the image; allowing the user to direct the visualization process on-the-fly. VIEW also goes beyond these systems by supporting new module development within the confines of the system (although IRIS Explorer has recently introduced several embedded languages [7]). The use of an interpreted language, with built-in graphical debugging, greatly facilitates tool development.

Several visualization programming languages and systems have been developed in recent years. Palmer's pdbq language [9] provides support for visualization of molecular structures. Hultquist's LISP-based system for flow-visualization [10] allows rapid prototyping of new algorithms. The VIEW language extends these systems by adding interaction with the image. With Hibbert's system for developing algorithms to process meteorological data [11], the user steps through an algorithm, choosing a variety of display representations for intermediate values. The selection of locations to be examined is performed on-screen. VIEW provides a similar facility, with the addition of user-specified geometries and interaction sequences. Gramps [12] is a general purpose graphics language which has been extended for molecular modeling [13]. VIEW goes beyond Gramps by providing a general-purpose programming language and scriptable interaction sequences.

The MAGE system, developed by D.C. and J.S. Richardson, pioneers a new concept in scientific visualization [14]. Authors in the journal *Protein Science* publish not only their visual images, but also the associated 3-D display lists on a diskette. The diskette also contains the MAGE software for the Macintosh and the PC. Animated visualizations are pre-scripted using a scripting language available to any reader. In addition to viewing the animation, the reader may use a fixed set of database query and visualization tools to explore the images.

WHAT'S NEW

In summary, the VIEW system goes beyond previous work by providing:

- data-drawing

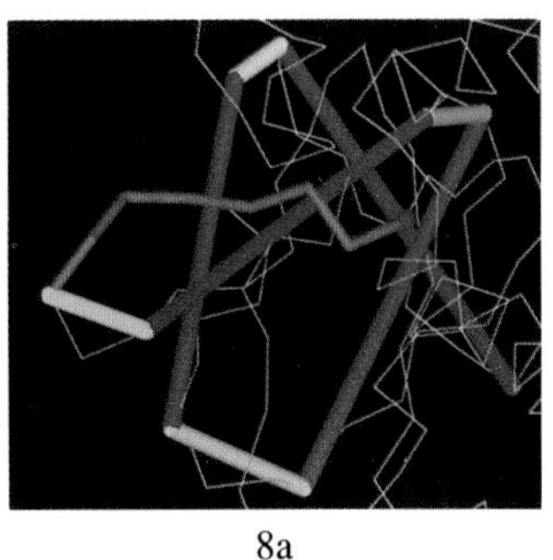

8a

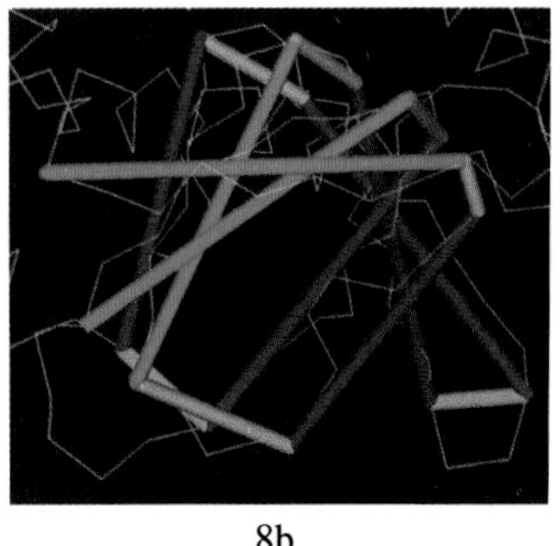

8b

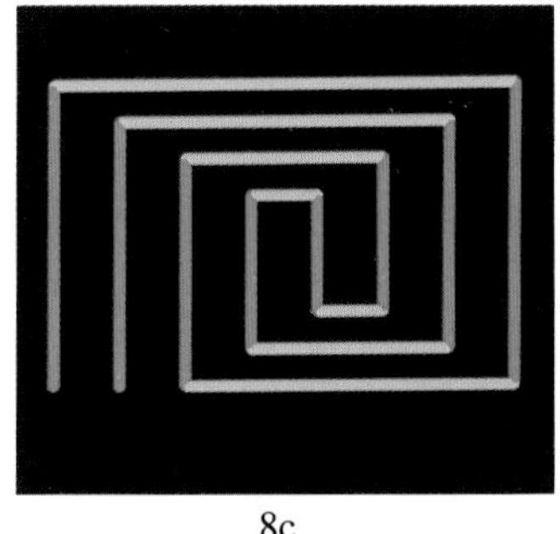

8c

Figure 8. Steps in tracing chain topology. The final figure shows a classic Greek-key barrel motif.

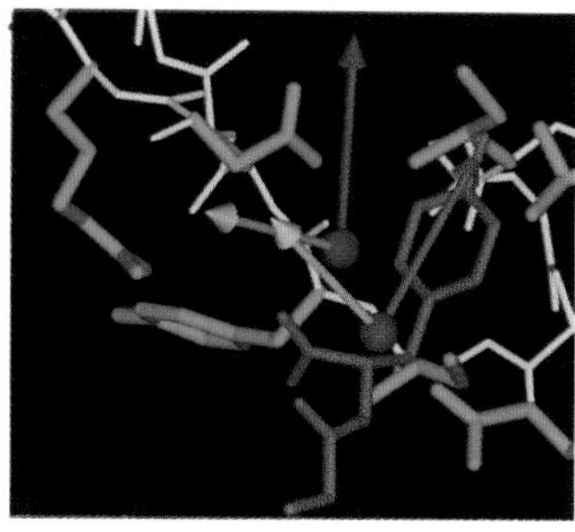
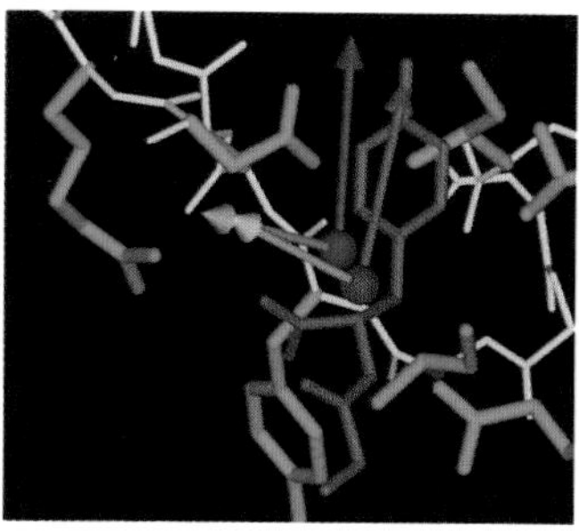
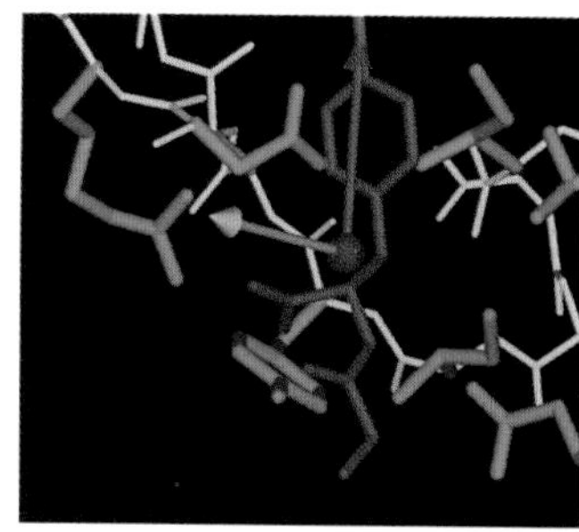

Figure 9. Interactive simulation of dipeptide binding

- image-based interaction in which the user changes the visualization by touching parts of it.
- user-customizable interaction sequences.
- conditional event-monitors that allow parts of the visualization to respond automatically to user actions on other parts.
- multiple event-monitors based on spatial search that allow simultaneous evaluation of potential actions at a large number of 3-D locations.
- graphical debugging in which the image is treated as a trace of a routine's execution state.

APPLICATION AND SYSTEM EXTENSIONS

The VIEW system as is could be readily applied to other datasets that are naturally represented by discrete geometric structures. Airframes or finite-element models are good examples. Users commonly superimpose analytical artifacts such as grids, region boundaries, and isovalue surfaces into scientific databases. These artifacts provide structured geometry to which the VIEW approach could be applied.

Volume data presents difficulties for current visualization systems; the sheer volume of information precludes real-time specification of parameters. An interactive exploratory system might provide a solution. We can imagine starting with a skeletal representation of a volume dataset, perhaps a sparse cloud of points. A flashlight tool could be used to produce a higher quality rendering for user-selected portions of the data set.

Selection of regions of interest is a common task in studying a dataset. A scripting capability would allow users to build tools to display anomalies in the data, search for and highlight extrema, and construct a variety of other interactive filters to limit the amount of visual information displayed. A language tailored to volume data, containing commonly used datatypes and operations, should provide powerful exploratory capabilities.

The ability to script interaction demonstrated in VIEW might prove extremely useful in dealing with fluid-flow data and other time-varying datasets. Interactive placement of trace particles and other types of probes is already common in systems for studying flow fields. The conformational animations produced using VIEW show simple cases of scripting interaction with time-varying datasets. Additional language support for handling time-varying data would greatly enhance this capability. Scientists would be able to readily tailor the visualization process to accommodate a variety of datasets and interaction styles.

A useful extension of VIEW would be an ability to sketch geometry into an animation. After a series of animation frames have been created, the user might wish to sketch new geometry into a single frame using any of the VIEW drawing tools. The tools would automatically add the same geometric forms to all frames, with geometric parameters properly updated to account for between-frame positional changes.

The conditional event-monitor mechanism has proved to be a powerful tool for specifying interaction sequences. The shortcoming of the technique, however, is that evaluation of the conditionals slows the overall response of the system. A natural solution would be to implement a multi-processor architecture for the system. Each processor would be assigned evaluation of one or more monitors, with access to the required symbol tables and parse trees through shared memory. Any processor that detects a monitor trigger would set a global flag, with an associated record indicating the event to be executed. The main control process would simply check the flag as part of its polling loop and when appropriate, would initiate event processing.

Conditional event-monitors are also limited by the restriction of the header to a single relational expression. We would like to specify an arbitrary code block to be evaluated continually, with some portion of that block serving as the conditional expression. We have not taken that approach in the current implementation because read-only relational expressions are easier to deal with than general blocks of code. In the latter case, we would need to implement a critical section mechanism, ensuring that only a single event-monitor or tool attempts to update the symbol table at a time. Doing so would make the conditional event-monitor mechanism much more powerful.

SYSTEM AVAILABILITY

VIEW is available for public use via anonymous ftp. The ftp site is ftp.cs.unc.edu (152.2.128.159). Executables, data files, and documentation are located in the pub/VIEW directory. More extensive documentation is available from the UNC Department of Computer Science.

ACKNOWLEDGMENTS

This work is supported by the Biotechnology Research Program, National Center for Research Resources, NIH, grant number RR02170. Our thanks to the many graduate research assistants who worked on previous versions of the VIEW system, and to Daniel Aliaga for assistance in implementing the current version. Tom Palmer and Dave Bock offered many useful suggestions on the applicability of VIEW concepts to other datatypes. Thanks to Amitabh Varshney, and Mike Bajura for assistance in preparing the manuscript, and to Laura Bollinger for careful editing. We especially thank collaborating biochemist Kim Gernert of Duke University, for numerous contributions to this research.

REFERENCES

[1] B.H. McCormick, T.A. DeFanti, and M.D. Brown, eds., "Visualization in Scientific Computing," *Computer Graphics*, Vol. 21, No. 6, Nov. 1987.

[2] M. Pique, J.S. Richardson, and F.P. Brooks, Jr., "What Does a Protein Look Like?" Invited videotape presented at 1982 SIGGRAPH Conference, July 1982.

[3] J.S. Richardson *et al*, "Looking at Proteins: Representations, Folding, Packing, and Design," *Biophys. J.*, Vol. 63, Nov. 1992, pp. 1186-1209.

[4] Bergman, *et al*, "VIEW – Visualization Impromptu Evaluation Workbench," abstract in *J. Mol. Graphics*, Vol. 6, Dec. 1988, pp. 223.

[5] C. Upson *et al*, "The Application Visualization System: A Computational Environment for Scientific Visualization," *IEEE Computer Graphics & Applications*, Vol. 9, No. 4, July 1989, pp. 30-42.

[6] D.S. Dyer, "A Dataflow Toolkit for Visualization," *IEEE Computer Graphics & Applications*, Vol. 10, No. 4, July 1990, pp. 60-69.

[7] *IRIS Explorer (TM) User's Guide*, Document Number 007-1371-010, Silicon Graphics, Inc., Mountain View, CA, Jan. 1992.

[8] B. Lucas *et al*, "An Architecture for a Scientific Visualization System," *Proc. Visualization '92* (Oct. 1992), pp. 107-114.

[9] T.C. Palmer, "A Language for Molecular Visualization," *IEEE Computer Graphics & Applications*, Vol. 12, No. 3, May 1992, pp. 23-32.

[10] J.P. Hultquist and E.L. Raible, "SuperGlue: A Programming Environment for Scientific Visualization," *Proc. Visualization '92* (Oct. 1992), pp. 243-251.

[11] W. Hibbert, C.R. Dyer, and B. Paul, "Display of Scientific Data Structures for Algorithm Visualization," *Proc. Visualization '92* (Oct. 1992), pp. 139-146.

[12] T.J. O'Donnell and A.J. Olson, "Gramps – A Graphics Language Interpreter for Real-Time Interactive Three-Dimensional Picture Editing and Animation," *Computer Graphics* (Proceedings of SIGGRAPH 1981), Vol. 15, No. 3, Aug. 1981, pp. 133-142.

[13] M.C. Connolly and A.J. Olson, "Granny, a Companion to Gramps for the Real-Time Manipulation of Macromolecular Models." *Computers and Chemistry*, Vol. 9, No. 1, 1985, pp. 1-6.

[14] D.C. Richardson and J.S. Richardson, "The Kinemage: A Tool for Scientific Communication," *Protein Science*, Vol. 1, 1992, pp. 3-9.

The Nanomanipulator: A Virtual-Reality Interface for a Scanning Tunneling Microscope

Russell M. Taylor II[1]
Warren Robinett[1]
Vernon L. Chi[1]
Frederick P. Brooks, Jr.[1]
William V. Wright[1]

Department of Computer Science
University of North Carolina, Chapel Hill

R. Stanley Williams[2]
Erik J. Snyder[3]

Department of Chemistry
University of California, Los Angeles

Abstract

We present an atomic-scale teleoperation system that uses a head-mounted display and force-feedback manipulator arm for a user interface and a Scanning Tunneling Microscope (STM) as a sensor and effector. The system approximates presence at the atomic scale, placing the scientist *on* the surface, *in* control, *while* the experiment is happening. A scientist using the Nanomanipulator can view incoming STM data, feel the surface, and modify the surface (using voltage pulses) in real time. The Nanomanipulator has been used to study the effects of bias pulse duration on the creation of gold mounds. We intend to use the system to make controlled modifications to silicon surfaces.

CR Categories: C.3 (Special-purpose and application-based systems), I.3.7 (Virtual reality), J.2 (Computer Applications Physical Sciences)

Keywords: haptic, force, scientific visualization, interactive graphics, virtual worlds, scanning tunneling microscopy, telepresence, teleoperation.

1. Introduction

We are just beginning to have fast enough graphics engines and acceptable trackers to allow us to provide scientists with a real-time immersive virtual-world interface to their instruments. We have brought this power to bear on the visualization of data from and control of a Scanning Tunneling Microscope with the UNC/UCLA Nanomanipulator system. The virtual-world interface demonstrably contributes to the power of the instrument.

The Scanning Tunneling Microscope (STM) was conceived in 1978 by G. Binnig and H. Rohrer at the IBM Zurich Research Laboratory and first demonstrated in 1981. It was originally designed to aid in understanding the growth, structures, and electrical properties of very thin oxide layers. [4] [5]

An STM consists of a piezoelectric positioning element, a conducting (usually metal) tip and a conducting sample (the surface under study). In our instrument, built by E.A. Eklund at UCLA, the piezoelectric crystal elements are arranged as three orthogonal bars, each of which controls one axis (see figure 1). As voltages are applied across the crystals, they change their lengths. Since the tip is rigidly attached to the crystals, they can be used to position the tip relative to the sample. Our STM can scan areas up to 200 nanometers (nm) on a side.

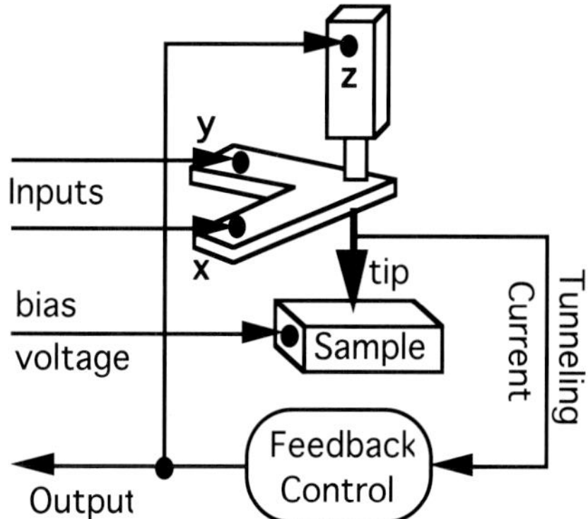

Figure 1: A Scanning Tunneling Microscope. The feedback control maintains the tip at a constant distance above the surface.

A bias voltage is applied to the sample with respect to the tip. At very close range (on the order of a few tenths of a nm), a tunneling current flows between the tip and the surface. This current decreases exponentially with increasing distance between the tip and the sample. In our configuration, the X and Y piezoelectric crystals are used to raster the tip back and forth across the surface in a boustrophedonic* pattern and the Z crystal is controlled by a feedback circuit that attempts to

---

[1] CB #3175, UNC, Chapel Hill NC 27599-3175. (919) 962-1701 taylorr@cs.unc.edu
(919) 967-6375 robinett@cs.unc.edu
(919) 962-1742 chi@cs.unc.edu
(919) 962-1931 brooks@cs.unc.edu
(919) 962-1838 wright@cs.unc.edu

[2] Chemistry Dept., UCLA, Los Angeles, CA 90024-1569. williams@uclach.bitnet

[3] Aono Atomcraft Project, 5-9-9 Tohkohdai, Tsukuba–shi, Ibaraki. 300-26 JAPAN. ejs@odysseus.chem.ucla.edu

*Literally, "as the ox plows."

maintain a fixed tunneling current and thus a constant distance between the tip and sample. A scan of the surface proceeds by repeatedly moving the tip in X and Y and then reading the voltage on the Z axis to determine surface height.

The STM is capable of resolving individual atoms in a sample. The radii of atoms range from 0.03 to 0.27 nm, or approximately 1 billionth the size of common objects, such as a golf ball or a basketball. Typical chemical bonds range from 0.15 to 0.25 nm. For comparison, a typical feature on a current integrated circuit might be 1 micron (1,000 nm) across. Optical microscopes are limited in resolving power to approximately the wavelength of the radiation used in imaging, which is 400-700 nm.

The STM uses a very sharp physical probe to gather information about the sample surface, rather than analyzing reflected photons or electrons. The key to the resolution of the STM is that the length of the piezoelectric positioners can be accurately controlled to 0.01 nm, and that the tunneling current is extremely sensitive to tip-to-sample separation (moving the tip 0.1 nm closer to the surface increases the tunneling current by a factor of 10).

Unlike other microscopes, the STM provides its information as an elevation map rather than a projected image. The scientist wants to understand the geometry of the three-dimensional surface, so these values must be interpreted. The most natural method of interpretation is to reconstruct the surface from the sampled height information, a common process in computer graphics.

In addition to its ability to map the surface, the tip of the STM can be used as a local probe to modify the surface. [2] This makes the STM useful for nanofabrication. There are at least two ways this can be accomplished. The first is to physically contact the surface with the tip, which causes large and unpredictable modifications to both the tip and the surface. The second, more controlled method is to apply a voltage pulse between the tip and the surface. Since the distance between the two is so small, even moderate voltages produce a strong electric field. Both Lyo and Avouris and Kobayashi et al. have shown that it is possible to alter the surface of a silicon crystal with such fields. The former authors have successfully removed clusters and even individual Si atoms from a surface by applying voltage pulses of +3V to the sample under study (with the tip grounded). The amount of material transferred in each pulse depended on the distance from the bottom of the tip to the sample surface (the smaller the distance, the larger the field and thus the more material transferred). They were also able to transfer atoms from the tip back onto the surface by applying voltage pulses of -3V to the sample. Kobayashi et al. have been able to form trenches only a few nanometers wide. They scanned the tip over the surface at a speed of 50 nm/s while holding the sample at a constant voltage of either polarity in the range from 4-10 volts. They used tip-sample separations significantly larger than those used by Lyo and Avouris. These studies have demonstrated the feasibility of altering the structure of a surface literally one atom at a time. What they lacked was the ability to interactively view the surface while it was being modified. [14] [11]

We have built a virtual-worlds interface that converts the STM from a remote batch data collector to a real-time user-guided data collector, and from a remote batch surface modifier to a real-time user-guided surface modifier. The material surface under the STM is sampled and then graphically reconstructed, lighted, and presented to the user at human scale, magnified approximately a billion times. In January 1992, an STM built at UCLA was brought to North Carolina and interfaced to the existing hardware and software of UNC's Head-Mounted Display project and the GROPE force display project. [18] We named the system the "Nanomanipulator" because it allows the user to see, feel, and manipulate matter at the nanometer scale.

The STM functions as both the imager and effector in this atomic-scale teleoperator system. The system operates in three modes. In *raster-scan mode*, the STM tip moves back and forth, continually streaming in new surface height data on a user-specified grid. This data updates the reconstructed surface model in real time. Independently and asynchronously, the viewer may fly about the surface, or hold it at arm's length and tilt it so that the directional illumination reveals and highlights surface detail. The surface model serves as the buffer converting between the back and forth slow scanning of the STM and the TV-like fast scanning of the display system.

In *feel mode*, the scientist uses the manipulator arm to move the STM tip directly (as the crow flies) over the surface, feeling the contours, and perceiving particular point heights, as the STM visual cursor traverses the surface image.

In *pulse mode*, the user also moves the tip directly over the surface, and, with a hand trigger, may select locations to fire bias pulses, modifying the surface.

The user interface through which the human user perceives the microscopic world consists of a stereoscopic head-mounted display and a force-feedback handgrip. The viewpoint changes of the user's head and control gestures of the user's hand are scaled down by the Nanomanipulator to control the viewpoint from which the microscopic world is seen by the user and to control surface modifications enacted by the STM.

Figure 2 shows the user interface for the Nanomanipulator.

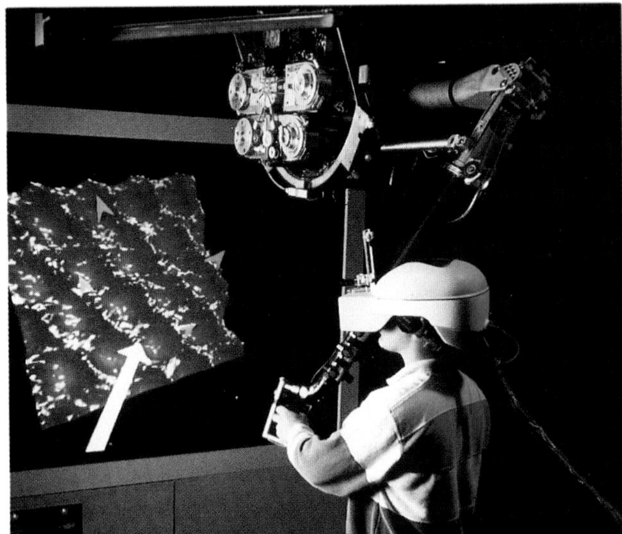

Figure 2: User interface for the Nanomanipulator system. The user can control the action of the STM tip with the force-feedback ARM, feel surface contours, and specify bias pulses by pressing the finger trigger. The user sees the sample surface through the head-mounted display.

The graphics system that generates the stereoscopic images for the HMD provides highly detailed shaded 3D color images in real time. The HMD and head-tracker allow the graphics to be generated in coordination with the user's voluntary head motions, so that users perceive themselves to be surrounded by the microscopic environment.

2. Previous STM Visualization

The standard method of STM data visualization during data collection is to construct gray scale images where dot brightness corresponds to surface height at each point in the image. For later offline viewing or publication, most visualization is done using various graphing routines on personal computers. These packages draw a connected line for each scanline the tip has made, possibly doing hidden line removal on areas that would be occluded. Color is used effectively to show either surface height or other surface properties. For presentation, shaded surface images are sometimes computed. [7] [15] [20] [21]

Dr. Joe Lyding at the Beckman Institute of the University of Illinois has produced an Application Visualization System (AVS) interface module that gives data from the STM scans to other AVS modules for high-quality interactive rendering of surfaces using Gouraud shading. This results in shaded images from a given point of view at rates on the order of one image per minute. Dr. Lyding has found that his interactive viewing system guides experiments by showing interesting areas of study while the data is still being collected. [personal communication] We have found the same effect in our system.

Dr. Besenbacher et al. at the University of Aarhus, Denmark, have taken another approach. They still draw the images on a personal computer, but they make images from successive scans and put them onto videotape for later viewing. This allows them to view surface dynamics that happened during the experiment. The dynamics cannot be viewed while the experiment is in progress, but nonetheless they have found the motion display to be very useful. Referring to his videotaped images of the scanned surface, Dr. Besenbacher writes "...one can record *STM movies* and thereby visualize in real time and space dynamical processes on metal and semiconductor surfaces. Such information, which cannot be obtained by any other means, is very decisive for a full understanding of both the growth mode of reconstructed phases and the resulting static structure." [3] We have also found this property of our system to be valuable.

3. The Nanomanipulator

The goal of this system is to approach an ideal interface for the scientist — presence on the surface itself, with the ability to interact with the surface in real time. The Nanomanipulator system mediates between the human-scale actions of the user and the atomic-scale actions of the STM. A Head-Mounted Display (HMD) and Force-Feedback Argonne-III Remote Manipulator (ARM) provide an immersive virtual environment in which the user is given the ability to act at the atomic scale. The purpose of this system is to scale the STM environment (nanometer scale) up to human size (meter scale) and to provide a means for making changes in this environment - it seeks to create teleoperation at the atomic scale, which requires a scaling factor of 10^9.

3.1 System Structure

The Nanomanipulator system comprises several parts, including the STM itself, the Pixel-Planes 5 graphics engine, a real-time control computer (currently an IRIS 240) to control the STM, and a user interface subsystem (running on a Sun 4). See figure 3 for a system diagram.

Due to the varying requirements of its different parts, the system has been segmented into a distributed set of heterogeneous processors. These subsystems act as communicating sequential processes. The ARM, STM, and user interface sections communicate over an ethernet. The user interface and Pixel-Planes 5 communicate over a VME bus. The various graphics processors within Pixel-Planes 5 communicate over a 640 MByte/s ring network.

Our ethernet LAN provides about a 1 megabit/second sustained path between hosts on the network. This bandwidth is adequate to handle the data coming from the STM, which is limited in scan rate by the electronics and piezoelectric crystal resonances to less than 50 kilobits/second.

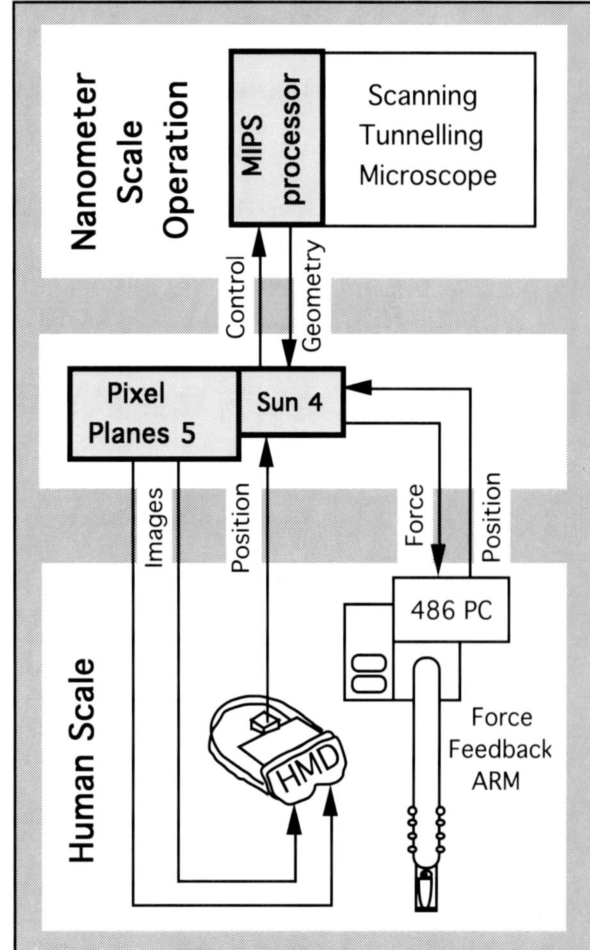

Figure 3: Nanomanipulator system diagram. User Interface code running on the Sun 4 mediates between the atomic-scale operations in the STM and the human-scale operations of the user. Pixel-Planes 5 provides real time shaded stereo images.

STM Controller Process The STM is controlled by one of the processors on an IRIS 240. The X and Y position are controlled by D/A cards and the Z value is read back in through an A/D card. The bias pulses are provided by an HP8131A pulse generator that is interfaced to the computer through an IEEE488.2 (HPIB) bus. The pulse generator is capable of producing controlled pulses as narrow as 500 ps. We have carefully controlled the impedance out to the end of the sample; however the tip side impedance is unknown. As a result, we expect the pulses to be repeatable but of unknown shape as they cross the sample-tip boundary.

The control process accepts commands from the user interface and produces geometry information. When the process is scanning, it streams data to the user interface continually, sending up to 30 packets per second with whatever results have accumulated from scanning during that time. The process is also capable of moving the tip to a given location and returning the height there immediately or applying a pulse there.

User Interface Process The user interface process routes information among the various parts of the system and translates user commands into system commands. It is built on top of several existing software systems that were developed at UNC. The tracking, display, virtual-world editing, menus, and force feedback ARM control were all provided by existing libraries. [10] [17]

The HMD that we currently use is made by Virtual Research. This is a stereo color display helmet that is tracked by a Polhemus tracker. The HMD group has written a software library to handle the interface between the Polhemus and user code. Several projects at UNC have designed virtual worlds for building walkthrough, radiation treatment planning, molecular visualization, and particle systems. [10] The Ultrasound project has interfaced incoming data to Pixel-Planes 5 and overlaid the data on the real world. [1]

The ARM is an Argonne III Remote Manipulator that is interfaced to an IBM PC through A/D and D/A cards. A control library has been written by the GROPE project to access the ARM. Several systems have been designed that use the ARM, leading to the force feedback molecular docking program. [6]

Pixel-Planes 5 The images that are generated for the HMD are produced by Pixel-Planes 5 (Pxpl5). This is a massively parallel graphics engine that was developed at UNC-CH under the direction of Henry Fuchs and John Poulton [9]. Along with the hardware itself, the Pixel-Planes team has created the PPHIGS library as a programmer's interface to the machine. This is a graphics library modeled after the PHIGS standard. Pxpl5 has dozens of I860 processors used as graphics processors (GPs). These processors run the display code and can also be programmed via C code callbacks within the display list.

Pixel-Planes 5 is optimized for drawing static display lists of triangles in real time; performing many updates to the display list ordinarily slows the update rate down unacceptably. New height data arrives from the STM at a rate of up to 500 samples per second, which is 25 data points per frame. Each data point affects the normals at the four surrounding points, and each normal affects up to six surrounding triangles. The system must therefore be able to perform about 600 triangle updates per frame while still maintaining the 20 Hz update rate.

Fortunately, it is possible to program the GPs on Pxpl5 directly, and the display list is split among the GPs. Each GP makes a list for each point of where it is stored in the display list (usually in 6 different triangles) and this list is used to propagate changes into the display list. We send the new point information to the GPs and each one modifies its portion of the display list in parallel. This provides sufficient speed to handle the changes.

3.2 Towards the ideal user interface

The data from the STM is presented to the user as a three-dimensional surface drawn in the head-mounted display. The surface appears to be made of shiny plastic and is colored according to height, with lower areas bluer and higher areas redder. The user sees a line sweeping across the surface as new position updates are received from the STM. The surface is sampled on a regular grid whose spacing is specified at run time. We typically use 80 samples per line and 80 lines on the surface, but the user can interactively trade speed for resolution by re-running the program.

The user's hand is tracked with the ARM. An icon is drawn at the hand location to graphically indicate the current mode of operation, much as the cursor on a Macintosh computer changes shape to indicate current mode. The user selects between modes using a pull-down menu system that is brought up by a thumb trigger on the ARM handgrip. The menu also allows saving the STM data to disk for later analysis.

The finger trigger on the handgrip has different behaviors depending on the mode the user is in. The modes dealing with viewing the virtual world are *fly*, *grab*, *scale up*, and *scale down*. [19] The modes dealing with controlling the STM are *feel*, *pulse*, *select part*, and *select all*.

Fly In *fly* mode, the user holds down the finger trigger to translate through the microscopic landscape in the direction pointed by the handgrip.

Grab In *grab* mode, the user can change the orientation of the virtual world by, in effect, grabbing the "fabric of space" and rotating it. The user moves the handgrip to the desired center of rotation and then holds the trigger down while rotating the handgrip.

Scale One wants to dynamically change the scale factor between the user's scale and the virtual world that represents the microscopic landscape. Such a change is perceived by the user as the virtual world expanding or shrinking. At a magnification of 10^9, a 10 cm gesture by the user would move the STM tip a distance of 0.1 nm on the sample surface, whereas at a magnification of 10^7 the same gesture would move the tip 10 nm. In *scale up* mode, when the user holds down the trigger, the virtual world expands at a fixed rate, using the handgrip location as the center of expansion. *Scale down* mode is similar.

Feel In *feel* mode, the user moves the handgrip around on the surface and feels a force that pulls it up or down to the surface. As the handgrip moves about in X and Y, the STM tip follows the motion. As the user moves, the height of the surface at the cursor location is sampled and a linear restoring force is applied to the handgrip in the Z direction towards the surface. The X and Y position do not have to correspond to grid locations in this mode, so it can be used to supersample the surface. At no time does the user actually control the Z motion of the tip; that is controlled by an electronic feedback circuit. This was a design choice that prevents the user from crashing the tip into the surface. The forces felt are simulated spring forces based on the handgrip height versus the surface height at the given (X,Y) location.

Pulse In *pulse* mode, the user can cause the STM to produce bias pulses. The user moves the handgrip cursor over the place on the surface where the pulse is to go and presses the finger trigger. The STM moves the tip to the indicated spot, pulses the bias, and then resumes scanning the image. This is the mode that allows surface modification; for example, placing blobs of gold from the tip onto the surface.

Select The *select* commands are used to examine part of the surface rapidly. The STM takes about 33 seconds to scan the whole surface, since the tip velocity is constrained. Faster updates for smaller surface areas are useful when making changes to the surface. The user can select a section of the grid to be scanned by pressing the finger trigger, dragging, and releasing to indicate a rectangle of interest. The faster updates allow the user to react to mistakes in the modifications as they occur and immediately see when modifications have been completed and with what result.

Since all of the above interaction is possible while the surface is still under the microscope and being scanned, the user can direct the study of the surface based on data just obtained. If part of the surface looks more interesting and merits further study, the user can select that region of interest and get faster scanning, since only part of the surface is scanned. If there is some question whether an area contains a certain feature or if it contains only noise, it can either be rapidly scanned multiple times or felt (and thereby resampled) by moving the tip over it to see if the apparent feature persists.

3.3 System Performance

Performance tests were run for the system on a Pixel-Planes machine with 41 GPs and 20 renderers. The region examined was a 200x200 nm area of gold scanned with a cut gold tip. We took a 100x100 grid of samples and tessellated each grid square with two triangles. For stereoscopic vision, this is 40,000 triangles each frame. The display rate was 20 frames/second when viewing the entire data set (800K triangles per second). For an 80x80 grid, the rate was 24 hz. These rates are sufficient to make the user feel present on the remote (in scale) surface.

The tip was acquiring new data at a rate of three grid lines per second. Since there were 100 lines in the grid, this means that the entire grid was scanned every 33 seconds. The world is updated as the samples come in, so the user sees a line of updates sweeping back and forth across the scene. Our scan rate is presently limited by the piezo resonance frequencies and the frequency response of our feedback circuit.

We were initially unable to maintain the desired update rate in the *feel surface* mode. In this mode, the position of the hand must be sensed, the tip moved to the correct location, and the force applied to the user. Doing all of this each frame halved the update rate until we pipelined the operation with the display operation. The user therefore feels the force for the previous video frame. When the user moves slowly over a surface, the effect of this lag is negligible.

4. Results

A prototype viewing system, called the Microscape, was set up at UNC before the actual STM was installed. This system allowed the user to fly around and feel a surface that was generated from STM data stored on disk. One of the data sets was an ion-bombarded graphite sample that contained several sheets of graphite that had been pushed upward out of the sample, much like the earth is pushed upwards along an earthquake fault. Previously, these features had been thought to be noise, but the real time shading of the Microscape system showed clearly that they were not aligned with the scan direction and that they were regularly spaced. This discovery convinced us of the power of the visualization and encouraged us to put the current system in place.

Once the UCLA STM had been set up at UNC and the system could modify surfaces, we duplicated the experiments discussed in [16], depositing gold from the tip onto a gold surface. We used a cut gold tip, rather than an etched tip. We used a bias voltage of 235 mV and a tunneling current of 1 nA. For 5V pulse heights, we found that 20 ns pulses repeatably moved material but that 10 and 15 ns pulses rarely did. We also found that the gold mounds we made would anneal as they were repeatedly scanned, often disappearing entirely within a few scans, even though they persisted for long periods if not scanned. More robust structures could be formed by repeatedly pulsing the same location after each scan. One such feature remained in place for the duration of several experiments - tens of scans. Figure 4 shows a gold surface before and after voltage pulses were applied.

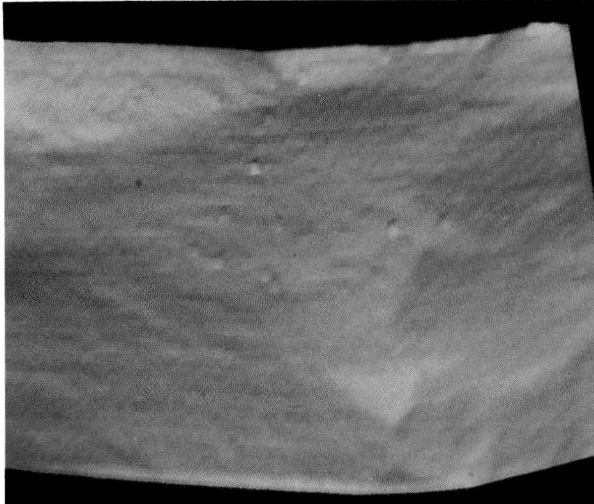

Figure 4a: Gold surface before bias pulses were applied. Surface is colored according to height, with higher areas being redder. Scan area is 100 by 100 nanometers. There are 80 samples each in x and y.

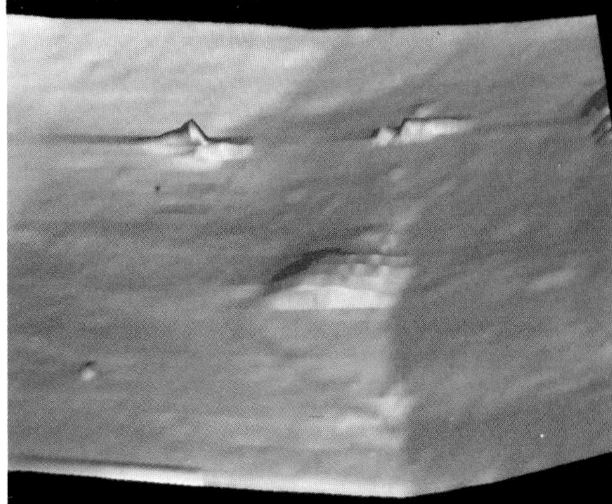

Figure 4b: Gold surface after bias pulses were applied. Several gold mounds have been deposited on the surface. The large mound in the center is about 20 nanometers wide. The smaller bumps were unintentional.

5. Significance

The significance of the virtual-reality interface to the STM is that it gives the scientist simulated *presence* on the sample surface. The benefits of this are: improved perception of 3D structures, more effective exploration of the sample, the ability to observe dynamic processes in near real time, and the ability to interactively modify the surface. To put it in plain language, when you are present somewhere, you can look around, you can look at things from different angles, you can feel interesting things at arm's length, you can watch the behavior of things that move or change, you can pick up things and rearrange them, and you can tweak things to see how they respond. People use all of these behaviors when they investigate places and things in the macroscopic world. Scientists, through the mediation of the Nanomanipulator, can engage in all these exploratory behaviors at the atomic scale, with their actions scaled down from meters to nanometers.

The scientist's ability to recognize specific molecular structures within the noisy, sampled data is improved by using stereoscopic, shaded 3D color graphics with specular highlights. This improved perception of 3D structures, in comparison with 2D gray-scale images with brightness coding height, was evident from the first month of the collaboration; The Williams team at UCLA recognized the up-tilted graphite planes on the first viewing of their STM data rendered as a fly-through with shaded 3D color graphics. They had puzzled over the data for months previously.

Providing stereoscopic, rather than monoscopic, viewing is useful to the scientist because the stereo provides a direct perception of depth for nearby virtual objects. Allowing accurate perception of the 3D spatial structure of STM data makes it possible for scientists to use their own specialized knowledge to recognize structures and features of interest in the data.

Displaying the STM data through a head-mounted display as an intuitively accessed surrounding virtual world allows the 3D graphical world seen by the scientist to be spatially superimposed with the force field felt through the force-feedback handgrip. This allows the user to see and feel a virtual object at a single location in space, just as occurs with real objects. This is harder to do without an HMD, since a large monitor screen tends to get in the way of the feeling gestures of the hand. Also, we believe that displaying the 3D data as a surrounding virtual world helps to better orient the scientist within the data.

The Nanomanipulator allows the scientist to interactively explore the sample in the STM in new ways. First, since the data produced by the STM is a grid of elevations, it can be graphically rendered from any viewpoint. This means that scientists, by means of gestural commands, can translate themselves over the sample surface, scale the surface up and down, and rotate the surface to any orientation. This allows the scientist to fly down into canyons on the surface, and even to fly beneath the surface and see it from below. This ability to see the sample from an arbitrary viewpoint is not possible with imaging-type microscopes, such as optical and scanning-electron microscopes.

The Nanomanipulator allows a second new type of interactive exploration of the sample: the user can interactively modify the scanning parameters of the STM. Current practice at most STM sites is to collect data with the STM first, and then to view and analyze it later, off-line. In such an arrangement, if a feature of interest lies halfway off the sample grid, or if the grid is too coarse to get a good look at the feature, there is not much to be done. But with the ability to scan different areas and at different scales as the exploration progresses, the scientist is empowered to explore more effectively. For example, if a feature of possible interest is seen in a wide-area coarse scan, the user can then interactively focus the scan on the feature of interest to get a high-resolution view of the feature. Having an expert human observer in the control loop makes this sort of interactive exploration very powerful.

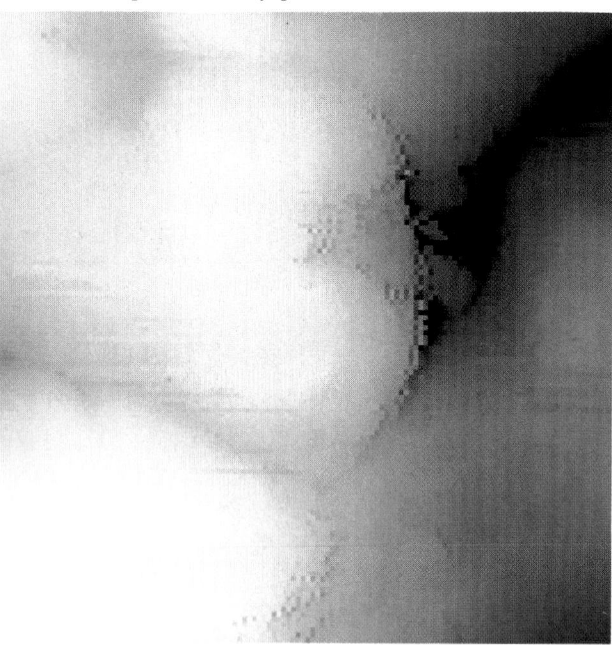

Figure 5a: Gray-scale image of ion-bombarded graphite sample. This is the standard representation given in real time by STM user interfaces.

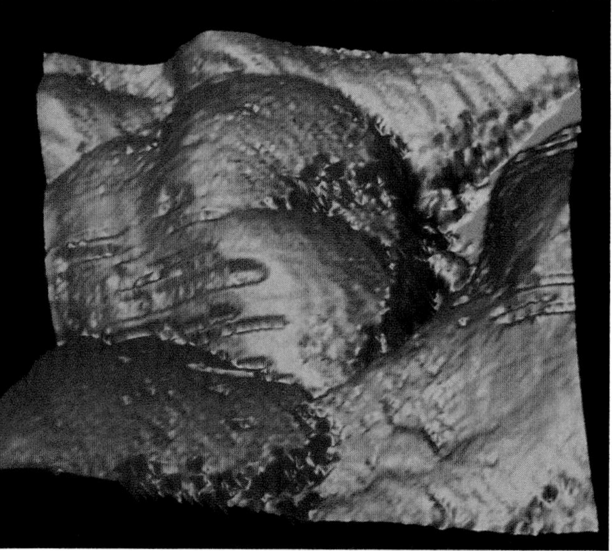

Figure 5b: Shaded image of the same sample. This image shows clearly the tip scratches on the lower left part of the sample and the ripples in the upper right corner caused by sheets of graphite pushing upward out of the surface.

Since the data from the STM comes in as the sampling occurs in real-time, the scientist can observe dynamic processes with time scales of seconds as they evolve on the surface.

The Nanomanipulator gives the scientist the ability to make controlled modifications to the sample surface. This capability takes the Nanomanipulator beyond being a mere passive observing instrument, and makes it rather a tool for conducting experiments on the atomic scale, for fabricating nanometer-scale structures, and perhaps ultimately for building molecular structures atom by atom. We foresee that this will allow the construction of new structures and materials, such as nanometer-scale electronic circuits, which are not now possible to fabricate in any way whatsoever. The advantage of using the Nanomanipulator in this process is that the operator can detect any mistakes or aberrations in the structure being built and correct them in real time. A skilled user can respond to surprise much more creatively than a computer algorithm, and when sculpting at atomic scale, there are bound to be many surprises.

6. Future Directions

The first applications of the Nanomanipulator will be for *nanomachining* of structures on surfaces. This will involve processes similar to those in present electronic device technology (which has about 1/2 micron feature size), where a thin film, in this case only a few monolayers thick, is deposited onto a substrate. The Nanomanipulator will then be used as a mill to directly remove material and pattern a structure on the deposited film, without going through the stages of resist deposition, exposure, and removal. Initially, these structures will be test devices, such as single-electron transistors or platforms for recognizing and immobilizing particular molecular species. The Nanomanipulator will also be used as a probe to study the properties of these devices.

In order for nanomachined devices to become useful tools rather than laboratory curiosities or atomic scale artworks, they will have to be manufactured in massively parallel processes. This will only be possible after we have learned how to manipulate atoms as reproducibly as quantum uncertainty and the second law of thermodynamics will allow. The experience gained in working with the Nanomanipulator may provide the basis for that understanding.

Acknowledgments

We keenly appreciate support for this research: from the National Institutes of Health, The Office of Naval Research, the Defense Advanced Research Projects Agency, and the National Science Foundation. Argonne National Laboratories furnished the force-feedback ARM.

The local projects at UCLA were supported in part by the Office of Naval Research and by NSF grant DMR-89-22027.

Thanks to Roberto Melo for help characterizing the system and for designing and building a new feedback circuit.

We appreciate the groundwork laid by other projects at UNC –the Pixel-Planes 5 group, the Head-Mounted Display group, the GROPE project, and the Tracker project – without which we would not have been able to get up and running.

Thanks to David Banks for his help and suggestions that made the paper twice as good as it was.

Thanks to UNC computer Facilities Group and to the Microelectronic Systems Lab for providing an environment where we can work on our project rather than just on our computers.

References

[1] Bajura, Michael, Henry Fuchs, and Ryutarou Ohbuchi. Merging Virtual Objects with the Real World: Seeing Ultrasound Imagery within the Patient. Proceedings of SIGGRAPH '92 (Chicago, Illinois, July 26-31, 1992), In *Computer Graphics* 26, 2 (July 1992), 203-210.

[2] Becker, R.S., J.A. Golovchenko and B.S. Swartzentruber. Atomic-Scale Surface Modifications Using a Tunnelling Microscope. *Nature* 325(1987), 419.

[3] Besenbacher, F., F. Jensen, E. Lægsgaard, K. Mortensen, and I. Stensgaard. Visualization of the Dynamics in Surface Reconstructions. *Journal of Vacuum Science Technology*. B 9 (2), Mar/Apr 1991, 874-877.

[4] Binnig, G. and H. Rohrer. Scanning Tunneling Microscopy. *Helvetica Physica Acta*. 55 (1982), 726-735.

[5] Binnig, G. and H. Rohrer. Scanning Tunneling Microscopy - From Birth to Adolescence. *Reviews of Modern Physics*, 59(3) July 1987, 615-625.

[6] Brooks, F. P., Jr., M. Ouh-Young, J. J. Batter, and P. J. Kilpatrick. Project GROPE - Haptic Displays for Scientific Visualization. Proceedings of SIGGRAPH '90. In *Computer Graphics* 24, 4 (August 1990), 177-185.

[7] Edstrom, Ronald D. and Maria A. Miller. Scanning Tunneling Microscopy and Atomic Force Microscopy Visualization of the Components of the Skeletal Muscle Glycogenolytic Complex. *Journal of Vacuum Science Technology, B* 9 (2) (Mar/Apr 1991), 1248-1252.

[8] Eklund, E.A.. Correlation from Randomness: Scanning Tunneling Microscopy Applied to the Quantitative Analysis of Sputtered Graphite Surfaces. *Ph. D. Thesis*, UCLA. 1991.

[9] Fuchs, Henry, John Poulton, John Eyles, Trey Greer, Jack Goldfeather, David Ellsworth, Steve Molnar, Greg Turk, Brice Tebbs, and Laura Israel. Pixel-Planes 5: A Heterogeneous Multiprocessor Graphics System Using Processor-Enhanced Memories. Proceedings of SIGGRAPH '89. In *Computer Graphics*, 19, 3 (1989). 79-88.

[10] Holloway, Richard, Henry Fuchs, and Warren Robinett. Virtual-Worlds Research at the University of North Carolina at Chapel Hill. *Proc. Computer Graphics '91*, London.

[11] Kobayashi, A., F. Grey, R. S. Williams, and M. Aono. Nanometer-Scale Silicon Groove Formation by STM. *Science*, in press, 1993.

[12] Komuro, M., S. Okayama, O. Kitamura, W. Mizutani, H. Tokumoto, and K. Kajimura. Nanometer Structure Fabricated by FIB and its Observation by STM. *Microelectronic Engineering* 6 (1987), 343-348.

[13] Lyding, J. W. , S. Skala, J. S. Hubacek, R. Brockenbrough, and G. Gammie. Variable-temperature scanning tunneling microscope. *Rev. Sci. Instrum.* 59 (9), (September 1988), 1897-1902.

[14] Lyo, I.W. and Ph. Avouris. Field-Induced Nanometer to Atomic Scale Manipulation of Si Surfaces with the Scanning Tunneling Microscope. *Science* 253 (1991), 173.

[15] Magonov, S. N., G. Bar, E. Keller, E. B. Yagubskii, and H. J. Cantow. Atomic Scale Surface Studies of Conductive Organic Compounds. *Synthetic Metals*, 40 (1991), 247-256.

[16] Mamin, H. J., S. Chiang, H. Birj, P. H. Guethner, and D. Rugar. Gold deposition from a scanning tunneling microscope tip. J. *Vac. Sci. Technol. B* 9 (2) (Mar/Apr 1991), 1398-1402.

[17] Ouh-young, Ming. Force Display In Molecular Docking. *Ph. D. Thesis*, University of North Carolina at Chapel Hill, 1990.

[18] Robinett, W., R. Taylor, V. Chi, W. V. Wright, F. P. Brooks Jr., R. S. Williams, and E. J. Snyder. The Nanomanipulator: An Atomic-Scale Teleoperator. *SIGGRAPH '92 course notes* for "Implementation of Immersive Virtual Environments."

[19] Robinett, W., and R. Holloway. Implementation of Flying, Scaling, and Grabbing in Virtual Worlds. *ACM Symposium on Interactive 3D Graphics,* Cambridge MA (1992).

[20] Snyder, Eric J., Mark S. Anderson, William M. Tong, R. Stanley Williams, Samir J. Anz, Marcos M. Alvarez, Yves Rubin, François N. Diederich, and Robert L. Whetten. Atomic Force Microscope Studies of Fullerene Films: Highly Stable C60 fcc (311) Free Surfaces. *Science*, 253, 12 (July 1991), 171-173.

[21] Stoll, E. P.. Picture processing and three-dimensional visualization of data from scanning tunneling and atomic force microscopy. *IBM Journal of Research and Development*, 35, . 1/2 (January/March 1991), 67-77.

Surround-Screen Projection-Based Virtual Reality: The Design and Implementation of the CAVE

Carolina Cruz-Neira†
Daniel J. Sandin
Thomas A. DeFanti
Electronic Visualization Laboratory (EVL)
The University of Illinois at Chicago

Abstract

This paper describes the CAVE (CAVE Automatic Virtual Environment) virtual reality/scientific visualization system in detail and demonstrates that projection technology applied to virtual-reality goals achieves a system that matches the quality of workstation screens in terms of resolution, color, and flicker-free stereo. In addition, this format helps reduce the effect of common tracking and system latency errors. The off-axis perspective projection techniques we use are shown to be simple and straightforward. Our techniques for doing multi-screen stereo vision are enumerated, and design barriers, past and current, are described. Advantages and disadvantages of the projection paradigm are discussed, with an analysis of the effect of tracking noise and delay on the user. Successive refinement, a necessary tool for scientific visualization, is developed in the virtual reality context. The use of the CAVE as a one-to-many presentation device at SIGGRAPH '92 and Supercomputing '92 for computational science data is also mentioned.

Keywords: Virtual Reality, Stereoscopic Display, Head-Tracking, Projection Paradigms, Real-Time Manipulation

CR Categories and Subject Descriptors: I.3.7 [Three-Dimensional Graphics and Realism]: Virtual Reality; I.3.1 [Hardware Architecture]: Three-Dimensional Displays.

1. Introduction

1.1. Virtual Reality Overview

Howard Rheingold [11] defines virtual reality (VR) as an experience in which a person is "surrounded by a three-dimensional computer-generated representation, and is able to move around in the virtual world and see it from different angles, to reach into it, grab it, and reshape it." The authors of this paper prefer a definition more confined to the visual domain: a VR system is one which provides real-time viewer-centered head-tracking perspective with a large angle of view, interactive control, and binocular display. A competing term, *virtual environments (VE),* chosen for "truth in advertising" [1], has a somewhat grander definition which also correctly encompasses touch, smell, and sound. Although VE is part of the CAVE acronym, we will use the initials VR herein to conform to mainstream usage.

† 851 S. Morgan, Room 1120 SEO (M/C 154). Chicago, IL 60607-7053. E-mail: cruz@bert.eecs.uic.edu

Several common systems satisfy some but not all of the VR definition above. Flight simulators provide vehicle tracking, not head tracking, and do not generally operate in binocular stereo. Omnimax theaters give a large angle of view [8], occasionally in stereo, but are not interactive. Head-tracked monitors [4][6] provide all but a large angle of view. Head-mounted displays (HMD) [7][13] and BOOMs [9] use motion of the actual display screens to achieve VR by our definition. Correct projection of the imagery on large screens can also create a VR experience, this being the subject of this paper.

Previous work in the VR area dates back to Sutherland [12], who in 1965 wrote about the "Ultimate Display." Later in the decade at the University of Utah, Jim Clark developed a system that allowed wireframe graphics VR to be seen through a head-mounted, BOOM-type display for his dissertation. The common VR devices today are the HMD and the BOOM. Lipscomb [4] showed a monitor-based system in the IBM booth at SIGGRAPH '91 and Deering [6] demonstrated the Virtual Portal, a closet-sized three-wall projection-based system, in the Sun Microsystems' booth at SIGGRAPH '92. The CAVE, our projection-based VR display [3], also premiered at SIGGRAPH '92. The Virtual Portal and CAVE have similar intent, but different implementation schemes.

To distinguish VR from previous developments in computer graphics, we list the depth cues one gets in the real world.

1 Occlusion (hidden surface)
2 Perspective projection
3 Binocular disparity (stereo glasses)
4 Motion Parallax (head motion)
5 Convergence (amount eyes rotate toward center of interest, basically your optical range finder)
6 Accommodation (eye focus, like a single-lens reflex as range finder)
7 Atmospheric (fog)
8 Lighting and Shadows

Conventional workstation graphics gives us 1, 2, 7, and 8. VR adds 3, 4, and 5. No graphics system implements accommodation clues; this is a source of confusion until a user learns to ignore the fact that everything is in focus, even things very close to the eyelash cutoff plane that should be blurry.

The name of our virtual reality theater, "CAVE," is both a recursive acronym (CAVE Automatic Virtual Environment) and a reference to "The Simile of the Cave" found in Plato's *Republic* [10], in which the philosopher discusses inferring reality (ideal forms) from projections (shadows) on the cave wall. The current CAVE was designed in early 1991, and it was implemented and demonstrated to visitors in late 1991. This paper discusses details of the CAVE design and implementation.

1.2. CAVE Motivation

Rather than having evolved from video games or flight simulation, the CAVE has its motivation rooted in scientific visualization and the SIGGRAPH '92 Showcase effort. The CAVE was designed to be a useful tool for scientific visualization. Showcase was an experiment; the Showcase chair, James E. George, and the Showcase committee advocated an environment for computational scientists to interactively present their research at a major professional conference in a one-to-many format on high-end workstations attached to large projection screens. The CAVE was developed as a "Virtual Reality Theater" with scientific content and projection that met the criteria of Showcase. The Showcase jury selected participants based on the scientific content of their research and the suitability of the content to projected presentations.

Attracting leading-edge computational scientists to use VR was not simple. The VR had to help them achieve scientific discoveries faster, without compromising the color, resolution, and flicker-free qualities they have come to expect using workstations. Scientists have been doing single-screen stereo graphics for more than 25 years; any VR system had to successfully compete. Most important, the VR display had to couple to remote data sources, supercomputers, and scientific instruments in a functional way. In total, the VR system had to offer a significant advantage to offset its packaging. The CAVE, which basically met all these criteria, therefore had success attracting serious collaborators in the high-performance computing and communications (HPCC) community.

To retain computational scientists as users, we have tried to match the VR display to the researchers' needs. Minimizing attachments and encumbrances have been goals, as has diminishing the effect of errors in the tracking and updating of data. Our overall motivation is to create a VR display that is good enough to get scientists to get up from their chairs, out of their offices, over to another building, perhaps even to travel to another institution.

1.3. CAVE Design

The CAVE we exhibit at conferences is a theater 10'x10'x10' made up of three rear-projection screens for walls and a down-projection screen for the floor, as shown in Figure 1. (Our development system at EVL is actually 7'x7'x7' due to ceiling height limitations.) Projectors throw full-color workstation fields (1280x512 stereo) at 120Hz onto the screens, giving between 2,000 and 4,000 linear pixel resolution to the surrounding composite image. Computer-controlled audio provides a sonification capability to multiple speakers. A user's head and hand are tracked with Polhemus or Ascension tethered electromagnetic sensors. Stereographics' LCD stereo shutter glasses are used to separate the alternate fields going to the eyes. Four Silicon Graphics high-end workstations create the imagery (one for each screen); they are tied to a fifth for serial communications to input devices and synchronization via fiber-optic reflective memory by Systran Corporation. The CAVE's theater area sits in a 30'x20'x13' room, provided that the projectors' optics are folded by mirrors. Conference use thus far has necessitated the building of a light-tight structure of this size on site to house the screens and projectors.

Goals that inspired the CAVE engineering effort include:

1. The desire for higher-resolution color images and good surround vision without geometric distortion.
2. Less sensitivity to head-rotation induced errors
3. The ability to mix VR imagery with real devices (like one's hand, for instance)
4. The need to guide and teach others in a reasonable way in artificial worlds
5. The desire to couple to networked supercomputers and data sources for successive refinement

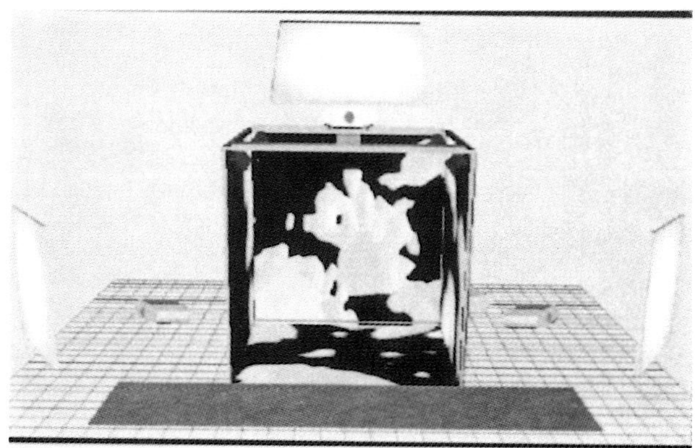

Figure 1: *CAVE diagram.* Graphics by Milana Huang, University of Illinois at Chicago

Significant barriers, now hurdled, include eliminating the lag inherent in common green video projector tubes, corner detailing, and frame accurate synchronization of the workstations; our solutions to these problems are described in detail in section 3. The electromagnetic trackers required building the CAVE screen support structure out of non-magnetic stainless steel (which is also relatively non-conductive), but non-linearities are still a problem, partially because conductive metal exists on the mirrors and in the floor under the concrete. Wheelchairs, especially electric ones, increase tracker noise and non-linearities as well.

Unsolved problems to date include removing the tracking tether so the user is less encumbered, moving the shutters from the eyes to the projectors so cheap cardboard polarizing glasses can be used, incorporating accurate directional sound with speakers, and bringing down the cost. These, and other problems we've encountered, are described in section 6.

The implementation details fall mainly into two categories: projection and stereo. These will be presented next.

2. Projection Details

2.1. Cube Sides As Projection Planes

One rarely noted fact in computer graphics is that the projection plane can be anywhere; it does not have to be perpendicular to the viewer (as typical on workstations, the HMD, and the BOOM). An example of an unusual projection plane is the hemisphere (like in Omnimax theaters or some flight simulators). However, projection on a sphere is outside the real-time capability of the ordinary high-end workstation. And, real-time capability is a necessity in VR.

The CAVE uses a cube as an approximation of a sphere. This simplification greatly aids people trying to stand in the space, and fits the capabilities of off-the-shelf graphics and high-resolution projection equipment, both of which are made to create and project imagery focused on flat rectangles. The defects one encounters in attempting to build a perfect cube are fortunately within the range of adjustment by standard video projectors; in particular, keystoning and pincushion corrections can be utilized. Thus, the ability to match projected images at the seams and corners is effectively perfect, with tuning effort.

2.2. Window Projection Paradigm

The most common computer graphics projection paradigm is the camera view. This type of projection simulates the way an image is captured on film, and includes the direction the camera is pointed and the focal length, position, and twist angle of the lens. In the camera paradigm, stereo is typically achieved by using two cameras; this is the technique used by the HMD and BOOM. The CAVE instead uses a window projection paradigm in which the projection plane and projection point relative to the plane are specified, thus creating an off-axis perspective projection.

Fortunately, the Silicon Graphics' Graphics Library (GL) [14] provides a window projection function. Since this function can also be performed by two shears and a standard perspective projection, or, alternatively, by a translation, a standard perspective projection and a translation back, the window projection function can easily be constructed from more primitive functions, if not available in another graphics library.

In the CAVE, the projection plane locations correspond to the locations of the actual walls. Therefore, as the viewer moves around in the environment, the off-axis stereo projection is calculated according to his/her position with respect to the walls (see Figure 2).

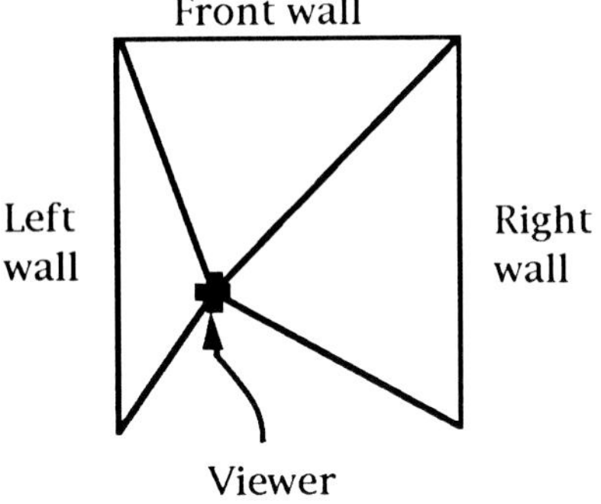

Figure 2: Off-axis projection

For the simplicity of the calculations, we assume that all the walls share the same reference coordinate system as shown in Figure 3. The origin of the coordinate system is placed in the center of the CAVE and it is a right-handed system with respect to the front wall. All the measurements from the trackers (position and orientation) are transformed to match this convention.

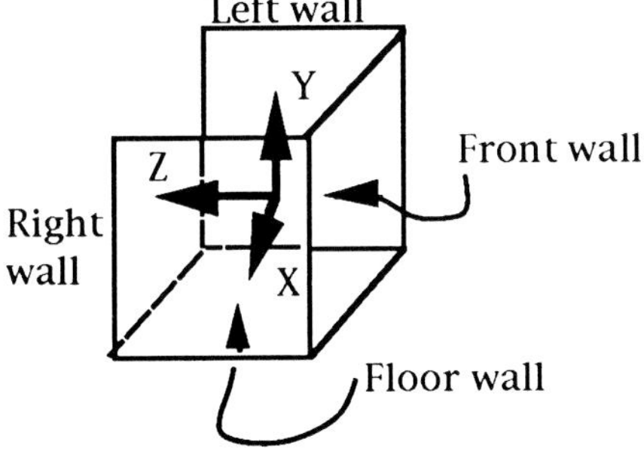

Figure 3: CAVE reference system.

Figure 4 shows a top diagram of the CAVE. The point Q' is the projection of the point Q. PP is the distance from the center of the CAVE to the front wall (5' for the 10'x10'x10' CAVE).

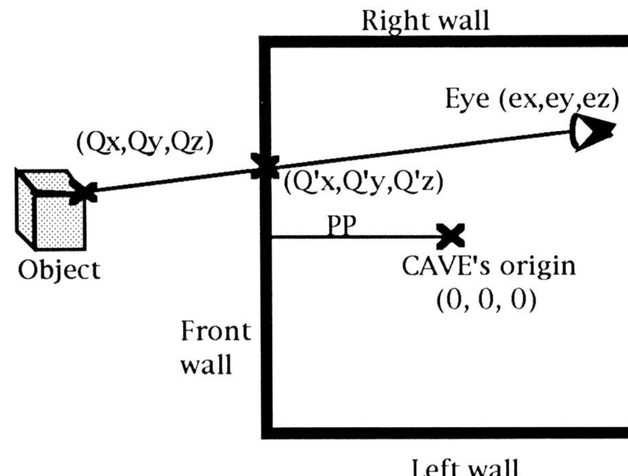

Figure 4: CAVE projection diagram

Using straightforward algebra and following the conventions in Figure 4, the projection Q' of a point Q(Q_x, Q_y, Q_z) on the front wall is given by:

$$Q'x = Qx + \frac{(PP - Qz)(ex - Qx)}{ez - Qz}$$

$$Q'y = Qy + \frac{(PP - Qz)(ey - Qy)}{ez - Qz}$$

Thus, the general projection matrix is:

$$\begin{pmatrix} 1 & 0 & 0 & 0 \\ 0 & 1 & 0 & 0 \\ -\frac{ex}{ez - PP} & -\frac{ey}{ez - PP} & 1 & -\frac{1}{ez - PP} \\ \frac{exPP}{ez - PP} & \frac{eyPP}{ez - PP} & 0 & \frac{ez}{ez - PP} \end{pmatrix}$$

One important issue to mention is that, in the CAVE, the eyes are not assumed to be horizontal and in a plane that is perpendicular to the projection plane. A clear example of this is a situation in which the viewer is looking at one of the corners of the CAVE with his/her head tilted. Our tracker is mounted on top of the stereo glasses; it is raised 5.5" from the glasses to minimize interference and centered between the eyes. From the values obtined from the tracker, and assuming an interpupilar distance of 2.75", we can determine the position of each eye and its orientation with respect to each one of the walls before applying the projection matrix.

The reader can easily derive the matrices for the other walls of the CAVE. Notice that, since the walls of the CAVE are at exactly 90° from each other, the viewer's position with respect to the other walls are:

Left wall: (e_z, e_y, e_x) Right wall: ($-e_z$, e_y, e_x)
Floor wall: (e_x, e_z, $-e_y$)

3. Stereo Vision Details

3.1. Convergence

To achieve stereo vision in the CAVE, we, in principle, do two off-axis stereo projections per screen, one for each eye. We need to obtain information from the tracker to accurately place each eye. We assume that the center of rotation of the eye is close enough to the nodal point (projection point) of the eye to not introduce significant error. Thus, as with other VR systems, where the eyes are looking does not enter into the calculations.

3.2. Frame Sequential Stereo

To get a different image to each eye, we use frame sequential stereo with synchronized shutter glasses. Infrared transmitters cause the lens for each eye to stay transparent for the proper 512 lines of the 1280x1024 image per screen, switching during vertical retrace time. We produce 120 fields per second, thus updating the whole image at 60Hz, producing a flicker-free image.

Note, however, that the green phosphor used in commercially available projection tubes has a persistence that is too long, so a user always sees both images anyway, destroying the stereo effect. Until Stereographics provided us with P43 coated green tubes by special order, we did our experiments (in 1991) in blue and red and shades of magenta. With luck, tube manufacturers will be motivated to add such tubes to their catalogs soon.

3.3. Distortion Correction

The HMD, BOOM, and monitor VR systems have significant geometric distortion inherent in their optics. Modern data projectors have extensive electronic adjustments to accurately correct geometric distortions.

3.4. Minimizing User Shadows

The three wall screens are rear projected so that the participants in the CAVE do not cast shadows. The floor is down projected so shadows are cast. We off-axis project the image from the front top instead of directly overhead, so the shadow of the user falls mainly behind him/her.

3.5. Frame Accurate Synchronization

Another problem we had to solve was the perfect synchronization of the screen updates. If the images are even one frame out of sync, the images in the corners crease and start to look sucked in like sofa cushions. We were unable to get adequate response from the UNIX system to synchronize within the 8ms needed, so (at the suggestion of Silicon Graphics staff) we went to reflective memory, a sort of shared cache arrangement among all the workstations. Reflective memory allows C-pointers to directly access chunks of memory, neatly bypassing the operating system. We intend to use the reflective memory for more sophisticated data sharing, including broadcasting of meshes, textures, and polygon lists. For now, however, reflective memory solves a nasty problem.

3.6. Edge Matching

Particular attention is paid to the edges and corners of the screen to avoid occlusion of stereo objects inside the room. We minimize the seams by stretching a 10'x30' plastic screen over 1/8" stainless steel cable under tension. This gives a seam of about a pixel or so in width, which can be seen but can also be easily ignored. Hence, the illusion of stereo in the CAVE is extremely powerful to the viewer. The floor butts up against the screen fairly perfectly (1/16") and presents no problem.

In the case of 3D movies and workstation screens, stereo objects in front of the screen (often the most interesting ones) have to stay pretty much centered. When a stereo object in front of a screen hits the edge (called "frame violation" in the jargon), it collapses the depth illusion since occlusion is a stronger depth cue than binocular disparity. The CAVE's screen edges are basically out of view (one can see the tops of the screens, but they are high up) so the stereo objects can be anywhere.

We were amazed at how much the floor adds to the experience; a user can walk around convincing objects that are being projected into the room. Since the tracker provides six degrees of information, the user's head can tilt as well, a natural way to look at objects. The HMD provides this capability, but BOOM hardware does not.

3.7 Minimizing Occlusion by Participants

A user's hand can cause stereo violation if an object is between the eyes and the hand, a rare enough situation. People are very eager to resolve stereo violation whenever it's easy so, in these instances, the user simply moves his/her hand out of the way.

A much more serious situation occurs with multiple people in the CAVE. If someone gets in the way of another viewer and an object is supposed to be projected between the two of them, the stereo collapses. We avoid this by having a "teacher" or "guide" control the navigation, but let the "student" or "tourist" be tracked and stand in front, thereby getting the best stereo experience without first having to learn to be an expert navigator of the data space, whatever it is. At conferences, we often jam a dozen people at a time in the CAVE and try to keep the images in front of the crowd. Since people more or less have to stay still or move together, the VR experience for all, however limited, is nevertheless pleasing.

3.8. Motion Sickness

Seeing one's own body or those of other people may in fact be a good idea. Of 9,000 or so people who have been in the CAVE, two have experienced enough nausea to complain about it, a very low ratio (apparently) for VR [1]. We don't yet know why the CAVE doesn't make people nauseous; perhaps it is content related. Our images primarily have to do with scientific data that changes over time, not roller coaster type motions with fast tilting horizons typical of many VR applications. Another explanation may be our better coping with fast head rotation (see next section).

4. Quantitative Analysis of the Effect of Tracking Noise and Latency

4.1. Introduction

Different VR modes have different responses to errors in tracking viewer position. One reason for the differences depends on whether the projection plane moves with the viewer (as with BOOMs and HMDs) or not (in the case of the monitor and CAVE). A second reason is the difference in the distance of the projection plane to the eye, which distinguishes the monitor implementation from the CAVE's.

4.2. Rotation errors

Tracking errors can be resolved into displacement errors and rotation errors. Actual problems are often a combination of the two. In the monitor and CAVE paradigms, since the projection plane does not move with the viewer's position and angle, a rotation about the projection point in the eye creates zero error. In the HMD/BOOM paradigm, a given rotational tracking error produces the same magnitude of rotational error in the image, but of opposite sign. This is a serious problem if the user's head rotates quickly because the whole visual scene first rotates with the head and then steps back into the proper place.

4.3. Analysis of displacement errors in the CAVE and monitor paradigms

The effect of displacement error for both the CAVE and the monitor paradigms is illustrated in Figure 8. The displacement error in eye tracking is ΔP (in a plane parallel to the projection plane), the distance from the eye to the projection plane is PD, and the distance to the object is Z. DISP is the distance error on the projection plane. α is the angular error.

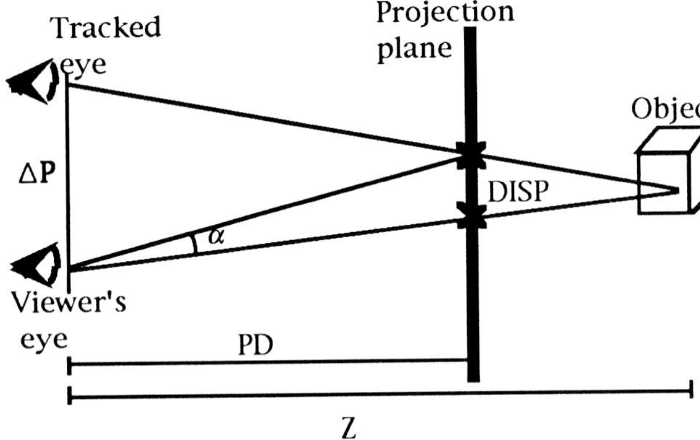

Figure 8: Effect of displacement error for both the CAVE and the monitor paradigms

$$DISP = \Delta P\left(\frac{Z-PD}{Z}\right)$$

$$\alpha = \arctan\left(\frac{DISP}{PD}\right)$$

$$\alpha \cong \frac{DISP}{PD} \text{ for small angles}$$

therefore,

$$(1)\ \alpha \cong \frac{\Delta P\frac{(Z-PD)}{Z}}{PD}$$

For large Z, $\frac{(Z-PD)}{Z} \cong 1$

therefore,

$$(2)\ \alpha \cong \frac{\Delta P}{PD}$$

For small Z, $\frac{(Z-PD)}{Z} \cong -\frac{PD}{Z}$

therefore,

$$(3)\ \alpha \cong -\frac{\Delta P}{Z}$$

For Z = PD (when the object is on the projection plane),

$$\frac{(Z-PD)}{Z} = 0$$

therefore,

$$(4)\ \alpha = 0$$

Equation (1) represents the approximate angular error α for a displacement tracking error ΔP in the monitor and CAVE paradigms.

Equation (2) shows that the larger projection distance PD associated with the CAVE, as compared to the monitor, makes angular error α due to displacement ΔP smaller for large distances Z to the object viewed.

Equation (3) shows that for very small Z values, the monitor and CAVE have similar responses.

Equation (4) shows that when objects are on the projection planes of the monitor or CAVE, the angular error α due to displacement is zero.

4.4. Analysis of displacement errors in the BOOM and HMD

A similar analysis for the BOOM and HMD is indicated in Figure 9.

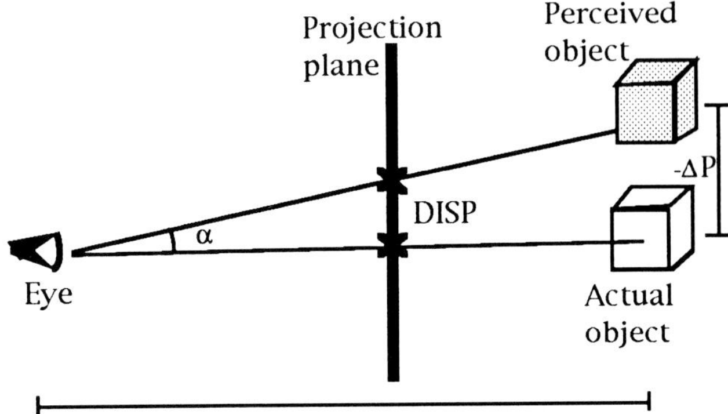

Figure 9: Effect of displacement error for both the HMD and the BOOM paradigms

A displacement error in tracking head position results in identical errors in both the eye position and the projection plane position. This results in a negative displacement of the object being viewed.

$$\alpha = \arctan\left(\frac{-\Delta P}{Z}\right)$$

For small angles,

$$(5)\quad \alpha \cong \frac{-\Delta P}{Z}$$

Equation (5) shows that the angular error α is independent of the projection distance PD to the projection plane. Comparing equation (5) with (2), we see that the BOOM and HMD have less angular error α for displacement errors ΔP for large object distances Z than the CAVE/monitor models. Comparing equation (5) with (3), we see that the BOOM and HMD have similar angular errors α for small object distance Z.

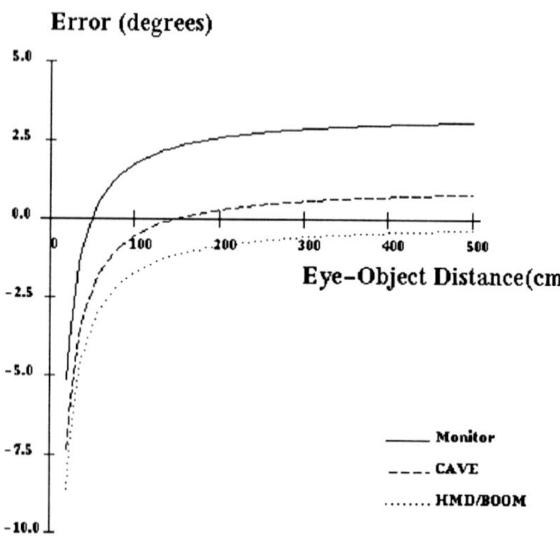

Figure 10: Angular error for a 3cm tracker displacement

Figure 10 graphs the angular error α due to a tracker displacement error ΔP of 3cm for object distances Z. This case represents a tracking error due to latency of a person moving 30cm/second combined with a display rate of 10 frames/second. For large object viewing distances (Z=500cm), the HMD/BOOM have the best performance, the CAVE has 2-1/2 times the error, and the monitor has 9 times the error. For small object viewing distances (Z=20cm), the monitor has the best performance, and the CAVE and HMD/BOOM have only slightly worse error magnitudes.

4.5. Examples of combined rotation and displacement tracking errors

Normal head motions like nodding and panning involve both rotation and displacement of the eyes. The combined effect of these errors may be approximated by summing the individual angular errors α. The assumed projection distances PD for the monitor and 10' CAVE are 50cm and 150cm, respectively.

Figure 11 graphs the angular error α as a function of eye/object distance Z due to a head rotation (pan) of 90 degrees/second and a display rate of 10 frames/second. It is assumed that the eyes are 5cm from the center of rotation. For large Z, the CAVE is 43 times better than the HMD/BOOM and 4 times better than the monitor. For small Z, the CAVE and monitor are 6 times better than the HMD/BOOM.

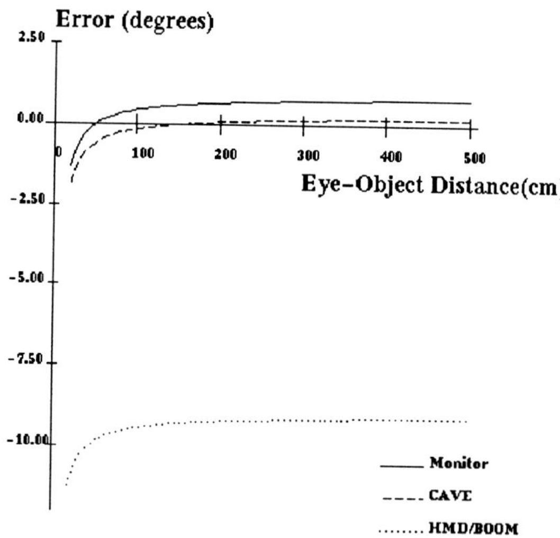

Figure 11: Tracking errors introduced by head panning

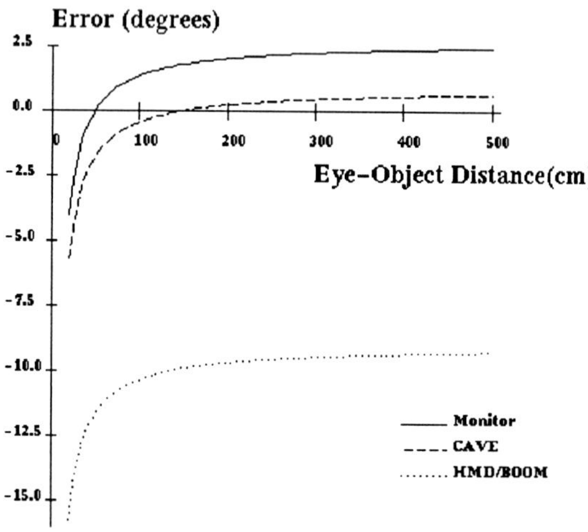

Figure 12: Tracking errors introduced by head nodding

Figure 12 graphs the angular error α as a function of eye/object distance Z due to a head rotation (nod) of 90 degrees/second and a display rate of 10 frames/second. It is assumed that the eyes are 15cm from the center of rotation. For large Z, the CAVE is 15 times better than the HMD/BOOM and 4 times better than the monitor. For small Z, the CAVE and monitor are 3 times better than the HMD/BOOM.

The examples above are all due to tracking errors caused by latency. Tracking errors from other sources, such as electrical interference, tend to be about an order of magnitude smaller, but the ratios are the same and we can draw the same conclusions. For the head-panning example in section 4.5, the problem was caused by normal head motion; if, however, we divide the angular error α by 20, we could interpret the graph as representing the case of a 0.5-degree tracking error combined with a tracking receiver mounted 5cm from the eye.

5. Successive Refinement

One benefit of the wrap-around screens in the CAVE is the potential for successive refinement of images. It is fair to say that we will never, in our lifetimes, have enough computing power to create complex models and display them in real time. Successive refinement trades off motion for time, freezing the image and filling it in, a now common computer graphics technique. Yet, one cannot freeze the image in a HMD without major disorientation. In the BOOM, successive refinement is possible but the user cannot look around. In the CAVE, one can navigate to a place in real time and then send off to a supercomputer for a highly detailed set of four images, still in stereo. When the images come back, the user can still pan around, although he/she cannot navigate while in this mode. The best stereo is achieved when looking in the last interactively tracked direction. Optimizing for this mode is the subject of active ongoing research.

Making VR usable in less-than-real-time situations is important. Supercomputers are essentially floating-point machines. One popular vector machine we use cannot create 1280x1024 pixel maps in real time because the floating-to-fixed conversions are done by non-vectorized subroutine calls (at three conversions, one for each pixel color component, it gets time consuming). There are no floating-point frame buffers for sale. In addition, the desire to transmit a 1280x1024 24-bit image to a workstation 60 times a second requires nearly 2 gigabits of network throughput! Multiply that by 4 for the CAVE screens. Since an update rate of only 10 times a second is closer to VR industry standards, divide by 6, which results in a need for 1.25 gigabits/second. Clearly, we try to transmit polygon lists and meshes in floating point and let the workstation's graphics engine do its job whenever possible.

Naturally, it is important to consider more than image complexity; the basic science being computed often is extremely complex and will not respond in real time. Sometimes large stores of precomputed data are meaningful to explore; perhaps disk-based playback will be useful. The CAVE is a research resource now being used by scientists at the University of Illinois at Chicago, the National Center for Supercomputing Applications, Argonne National Laboratory, University of Chicago, California Institute of Technology, and the University of Minnesota. The overall goal is to match the capabilities of supercomputing, high-speed networking, and the CAVE for scientific visualization applications.

6. CAVE Shortcomings

6.1. Cost

The CAVE is big and expensive, although, given inflation, it is no more expensive than the PDP-11/Evans & Sutherland single-user display system was 20 years ago. Also, considering that up to 12 people can space-share the CAVE, the cost per person comes down in some circumstances. Cheap wall-sized LCD screens with low latency that one could stand on would be great to have, if they only existed. The desire for the rendering afforded by $100,000 state-of-the-art graphics engines will not abate; however, current effects will be achievable at more modest cost as time goes on.

6.2. Ability to Project on All Six Sides of the CAVE

Six screens would make a better CAVE. We originally planned to do both floor and ceiling "rear" projections, which would have necessitated raising the CAVE structure 10'. A hole in the floor and a large sheet of strong glass or plastic would be a better solution, but not one easily achieved at conferences or universities.

A rear screen for the fourth wall might be possible, although the details for human entrance and exit would have to be worked out, especially if the cable-stretched screen technique were used. Four screens work very well, yielding large surround views for both panning actions and looking down. Consequently, objects inside the room can be walked around and virtually beg to be touched.

6.3. Light Spillage

One problem is the light spillage from the "screen" on the floor (the wall screens are fortunately not very reflective). Our floor screen is simply a painted floor board; the floor paint was quickly chosen by using the color-matching computer at the local paint distributor to duplicate the wall screens' color as a first approximation. The only time there would be a problem having one screen brighter than the others would be when the center of interest is not an object on the brightest screen, an unusual case. Very bright screens all around do tend to reduce image contrast somewhat, but this, too, has not been an issue. Naturally, good graphic design optimizes for the strengths and weaknesses of any medium.

6.4. Utilizing the CAVE Medium to Its Full Potential

The CAVE, like Omnimax, represents a different visual paradigm: inside out instead of outside in. From working with students and colleagues, we realize that getting people to design visualizations and think in terms of inside-out is difficult, especially since the CAVE simulator used in the early stages of application development has an outside-in presentation on the workstation screen. Nonetheless, it is a concept into which it is fairly easy to incorporate data.

6.5. Fragility

The CAVE is not "museum hardy." The screens, tracker, and glasses are not kid-proof, thereby limiting use in museums, malls, arcades, and so on. More research is needed.

6.6. New Control Paradigms

As the computing community went from command-line terminals to 2D raster systems, the pull-down menu and mouse provided an alternative to the command line and keyboard. The CAVE has not produced any significant new control paradigms to date, although "step-on" menus have been proposed. One graduate student (Randy Hudson) has achieved a nice way to control rotation by having the user stroke a barely perceptible tessellated wireframe sphere with his/her hand. We look forward to the challenge of finding the next control models and encourage anyone with ideas to come and discuss collaboration.

6.7. Directional Sound

Another issue to address is the effective implementation of directional sound. In theory, with speakers in all corners, one should be able to achieve good directionality with the proper audio synthesis gear. In practice, however, sound localization is compromised by reflections off the screens.

6.8. Ability to Document

The CAVE is very hard to photograph. Imaginations soar when readers are presented with excellent suggestive 2D photos of other VR devices in use. We have not been able to compete in this domain. However, the CAVE and monitor are both amenable to video documentation if the tracking device is attached to the camera and the interoccular distance is adjusted to zero.

7. Conclusions

The CAVE has proven to be an effective and convincing VR paradigm that widens the applicability and increases the quality of the virtual experience. The CAVE achieves the goals of producing a large angle of view, creating high-resolution (HDTV to twice HDTV) full-color images, allowing a multi-person (teacher/student or salesperson/client) presentation format, and permitting some usage of successive refinement. Furthermore, the flatness of the projection screens and the quality of geometric corrections available in projectors allow presentations of 3D stereo images with very low distortion as compared to monitor-based, HMD, and BOOM VR systems. The user is relatively unencumbered given that the required stereo glasses are lightweight and the wires to the head and hand trackers for the tracked individual are very thin. Since the projection plane does not rotate with the viewer, the CAVE has dramatically minimized error sensitivity due to rotational tracking noise and latency associated with head rotation, as compared to the HMD and BOOM.

At SIGGRAPH '92 and Supercomputing '92, more than a dozen scientists, in fields as diverse as neuroscience, astrophysics, superconductivity, molecular dynamics, computational fluid dynamics, fractals, and medical imaging, showed the potential of the CAVE for teaching and communicating research results. Collaborative projects are currently underway in non-Euclidean geometries, cosmology, meteorology, and parallel processing. The CAVE is proving itself a useful tool for scientific visualization, in keeping with our Laboratory's goal of providing scientists with visualization tools for scientific insight, discovery, and communication.

8. Future Work

Further research efforts will tie the CAVE into high-speed networks and supercomputers. We have interest in adding motion-control platforms and other highly tactile devices. Hardening and simplifying the CAVE's design for the nation's science museums, schools, and shopping malls is a goal as well. Design and implementation of quantitative experiments to measure CAVE performance are also planned.

9. References

[1] Bishop, G., Fuchs, H., et al. Research Directions in Virtual Environments. *Computer Graphics*, Vol. 26, 3, Aug. 1992, pp. 153--177.

[2] Brooks, F.P. Grasping Reality Through Illusion: Interactive Graphics serving Science. *Proc. SIGCHI ' 88*, May 1988, pp. 1-11.

[3] Cruz-Neira, C., Sandin, D.J., DeFanti, T.A., Kenyon, R., and Hart, J.C. The CAVE, Audio Visual Experience Automatic Virtual Environment. *Communications of the ACM*, June 1992, pp. 64-72.

[4] Codella, C., Jalili, R., Koved, L., Lewis, B., Ling, D.T., Lipscomb, J.S., Rabenhorst, D., Wang, C.P., Norton, A., Sweeny, P., and Turk, G. Interactive simulation in a multi-person virtual world. *ACM Human Factors in Computing Systems*, CHI '92 Conf., May 1992, pp. 329-334.

[5] Chung, J.C., Harris et al. Exploring Virtual Worlds with Head-Mounted Displays. *Proc. SPIE*, Vol. 1083-05, Feb.1990, pp. 42-52.

[6] Deering, M. High Resolution Virtual Reality. *Computer Graphics*, Vol. 26, 2, July 1992, pp.195-201.

[7] Fisher, S. The AMES Virtual Environment Workstation (VIEW). *SIGGRAPH '89, Course #29 Notes*, Aug. 1989.

[8] Max, N. SIGGRAPH'84 Call for Omnimax Films. *Computer Graphics*, Vol 16, 4, Dec. 1982, pp. 208-214.

[9] McDowall, I.E., Bolas, M., Pieper, S., Fisher, S.S. and Humphries, J. Implementation and Integration of a Counterbalanced CRT-based Stereoscopic Display for Interactive Viewpoint Control in Virtual Environments Applications. *Proc. SPIE*, Vol. 1256-16.

[10] Plato. *The Republic*. The Academy, Athens, c.375 BC.

[11] Rheingold, H. *Virtual Reality*. Summit, New York, 1991.

[12] Sutherland, I.E. The Ultimate Display. *Proc. IFIP* 65, 2, pp. 506-508, 582-583.

[13] Teitel, M.A. The Eyephone: A Head-Mounted Stereo Display. *Proc. SPIE*, Vol.1256-20, Feb. 1990, pp. 168-171.

[14] *Graphics Library Programming Guide*. Silicon Graphics, Inc. 1991.

Acknowledgments

CAVE research is being conducted by the Electronic Visualization Laboratory of the University of Illinois at Chicago, with extraordinary support from Argonne National Laboratory and the National Center for Supercomputing Applications at the University of Illinois at Urbana-Champaign. Equipment support is provided by Ascension Technology Company, DataDisplay Corporation, Electrohome Projection Systems, Polhemus, Silicon Graphics Computer Systems, Stereographics Corporation, and Systran Corporation. Major funding is provided by the National Science Foundation (NSF) grant ASC-92113813, which includes support from the Defense Advanced Research Projects Agency and the National Institute for Mental Health, NSF grant IRI-9213822, and the Illinois Technology Challenge Grant.

Painting with Light

Chris Schoeneman
Julie Dorsey
Brian Smits
James Arvo
Donald Greenberg

Program of Computer Graphics
Cornell University
Ithaca, NY 14853

ABSTRACT

We present a new approach to lighting design for image synthesis. It is based on the *inverse problem* of determining light settings for an environment from a description of the desired solution. The method is useful for determining light intensities to achieve a desired effect in a computer simulation and can be used in conjunction with any rendering algorithm. Given a set of lights with fixed positions, we determine the light intensities and colors that most closely match the target image painted by the designer using a constrained least squares approach. We describe an interactive system that allows flexible input and display of the solution.

CR Categories and Subject Descriptors: I.3.7 [**Computer Graphics**]: Three-Dimensional Graphics and Realism; I.3.3 [**Computer Graphics**]: Picture/Image Generation; I.3.6 [**Computer Graphics**]: Methodology and Techniques - Interaction techniques.

Additional Key Words: simulation, global illumination, radiosity, ray tracing, lighting design, inverse problems.

1 INTRODUCTION

Although global illumination algorithms can produce strikingly realistic images, these algorithms can be difficult to use for lighting design. Currently the only tools available to designers are based upon *direct* methods—those that determine an image from a complete description of an environment and its lighting parameters. This forces a designer to begin with a geometric model, position the lights, assign their colors and intensity distributions, and finally compute a solution. The process is repeated until the solution matches the desired effect. This method is generally time-consuming, tedious, and often counter-intuitive. Given that we usually begin with a notion of the final appearance, a more natural, albeit more difficult, approach is to solve the *inverse problem*—that is, to allow the user to create a *target image* and have the algorithm work backwards to establish the lighting parameters. Inverse problems infer parameters of a system from observed or desired data [1]—in contrast with direct problems, which simulate the effects given all parameters. Although inverse problems are common in radiative transfer, thus far the field of computer graphics has been almost exclusively concerned with direct problems. Yet, inverse problems match a central goal of lighting design—determining how to achieve a desired effect.

In this paper, we present an approach that allows a designer to "paint" a scene as it is desired to appear. Given static geometry and a set of lights with fixed positions, a *constrained least squares* approach is used to determine the light intensities and colors that most closely match the target image painted by the designer. In the domain of lighting design, geometry often constrains the placement of the lights [2]; the designers frequently know about where to put the lights but not how the lights will combine or how bright to make them. Consequently, the task of selecting appropriate intensities for static lights is a useful subproblem of lighting design, and this is our focus. We do not address the automatic placement of lights, nor the mapping of simulated intensities to physical properties of the lights [3, 9].

2 INVERSE PROBLEM

The problem can be phrased more formally as follows: given static scene geometry and a desired appearance, determine the lights that will most closely match the target. There are constraints on possible solutions: only certain objects can emit light and only positive energy can be emitted—keeping us in the realm of physically meaningful solutions. The existence of constraints implies that not every target is realizable. The most general problem of determining how many lights to use, where the lights should be placed, as well as the distribution, color, and intensity of the lights is a non-linear optimization problem. However, if all possible lights have been positioned, and their distributions have been fixed, the determination of which lights to use and what their colors and intensities should be is a linear optimization problem.

2.1 Constrained Least Squares

Suppose $\{\Phi^1, \ldots, \Phi^n\}$ is the set of functions resulting from n distinct light sources illuminating an environment independently. These functions can be computed by any illumination algorithm, including those that account for interreflection and shadows. For example, they may be ray traced images [10] of a scene for each light from the same viewpoint, or radiance functions over surfaces in the environment computed via radiosity [4]. Let Ψ be the target function we wish to approximate. To formulate the approximation problem we require some minimal structure on the space of functions. In particular, we require vector addition and scaling, which we define pointwise, as well as an inner product defined on pairs of functions (i.e. a symmetric positive definite bilinear form). From the inner product we gain the useful notion of the "size" of a function via the norm

$$||\Phi|| = \sqrt{\langle \Phi , \Phi \rangle}, \tag{1}$$

which provides a measure of error. The approximation problem can then be stated in terms of finding non-negative weights $w_1, \ldots, w_n$ such that the function

$$\widehat{\Psi} = \sum_{i=1}^{n} w_i \Phi^i \tag{2}$$

minimizes the objective function $||\Psi - \widehat{\Psi}||$. Stated in this way, the problem is one of least squares. Its unique solution is easily expressed in terms of the inner products:

$$\underbrace{\begin{bmatrix} \langle \Phi^1 , \Phi^1 \rangle & \cdots & \langle \Phi^1 , \Phi^n \rangle \\ \vdots & & \vdots \\ \langle \Phi^n , \Phi^1 \rangle & \cdots & \langle \Phi^n , \Phi^n \rangle \end{bmatrix}}_{M} \underbrace{\begin{bmatrix} w_1 \\ \vdots \\ w_n \end{bmatrix}}_{w} = \underbrace{\begin{bmatrix} \langle \Phi^1 , \Psi \rangle \\ \vdots \\ \langle \Phi^n , \Psi \rangle \end{bmatrix}}_{b} . \tag{3}$$

The $n \times n$ matrix M is the Gram matrix of the inner product, which consists of the coefficients of the normal equations [7]. The Gram matrix is non-singular if and only if the functions $\{\Phi^1, \ldots, \Phi^n\}$ are linearly independent, which will normally be the case if all n lights produce distinct effects on the environment. Naturally, this excludes coincident light sources.

The remaining task is to define an appropriate inner product on the space of functions. Here we make use of the exact nature of the functions. If the functions assign intensities to a set of p discrete points, such as images consisting of p pixels, then the natural inner product is the p-dimensional vector dot product.

Alternatively, if the functions define surface radiance, the most natural inner product is the integral of the pointwise product of the functions. We further assume that the functions are piecewise linear, defined by interpolating a finite set of patch vertices. This representation is easily integrated yielding

$$\langle \Phi^i , \Phi^j \rangle = \sum_{k=1}^{v} \Phi^i_k \alpha_k^2 \Phi^j_k \tag{4}$$

where v is the number of patch vertices, α_k is proportional to the sum of all patch areas adjacent to the kth vertex, and Φ^i_k is the radiosity at vertex k due to light i. Under these assumptions, the *normal equations* can be written

$$A^T D A w = A^T D \Psi \tag{5}$$

where A is the $v \times n$ matrix of the n vectors Φ^i, and D is the $v \times v$ diagonal matrix $\text{diag}(\alpha_1^2, \ldots, \alpha_v^2)$ of the weights used for the inner product. With this definition, $||\Phi||$ is proportional to the total power leaving all surfaces. Also, changes to the inner product are easily expressed as changes to D.

2.2 Solving the Normal Equations

The problem now is to solve the system of equations from Equation 5. This system contains n equations in n unknowns where n, the number of lights, is generally much smaller than the number of vertices in the environment or pixels in the image. Let $M = A^T D A$ and $b = A^T D \Psi$ as in Equation 3. We chose to solve the system $Mw = b$ using a modified Gauss-Seidel iteration.

There is no guarantee that the solution to the system has only positive entries. Simply clipping to zero after convergence is not a viable approach because negative values counteract some of the positive energy; ignoring them causes the environment to be too bright. To avoid this difficulty, we modify the Gauss-Seidel algorithm so that negative values are clipped to zero during each iteration. On the $k+1$ iteration of the modified algorithm, the updated value of w_i is

$$w_i^{(k+1)} = \max\left(\frac{b_i - \sum_{j=0}^{i-1} M_{ij} w_j^{(k+1)} - \sum_{j=i+1}^{n} M_{ij} w_j^{(k)}}{M_{ii}} , 0 \right) . \tag{6}$$

Since a zero value does not influence other entries of w, we are effectively ignoring that light while the iteration is producing a negative value for it. In practice, this approach always converges in the sense that the difference between two iterations goes to zero. An alternative method may be found in [6].

3 IMPLEMENTATION

Our implementation is based on surface radiance functions as opposed to images. The system is therefore view-independent, solving for light intensities that are meaningful in a global sense, not simply for a given view. Although the system does no automatic placement of lights, the user may modify light source positions and distributions at any time. However, any such change requires that a new solution Φ_i be computed. To keep these operations fast, we have currently limited the solutions to direct illumination from each of the lights, accounting for distance and visibility but not secondary reflections. Similarly we restrict surfaces to be ideal diffuse reflectors. Using more complex techniques to find the light source functions makes moving a light more expensive, but does not affect the algorithm. By solving for the intensity of each color channel separately, the colors are determined as well as the intensities.

The user modifies the radiance function of the target by "painting" light onto surfaces. We also adjust the matrix D so that painted surfaces have more weight (or more area) in the solution, causing the system to try harder to match painted surfaces than unpainted ones. This is necessary in complex environments where the large unpainted areas can overwhelm the effect of small painted areas.

To achieve interactive speeds while painting we use the method introduced by Hanrahan and Haeberli [5] to quickly find which patch the brush is currently affecting. Object id's and the patch uv coordinates are rendered into auxiliary buffers. A lookup at the paint brush position in these buffers quickly identifies the patch being painted. Only painted patches are redrawn. Since very few patches change at once, updates are easily made in real time.

The patch's reflectance function modifies the light as it gets painted on a surface. This prevents a surface from being painted with physically unattainable colors. For example, a purely red surface cannot be painted blue. The modified light then gets distributed to the patch's vertices according to their proximity to the paint brush. We restrict the radiosity at a vertex to between zero and one and linearly map this to the full dynamic range of the display.

The system recomputes the closest fitting combination of lights after each brush stroke. All vertices painted between a button press and release comprise a stroke. To maintain interactivity, we perform all the updates incrementally. Instead of completely rebuilding Ψ

(the target radiosities) and re-solving, however, we only change the elements corresponding to painted vertices and make incremental changes to the inner products. If $\Delta\Psi$ is a vector of the changes to the radiosities with p non-zero terms, then

$$b_{new} = A^{T}D(\Psi + \Delta\Psi) = b_{old} + A^{T}D\Delta\Psi. \tag{7}$$

Since $\Delta\Psi$ is typically very sparse, we can update b with $O(np)$ operations by ignoring all zero entries of $\Delta\Psi$. Since most of the environment hasn't changed, the old intensities provide a good initial guess for the modified Gauss-Seidel iteration and it converges quickly. We can similarly update the weight (i.e. effective area) of vertices. Consider changing the importance of one vertex. Let ΔD be the diagonal matrix with its sole non-zero entry being the change in weight of the vertex. Then

$$b_{new} = A^{T}(D + \Delta D)\Psi = b_{old} + A^{T}\Delta D\Psi. \tag{8}$$

Because ΔD has only one non-zero entry, $\Delta D\Psi$ has only one non-zero entry and b_{old} can be updated with $O(n)$ operations. Changing the inner product, though, requires that M be updated as well. This can be done incrementally, observing that

$$M_{new} = A^{T}(D + \Delta D)A = M_{old} + A^{T}\Delta DA. \tag{9}$$

Since ΔDA has only one non-zero row, we need to look at only one column of A^{T} so we can do the multiplication in $O(n^2)$ steps.

In addition to painting, the user can also interactively move and aim light sources. Changing a light requires recomputing the direct illumination due to that light. Since A changes, M must be recomputed as well; however the cost of recomputing a column of A greatly overshadows the matrix multiply used to determine M. Because this can take time for large environments, the user can defer these computations until all the lights have been satisfactorily placed.

The user may also move the camera interactively. Because we paint directly onto the geometry, painted surfaces are view-independent. Also, since no directional effects are accounted for, the functions Φ^{i} for each light are independent of the position and orientation of the camera. Therefore we need not recompute $A = |\Phi^{1} \cdots \Phi^{n}|$ or re-solve for the light intensities as a result of moving the camera.

4 RESULTS

We tested the system on a moderately complex environment consisting of polygonal meshes with about 19,000 polygons, 27,000 vertices, and 12 lights. Figure 1 shows the user's painted environment at the top and the system's solution on the bottom. A user can see both views at once while working to get immediate feedback on how closely the design is being met. Figure 2 shows the same environment with the same light positions but with different painted intensities and colors (left) and a distinct best approximation (middle). The lighting parameters determined by the interactive lighting design were then used to compute a ray traced solution, which is shown in Figure 2 (right). The large scale washes of color and illumination levels are captured well in the rendered image. The user can quickly and easily modify a design to have a very different appearance.

Figure 3 shows the screen during a painting session. The window in which the user paints is on the left and the best fit solution is on the right. Some of the support tools for choosing light to paint and positioning lights are also shown. In this design, 14 lights were placed in another environment of similar complexity.

Figure 1: Design (top) and associated best approximation (bottom).

5 CONCLUSIONS AND FUTURE WORK

We have created an interactive system to help with lighting design in image synthesis by solving a restricted inverse lighting problem. The user paints an approximation of the desired result and the system computes light intensities and colors to match it. This approach can be more intuitive and easier to use than the usual direct edit–render cycle.

Given fixed geometry and a desired target, the problem of determining light intensities and colors can be solved in the least squares sense using a modified Gauss-Seidel algorithm. The method can be made more interactive by using incremental updates to the matrices and vectors involved in the solution process. Magnifying the effect of each brush stroke by increasing the weight of the affected vertices allows the user to make changes to the environment with relatively little effort.

Although they have received little attention in computer graphics, inverse lighting algorithms have great potential as design tools. Clearly there is much to do beyond automatic selection of light source intensities. Automatic light source placement would greatly increase the utility of the technique, but will require more elabo-

Figure 2: Design (left); best approximation (middle); ray tracing (right).

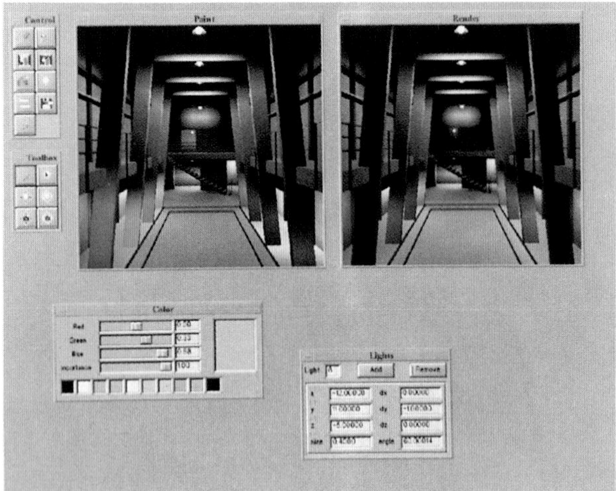

Figure 3: Interactive system.

rate optimization methods, as this requires solving non-linear constrained optimization problems.

Any rendering technique will work for determining the contributions from each of the lights. Our use of direct illumination only was motivated by a desire to allow interactive light placement. A more elaborate implementation might compute more accurate solutions for those lights that were unlikely to change position or distribution.

In order to make the system usable for lighting designers, some way of mapping screen intensities to physical units in the system must be found. Since the system is being driven by the user's perception of what is being painted, the lighting conditions of the user's environment must be accounted for, as well as the non-linearities of the monitor, the reproduction of color on the monitor, and most importantly, the extremely limited dynamic range of the monitor.

ACKNOWLEDGEMENTS

We would like to thank Jed Lengyel for his helpful comments and Kurk Dorsey and Suzanne Smits for their help assembling the paper. Much thanks to Matthew Bannister who created the model and the lighting designs. This work was supported by the NSF grant "Interactive Computer Graphics Input and Display Techniques" (CCR-8617880), and by the NSF/DARPA Science and Technology Center for Computer Graphics and Scientific Visualization (ASC-8920219). The authors gratefully acknowledge the generous equipment grant from Hewlett Packard Corporation on whose workstations the research was conducted.

REFERENCES

[1] Baltes, H. P., editor. *Inverse Source Problems in Optics*, Springer-Verlag, New York, 1978.

[2] Dorsey, Julie O'B., François X. Sillion, and Donald P. Greenberg. "Design and Simulation of Opera Lighting and Projection Effects," in *Computer Graphics*, 25(4), August 1991, pages 41–50.

[3] Evans, Ralph M. *Eye, Film, and Camera in Color Photography*, John Wiley & Sons, New York, 1959.

[4] Goral, Cindy M., Kenneth E. Torrance, Donald P. Greenberg, and Bennett Battaile. "Modeling the Interaction of Light Between Diffuse Surfaces," in *Computer Graphics*, 18(3), July 1984, pages 213–222.

[5] Hanrahan, Pat and Paul Haeberli. "Direct WYSIWYG Painting and Texturing on 3D Shapes," in *Computer Graphics*, 24(4), August 1990, pages 215–223.

[6] Lawson, Charles L. and Hanson Richard J. *Solving Least Squares Problems*, Prentice-Hall, Englewood Cliffs, 1974.

[7] Luenberger, David G. *Optimization by Vector Space Methods*, John Wiley & Sons, New York, 1969.

[8] Poulin, Pierre and Alain Fournier. "Lights from Highlights and Shadows," Proceedings of the 1992 Symposium on Interactive 3D Graphics, in *Computer Graphics*, April 1992, pages 31–38.

[9] Tumblin, Jack and Holly Rushmeier. "Tone Reproduction for Realistic Computer Generated Images," in Radiosity Course Notes of SIGGRAPH'91, ACM, August 1991, pages 229–257.

[10] Whitted, Turner. "An Improved Illumination Model for Shaded Display," *CACM*, 32(6), June 1980, pages 343–349.

Radioptimization — Goal Based Rendering

John K. Kawai
Department of Computer Science
University of Utah

James S. Painter
Department of Computer Science
University of Utah

Michael F. Cohen
Department of Computer Science
Princeton University

Abstract

This paper presents a method for *designing* the illumination in an environment using optimization techniques applied to a radiosity based image synthesis system. An optimization of lighting parameters is performed based on user specified constraints and objectives for the illumination of the environment. The *Radioptimization* system solves for the "best" possible settings for: light source emissivities, element reflectivities, and spotlight directionality parameters so that the design goals, such as to minimize energy or to give the room an impression of "privacy", are met. The system absorbs much of the burden for searching the design space allowing the user to focus on the goals of the illumination design rather than the intricate details of a complete lighting specification.

The system employs an object space perceptual model based on work by Tumblin and Rushmeier to account for psychophysical effects such as subjective brightness and the visual adaptation level of a viewer. This provides a higher fidelity when comparing the illumination in a computer simulated environment against what would be viewed in the "real" world. Optimization criteria are based on subjective impressions of illumination with qualities such as "pleasantness", and "privateness". The qualities were selected based on Flynn's work in illuminating engineering. These criteria were applied to the radiosity context through an experiment conducted with subjects viewing rendered images, and the respondents evaluated with a Multi-Dimensional Scaling analysis.

1 Introduction

Historically, lighting design has been a black art. The lighting designer first received a design specification of the customer's expectations and of the room's function. The designer then made a lighting lay out and from experience would sketch what the room would look like from rough lighting calculations. With the advent of computer aided rendering, this process has been simplified allowing the designer to model lighting specifications with a CAD system and have it simulate the lighting calculations giving the designer a quick design check of what the room would look like. This also provides the customer who has no experience with lighting units a realistic preview of the finished room early in the design cycle [16]. Progress in rendering to date has mainly focused on improving the realism of the physical simulation and the development of algorithms with faster performance. Although great advances have been made in these areas, little work has been done on addressing the design problems in creating better quality lighting, except for a few systems that determine lighting placement by indicating desired areas of highlights and/or shadow [12].

Lighting designers base their art on the belief that spatial lighting patterns are a visual communicative medium, in which some patterns of light suggest or reinforce shared attitudes and impressions to people of the same cultural background [5]. In addition, the designer must be aware of the need to conserve the electrical energy used in implementing their designs. An over-reaction to the wasteful energy consumption of the 1960s and 1970s often led to buildings which were inadequately lit for their designed purposes, hampering the productivity of the residents. A better balance of goals between energy conservation and the quality of the lighting is needed [10].

This paper proposes a goal based illumination design approach, that has been termed *Radioptimization*, to help a lighting designer search the space of possible lighting specifications. Though computers will never replace artists, the system may generate configurations not previous considered or optimize on an already considered configuration. The approach allows the designer to concentrate on high level goals such as "visual clarity" and specify constraints such as minimum lighting levels in specific locations. The system then determines optimal settings for the lighting parameters of the modeled environment by searching for the "best" possible settings for light source emissivities, surface reflectivities, and spotlight directionality. Unconstrained optimization techniques are employed in conjunction with classical radiosity [3, 2, 8] to simulate global illumination.

Creating an appropriate two-way link between the designer and the rendering system requires two important enhancements to basic rendering methods. First, since the designer is asked to iteratively evaluate the visual impression from a rendered image, the images must provide (as much as possible) a subjective match to a "real" environment. The work of Tumblin and Rushmeier [18] on the psycho-physical quantities of subjective brightness has been applied to map luminance values to brightness values to provide higher fidelity for comparing the illumination of a computer generated scene.

Secondly, the optimization objectives presented to the de-

© 1993 ACM-0-89791-601-8/93/008/0147 $01.50

signer are based on John Flynn's work [5] whose experiments allowed one to measure impressions of lighting patterns. To develop the objective functions, experiments were conducted with subjects viewing computer generated images to create a mapping from Flynn's criteria to quantifiable qualities in the radiosity simulations.

There are three bodies of technology and related literature that are central to the work reported here: numerical optimization, radiosity based image synthesis, and knowledge about human perception as it relates to subjective impressions of lighting and to subjective impressions from images presented on a CRT. We will briefly review each of these areas concentrating on the pertinent subtopics in each that relate directly to this work.

1.1 Optimization

The basic constrained optimization problem is to minimize the scalar quantity of an objective function of n system parameters while satisfying a set of constraints. Although this is a well researched area, to date there is no computational algorithm for optimization which will always find the global minimum of a general non-linear objective function.

Most methods for dealing with constraints transform the constrained problem to an (approximately) equivalent unconstrained optimization by either removing the constraints by explicitly solving for one optimization variable, or by adding a new function to the objective [14, 15]. In the simplest case a constraint can be transformed into a *penalty* function, which when added to the objective returns a high value on a constraint violation.

Once the constraints are removed or transformed, the problem reduces to finding a minimum of the objective. Most optimization methods are performed iteratively from a starting point, in the multidimensional search space. Local information about the value, gradient, and Hessian (matrix of second order partial derivatives) of the function is gathered and a search direction is selected to move the solution to a new guess. One such technique for selecting a search direction is Newton's Method which solves for a step direction as the inverse of the Hessian times the negative gradient, i.e, $\Delta \mathbf{X} = -(\nabla^2 f)^{-1} \cdot \nabla f$.

Although Newton's method can have great success, a number of Quasi-Newton methods have been developed to numerically approximate the Hessian from a series of gradients for applications where it is either inefficient or impossible to derive the Hessian directly. These include the Broyden-Fletcher-Goldfarb-Shanno (BFGS) method [13, 11], which due to non-linearities does a series of one dimensional line searches until it converges on a local minimum.

1.2 Radiosity

Radiosity methods simulate the illumination of Lambertian diffuse environments by deriving an energy balance equation. Discretizing the environment into a set of elements with an assumed functional form, typically a constant value, for the radiosity across the surface, the balance of energy between elements is defined as through a set of interdependent linear constraints in the form:

$$B_i = E_i + \rho_i \sum_{j=1}^{n} F_{i,j} B_j \qquad (1)$$

where B_i is the radiosity of element i, E_i is the emission of element i, ρ_i is the reflectivity of element i, and $F_{i,j}$ is the form factor from element i to element j.

The form factor is the fraction of light leaving one element (i) that arrives at another (j) and is given by:

$$F_{i,j} = \frac{1}{A_i} \int_{p_i \in A_i} \int_{p_j \in A_j} \delta(p_i, p_j) \frac{cos(\phi_i) cos(\phi_j)}{\pi r_{ij}^2} dA_i dA_j$$

where A_i and A_j are the area of the element surfaces, p_i and p_j are points on elements i and j respectively, $\delta(p_i, p_j)$ returns 1 if p_i and p_j are mutually visible and 0 otherwise, ϕ_i is the angle between the normal vector at p_i and the vector from p_i to p_j, ϕ_j is the angle between the normal vector at p_j and the vector from p_j to p_i, and r_{ij} is the distance from p_i to p_j. For an environment of n patches, equaton 1 can be expressed as a set of n simultaneous linear equations.

This system of equations can be solved numerically by "gathering" or "shooting" methods [3, 2]. The solution to this system yields the element radiosities, B_i, which can be projected from any view point onto the view plane for a final image. At first glance a direct solution to the radiosity equation appears to require at least $O(n^2)$ space and time, given n elements. Hanrahan *et al.* have shown, however, that an equivalent to the form factor matrix can be computed and stored in $O(n)$ space and time by exploiting the cohenerent structure of the matrix [8].

Directional lighting effects such as spotlights can be added to the radiosity equation by replacing the $cos(\phi_i)$ term in the form factor equation with a different distribution function:

$$F_{i,j} = \frac{1}{A_i} \int_{p_i \in A_i} \int_{p_j \in A_j} \delta(p_i, p_j) s(\phi_i) \frac{cos(\phi_j)}{\pi r_{ij}^2} dA_i dA_j$$

where $s(\phi_i)$ is the directionality distribution weight for the light source as a function of the angle between the direction vector of the light (element i) and the vector between the points p_i and p_j. Here we restrict ourselves to distributions of the form, $s_n(\phi) = w(n) \cos^n(\phi)$ for values $n >= 1$. It is useful to be able to change the beam width without affecting the total energy emitted by the light. This requires a normalization factor, $w(n)$, in the emission function s_n. The normalization factor $w(n)$ must be chosen so that the total energy emitted over the hemisphere is constant, independent of n, as the beam width is adjusted. The value of the constant is chosen so that $w(1) = 1$. That is, $\int_{\text{hemisphere}} s_n d\omega = \pi$, where $d\omega$ is the differential solid angle on the sphere. Carrying out the integration in spherical coordinates yields the normalization weight, $w(n) = (n+1)/2$.

1.3 Human Perception

1.3.1 Brightness

Brightness is a measure of the subjective sensation produced by visible light. Brightness, measured in units of brils, relates linearly to human visual response. For example, if two light sources are compared and one appears to be twice as bright as the other, the brightness of the first, in brils, will be twice that of the second.

The human eye is sensitive to a luminance range of approximately ten orders of magnitude. However, at any one time the eye can only detect a brightness range of 100 to 1 with good accuracy. The iris adjusts, limiting the amount of light entering the eye, in order to seek a state of equilibrium that is appropriate for the general brightness conditions. Tumblin and Rushmeier [18] studied work by Stevens [17] who theorized that the adaptation level of a scene can be estimated by the expected value (mean) of the log_{10} of the luminances visible on the retina, i.e., $EXP_{p \in retina}\{log_{10}(L(p))\}$ where $L(p)$ is the luminance at a point p on the retina. Miller *et al.* also theorized that differing adaptations of the eye result in a family of curves relating luminance and brightness values in the form, $log_{10}(P) = aa * log_{10}(L) + bb$ where P is the brightness value specified in *brils*, L is the luminance value specified in *nits*, bb is $-0.4(log_{10}(L_w))^2 + (-2.58 log_{10}(L_w)) + 2.02$, aa is $0.4 log_{10}(L_w) + 2.92$, and L_w is the white adapting luminance which can be approximated by the equation $log_{10}(L_w) = EXP\{log_{10}(L_i)\} + 0.84$.

This perceptual model accepts luminance values in units of *nits* which in photometric units are related to *lux* on a diffuse surface by, 1 lux = 1 nit / 10,000. Thus solving for brils in terms of an element radiosity of B lux yields:

$$P = 10^{aa * log_{10}(B/10{,}000) + bb} \tag{2}$$

Since the adaptation of the eye is affected only by what is visible to the retina, perceptual processing is usually done as a view dependent process in screen space. This assumes that the viewer adapts to a single view rather than to an entire environment. In practice, we are constantly moving our head and eyes to scan a room and hence adapt to the overall room lighting rather than to a single view. In our work we propose a view independent approach to lighting design, since the designer's goal is to optimize on the overall impression of a room rather than a particular view of the room. Therefore, the conversion from luminance units into perceptual units is performed in object space. Each element is considered to contribute to the adaptation proportional to its physical size. This neglects the view dependent effects of perspective foreshortening and occlusion but has the advantage that it yields view independent results. We have found that the object space, view independent, method gives results that are nearly identical to view dependent screen space methods for typical, single room, architectural models. In addition to the view independence, calculating perception in object space has the added advantage of faster performance if the number of elements is much smaller than the number of screen pixels.

1.3.2 Subjective Impressions of Illumination

In the 1970's, John Flynn published a series of articles [6, 4, 5], introducing a methodology with which to quantify parameters that elicit a shared human behavioral response and subjective impression. In particular, Flynn examined how non-uniform, peripheral, and bright lighting affects impressions of visual clarity, spaciousness, relaxation, and privacy. Flynn created six different light settings for a conference room and subjectively associated each room with a non-uniform, peripheral, and brightness value so that each room corresponded to a point in a 3 dimensional space of the different lighting characteristics. Flynn also associated a set of semantic differential (SD) rating scales such as large-small and spacious-cramped with each category of impression. Test subjects were then asked to make pair wise comparisons of the differences between each room from the set of SD rating scales where 0 meant no difference and 10 meant a large difference.

The data gathered resulted in a 6x6 symmetric dissimilarity matrix comparing the 6 rooms for each subject tested and each SD comparison made, *e.g.* large-small. The multidimensional scaling program INDSCAL [1, 7], was used to determine how each subjected weighted the non-uniformity, peripheral and brightness values in making each SD comparison. A weighting of each dimension for each subject was determined that best fit the data. The results showed a correlation between the room positions hypothesized by Flynn and the positions computed by INDSCAL, supporting Flynn's hypothesis that brightness, non-uniformity, and peripheral lighting reinforce particular impressions. In addition, there also was a correlation for the weights for each parameter among all the subjects, supporting the concept that particular lighting patterns elicit a shared impression. By this process, Flynn was not only able to demonstrate that there is a definite correlation between the measurable quantities (non-uniform, peripheral, and bright lighting) and the subjective impressions (visual clarity, spaciousness, and relaxation), but was able to quantify how much each of the measurable dimensions affects each subjective impression.

As described shortly, we have adapted this work through an additional level of experimentation in which subjects reported impressions from computer generated images.

2 Problem Formulation

To pose the illumination design task as a constrained optimization problem we must identify: the variables involved in the optimization process, the constraints that must be satisfied, and the objective function.

2.1 Optimization Variables

In a normal radiosity based renderer, the element radiosities B_i are the unknowns to be computed in terms of fixed material and light property parameters. In the optimization setting the material and light properties are no longer fixed and must also be considered as variables. Constraints may be imposed on any of these variables and the objective function may involve any or all of them.

In the illumination design problem the optimization variables are light source specification parameters (emissions, spotlight directions, spotlight focus), element radiosities, B_i, and element reflectivities, ρ_i. Two types of light sources are considered: diffusely emitting elements described by a single emissivity parameter E_i, and directional lights idealized as spotlights described by a position, direction, and a cos^n directional distribution. Light source positions are assumed to be fixed and only the direction and distribution pattern is allowed to change during optimization.

Every light source emission E_i, light direction vector $\mathbf{V}_i$, cosine distribution exponent n_i, element radiosity B_i and reflectivity ρ_i, has the potential to be a variable in the optimization problem. If all are treated explicitly as domain variables in the optimization an intractably large system will result. Fortunately, the B_i's can be eliminated by direct substitution of the radiosity equation, and typically only a small number of the elements will have variable emission, reflectivity or directionality parameters. These remaining variables are called the "free" variables of the optimization problem.

2.2 Constraints

Constraints fall into three categories.

Physical constraints specify the relationships between light emission and element radiosities that are dictated by the physics of light transport. The constraints are captured in the rendering equation [9]. We assume perfect diffuse surfaces and a discretized environment yielding the radiosity approximation given in equation 1.

Design goals are constraints provided by the user. These may be either equality or inequality constraints and may apply to a single element, or a conglomeration of elements. For example, the requirement that a particular element's radiosity is a given constant, $B_i = K$ for some constant K is an equality constraint on a single element that expresses a fixed radiosity for the element. Inequality constraints such as $K_{low} \leq B_i \leq K_{high}$ can also be specified (in essence two inequality constraints) requiring the radiosity of element i to stay within the bounds K_{low} and K_{high}.

Barrier constraints are hard bounds on the allowable ranges of the optimization variables that must be satisfied to insure that the model is physically realizable. For example, light emissions must remain positive and element reflectivities must remain in the range $0 <= \rho_i <= 1$. Barrier constraints are conceptually similar to inequality design goals. The main difference is that a barrier constraint *must* be satisfied in order to produce a valid model. Design goals are *desires* that need not be satisfied exactly.

2.3 Objective Function

In general, radioptimization problems are under-constrained. There may be an infinite number of possible solutions that satisfy the problem constraints. The *objective* function is used to select between the many possible solutions. The simplest, directly measurable objective is the minimization of energy, $f_{energy} = \sum_i B_i A_i$.

In theory, any user specified function of the optimization variables could be used as an objective function. An alternative is to provide a fixed library of objective functions and allow the user to construct an objective function via linear combinations of the library functions. Each individual objective function in the library has a well defined and intuitive behavior. The user can then control the weights of the individual objectives to determine the final objective function. This allows user control without an undo amount of complexity.

A variation of Flynn's work, described in the previous section, was used to develop a way of quantifying subjective impressions. Flynn's experiment was duplicated except, instead of having the subjects judge actual rooms with different lighting characteristics, they were shown rendered images of an identical room with different light patterns (see figure 4). Once the data set was collected, it was processed by INDSCAL with the brightness, non-uniform, and peripheral values for each room computed by the following functions:

$$f_{brightness}(P, A) = -\frac{\sum_{i\in\chi} P_i A_i}{\sum_{i\in\chi} A_i}$$

$$f_{non-uniform}(P, A) = -\left(\frac{\sum_{i\in\psi}(P_{avg,i}-P_i)^2 A_i}{\sum_{i\in\psi} A_i)}\right)^{\frac{1}{2}}$$

$$f_{peripheral}(P, A) = \frac{\sum_{i\in\mu} P_i A_i}{\sum_{i\in\mu} A_i} - \frac{\sum_{i\in\psi} P_i A_i}{\sum_{i\in\psi} A_i}$$

where χ is the set of all elements in the environment, ψ is the set of elements that make up the walls, μ is the set of all horizontally oriented elements, P_i is the brightness of element i, A_i is the area of element i, and $P_{avg,i}$ is the average brightness of the elements around element i. The functions are defined in terms of perceptual values because humans subjectively quantify illumination by brightness not by actual luminance.

The results from INDSCAL showed that there was a correlation among those tested in the relationship between the measurable quantities, brightness, non-uniform, and peripheral lighting, and the subjective impressions of visual clarity, privacy, and pleasantness. A linear transformation was fit to the INDSCAL data resulting in linear relationships between the subjective impressions and the measured values:

$$\begin{aligned} f_{clear} &= 0.90 \cdot f_{brightness} - 0.38 \cdot f_{non-uniform} - \\ &\quad 0.58 \cdot f_{peripheral} \\ f_{pleasant} &= 0.78 \cdot f_{brightness} - 0.53 \cdot f_{non-uniform} + \\ &\quad 0.24 \cdot f_{peripheral} \\ f_{private} &= 0.90 \cdot f_{brightness} + 0.32 \cdot f_{non-uniform} - \\ &\quad 0.09 \cdot f_{peripheral} \end{aligned}$$

2.4 Conversion of the Constrained Problem to an Unconstrained Problem

The design goal constraints can be included in the objective function through the *penalty method* [11] by penalizing deviations from constraints through explicit terms in the objective function. The penalty imposed on the objective is defined as the square of the constraint violation. For example, if the jth constraint, C_j, is an equality constraint specifying a particular radiosity[1] to be a given constant, $(B_{i_j} = K_j)$, this will result in a penalty term f_{C_j} in the cost function given by $f_{C_j} = A_{i_j}(K_j - B_{i_j})^2$. Inequality constraints can be handled through a penalty function that "turns on" when the constraint is not satisfied. For example, the inequality constraint C_j given by $(B_{i_j} < K_j)$ results in a penalty term $f_{C_j} = A_{i_j}(K_j - B_{i_j})^2$ when B_{i_j} is greater than K_j and is zero otherwise.

Barrier Constraints are handled in a similar fashion to impose hard physical restrictions on certain values, for example, the emission variables must always remain positive. Similarly, reflectivities must remain between 0 and 1. A barrier term is added to the objective function for each barrier constraint to avoid violations of these constraints. The barrier constraint G_j given by $(X_j > K_j)$ for some free variable X_j results in a barrier term $f_{G_j} = (X_j - K_j)^{-4}$ for $X_j > K_j$. In addition, the optimization search explicitly enforces the constraint $(X_j > K_j)$ by clamping the X_j to $K_j + \epsilon$ when X_j drops below K_j, where ϵ is a small positive constant. This will yield a large barrier term in the objective function tending to lead the search away from the barrier in the next iteration.

The remaining constraints are the "physical constraints" specified by the radiosity equation (equation 1). These are dealt with by direct substitution. The radiosity equation implicitly defines each B_i in terms of all the $E, \mathbf{V}, n$ and ρ's. The B_i's are calculated via a radiosity solution algorithm [8]. The values for the P_i's can then be computed directly from the B_i's by equation 2. The B_i and P_i values can be directly substituted into the objective function. This effectively eliminates all the B_i's and P_i's from the set of optimization domain variables.

Thus the modified optimization problem is given by:

[1] B_{i_j} indicates the radiosity of the ith element, where i was selected by the jth constraint, C_j.

$$
\begin{array}{rllr}
f(\mathbf{X}) = & W_{energy} & f_{energy} & + \\
& W_{brightness} & f_{brightness} & + \\
& W_{non-uniform} & f_{non-uniform} & + \\
& W_{peripheral} & f_{peripheral} & + \\
& W_{clear} & f_{clear} & + \\
& W_{pleasant} & f_{pleasant} & + \\
& W_{private} & f_{private} & + \\
& W_{designgoals} & \sum_j f_{C_j} & + \\
& & \sum_j f_{G_j} &
\end{array} \quad (3)
$$

where $\mathbf{X}$ is a point in the multidimensional space spanned by the remaining free variables, E_i, $\mathbf{V}_i$, n_i, and ρ_i.

Through the use of the penalty method, barrier functions, and substitution of physics constraints, the optimization problem can now be stated as a simple unconstrained, multidimensional minimization problem. Let $\mathbf{X}$ be a multidimensional vector in the "design space", the space spanned by the free variables in the design. We must identify a point in the design space, $\mathbf{X}^\star$, such that the objective function $f(\mathbf{X}^\star)$ is (at least locally) minimized. There are many solution methods for such a minimization problem. We use the well known BFGS method described above [13].

3 Implementation

The user provides an initial model that is rendered to provide a baseline rendering. The user can select elements interactively from an image generated from the baseline solution to specify the free variables in the optimization process. The user can also specify the objective function weights $W_{energy}, W_{brightness}, W_{non-uniform}$, etc. to direct the optimization process. After all the design goals and objective weights are specified, the optimization process is run until convergence is achieved.

This process can be described in Pseudo code by:

Compute baseline rendering.
Establish constraints and objectives.
REPEAT
  Evaluate partial derivatives.
  Compute search direction $\Delta\mathbf{X}$ *using BFGS.*
  Perform line search in the direction $\Delta\mathbf{X}$.
  Display results, and allow user to modify constraints and objectives
UNTIL convergence.

3.1 Baseline rendering

The initial model is rendered and displayed by the hierarchical radiosity solution algorithm of Hanrahan *et al.* [8]. During baseline rendering, the input model is subdivided into a hierarchical structure and links are established between nodes in the hierarchy to establish the block structured form factor matrix as described in [8].

3.2 Establishing Constraints and Objectives

Once an image is displayed the user can select elements directly from the screen with the mouse and set constraints via the user interface shown in figure 5. In this example, the desk top has been selected as indicated by the green outline. Current illumination information for the selected element is displayed in the lower right corner of the interface. Through a set of buttons in the interface, the user can elect to impose a constraint on the element radiosity, and/or specify that the element reflectivity or emission should be a free variable in the optimization process. Spot lights are handled with a similar interface that allows the light direction vector and/or distribution parameter n to be marked as free variables in the optimization. The objective function weights can also be adjusted with slider bars in this interface.

3.3 Partial Derivative Estimation

Evaluation of partial derivatives of the modified objective with respect to each free variables is required by the optimization process. For example, to compute the partial derivative of the objective function with respect to a light emission, E_k, we must evaluate:

$$
\begin{array}{rllr}
\partial f/\partial E_k = & W_{energy} & \sum_j \partial E_j/\partial E_k \; A_j & + \\
& W_{brightness} & \partial f_{brightness}/\partial E_k & + \\
& W_{non-uniform} & \partial f_{non-uniform}/\partial E_k & + \\
& W_{peripheral} & \partial f_{peripheral}/\partial E_k & + \\
& W_{clear} & \partial f_{clear}/\partial E_k & + \\
& W_{pleasant} & \partial f_{pleasant}/\partial E_k & + \\
& W_{private} & \partial f_{private}/\partial E_k & + \\
& W_{design} & \partial \sum_j f_{C_j}/\partial E_k & + \\
& & \partial \sum_j f_{G_j}/\partial E_k &
\end{array} \quad (4)
$$

The partial derivative of the constraint function f_{C_j} for an equality constraint $C_j : (B_{i_j} = K_j)$ is: $\frac{\partial f_{C_j}}{\partial E_k} = -2A_{i_j} \cdot (K_j - B_{i_j})\frac{\partial B_{i_j}}{\partial E_k}$. For an inequality constraint, the partial $\partial f_{C_j}/\partial E_k$ is zero when the constraint is satisfied and is given by the above equation otherwise. The partial of a barrier function f_{G_j} can also be expressed directly as: $\frac{\partial f_{G_j}}{\partial E_k} = -4(E_j - G_j)^{-5}\frac{\partial E_j}{\partial E_k}$.

The partials of the form $\partial E_j/\partial E_k$ are 1 if $j = k$ and zero otherwise. The partials in the form $\partial B_j/\partial E_k$ represent the "influence" that the free variable E_k has on each element radiosity B_j. These *influence factors* are equivalent to entries in the inverse of the form factor matrix. Once the influence factors are known, the scene can be rerendered with new light source emissivities without resolving the radiosity equations. Besides providing the partial derivatives necessary for the optimization process, explicit storage of the influence factors also allows interactive, near real time, user adjustments to the lighting.

Rather than perform an explicit inversion of the block structured system, the partial derivatives can be estimated

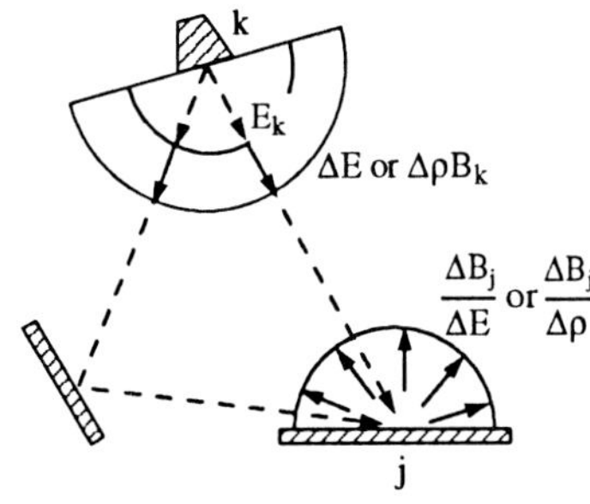

Figure 1: Estimation of $\partial B_j/\partial E_k$ or $\partial B_j/\partial\rho_k$ by shooting a delta emission from source k.

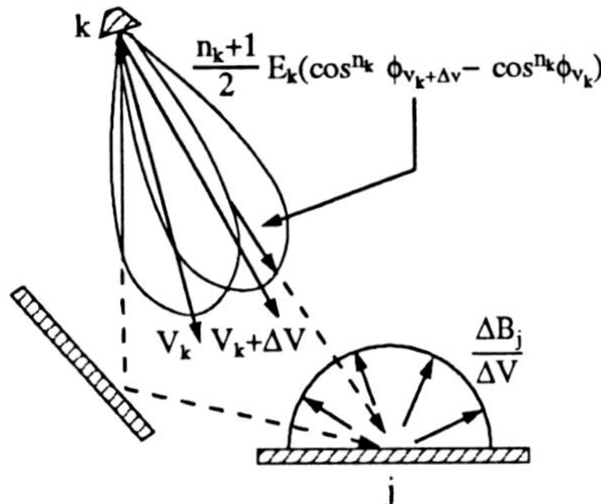

Figure 2: Estimation of $\partial B_j/\partial \mathbf{V}_k$ by shooting a delta emission from source k.

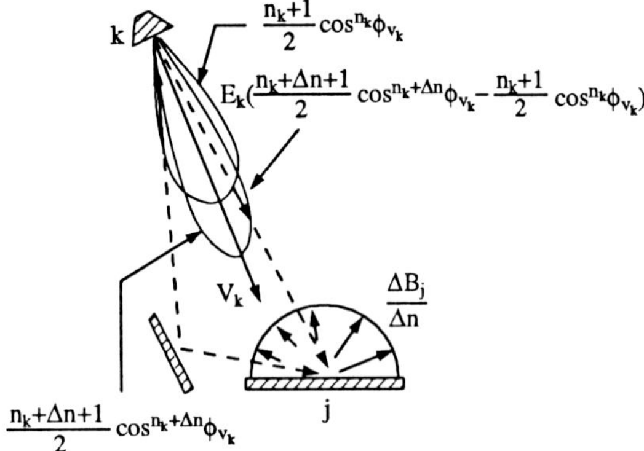

Figure 3: Estimation of $\partial B_j/\partial n_k$ by shooting a delta emission from source k.

by finite differences. A small "delta" emission, ΔE, is shot from the variable emission light source as indicated in figure 1 and allowed to interreflect. The iterative shooting operations are very rapid since the links representing the form factors are precomputed during the baseline rendering.

The result of shooting a small amount of energy through the network of links results in an effect on each element radiosity, ΔB_j, thus providing all the derivative estimates $\Delta B_j/\Delta E$. If the only free variables in the optimization are light emissions, these influence factors need only be evaluated once, due to linearity. On the other hand, if any spotlight directionality or element reflectance is allowed to be variable, light emission influence factors must be updated each iteration.

The partial derivative of the objective with respect to a variable element reflectivity is handled in a similar fashion. The element reflectivity ρ_k is adjusted by a small delta $\Delta\rho$. The effect on all other elements can be evaluated by "shooting" the unshot radiosity due to the change in reflectivity: $B_k\Delta\rho$. As with light sources, several shooting iterations may be necessary to account for multiple bounce effects. Once convergence has been achieved, the effect of $\Delta\rho$ on element radiosity ΔB_j is available and the influence factor estimate $\Delta B_j/\Delta\rho$ can be recorded.

Influence factors for spotlight directionality variables, $\mathbf{V}_k$ and n_k, are also approximated through finite differences. For example, a small change, $\Delta\mathbf{V}$, can be made to the direction vector $\mathbf{V}_k$ and the effect on each element radiosity can be determined by a series of shooting steps. The first shooting step, illustrated in figure 2, shoots a delta emission from the modified spotlight to all other elements. The delta emission is determined according to the change in the directionality parameter, in this case, $E_k\frac{(n_k+1)}{2}(cos^{n_k}(\phi_{v_k+\Delta v}) - cos^{n_k}(\phi_{v_k}))$ where ϕ_{v_k} is the angle between the original direction vector of the light and the direction of the element and $\phi_{v_k+\Delta v}$ is the angle between the *new* spotlight direction vector and the direction of the element. Subsequent shooting steps proceed in the normal fashion in order to handle multiple bounce effects. The same technique can be used when the distribution pattern parameter n_k is changed as illustrated in figure 3. In this case the radiosity cast is $E_k(\frac{(n_k+\Delta n+1)}{2}cos^{n_k}(\phi_{v_k}) - \frac{(n_k+1)}{2}cos^{n_k}(\phi_{v_k}))$.

The cost functions that measure patterns of light or subjective impressions are defined in terms of perception. The partial derivatives of the functions examining lighting patterns with respect to light emission E_k are:

$$\frac{\partial f_{brightness}}{\partial E_k} = -\frac{\sum_i \frac{\partial P_i}{\partial E_i} A_i}{\sum_i A_i}$$

$$\frac{\partial f_{non-uniform}}{\partial E_k} = -\left[\frac{\sum_i (P_{avg,i} - P_i)^2 A_i}{\sum_i A_i}\right]^{-\frac{1}{2}} * \left[\frac{\sum_i (P_{avg,i} - P_i)\left(\frac{\partial P_{avg,i}}{\partial E_k} - \frac{\partial P_i}{\partial E_k}\right)}{\sum_i A_i}\right]$$

$$\frac{\partial f_{peripheral}}{\partial E_k} = \left[\frac{\sum_i \frac{\partial P_i}{\partial E_k} A_i}{\sum_i A_i} - \frac{\sum_j \frac{\partial P_j}{\partial E_k} A_j}{\sum_j A_j}\right]$$

The partials of the subjective impressions are just a linear combination of the partial derivatives of $f_{brightness}$, $f_{non-uniform}$, and $f_{peripheral}$.

The partials $\partial P_j/\partial E_k$ are derived by differentiating equation 2 giving,

$$\frac{\partial P_j}{\partial E_k} = 10^{\gamma}\left[\frac{aa}{B_j}\frac{\partial B_j}{\partial E_k} + \frac{\partial \alpha}{\partial E_k}\zeta\right] \quad (5)$$

where α is the adaption level which can be approximated by $(\sum_i log_{10}(B_i/10,000)A_i)/\sum_i A_i$, γ is $aa * log_{10}(B_i/10,000) + bb$, and ζ is $0.4log_{10}(B_i/10,000) - ln(10)(0.8\alpha + 2.6)$.

If the the adaptation level is assumed constant with respect to a change in emission E_k, $\partial\alpha/\partial E_k = 0$, otherwise

$$\frac{\partial \alpha}{\partial E_k} = \frac{A_j}{B_j ln(10)\sum_i(A_i)}\frac{\partial B_j}{\partial E_k}$$

3.4 Optimization

The optimization process uses the BFGS algorithm, which evaluates the objective function and gradient at a current step in the design space in order to compute a search direction. Once a search direction is derived, a line search is performed in this direction. Each step in the line search involves a reevaluation of the objective function, hence a reevaluation of the element radiosities which are displayed, allowing the user to watch the progress of the optimization. This process is repeated until the system has converged to a minimum.

4 Experiences and Results

The first implementation of the Radioptimization system allowed an objective function based only on photometric measures and did not take into account the psychophysical properties of lighting. The system could successfully optimize lighting but required quite a bit of unintuitive "tweaking" of the objective function weights in order to achieve lighting that had the right subjective appearance. These early experiences led to the investigation of the psychophysical objective functions.

Figure 6 shows the effects that the subjective impressions have on an optimization. The top image constrains the table to have a small amount of illumination while conserving energy and creating an overall impression of visual clarity. To improve efficiency the optimization was run at a low resolution on a simplified model, without the chairs and television set. The optimization process took 1 minute and 21 seconds on an IBM Model 550 RISC System 6000. The bottom image has the same design goals as the top image except that it tries to elicit an impression of privateness. This optimization took 2 minutes and 11 seconds.

It took two or three hours of performing design iterations before developing an intuitive "feel" for the optimization process and the effects of the weights on the objective function. One of the problems with the design cycle is that there may be local minima of the specified objective that are visually unattractive. For example, in addition to the design goals mentioned above for figure 6, we needed to add an additional constraint limiting the illumination of the ceiling because pointing the lights directly at the ceiling was an optimal way of increasing the overall brightness of the room.

One drawback of the system at this point is that it is not fast enough to allow a highly interactive feedback cycle for complex models. However since the system allows a designer to think in terms of their own design goals, it requires fewer design iterations to achieve the desired result.

5 Conclusions

This paper has presented a new method of designing illumination in a computer simulated environment, based on goal directed modeling. A library of functions were developed that approximate a room's success in meeting certain lighting design goals such as minimizing energy or evoking an impression of privacy. The objective functions were developed through an experiment in which subjects ordered a set of images according to a particular impression. Processing this data with INDSCAL, showed a correlation between quantitative lighting patterns and subjective measures of visually clarity, pleasantness, and privacy. Once the lighting design goals have been set, the software system searches the space of lighting configurations for the illumination pattern that "best" meets the design specifications. The system absorbs much of the burden for searching the design space allowing the user to focus on the goals of the illumination design rather than the intricate details of a complete illumination specification.

The radioptimization system explores only one possible path in the application of optimization techniques to image synthesis design problems. Constrained optimization techniques may be more suitable than the unconstrained penalty method technique used here when the design goals must be satisfied precisely. Discrete optimization methods may be appropriate in some instances, for example when emissivities are constrained to a finite set, *e.g.* {60 Watts , 100 Watts , ⋯}. Geometric properties of the model, such as the position of the lights or the size and position of the windows, could be allowed as free variables. More general image synthesis methods could be applied to account for non-diffuse effects such as glare.

Acknowledgments

Pat Hanrahan, Larry Aupperle and David Salzman provided the radiosity software used as a basis for this work. Greg Ward offered suggestions on useful objective functions for lighting design. Shinichi Kasahara participated in discussions about the work as it developed.

The first and second author's work was supported by NFS (CCR-9210587). All opinions, findings, conclusions, or recommendations expressed in this document are those of the authors and do not necessarily reflect the views of the sponsoring agencies.

References

[1] J. J. Chang and J. D. Carroll. How to use INDSCAL: a computer program for canonical decomposition of N-way tables and individual differences in multidimensional scaling. Technical report, Bell Telephone Laboratories, 1972.

[2] M. F. Cohen, S. E. Chen, J. R. Wallace, and D. P. Greenberg. A progressive refinement approach to fast radiosity image generation. *Computer Graphics (SIGGRAPH '88 Proceedings)*, 22(4):75–82, July 1988.

[3] M. F. Cohen and D. P. Greenberg. The hemi-cube: A radiosity for complex environments. *Computer Graphics (SIGGRAPH '85 Proceedings)*, 19(3):31–40, July 1985.

[4] J. E. Flynn. A study of subjective responses to low energy and nonuniform lighting systems. *Lighting Design and Application*, Feb. 1977.

[5] J. E. Flynn, C. Hendrick, T. J. Spencer, and O. Martyniuk. A guide to methodology procedures for measuring subjective impressions in lighting. *Journal of the IES*, Jan. 1979.

[6] J. E. Flynn, T. J. Spencer, O. Martyniuk, and C. Hendrick. Interim study of procedures for investigating the effect of light on impression and behavior. *Journal of the IES*, Oct. 1973.

[7] P. E. Green, F. J. Carmone, Jr., and S. M. Smith. *Multidimensional Scaling Concepts and Applications.* Smith, Allyn, and Bacon, 1989.

[8] P. Hanrahan, D. Salzman, and L. Aupperle. A Rapid Hierarchical Radiosity Algorithm. *Computer Graphics (SIGGRAPH '91 Proceedings)*, 25(4):197–206, July 1991.

[9] J. T. Kajiya. The rendering equation. *Computer Graphics (SIGGRAPH '86 Proceedings)*, 20(4):143–150, Aug. 1986.

[10] H. N. McKay. Energy optimization and quality lighting design. *Lighting Design and Application*, Mar. 1986.

[11] P. Y. Papalambros and D. J. Wilde. *Principles of Optimal Design.* Cambridge University Press, Cambridge, England, 1988.

[12] P. Poulin and A. Fournier. Lights from highlights and shadows. *1992 Symposium on Interactive 3D Graphics*, pages 31–38, Mar. 1992.

[13] W. H. Press, B. P. Flannery, S. A. Teukolsky, and W. T. Vetterling. *Numerical Recipes*. Cambridge University Press, New York, 1986.

[14] J. B. Rosen. The gradient projection method for nonlinear programming, part i: Linear constraints. *SIAM*, 8:181–217, 1960.

[15] J. B. Rosen. The gradient projection method for nonlinear programming, part ii: Non-linear constraints. *SIAM*, 9:514–532, 1961.

[16] P. C. Sorcar. *Architectural Lighting for Commercial Interiors*. John Wiley and Sons Inc., 1987.

[17] S. S. Stevens and J. C. Stevens. Brightness function: Effects of adaptation. *Journal of the Optical Society of America*, 53(3), Mar. 1963.

[18] J. Tumblin and H. Rushmeier. Tone reproductions for realistic computer generated images. Technical Report GIT-GVU-91-13, Graphics, Visualization, and Usability Center, Georgia Institute of Technology, July 1991.

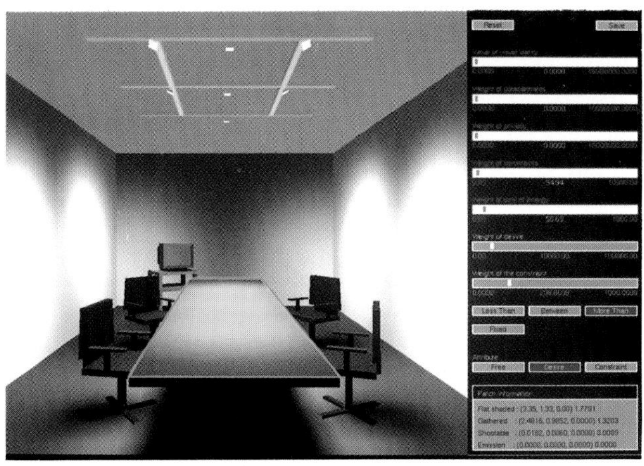

Figure 5: Sample interface which allows the user to set the weights of the objective and/or specify constraints.

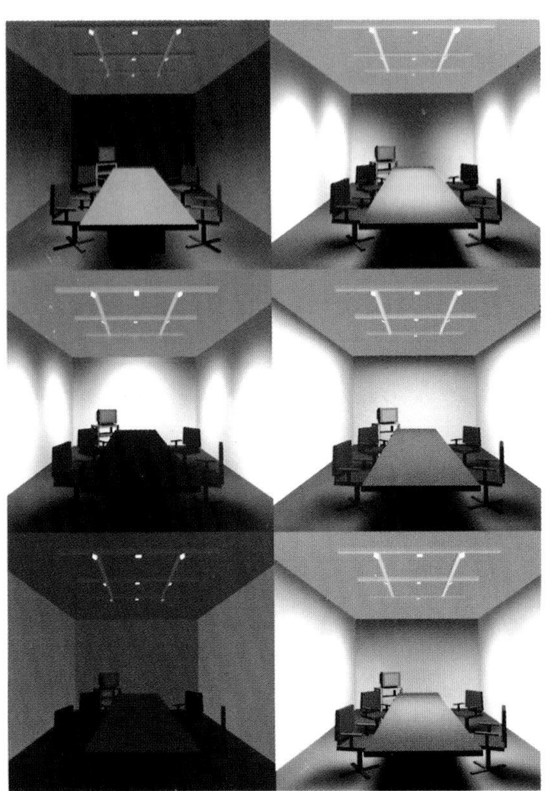

Figure 4: Computer generated rooms used to test subjects on which illumination patterns illicit particular subjective impressions.

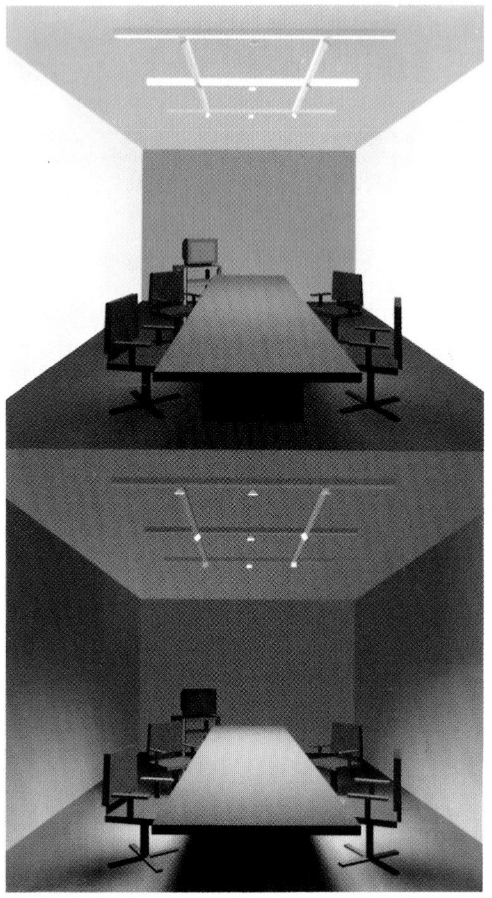

Figure 6: The top image constrains the table to have a small amount of illumination while preserving energy and creating an overall impression of visual clarity. The bottom image also constrains the table to have a small amount of illumination while preserving energy. In addition, it trys to create a feeling of privacy.

A Hierarchical Illumination Algorithm for Surfaces with Glossy Reflection

Larry Aupperle   Pat Hanrahan

Department of Computer Science
Princeton University

Abstract

We develop a radiance formulation for discrete three point transport, and a new measure and description of reflectance: *area reflectance*. This formulation and associated reflectance allow an estimate of error in the computation of radiance across triples of surface elements, and lead directly to a hierarchical refinement algorithm for global illumination.

We have implemented and analyzed this algorithm over surfaces exhibiting glossy specular and diffuse reflection. Theoretical growth in light transport computation is shown to be $O(n+k^3)$ for sufficient refinement, where n is the number of elements at the finest level of subdivision over an environment consisting of k input polygonal patches — this growth is exhibited in experimental trials. Naive application of three point transport would require computation over $O(n^3)$ element-triple interactions.

CR Categories and Subject Descriptors: I.3.7 [Computer Graphics]: Three-Dimensional Graphics and Realism.

Key Words: adaptive meshing, global illumination, radiosity, ray tracing.

1 Introduction

A major open problem in image synthesis is the efficient solution of the rendering equation. Radiosity methods have been quite successful over environments containing surfaces that exhibit only diffuse reflection. Unfortunately, very few materials are purely Lambertian reflectors, and efficient solution techniques have not yet been developed for more general specular or glossy reflection functions.

The rendering equation is an integral equation, and the solutions to complicated integral equations are generally obtained using either Monte Carlo or finite element techniques. Monte Carlo algorithms sometimes go under the name of distributed or stochastic ray tracing and are the most commonly employed in computer graphics (e.g. see [4, 5, 9, 12, 16]). Monte Carlo techniques have the advantage that they are easy to implement and can be used for complicated geometries and reflection functions. Unfortunately, their disadvantage is that they are notoriously inefficient. The second approach, the finite element method, has been very successfully applied to the rendering equation under the radiosity assumption, but has only begun to be employed in the general case, and with limited success. For example, Immel et al. [8] discretized radiance into a lattice of cubical environment maps, and solved the resulting system. More recently, Sillion et al. [13] used a mesh of spherical harmonic functions to represent radiance, and solved the resulting system using a shooting algorithm.

There are many ways to parameterize the rendering equation, and each leads to a different choice of basis functions. In the transport theory community two techniques are common: directional subdivision (the method of discrete ordinates or S_N), and spherical harmonics (P_N). These two techniques roughly correspond to the methods of Immel et al. and Sillion et al., although many interesting variations are possible. Our approach is somewhat different, and based on Kajiya's original formulation of the rendering equation [9]. Under this formulation, the rendering equation is expressed in terms of three point transport. That is, the kernel of the integral expresses the transport of light from a point on the source to a point on the receiver, via a point on a reflector. Given this formulation, the three point rendering equation can be discretized over pairs of elements to form a linear system of equations. Solving this system yields the radiance transported between elements. Note that this approach is very similar to the radiosity formulation.

The problem with finite element methods is that the matrix of interactions is very large for interesting environments. For a given environment of k input polygonal patches containing n elements at the finest level of refinement, the three point discretization that we are proposing generates an n^3 matrix of interactions. However, in this paper we show that we can accurately approximate the n^3 reflectance matrix with $O(n+k^3)$ blocks, in a way very similar to our recent hierarchical radiosity algorithm [7]. In that paper we showed how the n^2 form factor matrix could be approximated with $O(n+k^2)$ blocks, resulting in a very efficient algorithm in both space and time. Although the results presented in this paper are preliminary, we believe a hierarchical finite element approach along these lines will ultimately lead to a fast, efficient algorithm.

In the following section we describe our application of the finite element element method to the three point rendering equation, yielding a radiance formulation for discrete transport. In Section 3 we present a simple adaptive refinement algorithm for computation over this formulation, and the iterative solution technique employed for the actual calculation of transport. In Section 4 we discuss our implementation of the algorithm over glossy reflection, and in Section 5 we present some experiments and results. An appendix to this paper contains details of our error analysis for discrete transport under the glossy model.

2 Discrete Three Point Transport

The algorithm presented in this paper operates through two functions: refinement of the environment to form a hierarchy of discrete interactions, patches and elements, and the actual computation of illumination over this hierarchy.

In this section we develop the basis for both discretization and transport. We derive a radiance formulation for three point transport, and a new measure and description of reflectance, *area reflectance*. This radiance formulation and associated reflectance provide a natural criterion for discretization under illumination and reflection, and allow both the computation of radiance across triples of individual surface elements, and the expression and computation of all light transport over all surfaces.

 ACM-0-89791-601-8/93/008/0155 $01.50

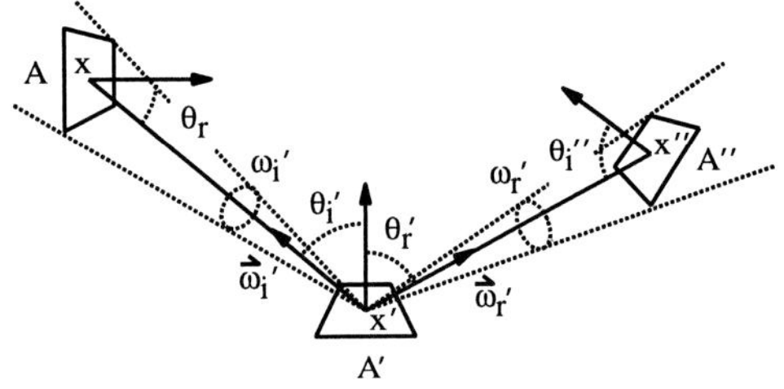

Figure 1: Geometry of Reflection

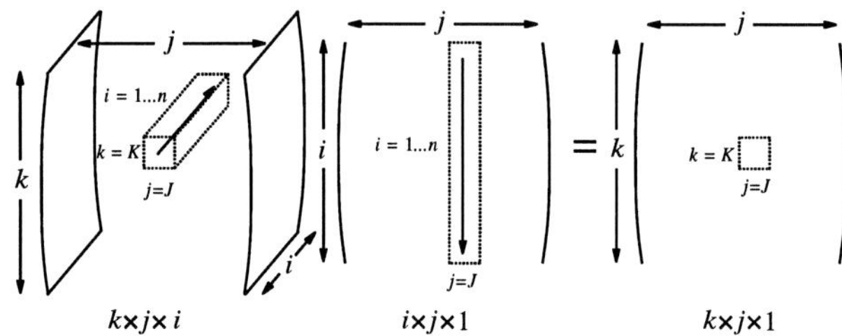

Figure 2: A Reflection Product

2.1 A Radiance Formulation for Three Point Transport

When computing and imaging illumination within an environment, we are interested in the transport of light from surface to surface — it is this interaction of surfaces that characterizes illumination, in the absence of participatory media. Reflection within an environment may thus be naturally expressed over triples of surfaces. Consider surfaces A, A', and A'' (Figure 1) — we will examine the transport of light incident at A' originating at A and reflected toward A''.

Let ω_i' and ω_r' be the solid angles subtended at point x' by A and A'', respectively. Consider differential solid angles at $\vec{\omega}_i'$ and $\vec{\omega}_r'$ — by definition of the bidirectional reflectance-distribution function (BRDF), f_r [11], the radiance $L(\vec{\omega}_r')$ along $\vec{\omega}_r'$ due to illumination through solid angle ω_i' is:

$$L(\vec{\omega}_r') = \int_{\omega_i'} f_r(\vec{\omega}_i', \vec{\omega}_r') L(\vec{\omega}_i') \cos\theta_i' d\omega_i'$$

Integrating this expression over ω_r', and introducing $\cos\theta_r'$, we have:

$$\int_{\omega_r'} L(\vec{\omega}_r') \cos\theta_r' d\omega_r' =$$
$$\int_{\omega_r'} \int_{\omega_i'} f_r(\vec{\omega}_i', \vec{\omega}_r') L(\vec{\omega}_i') \cos\theta_i' \cos\theta_r' d\omega_i' d\omega_r'$$

We may then reparameterize over A and A'' to yield:

$$\int_{A''} L(x', x'') G(x', x'') dx'' =$$
$$\int_A \int_{A''} f_r(x, x', x'') L(x, x') G(x, x') G(x', x'') dx'' dx$$

where

$$G(x, x') = \frac{\cos\theta_r \cos\theta_i'}{|x - x'|^2} v(x, x')$$

where $v(x, x')$ is 1 if points x, x', are mutually visible, and 0 otherwise. Note that G is very similar to a differential form factor.

We integrate over A', thus introducing all three areas into the formulation:

$$\int_{A'} \int_{A''} L(x', x'') G(x', x'') dx'' dx' = \tag{1}$$
$$\int_A \int_{A'} \int_{A''} f_r(x, x', x'') L(x, x') G(x, x') G(x', x'') dx'' dx' dx$$

We may now rewrite the equation in discrete form. Let A_j and A_k be subareas of A' and A'' such that $L(x', x'')$ is nearly constant over their surfaces. The left side of equation (1) may then be rewritten, bringing radiance out of the integral as L_{jk}:

$$L_{jk} \int_{A_j} \int_{A_k} G(x', x'') dx'' dx' = \pi L_{jk} A_j F_{jk}$$

by definition of the diffuse form factor, F_{jk}.

We may similarly discretize A as A_i, and rewrite the right side of equation (1) as:

$$L_{ij} \int_{A_i} \int_{A_j} \int_{A_k} f_r(x, x', x'') G(x, x') G(x', x'') dx'' dx' dx =$$
$$\sum_i \pi L_{ij} A_i F_{ij} R_{ijk}$$

where R_{ijk} is defined such that

$$\pi A_i F_{ij} R_{ijk} =$$
$$\int_{A_i} \int_{A_j} \int_{A_k} f_r(x, x', x'') G(x, x') G(x', x'') dx'' dx' dx$$

Note that, by the symmetry of f_r and G:

$$A_i F_{ij} R_{ijk} = A_k F_{kj} R_{kji}$$

We thus have:

$$\begin{aligned} \pi L_{jk} A_j F_{jk} &= \pi \sum_i L_{ij} A_k F_{kj} R_{kji} \\ &= \pi \sum_i L_{ij} A_j F_{jk} R_{kji} \end{aligned}$$

by the reciprocity of form factors, and thus:

$$L_{jk} = \sum_i L_{ij} R_{kji}$$

The three dimensional character of R_{kji} over indices i, j, k leads naturally to a three dimensional matrix formulation for the above system. Consider a product over an $n \times n \times n$ R_{kji} "matrix" and an $n \times n \times 1$ L_{ij} matrix producing an $n \times n \times 1$ matrix of reflected radiances, as shown in Figure 2. Note that the R_{kji} matrix is of size $O(n^3)$ — the hierarchical method discussed in subsequent sections of this paper addresses more tractable representation of this matrix.

Taking into account emission, we have derived a radiance formulation for three point transport:

$$L_{jk} = E_{jk} + \sum_i L_{ij} R_{kji} \tag{2}$$

This formulation states that:

> *The radiance at Area j in the direction of Area k is equal to the radiance emitted by j in the direction of k, plus, for every Area i, the radiance at i in the direction of j multiplied by the area reflectance R_{kji}.*

Note that equation (2) is very similar to the radiosity formulation:

$$B_j = E_j + \rho_j \sum_i B_i F_{ji}$$

2.2 Area Reflectance

The quantity R_{kji} has a natural and satisfying physical significance — it is an expression of reflectance over areas A_i, A_j, and A_k.

Consider the fraction of the radiant flux transported from A_i incident to A_j that is reflected in the direction of area A_k:

$$\frac{\int_{A_i}\int_{A_j}\int_{A_k} f_r(x,x',x'')L(x,x')G(x,x')G(x',x'')dx''dx'dx}{\int_{A_i}\int_{A_j} L(x,x')G(x,x')dx'dx}$$

If we assume that incident radiance is uniform and isotropic over both ω_i' (as induced by A_i) and A_j, we may divide through by $L(x,x')$, yielding:

$$\rho(A_i,A_j,A_k) \equiv \frac{\int_{A_i}\int_{A_j}\int_{A_k} f_r(x,x',x'')G(x,x')G(x',x'')dx''dx'dx}{\int_{A_i}\int_{A_j} G(x,x')dx'dx}$$

We define $\rho(A_i,A_j,A_k)$ to be *area reflectance*. Note that area reflectance is similar to biconical reflectance [11], save that it is also integrated over the reflecting surface.

By definition of R_{ijk}:

$$R_{ijk} = \rho(A_i,A_j,A_k)$$

Conservation of energy over reflection, and the reciprocity relation derived for R_{ijk} above, constitute fundamental properties of area reflectance:

1. $\sum_k R_{ijk} \le 1$, for fixed i, j.
2. $A_i F_{ij} R_{ijk} = A_k F_{kj} R_{kji}$.

where equality is achieved in property 1 over complete enclosures and perfect reflectivity.

2.3 Evaluation of R_{kji}

In this section we examine the evaluation of R_{kji} over given patches A_i, A_j, A_k.

Recall:

$$R_{kji} = \frac{\int_{A_k}\int_{A_j}\int_{A_i} f_r(x'',x',x)G(x'',x')G(x',x)dx dx' dx''}{\int_{A_k}\int_{A_j} G(x'',x')dx'dx''}$$

We assume that discrete areas A_i, A_j, A_k are of small enough scale that f_r and G are relatively constant over their surfaces. Then:

$$\begin{aligned} R_{kji} &= \frac{S_{kji}G_{kj}G_{ji}A_kA_jA_i}{G_{kj}A_kA_j} \\ &= S_{kji}G_{ji}A_i \end{aligned}$$

where S is the discretized value of f_r, $S_{ijk} = S_{kji} = S_{x_k x_j x_i}$.

Note that the average value of $G(x',x)$ over A_i and A_j is $\pi F_{ji}/A_i$ — we thus estimate $G_{ji}A_i$ by πF_{ji}, and compute R_{kji} as:

$$R_{kji} = \pi F_{ji} S_{kji}$$

In practice, it will not be possible to compute the exact values of F_{ji} and S_{kji} over A_i, A_j, A_k. We assume that we are able to estimate these values, along with error bounds for each estimation. Let ΔF_{ji} and ΔS_{kji} be error estimates for computed F_{ji} and S_{kji}, respectively. We then have an estimate for area reflectance in the form:

$$\begin{aligned} R_{kji} &= \pi(F_{ji}+\Delta F_{ji})(S_{kji}+\Delta S_{kji}) \\ &= \pi(F_{ji}S_{kji}+\Delta F_{ji}S_{kji}+\Delta S_{kji}F_{ji}+\Delta F_{ji}\Delta S_{kji}) \\ &\approx \pi(F_{ji}S_{kji}+\Delta F_{ji}S_{kji}+\Delta S_{kji}F_{ji}) \end{aligned}$$

Assuming $\Delta F_{ji} < F_{ji}$, $\Delta S_{kji} < S_{kji}$, we have neglected the last term and estimate the error in R_{kji} as $\pi(\Delta F_{ji}S_{kji} + \Delta S_{kji}F_{ji})$.

In general, and as is shown for glossy reflection in Section 4, the accuracy of estimators for F_{ji} and S_{kji} is dependent on the size of the patches over which reflectance is computed, relative to their distance apart. As relative size decreases, so does error in computation, leading directly to the adaptive refinement strategy for illumination presented in Section 3 below.

3 Algorithms for Three Point Transport

3.1 Introduction

Recall equation (2):

$$L_{jk} = E_{jk} + \sum_i L_{ij} R_{kji}$$

This equation suggests both a solution strategy for radiance under three point transport, and a natural representation for illumination within the solution system.

We may interpret equation (2) as a gathering iteration similar to that employed for radiosity under diffuse reflection: the radiance L_{jk} at patch A_j in the direction of patch A_k is found by gathering radiances L_{ij} in the direction of A_j at patches A_i. We may solve for transport by gathering radiance for each L_{jk}, and successively iterating to capture all significant re-reflection.

We are left with the question of what structure we are gathering over and iterating upon. Note that all illumination is expressed as the radiance at a given patch in the direction of another — it is these patch-patch interactions that form the primary structure within the solution system. All operation is over interactions: both the representation and transport of radiance, and the iteration and solution for illumination.
Consider the following structure:

```
typedef struct _interaction {

    Patch *from;
    Patch *to;

    Color  L;
    Color  Lg;

    List   *gather;

    struct _interaction *nw, *sw, *se, *ne;

} Interaction;
```

A given interaction ij is defined by two patches `ij->from` and `ij->to`, and represents the radiance at `from` in the direction of `to`. This radiance is stored within the interaction as attribute `L`. `Lg` is radiance gathered during the current solution iteration from interactions contained in the list `gather`. Subinteractions `nw`, `sw`, `se`, `ne` are the children of ij, induced by subdivision over either `from` or `to`. The structure assumes quadtree refinement, leaving northwest, southwest, southeast, and northeast descendants.

In the following sections we will present an algorithm for the refinement and computation of illumination over a hierarchy of interactions. The algorithm will operate by refining pairs of interactions ij, jk (such that `ij->to == jk->from`), to ensure that computed reflectance across the interaction pairs, and associated patch triples, satisfies user specified error bounds. If a given interaction pair ij, jk is satisfactory, the interactions are linked to record that radiance may be gathered from ij to jk, otherwise one or both interactions are subdivided and refinement applied to their descendants.

After refinement, a gathering iteration may be carried out, each interaction gathering radiance from interactions to which it has been linked. The gathered radiances are then distributed within each receiving interaction hierarchy, and subsequent iterations computed until satisfactory convergence has been achieved.

Note that, within this system, the eye may be regarded as simply another object with which patches may interact. The radiance along interactions to the eye provides the resulting view.

3.2 Adaptive Refinement

Consider the following procedure:

```
Refine(Interaction *ij, Interaction *jk,
       float Feps, float Seps, float Aeps)
{
    float feps, seps;

    feps = GeometryErrorEstimate(ij);
    seps = ReflectionErrorEstimate(ij, jk);

    if (feps < Feps && seps < Seps)
        Link(ij, jk);

    else if (seps >= Seps) {

        switch(SubdivS(ij, jk, Aeps)) {

        case PATCH_I:

            Refine(ij->nw, jk, Seps, Feps, Aeps);
            Refine(ij->sw, jk, Seps, Feps, Aeps);
            Refine(ij->se, jk, Seps, Feps, Aeps);
            Refine(ij->ne, jk, Seps, Feps, Aeps);

            break;

        case PATCH_J:
            /* refine over children of ij and jk */
        case PATCH_K:
            /* refine over children of jk        */
        case NONE:
            Link(ij, jk);
        }
    }

    else {    /* feps >= Feps */

        switch(SubdivG(ij, jk, Aeps)) {

        /* refine over children, or link, as    */
        /* directed by PATCH_I, J, K, or NONE.  */

        }
    }
}
```

This procedure computes over pairs of interactions, and associated patch triples, subdividing and recursively refining if estimated error exceeds user specified bounds, linking the interactions for gathering if the bounds are satisfied, or if no further subdivision is possible. `Feps` and `Seps` are the bounds for geometric and reflection error, respectively; `Aeps` specifies the minimum area a patch may possess and still be subdivided. `GeometryErrorEstimate` and `ReflectionErrorEstimate` provide estimations for $\pi \Delta F_{ji} S_{kji}$ and $\pi \Delta S_{kji} F_{ji}$.

`SubdivS` and `SubdivG` control refinement for reflection and geometry error, respectively. Both routines select a patch for refinement, subdividing the patch and associated interaction(s) if required. An identifier for the selected patch is returned — if no patch may be subdivided, then `NONE` is passed back. Note that a given interaction/patch may be refined against many different interactions within the system, and thus may have already been subdivided when selected by a `Subdiv` routine — in this case, the routine simply returns the proper identifier.

The `Subdiv` routines should select for refinement patches that are of large size relative to their distance from their partner(s) in the transport triple. Form factor estimation is a convenient criterion for the determination of such patches — a large differential to area form factor F_{dpq} indicates that patch q is of large relative size. Care must be taken in subdivision, however, to ensure that each interaction is always subdivided in the same way for all refinements involving that interaction.

The `Subdiv` routines thus choose for refinement the patch of size at least `Aeps` that is of greatest form factor within ij and/or jk that will not induce multiple sets of children over either interaction. If patch p_j is of greatest form factor over both ij and jk, and of area greater than `Aeps`, then it is chosen for refinement (Figure 3 at middle). Otherwise, if p_j is selected over one interaction, but p_i or p_k is selected over the other, then the "outside" patch is chosen for refinement. Given two selected outside patches, `SubdivS` selects the one of greater form factor relative to p_j; `SubdivG` selects p_i over p_k, as p_k has no direct effect on geometric accuracy. Note, however, that even under `SubdivG`, if only p_j and p_k are allowed subdivision, p_k will be selected, although with further subdivision the triple will eventually balance sufficiently to allow refinement over p_j.

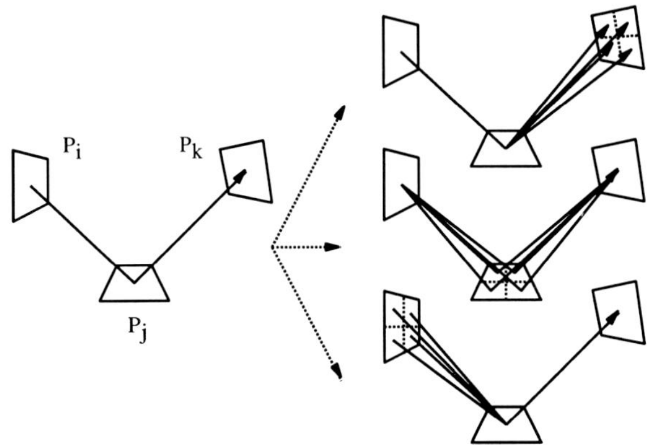

Figure 3: Refinement and Subdivision

3.3 Gathering Radiance

Gathering radiance over interactions may be written as a simple procedure:

```
Gather(Interaction *jk)
{
    Interaction *ij;

    if (jk) {

        jk->Lg = 0;

        ForAllElements(ij, jk->gather)
            jk->Lg += ij->L * Reflectance(ij, jk);

        Gather(jk->nw);
        Gather(jk->sw);
        Gather(jk->se);
        Gather(jk->ne);
    }
}
```

We gather radiance into `jk->Lg` rather than directly into `jk->L` to avoid the necessity of a push/pull with every invocation of the procedure (see Section 3.4). The solution method is thus simple Jacobi iteration, as opposed to Gauss-Seidel, as the hierarchical structure imposes simultaneous rather than successive displacement.

3.4 Radiance within a Hierarchy

A gathering iteration results in received radiance scattered throughout each interaction hierarchy. This gathered radiance must be distributed and accounted for over all ancestors and descendants of each receiving interaction, in order to maintain the consistency and correctness of the hierarchical representation of radiance between patches.

We employ a distribution algorithm similar to that presented in [7] for radiosity over patch/element hierarchies: gathered radiance is "pushed" to the leaf interactions within each hierarchy to ensure propagation to all descendants, and then "pulled" and distributed back up from the leaves through all higher level interactions to their common ancestor at the root. As is shown in [2], radiance may be pushed unchanged within the interaction hierarchy, and area averaged as it is pulled from child to parent.

4 Application over Glossy Reflection

In this section we discuss our implementation of the above algorithms over glossy reflection.

4.1 The Reflection Function

We employ a highly simplified Torrance-Sparrow [15] model for our glossy reflection function:

$$f_g(\vec{\omega}_i, \vec{\omega}_r) = \frac{\kappa + 2}{8\pi} \frac{\cos^\kappa \theta_m}{\cos\theta_i \cos\theta_r} sh(\theta_i, \theta_r)$$

This function incorporates the facet distribution function $\cos^\kappa \theta_m$ developed by Blinn [3], normalized for projected facet area under

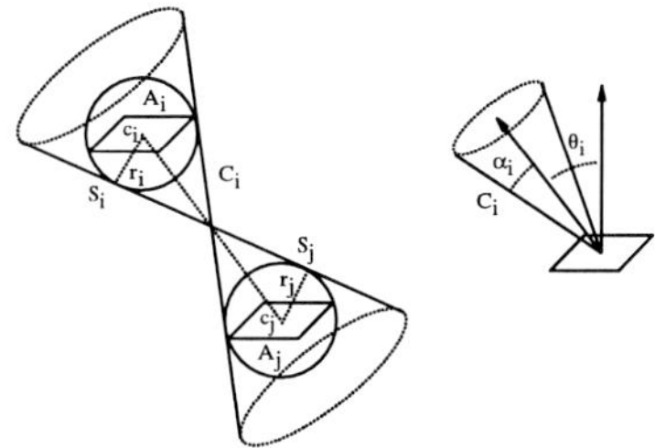

Figure 4: Estimating Cones

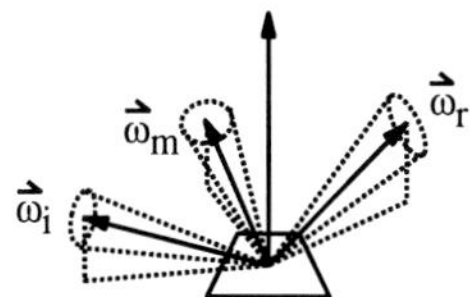

Figure 5: C_i, C_r, and C_m

[10]. Angle θ_m is that made to the mean surface normal by $\vec{\omega}_m$, the microfacet mirror orientation normal lying halfway between $\vec{\omega}_i$ and $\vec{\omega}_r$.

Function $sh(\theta_i, \theta_r)$ expresses self-shadowing over microfacets — for near specular surfaces, such self-shadowing or masking does not become critical until relatively high θ_i or θ_r [6]. The implemented system thus simply clamps sh from 1 to 0 when θ_i or θ_r exceeds a preset θ_{bound} near the horizon. This scheme serves as a crude approximation to the shadowing function; however, a better strategy would be to employ a much fuller tabulation of the function, incorporated into the error analysis presented below. A more complete discussion of shadowing and conservation of energy over f_g is presented in [2].

4.2 Error Estimation

Recall the general expression for error derived in Section 2.3:

$$\pi(\Delta F_{ji} S_{kji} + \Delta S_{kji} F_{ji})$$

In implementation we have estimated the form factor F_{ji} by F_{dji}, the form factor from a differential area at A_j to a disk of area A_i centered at A_i, as was employed in [7]. As discussed in [7], the relative error in this estimate is proportional to the estimate itself. In our implementation we have thus estimated absolute error ΔF_{ji} as at most proportional to F^2_{dji}.A brief discussion of relative and absolute error over hierarchical methods is presented in [2].

We now consider the error estimate ΔS_{kji}. As discussed in the appendix to this paper, we may compute bounding cones C_i, C_r, and C_m over all possible incident, reflected, and mirror orientation directions induced at A_j by A_i and A_k (Figures 4 and 5 — these figures are discussed more fully in the appendix). We may then compute maximum and minimum $\cos^\kappa \theta_m, \cos\theta_i, \cos\theta_r$ over these cones, and estimate error by interval width. The full expression for estimated error over transport is given in the appendix.

4.3 Clamping and Visibility

Evaluation of glossy reflectance over three surface areas, as required by the gather iteration, may be difficult, particularly if surface subdivision has been limited by Aeps rather than satisfaction of error bounds, and if κ, the facet distribution exponent, has high value. In this case we must estimate the integral of a spikey function over a relatively broad area.

Our solution is to band limit the BRDF in a fashion similar to that presented by Amanatides [1]. We employ the cone estimation techniques of the previous section to determine if the BRDF varies significantly over the given patches — if this variance exceeds a set bound, we "roughen" the reflecting surface, lowering κ to broaden the resulting reflection over the estimated cones. We then renormalize the resulting blurred function, as described in [1], to

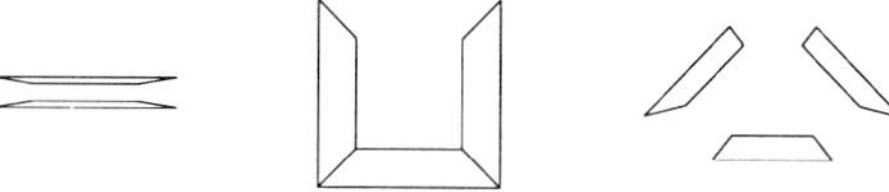

Figure 6: Geometric Configurations

prevent amplification of its low frequency components. We note that the resulting antialiasing is relatively aggressive, significantly dimming or eliminating reflections requiring overmuch blurring.

In implementation, we have computed visibility via jittered ray casting and inheritance similar to that of [7], storing visibility data in interactions as it is computed.

5 Results

5.1 Growth in Transport

We have measured the growth in transport triples (linked interactions) versus n, the maximum number of elements at the finest level of subdivision, over parallel, perpendicular, and "oriented" patches (Figure 7). The corresponding geometries are shown in Figure 6. The graphs show linear or near linear behavior over each range — the graph of triples vs. n for the perpendicular case is slightly concave over the lower data points, but subsides to linear with further refinement.

In previous work [7] on hierarchical refinement for radiosity, it was shown that for error estimate proportional to F_{dji}, and sufficient refinement, each subpatch may only interact with other patches in a limited local neighborhood. As discussed in [7], each patch may thus participate in at most c interactions, for some constant c independent of n and k. Adaptive refinement thus generates at most $O(n)$ transport interactions. We will show a similar bound for discrete three point transport under glossy reflection.

Recall that the estimate for error in computed transport is proportional to $\Delta F_{ji} S_{kji} + \Delta S_{kji} F_{ji}$. Our argument depends on two assumptions:

1. We may bound both ΔS_{kji} and S_{kji} by some S_{max}.

   As discussed below, the lower this S_{max}, the smaller the magnitude of the leading coefficient underling the resulting bound.

   Note that our argument thus does not apply to perfect specular reflection, as the corresponding BRDF incorporates the Dirac delta function [11]. Equivalently, the argument does not hold over f_g for $\kappa = \infty$ (inducing mirror reflection), as we can not provide a finite bound for S in this case.

   For finite κ, however, the desired bound over glossy reflection is achieved by:

$$\frac{\kappa+2}{8} \max(\cos^\kappa \theta_m) \max(\sec\theta_i) \max(\sec\theta_r)$$

   The maxima over the secant terms are bounded by microfacet self-shadowing.

2. ΔF_{ji} and F_{ji} within our error estimate are at most proportional to F_{dji}.

   Recall that we estimate F_{ji} as F_{dji}, and ΔF_{ji} as F^2_{dji}, thus satisfying this assumption.

Given these assumptions, estimated error is at most proportional to $S_{\text{max}} F_{dji}$.

We may now show $O(n)$ growth, for sufficient refinement. Consider refinement over interaction ij under an error estimate at worst proportional to $S_{\text{max}} F_{dji}$. The error estimate is thus proportional to F_{dji}, and therefore, for sufficient refinement, there are at most $O(n)$ such interactions, as discussed in [7].

Consider now an error satisfied link from ij to an interaction jk. For sufficient refinement under our subdivision scheme, we may assume that form factors F_{ij}, F_{ji}, F_{jk}, F_{kj} over p_i, p_j, and p_k are roughly equal. Furthermore, these satisfying form factors depend only on the error estimate, reflection function, and error bounds, not on n or k.

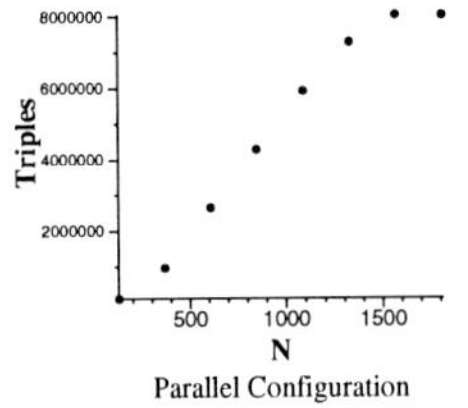

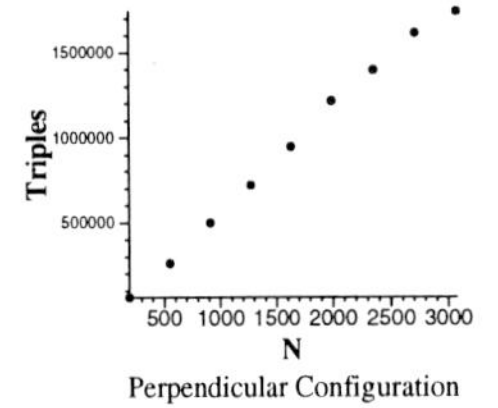

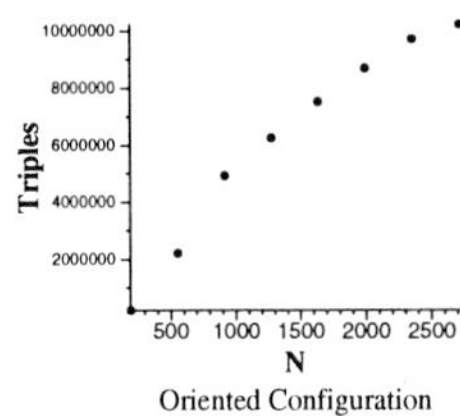

Figure 7: Triples vs. N over Geometry. Error bounds $e = 0.1$. Glossy exponent $\kappa = 25$. For oriented case $e = 0.005$.

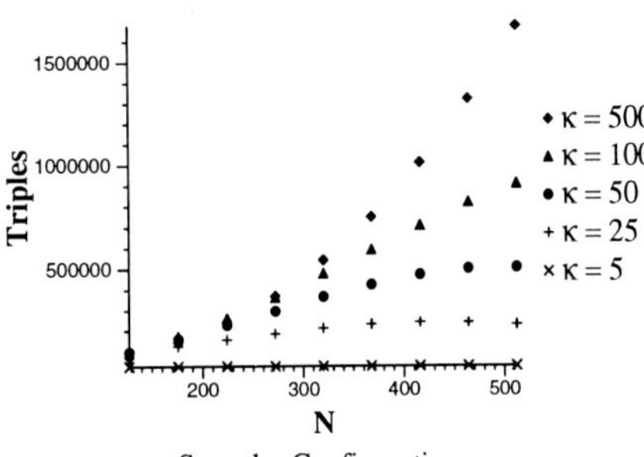

Figure 8: Triples vs. N over κ. The graph is over parallel polygons for which the error bounds and interpolygon distance have been doubled.

At worst the above form factors are such that $F_{**}S_{\max} < \texttt{Eps}$, where Eps is the most restrictive error bound. Note that, as stated above, F_{**} depends only on the error estimate, reflection function (ie. $S_{\max}$), and error bounds. Only some constant number of such form factors may be fitted over the directional hemisphere above p_j, and thus ij may only be linked to some constant number of interactions jk. The total number of linked interactions, and corresponding transport triples, is thus $O(n)$.

Note that the above argument, although it establishes the desired bound, may overstate the potential for links at a given interaction. For a given ij, much of the directional reflection into the hemisphere over p_j may not achieve $S_{\max}$, and may even be of maximum 0. That is, the analysis ignores the modulation between the paired error and value terms within the error estimate.

As κ increases in magnitude, the corresponding bound $S_{\max}$ must increase as well. We may thus expect greater growth in transport computation with higher specular exponent, as shown in Figure 8. Within this graph, growth is superlinear for $\kappa = 500$, though further trials over a higher range of $n = 500 \ldots 2000$ have shown that the rate subsides to linear as n increases, allowing sufficient refinement for the local neighborhood property to obtain.

Finally, we note that under specular reflection each element is reflected across every other element perfectly, and to a first approximation is visible from a constant number of other elements in the environment (at least in the case of a convex enclosed room; the analysis is complicated by occlusion and certain worst case alignments). Thus, the number of interactions is at least $O(n^2)$ — we conjecture that it is no worse than this bound.

5.2 Illumination and Refinement

Figure 9 shows illumination and meshing over surfaces of varying glossiness (specular exponent). Within each image, the reflecting surface is perpendicular to the diamond shaped light source, and we see the resulting reflection in the direction of the eye. Note the conformation of meshing to the highlight over each surface. The "stretched" nature of the highlight along the axis to the eye is characteristic of Torrance-Sparrow reflection over fairly oblique angles, and accounts for the increased sensitivity of meshing along this axis. The rightmost three images in the figure show the meshing from above. The illumination shown in these images is somewhat unusual - it shows the reflection to the eye as though it had been painted on the reflecting surface, and then viewed from a different location, directly above. The images in Figure 11 show similar eye/offset views for the reflection of a garish checkerboard.

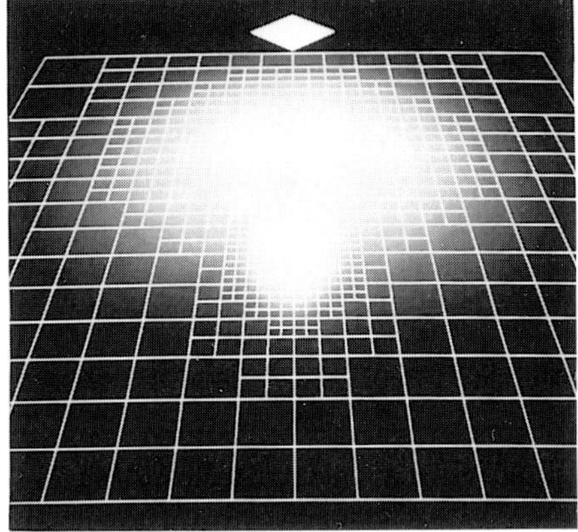

Figure 10: Meshing for glossy and diffuse reflection

Figure 9				
Max Elements		4160		
Max Triples		262144		
Computed	patches	elements	triples	time
$\kappa = 25$	790	593	6706 (2.6%)	2.2s
$\kappa = 100$	1290	968	24214 (9.2%)	8.0s
$\kappa = 500$	874	656	12106 (4.6%)	4.1s
Figure 10				
Max Elements		16448		
Max Triples		1048576		
Computed	patches	elements	triples	time
$\kappa = 500$	1578	1184	7834 (0.75%)	5.0s
Figure 12				
Max Elements		15138		
Max Triples		222385209344		
Computed	patches	elements	triples	time
$\kappa = 500$	6479	4866	70995 (0.00003%)	3m13s

Table 1: Image Statistics

The image in Figure 10 shows contrasting illumination and meshing induced by diffuse and glossy reflection. Note the distinct meshing for each highlight. Glossy reflection is at a less oblique angle, and thus both the highlight and meshing exhibit less distortion in the direction of the eye.

Note that these scenes are extremely simple — application to more complex environments is still very expensive, despite the employment of hierarchical methods. Motivated by the work of Smits et al. [14] in hierarchical radiosity, we are currently experimenting with importance and radiance weighting over three point transport — preliminary results of this work are shown in Figure 12. The given environment contains four reflectors: the broad face of each of the three "slabs" and the top of the central cube. In addition to the reflections seen in the slabs, note the play of light originating at the lamp at left, reflected off the cube top, and over the upper part of the green wall at right. Total potential transport triples over this environment at the finest level of subdivision is just over 222 billion — our system, under importance and radiance weighting, employs 70,995, a reduction to 3 hundred-thousandths of 1 percent.

Table 1 provides further statistics for the images. Timings are given for a Silicon Graphics indigo workstation with a single 50 MHz R4000 processor. The image shown in Figure 12 was generated after seven complete iterations (gathers to all interactions), and total time just over three minutes.

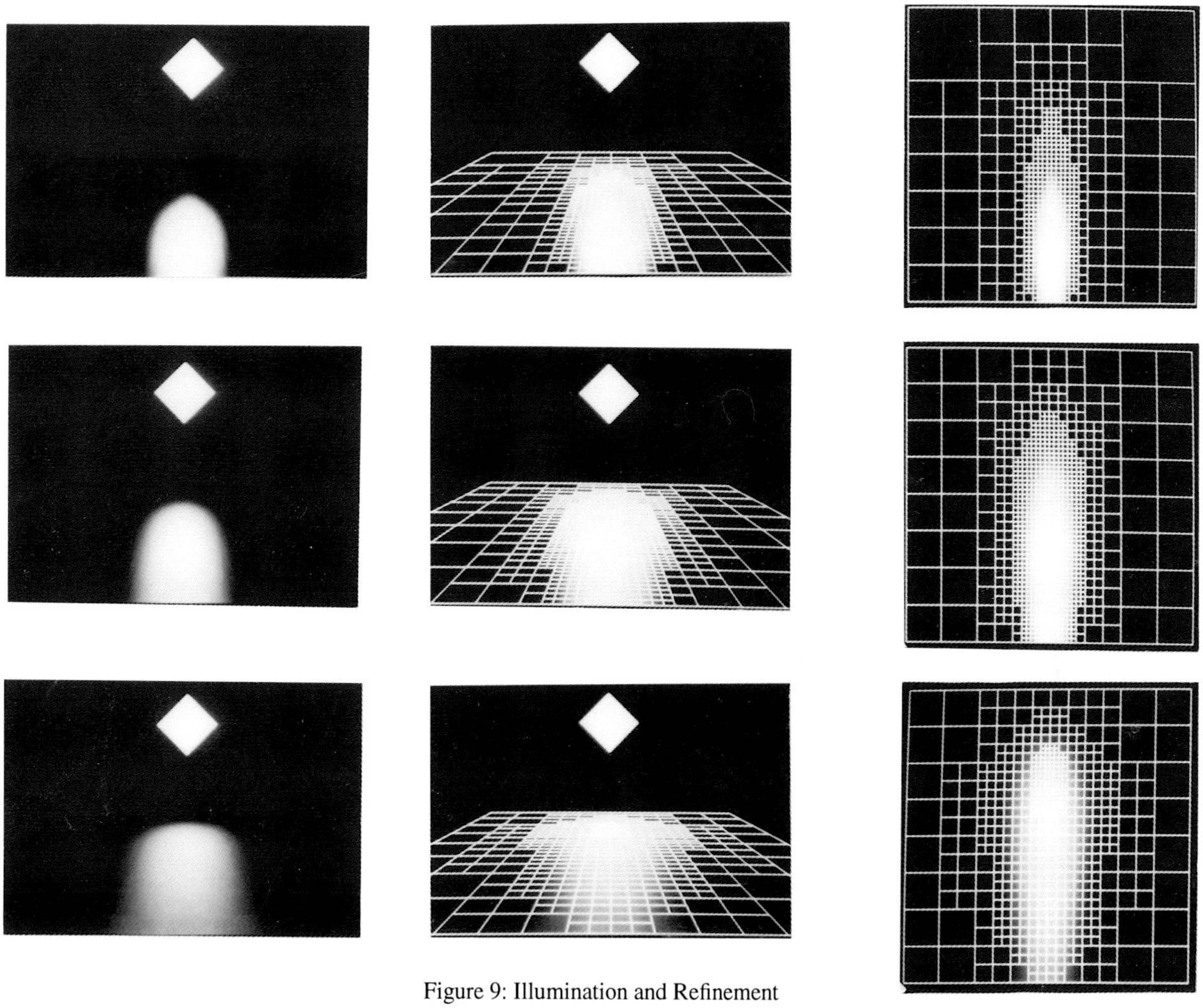

Figure 9: Illumination and Refinement

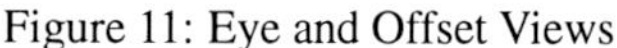

Figure 11: Eye and Offset Views

Figure 12: Cube and Slabs

6 Discussion

Recall the matrix formulation shown in Figure 2. For any n of reasonable size, the resulting n^3 matrix will be unmanageable — we have shown, however, that for sufficient refinement the n^3 entries in the matrix may be approximated to within user specified bounds by $O(n)$ subblocks. The gather and push/pull procedures described in preceding sections allow manipulation and solution over this representation. As discussed in [2], the resulting system may be shown to converge.

Growth in transport is more accurately described as $O(n + k^3)$, where k is the number of input polygonal patches within the environment, as opposed to elements. The k^3 term is generated by the initial examination of all polygon triples for reflection, and is subsumed by n as the number of elements increases. As the number of polygons in an environment grows, however, the k^3 term will become prohibitively large. As discussed in [14] with respect to the related problem under hierarchical radiosity, the capability to cluster as well as refine polygons would reduce the difficulty of unnecessary initial interactions. Clustering is arguably the most important open problem in the computation of global illumination.

The hierarchical approach described in this paper was derived by writing the rendering equation in a three point transport formulation. Another option would be to parameterize radiance by position and direction – we believe that a similar hierarchical approach could be employed with the method of discrete ordinates or spherical harmonics.

Finally, we note that, similarly to other algorithms for hierarchical illumination [7, 14], the algorithm described in this paper bounds estimated error over individual transport computations. As discussed in [14], bounding estimated error over individual transport does not easily or necessarily provide a rigorous bound for overall error in the solution. An analysis and means of computing such a bound over hierarchical illumination remains an interesting open problem.

7 Acknowledgements

This research was partially supported by equipment grants from Apple and Silicon Graphics Computer Systems and a research grant from the National Science Foundation (CCR 9207966). The authors would like to thank Dr. P. Prusinkiewicz for access to the graphics research facilities at the University of Calgary during the final stages of this work, and Deborah Fowler for her crucial assistance in shooting test images, paste up and much other support and encouragement. Thanks to Cullen Jennings and David Laur for all of their help recording images. We especially thank the anonymous referees for their many helpful comments and suggestions.

8 References

[1] Amanatides, J. (1992) Algorithms for the detection and elimination of specular aliasing. *Proc. Graphics Interface '92*, 86-93.

[2] Aupperle, L. (1993) Hierarchical algorithms for illumination. Doctoral Dissertation, Princeton University.

[3] Blinn, J.F. (1977) Models of light refection for computer synthesized pictures. *Computer Graphics* 11 (2), 192-198.

[4] Chen, S.E., Rushmeier, H.E., Miller, G., Turner, D. (1991) A progressive multi-pass method for global illumination. *Computer Graphics* 25 (4), 165-174.

[5] Cook, R.L. (1986) Stochastic sampling in computer graphics. *ACM Transactions on Graphics* 5 (1), 51-72.

[6] Hall, R. (1989) Illumination and color in computer generated imagery. Springer-Verlag, New York.

[7] Hanrahan, P., Salzman, D., Aupperle, L. (1991) A rapid hierarchical radiosity algorithm. *Computer Graphics* 25 (4), 197-206.

[8] Immel, D.S., Cohen, M.F., Greenberg, D.P. (1986) A radiosity method for non-diffuse environments. *Computer Graphics* 20 (4), 133-142.

[9] Kajiya, J.T. (1986) The rendering equation. *Computer Graphics* 20 (4), 143-150.

[10] Mitchell, D. (1992) Manuscript.

[11] Nicodemus, F.E., Richmond, J.C., Hsia, J.J., Ginsberg, I.W., Limperis, T. (1977) Geometrical considerations and nomenclature for reflectance. National Bureau of Standards monograph, no. 160.

[12] Shirley, P. (1990) A ray tracing method for illumination calculation in diffuse-specular scenes. *Proc. Graphics Interace '90*, 205-212.

[13] Sillion, F.X., Arvo, J.R., Westin, S.H., Greenberg, D.P. (1991) A global illumination solution for general reflectance distributions. *Computer Graphics* 25 (4), 187-196.

[14] Smits, B.E., Arvo, J.R., Salesin, D.H. (1992) An importance-driven radiosity algorithm. *Computer Graphics* 26 (2), 273-282.

[15] Torrance, K.E., Sparrow, E.M. (1967) Theory for off-specular reflection from roughened surfaces. *J. of the Optical Society of America* 57 (9), 1105-1114.

[16] Ward, G.J., Rubinstein, F.M., Clear, R.D. (1988) A ray tracing solution for diffuse environments. *Computer Graphics* 22 (3), 85-92.

Appendix: Error Analysis

Recall the error expression derived in Section 2.3:

$$\pi(\Delta F_{ji} S_{kji} + \Delta S_{kji} F_{ji})$$

In implementation, we have divided ΔS_{kji} into separate components for each subfactor of f_g. We thus have:

$$\frac{\kappa+2}{8}(\Delta F_{ji}\frac{\cos^\kappa \theta_m}{\cos\theta_i \cos\theta_r} + \Delta\cos^\kappa \theta_m F_{ji}\frac{1}{\cos\theta_i\cos\theta_r} + \Delta\sec\theta_i F_{ji}\frac{\cos^\kappa\theta_m}{\cos\theta_r} + \Delta\sec\theta_r F_{ji}\frac{\cos^\kappa\theta_m}{\cos\theta_i})$$

In implementation, the refinement procedure of Section 3.2 takes an additional argument, `Ceps`, against which the two estimates of error in reciprocal cosine are tested.

We are left with the computation of $\Delta\sec\theta_i$, $\Delta\sec\theta_r$, and $\Delta\cos^\kappa\theta_m$. The variance (and associated error) in these cosine terms over given patches A_i, A_j, A_k is determined by the set of possible $\vec{\omega}_i$, $\vec{\omega}_r$ lying between the patches (we dispense with $'$ notation in this section).

Consider patches A_i, and A_j (Figure 4): we enclose these patches in spheres S_i, S_j with centers c_i, c_j, and radii r_i, r_j, respectively. For the moment we will assume that the interiors of S_i and S_j do not intersect, and thus there exists a tangent cone lying between the spheres.

Note that this cone is a right circular cone centered on the line joining c_i and c_j. Consider the nappe containing S_i: it may be regarded as a cone of direction vectors centered about the vector $c_i - c_j$. We will call this vector cone C_i. If p_i and p_j are any two points on or in S_i, S_j, then the vector $p_i - p_j$ lies within C_i. C_i thus bounds the set of possible $\vec{\omega}_i$. We may characterize C_i by the angle α_i defined by its axis, $c_i - c_j$, and boundary — cone C_r and angle α_r may be similarly defined over A_j and A_k. If either pair of spheres intersect, we set the corresponding $\alpha = \pi$. We may easily compute maxima and minima for $\sec\theta_i$ and $\sec\theta_r$ given C_i and C_r, and may then compute error in estimation as $(\max - \min)/2$.

The cones C_i and C_r centered about $\vec{\omega}_i$ and $\vec{\omega}_r$ induce a similar cone of variation about $\vec{\omega}_m$ (Figure 5). Application of basic spherical trigonometry yields [2]:

$$\alpha_m \leq \arcsin\min(\frac{\sin(\alpha_i/2) + \sin(\alpha_r/2)}{\vec{\omega}_i \cdot \vec{\omega}_m}, 1.0)$$

Given α_m, determination of $\max(\cos^\kappa\theta_m)$, $\min(\cos^\kappa\theta_m)$, and thus $\Delta\cos^\kappa\theta_m$ immediately follows.

Having computed these estimates and maxima, and incorporating the estimates for form factor computation, we may bound and estimate error in transport as:

$$\frac{\kappa+2}{8}(F_{dji}^2 \max(\cos^\kappa\theta_m)\max(\sec\theta_i)\max(\sec\theta_r) + \Delta\cos^\kappa\theta_m F_{dji}\max(\sec\theta_i)\max(\sec\theta_r) + \Delta\sec\theta_i F_{dji}\max(\cos^\kappa\theta_i)\max(\sec\theta_r) + \Delta\sec\theta_r F_{dji}\max(\cos^\kappa\theta_i)\max(\sec\theta_i))$$

It is this error measure that we employ in our implementation.

On the Form Factor between Two Polygons

Peter Schröder **Pat Hanrahan**

Department of Computer Science
Princeton University

Abstract

Form factors are used in radiosity to describe the fraction of diffusely reflected light leaving one surface and arriving at another. They are a fundamental geometric property used for computation. Many special configurations admit closed form solutions. However, the important case of the form factor between two polygons in three space has had no known closed form solution. We give such a solution for the case of general (planar, convex or concave, possibly containing holes) polygons.

CR Categories and Subject Descriptors: I.3.7 [Computer Graphics]: *Three-Dimensional Graphics and Realism – Radiosity*; J.2 [Physical Sciences and Engineering]: *Engineering*.

Additional Key Words and Phrases: Closed form solution; form factor; polygons.

1 Introduction

When using the radiosity technique to create images the form factor plays a central role. It describes the fraction of radiation diffusely emitted from one surface reaching another surface. The accurate computation of form factors is the central theme in many recent papers. Goral et al. [4], who introduced radiosity to the computer graphics community, used numerical contour integration to compute form factors between polygons. Cohen and Greenberg [3] took visibility into account with their hemicube algorithm. More recent hierarchical and adaptive algorithms compute still more accurate form factors [10; 5]. Nishita and Nakamae [8] and Baum et al. [2] have used an exact solution for the form factor between a differential surface element and a polygon. Most radiosity algorithms are restricted to polygonal environments, and so a closed form solution for the form factor between polygons is potentially of great utility.

The history of computing form factors is very long. A closed form expression for the form factor between a differential surface element and a polygon was found by Lambert in 1760 [7]. Lambert proceeded to derive the form factor for a number of special configurations among them the form factor between two perpendicular rectangles sharing a common edge. He writes about the latter derivation:

> Although this task appears very simple its solution is considerably more knotted than one would expect. For it would be very easy to write down the differential expression of fourth order, which one would need to integrate four fold; but the highly laborious computation would fill even the most patient with disgust and drive them away from the task.

Other workers have derived closed form solutions for the form factors between many different geometric configurations and these can be found in standard textbooks. However, we are not aware of a closed form solution for the form factor between two general polygons. Thus, this problem has remained open for over 230 years.

In this paper we present a formula for the form factor integral between two general polygons. The derivation of this formula is quite involved, and the interested reader is referred to [9] for a detailed derivation. The purpose of this paper is to bring this result to the attention of the graphics community.

2 Closed form solution

The form factor integral can be reduced to a double contour integral by two applications of Stokes' theorem [6]

$$\begin{aligned}\pi A_1 F_{12} &= \int_{A_1}\int_{A_2} \frac{\cos\theta_1 \cos\theta_2}{\|\vec{r}\|^2}\, dA_2\, dA_1 \\ &= \frac{1}{4}\int_{\partial A_1}\int_{\partial A_2} \ln(\vec{r}\cdot\vec{r})\, d\vec{x}_2 \cdot d\vec{x}_1\end{aligned}$$

where θ_1, θ_2 are the angles between the normal vector of the respective surface and a radius vector $\vec{r}$, which connects two points on the surfaces. The above equation holds for all surfaces such that every point on either surface sees the same contour of the other surface.

In the case of polygons P_1 and P_2 the contour integral reduces to a sum of double line integrals over all pairwise combinations of edges

$$4\pi A_{P_1} F_{P_1 P_2} = \sum_{E_i\, E_j} \cos\angle E_i E_j \int_{E_i}\int_{E_j} \ln(\vec{r}\cdot\vec{r})\, ds_j\, dt_i$$

Ignoring the factor $\cos\angle E_i E_j$ we are left with the task of giving a solution to integrals of the general form $\int_0^{c_2}\int_0^{c_0} \ln f(s,t)\, ds\, dt$. c_0 and c_2 are the lengths of the edges over which a given double contour integral is taken and $f(s,t) = s^2 + c_1 st + t^2 + c_3 s + c_4 t + c_5$ is the bi-quadratic form which arises from the expansion of the dot product (see Table 2 for definitions of all variables). If the two line segments lie in a common plane we can factor $f(s,t)$ into two bi-linear forms and a solution is readily obtained with standard integration tables (see [9]). Lines in general position lead to the following result:

$$\begin{aligned}&\int_0^{c_2}\int_0^{c_0} \ln f(s,t)\, ds\, dt \\ &= \left\{ \left[(s + \frac{c_3}{2})\mathrm{G}(f(.,t))(s) + \frac{c_1}{2}\mathrm{H}(f(.,t))(s) \right] \Bigg|_{s=0}^{s=c_0} \right\} \Bigg|_{t=0}^{t=c_2} \\ &\quad -2c_0c_2 + c_{14}c_{15} \Bigg\{ \Bigg[\pi(2k(s)+1)\mathrm{M}(t) \\ &\quad -i \Big(\mathrm{L}(-c_{17}(s))(t) + \mathrm{L}(-c_{18}(s))(t) \\ &\quad -\mathrm{L}(c_{17}(s))(t) - \mathrm{L}(c_{18}(s))(t) \Big) \Bigg] \Bigg|_{s=0}^{s=c_0} \Bigg\} \Bigg|_{t=\sqrt{\frac{c_{13}}{\bar{c}_{13}}}}^{t=\sqrt{\frac{c_{13}+c_2}{\bar{c}_{13}+c_2}}}\end{aligned}$$

where $k(s) \in \{-1, 0, 1\}$ according to the particular branchcut of the complex logarithm choosen in L. The auxiliary functions G, H, L, and M are given in Table 1.

3 An example

We have implemented our closed form solution in Mathematica [11] (this code is available from `ps@princeton.edu`). The

 ACM-0-89791-601-8/93/008/0163 $01.50

$$
\begin{aligned}
\mathrm{L}(b)(y) &:= \int^y t^2(1-t^2)^{-3}\ln(b+t)\,dt = \tfrac{1}{16}\Big[\tfrac{-b\ln(y-1)}{(b+1)^2} - \tfrac{b\ln(1+y)}{(b-1)^2} + \Big(\tfrac{2(b+y)(1+by)[(b-y)^2+(by-1)^2]}{(b^2-1)^2(y^2-1)^2} + \ln\tfrac{(1-y)(1-b)}{(1+y)(1+b)}\Big)\ln(b+y) \\
&\qquad + \tfrac{2(b-y)}{(b^2-1)(y^2-1)} + \mathrm{Li}_2\left(\tfrac{1-y}{1+b}\right) - \mathrm{Li}_2\left(\tfrac{1+y}{1-b}\right)\Big] \\
\mathrm{M}(y) &:= \int^y t^2(1-t^2)^{-3}\,dt = \tfrac{1}{16}\left[4y(y^2-1)^{-2} + 2y(y^2-1)^{-1} + \ln\tfrac{y-1}{y+1}\right] \\
\mathrm{G}(q)(y) &:= \int^y \ln q(t)\,dt = \tfrac{q'(y)}{2a}\ln q(y) - 2y + \tfrac{d}{a}\tan^{-1}\tfrac{q'(y)}{d} \\
\mathrm{H}(q)(y) &:= \int^y t\ln q(t)\,dt = \left(\tfrac{y^2}{2} + \tfrac{c}{2a} - \tfrac{b^2}{4a^2}\right)\ln q(y) - \tfrac{y(ay-b)}{2a} - \tfrac{bd}{2a^2}\tan^{-1}\tfrac{q'(y)}{d}
\end{aligned}
$$

Table 1: Four auxiliary integrals needed in the solution. Notice that $\mathrm{L}(b)(y)$ uses the dilogarithm [1], $\mathrm{Li}_2(z) = \sum_1^\infty \frac{z^k}{k^2}$, $\frac{d}{dz}\mathrm{Li}_2(z) = -\frac{\ln(1-z)}{z}$. In G and H the argument q is an arbitrary quadratic polynomial $q(t) = at^2 + bt + c$ and $d = \sqrt{4ac - b^2}$.

$c_0 = \|E_j\|$	$c_{13} = \frac{c_{11} - \sqrt{c_{11}^2 - 4c_{10}c_{12}}}{2c_{10}}$
$c_1 = -2\vec{d}_i \cdot \vec{d}_j$	$c_{14} = \frac{\sqrt{c_{11}^2 - 4c_{10}c_{12}}}{c_{10}}$
$c_2 = \|E_i\|$	$c_{15} = \sqrt{c_{10}}c_{14}$
$c_3 = -2\vec{d}_j \cdot (\vec{p}_i - \vec{p}_j)$	$c_{16}(s) = c_1c_{13} - c_3 - 2s$
$c_4 = 2\vec{d}_i \cdot (\vec{p}_i - \vec{p}_j)$	$c_{17}(s) = \frac{-c_{15} + \sqrt{c_{15}^2 - 4\|c_{16}(s)\|^2}}{2i\bar{c}_{16}(s)}$
$c_5 = \|\vec{p}_i - \vec{p}_j\|^2$	$c_{18}(s) = \frac{-c_{15} - \sqrt{c_{15}^2 - 4\|c_{16}(s)\|^2}}{2i\bar{c}_{16}(s)}$
$c_{10} = 4 - c_1^2$	
$c_{11} = 4c_4 - 2c_1c_3$	
$c_{12} = 4c_5 - c_3^2$	

Table 2: All expressions for two edges E_{ij} with parameterization $\vec{x}_i(t) = \vec{p}_i + t\vec{d}_i$ and $\vec{x}_j(s) = \vec{p}_j + s\vec{d}_j$ ($\|\vec{d}_{i,j}\| = 1$).

implementation requires some care because of the complexities of the functions that are involved.

A simple example, which requires the full power of our formula, concerns the form factor between two equal width rectangles sharing an edge with an enclosing angle $\theta \in [0, \pi]$. The configuration is illustrated in Figure 1 together with the form factor as a function of θ for different aspect ratios $l = \frac{a}{b}$ (common edge length b).

4 Conclusion

We have given a closed form solution for the form factor between two general polygons. This solution is non-elementary since it involves the dilogarithm function. The principal value of our solution is in determining exact answers for general polygonal configurations. This can be used in practice for reference solutions to check more efficient approximations. Baum et al. [2] have also shown that the error in the computed solution can be reduced significantly when using a closed form solution near singularities of the integrand.

There has been a long history of computing closed form expressions for form factors starting with Lambert in 1760. The literature lists many special cases for which closed form solutions exist, but hitherto no solution had been given for general polygonal configurations. The present paper closes this gap.

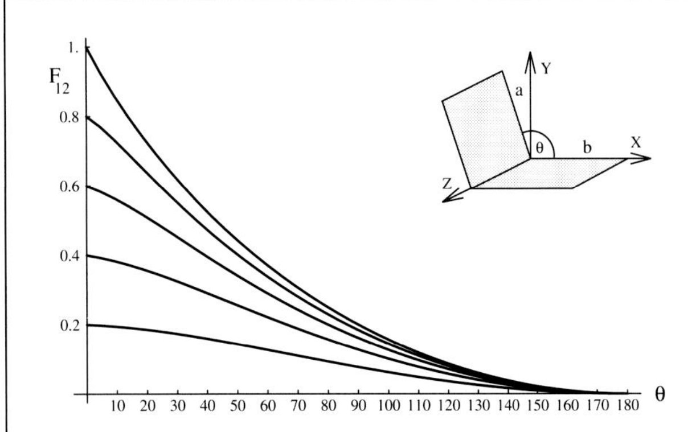

Figure 1: Geometry for two rectangles sharing a common edge with an enclosing angle of θ. The graphs show the form factor as a function of θ for edge ratios $l = \frac{a}{b}$ of .2, .4, .6, .8, and 1.0.

Acknowledgements

The first author would like to thank the Sci-Vis group at HLRZ for their support. Other support came from Apple, Silicon Graphics and the NSF (contract no. CCR 9207966).

References

[1] ABRAMOWITZ, M., AND STEGUN, I. A. *Handbook of Mathematical Functions*, 9th ed. Dover Publications, 1970.

[2] BAUM, D. R., RUSHMEIER, H. E., AND WINGET, J. M. Improving Radiosity Solutions Through the Use of Analytically Determined Form-Factors. *Computer Graphics 23*, 3 (July 1989), 325–334.

[3] COHEN, M. F., AND GREENBERG, D. P. The Hemi-Cube: A Radiosity Solution for Complex Environments. *Computer Graphics 19*, 3 (July 1985), 31–40.

[4] GORAL, C. M., TORRANCE, K. E., GREENBERG, D. P., AND BATTAILE, B. Modelling the Interaction of Light between Diffuse Surfaces. *Computer Graphics 18*, 3 (July 1984), 212–222.

[5] HANRAHAN, P., SALZMAN, D., AND AUPPERLE, L. A Rapid Hierarchical Radiosity Algorithm. *Computer Graphics 25*, 4 (July 1991), 197–206.

[6] HERMAN, R. A. *A Treatise on Geometrical Optics.* Cambridge University Press, 1900.

[7] LAMBERT. *Photometria sive de mensura et gradibus luminis, colorum et umbrae.* 1760. German translation by E. Anding in *Ostwald's Klassiker der Exakten Wissenschaften*, Vol. 31-33, Leipzig, 1892.

[8] NISHITA, T., AND NAKAMAE, E. Continuous Tone Representation of Three-Dimensional Objects Taking Account of Shadows and Interreflection. *Computer Graphics 19*, 3 (July 1985), 23–30.

[9] SCHRÖDER, P., AND HANRAHAN, P. A Closed Form Expression for the Form Factor between Two Polygons. Tech. Rep. CS-404-93, Department of Computer Science, Princeton University, January 1993.

[10] WALLACE, J. R., ELMQUIST, K. A., AND HAINES, E. A. A Ray Tracing Algorithm for Progressive Radiosity. *Computer Graphics 23*, 3 (July 1989), 315–324.

[11] WOLFRAM, S. *Mathematica.* Addison-Wesley, 1988.

Reflection from Layered Surfaces due to Subsurface Scattering

Pat Hanrahan

Department of Computer Science
Princeton University

Wolfgang Krueger

Department of Scientific Visualization
German National Research Center
for Computer Science

Abstract

The reflection of light from most materials consists of two major terms: the specular and the diffuse. Specular reflection may be modeled from first principles by considering a rough surface consisting of perfect reflectors, or micro-facets. Diffuse reflection is generally considered to result from multiple scattering either from a rough surface or from within a layer near the surface. Accounting for diffuse reflection by Lambert's Cosine Law, as is universally done in computer graphics, is not a physical theory based on first principles.

This paper presents a model for subsurface scattering in layered surfaces in terms of one-dimensional linear transport theory. We derive explicit formulas for backscattering and transmission that can be directly incorporated in most rendering systems, and a general Monte Carlo method that is easily added to a ray tracer. This model is particularly appropriate for common layered materials appearing in nature, such as biological tissues (e.g. skin, leaves, etc.) or inorganic materials (e.g. snow, sand, paint, varnished or dusty surfaces). As an application of the model, we simulate the appearance of a face and a cluster of leaves from experimental data describing their layer properties.

CR Categories and Subject Descriptors: I.3.7 [Computer Graphics]: *Three-Dimensional Graphics and Realism*.

Additional Key Words and Phrases: Reflection models, integral equations, Monte Carlo.

1 Motivation

An important goal of image synthesis research is to develop a comprehensive shading model suitable for a wide range of materials. Recent research has concentrated on developing a model of specular reflection from rough surfaces from first principles. In particular, the micro-facet model first proposed by Bouguer in 1759 [4], and developed further by Beckmann[1], Torrance & Sparrow[26], and others, has been applied to computer graphics by Blinn [2] and Cook & Torrance[8]. A still more comprehensive version of the model was recently proposed by He et al[12]. These models have also been extended to handle anisotropic microfacets distributions[24, 5] and multiple scattering from complex microscale geometries[28].

Another important component of surface reflection is, however, diffuse reflection. Diffuse reflection in computer graphics has almost universally been modeled by Lambert's Cosine Law. This law states that the exiting radiance is isotropic, and proportional to the surface irradiance, which for a light ray impinging on the surface from a given direction depends on the cosine of the angle of incidence. Diffuse reflection is qualitatively explained as due to subsurface scattering [18]: Light enters the material, is absorbed and scattered, and eventually exits the material. In the process of this subsurface interaction, light at different wavelengths is differentially absorbed and scattered, and hence is filtered accounting for the color of the material. Moreover, in the limit as the light ray is scattered multiple times, it becomes isotropic, and hence the direction in which it leaves the material is essentially random. This qualitative explanation accounts for both the directional and colormetric properties of diffuse materials. This explanation is also motivated by an early proof that there cannot exist a micro-facet distribution that causes equal reflection in all outgoing directions independent of the incoming direction [10].

The above model of diffuse reflection is qualitative and not very satisfying because it does not refer to any physical parameter of the material. Furthermore, there is no freedom to adjust coefficients to account for subtle variations in reflection from different materials. However, it does contain the essential insight: an important component of reflection can arise from subsurface scattering. In this paper, we present a model of reflection of light due to subsurface scattering in layered materials suitable for computer graphics. The only other work in computer graphics to take this approach is due to Blinn, who in a very early paper presented a model for the reflection and transmission of light through thin clouds of particles in order to model the rings of Saturn[2]. Our model differs from Blinn's in that it is based on one-dimensional linear transport theory—a simplification of the general volume rendering equation [19]— and hence is considerably more general and powerful. Of course, Blinn was certainly aware of the transport theory approach, but chose to present his model in a simpler way based on probabilistic arguments.

In our model the relative contributions of surface and subsurface reflection are very sensitive to the Fresnel effect (which Blinn did not consider). This is particularly important in biological tissues which, because cells contain large quantities of water, are translucent. A further prediction of the theory is that the subsurface reflectance term is not necessarily isotropic, but varies in different directions. This arises because the subsurface scattering by particles is predominantly in the forward direction. In fact, it has long been known experimentally that very few materials are ideal diffuse reflectors (for a nice survey of experiments pertaining to this question, see [18]).

We formulate the model in the currently emerging standard terminology for describing illumination in computer graphics [16, 11]. We also discuss efficient methods for implementation within the context of standard rendering techniques. We also describe how to construct materials with multiple thin layers. Finally, we apply the model to two examples: skin and leaves. For these examples, we build on experimental data collected in the last few years, and provide pointers to the relevant literature.

Another goal of this paper is to point out the large amount of recent work in the applied physics community in the application of linear transport theory to modeling appearance.

© 1993 ACM-0-89791-601-8/93/008/0165 $01.50

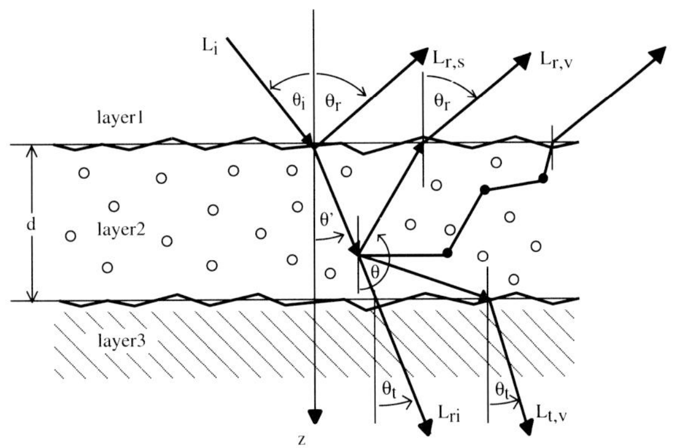

Figure 1: The geometry of scattering from a layered surface

(θ_i, ϕ_i)	Angles of incidence (incoming)
(θ_r, ϕ_r)	Angles of reflection (outgoing)
(θ_t, ϕ_t)	Angles of transmission
$L(z; \theta, \phi)$	Radiance [W / (m^2 sr)]
L_i	Incident (incoming) radiance
L_r	Reflected (outgoing) radiance
L_t	Transmitted radiance
L_+	forward-scattered radiance
L_-	backward-scattered radiance
$f_r(\theta_i, \phi_i; \theta_r, \phi_r)$	BRDF
$f_t(\theta_i, \phi_i; \theta_t, \phi_t)$	BTDF
$f_{r,s}(\theta_i, \phi_i; \theta_r, \phi_r)$	Surface or boundary BRDF
$f_{t,s}(\theta_i, \phi_i; \theta_t, \phi_t)$	Surface or boundary BTDF
$f_{r,v}(\theta_i, \phi_i; \theta_r, \phi_r)$	Volume or subsurface BRDF
$f_{t,v}(\theta_i, \phi_i; \theta_t, \phi_t)$	Volume or subsurface BTDF
n	Index of refraction
$\sigma_s(z; \lambda)$	Scattering cross section [mm^{-1}]
$\sigma_a(z; \lambda)$	Absorption cross section [mm^{-1}]
$\sigma_t(z; \lambda)$	Total cross section ($\sigma_t = \sigma_a + \sigma_s$) [mm^{-1}]
W	Albedo ($W = \frac{\sigma_s}{\sigma_t}$)
d	Layer thickness [mm]
$p(z; \theta, \phi; \theta', \phi'; \lambda)$	Scattering phase function ((θ', ϕ') to (θ, ϕ))

Table 1: Nomenclature

2 Reflection and Transmission due to Layered Surfaces

As a starting point we will assume that the reflected radiance L_r from a surface has two components. One component arises due to surface reflectance, the other component due to subsurface volume scattering. (The notation used in this paper is collected in Table 1 and shown diagramatically in Figure 1.)

$$L_r(\theta_r, \phi_r) = L_{r,s}(\theta_r, \phi_r) + L_{r,v}(\theta_r, \phi_r)$$

where:

$L_{r,s}$ - reflected radiance due to surface scattering

$L_{r,v}$ - reflected radiance due to volume or subsurface scattering

The models developed in this paper also predict the transmission through a layered surface. This is useful both for materials made of multiple layers, as well as the transmission through thin translucent surfaces when they are back illuminated. The transmitted radiance has two components. The first component is called the *reduced intensity*; this is the amount of incident light transmitted through the layer without scattering inside the layer, but accounting for absorption. The second is due to scattering in the volume.

$$L_t(\theta_t, \phi_t) = L_{ri}(\theta_t, \phi_t) + L_{t,v}(\theta_t, \phi_t)$$

where:

L_{ri} - reduced intensity

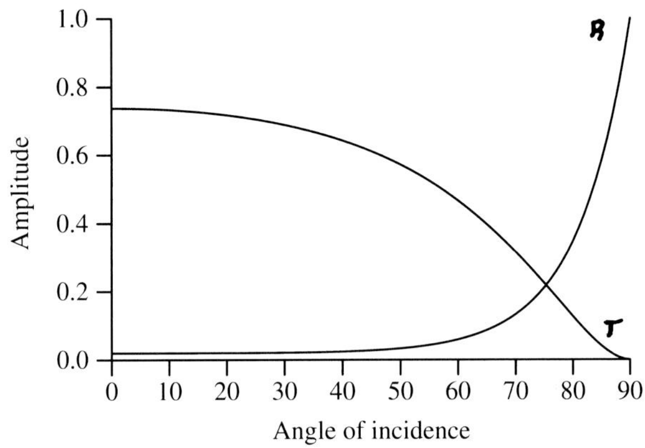

Figure 2: Fresnel transmission and reflection coefficients for a ray leaving air ($n = 1.0$) and entering water ($n = 1.33$).

$L_{t,v}$ - transmitted radiance due to volume or subsurface scattering

The bidirectional reflection-distribution function (BRDF) is defined to the differential reflected radiance in the outgoing direction per differential incident irradiance in the incoming direction [23].

$$f_r(\theta_i, \phi_i; \theta_r, \theta_r) \equiv \frac{L_r(\theta_r, \phi_r)}{L_i(\theta_i, \phi_i) \cos\theta_i d\omega_i}$$

The bidirectional transmission-distribution function (BTDF) has a similar definition:

$$f_t(\theta_i, \phi_i; \theta_t, \theta_t) \equiv \frac{L_t(\theta_t, \phi_t)}{L_i(\theta_i, \phi_i) \cos\theta_i d\omega_i}$$

Since we have separated the reflected and transmitted light into two components, the BRDF and BTDF also have two components.

$$\begin{aligned} f_r &= f_{r,s} + f_{r,v} \\ f_t &= f_{ri} + f_{t,v} \end{aligned}$$

If we assume a planar surface, then the radiance reflected from and transmitted across the plane is given by the classic Fresnel coefficients.

$$\begin{aligned} L_r(\theta_r, \phi_r) &= R^{12}(n_i, n_t; \theta_i, \phi_i \rightarrow \theta_r, \phi_r) L_i(\theta_i, \phi_i) \\ L_t(\theta_t, \phi_t) &= T^{12}(n_i, n_t; \theta_i, \phi_i \rightarrow \theta_t, \phi_t) L_i(\theta_i, \phi_i) \end{aligned}$$

where

$$\begin{aligned} R^{12}(n_i, n_t; \theta_i, \phi_i \rightarrow \theta_r, \phi_r) &= R(n_i, n_t, \cos\theta_i, \cos\theta_t) \\ T^{12}(n_i, n_t; \theta_i, \phi_i \rightarrow \theta_t, \phi_t) &= \frac{n_t^2}{n_i^2} T = \frac{n_t^2}{n_i^2}(1 - R) \end{aligned}$$

where R and T are the Fresnel reflection formulae and are described in the standard texts (e.g. Ishimura[14]) and θ_t is the angle of transmission. Besides returning the amount of reflection and transmission across the boundary, the functions R^{12} and T^{12}, as a side effect, compute the reflected and refracted angles from the Reflection Law ($\theta_r = \theta_i$) and Snell's Law ($n_i \sin\theta_i = n_t \sin\theta_t$). Note also the factor of $(n_t/n_i)^2$) in the transmitted coefficient of the above formula; this arises due to the change in differential solid angle under refraction and is discussed in Ishimura[pp. 154-155]. Plots of the Fresnel functions for the boundary between air and water are shown in Figure 2.

In our model of reflection, the relative contributions of the surface and subsurface terms are modulated by the Fresnel coefficients.

$$f_r = R f_{r,s} + T f_{r,v} = R f_{r,s} + (1 - R) f_{r,v}$$

Thus, an immediate prediction of the model is that reflection due to subsurface scattering is high when Fresnel reflection is low, since more light enters the surface layer. Notice in Figure 2 that the percentage of transmission is very high for a quite wide range of angles of incidence. Thus, the reflectance properties of materials impregnated with water or oil (dielectrics with low indices of refraction) are dominated by subsurface reflectance components at near perpendicular angles of incidence, and surface components at glancing angles of incidence.

Actually, light returning from the subsurface layers must refract across the boundary again. Thus, it will be attenuated by yet another Fresnel transmission factor. Recall that if light returns from a media with a higher index of refraction, then total internal reflection may occur. All light with an incident angle greater than the critical angle ($\theta_c = sin^{-1}\, n_i/n_t$) will not be transmitted across the boundary. By assuming an isotropic distribution of returning light, we can compute the percentage that will be transmitted and hence considered reflected. This sets an upper bound on the subsurface reflectance of $1 - (n_i/n_t)^2$ (remember, $n_t > n_i$). For example, for an air-water boundary, the maximum subsurface reflectance is approximately .44.

3 Description of Materials

The aim of this work is to simulate the appearance of natural materials such as human skin, plant leaves, snow, sand, paint, etc. The surface of these materials is comprised of one or more layers of material composed of a mixture of randomly distributed particles or inhomogeneities embedded in a translucent media. Particle distributions can also exist, in which case the properties are the material are given by the product of each particle's properties times the number of particles per unit volume.

The layers of such materials can be described by a set of macroscopic parameters as shown in the following table. Measurements of these properties have been made for a large variety of natural materials.

Symbol	Property
n	index of refraction
σ_a [mm^{-1}]	absorption cross section
σ_s [mm^{-1}]	scattering cross section
d [mm]	depth or thickness
$p(\cos j)$	scattering phase function
g	mean cosine of phase function

- *Index of Refraction*
  The materials considered are dielectrics where n is on the order of the index of refraction of water (1.33).
- *Absorption and scattering cross section*
  The intensity of the backscattered and transmitted light depends on the absorption and scattering properties of the material. The cross section may be interpreted as the probability per unit length of an interaction of a particular type. The total scattering cross section $\sigma_t = \sigma_a + \sigma_s$. The mean free path is equal to the reciprocal of the total cross section. An important quantity is the albedo, which equals $W = \sigma_s/\sigma_t$. If the albedo is close to 1, the scattering cross section is much greater than the absorption cross section, whereas if the albedo is close to 0, absorption is much more likely than scattering.
- *Scattering phase function*
  The phase function, $p(\vec{x};\theta,\phi;\theta',\phi')$ represents the directional scattering from (θ',ϕ') to (θ,ϕ) of the light incident onto a particle. This function depends on the nature of the scattering medium. The form of p is affected by the size, form and orientation of the suspended particles, the dielectric properties of the particles, and the wavelength of the incident light. The scattering of light from particles small compared to the wavelength of light is given by the Rayleigh scattering formula, and the scattering due to dielectric spheres of different radii by the Mie formula.

  However, most materials contain distributions of particles of many different sizes, so simple single particle phase functions are not applicable. For this reason, we describe the material phase function with the empirical formula, the Henyey-Greenstein formula[13].

  $$p_{HG}(\cos j) = \frac{1}{4\pi}\frac{1-g^2}{(1+g^2-2g\cos j)^{3/2}}$$

  where j is the angle between the incoming and the outgoing direction (if the phase function depends only on this angle the scattering is symmetric about the incident direction). The Henyey-Greenstein formula depends on a single parameter g, the mean cosine of the scattered light. The Henyey-Greenstein phase function for different values of g is shown in Figure 3. Note that if $g = 0$ the scattering is isotropic, whereas positive g indicates predominantly forward scattering and negative g indicates predominantly backward scattering.

Figure 3: Henyey-Greenstein phase function for $g = -.3$ and $g = .6$.

In the model employed in this paper, material properties are described macroscopically as averages over the underlying microscopic material property definitions. If the material is made of several components, the resulting properties of the composite materials can be computed by simple summation.

$$\sigma_a = \sum_{i=1}^{n} w_i\, \sigma_{a,i}$$

$$\sigma_s\, p(\cos j, g) = \sum_{i=1}^{n} w_i\, \sigma_{s,i}\, p(\cos j, g_i)$$

and so on. Here w_i is the volume fraction of the volume occupied by material i.

Another very important property of real materials is that the properties randomly vary or fluctuate. Such fluctuations cause variation in the appearance of natural surfaces. This type of fluctuation is easy to model with a random noise function or a texture map.

Optical propagation in random media has been studied in a variety of applications, including blood oximetry, skin photometry, plant physiology, remote sensing for canopies and snow, the paint and paper industry, and oceanic and atmospheric propagation. For many examples the macroscopic parameters have been measured across many frequency bands. A major attempt of our work is the simulation of the appearance of natural surfaces by using measured parameters to be inserted into the subsurface reflection and transmission formulas. This approach is similar to the attempt of Cook & Torrance [8] to simulate the appearance of metallic surfaces by using appropriate values for the refractive index and the roughness parameters.

4 Light Transport Equations

Linear transport theory is a heuristic description of the propagation of light in materials. Transport theory is an approximation to electromagnetic scattering theory, and hence cannot predict diffraction, interference or quantum effects. In particular, the specular reflection of light from rough surfaces whose height variation is comparable in size to the wavelength of incident light requires the full electromagnetic theory as is done in He et al[12]. A nice discussion of the derivation of transport theory from electromagnetism and the conditions under which it is valid is contained in an recent article by Fante[9]. The applicability of transport theory, however, has been verified by its application to a large class of practical problems involving turbid materials, including inorganic materials such as ponds, atmospheres, snow, sand and organic materials such as human skin and plant tissue[14].

Transport theory models the distribution of light in a volume by a linear integro-differential equation.

$$\frac{\partial L(\vec{x},\theta,\phi)}{\partial s} = -\sigma_t L(\vec{x},\theta,\phi) + \sigma_s \int p(\vec{x};\theta,\phi;\theta',\phi') L(\vec{x},\theta',\phi')\, d\theta'\, d\phi'$$

This equation is easily derived by accounting for energy balance within a differential volume element. It simply states that the change in radiance along a particular infinitesimal direction ds consists of two terms. The first term decreases the radiance due to absorption and scattering. The second term accounts for light scattered in the direction of ds from all other directions. Thus, it equals the integral over all incoming directions.

For layered media, the assumption is made that all quantities only depend on z and not on x and y. This assumption is valid if the incoming illumination is reasonably constant over the region of interest. It is also roughly equivalent to saying the reflected light emanates from the same point upon which it hits the surface. With this assumption, the above equation simplifies to

$$\cos\theta \frac{\partial L(\theta,\phi)}{\partial z} = -\sigma_t L(\theta,\phi) + \sigma_s \int p(z;\theta,\phi;\theta',\phi')\, L(\theta',\phi')\, d\theta'\, d\phi'$$

The above equation is an integro-differential equation. It can be converted to an equivalent double integral equation, whose solution is the same as the original integro-differential equation.

$$L(z;\theta,\phi) = \int_0^z e^{-\int_0^{z'} \sigma_t \frac{dz''}{\cos\theta}} \int \sigma_s(z')\, p(z';\theta,\phi;\theta',\phi')\, L(z';\theta',\phi')\, d\omega'\, \frac{dz'}{\cos\theta}$$

This is the basis of most current approaches to volume rendering.

The 1-dimensional linear transport equation must also satisfy certain boundary conditions. This is most easily seen by considering the forward and the backward radiance separately.

$$L(\theta,\phi) = L_+(\theta,\phi) + L_-(\pi-\theta,\phi)$$

Where L_+ is energy propagating in the positive z direction, and L_- in the negative direction. Note that L_- is defined to be a function of of $\pi-\theta$, the angle between the backward direction of propagation and the negative z axis. It is important to remember this convention when using formulas involving backward radiances.

At the top boundary the forward radiance is related to the incident radiance.

$$L_+(z=0;\theta',\phi') = \int f_{t,s}(\theta_i,\phi_i;\theta',\phi')\, L_i(\theta_i,\phi_i)\, d\omega_i$$

This simply states that the forward component of radiance entering the volume at the boundary is due to light transmitted across the surface. If we assume a planar surface and parallel incident rays, then $f_{t,s}$ equals the Fresnel transmission term times a δ-function that picks up the appropriate angle of incidence.

$$L_+(z=0;\theta',\phi') = T^{12}(n_i,n_t;\theta_i,\phi_i \rightarrow \theta',\phi') L_i(\theta_i,\phi_i)$$

In the more general case of a rough surface, $f_{t,s}$ is given by a transmission coefficient times the probability that light will refract in the desired direction.

The boundary conditions at the top let us formally state the contribution to reflection due to subsurface scattering in terms of the solution of the integral equation at the boundary $z=0$.

$$L_{r,v}(\theta_r,\phi_r) = \int f_{t,s}(\theta,\phi;\theta_r,\phi_r)\, L_-(z=0;\theta,\phi)\, d\omega$$

Assuming a planar surface, this integral simplifies to

$$L_{r,v}(\theta_r,\phi_r) = T^{21}(n_i,n_t;\theta,\phi \rightarrow \theta_r,\phi_r) L_-(z=0;\theta,\phi)$$

Similar reasoning allows the transmitted radiance to be determined from the boundary conditions at the bottom boundary.

$$L_{t,v}(\theta_t,\phi_t) = \int f_{t,s}(\theta,\phi;\theta_t,\phi_t)\, L_+(z=d;\theta,\phi)\, d\omega$$

Once again, assuming a smooth surface,

$$L_{t,v}(\theta_t,\phi_t) = T^{23}(n_2,n_3;\theta,\phi \rightarrow \theta_t,\phi_t) L_+(z=d;\theta,\phi)$$

Thus, the determination of the reflection functions has been reduced to the computation of $L_-(z=0)$ and $L_+(z=d)$—the solution of the one-dimensional transport equation.

5 Solving the Integral Equation

There are very few cases in which integro-differential equations can be directly solved. The most famous solution is for the case of isotropic scattering and was derived by Chandrasekhar[7, p. 124]. Even for this simple phase function the solution is anisotropic.

The classic way to solve such an equation is to write it in terms of the Neumann series. Physically, this can be interpreted as expanding the solution in terms of the radiance due to an integer number of scattering events. That is,

$$L = \sum_{i=0}^{\infty} L^{(i)}$$

where $L^{(0)}$ is the direct radiance assuming no scattering, $L^{(1)}$ is the radiance due to a single scattering event, and $L^{(i)}$ is the radiance due to i scattering events. Similar equations apply to the forward and backward radiances, $L_+^{(i)}$ and $L_-^{(i)}$.

The radiance due to the i scattering events can be written using the following recurrence.

$$L^{(i+1)}(z;\theta,\phi) = \int_0^z e^{-\int_0^{z'} \sigma_t \frac{dz''}{\cos\theta}} \int \sigma_s(z')\, p(z';\theta,\phi;\theta',\phi')\, L^{(i)}(z';\theta',\phi')\, d\omega'\, \frac{dz'}{\cos\theta}$$

This is the basis for most iterative approaches for numerically calculating transport quantities.

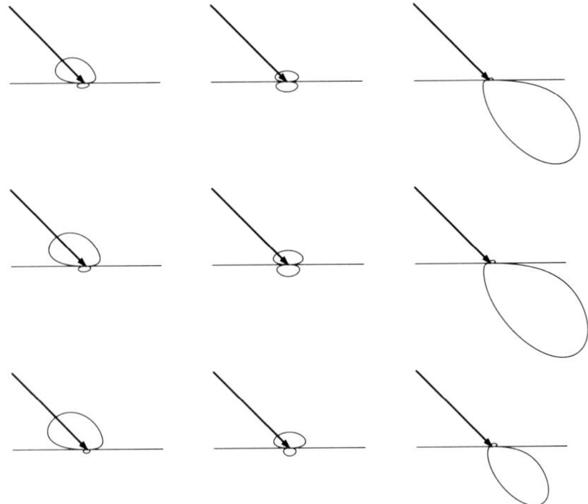

Figure 4: Solutions for $f^{(1)}_{r,v}$ and $f^{(1)}_{t,v}$ for different values of g and τ_d. From left to right the phase function shifts from predominately backward scattering ($g = -0.3$) to isotropic scattering ($g = 0.0$) to forward scattering ($g = 0.6$). From top to bottom the optical depth of the layer increases from 0.5 to 1.0 to 2.0.

5.1 First-Order Approximation

Another classic result in radiative transport, also derived by Chandrasekhar[7], is the analytic solution to the integral equation assuming only a single scattering event. As mentioned previously, this is equivalent to the method described by Blinn but derived using a completely different technique [2].

The 0th-order solution assumes that light is attenuated by the scattering and absorption, but not scattered. The attenuated incident light is called the *reduced intensity* and equals

$$L^{(0)}_{+}(z) = L_{+}(z = 0)e^{-\tau / \cos\theta}$$

Here,

$$\tau(z) = \int_0^z \sigma_t \, dz$$

is called the *optical depth*. If σ_t is constant, then $\tau_d = \sigma_t d$.

Using the boundary conditions for incident and reflected light, and also rewriting the above equation in terms of the angles of incidence and reflection, we arrive at the following formula for the 0th-order transmitted intensity

$$L^{(0)}_{t,v}(\theta_t, \phi_t) = T^{12}T^{23}e^{-\tau_d}L_i(\theta_i, \phi_i)$$

By substituting the 0th-order solution, or reduced intensity, into the integral equation, the 1st-order solutions for forward and backward scattering can be calculated. The details of this calculation are described in Chandrasekhar and Ishimura and there is no need to repeat them here.

Using the boundary conditions for incident and reflected light, and also rewriting in terms of the angles of incidence and reflection, we arrive at the following formula for the backscattered radiance:

$$L^{(1)}_{r,v}(\theta_r, \phi_r) =$$
$$WT^{12}T^{21}p(\pi-\theta_r,\phi_r;\theta_i,\phi_i)\frac{\cos\theta_i}{\cos\theta_i+\cos\theta_r}(1-e^{-\tau_d(1/\cos\theta_i+1/\cos\theta_r)})L_i(\theta_i,\phi_i)$$

This general formula shows that the backscattered light intensity depends on the Fresnel transmission coefficients, the albedo, the layer depth, and the backward part of the scattering phase function.

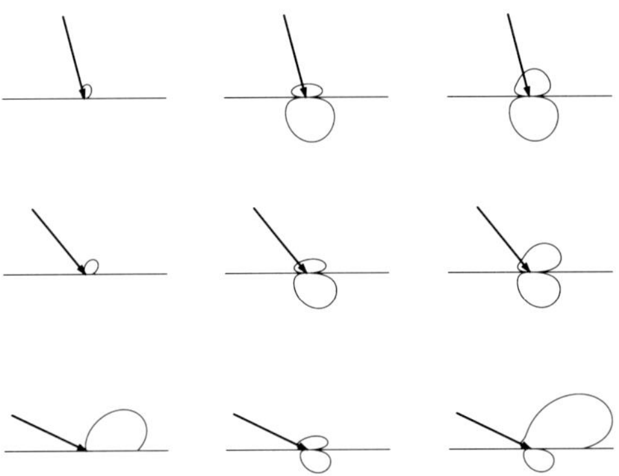

Figure 5: Solutions for f_r and f_t. In the left column is the surface specular reflection and in the middle is the subsurface reflection and transmission. On the right is the sum of surface and subsurface modulated by the Fresnel coefficients. From top to bottom the angle of incidence increases from 10 to 40 to 65 degrees.

A special case of this equation is Seeliger's Law, the first attempt to model diffuse reflection from first principles[25]. Seeliger's Law can be derived by assuming a semi-infinite layer ($\tau_d = \infty$) and ignoring Fresnel effects.

$$L_{r,v}(\theta_r, \phi_r) = \frac{\cos\theta_i}{\cos\theta_i + \cos\theta_r}L_i(\theta_i, \phi_i)$$

At the boundary $z = d$, the forward scattered radiance is given by

$$L^{(1)}_{t,v}(\theta_t, \phi_t) =$$
$$WT^{12}T^{23}p(\theta_t,\phi_t;\theta_i,\phi_i)\frac{\cos\theta_i}{\cos\theta_i-\cos\theta_t}(e^{-\tau_d/\cos\theta_i}-e^{-\tau_d/\cos\theta_t})L_i(\theta_i,\phi_i)$$

For $\cos\theta_t = \cos\theta_i$, the singular factors can be avoided by using L'Hospital's rule, yielding

$$L^{(1)}_{t,v}(\theta_t, \phi_t) = WT^{12}T^{23}p(\theta_t, \phi_t; \theta_t, \phi_t)\frac{\tau_d}{\cos\theta_t}e^{-\tau_d/\cos\theta_t}L_i(\theta_t, \phi_t)$$

Figure 4 shows $f_{r,v}$ and $f_{t,v}$ for various values of g and d. Figure 5 shows the surface and subsurface components of the reflection model for various angles of incidence. These reflection and transmission distribution functions have several interesting properties:

1. The reflection steadily increases as the layer becomes thicker; in contrast, the transmission due to scattering increases to a point, then begins to decrease because of further scattering events.
2. Subsurface reflection and transmission can be predominately backward or forward depending on the phase function.
3. As the angle of incidence becomes more glancing, the surface scattering tends to dominate, causing both the reflection and the transmission due to subsurface scattering to decrease.
4. Due to the Fresnel effect, the reflection goes to zero at the horizons. Also, the reflection function appears "flattened" relative to a hemicircle. Thus, reflection for near normal angles of incidence varies less than Lambert's Law predicts.
5. The distributions vary as a function of reflection direction. Lambert's Law predicts a constant reflectance in all directions (which would be drawn as a hemicircle in these diagrams).

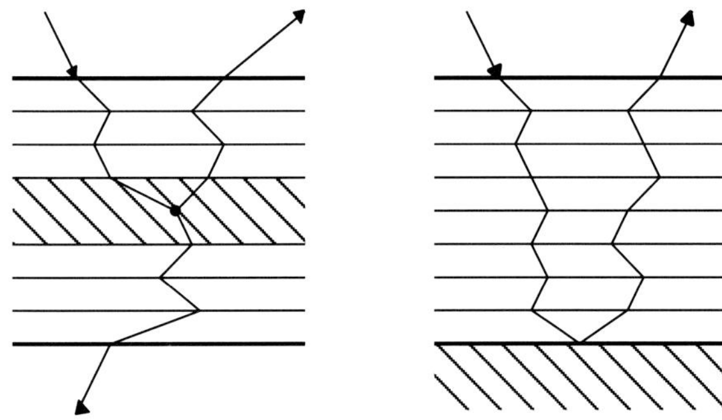

Figure 6: Determining first-order solutions for multiple layers. On the left, the contribution to the first order solution for a single layer. One the right, the contribution to the first order solution due to reflectance off a single layer.

The above formulas can be used to generate first-order solutions for multiple layers. (This is shown diagrammatically in Figure 6.) The total first-order scattering will be the sum of the first-order scattering from each layer, weighted by the percentage of light making it to the layer and returning from the layer. The percentage of light making it to the layer is the product of the 0th-order transmission functions (or reduced intensity) for a path through the layers above the reflecting layer. Similarly, the percentage of light leaving the entire layer after reflection is equal to the product of the 0th-order transmission functions for the path taken on the way out. Note that across each boundary the light may refract, and thus change direction and be attenuated by the Fresnel coefficient, but this is easy to handle. The process simplifies, of course, if each layer has the same index of refraction, since no reflection or change of direction occurs between layers. Given the above formulas it is very easy to construct a procedure to perform this calculation and we will make use of it in the results section.

The above formula can also be generalized to include reflection from a boundary between layers. In many situations reflection can only occur from the bottom layer. In this case, we add a single term accounting for the reduced intensity to reach the lower boundary, and also weight the returning light from that boundary. Such a model is commonly employed to model the reflection of light from a pool of water[15], and has been employed by Nishita and Nakamae[22]. Further generalizations of this type are described in Ishimura[14, p. 172].

6 Multiple Scattering

The above process of substituting the ith-order solution and then computing the integral to arrive at the (i+1)th-order solution can be repeated, but is very laborious. Note that subsequent integrals now involve angular distributions, because, although the input radiance is non-zero in only a single direction, the scattered radiance essentially comes from the directional properties of the phase function. Thus, this approach to solving the system analytically quickly becomes intractable.

We have implemented a Monte-Carlo algorithm for computing light transport in layered media. This algorithm is described in Figure 7. A thorough discussion of the application of Monte Carlo algorithms for layered media is discussed in the book [21], and the techniques we are using are quite standard.

To investigate the effects of multiple scattering terms, we simulated a semi-infinite turbid media with different albedos. The reflectance was computed and when the particles returning from the media are scored, we keep track of how many scattering events they underwent. Figure 8 shows the results of this experiment. The top curve is the total reflectance, and the lower curves represent scattering up to some order. Note that when the albedo is high, implying that $\sigma_s >> \sigma_a$, the first order term is only a small percentage of the total reflectance. However, as the albedo decreases, corresponding to greater absorption, a few low-order terms accurately approximate the reflectance. This effect can be explained by recalling that each term in the Neumann series representing the reflection is on the order of W^i, and since W is always less than one, the magnitude of higher-order terms quickly goes to zero.

1 *Initialize*: A particle enters the layer at the origin. Initialize $\vec{p}$ to the origin and the direction $\vec{s}$ to the direction at which the ray enters the layer. Set the weight $w = 1$.

2 *Events*: Repeat the following steps until the ray weight drops below some threshold or the ray exits the layer.

2A *Step*: First, estimate the distance to the next interaction:

$$d = -\frac{\log r}{\sigma_t}$$

Where r in this and the following formulas is a uniformly distributed random number between 0 and 1. Then, compute the new position:

$$\vec{p} = \vec{p} + d\,\vec{s}$$

And, finally set the particle weight to

$$w = w\frac{\sigma_s}{\sigma_s + \sigma_a}$$

Note: If d causes the particle to leave the layer, break from the repeat loop and adjust the weight using the distance to the boundary.

2B *Scatter*: First, estimate the cosine of the scattering angle for the Henyey-Greenstein phase function using the following formula.

$$\cos j = \frac{1}{|2g|}(1 + g^2 - (\frac{1 - g^2}{1 - g + 2gr})^2)$$

and $\cos\phi$ and $\sin\phi$ with $\phi = 2\pi r$. Then, compute the new direction:

$$\vec{t} = \begin{pmatrix} (\vec{s}.x\cos\phi\cos\theta - \vec{s}.y\sin\phi)/\sin\theta \\ (\vec{s}.y\cos\phi\cos\theta + \vec{s}.x\sin\phi)/\sin\theta \\ \sin\theta \end{pmatrix}$$

$$\vec{s} = \vec{s}\cos j + \vec{t}\sin j$$

Here, $\cos\theta = \vec{s}.z$ and $\sin\theta = \sqrt{1 - \vec{s}.z^2}$. Note: Care must be taken if $\sin\theta = 0$.

3 *Score*: Divide the sphere into regions of equal solid angle and add the weight of the particle to the weight associated with the bin in which it is contained.

Figure 7: Basic Monte Carlo algorithm for layered media

We have also computed the BRDF as a function of the angle of reflection using our Monte Carlo algorithm for the same configuration as described in the last experiment. The results are shown in Figure 9. Recall that the 1st-order reflection due to a semi-infinite media is given by Seeliger's Law: $\cos\theta_i/(\cos\theta_i + \cos\theta_r)$. The computed 1st-order BRDF matches the theoretical result quite well. In this figure we also plot the total BRDF due to any number of scattering events, and the difference between the total and the 1st-order BRDF. Note as in the previous experiment when the albedo W is small, the BRDF is closely approximated by the 1st-order term. However, note that the shape of the reflection function is also largely determined by the shape of the 1st-order reflection, which in turn is largely determined by the phase function. Fur-

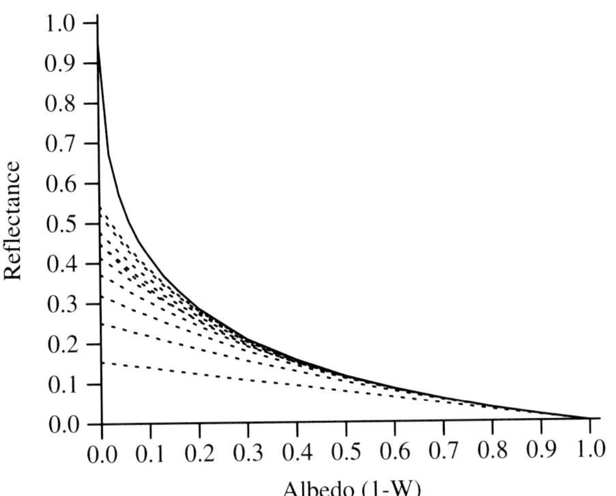

Figure 8: A plot of reflectance versus albedo for a semi-infinite media. The top curve is the total reflectance (the total radiant energy per unit area reflected divided by the incident irradiance). The bottom curve is the reflectance assuming only a single scattering event. Moving upward is a sequence of curves consisting of additional terms corresponding to a single additional scattering event. The first 10 terms in the solution are shown; In our simulations, we recorded terms involving thousands of scattering events.

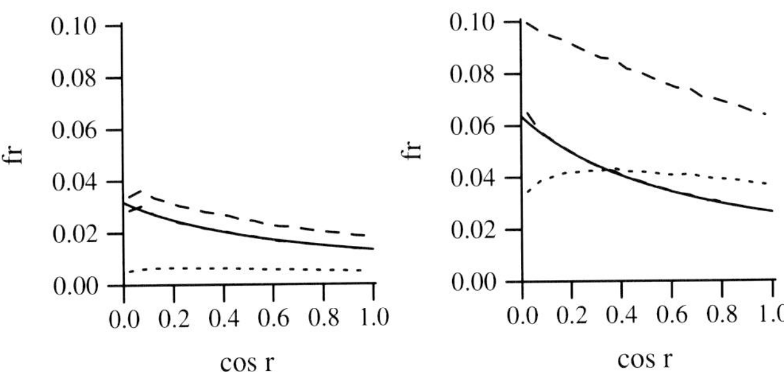

Figure 9: Graphs of the BRDF (f_r) as a function of the angle of reflection for a semi-infinite slab with different albedos (on the left $W = 0.4$ and on the right $W = 0.8$) and an angle of incidence of 45°. The solid line is the theoretical BRDF as given by Seeliger's Law (the superimposed dashed line is the computed 1st-order BRDF showing a good match). The top dashed curve is the total computed BRDF; The bottom dotted curve is the difference between the total BRDF due to multiple scattering events and the 1st-order BRDF.

Property	Epidermis	Dermis	Pigment	Blood
n	1.37-1.5	1.37-1.5	1.37-1.5	1.37-1.5
σ_a [mm^{-1}]	3.8	0.3		32.6
σ_s [mm^{-1}]	50.0	21.7		0.96
d [mm]	0.001-0.15	1-4		
g	0.79	0.81	.79	.0

Table 2: Two Layer Skin Model Properties. Pigment coefficients are mixed with epidermal coefficients to compute the properties of the outer layer. Blood coefficients are mixed with dermal coefficients to compute the properties of the inner layer.

ther, observe that the difference between the 1st-order solution and the full solution is approximately independent of the angle of reflection. Thus, the sum of the higher order terms roughly obeys Lambert's Law. For this reason it is often convenient to divide the subsurface reflection into two terms:

$$L_{r,v}(\theta_r, \phi_r) = L^{(1)}(\theta_r, \phi_r) + L^m$$

where L^m is constant and represents the sum of all the multiple scattering terms.

Finally, we have begun preliminary experiments where we incorporate a Monte Carlo subsurface ray tracer within a standard ray tracer. When the global ray tracer calls the subsurface ray tracer it attempts to estimate the BRDF and BTDF to a particular light source. This is done by *biasing* the Monte Carlo procedure to estimate the energy transported to the light. A simple method to do this is to send a ray to the light at each scattering event, as described in Carter and Cashwell[6]. This ray must be weighted by the phase function and the attenuation caused by the traversal through the media on the way to the light. If the albedo is less than 1, then only a few scattering events are important, and thus the subsurface ray tracer consumes very little time on average (the cost is proportional the the mean number of scattering events). Also, since the subsurface ray tracer does not consider the global environment when tracing its rays, the cost of subsurface Monte Carlo simulation at every shading calculation is relatively low. The advantage of this approach is that the BRDF's do not have to precomputed, and so if material parameters are varying across the surface, the correct answer is still estimated correctly at each point.

7 Results

The subsurface scattering models developed in this paper has been tested on two common natural surfaces: human skin and plant leaves. The goal of these experiments are twofold: First, to compare our anisotropic diffuse reflection model with Lambertian shading. Second, to attempt to simulate the optical appearance from measured parameters. Our experiments are meant to be suggestive of the power of this approach; we do not claim to have an experimentally validated model.

7.1 Skin

Human skin can be modeled as two layers with almost homogeneous properties. Both layers are assumed to have the same refractive index but a different density of randomly distributed absorbers and scatterers. The outer epidermis essentially consists of randomly sized tissue particles and imbedded pigment particles containing melanin. The pigment particles act as strongly wavelength dependent absorbers causing a brown/black coloration as their density increases. The inner dermis is considered to be a composition of weakly absorbing and strongly scattering tissue material and of blood which scatters light isotropically and has strong absorption for the green and blue parts of the spectrum. Experimental evidence also supports the hypothesis that light scattering in the skin is anisotropic with significant forward scattering. A comprehensive study of optical properties of human skin can be found in van Gemert et al.[27]. The values chosen for our test pictures are given in Table 2. We also add a thin outer layer of oil that reflects light using the Torrance-Sparrow model of rough surfaces.

A head data set was acquired using a medical MRI scanner. Unfortunately, the ears and the chin were clipped in the process, but enough of the head is visible to test our shading models. A volume ray tracer was adapted to output the position and normal vector of the skin layer for each pixel into a file, and this input was used to evaluate the shading models described in this paper.

The influence of the various factors appearing in the subsurface reflection formula are shown on Plate 1. These pictures are

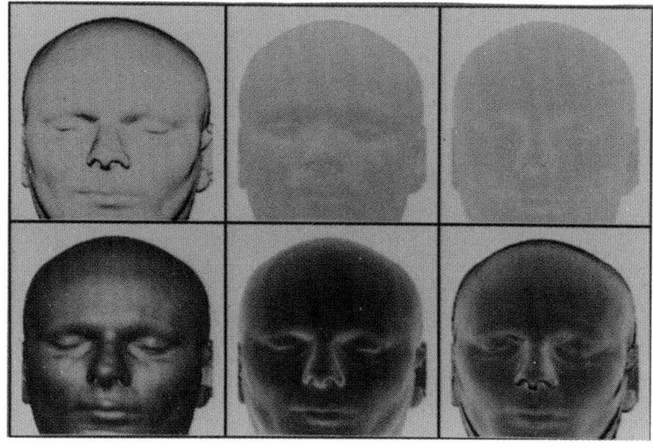

Plate 1.

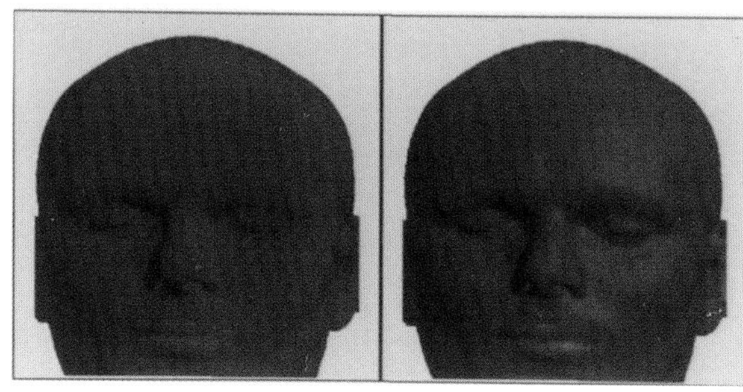

Plate 3: Dark complexion controlled by setting the concentration of melanin. On the left are images with just subsurface scattering. On the right, an specular surface term is added to simulate an oily coat. In these pictures $g = .65$.

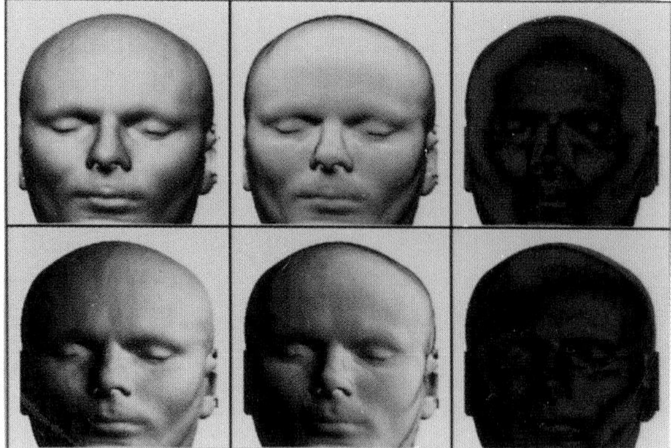

Plate 2.

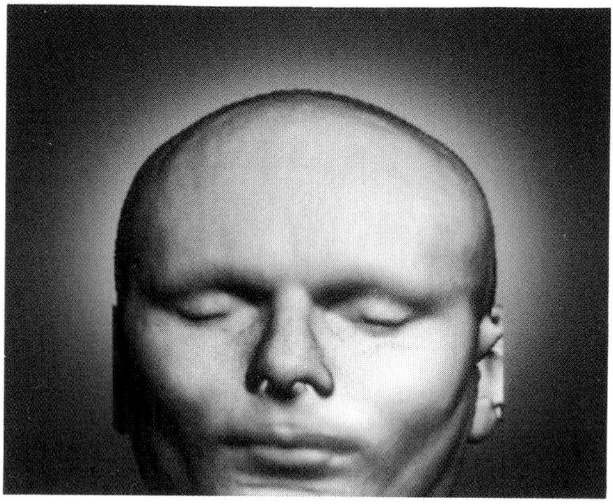

Plate 4: Human face with variation in subsurface blood concentration, an oily outer layer and Gaussian variation in parameters to create the "freckles."

not shaded in the conventional way. In particular, a Lambertian shading model would yield a constant image. The first picture (upper left) shows the influence of the Fresnel factors. Observe that the intensity is almost flat, but strongly attenuated for glancing incident and viewing angles. The second picture (upper middle) shows the action of Seeliger's Law alone. Seeliger's Law leads to very little variation in shading, which makes the surface appear even more chalky or dusty. The third picture (upper right) demonstrates the action of the factor accounting for the finite layer depth giving only weak enhancements for glancing angles. This is a minor effect. The fourth picture (lower left) shows the influence of the Henyey-Greenstein scattering phase function for small backward scattering ($g = -.25$) and the fifth picture (lower middle) shows the effect of large forward scattering ($g = .75$). The result is strong enhancement of glancing reflection for low angles of incidence and viewing, assuming they are properly aligned. The last picture (lower right) shows the superposition of these four factors with $g = .75$ giving a complex behavior. An overall smoothing of the reflection appears; the surface appears to be more "silk-like" (see also Plate 3). Although these effects are all subtle, their combination when controlled properly can create a wide variation in appearance.

The appearance of the face with the new subsurface reflection model is compared to the Lambertian diffuse reflection model for different angles of incidence in Plate 2. The left column shows the results for the Lambert scattering for angles 0 and 45 degrees, and the middle column is rendered for the new model. Again, notice a much smoother "silk-like" appearance. The right column gives the relative difference of both models, red indicates more reflection from the new model, and blue vice versa.

To illustrate the degrees of freedom of the model, we rendered several faces with their parameters controlled by texture maps. One texture map controls the relative concentration of blood in the dermis; another texture map controls the concentration of melanin in the epidermal layer. These faces are shown in Plates 3 and 4. To create a dark complexion we modulate the percentage of pigment in the otherwise transparent epidermis. This creates a dark brown appearance due to the strong absorption of melanin (in this case we set the absorption to .6). For the lips the epidermis is set to be very thin such that the appearance is dominated by the reflection from the dermis which has for the lips a large blood content (strong absorption for green and blue light component). The epidermis pigment part also has been varied locally with about 20% with a Gaussian process. This allows us to create a wide variety of skin colors, from black to suntanned to Caucasian, and from flushed to burnt to relaxed. The pictures in Plate 3 also show the effect of an additional specular term due to a thin layer of oil on the skin. Finally, Plate 4 shows another picture created by our program.

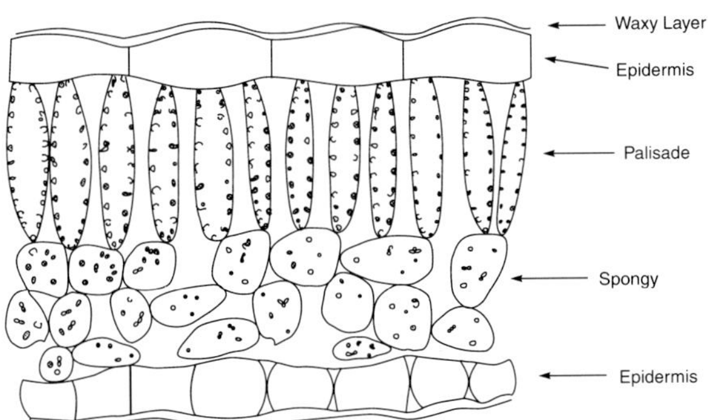

Figure 10: Typical leaf cross-section (Redrawn from [20]).

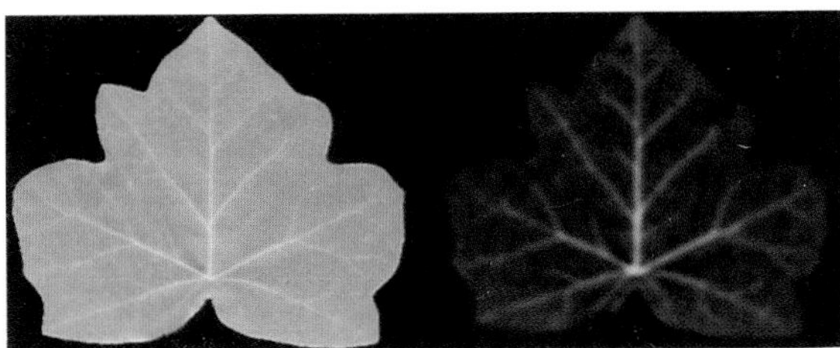

Plate 5: Leaf Model. On the left is the albedo image and on the right is a thickness image (white indicates thick)

This picture took approximately 20 seconds to render on a Silicon Graphics Personal Iris.

7.2 Leaves

Figure 10 shows an idealized leaf in cross-section. The leaf is composed of several layers of cells. On the top and bottom are epidermal cells with a thin smooth, waxy cuticular outer layer. The waxy cuticular layer is largely responsible for specularly reflected light. Below the upper epidermal cells there are a series of long palisaide cells which are highly absorbing due to the numerous chloroplasts contained within them. Below the palisaide cells are a loosely packed layer of irregularly shaped spongy cells. The spaces between the spongy cells are filled with air, which causes them to scatter light. Both the palisaide and the spongy cells are quite large (approximately 20 μm) compared to the wavelength, so their scattering phase function is forward directed. Furthermore, the cells are high in water content, so the index of refraction of the leaf is approximately equal to that of water—1.33. A typical leaf is .5 to 1 mm thick, with an optical depth of 5 to 10.

To test our model on a leaf, we constructed a leaf model using the technique described in Bloomenthal[3]. Although spectral transmission and reflectance curves are available for leaves[29], we have set the color of the leaf from an image acquired from a digital scanner. An albedo image is texture mapped onto a series of simply-shaped, bent polygons to create the leaf. Where the texture map is transparent the polygon is considered transparent and the leaf is not visible. We also modulate the thickness of the leaf with a thickness map drawn on top of the original leaf image. The texture maps we used are shown in Plate 5. The waxy cuticle is modeled using a rough specular surface with a specular exponent of 10. The interior of the leaf is modeled as a single homogeneous layer with an optical depth of 5 and a mean scattering cosine of .3[20].

Pictures were generated by modifying a conventional ray tracer to account for subsurface reflection and transmission. When a ray encounters a leaf, the BRDF and BTDF are evaluated for direct illumination from light sources. Shadow rays are cast to the light source, and if the ray stabs any other leaves the light intensity is attenuated by the 0th-order transmission function through each leaf. Plate 6 shows a picture of a cluster of leaves with the sun in different positions. Note that the reflection from leaves is largely determined by specular reflection due to the waxy cuticle; there is very little diffuse reflection and hence when the light source is on the same side of the leaf as the viewer, the leaf is quite dark. The transmission term, however, can be quite large, and therefore the leaves may actually be brighter when the are illuminated from behind. Note also that the increased thickness of the veins cause dark shadows to be cast on other leaves. The veins also appear dark when the leaf is back lit because they absorb more light, and bright when the leaf is front lit because their increased thickness causes more light to be reflected.

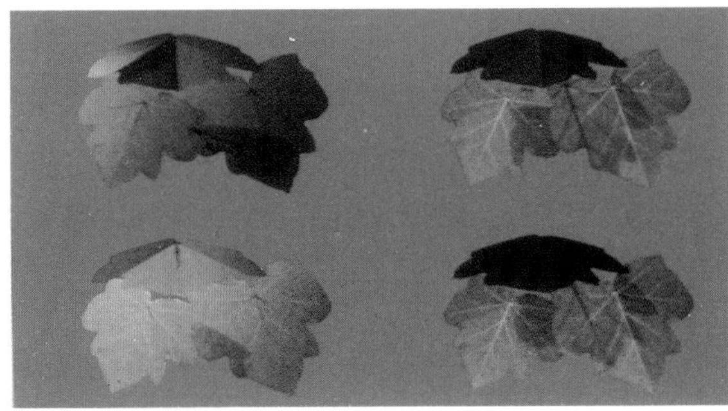

Plate 6: A cluster of leaves. A series of leaf images under different simulated lighting conditions. On the left are two backlit images, on the right, front lit.

8 Summary and Discussion

We have presented a reflectance model consisting of two terms: the standard surface reflectance and a new subsurface reflectance due to backscattering in a layered turbid media. This model is applicable to biological and inorganic materials with low indices of refraction, because their translucent nature implies that a high percentage of the incident light enters the material, and so the subsurface reflection is quite large. This model incorporates directional scattering within the layer, so the resulting subsurface reflection is not isotropic. This model can be interpreted as a theoretical model of diffuse reflectance. Thus, this model predicts a directionally varying diffuse reflection, in contrast to Lambert's Law. However, if multiple scattering contributes significantly to the reflection, then the higher scattering terms contribute to a reflection function with roughly the same shape.

As in any model, our model makes many assumptions. The two most important are that the physical optics may be approximated with transport theory, and that the material can be abstracted into layered, turbid media with macroscopic scattering and absorption properties. An "exact" model of biological tissues would explicitly model individual cells, organelles and so on, in considerably more detail. The Monte-Carlo algorithm for simulating reflection by Westin et al.[28] is an example of such an approach. Although such an approach may seem more accurate, often the experimental data needed to describe the arrangements of these structures is simply not available, and so in the end the results may be difficult to validate. An advantage of the transport theory approach is that the parameters of the model often may be directly extracted from experimental data.

A legitimate criticism of our work is that we did not directly compare the predictions of our model with experiment. The predictions of our model and the influence of measured material parameters should be checked carefully. However, we believe that this model has many applications in computer graphics even if it does not perfectly predict measured reflection functions. The metaphor of layered surfaces is very easy for users to understand because is a natural way to describe phenomenologically the appearance of many materials. It also fits easily into most rendering systems and can be implemented efficiently.

Finally, transport theory is a heuristic theory based on abstracting microscopic parameters into statistical averages. Transport theory is also the basis of the rendering equation, which is widely viewed as the correct theoretical framework for global illumination calculations. In this paper we propose to model surface reflection from layered surfaces with transport theory. Thus, when our reflectance model for layered surfaces is incorporated into a ray tracer, there is a hierarchy of transport calculations being performed. Within this hierarchy, the lower level transport equation computes the reflectance for the higher level transport equation. When performing this calculation, the lower level transport equation uses as its initial conditions the values from the higher level transport solution. Thus the two levels are coupled in a very simple way. In fact, it is possible to reformulate transport theory entirely in terms of reflection functions, the result is an integral equation for the reflection function itself; in this formulation the radiance does not appear at all. Coupling transport equations at different levels of detail in this manner is a promising approach to tackling the problem of constructing representations with many different levels of detail as proposed by Kajiya[17].

9 Acknowledgements

We would like to thank Craig Kolb for his help with RayShade and the leaf pictures. We would also like to thank David Laur for his help with the color plates. This research was partially supported by Apple, Silicon Graphics Computer Systems, David Sarnoff Research Center, and the National Science Foundation (CCR 9207966).

References

[1] BECKMANN, P., AND SPIZZICHINO, A. *The scattering of electromagnetic waves from rough surfaces*. Pergamon, Oxford, 1963.

[2] BLINN, J. F. Light Reflection Functions for Simulation of Clouds and Dusty Surfaces. *Computer Graphics 16*, 3 (July 1982), 21–29.

[3] BLOOMENTHAL, J. Modeling the Mighty Maple. *Computer Graphics 19*, 3 (July 1985), 305–311.

[4] BOUGUER, P. *The Gradation of Light*. University of Toronto Press, 1960.

[5] CABRAL, B., MAX, N., AND SPRINGMEYER, R. Bidirectional reflection functions from surface bump maps. *Computer Graphics 21*, 4 (July 1990), 273–281.

[6] CARTER, L., AND CASHWELL, E. *Particle Transport Simulation with the Monte Carlo Method*. Energy Research and Development Administration, 1975.

[7] CHANDRASEKHAR, S. *Radiative Transfer*. Dover, New York, 1960.

[8] COOK, R. L., AND TORRANCE, K. E. A Reflection Model for Computer Graphics. *ACM Transactions on Graphics 1*, 1 (1982), 7–24.

[9] FANTE, R. Relationship between Radiative Transport Theory and Maxwell's Equations in Dielectric Media. *J. Opt. Soc. Am. 71*, 4 (April 1981), 460–468.

[10] GRAWBOSKI, L. *Astrophysics J. 39* (1914), 299.

[11] HANRAHAN, P. From Radiometry to the Rendering Equation. *SIGGRAPH Course Notes: An Introduction to Radiosity* (1992).

[12] HE, X. D., TORRANCE, K. E., SILLION, F. X., AND GREENBERG, D. P. A Comprehensive Physical Model for Light Reflection. *Computer Graphics 25*, 4 (July 1991), 175–186.

[13] HENYEY, L. G., AND GREENSTEIN, J. L. Diffuse radiation in the galaxy. *Astrophysics J. 93* (1941), 70–83.

[14] ISHIMURA, A. *Wave Propagation and Scattering in Random Media*. Academic Press, New York, 1978.

[15] JERLOV, N. G. *Optical Oceanography*. Elsevier, Amsterdam, 1968.

[16] KAJIYA, J. Radiometry and Photometry for Computer Graphics. *SIGGRAPH Course Notes: State of the Art in Image Synthesis* (1990).

[17] KAJIYA, J. Anisotropic Reflection Models. *Computer Graphics 19*, 3 (July 1985), 15–22.

[18] KORTUM, G. *Reflectance Spectroscopy*. Springer-Verlag, Berlin, 1969.

[19] KRUEGER, W. The Application of Transport Theory to the Visualization of 3-D Scalar Fields. *Computers in Physics 5* (April 1991), 397–406.

[20] MA, Q., ISHIMURA, A., PHU, P., AND KUGA, Y. Transmission, Reflection and Depolarization of an Optical Wave For a Single Leaf. *IEEE Transactions on Geoscience and Remote Sensing 28*, 5 (September 1990), 865–872.

[21] MARCHUK, G., MIKHAILOV, G., NAZARALIEV, M., DARBINJAN, R., KARGIN, B., AND ELEPOV, B. *The Monte Carlo Methods in Atmospheric Optics*. Springer Verlag, Berlin, 1980.

[22] NAKAMAE, E., KANEDA, K., OKAMOTO, T., AND NISHITA, T. A Lighting Model Aiming at Drive Simulators. *Computer Graphics 24*, 4 (August 1990), 395–404.

[23] NICODEMUS, F. E., RICHMOND, J. C., AND HSIA, J. J. *Geometrical Considerations and Reflectance*. National Bureau of Standards, October 1977.

[24] POULIN, P., AND FOURNIER, A. A Model for Anisotropic Reflection. *Computer Graphics 24*, 4 (August 1990), 273–282.

[25] SEELIGER, R. *Munch. Akad. II. Kl. Sitzungsber 18* (1888), 201.

[26] TORRANCE, K. E., AND SPARROW, E. M. Theory of Off-Specular Reflection From Roughened Surfaces. *Journal of the Optical Society of America 57* (September 1967), 1104–1114.

[27] VAN GEMERT, M. F. C., JACQUES, S. L., STERENBERG, H. J. C. M., AND STAR, W. M. Skin Optics. *IEEE Transactions on Biomedical Engineering 36*, 12 (December, 1989), 1146–1154.

[28] WESTIN, S. H., ARVO, J. R., AND TORRANCE, K. E. Predicting Reflectance Functions from Complex Surfaces. *Computer Graphics 26*, 2 (July 1992), 255–264.

[29] WOOLLEY, J. T. Reflectance and Transmittance of Light by Leaves. *Plant Physiology 47* (1971), 656–662.

Display of The Earth Taking into Account Atmospheric Scattering

Tomoyuki Nishita **Takao Sirai**
Fukuyama University
Higashimura-cho, Fukuyama, 729-02 Japan

Katsumi Tadamura **Eihachiro Nakamae**
Hiroshima Prefectural University
Nanatsuka-cho, Shoubara City, 727 Japan

Abstract

A method to display the earth as viewed from outer space (or a spaceship) is proposed. The intention of the paper is application to space flight simulators (e.g., reentry to the atmosphere) and the simulation of surveys of the earth (comparisons with observations from weather satellites and weather simulations); it is not for geometric modeling of terrains and/or clouds viewed from the ground, but for displaying the earth including the surface of the sea viewed from outer space taking into account particles (air molecules and aerosols) in the atmosphere and water molecules in the sea.

The major points of the algorithm proposed here are the efficient calculation of optical length and sky light, with lookup tables taking advantage of the facts that the earth is spherical, and that sunlight is parallel.

CR Categories and Subject Descriptors:
I.3.3 [**Computer Graphics**]:Picture/Image Generation
I.3.7 [**Computer Graphics**]: Three-Dimensional Graphics and Realism
Key Words: Earth, Atmospheric Scattering, Optical Length, Sky light, Color of Water, Photo-realism, Radiative Transfer

1 INTRODUCTION

Research on image synthesis of realistic 3-D models is one of the most popular fields these days. Displays of natural scenes such as mountains, trees, sea, clouds have been attractively rendered, and an image synthesis of the earth has also been developed. Images of the earth are widely used in movies or TV commercials, e.g., the CG library of earth images[6] was recently released for use in this field. These images, however, are focused on how to create attractive images without any requirement of physical based accuracy. However, physically-based images are required for the study of the simulation of surveys of the earth, such as observation from weather satellites in comparison to weather simulation, and flight simulators in space. The color of the earth when viewed from space varies according to the relationship between the view direction and the position of the sun. In the famous words of the astronaut, "the earth was blue". When we observe the earth from relatively close to the atmosphere, the atmosphere surrounding the earth appears as blue, and the atmosphere near the boundary of the shadow due to the sun appears red (i.e., sunset). The color of clouds also varies according to the sun's position. These phenomena are optical effects caused by particles in the atmosphere, and cannot be ignored. The color of the surface of the sea is not uniform, such as navy blue; it has various colors which depend on incident light to the sea and absorption/scattering effects due to water molecules.

This paper proposes an algorithm of physically-based image synthesis of the earth viewed from space. The method proposed here has the following advantages:

(1) Calculation of the spectrum of the earth viewed through the atmosphere; the earth is illuminated by direct sunlight and sky light affected by atmospheric scattering.

(2) Calculation of the spectrum of the atmosphere taking account of absorption/scattering due to particles in the atmosphere.

(3) Calculation of the spectrum on the surface of the sea taking into account radiative transfer of water molecules.

The major parts in 1) and 2) are concerned with the calculation of optical length and sky light. For these calculations, numerical integrations taking into account atmospheric scattering are required, but they are effectively solved by using several (various) lookup tables making good use of the facts that the shape of the earth is a sphere and that sunlight is a parallel light. For 3), we show that an analytical solution is available instead of numerical integrations.

In the following sections, the basic idea of the lighting model for rendering the color of the earth taking into account atmospheric scattering, rendering the color of clouds, and spectrum calculation of the sea is described. Finally, several examples are demonstrated in order to show the effectiveness of the method proposed here.

2 BASIC IDEAS

In order to render the earth, the following elements should be taken into account: a geometric model of the earth, the atmosphere (air molecules, aerosols), sea, clouds, and the spectrum of the sunlight.

This paper discusses rendering an algorithm of the earth, the atmosphere, sea, and clouds viewed from outer space or various positions within the atmosphere; the following optical characteristics should be considered:

(1) The color of the atmosphere: the atmosphere contains air molecules and aerosols, and scattered sunlight from those particles reaches the viewpoint; the intensity of the light reaching the viewpoint is obtained by integrating scattered light from every particle on the ray, and the light scattered from the atmosphere around the earth also reaches this viewpoint.

(2) The color of the earth's surface: the earth is illuminated by both direct sunlight and sky light. Sunlight is absorbed when light passes through the atmosphere, and sky light consists of light scattered by particles in the air. On the way, passing through the atmosphere the light is attenuated, and its spectrum changes.

© 1993 ACM-0-89791-601-8/93/008/0175 $01.50

(3) The color of the sea: sunlight reaching the surface of the sea is divided into reflected light at the surface and light scattered from water molecules. Both of them pass through the atmosphere and reach the viewpoint.

(4) The color of clouds: sunlight is scattered from particles of clouds, the scattered light is attenuated and reaches the viewpoint.

These phenomena should be simulated as precisely as possible in the calculation of the spectrum of the earth and the atmosphere. As we intend to concentrate on close views of the earth, the bumped terrain model of the earth is used instead of a simple sphere; the continents are modeled by 3D fractals, and the sea is expressed by a sphere consisting of some curved surfaces. Geometric models such as a spaceship are also dealt with.

For hidden surface removal, the scanline algorithm for free form surfaces developed by the authors is employed[11]; the surfaces are expressed by Bézier surfaces.

3 MODELING OF THE EARTH

Even though we may use a modeling in which the earth is treated as a sphere and the land is modeled by bump mapping, we consider the earth as having two components, land and sea: the sea consist of eight cubic Bézier patches, and the land consists of a set of curved surfaces.

The land data is made by mapping small patches onto the sphere, which are subdivided by using fractals after giving the altitude data for each mesh point overlapped onto a world map: the random midpoint displacement algorithm is employed as a fractal.

A scanned image of the map is used as the texture of the land. Therefore the color is not the real color of the earth.

4 SPECTRUM OF THE ATMOSPHERE

Previous work taking account scattering/absorption due to particles include; a) the display of Saturn's rings (reflective ice particles)[1], b) for light scattering from particles in the air, shafts of light caused by spot lights[12], and light beams passing through gaps in the clouds or through trees[8], c) scattered light due to nonuniform density particles such as clouds and smoke[12][4], d) sky color taking account atmospheric scattering[5]. In this paper we focus our discussion on the atmosphere. On this topic, Klassen[5] approximated the atmosphere as multiple layers of plane-parallel atmosphere with uniform density; however, this method results in a large error near the horizon. We discuss here a spherical-shell atmosphere with continuous variation of density in order to improve accuracy. Though his method can only render the color of the sky viewed from a point on the earth, the method discussed here can render the color of the atmosphere viewed from space.

The color of the atmosphere is much influenced by the spectrum of the sunlight, scattering/absorption effects due to particles in the air, reflected light from the earth's surface, and the relationship between the sun's position and the viewpoint (and direction). The sunlight entering the atmosphere is scattered/absorbed by air molecules and aerosol, and ozone layers. The characteristics of scattering depend on the size of particles in the atmosphere. Scattering by small particles such as air molecules is called Rayleigh scattering, and scattering by aerosols such as dust is called Mie scattering. Light is attenuated by both scattering and absorption.

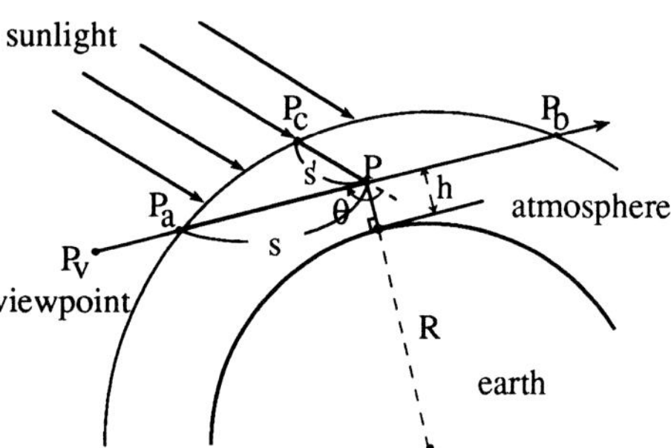

Figure 1: Intensity calculation for the ray intersecting only with the atmosphere.

4.1 Assumptions for Spectrum Calculation

For the spectrum calculation, we use the following assumptions:

(1) The multiple scattering of light between air molecules and aerosols in the atmosphere is ignored because of its negligible values and large computational cost, so only single scattering is considered. The interreflection of light between the earth's surface and particles in the air is also neglected because of the same reasons.

(2) For visible wavelengths, absorption in the ozone layer is negligible compared to absorption by air molecules and aerosols.

(3) The density distributions of air molecules and aerosols are taken into account; their densities vary exponentially with altitude[16].

(4) It is assumed that light travels in a straight line even though the actual path is curved due to the variation of index of refraction with altitudes.

4.2 Atmospheric Scattering

Let's consider scattering due to air molecules and aerosols.

First, single scattering due to air molecules is described. The light reflected due to Rayleigh scattering, I, is generally given by the following equation;

$$I(\lambda,\theta) = I_0(\lambda)K\rho F_r(\theta)/\lambda^4$$
$$K = \frac{2\pi^2(n^2-1)^2}{3N_s} \quad (1)$$

where I_o is the intensity of incident light, K is a constant for the standard atmosphere (molecular density at sea level), θ the scattering angle (see Fig. 1), F_r the scattering phase function indicating the directional characteristic of scattering (given by $3/4(1+cos^2(\theta))$), λ the wavelength of incident light, n the index of refraction of the air, N_s the molecular number density of the standard atmosphere, and ρ the density ratio. ρ depends on the altitude h ($\rho = 1$ at sea level) and is given by

$$\rho = exp(\frac{-h}{H_0}), \quad (2)$$

where H_0 is a scale height ($H_o = 7994$m), which corresponds to the thickness of the atmosphere if the density were uniform.

Eq. (1) indicates that the intensity of scattering is inversely proportional to the 4th power of the wavelength. Short wavelength light is very strongly attenuated by traversing the atmosphere, but long wavelength light is scarcely affected. This is why the sky appears blue in the daytime. Conversely, at sunset or sunrise, the distance traversed by the light increases, and the color of sky changes to red because of increased scattering of short wavelengths. The attenuation coefficient β (i.e., the extinction ratio per unit length) is given by

$$\beta = \frac{8\pi^3(n^2-1)^2}{3N_s\lambda^4} = \frac{4\pi K}{\lambda^4} \quad (3)$$

As shown in Fig.1, the light reaching viewpoint P_v can be obtained as the remainder after scattering and absorption due to air molecules along the path between P_b and P_v. The light at P has been attenuated due to travel in the atmosphere (P_cP), and the light scattering from P is also attenuated before reaching P_v.

To calculate the attenuation caused by particles for light of wavelength λ traversing distance s, we use the optical depth, which is obtained by integrating β of Eq. (3) along the path s. Let's denote the integration variable s and the distance S, then the optical depth is given by

$$t(S,\lambda) = \int_0^S \beta(s)\rho(s)ds = \frac{4\pi K}{\lambda^4}\int_0^S \rho(s)ds \quad (4)$$

Next, single scattering due to aerosols is described. Scattering optics and the density distribution for aerosols differ from air molecules; Eq. (4) is different, too. Because the size range of particles of aerosols is very great, Mie scattering is applied for the phase function in Eq. (1) which exhibits a strong forward directivity. The Henyey-Greenstein function is well known as a phase function. Recently, Cornette[18] improved it, which gives a more reasonable physical expression:

$$F(\theta,g) = \frac{3(1-g^2)}{2(2+g^2)}\frac{(1+cos^2\theta)}{(1+g^2-2gcos\theta)^{3/2}}, \quad (5)$$

where g is an asymmetry factor and given by

$$g = \frac{5}{9}u - (\frac{4}{3} - \frac{25}{81}u^2)x^{-1/3} + x^{1/3},$$

$$x = \frac{5}{9}u + \frac{125}{729}u^3 + (\frac{64}{27} - \frac{325}{243}u^2 + \frac{1250}{2187}u^4)^{1/2},$$

where if $g = 0$ then this function is equivalent to Rayleigh scattering. u is determined by the atmospheric condition (e.g., haze) and wavelength; u varies from 0.7 to 0.85(see [18]).

Like the density distribution of air molecules, the density of aerosols decreases exponentially with altitude, but the rate of decrease is different from that of air molecules. The density can be obtained by setting the scale height, H_o, of Eq. (2) to 1.2km[16].

4.3 Intensity Calculation due to Atmospheric Scattering

Let's discuss a ray from viewpoint P_v to the earth, the light reaching the viewpoint has the following three passes: a) the ray passing through only the atmosphere, b) the ray intersecting with the earth, c) the ray passing through only space. For c) intensity calculation is not required. The calculation methods for a) and b) are described in the following.

4.3.1 Spectrum calculation for only the atmosphere

Let's discuss light scattering due to air molecules on the ray passing just through the atmosphere. The discussion for aerosols is omitted because the optics is similar except for $1/\lambda^4$ dependence. As shown in Fig.1, the light reaching P_v can be obtained as the remainder after scattering and absorption due to air molecules along the intersection line between the ray and the atmosphere, P_bP_a. The intensity of the light scattered at point P (at distance s from P_v) in the direction of P_v, I_p, is obtained by Eq.(1). The light scattered at P is attenuated before arriving at P_v. The intensity of the light arriving at P, I_p, can be obtained by setting the integration interval to P_cP in Eq. (4) of optical depth, that is

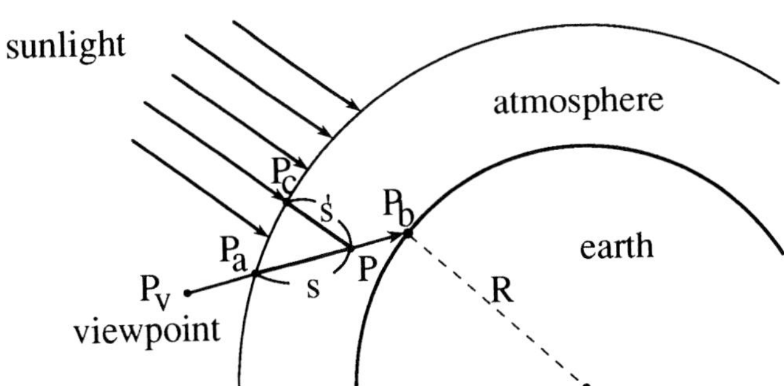

Figure 2: Intensity calculation for the ray intersecting with the earth.

$$I_p(\lambda) = I_s(\lambda)KF_r(\theta)\rho\frac{1}{\lambda^4}exp(-t(PP_c,\lambda)), \quad (6)$$

where I_s is the solar radiation at the top of the atmosphere, and $t(PP_c,\lambda)$ the optical depth from the top of the atmosphere to point P (l is the integration variable) and given by

$$t(PP_c,\lambda) = \int_P^{P_c} \beta(l)\rho(l)dl.$$

As the light scattering from P is also attenuated before reaching P_v, the intensity of the light reaching P_v, I_{pv}, can be obtained by multiplying the attenuation by the intensity at P, that is

$$I_{pv}(\lambda) = I_p(\lambda)exp(-t(PP_a,\lambda)). \quad (7)$$

As the distance to the sun can be considered almost infinite, the sunlight can be assumed to be a parallel beam. Thus the scattering angle at every point along P_aP_b can be considered constant. That is, I_v reaching P_v can be obtained by integrating scattered light due to air molecules on P_aP_b:

$$I_v(\lambda) = \int_{Pa}^{Pb} I_{pv}(\lambda)ds$$

$$= I_s(\lambda)\frac{KF_r(\theta)}{\lambda^4}\int_{P_a}^{P_b} \rho\ exp(-t(PP_c,\lambda) - t(PP_a,\lambda))ds \quad (8)$$

4.3.2 Spectrum calculation of the earth

Let's consider the ray intersecting with the earth as shown in Fig.2. The intensity scattered due to particles on the path, P_aP_b, can be obtained in the same manner as the description in 4.3.1. When point P coincides with point P_b (i.e., on the earth surface), the light reaching the viewpoint is obtained by adding reflected light from the earth to the light scattered due to molecules on P_aP_b. The intensity of light reaching viewpoint P_v, I'_v, is expressed by

$$I'_v(\lambda) = I_v(\lambda) + I_e(\lambda)exp(-t(P_aP_b,\lambda)), \quad (9)$$

where I_v is the scattered light of Eq. (8). I_e is reflected light at the earth;the direct component of sunlight and ambient light. The ambient light is mainly sky light. By considering

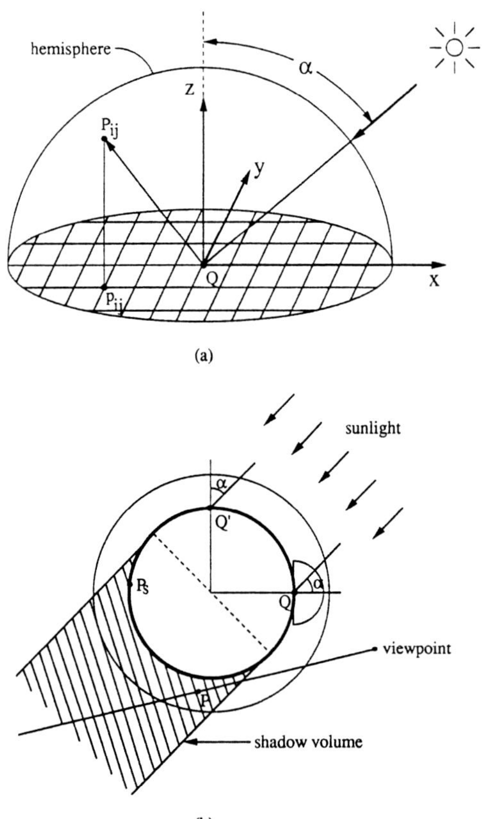

Figure 3: Calculation of sky light and shadow detection due to the earth.

attenuation of sunlight reaching the earth surface, I_e is given by

$$I_e(\lambda) = r(\lambda)(cos\alpha\ I_s(\lambda)\ exp(-t(P_cP_b, \lambda)) + I_{sky}(\lambda, \alpha)), \tag{10}$$

where $r(\lambda)$ is the diffuse reflection of the earth, α the angle between the normal vector of the earth and light vector (sunlight), and I_{sky} sky light. The direct component is small at the region where α is large (i.e., nearby the boundary of shadow) and tends to be reddish because of its long optical length.

Sky light is scattered light due to particles in the atmosphere. The radiance distribution of sky light can be obtained by setting the viewpoint on the earth in Eq.(8). As we are discussing the earth as viewed from space, shadows caused by obstacles on the surface are ignored, even though we take into account shadows due to the earth itself. That is, for shadow calculation, the earth is assumed to be a sphere with a smooth surface. Sky light due to scattered light from clouds is also ignored here. The illuminance at point Q on the earth due to the whole sky is obtained by using the following method: let's consider an element on a hemisphere whose center is Q (see Fig.3), calculate the intensity at each element on the hemisphere, and project each element onto the base of the hemisphere, then the illuminance is obtained by integrating the intensity of each element by weighting its projected area[13].

I_{sky} is calculated as follows: as shown in Fig.3 (a), the base of the hemisphere is divided into a mesh. Let's consider point P_{ij} on the hemisphere, which is mapped onto the hemisphere of the mesh point p_{ij} inversely, and calculate the intensity in the direction of QP_{ij}. The illuminance due to the whole sky is obtained by adding intensities at every mesh point within the base circle of the hemisphere. As shown in Fig. 3(a), the x-axis is set so that the sun exists on the $x - z$ plane; the region in the half circle (e.g., $y > 0$) is enough to get I_{sky} because of symmetry.

The radiance distribution of the sky is determined by angle α between the normal of the surface of the earth and the direction of the sunlight. Even though the direction of the sunlight is different at each point on the earth, the illuminance due to sky light (integrated values) at any point with the same angle α has the same value (e.g., Q and Q' in Fig.3). This means that the illuminance due to sky light at arbitrary angle α can be obtained by linear interpolation of a precalculated lookup table of I_{sky}. Note that I_{sky} is not zero at regions where there is no direct sunlight ($\alpha > 90$ degrees, e.g., P_s in Fig.3), so that I_{sky} for $\alpha = 0$ to $\alpha = 110$ degrees must be prepared in the lookup table.

4.3.3 Detection of shadow caused by the earth

As shown in Fig.3 (b), point P on the ray exists in the shadow region caused by the earth (we refer to it as a *shadow volume*), the scattered light in this region is zero because there is no incident light. Therefore it is sufficient to consider only attenuation in this region.

As the shadow volume is expressed by a cylinder, which is obtained by sweeping the circle (i.e., the contour of the earth viewed from the sun), the shadow segment on the ray can be calculated as the intersection segment between the cylinder and the ray.

4.3.4 Calculation of optical depth

The optical length of air molecules is calculated by numerical integration of Eq. (4) (in the case of aerosols, the density distribution and the extinction coefficient are different). The optical length is calculated by trapezoidal integration of sampled density. The optical length at sampling point P_i on the ray is obtained by adding the optical length of interval $P_{i-1}P_i$ to the optical length at P_{i-1}. Therefore the integration of the optical depth should start from the viewpoint. The optical length between the light source and point P_i on the ray is also required (e.g., PP_c in Fig.1). This calculation is required at every sampling point on the ray; optimization should be considered because of computational expense. We use a lookup table to save on computation time.

The density distribution of particles in the atmosphere varies exponentially with altitude. This means that the errors in the numerical integration become large when it is performed with a constant interval. Intervals which are inversely proportional to the density are desired; that is small intervals for low altitude and long intervals for high altitude. In order to realize this condition, the atmosphere is assumed as multiple spherical-shells. The radius of each sphere is set so that the difference in density between every adjacent sphere is within a given value. As a result, the difference between the radii of the shell is small for low altitude, and is large for high altitude, as shown in Fig.4. As Rayleigh scattering governs the calculation of optical length, the radius of each sphere is determined by the density distribution of air molecules. Let's consider N layers of spheres. The radius is given by(see Fig. 4)

$$r_i = H_0 log(\rho_i) + R, \quad \rho_i = 1. - i/N, \tag{11}$$

where R is the radius of the earth. For $i = N$, r_N is set to the radius of the atmosphere. For aerosols, the scale height is smaller than that for air molecules; aerosols mainly exist at low altitude. Therefore aerosols exist in the dense radii of shells; this fact assures the correctness of the above mentioned algorithm.

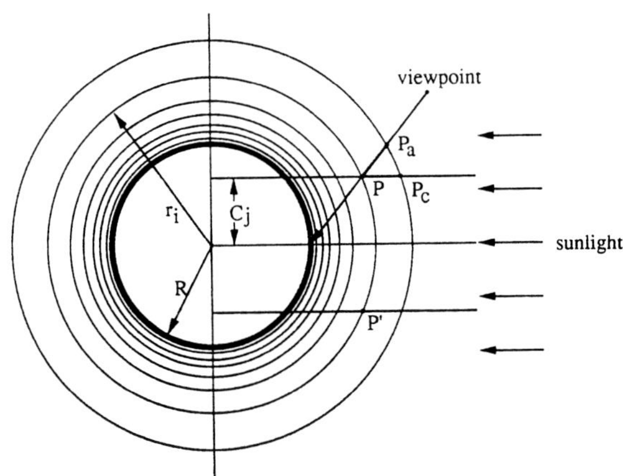

Figure 4: Calculation of optical depth.

The sampling points used in the integration are employed as the intersection points between the ray (view sight or light ray) and the multi-imaginary spheres and these intersection are easily obtained. The density at every sampling point is easily found from the lookup table indexed by the index numbers of the sphere, which is easily get from the altitude of the point.

The optical length between the sun and an arbitrary point on the ray can easily be precalculated because the earth is a sphere and sunlight is parallel light. As shown in Fig.4, let's consider a cylinder defined by sweeping the circle which passes through the center of the earth and is perpendicular to the light direction. Every optical length at the intersection (i.e. circle) between the cylinder and each one of the multi-imaginary spheres is equal (e.g., P and P' in figure). The optical lengths at the intersection points between the cylinders with radius C_j and the spheres with radius r_i is calculated(e.g.,P_aP in fig.) and are stored in the lookup table. The optical depth at arbitrary point P on the ray is easily calculated by linear interpolation, after the radius of the cylinder including P and the radius of the sphere are calculated. The lookup table here is 2D array: $[r_i, C_j]$. After getting indeces i and j from point P, the optical depth can be obtained by linear interpolation from $[r_i, C_j]$,$[r_{i+1}, C_j]$, $[r_{i+1}, C_{j+1}]$,$[r_i, C_{j+1}]$.

As described above, the light intensity of one wavelength reaching the viewpoint can be calculated by numerical integration with respect to pass length. Therefore the light intensity in the range of visible wavelengths (r, g, b in this paper) can be calculated.

5 THE COLOR OF CLOUDS

Since the geometric modeling of clouds is not our main subject, we are displaying the earth as viewed from space, clouds are simply modeled by applying 2D fractals. That is, the density distribution of clouds is expressed by mapping the fractal images of the necessary Mandelbrot set (0.39032+ 0.23775i is used in this paper)[15]. To take into account clouds with various altitudes, multiple imaginary spheres are employed to map fractal images on them.

Their color is determined by the following two light paths. One is on the light which passes through the atmosphere of scattered light due to cloud particles, again passing through the atmosphere, and reaches the viewpoint. Another one is on the light which passes through the atmosphere, reflected light at the earth's surface is attenuated by cloud particles,

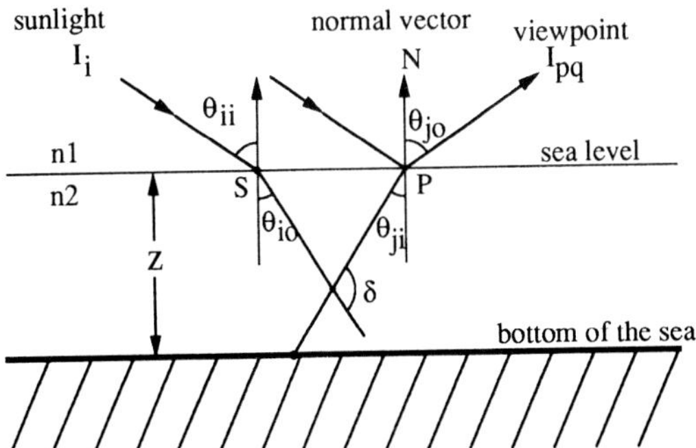

Figure 5: Calculation of color of water surface.

again passing through the atmosphere. Multiple scattering in clouds is ignored here.

The size of particles in clouds is larger than that of air molecules or of aerosols. Light scattered by such large particles is little influenced by wavelength. (However, the spectrum of incident sunlight onto clouds depends fairly strongly on the sun position.) The light reflected from clouds depends on the phase function (the angle between the view vector and light vector); the phase function is expressed by Eq.(5) (see reference[18] on the value u). In the case of clouds not being illuminated by the sunlight because of the shadow due to the earth; the shadow detection is executed by using the shadow volume described before. The shadows on the earth due to clouds are ignored in this paper. In the near future, a more precise model for clouds is slated in order to get images of the earth viewed from relatively close to the earth's surface.

6 COLOR OF THE SEA

Let's consider the light reaching a viewpoint from the surface of the sea, There are three paths (see Fig. 5): (1) reflected light on the water surface, (2) scattered light due to particles within the water leaving the water surface (3) attenuated light passing through the sea after reaching the bottom of water.

Calculation methods of the color of water have been developed by Max[8], Fournier[2], Ts'o[17], and Mastin[7] . However their methods focused on (1) and shapes of waves, and did not refer to (2)(scattered light due to particles in the water). The method proposed here takes into account (1) and (2). Furthermore the attenuation of the light passing through the atmosphere is taken into account. For (3), the light from the bottom of the sea can be neglected because of the depth of the sea.

When the light is incident to the water surface, the light path is divided into reflection and refraction. The relation between the reflection and refraction on the water surface obeys Fresnel's law of reflection. Incident light is refracted at the water surface; the relation between the incident angle and reflection angle obeys Snell's law. The refracted light is scattered/absorbed by water molecules in the sea, and reaches the viewpoint after refracting at the water surface again. For this phenomena, Gordon and McCluney [3, 9] proposed a quasi-single-scattering (QSS) model based on the radiative transfer equation. However, in the model the sun's position is limited to the zenith. We improved upon this. The light intensity transmitted in water, I_{PQ}, is given by

$$I_{PQ}(\theta_{ii}, \theta_{io}, z) = \frac{I_i(\lambda)T_i(\theta_{ii}, \theta_{i0})T_o(\theta_{ji}, \theta_{jo})\beta(\delta, \lambda)}{n^2(\cos\theta_{io} + \cos\theta_{ji})c(\lambda)[1 - \omega_0(\lambda)F(\lambda)]}$$
$$\times(1 - exp(-zc(\lambda)[1 - \omega_0(\lambda)F(\lambda)](\sec\theta_{ji} + \sec\theta_{io})),$$

(12)

where λ is wave length, z the depth of the sea, θ_{ii} the angle between the surface normal at point P and the direction of the viewing direction, θ_{io} the angle between the direction of the zenith and the direction of incident sunlight, θ_{jo} the angle between the reverse direction of the zenith and the sunlight after refraction, $I_i(\lambda)$ the irradiance of sunlight just above the water surface, n the refractive index of water, T_i and T_o the transmittance of the incident light at point S and P, respectively, $c(\lambda)$ the attenuation coefficient of light which expresses the ratio of lost energy of light when the light travels a unit length, β a volume scattering function ω_0 the albedo of water , and F the fraction of the scattering coefficient in a forward direction. Data of β, ω_0, and F used in this paper is obtained from [10]. Eq. (12) shows that the color of water depends on the depth, the incident angles and viewing direction. The surface of the sea is not flat, and is a spherical surface (i.e., the normal vector of each point on the surface is different); the color of the sea varies according to the position because the incident and viewing angles to the surface normal at each position are different.

As described above, both the incident light to the sea and the color (intensity) of the sea are attenuated by the atmosphere. By using the same method as described in 4.3.2, this effect can be calculated by taking into account two optical lengths; from the sun to the surface and from the surface to the viewpoint.

7 EXAMPLES

Fig. 6 shows an example of the color of the atmosphere. The color of the earth is assumed to be black in order to demonstrate the atmospheric color only. The position of the sun is behind and to the left of the observation point. Even though the earth is assumed to be a black body, it looks blue, and the boundary of the earth is white.

Fig. 7 shows the images of the earth with texture-mapped continents viewed from space; the location of the observation is at altitude 36,000 km, which corresponds to the altitude of the Japanese weather satellite called *Himawari*, at 135°E 0° N and the direction of the sun is 70° E 20° N. In Fig. (a), the color of the sea, direct sunlight, and sky light are taken into account, but the attenuation from the earth to the viewpoint is ignored(i.e., it corresponds to the color when the observer stands on the earth). In Fig. (b), atmospheric scattering/absorption is also taken into account (i.e., the color of the atmosphere is added). In Fig. (c), clouds are added.

Figs. 8,9 show examples of the earth viewed from relatively close-by; the viewpoint is at altitude 500km at 0° E 60° N. The direction of the sun in Fig. 8 is 0° E 20N, and the directions of the sun in Fig. 9 are 200° E 20°N and 240° E 15°N. Fig. 8 corresponds to noon(daytime), and Fig. 9 correspond to evening or dawn sky. In Fig. 9(b), one can observe the shadow (the dark part in the red atmosphere) due to the earth. The color of clouds changes to red due to the change of color of direct sunlight. These examples depict beautiful variations in color of the earth and the atmosphere. The space shuttle in the figure consists of 178 Bézier patches.

Let's show the photographs taken by the first Japanese astronaut aboard space shuttle, Dr. M. Mouri(NASDA), in Fig.10 (altitude 300km, September, 1992). Fig.11 displays the results of our simulation. One may observe differences between the photos and the simulation results. One of the reasons on Fig.11(a) may be due to the poor modeling of clouds and lands. In Fig.(b) some horizontal layers(e.g., orange color) are observed, one of them may be aerosols due to explosion of Volcano in Philippine. These facts suggest the necessity for further researching.

For hidden surface removal, the scanline algorithm for curved surfaces [11] is employed, and for anti-aliasing the multi-scanning algorithm[14] is employed. The calculation was done on an IRIS Indigo Elan. The computation times for Fig.7 (c) and Fig. 9 were 3.8 minutes and 12.0 minutes, respectively(image size=500 x 490).

8 CONCLUSION

We have proposed an algorithm for physically-based image synthesis of the earth viewed from space. As shown in the examples, the proposed method gives us photo-realistic images taking into account the color of the earth, clouds, and the sea. The advantages of the proposed method are as follows:

(1) The spectrum of the surface of the earth is calculated by taking into account direct sunlight and sky light as affected by atmospheric scattering.

(2) The spectrum of the atmosphere is calculated by taking into account absorption/scattering due to particles in the atmosphere.

(3) The spectrum on the surface of the sea is calculated by taking into account radiative transfer of water molecules.

(4) The optical depth and illuminance due to sky light are efficiently calculated by using several lookup tables taking advantages of the facts that the earth is spherical and that sunlight is parallel.

Acknowledgment : The authors would like to acknowledge A. Wakayama (currently Fujitsu Co.) for his help in coding of the prototype of our program.

References

[1] J.F. Blinn, "Light Reflection Functions for Simulation of Clouds and Dusty Surfaces," *Computer Graphics*, Vol. 16, No. 3 (1982),pp. 21-29.

[2] A. Fournier, " A Simple Model of Ocean Waves," *Computer Graphics*, Vol. 20, No. 4,(1986),pp. 75-84.

[3] H.R, Gordon, ' Simple Calculation of the Diffuse Reflectance of the Ocean," *Applied Optics*, Vol. 12, No. 12,(1973),pp. 2803-2804.

[4] J.T. Kajiya, "Ray tracing Volume Densities," *Computer Graphics*, Vol.18, No.3 (1984) pp.165-174.

[5] RV Klassen, "Modeling the Effect of the Atmosphere on Light," *ACM Transaction on Graphics*, Vol. 6, No. 3,(1987),pp. 215-237.

[6] LINKS Corporation, leaflet of "LINKS CG LIBRARY", (1991)

[7] G. A. Mastin, P. A. Watterberg, and J. F. Mareda,. " Fourier Synthesis of Ocean Scenes," *IEEE Computer Graphics & Applications*, Vol. 7, No. 3,(1987),pp. 16-23.

[8] N. Max, "Light Diffusion through Clouds and Haze," *Graphics and Image Processing*, Vol.33, No.3 (1986) pp.280-292.

[9] McCluney, W.R. Ocean Color Spectrum Calculations. *Applied Optics*, Vol. 13, No. 10,(1974),pp. 2422-2429.

[10] N. G. Jerlov, "Optical Oceanography," *Elsevier, Amsterdom* (1968).

[11] T. Nishita, K. Kaneda, E. Nakamae, " A Scanline Algorithm for Displaying Trimmed Surfaces by Using Bézier Clipping," *The Visual Computer*, Vol.7, No.5 (1991) pp.269-279.

[12] T. Nishita, Y. Miyawaki, E. Nakamae, "A Shading Model for Atmospheric Scattering Considering Distribution of Light Sources," *Computer Graphics*, Vol. 21, No. 4,(1987),pp. 303-310.

[13] T. Nishita, E. Nakamae, "Continuous tone Representation of Three-Dimensional Objects Illuminated by Sky Light," *Computer Graphics*, Vol. 20, No. 4,(1986),pp. 125-132.

[14] T. Nishita, E. Nakamae, "Half-Tone Representation of 3D Objects with Smooth Edge by Using a Multi-Scanning Method," *J.Information Processing(in Japanese)*, Vol.25, No.5,(1984), pp.703-711.

[15] K. Sato, "Fractal Graphics," *Rassel Co.(in Japanese)* (1989) p.74

[16] S. Sekine, "Optical characteristics of turbid atmosphere," *J Illum Eng Int Jpn*, Vol.71, No.6, (1987) pp.333

[17] P. Y. Ts'o, B. A Barsky,. " Modeling and Rendering Waves: Wave-Tracing Using Beta-Splines and Reflective and Refractive Texture Mapping," *ACM Transactions on Graphics*, Vol. 6, No. 3,(1987),pp. 191-214.

[18] W.M. Cornette, J.G. Shanks, "Physical reasonable analytic expression for the single-scattering phase function," *Applied Optics*, Vol.31, No.16 (1992), pp.3152-

Figure 6: The color of the atmosphere.

Figure 8: The earth viewed from relatively close-by.

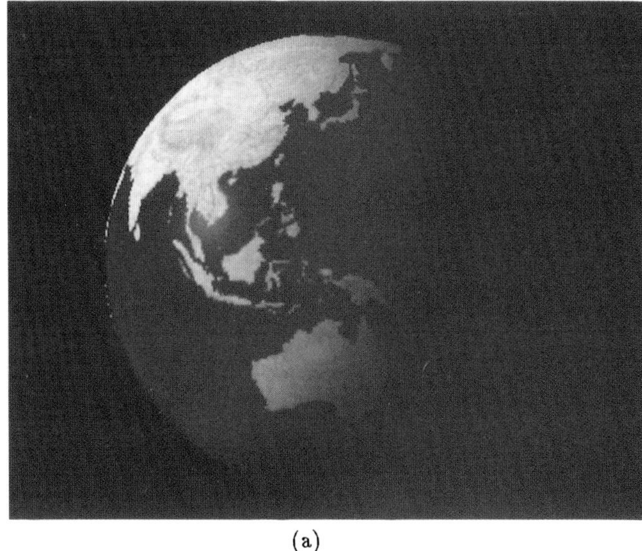

(a)

(b)

(c)

Figure 7: The earth viewed from space.

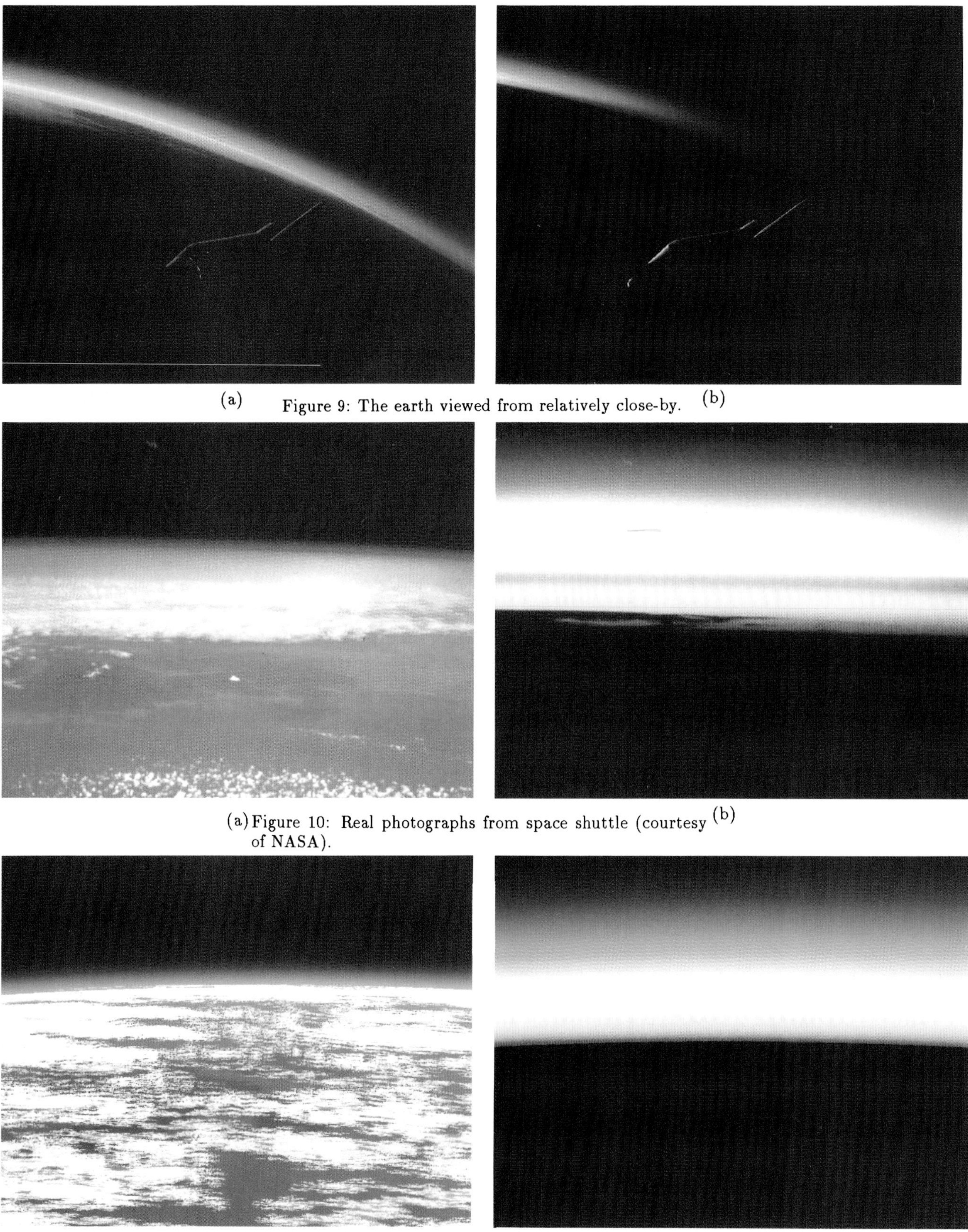

(a) Figure 9: The earth viewed from relatively close-by. (b)

(a) Figure 10: Real photographs from space shuttle (courtesy of NASA). (b)

(a) Figure 11: Comparisons with simulation. (b)

Smooth Transitions between Bump Rendering Algorithms

Barry G. Becker[1]
Nelson L. Max[2]

University of California, Davis
and
Lawrence Livermore National Laboratory

ABSTRACT

A method is described for switching smoothly between rendering algorithms as required by the amount of visible surface detail. The result will be more realism with less computation for displaying objects whose surface detail can be described by one or more bump maps. The three rendering algorithms considered are a BRDF, bump-mapping, and displacement-mapping. The bump-mapping has been modified to make it consistent with the other two. For a given viewpoint, one of these algorithms will show a better tradeoff between quality, computation time, and aliasing than the other two. The decision as to which algorithm is appropriate is a function of distance, viewing angle, and the frequency of bumps in the bump map.

CR Categories: I.3.3 [Computer Graphics]: Picture/Image Generation; I.3.5 [Computer Graphics]: Three-Dimensional Graphics and Realism.

Keywords: animation, BRDF, bump map, displacement map, rendering, surface detail, volume texture.

1. INTRODUCTION

Objects in animation are sometimes distant specks; at other times a tiny part of one will fill the whole screen. If these objects have rough surfaces, the same rendering algorithm should not be used in both cases. Almost all real materials have a hierarchy of surface detail. We assume that the macro-structure of all objects is described by parameterized patches or a polygonal mesh. The micro-structure is then described by one or more bump tables for each level of detail below the geometrical, each giving bump height as a function of the 2-D surface parameters. An alternative way to describe the surface detail is through the use of volume textures to specify bump height as a function of 3-D coordinates[10, 12].

LLNL, P.O. Box 808/L-301, Livermore, CA 94550
1. (510)422-3724 becker@mozart.llnl.gov
2. (510)422-4074 max2@llnl.gov

The Bidirectional Reflection Distribution Function or BRDF[13, 14, 6] captures the surface properties which are too small to be visible. Most real surfaces are neither purely specular (mirror-like) nor purely diffuse, but rather somewhere in between. To represent this non-trivial distribution of light reflectance a BRDF is used. It can be represented by a table indexed by a lighting direction and a viewing direction, to give the reflectance as a function of these directions. The BRDF used for this research is constructed from distributions of normals recorded from various views of a single displaced surface patch.

Bump-mapping[2] is an inexpensive way to achieve a good approximation to macroscopic surface roughness. The parameterized surface is treated as smooth for the purpose of visible surface determination, while the surface normals are perturbed to a first order approximation of what the actual bump normals would be.

The third algorithm, displacement-mapping[4, 5], is used when any shortcut in computation will be noticeable to the eye. Displacement-mapping is different in that the surface is actually offset by the appropriate bump height so that the full 3-D geometry can be rendered. For purposes of maintaining consistent shading, the same approximated normal is used to shade the displaced surface as was used in the bump map. However, now it is applied to the displaced surface rather than to the flat parametric one.

Bump-mapping is good for economically rendering bumps which can be described as a height field. Unfortunately it does not account for occlusion. It is necessary to modify flat bump-mapping so that it yields images statistically similar to images produced by the other two methods. This revised procedure will be termed 'redistribution bump-mapping' because it redistributes the normals in a way that is statistically similar to those seen on the displaced surface viewed from a specific direction.

The three methods are blended together so that the parts of the scene which are close to the viewer, or close to the extreme edge (silhouette), would be displacement-mapped, since this is where missing detail would be noticed most. Smooth silhouette edges are an artifact of bump mapping which is easy to detect. Parts farther away, or whose normals are parallel to the viewing direction, will be bump-mapped. When surfaces have microscopic material-specific qualities or are very far from the viewer, they are rendered using a BRDF. More

 ACM-0-89791-601-8/93/008/0183

specifically, for a given scene, those features with a spatial frequency higher than one half cycle per pixel (the Nyquist limit) are considered in the BRDF. At the other end of the spectrum, features that are large enough to cause noticeable occlusion need to be displacement-mapped. The parts in between are rendered with varying degrees of redistributed bump-mapping. Most importantly, there is a smooth transition among the three. The effect is that the whole scene looks as if it were displacement-mapped, when in fact much of it was rendered with cheaper algorithms. Extending this concept we can have high frequency rough surfaces on top of low frequency rough surfaces, each bumpy level of detail having three rendered representations.

In Figure 1 we see a teapot rendered in the four different ways. All renderings are based on the same height function. A major consideration for a smooth transitions among these is the consistency of the shading between methods. The amount of light emitted by a surface rendered with one method does not necessarily equal that amount emitted by the same surface rendered with another. Nor is the distribution of that light necessarily equivalent. A key aspect of this research is the determination of how the varying algorithms need to be modified in order to have their overall area-averaged light intensity contributions consistent.

There are five reasons why the average reflected intensity from a bump-mapped image is inconsistent with the reflected intensity from either the BRDF rendered image or the displacement-mapped image of the same object. Usually the BRDF is constructed under the assumption that the microfeatures of the surface are composed entirely of specular, mirrored facets. Bump- and displacement-mapping contain both specular and diffuse components. The easy solution to this inconsistency is to include a diffuse component for each microfacet when constructing the BRDF for the highest frequency bumps. Usually there is an inconsistency between bump- and displacement-mapping because actual surface displacement creates a geometrically computed facet normal for the shader while the perturbed normals for bump maps are only approximations. As previously mentioned this is overcome by using the approximated bump-mapped normals on the displaced surface. The approximated bump normals also vary more smoothly than the facet normals, especially with our quadratic interpolation, which is smoother than Blinn's approximation[2]. Note that if a procedural displacement function is employed, it is possible to compute the surface normal analytically. Since the BRDF is constructed from a displacement-mapped patch, the same inconsistency may arise for it. Again the solution is remedied by using the bump normal for tabulating the BRDF. The most difficult consistency problem is caused by occlusion. Occlusion, which is the hiding of some bumps by others, can change the distribution of visible surface normals. A solution is presented which redistributes bump normals so they match a distribution of normals similar to one derived from displacement-mapping. Lastly, there is the problem of consistency of shadowing. We have not yet found a general solution for shadowing, so we draw our images and compute our BRDF without it.

The concept of blending between methods is not new. The difficulty in overcoming the intensity distribution inconsistencies is perhaps the main reason why there are few coded examples. Kajiya[8] mentioned a hierarchy of scale which is appropriate for modelling the complexity of nature. He states that each level of detail contains the three subscales discussed above. Westin *et al.*[14] describes these levels as the geometrical, milliscale, and microscale. Perlin[11] proposed a method to shift between the BRDF and perturbed normals. Perlin's method does not include an explicit height table for determining the new normals, making displacement-mapping difficult. Fournier[7] has presented a promising approach for filtering normal maps by recording a discrete number of Phong peaks.

The software for each of the three algorithms described in this paper has been combined according to the previously discussed considerations. The result is an animation which explores a surface from changing distances and directions, showing that there are no significant side effects while transitioning between renderers. For more detail concerning the implementation refer to Becker[1].

2. BASIC ALGORITHMS

2.1 Bidirectional Reflection Distribution Functions

The BRDF is used to capture the microscopic reflectance properties of a surface. The BRDF itself can be a table of reflectivities or it can be represented by a spherical harmonic series approximation[3, 14]. It is a function of either three or four variables representing the polar and azimuthal angles of the light rays. The polar angle is called θ and it measures the angle away from the normal. Its domain is $[0, \pi/2]$. The azimuthal angle is denoted by ϕ and has domain $[0, 2\pi)$, with 0 and 2π both in the direction of the viewer. An isotropic surface is one for which the emitted intensity does not vary as the surface is rotated radially about its surface normal. If only isotropic textures are used, then the arguments to the BRDF reduce to the two polar viewing directions and the difference in the azimuthal angle between the viewing and lighting directions. In the most general anisotropic case, the BRDF is a function of viewing direction and lighting directions, requiring all four angles.

There are several different ways to construct a BRDF. Cabral[3] constructed the BRDF directly from a bump map using horizon tables. Westin *et al.*[14] ray traced a generalized 3-D surface sample in order to calculate the intensities for their BRDF. Our method uses normal distributions. They are already required in order to create redistribution functions for the new bump-mapping method. The same normal distributions are used to create the BRDF. Fournier[7] has also discussed normal distributions.

A normal distribution is obtained by tabulating sampled normals from a projected displacement-mapped flat patch. The range of normals is a hemisphere. The hemisphere can be discretized into a finite number of (θ_N, ϕ_N) bins. When the displacement map is projected, each pixel of the projected image represents a sample normal, and the count for the bin containing that normal is incremented. If bump-mapping is used to draw the flat patch, then the approximated normal distribution is independent of θ. However, when looking from some direction with $\theta > 0$, self-occlusion may occur in the displacement-mapped image. This occlusion is accounted for by rendering the displacement-mapped geometry with a hardware z-buffer, coding the normal directions into the pixel colors. For grazing angles many potentially occluding patches may have to be rendered in order to get the occlusion correct on a single patch. The problem is solved by rendering a single patch using parallel projection, and then using a block read from the screen buffer to copy the patch to all the positions where it is needed, in a back to front ordering. In a postprocess the sample normals are scanned in and the distributions are created. These distributions will be used to find the redistribution functions and to make the BRDF. The normal distributions are stored in a 3-D table. The first index is the viewing polar angle θ_V. The second and third indices are the θ_N, ϕ_N angles specifying the normal direction. For simplicity a table access is described by $distr[\theta_V, N]$, where $N = (\theta_N, \phi_{N-V})$, and ϕ_{N-V} denotes $\phi_N - \phi_V$. The difference between viewing and lighting ϕ's is denoted by ϕ_{V-L}. To improve the statistics of the distribution, the patch is viewed in many ϕ_V directions for each θ_V. The result is normal distributions for each θ_V which account for proper occlusion. To use these distributions in constructing the BRDF, the algorithm in Figure 2 is used.

```
for each level n from highest to lowest frequency
 for each θ_V
   for each θ_L
     for each φ_{V-L}
      {H = (V + L)/|V + L|
       for each θ_N
         for each φ_{N-V}
          if highest frequency BRDF
             { increment BRDF^n_diff[θ_V, θ_L, φ_{V-L}] by
                (L · N)distr^n[θ_V, N]
               increment BRDF^n_spec[θ_V, θ_L, φ_{V-L}] by
                (H · N)^Phong distr^n[θ_V, N]
             }
          else
             { compute θ'_V, θ'_L and φ'_{V-L}
               increment BRDF^n_diff[θ_V, θ_L, φ_{V-L}] by
                 BRDF^{n-1}_diff[θ'_V, θ'_L, φ'_{V-L}]distr^n[θ_V, N]
               increment BRDF^n_spec[θ_V, θ_L, φ_{V-L}] by
                 BRDF^{n-1}_spec[θ'_V, θ'_L, φ'_{V-L}]distr^n[θ_V, N]
             }
      }
```

Figure 2. The algorithm to compute the BRDF using a table of normal distributions.

Note that there are two components to the BRDF, one for the diffuse information and one for the specular. This way the amount of diffusivity and specularity chosen can be used as a parameter later. The θ'_V and θ'_L represent the angles between the viewing or lighting direction and the bin normal N, rather than with the flat surface patch normal. The angle ϕ'_{V-L} is the difference between L and V when projected to the plane perpendicular to the bump normal. It is computed by

$$\phi'_L = \arctan((L \cdot (N \times x)), (L \cdot (y \times N)))$$

$$\phi'_V = \arctan((V \cdot (N \times x)), (V \cdot (y \times N)))$$

$$\phi'_{V-L} = mod((\phi'_V - \phi'_L + \pi), 2\pi) - \pi \qquad (1)$$

where $x = (1,0,0)$ and $y = (0,1,0)$ are the axis directions of the bump table. This technique will give the same BRDF as if the combined displacement maps were used, as long as there is no correlation between the bumps at the different levels.

A smooth surface patch is rendered by interpolating the BRDF trilinearly in the angles θ_V, θ_L, and ϕ_{V-L}. The indices for the table are computed from a local coordinate on the patch surface. The smooth surface normal points in the direction of $\theta = 0$. The origin of the azimuthal angle is the projection of the viewing direction onto the surface.

For a given patch parameterization, $P(u,v)$, the partial derivatives, $P_u = \frac{\partial P}{\partial u}$ and $P_v = \frac{\partial P}{\partial v}$, are rarely the same length (causing stretching), and not always perpendicular (causing warping). For these reasons special care must be taken when indexing the BRDF to determine an intensity. The method for computing the difference in azimuthal angle is as follows:

$$V_n = [V \cdot P_u, V \cdot P_v, 0]$$

$$L_n = [L \cdot P_u, L \cdot P_v, 0]$$

$$\Phi_{V-L} = \arccos(\frac{V_n}{|V_n|} \cdot \frac{L_n}{|L_n|}) \qquad (2)$$

The stretching will actually change the normal directions making the BRDF inaccurate. The BRDF would need to be recalculated to yield a theoretically correct result, but equation (2) does get the occlusion correct and gives nice anisotropic highlight effects in places where they would be expected.

2.2 Bump-Mapping

In Blinn's bump-mapping[2], the surface is not actually altered from its smooth parametric form, but it is shaded as though it were.

Blinn used a bump height table B to calculate a linear approximation to the bump normal at a point P on an object surface. If $\vec{P}_u$ and $\vec{P}_v$ are the partial derivatives as above, the unnormalized surface normal is $\vec{N} = \vec{P}_u \times \vec{P}_v$. In the bump map B, the partial derivatives B_u and B_v at the interpolated point corresponding to P can also be computed using finite differences.

$$B_u = (B[u+\epsilon, v] - B[u-\epsilon, v])/(2 * \epsilon) \qquad (3)$$

and B_v is similar. Each evaluation of B uses bilinear interpolation.

Truncating insignificant terms, Blinn[2] has showed that the new normalized normal is very close to

$$\vec{N}' = \frac{\vec{N} + B_u(\vec{N} \times \vec{P}_v) - B_v(\vec{N} \times \vec{P}_u)}{|\vec{N} + B_u(\vec{N} \times \vec{P}_v) - B_v(\vec{N} \times \vec{P}_u)|} \qquad (4)$$

We have chosen to compute the bump map derivatives by a quadratic rather than linear scheme. Mach bands are eliminated by replacing Blinn's linear formula by a C^1 partial derivative formula, defined by taking the derivative of the C^2 cubic B spline curve approximation to the bump heights as a function of u or of v. Let $du = u - \lfloor u \rfloor$, then

$$B_u = (-du^2/2 + du - .5)B[\lfloor u \rfloor - 1, v] + (3du^2/2 - 2du)B[\lfloor u \rfloor, v]$$

$$+(-3du^2/2 + du + .5)B[\lfloor u \rfloor, v] + (du^2/2)B[\lfloor u \rfloor + 2, v]$$

and B_v is similar. Here each function evaluation requires only a linear interpolation in v. This method uses the same eight neighboring values in the height table as does (3), but with quadratic rather than linear weights.

The normals generated by this process do not lie in a distribution consistent with the other two algorithms. As previously discussed, $\vec{N}'$ must be further modified so that on average it will contribute to a normal distribution similar to displacement-map normals. This new algorithm, redistribution bump-mapping, is described in detail in Section 3.

It should also be noted that Perlin's volume textures[12], with the improvement by Max and Becker[10], can be substituted for bump maps when computing height values. The advantage of this is that there is no explicit parameterization to be concerned with, and thus no stretching to cause singularities or anisotropy. If a square patch has an isotropic texture mapped onto it, the texture becomes anisotropic as soon as the patch is stretched unevenly. Many parameterizations have singularities which lead to degenerate patches. If anisotropy is undesirable, then volume textures should be used. Perlin also used volume textures, and redistributed the normals to make them gaussian (personal communication) in his implementation of [11].

2.3 Displacement-Mapping

Displacement-mapping is the direct approach to rendering surface detail. For parameterized surfaces, each patch in the object has a u and v parameterization. The u and v coordinates are used as indices to look up height values in the bump height table. The corresponding vertex is then displaced along its normal vector by that height[4]. The normal generated from the bump approximation is also used on the displaced vertices. There is little loss of accuracy in doing this, and continuity during the transition is assured. Occlusion, the main problem with bump-mapping, is accounted for automatically when the vertices are displaced.

Having multiple bump maps for many levels of detail means the displaced bumps will be rendered with the BRDF constructed from the next bump map of higher frequency. To keep combined displacements consistent with BRDFs representing several combined bump maps, surface perturbations for the ith level must be perpendicular to the $(i-1)^{th}$ displaced surface. This means that for each vertex, P_u and P_v vectors must be computed for each level of detail which has been displaced. Since P_u and P_v are not necessarily perpendicular it is recommended that the following formula be used to compute them, given that the surface normal is N.

$$P_u[level+1] = P_u[level] + B_u[level]N[level]$$

where $B_u[i], B_v[i]$ are the ith bump map partial derivatives. The equation for P_v is similar.

3. REDISTRIBUTION BUMP-MAPPING

3.1 Normal Redistribution

The problem of eliminating inconsistencies between the different rendering models lies at the heart of making smooth transitions from one algorithm to another. Primarily we are concerned with keeping the integral of intensities equal over a small area on the surface while the rendering method changes.

Unfortunately, normals from bump-mapping do not yield a distribution similar to that of displacement-mapping or the BRDF. Since the polygon or patch itself is not displaced, it is possible to see normals which ought to be hidden by occluding bumps. In order to overcome this problem a redistribution function q is created. This is a function which accepts as input a normal generated by Blinn's[2] bump approximation, and outputs a normal which is statistically consistent with the distribution used to form the BRDF.

Since the distribution of normals on a displacement-mapped flat patch is different for each viewing angle, it is necessary to have redistribution functions for each one. When the viewing angle is vertical, the identity function is used. When the viewing angle is just above the horizon, the redistribution of bump normals is necessarily quite drastic. The effect is to pull forward normals that might be facing away, and push upward those that might be hidden. This new scheme for doing bump-mapping might appropriately be termed redistribution bump-mapping.

3.2 Redistribution Function Construction

Suppose a bumpy surface is viewed from a direction with polar angle θ_V. Let g denote the distribution of normals $distr(\theta, N)$ at this fixed θ_V, computed as above from the displacement map. Let f denote the distribution of normals in a (non-displaced) bump-mapped image. Note that f is the same as $distr(0, N)$. If q is the redistribution function described above, then the requirement that q take the distribution f to the distribution g is that for any region R in the hemisphere H of possible normals,

$$\int_{q(R)} f(\theta,\phi)d\omega = \int_R g(\theta,\phi)d\omega \tag{5}$$

It is easier to explain how to specify q in a 1-D case. So suppose $f(x)$ and $g(x)$ are two distributions on $[0,1]$, such that

$$\int_0^1 f(x)dx = \int_0^1 g(x)dx = 1 \tag{6}$$

The problem is to find $q : [0,1] \rightarrow [0,1]$ such that

$$\int_{q(a)}^{q(b)} f(x)dx = \int_a^b g(x)dx \tag{7}$$

where a and $b \in [0,1]$. It is enough to guarantee that

$$\int_0^{q(b)} f(x)dx = \int_0^b g(x)dx. \tag{8}$$

Let

$$G(b) = \int_0^b g(x)dx$$

and

$$F(b) = \int_0^b f(x)dx.$$

Then

$$G(b) = F(q(b))$$

hence

$$q(b) = F^{-1}(G(b)). \tag{9}$$

The redistribution function q maps a point b so that the area under the curve before b in g is equal to the area under the curve before the point $q(b)$ in f.

The problem in 2-D can be handled similarly. One method is to define 1-D redistribution functions separately for θ and ϕ. This gives adequate results for most bump maps, whose θ and ϕ distributions are fairly independent. This independence assumption is confirmed by the animation. For a more precise redistribution function, one can first redistribute ϕ, and then for each fixed ϕ, establish a separate redistribution function for θ. For details see Becker[1].

4. TRANSITIONS

4.1 Partial Bump Displacement

For control of appearance and for smooth transitions we want the ability to change the height of the bumps in the bump map. This will alter the normal distribution and occlusion information. By close consideration we can see that the change can be accounted for without having to recalculate the redistribution functions every time the bump heights are altered. If the heights are multiplied by a factor t, then the tangent of the angle between the bump normal and the smooth surface normal should also change by a factor t; i.e., $\tan(\theta_{N_t}) = t \cdot \tan(\theta_N)$. The normal, $N = (\theta_N, \phi_N)$, needs to be replaced by $N_t = (\arctan(t \cdot \tan(\theta_N)), \phi)$. In order to keep the visibility information the same, the viewing angle, θ_V, must be replaced with $\theta_W = \text{arccot}(\cot(\theta_V)/t)$. See discussion below concerning Figure 3.

The height of the bumps used to calculate the BRDF and redistribution functions must be the same as that of the bumps being rendered. This is because the BRDF is changed in a non-trivial way as the bump heights change. If we were only concerned with bump- and displacement-mapping, we could change the indexing on the redistribution functions to get the occlusion correct for changing bump heights. Unfortunately there is no easy way to re-index the BRDF to account for scale changes. Between the BRDF and redistribution bump-mapping, an intensity is computed for both methods. The resulting intensity is an interpolation of the two.

For the transition between bump- and displacement-mapping, intensity interpolation is not used, since it would cause the bump shading (particularly the highlights) to cross-dissolve rather than correctly adjust in position. As the bumps go from no displacement to full displacement the surface normals do not change, since they are always represented by Blinn's bump normal. The visible subset of bump normals does change, however, due to changing occlusion. Let $disp$ be the transition parameter which gives the fraction of the full bump height. With $disp = 0$ all normals are seen, even those on the back of bumps. With $disp = 1$, only the visible subset of these normals are seen. In Figure 3 the segments of the visible surface are shown in bold. The redistribution of normals takes normals from standard bump-mapping into this visible subset. For partially displaced bumps there is a different subset of visible normals, but there is a relationship between the bump height and this subset which can be exploited to give the necessary redistribution.

Different redistribution functions for varying heights are not stored, only different functions for different viewing θ's. Fortunately the two are equivalent. For the fractional bump height, $disp$, we can determine a new θ_W for which the same distribution of full height bump normals will be seen. Figure 3 shows that the distribution of normals for this partially displaced surface, viewed from θ_V, is identical to the distribution of visible normals for the fully displaced surface viewed from θ_W. The slope of the line V in Figure 3 is $disp$ times the slope of line W, so $\cot(\theta_V) = disp \cdot \cot(\theta_W)$ and the formula for finding θ_W is:

$$\theta_W = \text{arccot}(\cot(\theta_V)/disp).$$

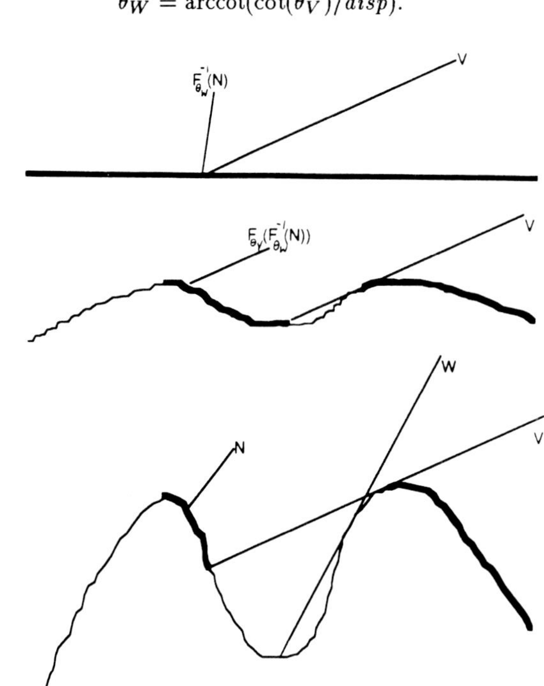

Figure 3 Top: the non-displaced surface. Middle: surface displaced by bump height fraction $disp$. Bottom: Fully displaced surface.

The inverse redistribution function for θ_W is applied to take the visible bump normal from the partially displaced surface into a distribution similar to one from a flat bump-mapped surface. Next the redistribution function for θ_V is applied to that normal to take it all the way forward to match statistically a full displacement-mapped normal. Thus the change from bump-mapping to displacement-mapping is done through two table based function evaluations. Notice that as the bumps decrease in height, the new viewing θ_W approaches vertical. This means that the inverse function needs to alter the normals less in order to get them back to the bump-map distribution.

4.2 Algorithm Selection Criterion

Now that it is known how to modify the algorithms so that they will not deviate from a fundamental reflection model, it must be decided when to apply which algorithm. Clearly displacement-mapping should be applied when the view is close, and the BRDF when the view is far. The relationship is $1/d$, where d is distance, since that is how the projected size of an object relates to distance. Another variable to consider is viewing angle, θ_V. If f is the wavelength of a feature then $f\cos(\theta_V)/d$ is the wavelength of the projected feature (in the direction of maximum foreshortening), and should be no smaller than two pixels. When the object is close, we would like to see a rough silhouette; when it is far, aliasing becomes a problem on the edge so use of the BRDF is desirable. This implies that as the object moves away from the viewer, the transition from displaced bumps to BRDF will be far more rapid on the object silhouette than on that area where the patch normal points toward the viewer. The threshold at which the switch occurs is determined by a constant D. Summarizing these properties, we define a transition parameter

$$T(d, \theta_V) = (1/d - D)/(\cos(\theta_V) + \epsilon). \quad (10)$$

Here d is the distance from the viewpoint to the surface, θ_V is the angle between the viewing ray and the surface normal, and D is dependent on individual bump maps. To avoid an instantaneous transition on the silhouette an ϵ is added to the cosine term in the denominator. The constant D should be large if the highest frequency component of the bump map is large. Note that D controls where the function changes from positive to negative, and thus lies midway between displacement-mapping and the BRDF. The formula for determining D is

$$D = c \cdot freq \cdot S$$

where $freq$ is the highest frequency in the bump map and S is the amount the u and v values are scaled. If S is large, then the bump map will be repeated more times over the same area, and the partial derivatives, P_u and P_v, are made shorter by a factor of S. The constant c controls computational effort by globally shifting the scene toward more BRDF or alternatively more displacement. If shadows are included, the shadow terminator should be treated just like the silhouette. Areas far from the terminator are likely to be completely illuminated or shadowed, but on the terminator, displacement-mapping will make the shadowing exact. The parameter given by equation (10) determines the algorithm or algorithms used for rendering. Let the threshold values for choice of renderer be $e1 < e2 < 0 < e3 < e4$. If $T < e1$ then use the BRDF, if $T > e4$ then use displacement mapping, and if $e2 < T < e3$ use redistribution bump mapping. Values of T other than these indicate regions where algorithms are blended. Values of -1, -.3, .3, and 1 respectively, were found to give good results.

4.3 Multiple Levels of Detail

With multiple levels of detail there are many more than two possible transition points. Many other cases need to be considered. The displacement-mapped image of the ith layer is rendered using the BRDF for the $(i-1)^{th}$ layer. As the camera continues to zoom in, the BRDF will switch to bump-mapping and then again to displacement-mapping.

Since each bump map has its own independent transition regions, some areas may have bump-mapping from two or more different levels. Perlin [11] suggests that each set of bumps be limited to a narrow range of frequencies. The result of implementing two levels of detail is shown in Figure 4. The bump map describing the surface detail is broken up into high and low order band-limited frequencies. The low frequencies compose the first level bump map and the high frequencies compose the second level. The left half of Figure 4 is color coded according to the algorithm used to render the most refined level of detail visible. Hence one can see bumpy sections colored yellow to indicate the BRDF from the next lower level was used to render the displaced bumps.

5. RESULTS

5.1 Consistency Comparison

In Figure 5 we can see the four rendering methods compared. The difference between the lighting and viewing ϕ is zero. Note that since the lighting and viewing directions are in alignment the patch becomes brighter for grazing angles. The rows are rendered with bump-mapping, redistribution bump-mapping, BRDF, and displacement mapping respectively. Note that redistribution bump-mapping is far more consistent with the BRDF and displacement-mapping than is ordinary bump-mapping. Figure 6 is a table which shows quantitative results for viewing angles corresponding to those shown in Figure 5.

Figure 5 Intensity comparisons. The lighting direction is consistently $\theta_L = \pi/4$. The rows from top to bottom represent bump-mapping, redistribution bump mapping, BRDF, and displacement mapping.

	$\theta_v=0$	$\theta_v=\pi/6$	$\theta_v=\pi/3$	$\theta_v=4\pi/9$
Bump	128	129	129	129
Redistribution	128	143	170	194
BRDF	129	146	172	192
Displacement	128	146	175	194

Figure 6 Area averaged intensities for the diffuse component.

In Figure 7, a single flat patch is drawn in perspective. Regions in the foreground are clearly displacement-mapped. The middle region is redistribution bump-mapped, and the furthest edge is almost completely shaded with the BRDF. It should be apparent that there is no intensity inconsistency between methods and that the transition is smooth.

5.2 Conclusions

Combining displacement-mapping, bump-mapping and a BRDF into one algorithm makes it possible to explore great scale changes, without changing the geometrical data base. Using a series of bump maps we can generate a variety of rough surfaces simulating different material properties. Objects in the scene will have a complex underlying structure but only the minimum amount of effort necessary to give the impression of complete geometrical representation will be expended. Current animations are restricted by the amount of geometrically represented detail. If the view gets too close to a feature, large drab polygons fill the display. With hierarchy of detail, the polygon level need never be reached, no matter how close the viewer gets. Even at intermediate and far distances the light interacts with flat polygonal surfaces as if they were truly composed of millions of smaller micro-polygons. As a result the otherwise drab polygons become alive with texture and interesting highlights. Those smaller micro-polygons may actually get rendered, but only if the viewer zooms in much closer.

5.3 Future Research

Shadowing is the main enhancement yet to be considered. One way to do the shadowing of displaced bumps is to use the two-pass z-buffer method developed by Williams[15]. Horizon mapping[9] has been shown to generate shadows for bump-mapped images. It will also work for redistribution bump-mapping since the horizon is determined by the u and v parameterization, not the normal. However, this may cause a problem since the rendering is according to a redistributed normal, and the shadows are according to the parameterization. The shadowing may look inappropriate for the rendered bumps. The shadowing for BRDFs can be done using horizon mapping, as was demonstrated by Cabral[3]. Another possibility is to use only the unshadowed normals from a displaced, rendered, and shadowed flat patch to generate the distributions for the BRDF and the redistribution function. The result should be consistent in terms of average intensity, but may not look qualitatively correct.

5.4 Acknowledgements

This work was performed under the auspices of the U.S. Department of Energy by Lawrence Livermore National Laboratory under contract No. W-7405-Eng-48.

BIBLIOGRAPHY

1. Becker, Barry, "Smooth Transitions Between Rendering Algorithms During Animation", Master's thesis, University of California at Davis, Davis, CA, December, 1992.
2. Blinn, James F., "Models of Light Reflection for Computer Synthesized Pictures", *Proceedings of SIGGRAPH '77, Computer Graphics*, Vol. 11, No. 2, July, 1977, pp192-198.
3. Cabral, Brian, Nelson Max, and Rebecca Springmeyer, "Bidirectional Reflection Functions from Surface Bump Maps", *Proceedings of SIGGRAPH '87, Computer Graphics*, Vol. 21, No. 4, July, 1987, pp273-281.
4. Cook, Robert L., "Shade Trees", *Proceedings of SIGGRAPH '84, Computer Graphics*, Vol. 18, No. 3, July, 1984, pp223-231.
5. Cook, Robert L., Loren Carpenter, and Edwin Catmull, "The Reyes Image Rendering Architecture", *Proceedings of SIGGRAPH '87, Computer Graphics*, Vol. 21, No. 4, July, 1987, pp95-102.
6. Cook, Robert L, and Kenneth Torrance,"A Reflectance Model for Computer Graphics",*Proceedings of SIGGRAPH '81, Computer Graphics*, Vol. 15, No. 3, August, 1981, pp307-316.
7. Fournier, Alain, "Normal Distribution Functions and Multiple Surfaces",*GI '92 Workshop on Local Illumination*, 1992, pp 45-52.
8. Kajiya, James, "Anisotropic Reflection Models", *Proceedings of SIGGRAPH '85, Computer Graphics*, Vol. 19, No. 3, July, 1985, pp15-21.
9. Max, Nelson L., "Horizon Mapping: Shadows for Bump-mapped Surfaces", *The Visual Computer*, Springer-Verlag, Vol. 4, No. 2, 1988, pp109-117.
10. Max, Nelson L., and Barry Becker, "Bump Shading for Volume Textures", to appear in *IEEE Computer Graphics and Applications*, 1993.
11. Perlin, Kenneth, "A Unified Textural Reflectance Model", *Advanced Image Synthesis course notes, Proceedings of SIGGRAPH '84, Computer Graphics*, July, 1984.
12. Perlin, Kenneth, "An Image Synthesizer", *Proceedings of SIGGRAPH '85, Computer Graphics*, Vol. 19, No. 3, July, 1985, pp287-296.
13. Torrance, Kenneth, and Ephraim Sparrow, "Theory for Off-Specular Reflection from Roughened Surfaces", *Journal of the Optical Society of America*, 57(9), 1967, pp1105-1114.
14. Westin, Stephen H., James R. Arvo, and Kenneth E. Torrance, "Predicting Reflectance Functions from Complex Surfaces", *Proceedings of SIGGRAPH 92, Computer Graphics*, Vol. 26, No. 2, July, 1992.
15. Williams, Lance, "Casting Curved Shadows on Curved Surfaces",*Proceedings of SIGGRAPH '78, Computer Graphics*, Vol. 12, No. 3, July, 1978, pp270-274.

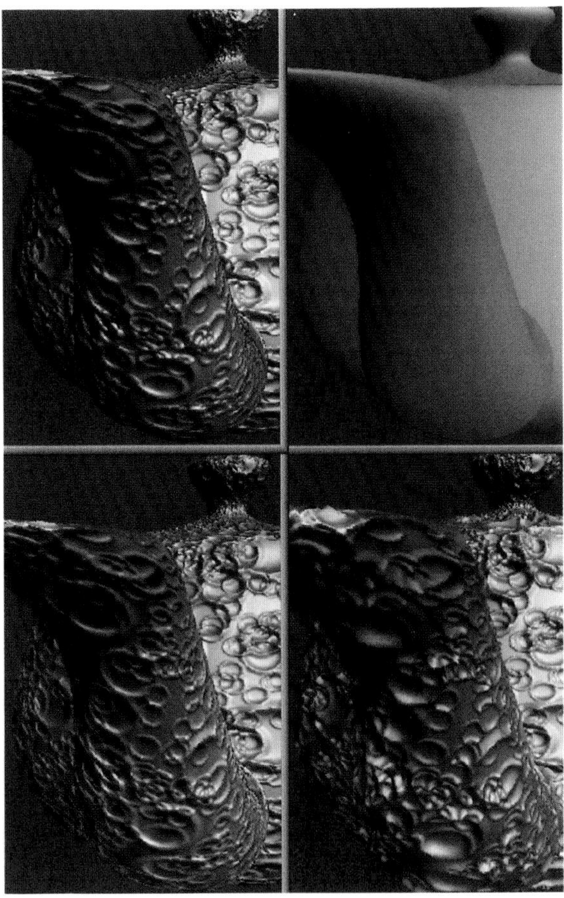

Figure 1. Counter-clockwise from upper left: bump-mapping, redistribution bump-mapping, displacement-mapping, BRDF. The difference between redistribution bump-mapping and plain bump-mapping is apparent near the bottom of the spout.

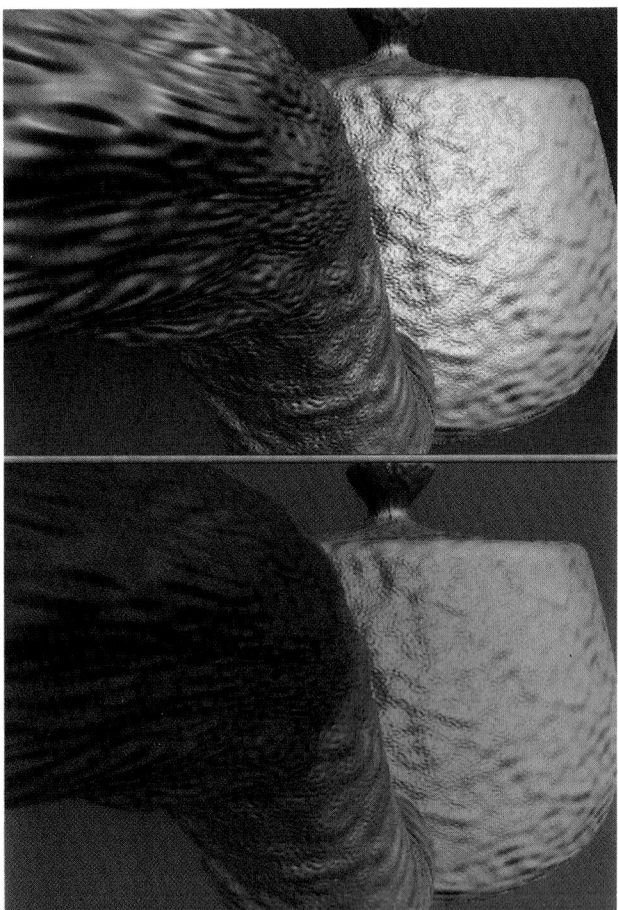

Figure 4. Two levels of bumpy detail. Colors in the bottom half indicate BRDF(yellow), redistribution bump-mapping(blue), and displacement-mapping(red) for the higher frequency bumps.

Figure 7. Transitions on a flat surface. BRDF(yellow) in the back, redistribution bump-mapping(blue) in the middle, and displacement-mapping(red) in the foreground.

Linear Color Representations for Full Spectral Rendering

Mark S. Peercy
Department of Applied Physics
Stanford University

Abstract

We present a general linear transform method for handling full spectral information in computer graphics rendering. In this framework, any spectral power distribution in a scene is described with respect to a set of fixed orthonormal basis functions. The lighting computations follow simply from this decision, and they can be viewed as a generalization of point sampling. Because any basis functions can be chosen, they can be tailored to the scenes that are to be rendered. We discuss efficient point sampling for scenes with smoothly varying spectra, and we present the use of characteristic vector analysis to select sets of basis functions that deal efficiently with irregular spectral power distributions. As an example of this latter method, we render a scene illuminated with fluorescent light.

CR Categories and Subject Descriptors: I.3.3 [**Computer Graphics**]: Picture/Image Generation–Display Algorithms; I.3.7 [**Computer Graphics**]: Three-Dimensional Graphics and Realism.

Additional Keywords: linear color representations, full spectral rendering, linear models, tristimulus values.

1 Introduction

Accurate color rendering in computer graphics must account for the full spectral character of the lights and surfaces within a scene. The rendering procedure must preserve enough spectral information to compute final values for output to some display device, such as an *RGB* monitor. However, one wishes to minimize the computational cost of the rendering to reduce the time required to create an image. Therefore, one desires efficient methods of handling full spectral information during image synthesis.

Author's address: Dept. of Applied Physics, Stanford University
Stanford, CA 94305-4090
peercy@kaos.stanford.edu (415)725-3301

Some suggested techniques in dealing with full spectral information include the use of the tristimulus values for the lights and surfaces [1], the use of polynomial representations of spectra [16], and the use of linear models of surfaces and lights [20] [12]. The typical method employed is point sampling of the surfaces and the lights at a given number of wavelengths. These point samples are used in a numerical integration method to compute approximate tristimulus values before being transformed to values appropriate for display. To minimize the total number of samples, one seeks an efficient integration approximation; one approximation that has been studied in various forms is Gaussian quadrature [14] [19] [2].

In this paper, we consider a more general method for handling full spectral information in synthetic image generation; our technique is closely related to the use of linear models presented in [20]. The principal idea is that we describe the spectral power distribution of the light at every step of the rendering procedure with respect to a single collection of orthonormal basis functions. This formalism encompasses point sampling, which uses delta functions as its basis functions.

The constraint of describing all of the spectral power distributions with respect to the basis functions is advantageous for two reasons. First, it makes the rendering process completely linear. Therefore, this technique can be considered a generalization of point sampling and can be readily incorporated into standard renderers. Second, one has the freedom to select any orthonormal set of basis functions. This freedom can be exploited to increase the efficiency of the rendering process.

The body of this paper is divided into two main sections. In Section 2 we discuss the mathematical formalism of linear color representations of the lights and surfaces, and in Section 3 we address the problem of selecting appropriate basis functions. In this latter section, we discuss Riemann summation for efficient point sampling in scenes with smoothly varying spectra, and we present the use of characteristic vector analysis to provide efficient basis functions for scenes with complex spectra.

2 Linear Color Representations

During the rendering process, we demand that any spectral power distribution in the scene be described by m orthonormal basis functions $E_i(\lambda); i = 1, ..., m$. By any distribution, we mean not only the light coming directly from a light source but also light that has been once, twice, or an arbitrary number of times reflected from surfaces in the scene. In this section, we use this restriction to derive the color representations of both the spectral power distributions and the surfaces, and we discuss the transformation of this color information to values appropriate for display.

2.1 Spectral Power Distributions

To obtain a representation for the spectral power distributions in a scene, we can project the spectral power distribution, $I(\lambda)$, of any light source onto the subspace spanned by the basis functions;

$$I(\lambda) = \sum_{i=1}^{m} \epsilon_i E_i(\lambda), \tag{1}$$

where

$$\epsilon_i = \int_\lambda I(\lambda) E_i(\lambda) d\lambda. \tag{2}$$

follows from the orthonormality condition. Thus, any light within the scene can be described with the m elements ϵ_i. These elements are simply the coefficients of the linear transformation defined by the set of basis functions, so we refer to this method as a general linear transform method.

2.2 Surface Reflectances

To obtain a representation for the surfaces, we project the spectral power distribution of the light reflected from those surfaces onto the set of basis functions (for clarity and without loss of generality, we neglect transmission and attenuation in this discussion). Lighting models typically divide the reflected light into three terms: ambient, diffuse, and specular ([6] discusses lighting models in detail); the spectral power distribution of light reflected from a surface, I_o, is given by

$$\begin{aligned} I_o(\Omega, \lambda) &= R_a(\lambda) I_a(\lambda) + G_d(\Omega) R_d(\lambda) I_s(\lambda) \\ &\quad + R_s(\Omega, \lambda) I_s(\lambda). \end{aligned} \tag{3}$$

Here, Ω denotes a general dependence on the geometry of the reflection, and λ denotes a general dependence on wavelength. $I_a(\lambda)$ is the distribution of the ambient light, $I_s(\lambda)$ is the distribution of directional incoming light, and $G_d(\Omega)$ is the diffuse geometry term. $R_a(\lambda)$, $R_d(\lambda)$, and $R_s(\Omega, \lambda)$ are the ambient, diffuse, and specular reflectances of the surface, respectively. In general, the specular reflectance is a function both of geometry and wavelength. However, empirical models often replace the specular reflectance with a separable term, resulting in a *piecewise separable* lighting model

$$\begin{aligned} I_o(\Omega, \lambda) &= R_a(\lambda) I_a(\lambda) + G_d(\Omega) R_d(\lambda) I_s(\lambda) \\ &\quad + G_s(\Omega) R_s(\lambda) I_s(\lambda). \end{aligned} \tag{4}$$

As described in Section 2.1, the ambient light and directional light are represented by their transform coefficients,

$$I_a(\lambda) = \sum_{i=1}^{m} \epsilon_i^a E_i(\lambda) \tag{5}$$

$$I_s(\lambda) = \sum_{i=1}^{m} \epsilon_i^s E_i(\lambda). \tag{6}$$

By using Equations 5 and 6 in Equation 3, the spectral power distribution reflected from a surface is

$$\begin{aligned} I_o(\Omega, \lambda) &= \sum_{i=1}^{m} \epsilon_i^a R_a(\lambda) E_i(\lambda) + \sum_{i=1}^{m} \epsilon_i^s G_d(\Omega) R_d(\lambda) E_i(\lambda) \\ &\quad + \sum_{i=1}^{m} \epsilon_i^s R_s(\Omega, \lambda) E_i(\lambda). \end{aligned} \tag{7}$$

To obtain the surface representations, we project this result back onto the the basis functions as in Equation 1;

$$I_o(\Omega, \lambda) = \sum_{j=1}^{m} \epsilon_j^o E_j(\lambda). \tag{8}$$

From Equation 2 and Equation 7,

$$\begin{aligned} \epsilon_j^o &= \int_\lambda I_o(\Omega, \lambda) E_j(\lambda) d\lambda && (9) \\ &= \sum_{i=1}^{m} R_{ij}^a \epsilon_i^a + G_d(\Omega) \sum_{i=1}^{m} R_{ij}^d \epsilon_i^s + \sum_{i=1}^{m} R_{ij}^s(\Omega) \epsilon_i^s && (10) \end{aligned}$$

where

$$\begin{aligned} R_{ij}^a &= \int_\lambda R_a(\lambda) E_i(\lambda) E_j(\lambda) d\lambda && (11) \\ R_{ij}^d &= \int_\lambda R_d(\lambda) E_i(\lambda) E_j(\lambda) d\lambda && (12) \\ R_{ij}^s(\Omega) &= \int_\lambda R_s(\Omega, \lambda) E_i(\lambda) E_j(\lambda) d\lambda. && (13) \end{aligned}$$

R_{ij}^a is the projection onto the jth basis function of the spectral power distribution obtained from the reflection of the ith basis function from the ambient reflectance of the surface. R_{ij}^d and $R_{ij}^s(\Omega)$ are analogous terms for the diffuse and specular reflections, respectively.

Writing Equation 10 in matrix form, we obtain

$$\begin{aligned} \begin{pmatrix} \epsilon_1^o \\ \vdots \\ \epsilon_m^o \end{pmatrix} &= \begin{pmatrix} R_{11}^a & \cdots \\ \vdots & \ddots \end{pmatrix} \begin{pmatrix} \epsilon_1^a \\ \vdots \\ \epsilon_m^a \end{pmatrix} + \\ &\quad G_d(\Omega) \begin{pmatrix} R_{11}^d & \cdots \\ \vdots & \ddots \end{pmatrix} \begin{pmatrix} \epsilon_1^s \\ \vdots \\ \epsilon_m^s \end{pmatrix} + \\ &\quad \begin{pmatrix} R_{11}^s(\Omega) & \cdots \\ \vdots & \ddots \end{pmatrix} \begin{pmatrix} \epsilon_1^s \\ \vdots \\ \epsilon_m^s \end{pmatrix} \end{aligned} \tag{14}$$

In vector notation, this equation can be written

$$\vec{\epsilon^o} = R^a \vec{\epsilon^a} + G_d(\Omega) R^d \vec{\epsilon^s} + R^s(\Omega) \vec{\epsilon^s}. \tag{15}$$

This final equation reveals the mathematical formalism behind the linear transform method. The spectral power distributions ($I_a(\lambda)$, $I_s(\lambda)$, and $I_o(\Omega, \lambda)$) are represented by column vectors of length m containing the transform coefficients ($\vec{\epsilon^a}, \vec{\epsilon^s}$, and $\vec{\epsilon^o}$, respectively). Each component of the surface reflectance ($R_a(\lambda), R_d(\lambda)$, and $R_s(\Omega, \lambda)$) is represented by a single $m \times m$ matrix (R^a, R^d, and $R^s(\Omega)$, respectively). The interaction of light with a surface component assumes the form of simple matrix multiplication, converting the coefficients of the incoming light into the coefficients of the outgoing light. This result is a generalization of the point sampling case; with point samples, the surface matrices are diagonal, and the matrix product multiplies respective sample values. Because this technique is linear, it can be included without difficulty in standard renderers.

For the general lighting model case, the specular matrix is a function of the geometry. Because the elements of the surface matrices are obtained through integration over the basis functions, this integration must be performed for each geometry configuration. If, however, one uses a piecewise separable lighting model, the geometry and wavelength dependence separate in the specular term,

$$\vec{\epsilon^o} = R^a \vec{\epsilon^a} + G_d(\Omega) R^d \vec{\epsilon^s} + G_s(\Omega) R^s \vec{\epsilon^s}, \qquad (16)$$

and the three surface matrices, R^a, R^d, and R^s, can be precomputed.

The above discussion addresses only surface reflection, but effects such as transmission and attenuation can be included straightforwardly in this framework. As with the reflectance components, these terms take the form of $m \times m$ matrices that act on the coefficients of the incoming light.

2.3 Conversion to RGB

The rendering algorithm determines the spectral contributions to a pixel by computing multiple reflection paths from each of the light sources to the viewer. These contributions are transform coefficients, and by linearity they can be combined to provide a final set of coefficients for that pixel, $\epsilon_i^p; i = 1, ..., m$. Equation 1 gives the approximation to the spectral power distribution arriving at the pixel,

$$I_p(\lambda) = \sum_{i=1}^{m} \epsilon_i^p E_i(\lambda). \qquad (17)$$

To compute appropriate values for display, one first computes the tristimulus values, XYZ, for the pixel by integrating the final spectrum over the three color matching functions [21]

$$\begin{aligned} X = \int \bar{x}(\lambda) I_p(\lambda) d\lambda &= \int \sum_{i=1}^{m} \epsilon_i^p \bar{x}(\lambda) E_i(\lambda) d\lambda \\ &= \sum_{i=1}^{m} T_{xi} \epsilon_i^p \qquad (18) \end{aligned}$$

$$\begin{aligned} Y = \int \bar{y}(\lambda) I_p(\lambda) d\lambda &= \int \sum_{i=1}^{m} \epsilon_i^p \bar{y}(\lambda) E_i(\lambda) d\lambda \\ &= \sum_{i=1}^{m} T_{yi} \epsilon_i^p \qquad (19) \end{aligned}$$

$$\begin{aligned} Z = \int \bar{z}(\lambda) I_p(\lambda) d\lambda &= \int \sum_{i=1}^{m} \epsilon_i^p \bar{z}(\lambda) E_i(\lambda) d\lambda \\ &= \sum_{i=1}^{m} T_{zi} \epsilon_i^p. \qquad (20) \end{aligned}$$

In matrix form, this set of equations can be written

$$\begin{pmatrix} X \\ Y \\ Z \end{pmatrix} = \begin{pmatrix} T_{x1} & T_{x2} & \cdots & T_{xm} \\ T_{y1} & T_{y2} & \cdots & T_{ym} \\ T_{z1} & T_{z2} & \cdots & T_{zm} \end{pmatrix} \begin{pmatrix} \epsilon_1^p \\ \epsilon_2^p \\ \vdots \\ \epsilon_m^p \end{pmatrix}. \qquad (21)$$

With $\vec{x} = (X, Y, Z)^T$, this equation yields

$$\vec{x} = T\vec{\epsilon^p}. \qquad (22)$$

The elements T_{xi}, T_{yi}, and T_{zi} of the matrix T are coefficients that result from integration of the ith basis function over the three color matching functions. For point sampling, these elements are modified based on the method of numerical integration. For example, common Riemann summation over evenly spaced samples includes the distance between the sample points [17], and Gaussian quadrature has its own unique weights [5].

Assuming that an RGB display monitor is properly gamma-corrected [4], the color values, $\vec{c} = (R, G, B)^T$, of a given pixel are computed from the tristimulus values by applying a 3×3 matrix, M, derived from the chromaticities of the phosphors of the monitor [6]

$$\begin{aligned} \vec{c} &= M\vec{x} \qquad (23) \\ &= MT\vec{\epsilon^p} \qquad (24) \\ &= C\vec{\epsilon^p}. \qquad (25) \end{aligned}$$

Therefore, the RGB values can be obtained directly through a linear transformation of the final coefficient values by a $3 \times m$ matrix C. Because this step is linear, it can be applied at any time to the separate contributions to the final pixel values.

3 Selection of Basis Functions

It is in the selection of the basis functions that the flexibility of the general transform method is demonstrated. In this section, we describe some factors that determine the effective selection of basis functions, and we present two methods for determining basis functions that are tailored to the spectral power distributions in a scene.

As mentioned in Section 2, the lighting model is a significant influence on the choice of basis functions. If the lighting model is not piecewise separable, the surface matrices must be computed for each geometry configuration, so the most efficient basis functions are most likely point samples. If, however, the lighting model is piecewise separable, we have another consideration. The components of the surface reflectances are represented by $m \times m$ matrices. Therefore, the reflection of light from a surface requires, in general, m^2 multiplies. If the basis functions are point samples, though, the surface matrices are diagonal, and the reflection requires only m multiplies. Indeed, only m multiplies are required for any set of non-overlapping basis functions. Consequently, the computational intensiveness of the general transform rises more rapidly than that of point sampling as the number of basis functions increases.

A third consideration when selecting basis functions is the nature of the spectral power distributions in the scene to be rendered. For smoothly varying distributions, point sampling can be quite efficient, but for complicated spectra, a set of general basis functions can be more appropriate. We discuss each of these methods in the following sections.

3.1 Point Sampling

Point sampling is typically linked to a numerical integration method used in approximating the tristimulus integrals, Equations 18-20. Gaussian quadrature, which is optimal for integrating polynomials over general weighting functions [5], has been applied to this problem [14] [19] [2]. If the spectral power distributions are well described by lower order polynomials, Gaussian quadrature can provide sufficient accuracy with a small number of sample points; it was shown in [14] that as few as four point samples are adequate for many rendering applications.

Here, we discuss the use of simple Riemann summation for approximating the tristimulus integrals. Rather than being efficient for polynomial functions, Riemann summation is efficient when integrating functions that contain a small number of Fourier coefficients.

Riemann Summation

Riemann summation is the sum over evenly spaced sample values weighted by the distance between the sample wavelengths [17]. Given $N+2$ evenly spaced sample points $\lambda_0, \lambda_1, ..., \lambda_{N+1}$ separated by a distance $\Delta\lambda = (\lambda_{N+1} - \lambda_0)/(N+1)$ and a spectral power distribution $I(\lambda)$, Riemann summation gives

$$
\begin{aligned}
X &= \int_\lambda \bar{x}(\lambda) I(\lambda) d\lambda \approx \Delta\lambda \sum_{i=0}^{N+1} \bar{x}(\lambda_i) I(\lambda_i) \\
Y &= \int_\lambda \bar{y}(\lambda) I(\lambda) d\lambda \approx \Delta\lambda \sum_{i=0}^{N+1} \bar{y}(\lambda_i) I(\lambda_i) \\
Z &= \int_\lambda \bar{z}(\lambda) I(\lambda) d\lambda \approx \Delta\lambda \sum_{i=0}^{N+1} \bar{z}(\lambda_i) I(\lambda_i).
\end{aligned} \tag{26}
$$

An appropriate choice of endpoints, λ_0 and λ_{N+1}, is the most closely spaced pair of wavelengths that can be chosen such that the color matching functions at these wavelengths can be taken to be zero. We found that $\lambda_0 = 400nm$ and $\lambda_{N+1} = 700nm$ are often reasonable choices; truncation at these limits results in errors significantly smaller than those incurred by undersampling the spectra [17] [18]. Taking $\bar{x}(\lambda_0) = \bar{y}(\lambda_0) = \bar{z}(\lambda_0) = 0$ and $\bar{x}(\lambda_{N+1}) = \bar{y}(\lambda_{N+1}) = \bar{z}(\lambda_{N+1}) = 0$, only the N interior points, $\lambda_1, ..., \lambda_N$, need to be preserved during the rendering process; the basis functions for the spectral power distributions are given by delta functions at these wavelengths.

With the endpoints of the integrands equal to zero, Riemann summation with N points is exact for any linear combination of the first $2N+2$ Fourier functions 1, $sin(2\pi\frac{\lambda-\lambda_0}{\lambda_{N+1}-\lambda_0})$, $cos(2\pi\frac{\lambda-\lambda_0}{\lambda_{N+1}-\lambda_0})$, ..., $sin(2\pi N\frac{\lambda-\lambda_0}{\lambda_{N+1}-\lambda_0})$, $cos(2\pi N\frac{\lambda-\lambda_0}{\lambda_{N+1}-\lambda_0})$, $sin(2\pi(N+1)\frac{\lambda-\lambda_0}{\lambda_{N+1}-\lambda_0})$. Therefore, if the products of the spectral power distributions with each of the color matching functions are well described by a small number of Fourier coefficients, Riemann summation provides an efficient method for integration. For the set of spectral power distributions obtained from the Macbeth Color Checker [13] under CIE Standard Illuminant C [21], Riemann summation with four point samples at 460nm, 520nm, 580nm, and 640nm results in an average error of less than 5% in the tristimulus values. Rendering with these four sampling points is often sufficient; if it is not, selecting five, six, or more evenly spaced samples is straightforward.

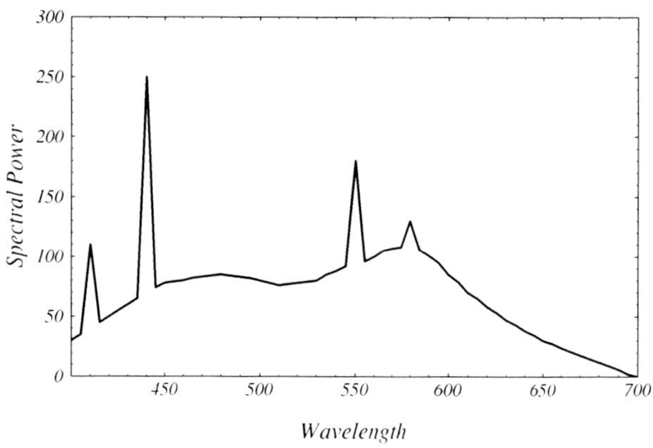

Figure 1: Spectral power distribution of a fluorescent light

3.2 General Basis Functions

For scenes with complicated spectral power distributions or surface properties, naive point sampling is insufficient. One notable example is the spectral power distribution of fluorescent light, which is ubiquitous in indoor scenes. Fluorescent light, an example of which is shown in Figure 1 [21], is characterized by narrow emission lines at several wavelengths, a factor leading to aliasing with a small number of point samples. For these complicated cases, one would like to be able to tailor the basis functions to the complex spectra. One attempt in this direction is the use of abutting box functions over the range of wavelengths whose widths are chosen based on the spectra within the scene [7] [6]. Another technique for dealing with these scenes is hand-selecting the basis functions using knowledge of the spectra in the scene. For example, for fluorescent lights, one could ensure that point samples were positioned at the emission lines.

Here, we present an alternative method for the selection of basis functions, gaining insight from studies done on the construction of linear models of surface reflectances and spectral power distributions [3] [8] [9] [15] [12]. Most of these studies have stressed the use of characteristic vector analysis or principal component analysis to characterize lights and surfaces. This technique can be applied to the rendering problem to provide an automated method for selecting an efficient set of basis functions.

Characteristic Vector Analysis

Given a set of spectral power distributions, characteristic vector analysis computes an ordered set of functions such that the first m functions are the "best" m functions for approximating the distributions. Here, "best" is measured in terms of least squared error between the actual and the approximating spectra. Formally, for the approximation of the spectral power distribution

$$I(\lambda) \approx \sum_{i=1}^{m} \epsilon_i E_i(\lambda), \tag{27}$$

the basis functions, $E_i(\lambda)$, are computed such that the sum of the approximation error over all of the lights in the set is minimized

$$Err = \sum_{I} \int [I(\lambda) - \sum_{i=1}^{m} \epsilon_i E_i(\lambda)]^2 d\lambda. \tag{28}$$

In practice, this set can be determined by placing the representative spectra in the columns of a matrix and performing a singular value decomposition [10] [11].

The task is then to find a representative set of spectra on which to perform the analysis. For the rendering problem, the basis functions should describe any spectral power distribution within the scene. The distributions contain contributions from the light sources themselves, from once-reflected light, and from multiply-reflected light. Therefore, an appropriate set of spectra is that set derived from possible interreflections within the scene. Given the spectral power distributions of the lights and the components of the surface reflectances in a scene, one can construct a tree of possible interreflection spectra (disregarding any geometry). The lights themselves would be included, and any number of reflections and interreflections could be included. The basis functions computed from a characteristic vector analysis of this set would then approximate these spectral power distributions.

If the number of spectral power distributions to fit is too large, this technique can become inefficient; the cost of computing the basis functions may exceed the savings in rendering time. Also, this method is inapplicable if one does not know *a priori* the spectral character of the surfaces and lights in the scene. However, for many scenes, this technique can readily be applied.

3.3 Examples

To demonstrate the use of characteristic vector analysis in selecting basis functions, we present two related examples. Both examples use the fluorescent light in Figure 1 to show the ability of this technique to handle complex spectra. In the first example, we determine the efficiency in computing the tristimulus values of a set of spectral power distributions, and in the second, we render a simple scene.

Tristimulus Values of Test Spectra

We select as sample spectra the twenty-four squares of the Macbeth Color Checker under the fluorescent light. A set of basis functions can be computed by performing a characteristic vector analysis on the set of twenty-five spectral power distributions given by the light itself and the light reflected from the twenty-four samples. Figure 2 shows the first three basis functions for this set; as can be seen, characteristic vector analysis preserves the narrow peaks that are found in the spectral power distribution of the light source.

From these basis functions, we compute the transform coefficients of the fluorescent light with Equation 2. Assuming only diffuse reflection and ignoring geometry, we use Equation 12 to compute a single matrix for each of the twenty-four

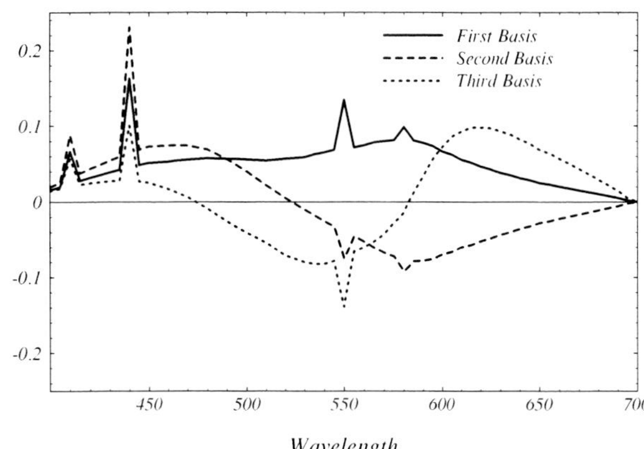

Figure 2: First three basis functions computed with characteristic vector analysis for fluorescent light reflected from the twenty-four squares of the Macbeth Color Checker.

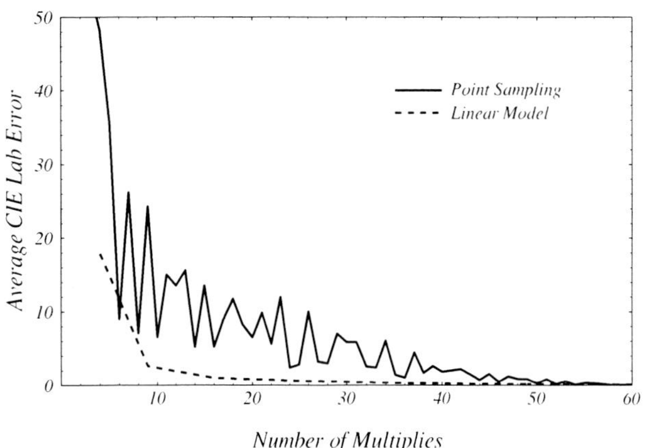

Figure 3: Average CIE Lab Error for set of spectra as a function of the number of multiplies per reflection for evenly spaced point samples and for the general linear transform computed with characteristic vector analysis.

surfaces in the color checker. The product of the vector of coefficients with each of these matrices gives column vectors containing the coefficients of the reflected light. From these vectors, we compute the linear model approximation to the tristimulus values of each of the twenty-four patches with Equations 18-20. The average CIE Lab error in units of ΔE [21] can then be calculated as a function of the number of basis functions. For reference, we also compute this error as a function of the number of evenly spaced point samples for Riemann summation. To compare the two methods in terms of their computational intensiveness, we plot in Figure 3 the errors as a function of the number of multiplies per reflection.

The general linear model is significantly more efficient than point sampling; the latter shows severe oscillations from the sampling error in computing the narrow peaks in the fluorescent light. Clearly, the point sampling method should (and would) be amended for the fluorescent light case. The most natural method is to ensure point samples lie on the narrow peaks and are weighted appropriately during the integration. This is tantamount to hand-selecting a general

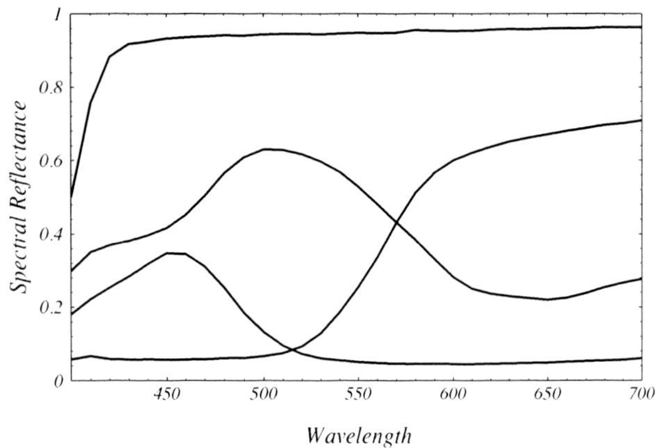

Figure 4: Four surface reflectances from the Macbeth Color Checker used in the example image.

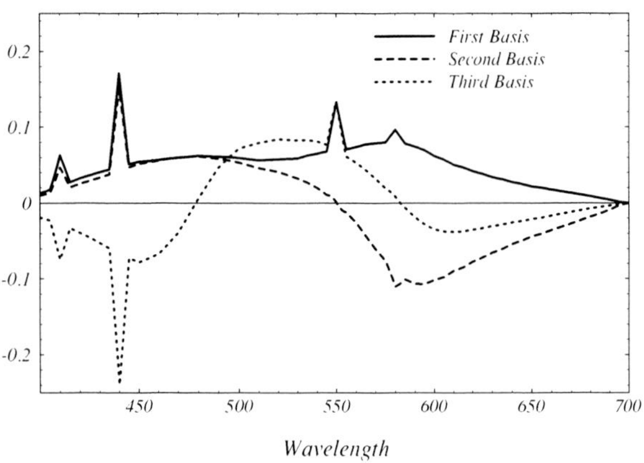

Figure 5: First three basis functions of the general linear model computed with characteristic vector analysis for the example image.

linear model. Characteristic vector analysis is attractive because it matches most anomalies in the spectra without the user being required to address each one distinctly.

Image Generation

We now apply characteristic vector analysis to select basis functions for ray tracing of a simple scene under fluorescent light. The four distinct surface reflectances in the scene are taken from the Macbeth Color Checker and are shown in Figure 4. To compute the basis functions, we perform a characteristic vector analysis on the set of spectra consisting of the light source itself, all single reflections, and all second interreflections from the four surface samples; the first three basis functions are shown in Figure 5. These functions are used to compute the column vector of the light source and the ambient, diffuse, and specular reflectance matrices for each of the surfaces in the scene.

Figure 6 shows the resultant images for four different numbers of basis functions. The top left image in the figure displays the full resolution rendering of the scene computed at one nanometer intervals. The two columns display the general linear model and evenly spaced point sampling for the same number of multiplies per reflection. The left column shows the general model with 2, 3, 4, and 5 basis functions from top to bottom, and the right column shows 4, 9, 16, and 25 evenly spaced point samples from top to bottom. The linear model based on characteristic vector analysis is superior for all images; with just three basis functions, it is virtually identical to the full resolution image.

5 Conclusions

We have presented a general description of the use of linear transform methods in synthetic image generation. This formalism requires that all spectral power distributions be described with respect to a set of orthonormal basis functions. The spectral power distributions are represented by column vectors, and the surfaces are described by matrices. Reflection during the rendering procedure takes the form of matrix multiplication. Because this process is linear, it allows for easy implementation. In addition, this framework guides the choice of basis functions for efficient rendering.

We have discussed two possibilities for the selection of the basis functions, Riemann summation for efficient point sampling and characteristic vector analysis of a representative set of spectra in the scene. Point sampling based on Riemann summation is effective when the spectral power distributions in a scene are well described with low-order Fourier components. The method based on characteristic vector analysis is of comparable efficiency to point sampling techniques when the scenes contain smoothly varying spectra, and it can be significantly more efficient for scenes with complex spectra. We demonstrated this by rendering a scene illuminated by fluorescent light.

A promising direction of future work is the investigation of basis functions that make the rendering procedure more efficient; the techniques in [12] are potentially useful to this end. In addition, we have focussed in this paper on minimizing the cost of full spectral rendering, but the flexibility of the general method might be useful for other issues in computer graphics, such as texturing, that deal with spectral information during rendering.

Acknowledgements

This material is based upon work supported under a National Science Foundation Graduate Fellowship and partially supported by the National Science Foundation under Grant NSF ECS 88-15815. The author would like to thank Lambertus Hesselink, Marc Levoy, and Paul Ning for helpful discussions. He especially would like to thank Brian Wandell for helpful discussions and for providing the spectral data used in this work.

References

[1] Borges, Carlos. Trichromatic Approximation for Computer Graphics Illumination Models. Proceedings of SIGGRAPH '91 (Las Vegas, Nevada, July 28-August 2, 1991). In *Computer Graphics 25*,4 (July 1991),101-104.

[2] Borges, Carlos. *Numerical Methods for Illumination Models in Realistic Image Synthesis.* PhD dissertation, University of California, Davis, 1990.

Figure 6: Comparison of general linear model with evenly spaced point sampling. The top left image is a full resolution image computed at one nanometer steps; the left image in each row is the general model with 2, 3, 4, and 5 basis functions from top to bottom; the right image is evenly spaced point sampling with 4, 9, 16, and 25 samples.

[3] Cohen, Jozef. Dependency of the Spectral Reflectance Curves of the Munsell Color Chips. *Psychon. Sci. 1* (1964), 369-370.

[4] Cowan, William. An Inexpensive Scheme for Calibration of a Color Monitor in Terms of CIE Standard Coordinates. Proceedings of SIGGRAPH '83 (Detroit, Michigan, July 25-29, 1983). In *Computer Graphics 17*,3 (July 1983), 315-321.

[5] Davis, P. and Rabinowitz, P. *Methods of Numerical Integration.* Academic Press, New York, 1975.

[6] Hall, Roy. *Illumination and Color in Computer Generated Imagery.* Springer-Verlag, New York, 1989.

[7] Hall, Roy and Greenberg, Donald. A Testbed for Realistic Image Synthesis. *IEEE Computer Graphics and Applications 3* (1983), 10-20.

[8] Judd, Deane, MacAdam, David, and Wyszecki, Gunter. Spectral Distribution of Typical Daylight as a Function of Correlated Color Temperature. *J. Opt. Soc. Am. 54*,8 (1964), 1031-1040.

[9] Maloney, Laurence. Evaluation of linear models of surface spectral reflectance with small numbers of parameters. *J. Opt. Soc. Am. A 3*,10 (1986), 1673-1683.

[10] Maloney, Laurence. *Computational Approaches to Color Constancy.* PhD dissertation, Stanford University, 1985.

[11] Mardia, K., Kent, J., and Bibby, J. *Multivariate Analysis.* Academic, London, 1979.

[12] Marimont, David and Wandell, Brian. Linear models of surface and illuminant spectra. *J. Opt. Soc. Am. A 9*,11 (1992), 1905-1913.

[13] McCamy, C., Marcus, H., and Davidson, J. A Color Rendition Chart. *J. Appl. Photographic Engrg. 11*,3 (1976), 95-99.

[14] Meyer, Gary. Wavelength Selection for Synthetic Image Generation. *Computer Vision, Graphics, and Image Processing 41* (1988), 57-79.

[15] Parkkinen, J., Hallikainen, J., and Jaaskelainen, T. Characteristic Spectra of Munsell Colors. *J. Opt. Soc. Am. A 6*,2 (1989), 318-322.

[16] Raso, Maria, and Fournier, Alain. A Piecewise Polynomial Approach to Shading Using Spectral Distributions. Proceedings of Graphics Interface '91. (Calgary, Alberta, June 3-7, 1991), 40-46.

[17] Smith, Brent, Spiekermann, Charles, and Sember, Robert. Numerical Methods for Colorimetric Calculations: A Comparison of Integration Methods. *COLOR Research and Application 17*,6 (1992), 384-393.

[18] Smith, Brent, Spiekermann, Charles, and Sember, Robert. Numerical Methods for Colorimetric Calculations: Sampling Density Requirements. *COLOR Research and Application 17*,6 (1992), 394-401.

[19] Wallis, Robert. Fast computation of tristimulus values by use of Gaussian quadrature. *J. Opt. Soc. Am. 65*,1 (1975), 91-94.

[20] Wandell, Brian. The Synthesis and Analysis of Color Images. *IEEE Trans. on Pattern Analysis and Machine Intelligence, PAMI-9*,1 (1987), 2-13.

[21] Wyszecki, Gunter and Stiles, W.S. *Color Science: Concepts and Methods, Quantitative Data and Formulae.* John Wiley and Sons, 1982.

Combining Hierarchical Radiosity and Discontinuity Meshing

Dani Lischinski *Filippo Tampieri* *Donald P. Greenberg*

Program of Computer Graphics
Cornell University
Ithaca, NY 14853

ABSTRACT

We introduce a new approach for the computation of view-independent solutions to the diffuse global illumination problem in polyhedral environments. The approach combines ideas from hierarchical radiosity and discontinuity meshing to yield solutions that are accurate both numerically and visually. First, we describe a modified hierarchical radiosity algorithm that uses a discontinuity-driven subdivision strategy to achieve better numerical accuracy and faster convergence. Second, we present a new algorithm based on discontinuity meshing that uses the hierarchical solution to reconstruct an object-space approximation to the radiance function that is visually accurate. Our results show significant improvements over both hierarchical radiosity and discontinuity meshing algorithms.

CR Categories and Subject Descriptors: I.3.3—[**Computer Graphics**]: Picture/Image Generation; I.3.7—[**Computer Graphics**]: Three-Dimensional Graphics and Realism.

Additional Key Words and Phrases: diffuse reflector, discontinuity meshing, global illumination, hierarchical radiosity, Mach bands, photorealism, quadratic interpolation, radiance function, radiosity, reconstruction, shadows, view-independence.

1 INTRODUCTION

Computing solutions to the global illumination problem is an essential part of photorealistic image synthesis. In this paper, we are interested in computing *view-independent* (or *object-space*) solutions for global illumination. Such solutions provide an approximation to the radiance function across each surface in the environment. Once a solution is computed, images from any viewpoint can be rendered with a relatively small additional effort. These methods are particularly attractive for applications such as architectural design, interior design, lighting design, illumination engineering, and virtual reality, in which the need for multiple views or walk-throughs of static environments arises.

So far, most view-independent methods have been derived from the radiosity method that was originally developed to solve radiative heat transfer problems [23]. Computer graphics researchers adopted this method to compute the global illumination of diffuse polyhedral environments [10, 7, 19]. Radiosity has been extended and improved dramatically since, but there is still much to be done before the method can become a useful tool for its intended users.

The goal of our research is to develop an efficient radiosity system that satisfies the following requirements:

Objective (numerical) accuracy: Solutions produced by the system should converge rapidly to the exact solution. This requirement may seem obvious, however, in the computer graphics community results of simulations are too often judged solely by their visual appearance.

Subjective (visual) accuracy: While visual appearance should not be used to judge the objective accuracy of the simulation, it is still very important, since the image is the final product. Clearly, accurate visual appearance can be achieved through numerically accurate simulation (if the underlying model is physically accurate.) Unfortunately, experience has shown that the human visual system is extremely sensitive to small perceptual errors that are difficult to quantify. The simulated environments can be very complex and, therefore, the computation of ultra-accurate solutions is generally impractical. Thus, we must have means of producing visually acceptable images even from coarse solutions.

Ease of control: (i) The system should be controllable by users who are not necessarily familiar with its inner workings. Therefore, the control parameters should be intuitive and small in number. (ii) In many cases (such as early design stages) the user is interested in a quick solution, even if not exceedingly accurate. At other times, one might be willing to wait overnight for a reliable solution. Therefore, the system should provide the user with the option to trade speed for accuracy.

Most radiosity systems do not satisfy any of these requirements. There are no error bounds on the solutions, because approximations are often used without justifications regarding their impact on the accuracy of the results. The resulting images typically exhibit many visual artifacts such as Mach bands, light and shadow leaks, jagged shadow boundaries, and missing shadows. Radiosity systems are seldom user-friendly and require massive user intervention: typically, a time consuming trial-and-error process is required to produce an image that looks right. Baum *et al.* [1] and Haines [12] provide good discussions of the various pitfalls of radiosity.

In this paper we present a new radiosity method, which comes closer to satisfying our goals. The new method combines two recently developed approaches: hierarchical radiosity [14] and discontinuity meshing [15, 18]. First, we present an improved hierarchical radiosity algorithm that uses a discontinuity-driven subdivision strategy to achieve better numerical accuracy and faster convergence. Second, we describe a new algorithm based on discontinuity meshing that uses the hierarchical solution to reconstruct a visually accurate approximation to the radiance function. Thus, results of high visual quality can be obtained even from coarse global illumination simulations. Previous attempts to improve the visual quality of radiosity solutions were described by Nishita and Nakamae [19], Kok and Jansen [17], Chen *et al.* [4], and Reichert [20]. In all of these cases, however, the improvement takes place in image space, after the view and the resolution have been specified. Our method, instead, operates entirely in object space, and the improved solution is view-independent.

2 HIERARCHICAL RADIOSITY

The traditional radiosity approach [10, 7] discretizes the environment into n elements and solves a linear system of n equations, where the radiosities of the elements are the unknowns. The most serious drawback of this approach is the need to compute the $O(n^2)$ coefficients of the linear system, corresponding to the interactions (transfers of light energy) between pairs of elements. In addition to the overwhelming computational complexity, most of these computations are performed to unnecessarily high accuracy, while some are not sufficiently accurate.

Hierarchical radiosity (HR) [14] overcomes these problems by decomposing the matrix of interactions into $O(n)$ blocks, for a given accuracy. These blocks correspond to interactions of roughly equal magnitude, and the same computational effort is required for computing each block. HR operates by constructing a hierarchical subdivision of each input surface. Each node in the hierarchy represents some area on the surface. Two nodes are linked together if the interaction between their corresponding areas can be computed within the required accuracy; otherwise, the algorithm attempts to link their children with each other. Each link corresponds to a block in the interaction matrix.

HR has several important advantages: it is fast, the errors in its approximations are bounded, and it is controlled by only two parameters: the error tolerance and the minimum node area. The smaller the values of these parameters, the more accurate (and expensive) the solution becomes. Thus, HR satisfies our goals of objective accuracy and ease of control.

However, the HR algorithm still suffers from shadow leaks and jagged shadow boundaries. This occurs because surfaces are subdivided regularly, not taking into account the geometry of the shadows. HR uses point sampling to classify the inter-visibility between two surfaces, so it is prone to missing small shadows altogether. Of course, as the user-specified tolerance becomes smaller, the solution becomes more accurate, and the visual artifacts decrease. Nevertheless, images of high visual quality can require solutions of prohibitively high accuracy.

The number of links created by HR is $O(n + m^2)$ where n is the final number of nodes and m is the number of input surfaces. As the complexity of the environment increases, the m^2 term eventually becomes dominant, drastically reducing the efficiency of the algorithm. As pointed out by Smits *et al.* [22], this problem could be solved by grouping the input surfaces into higher level clusters. This is an interesting research topic by itself, and it will not be pursued in this paper.

3 DISCONTINUITY MESHING

Radiosity methods typically attempt to approximate the radiance function with constant elements and use linear interpolation to display the result. The actual radiance function, however, is neither piecewise constant nor piecewise linear. It is usually smooth, except along certain curves across which discontinuities in value or in derivatives of various order may occur. Discontinuities in radiance functions are discussed in detail elsewhere [16, 15, 18]; what follows is a brief summary of the various types of discontinuity and their causes.

The most significant discontinuities are discontinuities in the radiance function itself (denoted D^0). They occur along curves of contact or intersection between surfaces. Discontinuities in the first and the second derivatives (D^1 and D^2, respectively) occur along curves of intersection between surfaces in the environment and *critical surfaces* corresponding to qualitative changes in visibility, or *visual events*. Visual events in polyhedral environments can be classified into two types [9]: EV events defined by the interaction of an edge and a vertex, where the critical surface is a planar wedge; and EEE events defined by the interaction of three edges, where the critical surface is a part of a quadric. Discontinuities of higher than second order are also possible [16].

Discontinuities are very important both numerically and visually: all the boundaries separating unoccluded, penumbra, and umbra regions correspond to various discontinuities. When a discontinuity curve crosses a mesh element, the approximation to the radiance function over that element becomes less accurate. The resulting errors usually correspond to the most visually distracting artifacts in radiosity images. The traditional radiosity approach uses adaptive subdivision [8] to reduce these errors, however there are several problems with this approach. First, the user must specify an initial mesh that is sufficiently dense, or features will be lost. Second, the shape of the mesh is determined by the geometry of the surface being meshed, and the discontinuities are not resolved exactly. As a result, many small elements are created as the method attempts to converge to shadow boundaries. Furthermore, although the resulting solution may be of adequate visual quality for some views, artifacts may become visible as the view changes (e.g., when we zoom in on a surface.)

Discontinuity meshing (DM) algorithms compute the location of certain discontinuities and represent them explicitly, as boundaries, in the mesh. This leads to solutions which are both numerically and visually more accurate. Another advantage is that higher order elements can be used much more effectively in conjunction with discontinuity meshes [16]. Several algorithms have been described that use the idea of discontinuity meshing to various extents [1, 3, 6, 15].

Recently, a progressive radiosity DM algorithm was described by the authors [18]. The meshing in this algorithm is automatic. Using analytical visibility and form factor computations followed by quadratic interpolation it has produced radiosity solutions of impressive visual accuracy. This algorithm was also shown to be numerically accurate [24].

However, this method is too expensive for computing converged solutions of complex environment and only offers limited user control in trading off speed for accuracy. The main reason for this is that all energy transfers are computed very accurately, regardless of their magnitude.

4 A COMBINED APPROACH

Hierarchical radiosity and discontinuity meshing seem to complement each other in their strengths and weaknesses: HR is fast, but the visual appearance of the results can be disappointing; DM, on the other hand, has produced visually accurate results, but so far it has been too expensive for simulation of complex environments. This observation motivated us to look for ways of merging the two methods. Our investigation resulted in the following two-pass approach:

The global pass uses a modified HR algorithm to compute a radiosity solution within a prespecified tolerance. Instead of regular quadtree subdivision, the modified algorithm subdivides surfaces along discontinuity segments. This improves the numerical accuracy and results in faster convergence.

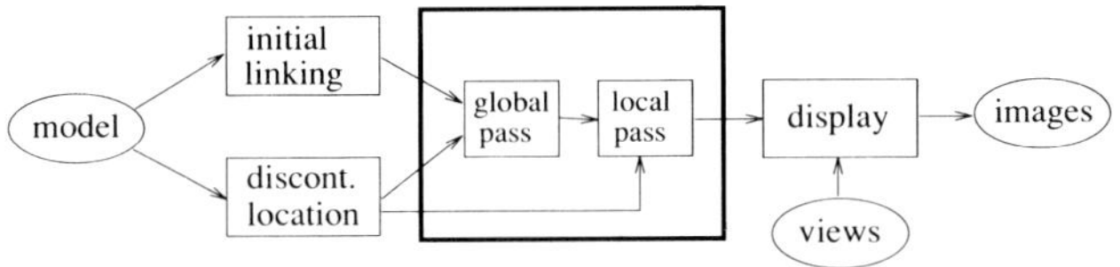

Figure 1: The structure of the new radiosity system

The local pass uses DM and quadratic interpolation to refine the approximation to the radiance function locally on each surface in the environment. Thus, the solution computed by the global pass is transformed into a more visually accurate form.

When the computation is arranged in this way the simulation becomes more efficient. The global pass need not be concerned with visual accuracy. This eliminates the need to maintain a topologically connected mesh, to prevent T-vertices, or to use extremely fine subdivision around shadow boundaries, since this has little effect on the global distribution of light in the environment. The local pass, on the other hand, can create as many elements as necessary for a high quality reconstruction of the radiance function, without overburdening the global illumination simulation. As a result, it is possible to produce images of high visual accuracy even from quick simulations.

To test our approach we have implemented a new radiosity system whose overall structure is shown in Figure 1. The global and the local passes are discussed in detail in the next two sections. In the rest of this section we briefly describe the remaining parts.

The initial linking stage creates for each input polygon a list of links to all the polygons that are visible from it. For each link it is determined whether the two polygons are completely or partially visible to each other. This creates a starting point for the global pass, which proceeds to refine these links as needed. We test visibility between two polygons using a combination of shaft-culling [13] and the ray-tracing algorithm that Hanrahan *et al.* [14] used.

The discontinuity location stage computes the location of all the D^0 discontinuities, since these are typically responsible for the most severe errors (both numerically and visually.) In most environments the direct illumination by primary light sources is responsible for the most perceptible illumination details. Therefore, all of the D^1 and D^2 discontinuities caused by EV events involving the primary light sources are computed as well. The computed discontinuities are henceforth collectively referred to as *primary* discontinuities.

EEE events are more difficult to handle because their corresponding critical surfaces are curved, rather than planar. However, the resulting discontinuities always lie within penumbra regions, and never define the outer boundaries of a shadow. For these reasons, we excluded EEE events from our current implementation.

We described the discontinuity location algorithm in a previous paper [18]. Tampieri [24] provides a more detailed description of this algorithm. Heckbert [15] and Teller [25] describe alternative algorithms for locating discontinuities. Teller's algorithm is the only one capable of handling EEE events.

5 THE GLOBAL PASS

In order to understand how the accuracy of HR can be improved, we must examine its sources of error. Consider two nodes s and r linked together by the HR algorithm. Let $B_{rs}(x)$ denote the actual radiosity due to node s at point x on node r. The algorithm approximates this radiosity by a constant function

$$B_{rs}(x) \sim \hat{B}_{rs} = \rho_r B_s F_{rs} V_{rs}$$

where ρ_r is the reflectivity of node r; B_s is the average radiosity of node s; F_{rs} is the form factor from r to s; and V_{rs} is the inter-visibility factor between r and s (the visible fraction of the area of s, averaged over r).

We are interested in bounding the error between the computed and the actual radiosities

$$E_{rs} = \sup_{x \in r} \left| B_{rs}(x) - \hat{B}_{rs} \right| \qquad (1)$$

To that end, we define the following upper and lower bounds:

$$\begin{array}{ll} B_s^{\min} = \inf_{x \in s} B_s(x) & B_s^{\max} = \sup_{x \in s} B_s(x) \\ F_{rs}^{\min} = \inf_{x \in r} F_{xs} & F_{rs}^{\max} = \sup_{x \in r} F_{xs} \\ V_{rs}^{\min} = \inf_{x \in r} V_{xs} & V_{rs}^{\max} = \sup_{x \in r} V_{xs} \end{array}$$

where $B_s(x)$ is the radiosity at point x on s; F_{xs} is the form factor from point x to s; and V_{xs} is the fraction of the area of s visible from x. Clearly, both $B_{rs}(x)$ and $\hat{B}_{rs}$ lie in the interval

$$\left[\rho_r B_s^{\min} F_{rs}^{\min} V_{rs}^{\min}, \rho_r B_s^{\max} F_{rs}^{\max} V_{rs}^{\max} \right]$$

Therefore, the error E_{rs} is bounded by the width of the interval

$$E_{rs} \leq \rho_r \left(B_s^{\max} F_{rs}^{\max} V_{rs}^{\max} - B_s^{\min} F_{rs}^{\min} V_{rs}^{\min} \right) \qquad (2)$$

Three main factors affect the magnitude of the error:

1. the variation of the radiosity on the source node s
2. the variation of the form factor across the receiver node r
3. the variation in the visibility of the source from the receiver

Therefore, if we find the potential error in the transfer of light energy from s to r too large, we can try to reduce the error by reducing any of these factors. For instance, subdividing the receiving node will reduce the variation of the form factor. Subdividing the source will reduce the variation of the radiosity on the source. Subdividing either of the two may reduce the variation in the visibility.

Unfortunately, errors due to visibility are more difficult to handle than errors of the other two types. If the two nodes are completely visible to each other, the error usually decreases rapidly as the nodes are subdivided. When the two nodes are completely occluded from each other no light energy transfer occurs, and the error is zero. Partial visibility, on the other hand, often results in very fine subdivisions, primarily because of loose bounds on the variation in visibility between two finite areas. In HR, visibility is estimated by casting a number of rays between the two nodes. Thus, if partial visibility is detected, all we know is that the actual visibility is in the interval $(0, 1)$.

Clearly, it would be to our advantage to use a subdivision strategy that would result in as many totally visible or totally occluded pairs, as quickly as possible. Since discontinuity lines on the receiver correspond to abrupt changes in the visibility of the sources [16, 18], subdividing the receiver along these lines should quickly resolve partial occlusion.

We have modified the HR algorithm to perform discontinuity-driven subdivision instead of regular subdivision. There are two main changes in the data structures used by the new algorithm: first, we store with each node a list of all the discontinuity segments on the corresponding polygon; second, we use a 2D binary space partitioning (BSP) tree [3] instead of a quadtree to represent the hierarchical subdivision of each initial polygon, since BSP trees allow for subdivision of polygons along arbitrarily oriented lines. Pseudocode for subdividing a node is given in Figure 2.

When a node is subdivided we choose one of its discontinuity segments and split the node using the corresponding line equation. The segment is chosen such that the split is as balanced as possible.

```
Boolean Subdivide(node)
if not IsLeaf(node) then
    return TRUE
end if
if node.area < minNodeArea then
    return FALSE
end if
if node.DSegments ≠ NIL then
    DSegment s ← ChooseBestSegment(node)
    (left, right) ← SplitNode(node, s)
    (leftList, rightList) ← SplitSegmentList(node, s)
else
    (left, right) ← SplitEqual(node)
    (leftList, rightList) ← (NIL, NIL)
end if
node.left ← CreateNode(left, leftList)
node.right ← CreateNode(right, rightList)
return TRUE
```

Figure 2: Pseudocode for the *Subdivide* routine

Priority is given to D^0 discontinuities over higher order ones, since the former typically bound areas totally occluded from the rest of the environment. The subdivision is completed by splitting the list of segments into two new lists, one for each child. If no segments are stored with the node, we split the node by connecting the midpoint of the longest edge to a vertex or another midpoint chosen so that the resulting children have roughly equal areas.

5.1 Results

Figure 4 demonstrates the improved hierarchical algorithm using a simple environment illuminated by two small triangular light sources. A 3D view of the environment is shown in image a1. The radiance function on the floor polygon is shown in image a2. Image a3 shows the discontinuity segments on the floor. D^0 discontinuities are drawn in red; D^1 and D^2 discontinuities in yellow. In rows b and c, we compare the subdivision produced by the discontinuity-driven algorithm to the one produced by regular subdivision. The level of subdivision shown increases from left to right: the leftmost pair shows the subdivision at level 2, then level 4, 6, and 8.

The new algorithm is much quicker to correctly separate regions corresponding to complete occlusion, partial visibility, and complete visibility. Already at subdivision level 4 (image b2), most of the nodes can be classified as either totally visible or totally occluded with respect to each of the light sources. For these areas there are no more visibility errors. At subdivision level 6 (image b3) all of the discontinuities have been used, and the partially visible nodes are now confined exactly to the areas of penumbra.

In order to compare the rates of convergence of the two strategies we computed a set of approximations to the direct illumination on the floor using a successively larger number of elements. Figure 3 shows the RMS and the maximum absolute errors versus the number of elements for the two strategies. These errors were computed with respect to an analytical solution at the vertices of a 400 by 400 grid on the floor. All the values were scaled to set the maximum brightness on the floor to 1.

Our algorithm converges faster in both error metrics. Note that the convergence of the regular subdivision is particularly poor in the maximum absolute error metric. The reason is that there are D^0 segments on the floor that are not aligned with the subdivision axes. Thus, there are always elements that are partially covered by the pyramid while the remaining part is brightly illuminated by the

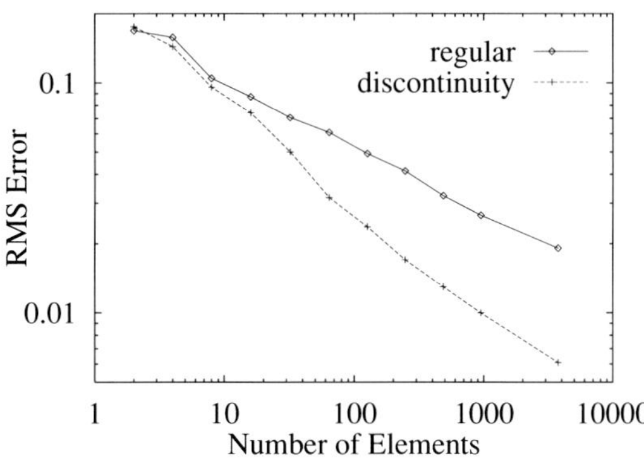

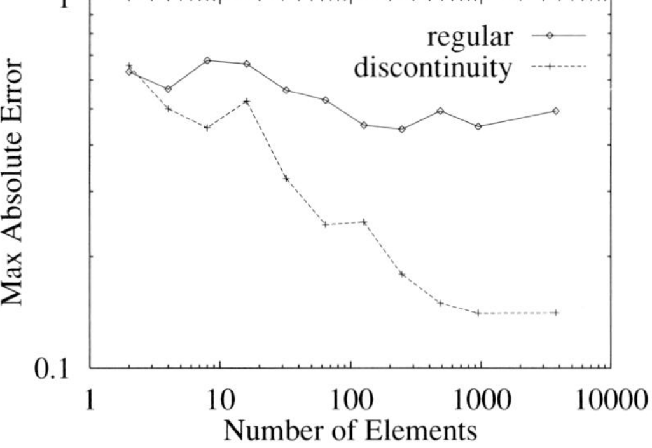

Figure 3: A comparison of errors between the two subdivision strategies using log-log plots

light sources. The algorithm assigns a single constant value to each such element, and this results in a large error there. Our algorithm, on the other hand, resolves D^0 discontinuities and therefore does not suffer from this problem.

In the RMS error metric regular subdivision does converge, because the elements that contain the errors become progressively smaller, and this is accounted for by the metric; however, the convergence is slower.

6 THE LOCAL PASS

The global pass results in a hierarchical solution that is essentially a piecewise constant approximation to the radiance function on each polygon in the environment. Often, this approximation is quite coarse. Now our goal is to convert this solution into a form more suited for producing visually accurate images. To that end, we need to locally refine the radiance approximation on each polygon.

Our experience with discontinuity meshing [18] has shown that reproducing the discontinuities in the radiance function, while maintaining a smooth approximation elsewhere is key to achieving visual accuracy, especially when multiple views of the same solution are to be rendered. Therefore, we construct a discontinuity mesh containing the precomputed primary discontinuities for each polygon. Mesh nodes are assigned radiance values using the hierarchical solution. This mesh is then used for the shaded display of the environment. Thus, the local pass essentially performs an additional light gathering operation over the environment. However, instead of gathering to the nodes in the hierarchy, we gather to the elements of the discontinuity mesh.

The discontinuity mesh is constructed using constrained Delaunay triangulation (CDT) [5]. The Delaunay triangulation (DT) of a point set maximizes the minimum angle over all possible triangula-

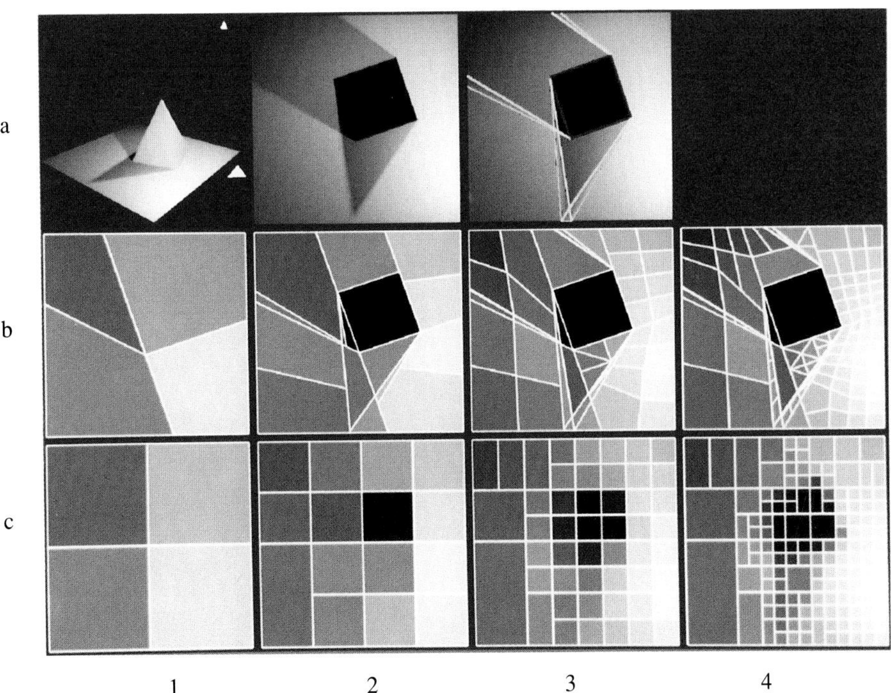

Figure 4: Discontinuity-driven vs. regular subdivision

tions of that set and has a number of other desirable properties [2]. These properties are important because they result in well-shaped elements that yield more accurate approximations and reduce visual artifacts during display [1]. CDT takes as input a point set and a set of edges connecting some of the points, and creates a triangulation of the points that is constrained to include all the input edges. CDT preserves the properties of DT over all the constrained triangulations. We have implemented an incremental CDT algorithm that is a simple extension of the incremental DT algorithm described by Guibas and Stolfi [11]. An alternative easy-to-implement algorithm is described in the excellent survey by Bern and Eppstein [2].

For each input polygon we provide the CDT routine with all of its boundary edges and discontinuity segments. The corners of all the leaf nodes in the corresponding hierarchy are given as well. Thus, the resulting mesh is dense enough to adequately sample the solution computed by the global pass. As a result of the properties of the CDT, most of the triangles are well shaped unless the hierarchy is very coarse.

The radiance across each triangle is approximated using a standard quadratic element commonly used in finite element methods [27]. Six radiance values are computed for each element: three at the vertices, and three at the edge midpoints. Except for D^0 edges, these values are shared between adjacent faces (our CDT algorithm constructs a topological data structure suitable for such information sharing [11].) The six values are then interpolated by a quadratic bivariate polynomial. This scheme yields a C^0 piecewise quadratic interpolant to the radiance on each polygon. This interpolant was found to provide approximations that look smoother and are less prone to Mach bands than the traditional piecewise linear interpolation [18]. Salesin *et al.* [21] describe a piecewise cubic interpolant that can be used instead, if C^1 interpolation is desired.

To obtain a radiance value at a point x we use the information available to us from the hierarchical solution. Below we describe four different methods that we have experimented with. Pseudocode for the last three methods is given in Figure 5.

Method A. The simplest approach is to use the radiance value stored in the hierarchy leaf that contains x. If x is on the boundary between two or more leaves, their values are averaged to yield the radiance at x. This method has no overhead other than locating the containing leaves.

The accuracy of the resulting value depends on the accuracy of the global pass solution. Consider the path from the root of the hierarchy to the leaf containing the point x. Every node along this pass has zero or more links to other nodes, representing areas on primary or secondary sources that illuminate x. The error at x due to one such link between a containing node r and an illuminating node s is bounded by equation (2). The total error at x is the sum of the errors over all the contributing links.

Method B. Each contributing link stores the unoccluded form factor from the center of its node to the corresponding source, as well as the visibility factor. To obtain a more accurate radiance value for x we can recompute the unoccluded form factor to each source at point x. Each form factor is multiplied by the visibility stored with the link and by the radiosity of the source. This results in a smaller bound on the error due to a link between r and s

$$E_{rs}(x) \leq \rho_r F_{xs} \left(B_s^{\max} V_{rs}^{\max} - B_s^{\min} V_{rs}^{\min} \right) \quad (3)$$

Method C. The next logical step is to recompute both the form factor and the visibility of each source as seen from x. In order to obtain an accurate visibility value the visible parts of the source are computed analytically [18]. As a result, the error bound shrinks further:

$$E_{rs}(x) \leq \rho_r F_{xs} V_{xs} \left(B_s^{\max} - B_s^{\min} \right) \quad (4)$$

However, the computation becomes more expensive.

Method D. To reduce the cost, we can recompute the visibility for links to primary light sources only. This is justified by the fact that primary sources are typically responsible for the most noticeable shadows. Moreover, these are precisely the sources for which discontinuities have been computed and inserted into the mesh. Thus, we obtain the same accuracy as in method C for links to primary sources, while the error due to other links remains the same as in method B.

```
Spectrum Shade(node, x)
rad ← 0
foreach l ∈ node.links do
    ff ← FormFactor(x, l.source)
    v ← Visibility(x, l)
    rad ← rad + ff * v * l.source.radiosity
end for
if IsInterior(node) then
    if Contains(node.left, x) then
        rad ← rad + Shade(node.left, x)
    else if Contains(node.right, x) then
        rad ← rad + Shade(node.right, x)
    else
        rad ← rad + 0.5 * (Shade(node.left, x)
                          +Shade(node.right, x))
    end if
end if
return rad

Real Visibility(x, link)
case ShadingMethod in
  B: v ← link.visibility
  C: v ← RecomputeVisibility(x, link.source)
  D: if IsPrimary(link.source) then
         v ← RecomputeVisibility(x, link.source)
     else
         v ← link.visibility
     end if
end case
return v
```

Figure 5: Pseudocode for the *Shade* routine

6.1 Results

We compared methods A, B, C, and D using a simple model of a square exhibit room displaying a modern sculpture illuminated by two small square light sources.

Three global pass solutions of the exhibit room are shown at the top row of Figure 6, in order of increasing accuracy starting from the left. For each solution, the elements (leaf nodes) of the hierarchical subdivision are shown as flat shaded, outlined polygons. The bottom row of the same figure shows the corresponding local pass meshes. Table 1 reports statistics for both passes.

The results of the global pass were fed to the local pass four times, once for each of the methods A, B, C, and D, yielding a total of twelve radiosity solutions shown in Figure 7. Columns 1, 2, and 3 were computed respectively from the low, medium, and high accuracy global pass solutions shown in Figure 6. Each row corresponds to a different shading strategy starting with method A for the top row.

As demonstrated in the top row, method A is prone to visual artifacts: the shading on walls is flat or not sufficiently smooth; some shadows are entirely missing (image A1), while others have incorrect boundaries. These artifacts are the result of interpolating radiance values obtained by sampling the piecewise constant global pass solution.

Method B reduces some of these artifacts. The appearance of unoccluded areas is greatly improved, since accurate form factor are recomputed at every interpolated point in the mesh. However, the penumbra regions of the shadows cast by the sculpture are still incorrect and shadows are still missing from the coarse solution (image B1.) The reason is that Method B still uses node-to-node visibility factors to approximate node-to-point visibility.

	Solution Accuracy		
	low	medium	high
input polygons	47	47	47
disc. segments	559	559	559
initial links	652	652	652
total links	720	1316	21805
total nodes	147	803	6041
total leaf nodes	97	425	3044
CDT elements	1538	2384	8177
shading calls	3799	5674	17984
initial linking	6	6	6
discontinuity comp.	1	1	1
hierarchical sol.	1	4	60
triangulation	0.53	0.81	2.78
method A	1	2	13
method B	6	10	80
method C	405	624	2633
method D	20	26	110

Table 1: Statistics for images in Figures 6 and 7. Timings are in seconds for execution on an HP 9000/720 workstation.

As shown in row C, method C correctly reconstructs all of the shadows. In particular, note the appearance of the shadows in the coarse solution (image C1.) This method results in the best visual accuracy we were able to obtain, given a global solution.

Method D yields results that are almost indistinguishable from those given by method C. However, as can be seen from the timings reported in Table 1, method D takes only a fraction of the time required by method C. In fact, it is not much more expensive than method B.

When using methods C or D, little difference can be seen between the medium and high accuracy solutions (columns 2 and 3). Although the latter solution is objectively more accurate, from a visual standpoint, the former solution is almost as good. If fact, it is apparent that even very low accuracy global pass solutions can yield results of reasonable visual quality when followed by a local pass using method D (image D1.)

When comparing the computation times reported in Table 1, it can be seen that the local pass is in most cases costlier than the global pass. It may be argued that the time used by the local pass could be better spent in further refinement of the subdivision hierarchy in the global pass. One might expect that if the hierarchy were sufficiently refined, even a very simple shading strategy would have sufficed for visually accurate results. Figure 7, however, demonstrates that this is not the case. Image D2, computed from the medium accuracy global pass followed by method D for the local pass, is visually more accurate than images A3 and B3; yet, it took considerably less time to compute (38 versus 83 and 150 seconds, respectively.)

Another set of comparisons was made to illustrate the importance of including discontinuity segments in the mesh for the local pass. Figure 8 shows a view of the floor of the exhibit room. The top row shows the mesh in wireframe with D^0 discontinuities in red and D^1 and D^2 discontinuities in yellow. The bottom row shows the shaded floor as reconstructed by the local pass. All images were computed from the medium accuracy global pass solution shown in image a2 of Figure 6 and all of them used method D in the local pass. As can be seen from the top row of Figure 8, no discontinuity segments were included in the left mesh, only D^0 discontinuities were included in the middle mesh, and all the discontinuity segments were included in the right mesh.

When comparing the corresponding images in the bottom row, the higher quality of the right image stands out. Image b1 presents

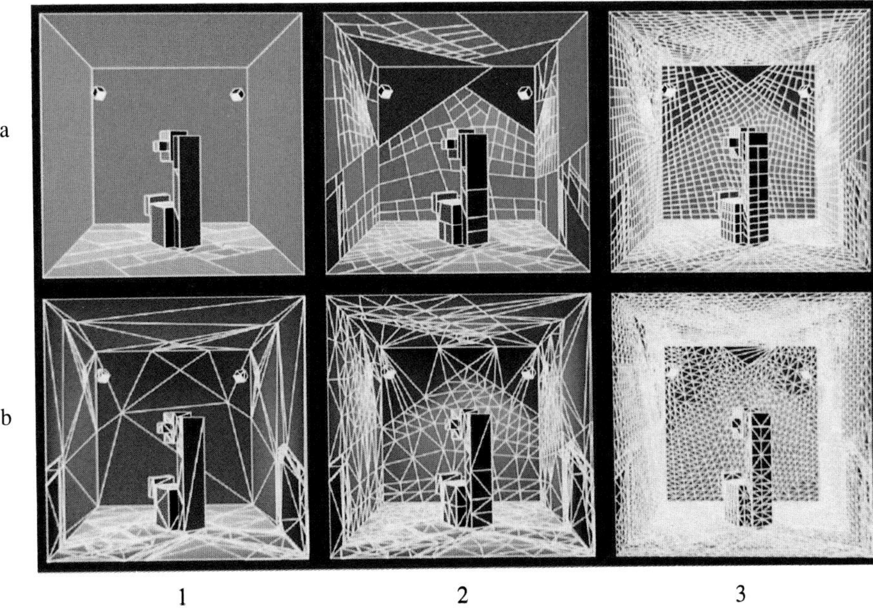

Figure 6: Exhibit Room. Global pass solutions (top row) and the corresponding local pass meshes (bottom row). The accuracy of the solutions increases from left to right.

many of the visual artifacts typical of conventional radiosity methods: shadow and light leaks, fuzzy shadow boundaries, and incorrectly shaped shadows. Image b2 shows how including D^0 discontinuities greatly reduces shadow and light leaks, but still has problems reproducing shadow boundaries and penumbra areas. Finally, image b3, correctly captures all shadow boundaries. We conclude, therefore, that it is necessary to represent discontinuities explicitly in the local pass mesh, even though some or all of them may have been resolved by the subdivision in the global pass.

	Discontinuities in the Mesh		
	none	D^0	$D^0\ D^1\ D^2$
triangulation	0.39	0.39	0.81
shading	9	10	26
disc. segments	0	36	559
CDT elements	1170	1190	2384
shading calls	2739	3027	5674

Table 2: Statistics for the comparison of meshing strategies shown in Figure 8. Timings are in seconds for execution on an HP 9000/720 workstation.

As the statistics reported in Table 2 show, building a mesh that incorporates discontinuity segments takes longer than building one without discontinuities. Furthermore, including the discontinuities generally results in a larger number of elements and consequently shading the mesh takes longer. We believe, however, that the increased computation time is well justified.

7 A FINAL COMPARISON

In this section we demonstrate the performance of our combined approach on an environment of moderate complexity (1,688 input polygons.) Figure 9 shows a rendered view of the scene. There are two primary light sources: a small distant polygonal source outside the room simulates sunlight, and another polygonal source close to the ceiling provides the artificial illumination.

The figure shows two images of the same environment. The left image (HDMR) was generated using primary discontinuity segments in both passes with shading method D in the local pass. To generate the right image (HR) we modified our algorithm to essentially emulate regular HR: discontinuities were not used in either pass, the vertices of the triangles were shaded using method A, and linear interpolation was used for display.

As can be expected in a complex environment, the initial linking stage results in a very large number of initial links, most of which represent interactions of very small magnitude. For efficiency, we use a simple culling strategy: we ignore all the initial links that do not involve a primary light source and whose form factor falls below a user specified threshold. We found that by using a small threshold it is possible to eliminate most of the initial links, without any noticeable change in the resulting images. As was mentioned in Section 2, clustering of input surfaces in the initial linking stage should provide a more comprehensive solution to this problem.

Table 3 reports various statistics for the two solutions from which the images in Figure 9 were rendered. The two solutions have roughly the same number of final triangles, yet the HDMR solution looks dramatically better than the HR solution; while the latter exhibits many of typical problems of radiosity images, HDMR produces sharp shadow boundaries and correct penumbrae, eliminates shadow and light leaks, and captures some small features that are entirely missed by HR. Furthermore, the total computation time was almost twice as long for the HR solution.

We attempted to perform a similar comparison with our progressive DM algorithm [18]. However, we were not able to obtain a converged solution for this environment: after four hours of computation the DM algorithm was still in its fourth iteration.

7.1 Complexity of Discontinuity Meshing

A legitimate concern regarding discontinuity meshing is that, in theory, l light source edges and m polygon edges can result in $O(lm)$ distinct EV visual events. In the worst case, each event intersects $O(m)$ polygons, resulting in a total number of $O(lm^2)$ discontinuity segments. In such a case each polygon has $O(lm)$ discontinuity segments, which can result in as many as $O(l^2m^2)$ elements in the discontinuity mesh for that polygon.

We have found that this worst case analysis is too pessimistic in practice. Consider, for example, the environment shown in

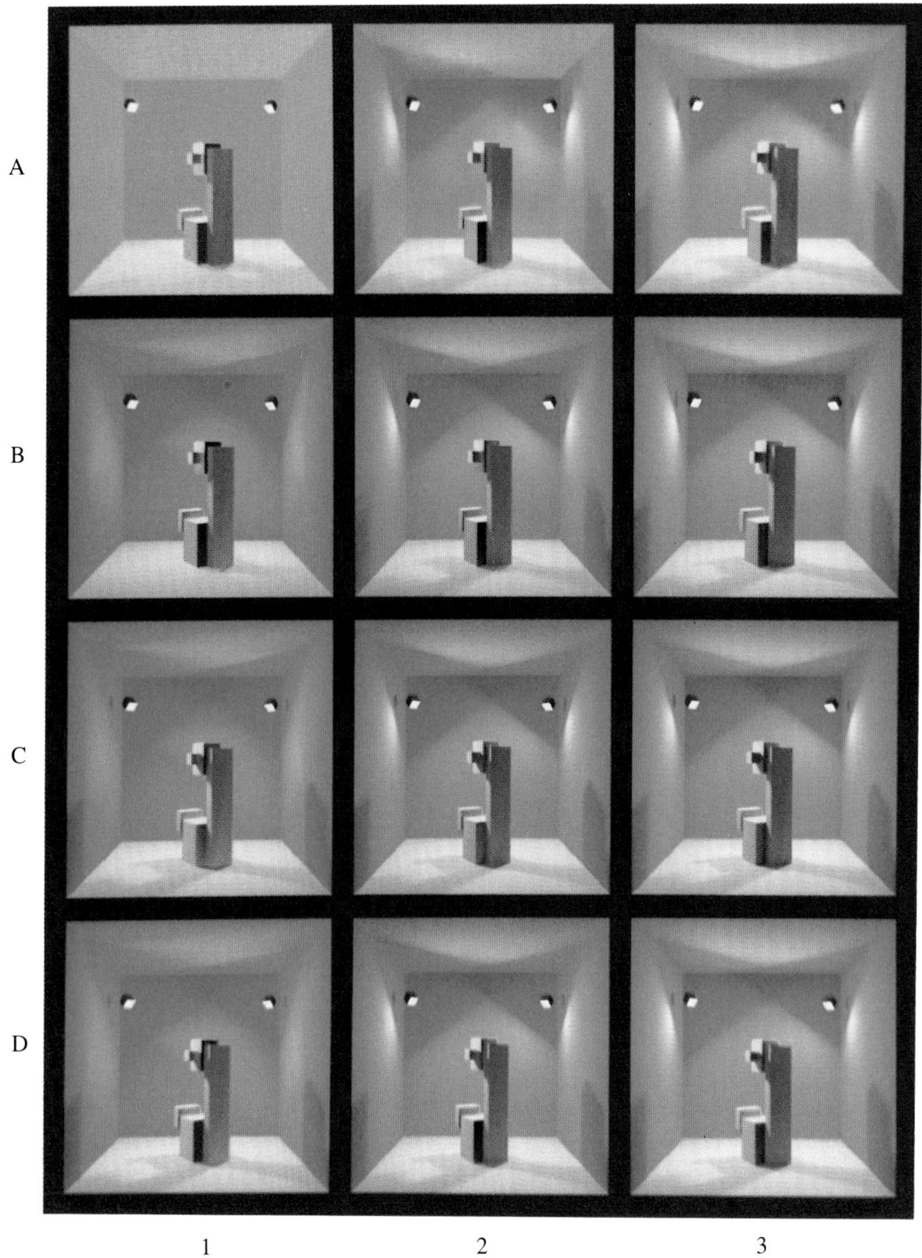

Figure 7: Exhibit Room. A comparison of shading strategies. Columns 1, 2, and 3 were computed respectively from the low, medium, and high accuracy global pass solutions shown in Figure 6. Each row corresponds to a different shading strategy; starting from the top: method A, method B, method C, and method D.

Figure 9. In this environment l is 8, and m is 6,744. The worst case upper bound on the number of discontinuity segments on a single polygon is 215,808. In practice, there were 18,664 discontinuity segments in the entire environment, an average of roughly 11 segments per polygon. The highest number of segments on a single polygon (the floor) is 2,175, resulting in only 7,627 triangles in the floor's discontinuity mesh.

8 CONCLUSIONS

By combining hierarchical radiosity with discontinuity meshing we have created a new radiosity method that is superior to both of its ancestors: it is more accurate than the HR algorithm, both numerically and visually, and it is faster and more flexible than DM algorithms. The new algorithm is capable of producing high quality images even from quick simulations.

Hierarchical radiosity has been recently extended to deal with very complex environments by introducing the notion of importance into the solution process [22]. This improvement is readily applicable to our algorithm as well: the global pass would simultaneously solve for radiosity and for importance as described by Smits *et al.* [22]; the local pass would only reconstruct the radiance on surfaces which are direct receivers (or emitters) of importance.

There are several aspects of our algorithm that can be substantially improved:

Visibility computations. Our implementation uses shaft culling [13] to reliably determine complete visibility between polygons, but point sampling is used to determine whether two polygons are entirely occluded from each other. Our method could be improved by using the accurate and reliable visibility algorithms described by

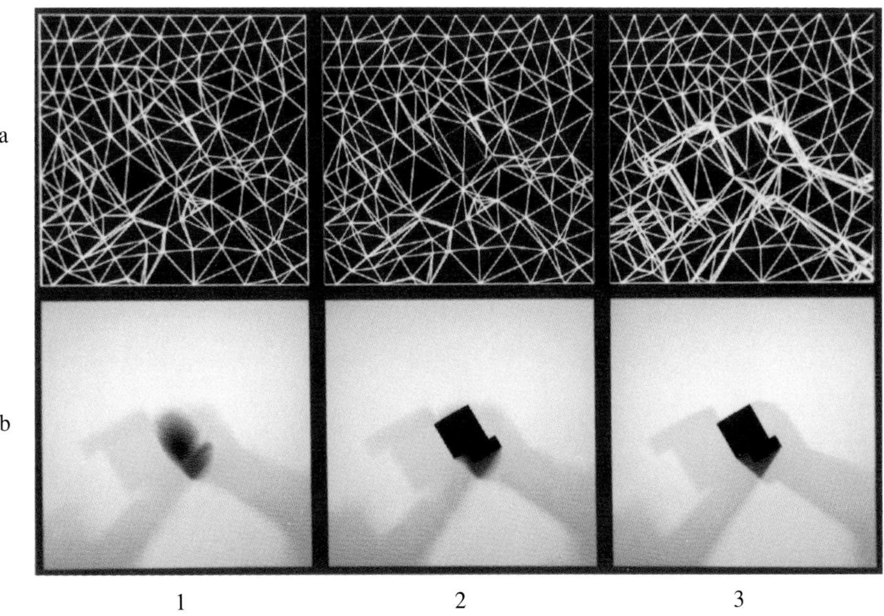

Figure 8: Exhibit Room Floor. A comparison of meshing strategies. Mesh (top row) and computed radiance (bottom row) on the floor using simple CDT (left), CDT with D^0 discontinuity segments (middle), and CDT with D^0, D^1, and D^2 discontinuity segments (right).

Figure 9: A comparison of Hierarchical Discontinuity Meshing Radiosity (left) vs. Hierarchical Radiosity (right)

	Radiosity Algorithm	
	HDMR	HR
initial linking	2 : 16 : 27	2 : 16 : 27
discontinuity computations	0 : 09 : 06	0 : 00 : 00
hierarchical solution	0 : 16 : 42	3 : 58 : 01
triangulation	0 : 00 : 21	0 : 00 : 16
shading computations	0 : 33 : 49	0 : 00 : 51
total time (hr:min:sec)	3 : 16 : 56	6 : 15 : 35
input polygons	1,688	1,688
discontinuity segments	18,664	0
initial links	165,814	165,814
links after culling	27,002	27,002
total links	39,056	161,668
total nodes	5,778	35,454
total leaf nodes	3,733	18,571
avg. depth of hierarchy	1.31	2.04
CDT elements	41,090	41,284
shading calls	109,885	101,208
recomputed form factors	3,609,941	0
recomputed visibility terms	128,705	0

Table 3: Statistics for the comparison of hierarchical discontinuity meshing radiosity (HDMR) vs. hierarchical radiosity (HR) shown in Figure 9. All timings are for execution on an HP 9000/720 workstation.

Teller and Hanrahan [26].

We need to be able to compute tight bounds on the visibility between two partially occluded polygons. This would improve the efficiency of the global pass by eliminating unnecessary subdivision in penumbral areas.

Choice of sources. Our algorithm is particularly effective for environments with a few primary light sources that are responsible for the most noticeable shadows. In general, however, primary light sources do not dominate the illumination on all the surfaces in an environment. Our algorithm should be extended to compute a set of the most dominant sources, primary or secondary, with respect to each receiving surface. This set should be used both for computing the discontinuities on that surface and for determining when visibility should be recomputed in the local pass.

Choice of discontinuities. Not all the discontinuities are equally significant. In the global pass, for example, we should choose discontinuities that would resolve partial visibility most effectively, rather than ones that split the node most evenly. In the local pass we need to identify the discontinuities that are visually significant and insert only these discontinuities into the mesh.

ACKNOWLEDGEMENTS

We would like to thank Brian Smits, Jim Arvo, and Kevin Novins for helpful discussions and for reviewing the manuscript. Ben Trumbore assembled and submitted the review draft when the authors were away on vacation. Suzanne Smits modeled the sculpture used in the examples in Section 6, and Matt Hyatt modeled the room used in the final comparison. This work was supported by the NSF grant, "Interactive Computer Graphics Input and Display Techniques" (CCR-8617880), by the NSF/DARPA Science and Technology Center for Computer Graphics and Scientific Visualization (ASC-8920219), and by generous donations of equipment from Hewlett-Packard.

REFERENCES

[1] Baum, Daniel R., Stephen Mann, Kevin P. Smith, and James M. Winget. "Making Radiosity Usable: Automatic Preprocessing and Meshing Techniques for the Generation of Accurate Radiosity Solutions," *Computer Graphics*, 25(4), July 1991, pages 51–60.

[2] Bern, Marshall and David Eppstein. "Mesh Generation and Optimal Triangulation," in Hwang, F.K. and D.-Z. Du, editors, *Computing in Euclidian Geometry*, World Scientific, 1992.

[3] Campbell, III, A. T. *Modeling Global Diffuse Illumination for Image Synthesis*, PhD dissertation, U. of Texas at Austin, Texas, December 1991.

[4] Chen, Shenchang Eric, Holly E. Rushmeier, Gavin Miller, and Douglass Turner. "A Progressive Multi-Pass Method for Global Illumination," *Computer Graphics*, 25(4), July 1991, pages 165–174.

[5] Chew, L. Paul. "Constrained Delaunay Triangulations," *Algorithmica*, 4, 1989, pages 97–108.

[6] Chin, Norman and Steven Feiner. "Fast Object-Precision Shadow Generation for Area Light Sources Using BSP Trees," in Proceedings of 1992 Symposium on Interactive 3D Graphics, March 1992.

[7] Cohen, Michael F. and Donald P. Greenberg. "The Hemi-Cube: A Radiosity Solution for Complex Environments," *Computer Graphics*, 19(3), July 1985, pages 31–40.

[8] Cohen, Michael F., Donald P. Greenberg, and David S. Immel. "An Efficient Radiosity Approach for Realistic Image Synthesis," *IEEE Computer Graphics and Applications*, 6(2), March 1986, pages 26–35.

[9] Gigus, Ziv and Jitendra Malik. "Computing the Aspect Graph for Line Drawings of Polyhedral Objects," *IEEE Transactions on Pattern Analysis and Machine Intelligence*, 12(2), February 1990, pages 113–122.

[10] Goral, Cindy M., Kenneth E. Torrance, Donald P. Greenberg, and Bennett Battaile. "Modeling the Interaction of Light Between Diffuse Surfaces," *Computer Graphics*, 18(3), July 1984, pages 213–222.

[11] Guibas, Leonidas and Jorge Stolfi. "Primitives for the Manipulation of General Subdivisions and the Computation of Voronoi Diagrams," *ACM Transactions on Graphics*, 4(2), April 1985, pages 74–123.

[12] Haines, Eric A. "Ronchamp: A Case Study for Radiosity," SIGGRAPH'91 Frontiers in Rendering Course Notes, July 1991.

[13] Haines, Eric A. and John R. Wallace. "Shaft Culling for Efficient Ray-Traced Radiosity," in Proceedings of the Second Eurographics Workshop on Rendering, May 1991.

[14] Hanrahan, Pat, David Salzman, and Larry Aupperle. "A Rapid Hierarchical Radiosity Algorithm," *Computer Graphics*, 25(4), July 1991, pages 197–206.

[15] Heckbert, Paul S. "Discontinuity Meshing for Radiosity," in Proceedings of the Third Eurographics Workshop on Rendering, May 1992, pages 203–216.

[16] Heckbert, Paul S. *Simulating Global Illumination Using Adaptive Meshing*, PhD dissertation, UC Berkeley, California, June 1991.

[17] Kok, Arjan J. F. and Frederik Jansen. "Source Selection for the Direct Lighting Computation in Global Illumination," in Proceedings of the Second Eurographics Workshop on Rendering, May 1991.

[18] Lischinski, Dani, Filippo Tampieri, and Donald P. Greenberg. "Discontinuity Meshing for Accurate Radiosity," *IEEE Computer Graphics and Applications*, 12(6), November 1992, pages 25–39.

[19] Nishita, Tomoyuki and Eihachiro Nakamae. "Continuous Tone Representation of Three-Dimensional Objects Taking Account of Shadows and Interreflections," *Computer Graphics*, 19(3), July 1985, pages 23–30.

[20] Reichert, Mark C. *A Two-Pass Radiosity Method Driven by Lights and Viewer Position*, Master's thesis, Cornell University, Ithaca, New York, January 1992.

[21] Salesin, David, Dani Lischinski, and Tony DeRose. "Reconstructing Illumination Functions with Selected Discontinuities," in Proceedings of the Third Eurographics Workshop on Rendering, May 1992, pages 99–112.

[22] Smits, Brian E., James R. Arvo, and David H. Salesin. "An Importance-Driven Radiosity Algorithm," *Computer Graphics*, 26(4), July 1992, pages 273–282.

[23] Sparrow, Ephraim M. "On the Calculation of Radiant Interchange between Surfaces," in Ibele, Warren E., editor, *Modern Developements in Heat Transfer*, Academic Press, New York, 1963.

[24] Tampieri, Filippo. *Discontinuity Meshing for Radiosity Image Synthesis*, PhD dissertation, Cornell University, Ithaca, New York, May 1993.

[25] Teller, Seth J. "Computing the Antipenumbra of an Area Light Source," *Computer Graphics*, 26(4), July 1992, pages 139–148.

[26] Teller, Seth and Pat Hanrahan. "Global Visibility Algorithms for Illumination Computations," *Computer Graphics*, 27(4), August 1993.

[27] Zienkiewicz, O. C. and R. L. Taylor. *The Finite Element Method*, pages 128–132, Vol. 1, McGraw-Hill, London, 4th edition, 1989.

Radiosity Algorithms Using Higher Order Finite Element Methods

Roy Troutman, Nelson L. Max

Lawrence Livermore National Laboratory

Abstract

Many of the current radiosity algorithms create a piecewise constant approximation to the actual radiosity. Through interpolation and extrapolation, a continuous solution is obtained. An accurate solution is found by increasing the number of patches which describe the scene. This has the effect of increasing the computation time as well as the memory requirements. By using techniques found in the finite element method, we can incorporate an interpolation function directly into our form factor computation. We can then use less elements to achieve a more accurate solution. Two algorithms, derived from the finite element method, are described and analyzed.

CR Categories and Subject Descriptors: I.3.3 [Computer Graphics]: Picture/Image Generation - Display Algorithms. I.3.7 [Computer Graphics]: Three-Dimensional Graphics and Realism.

Additional Key Words and Phrases: finite elements, form-factor, global illumination, radiosity.

1 Introduction

The traditional radiosity algorithm computes the form factors at a collection of points [5]. There have been several techniques used to enhance and speed up the algorithm. Cohen described an algorithm which enabled more complex environments to be rendered by placing a half cube or "hemicube" at each evaluation point and sampling through pixels on the hemicube surface [3]. We can improve the accuracy of the solution by increasing the resolution of the hemicube or by analytically determining the form factors [1], [13]. Further improvements can be made by producing a mesh which follows the discontinuities introduced by shadow boundaries and surface intersections [9], [10].

Rather than assuming the radiosity arrives from piecewise constant patches, Max and Allison introduced an algorithm which assumed a piecewise linear approximation [11]. This algorithm works by placing an interpolation function directly into the form factor computation. Using this technique, a more accurate solution can be obtained with less patches [9]. An extension to this algorithm is to increase the order of the interpolation function to quadratic, cubic or even higher [16]. These interpolation functions are what the finite element method refers to as basis functions [2].

2 Basis Functions

The details of the basis functions, elements and nodes can be found in [2]. We will only give a brief overview to establish our terminology.

2.1 Approximation Function

The finite element method associates a basis function for each of the local nodes in a representative element. The basis function for a global node becomes a combination of basis functions defined on the local nodes of all elements which contain the global node [2], [9], [14]. In this paper a node is "contained" or "in" an element if it is on the boundary or interior of the element. Using the basis function f_i and radiosity B_i associated with each node i, we can approximate the radiosity at a point x in our environment as a linear combination of the radiosities of each node or

$$\tilde{B}(x) = \sum_{i=1}^{n} B_i f_i(x) \qquad \textbf{(EQ 1)}$$

2.2 Element Construction

Due to its compatibility with triangulation and orientation independence using Gouraud shading, we have chosen the triangle as our element. We also need to concern ourselves with the connectivity of this element. Our solution will be much more accurate if we align our mesh to the D^0 and D^1 discontinuities as described by [9] and [10]. We can obtain elements with C^0 continuity by using the same nodes on the boundary of adjacent elements [2], [4]. By definition, the C^0 elements can accurately model D^1 discontinuities. A D^0 discontinuity would result from surface intersection, discrete changes in emissivity or discrete changes in reflectivity. These can be modeled by aligning our edges to the discontinuities and duplicating the nodes along the edge [9]. Higher order discontinuities could be modeled by selectively enforcing higher derivative continuity across the common edges between adjacent elements, but this is quite complex [12] so we approximate them by using smaller elements.

3 Finite Element Methods

This section will give a very brief introduction to finite element mathematics to provide us with modifications needed for the radiosity algorithm to incorporate higher order elements and the previously discussed basis functions.

3.1 Residual Error

We start by reiterating an equation from [8] which describes the radiosity for all points in the environment

$$B(x) = E(x) + \rho(x) \int_{\Omega} ds\, \kappa(x, s)\, B(s) \qquad \textbf{(EQ 2)}$$

where

$$\kappa(x, s) = V(x, s) \frac{\cos\theta_i \cos\theta_j}{\pi r^2} \qquad \textbf{(EQ 3)}$$

Exact solutions to (EQ 2) are known only in the simplest of geometries [8]. The exact solution can be approximated using the linear combination in (EQ 1). Traditional radiosity methods can be thought of as having a constant basis function of $f_i(x) = 1$ for all points x inside patch i. These *constant basis* radiosity algorithms will not be reiterated. The method introduced in [11] uses linear basis functions centered on the vertices. We will be presenting algorithms for extending *polynomial basis* radiosity to higher order polynomials.

The traditional radiosity method assigns an emissivity and reflectivity to each patch. We can enhance our radiosity algorithms by claiming that the exact emissivity and reflectivity are also defined by an approximation function similar to (EQ 1). This would allow us to describe variations in emissivity and reflectivity up to the degree of the basis function. For the sake of brevity, we will assume that the

Address: P.O. Box 808, Livermore, Ca. 94550
email: roy@nersc.gov, max2@llnl.gov

 ACM-0-89791-601-8/93/008/0209

emissivity e_k and reflectivity ρ_k are constant across each individual surface, k.

We can replace $B(s)$ in (EQ 2) by our approximation function to obtain an approximate solution for $B(x)$. If our approximation is good, then the approximate solution for $B(x)$ and the value obtained by applying (EQ 2) at point x should be close. If our approximate solution is exact, the difference between these two approximations will be zero. This gives us a measure of the accuracy of our approximation and is defined as the *residual error*. More specifically, it is expressed as

$$r(x) = E(x) + \rho(x)\int_{\Omega} ds\, \kappa(x,s)\tilde{B}(s) - \tilde{B}(x) \quad \text{(EQ 4)}$$

3.2 Method of Weighted Residuals

A general approximation technique is the method of weighted residuals. This technique requires the residual error to be orthogonal to a set $\{w_i(x)\}$ of weighting functions over the domain Ω. It was shown in [8] that the resulting equations could be expressed in matrix form as

$$[\mathbf{M} - \mathbf{K}]\,\mathbf{B} = \mathbf{E} \quad \text{(EQ 5)}$$

where **B** is a column vector containing the coefficients to our approximation and

$$M_{ij} = \int_{\Omega} dx\; w_i(x) f_j(x)$$

$$K_{ij} = \rho_k \int_{\Omega} dx\; w_i(x) \int_{\Omega} ds\, \kappa(x,s) f_j(s) \quad \text{(EQ 6)}$$

$$E_i = e_k \int_{\Omega} dx\; w_i(x)$$

where k is the index of the surface supporting weight function w_i.

4 Higher Order Algorithms

We have presented a set of interpolation functions in section 2 and combined them with our radiosity integral using the finite element method in section 3. This gave us a matrix equation where each component of the matrix contained a weighting function. By replacing the weights with different functions we obtain the point collocation and Galerkin methods [8].

4.1 Point Collocation Method

The traditional gathering algorithm as well as the linear vertex radiosity method introduced in [11] are examples of the point collocation method. This method replaces the weighting function in (EQ 6) with the dirac delta [8]. This simplifies the $\mathbf{M}$ in (EQ 5) to be the identity matrix and $\mathbf{E}$ to be a column vector containing the emissivities at each node. The elements of $\mathbf{K}$ have the value

$$K_{ij} = \rho_k \int_{\Omega} ds\, \kappa(x_i, s) f_j(s) \quad \text{(EQ 7)}$$

The contents of the integral describes a differential area to weighted area form factor where the area is defined by the domain of the basis associated with node j. We will call this a differential area to basis form factor. This integral can be solved using the approach specified in [11]. The pseudocode is as follows

```
Initialize F to 0
For each pixel h in hemicube
    k = index of patch at h
    Q = point on surface of k
    For each node j in patch k
        F_ij = F_ij + f_j(Q)Δ_h
    EndFor
EndFor
```

4.2 Galerkin Method

The Galerkin method replaces the weighting functions with the basis functions giving us the following definitions for the matrices of (EQ 5).

$$M_{ij} = \int_{\Omega} dx\; f_i(x) f_j(x)$$

$$K_{ij} = \rho_k \int_{\Omega} dx\; f_i(x) \int_{\Omega} ds\, \kappa(x,s) f_j(s) \quad \text{(EQ 8)}$$

$$E_i = e_k \int_{\Omega} dx\; f_i(x)$$

We'll start by looking at the equation for M_{ij}. We only need to concern ourselves with the area where f_i and f_j are both non-zero. This will only occur if an element can be found which has the nodes i and j on the boundary or interior. Clearly this occurs if i equals j. We can easily compute M_{ij} by considering only the elements which contain node i and looking through that small set of elements for the elements which also contain node j. We then integrate across these elements individually and sum the results. The formula for 2-D change of variables from the global triangle to the representative element gives us the Jacobian determinant which is the area of the global element. Therefore, the integral across an element is the same as the integral across the representative element multiplied by the area of the element. The final result is a constant multiplied by the area of the global element. The constant is dependent upon the relative positions of the local nodes corresponding to i and j. We can store these constants in a matrix $\mathbf{M}_c$. This matrix is symmetrical, which is what we would expect by looking at the equation. The local node numbers for i and j correspond to the row and column of a location this matrix.

Solving for E_i follows a similar path. In this case, we must integrate across the domain of the basis function. We can form a vector $\mathbf{E}_c$ which contains the integral of all of the local nodes across the representative element. To compute E_i, we look at each element which has node i, use the local node number as an index into $\mathbf{E}_c$, multiply that array element by the area and then add it to the current value of E_i. After we visit each element, we multiply our result by the node emission e_i.

Computing K_{ij} is slightly more involved. We know from (EQ 7) that the inner integral is a differential area to weighted area form factor. In the Galerkin case, the weighted area still corresponds to the domain of a basis function, but the differential area corresponds to some point x in the domain of f_i. We will express this differential area to basis form factor as F_{xj}. Our equation simplifies to

$$K_{ij} = \rho_k \int_{\Omega} dx\; f_i(x) F_{xj} \quad \text{(EQ 9)}$$

The contents of the integral describe a basis to basis form factor. This integral is in a form that is appropriate for Gaussian quadrature [2], [16]. The problem of computing K_{ij} is now reduced to computing a set of form factors, adding the results multiplied by the appropriate weight and multiplying by the reflectivity.

To compute the basis to basis form factor with gaussian quadrature we start by specifying the degree of precision [2]. This provides us with a collection of gauss points on each element. We compute an array of differential area to basis form factors FF (computed by the algorithm in section 4.1) at each of the gauss points. This hemicube will affect the basis to basis form factors associated with each node in the element. After we have completed computing the entire matrix of form factors, we multiply each row by the reflectivity to obtain $\mathbf{K}$. This gives us the following algorithm

```
Initialize F to 0
For each patch p
    a_p = area of patch p
    For each gauss point l
        Q_l = global coordinate of point l
        w_l = weight assigned to point l
        FF = array of form factors computed at Q_l
        For each node i in p
            For j = 1 to total number of nodes
                F_ij = F_ij + a_p × w_l × f_i(Q_l) × FF(j)
            Endfor
        Endfor
    Endfor
Endfor
```

The matrix **M** is very sparse. To avoid using an excessive amount of memory due to random access, the matrix is computed one row at a time. This requires us to visit a node and find the patches which share this node. The winged edge data structure allows us to easily determine adjacent elements. The algorithm for computing **M** and **E** is as follows.

```
Initialize M and E to 0
For each node i
    P = set of patches containing i
    For each patch p ∈ P
        a_p = area of patch p
        J = set of nodes in p
        l_i = local node number of node i
        For each j ∈ J
            l_j = local node number of node j
            M_ij = M_ij + a_p × M_c(l_i, l_j)
        Endfor
        E_i = E_i + a_p × E_c(l_i)
    Endfor
Endfor
```

To solve for **B**, we multiply each row of the form factor matrix by the reflectivities and solve the matrix using the Gauss-Seidel iteration method.

5 Analysis

A quantitative measurement of the accuracy of our algorithms are obtained by applying an error metric. We will apply this metric to images generated by our collocation and Galerkin algorithms.

5.1 Error Metric

We determine the RMS radiosity reconstruction error by rendering each surface individually at the same distance. Our reference image was obtained by using quadratic basis elements on a discontinuity meshed version of our scene and applying a hemicube with a resolution of 314 x 314 x 157. Since 157 is a prime number, the chance of a correlation with a lower resolution hemicube is reduced. The floating point radiosity of each pixel is compared to the same pixel in each rendered surface of the reference. The error is measured using

$$\sqrt{\frac{\sum_{i=1}^{n}\left(\frac{r_i - e_i}{r_i}\right)^2}{n}} \qquad \textbf{(EQ 10)}$$

where r_i is the radiosity value at pixel i in the reference scene, e_i is the radiosity at pixel i in a test scene and n is the total number of pixels occupied by a rendered image of every surface. Computing the error in this manner reduces the chance of bias since it is improbable that any particular node in our scene will be on a pixel center.

5.2 Collocation Results

The collocation algorithm was implemented on a Cray YMP/C90. Timing information was obtained using the Unix *times* function. The computation time was considered to be the time spent executing the code added to the time spent completing system calls. The total time includes the time spent generating and solving the matrix. We do not include I/O times. We could not include the time spent generating the mesh since some of the following meshes were generated by hand. Because of its flexibility, Heckbert's software z-buffer [7] was used to project the environment onto the hemicube. Although the program computed the radiosity for the red, green and blue components, only the blue component was used to determine the error.

We start by analyzing the source of error in Figure 1. Most of the error in this image is due to the shadow edges on the floor. By rendering the radiosity of the floor as a 3-D shaded surface, we enhance the radiosity discontinuities that would not be visible when the scene is rendered as an image. Figure 1 also shows the radiosity of the floor of the reference scene rendered in this manner. This gives us more information about where errors occur as well as how close our approximation is to a converged reference.

The reference image appeared to be extremely smooth. However, when we looked at the floor rendered as a shaded surface, slight discontinuities due to hemicube aliasing were detected. These artifacts are referred to as plaid patterns in [1] and [15]. When the edge of a light source is parallel or at a 45 degree angle to the edge of the hemicube, the amount of aliasing is greatly enhanced. In some scenes it may be possible to determine an ideal rotation for the hemicube in order to reduce aliasing, but when we introduce occlusion, the apparent edge of a source changes. In general, we can reduce the chance of a poor alignment by introducing a random rotation to the hemicube. This gives a slight improvement in terms of numerical error and a big improvement in terms of visually perceptible error. To improve our reference even further, we solved for the radiosity several times and averaged the results.

We applied a uniform and discontinuity mesh to Figure 1. By increasing the resolution of a mesh, the amount of computation time increases as the error decreases. We did not have access to triangulation software that would easily allow us to create a variable sized discontinuity mesh. An interactive mesh generator called Maze [6] was used to produce a set of quadrilaterals which were then split into triangles. One of the goals used in producing this mesh was to limit the number of slices or poorly formed elements. Once the mesh was created, we were easily able to further subdivide the resulting triangles to improve the accuracy of our solution.

Figure 2 shows the results of the algorithm when applied to the scene shown in Figure 1 with a 100 x 100 x 50 hemicube. A log error of less than -1.3 generated an image which was very difficult to distinguish from the reference. A log error of less than -1.6 generated an image which could not be distinguished from the reference even with high quality display devices. A log error of approximately -2 was mostly due to hemicube aliasing. Note that the linear and constant uniform elements did not obtain these error levels in the time frame shown. The effect on the form factors due to visibility changes is basically quadratic, so we did not expect or see a great deal of improvement in the cubic element over the quadratic element. Discontinuity meshing showed the most impressive results. The linear discontinuity elements produced the same error as the best uniform elements in half the time. The quadratic and cubic discontinuity elements produced an error level so small that further reduction could only be obtained by increasing the resolution of the hemicube.

The collocation algorithm was applied to other simple scenes. In some cases, even the higher order C^0 elements did not conform well to the radiosity solution along edges of high variance. These edges can be found near dimly lit corners of a closed room.

5.3 Galerkin Results

The Galerkin method was also implemented on the Cray YMP/C90. This method required only minor modifications to the existing collocation algorithm. The program was implemented so that the user could specify the number of degrees of precision. It was shown in [14] that in the case of the uniform mesh, the optimal degrees of precision for the constant, linear, quadratic and cubic basis were one, one, four and four, respectively. At these levels the algorithm produced less error in less time. We also found that the discontinuity mesh produced these same optimal degrees of precision. The constant basis Galerkin algorithm is identical to the constant basis collocation algorithm [14], so we don't present these results.

Figure 2 shows the results of applying the Galerkin method using a uniform and discontinuity mesh for the scene in Figure 1. We used the same 100 x 100 x 50 resolution hemicube for these tests. The quadratic and cubic basis achieved a lower error than the linear for both meshes. The quadratic and cubic discontinuity mesh again produced very small error levels immediately. In comparison to the collocation method, the Galerkin method as we implemented it took considerably more time to achieve the same error level.

In general, the number of patches for a scene with triangular elements is larger than the number of vertices. Since the number of hemicubes used in Gaussian quadrature depends on the number of patches, our Galerkin implementation required many more hemicubes to compute the matrices for the same scene. Figure 1 was computed using the collocation method with a quadratic basis. This required 2282 hemicubes. Our Galerkin implementation would require 3042 hemicubes if we used just 2 degrees of precision.

6 Conclusions and Future Work

We have presented two radiosity algorithms which use the finite element method and higher order basis functions to produce a more accurate solution in less time. The collocation method proved to be easier to implement and converged faster than the Galerkin method for the scenes presented. By applying discontinuity meshing, our algorithms computed an accurate solution in only a fraction of the time used by traditional methods.

Applying adaptive meshing to these algorithms could present a challenging problem. In a more traditional approach, we would subdivide our patches if the gradient became too large. The higher order elements can model these large gradients. The criteria for subdivision would require some investigation [10].

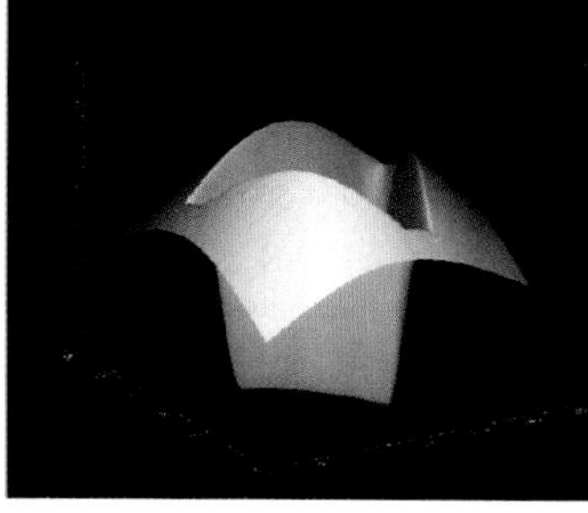

Figure 1 Reference scene used for convergence test. On the left is the rendered scene. On the right is a height field showing the radiosity of the floor.

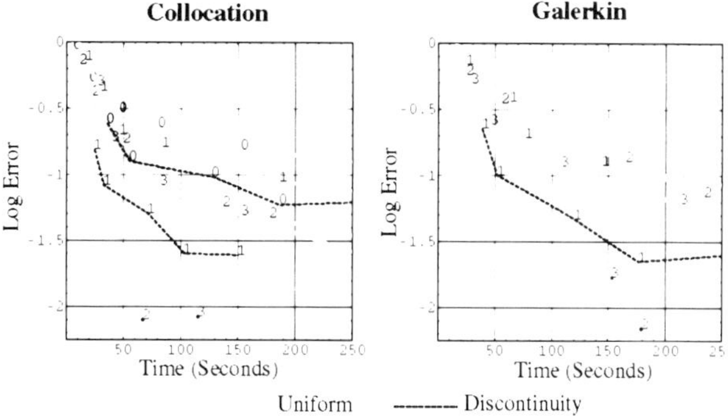

Figure 2 Error plots. The solid lines are the results from the uniform mesh. The dashed lines and single points are from the discontinuity mesh. The numbers indicate the degree of the basis functions. The error is reduced by increasing the number of elements.

We restricted our elements to planar C^0 triangles. We could use square or even curved elements. The curved element may require ray tracing for computing the form factors, but it would allow us to use exact geometries. An additional improvement to the accuracy might be possible by using C^1 reconstruction technique [12].

Modifications to the algorithms for progressive radiosity is possible. The collocation method could be used with a ray tracing algorithm similar to [15]. In this case we would have to sample the entire basis domain rather than a single patch. Creating an efficient algorithm would be another puzzle.

Acknowledgments

This work was performed under the auspices of the U.S. Department of Energy by Lawrence Livermore National Laboratory under contract No. W-7405-Eng-48.

References

[1] Baum, Daniel R., Holly E. Rushmeier, James M. Winget, *Improving Radiosity Solutions Through the Use of Analytically Determined Form-Factors*, Computer Graphics 23(3), July 1989

[2] Burnett, David S., *Finite Element Analysis*, Addison Wesley Publishing Co., Reading, Massachusetts, May 1988

[3] Cohen, Michael F., Donald P. Greenberg, *The Hemicube: A Radiosity Solution for Complex Environments*, Computer Graphics 19(3), July 1985

[4] Farin, Gerald, *Curves and Surfaces for Computer Aided Geometric Design*, Academic Press, 1990.

[5] Goral, Cindy M., Kenneth E. Torrance, Donald P. Greenberg, Bennett Battaile, *Modeling the Interaction of Light Between Diffuse Surfaces*, Computer Graphics 18(3), July 1984

[6] Hallquist, John O., *MAZE - An Input Generator for DYNA2D and NIKE2D*, LLNL Tech. Report, UCID-19029, Rev. 2.

[7] Heckbert, Paul S., *Generic Convex Polygon Scan Conversion and Clipping*, Graphics Gems, Academic Press, 1990

[8] Heckbert, Paul S., James M. Winget, *Finite Element Methods for Global Illumination*, U.C. Berkeley, Jan. 1991

[9] Heckbert, Paul S., *Discontinuity Meshing for Radiosity*, Third Eurographics Workshop on Photorealism, Consolidation Express, Bristol, England, May 1992

[10] Lischinski, Dani, Filippo Tampieri, Donald P. Greenberg, *Combining Hierarchical Radiosity and Discontinuity Meshing*, Computer Graphics, Annual Conf. Series, Aug. 1993

[11] Max, Nelson L., Michael J. Allison, *Linear Radiosity Approximations using Vertex-to-Vertex Form Factors*, Graphics Gems III, Academic Press, 1992

[12] Salesin, David, Dani Lischinski, Tony DeRose, *Reconstructing Illumination Functions with Selected Discontinuities*, Third Eurographics Workshop on Photorealism, Consolidation Express, Bristol, England, May 1992

[13] Siegel, Robert, John R. Howell, *Thermal Radiation Heat Transfer*, McGraw-Hill Book Co., N.Y., 1972

[14] Troutman, Roy, *Parallel Radiosity Algorithms using Higher Order Finite Elements*, Master's thesis, U.C. Davis, Dec. 1992

[15] Wallace, John R., Kells A. Elmquist, Eric A. Haines, *A Ray Tracing Algorithm For Progressive Radiosity*, Computer Graphics 23(3), July 1989

[16] Zats, Harold R., *Galerkin Radiosity: Higher Order Global Illumination*, Computer Graphics, Annual Conf. Series, Aug. 1993

Galerkin Radiosity:

A Higher Order Solution Method for Global Illumination

Harold R. Zatz[1]
Cornell Program of Computer Graphics

Abstract

This paper presents an alternative radiosity formulation using piecewise smooth radiance functions that incorporates curved surfaces directly. Using the Galerkin integral equation technique as a mathematical foundation, surface radiance functions are approximated by polynomials. This model eliminates the need for *a posteriori* rendering interpolation, and allows the direct use of non-planar parametric surfaces. Convergence problems due to singularities in the radiosity kernel are analyzed and rectified, and sources of approximation error are examined. The incorporation of a shadow masking technique vastly reduces the need for meshing and associated storage space—accurate radiosity calculations can often be made with no meshing. The technique is demonstrated on traditional radiosity scenes, as well as environments with untessellated curved surfaces.

CR Categories and Subject Descriptors: I.3.7 [**Computer Graphics**]: Three-Dimensional Graphics and Realism; I.3.3 [**Computer Graphics**]: Picture/Image Generation.

Additional Keywords and Phrases: global illumination, radiosity, integral equations, Galerkin methods, curved surfaces, progressive refinement.

1 Introduction

The behavior of light interacting with a macroscopic environment is extremely complex. Despite considerable effort spent searching for a closed-form solution to global illumination problems [10, 22], it seems unlikely that such an approach will be found. To produce computer-generated pictures in a reasonable amount of time, approximations must be used. Typical approximation techniques include the use of direct lighting only, tessellation of the simulated environment into polygonal surfaces, constant or linear shading of surfaces, and sampling the intensity distribution at a limited number of points.

Goral *et al.* [7] introduced the conventional radiosity approximations to computer graphics, assuming surfaces have purely diffuse reflectance distributions, and that finite regions on these surfaces have locally constant radiosity values. Intensity variations across a surface are accounted for by meshing it into a large number of smaller pieces.

Although these assumptions are effective, recent research has demonstrated their limitations. Conventional radiosity techniques generally require that objects be flat or polygonal [1, 7, 3], even though Wallace has demonstrated [21] that radiosity transfers can be computed between non-planar surfaces. Generating images with accurately placed shadows involves a lengthy meshing process, whether surfaces are divided along arbitrary lines [15, 2, 9] or along actual lines of shadow discontinuity [13, 12].

In finite element analysis, it is often possible to trade off a large number of lower-order elements for a smaller number of higher-order elements. Sparrow [18] and Heckbert [10, 11] have successfully applied higher-order radiosity techniques to special-case geometries. Max and Allison [14] explored some of the difficulties of using a linear elements in more general radiosity meshes. In this paper we reformulate the radiosity equations with the goal of applying higher-order *Galerkin* techniques to more general environments, paying particular attention to the difficulties caused by singularities and shadow discontinuities. Benefits of this approach include the direct incorporation of curved surfaces into the solution technique, as well as a significant memory savings due to a drastic reduction of mesh size.

The Galerkin method does have its disadvantages; dealing with shadows and extremely bright light sources can be tricky, and computationally expensive singularities can appear in many places in a complex environment. However, the use of higher-order functions to replace meshing provides a different perspective on the difficulties of the global illumination problem, avoiding some of the difficulties of conventional methods.

2 Background

The radiosity model of global illumination is based on the principle of energy conservation. All light energy emitted within an enclosure is tracked as it reflects off surfaces within that environment, until it dissipates into heat. Conventional radiosity methods [1, 2, 3, 4, 7, 9, 15, 21] generally simplify the solution procedure by using the Constant Radiosity Assumption [20]—the primary assumption that radiosity values are constant over finite regions, and subsidiary assumptions that emittance, reflectivity, and surface normals are also constant over finite regions. Unfortunately, this constant, polygonal approach to the radiosity problem limits the solution accuracy. Conventional radiosity methods attempt to compensate by increasing the mesh density, assuming that the environment can be accurately approximated if enough polygons. However, the number of polygons needed often exceeds the memory and computational resources available.

Tampieri and Lischinski [20] further explain that the Constant Radiosity Assumption leads to fundamental errors in radiosity computations. A solution computed on a tessellated surface can only be as accurate as the tessellation. The Constant Radiosity Assumption also presents inconsistency between its illumination and rendering phases. During the energy transfer phase, radiosity is assumed constant across each polygon. However, radiosity renderings are made by sampling each polygon at a few points and then interpolating brightness values between these points. Basic signal processing shows that while interpolating a solution may make an image look more accurate, all such interpolation can do is mask error by blurring the image. A consistent radiosity solution must incorporate the interpolation into the energy transfer calculations.

2.1 The Radiosity Integral Equation

In order to apply the appropriate mathematical tools to the solution of radiosity problems, it is convenient to express the radiosity equation in parametric form. Parametrically, the key radiosity variables (radiosity, emittance, reflectivity, *etc.*) are represented as functions of two variables, (s, t) or (u, v), over each surface i or j. By abstracting all the complexity of surface interaction into a single kernel function $K_{ij}(s, t, u, v)$, the radiosity equation can be written as an integral equation,

$$B_i(s, t) = E_i(s, t) + \sum_j \int\int K_{ij}(s, t, u, v) B_j(u, v) du\, dv, \quad (1)$$

where the kernel function $K_{ij}(s, t, u, v)$ is the product of the double-differential form factor $F_{i-j}(s, t, u, v)$, reflectivity $\rho_i(s, t)$, area $A_i(s, t)$, and visibility $\mathrm{VIS}_{ij}(s, t, u, v)$

$$K_{ij}(s, t, u, v) = \rho_i(s, t) F_{i-j}(s, t, u, v) \mathrm{VIS}_{ij}(s, t, u, v) A_j(u, v). \quad (2)$$

---

[1]now at Rhythm and Hues Studios, Inc., 910 North Sycamore Ave., Hollywood, CA 90038. E-mail: hzatz@rhythm.com or hzatz@alumni.caltech.edu

The form factor and area functions can be further expanded in terms of the functions describing surface geometry $\vec{x}_i(s,t)$ and normals $\hat{n}_i(s,t)$:

$$F_{i-j}(s,t,u,v) = \frac{(\hat{n}_i(s,t) - \hat{n}_j(u,v)) \cdot (\vec{x}_j(u,v) - \vec{x}_i(s,t))}{\pi \|\vec{x}_i(s,t) - \vec{x}_j(u,v)\|^4}$$

$$A_j(u,v) = \left\| \frac{\partial \vec{x}_j(u,v)}{\partial u} \times \frac{\partial \vec{x}_j(u,v)}{\partial v} \right\| \tag{3}$$

3 Mathematical Background

The Galerkin method provides a method for solving integral equations in terms of a basis set of non-constant functions across each surface. This section provides the mathematical background necessary to apply the Galerkin method to the radiosity equation.

3.1 Basis Set Projection

To approximate the radiosity distribution by a combination of functions, we first need formal tools to manipulate an appropriate two-dimensional basis set. We denote this basis set $\{\mathcal{T}_k(s,t) | k = 0, 1, \ldots\}$, where s and t are the parametric variables across a surface, and k specifies a particular function in the set.

Just as geometric vectors have a dot product that projects one onto the other, the inner product of two functions $f(s,t)$ and $g(s,t)$ can be defined,

$$\langle f | g \rangle_{\mathcal{W}} = \int_{-1}^{1} \int_{-1}^{1} f(s,t) g(s,t) \mathcal{W}(s,t) ds\, dt. \tag{4}$$

$\mathcal{W}(s,t)$ is some weighting function that describes the importance of different positions to the inner product. To apply the Galerkin method to radiosity, we use an orthonormal set of basis functions, $\{\mathcal{T}_k(s,t)\}$—a set designed so that for a particular inner product weight function $\mathcal{W}(s,t)$,

$$\forall_{k,l} \quad \langle \mathcal{T}_k | \mathcal{T}_l \rangle_{\mathcal{W}} = \delta_{kl}. \tag{5}$$

Finding the combination of orthonormal basis functions closest to some particular function is relatively simple. Given that the radiosity function over surface i is $B_i(s,t)$, we define the coefficients B_i^k

$$B_i^k = \langle B_i | \mathcal{T}_k \rangle_{\mathcal{W}}. \tag{6}$$

The original function can be approximated by the weighted sum,

$$B_i(s,t) \approx \sum_k B_i^k \mathcal{T}_k(s,t). \tag{7}$$

3.2 Legendre and Jacobi Polynomials

The Galerkin method is usually solved using an orthonormal polynomial basis set, defined on the interval $[-1, 1]$. Legendre and Jacobi polynomials are one-dimensional, orthonormal polynomials which can be combined into a two-dimensional basis set by multiplying two polynomials in different variables. We limit our analysis in the next two sections to polynomials of one variable.

When the inner product has a weight function equal to one, the polynomials formed are the Legendre polynomials. The unnormalized Legendre polynomials are generated by a recursion rule [8],

$$P_0(x) = 1 \qquad P_1(x) = x$$

$$(n+1)P_{n+1}(x) = (2n+1)xP_n(x) - nP_{n-1}(x). \tag{8}$$

The normalized Legendre polynomials are

$$\bar{P}_n(x) = \sqrt{n + \frac{1}{2}} P_n(x) \tag{9}$$

Polynomial sets can also be created with non-constant inner product weight functions $\mathcal{W}(x)$. Later in this paper (section 4.2), a set of polynomials will be needed with a weight function that has a multiple zero at its endpoints. The Jacobi polynomials $P_i^{(\alpha,\beta)}$ have such behavior, with the weight function,

$$\mathcal{W}(x) = (1-x)^{\alpha}(1+x)^{\beta}, \tag{10}$$

where α and β are the degree of multiplicity.

The unnormalized Jacobi polynomials have a more complex recursion rule than the Legendre polynomials [5]:

$$P_0^{(\alpha,\beta)}(x) = 1 \qquad P_1^{(\alpha,\beta)}(x) = \frac{\alpha-\beta}{2} + \frac{2+\alpha+\beta}{2}x$$

$$P_{n+1}^{(\alpha,\beta)}(x) = \frac{A_n^{(\alpha,\beta)}x - B_n^{(\alpha,\beta)}}{C_n^{(\alpha,\beta)}} \tag{11}$$

where

$$\begin{aligned} A_n^{(\alpha,\beta)} &= (2n+\alpha+\beta+1)(\alpha^2-\beta^2+2n+\alpha+\beta+2) \\ &\quad \times (2n+\alpha+\beta)P_n^{(\alpha,\beta)}(x) \\ B_n^{(\alpha,\beta)} &= 2(n+\alpha)(n+\beta)(2n+\alpha+\beta+2)P_{n-1}^{(\alpha,\beta)}(x) \\ C_n^{(\alpha,\beta)} &= 2(n+1)(n+\alpha+\beta+1)(2n+\alpha+\beta) \end{aligned} \tag{12}$$

These polynomials can be normalized by the factor [8]:

$$\sqrt{\frac{\Gamma(n+1)\Gamma(\alpha+\beta+1+n)(\alpha+\beta+1+2n)}{\Gamma(\alpha+1+n)\Gamma(\beta+1+n)2^{\alpha+\beta+1}}} \tag{13}$$

3.3 Quadrature Rules

An informative explanation of one-dimensional quadrature rules has been compiled by Delves and Mohamed [6]. A condensed version is presented here.

A quadrature rule is a method for approximating the integral of a function by a weighted sum of function samples at particular points. Quadrature rules can be used to approximate inner product integrals, like that in (4). Given a fixed function $\mathcal{W}(x)$ and another function $f(x)$, we can choose points ξ_i and weights w_i such that:

$$\int_a^b f(x)\mathcal{W}(x)dx \approx \sum_i w_i f(\xi_i) \tag{14}$$

Quadrature rules can be designed to be exact for a certain class of functions. The Gaussian quadrature rules, by computing optimal positions for the N sample points ξ_i, are exact for polynomials up to order $2N-1$. The Gauss quadrature rule with weight function $\mathcal{W}(x)$ is closely tied to the set of orthogonal polynomials with the same weight function.

To develop an N-point Gauss quadrature rule for the integral

$$\int_{-1}^{1} \mathcal{W}(x) f(x)\, dx \approx \sum_{i=1}^{N} w_i f(\xi_i), \tag{15}$$

start by choosing a set of orthogonal polynomials $\mathcal{T}_i(x)$ with the same weight function $\mathcal{W}(x)$, and expressed in terms of recursion rules [17] so that:

$$\mathcal{T}_{-1}(x) \equiv 0, \qquad \mathcal{T}_0(x) \equiv 1,$$

$$\mathcal{T}_{i+1}(x) \equiv (x - \delta_{i+1})\mathcal{T}_i(x) - \gamma_{i+1}^2 \mathcal{T}_{i-1}(x). \tag{16}$$

Take these δ_i and γ_i coefficients, and construct a tridiagonal symmetric matrix:

$$\begin{bmatrix} \delta_1 & \gamma_2 & & 0 \\ \gamma_2 & \delta_2 & \ddots & \\ & \ddots & \ddots & \gamma_N \\ 0 & & \gamma_N & \delta_N \end{bmatrix} \tag{17}$$

The eigenvalues of this matrix, which are also the roots of the polynomial $\mathcal{T}_N(x)$, are the quadrature rule's positions ξ_i. The square of the first coefficient of the ith eigenvector is the quadrature weight w_i. The eigenvectors and eigenvalues for tridiagonal symmetric matrices can be found using QR factorization [17].

To create the Gauss-Legendre rule of order N, exact for polynomials up to degree $2N-1$, the γ_i and δ_i coefficients are [22]:

$$\delta_{i+1} = 0, \qquad \gamma_{i+1} = \sqrt{\frac{i^2}{(2i+1)(2i-1)}}, \tag{18}$$

and for general Jacobi polynomials $P_i^{(\alpha,\beta)}$:

$$\begin{aligned} \delta_{i+1} &= \frac{(\alpha+\beta)(\beta-\alpha)}{(2i+\alpha+\beta+2)(2i+\alpha+\beta)}, \\ \gamma_{i+1} &= \sqrt{\frac{4(i+\alpha)(i+\beta)i(\alpha+\beta+i)}{(\alpha+\beta+2i)^2(\alpha+\beta+2i+1)(\alpha+\beta+2i-1)}}. \end{aligned} \tag{19}$$

When using these quadrature rules to project a function into a basis set using (6), it is important to use a sufficiently accurate quadrature rule. If a one-dimensional polynomial basis set includes terms up to order n, the projection integral (6) must be accurate up to order $2n$—since the function is represented as a polynomial of order n, the projection integrand will be a polynomial of order $2n$. Therefore, a one-dimensional Gaussian quadrature rule must have at least $N+1$ sample points to integrate accurately [6].

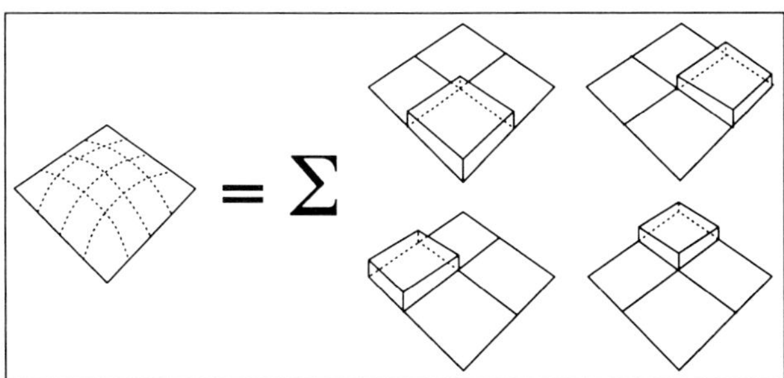

Figure 1: Conventional radiosity methods approximate a surface's radiosity by meshing it into a large number of constant intensity patches. Radiosity is represented by height above the surface.

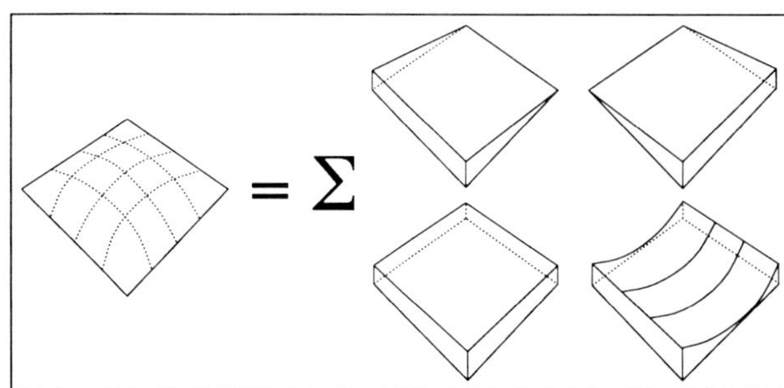

Figure 2: Higher-order radiosity approximates a surface's radiosity by dividing it into several different smooth functions. These smooth functions are scaled and combined to approximate the original radiosity distribution.

4 Non-Constant Radiosity

Consider the effect of meshing a single surface into constant radiosity patches (Figure 1). Although the radiosity is smooth on individual patches, combinations describe a discontinuous, stair-step radiosity function. To produce a smooth, consistent solution, we need to formulate radiosity in terms of smooth functions across an entire surface, instead of disjoint patches on parts of a surface.

Figure 2 shows a hypothetical decomposition of a radiosity function. Constant, linear, and higher-order functions are combined to produce a smooth approximation to the radiosity function. If the radiosity of every surface were represented by a combination of these functions, the radiosity problem would reduce to finding their relative weights.

To properly compute these proportions, we use a radiosity formulation based on a linear combination of orthonormal basis functions $\{\mathcal{T}_l(s,t)\}$. Instead of radiosity values, we use radiosity coefficients $\{B^l\}$—the relative contribution of each function $\mathcal{T}_l(s,t)$. The full radiosity distribution on a surface becomes the function

$$B_{\text{total}}(s,t) = \sum_l B^l \mathcal{T}_l(s,t). \tag{20}$$

Functions on different surfaces must interact in a manner analogous to the way conventional patches interact through form factors. Just as conventional radiosity uses form factors to describe the interaction between patches, here the kernel function $K_{ij}(s,t,u,v)$ from (1) details how energy is transferred between functions on different surfaces. When two constant functions on different surfaces interact, the kernel function interaction is equivalent to a classical form factor. Other kernel functions describe higher-order interactions.

4.1 The Galerkin Method

Given an orthonormal basis set, the Galerkin technique finds a good [6] fit to the integral equation's solution within that set. Heckbert [10, 11] suggested that the Galerkin method and meshing could be used to solve the radiosity integral equation in a plane. This and subsequent sections demonstrate how it can be applied to three-dimensional radiosity.

Starting with the parametric radiosity equation (1),

$$B_i(s,t) = E_i(s,t) + \sum_j \int\!\!\int K_{ij}(s,t,u,v) B_j(u,v)\,du\,dv, \tag{21}$$

expand the $B_j(u,v)$ term inside the integral in terms of the basis set $\{\mathcal{T}_l(u,v)\}$ using (7). The B_j^l coefficient can be moved outside of the integral, and the summations over j and l can be combined to produce the equation

$$B_i(s,t) = E_i(s,t) + \sum_{j,l} B_j^l \int\!\!\int K_{ij}(s,t,u,v)\mathcal{T}_l(u,v)\,du\,dv. \tag{22}$$

Now, take the inner product of both sides with the kth basis set function $\mathcal{T}_k(s,t)$. Using bilinearity and the relation described in (6),

$$B_i^k = E_i^k + \sum_{j,l} B_j^l \left\langle \int\!\!\int K_{ij}(s,t,u,v)\mathcal{T}_l(u,v)\,du\,dv \,\middle|\, \mathcal{T}_k(s,t) \right\rangle_{\mathcal{W}}. \tag{23}$$

The inner product now depends only on known information; the kernel function K_{ij} is a function of the environment, and $\{\mathcal{T}_l(u,v)\}$ is a precomputed basis set. The result of that inner product is denoted K_{ij}^{kl}, the kernel matrix. Evaluating this inner product is the most difficult part of a radiosity solution, requiring four integrations—two explicit, and two in the inner product. However, once the kernel matrix has been computed for each value of i, j, k, and l, the radiosity equation can be written as a matrix equation,

$$B_i^k - E_i^k = \sum_{j,l} B_j^l K_{ij}^{kl}. \tag{24}$$

Just as a conventional form factor matrix relates constant radiosities on different elements, the kernel matrix relates radiosity functions across different surfaces. The K_{ij}^{kl}, B_i^k and E_i^k values are analogous to classical form factors, patch radiosities, and emittances, respectively. However, each of these coefficients refers to some function representing part of the distribution of radiosity across a surface, as opposed to a constant value across a surface. Note also that even though (24) is written in terms of four indices, since the surface indices i, j and function indices k, l are independent of each other, (24) is still a two-dimensional matrix equation.

This equation can be solved using any standard matrix technique, such as Gaussian elimination, or progressive refinement techniques [4]. Cohen *et al*'s progressive refinement technique requires slight modification with Galerkin radiosity, because the radiosity coefficients B_j^l may have negative values. These negative values do not indicate negative energies; they are a weight applied to the basis function. The shooting order should be based on unshot magnitude:

$$M_j^l = \|B_j^l\| \int\!\!\int |\mathcal{T}_l(u,v)|\, dA_j(u,v)\,du\,dv. \tag{25}$$

4.2 Edge Singularities

Near the common edge of two non-coplanar surfaces, the double-differential form factor approaches infinity as a pole of order two[22]. Although the function still has a finite integral, the singularity can cause serious convergence problems. If the singularity is ignored, Galerkin solution methods converge extremely slowly for a mediocre basis set, and may fail entirely for a bad basis set.

To insure reasonable convergence, the basis set must compensate for the singularity. In (23), the singularity appears inside the quadruple integral that generates K_{ij}^{kl}. This integral also includes the inner product weight function $\mathcal{W}(s,t)$. If the weight function $\mathcal{W}$ is chosen with zeroes of sufficiently high multiplicity where the kernel function K_{ij} goes to infinity, the two features can cancel and the integral will converge. Since the kernel singularity grows as a pole of order two, the weight function should have zeroes of multiplicity two at its edges. The Jacobi polynomial sets $\mathcal{P}^{(0,2)}$ and $\mathcal{P}^{(2,0)}$ (see section 3.2), have appropriate weight functions.

By using a hybrid Galerkin method, the edge singularities are cancelled. For non-singular light transfers between surfaces that do not touch, a Legendre basis set is used. For the few transfers that are singular, a basis set of Jacobi polynomials is used, either $\mathcal{P}^{(0,2)}$ or $\mathcal{P}^{(2,0)}$ depending on the singularity's location. After computing the K_{ij}^{kl} coefficients and the associated radiosity transferred in a singular shot, project this polynomial function in s and t is back into a Legendre basis set for storage. An empty box computed with this hybrid method is shown in Figure 6.

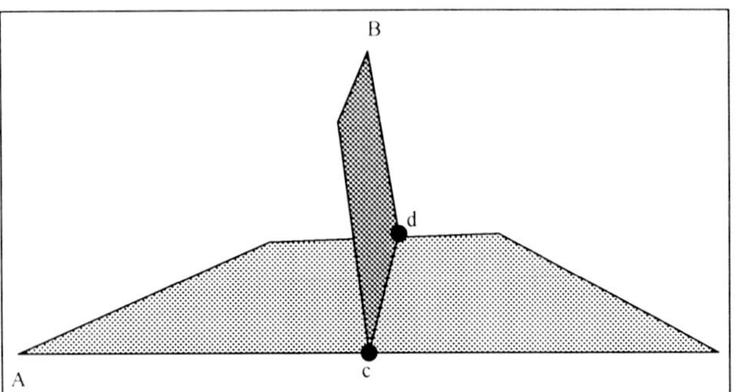

Figure 3: Surfaces A and B meet in a T-intersection; surface B divides surface A into two regions along the line $\overline{cd}$.

Because singularities can be produced at any non-parallel intersection, geometries with T-intersections (the three-dimensional analog to Heckbert's T-corners [11]) like those in Figure 3 make singularities difficult to handle. Although such geometries could be handled by using a basis set with a two-dimensional weight function containing a double zero in the middle of the surface along the curve of intersection, constructing such basis sets would be relatively difficult even for polygonal surfaces. More effective approaches include subdividing significant T-intersections into distinct singular intersections, or ignoring the singularity altogether when possible.

4.3 Computing the Energy Transfers

In order to generate radiosity solutions, entries in the kernel matrix (24) must be computed. Each entry is computed by applying a quadrature rule (15) to approximate the inner product of (23) for particular values of i, j, k and l. For non-singular energy transfers—those between surfaces that do not share a common edge—the inner product weight function is unity, and the quadrature rule is a Gauss-Legendre quadrature rule constructed with (17) and (18). If the Gauss-Legendre quadrature points and weights are denoted p^{L}_{α} and w^{L}_{α} respectively, then each kernel matrix element is approximated by the summation,

$$K_{ij}^{kl} \approx \sum_{\alpha,\beta,\gamma,\delta} K_{ij}(p^{L}_{\alpha}, p^{L}_{\beta}, p^{L}_{\gamma}, p^{L}_{\delta}) T_k^{L}(p^{L}_{\alpha}, p^{L}_{\beta}) T_l^{L}(p^{L}_{\gamma}, p^{L}_{\delta}) w^{L}_{\alpha} w^{L}_{\beta} w^{L}_{\gamma} w^{L}_{\delta}. \tag{26}$$

Since each kernel sample requires a full intersection test with the environment, caching samples $K_{ij}(p^{L}_{\alpha}, p^{L}_{\beta}, p^{L}_{\gamma}, p^{L}_{\delta})$ or results of the associated intersection tests can save significant CPU time, at the expense of additional storage.

Singular energy transfers—those between two surfaces that meet in a singular edge—require additional processing. Kernel matrix elements for a singular transfer are computed using a Gauss-Jacobi quadrature rule matching the Jacobi basis set. Once the quadrature rule's points p^{J}_{α} and weights w^{J}_{α} have been computed using (17) and (19), the kernel matrix elements can be computed by the summation,

$$K'^{kl}_{ij} \approx \sum_{\alpha,\beta,\gamma,\delta} K_{ij}(p^{J}_{\alpha}, p^{J}_{\beta}, p^{L}_{\gamma}, p^{L}_{\delta}) T_k^{J}(p^{J}_{\alpha}, p^{J}_{\beta}) T_l^{L}(p^{L}_{\gamma}, p^{L}_{\delta}) w^{J}_{\alpha} w^{J}_{\beta} w^{L}_{\gamma} w^{L}_{\delta}. \tag{27}$$

When this weighted sum is evaluated, the resulting matrix entries K'^{kl}_{ij} are in terms of a Jacobi basis set, while the E_i^k and B_i^k values in storage are in terms of a Legendre basis set. The Jacobi matrix entries must be projected into the Legendre basis set before they can be combined with the other coefficients. Since the K'^{kl}_{ij} coefficients are simply leading multipliers for polynomials, they can be converted from Jacobi coefficients to Legendre coefficients by expanding the Jacobi coefficients into an ordinary polynomial in s and t, and then converting that polynomial back into a sum of Legendre polynomials.

5 Shadow Discontinuities

As with any illumination algorithm, dealing with occlusions presents a special challenge. The easiest way to deal with shadows is to let the basis functions find a best fit. Unfortunately, shadows produce sharp edges which cannot be expressed in terms of a few polynomials. Attempting to model such edges with a small polynomial basis set produces a fuzzy shadow with ripples around it—the Gibbs behavior visible in Figure 7.

Shadow edges come from discontinuities in the radiosity function [10]. One way to remove these discontinuities is to mesh the environment along curves of discontinuity [13, 12], a process which eliminates the occlusion difficulties of Galerkin radiosity. Unfortunately, discontinuity meshing methods magnify the number of surfaces in the scene, vastly increasing computation time. Even though shadows are primarily an interaction between a light source and a receiving surface, subdividing the receiving surface to produce accurate shadows complicates interactions with the rest of the environment.

5.1 Shadow Masking

To smooth the shadow discontinuities out of the radiosity distribution seen by the Galerkin method, we propose using a *shadow mask* approximation. For the majority of emitter-receiver pairs, where shadows do not have a high-frequency effect on the solution, traditional visibility calculations can be used. However, for a select group of emitter-receiver pairs, we move the visibility term $\mathrm{VIS}_{ij}(s, t, u, v)$ out of the kernel function and integral in equations (2) and (1), and replace it with a normalized shadow mask function $M_{i\leftarrow j}(s, t)$,

$$M_{i\leftarrow j}(s, t) = \frac{\iint \mathrm{VIS}_{ij}(s, t, u, v)\,du\,dv}{\iint du\,dv}. \tag{28}$$

This function approximates the fraction of the light originating from emitter j that arrives at a particular location on receiving surface i. The shadow mask is one where the emitter is fully visible, zero where the emitter is fully occluded, and takes on intermediate values when the light is partially occluded. It is essentially a texture map for painting the shadow onto the receiving surface.

During the radiosity pass, if the energy transfer from emitter j to receiver i involves a shadow mask, the radiosity is accumulated without visibility calculations in the special coefficients $B^k_{i\leftarrow j}$ instead of B_i^k. When light is re-emitted from surface i's basis functions, the kernel samples are multiplied by the shadow mask across surface i, restoring some of the occlusion information. The radiosity across a surface, $B_i(s, t)$, becomes the combination of ordinary Galerkin basis functions and shadow mask-weighted basis functions. If h represents all light sources casting a shadow on surface i,

$$B_i(s, t) = \sum_k B_i^k T_k(s, t) + \sum_{h,k} M_{i\leftarrow h}(s, t) B^k_{i\leftarrow h} T_k(s, t). \tag{29}$$

By using coefficients $B^k_{i\leftarrow h}$, radiosity in the shadow mask is maintained separately from radiosity coming from other parts of the environment. When a receiving surface has shadow masks associated with it, every surface interacts either with a shadow mask, or with the standard surface description—not both.

In this implementation, shadow masks were computed from equation (28) using multiple point-to-point visibility samples regularly spaced in the parametric dimensions. Values of $M_{i\leftarrow j}(s, t)$ were computed by linear interpolation between these sample points. Shadow mask samples could conceivably be taken along lines of discontinuity, or in some more complicated non-regular structure to improve efficiency or accuracy.

In all environments tested, even accounting for the time spent constructing shadow masks, the time required to compute a radiosity solution using shadow masks was significantly smaller than that for a full discontinuity mesh. For the simple environment in Figure 8, the shadow mask was a regular 40 by 40 grid of sample points on the floor. Without Gibbs phenomena to transfer energy into higher order basis functions as in Figure 7, the radiosity pass actually required fewer shots and less time to converge than the non-shadow masked version.

Since a shadow mask only adds one surface to the rows (but not the columns) of the radiosity matrix for each associated emitter-receiver pair in the environment, shadow masks add relatively little to radiosity solution time compared to discontinuity meshing methods. Shadow masks can be precomputed for portions of the environment where shadow details are expected to be significant. Furthermore, since shadow masks are defined in parametric space, a single implementation can cast shadows to and from any type of surface.

Unfortunately, shadow masks also have significant disadvantages. By moving the visibility term out of the radiosity equation's integral, any correlation between the emitter's light distribution and the shape of the occluding

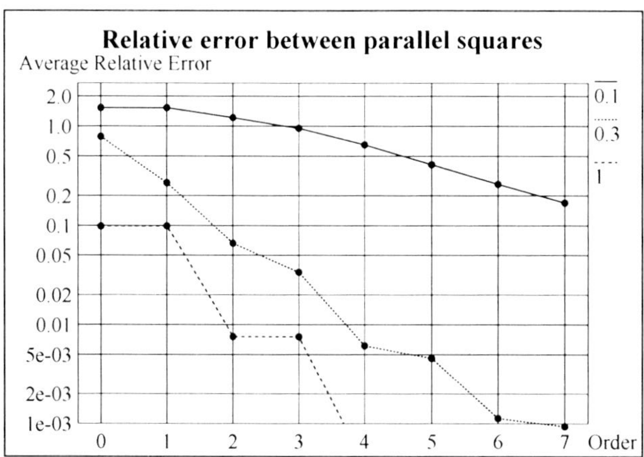

Figure 4: Average relative error for Galerkin radiosity transfers between two parallel squares of width l, distance l, $0.3l$, and $0.1l$ apart.

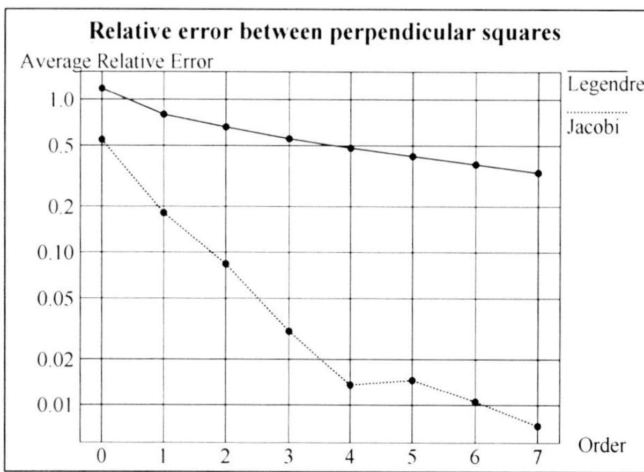

Figure 5: Average relative error for Galerkin radiosity transfers between two adjacent perpendicular squares at a corner. The Jacobi basis set computation produces significantly less error for this singular transfer than the Legendre basis set.

surface is destroyed. Because of this, a shadow mask solution will not converge to the "true" solution. Placement of the shadow masks is currently left to the user; some criteria is needed for determining whether or not to use shadow masks. Although shadow masks can be stored in a simple grid fashion, such a grid may not produce the best results when used with a particular quadrature rule. Finally, any attempt at increasing the spatial accuracy of shadow masks can duplicate many of the difficulties of storing a mesh on a surface.

However, there is a significant difference between increasing the density of a mesh and increasing the density of a shadow mask—every element of a mesh becomes another surface interacting with the environment, while even the most complex shadow mask is still only part of one surface. Shadow masks do facilitate the generation of approximate radiosity solutions with the Galerkin method, by smoothing out shadow discontinuities. Further research may suggest ways to avoid their associated disadvantages.

6 Sources of Error

The principal cause of error is not using a large enough basis set; as more basis functions are used, the Galerkin method produces a more accurate solution. Improper treatment of shadows can also cause significant inaccuracies in a Galerkin solution; if shadow discontinuities are ignored, they produce Gibbs-behavior ripples, and if shadow masks are used, they introduce approximation error. Additional errors come from inaccuracies in the quadrature rule used to evaluate kernel matrix integrals, or from approximate matrix solution techniques like progressive radiosity.

In this section, error analysis is provided at two different scales. At the level of surface-to-surface energy transfer, Galerkin radiosity results are examined for a few simple cases where comparison with an exact analytical solution is possible. At the level of picture generation, conventional and Galerkin radiosity solutions are compared for a standard radiosity test environment.

6.1 Energy Transfer Error

For the simple environment used by Sparrow's variational radiosity solution [18], a fourth-order solution produced a relative error of less than one percent. Using the method of this paper, error computations for a single energy transfer between parallel and perpendicular squares produce similar levels of accuracy. All comparisons in this section are made against an analytic solution using the formulation of Sparrow and Cess [19]. The relative error metric used is

$$E = \left\langle \frac{|B_{\text{Galerkin}}(s,t) - B_{\text{exact}}(s,t)|}{B_{\text{exact}}(s,t)} \right\rangle_{s,t}, \qquad (30)$$

where the error is evaluated on a 500 by 500 grid of sample points on the receiving surface. Transmitting and receiving squares are the same size, and are computed at the same solution order (although for numeric reasons, this often produces the worst results [22]).

The simplest case is for a radiosity transfer between parallel squares with sides of length l, as shown in Figure 4. With the distance between the squares equal to their size, the fourth-order transfer gives a relative error of only 0.04%. Since the accuracy increases as the squares are placed farther away with respect to their size, a fourth or fifth order transfer should produce reasonable accuracy for computer graphics applications.

As the squares move closer, the relative error becomes much higher. When the distance between the squares is reduced to one-tenth their width, even a seventh order solution produces an average relative error of 16.9%. Unfortunately, when surfaces are extremely close relative to their size, to achieve reasonable accuracy, the surfaces must still be subdivided.

Experiments with perpendicular rectangles (Figure 5) illustrate the importance of proper treatment of singularities. Using a non-singular Legendre basis set to compute the energy transfer produced large error even at high order; a seventh order transfer produced a relative error of 33.2%. Using a singular Jacobi basis set, results are much more accurate. Fourth and fifth order transfers both produce about 1.4% relative error.

6.2 Comparison with Conventional Radiosity

Lischinski and Tampieri provided a reference solution to a two-box radiosity environment. This solution was computed using the discontinuity meshing techniques of [13], with adaptive integration using Wallace [21] point-to-point form factors. Individual triangles in the mesh were treated consistently as quadratic elements, limiting error in their reference solution to a few meshing artifacts, visible near the corners of the top wall. This solution is used as a comparison baseline for images generated with Galerkin radiosity.

The *order* of a solution is the highest total polynomial order used as a basis function for the solution. A zeroth-order solution would be equivalent to a conventional radiosity solution, with radiosity constant across a surface. A first-order solution would have linear radiosity variation, a second-order solution would have quadratic variation, and so on. Note that a basis function's order depends on the sum of the highest orders used in each dimension. Different surfaces in a solution can be different orders; a high order basis could be used for large, visible areas, while a low order basis may be sufficient for shadowed regions.

Figure 9 shows pictures of a simple test environment solved with different solution orders. Shadows were created using a 20 by 20 grid shadow mask. Notice how the floor appears smoother at higher order, even though no post-processing interpolation was used to smooth the meshing. Meshing (Figure 10) was only performed to eliminate T-intersections; the three boxes and light were meshed to 26 polygons.

Figure 11 shows difference images between the different order Galerkin solutions of the test environment and the reference solution. These images were created by converting the Galerkin and conventional radiosity solution images to black and white, and then computing the absolute value of the intensity difference at each pixel. Dark regions of these images are where the two solutions agree; bright regions are where the two solutions differ. The Galerkin image was translated slightly before comparison, so that outlines of the boxes and floors would be visible in the difference images. As would be expected, the difference images get progressively darker as the solution

Figure	Description	CPU time	Shots
6	Empty box	5.4s	7
7	Box with single occluder	59.7 s	33
8	Shadow masked box	42.8 s	22
12	Clay teapot	6.71 h	53

Table 1: Timings for the shadow generation and radiosity pass combined for various pictures computed with this algorithm. All timings are for an HP 9000/720 workstation.

order increases; the regions where the solution is least accurate tend to be near singular edges.

In this particular test case, the method of [13] took about the same amount of time as the highest-order Galerkin solution. However, the Galerkin method only required 6.5 Megabytes of memory, compared to 75 Megabytes for a more conventional, meshing approach. For all environments tested in this paper, Galerkin and conventional radiosity methods tend to take about the same amount of time to produce equivalent pictures. However, the Galerkin radiosity technique's lower memory usage is maintained in more complex environments.

7 Results

The radiosity solution computed by this method is a list of basis set expansion coefficients B_i^k for each surface i and basis function k. The actual radiance at a given point (s, t) on surface i is recovered from these coefficients using (7). If shadow masks were used, the additional coefficients B_{ih}^k are incorporated with (29).

In this implementation, environments are rendered by a simple ray-tracing/scanline technique. When a ray intersects a surface, that intersection point is projected back into the surface's parametric space, and the result is used to compute a radiosity value for the appropriate pixel.

7.1 Curved Surfaces

Curved surfaces can be easily incorporated into Galerkin radiosity; the kernel term's form factor as expressed in (3), includes surface normals explicitly. To implement curved surfaces, replace the traditional constant surface normal value with a function, computable at any parametric location. Sample pictures are shown with bicubic patches (Figure 12) and other curved surfaces (Figure 13). The Galerkin radiosity method was applied directly to these environments; the curved surfaces were *not* tiled.

For comparison purposes, the teapot environment was also computed using a commercially-available radiosity package [16]. This package uses the point-sampling algorithm of Wallace *et al.* [21] to compute form factors, but does not perform adaptive meshing. Since this radiosity package cannot use bicubic patches directly, each of the teapot's patches were tessellated with a 20 by 20 grid. The radiosity solution took 6.2 hours, and over 54 megabytes of memory to compute; this simple forty-patch scene became a relatively complex, eight thousand polygon environment. In contrast, the Galerkin computation took 6.7 hours, but only required 3.9 megabytes of memory during the radiosity pass. Over 90% of this computation time was spent computing visibility samples.

The significant point of this comparison is that given approximately equivalent amounts of time to produce a solution, conventional and Galerkin methods produced similar results. But since Galerkin methods needn't maintain the detailed geometric structure of a mesh, they use significantly less memory.

7.2 Parallelization

Galerkin radiosity environments are not meshed into large, complicated data structures, so it is relatively easy to maintain copies of the environment in memory on multiple hosts. Since each individual light transfer between two surfaces depends only on the geometry and shadow masks, they can be computed on independent machines. Such a parallelization scheme was implemented, running concurrently on DECstations, HP 700's and 800's, and on multiple processors of an Apollo DN10000. The image of Figure 13 was computed in parallel on five DECstations and five HP 700's as a background process over two days.

8 Conclusions

Using the Galerkin method, this paper has presented an alternative method for producing radiosity simulations. Through special treatment of the radiosity equation's singularities and discontinuities, the Galerkin technique's dependency on smooth kernels can be overcome. Although the resulting pictures are similar to those produced by conventional radiosity methods, the method used to generate them is fundamentally different:

- The radiosity across a surface is represented as a smoothly varying function. Pictures are rendered directly from the radiosity solution, without an additional blurring step.
- Adequately sampled curved surfaces can be used directly. Since curved surfaces don't need to be tessellated, they can be incorporated into a scene cheaply. Issues of approximating a surface's geometry and approximating a surface's radiosity are separated.
- Energy transfer error analysis shows that meshing is only essential when two surfaces are extremely close to each other relative to their size. Meshing is *not* needed to model variations in intensity across a surface.
- By using shadow masks, the local details of shadow edge generation are separated from the global issues of energy balance.

9 Deficiencies of the Method

As with any rendering algorithm, Galerkin radiosity has its own particular disadvantages. Problems with the treatment of shadows are the most significant; if important shadows are missed, a solution will contain significant Gibbs ringing behavior. It may not always be easy to determine ahead of time where detailed shadow masking or meshing will be necessary, possibly requiring multiple solution attempts before all shadows are properly accounted for.

Shadow masking is only a rough approximation to the true occlusion behavior; it eliminates any correlation between variations in light source intensity and the intensity of the shadow, virtually returning to the Constant Radiosity Assumption for a shadow's light source. Furthermore, the distribution of the shadow mask sample points can have a significant impact on the accuracy of the shadow they generate.

Higher order methods also have the potential to be computationally expensive. Because of the $(N + 1)^4$ samples required to transfer radiosity between surfaces of order N, radiosity calculations can become extremely expensive if too high a solution order is used. In general, an order of 4 or 5 is sufficient, but self-intersecting or highly curved surfaces may require a higher-order solution.

The method does not mathematically guarantee radiosity continuity between adjacent coplanar surfaces. However, such surfaces appear much less frequently in a shadow masked environment than in a meshed environment. If such continuity is needed, it can be generated by using a high enough order on the adjacent surfaces that the error on each surface is reduced until their radiosity values along their common boundaries match visibly—usually 8 or 9 in our tests.

Finding all the singularities in a system can also be difficult. Environments usually have a large number of T-intersections (see Figure 3), each of which could require a separate meshing step. Although T-intersections can often be ignored, there's always a risk that the ignored singularity will cause the solution to fail to converge, requiring recomputation.

10 Future Work

Shadow masks are currently implemented using bilinear interpolation on a simple grid of sample points. Many more efficient sampling schemes are possible, such as adaptive quadtrees, or some method that directly computes the location of shadow discontinuities. Additionally, some method should be developed for automatically determining where shadow masks are needed. Some generalization of shadow masks is needed to account for variations in light source intensity.

A means for enforcing continuity between adjacent surfaces, possibly by using some sort of modified patch/element method could lower the required solution order, and significantly accelerate the algorithm when such surfaces are present. A method combining adaptive meshing and a low order Galerkin solution might produce reasonable images rapidly. Extending

Figure 6: An empty box computed with up to fourth order polynomials, or 15 basis functions across each surface. On an HP 9000/720, the radiosity pass took 5.4 CPU seconds.

Figure 7: A box with an occluding rectangle computed with a fourth order basis on all surfaces except the floor, which has an eighth order basis. The ripples on the floor of the box appear because shadow discontinuities cannot be accurately described by a low frequency Galerkin basis set.

Hanrahan's hierarchical multigridding technique [9] to higher order functions could produce a means to do this. Some method must also be found to automatically determine an appropriate solution order for each surface, instead of the current area-based heuristic.

The method of this paper uses a Legendre basis set for non-singular energy transfers. Galerkin methods frequently use a Chebyshev basis; by examining the relative accuracy of different basis sets, it may be possible to find a better basis set for the radiosity problem.

This paper is only a first attempt at applying higher order solution methods to the radiosity problem. Much work remains to fully integrate this approach into the general framework of global illumination and radiosity.

Acknowledgements

The Program of Computer Graphics at Cornell is one of five sites of the NSF/DARPA Science and Technology Center for Computer Graphics and Scientific Visualization (Grant # ASC-8920219). Thanks to HP/Apollo and DEC for equipment donations. This research was partially conducted under a National Science Foundation grant entitled "Interactive Input and Display Techniques." The author was funded by a National Science Foundation Graduate Student Fellowship, a Dabnicorp Computer Graphics award, and by a Cornell University Sage Fellowship. I would like to thank Don Greenberg for providing insightful comments as to what was needed to write up this research, Dani Lischinski and Filippo Tampieri for providing the reference solution of Section 6, and especially Jim Arvo for his advice in developing the research and this text. I'd also like to thank everyone at the Cornell Program of Computer Graphics, Rhythm and Hues, Inc., and the Caltech Graphics Lab for their support and encouragement.

References

[1] Daniel Baum, Holly Rushmeier, and James Winget, "Improved Radiosity Solutions Through the Use of Analytically Determined Form-Factors", *Computer Graphics*, 23(3), pp. 325-334, 1989.

[2] A. T. Campbell, III and Donald Fussell, "Adaptive Mesh Generation for Global Diffuse Illumination", *Computer Graphics*, 24(4), pp. 155-164, 1990.

[3] Michael Cohen and Donald Greenberg, "The Hemi-Cube: A Radiosity Solution For Complex Environments", *Computer Graphics*, 19(3), 1985, pp. 31-40.

[4] Michael Cohen, Shenchang Chen, John Wallace, Donald Greenberg, "A Progressive Refinement Approach to Fast Radiosity Image Generation", *Computer Graphics*, 22(4), 1988, pp. 75-84.

[5] Philip Davis, *Interpolation and Approximation*, Blaisdell, New York, 1963.

[6] L. M. Delves and J. L. Mohamed, *Computational Methods for Integral Equations*, Cambridge University Press, New York, 1985.

[7] Cindy Goral, Kenneth Torrance, Donald Greenberg, and Bennett Battaile, "Modeling the Interaction of Light Between Diffuse Surfaces", *Computer Graphics*, 18(3), July 1984, pp. 213-222.

[8] I. S. Gradshteyn and I. M. Ryzhik, *Table of Integrals, Series, and Products*, 4th edition, Academic Press, Inc., New York, 1965.

[9] Pat Hanrahan, David Salzman, and Larry Aupperle, "A Rapid Hierarchical Radiosity Algorithm", *Computer Graphics*, 25(4), pp. 197-206, 1991.

[10] Paul Heckbert, *Simulating Global Illumination Using Adaptive Meshing*, Report No. UCB/CSD 91/636, University of California, Berkeley, 1991.

[11] Paul Heckbert and James Winget, *Finite Element Methods for Global Illumination*, Report No. UCB/CSD 91/643, University of California, Berkeley, 1991.

[12] Paul Heckbert, "Discontinuity Meshing for Radiosity", *Third Eurographics Worshop on Rendering*, Bristol, UK, May 1992.

[13] Dani Lischinski, Filippo Tampieri, and Donald Greenberg, "Discontinuity Meshing for Accurate Radiosity", IEEE CG&A, 12(6), Nov. 1992.

[14] Nelson Max and Michael Allison, "Linear Radiosity Approximations using Vertex-to-Vertex Form Factors", *Graphics Gems III*, Academic Press, 1992, p. 319

[15] Tomoyuki Nishita and Eihachiro Nakamae, "Continuous Tone Representation of Three-Dimensional Objects Taking Account of Shadows and Interreflection", *Computer Graphics*, 19(3), 1985, pp. 23-30.

[16] *Starbase Radiosity and Ray Tracing Programmer's Manual*, Hewlett Packard Co., USA, 1990.

[17] J. Stoer and R. Bulirsch, *Introduction to Numerical Analysis*, Springer-Verlag, New York, 1980.

[18] E. M. Sparrow, "Application of Variational Methods to Radiation Heat-Transfer Calculations", *Journal of Heat Transfer*, November 1960, pp. 375-380.

[19] E. M. Sparrow and R. D. Cess, *Radiation Heat Transfer— Augmented Edition*, Hemisphere Publishing Corp., Washington, 1978.

[20] Filippo Tampieri and Dani Lischinski, "The Constant Radiosity Assumption Syndrome", in the Proceedings of the Second Eurographics Workshop on Rendering, Barcelona, 1991.

[21] John Wallace, Kells Elmquist, Eric Haines, "A Ray Tracing Algorithm for Progressive Radiosity", *Computer Graphics*, 23(3), 1989, pp. 315-324.

[22] Harold Zatz, *Galerkin Radiosity: A Higher Order Solution Method for Global Illumination*, Master's Thesis, Cornell University, Ithaca, New York, 1992.

Figure 8: A box with the transfer from light source to floor shadow masked, computed to fourth order on all surfaces except the floor and light source, which are computed to eighth order.

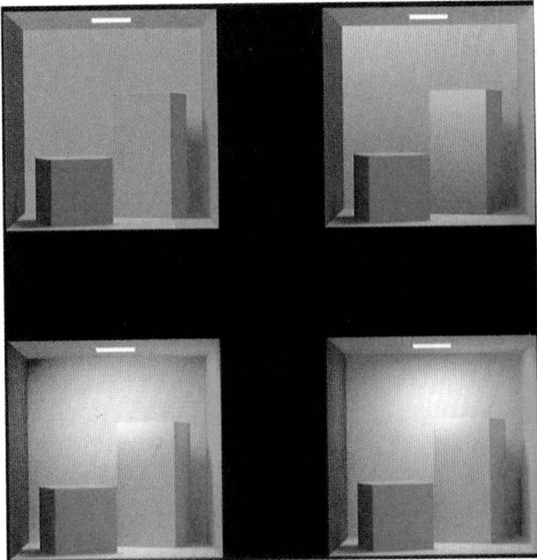

Figure 9: Solving the two box test environment, with solution orders zero, one, three, and seven.

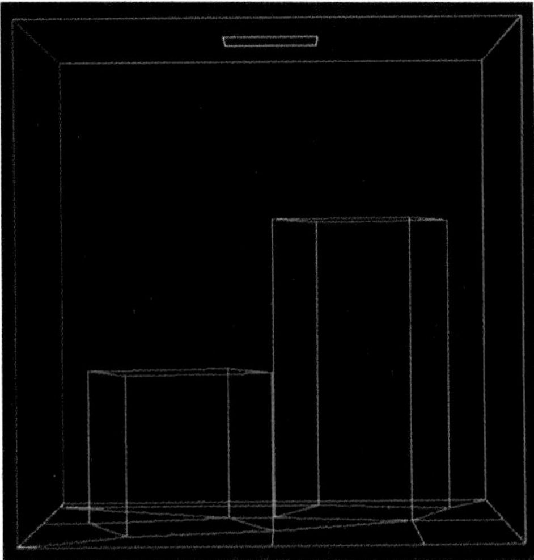

Figure 10: Mesh used for Figure 9. Only the floor has been meshed, to eliminate T-intersections. The boxes, walls, and ceilings were each solved using functions over the entire surface.

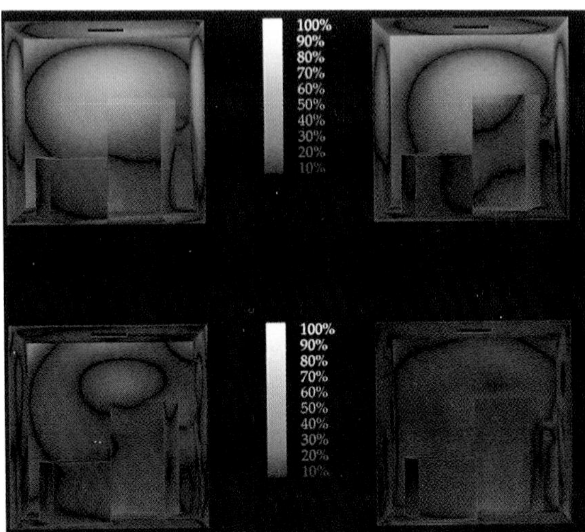

Figure 11: Difference images between the two box test environment and the reference solution, with solution orders zero, one, three, and seven.

Figure 12: The radiosity function across the clay teapot was solved directly, with a sixth-order basis set for each bicubic patch. The floor, walls, and portions of the teapot received shadow masks from the four lights.

Figure 13: This picture shows the interior of a temple containing 607 parametrically defined, non-meshed surfaces, including polygons, bicubic patches, cylinders, and cubic extrusions. Most surfaces were computed with a fourth or fifth order solution, except for the walls and roof at seventh order, and the cylindrical light fixtures at thirteenth order.

Wavelet Radiosity

Steven J. Gortler Peter Schröder Michael F. Cohen Pat Hanrahan

Department of Computer Science
Princeton University

Abstract

Radiosity methods have been shown to be an effective means to solve the global illumination problem in Lambertian diffuse environments. These methods approximate the radiosity integral equation by projecting the unknown radiosity function into a set of basis functions with limited support resulting in a set of n linear equations where n is the number of discrete elements in the scene. Classical radiosity methods required the evaluation of n^2 interaction coefficients. Efforts to reduce the number of required coefficients without compromising error bounds have focused on raising the order of the basis functions, meshing, accounting for discontinuities, and on developing hierarchical approaches, which have been shown to reduce the required interactions to $O(n)$.

In this paper we show that the hierarchical radiosity formulation is an instance of a more general set of methods based on *wavelet* theory. This general framework offers a unified view of both higher order element approaches to radiosity and the hierarchical radiosity methods. After a discussion of the relevant theory, we discuss a new set of linear time hierarchical algorithms based on wavelets such as the multiwavelet family and a flatlet basis which we introduce. Initial results of experimentation with these basis sets are demonstrated and discussed.

CR Categories and Subject Descriptors: I.3.7 [Computer Graphics]: *Three-Dimensional Graphics and Realism – Radiosity*; G.1.9 [Numerical Analysis]: *Integral Equations – Fredholm equations*.

Additional Key Words and Phrases: global illumination, wavelets, hierarchical radiosity.

1 Introduction

In computer graphics, radiosity methods have been used to solve the global illumination problem in environments consisting entirely of Lambertian (diffuse) reflectors and emitters. The solution is a radiosity function over the domain of the surfaces in the scene. Classical radiosity [9, 6] (CR), derived from the radiative heat transfer literature, approximates the radiosity function as piecewise constant. An energy balance argument gives rise to a linear system. This system has n^2 coefficients called *form factors*. Here n is the number of discrete areas, or *elements*, over which the radiosity function has been assumed to be constant. The form factor describes the fraction of the energy leaving one element and arriving at another. Typically, an iterative algorithm such as Gauss-Seidel iteration [22] or progressive radiosity [5, 10] is used to solve the system of linear equations for the radiosities.

An integral equation called the rendering equation was proposed by Kajiya to model the global illumination problem [14]. He showed that CR is a particular approximation to this equation. By casting the problem in this form, techniques developed for the solution of integral equations [8] can be exploited to solve the radiosity equation.

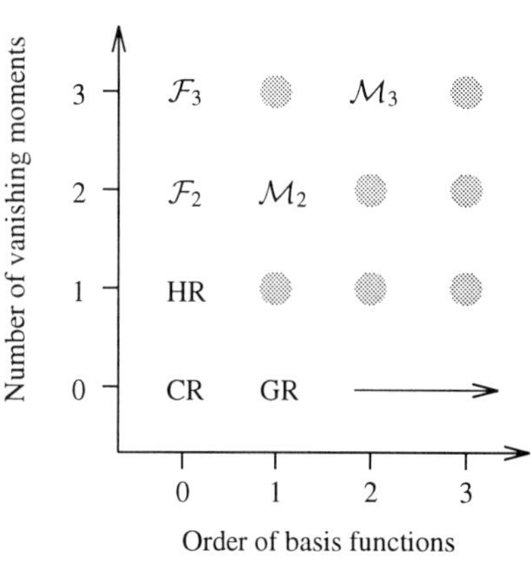

Figure 1: The space of projection methods for radiosity.

In particular, Heckbert [12, 13] has demonstrated that the linear system in radiosity can be derived by *projecting* the radiosity integral into a finite dimensional function space. The CR algorithm results from using the *space of piecewise constant functions*, (i.e., projecting the function into a set of constant (or "box") *basis* functions). In general, a function can be projected into any finite dimensional function space. A desirable finite dimensional space is one that can represent the function accurately with as few terms as possible. In his studies, Heckbert considered radiosity functions that are piecewise linear. Zatz [25] has used Legendre polynomials to arrive at solutions that are piecewise polynomial of higher order. Other researchers have explored the use of higher order bases in the mesh construction and reconstruction phases of the algorithm [18] as well as discontinuity meshing [15, 13]. The use of higher order bases, which we will refer to as galerkin radiosity (GR), has been shown to lower the number of basis functions needed to obtain a particular level of accuracy, albeit at a higher cost per basis.

A second avenue of research has attempted to lower the computational complexity of solving the linear system which arises in CR. Hanrahan et al. [11] presented a hierarchical radiosity method (HR) modeled after recent advances in n-body algorithms. HR exploits the fact that neighboring patches in the environment often have similar form factors to distant patches. This reasoning is extended to form a hierarchy of patches, (i.e., a hierarchy of basis functions) in a straightforward manner.

While the methods using higher order bases try to exploit *coherence* in the illumination function, HR tries to exploit the coherence in the form factor itself, more precisely, in the kernel of the radiosity integral. In particular, HR is based on approximating the kernel as a constant function over intervals of varying sizes. In places that the kernel varies slowly, large intervals are used. Where the kernel varies quickly, smaller intervals are needed.

Recently Beylkin et al. [3] made the observation that integral operators satisfying very general smoothness conditions can be approximated to any finite precision with only $O(n)$ coefficients when projected into a wavelet basis instead of the usual $O(n^2)$. This remarkable result means that, in practice, integral equations governed by smooth kernels lead to sparse matrices that can be solved in linear time. Since the radiosity kernel is, in general, a smooth function of the type required by this theorem, wavelet methods can be used to obtain $O(n)$ complexity radiosity algorithms. We call this *wavelet radiosity*.

Hierarchical basis functions have been used before with finite-element methods [24] and applied to problems such as surface interpolation [23]. In those instances, hierarchical basis functions were used to improve the condition number of the matrix. In our context, the hierarchical basis functions (wavelets) are used because many of the resulting matrix coefficients are small enough to be ignored while still allowing for an accurate answer. In some sense we are regarding the matrix as an image on which we are able to perform lossy compression. Coefficients are negligible because over many regions the kernel can be well approximated by a low order polynomial.

The mathematical tools of wavelet analysis provide a general framework offering a unified view of both higher order element approaches to radiosity, and the hierarchical radiosity methods. Figure 1 places earlier algorithms plus the new methods we investigate here into a matrix relating hierarchy versus the order of the underlying basis. CR uses zero order polynomials, while GR uses higher order polynomials (indicated by the arrow). The vertical axis represents the sparseness obtained by exploiting smoothness of some order in the kernel. HR exploits "constant" smoothness in the kernel. Within this context, we recognize HR as a first order wavelet. Higher order wavelets can be used that result in an even sparser matrix. One such family of higher order wavelets is the multiwavelet family of [1] ($\mathcal{M}_{2,3}$ in Figure 1). We will also introduce a new family of wavelets, which we have dubbed *flatlets* ($\mathcal{F}_{2,3}$ in Figure 1) that require only low order quadrature methods while maintaining most of the benefits of other wavelet sets.

This paper proceeds with a review of projection methods for solving integral equations followed by a discussion of recent advances concerning the solution of integral equations using wavelets. Finally we discuss our implementation and report experimental findings. Some of the more technical details of wavelet projections, as well as a detailed analysis of the underlying mathematical framework, are described in [20].

2 The Radiosity Integral Equation

If all surfaces and emitters are Lambertian diffuse, the rendering equation can be written as,

$$B(s_1, s_2) = E(s_1, s_2) + \rho(s_1, s_2) \int\int dt_1 dt_2 \frac{\cos\theta_s \cos\theta_t}{\pi r_{st}^2} V_{st} B(t_1, t_2) \quad (1)$$

where $B(s_1, s_2)$ gives the radiosity at a point specified by the surface parameters s_1, s_2, E the emission, and ρ the reflectivity[1]. The *kernel* of the integral,

$$k(s_1, s_2, t_1, t_2) = \rho(s_1, s_2) \frac{\cos\theta_s \cos\theta_t}{\pi r_{st}^2} V_{st}$$

is a function describing the geometric and visibility relationship between two points in the domain; θ_s and θ_t are the angles between the surface normals and the line between **s** and **t**; r_{st} is the distance between the two points; V_{st} is 1 if point **s** is visible to point **t** and 0 otherwise.

Over many large intervals, where r is large relative to the size of the patches, the kernel is well represented by a low order polynomial. Notable exceptions include the corners of the environment where r^2 goes to 0 and the kernel is singular, and shadow discontinuities where the visibility switches abruptly from 0 to 1.

3 Projections

After a short review of function projections we will show how projections can be used to find approximate solutions to integral equations such as the radiosity equation. The ideas presented here can be found in greater detail in [12, 25].

We begin by writing the approximation of a function $B(s)$ in a finite dimensional function space where all functions $\hat{B}(s)$ can be expressed as a linear combination of n *basis functions* $N_i(s)$

$$B(s) \approx \hat{B}(s) = \sum_{i=1}^{n} B_i N_i(s)$$

where the B_i are scalar coefficients with respect to the chosen bases. For example, the space of piecewise constant functions is spanned by a basis of translated "box" functions, and the space of piecewise linear functions is spanned by a basis of translated "hat" functions.

To complete the approximation, we must find a way to derive the coefficients. For this, we define an inner product of two functions $f(s)$ and $g(s)$ as $\langle f, g\rangle = \int ds\, f(s)g(s)$. Two functions are orthogonal iff $\langle f, g\rangle = 0$. We then say that a function $\hat{B}(s)$ is the orthogonal projection of $B(s)$ into the finite dimensional function space if $\langle B - \hat{B}, N_i\rangle = 0$ for all basis functions $N_i(s)$.

If the original basis functions are orthonormal we can find the coefficients of a function $B(s)$ with respect to the basis $\{N_i\}$ by performing inner products

$$\hat{B}(s) = \sum_i B_i N_i(s) = \sum_i \langle B, N_i\rangle N_i(s)$$

In the case of bases which are not orthonormal we must use inner products with the *dual* basis functions (see [20]) to find the coefficients.

Using projection methods, instead of solving the integral equation (1), we solve the related integral equation[2]

$$\hat{B}(s) = \hat{E}(s) + \sum_i \left\langle \int dt\, k(s,t)\hat{B}(t),\ N_i(s) \right\rangle N_i(s) \quad (2)$$

In words, we *operate* on (integrate against the kernel) the projected function $\hat{B}(t)$. After having been operated on, the resulting function generally no longer lies in the finite dimensional function space, so the function is reprojected against the $N_i(s)$. $\hat{B}$ can be obtained by solving the linear system

$$B_i = E_i + \sum_j B_j K_{ij}$$

$$K_{ij} = \int ds \int dt\, k(s,t) N_j(t) N_i(s) \quad (3)$$

To compute the integrals K_{ij} some form of numerical quadrature or closed form solution [21] must be employed. If the basis functions are piecewise constant, these integrals are related to the well known form factors.

[1] The reflectivity, ρ, is actually a function of wavelength. Without loss of generality, we will consider only a monochromatic world for the remainder of this paper.

[2] In order to simplify the presentation we will write the radiosity function as having one variable, and the kernel function as having two variables. In the text we will explain what needs to be done for a 3D radiosity implementation.

It is important to remember that the projected equation is only an approximation to the original integral equation. Projections into different finite dimensional spaces will result in different approximations with differing amounts of error and different types of error. In general the projection error is $O(h^{p+1})$ where h is the resolution of the grid, and p the degree of the polynomial used which favors higher order basis functions. Higher order basis functions also result in smoother reconstructed radiosity solutions leading to fewer visual artifacts. However, higher order basis functions require more work to evaluate the associated inner products, possibly offsetting potential savings.

One set of choices for basis functions is given by the family of functions called wavelets.

4 Wavelets

Wavelet theory is a rapidly developing field that has its roots in pure mathematics [7] and signal processing [16]. Good introductions to the topic can be found in [17, 4]. In this section we review some wavelet theory focusing on the relevant issues for radiosity.

Wavelets form hierarchical bases which can offer alternative bases for familiar finite dimensional function spaces. The simplest wavelet construction is the Haar construction shown in Figure 2. In the upper left is a set of basis functions which span all piecewise constant functions at resolution 8 on the interval. Using the operators g (pairwise differencing) and h (pairwise averaging) we can construct another basis for the same space (upper right). Four of these functions are just like the original basis, only wider, thus we can repeat the construction (middle right). Repeating once more we finally have a basis for the original space of functions consisting of the overall average ϕ_0 and the difference functions $\psi_{i,j}$ from all the lower levels. The last set of functions is known as the Haar *wavelet basis*. This construction is very similar to an image pyramid that one might use for texture mapping. In such a pyramid the image (function in our case) is represented at different levels of resolution by successive averaging steps. In the Haar pyramid we only remember the overall average and all the *differences* between successive levels of the pyramid.

The Haar basis is only the simplest example of an infinite family of such constructions, however the basic principles are the same for all wavelet bases. More formally we start with two functions $\psi(s)$ (sometimes called the *detail* function) and $\phi(s)$ (the *smooth* function) defined on the unit interval $s \in [0, 1]$. Scales (or levels) i and translates j of $\phi(s)$ and $\psi(s)$ are expressed as

$$\phi_{i,j}(s) = 2^{i/2}\phi(2^i s - j)$$
$$\psi_{i,j}(s) = 2^{i/2}\psi(2^i s - j)$$

with $j = 0, \ldots, 2^i - 1$. According to this indexing, the function $\phi_{i,j}$ is just like the function $\phi_{i-1,j}$ except that $\phi_{i-1,j}$ is twice as wide, and $1/\sqrt{2}$ times as tall (the wider functions are shorter so that $\langle\phi_{i,j}, \phi_{i,k}\rangle$ remains constant independent of i). Similarly, $\phi_{i,j}$ is just like the function $\phi_{i,j+1}$ except it is translated. To create an $n = 2^L$ dimensional function space we construct an L level hierarchy of functions that are scales and translates of ϕ and ψ (Figure 2 illustrates $L = 3$). We obtain the wavelet basis for the hierarchy by choosing only the detail shapes on all levels plus the smooth shape on the top level, $\psi_{i,j}$, $i = 0, \ldots, L-1$ and ϕ_0. Between levels there is the so called *two-scale* relationship

$$\phi_{i-1,j} = \sum_k h_{k-2j}\phi_{i,k}$$

$$\psi_{i-1,j} = \sum_k g_{k-2j}\phi_{i,k}$$

In words the ϕ functions at a given level can be linearly combined to yield ϕ and ψ functions at the next coarser level. This combination can be expressed as a convolution with some sequences h and g with the result subsampled by 2 (expressed by the factor 2 in the index "$k - 2j$" of h and g). The sequences h and g can be thought of as a low pass filter and high pass filter respectively.

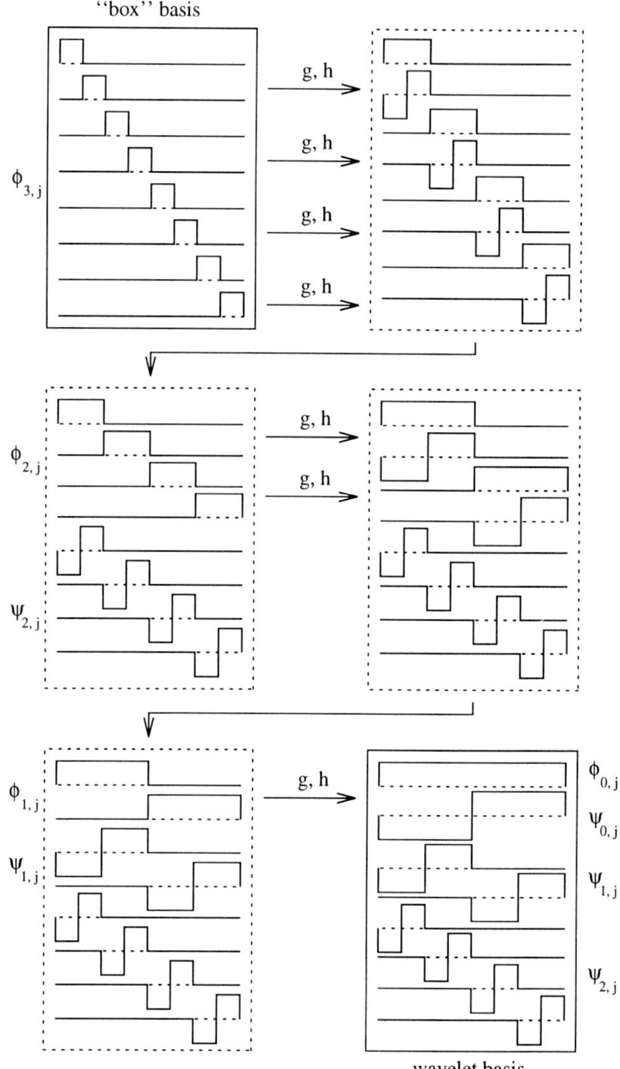

Figure 2: Transformation of a piecewise constant basis into the Haar wavelet basis.

The projection of an arbitrary function $B(s)$ into a wavelet[3] basis can be formally written as

$$\hat{B}(s) = \langle B, \phi_0\rangle\phi_0(s) + \sum_{ij}\langle B, \psi_{i,j}\rangle\psi_{i,j}(s) \qquad (4)$$

Instead of computing all the above inner products, we can find the coefficients efficiently by exploiting the two-scale relationship. Given the projection of some arbitrary function $B(s)$ with respect to the lowest level basis $\phi_{L,j}$ the wavelet coefficients can be found using a pyramid algorithm [16]. Each stage of this algorithm takes a vector of coefficients and convolves it with the filters h and g, returning the smooth and detail coefficients one level up

[3] To simplify the discussion we are assuming that we have an orthonormal wavelet basis. We discuss the non orthonormal case in [20].

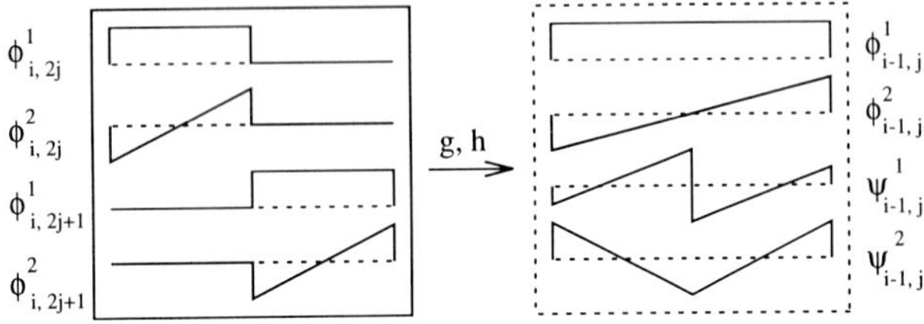

Figure 3: The $\mathcal{M}_2$ wavelet construction whose smooth shapes are the first two Legendre polynomials. Both of the detail shapes (lower right) have two vanishing moments.

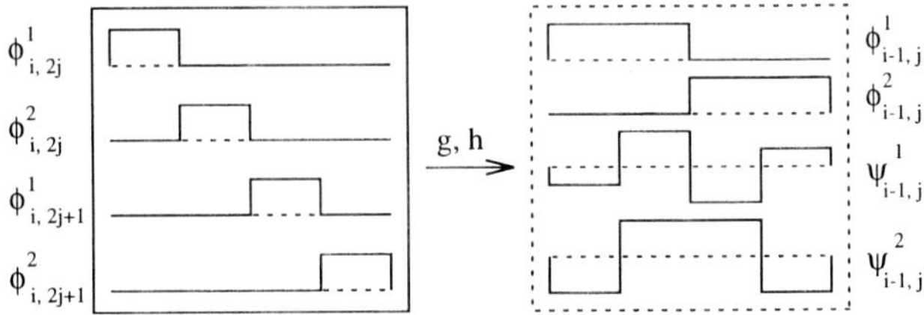

Figure 4: The $\mathcal{F}_2$ wavelet construction. $\mathcal{F}_2$ bases have two different detail shapes. Both of the detail shapes have two vanishing moments.

```
XformUp( vector B_φ, int i )
  for( j = 0; j < 2^i/2; j++)
    B_φ^up[j] = Σ_k h_{k-2j} B_φ[k];
    B_ψ^up[j] = Σ_k g_{k-2j} B_φ[k];
  return (B_φ^up, B_ψ^up);
```

The entire one dimensional pyramid transform is then stated as

```
PyramidUp( vector B_{φ_{L,k}} )
  for( i = L; i > 0; i-- )
    (B_{φ_{i-1,k}}, B_{ψ_{i-1,k}}) = XformUp( B_{φ_{i,k}} , i );
  return (B_{φ_0}, B_{ψ_{i,k}}, i = 0,...,L-1);
```

If the h and g convolutions have constant width (with respect to i) then each call to **XformUp** has cost linear in the length of the array passed in. Since each successive call in **PyramidUp** works on only the smooth half left by the previous call the overall runtime to build the pyramid is $O(n + \frac{n}{2} + \frac{n}{4} + \ldots + 1) = O(n)$.

A similar algorithm **PyramidDown** reverses this process using **XformDown** for successive calls

```
XformDown( vector B_φ, vector B_ψ, int i )
  for( j = 0; j < 2*2^i; j++ )
    B_φ^down[j] = Σ_k h_{j-2k} B_φ[k] + Σ_k g_{j-2k} B_ψ[k];
  return B_φ^down ;

PyramidDown( B_{φ_0}, B_{ψ_{i,k}}, i = 0,...,L-1 )
  for( i = 0; i < L; i++ )
    B_{φ_{i+1,k}} = XformDown( B_{φ_{i,k}}, B_{ψ_{i,k}} , i );
  return B_{φ_{L,k}} ;
```

A key property of wavelets essential to this work is that a sufficiently smooth function $B(s)$, when expressed in a wavelet basis (Equation 4) will have many small coefficients. By ignoring these negligible coefficients we are left with a sparse, approximate representation. The negligible coefficients occur because wavelet functions have *vanishing moments*. We say that a function $\psi(s)$ has M vanishing moments if

$$\int ds\, \psi(s) s^i = 0, \quad i = 0, \ldots, M-1$$

The Haar wavelet (Figure 2) has one vanishing moment, thus the projection of a nearly constant function into the Haar basis will have wavelet coefficients near 0. Similarly, if a wavelet basis function has two vanishing moments, the projection of a linear function will vanish. Figures 3 and 4 show examples of wavelets, ψ, with two vanishing moments.

5 Wavelets In Higher Dimensions

Wavelet bases for functions of two or more variables are required for radiosity. Our goal is to project the kernel, which is a four dimensional function, into a basis set in which it has a sparse representation.

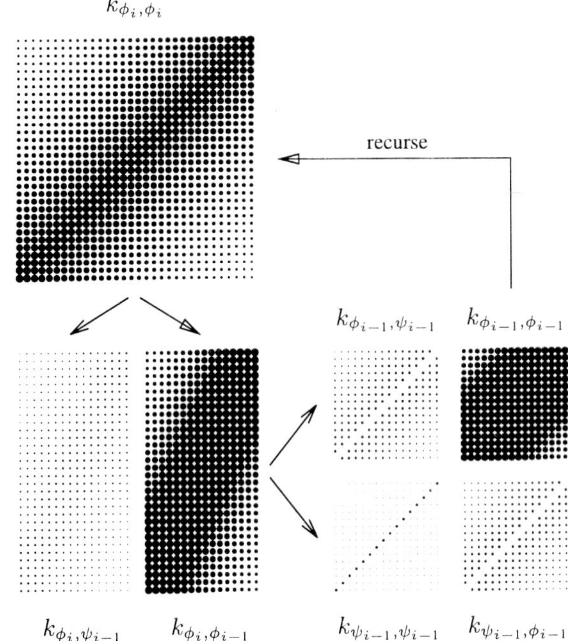

Figure 5: The 2D Pyramid Algorithm is applied to form factors taken from the flatland radiosity environment consisting of two parallel line segments. (Flatland [13] is radiosity in a plane). The dot size indicates the magnitude of a given entry in the matrix.

An arbitrary function $k(s,t)$ of two variables on a finite two dimensional interval can be approximated by some function $\hat{k}(s,t)$ that lies in a two variable finite dimensional function space. Given a particular one dimensional wavelet, a 2D wavelet basis[4] is made up of the functions

$$\phi_0(s)\phi_0(t)$$
$$\psi_{i,j}(s)\psi_{i,k}(t)$$
$$\psi_{i,j}(s)\phi_{i,k}(t)$$
$$\phi_{i,j}(s)\psi_{i,k}(t)$$

where we only couple functions on the same scale i, where $i = 0, \ldots, L-1$ and $j,k = 0, \ldots, 2^i - 1$.

The 2D wavelet coefficients may be obtained from the finest resolution coefficients $B_{\phi_{L,j},\phi_{L,k}}$ using a 2D **PyramidUp** algorithm. This algorithm begins with the $B_{\phi_{L,j},\phi_{L,k}}$ written in a 2D matrix tableau. It then applies **XformUp** once to each row, followed by an application of **XformUp** to each resulting column. This procedure is applied recursively to the $B_{\phi_{L-1,j},\phi_{L-1,k}}$ quar-

[4] Another 2D wavelet basis could be constructed from the tensor product of a 1D wavelet basis. The different forms of multidimensional wavelet bases are discussed in [3, 20].

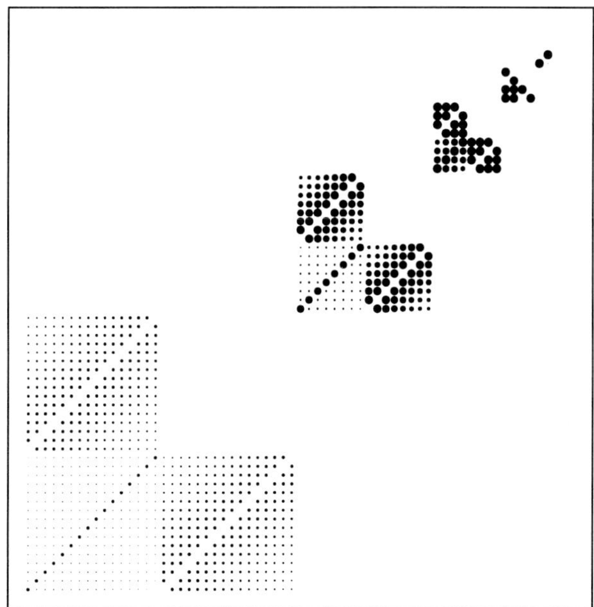

Figure 6: To illustrate the sparseness of the kernel matrix we transform the flatland radiosity matrix from Figure 5 into the 2D Haar basis. Many of the coefficients are small in magnitude (small dots).

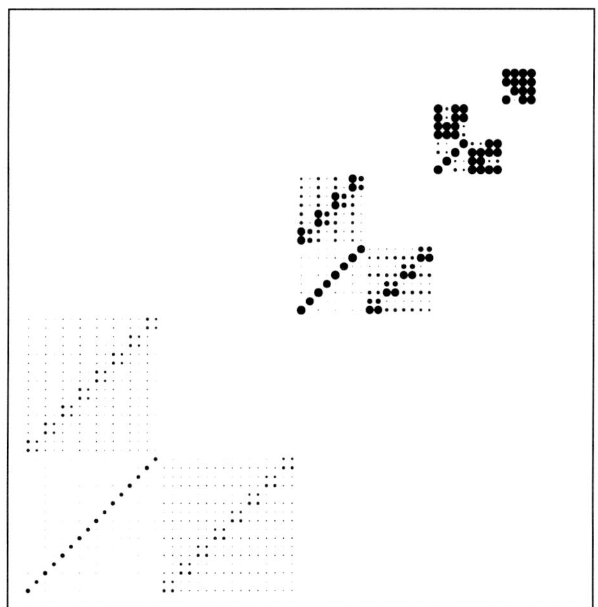

Figure 7: We transform the same matrix into the $\mathcal{F}_2$ basis. Notice that even more of the coefficients are negligible now.

ter (Figure 5). The construction of a 2D **PyramidDown** follows analogously from the one dimensional **PyramidDown**.

This construction can be extended to functions of four variables such as the kernel in 3D radiosity $k(s_1, t_1, s_2, t_2)$. For this case, there are sixteen combinations of ϕ and ψ functions in four variables. The basis is made up of all fifteen combinations on the same scale i which involve ψ functions. The corresponding pyramid transformation functions are constructed as in the two dimensional case by applying **XformUp** and **XformDown** respectively to each dimension in turn.

For this type of multidimensional wavelet basis Beylkin et al. [3] show that for a given error tolerance, only $O(n)$ coefficients need to be used to attain the prescribed error tolerance in the results of our computations. Figures 6 and 7 visualize the sparseness of a flatland radiosity kernel when written in two wavelet bases with one and two vanishing moments respectively.

6 Radiosity with Wavelets

To obtain an efficient radiosity algorithm, we project the kernel by taking inner products with the wavelet basis functions. The coefficients of the kernel with respect to the basis are given by

$$\begin{aligned}
k^{\phi} = k_{\phi_0,\phi_0} &= \int dt \int ds\, k(s,t)\phi_0(s)\phi_0(t) \\
k^{\alpha}_{ijk} = k_{\psi_{i,j},\psi_{i,k}} &= \int dt \int ds\, k(s,t)\psi_{i,j}(s)\psi_{i,k}(t) \\
k^{\beta}_{ijk} = k_{\phi_{i,j},\psi_{i,k}} &= \int dt \int ds\, k(s,t)\phi_{i,j}(s)\psi_{i,k}(t) \\
k^{\gamma}_{ijk} = k_{\psi_{i,j},\phi_{i,k}} &= \int dt \int ds\, k(s,t)\psi_{i,j}(s)\phi_{i,k}(t)
\end{aligned}$$

Because of the vanishing moment properties of the wavelets and the smoothness properties of the kernel, many of these terms are nearly zero.

A projected version of the integral operator can now be derived by projecting the kernel itself. This derivation which we only sketch here is described in greater detail in Beylkin et al. [3]. The k^{α}, k^{β} and k^{γ} coefficients are used to represent the kernel which has been approximated with respect to the wavelet basis. Given this projection, after performing the necessary algebra, the approximate operator can be written as

$$\begin{aligned}
&\int dt\, \hat{k}(s,t)B(t) = \\
&\quad B^{\phi}k^{\phi}\phi_0(s) + \sum_{ij}(\sum_k B^{\alpha}_{ik}k^{\alpha}_{ijk})\psi_{i,j}(s) \\
&\quad + \sum_{ij}(\sum_k B^{\beta}_{ik}k^{\beta}_{ijk})\phi_{i,j}(s) + \sum_{ij}(\sum_k B^{\gamma}_{ik}k^{\gamma}_{ijk})\psi_{i,j}(s)
\end{aligned} \tag{5}$$

where

$$\begin{aligned}
B^{\alpha}_{ik} = B^{\gamma}_{ik} = B_{\psi_{i,k}} &= \int dt\, \psi_{i,k}(t)B(t) \\
B^{\beta}_{ik} = B_{\phi_{i,k}} &= \int dt\, \phi_{i,k}(t)B(t) \\
B^{\phi} = B_{\phi_0} &= \int dt\, \phi_0(t)B(t)
\end{aligned}$$

6.1 The Basic Algorithm

Equation 5 suggests the following three phase algorithm to approximate the kernel operating on a radiosity function.

Step 1 *Pull*: Obtain the n (n = number of bases of the radiosity function) coefficients B^{α} and the n coefficients B^{β} of the radiosity function. If we are initially given the coefficients $B_{\phi_{L,j}}$, the $2n$ needed coefficients can be obtained by calling a procedure **Pull** which is just like **PyramidUp** except it returns *both* the ϕ and ψ coefficients. This step transforms n coefficients into $2n$

coefficients. A 1D **Pull** would then be

```
Pull( vector $B_{\phi_{L,k}}$ )
  for( $i = L$; $i > 0$; $i--$ )
    ($B_{\phi_{i-1,k}}$, $B_{\psi_{i-1,k}}$) = XformUp( $B_{\phi_{i,k}}$ , i );
  return ( $B_{\phi_{i,k}}$, $B_{\psi_{i,k}}$, $i = 0, \ldots, L-1$ ) ;
```

Step 2 *Gather*: Let the projected kernel operate on the projected radiosity function. This means that we sum over the index k, and is equivalent to a matrix multiply. Because of the vanishing moments of the wavelet functions most of the n^2 kernel coefficients will be near zero and may be ignored if the action of the kernel is desired to finite precision. The procedure **Gather** results in $2n$ coefficients $G_{\phi_{i,j}}$ and $G_{\psi_{i,j}}$ that represent the resultant radiosity function as a combination of $\phi_{i,j}(s)$ and $\psi_{i,j}(s)$.

Step 3 *Push*: Reconstruction of the radiosity function using the $2n$ functions $\phi_{i,j}(s)$ and $\psi_{i,j}(s)$ is done with the procedure **Push** which is similar to **PyramidDown** but takes as arguments *both* the ϕ and ψ coefficients. A 1D **Push** would then be

```
Push( $B_{\phi_{i,k}}$, $B_{\psi_{i,k}}$, $i = 0, \ldots, L-1$ )
  for( $i = 0$; $i < L$; $i++$ )
    $B_{\phi_{i+1,k}}$ += XformDown( $B_{\phi_{i,k}}$, $B_{\psi_{i,k}}$ , i );
  return $B_{\phi_{L,k}}$ ;
```

Wrapping this projected operator within a Jacobi iteration loop results in the following algorithm

```
($k^\alpha$,$k^\beta$,$k^\gamma$) = ProjectKernel();
$B_{\phi_{L,k}}$ = $E_{\phi_{L,k}}$;
while( !converged )
  $G$ = 0;
  ($B_{\phi_{i,k}}$, $B_{\psi_{i,k}}$) = Pull( $B_{\phi_{L,k}}$ );
  ($G_{\phi_{i,j}}$, $G_{\psi_{i,j}}$) = Gather( $B_{\phi_{i,k}}$, $B_{\psi_{i,k}}$, $k^\alpha$, $k^\beta$, $k^\gamma$ );
  $G_{\phi_{L,k}}$ = Push( $G_{\phi_{i,j}}$, $G_{\psi_{i,j}}$ );
  $B_{\phi_{L,k}}$ = $G_{\phi_{L,k}} + E_{\phi_{L,k}}$;
Display();
```

The push and pull can be done in $O(n)$ (linear in the number of elements) steps. The gather step (this is a complete gather sweep which updates all of the entries) can be done in $O(m)$ time where m is the number of terms in the kernel expansion (matrix) that are significant. We want m to be as small as possible. Wavelet bases will lead to $m = O(n)$ where the constant factor in $O(n)$ decreases with the number of vanishing moments.

What remains is to project the kernel into the wavelet basis, which may be done as follows

```
ProjectKernel()
  $k_{\phi_{L,j},\phi_{L,k}}$= Quadrature( $k$, $\phi_{L,j}$, $\phi_{L,k}$ );
  ($k^\alpha$, $k^\beta$, $k^\gamma$) = PyramidUp( $k_{\phi_{L,j},\phi_{L,k}}$);
  where( ($k^\alpha$, $k^\beta$, $k^\gamma$) < $\epsilon$ )
    ($k^\alpha$, $k^\beta$, $k^\gamma$) = 0 ;
```

6.2 The Top Down Approach

Unfortunately, this bottom up **ProjectKernel** is an expensive implementation requiring quadratic time and space. The costs can be dramatically cut by using an *oracle* which predicts which m of the n^2 coefficients of the projected kernel are significant. Then, these m values are computed directly by quadrature or symbolic integration.

Assuming that the oracle can estimate the smoothness of the kernel for a given region (vis-a-vis a given number of vanishing moments), an efficient top down recursive version of **ProjectKernel** can be written as follows

```
ProjectKernel( i, patch p, patch q )
  smooth = AskOracle( p, q );
  if( smooth ) return;
  else
    ($k^\alpha_{i,j(p),k(q)}$, $k^\beta_{i,j(p),k(q)}$, $k^\gamma_{i,j(p),k(q)}$)
      = Quadrature( k, p, q );
  if( i == L-1 ) return;
  else
    ProjectKernel( i+1, left(p), left(q) );
    ProjectKernel( i+1, left(p), right(q) );
    ProjectKernel( i+1, right(p), left(q) );
    ProjectKernel( i+1, right(p), right(q) );
```

If the oracle finds the region under consideration sufficiently smooth no more recursive calls need be executed, since the coefficients at lower levels will be insignificant by assumption. The function **Quadrature()** computes the projection of the kernel function onto the basis functions at the given level.

6.3 3D Radiosity

In 3D radiosity B is a function of two variables so in the main program we use a 2D **Pull** and a 2D **Push** respectively. k is a function of four variables so in the bottom up **ProjectKernel** we use a 4D **PyramidUp** function. In the top down approach to **ProjectKernel** there are fifteen not three quadratures and sixteen recursive calls for all combinations of four children of **p** and **q**.

7 Implementation

The top down algorithm described above has been implemented by extending the implementation of hierarchical radiosity described in Hanrahan et al. [11].

7.1 Choice of Basis

Two families of wavelets have been explored, multiwavelets [1] and a family of wavelets that we call flatlets. Each of these families have members with any number of vanishing moments.

The construction of $\mathcal{M}_M$ (multiwavelet with M vanishing moments) begins with M smooth functions which are the first M Legendre Polynomials, $\phi^m(s) = L_m(s)$, and M detail functions $\psi^m(s)$ that are piecewise polynomials of degree $M-1$, and have M vanishing moments. A hierarchy is then constructed from these shapes. $\mathcal{M}_1$ is the Haar basis, however, for M greater than 1, $\mathcal{M}_M$ is technically speaking not a true wavelet since it begins with a collection of ϕ and ψ functions instead of a single pair.

Multiwavelets form an orthonormal basis. Figure 3 shows the basis functions for the $\mathcal{M}_2$ hierarchy. The two-scale relationship for $\mathcal{M}_2$ is expressed concisely as

$$\frac{1}{\sqrt{8}} \begin{bmatrix} 2 & 0 & 2 & 0 \\ -\sqrt{3} & 1 & \sqrt{3} & 1 \\ 0 & -2 & 0 & 2 \\ 1 & \sqrt{3} & -1 & \sqrt{3} \end{bmatrix} \begin{bmatrix} \phi^1_{i,2j} \\ \phi^2_{i,2j} \\ \phi^1_{i,2j+1} \\ \phi^2_{i,2j+1} \end{bmatrix} = \begin{bmatrix} \phi^1_{i-1,j} \\ \phi^2_{i-1,j} \\ \psi^1_{i-1,j} \\ \psi^2_{i-1,j} \end{bmatrix}$$

Using this relationship the push and pull operations can be computed using a binary tree, instead of as a subsampled vector convolution. A node stores the four coefficients of the functions $\phi^1_{i-1,j}$, $\phi^2_{i-1,j}$, $\psi^1_{i-1,j}$, $\psi^2_{i-1,j}$. During a pull, a node computes the values of its coefficients as a linear combination of the $\phi^1_{i,2j}$, $\phi^2_{i,2j}$ coefficients obtained from its left child, and the $\phi^1_{i,2j+1}$, $\phi^2_{i,2j+1}$ coefficients obtained from its right child. To represent the radiosity function over a patch we need a 2D $\mathcal{M}_2$ basis for which we use a quad-tree where each node stores sixteen coefficients. During a pull, a node computes its coefficients as a linear combination of the sixteen $\phi\phi$ coefficients from its children (four from each child).

The flatlet basis $\mathcal{F}_M$ is made up entirely of piecewise constant functions. The ϕ^m are M adjacent box functions, and the ψ^m are M piecewise constant functions that have M vanishing moments. Figure 4 shows the $\mathcal{F}_2$ hierarchy.

For $\mathcal{F}_2$, the two-scale relationship is given by

$$\frac{1}{\sqrt{2}}\begin{bmatrix} 1 & 1 & 0 & 0 \\ 0 & 0 & 1 & 1 \\ -1 & 3 & -3 & 1 \\ -1 & 1 & 1 & -1 \end{bmatrix}\begin{bmatrix} \phi^1_{i,2j} \\ \phi^2_{i,2j} \\ \phi^1_{i,2j+1} \\ \phi^2_{i,2j+1} \end{bmatrix} = \begin{bmatrix} \phi^1_{i-1,j} \\ \phi^2_{i-1,j} \\ \psi^1_{i-1,j} \\ \psi^2_{i-1,j} \end{bmatrix} \quad (6)$$

The top two rows of the matrix in the above equation are chosen to give us box functions twice as wide. The bottom two rows are chosen to be orthogonal to constant and linear variation, (the vectors $[1,1,1,1]$, $[0,1,2,3]$)[5]. For a discussion of a similar construction see [2].

Both flatlets and multiwavelets can be constructed to have any number of vanishing moments to increase the sparseness of the integral operator representation. For both bases, the case $M = 1$ reduces to the Haar basis. For $M > 1$ multiwavelets offer the benefits of projecting into a higher order space, resulting in increased convergence rates and smoother basis functions to represent the answer. These benefits come at the expense of higher order quadratures necessary for the inner products. Flatlets for $M > 1$ also offer accelerated convergence while the quadratures remain equivalent to form factor computations for which there exits a large body of literature and code, and for which some closed form solutions are known. The final answer is still represented as a piecewise constant function, albeit at the finest resolution $\phi_{L,j}$. Since the degree of the basis functions does not go up in the flatlet case the width of support needs to be increased as M increases.

With multiwavelets and flatlets there is also a cost incurred by increasing the number of vanishing moments. Larger M will result in h and g filters with wider support. Thus any non-smoothness in $k(s,t)$, such as a shadow discontinuity, will fall under the support of more basis functions. This increases the number of significant terms in the integral operator.

[5] A technical detail concerns the fact that flatlets for $M > 1$ are not orthonormal and thus require the dual basis functions to compute `PyramidUp` (see [20]).

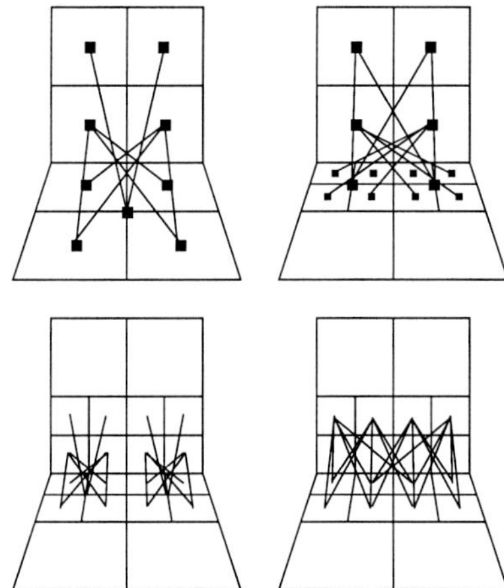

Figure 8: Two different oracles and the interaction patterns they generate.

7.2 Pull, Push and Gather

Both multiwavelets and flatlets are instances of *tree* wavelets. A tree wavelet has the property that the convolution sequences h and g for two neighboring elements do not overlap. This property allows us to organize all computations along a tree which does not need to have uniform depth. Tree wavelets also allow for another simplification. Since all necessary coefficients reside in the immediate children of a node we can use the two-scale relationship to store only the $\phi\phi$ coefficients and need not represent the $\phi\psi$, $\psi\phi$, and $\psi\psi$ coefficients explicitly. With this simplification **ProjectKernel** is implemented as follows

```
ProjectKernel( i, patch p, patch q )
  ParentLevelsmooth = AskOracle( p, q );
  if( ParentLevelsmooth || i == L )
    k_φ,φ = Quadrature( k, p, q );
    CreateLink( k_φ,φ, p, q );
  else
    ProjectKernel( i+1, left(p), left(q) );
    ProjectKernel( i+1, left(p), right(q) );
    ProjectKernel( i+1, right(p), left(q) );
    ProjectKernel( i+1, right(p), right(q) );
```

In our implementation of radiosity using the $\mathcal{M}_M$ and $\mathcal{F}_M$ bases, the radiosity function over each polygon is represented by $B_{\phi\phi}$ coefficients that are stored in a quad-tree. Each node holds M^2 $B_{\phi\phi}$ coefficients. Pulling and pushing are done in the quad-tree as in [11] except that for different bases, we use different two-scale relationships. The kernel is represented by its $k_{\phi\phi\phi\phi}$ coefficients that are stored on links created between nodes of different polygons' quad-trees. Each such link caries M^4 interaction terms. For the $\mathcal{F}_M$ bases the interaction terms are still form factors, but for $\mathcal{M}_M$ the coefficients on the links represent higher order interactions which require quadrature computations of the appropriate order. Gathering is done by moving B values across the links, weighted by the k values on the link. In this context, HR can be viewed as wavelet radiosity using the Haar basis.

7.3 Oracle

The oracle must decide whether the kernel is sufficiently smooth over two patches in the environment i.e., resembles a polynomial of degree $M - 1$ or less. If the kernel is smooth, all ψ terms will (sufficiently) vanish and thus any work to evaluate the lower interaction terms can be avoided.

The most accurate approach to measure the kernel smoothness is to directly evaluate the integrals of the kernel against the ψ on this and all lower levels and verify that they are below the required threshold. This is computationally too expensive and we approximate this computation in the following way. The kernel is sampled at the points required by a Gauss-Legendre quadrature rule of the appropriate order and an interpolating polynomial of degree $M - 1$ is constructed using Neville's algorithm [22]. Given this interpolating polynomial k_P we compute the L_1 error $\int |k_P - k|$ with a quadrature rule which places sample points in-between the previously chosen points. If the value of this integral is small we conclude that our current level of (smooth) approximation matches the kernel function well and the **AskOracle** function returns **True**. Note that the sample points for the interpolating polynomial are chosen so that they can be used directly in the computation of the interaction link values. If the **AskOracle** function returns **False** these samples are discarded. A less costly approach could use geometric information, such as the size, orientation, and distance between two patches. In effect this was done in the original HR implementation. However for the $\mathcal{F}_M$ and $\mathcal{M}_M$, $M > 1$ bases it is not immediately clear what the corresponding geometric reasoning would be.

It is important to realize that any such implementation of an oracle will introduce errors due to its approximate nature. If the oracle is not stringent enough, and necessary terms are neglected, artifacts will appear in the image. Figure 8 shows two different oracles and the interactions they force. Two successive levels of interactions are shown (top to bottom). On the left is an oracle allowing patches close to the singularity (where the kernel varies rapidly) to be linked (meaning no further subdivision will be done). For this oracle the interaction patterns separate on the lower level. On the right is a more stringent oracle which does not allow singular interactions until patches have become very small. As a result we do not see the separation.

As in [11] we use *brightness refinement* which means that the stringency of the oracle is weighted by the brightness of the involved patches. Also as in [11] a fast partial visibility test is performed by using a constant number of jittered rays. If two patches are partially occluded and there is sufficient energy being transferred between the two patches the oracle returns **False**.

7.4 Quadrature

If the oracle returns **True**, numerical integrations must be performed to compute the $k_{\phi\phi\phi\phi}$ terms associated with the link to be created. Our implementation uses Gauss-Legendre quadrature [22] for this purpose. A Gauss-Legendre quadrature rule provides an accurate integration for polynomials up to order $2p - 1$, where p is the number of sample points. The order of the quadrature and the related number of sample points required depends on the sum of the order of the wavelet bases, and the assumed order of the kernel itself.

For the projection of the kernel against a flatlet basis, a two point rule is used for each constant section of the basis function. In the case of multiwavelets $\mathcal{M}_M$, $M > 1$, M points are chosen along each coordinate axis since we need to have a high enough order of integration to account for the polynomial variance in the kernel and the polynomial basis functions themselves. For example, for $M = 3$ we compute coefficients when the kernel varies approximately up to 2nd by projecting onto basis functions up to 2nd order. Thus the integrand is approximately 4th order, and we can use a three point Gauss rule.

The number of integrals which need to be computed for a link is M^4, however for all these integrals only a total of M^4 samples of the kernel function are required. Using precomputed weights, these samples are combined to give all the desired integrals.

We treat visibility following [11] by casting a constant number of jittered rays between two patches to estimate the fraction of visibility. This is then used to attenuate the quantity returned by the Gauss-Legendre quadrature. This technique relies on the fact that we always subdivide in the vicinity of a shadow discontinuity limiting errors due to the non-smooth nature of the kernel to a small region.

When the two patches that are linked up are close to the singularity in k, quadratures will encounter numerical difficulties if they are not properly adapted to the singularity. In particular a Gauss-Legendre rule will produce large errors and an adapted quadrature rule is required. This phenomenon is not unique to wavelet radiosity but applies to all GR methods. Special Gauss rules can be designed for the particular singularity found in the radiosity kernel. Zatz [25] uses such custom rules and notes the need for an automatic decision procedure as to when to switch the type of integration. In our implementation of flatlets, we use a closed form solution for the form factor [21] whenever the patches border on the singularity. While this computation is expensive, it only needs to be invoked in a small fraction of interaction computations and contributes little to overall runtime. For multiwavelets we have no such closed form available. In this case the oracle forces subdivision to small enough patches at the singularity that the resulting errors contribute very little to the overall error. Alternative constructions for singular transports are discussed in [19].

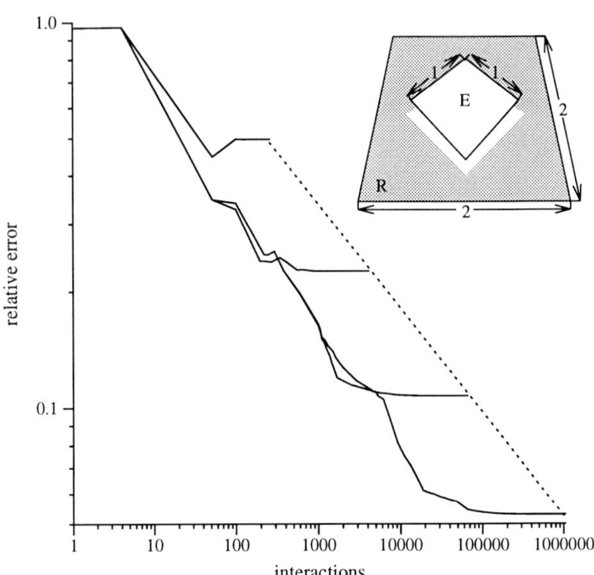

Figure 9: Relative L_1 error as a function of the number of interaction links for the haar basis with $h = \frac{1}{4}, \frac{1}{8}, \frac{1}{16}, \frac{1}{32}$ (top to bottom). The test configuration is depicted in the upper right corner.

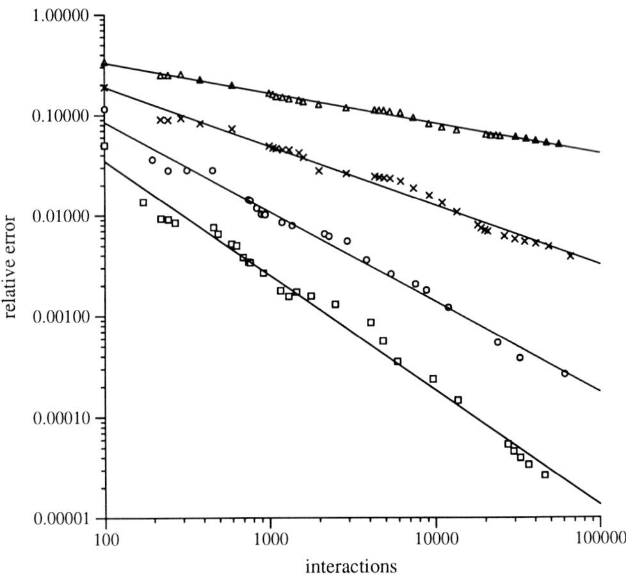

Figure 10: Relative L_1 error as a function of the number of interactions for the wavelet bases $\mathcal{M}_1$, $\mathcal{M}_2$, $\mathcal{M}_3$, and $\mathcal{M}_4$ (top to bottom) using the same test configuration as in Figure 9. Here $h = \frac{1}{32}$.

8 Experimental Results

In this section we present findings that compare how radiosity behaves using different wavelet bases. We give results from the analysis of a simple 3D configuration, for which we have an analytic solution against which to check our results. We finish with an image of a full environment.

One test case used the configuration depicted in the inset in

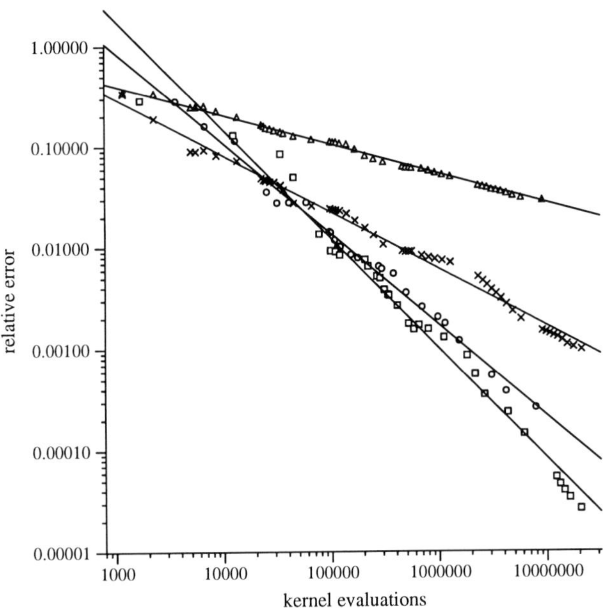

Figure 11: Relative L_1 error as a function of work.

Figure 12: Computed image of perpendicular emitter and receiver. for the Haar basis (left), and $\mathcal{F}_2$ basis (right) using same amount of work. Note that we have not performed any post processing such as Gouraud shading.

Figure 9. A pure emitter of side length 1 is placed 0.1 units above a pure receiver of side length two. For this particular configuration the radiosity on the receiver is given by the differential area to finite area form factor at every point. Figure 9 shows the behavior of the relative L_1 error for the Haar basis as a function of the number of interactions for various grid sizes h. The far point on each of the lines corresponds to a full matrix solution. Note in particular that the final accuracy is reached well before all matrix elements are computed. Plots for higher order basis functions exhibit the same overall shape but with steeper slopes and overall lesser error. Figure 10 shows the behavior of the $\mathcal{M}_M$ bases for $M = 1, \ldots, 4$ and $h = \frac{1}{32}$. The ratio of successive slopes (as fitted to the points) is almost precisely $1 : 2 : 3 : 4$, as one would expect from the order of basis functions employed. For both plots we have depicted error as a function of number of interactions. However a user experiences error as a function of work which is more accurately measured by the number of kernel evaluations. Since the amount of work increases for higher order methods it is not clear a priori whether a higher order method will always yield better results in a shorter time. Figure 11 shows error as a function of kernel evaluations for the same data as that used in Figure 10. The plot for $M = 1$ is translated with respect to all others since we always use at least a two point quadrature rule even if the basis functions are constant. The plot shows that if sufficient accuracy is required higher order basis functions achieve lower error for the same amount of work.

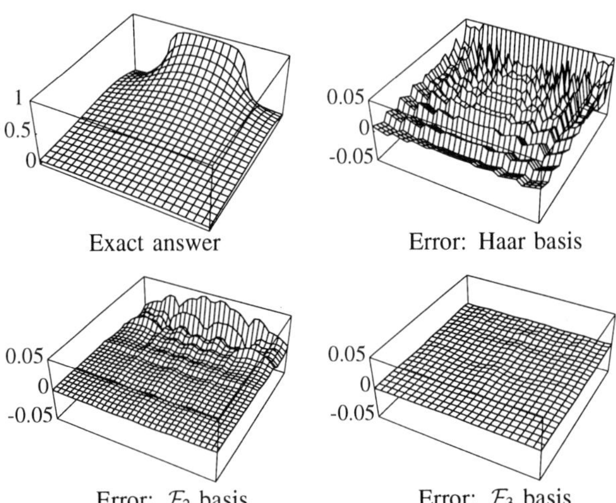

Figure 13: Heightfield error plots for perpendicular emitter and receiver.

Figure 14: Architectural scene computed with the $\mathcal{M}_2$ basis and rendered directly from the basis functions.

We have also examined the behavior of our methods near the singularity of an environment consisting of perpendicular polygons (Figure 12). The emitter was chosen to be half as wide as the receiver to create more variation in the radiosity function. The grid size was set to $\frac{1}{32}$. The upper left plot in Figure 13 shows the exact solution plotted as a height field over the receiver. On the top right is a plot of the difference between exact solution and the computed solution for the Haar basis. On the bottom are similar error surfaces for the $\mathcal{F}_2$ and $\mathcal{F}_3$ bases (left and right respectively). The amount of work was approximately constant (8000 interactions) for all three solutions. The graphs show clearly the lesser and smoother error for the $\mathcal{F}_2$ and $\mathcal{F}_3$ bases demonstrating the effectiveness of bases with more vanishing moments. This is also illustrated by the rendered images in Figure 12.

The algorithm has also been run on a more complex environment (Figure 14). This picture, as well as Figure 12, does not use any postprocessing such as Gouraud shading. Instead the surface brightness is computed directly from the basis functions and associated coefficients.

9 Conclusion and Future Work

In this paper we have presented the basic theory of projections of integral operators into hierarchical bases, and laid out the theoretical foundation of a new set of techniques involving wavelets. With this in hand, we introduced a new set of linear time algorithms we have called *wavelet radiosity*, and shown that the hierarchical radiosity described by Hanrahan et al. was an instance of a first order wavelet approach.

We have introduced a new family of wavelets, dubbed flatlets and also experimented with a second family of wavelets, multiwavelets. Both lead to efficient algorithms. Future work includes examining various wavelet bases which may have better properties than the multiwavelets and flatlets. For example the Coiflet functions of [7, 3] allow for fast one point quadrature methods. The tree wavelets that we implemented do not enforce any kind of continuity at element boundaries, possibly leading to blocky artifacts. Spline wavelets [4] might provide a basis which would alleviate this.

While our initial implementation was limited to quadrilateral polygons there is nothing in the underlying algorithms that prevents the use of any surface whose parameter domain is rectilinear, such as for example bicubic patches. The only change involves the reparameterization (change of variable) in the coupling integrals. It would be very desirable to design bases which work with triangular domains since triangles are a common primitive in meshing algorithms.

There are still fundamental questions that have yet to be addressed. We would like to gain a better understanding of how wavelet expansions interact with the visibility term in the kernel. It is also important to find methods that remain efficient when the environment consists of a large number of small polygons.

Acknowledgements

The research reported here was partially supported by Apple, Silicon Graphics Computer Systems, and the National Science Foundation (CCR 9207966). We would like to thank S. V. Krishnan for his useful comments. We would also like to thank Ju-sung Lee, Jonathan McAllister, and Michael Neufeld for creating the model of the room.

References

[1] ALPERT, B. A Class of Bases in L^2 for the Sparse Representation of Integral Operators. *SIAM Journal on Mathematical Analysis 24*, 1 (Jan 1993).

[2] ALPERT, B., BEYLKIN, G., COIFMAN, R., AND ROKHLIN, V. Wavelet-like Bases for the Fast Solution of Second-kind Integral Equations. *SIAM Journal on Scientific Computing 14*, 1 (Jan 1993).

[3] BEYLKIN, G., COIFMAN, R., AND ROKHLIN, V. Fast Wavelet Transforms and Numerical Algorithms I. *Communications on Pure and Applied Mathematics 44* (1991), 141–183.

[4] CHUI, C. K. *An Introduction to Wavelets*, vol. 1 of *Wavelet Analysis and its Applications*. Academic Press Inc., 1992.

[5] COHEN, M., CHEN, S. E., WALLACE, J. R., AND GREENBERG, D. P. A Progressive Refinement Approach to Fast Radiosity Image Generation. *Computer Graphics 22*, 4 (August 1988), 75–84.

[6] COHEN, M. F., AND GREENBERG, D. P. The Hemi-Cube: A Radiosity Solution for Complex Environments. *Computer Graphics 19*, 3 (July 1985), 31–40.

[7] DAUBECHIES, I. *Ten Lectures on Wavelets*, vol. 61 of *CBMS-NSF Regional Conference Series in Applied Mathematics*. SIAM, 1992.

[8] DELVES, L. M., AND MOHAMED, J. L. *Computational Methods for Integral Equations*. Cambridge University Press, 1985.

[9] GORAL, C. M., TORRANCE, K. E., GREENBERG, D. P., AND BATTAILE, B. Modelling the Interaction of Light between Diffuse Surfaces. *Computer Graphics 18*, 3 (July 1984), 212–222.

[10] GORTLER, S. J., COHEN, M. F., AND SLUSALLEK, P. Radiosity and Relaxation Methods; Progressive Refinement is Southwell Relaxation. Tech. Rep. CS-TR-408-93, Department of Computer Science, Princeton University, February 1993.

[11] HANRAHAN, P., SALZMAN, D., AND AUPPERLE, L. A Rapid Hierarchical Radiosity Algorithm. *Computer Graphics 25*, 4 (July 1991), 197–206.

[12] HECKBERT, P. S. *Simulating Global Illumination Using Adaptive Meshing*. PhD thesis, University of California at Berkeley, January 1991.

[13] HECKBERT, P. S. Radiosity in Flatland. *Computer Graphics Forum 2*, 3 (1992), 181–192.

[14] KAJIYA, J. T. The Rendering Equation. *Computer Graphics 20*, 4 (1986), 143–150.

[15] LISCHINSKI, D., TAMPIERI, F., AND GREENBERG, D. P. A Discontinuity Meshing Algorithm for Accurate Radiosity. *IEEE CG&A 12*, 4 (July 1992).

[16] MALLAT, S. G. A Theory for Multiresolution Signal Decomposition: The Wavelet Representation. *IEEE Transactions on Pattern Analysis and Machine Intelligence 11* (July 1989), 674–693.

[17] PRESS, W., TEUKOLSKI, S., VETTERLING, W., AND FLANNERY, B. *Numerical Recipies in C, The Art of Scientific Computing*, 2 ed. Cambridge University Press, 1992.

[18] SALESIN, D., LISCHINSKI, D., AND DEROSE, T. Reconstructing Illumination Functions with Selected Discontinuities. *Third Eurographics Workshop on Rendering* (1992), 99–112.

[19] SCHRÖDER, P. Numerical Integration for Radiosity in the Presence of Singularities. In *Fourth Eurographics Workshop on Rendering* (1993).

[20] SCHRÖDER, P., GORTLER, S. J., COHEN, M. F., AND HANRAHAN, P. Wavelet Projections For Radiosity. In *Fourth Eurographics Workshop on Rendering* (June 1993).

[21] SCHRÖDER, P., AND HANRAHAN, P. On The Form Factor Between Two Polygons. In *Computer Graphics, Annual Conference Series, 1003* (August 1993), Siggraph.

[22] STOER, J., AND BULIRSCH, R. *Introduction to Numerical Analysis*. Springer Verlag, New York, 1980.

[23] SZELISKI, R. Fast Surface Interpolation Using Hierarchical Basis Functions. *IEEE Trans. PAMI 12*, 6 (June 1990), 513–439.

[24] YSERENTANT, H. On the Multi-level Splitting of Finite Element Spaces. *Numerische Mathematik 49* (1986), 379–412.

[25] ZATZ, H. R. Galerkin Radiosity: A Higher-order Solution Method for Global Illumination. In *Computer Graphics, Annual Conference Series, 1003* (August 1993), Siggraph.

Hierarchical Z-Buffer Visibility

Ned Greene* Michael Kass† Gavin Miller†

Abstract

An ideal visibility algorithm should a) quickly reject most of the hidden geometry in a model and b) exploit the spatial and perhaps temporal coherence of the images being generated. Ray casting with spatial subdivision does well on criterion (a), but poorly on criterion (b). Traditional Z-buffer scan conversion does well on criterion (b), but poorly on criterion (a). Here we present a hierarchical Z-buffer scan-conversion algorithm that does well on both criteria. The method uses two hierarchical data structures, an object-space octree and an image-space Z pyramid, to accelerate scan conversion. The two hierarchical data structures make it possible to reject hidden geometry very rapidly while rendering visible geometry with the speed of scan conversion. For animation, the algorithm is also able to exploit temporal coherence. The method is well suited to models with high depth complexity, achieving orders of magnitude acceleration in some cases compared to ordinary Z-buffer scan conversion.

CR Categories and Subject Descriptors: I.3.7 [Computer Graphics]: Three-Dimensional Graphics and Realism - Hidden line/surface removal; J.6 [Computer-Aided Engineering]: Computer-Aided I.3.1 [Computer Graphics]: Hardware Architecture - Graphics Processors

Additional Key Words and Phrases: Octree, Pyramid, Temporal Coherence, Spatial Coherence, Z Buffer.

1 Introduction

Extremely complex geometric databases offer interesting challenges for visibility algorithms. Consider, for example, an interactive walk-through of a detailed geometric database describing an entire city, complete with vegetation, buildings, furniture inside the buildings and the contents of the furniture. Traditional visibility algorithms running on currently available hardware cannot come close to rendering scenes of this complexity at interactive rates and it will be a long time before faster hardware alone will suffice. In order to get the most out of available hardware, we need faster algorithms that exploit properties of the visibility computation itself.

There are at least three types of coherence inherent in the visibility computation which can be exploited to accelerate a visibility algorithm. The first is object-space coherence: in many cases a single computation can resolve the visibility of a collection of objects which are near each other in space. The second is image-space coherence: in many cases a single computation can resolve the visibility of an object covering a collection of pixels. The third is temporal coherence: visibility information from one frame can often be used to accelerate visibility computation for the next frame. Here we present a visibility algorithm which exploits all three of these types of coherence and sometimes achieves orders of magnitude acceleration compared with traditional techniques.

The dominant algorithms in use today for visibility computations are Z-buffer scan conversion and ray-tracing. Since Z buffers do not handle partially transparent surfaces well, we will restrict the discussion to models consisting entirely of opaque surfaces. For these models, only rays from the eye to the first surface are relevant for visibility, so the choice is between Z buffering and ray-casting (ray-tracing with no secondary rays).

Traditional Z buffering makes reasonably good use of image-space coherence in the course of scan conversion. Implementations usually do a set-up computation for each polygon and then an incremental update for each pixel in the polygon. Since the incremental update is typically much less computation than the set-up, the savings from image-space coherence can be substantial. The problem with the traditional Z-buffer approach is that it makes no use at all of object-space or temporal coherence. Each polygon is rendered independently, and no information is saved from prior frames. For extremely complex environments like a model of a city, this is very inefficient. A traditional Z-buffer algorithm, for example, will have to take the time to render every polygon of every object in every drawer of every desk in a building even if the whole building cannot be seen, because the traditional algorithm can resolve visibility only at the pixel level.

Traditional ray-tracing or ray-casting methods, on the other hand, make use of object-space coherence by organizing the objects in some type of spatial subdivision. Rays from the eye are propagated through the spatial subdivision until they hit the first visible surface. Once a ray hits a visible surface, there is no need to consider any of the surfaces in the spatial subdivisions further down along the ray, so large portions of the geometry may never have to be considered during rendering. This is an important improvement on Z buffering, but it makes no use of temporal or image-space coherence. While ray-casting algorithms that exploit temporal coherence have been explored, it seems extremely difficult to exploit image-space coherence in traditional ray casting algorithms.

Here we present a visibility algorithm which combines the strengths of both ray-casting and Z buffering. To exploit object-

*Apple Computer, U.C. Santa Cruz

†Apple Computer

space coherence, we use an octree spatial subdivision of the type commonly used to accelerate ray tracing. To exploit image-space coherence, we augment traditional Z-buffer scan conversion with an image-space Z pyramid that allows us to reject hidden geometry very quickly. Finally, to exploit temporal coherence, we use the geometry that was visible in the previous frame to construct a starting point for the algorithm. The result is an algorithm which is orders of magnitude faster than traditional ray-casting or Z buffering for some models we have tried. The algorithm is not difficult to implement and works for arbitrary polygonal databases.

In section II, we survey the most relevant prior work on accelerating ray casting and scan conversion. In section III, we develop the data structures used to exploit object-space, image-space and temporal coherence. In section IV, we describe the implementation and show results for some complex models containing hundreds of millions of polygons.

2 Prior Work

There have been many attempts to accelerate traditional ray-tracing and Z buffering techniques. Each of these attempts exploits some aspect of the coherence inherent in the visibility computation itself. None of them, however, simultaneously exploits object-space, image-space and temporal coherence.

The ray-tracing literature abounds with references to object-space coherence. A variety of spatial subdivisions have been used to exploit this coherence and they seem to work quite well (e.g. [1, 2, 3, 4, 5]). Temporal coherence is much less commonly exploited in practice, but various techniques exist for special cases. If all the objects are convex and remain stationary while the camera moves, then there are constraints on the way visibility can change[6] which a ray tracer might exploit. On the other hand, if the camera is stationary, then rays which are unaffected by the motion of objects can be detected and used from the previous frame[7]. When interactivity is not an issue and sufficient memory is available, it can be feasible to render an entire animation sequence at once using spacetime bounding boxes[8, 9]. While these techniques make good use of object-space coherence and sometimes exploit temporal coherence effectively, they unfortunately make little or no use of image-space coherence since each pixel is traced independently from its neighbors. There are heuristic methods which construct estimates of the results of ray-tracing a pixel from the results at nearby pixels (e.g. [10]), but there seems to be no guaranteed algorithm which makes good use of image-space coherence in ray tracing.

With Z-buffer methods (and scan conversion methods in general) the problems are very different. Ordinary Z-buffer rendering is usually implemented with an initial set-up computation for each primitive followed by a scan-conversion phase in which the affected pixels are incrementally updated. This already makes very good use of image-space coherence, so the remaining challenge with Z-buffer methods is to exploit object-space and temporal coherence effectively.

A simple method of using object-space coherence in Z-buffer rendering is to use a spatial subdivision to cull the model to the viewing frustum [11]. While this can provide substantial acceleration, it exploits only a small portion of the object-space coherence in models with high depth complexity. In architectural models, for example, a great deal of geometry hidden behind walls may lie within the viewing frustum.

In order to make use of more of the object-space coherence in architectural models, Airey et. al. [12, 13] and subsequently Teller and Sequin[15] proposed dividing models up into a set of disjoint cells and precomputing the potentially visible set (PVS) of polygons from each cell. In order to render an image from any viewpoint within a cell, only the polygons in the PVS need be considered. These PVS schemes are the closest in spirit to the visibility algorithm presented here since they attempt to make good use of both object-space and image-space coherence. Nonetheless, they suffer from some important limitations. Before they can be used at all, they require an expensive precomputation step to determine the PVS and a great deal of memory to store it. Teller and Sequin, for example, report over 6 hours of precomputation time on a 50 MIP machine to calculate 58Mb of PVS data needed for a model of 250,000 polygons[15]. Perhaps more importantly, the way these methods make use of cells may limit their appropriateness to architectural models. In order to achieve maximum acceleration, the cells must be 3D regions of space which are almost entirely enclosed by occluding surfaces, so that most cells are hidden from most other cells. For architectural models, this often works well since the cells can be rooms, but for outdoor scenes and more general settings, it is unclear whether or not PVS methods are effective. In addition, the currently implemented algorithms make very special use of axially-aligned polygons such as flat walls in rectilinear architectural models. While the methods can in principle be extended to use general 3D polygons for occlusion, the necessary algorithms have much worse computational complexity[15]. Finally, although the implementations prefetch PVS data for nearby cells to avoid long latencies due to paging, they cannot be said to exploit temporal coherence in the visibility computation very effectively.

The algorithm presented here shares a great deal with the work of Meagher[16] who used object-space octrees with image-space quadtrees for rendering purposes. Meagher tried to display the octree itself rather than using it to cull a polygonal database, so his method is directly applicable to volume, rather than surface models. Nonetheless his algorithm is one of the few to make use of both object-space and image-space coherence. The algorithm does not exploit temporal coherence.

3 Hierarchical Visibility

The hierarchical Z-buffer visibility algorithm uses an octree spatial subdivision to exploit object-space coherence, a Z pyramid to exploit image-space coherence, and a list of previously visible octree nodes to exploit temporal coherence. While the full value of the algorithm is achieved by using all three of these together, the object-space octree and the image-space Z pyramid can also be used separately. Whether used separately or together, these data structures make it possible to compute the same result as ordinary Z buffering at less computational expense.

3.1 Object-space octree

Octrees have been used previously to accelerate ray tracing[5] and rendering of volume data sets[16] with great effectiveness. With some important modification, many of the principles of these previous efforts can be applied to Z-buffer scan conversion. The result is an algorithm which can accelerate Z buffering by orders of magnitude for models with sufficient depth complexity.

In order to be precise about the octree algorithm, let us begin with some simple definitions. We will say that a polygon is hidden with respect to a Z buffer if no pixel of the polygon is closer to the observer than the Z value already in the Z buffer. Similarly, we will say that a cube is hidden with respect to a Z buffer if all of its faces are hidden polygons. Finally, we will call a node of the octree hidden if its associated cube is hidden. Note that these definitions depend on the sampling of the Z buffer. A polygon which is hidden at one Z-buffer resolution may not be hidden at another.

With these definitions, we can state the basic observation that makes it possible to combine Z buffering with an octree spatial subdivision: If a cube is hidden with respect to a Z buffer, then all polygons fully contained in the cube are also hidden. What this means is the following: if we scan convert the faces of an octree cube and find that each pixel of the cube is behind the current surface in the Z buffer, we can safely ignore all the geometry contained in that cube.

From this observation, the basic algorithm is easy to construct. We begin by placing the geometry into an octree, associating each primitive with the smallest enclosing octree cube. Then we start at the root node of the octree and render it using the following recursive steps: First, we check to see if the octree cube intersects the viewing frustum. If not, we are done. If the cube does intersect the viewing frustum, we scan convert the faces of the cube to determine whether or not the whole cube is hidden. If the cube is hidden, we are done. Otherwise, we scan convert any geometry associated with the cube and then recursively render its children in front-to-back order.

We can construct the octree with a simple recursive procedure. Beginning with a root cube large enough to enclose the entire model and the complete list of geometric primitives, we recursively perform the following steps: If the number of primitives is sufficiently small, we associate all of the primitives with the cube and exit. Otherwise, we associate with the cube any primitive which intersects at least one of three axis-aligned planes that bisect the cube. We then subdivide the octree cube and call the procedure recursively with each of the eight child cubes and the portion of the geometry that fits entirely in that cube.

The basic rendering algorithm has some very interesting properties. First of all, it only renders geometry contained in octree nodes which are not hidden. Some of the rendered polygons may be hidden, but all of them are "nearly visible" in the following sense: there is some place we could move the polygon where it would be visible which is no further away than the length of the diagonal of its containing octree cube. This is a big improvement over merely culling to the viewing frustum. In addition, the algorithm does not waste time on irrelevant portions of the octree since it only visits octree nodes whose parents are not hidden. Finally, the algorithm never visits an octree node more than once during rendering. This stands in marked contrast to ray-tracing through an octree where the root node is visited by every pixel and other nodes may be visited tens of thousands of times. As a result of these properties, the basic algorithm culls hidden geometry very efficiently.

A weakness of the basic algorithm is that it associates some small geometric primitives with very large cubes if the primitives happen to intersect the planes which separate the cube's children. A small triangle which crosses the center of the root cube, for example, will have to be rendered anytime the entire model is not hidden. To avoid this behavior, there are two basic choices. One alternative is to clip the problematic small polygons so they fit in much smaller octree cells. This has the disadvantage of increasing the number of primitives in the database. The other alternative is to place some primitives in multiple octree cells. This is the one we have chosen to implement. To do this, we modify the recursive construction of the octree as follows. If we find that a primitive intersects a cube's dividing planes, but is small compared to the cube, then we no longer associate the primitive with the whole cube. Instead we associate it with all of the cube's children that the primitive intersects. Since some primitives are associated with more than one octree node, we can encounter them more than once during rendering. The first time we render them, we mark them as rendered, so we can avoid rendering them more than once in a given frame.

3.2 Image-space Z pyramid

The object-space octree allows us to cull large portions of the model at the cost of scan-converting the faces of the octree cubes. Since the cubes may occupy a large number of pixels in the image, this scan conversion can be very expensive. To reduce the cost of determining cube visibility, we use an image-space Z pyramid. In many cases, the Z pyramid makes it possible to conclude very quickly a large polygon is hidden, making it unnecessary to examine the polygon pixel by pixel.

The basic idea of the Z pyramid is to use the original Z buffer as the finest level in the pyramid and then combine four Z values at each level into one Z value at the next coarser level by choosing the farthest Z from the observer. Every entry in the pyramid therefore represents the farthest Z for a square area of the Z buffer. At the coarsest level of the pyramid there is a single Z value which is the farthest Z from the observer in the whole image.

Maintaining the Z pyramid is an easy matter. Every time we modify the Z buffer, we propagate the new Z value through to coarser levels of the pyramid. As soon as we reach a level where the entry in the pyramid is already as far away as the new Z value, we can stop.

In order to use the Z pyramid to test the visibility of a polygon, we find the finest-level sample of the pyramid whose corresponding image region covers the screen-space bounding box of the polygon. If the nearest Z value of the polygon is farther away than this sample in the Z pyramid, we know immediately that the polygon is hidden. We use this basic test to determine the visibility of octree cubes by testing their polygonal faces, and also to test the visibility of model polygons.

While the basic Z-pyramid test can reject a substantial number of polygons, it suffers from a similar difficulty to the basic octree method. Because of the structure of the pyramid regions, a small polygon covering the center of the image will be compared to the Z value at the coarsest level of the pyramid. While the test is still accurate in this case, it is not particularly powerful.

A definitive visibility test can be constructed by applying the basic test recursively through the pyramid. When the basic test fails to show that a polygon is hidden, we go to the next finer level in the pyramid where the previous pyramid region is divided into four quadrants. Here we attempt to prove that the polygon is hidden in each of the quadrants it intersects. For each of these quadrants, we compare the closest Z value of the polygon in the quadrant to the value in the Z pyramid. If the Z-pyramid value is closer, we know the polygon is hidden in the quadrant. If we fail to prove that the primitive is hidden in one of the quadrants, we go to the next finer level of the pyramid for that quadrant and try again. Ultimately, we either prove that the entire polygon is hidden, or we recurse down to the finest level of the pyramid and find a visible pixel. If we find all visible pixels this way, we are performing scan conversion hierarchically.

A potential difficulty with the definitive visibility test is that it can be expensive to compute the closest Z value of the polygon in a quadrant. An alternative is to compare the value in the pyramid to the closest Z value of the entire polygon at each step of the recursion. With this modification, the test is faster and easier to implement, but no longer completely definitive. Ultimately, it will either prove that the entire polygon is hidden, or recurse down to the finest level of the pyramid and find a pixel it cannot prove is hidden. Our current implementation uses this technique. When the test fails to prove that a polygon is hidden, our implementation reverts to ordinary scan conversion to establish the visibility definitively.

3.3 Temporal coherence list

Frequently, when we render an image of a complex model using the object-space octree, only a small fraction of the octree cubes are visible. If we render the next frame in an animation, most of the cubes visible in the previous frame will probably still be visible. Some of the cubes visible in the last frame will become hidden and some cubes hidden in the last frame will become visible, but frame-to-frame coherence in most animations ensures that there will be relatively few changes in cube visibility for most frames (except scene changes and camera cuts). We exploit this fact in a very simple way with the hierarchical visibility algorithm. We maintain a list of the visible cubes from the previous frame, the *temporal coherence list*, and simply render all of the geometry on the list, marking the listed cubes as rendered, before commencing the usual algorithm. We then take the resulting Z buffer and use it to form the initial Z pyramid. If there is sufficient frame-to-frame coherence, most of the visible geometry will already be rendered, so the Z-pyramid test will be much more effective than when we start from scratch. The Z-pyramid test will be able to prove with less recursion that octree cubes and model polygons are hidden. As we will see in section IV, this can accelerate the rendering process substantially. After rendering the new frame, we update the temporal coherence list by checking each of the cubes on the list for visibility using the Z-pyramid test. This prevents the temporal coherence list from growing too large over time.

One way of thinking about the temporal coherence strategy is that we begin by guessing the final solution. If our guess is very close to the actual solution, the hierarchical visibility algorithm can use the Z pyramid to verify the portions of the guess which are correct much faster than it can construct them from scratch. Only the portions of the image that it cannot verify as being correct require further processing.

4 Implementation and Results

Our initial implementation of the hierarchical visibility algorithm is based on general purpose, portable C code and software scan conversion. This implementation uses the object-space octree, the image-space Z pyramid and the temporal coherence list. Even for relatively simple models the pure software algorithm is faster than traditional software Z buffering, and for complex models the acceleration can be very large.

In order to test the algorithm, we constructed an office module consisting of 15K polygons and then replicated the module in a three dimensional grid. Each module includes a stairway with a large open stairwell making it possible to see parts of the neighboring floors. None of the office walls extends to the ceiling, so from a high enough point in any of the cubicles, it is possible to see parts of most of the other cubicles on the same floor.

For simple models with low depth complexity, the hierarchical visibility method can be expected to take somewhat longer than traditional scan conversion due to the overhead of performing visibility tests on octree cubes and the cost of maintaining a Z pyramid. To measure the algorithm's overhead on simple models, we rendered a single office module consisting of 15K polygons at a viewpoint from which a high proportion of the model was visible. Rendering time for a 512 by 512 image was 1.52 seconds with the hierarchical visibility method and 1.30 seconds with traditional scan conversion, indicating a performance penalty of 17%. When we rendered three instances of the model (45K polygons), the running time was 3.05 seconds for both methods indicating that this level of complexity was the breakeven point for this particular model. Hierarchical visibility rendered nine instances of the same model (105K polygons) in 5.17 seconds, while traditional scan conversion took 7.16 seconds.

The chief value of the hierarchical visibility algorithm is, of course, for scenes of much higher complexity. To illustrate the point, we constructed a 33 by 33 by 33 replication of the office module which consists of 538 million polygons. The model is shown rendered in figure 1. 59.7 million polygons lie in the viewing frustum from this viewpoint, about one tenth of the entire model. Using the hierarchical visibility method, the Z-pyramid test was invoked on 1746 octree cubes and culled about 27% of the polygons in the viewing frustum. The bounding boxes of 687 cubes were scan converted which culled nearly 73% of the model polygons in the viewing frustum, leaving only 83.0K polygons of which 41.2K were front facing (.000076 of the total model) to be scan converted in software. On an SGI Crimson Elan, the entire process took 6.45 seconds. Rendering this model using traditional Z buffering on the Crimson Elan hardware took approximately one hour and fifteen minutes. Rendering it in software on the Crimson would probably take days.

The center left panel of figure 1 shows the depth complexity processed by the algorithm for the image in the upper left. The depth complexity displayed in this image is the number of times each pixel was accessed in a box visibility test or in Z-buffer polygon scan conversion. Note the bright regions corresponding to portions of the image where it is possible to see far into the model; these are regions where the algorithm has to do the most work. In this image, the average depth complexity due to box scans is 7.23, and due to polygon scan-conversion is 2.48 for a total of 9.71. The maximum depth complexity is 124. Dividing the number of times the Z pyramid is accessed by the number of pixels on the screen lets us assign a value of .43 for the "depth complexity" of the Z-pyramid tests. Thus, the total average depth complexity of Z-pyramid tests, box scans and polygon scans is 10.14. Note that this is not the depth complexity of the model itself, but only the depth complexity of the hierarchical visibility computation. Computing the true depth complexity of the scene would require scan converting the entire model of 538 million polygons in software, which we have not done. In the lower left of figure 1, we show the viewing frustum and the octree subdivision. The two long strings of finely divided boxes correspond to the two brightest regions in the depth complexity image. Note that the algorithm is able to prove that large octree nodes in the distance are hidden. In the lower right, we show the Z pyramid for the scene. Even at fairly coarse resolutions, the Z pyramid contains a recognizeable representation of the major occluders in the scene.

The office environment of figure 1 was chosen in part because it is a particularly difficult model for PVS methods. From every office cubicle in this environment, there are points from which almost every other cubicle on the same floor is visible. As a result, if the cubicles were used as cells in a PVS method, the potentially visible set for each cell would have to include nearly all the cells on its floor and many on other floors. Since each floor contains about 4 million polygons, the PVS methods would probably have to render many more polygons than the hierarchical method. In addition, the precomputation time for published PVS methods would be prohibitive for a model of this complexity. This model has 2000 times as many polygons as the model described by Teller and Sequin[15] which required 6 hours of pre-processing.

Admittedly, the replication of a single cell in the model means that it may not be a representative example, but it will be some time before people use models of this complexity without a great deal of instancing. The hierarchical visibility program we used for this example makes use of the replication in only two ways. First, the algorithm does not need to store half a billion polygons in main memory. Second, the algorithm only needs to consider a single cell in constructing the octree. These same simplifications would

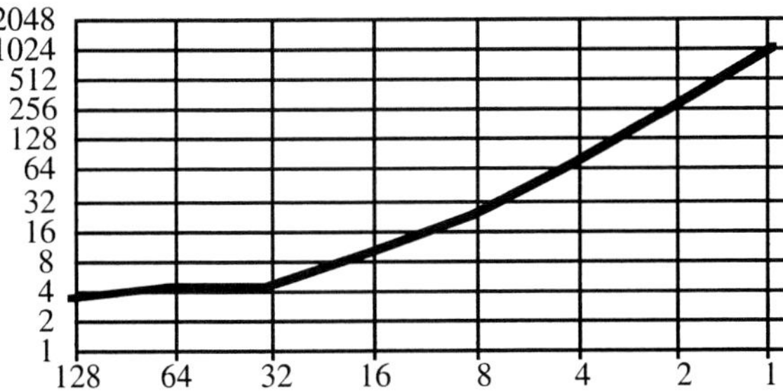

Fig. 3: Total time in seconds to render all windows as a function of the number of pixels on the side of each window.

apply to any complex model using a great deal of instancing.

Figure 2 shows the hierarchical visibility method applied to an outdoor scene consisting of a terrain mesh with vegetation replicated on a two-dimensional grid. The model used for the lower left image consists of 53 million polygons, but only about 25K polygons are visible from this point of view. Most of the model is hidden by the hill or is outside the viewing frustum. The corresponding depth complexity image for hierarchical visibility computations is shown at the top left. The algorithm works hardest near the horizon where cube visibility is most difficult to establish. This frame took 7 seconds to render with software scan conversion on an SGI Crimson. In the lower right, we show a model consisting of 5 million polygons. Even though the model is simpler than the model in the lower left, the image is more complicated and took longer to render because a much larger fraction of the model is visible from this point of view. This image took 40 seconds to render with software scan conversion on an SGI Crimson. The average depth complexity for the scene is 7.27, but it reaches a peak of 85 in the bright areas of the depth complexity image in the upper right. These outdoor scenes have very different characteristics from the building interiors shown in figure 1 and are poorly suited to PVS methods because (a) very few of the polygons are axis-aligned and (b) the cell-to-cell visibility is not nearly as limited as in an architectural interior. Nonetheless, the hierarchical visibility algorithm continues to work effectively.

4.1 Parallelizability and Image-space coherence

We have made our hierarchical visibility implementation capable of dividing the image into a grid of smaller windows, rendering them individually and compositing them into a final image. The performance of the algorithm as the window size is varied tells us about the parallel performance of the algorithm and the extent to which it makes use of image-space coherence. If, like most ray tracers, the algorithm made no use of image-space coherence, we could render each pixel separately at no extra cost. Then it would be fully parallelizable. At the other extreme, if the algorithm made the best possible use of image-space coherence, it would render a sizeable region of pixels with only a small amount more computation than required to render a single pixel. Then it would be difficult to parallelize. Note that if we shrink the window size down to a single pixel, the hierarchical visibility algorithm becomes a ray caster using an octree subdivision.

Figure 3 graphs the rendering time for a frame from a walk-through of the model shown in figure 1 as a function of the window size. For window sizes from 32 by 32 on up, the curve is relatively flat, indicating that the algorithm should parallelize fairly well. For window sizes below 32 by 32, however, the slope of the curve indicates that the time to render a window is almost independent of the window size. The algorithm can, for example, render a 32 by 32 region for only slightly more than four times the computational expense of ray-casting a single pixel with this algorithm. Comparing the single pixel window time to the time for the whole image, we find that image-space coherence is responsible for a factor of almost 300 in running time for this example.

4.2 Use of graphics hardware

In addition to the pure software implementation, we have attempted to modify the algorithm to make the best possible use of available commercial hardware graphics accelerators. This raises some difficult challenges because the hierarchical visibility algorithm makes slightly different demands of scan-conversion hardware than traditional Z buffering. In particular, the use of octree object-space coherence depends on being able to determine quickly whether any pixel of a polygon would be visible if it were scan converted. Unfortunately, the commercial hardware graphics pipelines we have examined are either unable to answer this query at all, or take milliseconds to answer it. One would certainly expect some delay in getting information back from a graphics pipeline, but hardware designed with this type of query in mind should be able to return a result in microseconds rather than milliseconds.

We have implemented the object-space octree on a Kubota Pacific Titan 3000 workstation with Denali GB graphics hardware. The Denali supports an unusual graphics library call which determines whether or not any pixels in a set of polygons are visible given the current Z buffer. We use this "Z query" feature to determine the visibility of octree cubes. The cost of a Z query depends on the screen size of the cube, and it can take up to several milliseconds to determine whether or not a cube is visible. Our implementation makes no use of the Z pyramid because the cost of getting the required data to and from the Z buffer would exceed any possible savings. On a walk-through of a version of the office model with 1.9 million polygons, the Titan took an average of .54 seconds per frame to render 512 by 512 images. Because of the cost of doing the Z query, we only tested visibility of octree cubes containing at least eight hundred polygons. Even so, 36.5% of the running time was taken up by Z queries. If Z query were faster, we could use it effectively on octree cubes containing many fewer polygons and achieve substantial further acceleration. The Titan implementation has not been fully optimized for the Denali hardware and makes no use of temporal coherence, so these performance figures should be considered only suggestive of the machine's capabilities.

The other implementation we have that makes use of graphics hardware runs on SGI workstations. On these workstations, there is no way to inquire whether or not a polygon is visible without rendering it, so we use a hybrid hardware/software strategy. We do the first frame of a sequence entirely with software. On the second frame, we render everything on the temporal coherence list with the hardware pipeline. Then we read the image and the Z buffer from the hardware, form a Z pyramid and continue on in software. With this implementation, on the models we have tried, temporal coherence typically reduces the running time by a factor of between 1.5 and 2.

In the course of a walk-through of our office model, we rendered the frame in the upper left of figure 1 without temporal coherence, and then the next frame shown in the upper right of figure 1 using temporal coherence. The new polygons rendered in software are shown in magenta for illustration. For the most part, these are polygons that came into view as a result of panning the camera. The center right shows the depth complexity of the hierarchical computation for this frame. The image is much darker in most regions because the algorithm has much less work to do given the previous frame as a starting point. This temporal coherence frame took 3.96 seconds to render on a Crimson Elan, as compared with 6.45 seconds to render the same frame without temporal coherence.

Current graphics accelerators are not designed to support the rapid feedback from the pipeline needed to realize the full potential of octree culling in the hierarchical visibility algorithm. Hardware designed to take full advantage of the algorithm, however, could make it possible to interact very effectively with extremely complex environments as long as only a manageable number of the polygons are visible from any point of view. The octree subdivision, the Z pyramid and the temporal coherence strategy are all suitable for hardware implementation.

5 Conclusion

As more and more complex models become commonplace in computer graphics, it becomes increasingly important to exploit the available coherence in the visibility computation. Here we present an algorithm which combines the ability to profit from image-space coherence of Z-buffer scan conversion with the ability of ray tracing to avoid considering hidden geometry. It appears to be the first practical algorithm which materially profits from object-space, image-space and temporal coherence simultaneously. The algorithm has been tested and shown to work effectively on indoor and outdoor scenes with up to half a billion polygons.

The hierarchical visibility algorithm can make use of existing graphics accelerators without modification. Small changes in the design of graphics accelerators, however, would make a large difference in the performance of the algorithm. We hope that the appeal of this algorithm will induce hardware designers to alter future graphics hardware to facilitate hierarchical visibility computations.

Acknowledgements

We thank Frank Crow and the Advanced Technology Group at Apple Computer for supporting this research. We also thank Mike Toelle, Avi Bleiweiss, Helga Thorvaldsdottir and Mike Keller of Kubota Pacific Corporation for helping us test our algorithm on a Titan workstation.

References

[1] S. M. Rubin and T. Whitted. A 3-dimensional representation for fast rendering of complex scenes. *Computer Graphics*, 14(3):110–116, July 1980.

[2] A. Glassner. Space subdivision for fast ray tracing. *IEEE CG&A*, 4(10):15–22, Oct. 1984.

[3] D. Jevans and B. Wyvill. Adaptive voxel subdivision for ray tracing. *Proc. Graphics Interface '89*, 164–172, June 1989.

[4] T. Kay and J. Kajiya. Ray tracing complex surfaces. *Computer Graphics*, 20(4):269–278, Aug. 1986.

[5] M. Kaplan. The use of spatial coherence in ray tracing. In *Techniques for Computer Graphics, etc.*, D. Rogers and R. A. Earnshaw, Springer-Verlag, New York, 1987.

[6] H. Hubschman and S. W. Zucker. Frame to frame coherence and the hidden surface computation: constraints for a convex world. *ACM TOG*, 1(2):129–162, April 1982.

[7] D. Jevans. Object space temporal coherence for ray tracing. *Proc. Graphics Interface '92*, Vancouver, B.C., 176–183, May 11-15, 1992.

[8] A. Glassner. Spacetime ray tracing for animation. *IEEE CG&A*, 8(3):60–70, March 1988.

[9] J. Chapman, T. W. Calvert, and J. Dill. Spatio-temporal coherence in ray tracing. *Proceedings of Graphics Interface '90*, 196–204, 1990.

[10] S. Badt, Jr. Two algorithms for taking advantage of temporal coherence in ray tracing *The Visual Computer*, 4:123–132, 1988.

[11] B. Garlick, D. Baum, and J. Winget. Interactive viewing of large geometric databases using multiprocessor graphics workstations. *SIGGRAPH '90 Course Notes: Parallel Algorithms and Architectures for 3D Image Generation*, 1990.

[12] J. Airey. Increasing update rates in the building walkthrough system with automatic model-space subdivision. Technical Report TR90-027, The University of North Carolina at Chapel Hill, Department of Computer Science, 1990.

[13] J. Airey, J. Rohlf, and F. Brooks. Towards image realism with interactive update rates in complex virtual building environments. *ACM SIGGRAPH Special Issue on 1990 Symposium on Interactive 3D Graphics*, 24(2):41–50, 1990.

[14] S. Teller and C. Sequin. Visibility preprocessing for interactive walkthroughs. *Computer Graphics*, 25(4):61–69, 1991.

[15] S. Teller and C. Sequin. Visibility computations in polyhedral three-dimensional environments. U.C. Berkeley Report No. UCB/CSD 92/680, April 1992.

[16] D. Meagher. Efficient synthetic image generation of arbitrary 3-D objects. *Proc. IEEE Conf. on Pattern Recognition and Image Processing*, 473–478, June 1982.

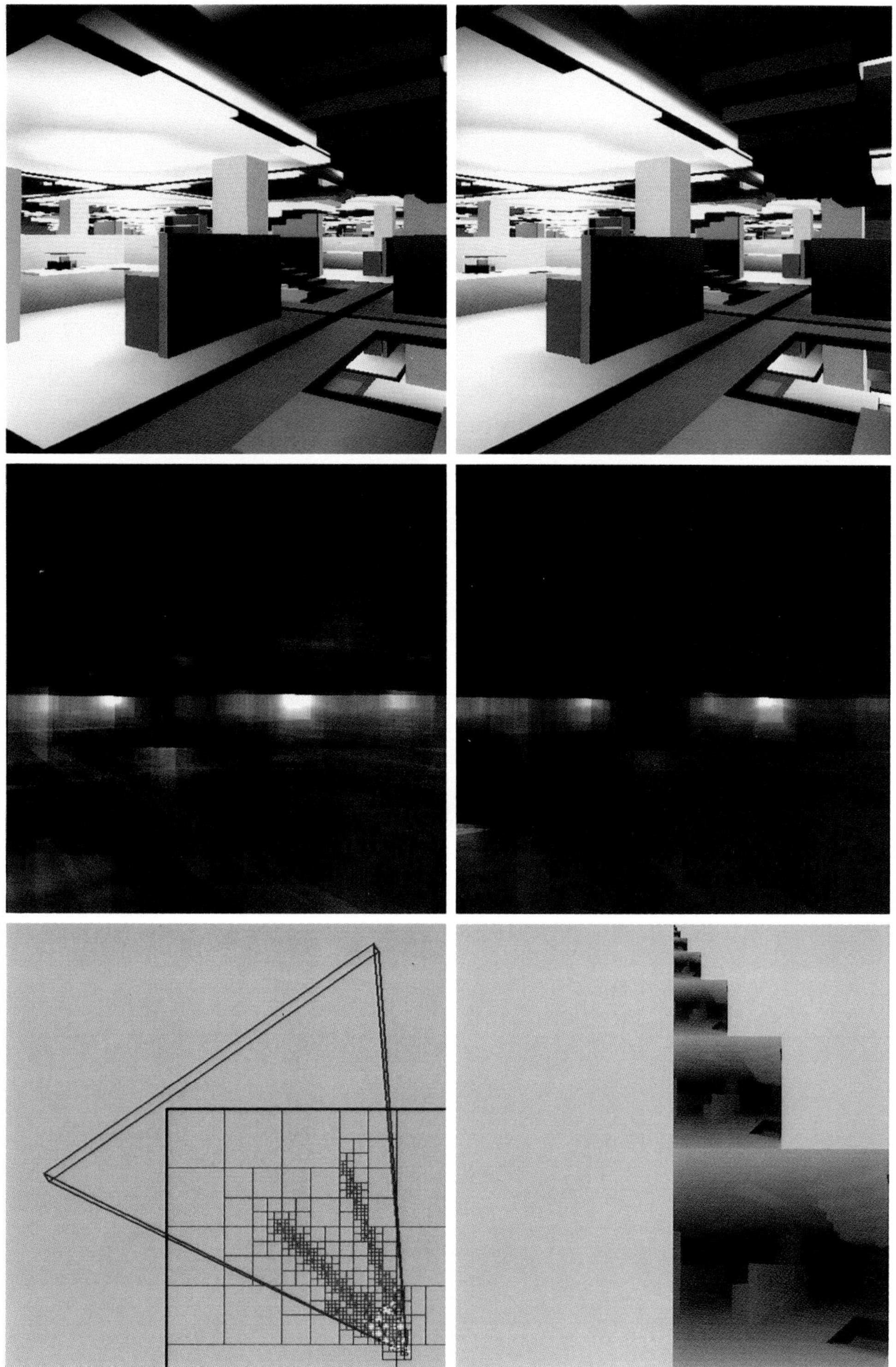

Figure 1: A 538 million polygon office environment rendered with hierarchical visibility. Upper left: Rendered image. Center left: Depth complexity of the hierarchical visibility computation. Lower Left: Viewing frustum and octree cubes examined while rendering the image in the upper left. Lower right: Z pyramid used to cull hidden geometry. Upper right: Image rendered with temporal coherence. Polygons not rendered in the previous frame are shown in magenta. Center right: Depth complexity of the hierarchical visibility computation for the frame rendered using temporal coherence.

Figure 2: Lower left: Image of a 53 million polygon model (mostly hidden) rendered using hierarchical visibility. Upper left: Corresponding depth complexity for the hierarchical visibility computation. Lower right: Image of a 5 million polygon model. Upper right: Corresponding depth complexity for the hierarchical visibility computation.

Global Visibility Algorithms for Illumination Computations

Seth Teller
Institute of Computer Science
Hebrew University of Jerusalem

Pat Hanrahan
Department of Computer Science
Princeton University

Abstract

The most expensive geometric operation in image synthesis is visibility determination. Classically this is solved with hidden surface removal algorithms that render only the parts of the scene visible from a point. Global illumination calculations, however, may require information between any two points in the scene. This paper describes global visibility algorithms that preprocess polygon databases in order to accelerate visibility determination during illumination calculations. These algorithms are sensitive to the output complexity in visibility space; that is, how many pairs of objects are mutually visible. Furthermore, the algorithms are incremental so that they work well with progressive refinement and hierarchical methods of image synthesis. The algorithms are conservative, but exact; that is, when they return visibility predicates they can be proved true. However sometimes they do not return either totally visible or totally invisible, but partially visible, even though in the same situation a better algorithm might return the exact answer. In this paper we describe the algorithms and their implementation, and show that, in a scene with low average visual complexity, they can dramatically accelerate conventional radiosity programs.

CR Categories and Subject Descriptors: I.3.5 [Computational Geometry and Object Modeling]: *Geometric Algorithms, Languages, and Systems*; I.3.7 [Computer Graphics]: *Three-Dimensional Graphics and Realism — Radiosity*; J.2 [Physical Sciences and Engineering]: *Engineering*.

Additional Key Words: Hidden surface removal, visibility space, radiosity, global illumination, algorithmic triage.

1 Introduction

In the early days of image synthesis a central geometric problem was hidden surface removal. With the advent of z-buffering, modern workstations can display pictures of 3D scenes containing millions of polygons in real-time. However, such workstations have limited shading capabilities because they make the assumption that all light sources illuminate every object. One major thrust of current research in image synthesis is to remove this restriction so that the shading correctly accounts for the illumination incident on every object. To do this every surface element must assess what light sources, or more generally, what surfaces reflecting light towards it, are visible to it. This type of illumination calculation is termed global, in contrast to local, because the entire scene must be analyzed to determine if there are any occluders interfering with the transfer of light between objects. Collating such visibility information is more difficult than determining merely what is visible from a single vantage point, as is done in hidden surface removal. For example, the fastest algorithm currently known for computing a complete description of the interocclusion due to a polyhedral object of n vertices can take $O(n^6 \lg n)$ time [9].

This paper describes global visibility algorithms that analyze the entire visibility space, and are applicable to a range of illumination problems. Here, we apply them to a hierarchical radiosity algorithm. We have implemented several practical algorithms, and show that they allow efficient global visibility calculations for scenes of low visual complexity. The algorithms are based on three simple ideas:

Visibility preprocessing. To compute what is visible from all points on the surfaces of the objects being shaded, we preprocess the scene to speed future visibility tests. For the purposes of global illumination we need only consider all pairwise interactions between objects. Preprocessing removes totally invisible pairs from consideration, and accelerates later queries regarding visibility between points on partially visible pairs.

Incremental visibility maintenance. The most efficient global illumination algorithms operate iteratively based on error criteria. Examples are hierarchical radiosity, where surfaces are subdivided with respect to each other according to potential light transfers between them [11], and progressive refinement methods where light is transferred among surfaces in order of brightness [5]. Thus, the visibility algorithms should be lazy and sensitive to required precision. They should also allow refinement so that more precise determinations can be made as needed.

Conservative triage. Both the preprocessing and maintenance methods use conservative triage to avoid the combinatorial complexity of exact visibility determination. We classify visibility into three categories: totally INVISIBLE, totally VISIBLE, and PARTIAL (partially visible). The classification is conservative in that all interactions classified as INVISIBLE or VISIBLE are correct; however, it is acceptable for the classification to return PARTIAL when the correct result is either VISIBLE or INVISIBLE. This allows us to forego complex analysis or "punt" if such analysis will take too long to determine the exact answer. Of course, for this to work we need either another visibility algorithm to complete the analysis, or we must expect the situation to simplify eventually (e.g., through subdivision).

The visibility algorithms presented here generalize previous work on preprocessing environments for interactive walkthroughs. In [24], an algorithm was given to preprocess a 2D environment of axial line segments, such as floorplans. This was extended to 3D axial rectangles in [22]. This paper treats the case of convex polygons in general position.

The global visibility algorithms described here have been implemented with a global illumination system that computes radiosity values for polygonal scenes [11]. The algorithm maintains a hierarchy of interactions between subdivided polygons at different levels of detail. A key feature of the algorithm is that only $O(k^2 + n)$ interactions are ever examined (with k the number of input polygons, and n the number of elements created by subdividing those polygons). The hierarchical radiosity algorithm, as originally designed, used pairwise visibility information between polygons. In the original implementation, however, this visibility information was *inexact*. Visibility status was determined by shooting a constant number of rays between two polygons. If all of the rays reached from one polygon to the other, the polygons were considered totally visible, whereas if none of the rays reached, the polygons were considered totally invisible. The conservative algorithms described in this paper, in contrast, are provably more precise.

2 Overview

We present novel algorithms that subdivide space, construct a *conservative visibility graph* over the polygons in a geometric model, then maintain the correctness of the graph under recursive subdivision of the polygons. In the context of the hierarchical radiosity computation, this conservative visibility graph guarantees that throughout the computation, all polygons that potentially interact (e.g., exchange energy) will be known. The construction and maintenance of the graph occurs in four stages.

1. Spatial Subdivision. The geometric model is first *spatially subdivided* into convex polyhedral cells, linked across shared boundaries only when some *portal*, or transparent region, exists on the boundary. For a large class of models, and particularly for architectural models, the subdivision proves a natural way of hierarchically capturing the geometric and occlusive characteristics of the model.

2. Visibility Propagation. Each cell of the spatial subdivision encloses some portion of the geometric model. Clearly, only when two *cells* are mutually visible can their contents (i.e., model polygons) interact. Consequently, we hierarchically enumerate all visibility between portions of the model by first establishing *inter-cell* visibility, then establishing *inter-polygon* visibility only where cells are mutually visible. This is accomplished by *propagating* incremental visibility information through the cells of the spatial subdivision; as each cell "sees" into increasingly distant cells, the visibility graph is augmented to record any previously unknown interactions. (Portal enumeration is simply the first and crudest record of visibility propagation.)

Visibility propagation provably discovers all partially or totally visible cell (polygon) pairs, at the cost of occasionally misclassifying an invisible cell (polygon) pair as visible. The alternative, misclassification of some mutually visible interaction as invisible, is plainly unacceptable, since it may omit from consideration an interaction later to prove important.

3. Blocker Detection. In an exacting illumination computation such as global illumination, it is not sufficient to determine simply that two polygons are partially visible; some estimation must be made of the extent to which they are visible, as well as how much error might be incurred by the estimation. Therefore, once potential visibility between a pair of polygons is established, a set of *interfering polygons* or *blockers* is determined that may occlude part of one polygon as seen from some point on the other. This interference computation is again *conservative*; a non-interfering polygon may occasionally be classified as a blocker, but a blocker will *never* be classified as non-interfering. In the visibility graph, *blocker lists* augment existing links between mutually visible polygons; total visibility is established whenever the blocker list is empty. Perhaps surprisingly, we show that these conservative overestimated blocker lists are generally *smaller* than those maintained by existing algorithms.

4. Blocker Maintenance. In a hierarchical radiosity algorithm, polygons (*patches*, in radiosity parlance) are allowed to exchange radiant energy only when the interaction satisfies some specified global error bound [11]. Otherwise, the patches are subdivided, and interaction is recommenced among the child patches. It is natural to consider how the conservative visibility graph among the patches can be *incrementally maintained* under subdivision. Each child patch may be partially or totally visible, or completely invisible, to its child counterparts on the other polygon. We show how, given the parent interaction, conservative blocker lists for the children can be determined incrementally. We present a novel blocker maintenance technique involving *linespace*, a five-dimensional representation of 3D lines (i.e., light rays).

The algorithms we present are of interest in several ways. First, they comprise a practical treatment of visibility issues for unrestricted (i.e., non-axial) three-dimensional environments, in contrast to previous work [1, 8, 24]. Second, the conservative visibility description we compute – identification of all mutually visible pairs, and the blocker set for each pair – is a natural, output-sensitive way of characterizing visibility among polygons or more general objects, for any algorithms that require information about occlusion and/or illumination. Finally, we show that the use of these algorithms dramatically improves the time and space efficiency of an existing radiosity computation [11].

3 Spatial Subdivision

The geometric model is specified as a set P of convex polygons (Figure 1). The space embedding the geometric model is subdivided into convex polyhedral *cells*, typically separated by polygons (Figure 2). The construction is based on BSP trees [7], but the visibility algorithms we subsequently present are provably correct for any spatial subdivision satisfying a few geometric criteria [22].

Figure 1: A geometric model comprised of polygons.

First, a polyhedral *root volume* is constructed as the convex hull of P. While polygons of sufficient size are present, a polygon is chosen whose support plane is to partition the remainder of the set. The choice is made using a simple heuristic that determines the polygon whose cross-section in the current cell is largest, when expressed as a fraction of the cell's areal intersection with the polygon's support plane; if any polygons separate the cell into mutually invisible parts, one such polygon is chosen. This heuristic tends to yield effective splitting trees in practice.

Figure 2: Subdivision of the model into cells and portals.

Next, the *portals*, or transparent portions, of each cell boundary are explicitly constructed. Since cell boundaries are induced on the support planes of polygons, these boundaries are typically partially or completely obscured. Each boundary stores a list of coaffine and incident polygons. The portals on each boundary comprise a convex decomposition of the set difference of the cell boundary with the union of these polygons. Each portal stores identifiers for the cells which it connects. The spatial subdivision therefore comprises an *adjacency graph* over the cells, since two cells are adjacent in this graph iff they share a boundary that is not completely opaque.

4 Visibility Propagation

Once a conforming spatial subdivision is built, visibility propagation commences. The propagation algorithm operates in object space, and performs a *constrained traversal* of the adjacency graph outward from each *source* cell. Whenever a cell is reached by this traversal, its associated polygons are examined pairwise with those in the source for mutual visibility; unreached entities are definitely invisible from the source.

A given cell can see into its neighbors only through portals, and into more distant cells only through *portal sequences*; i.e., ordered lists of portals such that each consecutive pair of portals lead into and out of the same cell. The cell adjacency graph is searched by determining cells between which an unobstructed *sightline* exists. A sightline must be disjoint from any occluders and thus must intersect, or *stab*, a portal in order to pass from one cell to the next. To establish inter-cell visibility, it is sufficient to find a stabbing line through a particular portal sequence; since if some point in the *interior* of one cell can see a point in the interior of another, a sightline must exist between the boundaries of the source cell and the reached cell.

Thus, the problem of finding sightlines between cell interiors reduces to finding sightlines through portal sequences of increasing length. Consequently, the primitive visibility operation in a conforming spatial subdivision is the determination of a stabbing line, given a portal sequence, or the determination that no such stabbing line exists. The portal sequences are generated incrementally by a depth-first search (DFS) emanating from a particular cell boundary; when a sequence no longer admits a sightline, the active branch of the DFS terminates.

4.1 Inter-Cell Visibility

Sightline determination is an *existence* predicate, in that it merely establishes visibility between two points on different cells. Suppose two cells are mutually visible through a portal sequence. In general, only a portion of each cell is visible to the other, due to occlusion by opaque material abutting the edges of intervening portals (Figures 3, 4). Whenever inter-cell visibility is established, mutually visible *volumes* are constructed for the cell pair; these volumes and the reaching portal sequence are then used to determine inter-polygon visibility among the cells' associated polygons.

Figure 3: Visibility propagation from a source cell S_1.

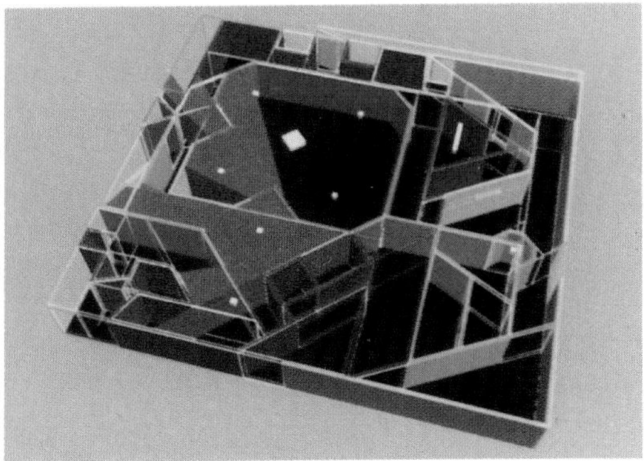

Figure 4: Visibility propagation from a source cell S_2.

The volume visible to a polygon in the presence of polygonal occluders is, in general, bounded by quadratic surfaces [18]. An algorithm for computing this volume was implemented and described in [21], but is not yet sufficiently robust for use on complex models. Consequently, we have developed a simpler algorithm that computes a polyhedral volume guaranteed to enclose the exact visible region. The algorithm is a straightforward construction that, using separating tangent planes, performs a kind of internal pivoting over the edges and vertices occurring along the portal sequence. We treat the algorithm briefly here; details can be found in [22].

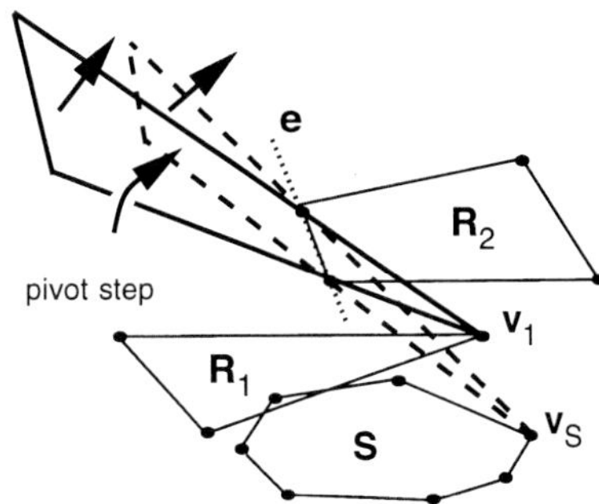

Figure 5: A pivoting step on edge $\mathbf{e}$, from $\mathbf{v}_1$ to $\mathbf{v}_S$.

The algorithm exploits the fact that for each portal edge, at most two separating planes can contribute a face to polyhedral bounds on the illuminated volume (Figure 5), since at most one vertex from each halfspace of the associated portal can span a relevant plane with the edge. Consider some edge $\mathbf{e}$ on a portal $\mathbf{R}_2$, and the portals occurring before $\mathbf{R}_2$. Each of these portals has at most one *extremal* vertex that spans a separating plane with $\mathbf{e}$ (in the figure, $\mathbf{R}_1$ has extremal vertex $\mathbf{v}_1$ and $\mathbf{S}$ has extremal vertex $\mathbf{v}_S$). Together with $\mathbf{e}$, only one of these (at most $\frac{n}{3}$) extremal vertices can span a plane that contains all the other extremal vertices in the same halfspace as the portal $\mathbf{R}_2$. This single plane is the only one of the n candidate planes that can contribute faces to the boundary of the illuminated volume. Therefore, for any n portal edges there are at most $2n$ boundary planes, each of which can be identified in $O(n)$ time by pivoting over the vertices of the other portals. The total time to identify the $2n$ relevant planes is therefore $O(n^2)$. Moreover, the set of $O(n)$ planes can be updated incrementally whenever a new portal is encountered, simply by updating the existing halfspaces with respect to the new portal vertices, and introducing planes tight on the new portal edges. The $O(n)$ positive halfspaces of the planes are inspected for an intersection with the c BSP halfspaces bounding the reached cell in time $O(n+c)$ with a linear programming algorithm [15, 19]. If no such intersection exists then the reached cell can not be visible to the source through the active portal sequence.

4.2 Inter-Polygon Visibility

Whenever a cell is reached by the graph propagation, an *active set* of halfspaces bounds the volume in the reached cell visible to the source. The orientations of each of these halfspaces are reversed to bound the volume illuminated by the *reached* cell in the *source*. Only polygons in these respective volumes can be mutually visible. Each incident source polygon is prefixed to the front of the active portal sequence (Figure 6). The visible volume in the reached cell due to the augmented sequence is then tested for incidence with the appropriate subset of polygons stored in the reached cell. (The notion of conservative inter-polygon visibility can be simply extended to treat visibility between general objects [22].)

Figure 6 depicts this mechanism for an analogous 2D situation, in which "polygons" and "portals" are line segments. A source cell S (Figure 6-i) establishes inter-cell visibility to a cell R via some portal sequence. The polygon B in S can have no interaction with R's interior, and it is not considered further. Polygon C is incident on the inter-cell visibility volume, and therefore potentially visible from some point in S. However, when the portal sequence is augmented with the constraints due to A (Figure 6-ii), polygon C is found to be invisible from A. Finally, D is found to intersect A's visible region in R, and A and D are established to be mutually

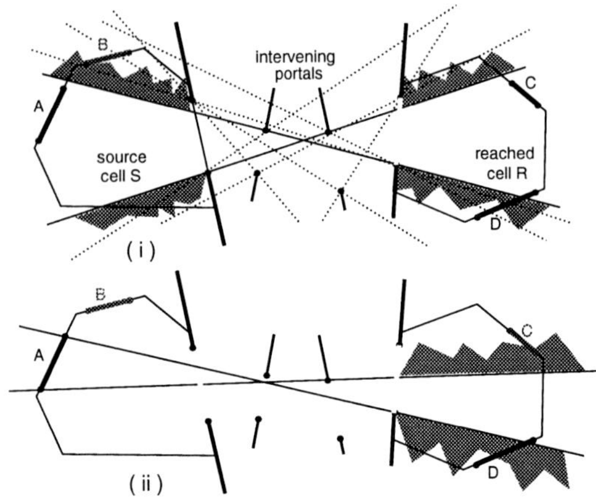

Figure 6: Establishing visibility of 2D "polygons" A and D.

visible.

The convexity of spatial subdivision cells allows an important optimization. Any two polygons entirely incident on the boundaries of the same cell can have blockers only in the relative interior of that cell. When the cell interior is empty (as it typically will be), the polygons can be immediately classified as entirely mutually visible. Thus, the spatial subdivision quickly identifies many instances of complete mutual visibility between nearby polygons.

Figures 7 and 8 depict the output of the inter-polygon visibility computation in three dimensions, for two polygons incident on different source cells. Display of the spatial subdivision has been suppressed for clarity.

Figure 7: Visibility propagation from a polygon in cell S_1.

Figure 8: Visibility propagation from a polygon in cell S_2.

5 Blocker Detection

When a pair (S, R) of polygons is found to be mutually visible, we record a visibility *interaction* $I(S, R)$, and proceed to identify the *blocker list* $B(S, R)$ of the pair. One could simply compute the set of blockers as those polygons incident on a convex volume containing S and R (as in [10]). However, the visibility graph and reaching portal sequence generally yield a better (i.e., smaller) blocker list. Denote the convex hull of all vertices of S and R as $conv(S, R)$. Clearly any blocker B must be incident on $conv(S, R)$ to contribute to $B(S, R)$. Moreover, observe that *only polygons visible to S along a sequence reaching R, or to R along a sequence reaching* S need be considered as blockers of S and R. For, if some polygon C is *not* visible to S, then *every* ray leaving S (including those rays to any point on R) must stab some polygon other than C before stabbing C.

The polygons S and R do not generally *see* the same set of blockers (Figures 7 and 8). Therefore, $B(S, R)$ is augmented whenever a search from S (R) to R (S) discovers a previously unknown blocker. Figure 9 depicts the result of the blocker computation, where all polygons except S, R, and $B(S, R)$ have been removed. Note that, of the polygons from the large central room, neither the large blue interior wall panels nor the thin blue doorjambs (cf. Figure 1) are classified as blockers. Thus the purely spatial (shaft) cull produces a blocker list of size 12 or more, whereas the blocker detection algorithm presented here computes a list of 6 blockers.

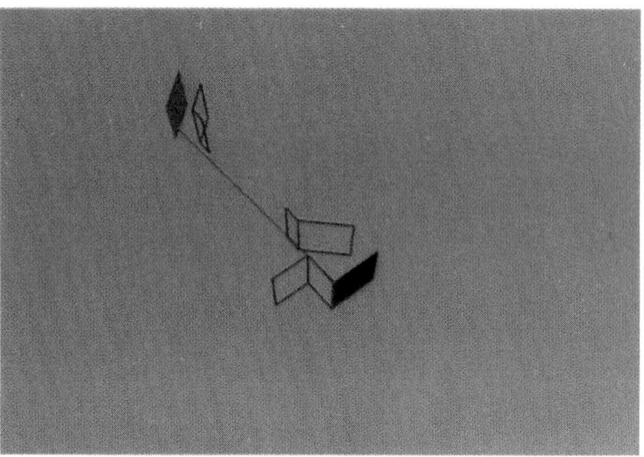

Figure 9: The final blocker list of S and R.

Finally, the blocker criterion presented above is conservative, since $B(S, R)$ may include polygons that are visible to S or to R but do not affect occlusion between them. The *exact* determination of the blocker list is computationally involved; a polygon B is a blocker of S and R only if some ray from S to R exists whose only front-facing polygon intersection, aside from that with R, is with B. (The asymmetry of the definition arises from the fact that, in a manifold polyhedral environment of oriented polygons, only front faces can be visible to front faces.)

6 Blocker Maintenance

Given a set of polygons P, the visibility preprocessing scheme produces, for every polygon $S \in P$, a set of visible polygons $V(S)$. For each polygon $R \in V(S)$, the *blocker list* $B(S, R)$ enumerates all polygons $B \in P \setminus \{S, R\}$ that potentially impede visibility between S and R. $B(S, R)$ points only to top-level patches; this makes sense, since blockers should be as large as possible to cause maximal occlusion. For each interaction $I(S, R)$, we store a *tube* data structure, which associates an interacting patch pair, a blocker list, the *visibility status* $V(S, R)$ of the interaction (i.e., VISIBLE or PARTIAL), and some additional geometric information used for incremental visibility tests.

In the hierarchical radiosity algorithm, when the energetic interaction between two patches can not be characterized to within the global error bound, one of the patches of the interaction is symmetrically *subdivided*, and its children are allowed to interact with the other patch [11]. Clearly, interactions between either patch and the children of its counterpart are highly coherent. The tube data structure exploits this coherence to perform efficient and accurate visibility reclassification after subdivision.

Each child interaction's blocker list is necessarily a subset of the parent's blocker list; we wish to efficiently, and incrementally, determine the child tube's blockers. We say that a blocker B *impinges* on $I(S,R)$ if it occludes S from R, and that B is *disjoint* from $I(S,R)$ if B can not cause occlusion. Whenever a blocker list is discovered to be *empty* (i.e., to contain no impinging blockers), complete visibility between the interacting patches will be established, and no further visibility computations need be done for any children of this interaction. Conversely, whenever the blocker list is discovered to be *completely occluding*, there can be no energy transport between S and R, and the interaction is discarded (alternatively, the culprit blocker(s) can be retained as "proof" that the patches cannot interact). Finally, when neither complete visibility nor complete occlusion can be quickly determined, the status of the child interaction remains partially visible.

6.1 Linespace

The tube structure efficiently encodes the set of all lines between S and R, using a five-dimensional line representation known as Plucker coordinates [20], or simply *linespace*. Lines in three dimensions correspond to hyperplanes and points in linespace. Any two 3D rays a and b can be *oriented* by considering their linespace counterparts Λ_a, a 5D hyperplane, and Π_b, a 5D point (details of the mapping can be found in [21]).

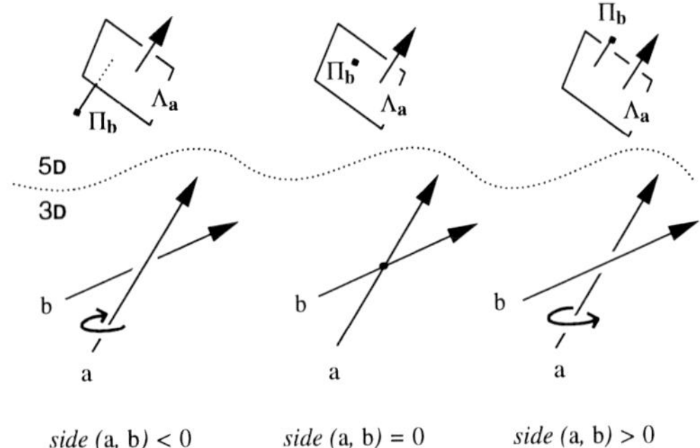

The signed distance of Π_b from Λ_a determines the sense in which the lines "go around" each other in 3D; if Π_b lies on Λ_a the lines a and b are coplanar. This "sidedness" property can be used to represent the set of lines through a collection of convex polygons. In practice, there is one caveat to using the linespace representation [23]. The only portion of linespace corresponding to 3D lines with real coefficients are those linespace points lying on a 4D manifold known as the Plucker quadric [20]; all other linespace points correspond to 3D lines with complex coefficients. Fortunately, the algorithms used in this paper need never consider the Plucker quadric, since they manipulate only lines known *a priori* to have real coefficients.

Consider two convex polygons S and R, comprised of sets of oriented edges S_k and R_k, respectively. For there to exist some line $\mathbf{L}$ that stabs the interiors of S and R, $\Pi_{\mathbf{L}}$ must lie in the appropriate signed halfspaces h_k of the hyperplanes $\Lambda_{\mathbf{S}_k}$ and $\Lambda_{\mathbf{R}_k}$.

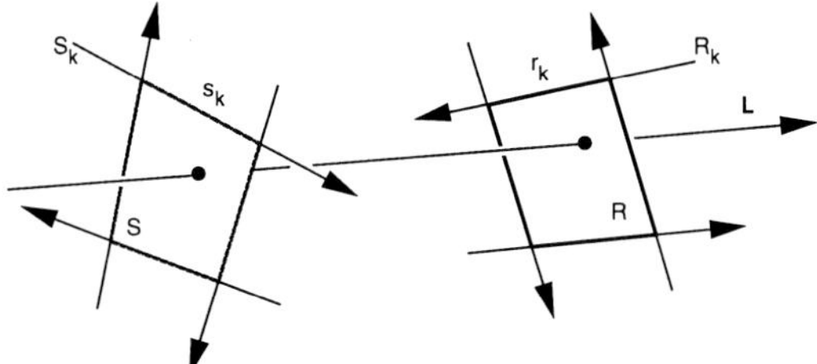

Thus, the set of all lines through S and R corresponds to the interior of a five-dimensional convex polytope $\cap_k h_k$ [21]. Rather than attempt to compute this polytope directly, we can manipulate the vertices of its intersection with the Plucker quadric, which are comparatively easy to generate. Each such vertex corresponds to a collection of four support lines from S and R, since four 5D hyperplanes must intersect with the Plucker quadric to generate each such vertex. These vertices must correspond to stabbing lines tight on four edges of S and R in 3D; i.e., lines through a vertex of S and a vertex of R (note that these lines necessarily have real 3D coefficients). In our implementation, there are at most sixteen such lines, since all patches are quadrilaterals.

There are several advantages to performing blocker analysis in linespace. The data structure for a single blocker is constant size, and for a single patch interaction is linear in the number of blockers. The linespace analysis obviates complicated 3D topological and numerical computations. The only operations required by the linespace representation are mapping from 3D lines to 5D points and hyperplanes, and computing inner products between points and hyperplanes.

6.2 Incremental Blocker Maintenance

The tube data structure, and incremental visibility maintenance, can now be fully described. Suppose patch R is subdivided against patch S into child elements $C(R) \subset R$. The tube for S and each $C_R \in C(R)$ stores S, C_R, and a constant number of linespace points $\Pi(S,R)$ whose convex hull $conv(\Pi(S,R))$ includes the set of all lines through S and C_R. Finally, each blocker in $B(S,R)$ is reclassified with respect to the child tube to produce $B(S,C_R)$, and the visibility status $V(S,C_R)$ of each interaction $I(S,C_R)$ is determined. As before, many instances of total invisibility, partial visibility, and total visibility are discovered quickly. Other situations are considered too complex to analyze completely, and we "punt" and classify the interaction as partially visible (perhaps causing further subdivision [11]).

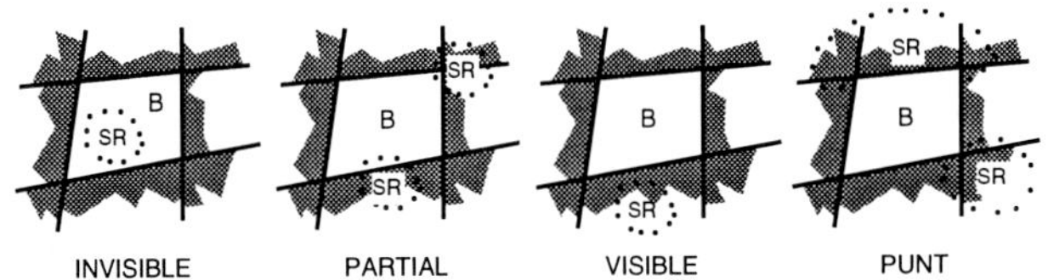

Figure 10: Performing 3D triage in 5D linespace.

Consider an interaction (S,R) and a single potential blocker B (Figure 10). We wish to determine, without extensive analysis, whether all, none, or some of the lines through S and R stab the blocker B. Respectively, this is equivalent to determining whether $conv(\Pi(S,R))$ lies entirely inside, is disjoint from, or has some intersection with $\cap_k \Lambda_k(B)$, the set of lines through the blocker (Figure 11). We exploit the fact that, in linespace, both sets of lines are convex.

The points in $\Pi(S,R)$ are first classified with respect to the blocker hyperplanes $\Lambda_k(B)$. If all of the points lie inside the $\Lambda_k(B)$, then $conv(\Pi(S,R)) \subset \cap_k \Lambda_k(B)$, by convexity. B is therefore completely occluding and $V(S,R)$ is INVISIBLE. If some of the points lie inside the $\Lambda_k(B)$, and some lie outside, some lines through S and R stab B, and $V(S,R)$ is PARTIAL. If *all* of the points lie outside some *single* $\Lambda_k(B)$, $V(S,R)$ is VISIBLE. Finally, the complex case occurs when *all* of the points lie outside *all* of the $\Lambda_k(B)$. This does not guarantee total visibility, since $conv(\Pi(S,R))$ may still have some intersection with $\cap_k \Lambda_k(B)$ (this case is labeled PUNT in Figures 10 and 11); accordingly, $V(S,R)$ is classified as PARTIAL.

The logic for multiple blockers is straightforward; any single blocker can cause $V(S,R)$ to be INVISIBLE, but all blockers must be disjoint in order for $V(S,R)$ to be VISIBLE. Otherwise, any impinging blocker causes $V(S,R)$ to become PARTIAL.

6.3 Evolution

Figure 12 depicts an example of blocker list evolution and incremental reclassification of child interactions. White lines connecting quadrilateral centroids represent VISIBLE interactions; green lines represent PARTIAL interactions, and red lines represent the tube

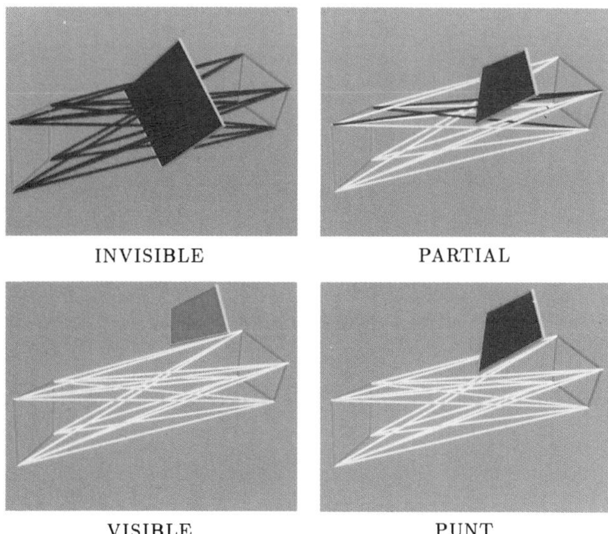

Figure 11: The four possible outcomes of a blocker classification.

between two interacting polygons. (INVISIBLE interactions are not shown.) In Figure 12-i, two red polygons interact via a blocker list containing the orange polygon. In Figure 12-ii, the large red polygon is subdivided into quadrants, and its child interactions with the small red polygon are shown. One of these interactions is INVISIBLE. The other three are PARTIAL; the tube for one of them is shown. Finally, in Figure 12-iii, the child polygon is subdivided; three of *its* children become VISIBLE to the polygon at right, but one (shown) remains PARTIAL.

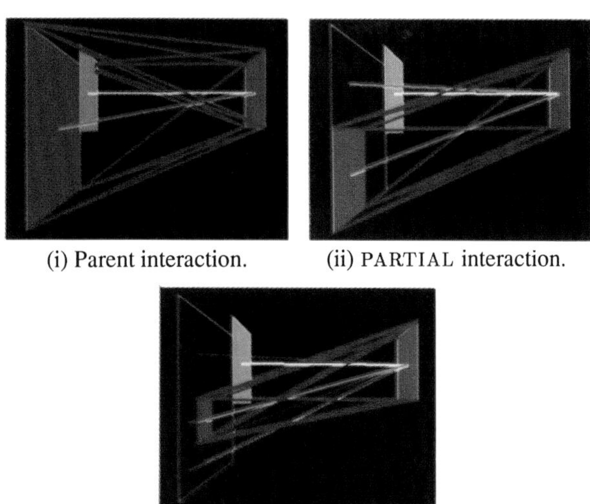

(i) Parent interaction. (ii) PARTIAL interaction.

(iii) VISIBLE interaction.

Figure 12: Reclassification of child interactions after subdivision.

The linespace algorithms guarantee conservative visibility, in that blockers are only discarded from interactions if they are definitely known to be disjoint. Existing algorithms use point-sampling [2, 6, 11, 16] or point-to-area visibility [3, 4] techniques and therefore do not guarantee correct inter-area visibility determination. In contrast, we establish exact visibility information where possible, and adaptively subdivide until the uncertainty of visibility estimation in the remaining cases is so small as to be unimportant.

The linespace blocker maintenance algorithms are simple and fast, although they sometimes overestimate occlusion by classifying disjoint blockers as impinging, and may not identify INVISIBLE interactions as early as might a more sophisticated algorithm. Establishment of improved algorithms for the determination of inter-polygon visibility in the presence of multiple blockers is an active area of research [17, 21, 25]. An exact algorithm was presented in [21], but is not yet sufficiently robust for application here.

The work and storage expended for the incremental visibility maintenance also serves to accelerate the sampling done to establish inter-patch energy transfer (i.e., to estimate form factors). The ray/blocker machinery is simply applied to random sample rays (as used in [11]). The cost of each ray/blocker test is four 5D inner products.

7 Results

7.1 Spatial Subdivision

We implemented the spatial subdivision, propagation, interference, and maintenance algorithms described, and instrumented their execution for the data set shown in Figure 1. All execution was on a lightly loaded 50-MIP Silicon Graphics VGX. The input model comprised 403 patches. Constructing the BSP tree required about thirty CPU seconds; the resulting tree contained 220 leaf cells. Each cell had 5.99 boundary faces, and 5.87 patches coaffine with some boundary face, on average (thus the spatial subdivision heuristics produced fairly local partitioning behavior). Another seven CPU seconds were absorbed by cell neighbor-finding and enumeration of the 525 portals between leaf cells of the subdivision.

7.2 Visibility Propagation

Computing inter-cell and inter-patch visibility for the model absorbed five CPU minutes. Of the $81003 = (403 \times 402)/2$ patch pairs in the model, 4,391, or 5.4%, were classified as mutually visible. (Thus preprocessing obviated nearly 95% of the potential patch-patch interactions). Of these 4,391 patch pairs, 2,814 (64.1%) were partially visible, and 1,577 (35.9%) were totally visible. Each patch saw, on average, 22 other patches.

The inter-cell traversals performed 10,128 stabbing tests of portal sequences, or about 46 tests per cell. The inter-polygon traversals performed 16,055 further incremental stabbing tests, one for each successfully reached cell and potentially visible patch pair. Thus, about 40 tests per patch were required to establish inter-patch visibility for all patches. The average length of a tested inter-cell portal sequence was just over 5 portals. This is consistent with our experience using a ten-thousand polygon, five-thousand cell axial model, in which the average portal sequence length was less than ten [8, 22]. A histogram of observed portal sequence lengths and stabbing percentages is shown in Figure 13.

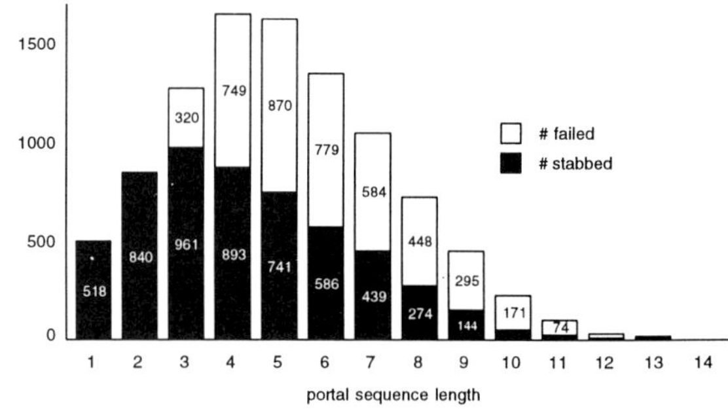

Figure 13: Stabbing successes and failures, by sequence length.

The inter-cell visibility determination uses a depth-first-search through the cell adjacency graph, applying an incremental stabbing predicate and visible volume computation at each step. The incremental operation expends linear time in the number of portals currently in the sequence, assuming a constant number of edges per portal, and so requires $O(n^2)$ time to stab a sequence of n portals. In practice, this seems not to prohibit use of the algorithms on real data sets, since most portal sequences are short (less than ten portals), and the algorithmic constants are therefore more important than the asymptotic complexity measure.

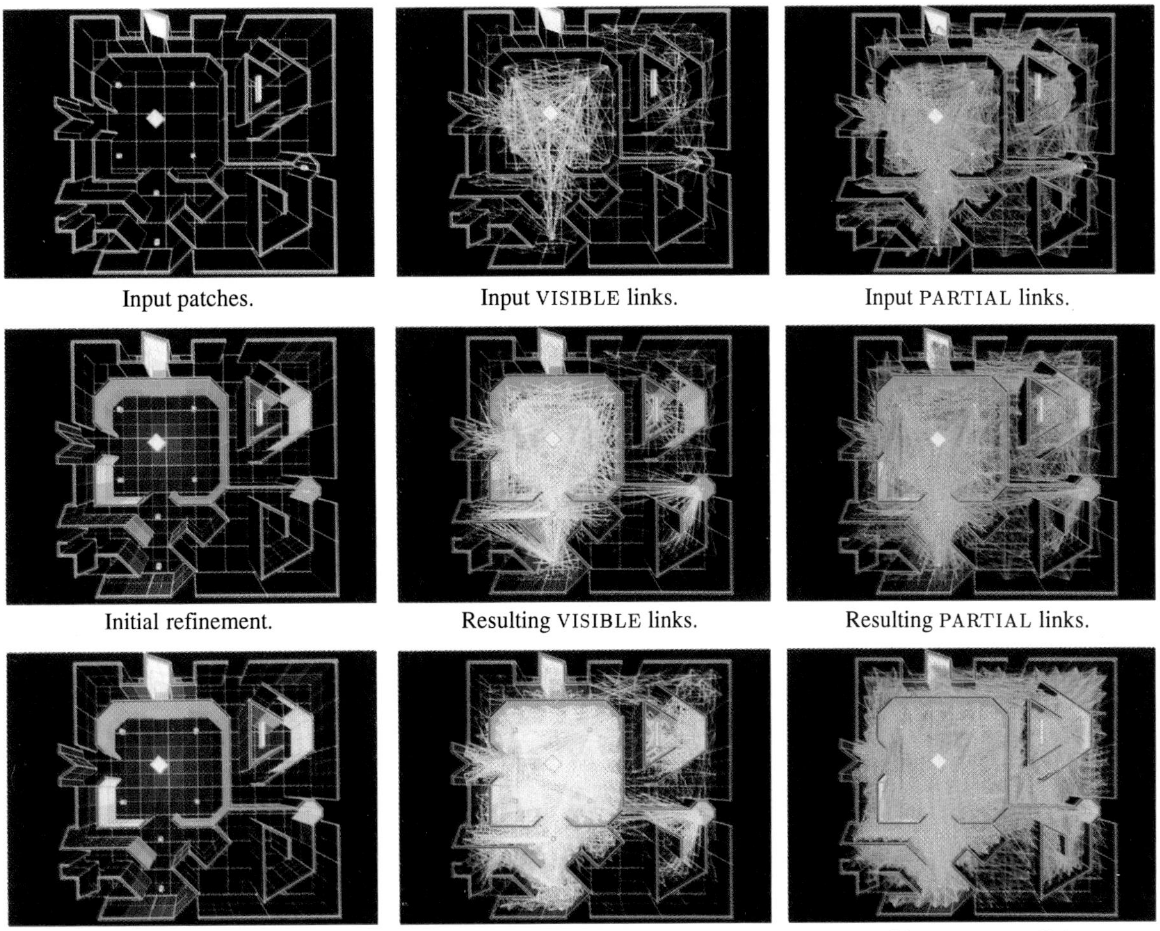

Input patches. Input VISIBLE links. Input PARTIAL links.

Initial refinement. Resulting VISIBLE links. Resulting PARTIAL links.

Second refinement. Resulting VISIBLE links. Resulting PARTIAL links.

Figure 14: Refinement of the input patches (left), VISIBLE links (middle), and PARTIAL links (right).

7.3 Blocker Detection

There were 5 blockers between partially visible patches, on average, reached through portal sequences of average length five. The subdivision heuristic was effective; the BSP tree did not suffer from excessive "free-space" splitting, or regions in which subdivision planes were induced due to far away polygons.

The visibility analysis communicated its results to the radiosity computation via an ASCII file. Each file line recorded an interaction $I(S, R)$ between two polygons, the length of the associated blocker list $B(S, R)$, and the blockers themselves. A zero-length blocker list implied total visibility between S and R, i.e., $V(S, R)$ =VISIBLE; otherwise the visibility status was PARTIAL.

7.4 Blocker Maintenance

The model input to the radiosity computation is shown at the upper left of Figure 14. The input patches form the radiosity program's initial mesh. The 4,391 initial VISIBLE and PARTIAL links are shown, respectively, in white (middle column) and green (right column). Two iterations of patch-patch refinement were performed. The resulting model mesh, PARTIAL and VISIBLE interactions are displayed in the second and third rows of Figure 14. The number of VISIBLE links drastically increases after the first iteration. Their increased density naturally indicates unoccluded regions of the model. Similarly, the green PARTIAL links indicate occlusion. INVISIBLE links are not shown, as they were discarded by the radiosity program upon detection.

Using the results of the visibility preprocessing, the initial refine took only 11 seconds, performing 145,846 interactions. The second refinement stage required 50 seconds, and performed 186,703 interactions. About 90% of the refined interactions were VISIBLE, thus requiring no sampling for form-factor estimation. Table 1 charts the evolution of each link type, the number of elements, and the number of interactions at each refine.

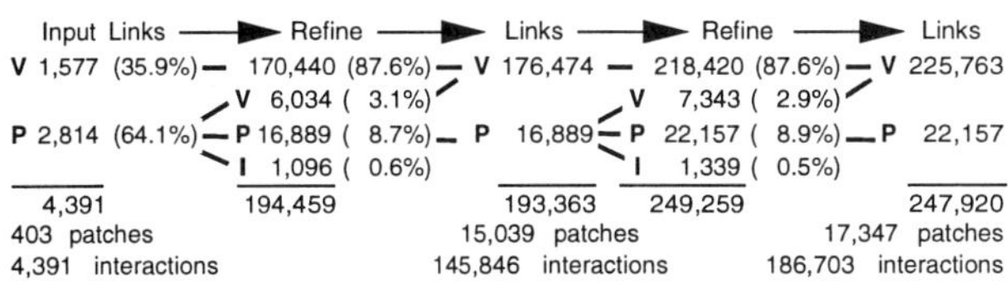

Input Links	Refine	Links	Refine	Links
V 1,577 (35.9%)	170,440 (87.6%)	V 176,474	218,420 (87.6%)	V 225,763
	V 6,034 (3.1%)		V 7,343 (2.9%)	
P 2,814 (64.1%)	P 16,889 (8.7%)	P 16,889	P 22,157 (8.9%)	P 22,157
	I 1,096 (0.6%)		I 1,339 (0.5%)	
4,391	194,459	193,363	249,259	247,920
403 patches		15,039 patches		17,347 patches
4,391 interactions		145,846 interactions		186,703 interactions

Table 1: Link evolution by type, with patch and interaction counts.

Since the time complexity of the radiosity algorithm is proportional to the number of interactions, the visibility preprocessing significantly decreased the computation done by the radiosity algorithm. Moreover, the modified radiosity algorithm was more accurate, since no partially visible interactions were missed due to sampling errors (as in [11]).

7.5 Blocker Visualization

All of the algorithms described in this paper were implemented using visualization tools that allowed interactive inspection of complex data structures. Figures 15 through 17 depict the use of this tool to investigate some interesting PARTIAL interactions. Again, the white and green line segments represent VISIBLE and PARTIAL interactions, respectively; for a particular partial interaction in each figure, the tube is shown (in red), and the blockers for the interaction

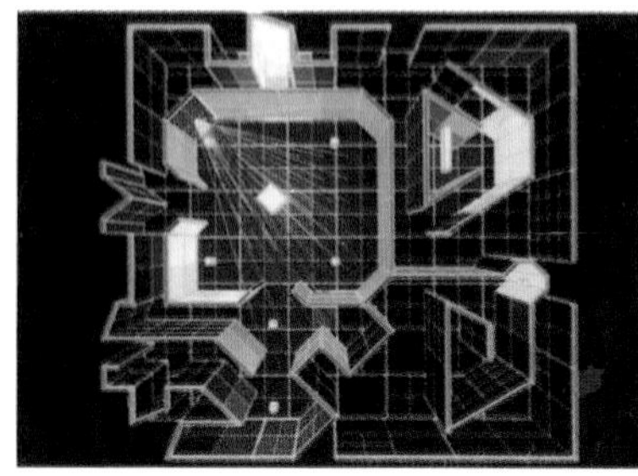

Figure 15: The tube data structure (red, orange) for an ordinary PARTIAL interaction.

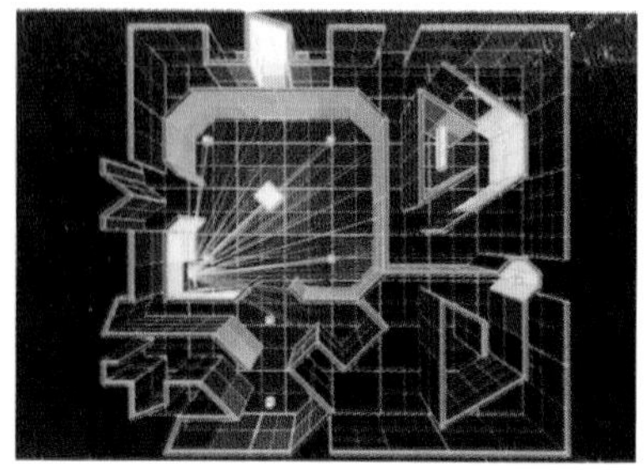

Figure 16: Spatially incident polygons that have not been classified as blockers.

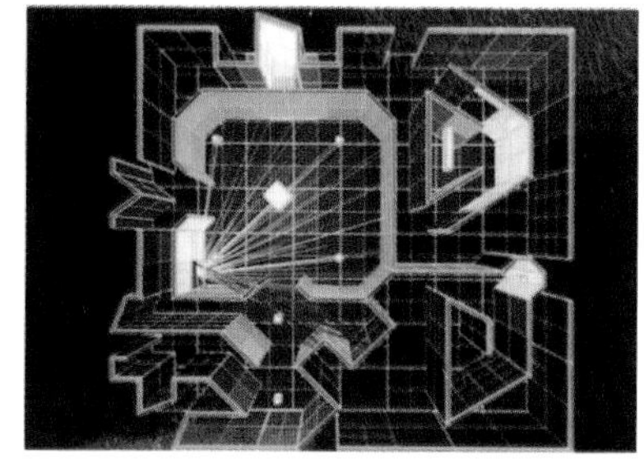

Figure 17: A PARTIAL interaction that could be classified as INVISIBLE.

are highlighted in orange. Figure 15 depicts an ordinary PARTIAL interaction. Figure 16 depicts spatially incident polygons that (correctly) have not been classified as blockers. Figure 17 depicts a PARTIAL interaction for which no single blocker occludes the source and receiver; a more sophisticated algorithm could classify this interaction as INVISIBLE.

8 Summary and Conclusion

We have presented several novel algorithms that represent an effective application of global visibility analysis to radiosity computations, an important problem in image synthesis. Given the complexity of both the visibility and radiosity approaches used, it was surprisingly easy to couple the two processes. We did so using an abstraction in which interactions between polygons were maintained along with all potentially blocking polygons. We argue that, for an interesting class of large models, inter-polygon visibility has roughly constant complexity throughout the interior of the model. After construction of a spatial subdivision for the model, the visibility algorithms we present are output sensitive; they expend work proportional to the amount of inter-polygon visibility present.

None of the visibility algorithms attempt to compute exact visibility information. However, they achieve precision in a different sense, by reporting all visibilities conservatively; potentially visible interactions are always reported.

Only blockers can occlude a specified source from a specified emitter. Thus, the blocker list formulation is applicable to the problem of discontinuity meshing in the presence of area light sources [12, 13, 14, 21], as well as to the construction of an "oracle" to decide which, if any, among a collection of discontinuities should be meshed upon earliest.

We showed that the visibility analysis significantly accelerated a radiosity computation in a polygonal environment. Finally, we demonstrated the successful application of some elegant concepts such as linespace and algorithmic triage to the concrete problem of construction and incremental maintenance of blocker lists.

Acknowledgments

The authors are grateful to David Laur for his assistance with the geometric model and the color plates, and to Dani Lischinski for his valuable comments. This work was begun during a visit to the NSF Science and Technology Center for the Visualization of Geometric Structures, in Minneapolis, and partially supported by Apple, Silicon Graphics Computer Systems, and the National Science Foundation (CCR 9207966).

References

[1] AIREY, J. M. *Increasing Update Rates in the Building Walkthrough System with Automatic Model-Space Subdivision and Potentially Visible Set Calculations*. PhD thesis, UNC Chapel Hill, 1990.

[2] BAUM, D. R., MANN, S., SMITH, K. P., AND WINGET, J. M. Making Radiosity Usable: Automatic Preprocessing and Meshing Techniques for the Generation of Accurate Radiosity Solutions. *Computer Graphics (Proc. SIGGRAPH '91) 25*, 4 (1991), 51–60.

[3] CAMPBELL III, A., AND FUSSELL, D. S. An Analytic Approach to Illumination with Area Light Sources. Tech. Rep. TR-91-25, Department of Computer Sciences, UT Austin, 1991.

[4] CHIN, N., AND FEINER, S. Fast Object-Precision Shadow Generation for Area Light Sources Using BSP Trees. In *Proc. 1992 Symposium on Interactive 3D Graphics* (1992), pp. 21–30.

[5] COHEN, M. F., CHEN, S. E., WALLACE, J. R., AND GREENBERG, D. P. A Progressive Refinement Approach to Fast Radiosity Image Generation. *Computer Graphics (Proc. SIGGRAPH '88) 22*, 4 (1988), 75–84.

[6] COHEN, M. F., AND GREENBERG, D. P. The Hemi-Cube: A Radiosity Solution for Complex Environments. *Computer Graphics (Proc. SIGGRAPH '85) 19*, 3 (1985), 31–40.

[7] FUCHS, H., KEDEM, Z., AND NAYLOR, B. On visible surface generation by a priori tree structures. *Computer Graphics (Proc. SIGGRAPH '80) 14*, 3 (1980), 124–133.

[8] FUNKHOUSER, T. A., SÉQUIN, C. H., AND TELLER, S. Management of Large Amounts of Data in Interactive Building Walkthroughs. In *Proc. 1992 Workshop on Interactive 3D Graphics* (1992), pp. 11–20.

[9] GIGUS, Z., CANNY, J., AND SEIDEL, R. Efficiently Computing and Representing Aspect Graphs of Polyhedral Objects. *IEEE Transactions on Pattern Analysis and Machine Intelligence 13*, 6 (1991), 542–551.

[10] HAINES, E. A., AND WALLACE, J. R. Shaft Culling for Efficient Ray-Traced Radiosity. In *Proc. 2nd Eurographics Workshop on Rendering* (May 1991).

[11] HANRAHAN, P., SALZMAN, D., AND AUPPERLE, L. A Rapid Hierarchical Radiosity Algorithm. *Computer Graphics (Proc. SIGGRAPH '91) 25*, 4 (1991), 197–206.

[12] HECKBERT, P. S. *Simulating Global Illumination Using Adaptive Meshing*. PhD thesis, Computer Sciences Department, UC Berkeley, June 1991.

[13] LISCHINSKI, D., TAMPIERI, F., AND GREENBERG, D. P. Discontinuity Meshing for Accurate Radiosity. *IEEE Computer Graphics and Applications 12*, 6 (1992), 25–39.

[14] LISCHINSKI, D., TAMPIERI, F., AND GREENBERG, D. P. Combining Hierarchical Radiosity and Discontinuity Meshing. *Computer Graphics (Proc. SIGGRAPH '93) 27* (1993).

[15] MEGIDDO, N. Linear programming in linear time when the dimension is fixed. *Journal of the ACM 31* (1984), 114–127.

[16] NISHITA, T., AND NAKAMAE, E. Half-Tone Representation of 3-D Objects Illuminated by Area Sources or Polyhedron Sources. In *Proc. IEEE COMPSAC, 1983* (1983), pp. 237–242.

[17] PLANTINGA, H. An algorithm for finding the weakly visible faces from a polygon in 3D. Tech. Rep. 92–11, U of Pittsburgh, 1992.

[18] PLANTINGA, W., AND DYER, C. An algorithm for constructing the aspect graph. In *Proc. 27th Annual IEEE Symposium on Foundations of Computer Science* (1986), pp. 123–131.

[19] SEIDEL, R. Small-dimensional linear programming and convex hulls made easy. *Discrete and Computational Geometry* (1991), 423–434.

[20] SOMMERVILLE, D. *Analytical Geometry of Three Dimensions*. Cambridge University Press, 1959.

[21] TELLER, S. Computing the Antipenumbra Cast by an Area Light Source. *Computer Graphics (Proc. SIGGRAPH '92) 26*, 2 (1992), 139–148.

[22] TELLER, S. *Visibility Computations in Densely Occluded Polyhedral Environments*. PhD thesis, CS Dept., UC Berkeley, 1992.

[23] TELLER, S., AND HOHMEYER, M. E. Computing the Lines Piercing Four Lines. Tech. Rep. UCB/CSD 91/665, Computer Science Department, UC Berkeley, 1991.

[24] TELLER, S., AND SÉQUIN, C. H. Visibility Preprocessing for Interactive Walkthroughs. *Computer Graphics (Proc. SIGGRAPH '91) 25*, 4 (1991), 61–69.

[25] ZHAO, J., AND DOBKIN, D. Personal communication, 1992.

Adaptive Display Algorithm for Interactive Frame Rates During Visualization of Complex Virtual Environments

Thomas A. Funkhouser and Carlo H. Séquin
University of California at Berkeley‡

Abstract

We describe an adaptive display algorithm for interactive frame rates during visualization of very complex virtual environments. The algorithm relies upon a hierarchical model representation in which objects are described at multiple levels of detail and can be drawn with various rendering algorithms. The idea behind the algorithm is to adjust image quality adaptively to maintain a uniform, user-specified target frame rate. We perform a constrained optimization to choose a level of detail and rendering algorithm for each potentially visible object in order to generate the "best" image possible within the target frame time. Tests show that the algorithm generates more uniform frame rates than other previously described detail elision algorithms with little noticeable difference in image quality during visualization of complex models.

CR Categories and Subject Descriptors:
[Computer Graphics]: I.3.3 Picture/Image Generation – *viewing algorithms*; I.3.5 Computational Geometry and Object Modeling – *geometric algorithms, object hierarchies*; I.3.7 Three-Dimensional Graphics and Realism – *virtual reality*.

1 Introduction

Interactive computer graphics systems for visualization of realistic-looking, three-dimensional models are useful for evaluation, design and training in virtual environments, such as those found in architectural and mechanical CAD, flight simulation, and virtual reality. These visualization systems display images of a three-dimensional model on the screen of a computer workstation as seen from a simulated observer's viewpoint under interactive control by a user. If images are rendered smoothly and quickly enough, an illusion of real-time exploration of a virtual environment can be achieved as the simulated observer moves through the model.

‡Computer Science Division, Berkeley, CA 94720

It is important for a visualization system to maintain an interactive frame rate (e.g., a constant ten frames per second). If frame rates are too slow, or too jerky, the interactive feel of the system is greatly diminished [3]. However, realistic-looking models may contain millions of polygons – far more than currently available workstations can render at interactive frame rates. Furthermore, the complexity of the portion of the model visible to the observer can be highly variable. Tens of thousands of polygons might be simultaneously visible from some observer viewpoints, whereas just a few can be seen from others. Programs that simply render all potentially visible polygons with some predetermined quality may generate frames at highly variable rates, with no guaranteed upper bound on any single frame time.

Using the UC Berkeley Building Walkthrough System [5] and a model of Soda Hall, the future Computer Science Building at UC Berkeley, as a test case, we have developed an adaptive algorithm for interactive visualization that guarantees a user-specified target frame rate. The idea behind the algorithm is to trade image quality for interactivity in situations where the environment is too complex to be rendered in full detail at the target frame rate. We perform a constrained optimization that selects a level of detail and a rendering algorithm with which to render each potentially visible object to produce the "best" image possible within a user-specified target frame time. In contrast to previous culling techniques, this algorithm guarantees a uniform, bounded frame rate, even during visualization of very large, complex models.

2 Previous Work

2.1 Visibility Determination

In previous work, visibility algorithms have been described that compute the portion of a model potentially visible from a given observer viewpoint [1, 11]. These algorithms cull away large portions of a model that are occluded from the observer's viewpoint, and thereby improve frame rates significantly. However, in very detailed models, often more polygons are visible from certain observer viewpoints than can be rendered in an interactive frame time. Certainly, there is no upper bound on the complexity of the scene visible from an observer's viewpoint. For instance, consider walking through a very detailed model of a fully stocked department store, or viewing an assembly of a complete airplane engine. In our model of Soda Hall, there are some viewpoints from which an observer can see more than eighty thousand polygons. Clearly, visibility processing alone is not sufficient to guarantee an interactive frame rate.

 ACM-0-89791-601-8/93/008/0247 $01.50

2.2 Detail Elision

To reduce the number of polygons rendered in each frame, an interactive visualization system can use *detail elision*. If a model can be described by a hierarchical structure of *objects*, each of which is represented at multiple *levels of detail* (LODs), as shown in Figure 1, simpler representations of an object can be used to improve frame rates and memory utilization during interactive visualization. This technique was first described by Clark [4], and has been used by numerous commercial visualization systems [9]. If different representations for the same object have similar appearances and are blended smoothly, using transparency blending or three-dimensional interpolation, transitions between levels of detail are barely noticeable during visualization.

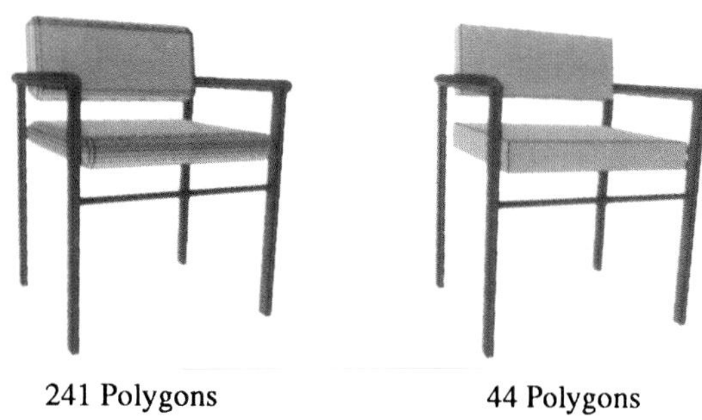

Figure 1: Two levels of detail for a chair.

Previously described techniques for choosing a level of detail at which to render each visible object use static heuristics, most often based on a threshold regarding the size or distance of an object to the observer [2, 8, 9, 13], or the number of pixels covered by an average polygon [5]. These simple heuristics can be very effective at improving frame rates in cases where most visible objects are far away from the observer and map to very few pixels on the workstation screen. In these cases, simpler representations of some objects can be displayed, reducing the number of polygons rendered without noticeably reducing image quality.

Although static heuristics for visibility determination and LOD selection improve frame rates in many cases, they do not generally produce a *uniform* frame rate. Since LODs are computed independently for each object, the number of polygons rendered during each frame time depends on the size and complexity of the objects visible to the observer. The frame rate may vary dramatically from frame to frame as many complex objects become visible or invisible, and larger or smaller.

Furthermore, static heuristics for visibility determination and LOD selection do not even guarantee a *bounded* frame rate. The frame rate can become arbitrarily slow, as the scene visible to the observer can be arbitrarily complex. In many cases, the frame rate may become so slow that the system is no longer interactive. Instead, a LOD selection algorithm should adapt to overall scene complexity in order to produce uniform, bounded frame rates.

2.3 Adaptive Detail Elision

In an effort to maintain a specified *target frame rate*, some commercial flight simulators use an adaptive algorithm that adjusts the size threshold for LOD selection based on feedback regarding the time required to render previous frames [9]. If the previous frame took longer than the target frame time, the size threshold for LOD selection is increased so that future frames can be rendered more quickly.

This adaptive technique works reasonably well for flight simulators, in which there is a large amount of coherence in scene complexity from frame to frame. However, during visualization of more discontinuous virtual environments, scene complexity can vary radically between successive frames. For instance, in a building walkthrough, the observer may turn around a corner into a large atrium, or step from an open corridor into a small, enclosed office. In these situations, the number and complexity of the objects visible to the observer changes suddenly. Thus the size threshold chosen based on the time required to render previous frames is inappropriate, and can result in very poor performance until the system reacts. Overshoot and oscillation can occur as the feedback control system attempts to adjust the size threshold more quickly to achieve the target frame rate.

In order to *guarantee* a bounded frame rate during visualization of discontinuous virtual environments, an adaptive algorithm for LOD selection should be *predictive*, based on the complexity of the scene to be rendered in the current frame, rather than *reactive*, based only on the time required to render previous frames. A predictive algorithm might estimate the time required to render every object at every level of detail, and then compute the largest size threshold that allows the current frame to be rendered within the target frame time. Unfortunately, implementing a predictive algorithm is non-trivial, since no closed-form solution exists for the appropriate size threshold.

3 Overview of Approach

Our approach is a generalization of the predictive approach. Conceptually, every potentially visible object can be rendered at any level of detail, and with any rendering algorithm (e.g., flat-shaded, Gouraud-shaded, texture mapped, etc.). Every combination of objects rendered with certain levels of detail and rendering algorithms takes a certain amount of time, and produces a certain image. We aim to find the combination of levels of detail and rendering algorithms for all potentially visible objects that produces the "best" image possible within the target frame time.

More formally, we define an *object tuple*, (O, L, R), to be an instance of object O, rendered at level of detail L, with rendering algorithm R. We define two heuristics for object tuples: $Cost(O, L, R)$ and $Benefit(O, L, R)$. The *Cost* heuristic estimates the time required to render an object tuple; and the *Benefit* heuristic estimates the "contribution to model perception" of a rendered object tuple. We define S to be the set of object tuples rendered in each frame. Using these formalisms, our approach for choosing a level of detail and rendering algorithm for each potentially visible object can be stated:

$$\begin{aligned} &\text{Maximize :} \\ &\qquad \textstyle\sum_S Benefit(O, L, R) \\ &\text{Subject to :} \\ &\qquad \textstyle\sum_S Cost(O, L, R) \leq TargetFrameTime \end{aligned} \tag{1}$$

This formulation captures the essence of image generation with real-time constraints: "do as well as possible in a given amount of time." As such, it can be applied to a wide variety of problems that require images to be displayed in a fixed amount of time, including adaptive ray tracing (i.e., given a fixed number of rays, cast those that contribute most to the image), and adaptive radiosity (i.e., given a fixed number of form-factor computations, compute those that contribute most to the solution). If levels of detail representing "no polygons at all" are allowed, this approach handles cases where the target frame time is not long enough to render all potentially visible objects even at the lowest level of detail. In such cases, only the most "valuable" objects are rendered so that the frame time constraint is not violated. Using this approach, it is possible to generate images in a short, fixed amount of time, rather than waiting much longer for images of the highest quality attainable.

For this approach to be successful, we need to find *Cost* and *Benefit* heuristics that can be computed quickly and accurately. Unfortunately, *Cost* and *Benefit* heuristics for a specific object tuple cannot be predicted with perfect accuracy, and may depend on other object tuples rendered in the same image. A perfect *Cost* heuristic may depend on the model and features of the graphics workstation, the state of the graphics system, the state of the operating system, and the state of other programs running on the machine. A perfect *Benefit* heuristic would consider occlusion and color of other object tuples, human perception, and human understanding. We cannot hope to quantify all of these complex factors in heuristics that can be computed efficiently. However, using several simplifying assumptions, we have developed approximate *Cost* and *Benefit* heuristics that are both efficient to compute and accurate enough to be useful.

4 Cost Heuristic

The $Cost(O, L, R)$ heuristic is an estimate of the time required to render object O with level of detail L and rendering algorithm R. Of course, the actual rendering time for a set of polygons depends on a number of complex factors, including the type and features of the graphics workstation. However, using a model of a generalized rendering system and several simplifying assumptions, it is possible to develop an efficient, approximate *Cost* heuristic that can be applied to a wide variety of workstations. Our model, which is derived from the *Graphics Library Programming Tools and Techniques* document from Silicon Graphics, Inc. [10], represents the rendering system as a pipeline with the two functional stages shown in Figure 2:

- *Per Primitive:* coordinate transformations, lighting calculations, clipping, etc.
- *Per Pixel:* rasterization, z-buffering, alpha blending, texture mapping, etc.

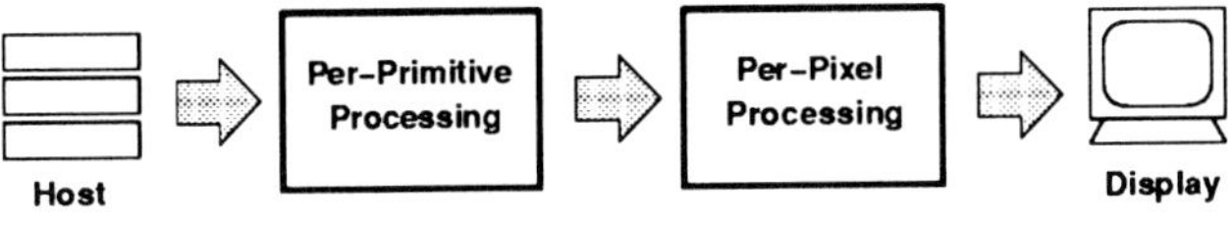

Figure 2: Two-stage model of the rendering pipeline.

Since separate stages of the pipeline run in parallel, and must wait only if a subsequent stage is "backed up," the throughput of the pipeline is determined by the speed of the slowest stage – i.e., the bottleneck. If we assume that the host is able to send primitives to the graphics subsystem faster than they can be rendered, and no other operations are executing that affect the speed of any stage of the graphics subsystem, we can model the time required to render an object tuple as the maximum of the times taken by any of the stages.

We model the time taken by the *Per Primitive* stage as a linear combination of the number of polygons and vertices in an object tuple, with coefficients that depend on the rendering algorithm and machine used. Likewise, we assume that the time taken by the *Per Pixel* stage is proportional to the number of pixels an object covers. Our model for the time required to render an object tuple is:

$$Cost(O, L, R) = max \left\{ \begin{array}{c} C_1 Poly(O, L) + C_2 Vert(O, L) \\ C_3 Pix(O) \end{array} \right\}$$

where O is the object, L is the level of detail, R is the rendering algorithm, and C_1, C_2 and C_3 are constant coefficients specific to a rendering algorithm and machine.

For a particular rendering algorithm and machine, useful values for these coefficients can be determined experimentally by rendering sample objects with a wide variety of sizes and LODs, and graphing measured rendering times versus the number of polygons, vertices and pixels drawn. Figure 3a shows measured times for rendering four different LODs of the chair shown in Figure 1 rendered with flat-shading. The slope of the best fitting line through the data points represents the time required *per polygon* during this test. Using this technique, we have derived cost model coefficients for our Silicon Graphics VGX 320 that are accurate within 10% at the 95% confidence level. A comparison of actual and predicted rendering times for a sample set of frames during an interactive building walkthrough is shown in Figure 3b.

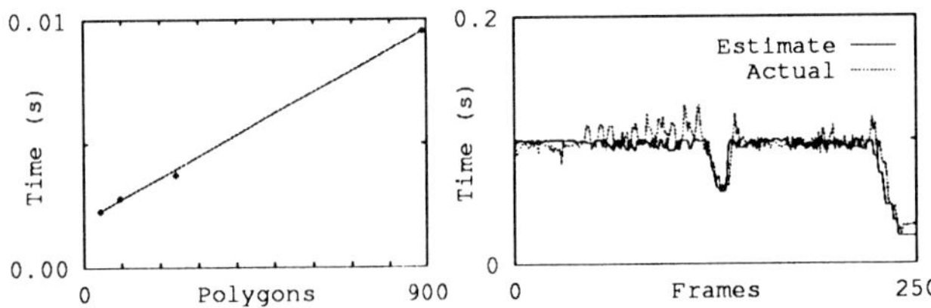

Figure 3: Cost model coefficients can be determined empirically. The plot in (a) shows actual flat-shaded rendering times for four LODs of a chair, and (b) shows a comparison of actual and estimated rendering times of frames during an interactive building walkthrough.

5 Benefit Heuristic

The $Benefit(O, L, R)$ heuristic is an estimate of the "contribution to model perception" of rendering object O with level of detail L and rendering algorithm R. Ideally, it predicts the amount and accuracy of information conveyed to a user due to rendering an object tuple. Of course, it is extremely difficult to accurately model human perception and understanding, so we have developed a simple, easy-to-compute heuristic based on intuitive principles.

Our *Benefit* heuristic depends primarily on the size of an object tuple in the final image. Intuitively, objects that appear larger to the observer "contribute" more to the image (see Figure 4). Therefore, the base value for our *Benefit* heuristic is simply an estimate of the number of pixels covered by the object.

Our *Benefit* heuristic also depends on the "accuracy" of an object tuple rendering. Intuitively, using a more detailed representation or a more realistic rendering algorithm for an object generates a higher quality image, and therefore conveys more accurate information to the user. Conceptually, we evaluate the "accuracy" of an object tuple rendering by comparison to an *ideal image* generated with an

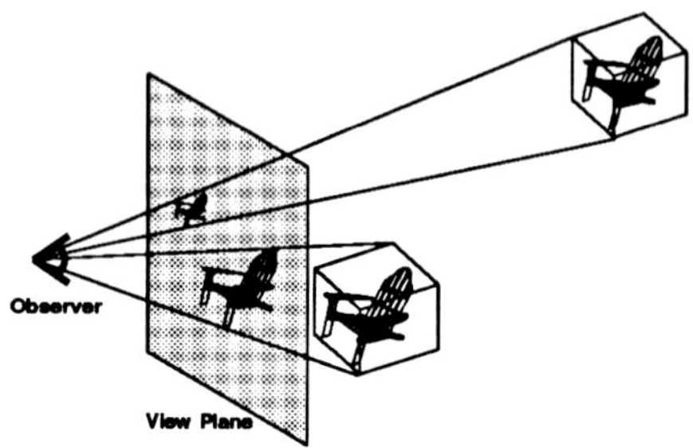

Figure 4: Objects that appear larger "contribute" more to the image.

ideal camera. For instance, consider generating a gray-level image of a scene containing only a cylinder with a diffusely reflecting Lambert surface illuminated by a single directional light source in orthonormal projection. Figure 5a shows an intensity plot of a sample scan-line of an ideal image generated for the cylinder.

First, consider approximating this ideal image with an image generated using a flat-shaded, polygonal representation for the cylinder. Since a single color is assigned to all pixels covered by the same polygon, a plot of pixel intensities across a scan-line of such an image is a stair-function. If an 8-sided prism is used to represent the cylinder, at most 4 distinct colors can appear in the image (one for each front-facing polygon), so the resulting image does not approximate the ideal image very well at all, as shown in Figure 5b. By comparison, if a 16-sided prism is used to represent the cylinder, as many as 8 distinct colors can appear in the image, generating a closer approximation to the ideal image, as shown in Figure 5c.

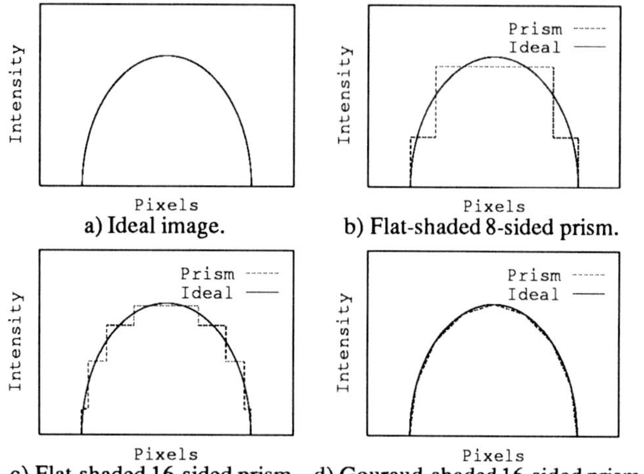

a) Ideal image. b) Flat-shaded 8-sided prism.

c) Flat-shaded 16-sided prism. d) Gouraud-shaded 16-sided prism.

Figure 5: Plots of pixel intensity across a sample scan-line of images generated using different representations and rendering algorithms for a simple cylinder.

Next, consider using Gouraud shading for a polygonal representation. In Gouraud shading, intensities are interpolated between vertices of polygons, so a plot of pixel intensities is a continuous, piecewise-linear function. Figure 5d shows a plot of pixel intensities across a scan line for a Gouraud shaded 16-sided prism. Compared to the plot for the flat-shaded image (Figure 5b), the Gouraud shaded image approximates the ideal image much more closely.

More complex representations (e.g., parametric or implicit surfaces) and rendering techniques (e.g., Phong shading, antialiasing or ray tracing) could be used to approximate the ideal image even more closely. Based on this intuition, we assume that the "error," i.e., the difference from the ideal image, decreases with the number of samples (e.g., rays/vertices/polygons) used to render an object tuple, and is dependent on the type of interpolation method used (e.g., Gouraud/flat). We capture these effects in the ***Benefit*** heuristic by multiplying by an "accuracy" factor:

$$Accuracy(O, L, R) = 1 - Error = 1 - \frac{BaseError}{Samples(L, R)^m}$$

where Samples(L, R) is #pixels for ray tracing, or #vertices for Gouraud shading, or #polygons for flat-shading (but never more than #pixels); and m is an exponent dependent on the interpolation method used (flat = 1, Gouraud = 2). The ***BaseError*** is arbitrarily set to 0.5 to give a strong error for a curved surface represented by a single flat polygon, but still account for a significantly higher benefit than not rendering the surface at all.

In addition to the size and accuracy of an object tuple rendering, our ***Benefit*** heuristic depends on on several other, more qualitative, factors, some of which apply to a static image, while others apply to sequences of images:

- **Semantics:** Some types of object may have inherent "importance." For instance, walls might be more important than pencils to the user of a building walkthrough; and enemy robots might be most important to the user of a video game. We adjust the ***Benefit*** of each object tuple by an amount proportional to the inherent importance of its object type.

- **Focus:** Objects that appear in the portion of the screen at which the user is looking might contribute more to the image than ones in the periphery of the user's view. Since we currently do not track the user's eye position, we simply assume that objects appearing near the middle of the screen are more important than ones near the side. We reduce the ***Benefit*** of each object tuple by an amount proportional to its distance from the middle of the screen.

- **Motion Blur:** Since objects that are moving quickly across the screen appear blurred or can be seen for only a short amount of time, the user may not be able to see them clearly. So we reduce the ***Benefit*** of each object tuple by an amount proportional to the ratio of the object's apparent speed to the size of an average polygon.

- **Hysteresis:** Rendering an object with different levels of detail in successive frames may be bothersome to the user and may reduce the quality of an image sequence. Therefore, we reduce the ***Benefit*** of each object tuple by an amount proportional to the difference in level of detail or rendering algorithm from the ones used for the same object in the previous frame.

Each of these qualitative factors is represented by a multiplier between 0.0 and 1.0 reflecting a possible reduction in object tuple benefit. The overall ***Benefit*** heuristic is a product of all the aforementioned factors:

$$Benefit(O, L, R) = Size(O) * Accuracy(O, L, R) * \\ Importance(O) * Focus(O) * Motion(O) * Hysteresis(O, L, R)$$

This ***Benefit*** heuristic is a simple experimental estimate of an object tuple's "contribution to model perception." Greater ***Benefit*** is assigned to object tuples that are larger (i.e., cover more pixels in the image), more realistic-looking (i.e., rendered with higher levels of detail, or better rendering algorithms), more important (i.e., semantically, or closer to the middle of the screen), and more apt to blend with other images in a sequence (i.e., hysteresis). In our implementation, the user can manipulate the relative weighting of these factors interactively using sliders on a control panel, and observe their effects in a real-time walkthrough. Therefore, although our current *Benefit* heuristic is rather ad hoc, it is useful for experimentation until we are able to encode more accurate models for human visual perception and understanding.

6 Optimization Algorithm

We use the *Cost* and *Benefit* heuristics described in the previous sections to choose a set of object tuples to render each frame by solving equation 1 in Section 3.

Unfortunately, this constrained optimization problem is NP-complete. It is the Continuous Multiple Choice Knapsack Problem [6, 7], a version of the well-known Knapsack Problem in which elements are partitioned into candidate sets, and at most one element from each candidate set may be placed in the knapsack at once. In this case, the set S of object tuples rendered is the knapsack, the object tuples are the elements to be placed into the knapsack, the target frame time is the size of the knapsack, the sets of object tuples representing the same object are the candidate sets, and the *Cost* and *Benefit* functions specify the "size" and "profit" of each element, respectively. The problem is to select the object tuples that have maximum cumulative benefit, but whose cumulative cost fits in the target frame time, subject to the constraint that only one object tuple representing each object may be selected.

We have implemented a simple, greedy approximation algorithm for this problem that selects object tuples with the highest *Value* ($Benefit(O, L, R)/Cost(O, L, R)$). Logically, we add object tuples to S in descending order of *Value* until the maximum cost is competely claimed. However, if an object tuple is added to S which represents the same object as another object tuple already in S, only the object tuple with the maximum benefit of the two is retained. The merit of this approach can be explained intuitively by noting that each subsequent portion of the frame time is used to render the object tuple with the best available "bang for the buck." It is easy to show that a simple implementation of this greedy approach runs in $O(n \log n)$ time for n potentially visible objects, and produces a solution that is at least half as good as the optimal solution [6].

Rather than computing and sorting the *Benefit*, *Cost*, and *Value* for all possible object tuples during every frame, as would be required by a naive implementation, we have implemented an incremental optimization algorithm that takes advantage of the fact that there is typically a large amount of coherence between successive frames. The algorithm works as follows: At the start of the algorithm, an object tuple is added to S for each potentially visible object. Initially, each object is assigned the LOD and rendering algorithm chosen in the previous frame, or the lowest LOD and rendering algorithm if the object is newly visible. In each iteration of the optimization, the algorithm first increments the accuracy attribute (LOD or rendering algorithm) of the object that has the highest subsequent *Value*. It then decrements the accuracy attributes of the object tuples with the lowest current *Value* until the cumulative cost of all object tuples in S is less than the target frame time. The algorithm terminates when the same accuracy attribute of the same object tuple is both incremented and decremented in the same iteration.

This incremental implementation finds an approximate solution that is the same as found by the naive implementation if *Values* of object tuples decrease monotonically as tuples are rendered with greater accuracy (i.e., there are diminishing returns with more complex renderings). In any case, the worst-case running time for the algorithm is $O(n \log n)$. However, since the initial guess for the LOD and rendering algorithm for each object is generated from the previous frame, and there is often a large amount of coherence from frame to frame, the algorithm completes in just a few iterations on average. Moreover, computations are done in parallel with the display of the previous frame on a separate processor in a pipelined architecture; they do not increase the effective frame rate as long as the time required for computation is not greater than the time required for display.

7 Test Methods

To test whether this new cost/benefit optimization algorithm produces more uniform frame rates than previous LOD selection algorithms, we ran a set of tests with our building walkthrough application using four different LOD selection algorithms:

a) **No Detail Elision:** Each object is rendered at the highest LOD.

b) **Static:** Each object is rendered at the highest LOD for which an average polygon covers at least 1024 pixels on the screen.

c) **Feedback:** Similar to *Static* test, except the size threshold for LOD selection is updated in each frame by a feedback loop, based on the difference between the time required to render the previous frame and the target frame time of one-tenth of a second.

d) **Optimization:** Each object is rendered at the LOD chosen by the cost/benefit optimization algorithm described in Sections 3 and 6 in order to meet the target frame time of one-tenth of a second. For comparison sake, the *Benefit* heuristic is limited to consideration of *object size* in this test, i.e., all other *Benefit* factors are set to 1.0.

All tests were performed on a Silicon Graphics VGX 320 workstation with two 33MHz MIPS R3000 processors and 64MB of memory. We used an *eye-to-object* visibility algorithm described in [12] to determine a set of potentially visible objects to be rendered in each frame. The application was configured as a two-stage pipeline with one processor for visibility and LOD selection computations and another separate processor for rendering. Timing statistics were gathered using a $16\mu s$ timer.

In each test, we used the sample observer path shown in Figure 6 through a model of an auditorium on the third floor of Soda Hall. The model was chosen because it is complex enough to differentiate the characteristics of various LOD selection algorithms (87,565 polygons), yet small enough to reside entirely in main memory so as to eliminate the effects of memory management in our tests. The test path was chosen because it represents typical behavior of real users of a building walkthrough system, and highlights the differences between various LOD selection algorithms. For instance, at the observer viewpoint marked 'A', many complex objects are simultaneously visible, some of which are close and appear large to the observer; at the viewpoint marked 'B', there are very few objects visible to the observer, most of which appear small; and at the viewpoint marked 'C', numerous complex objects become visible suddenly as the observer spins around quickly. We refer to these marked observer viewpoints in the analysis, as they are the viewpoints at which the differences between the various LOD selection algorithms are most pronounced.

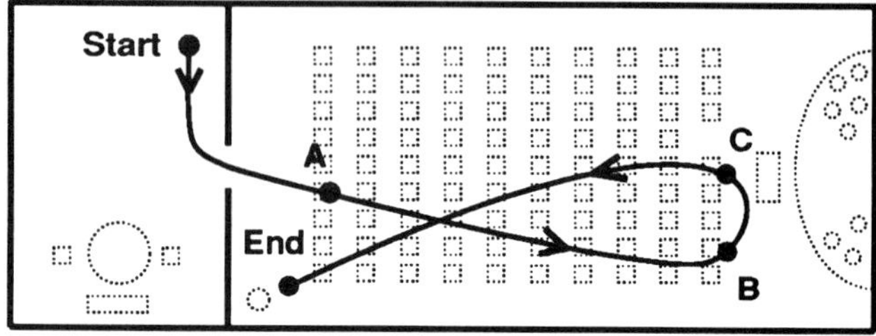

Figure 6: Test observer path through a model of an auditorium.

LOD Selection Algorithm	Compute Time		Frame Time		
	Mean	Max	Mean	Max	StdDev
None	0.00	0.00	0.43	0.99	0.305
Static	0.00	0.01	0.11	0.20	0.048
Feedback	0.00	0.01	0.10	0.16	0.026
Optimization	0.01	0.03	0.10	0.13	0.008

Table 1: Cumulative statistics for test observer path (in seconds).

8 Results and Discussion

Figure 7 shows plots of the frame time (seconds per frame) for each observer viewpoint along the test path for the four LOD selection algorithms tested. Table 1 shows cumulative compute time (i.e., time required for execution of the LOD selection algorithm) and frame time statistics for all observer viewpoints along the test path.

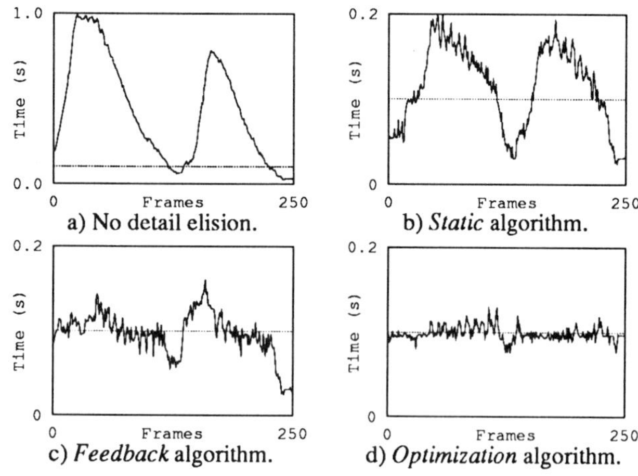

a) No detail elision. b) *Static* algorithm. c) *Feedback* algorithm. d) *Optimization* algorithm.

Figure 7: Plots of frame time for every observer viewpoint along test observer path using a) no detail elision, b) static algorithm, c) feedback algorithm, and d) optimization algorithm. Note: the "Frame Time" axis in plot (a) is five-times larger than the others.

If no detail elision is used, and all potentially visible objects are rendered at the highest LOD, the time required for each frame is generally long and non-uniform, since it depends directly on the number and complexity of the objects visible to the observer (see Figure 7a). In our test model, far too many polygons are visible from most observer viewpoints to generate frames at interactive rates without detail elision. For instance, at the observer viewpoint marked 'A' in Figure 6, 72K polygons are simultaneously visible, and the frame time is 0.98 seconds. Overall, the mean frame time for all observer viewpoints on the test path is 0.43 seconds per frame.

If the *Static* LOD selection algorithm is used, objects whose average polygon is smaller than a size threshold fixed at 1024 pixels per polygon are rendered with lower LODs. Even though the frame rate is much faster than without detail elision, there is still a large amount of variability in the frame time, since it depends on the size and complexity of the objects visible from the observer's viewpoint (see Figure 7b). For instance, at the observer viewpoint marked 'A', the frame time is quite long (0.19 seconds) because many visible objects are complex and appear large to the observer. A high LOD is chosen for each of these objects independently, resulting in a long overall frame time. This result can seen clearly in Figure 8a which depicts the LOD selected for each object in the frame for observer viewpoint 'A' – higher LODs are represented by darker shades of gray. On the other hand, the frame time is very short in the frame at the observer viewpoint marked 'B' (0.03 seconds). Since all visible objects appear relatively small to the observer, they are rendered at a lower LOD even though more detail could have been rendered within the target frame time. In general, it is impossible to choose a single size threshold for LOD selection that generates uniform frame times for all observer viewpoints.

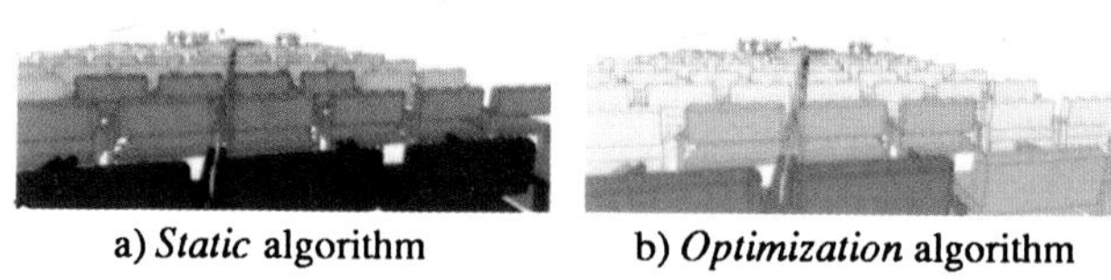

a) *Static* algorithm b) *Optimization* algorithm

Figure 8: Images depicting the LODs selected for each object at the observer viewpoints marked 'A' using the *Static* and *Optimization* algorithms. Darker shades of gray represent higher LODs.

The *Feedback* algorithm adjusts the size threshold for LOD selection adaptively based on the time taken to render previous frames in an effort to maintain a uniform frame rate. This algorithm generates a fairly uniform frame rate in situations of smoothly varying scene complexity, as evidenced by the relatively flat portions of the frame time curve shown in Figure 7c (frames 1–125). However, in situations where the complexity of the scene visible to the observer changes suddenly, peaks and valleys appear in the curve. Sometimes the frame time generated using the *Feedback* algorithm can be even longer than the one generated using the *Static* algorithm, as the *Feedback* algorithm is lured into a inappropriately low size threshold during times of low scene complexity. For instance, just before the viewpoint marked 'C', the observer is looking at a relatively simple scene containing just a few objects on the stage, so frame times are very short, and the size threshold for LOD selection is reduced to zero. However, at the viewpoint marked 'C', many chairs become visible suddenly as the observer spins around quickly. Since the adaptive size threshold is set very low, inappropriately high LODs are chosen for most objects (see Figure 9a), resulting in a frame time of 0.16 seconds. Although the size threshold can often adapt quickly after such discontinuities in scene complexity, some effects related to this feedback control (i.e., oscillation, overshoot, and a few very slow frames) can be quite disturbing to the user.

In contrast, the *Optimization* algorithm predicts the complexity of the model visible from the current observer viewpoint, and chooses an appropriate LOD and rendering algorithm for each object to meet the target frame time. As a result, the frame time generated using the *Optimization* algorithm is much more uniform than using any of

a) *Feedback* algorithm

b) *Optimization* algorithm

Figure 9: Images depicting the LODs selected for each object at the observer viewpoints marked 'C' using the *Feedback* and *Optimization* algorithms. Darker shades of gray represent higher LODs.

the other LOD selection algorithms (see Figure 7d). For all observer viewpoints along the test path, the standard deviation in the frame time is 0.008 seconds, less than one third of any of the other three algorithms tested. The longest frame time is 0.13 seconds, and the shortest is 0.075 seconds.

As the *Optimization* algorithm adjusts image quality to maintain a uniform, interactive frame rate, it attempts to render the "best" image possible within the target frame time for each observer viewpoint. As a result, there is usually little noticeable difference between images generated using the *Optimization* algorithm and ones generated with no detail elision at all. A comparison of images for observer viewpoint 'A' generated using a) no detail elision, and b) using the *Optimization* algorithm to meet a target frame time of one tenth of a second are shown in Figure 10. Figure 10a has 72,570 polygons and took 0.98 seconds to render, whereas Figure 10b has 5,300 polygons and took 0.10 seconds. Even though there are less than a tenth as many polygons in Figure 10b, the difference in image quality is barely noticeable. For reference, the LOD chosen for each object in Figure 10b is shown in Figure 8b. Note that reduction in rendering time does not map to a linear reduction in polygon count since polygons representing lower levels of detail tend to be bigger on average.

The *Optimization* algorithm is more general than other detail elision algorithms in that it also adjusts the rendering algorithm (and possibly other attributes in the future) for each object independently. Examine Figure 11, which shows three images of a small library on the sixth floor of Soda Hall containing several textured surfaces. Figure $11a_1$, shows an image generated using no detail elision – it contains 19,821 polygons and took 0.60 seconds to render. Figures $11b_1$ and $11c_1$ show images generated for the same observer viewpoint using the *Optimization* algorithm with target frame times of b) 0.15 seconds (4,217 polygons), and c) 0.10 seconds (1,389 polygons). Although the *Optimization* algorithm uses lower levels of detail for many objects (see Figures $11b_1$ and $11c_1$), and generates images that are quite different than the one generated with no detail elision (see Figures $11b_2$ and $11c_2$), all three images look very similar. Notice the reduced tessellation of chairs further from the observer, and the omission of texture on the bookshelves in Figure $11b_1$. Similarly, notice the flat-shaded chairs, and the omission of books on bookshelves and texture on doors in Figure $11c_1$.

Having experimented with several LOD selection algorithms in an interactive visualization application, we are optimistic that variation in image quality is less disturbing to a user than variation in the frame times, as long as different representations for each object appear similar, and transitions between representations are not very noticeable. Further experimentation is required to determine which types of rendering attributes can be blended smoothly during interactive visualization.

9 Conclusion

We have described an adaptive display algorithm for fast, uniform frame rates during interactive visualization of large, complex virtual environments. The algorithm adjusts image quality dynamically in order to maintain a user-specified frame rate, selecting a level of detail and an algorithm with which to render each potentially visible object to produce the "best" image possible within the target frame time.

Our tests show that the *Optimization* algorithm generates more uniform frame rates than other previously described detail elision algorithms with little noticeable difference in image quality during visualization of complex models. Interesting topics for further study include algorithms for automatic generation of multiresolution models, and experiments to develop measures of *image quality* and *image differences*.

10 Acknowledgements

We are grateful to Thurman Brown, Delnaz Khorramabadi, Priscilla Shih and Maryann Simmons for their efforts constructing the building model. Silicon Graphics, Inc. has been very generous, allowing us to use equipment, and donating a VGX 320 workstation to this project as part of a grant from the Microelectronics Innovation and Computer Research Opportunities (MICRO 1991) program of the State of California. We appreciate the assistance of Greg Ward, Sharon Fischler, and Henry Moreton who helped generate the color prints for this paper. Finally, we thank Seth Teller for his spatial subdivisions, visibility algorithms, and other important contributions to this project.

References

[1] Airey, John M., Rohlf, John H., and Brooks, Jr., Frederick P. Towards Image Realism with Interactive Update Rates in Complex Virtual Building Environments. *ACM SIGGRAPH Special Issue on 1990 Symposium on Interactive 3D Graphics*, 24, 2 (1990), 41-50.

[2] Blake, Edwin H. A Metric for Computing Adaptive Detail in Animated Scenes using Object-Oriented Programming. *Eurographics '87*. G. Marechal (Ed.), Elsivier Science Publishers, B.V. (North-Holland), 1987.

[3] Brooks, Jr., Frederick P. Walkthrough - A Dynamic Graphics System for Simulating Virtual Buildings. *Proceedings of the 1986 Workshop on Interactive 3D Graphics*.

[4] Clark, James H. Hierarchical Geometric Models for Visible Surface Algorithms. *Communications of the ACM*, 19, 10 (October 1976), 547-554.

[5] Funkhouser, Thomas A., Séquin, Carlo H., and Teller, Seth J. Management of Large Amounts of Data in Interactive Building Walkthroughs. *ACM SIGGRAPH Special Issue on 1992 Symposium on Interactive 3D Graphics*, 11-20.

[6] Garey, Michael R., and Johnson, David S. Computers and Intractibility: A Guide to the Theory of NP-Completeness. W.H. Freeman and Company, New York, 1979.

[7] Ibaraki, T., Hasegawa, T., Teranaka, K., and Iwase J. The Multiple Choice Knapsack Problem. *J. Oper. Res. Soc. Japan* 21, 1978, 59-94.

[8] Rossignac, Jarek, and Borrel, Paul. Multi-resolution 3D approximations for rendering complex scenes. *IFIP TC 5.WG 5.10 II Conference on Geometric Modeling in Computer Graphics*, Genova, Italy, 1993. Also available as IBM Research Report RC 17697, Yorktown Heights, NY 10598.

[9] Schachter, Bruce J. (Ed.). *Computer Image Generation.* John Wiley and Sons, New York, NY, 1983.

[10] *Graphics Library Programming Tools and Techniques*, Document #007-1489-01, Silicon Graphics, Inc., 1992.

[11] Teller, Seth J., and Séquin, Carlo H. Visibility Preprocessing for Interactive Walkthroughs. Proceedings of SIGGRAPH '91. In *Computer Graphics* 25, 4 (August 1991), 61-69.

[12] Teller, Seth J. *Visibility Computations in Densely Occluded Polyhedral Environments*. Ph.D. thesis, Computer Science Division (EECS), University of California, Berkeley, 1992. Also available as UC Berkeley technical report UCB/CSD-92-708.

[13] Zyda, Michael J. Course Notes, Book Number 10, Graphics Video Laboratory, Department of Computer Science, Naval Postgraduate School, Monterey, California, November 1991.

a) No detail elision

b) *Optimization* algorithm (0.10 seconds)

Figure 10: Images for observer viewpoint 'A' generated using a) no detail elision (72,570 polygons), and b) the *Optimization* algorithm with a 0.10 second target frame time (5,300 polygons).

a_1

a) No detail elision

b_1

b_2

b) *Optimization* algorithm (0.15 seconds)

c_1

c_2

c_3

c) *Optimization* algorithm (0.10 seconds)

Figure 11: Images of library generated using a) no detail elision (19,821 polygons), and the *Optimization* detail elision algorithm with target frame times of b) 0.15 seconds (4,217 polygons), and c) 0.10 seconds (1,389 polygons). LODs chosen for objects in b_1 and c_1 are shown in b_2 and c_c – darker shades of gray represent higher LODs. Pixel-by-pixel differences $abs(a_1 - b_1)$ and $abs(a_1 - c_1)$ are shown in b_3 and c_3 – brighter colors represent greater difference.

Discrete Groups and Visualization of Three-Dimensional Manifolds

Charlie Gunn
The Geometry Center, The University of Minnesota *

Abstract

We describe a software implementation for interactive visualization of a wide class of discrete groups. In addition to familiar Euclidean space, these groups act on the curved geometries of hyperbolic and spherical space. We construct easily computable models of our geometric spaces based on projective geometry; and establish algorithms for visualization of three-dimensional manifolds based upon the close connection between discrete groups and manifolds. We describe an object-oriented implementation of these concepts, and several novel visualization applications. As a visualization tool, this software breaks new ground in two directions: interactive exploration of curved spaces, and of topological manifolds modeled on these spaces. It establishes a generalization of the application of projective geometry to computer graphics, and lays the groundwork for visualization of spaces of non-constant curvature.

CR Categories and Subject Descriptors: I.3.3 [Picture/Image Generation] display algorithms I.3.5 [Computational Geometry and Object Modeling Graphics]: geometric algorithms, hierarchy and geometric transformations, I.3.7 [Three dimensional Graphics and Realism] color, shading, shadowing, and texture

Additional Key Words and Phrases: discrete group, tessellation, quotient space, projective geometry, hyperbolic geometry, spherical geometry, curvature, geodesic.

1 Discrete Groups

Symmetry, broadly speaking, implies a redundant supply of information. A mirror image contains the same information as the scene that it mirrors. The theory of discrete groups has been developed over the past 100 years as a formalization of the process of extracting a single copy of the information present in symmetric configurations. The discrete groups which we study here are groups of motions which act on a geometric space, such as Euclidean space, to produce tessellations by congruent non-overlapping cells. Familiar examples include wallpaper patterns, and the interlocking designs of M. C. Escher. We consider two simple examples before introducing mathematical definitions.

*Current address: SFB 288, MA 8-5, Technische Universität, Strasse des 17 Juni 136, 1 Berlin 12, Germany, gunn@sfb288.math.tu-berlin.de

1.1 The circle and the line

When we evaluate the expression $\sin(2\pi x)$ we are only interested in x mod 1, since sin is a periodic function: $\sin(2\pi x) = \sin(2\pi(x+k))$, where k is an integer. The set of all motions of the real line R by integer amounts forms a group Γ, which leaves invariant the function $\sin(2\pi x)$. We can form the *quotient* R/Γ, which is the set of equivalence classes with respect to this group. This quotient can be represented by the closed interval $[0,1]$, with the understanding that we identify the two endpoints. But identifying the two endpoints yields a circle. Once we know the values of $\sin(2\pi x)$ on the circle, we can compute it for any other value y, simply by subtracting or adding integers to y until the result lies in the range $[0,1)$.

In this example the *discrete group* Γ is the set of transformations of R given by all translations $x \rightarrow x+k$, where k is an integer. Γ is *discrete* since no non-trivial sequence in Γ converges to the the identity element. The *quotient* of R under this action is S^1, the unit circle. We write $R/\Gamma = S^1$.

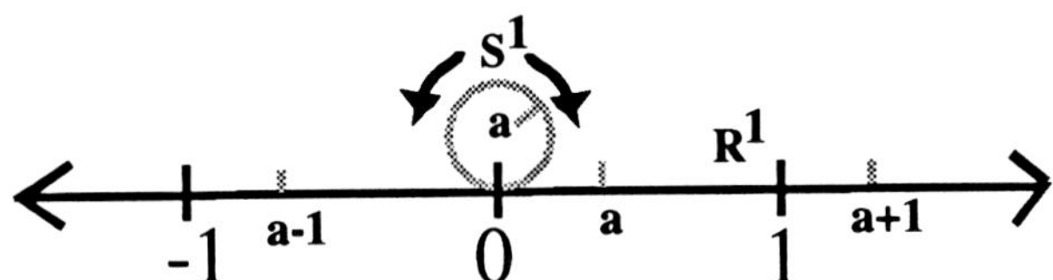

Figure 1: The circle is the quotient of R by the integers.

$I = [0,1)$ is a *fundamental domain* for this group action. We can recover R from the fundamental domain and Γ: the union

$$\bigcup_{g\in\Gamma} gI$$

covers R without overlap.

We move into two dimensions to bring out other features of the concepts introduced in this example.

1.2 The torus and the plane

Instead of R we now work with R^2. Let Γ be the group of translations of R^2 generated by $(x,y) \rightarrow (x+1,y)$ and $(x,y) \rightarrow (x,y+1)$, that is, unit translations in the coordinate directions. What is the quotient R^2/Γ? Instead of the unit interval with its endpoints identified, we are led to a unit square that has its edges identified in pairs. If we imagine the square is made of rubber and that we can perform the identifications by bending the square and gluing, we find that the resulting surface is the torus T^2. See Figure 2.

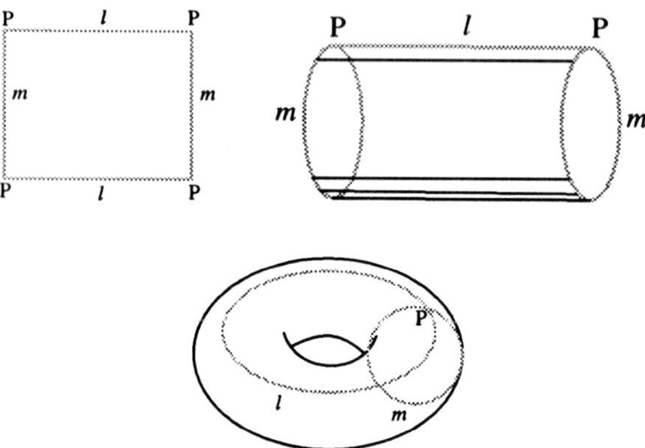

Figure 2: Making a torus from a square

1.3 Algebra and geometry: the fundamental group

A key element of this approach is the interplay of algebraic and geometric viewpoints. To clarify this, we introduce the *fundamental group* of a space, formed by taking all the closed paths based at some point P in the space. We get a group structure on this set: we can add paths by following one and then the other, and subtract by going around the second path in the reverse order. The zero-length path is the identity element. If one path can be moved or deformed to another path, the two paths correspond to the same group element. It is easy to check that different P's yield isomorphic groups. We say a space is *simply connected* if every closed path can be smoothly shrunk to a point, like a lasso, without leaving the space. [Mun75] The fundamental group of a simply connected space consists of just the identity element.

In the above example R^2 is simply connected; while T^2, the quotient, isn't. When X is the quotient of a simply connected space Y, we say that Y is the *universal covering space* of X. The importance of simply connected spaces in the study of discrete groups is due to a basic result of topology that (subject to technical constraints which we will consider satisfied) every space has a unique universal covering space [Mun75]. So in considering group actions, we need only consider actions on simply connected spaces.

The interplay of algebra and geometry reveals itself in the fact that the fundamental group of the quotient, a purely *topological* object, is isomorphic to the group of symmetries Γ, which arises in a purely *geometric* context.

1.4 Inside versus Outside Views

In the cases we will consider, the universal covering space X is a *geometric* space, that is, it comes equipped with a metric that determines distance between points and angles between tangent vectors. In this case we sometimes refer to X as a *model geometry.* This metric allows us to compute geodesics, or shortest paths, between points in the space [Car76]. The quotient space inherits this metric. R^2 is the universal covering space of T^2: if we unroll T^2 onto R^2, the copies of the torus will cover the plane completely, without overlap. We say these copies *tessellate* the plane. For some purposes the rolled-up torus sitting in R^3 is useful, but to gain the experience of what it is like to live *inside* the surface, we are better served by examining the *tessellation* of the universal covering space produced by the group.

For example, if we want to make pictures of what an inhabitant of T^2 sees, we will make them in R^2: Light follows geodesics, which appear to be very complicated on the rolled-up torus, but in R^2 are just ordinary straight lines. A complicated closed path based at P which wraps around the torus several times unrolls in the universal cover to be an ordinary straight line connecting P and hP for some $h \in \Gamma$. See Figure 3. An immediate consequence of this is that an observer on the torus based at P sees many copies of himself, one for every closed geodesic on the surface passing through P. See [Wee85] for a complete and elementary description of this phenomenon. We say the rolled-up torus represents the *outsider's* view; while the unrolled view we term the *insider's* view, since it shows what someone living inside the space would see. The importance of the insider's view becomes more telling in three dimensional spaces, since to "roll up" our fundamental domains requires four or more dimensions. In this case the insider's view becomes a practical necessity.

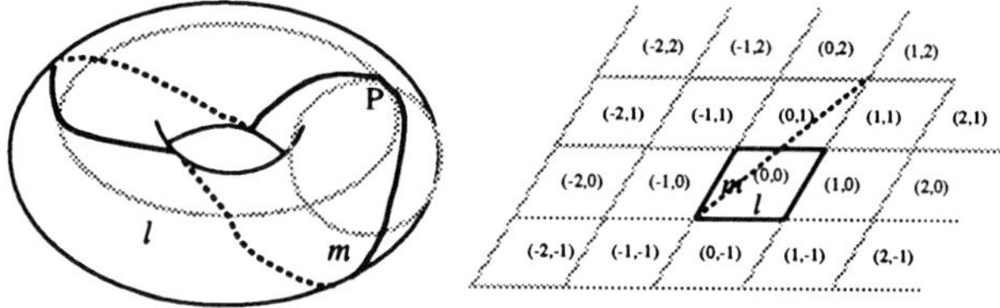

Figure 3: Outside and inside views of a complicated torus path

When we try to perform the analogous construction for the two-holed torus, instead of a square in the Euclidean plane R^2, we are led to a regular octagon in the hyperbolic plane H^2[FRC92]. We describe hyperbolic geometry in more detail below.

1.5 Definition of discrete group

A discrete group is a subgroup Γ of a continuous group G such that there is a neighborhood U of the identity in G with $U \cap \Gamma = I$, the identity element.

In the example of the torus above, the group Γ *acts* on R^2. Such an action on a topological space X is called *properly discontinuous* if for every closed and bounded subset K of X, the set of $\gamma \in \Gamma$ such that $\gamma K \cap K \neq \phi$ is finite. In the cases to be discussed here, Γ is discrete if and only if the action of Γ is properly discontinuous.

If in addition the quotient space X/Γ is compact, we say that Γ is a *crystallographic*, or *crystal*, group.

The group of the torus discussed in 1.2 above is a crystallographic group, the simplest so-called *wallpaper* group. There are exactly 17 wallpaper groups of the Euclidean plane. See [Gun83] for a full discussion of this case and the details of a computer implementation.

1.6 Dirichlet domains

Given a discrete group, there is a technique for constructing a fundamental domain, known as a Dirichlet domain. We define it now for future reference. Given a discrete group Γ acting on a space X and a point $P \in X$, the orbit $O(P)$ of P under Γ is $\bigcup_{g \in \Gamma} gP$. Then the Dirichlet domain with respect

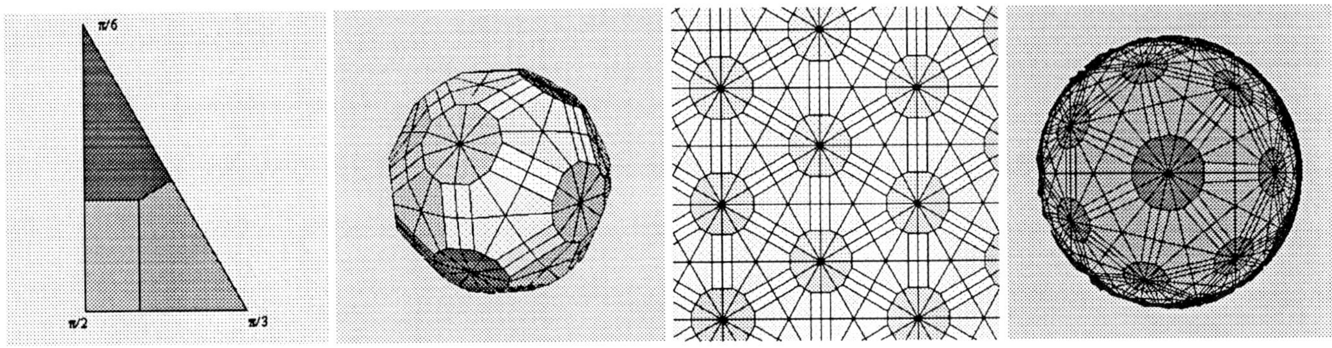

Figure 4: (235), (236) and (237) triangle groups tessellate S^2, R^2, and H^2.

to P is the set of points in X which are closer to P than to any other point of $O(P)$. We can be more precise. For each $Q \in O(P)$, construct the perpendicular bisector M of the segment PQ. Denote by H_Q the half-space containing P bounded by M. Then the Dirichlet domain D_P determined by Γ and P is

$$\bigcap_{Q \in O(P)} H_Q$$

In practice, for many of the groups the intersection can be assumed to involve only finitely many H_Q's. The resulting polyhedron is convex. If a face F is determined by $g \in \Gamma$, then $g^{-1}F$ will be a congruent face F' determined by g^{-1}. This face pairing is used in the sequel. Note that, since D_P depends upon P, there are potentially many different shapes for the Dirichlet domain for a given group. [Bea83] Computational geometers may recognize that a Dirichlet domain with respect to P is a *Voronoi cell* with respect to the orbit of P.

2 Non-Euclidean Geometries

In the examples above, the model geometry was Euclidean. There are two other simply connected two-dimensional spaces in addition to R^2 which can serve as our model geometries: the sphere S^2 and the hyperbolic plane H^2. They have geometries (to be described in more detail below) which satisfy all the postulates of Euclidean geometry except for the Parallel Postulate: Given a line L and a point P not on L, there is a unique line M passing through P which is parallel to L. The sphere has no parallel lines; while H^2 has infinitely many for a given L and P. See [Cox65] for an account of the discovery and development of these non-Euclidean geometries.

An equivalent characterization of Euclidean, spherical, and hyperbolic geometry is that the sum of the angles of a triangle is, respectively, equal to, greater than, or less than, π. Figure 4 shows tessellations of these three spaces by triangles with angles $(\pi/2, \pi/3, \pi/n)$, where $n = (5, 6, 7)$ yields spherical, Euclidean, and hyperbolic space.

We now turn to demonstrating models for these three geometries which share a common root in projective geometry. This will lead directly to techniques for visualizing discrete groups which act on these spaces.

2.1 Projective geometry

Projective geometry is the geometry of lines without regard to distance or measure. It was discovered at roughly the same time as the the non-Euclidean geometries discussed above; we show in the sequel how it can be considered to be the fundamental geometry out of which the other geometries arise.

The projective plane P^2 is gotten from the ordinary plane by adjoining a *line at infinity.* Projective space P^n can be constructed in every dimension n by adjoining an $n-1$ dimensional hyperplane at infinity. We assume the reader is familiar with homogeneous coordinates for projective space [Cox65]. The group of self-mappings of projective space P^n can then be represented via homogeneous coordinates as elements of the matrix group $PGL(R, n+1)$, the projective general linear group. This group consists of all invertible matrices of dimension $(n+1) \times (n+1)$, where two matrices are equivalent if one is a scalar multiple of the other [Cox87]. Much of the success of the approach described in this paper is due to the circumstance that many computer graphics rendering transformation pipelines support $PGL(R, 4)$.

2.2 From projective to metric geometry

Projective geometry does not include a notion of distance or angle measure. However, every projective transformation preserves a quantity known as the **cross ratio** . The cross ratio is a function of four collinear points:

$$\lambda(AB, CD) = \frac{(A-C)(B-D)}{(B-C)(A-D)}$$

Here the points are represented by a homogeneous coordinate system on their common line; for convienience we can assume this is ordinary Euclidean measure on the line. This invariant has been used by Cayley to construct metric geometries on the foundation of projective geometry [Cay59].

First choose a homogeneous conic Q which is to be invariant. The conic is known as the Absolute for the associated geometry. The projective transformations preserving Q form a subgroup H of the full projective group. Two given points P_0 and P_1 determine a line, which intersects the conic Q in a pair of points T_0 and T_1, whose coordinates may be complex numbers. Then define a distance function

$$d(P_0, P_1) = K \log \lambda(T_0T_1, P_0P_1) \tag{1}$$

where the constant K is determined according to the nature of Q in order to make the distance function real. Since the cross ratio is a multiplicative function, use of the log function yields an additive function. Measurement of angles between lines L_0 and L_1 proceeds in like manner, by determining the two tangent lines to Q which lie in the pencil of lines determined by L_0 and L_1.

This yields models for spherical, hyperbolic, and Euclidean geometry which share the same straight lines; what is different is how distance along them and between them is measured. The subgroup H becomes the isometry group for the metric geometry.

We will for simplicity's sake work in two dimensions, that is, with homogeneous coordinates (x, y, w), and consider only distance measurement, not angle measurement. All our results generalize directly to arbitrary higher dimension. Since the cases of spherical and hyperbolic geometry are more straightforward, we begin with them.

2.2.1 Spherical geometry

For the spherical case, we choose Q to be the totally imaginary conic $x^2 + y^2 + w^2 = 0$. The proper choice for K is $i/2$. We can derive from Q an *inner product* between pairs of points: if $P_0 = (x_0, y_0, w_0)$ and $P_1 = (x_1, y_1, w_1)$ then $P_0.P_1 = x_0x_1 + y_0y_1 + w_0w_1$. Then (1) reduces to:

$$d(P_0, P_1) = \arccos(\frac{P_0.P_1}{\sqrt{(P_0.P_0)(P_1.P_1)}})$$

This is the familiar measurement between points on the unit sphere. Projective transformations which preserve Q constitute the special orthogonal group SO(3), the group of rotations of three-dimensional Euclidean space. Although it is tempting to consider the familiar picture of S^2 sitting isometrically in R^3, it is more appropriate to think of the model presented purely in terms of P^2. In this model, to each point of P^2 we assign two antipodal points of S^2.

2.2.2 Hyperbolic geometry

For the hyperbolic case, we choose Q to be the totally real conic $x^2 + y^2 - w^2 = 0$, a cone aligned with the w-axis. The correct choice for K is $\frac{1}{2}$. The derived inner product of two points $P_0 = (x_0, y_0, w_0)$ and $P_1 = (x_1, y_1, w_1)$ is then $P_0.P_1 = x_0x_1 + y_0y_1 - w_0w_1$, sometimes called the Minkowski inner product. Our model for hyperbolic geometry will consist of the interior of this cone, where $P.P < 0$. Then (1) reduces to:

$$d(P_0, P_1) = \operatorname{arccosh}(\frac{P_0.P_1}{\sqrt{(P_0.P_0)(P_1.P_1)}})$$

where P_0 and P_1 lie in the interior of the cone. The isometry group is SO(2,1), the so-called Minkowski group.

Consider the hyperboloid of two sheets H, defined by the condition $P.P = -1$. Just as the unit sphere is a model for spherical geometry, the upper sheet of H is a model for hyperbolic geometry. The most convenient model for H^2 is hidden within H. Consider the plane $w = 1$. It intersects Q in a circle that bounds a disk D. We can project our hyperboloid H onto D from the origin. This projection respects the distance function defined above (it is, after all, a projective invariant). Then D is a model of hyperbolic geometry, the so-called Klein or projective model. It is shown in the right-most figure in Figure 4. In three dimensions, this yields a model of H^3 as the interior of the unit ball in R^3. There are several other commonly used models of hyperbolic geometry, most notably the Poincaré or conformal model [Bea83]. Our choice of the projective model here was determined by the fact that it yields the correct results for visualizing the insider's view.

2.2.3 Euclidean geometry

Euclidean, or parabolic, geometry arises when apply a limiting process to the conic $\epsilon(x^2 + y^2) + w^2 = 0$. As $\epsilon \to 0$, the expression for distance reduces to

$$d(P_0, P_1) = \sqrt{(x_0 - x_1)^2 + (y_0 - y_1)^2}$$

where P_0 and P_1 have been dehomogenized. The isometry group of this geometry $E(2)$ is the semi-direct product of $SO(2)$, the circle, and $R(2)$, the two-dimensional Euclidean translation group.

2.3 Comments

This development in terms of projective geometry is given fully in [Woo22] and is due to Cayley and Klein. For a treatment derived from the modern differential geometric viewpoint see [Car76]; for an implementation description following this viewpoint see [Gun92].

To justify the use of the names spherical and hyperbolic it is worthwhile to verify that the geometries induced by the indicated metrics on the indicated subspaces in fact yield geometries which behave correctly with respect to parallel lines and sums of angles of triangles.

For a detailed discussion of how to construct isometries of hyperbolic 3-space in the projective model discussed here see [PG92].

The above results, stated for the two-dimensional case, can be extended to arbitrary dimension.

3 Manifolds and Discrete Groups

An n-dimensional *manifold*, or n-manifold, is a topological space X such that X is locally homeomorphic to R^n, that is, every point of X has a neighborhood that can be mapped 1-1 and continuously onto a small ball in R^n. If in addition we can realize X as the quotient of a geometric space M by a discrete group, we say that X has a *geometric structure* modeled on M. A related concept to that of manifold is *orbifold*. An orbifold is like a manifold, but it may have singular points where it is locally homeomorphic not to R^n but rather to the quotient of R^n by a finite group. Orbifolds arise, generally speaking, when the elements of the discrete group have fixed points, such as rotations or reflections.

Initial work on the connection of discrete groups and theory of manifolds was done by Henri Poincaré in the 1880's. To this day much research in this field is driven by the Poincaré Conjecture, which asserts that a closed, connected, simply connected 3-dimensional manifold is homeomorphic to the 3-dimensional sphere S^3. This conjecture is closely related to the classification problem: making a list of all 3-manifolds. For example, in dimension 2, there is a uniformization theorem which says that any closed 2-dimensional manifold has a geometric structure modeled on one of S^2, R^2, or H^2. Recent work by Thurston and others has shown that many (possibly all) 3-manifolds have essentially unique geometric structures. That is, there are good reasons to believe that to every 3-manifold there corresponds an essentially unique discrete group [Thu82].

The geometric structures for 3-manifolds come from eight model geometries: R^3, S^3, and H^3 plus five additional simply connected spaces. The additional five are not as nice as the first three, since they are not *isotropic*: not all directions in space are the same. In any case, the most prevalent geometric structure is hyperbolic. For a description of these eight geometries, see [Thu82], [Thuar]. The current software implementation does not support these five additional geometries.

In the discussion that follows, we will concentrate on the insider's, rather than the outsider's, view of three dimensional orbifolds. That is, we will look at the tessellations of the simply connected space (Euclidean, hyperbolic, or spherical) induced by discrete groups.

4 Software Implementation

4.1 OOGL

In order to visualize the spaces under consideration, we have developed an implementation within an object-oriented graphics library, OOGL. The generic OOGL class is `Geom`. Subclasses include include geometric primitives such as `PolyList`, `Vect`, `Bezier`, and `Mesh`; and organizational objects such as `List` and `Inst` (for instancing geometry). Methods with which `Geoms` come equipped include: `Bound, Create, Copy, Delete, Save, Load, Pick, and Draw` .

An interactive viewer, `Geomview` [MLP+], has been constructed based upon OOGL. It supports viewing in the three geometries discussed above: Euclidean, hyperbolic, and spherical. This is possible since as noted above isometries in the three geometries can be expressed as elements of $PGL(R,4)$. The underlying low-level graphics libraries (in the case of OOGL, GL or Renderman [1]) support the use of elements of $PGL(R,4)$ for modeling and viewing transformations. This is a result of the fact that $PGL(R,4)$ is the smallest group which contains both the Euclidean isometries and the perspective transformation. The visualization task is also made easier by the fact that OOGL supports 4-dimensional vertices within all primitives. This provides a base for creating geometric models in hyperbolic and spherical space using homogeneous coordinates.

4.2 Shading

We have established how it is possible to implement non-Euclidean isometries using standard projective transformations. We have not addressed the question of correct lighting and shading of surfaces in these spaces. Indeed, the standard shading algorithms (in contrast to the standard transformations) are implicitly Euclidean. In order to model the behavior of light correctly in these non-Euclidean spaces, it is necessary to provide customized shaders which replace the default ones. This has been successfully achieved within the Renderman shading language [Ups89],[Gun92]. Figure 5 shows a view inside hyperbolic space from the movie "Not Knot". Interactive software shaders for OOGL for hyperbolic and spherical space have also been written.

These custom shaders use the expressions for distance and angle described in 2.2 to replace the Euclidean ones. Additionally, the decay of light intensity as a function of distance depends on the formula for the surface area of a sphere in each space. That is, the amount of light falling on an area element at distance d from a light source will be inversely proportional to the total area of the sphere with radius d. For example, in hyperbolic space light decays exponentially: the area of a sphere of radius r is given by $k \sinh(r)$ and $\sinh(r) \approx \exp(r)$ for large r. The shaders used to create figures 7 and 9 also involve a term to model fog.

[1] GL is a trademark of Silicon Graphics, Inc.; and Renderman, of Pixar.

5 The `DiscreteGroup` class

The `DiscreteGroup` class is a subclass of `Geom`. The minimal data includes a set of generating isometries represented by elements of $PGL(R,4)$ and some geometric data, represented by other OOGL objects. The `DiscreteGroup` class supports the standard methods listed above, and other methods of its own.

Because of the close connection to manifolds outlined in Section 3, it can also be thought of as a `Manifold` class. Many design decisions were made to support visualization of the insider's view of a manifold. From this point of view, every element of the scene description belongs to the manifold and hence should be tessellated by the group in the process of creating the insider's view. We have departed from this philosophy in one important respect: we do not tessellate the lights contained in the scene description. To do so would have sacrificed interactivity for a questionable increase in authenticity.

Points of interest among `DiscreteGroup` methods include:

5.1 File format

There is an ascii file format for loading and saving discrete groups. This format supports the three geometries described above, and includes lists of generators and group elements and also geometric objects for display within the tessellation.

5.2 `DiscreteGroupDraw`

Each `DiscreteGroup` instance includes a list of group elements and a collection of other `Geoms`. The general algorithm transforms each `Geom` by each group element and then draws it. There are some subtleties. Most of these groups are infinite, but we only compute and store a finite list of elements at any time. One of the difficulties of navigating in the tessellations produced by discrete groups is that normal flight tends to wander to the edge of the computed tessellation. To solve this problem, the `DiscreteGroup` object is provided with an automatic centering mechanism. It detects when the camera leaves the Dirichlet domain defined by the group, and moves the camera by an isometry (determined by the face-pairings), to stay within this central region. Note that since lighting is not tessellated, lights must be defined within the camera coordinate system in order that lighting is invariant under this movement.

Another added feature is that there is a separate associated `Geom` which represents the camera, or observer. Before being tessellated it is moved to the location of the camera, which as described above is constrained to stay within the Dirichlet domain. The observer then becomes aware of his own movement in the space. This is an important feature especially for detecting the singular locus of orbifolds. For example, when the camera approaches a axis of symmetry of order n in an orbifold, this fact is made clear by the approach of $n-1$ other copies of the camera to the same axis, a symmetry which the geometry of the Dirichlet domain alone may not reveal.

5.3 `DiscreteGroupEnum(int constraint() )`

is a method for enumerating lists of group elements given the generators. One such list is used by the draw routine: it defines which copies of the fundamental domain to draw. The constraint function accepts a single group element and returns 0 or 1 according to whether it satisfies its criteria. For example, a matrix may be rejected if it moves the origin far, its determinant is small, or its expression as a word in the generating elements is long. This enumeration software uses software acceleration provided by the theory of automatic groups [ECH+91], [Lev92] if an automatic structure has been provided for the discrete group.

5.4 `DiscreteGroupDirDom`

creates a fundamental domain using the Dirichlet domain algorithm described above. This is useful for exploring groups for which no other geometry has been provided. For display purposes, both a wire-frame of the full polyhedron and a possibly scaled version with faces colored to reflect the face-pairing identities are drawn. See Figure 9. The user can deduce features of the group by examining the face-pairing patterns, or by moving the distinguished point P.

6 Example applications

A variety of applications have been developed based on the `DiscreteGroup` software class.

`Maniview` is short for *Manifold Viewer*. In the paradigm of object-oriented software tools, it is essentially an Inspector for the class `DiscreteGroup` . `Maniview` communicates with `Geomview` via a two-way pipe. `Geomview` reads the description of the discrete group output by `Maniview` and displays it. The user typically loads a discrete group into `Maniview`, and then manipulates the discrete group via a set of control panels. These panels are grouped into: display settings, enumeration of group elements, choice of fundamental tile, and saving and loading various elements. A typical snapshot of a `Maniview` session is shown in Figure 8.

One of the milestones in the theory of discrete groups was the enumeration of the 230 crystal groups in three dimensional Euclidean space at the end of the nineteenth century. For a survey see [LM78],[Sch80]. `eucsyms`, an interactive application which allows the exploration of these groups has been developed by Olaf Holt at the Geometry Center, and adapted to use the `DiscreteGroup` software. `eucsyms` is connected by a two-way pipe with `Maniview`. Figure 6 shows a view inside the symmetry group *r3*.

We have also hooked up `Maniview` to a powerful program for computing hyperbolic structures on three dimensional manifolds, `snappea` by Jeff Weeks [Wee93]. This is a popular tool used by research topologists to construct and examine three dimensional manifolds.

`Geomview`, `Maniview`, `eucsyms`, and `snappea` are all available via anonymous ftp from geom.umn.edu [128.101.25.35]. Some of the computation of the groups and geometrical models shown in the figures have been computed using a Mathematica [2] package developed at the Geometry Center, also available via anonymous ftp from the same site.

[2] Mathematica is a trademark of Wolfram Research, Inc

7 Example spaces

7.1 "Not Knot"

The mathematical animation "Not Knot" [GM91] pioneered the visualization of the insider's view of hyperbolic space. It features one Euclidean orbifold (see Figure 7) and a series of hyperbolic orbifolds converging to a hyperbolic manifold that is the complement of the three linked circles known as the Borromean rings. Figure 5 shows one of these orbifolds, which tessellates H^3 with right-angled dodecahedra. One of the six generators is a rotation of $\frac{\pi}{2}$ around the large red axis. As a matrix this generator is:

$$\begin{pmatrix} -1.618033 & 1.618033 & 0 & -2.058171 \\ -1.618033 & 0 & 0 & -1.272019 \\ 0 & 0 & 1. & 0 \\ 2.058171 & -1.272019 & 0 & 2.618033 \end{pmatrix}$$

Note that all the non-zero entries are powers of the golden ratio. This is an example of an *arithmetic* group and is of particular mathematical interest.

The discrete groups underlying "Not Knot" have been converted into the `DiscreteGroup` format. Now, viewers interested in exploring the spaces depicted in "Not Knot" can do so.

7.2 The Poincaré homology sphere

Possibly the most famous three dimensional spherical manifold is the so-called Poincaré homology sphere. It arises abstractly by identifying the opposite faces of a regular dodecahedron with a twist of $\pi/5$. The tessellation of S^3 corresponding to this manifold consists of 120 regular dodecahedra, which meet 3 around each edge, and is known as the 120-cell or dodecahedral honeycomb [Cox73]. In contrast to the right-angled dodecahedron of hyperbolic space, these dodecahedra have dihedral angles of $\frac{2\pi}{3}$.

An inside view of this manifold appears in Figure 9. Note that the largest dodecahedron, which completely fills the view as if it surrounds the viewer, is also the farthest away. This is a typical feature of life in spherical space; as objects move away they decrease in size until they reach a maximum distance of $\pi/2$, then they begin to increase in size until they reach the antipodal point of the viewer at a distance of π, where they expand to fill completely the field of view, since every geodesic leaving the observer also passes through the antipodal point. Stereo viewing in spherical space would place great strain on Euclidean trained eyes: when an object is exactly at the equator, the lines of sight from an observer's eyes are parallel; as an object moves beyond the equator, the observer must look "anti-crosseyed" at it.

8 Directions for further work

Common ancestry in projective geometry means that some important procedures can be shared with traditional Euclidean systems. However, there remain a host of computer graphics issues related to modeling and animation in non-Euclidean spaces to be addressed. Many geometric constructions are very different. For example, consider a equidistant curve, that is, the set of points equidistant from a line. In the Euclidean plane an equidistant curve is a parallel line. But equidistant curves in spherical and hyperbolic space are not straight lines. What, then, is the proper generalization

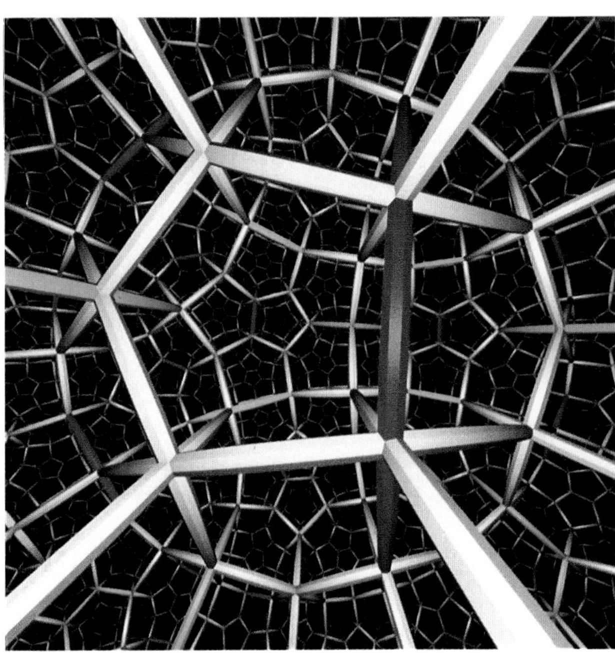

Figure 5: A view of the tessellation of hyperbolic space by regular right-angled dodecahedra, as in the movie "Not Knot". This image was rendered using Renderman.

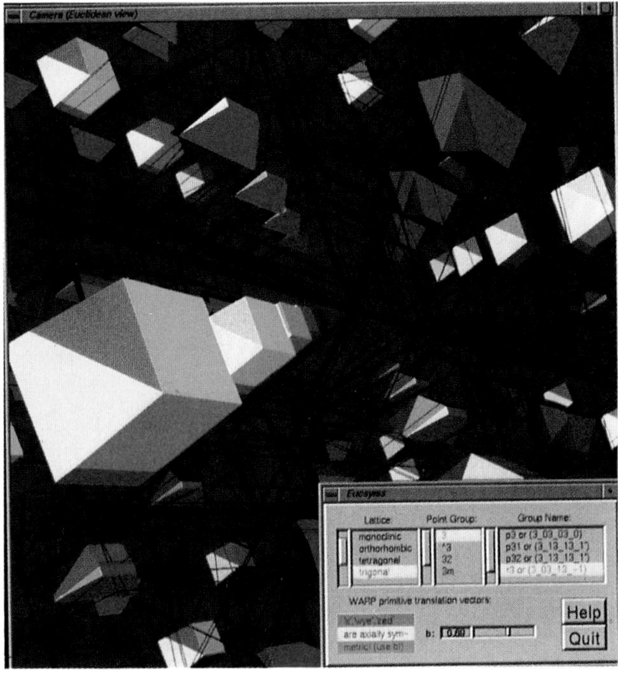

Figure 6: A snapshot of a session using **eucsyms**, an application for exploring the 230 Euclidean crystal groups.

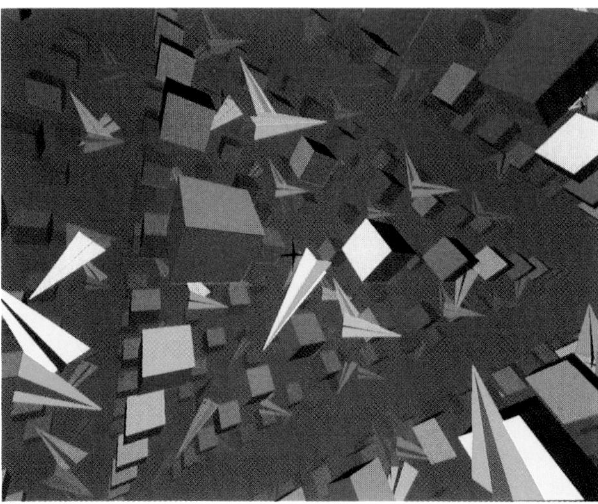

Figure 7: A view inside the Euclidean orbifold from "Not Knot" with the camera as a paper airplane.

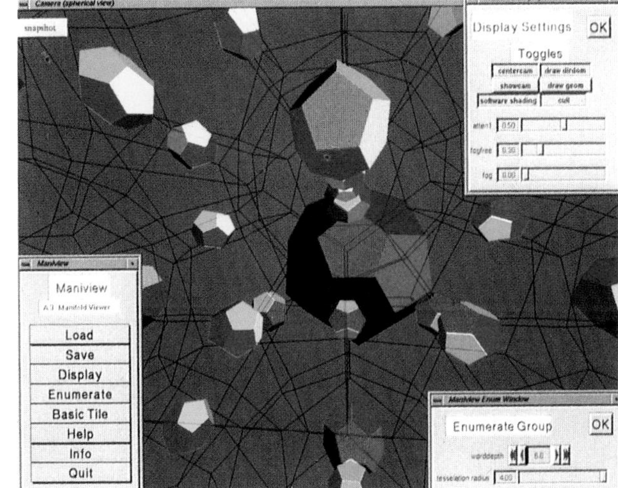

Figure 8: A typical session of **Maniview** showing some of its panels but hiding **Geomview** panels.

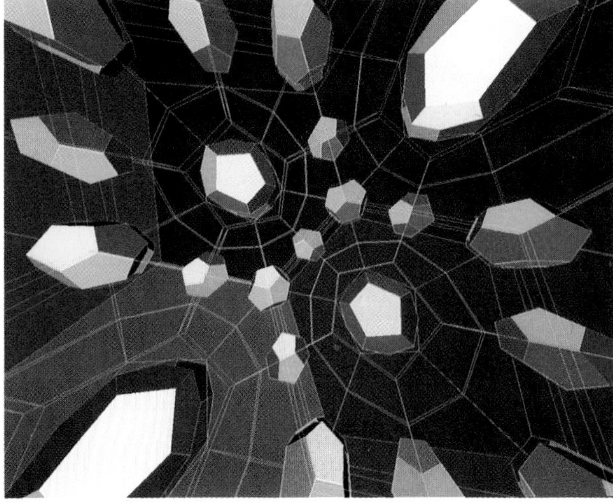

Figure 9: A view of the 120-cell. We reduce the size of the shaded polyhedra but draw the original edges.

of a cylinder in these spaces? Also, neither space allows similarity transformations: changing the size of an object changes its shape! Other questions arise. What sort of harmonic analysis is available to synthesize fractal terrains and textures in these spaces? If we hope to do physically-based modeling in these spaces, we need to expand our understanding of the laws of physics beyond the behavior of light described above in relation to shading. Finally, the theory of splines in non-Euclidean spaces was explored in [GK85].

In the area of topological content, one obvious goal is to implement the five non-isotropic three dimensional model geometries. Also, there are many sorts of discrete groups, particularly those that create fractal patterns, which do not fit neatly into the current framework.

In the direction of mathematical research and user interface, the efforts described here suggest various techniques for exploring 3-manifolds. Connecting this software with virtual reality technology would allow the researcher to perform a variety of explorations of the space. The use of sound also promises to yield useful evidence.

Looking at the wider world of Riemannian geometry, this work is one step in the direction of visualizing arbitrary curved spaces, the Riemannian manifolds that figure centrally in relativity and cosmology. For related work see [HD89].

Finally, this work opens a new domain for artistic creativity, three dimensional analogues of M. C. Escher's dramatic interlocking planar tessellations.

9 Conclusions

Approaching metric geometries via their common ancestry in projective geometry yields simple models which can be directly implemented in existing rendering systems. The resulting systems allow interactive navigation of curved spaces for the first time. Custom shaders provide realistic rendering of the insider's view. Methods for manipulating and displaying discrete groups allow interactive exploration of a wide class of topological manifolds modeled on these spaces, that have never been visualized before. The resulting system provides a unique tool for mathematicians, educators, and scientists and artists whose work is related to spatial symmetry.

Acknowledgements

I would like to acknowledge valuable ideas, comments, suggestions, and assistance from Bill Thurston, Jeff Weeks, Silvio Levy, Stuart Levy, Mark Phillips, John Sullivan, David Banks, and the reviewers.

References

[Bea83] Alan F. Beardon. *The Geometry of Discrete Groups.* Springer-Verlag, 1983.

[Car76] Manfredo P. Do Carmo. *Differential Geometry of Curves and Surfaces.* Prentice-Hall, 1976.

[Cay59] A. Cayley. A sixth memoir upon quantics. *Philosophical Transactions of the Royal Society of London*, 149:61–90, 1859.

[Cox65] H.M.S. Coxeter. *Non-Euclidean Geometry.* University of Toronto Press, 1965.

[Cox73] H.M.S. Coxeter. *Regular Polytopes.* Dover, 1973.

[Cox87] H.M.S. Coxeter. *Projective Geometry.* Springer Verlag, 1987.

[ECH+91] D. B. A. Epstein, Jim Cannon, Derek Holt, Silvio Levy, Mike Patterson, and William Thurston. *Word Processing in Groups.* Jones and Bartlett, 1991.

[FRC92] Helaman Ferguson, Alyn Rockwood, and Jordan Cox. Topological design of sculptural surfaces. *Computer Graphics*, 26:149–156, July, 1992. Proceedings of SIGGRAPH 1992.

[GK85] S. Gabriel and J. Kajiya. Spline interpolation in curved space. In *State of the Art Image Synthesis*, 1985. Course notes for SIGGRAPH 1985.

[GM91] Charlie Gunn and Delle Maxwell. *Not Knot.* Jones and Bartlett, 1991.

[Gun83] Charlie Gunn. A computer implementation of the two-dimensional euclidean crystallographic groups. Master's thesis, UNC, Chapel Hill, 1983.

[Gun92] Charlie Gunn. Visualizing hyperbolic geometry. In *Computer Graphics and Mathematics*, pages 299–313. Eurographics, Springer Verlag, 1992.

[HD89] Ping-Kang Hsiung and Robert H.P. Dunn. Visualizing relativistic effects in spacetime. In *Supercomputing 89.* IEEE/ACM, Nov, 1989.

[Lev92] Silvio Levy. Automatic generation of hyperbolic tilings. *Leonardo*, 35:349–354, 1992.

[LM78] E. H. Lockwood and R. H. Macmillan. *Geometric symmetry.* Cambridge University Press, 1978.

[MLP+] Tamara Munzner, Stuart Levy, Mark Phillips, Nathaniel Thurston, and Celeste Fowler. Geomview — an interactive viewing program for sgi workstations. ftp@geom.umn.edu.

[Mun75] James Munkres. *Topology: A First Course*, chapter 8. Prentice-Hall, 1975.

[PG92] Mark Phillips and Charlie Gunn. Visualizing hyperbolic space: Unusual uses of 4x4 matrices. In *1992 Symposium on Interactive 3D Graphics*, pages 209–214. ACM SIGGRAPH, ACM, 1992.

[Sch80] R.L.E. Schwarzenberger. *N-Dimensional Crystallography.* Pitman Publishing, 1980. chapters 13-16.

[Thu82] William Thurston. Three dimensional manifolds, kleinian groups and hyperbolic geometry. *BAMS*, 19:417–431, 1982.

[Thuar] William Thurston. *The Geometry and Topology of Three-Manifolds*, volume 1. to appear.

[Ups89] Steve Upstill. *The Renderman Companion.* Addison-Wesley, 1989. chapters 13-16.

[Wee] Jeff Weeks. snappea — a macintosh application for computing 3-manifolds. ftp@geom.umn.edu.

[Wee85] Jeff Weeks. *The Shape of Space.* Marcel Dekker, 1985.

[Woo22] Frederick Woods. *Higher Geometry.* Dover, 1961 (1922).

Imaging Vector Fields Using Line Integral Convolution

Brian Cabral
*Leith (Casey) Leedom**

Lawrence Livermore National Laboratory

ABSTRACT

Imaging vector fields has applications in science, art, image processing and special effects. An effective new approach is to use linear and curvilinear filtering techniques to locally blur textures along a vector field. This approach builds on several previous texture generation and filtering techniques[8, 9, 11, 14, 15, 17, 23]. It is, however, unique because it is local, one-dimensional and independent of any predefined geometry or texture. The technique is general and capable of imaging arbitrary two- and three-dimensional vector fields. The local one-dimensional nature of the algorithm lends itself to highly parallel and efficient implementations. Furthermore, the curvilinear filter is capable of rendering detail on very intricate vector fields. Combining this technique with other rendering and image processing techniques — like periodic motion filtering — results in richly informative and striking images. The technique can also produce novel special effects.

CR categories and subject descriptors: I.3.3 [Computer Graphics]: Picture/Image generation; I.3.7 [Computer Graphics]: Three-Dimensional Graphics and Realism; I.4.3 [Image Processing]: Enhancement.

Keywords: convolution, filtering, rendering, visualization, texture synthesis, flow fields, special effects, periodic motion filtering.

1. INTRODUCTION

Upon first inspection, imaging vector fields appears to have limited application — confined primarily to scientific visualization. However, much of the form and shape in our environment is a function of not only image intensity and color, but also of directional information such as edges. Painters, sculptors, photographers, image processors[16] and computer graphics researchers[9] have recognized the importance of direction in the process of image creation and form. Hence, algorithms that can image such directional information have wide application across both scientific and artistic domains.

Such algorithms should possess a number of desirable and sometimes conflicting properties including: accuracy, locality of calculation, simplicity, controllability and generality. Line Integral Convolution (LIC) is a new technique that possesses many of these properties. Its generality allows for the introduction of a completely new family of periodic motion filters which have wide application (see section 4.1). It represents a confluence of signal and image processing and a variety of previous work done in computer graphics and scientific visualization.

* Authors' current e-mail addresses are: *cabral@llnl.gov* and *casey@gauss.llnl.gov*.

2. BACKGROUND

There are currently few techniques which image vector fields in a general manner. These techniques can be quite effective for visualizing vector data. However, they break down when operating on very dense fields and do not generalize to other applications. In particular, large vector fields (512x512 or greater) strain existing algorithms.

Most vector visualization algorithms use spatial resolution to represent the vector field. These include sampling the field, such as with stream lines[12] or particle traces, and using icons[19] at every vector field coordinate. Stream lines and particle tracing techniques depend critically on the placement of the "streamers" or the particle sources. Depending on their placement, eddies or currents in the data field can be missed. Icons, on the other hand, do not miss data, but use up a considerable amount of spatial resolution limiting their usefulness to small vector fields.

Another general approach is to generate textures via a vector field. Van Wijk's *spot noise* algorithm[23] uses a vector field to control the generation of bandlimited noise. The time complexity of the two types of implementation techniques presented by Van Wijk are relatively high. Furthermore the technique, by definition, depends heavily on the form of the texture (spot noise) itself. Specifically, it does not easily generalize to other forms of textures that might be better suited to a particular class of vector data (such as fluid flow versus electromagnetic).

Reaction diffusion techniques[20, 24] also provide an avenue for visualizing vector fields since the controlling differential equations are inherently vector in nature. It is possible to map vector data onto these differential equations to come up with a vector visualization technique. Here too however, the time complexity of these algorithms limit their general usefulness.

Three-dimensional vector fields can be visualized by three-dimensional texture generation techniques such as texels and hypertextures described in [11, 15]. Both techniques take a texture on a geometrically defined surface and project the texture out some distance from the surface. By definition these techniques are bound to the surface and do not compute an image for the entire field as is done by Van Wijk[23]. This is limiting in that it requires a priori knowledge to place the surface. Like particle streams and vector streamers these visualization techniques are critically dependent on the placement of the sampling surface.

The technique presented by Haeberli[9] for algorithmicly generating "paintings" via vector-like brush strokes can also be thought of as a vector visualization technique. Crawfis and Max[5] describe a three-dimensional variation on this in which blurred cylinders represent three-dimensional brush strokes whose directions and colors are controlled by a three-dimensional vector field. Both techniques represent a conceptual extension of traditional icon placement, where the icons are more sophisticated shapes. However, these techniques break down as the density of the field increases since they require spatial resolution to work.

What is needed is a technique that can image dense vector fields, is independent of both predefined sampling placement constraints and texture generation techniques and can work in two and three dimensions. Such a technique would be very general and have wide application.

3. DDA CONVOLUTION

One approach is a generalization of traditional DDA line drawing techniques[1] and the spatial convolution algorithms described by Van Wijk[23] and Perlin[14]. Each vector in a field is used to define a long, narrow, DDA generated filter kernel tangential to the vector and going in the positive and negative vector direction some fixed distance, *L*. A texture is then mapped one-to-one onto the vector field. The input texture pixels under the filter kernel are summed, normalized by the length of the filter kernel, *2L*, and placed in an output pixel image for the vector position. Figure 1, illustrates this operation for a single vector in a field.

This effectively filters the underlying texture as a function of the vector field. The images in figure 2 are rendered using the DDA convolution algorithm. On the left is a simple circular vector field; to its right is the result of a computational fluid dynamics code. The input texture image in these examples is white noise. Although the description above implies a box filter, any arbitrary filter shape can be used for the filter convolution kernel. It is important to note that this algorithm is very sensitive to symmetry of the DDA algorithm and filter. If the algorithm weights the forward direction more than the backward direction, the circular field in figure 2 appears to spiral inward implying a vortical behavior that is not present in the vector field.

3.1 LOCAL FIELD BEHAVIOR

The DDA approach, while efficient, is inherently inaccurate. It assumes that the local vector field can be approximated by a straight line. For points in vector fields where the local radius of curvature is large, this assumption is valid. However, where there are complex structures smaller than the length of the DDA line, the local radius of curvature is small and is not well approximated by a straight line. In a sense, DDA convolution renders the vector field unevenly, treating linear portions of the vector field more accurately than small scale vortices. While this graceful degradation may be fine or even desirable for special effects applications, it is problematic for visualizing vector fields such as the ones in figure 2, since detail in the small scale structures is lost.

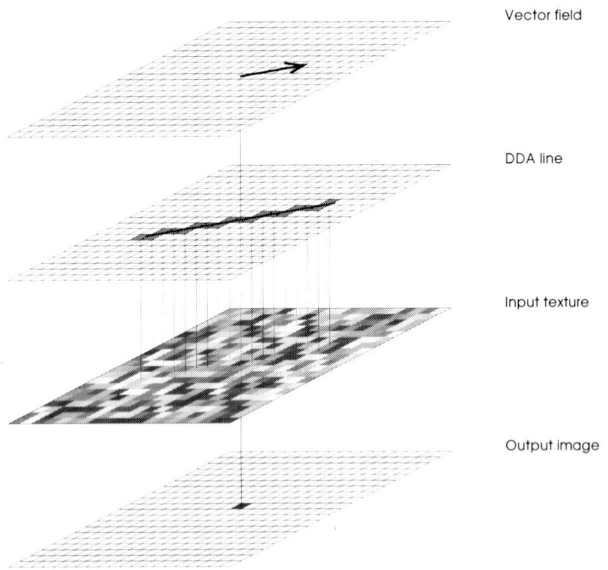

Figure 1: The mapping of a vector onto a DDA line and input pixel field generating a single output pixel.

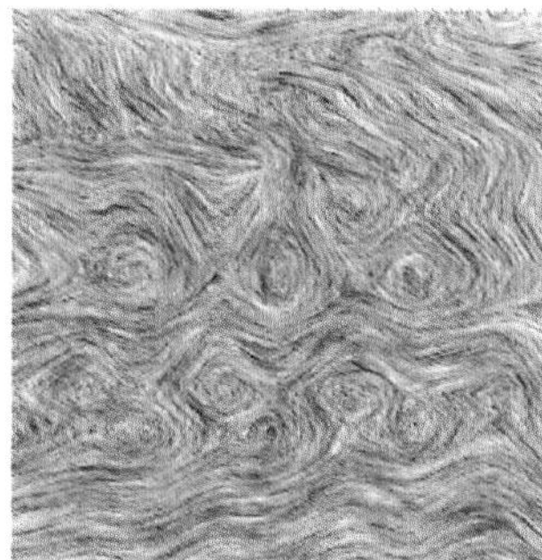

Figure 2: Circular and turbulent fluid dynamics vector fields imaged using DDA convolution over white noise.

Van Wijk's spot noise algorithm[23] also suffers from this problem since the spots are elliptically stretched along a line in the direction of the local field. If the ellipse major axis exceeds the local length scale of the vector field, the spot noise will inaccurately represent the vector field. An accurate measure of local field behavior would require a global analysis of the field. Such techniques currently do not exist for arbitrary vector fields, would most likely be expensive to calculate[13] and are an area of active research[7].

4. LINE INTEGRAL CONVOLUTION

The local behavior of the vector field can be approximated by computing a local stream line that starts at the center of pixel (x, y) and moves out in the positive and negative directions.[1] The forward coordinate advection is given by equation (1).

$$P_0 = (x + 0.5, y + 0.5)$$

$$P_i = P_{i-1} + \frac{V(\lfloor P_{i-1} \rfloor)}{\| V(\lfloor P_{i-1} \rfloor) \|} \Delta s_{i-1} \tag{1}$$

$V(\lfloor P \rfloor)$ = the vector from the input vector field at lattice point $(\lfloor P_x \rfloor, \lfloor P_y \rfloor)$

$$s_e = \begin{cases} \infty \text{ if } V \parallel e \\ 0 \text{ if } \dfrac{\lfloor P_c \rfloor - P_c}{V_c} < 0 \\ \dfrac{\lfloor P_c \rfloor - P_c}{V_c} \text{ otherwise} \end{cases} \quad \text{for } (e, c) \in \begin{Bmatrix} (top, y) \\ (bottom, y) \\ (left, x) \\ (right, x) \end{Bmatrix} \tag{2}$$

$$\Delta s_i = \min(s_{top}, s_{bottom}, s_{left}, s_{right})$$

[1] Vector field lattice and image coordinates are usually specified in a left-handed coordinate system while vector components are usually specified in a right-handed coordinate system. In this case, the *y*-component of the lattice coordinate in equation (1) must be reflected about the vertical center of the lattice to operate in a consistent coordinate system. This reflection has been omitted to preserve simplicity of presentation.

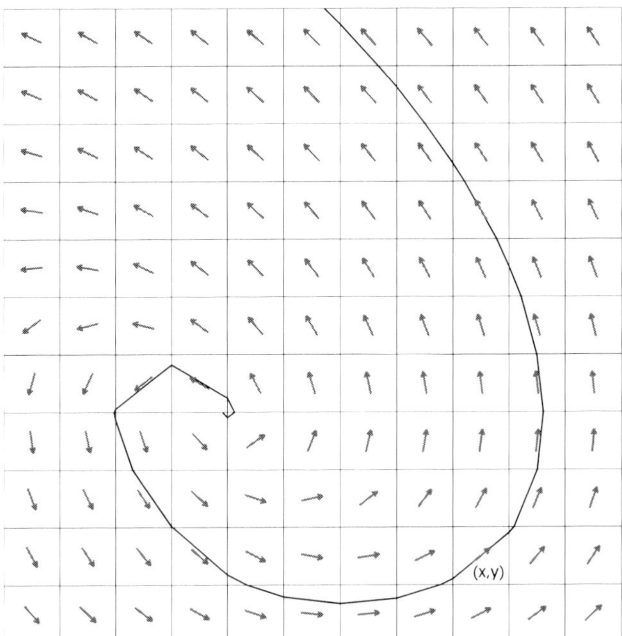

Figure 3: A two-dimensional vector field showing the local stream line starting in cell (x, y). The vector field is the upper left corner of the fluid dynamics field in figures 2 and 4.

Only the directional component of the vector field is used in this advection. The magnitude of the vector field can be used later in post processing steps as explained in section 4.3.1. Δs_i is the positive parametric distance along a line parallel to the vector field from P_i to the nearest cell edge.

As with the DDA algorithm, it is important to maintain symmetry about a cell. Hence, the local stream line is also advected backwards by the negative of the vector field as shown in equation (3).

$$P'_0 = P_0$$

$$P'_i = P'_{i-1} - \frac{V(\lfloor P'_{i-1} \rfloor)}{\| V(\lfloor P'_{i-1} \rfloor) \|} \Delta s'_{i-1} \quad (3)$$

Primed variables represent the negative direction counterparts to the positive direction variables and are not repeated in subsequent definitions. As above $\Delta s'_i$, is always positive.

The calculation of Δs_i in the stream line advection is sensitive to round off errors. Δs_i must produce advected coordinates that lie within the i+1th cell, taking the stream line segment out of the current cell. In the implementation of the algorithm a small round off term is added to each Δs_i to insure that entry into the adjacent cell occurs. This local stream line calculation is illustrated in figure 3. Each cell is assumed to be a unit square. All spatial quantities (e.g., Δs_i) are relative to this measurement. However, the cells need not be square or even rectangular (see section 6) for this approximation to work. So, without loss of generality, descriptions are given relative to a cubic lattice with unit spacing.

Continuous sections of the local stream line — i.e. the straight line segments in figure 3 — can be thought of as parameterized space curves in s and the input texture pixel mapped to a cell can be treated as a continuous scalar function of x and y.[2] It is then possible to integrate over this scalar field along each parameterized space curve. Such integrals can be summed in a piecewise $\mathbf{C}^1$ fashion and are known as line integrals of the first kind (LIFK)[2]. The convolution concept used in the DDA algorithm can now be combined with LIFK to form a Line Integral Convolution (LIC). This results in a variation of the DDA approach that locally follows the vector field and captures small radius of curvature features. For each continuous segment, i, an exact integral of a convolution kernel $k(w)$ is computed and used as a weight in the LIC as shown in equation (4).

$$h_i = \int_{s_i}^{s_i + \Delta s_i} k(w)\, dw \quad (4)$$

where

$$s_0 = 0$$

$$s_i = s_{i-1} + \Delta s_{i-1}$$

The entire LIC for output pixel $F'(x, y)$ is given by equation (5).

$$F'(x, y) = \frac{\sum_{i=0}^{l} F(\lfloor P_i \rfloor) h_i + \sum_{i=0}^{l'} F(\lfloor P'_i \rfloor) h'_i}{\sum_{i=0}^{l} h_i + \sum_{i=0}^{l'} h'_i} \quad (5)$$

where

$F(\lfloor P \rfloor)$ is the input pixel corresponding to the vector at position $(\lfloor P_x \rfloor, \lfloor P_y \rfloor)$

$$l = i \text{ such that } s_i \le L < s_{i+1} \quad (6)$$

The numerator of equation (5) represents the line integral of the filter kernel times the input pixel field, F. The denominator is the line integral of the convolution kernel and is used to normalize the output pixel weight (see section 4.2).

The length of the local stream line, $2L$, is given in unit pixels. Depending on the input pixel field, F, if L is too large, all the resulting LICs will return values very close together for all coordinates (x, y). On the other hand, if L is too small then an insufficient amount of filtering occurs. Since the value of L dramatically affects the performance of the algorithm, the smallest effective value is desired. For most of the figures, a value of 10 was used.

Singularities in the vector field occur when vectors in two adjacent local stream line cells geometrically "point" at a shared cell edge. This results in Δs_i values equal to zero leaving l in equation (6) undefined. This situation can easily be detected and the advection algorithm terminated. If the vector field goes to zero at any point, the LIC algorithm is terminated as in the case of a field singularity. Both of these cases generate truncated stream lines. If a zero field vector lies in the starting cell of the LIC, the input pixel value for that cell, a constant or any other arbitrary value can be returned as the value of the LIC depending on the visual effect desired for null vectors.

Using adjacent stream line vectors to detect singularities can however result in false singularities. False singularities occur when the vector field is nearly parallel to an edge, but causes the LIC to cross over that edge. Similarly, the cell just entered also has a near parallel vector which points to this same shared edge. This artifact can be remedied by adjusting the parallel vector/edge test found in equation (2), to test the angle formed between the vector and the edge against some small angle *theta*, instead of zero. Any vector which forms an angle less than *theta* with some edge is deemed to be "parallel" to that edge. Using a value of 3° for *theta* removes these artifacts.

The images in figure 4 were rendered using LIC and correspond to the same two vector fields rendered in figure 2. Note the increased amount of detail present in these images versus their DDA counterparts. In particular the image of the fluid dynamics vector field in figure 4 shows detail incorrectly rendered or absent in figure 2.

[2] Bilinear, cubic or Bezier splines are viable alternatives to straight line segments. However, these higher order curves are more expensive to compute.

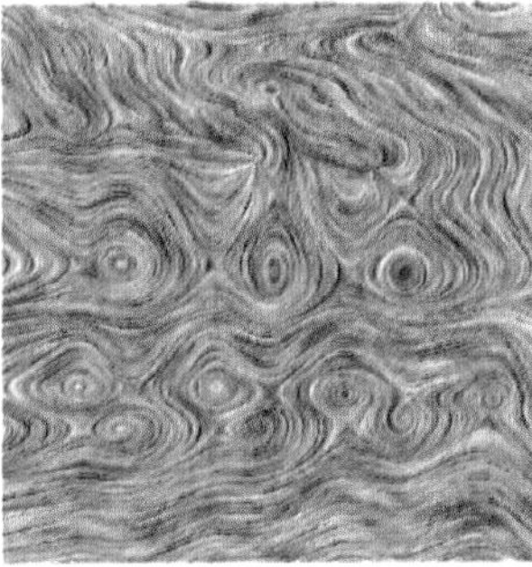

Figure 4: Circular and turbulent fluid dynamics vector fields imaged using LIC over white noise.

The images in figure 5 show the effect of varying L. The input texture is a photograph of flowers. The input vector field was created by taking the gradient of a bandlimited noise image and rotating each of the gradient vectors by 90°, producing vectors which follow the contours of the soft hills and valleys of the bandlimited noise. With L equal to 0, the input image is passed through unchanged. As the value of L increases, the input image is blurred to a greater extent, giving an impressionistic result. Here, a biased ramp filter[10] is used to roughly simulate a brush stroke.

Figures 2, 4, 8, 9 and 11 were generated using white noise input images. Aliasing can be a serious problem when using LIC with a high frequency source image such as white noise. The aliasing is caused by the one-dimensional point sampling of the infinitely thin LIC filter. This aliasing can be removed by either creating a thick LIC filter with a low-pass filter cross section or by low-pass filtering the input image. This second alternative is preferable since it comes at no additional cost to the LIC algorithm. The images in figure 6 show the effect of running LIC over 256x256 white noise which has been low-pass filtered using a fourth order Butterworth filter with cutoff frequencies of 128, 84, 64, and 32.

It is worth noting that Van Wijk's spot noise algorithm[23] can be adapted to use the local stream line approximation to more accurately represent the behavior of a vector field. Instead of straight line elliptical stretching, each spot could be warped so that the major axis follows the local stream line. Furthermore, the minor axis could either be perpendicular to the warped major axis or itself could be warped along transverse field lines. However, an algorithm to perform this task for an arbitrary local stream line would be inherently more expensive and complex than the LIC algorithm.

Sims[18] describes an alternative technique which produces results similar to LIC. This alternative approach warps or advects texture coordinates as a function of a vector field. The similarity between the two techniques is predictable even though the techniques are quite different. The dilation and contraction of the texture coordinate system warping has the visual effect of blurring and sharpening the warped image. This is due to the resampling and reconstruction process necessary when warping from one coordinate system to another. Thus, for regions where the source image is stretched along the vector field an apparent blurring will occur similar to those seen with LIC. However, the techniques are completely different in two fundamental ways. First, LIC is a local operator, meaning no information outside of a fixed area of interest is needed. Warping even when done locally requires maintaining global consistency to avoid tearing holes in the warped image. This increases the complexity of the warping operation when compared to LIC. Second, LIC is a spatially varying filtering operation and does not warp or transform any texture coordinates.

4.1 PERIODIC MOTION FILTERS

The LIC algorithm visualizes local vector field tangents, but not their direction. Freeman, et al[8] describe a technique which simulates motion by use of special convolutions. A similar technique is used by Van Gelder and Wilhelms[22] to show vector field flow. This technique can be extended and used to represent the local vector field direction via animation of successive LIC imaged vector fields using varying phase shifted periodic filter kernels.

The success of this technique depends on the shape of the filter. In the previous examples (figures 2 and 4), a constant or box filter is used. If the filter is periodic like the filters used in [8], by changing the phase of such filters as a function of time, apparent motion

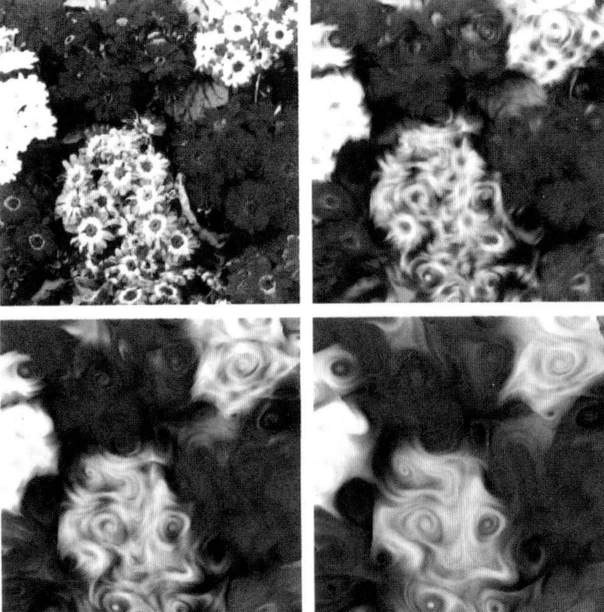

Figure 5: Photograph of flowers processed using LIC with L equal to 0, 5, 10 and 20 (left to right, top to bottom).

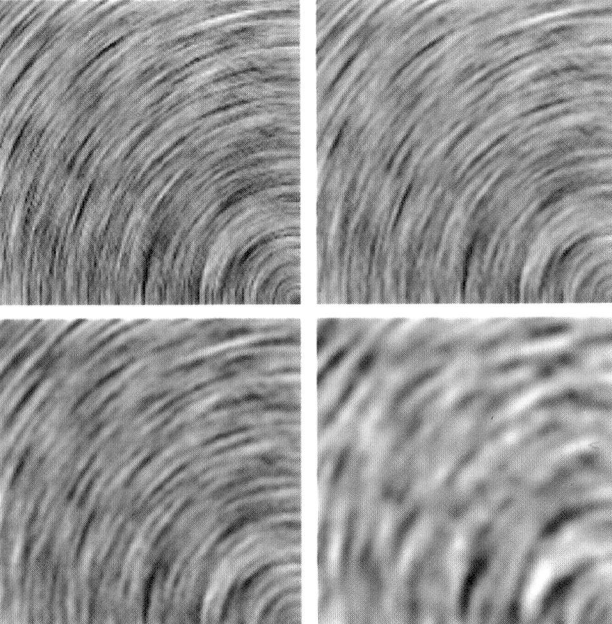

Figure 6: The upper left hand quarter of the circular vector field is convolved using LIC over Butterworth low-pass filtered white noise with cutoff frequencies of 128, 86, 64, and 32 (left to right, top to bottom).

in the direction of the vector field is created. However, the filters used in [8] were, by design, high-pass Laplacian edge enhancing filters. Using this filter over a bandlimited noise texture produces very incoherent images since the high frequency components of the noise are accentuated. Instead, it is possible, and desirable, to create periodic low-pass filters to blur the underlying texture in the direction of the vector field. A Hanning filter, $1/2(1 + \cos(w+\beta))$, has this property. It has low band-pass filter characteristics, it is periodic by definition and has a simple analytic form. This function will be referred to as the *ripple* filter function.

Since the LIC algorithm is by definition a local operation, any filter used must be windowed. That is, it must be made local even if it has infinite extent. In the previous section we used a constant filter implicitly windowed by a box of height one. Using this same box window on a phase shifted Hanning filter we get a filter with abrupt cutoffs, as illustrated in the top row of figure 7.

This abrupt cutoff is noticeable as spatio-temporal artifacts in animations that vary the phase as a function of time. One solution to this problem is to use a Gaussian window as suggested by Gabor[4].[3] By multiplying, or windowing, the Hanning function by a Gaussian, these cutoffs are smoothly attenuated to zero. However, a Gaussian windowed Hanning function does not have a simple closed form integral. An alternative is to find a windowing function with windowing properties similar to a Gaussian and which has a simple closed form integral. Interestingly, the Hanning function itself meets these two criteria. In the bottom row of figure 7, the five phase shifted Hanning filter functions in the top row are multiplied by the Hanning window function in the middle row. The general form of this function is shown in equation (7). In this equation c and d represent the dilation constants of the Hanning window and ripple functions respectively. β is the ripple function phase shift given in radians. The integral of $k(w)$ from a to b used in equation (4) is shown in equation (8).

$$k(w) = \frac{1 + \cos(cw)}{2} \times \frac{1 + \cos(dw + \beta)}{2} \qquad (7)$$

$$= \frac{1}{4}\left(1 + \cos(cw) + \cos(dw + \beta) + \cos(cw)\cos(dw + \beta)\right)$$

$$\int_a^b k(w)\,dw \qquad (8)$$

$$= \frac{1}{4}\left(\begin{array}{c} b - a + \dfrac{\sin(bc) - \sin(ac)}{c} \\ + \dfrac{\sin(bd + \beta) - \sin(ad + \beta)}{d} \\ + \dfrac{\sin(b(c-d) - \beta) - \sin(a(c-d) - \beta)}{2(c-d)} \\ + \dfrac{\sin(b(c+d) + \beta) - \sin(a(c+d) + \beta)}{2(c+d)} \end{array}\right)$$

As mentioned above, both the Hanning window and the Hanning ripple filter function can be independently dilated by adjusting c and d to have specific local support and periodicity. The window function has a fixed period of 2π.

Choosing the periodicity of the ripple function represents making a design trade-off between maintaining a nearly constant frequency response as a function of phase shift and the quality of the apparent motion[3]. A low frequency ripple function results in a windowed filter whose frequency response noticeably changes as a function of phase. This appears as a periodic blurring and sharpening of the image as the phase changes. Higher frequency ripple functions produce windowed filters with a nearly constant frequency response since the general shape of the filter doesn't radically change. However, the feature size picked up by the ripple filter is smaller and the result is less apparent motion. If the ripple frequency exceeds the Nyquist limit of the pixel spacing the apparent motion disappears. Experimentation shows that a ripple function frequency between 2 and 4 cycles per window period is reasonable. One can always achieve both good frequency response and good feature motion by increasing the spatial resolution. This comes, of course, at a cost of increased computation[16].

[3] D. Gabor in 1946 created a localized form of the Fourier transform known as the Gabor transform. This transform is the Fourier transform of an input signal multiplied by a Gaussian window translated along the signal as a function of time. The net result is a signal which is spatially and frequency localized. Wavelet theory is based on a generalization of this type of spatial and frequency localization.

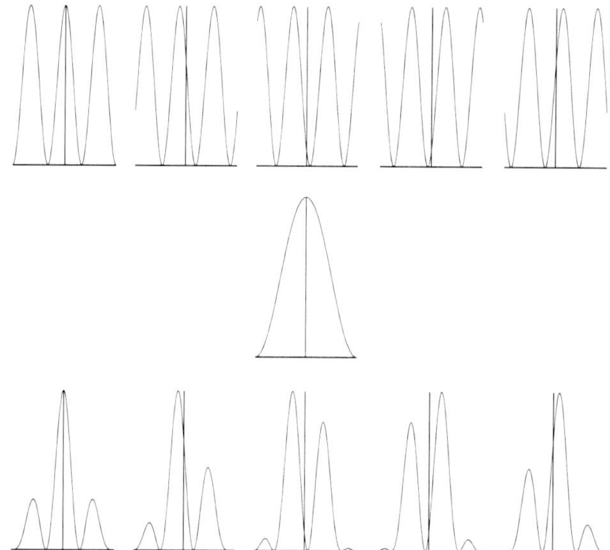

Figure 7: Phase shifted Hanning ripple functions(top), a Hanning windowing function(middle), and Hanning ripple functions multiplied by the Hanning window function(bottom).

4.2 NORMALIZATION

A normalization to the convolution integral is performed in equation (5) to insure that the apparent brightness and contrast of the resultant image is well behaved as a function of kernel shape, phase and length. The numerator in equation (5) is divided by the integral of the convolution kernel. This insures that the normalized area under the convolution kernel is always unity resulting in a constant overall brightness for the image independent of the filter shape and LIC length.

Because the actual length of the LIC may vary from pixel to pixel, the denominator can not be precomputed. However, an interesting effect is observed if a fixed normalization is used. Truncated stream lines are attenuated which highlights singularities. The images in figure 8 a show another section of the fluid dynamics vector field imaged with variable and constant kernel normalization. The implementation of the LIC algorithm uses precomputed sum tables for the integral to avoid costly arithmetic in the innermost loop.

A second normalization may be done to insure the output image retains the input image's contrast properties. The LIC algorithm reduces the overall image contrast as a function of L. In fact, in the case of the box filter, as L goes to infinity the entire output image goes to the average of the input image. This can be ameliorated by amplifying the input or contrast stretching the output image as a function of L. Clearly as L goes to infinity the amplification or con-

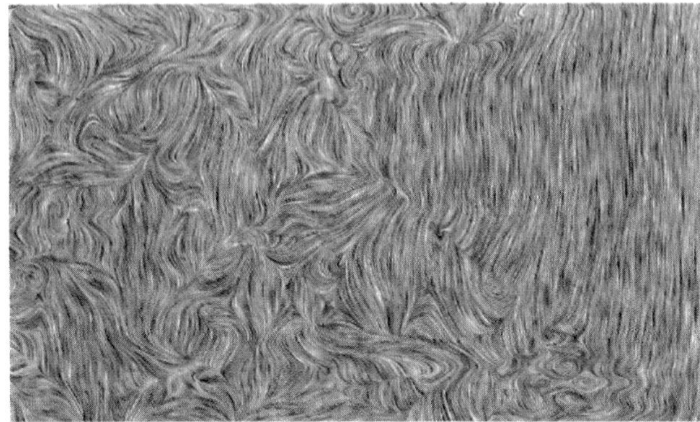

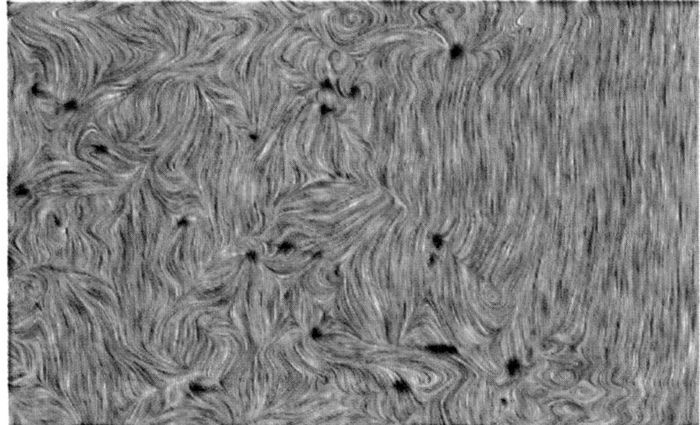

Figure 8: White noise convolved with fluid dynamics vector field using variable normalization (top) versus fixed normalization (bottom).

trast stretching must go to infinity as well. The images in all the figures are contrast stretched.

4.3 IMPLEMENTATION AND APPLICATION

The LIC algorithm is designed as a function which maps an input vector field and texture to a filtered version of the input texture. The dimension of the output texture is that of the vector field. If the input texture is smaller than the vector field the implementation of the algorithm wraps the texture using a toroidal topology. That is, the right and left edges wrap as do the top and bottom edges. If the texture is too large it is cropped to the vector field dimensions. Careful attention must be paid to the size of the input texture relative to that of the vector field. If too small a texture is used, the periodicity induced by the texture tiling will be visible. For scientific applications this is unacceptable. One must insure that the input texture is large enough so that the periodicity induced by the coordinate wrapping is not apparent.

Figure 9: White noise convolved with checkerboard vector field using fixed normalization (left), and then gradient shaded (right) to give the appearance of a rough woven surface texture.

The algorithm can be used as a data operator in conjunction with other operators much like those of Sims[17] and Perlin[14]. Specifically, both the texture and the vector field can be preprocessed and combined with post processing on the output image. The LIC implementation is a module in a data flow system like that found in a number of public domain and commercial products. This implementation allows for rapid exploration of various combinations of operators.

4.3.1 POST PROCESSING

The output of the LIC algorithm can be operated on in a variety of ways. In this section several standard techniques are used in combination with LIC to produce novel results.

An interesting example of constant kernel normalization is shown in figure 9. A simple basket weave pattern is generated by alternating vector directions in a checkerboard fashion. Each checker is surrounded by null vectors. This vector field is then used to convolve white noise. The LIC is truncated as it nears the edges of the checkers which results in a gradual attenuation. When that output is gradient shaded, the basket weave becomes very realistic. While other techniques could be used to generate such a texture, the simplicity of the source data illustrates the versatility of LIC.

A surface wind velocity field is imaged in figure 10 using LIC to blur $1/f$ noise. The resulting image is composed over an image of North America to present scale and location. The LIC algorithm is slightly modified to image vector magnitude by varying the length of the line integral, $2L$, as a function of the vector field magnitude. In figure 10 this effect is seen as clumpiness in $1/f$ cloud-like structures where the wind velocity field is small.

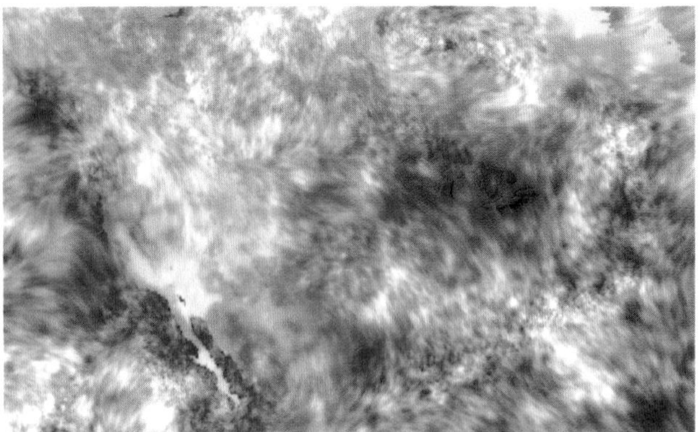

Figure 10: A wind velocity visualization is created by compositing an image of North America under an image of the velocity field rendered using variable length LIC over $1/f$ noise.

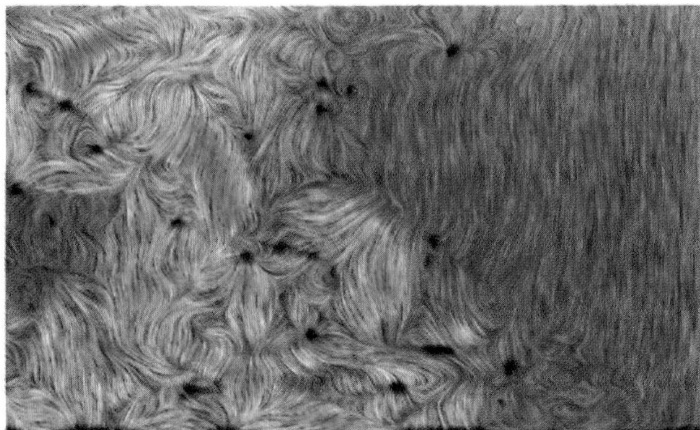

Figure 11: The fixed normalization fluid dynamics field imaged in figure 8 is multiplied by a color image of the magnitude of the vector field.

Figure 12: A photograph (top) of the Flavian Amphitheater is used to create a vector field. The field is then used to image a "painted" version of the same photograph (bottom).

Another method to add vector magnitude information is seen in figure 11. The [fixed normalization] fluid dynamics field of figure 8 is multiplied by a color image of the vector magnitude. The advantage of this approach over variable length LIC is that the fine grained detail generated by fixed length LIC is retained even in low magnitude areas.

The LIC algorithm can be used to process an image using a vector field generated from the image itself. In figure 12, a vector field is generated from the input image by low-pass filtering the image, taking the gradient of the resulting image and rotating the vectors by 90°.

The LIC algorithm can also be used to post process images to generate motion blur. A rendering algorithm or paint system can easily specify a pixel by pixel velocity field for objects. By using a biased triangle filter[10] and variable length LIC the input image can be motion blurred in the direction of apparent motion. This has precisely the desired results for motion blurring as seen in figure 13.

Figure 13: The original photo on the left shows no motion blurring The photo on the right uses variable length LIC to motion blur Boris Yeltsin's waving arm, simulating a slower shutter

4.4 THREE-DIMENSIONAL LIC

The LIC algorithm easily generalizes to higher dimensions. Equations (1), (3) and (5) trivially extend to three dimensions. In the three-dimensional case, cell edges are replaced with cell faces. Both the input vector field and input texture must be three-dimensional. The output of the three-dimensional LIC algorithm is a three-dimensional image or scalar field. This field is rendered using volume rendering techniques such as those found in [21] and [6].

Figure 14 is a three-dimensional rendering of an electrostatic field with two point charges placed a fixed distance apart from one another. In this volumetric rendering, the magnitude of the vector field is used to control the opacity transfer functions. Great efficiency gains can be achieved if the LIC algorithm exploits this by avoiding rendering for vector field cells whose magnitude is outside of the volume renderer's min/max threshold window.

5. PERFORMANCE

There is a distinct performance and quality trade-off between the DDA convolution algorithm and LIC. LIC is roughly an order of magnitude slower than the DDA method. Both algorithms were timed using cells processed per second (CPS) as the figure of merit. The tests were run on an unloaded IBM 550 RISC 6000. The DDA algorithm averages about 30,000 CPS while LIC averages about 3,000 CPS.

The three-dimensional algorithm only marginally degrades in performance with the increase in dimensionality, processing some 1,200 CPS. Since the algorithm remains one-dimensional in nature, the cost per cell only increases by a factor of three as a function of dimension. Using the thresholding described above, the performance of the three-dimensional LIC algorithm has exceeded 30,000 CPS.

6. FUTURE WORK

A number of research directions relating to LIC remain outstanding.

Currently no methods exist for determining the accuracy of a vector field representation, such as those created by LIC or any other method. These accuracy metrics would necessarily be related

Figure 14: A three-dimensional 512^3 electrostatic field is imaged by volumetrically ray tracing a three-dimensional scalar field produced using LIC over white noise.

to the differential topology of the entire vector field. As mentioned above, much work in theoretical and applied mathematics has been done in this area. This work needs to be studied and applied to efficient vector field imaging algorithms.

LIC is conceptually independent of the advection algorithm used to define the parametric support used by the convolution operation. The method described here might be best characterized as a variable step Euler's method. Other techniques such as a fourth order Runge-Kutta could produce differing or improved results. A thorough investigation into this issue is beyond the scope of this paper. It does, however, represent an area deserving special attention.

Visualizing the orthogonal complement of a two-dimensional vector field is accomplished by rotating the individual vectors 90°. However, in three-dimensional vector fields the orthogonal complement of a vector is a plane. This suggests that a generalization of the one-dimensional LIC filter would be a two-dimensional surface filter. This filter would have as its geometric support a differential surface whose normals would be defined by the vector field, thus creating a Surface Integral Convolution (SIC). As with the LIC, an arbitrary two-dimensional filter could then be used to filter the three-dimensional input image.

Another direction for generalization is to develop versions of the algorithm which operate directly on curvilinear and arbitrarily grided vector fields without resampling the input data. The LIC algorithm could easily be modified to handle arbitrary line intersections and topologies of both type of grids. As with the rectilinear LIC, it would have an analogous three-dimensional generalization. Two additional problems remain however: generating curvilinear and arbitrarily girded textures and output resampling.

One possible image processing application of LIC is the deblurring of motion blurred images. Images acquired with a moving CCD camera often exhibit such blurring. If the CCD frequency response curves and the camera motion are known, one-dimensional deconvolution techniques could be used in conjunction with LIC to deblur the images.

The local nature of the LIC algorithm suggests a parallel implementation. Such an implementation could, in principle, compute all pixels simultaneously. This would allow for interactive generation of periodic motion animations and special effects.

7. SUMMARY

Line integral convolution represents a new and general method for imaging two- and three-dimensional vector fields. The algorithm filters an input image along local stream lines defined by an input vector field and generates an output image. The one-dimensional filter shape is independent of either input and can be arbitrary. To indicate directional flow of the vector field, a whole family of continuous motion filters has been introduced. These filters give apparent motion in the direction of the vector field. The technique can also be used to create special effects. Additionally, the local nature of the algorithm lends itself to efficient and simple implementations.

8. ACKNOWLEDGMENTS

This work was performed under the auspices of the U.S. Department of Energy by Lawrence Livermore National Laboratory under contract W-7405-ENG-48. The SIGGRAPH '93 reviewers provided many helpful comments and suggestions. Thanks to Nelson Max who suggested using higher order functions within a cell and who provided critical assessment all along the way. Roger Crawfis deserves special thanks for various conversations over the past couple of years on the topic of vector visualization. Chuck Grant provided helpful suggestions clarifying the language used to discuss periodic motion filters. John Bell and Jeff Greenough provided the turbulent computational fluid dynamics data used in figures 2, 4, 8 and 11 and for using the algorithm in their work. Dean Williams and Jerry Potter provided the North America wind velocity data. Lastly, thanks to John Zych who helped with the rendering of the North America image.

REFERENCES

1. Bresenham, J. Algorithm for Computer Control of a Digital Plotter. In *IBM Systems Journal* 4, 1 (1965), 25-30.
2. Bronstein, I. and Semendyayev, K. *Handbook of Mathematics*. Van Norstrand Reinholt (1985), 291-293.
3. Chang, S. *Fundamentals Handbook of Electrical Engineering and Computer Engineering*. John Wiley & Sons, Inc. (1982), 264-266.
4. Chui, K. *An Introduction to Wavelets*. Academic Press, Inc. (1992), 49-60.
5. Crawfis, R. and Max, M. Direct Volume Visualization of Three-Dimensional Vector Fields. *Proceedings of the Workshop on Volume Visualization*, Kaufman and Lorensen Eds (1992).
6. Drebin, R., Carpenter, L. and Hanaran, P. Volume Rendering. *Computer Graphics* 22, 4 (August 1988), 65-74.
7. Dumortier, F., Roussarie, R., Sotomayor, J. and Zoladek, H., Study of Field Bifurcations. *Lecture Notes in Mathematics*, Springer-Verlag (1991).
8. Freeman, W., Adelson, E. and Heeger, D. Motion without Movement. *Computer Graphics* 25, 4 (July 1991), 27-30.
9. Haeberli, P. Paint By Numbers: Abstract Image Representation. *Computer Graphics* 24, 4 (August 1990), 207-214.
10. Heckbert, P. Filtering by Repeated Integration. *Computer Graphics* 20, 4 (August 1986), 315-321.
11. Kajiya, J. and Kay, T. Rendering Fur with Three Dimensional Textures. *Computer Graphics* 23, 3 (July 1989), 271-280.
12. Kenwright, D. and Mallinson, G. A 3-D Streamline Tracking Algorithm Using Dual Stream Functions. *IEEE Visualization '92 Conference Proceedings* (October 1992), 62-68.
13. Max, Nelson. Personal Communication (1992).
14. Perlin, K. An Image Synthesizer. *Computer Graphics* 19, 3 (August 1985), 287-296.
15. Perlin, K. Hypertexture. *Computer Graphics* 23, 3 (July 1989), 253-262.
16. Pratt, W. *Digital Image Processing*. 2nd ed. John Wiley & Sons, Inc. (1991), 243-245.
17. Sims, K. Artificial Evolution for Computer Graphics. *Computer Graphics* 25, 4 (August 1991), 319-328.
18. Sims, K. Choreographed Image Flow. *The Journal of Visualization and Computer Animation* 3, 1 (January-March 1992), 31-43.
19. Tufte, E. The Visual Display of Quantitative Information. *Chesire, CT: Graphics Press* (1983).
20. Turk, G. Generating Textures on Arbitrary Surfaces Using Reaction-Diffusion Textures. *Computer Graphics* 25, 4 (July 1991), 289-298.
21. Upson, C. and Keeler, M. V-Buffer: Visible Volume Rendering. *Computer Graphics* 22, 4 (August 1988), 59-64.
22. Van Gelder, A. and Wilhelms, J. Interactive Animated Visualization of Flow Fields. *Proceedings of the Workshop on Volume Visualization*, Kaufman and Lorensen Eds. (1992).
23. Van Wijk, J. Spot Noise Texture Synthesis for Data Visualization. *Computer Graphics* 25, 4 (July 1991), 309-318.
24. Witkin, A. and Kass, M. Reaction-Diffusion Textures. *Computer Graphics* 25, 4 (July 1991), 299-308.

Frequency Domain Volume Rendering

*Takashi Totsuka** *Marc Levoy*†

*SONY Corporation
†Computer Science Department, Stanford University

Abstract

The Fourier projection-slice theorem allows projections of volume data to be generated in $O(n^2 \log n)$ time for a volume of size n^3. The method operates by extracting and inverse Fourier transforming 2D slices from a 3D frequency domain representation of the volume. Unfortunately, these projections do not exhibit the occlusion that is characteristic of conventional volume renderings. We present a new frequency domain volume rendering algorithm that replaces much of the missing depth and shape cues by performing shading calculations in the frequency domain during slice extraction. In particular, we demonstrate frequency domain methods for computing linear or nonlinear depth cueing and directional diffuse reflection. The resulting images can be generated an order of magnitude faster than volume renderings and may be more useful for many applications.

CR Categories: I.3.7 [Computer Graphics]: Three-dimensional Graphics and Realism.; I.3.3 [Computer Graphics]: Picture/Image Generation; Display Algorithms.

Additional Keywords: Volume rendering, Fourier transform, Shading models, Scientific visualization, Medical imaging, Digital signal processing.

1 Introduction

Volume rendering is an important tool for visualizing 3D scalar fields. Most existing algorithms operate in the spatial domain. They can be classified as either image space algorithms (e.g. [7]) or object space algorithms (e.g. [4], [15]) depending on the order in which the data is traversed: along each ray cast from the image plane or along X, Y, and Z axis of the volume data. The complexity of these algorithms is $O(n^3)$ since all voxels must be visited to render an image. This high cost limits the use of these algorithms in interactive environments. Although efficient algorithms exist for sparse data sets [8], [14],[16], such optimization is data dependent.

In an effort to drastically reduce rendering costs, frequency domain algorithms based on the Fourier projection slice theorem have been proposed [5], [10]. It is well known that the integral of a 1D signal is equal to the value of its spectrum at the origin. The Fourier projection slice theorem extends this notion to higher dimensions. For a 3D volume, the theorem states that the following two are a Fourier transform pair:

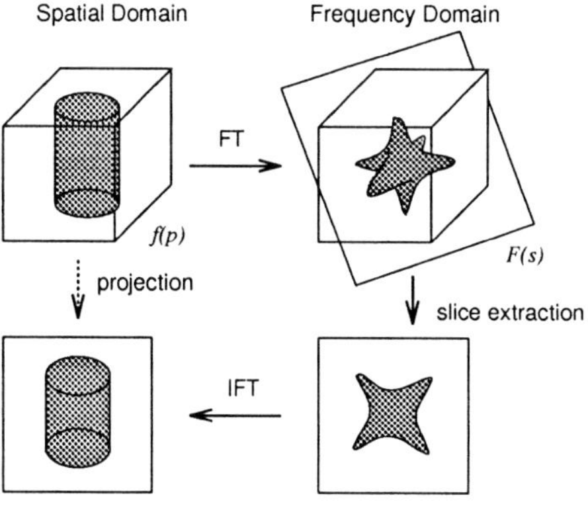

Figure 1: Volume rendering using Fourier projection slice theorem

- The 2D image obtained by taking line integrals of the volume along rays perpendicular to the image plane.
- The 2D spectrum obtained by extracting a slice from the Fourier transform of the volume along a plane which includes the origin and is parallel to the image plane.

Using this theorem, once a volume data is Fourier transformed, an (orthographic) image for any viewing direction can be obtained by extracting a 2D slice of the 3D spectrum at the appropriate orientation and then inverse Fourier transforming it (figure 1). The cost of this approach is dominated by the 2D inverse fast Fourier transform (IFFT) which is $O(n^2 \log n)$. Hence, the overall cost is also $O(n^2 \log n)$. Since $\log n$ grows slowly, the advantage of this approach over spatial domain algorithms is greater at large data sizes.

Despite their theoretical speed advantage, frequency domain volume rendering algorithms suffer from several well-known problems:

High interpolation cost: Because the sample points of the 3D spectrum and those of the 2D slice do not coincide except at the origin, the 3D spectrum must be interpolated and then resampled in order to extract a 2D slice. Since this interpolation is imperfect, replicas of the volume data are not fully suppressed, causing ghosts to appear on the projection image. Because any

* Sony Corporation. 6-7-35 Kitashinagawa, Shinagawa Tokyo 141, Japan (totsuka@av.crl.sony.co.jp)
† Center for Integrated Systems, Stanford University Stanford, CA 94305 (levoy@cs.stanford.edu)

filter that provides a sharp cutoff in the spatial domain also has wide support, high-quality interpolation is expensive. As the interpolation is $O(n^2)$, the FFT is still asymptotically dominant. However, due to a large constant factor associated with the interpolation, current implementations spend the majority of their running time in interpolation, making the algorithm not attractive for practical data sizes (128^3 or 256^3).

Memory cost: Due to the wide dynamic range and complex arithmetic associated with Fourier transforms, a pair of floating point numbers is required for each voxel. Assuming a 64-bit double precision representation, 16 bytes are required per voxel. By contrast, only 1 byte per voxel is necessary in spatial domain algorithms.

Lack of depth information: The projection obtained by the Fourier projection slice theorem is a line integral normal to the direction of view. Voxels on a viewing ray contribute equally to the image regardless of their distance from the eye. The image therefore lacks occlusion, an important visual cue. While some users (diagnostic radiologists in particular) prefer integral projections since nothing is hidden from view, this characteristic would be considered a drawback in most applications.

The first two problems listed above are technical in nature, and several promising solutions are proposed later in this paper. The lack of occlusion is fundamental, however, in so far as no projection-slice theorem is known that mimics the integro-differential equation ([6]) approximated by volume rendering algorithms. Fortunately, occlusion is only one of many cues employed by the human visual system to determine the shape and spatial relationships of objects. Other available cues include perspective, shading, texture, shadows, atmospheric attenuation, stereopsis, ocular accommodation, head motion parallax, and the kinetic depth effect.

It is possible, of course, to apply any shading technique in the spatial domain before the volume is Fourier transformed. However, such a naive approach would require recomputation of the volume followed by an expensive 3D forward FFT each time the view or the lighting condition is changed.

In an earlier paper [9], we instead showed that for a limited class of shading models, the dependence on viewing direction and lighting direction could be factored out of the projection integral, yielding equations of the form

$$I = \sum_{i=0}^{n} w_i \left(\int_{-\infty}^{+\infty} f_i\left(x(t), y(t), z(t)\right) dt \right). \quad (1)$$

Here, effects of viewing and lighting direction are solely expressed by weights w_i while the volumes f_i are independent of them. The indicated integration can be evaluated efficiently using the projection slice theorem. For example, linear depth cueing can be computed as the weighted sum of projections through three volumes that are depth cued before 3D forward FFT along X, Y, and Z directions, respectively.

The obvious disadvantage of this hybrid spatial-frequency domain approach is that it requires multiple copies of the volume. While still asymptotically faster than conventional spatial domain volume rendering, implementation considerations (problems one and two above) make it barely superior in practice.

In the present paper, we describe methods for rendering volumes with depth cueing and directional shading that operate entirely within the frequency domain. They are based on two well-known properties of the Fourier transform.

- Multiplication by a linear ramp in the spatial domain is equivalent to differentiation in the Fourier domain.
- Differentiation in the spatial domain is equivalent to multiplication by a linear ramp in the Fourier domain.

Using these properties, depth cueing implemented in [9] as spatial domain multiplication, is implemented in the present paper using frequency domain differentiation. Similarly, directional shading, implemented in [9] using spatial domain differentiation, is implemented in the present paper using frequency domain multiplication.

The remainder of the paper is organized as follows. Section 2 reviews the previous works. Section 3 presents our new frequency domain shape cueing techniques. Sections 4 and 5 refer to solutions to the interpolation and the memory cost problems, respectively. Section 6 shows results from our implementation, and section 7 gives conclusions and possible future directions.

2 Base Algorithm

We begin by briefly reviewing current frequency domain volume rendering algorithms. In the following discussion, small letters ($f, g, \ldots$) represent data in the spatial domain and capital letters ($F, G, \ldots$) represent data in the frequency domain. We also assume that the transform between the two domains is the Fourier transform which is denoted by $\mathcal{F}$.

Let $f(\boldsymbol{x})$ be a volume and $F(\boldsymbol{s})$ be its Fourier transform. $\boldsymbol{x}$ and $\boldsymbol{s}$ are 3D vectors in the spatial and frequency domain, respectively. Given $f(\boldsymbol{x})$, the algorithm first transforms it into the frequency domain to yield $F(\boldsymbol{s})$. This is done only once. For each view, the discrete spectrum $F(\boldsymbol{s})$ is interpolated along the extraction plane (parallel to the image plane and passing through the origin) using a filter $H(\boldsymbol{s})$. The interpolated spectrum is resampled to obtain a 2D spectrum which is then inverse transformed to obtain a spatial domain projection.

By the convolution theorem, interpolation $F(\boldsymbol{s}) * H(\boldsymbol{s})$ corresponds to $f(\boldsymbol{x}) \cdot h(\boldsymbol{x})$ in the spatial domain. Here, $h(\boldsymbol{x})$ is the response of the filter. Unless $H(\boldsymbol{s})$ is an ideal lowpass filter, its response has a smooth shoulder. Thus, the periphery of the volume and consequently the periphery of the projected image is attenuated. To cope with this "vignetting" problem, the volume data $f(\boldsymbol{x})$ can be premultiplied by the reciprocal of the response, $p_m(\boldsymbol{x}) = \frac{1}{h(\boldsymbol{x})}$ before its forward transformation [10]. As H and P_m cancel during interpolation, we obtain a correct slice of F (figure 2). We have implemented this method using filters obtained from Malzbender and have obtained excellent results, as documented in section 4 and 6.

3 Shape Cueing Techniques

3.1 Depth Cueing

Depth cueing is obtained by weighting voxels according to their distance from the observer. Let $d(\boldsymbol{x})$ be the weighting function or depth cueing function for a given eye position. Then, a depth-cued volume is expressed as $f(\boldsymbol{x}) \cdot d(\boldsymbol{x})$. By transforming it to the frequency domain and extracting a slice, we obtain a depth cued projection. As stated earlier, this straightforward approach requires an expensive 3D FFT ($n^3 \log n$) for each view. There is, however, an elegant and inexpensive equivalent operation in frequency domain.

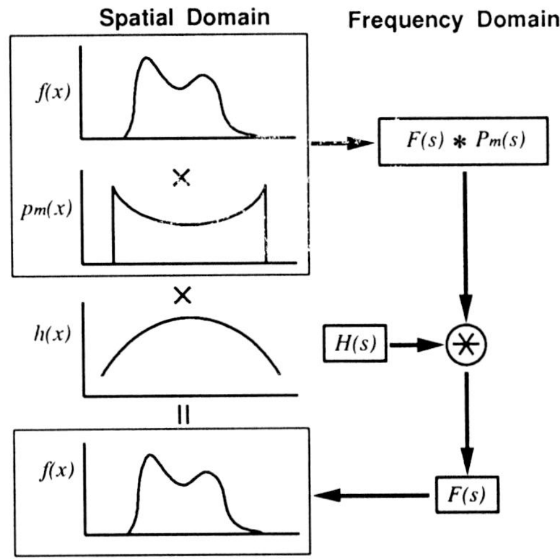

Figure 2: Premultiplication of the volume data

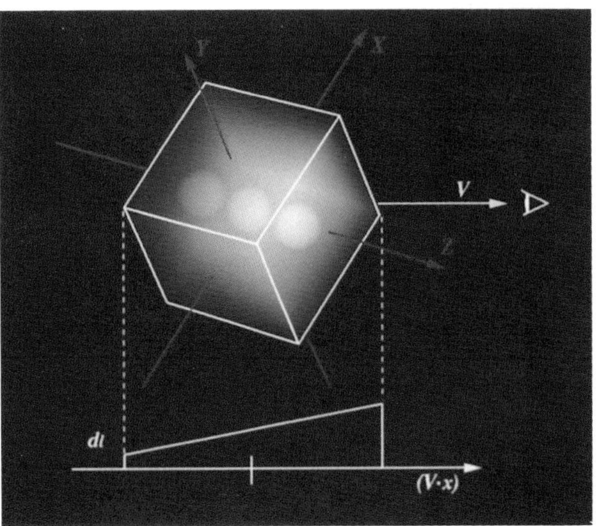

Figure 3: Linear depth cueing

Including the compensation $p_m(\boldsymbol{x})$ for the filter response, spatial domain depth cueing can be expressed as $f(\boldsymbol{x})\cdot d(\boldsymbol{x})\cdot p_m(\boldsymbol{x})$. By transforming and interpolating, this corresponds to $\mathcal{F}\{f(\boldsymbol{x})\cdot d(\boldsymbol{x})\cdot p_m(\boldsymbol{x})\} * H(\boldsymbol{s})$ at sample points on the slice in the frequency domain. Using the convolution theorem, this expression can be rewritten as follows:

$$\begin{aligned} & \mathcal{F}\{f(\boldsymbol{x})\, d(\boldsymbol{x})\, p_m(\boldsymbol{x})\} \ * \ H(\boldsymbol{s}) \\ = \ & (F(\boldsymbol{s}) * D(\boldsymbol{s}) * P_m(\boldsymbol{s})) \ * \ H(\boldsymbol{s}) \\ = \ & (F(\boldsymbol{s}) * P_m(\boldsymbol{s})) \ * \ (H(\boldsymbol{s}) * D(\boldsymbol{s})) \\ = \ & \mathcal{F}\{f(\boldsymbol{x})\, p_m(\boldsymbol{x})\} \ * \ H'(\boldsymbol{s}) \end{aligned} \tag{2}$$

where $H'(\boldsymbol{s}) = H(\boldsymbol{s}) * D(\boldsymbol{s})$.

Thus, merely by replacing the interpolation filter H with H', we have obtained depth cueing. Note that the above expression operates entirely in the frequency domain, and moreover is evaluated only on the plane of the slice being extracted. Hence, it is a 2D operation. Note also that because $\mathcal{F}\{f(\boldsymbol{x})\cdot p_m(\boldsymbol{x})\}$ is independent of the eye position, the 3D forward transform is performed only once.

Although H' must be computed for each view, the cost of recomputation is small because the support of filter H is small ($3^3 \sim 5^3$) and $D(\boldsymbol{s})$ is usually a simple expression. In practice, the recomputation is negligible compared with the cost of interpolation itself.

This frequency domain depth cueing method applies to any depth cueing function $d(\boldsymbol{x})$. Indeed, the method can be designed to highlight the middle portion of the volume while attenuating the front and back portions.

By way of example, we first consider simple linear depth cueing, $d_l(\boldsymbol{x})$. Let the view vector be $\boldsymbol{V}$. The signed depth measured from the origin of the volume is thus given by $(\boldsymbol{V}\cdot\boldsymbol{x})$, and $d_l(\boldsymbol{x})$ can be written as

$$d_l(\boldsymbol{x}) = C_{cue}(\boldsymbol{V}\cdot\boldsymbol{x}) + C_{avg} \tag{3}$$

where C_{cue} is the strength of the depth cueing effect and C_{avg} is a constant (see figure 3). Taking Fourier transforms, we obtain

$$D_l(\boldsymbol{s}) = -\frac{C_{cue}}{i2\pi}(\boldsymbol{V}\cdot\boldsymbol{\Delta}) + C_{avg}\,\delta(\boldsymbol{s}) \tag{4}$$

where $\boldsymbol{\Delta} = [\Delta_x, \Delta_y, \Delta_z]$ is the differential operator of convolution ($\Delta_x * f = \frac{\partial}{\partial x} f$). Substituting the interpolation filter with depth cueing (H') yields

$$\begin{aligned} H'(\boldsymbol{s}) &= H(\boldsymbol{s}) * D_l(\boldsymbol{s}) \\ &= -\frac{C_{cue}}{i2\pi}(\boldsymbol{V}\cdot\nabla H(\boldsymbol{s})) + C_{avg}\, H(\boldsymbol{s}) \end{aligned} \tag{5}$$

The first term exhibits the depth cueing effect. Since ∇H can be precomputed and stored in a table, computation of H' is of insignificant cost. An example of frequency domain linear depth cueing and projection is shown in figure 6(b). As a reference, the same volume rendered without depth cueing is shown in figure 6(a).

Although any function can be used for D, finding one that has a simple form reduces the cost of computing H'. The size of H' is also a consideration, since it directly impacts rendering time. To illustrate this important issue, let us employ a half period of a sine wave as $d(\boldsymbol{x})$. Since the transform of a sine function is two impulses, H' can be computed by shifting H and adding three copies[1] with complex weights. Note that this considerably increases the size of the filter kernel. By adjusting the origin, amplitude, and period such that the value is zero at the farthest voxel and unity at the closest voxel, we eliminate the need for a DC term. D now has the form $C_1\,\delta(\boldsymbol{s}-\boldsymbol{s}_w) + C_2\,\delta(\boldsymbol{s}+\boldsymbol{s}_w)$ where C_1 and C_2 are complex constants determined by the amplitude and the shift of the wave and $\boldsymbol{s}_w$ is determined by the period of the wave. The period is typically made long enough so that the depth cueing appears almost linear. We can further remove one of the impulses by doubling the weight of the remaining impulse. By removing one of the impulses, the projection image is no longer a real[2]. However, the real part of the result still contains the correct projection image. With this technique, depth cueing is implemented by an interpolation with a shifted H, which is practically free.

The notion of a shifted H gives us an alternative way to look at the process. Extracting a slice from a spectrum at a position translated from the origin by a distance d in a

[1] Two for the impulses of the sine wave term and one for the constant term of $d(\boldsymbol{x})$.

[2] The imaginary part is a cosine wave since we are using the analytic signal of the depth cueing function. See the discussion on the Hilbert transform in [1].

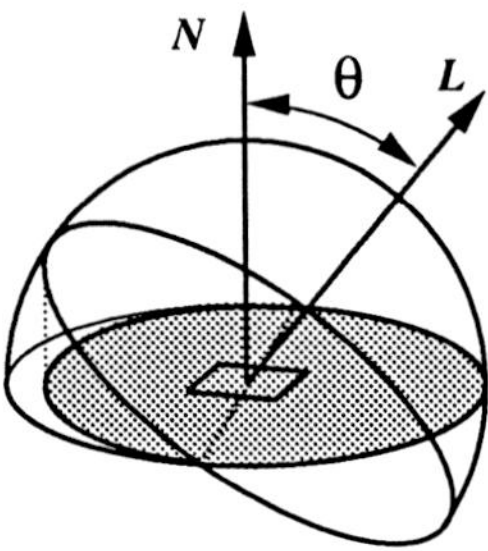

Figure 4: Hemispherical light source

direction $\boldsymbol{V}$ corresponds to phase-shifting the spatial domain projection by $e^{i2\pi d\,t}$ at distance t in the same direction $\boldsymbol{V}$. The real part of such a phase-shifted projection appears to fade in and out as a function of position in direction $\boldsymbol{V}$ and, for appropriate values of d, the visual effect is that of depth cueing.

3.2 Directional Shading

In a scene composed of surfaces, directional shading using the well-known Lambertian reflection model is given by

$$C_{amb}\, O_c L_{amb} + C_{dif}\, O_c L_{dif}\, \mathrm{MAX}\,(0, (\boldsymbol{N}\cdot\boldsymbol{L})) \qquad (6)$$

where C_{amb} and C_{dif} are constants defining the strength of ambient and directional shading terms, O_c is an object color, L_{amb} and L_{dif} are constants defining the color of ambient and directional lights, and $\boldsymbol{N}$ and $\boldsymbol{L}$ are unit surface normal and light vectors, respectively.

Ignoring the attenuation of light inside the volume, the ambient term can be approximated using

$$C_{amb}\, L_{amb}\, f(\boldsymbol{x}) \qquad (7)$$

The diffuse term, however, must be handled carefully because the nonlinear function MAX does not have a simple frequency domain representation. Note that the frequently used alternative, $|\boldsymbol{N}\cdot\boldsymbol{L}|$, which shades surfaces as if they are two-sided rather than the bounding surface of a solid, is also nonlinear and cannot be handled directly in the frequency domain.

To avoid this problem, we employ a hemispherical light source [12], [9]. The irradiance E_i on a surface having normal vector $\boldsymbol{N}$ illuminated by a hemisphere whose pole points in direction $\boldsymbol{L}$ as shown in figure 4 is proportional by Nusselt's analog (as described in [3]) to the projection of the visible portion of the hemisphere down onto the plane containing the surface, or

$$E_i \;=\; L_{dif}\,\frac{1}{2}(1 + \cos\theta) \;=\; L_{dif}\,\frac{1}{2}\big(1 + (\boldsymbol{N}\cdot\boldsymbol{L})\big) \qquad (8)$$

With this shading model, the diffuse term in a surface model is expressed as

$$C_{dif}\, O_c L_{dif}\,\frac{1}{2}\big(1 + (\boldsymbol{N}\cdot\boldsymbol{L})\big) \qquad (9)$$

For volumes, we have

$$C_{dif} L_{dif}\,\frac{1}{2}\,|\nabla f(\boldsymbol{x})| \left(1 + \frac{(\nabla f(\boldsymbol{x})\cdot\boldsymbol{L})}{|\nabla f(\boldsymbol{x})|}\right)$$
$$= \; C_{dif} L_{dif}\,\frac{1}{2}\big(|\nabla f(\boldsymbol{x})| + (\nabla f(\boldsymbol{x})\cdot\boldsymbol{L})\big) \qquad (10)$$

Since volume datasets do not have explicitly defined surfaces, $\nabla f(\boldsymbol{x})$ is used as the normal vector at each location. The strength of directional shading in volume rendering algorithms is commonly made proportional to the gradient magnitude as a simulation of the *surface-ness* of the volume [4],[7]. Locales having high gradient magnitudes (i.e., steep jumps in density) reflect more light.

Equation (10) can be computed entirely in the frequency domain. By the derivative theorem, the gradient in one domain is the first moment in the other domain. Thus, the shading computation can be performed as a moment computation in the frequency domain. This useful property of linear shading can also be exploited in image understanding algorithms. For example, [13] uses the moment to estimate the orientation of surfaces assuming that the reflectance function is linear with respect to the slope of the surfaces.

Transforming equations (7) and (10) to the frequency domain and including compensation for the filter response, we obtain

$$\begin{aligned}
&\mathcal{F}\big\{C_{amb}\, L_{amb}\, f(\boldsymbol{x}) \\
&\qquad + C_{dif} L_{dif}\,\frac{1}{2}\big(|\nabla f(\boldsymbol{x})| + (\nabla f(\boldsymbol{x})\cdot\boldsymbol{L})\big)\big\} \\
&= \big(C_{amb}\, L_{amb} + i\pi C_{dif}\, L_{dif}\,(\boldsymbol{s}\cdot\boldsymbol{L})\big) \\
&\qquad \times\big(\mathcal{F}\{f(\boldsymbol{x})\, p_m(\boldsymbol{x})\} * H(\boldsymbol{s})\big) \\
&\quad + \frac{1}{2}C_{dif}\, L_{dif}\,\big(\mathcal{F}\{\,|\nabla f(\boldsymbol{x})|\, p_m(\boldsymbol{x})\,\} * H(\boldsymbol{s})\big)
\end{aligned} \qquad (11)$$

The first term corresponds to the ambient term and the $(\boldsymbol{N}\cdot\boldsymbol{L})$ part of equation (9) while the second term corresponds to the accompanying constant 1. Once $f(\boldsymbol{x})p_m(\boldsymbol{x})$ and $|\nabla f(\boldsymbol{x})|\, p_m(\boldsymbol{x})$ are Fourier transformed, the shading computation can be performed during slice extraction (figure 5). Note that the interpolation filter H is applied first in order to reconstruct the pure spectrum of $f(\boldsymbol{x})$ from the premultiplied volume. Then, the first moment of the spectrum is computed to apply the directional shading.

Although computing a moment incurs a few additional floating point operations per sample on the slice, the additional expense is small relative to the number of operations that are required to evaluate the convolution at the sample point. It should also be noted that equation (11) can be easily extended to multiple light sources. In this case, we only have to add the moment terms for additional light sources. The increase in the computation cost is minor.

Figure 6(c) shows a projection shaded using this technique. As before, the method operates entirely in the frequency domain and requires computations only on the plane of the slice being extracted

The major drawback of this shading model is that it requires a second spectrum, $\mathcal{F}\{|\nabla f(\boldsymbol{x})|\, p_m(\boldsymbol{x})\}$ since there is no simple way to compute a gradient magnitude in the frequency domain. Hence, two slices must be extracted from two volumes. A linear shading equation such as $C_{amb}\, L_{amb}\, f(\boldsymbol{x}) + C_{dif}L_{dif}\,\nabla f(\boldsymbol{x})$ that requires only one volume can be derived under an appropriate interpretation. However, the upper bound of C_{dif} is restricted in order not to generate negative values and consequently the shading effect is restricted.

3.3 Combining Depth Cueing and Shading

It is possible to combine the depth cueing and directional shading techniques described in the foregoing section. When the two techniques are used together, the shading must be

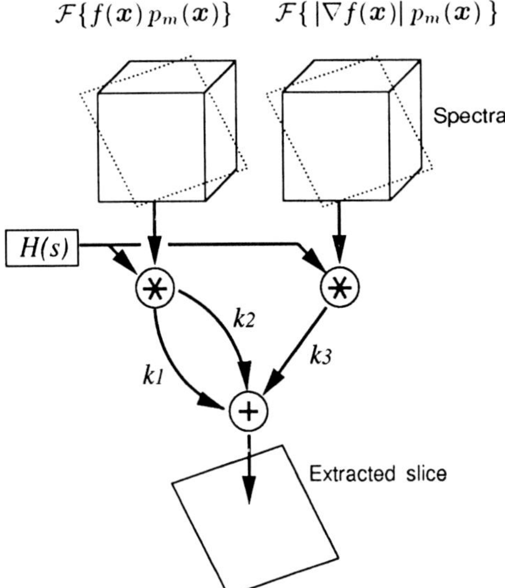

Figure 5: Shading computation in frequency domain. $k_1 = C_{amb}\,L_{amb}$ (ambient term), $k_2 = i\pi C_{dif}\,L_{dif}\,(\boldsymbol{s}\cdot\boldsymbol{L})$ (shading term), $k_3 = \frac{1}{2}C_{dif}\,L_{dif}$ (constant term).

applied first. Otherwise, distortion by the depth cueing would result in incorrect gradient vector by which the shading effect is computed. However, this order of operation requires two convolutions: one performed before the shading computation to recover F by interpolation filter H and one performed after shading in order to apply the depth cueing function. This approach makes depth cueing no longer an inexpensive operation since we can't use the composite filter H'.

We can work around this problem by reversing the order of shading and depth cueing and then adjusting the result to get the desired effect. Using this ordering, we employ the composite filter H' to perform the interpolation and the depth cueing at once. As we will see, for practical settings, even this adjustment is not necessary.

Here, we will examine the effect of reversed order operation in spatial domain. We focus on the gradient term of the shading equation (second term of equation (10)) since other terms are not affected by the order. Applying depth cueing function $d(\boldsymbol{x})$ to equation (10), we obtain the shaded and depth cued term. Omitting the coefficient $\frac{1}{2}C_{dif}\,L_{dif}$, the gradient term is $(\nabla f(\boldsymbol{x})\cdot\boldsymbol{L}\,)\,d(\boldsymbol{x})$. Reversing the order of computation, we get

$$\begin{aligned}&(\nabla[f(\boldsymbol{x})\,d(\boldsymbol{x})]\cdot\boldsymbol{L}\,)\\ =\;&(\nabla f(\boldsymbol{x})\cdot\boldsymbol{L}\,)\,d(\boldsymbol{x}) + f(\boldsymbol{x})\,(\nabla d(\boldsymbol{x})\cdot\boldsymbol{L}\,)\end{aligned}\tag{12}$$

The second term is the difference from the correct value. Since $d(\boldsymbol{x})$ is a function of depth $(\boldsymbol{V}\cdot\boldsymbol{x})$, the difference can be rewritten as

$$\begin{aligned}&f(\boldsymbol{x})\,(\nabla[d_{1D}\,(\boldsymbol{V}\cdot\boldsymbol{x})]\cdot\boldsymbol{L}\,)\\ =\;&f(\boldsymbol{x})\,d'_{1D}\,(\boldsymbol{V}\cdot\boldsymbol{x})\,(\,\boldsymbol{V}\cdot\boldsymbol{L}\,)\end{aligned}\tag{13}$$

where $d_{1D}(t)$ is a 1D depth cueing function. To maximize the shading effect, $\boldsymbol{L}$ is usually set perpendicular to $\boldsymbol{V}$ (i.e., the scene is illuminated from the side). In this case, the difference term becomes zero and the adjustment is not necessary. An example of this common special case is shown in figure 6(d).

If $(\boldsymbol{V}\cdot\boldsymbol{x})$ is non-zero, we need an adjustment. For linear depth cueing, the difference term including all the coefficients is

$$\frac{1}{2}C_{cue}C_{dif}\,L_{dif}\,f(\boldsymbol{x})\,(\boldsymbol{V}\cdot\boldsymbol{L})\tag{14}$$

which we can compute during slice extraction without convolution. For a more complex depth cueing function, a convolution is necessary.

4 Reducing Rendering Time

Although the interpolation required in order to extract an arbitrarily oriented slice from the 3D spectrum is $O(n^2)$, it consumes most of the running time. As might be expected, the cost of this interpolation step is almost entirely determined by the size of the filter. For the $3\times3\times3$ filter we employ, 27 input samples contribute to each output sample. If we instead employed a $1\times1\times1$ filter, only one input sample would contribute to each output sample, a great saving in time. Because a smaller filter has less sharp cut off in spatial domain, the resulting image would contain strong ghosts if it were used uniformly over the entire interpolation process. However, by adaptively changing the filter size, we can reduce rendering time while maintaining high image quality.

Most of the energy in a spectrum usually resides in a small number of low frequency components, while the vast majority of high frequency components are nearly zero. We have observed that usually 99% of the energy is contained by about 10% of the frequency components.

This property makes an adaptive scheme which selects an inexpensive filter for weak frequency components very attractive. For simplicity, let us consider interpolation of a 1D spectrum F by two filters; a larger filter H_1 and a smaller filter H_2. Each input sample component is filtered or scattered by either H_1 or H_2 according to its strength. Let F_1 be the set of those samples that are filtered by H_1 and F_2 be those filtered by H_2. Obviously, $F_1+F_2=F$. The correct result we want is $F*H_1$ or in the spatial domain, $f\,h_1$. The adaptive scheme can thus be written as follows:

$$\begin{aligned}&\mathcal{F}^{-1}\{\,F_1*H_1\;+\;F_2*H_2\,\}\\ =\;&\mathcal{F}^{-1}\{\,F*H_1\;+\;F_2*(H_2-H_1)\,\}\\ =\;&f\,h_1+f_2\,(h_2-h_1)\end{aligned}\tag{15}$$

The term $f_2\,(h_2-h_1)$ denotes the difference between the adaptively filtered image and the correct image. The mean square error is given by integrating the power of this error term. Using Rayleigh's theorem, its upper bound is given in the frequency domain as follows.

$$\begin{aligned}&\frac{1}{L}\int_{-\infty}^{+\infty}|\,f_2\,(h_2-h_1)\,|^2\,dx\\ \le\;&\frac{1}{L}\,h_{d\text{-}max}^2\int_{-\infty}^{+\infty}|\,f_2\,|^2\,dx\\ =\;&\frac{1}{L}\,h_{d\text{-}max}^2\int_{-\infty}^{+\infty}|\,F_2\,|^2\,ds\end{aligned}\tag{16}$$

where L is the length of the non-zero region of f and $h_{d\text{-}max}$ is the maximum of $|h_2-h_1|$. This upper bound allows us to select input samples to be filtered by H_2 such that the mean square error of the rendered image is below a user defined tolerance. Similar analysis provides an upper bound for the mean square error when more than 2 filters are employed. The idea extends straightforwardly to 3D discrete signals.

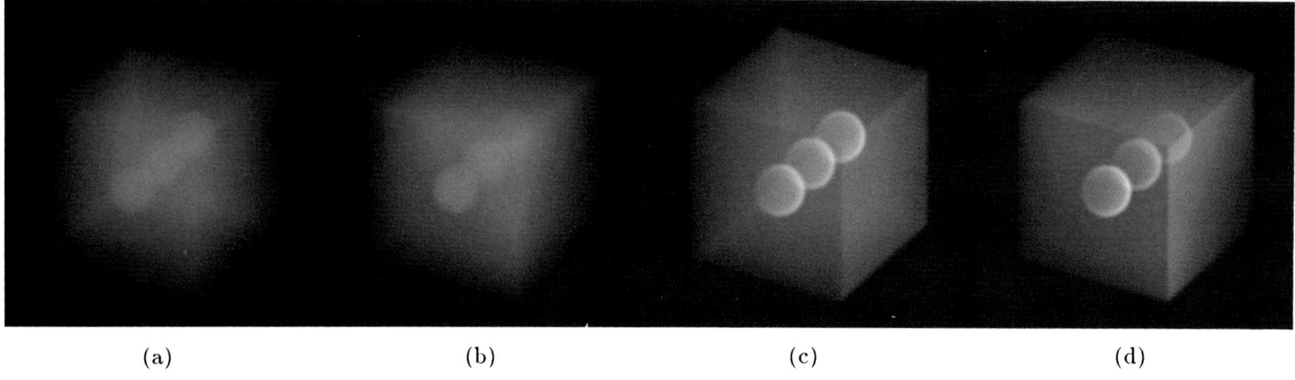

(a) (b) (c) (d)

Figure 6: Examples of frequency domain depth cueing and shading. (a) projection without depth cueing, (b) linear depth cueing, (c) directional shading without depth cueing, (d) directional shading with depth cueing.

This adaptive scheme is incorporated to the slice extraction as follows. First, each sample in the 3D spectrum is examined, and those whose magnitude is small enough to satisfy equation (16) are marked. This process is done only once after a volume data is transformed to the frequency domain. During slice extraction, each sample point on the slice plane is visited. If for a given sample point all of the 3D spectrum voxels that fall within the support of the larger filter are marked, the smaller filter is employed instead.

It is possible to improve this scheme further. To avoid testing all voxels falling within the support of the larger filter, we modify the preprocess to mark only those voxels that themselves satisfy equation (16) and for which all neighboring voxels lying within a distance from them equal to one-half of the support of the larger filter satisfy the equation. Given this more conservative marking, it is sufficient during slice extraction to test the spectrum voxel closest to the slice sample position. If that voxel is marked, we know without visiting any other voxels that it is safe to employ the smaller filter.

5 Reducing Memory Cost

Because the 3D spectrum is complex and requires a floating point representation due to its large dynamic range, a straightforward implementation using a double precision format consumes 16 times more memory than a spatial domain algorithm[3]. This explosion in memory cost can be controlled by using the Hartley transform [10] and a shorter number representation.

The Hartley transform is a direct relative of the Fourier transform [2]. The transform is defined as follows:

$$\mathcal{H}\{f(x)\} = F_H(s) = \int_{-\infty}^{+\infty} f(x)\,\mathrm{cas}2\pi sx\,dx \tag{17}$$

where $\mathrm{cas}2\pi sx = \cos 2\pi sx + \sin 2\pi sx$. Since the kernel is a real function, this transform maps a real function $f(x)$ to a real spectrum $F_H(s)$. Use of the Hartley transform, therefore, eliminates the need for a complex number. Since the Fourier spectrum of a real signal is hermitian[4], the same amount of memory saving is possible with the Fourier transform by dropping half of the spectrum (e.g., store only the positive coefficients along the S_x axis). However, such implementation would unnecessarily complicate the slice extraction process.

Due to wide dynamic range of spectra, a floating point format is necessary. Considering the necessity of premultiplying the volume before transforming, a 64-bit double precision format is a safe choice to represent a spectrum of a 256^3 volume. However, even using the Hartley transform, this occupies 8 times more memory than the original volume. This problem can be minimized by using a shorter floating point format. We have defined and used a 16-bit floating point format which reduces the memory cost factor to two.

6 Results

Figures 7-9 show images rendered using the algorithms we have described. The shading, depth cueing, adaptive filtering, the Hartley transform, and the 16-bit floating point format are all used in rendering these three images.

Figure 7 shows a human skull mounted in a lucite head cast. The data was acquired using computed tomography (CT). Zeros are padded to the original data (106^3) and resulting 128^3 volume data was rendered. The volume is shaded by a hemispherical light source located to the right and is also linearly depth cued with respect to the observer's position.

The use of multiple light sources is shown in figure 8. A polygonalization of the Utah teapot has been 3D scan-converted into a 256^3 volume data which is then shaded by a red, a green, and a blue light located perpendicular to the observer and 120 degrees apart. The resulting color on the surface provides some intuition for the orientation of the gradient vector.

Figures 9 and 10 compare the frequency domain rendering technique with a conventional spatial domain volume rendering. These images were generated using identical shading and depth cueing. There is no visible difference between the two images.

[3]Assuming each voxel is represented by one byte in the spatial domain algorithm. With shading, spatial domain algorithms require more memory.

[4]A signal whose real part is even and whose imaginary part is odd, i.e. $f(x) = f^*(-x)$.

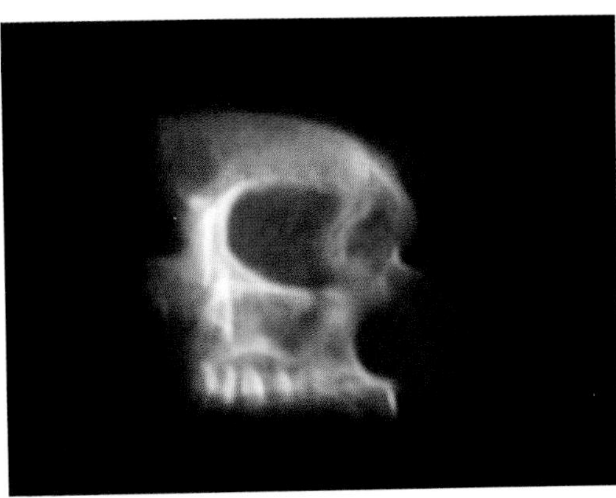

Figure 7: Human head. Frequency domain volume rendering. Data courtesy of North Carolina Memorial Hospital.

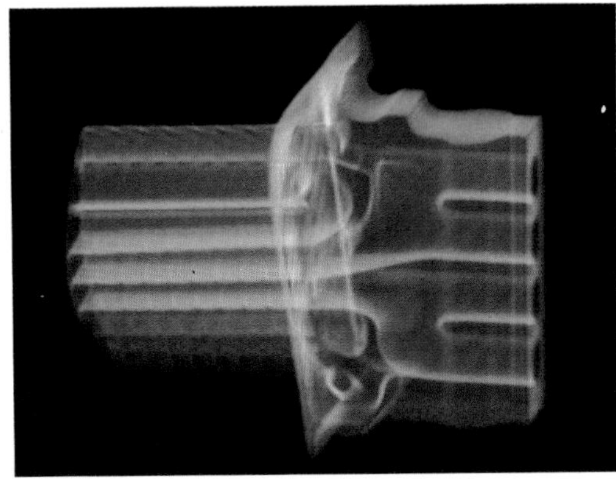

Figure 9: Turbine blade. Frequency domain volume rendering. The blade is lit by a green light (top), a blue light (bottom), and a dim red light (right). Data courtesy of General Electric.

Figure 8: Utah teapot. Frequency domain volume rendering. The pot is lit by a red light (right), a green light (upper left), and a blue light (lower left).

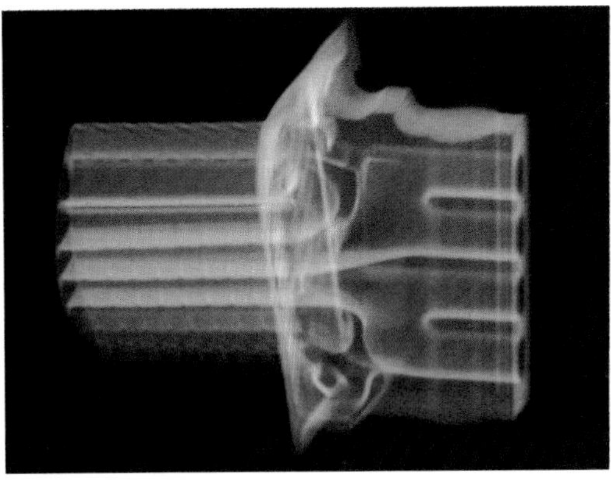

Figure 10: Same dataset as figure 9. Rendered with identical shading and depth cueing but using a spatial domain volume renderer.

The adaptive filtering scheme described in section 4 was implemented using a $3 \times 3 \times 3$ and a $1 \times 1 \times 1$ filter with the maximum difference in response set to ($h_{d\text{-}max}$) 0.3. Figures 7-9 were generated using this scheme. As shown in table 1, the scheme reduced the cost of interpolation to about 15% of the non-adaptive case. Relative error was always below 40dB, a level at which image differences are not visible.

Table 1 also shows rendering times to generate figures 7-9. Rendering times by a spatial domain renderer are also shown for comparison. These times include all necessary operations to create a 2D projection. For the frequency domain rendering technique, it consists of slice extraction (interpolation and resampling), inverse Harteley transform, and format conversion to and from the 16-bit floating point format and the machine's native format. Times were measured on an IRIS Crimson with a 50Mhz R4000 processor using non-optimized code. As the table shows, the running time of the frequency domain method grows much slower than the spatial domain method, which grows at $O(n^3)$.

The effect of round off error caused by the 16-bit floating format was very small. Relative difference from images generated using a 64-bit double precision representation were below 50dB. Figures 7-9 were generated using this format.

7 Conclusions

The use of the Fourier projection slice theorem allows us to replace the $O(n^3)$ spatial domain projection computation that arises in volume rendering with an $O(n^2 \log n)$ frequency domain computation, although the frequency domain projection operator is non-occluding, resulting in a loss of realism. In this paper, we have shown that other $O(n^3)$ spatial domain rendering computations that arise in volume rendering (i.e., shading and depth cueing) can be replaced with $O(n^2)$ frequency domain methods, and we propose that a judicious selection of these methods can restore much of the realism lost by using a non-occluding projection.

The speed advantage of our algorithm over volume rendering is considerable. As our experiments show, a 128^3 volume can be rendered in a fraction of a second on a conventional workstation. Further optimization of the code should achieve interactive rendering without specialized hardware.

Besides its speed advantage, the frequency domain approach lends itself to simple and elegant speed-accuracy tradeoffs. By extracting only the central portion of the 3D spectrum present on a slice, a renderer could provide a low resolution image quickly while the user is rotating the vol-

Volume data	Size	Adaptive filtering			Rendering time	
		Non adaptive	Adaptive			
		Num. ops.†	Num. ops.†	(Ratio)	Freq. domain	Spatial domain
Head	128^3	5.92×10^5	1.01×10^5	(17.1%)	0.54 sec	3.15 sec
Teapot	256^3	1.81×10^6	2.33×10^5	(12.9%)	1.77	24.29
Turbine	256^3	1.85×10^6	3.00×10^5	(16.2%)	2.03	24.38

†A filtering operation consists of a filter table look up, a reference to a voxel, a multiplication, and an addition.

Table 1: Effect of adaptive filtering

ume, to be replaced with a higher quality image when the mouse button or joystick is released.

Since the core computations of the algorithm are convolution and the FFT, an implementation using digital signal processors (DSPs) obviously suggests itself. With the growth of multimedia applications involving video and sound encoding and decoding, such processors are becoming a standard part of most graphics workstations. It should also be noted that these computations exhibit high data level parallelism and can be parallelized in any one of several ways.

With regard to limitations and improvements, further effort should be made to relax the limitations imposed by the linear nature of the Fourier/Hartley transform. The algorithm currently does not allow non-linear attenuation.

Acknowledgements

The authors wish to thank Tom Malzbender for helpful suggestions and his interpolation filter coefficients and Ronald Bracewell for useful hints on the use of the Hartley transform. The notion that shading could be factored with respect to digital compositing, an idea that inspired the present work, was suggested by Brice Tebbs. Discussions with Adam Levinthal were useful in the early stages of this project. Hide Hirase's volume modeling toolkit helped us creating test datasets.

This research was supported by the National Science Foundation (NSF), the National Aeronautics and Space Administration (NASA), and the sponsoring companies of the Stanford Center for Integrated Systems (CIS).

References

[1] Bracewell, Ronald, *The Fourier Transform and its Applications, revised second edition*, McGraw-Hill, 1986.

[2] Bracewell, Ronald, *The Hartley Transform*, Oxford University Press, 1986.

[3] Cohen, Michael and Greenberg, Donald, "The Hemicube: A Radiosity Solution for Complex Environments", *Computer Graphics*, Vol.19, No.3, pp.31-40, 1985.

[4] Drebin, Robert, Carpenter, Loren, and Hanrahan, Pat, "Volume Rendering", *Computer Graphics*, Vol.22, No.4, pp.65-74, 1988.

[5] Dunne, Shane, Napel, Sandy, and Rutt, Brian, "Fast Reprojection of Volume Data", *Proceedings of the First Conference on Visualization in Biochemical Computing*, IEEE Computer Society Press, pp.11-18, 1990.

[6] Hottel, Hoyt, and Sarofim, Adel, "Radiative Transfer", McGraw-Hill, 1967.

[7] Levoy, Marc, "Display of Surfaces from Volume Data", *IEEE Computer Graphics and Applications*, Vol.8, No.3, pp.29-37, 1988.

[8] Levoy, Marc, "Efficient Ray Tracing of Volume Data", *ACM Transactions on Graphics*, Vol.9, No.3, pp.245-261, 1990.

[9] Levoy, Marc, "Volume Rendering using the Fourier Projection-Slice Theorem", *Proceedings of Graphics Interface '92*, Canadian Information Processing Society, pp.61-69, 1992.

[10] Malzbender, Tom, "Fourier Volume Rendering", *ACM Transactions on Graphics*, Vol.12, No.3, July 1993.

[11] Napel, Sandy, Dunne, Shane, and Rutt, Brian, "Fast Fourier Projection for MR Angiography", *Magnetic Resonance in Medicine*, Vol.19, pp.393-405, 1991.

[12] Nishita, Tomoyuki and Nakamae, Eihachiro, "Continuous Tone Representation of Three-Dimensional Objects", *Computer Graphics*, Vol.20, No.4, pp.125-132, 1986.

[13] Pentland, Alex, "Linear Shape from Shading", *International Journal of Computer Vision*, Vol.4, pp.153-162, 1990.

[14] Subramanian, K.R. and Fussel, Donald, "Applying space subdivision techniques to volume rendering", *Proceedings of the First IEEE Conference on Visualization. (Visualization '90)*, IEEE Computer Society Press, pp.150-159, 1990.

[15] Westover, Lee, "Footprint Evaluation for Volume Rendering", *Computer Graphics*, Vol.24, No.4, pp.367-376, 1990.

[16] Zuiderveld, Karel, Koning, Anton, and Viergever, Max, "Acceleration of ray-casting using 3D distance transforms", *Proceedings of the SPIE – Visualization in Biomedical Computing 1992*, Vol.1808, pp.324-335, 1992.

View Interpolation for Image Synthesis

Shenchang Eric Chen, Lance Williams

Apple Computer, Inc.

ABSTRACT

Image-space simplifications have been used to accelerate the calculation of computer graphic images since the dawn of visual simulation. Texture mapping has been used to provide a means by which images may themselves be used as display primitives. The work reported by this paper endeavors to carry this concept to its logical extreme by using interpolated images to portray three-dimensional scenes. The special-effects technique of morphing, which combines interpolation of texture maps and their shape, is applied to computing arbitrary intermediate frames from an array of prestored images. If the images are a structured set of views of a 3D object or scene, intermediate frames derived by morphing can be used to approximate intermediate 3D transformations of the object or scene. Using the view interpolation approach to synthesize 3D scenes has two main advantages. First, the 3D representation of the scene may be replaced with images. Second, the image synthesis time is independent of the scene complexity. The correspondence between images, required for the morphing method, can be predetermined automatically using the range data associated with the images. The method is further accelerated by a quadtree decomposition and a view-independent visible priority. Our experiments have shown that the morphing can be performed at interactive rates on today's high-end personal computers. Potential applications of the method include virtual holograms, a walkthrough in a virtual environment, image-based primitives and incremental rendering. The method also can be used to greatly accelerate the computation of motion blur and soft shadows cast by area light sources.

CR Categories and Subject Descriptors: I.3.3 [Computer Graphics]: Picture/Image Generation; I.3.7 [Computer Graphics]: Three-Dimensional Graphics and Realism.

Additional Keywords: image morphing, interpolation, virtual reality, motion blur, shadow, incremental rendering, real-time display, virtual holography, motion compensation.

1 INTRODUCTION

Generating a large number of images of an environment from closely spaced viewpoints is a very useful capability. A traditional application is a flight in the cabin of an aircraft simulator, whereas the contemporary model is perhaps a walk through a virtual environment; in both cases the same scene is displayed from the view of a virtual camera controlled by the user. The computation of global illumination effects, such as shadows, diffuse and specular inter-reflections, also requires a large number of visibility calculations. A typical approach to this problem is to rely on the computer to repetitively render the scene from different viewpoints. This approach has two major drawbacks. First, real-time rendering of complex scenes is computationally expensive and usually requires specialized graphics hardware. Second, the rendering time is usually not constant and is dependent on the scene complexity. This problem is particularly critical in simulation and virtual reality applications because of the demand for real-time feedback. Since scene complexity is potentially unbounded, the second problem will always exist regardless of the processing power of the computer.

A number of approaches have been proposed to address this problem. Most of these approaches use a preprocess to compute a subset of the scene visible from a specified viewing region[AIRE91, TELL92]. Only the potentially visible objects are processed in the walkthrough time. This approach does not completely solve the problem because there may be viewing regions from which all objects are visible. Greene and Kass[GREE93] developed a method to approximate the visibility at a location from adjacent environment maps. The environment maps are Z-buffered images rendered from a set of discrete viewpoints in 3D space. Each environment map shows a complete view of the scene from a point. An environment map can take the form of a cubic map, computed by rendering a cube of 90° views radiating from that point [GREE86]. The environment maps are pre-computed and stored with viewpoints arranged in a structured way, such as a 3D lattice. An image from a new viewpoint can be generated by re-sampling the environment maps stored in adjacent locations. The re-sampling process involves rendering the pixels in the environment maps as 3D polygons from the new viewpoint. The advantage of this approach is that the rendering time is proportional to the environment map resolutions and is independent of the scene complexity. However, this method requires Z-buffer hardware to render a relatively large number of polygons interactively, a feature still not available on most low-end computers.

This paper presents a fast method for generating intermediate images from images stored at nearby viewpoints. The method has advantages similar to those of Greene and Kass' method. The generation of a new image is independent of the scene complexity. However, instead of drawing every pixel as a 3D polygon, our method uses techniques similar to those used in image morphing[BEIE92]. Adjacent images are "morphed" to create a new image for an in-between viewpoint. The morphing makes use of pre-computed correspondence maps and, therefore, is very efficient. Our experiments with the new method have shown that it can be performed at interactive rates on inexpen-

© 1993 ACM-0-89791-601-8/93/008/0279 $01.50

sive personal computers without specialized hardware.

The new method is based on the observation that a sequence of images from closely spaced viewpoints is highly coherent. Most of the adjacent images in the sequence depict the same objects from slightly different viewpoints. Our method uses the camera's position and orientation and the range data of the images to determine a pixel-by-pixel correspondence between images automatically. The pairwise correspondence between two successive images can be pre-computed and stored as a pair of morph maps. Using these maps, corresponding pixels are interpolated interactively under the user's control to create in-between images.

Pixel correspondence can be established if range data and the camera transformation are available. For synthetic images, range data and the camera transformation are easily obtainable. For natural images, range data can be acquired from a ranging camera [BESL88], computed by photogrammetry [WOLF83], or modeled by a human artist [WILL90]. The camera transformation can be found if the relative positions and orientations of the camera are known.

The idea of using images to represent a virtual environment has been presented previously. An earlier approach uses computer controlled videodiscs to perform surrogate travel [LIPP80]. A more recent approach uses digital movie technologies to construct a virtual museum [MILL92]. In both systems, a user navigates a finite set of routes and directions that have been pre-determined. Our method allows greater flexibility in the navigation because the stored frames can be interpolated smoothly to synthesize arbitrary intermediate points of view.

A static subject or environment portrayed by a restricted set of images indexed by the user's point of view supports a form of "desktop virtual reality" termed "virtual integral holography" [VENO90]. In this context also, our method permits smooth interpolation of the images to present a continuous display sequence, rather than quantizing the user's point of view and jumping to the closest prestored image.

The morphing method can be used to interpolate a number of different parameters, such as camera position, viewing angle, direction of view and hierarchical object transformation. The modeling and viewing transformations can be concatenated to compute the correspondence mapping between two images. Generally, the images can be arranged in an arbitrary graph structure. The nodes of the graph are the images. Each arc in the graph represents a correspondence mapping, which is bi-directional, and two maps are associated with each arc. The number of interpolation parameters determines the dimensionality of the graph. For instance, the graph for a virtual camera moving with two degrees of freedom (the latitudes and longitudes of a sphere bounding an object at a central "look-at" point, for example) is a simple polyhedron (rendering of objects rather than environments will be discussed in more detail in Section 4.4, Image-based Primitives.) The camera's location coordinates index a point on a face of the polyhedron, and the desired view is synthesized by interpolating the images and mappings stored with the vertices and edges of the face. Note that if each image is of the form of an environment map, view angle and direction also can be interpolated by re-projecting the environment map to the desired view orientation [MILL93] without increasing the dimensionality of the graph. Similarly, a camera moving in 3D is supported by a graph which takes the form of a 3D space lattice. The barycentric coordinates of the view location can be used to interpolate among the images attached to the vertices of the enclosing tetrahedron in a lattice of tetrahedra.

For the representation of scenes with objects moving or changes other than those consequent to a change in viewpoint, the graph becomes a general polytope. Generally, arbitrary distortions of surfaces are accommodated by the mapping, as are hierarchical motions of linkages or the limbs of animated characters[1]. To index such an elaborate set of mappings by the various parameters can be an arbitrarily complex process, requiring multivariate interpolation of a multidimensional graph.

Without loss of generality, this paper will concentrate on the interpolation of the camera position in 1D and 2D space (accommodating "virtual holograms" of objects as well as restricted navigation in 3D scenes). The scene is assumed to be static, and all the image changes are as a result of camera movement. Although the method can be applied to natural images, only synthetic ones have been attempted in the work described here. Interpolation of images accurately supports only view-independent shading. Reflection mapping or Phong specular reflection could be performed with separate maps for reflection map coordinates or normal components, but only diffuse reflection and texture mapping have been presented here.

Section 2 introduces the basic algorithms of the method as well as its limitations and optimizations. Section 3 gives implementation details and shows some examples. Section 4 shows applications of the method to virtual reality, temporal anti-aliasing, generating shadows from area lights, image-based display primitives and incremental rendering ("progressive refinement"). Conclusions and future directions are discussed in the last section.

2 VISIBILITY MORPHING

Image morphing is the simultaneous interpolation of shape and texture. The technique generally involves two steps. The first step establishes the correspondence between two images and is the most difficult part of most morphing methods. The correspondence is usually established by a human animator. The user might, for example, define a set of corresponding points or line segments within a pair or set of images. An algorithm is then employed to determine the correspondence (mapping) for the remainder of the images[BEIE92]. The second step in the process is to use the mapping to interpolate the shape of each image toward the other, according to the particular intermediate image to be synthesized, and to blend the pixel values of the two warped images by the same respective coefficients, completing the morph.

Our method uses the camera transformation and image range data to automatically determine the correspondence between two or more images. The correspondence is in the form of a "forward mapping." The mapping describes the pixel-by-pixel correspondence from the source to the destination image. The mapping is also bi-directional since each of the two images can act as the source and the destination. In the basic method, the corresponding pixels' 3D screen coordinates are interpolated and the pixels from the source image are moved to their interpolated locations to create an interpolated image. For pixels which map to the same pixel in the interpolated image, their Z-coordinates are compared to resolve visibility. Cross-dissolving the overlapping pixels' colors may be necessary if the image colors are not view-independent. This process is repeated for each of the source images.

This method is made more efficient by the following two properties. First, since neighboring pixels tend to move together in the mapping, a quadtree block compression is employed to exploit this coherence. Adjacent pixels which move in a similar manner are grouped in blocks and moved at the same time. This compression is particularly advantageous since a view-independent visible priority among the pixel blocks can be established. The pixel blocks are sorted once by their Z-co-

[1]Establishing such elaborate mappings is straightforward for synthetic images, a classic vision problem for natural ones.

ordinates, when the maps are created, and subsequently displayed from back to front to eliminate the overhead of a Z-buffer for visibility determination.

We will describe our method in terms of the morphing between two images first. Generalization of the method to more images is straightforward and will be discussed later.

2.1 Establishing Pixel Correspondence

As a camera moves, objects in its field of view move in the opposite direction. The speed of each object's apparent movement is dependent on the object's location relative to the camera. Since each pixel's screen coordinates (x, y and z) and the camera's relative location are known, a 4x4 matrix transformation establishes a correspondence between the pixels in each pair of images. The transformations can be pre-computed and reduced to a 3D spatial offset vector for each of the pixels. The offset vector indicates the amount each of the pixels moves in its screen space as a result of the camera's movement. The offset vectors are stored in a "morph map," which represents the forward mapping from one image to another. This map is similar in concept to a disparity map computed from a stereo pair[GOSH89], the field of offset vectors computed for "optical flow" analysis[NAGE86], or motion compensation in video compression and format conversion[MPEG90]. For a computed image or range image, an exact pixel-by-pixel map can be created. The mapping is many-to-one because many pixels from the first image may move to the same pixel in the second image. Therefore, the morph map is directional and two morph maps are needed for a pair of images.

The use of a pre-computed spatial look-up table for image warping has been presented in [WOLB89]. Wolberg used the look-up table to implement arbitrary forward mapping functions for image warping. Wolberg's maps contained absolute coordinates rather than offset vectors.

In a typical image morph, as described in the beginning of this section, a sparse correspondence provided by a human operator is used to perform strictly two-dimensional shape interpolation. Such a morph can also be used to interpolate stored images in order to represent 3D scenes or objects, as suggested in [POGG91]. The advantages of our method are that the correspondence is dense (every pixel has an explicitly computed map coordinate), the correspondence is automatic (rather than relying on human effort), and the explicit prestored maps permit the image deformations to be generated very quickly.

2.2 Interpolating Correspondences

To generate an in-between view of a pair of images, the offset vectors are interpolated linearly and the pixels in the source image are moved by the interpolated vector to their destinations. Figure 1 shows the offset vectors, sampled at twenty-pixel intervals, for the camera motion sequence in Figure 3.

The interpolation is an approximation to the transformation of the pixel coordinates by a perspective viewing matrix. A method which approximates the perspective changes with local frame shifting and scaling is presented in [HOFM88]. Perspective transformation requires multiplication of the pixel coordinates by a 4x4 matrix and division by the homogeneous coordinates, a rather computationally taxing process, although bounded by image resolution rather than scene complexity. Linear interpolation of pixel coordinates using the morph maps, on the other hand, is very efficient and can be performed incrementally using forward differencing.

If the viewpoint offset is small, the interpolation is very close to the exact solution. Moreover, quadratic or cubic interpolation, though slightly more expensive to perform, can be used to improve the accuracy of the approximation. When the viewpoint moves parallel to the viewing plane, the linear interpolation produces an exact solution. This case is demonstrated in Figure 2a, which traces the paths of mapped pixels in the interpolated image as the viewpoint traverses the four corners of a square parallel to the viewing plane. The squares in the figure are the extents of the pixel movement. Because the squares are parallel to the viewing plane, the linear interpolation of the square corners produces the same result as perspective transformation. Another special case is when the viewpoint moves perpendicular to the viewing plane along a square parallel to the ground(Figure 2b). The resulting pixel locations form trapezoids, which are the projections of squares parallel to the ground. The trapezoids can be interpolated linearly in the horizontal direction. The vertical direction requires perspective divisions. The divisions can be avoided if a look-up table indexed by the vertical offset is pre-computed for each possible integer height of the trapezoids. The second case can be generalized to include the case when the squares are perpendicular to both the ground and the viewing plane. If the viewpoints are aligned with a 3D lattice, the result will always fall into one of the above two cases, which allows us to use linear interpolation to generate an exact solution.

2.3 Compositing Images

The key problem with forward mapping is that overlaps and holes may occur in the interpolated image.

2.3.1 Overlaps

One reason overlaps occur is due to local image contraction. Local image contraction occurs when several samples in a local neighborhood of the source image move to the same pixel in the interpolated image. A typical example of this case is when our view of a plane moves from perpendicular to oblique. Perspective projection causes the image to contract as the plane moves away from the point of view. In the mapping, the samples on the far side of the plane contract while the samples on the near side expand. Contraction causes the samples to overlap in the target pixels.

Multiple layers of pixel depths also will cause the samples to overlap, as in the case of the foreground sculpture in Figure 3. Resolving this case is really a hidden surface problem. One way of solving this problem is to use the Z-buffer algorithm to determine the frontmost pixel. A more efficient way of determining the nearest pixel is presented in the Optimization Section.

2.3.2 Holes

Holes between samples in the interpolated image may arise from local image expansion when mapping the source image to the destination image. This case is shown in Figure 3 where a source image is viewed from viewpoints rotated to the right. The cyan regions indicate holes. Generally, a square pixel in the source image will map to a quadrilateral in the destination image. If we interpolate the four corners of the square instead of the pixel's center, the holes can be eliminated by filling and filtering the pixels in the destination quadrilateral.

A more efficient, though less accurate, method to fill the holes is to interpolate the adjacent pixels' colors or offset vectors. The holes are identified by filling the interpolated image with a reserved "background" color first. For those pixels which still retain the background color after the source to target mapping, new colors are computed by interpolating the colors of adjacent non-background pixels. Alternatively, we can interpolate the offset vectors of the adjacent pixels. The interpolated offset is used to index back to the source image to obtain the new sample color. Note that using a distinguished background color may not identify all the holes. Some of the holes may be created by a foreground object and are filled by a background object behind it (e.g., the holes in the sculpture in the rightmost image in Figure 3). This problem is alleviated, though not completely eliminated, when more source images are added as described below (e.g. Figure 5d).

Holes may also arise from sample locations invisible in each of the source images but visible in the interpolated image. The hole region, as shown in Figure 4, is the intersection of the umbra regions cast by viewpoints A and B and the visible region from point M. The small circle in the hole region is completely missed by the two source images from points A and B. One way of solving this problem is to use multiple source images to minimize the umbra region. Figure 5a shows the holes (cyan pixels) created by rotating one source image. Figure 5b shows that the number of holes is significantly less when two sources images are used. The number of holes can be reduced further if we place the two source viewpoints closer (Figure 5c). The remaining holes can be filled by interpolating the adjacent pixels(Figure 5d). If the images are computer-generated, a ray-tracing type of rendering can be used to render only those missing pixels.

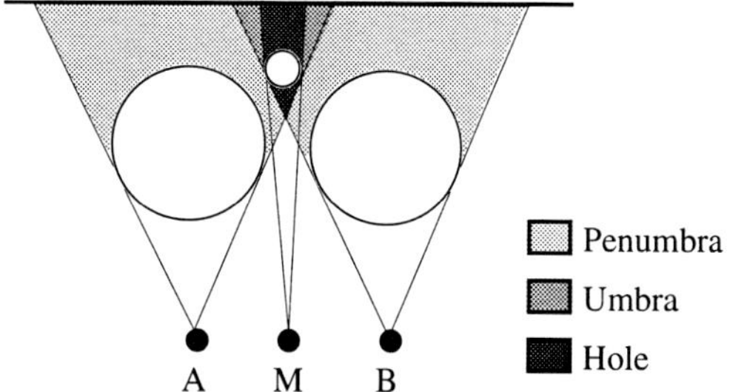

Fig. 4 Penumbra, umbra and hole regions

2.4 Optimization

The basic method is made more efficient by the following two steps.

2.4.1 Block Compression

Since adjacent pixels tend to move together in the mapping, a block compression scheme such as a quadtree can be applied to compress the morph map. The compression serves two purposes. First, it reduces the size of the morph map. Second, it allows us to interpolate offsets for entire blocks instead of pixel-by-pixel. The second aspect greatly accelerates the interpolation process as the main cost in the process is the interpolation of the offset vectors.

The compression ratio is related to the image depth complexity and the viewpoint movement. For images with high depth complexity, the compression ratio is usually low. The ratio is also lower if the viewpoint's movement results in greater pixel depth change. Figure 6 shows the quadtree decomposition of the morph map for the image sequence in Figure 3. The maximal offset threshold within a block is one pixel in Figure 6a and two pixels in Figure 6c, which means the offset vector coordinates within a block do not differ more than one or two pixel units. The compression ratio in Figure 6a is 15 to 1 and in Figure 6b is 29 to 1 (i.e., the number of blocks vs. the number of pixels).

The threshold provides a smooth quality degradation path for increased performance. Large threshold factors result in fewer quadtree blocks and, therefore, reduce the interpolation time. The performance gain is at the expense of increasing blockiness in the interpolated image. The interpolation times in Figure 6b and 6d are accelerated by a factor of 6 and 7 respectively. Note that the speedup factor does not grow linearly with the compression ratio because the same number of pixels still need to be moved.

2.4.2 View-Independent Visible Priority

In the basic method, the Z-buffer algorithm is used to resolve visibility. However, as shown in Figure 7, the A-closer-than-B priority established in View1 is still valid in View2, since Point A and Point B do not overlap in View2. The priority is incorrect in View3 when A and B overlap. As long as the angle θ in the figure is less than 90 degrees, the A-B priority does not need to be changed when the viewpoint is moved. This observation allows us to establish a view-independent visible priority for every source pixel for a viewing range. The pixels are ordered from back to front based on their original Z-coordinates when the morph maps are created, and are subsequently drawn in a back-to-front order in the interpolation process. This ordering of the samples, or sample blocks, eliminates the need for interpolating the Z-coordinates of every pixel and updating a Z-buffer in the interpolation process.

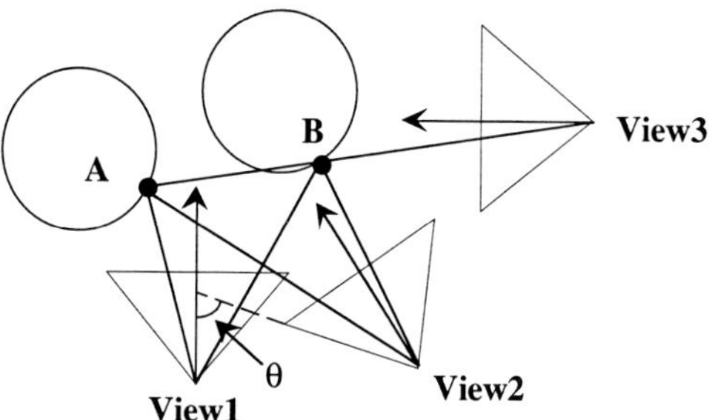

Fig. 7 View-independent visible priority

Note that the priority established here is for image pixels rather than for the underlying objects, unlike list-priority algorithms for hidden-surface removal[SCHU69].

This method applies to multiple source images as well. The source images' pixel Z-coordinates are transformed to a single coordinate system for establishing the Z-priority. All the pixels in the source images are sorted into the same priority list.

The priority can be assigned to every quadtree pixel block. With static objects and a moving camera, pixel offsets are directly related to Z-coordinates. Since the pixels within a block have similar offsets, they also have similar Z-coordinates. The Z-coordinates within a block are filtered to determine a Z value for the priority sort. The result is a sorted list of pixel blocks valid for the entire range between views.

3 IMPLEMENTATIONS

The method presented above can be summarized as follows.

3.1 Preprocessing

The preprocessing stage establishes the correspondence between each pair of source and destination images. As mentioned in Section 1, the source images are connected to form a graph structure. Each node of the graph contains a source image, its range data and camera parameters (i.e., camera's position, orientation). For each set of adjacent nodes in the graph, a sorted list of quadtree blocks is created (e.g., a block list is created for every triangle in a 2D lattice structure). Each block in the list contains a pointer to a pixel block in a source image, the size, the screen coordinates and the offset vectors of the block. The block list is created in the following steps:

Step 1. Get input data: a source node (image, range data and camera parameters), a destination node (only the camera parameters are needed) and a threshold factor for the quadtree decomposition.

Step 2. Create a morph map from the source to the destination (Section 2.1).

Step 3. Decompose the morph map into quadtree blocks and add the blocks to a block list (Section 2.4.1).

Step 4. Repeat Step 1 to 3 for each directional arc connecting the set of nodes.

5. Sort the block list from back to front by the blocks' Z-coordinates.

3.2 Interactive Interpolation

In the interactive interpolation stage, the block list corresponding to a new viewing location is retrieved. The parametric coordinates of the location with respect to the adjacent nodes are used as interpolation parameters. An interpolated image for the new location is generated in the following steps:

Step 1. Get input data: interpolation parameters and a sorted block list.

Step 2. Fill the interpolated image with a distinguished background color.

Step 3. For every block in the list in back-to-front order, compute its new location from the offset vectors and the interpolation parameters. Copy the pixel block from the source image to its new location in the interpolated image (Section 2.2).

Step 4. For every pixel in the interpolated image that still retains the background color, compute its color by filtering the colors of the adjacent non-background pixels (Section 2.3.2).

3.3 Examples

Figure 8 shows a sequence of images generated by moving the viewpoint to the right. The images were rendered at 256x256 resolution using progressive radiosity [COHE88] from a model created for the Virtual Museum project[MILL92].

Figure 9 shows two intermediate images created by morphing the leftmost and rightmost images. Each image took 0.17 second to generate (excluding the preprocessing time) on a Macintosh Quadra 950.

Note that for the interpolation to work properly, the source image cannot be anti-aliased. Anti-aliasing is view-dependent. It blends silhouette pixel colors from a particular viewpoint. Since the Z-buffer cannot be anti-aliased in the same way, the anti-aliased silhouette pixels may attach to either the foreground or the background objects depending on the quantization of the Z-buffer. This problem can be solved by morphing high-resolution unfiltered source images and then filtering the interpolated image.

The method can be applied to interpolating more than two source images. Figure 10 shows a sequence of images interpolated from the four source images in the corners. The viewpoints of the source images form a square parallel to the viewing plane. Therefore, as discussed before, linear interpolation is an exact solution to the perspective transformation. New images are computed from the nearest three corner images. The barycentric coordinates of the new viewpoint are used to interpolate the three images. Dividing the lattice into simplices minimizes the cost of interpolation.

4 APPLICATIONS

The morphing method can be used in a wide variety of applications which require fast visibility computations of a predefined static scene. Simulation and virtual reality applications typically require a scene to be displayed interactively from different viewpoints. Temporal anti-aliasing, or motion blur, can be accelerated by using morph maps to integrate image samples over time. The image samples are interpolated from key images using the morphing method. We also present an application of morph mapping to compute shadows from area lights using the shadow buffer method [WILL78]. The morphing method makes it possible to define a new class of graphic display primitives based on images. This approach is also useful in incremental rendering as it provides a way to reuse the pixels computed for previous images.

4.1 Virtual Reality

Instead of representing a virtual environment as a list of 3D geometric entities, the morphing method uses images (environment maps). To perform a walkthrough, the images adjacent to the viewpoint are interpolated to create the desired view.

In addition to supporting walkthroughs in virtual environments, the method can be used to create virtual holograms, where the display on the screen will change with respect to the user's viewpoint to provide 3D motion parallax. One existing approach uses 3D rendering to display the scene from the viewpoint obtained by a head location sensor[DEER92]. Another approach uses a finite set of pre-rendered frames, each corresponding to a particular viewing location[VENO90]. With the morphing method, only a few key images are required. The interpolation can generate the in-between frames. Figure 10 shows a sequence of images with vertical and horizontal motion parallax.

The image-based morphing method is inexpensive computationally and provides a smooth quality-speed tradeoff. Although the total storage requirement may be large, the amount of data needed to compute a frame is relatively small and can be read from secondary storage as needed. This approach is very appropriate for CD-ROM based devices because of their large storage capability. As the complexity of geometrical models increases, the advantage of image-based approaches will be more significant because of their bounded overhead.

Another advantage of using the image-based approach is that a real environment can be digitized by photographic means. Using a camera to capture the environment usually is much easier than modeling it geometrically. Although our method relies on range data to establish the correspondence between images, range data should be easier to obtain than the complete 3D geometry of the environment.

4.2 Motion Blur

If an image in a motion sequence is a sample at an instant of time instead of over a time interval, the motion will appear to be jerky and the image is said to be aliased in the temporal domain. One way to perform temporal anti-aliasing is super-sampling. The motion is sampled at a higher rate in the temporal domain and then the samples are filtered to the displayed rate. Super-sampling requires the computation of many more samples. For images which are expensive to render, this technique is very inefficient.

The morphing method allows additional temporal samples to be created by interpolation. The interpolation time is constant regardless of the rendering time for each frame. The sampling rate is determined by the largest offset vector from the morph map in order to perform proper anti-aliasing. Figure 11a is a motion blurred image computed from 32 source images for the camera motion in Figure 8. The images were first rendered at 512x512 resolution and then filtered down to 256x256 resolution before temporal anti-aliasing was performed. The temporal samples were anti-aliased with a box filter. Each image took around 5 seconds to render on a high-end workstation with 3D graphics hardware support. Figure 11b was computed from the same number of images interpolated from three of the source images. Each interpolated image took 0.6 second to compute on a Macintosh Quadra950. The only minor visible difference between the two images is the top of the inside loop of the foreground sculpture, due to the holes created from the interpolation as discussed previously.

The super-sampling approach requires the sampling rate to be determined based on the worst case. For images with fast moving objects and slowly moving backgrounds, this method is not very efficient. One way to solve this problem is to segment the images based on object movement and use different sampling rates for each segment. For instance, the foreground sculpture in this figure needs to be sampled at the highest rate while the wall behind it needs only a few samples. In the case of motion caused by viewpoint changes as in this figure, the segments can be sorted in order of depth as discussed in Section 2.4.2. Each segment is filtered independently and a temporal coverage value for each pixel is kept to indicate the ratio of background samples vs. all samples. The multiple segment layers are then composited in front-to-back order with each segment's pixel colors attenuated by the coverage value from the previous segment.

4.3 Shadows

A very general and efficient way of rendering shadows is the shadow buffer algorithm [WILL78]. The algorithm computes a Z-buffer (i.e., shadow map) from the point of view of the light source. To compute shadows, a surface point's coordinates are transformed to the light source's space and its Z-coordinate is compared to the corresponding Z-coordinate in the shadow map. If the point is further away then it is in shadow.

The algorithm only works for point light sources. To approximate a linear or an area source, many point lights may be needed [SHAP84]. The cost of computing the shadows is proportional to the number of point sources used.

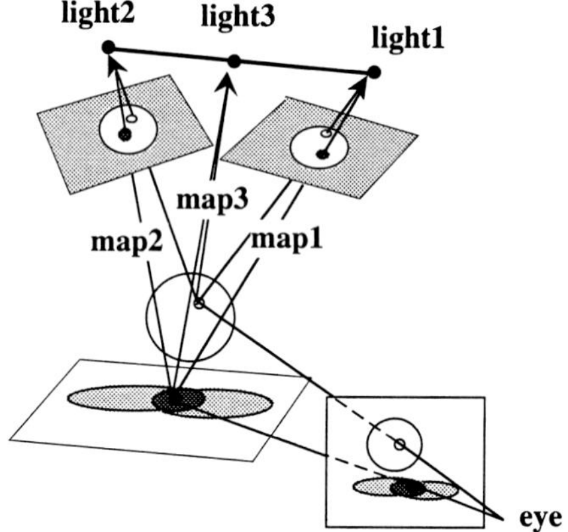

Fig. 12 Shadow buffer interpolation for a linear light source

The morphing method can be used to significantly reduce the cost of computing the shadow map for each of the point sources. Figure 12 illustrates the process of using the method to compute shadows from a linear light source. A shadow map is computed first for each of the two end points of the source (i.e., light1 and light2) using the conventional rendering method. A morph map from the viewpoint to each of the two end points is also computed to transform the screen coordinates to each point source's coordinate space (i.e., map1 and map2). The shadow map for an in-between point (e.g., light3) on the linear source is interpolated from the corner shadow maps using the morphing method. The same interpolation factor is used to interpolate the two morph maps (map1 and map2) to create a morph map from the viewpoint to the in-between light source point (map3). The standard shadow buffer algorithm is then used to compute shadows for the in-between point source. The process is repeated for all the in-between points at a desired interval. The resulting shadow images are composited to create the soft shadow of the linear source. This method can be generalized to any area or volume light source.

Figure 13 shows the result after compositing 100 in-between shadow images generated by randomly distributed points on a rectangular light source above the triangle. Four source shadow maps located at the corners of the rectangle were created for the interpolation. The shadow maps were rendered at 512x512 resolution and the shadow image resolution is 256x256. Percentage closer filtering [REEV87] was used to anti-alias the shadows for each image. Each shadow image took 1.5 seconds to compute. Shading for the illuminated pixels was computed by Lambert's Law weighted by the projected size of the rectangle source over the pixel.

4.4 Image-Based Primitives

A 3D object is perceived on a flat display screen through a series of 2D images. As long as we can generate the images from any viewpoint, it does not matter if a 3D description of the object is available. The morphing method permits any view of an object to be generated by interpolation from some key images. Therefore, a new class of primitives based on images can be defined. These image-based primitives are particularly useful for defining objects of very high complexity since the interpolation time is independent of the object complexity.

Figure 14 shows a sequence of images of a rotating teapot generated by the morphing method. The middle images were generated by interpolating the two key images at the extreme left and right. The key images were rendered with viewpoints rotated 22.5 degrees around the center of the teapot. A larger angular increment of the key images may result in holes and distortions as a result of the linear interpolation. Figure 15 is the same source images extrapolated to show the pixel blocks which compose the teapot.

Rendering an object using the morphing method is really not different from rendering a complete scene as described previously. The image-based object or scene can be treated as a "sprite" that can be composited with images generated by other means.

4.5 Incremental Rendering

Adjacent images in an animation sequence usually are highly coherent. Therefore, it's desirable to perform the rendering incrementally. Ideally, the rendering should be limited to only the pixels which are different from the previous frame. However, searching for the pixels that change is not always trivial. Some incremental rendering approaches which make use of frame-to-frame coherence were presented in [CHEN90], [JEVA92].

The morphing method provides a natural way of making use of frame coherence. For an animation sequence where the motion of every frame is known in advance, the frames can be rendered initially at a coarse temporal sampling rate. The remaining frames can then be computed by the morphing method. The missing samples or view-dependent shading, such as highlights, of the interpolated frames can be computed by additional rendering. If accuracy rather than speed is the main concern, the map-based interpolation or extrapolation of pixel coordinates can be replaced by perspective transformation.

5 CONCLUSIONS AND FUTURE DIRECTIONS

The interactive speed which the image-based display has achieved on modest computing platforms has fulfilled our primary goal in pursuing this research. In addition to this primary objective, we have demonstrated effective application of the view interpolation approach to computing some of the more complex rendering effects. Image-based computer graphics promises to be a productive area of research for some time. A number of intriguing research problems suggest themselves:

An automatic camera has been developed to record an array

of images of an object from viewpoints surrounding it [APPL92]. What are the prospects for automatic camera location selection to minimize the number of holes in the interpolated images? Similarly, what arc good algorithmic criteria for dispensing with as many recorded images as possible, or selecting the best subset of images to represent the object?

By modeling the 3D transformation from one image to the next by a field of straight-line offsets, we introduce an approximation analogous to polygonization (except in the restricted cases mentioned in Section 2.2). Higher-dimensional, rather than linear, interpolation might be expected to better approximate the arcs traversed by objects rotating between views. Curved motion blur is another possible benefit of higher-order interpolation.

View-dependent shading such as specular reflection would extend the useful range of morphing as a display technique. One possibility mentioned previously is to define additional maps for specular surfaces, which specify normal components or reflection map coordinates.

Special-purpose image compression might profit greatly from morph-mapping algorithms. The resemblance of the morph maps to motion-compensation vectors commonly used in video sequence compression has been mentioned. These vectors, used in format conversion to address the interlace problem, and in compression to squeeze a little more redundancy out of the signal, also find application in optical flow algorithms for tracking objects in the visual field. The redundancy removed from the video sequence by motion compensation is limited, as it applies only between successive frames. In a morph mapping encoder, objects which appear and disappear repeatedly could be encoded with a small set of maps. The decoder, a hybrid of an image warper and a graphics pipeline, would use them as "sprites" from a catalog of maps.

The representation of objects and surfaces as sets of images and maps, possibly pyramidal maps, suggests the application of morph mapping to more general global illumination models. The approach of determining visibility to an area light source to compute soft shadows can be extended to treating all surfaces as sources of radiosity. For many global illumination problems, a few images and morph maps can serve to represent hundreds or thousands of computed images.

6. ACKNOWLEDGMENTS

Thanks to the Virtual Museum team for the museum model and images. Dan Venolia anticipated the use of range images as display primitives (without interpolation) in his virtual holography work. Ken Turkowski contributed the teapot images. Ned Greene, Nelson Max and members of the Advanced Technology Computer Graphics Group have offered useful ideas and criticism. Frank Crow and Apple Computer's continuous support of this research is highly appreciated.

REFERENCES

[AIRE91] Airey, J., J. Rohlf and F. Brooks. Towards Image Realism with Interactive Update Rates in Complex Building Environments. ACM SIGGRAPH Special Issue on 1990 Symposium on Interactive 3D Graphics, 41-50.

[APPL92] Apple Human Interface Group. Object Maker. [exhibit] In Interactive Experience, CHI'92, Monterey CA.

[BESL88] Besl, P.J. Active Optical Range Imaging Sensors. Machine Vision and Applications Vol. 1, 1988, 127-152.

[BEIE92] Beier, T. and S. Neely. Feature-Based Image Metamorphosis. SIGGRAPH'92 Proceedings, 35-42.

[CHEN90] Chen, S. E. Incremental Radiosity: An Extension of Progressive Radiosity to an Interactive Image Synthesis System. SIGGRAPH'90 Proceedings, 135-144.

[COHE88] Cohen, M. F., S. E. Chen, J. R. Wallace and D. P. Greenberg. A Progressive Refinement Approach to Fast Radiosity Image Generation. SIGGRAPH'88 Proceedings, 75-84.

[DEER92] Deering, M. High Resolution Virtual Reality. SIGGRAPH'92 Proceedings, 195-202, 1992.

[GOSH89] Goshtasby, A. Stereo Correspondence by Selective Search. Proc. Japan Computer Vision Conf., 1-10, July, 1989.

[GREE86] Greene, N. Environment Mapping and Other Applications of World Projections. IEEE CG&A, Vol. 6, No. 11, November, 1986.

[GREE93] Greene, N. and M. Kass. Approximating Visibility with Environment Maps. Technical Report 41, 1993, Apple Computer, Inc.

[HOFM88] Hofman, G. R. The Calculus of the Non-Exact Perspective Projection. Eurographics'88 Proceedings, 429-442

[JEVA92] Jevans, D. Object Space Temporal Coherence for Ray Tracing. Graphics Interface'92 Proceedings, 176-183, 1992.

[LIPP80] Lippman, A. Movie Maps: An Application of the Optical Videodisc to Computer Graphics. SIGGRAPH'80 Proceedings, 32-43.

[MILL92] Miller, G., E. Hoffert, S. E. Chen, E. Patterson, D. Blacketter, S. Rubin, S. A. Applin, D. Yim and J. Hanan. The Virtual Museum: Interactive 3D Navigation of a Multimedia Database. The Journal of Visualization and Computer Animation, Vol. 3, No. 3, 183-198, 1992.

[MILL93] Miller, G.and S. E. Chen. Real-Time Display of Surroundings Using Environment Maps. Technical Report 42, 1993, Apple Computer, Inc.

[MPEG90] MPEG Video Committee Draft, December, 1990.

[NAGE86] Nagel, H.-H. Image Sequences - Ten (octal) Years from Phenomenology to a Theoretical Foundation. Proc. 8th ICPR, Paris 1986, 1174-1185.

[POGG91] Poggio, T. and R. Brunelli. A Novel Approach to Graphics. MIT A.I. Memo No. 1354, C.B.I.P. Paper No. 71, February, 1992.

[REEV87] Reeves, W. T., D. H. Salesin and R. L. Cook. Rendering Antialiased Shadows with Depth Maps. SIGGRAPH'87 Proceedings, 283-291.

[SCHU69] Schumacker, R., B. Brand, M. Gilliland, and W. Sharp. Study for Applying Computer-Generated Images to Visual Simulation, Technical Report AFHRL-TR-69-14, NTIS AD700375, U.S. Air Force Human Resources Lab., Air Force Systems Command, Brooks AFB, TX, September, 1969.

[SHAP84] Shapiro, B. L., N. I. Badler. Generating Soft Shadows with a Depth Buffer Algorithm. IEEE CG&A, Vol. 4, No. 10, 5-38, 1984.

[TELL92] Teller, S and C. Sequin. Visibility Preprocessing for Interactive Walkthroughs. SIGGRAPH'91 Proceedings, pp.61-69, 1991.

[VENO90] Venolia, D. and L. Williams. Virtual Integral Holography. Proc. SPIE-Extracting Meaning from Complex Data: Processing, Display, Interaction (Santa Clara, CA, February, 1990), 99-105.

[WILL78] Williams, L. Casting Curved Shadows on Curved Surfaces. SIGGRAPH'78 Proceedings, 270-274.

[WILL90] Williams, L. 3D Paint. ACM SIGGRAPH Special Issue on 1990 Symposium on Interactive 3D Graphics, 225-233.

[WOLB89] Wolberg, G. and T. E. Boult. Separable Image Warping with Spatial Lookup Tables. SIGGRAPH'89 Proceedings, 369-377.

[WOLF83] Wolf, P. R. Elements of Photogrammetry, McGraw-Hill, New York, 1983.

Fig. 1 *Offset vectors for the camera motion in Figure 3.*

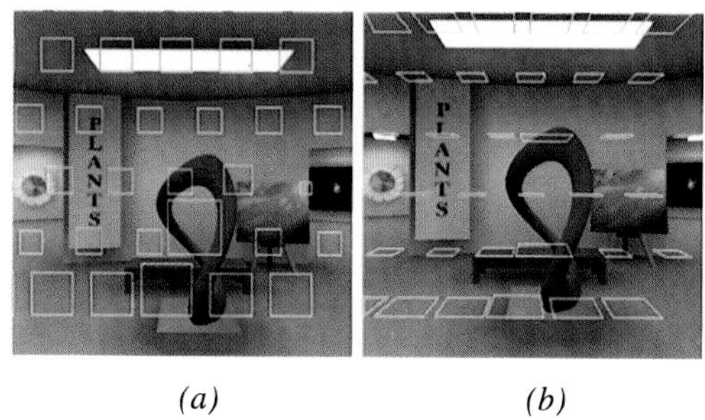

(a) *(b)*

Fig. 2 *Extents of pixel movement for 2D viewpoint motions: a) viewpoints parallel to the viewing plane, b) viewpoints parallel to the ground. (Source pixels are in the lower right corner of each extent.)*

Fig. 3 *A source image viewed from a camera rotated to the right.*

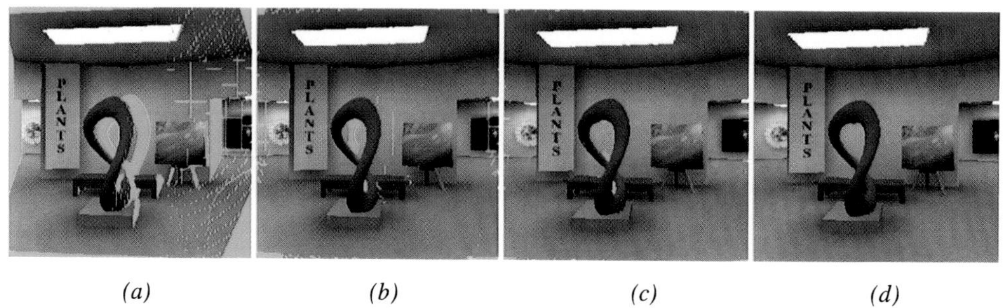

(a) *(b)* *(c)* *(d)*

Fig. 5 *(a) Holes from one source image, (b) holes from two source images, (c) holes from two closely spaced source images, (d) filling the holes with interpolation.*

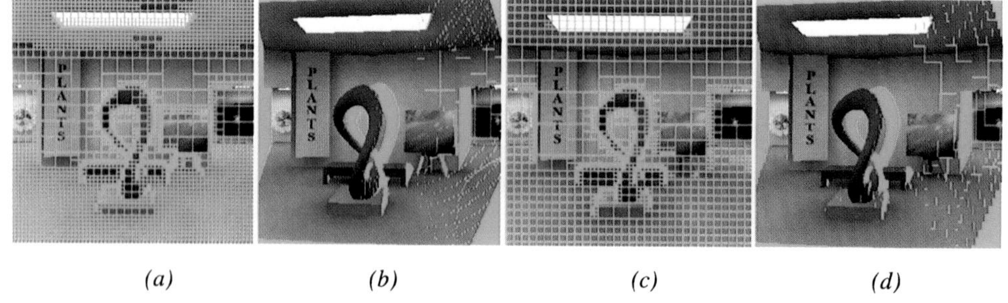

(a) *(b)* *(c)* *(d)*

Fig. 6 *Quadtree decompositions of a morph map: (a) compression ratio: 15 to 1, speedup factor: 6; (b) interpolated image from (a); (c) compression ratio: 29 to 1, speedup factor: 7; (d) interpolated image from (c).*

Fig. 8 *Rendered Virtual Museum images.*

Fig. 9 *Interpolated Virtual Museum images (two middle ones).*

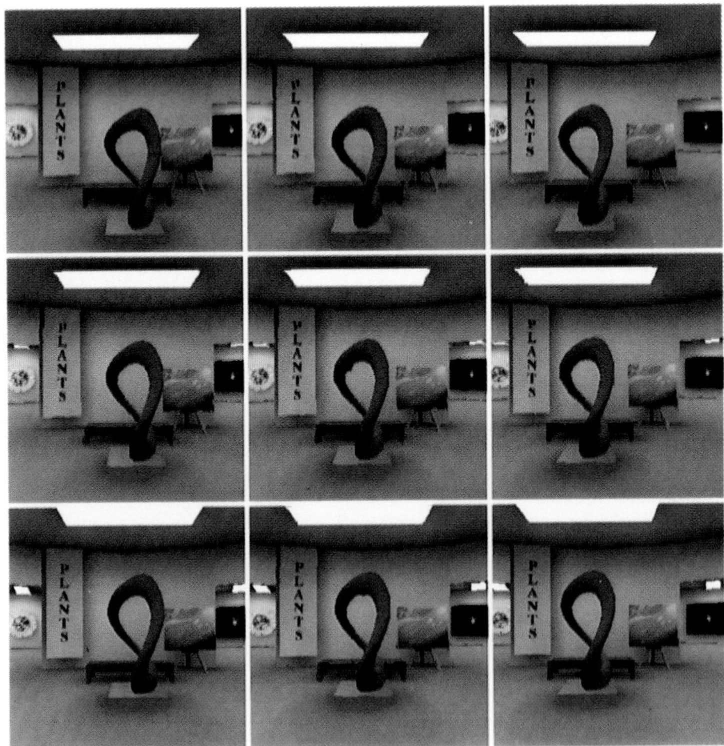

Fig. 10 *2D interpolation. The source images are in the corners. All the other images are interpolated from their nearest three source images. (The center one is interpolated from the upper two and the lower left corners.)*

(a) *(b)*

Fig.11 (a) Motion blur computed from source images, (b) motion blur computed from interpolated images[2].

Fig.13 Shadow from a rectangular area light computed with the shadow map interpolation.

Fig.15 Teapot extrapolated to show the quadtree pixel blocks.

Fig.14 Teapot images generated by interpolation (two middle ones).

[2]Figure 11 and 13 images were digitally enlarged 200% with bicubic interpolation.

Spatial Anti-aliasing for Animation Sequences with Spatio-temporal Filtering

Mikio Shinya
NTT Human Interface Laboratories
3-9-11 Midori-cho, Musashino-shi
Tokyo 180, Japan
email: shinya@nttarm.ntt.jp
tel: +81 422 59 2648

Abstract

Anti-aliasing is generally an expensive process because it requires super-sampling or sophisticated rendering. This paper presents a new type of anti-aliasing filter for animation sequences, the *pixel-tracing filter*, that does not require any additional sample nor additional calculation in the rendering phase. The filter uses animation information to calculate correlation among the images, and sub-pixel information is extracted from the sequence based on the correlation. Theoretical studies prove that the filter becomes an ideal anti-aliasing filter when the filter size is infinite.

The algorithm is simple image processing implemented as post-filtering. The computational cost is independent of the complexity of the scene. Experiments demonstrate the efficiency of the filter. Almost complete anti-aliasing was achieved at the rate of about 30 seconds per frame for very complex scenes at a resolution of 256×256 pixels. The pixel tracing filter provides effective anti-aliasing for animation sequences at a very modest computational cost.

CR Categories and Subject Descriptors: I.3.3 [Computer Graphics]: Picture/Image Generation; I.3.7 [Computer Graphics]: Three-Dimensional Graphics and Realism

Additional Keywords and Phrases: Anti-aliasing, Spatio-temporal filtering, Computer Animation

1 Introduction

Aliasing artifacts have been troublesome in the field of graphics for a long time. These problems are particularly bad in animation sequences, since flickering thin objects and traveling jaggies are very noticeable.

For viewers in general, these spatio-temporal artifacts are more noticeable than the purely spatial ones in still images. To detect spatial aliasing, the *true* images (e.g., continuous lines or checker board patterns) should be inferred from the sampled image by intelligent, high-level visual processing. On the other hand, spatio-temporal aliasing can be detected by low-level vision processes (e.g., flicker detection and optical flow segmentation) without deep knowledge. This may seem rather negative, but it also implies a positive aspect: there may be easier ways to detect and remove aliasing in animation sequences.

Usually, there is strong correlation among the successive frames of motion pictures. This correlation allows efficient image compression in video codecs (coder/decoder) [NETRA]. This motivates us to extract sub-pixel information from image sequences, which could reduce aliasing artifacts.

This paper mathematically analyzes spatio-temporal characteristics of motion image sequences, and clarifies the useful features of their spectrum. Based on the analysis, a new type of anti-aliasing algorithm is proposed. In the algorithm, the image sequences are filtered with a linear shift-variant spatio-temporal filter called the *pixel-tracing filter*. Through the image sequence, the filtering process traces the pixels corresponding to the same object point, and the weighted sum of their colors is calculated. Theoretical studies prove that the filter acts as an ideal anti-aliasing filter when the filter size is infinite.

Unlike most anti-aliasing algorithms, this algorithm is achieved by post-filtering. The advantages are:

- fast execution independent of the scene complexity (e.g., number of polygons),
- simplicity of implementation,
- no dependence on the rendering process.

Experiments showed that the algorithm was efficient in terms of computational cost and provided effective image improvement.

2 Related Work

There are too many studies of anti-aliasing to review exhaustively, so only spatio-temporal approaches are briefly mentioned here. There are two major methods of spatio-temporal anti-aliasing: super-sampling and analytic calculation. In the super-sampling scheme, distributed ray tracing [COOK84] and alpha-blending [HAEBERLI] with stochastic sampling [DIPPE,COOK86] are the most successful and commonly used. Their advantages are simplicity and generality, but the disadvantage is a computational cost that is proportional to the rate of super-sampling. Although adaptive sampling [LEE] and optimal sampling patterns [MITCHELL] have been investigated, image improvement by super-sampling is generally computationally expensive. The analytic approach, on the other hand, is attractive because an exact solution can be calculated in relatively modest computation time. However, algorithms usually involve rather complicated processes, such as three-dimensional scan-conversion [GRANT] and analytic filtering of polygons [CATMULL84], and are only applicable to particular object primitives (typically polygons). In short, both approaches directly calculate sub-pixel or sub-frame information and then apply local filters.

Our approach differs from the above methods in three ways. First, our approach does not require any additional sample or additional calculation in the rendering phase. Second, it evaluates sub-pixel information from the image sequences themselves, taking the advantage of global spatio-temporal correlation. Third, our method uses a temporally global filter to removes spatial aliasing while other methods attempt to produce motion-blur by local temporal filtering.

3 Fourier Analysis

Temporal variation in animation sequences is usually due to the motion of the camera and objects. In this section, we mathematically analyze the spatio-temporal spectra of image sequences of moving objects. The velocity on the image plane is first assumed to be constant in time and space; analyses with spatial and temporal variation follow. The analyses provide an ideal anti-aliasing filter with infinite integral under certain conditions. Throughout this section, a one-dimensional space (image) is assumed for simplicity, but extension to two-dimensional images is mathematically straightforward.

3.1 Preparation

Let x be the image coordinate in pixels and t be the time in frames. Let a real function $f_0(x)$ be the image at $t = t_0$, and $f(x;t)$ be the image sequence. The spatial Fourier transform of f is defined by

$$F_0(\xi) = \int f_0(x)\exp(\imath\xi x)dx,$$
$$F(\xi;t) = \int f(x;t)\exp(\imath\xi x)dx,$$

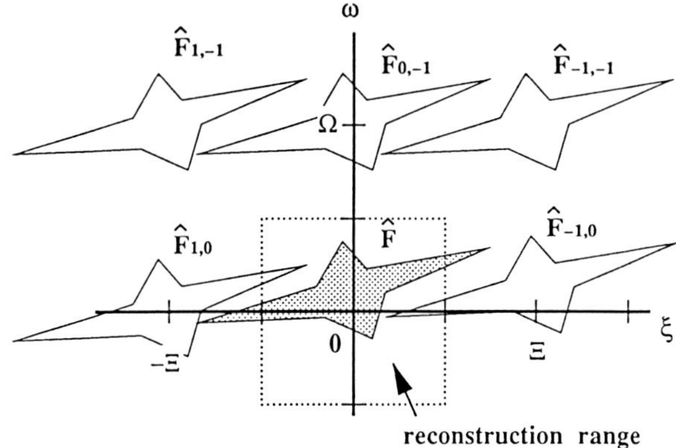

Figure 1: Aliasing in the Fourier Domain.

where ξ denotes the spatial angular frequency (rad/pixel), and $\imath$ is the imaginary unit, $\imath^2 = -1$. Similarly, the temporal Fourier transform is defined by

$$\hat{F}(\xi,\omega) = \int F(\xi;t)\exp(\imath\omega t)dt,$$

where ω is the temporal angular frequency in rad/frame.

The sampled image sequence $f_s(x,t)$ is represented by

$$f_s(x;t) = f(x;t)\sum_{k,l}\delta(x - 2\pi k/\Xi)\delta(t - 2\pi l/\Omega),$$

where Ξ and Ω are the sampling frequencies in space and time. When one point per pixel per frame is sampled, $\Xi = 2\pi$, and $\Omega = 2\pi$. The Fourier transform of f_s is

$$\hat{F}_s(\xi,\omega) = \sum_{n,m}\hat{F}_{n,m}(\xi,\omega), \quad (1)$$

where

$$\hat{F}_{n,m}(\xi,\omega) = \hat{F}(\xi + n\Xi, \omega + m\Omega).$$

Equation 1 indicates that replicas of $\hat{F}$ appear, centered at the grid points $(-n\Xi, -m\Omega)$, as illustrated in Figure 1.

When $\hat{F}(\xi,\omega) \neq 0$ outside the Nyquist frequencies $(\pm\Xi/2, \pm\Omega/2)$, some replicas intrude on the reconstruction range, causing aliasing artifacts. In other words, anti-aliasing can be achieved if replicas $\hat{F}_{n,m}$ can be filtered out. Therefore, anti-aliasing can be regarded as a process which calculates filtered images from the sampled images, and consequently, our objective is to find some mapping

$$f_s \longmapsto \int f_0(x)w(x_0 - x)dx$$

for any x_0. Here, $w(x)$ denotes some desirable spatial anti-aliasing filter.

The notation defined here is listed in Table 1. An introduction to sampling theory and aliasing can be found in [FOLEY].

Table 1: Symbols and notation

x	position on the image (pixel)
t	time (frame)
ξ	spatial angular frequency (rad/pixel)
ω	temporal angular frequency (rad/frame)
$f_0(x)$	image at $t = t_0$
$f(x;t)$	image at t
$f_s(x;t)$	sampled image sequence
$F_0(\xi)$	the spatial spectrum of f_0
$\hat{F}(\xi,\omega)$	the spatio-temporal spectrum of f.
$\hat{F}_s(\xi,\omega)$	the spatio-temporal spectrum of f_s.
Ξ	spatial sampling frequency
Ω	temporal sampling frequency
$\hat{F}_{n,m}$	the replica of $\hat{F}$ centered at $(-n\Xi, -m\Omega)$
$w(x)$	spatial anti-aliasing filter
$g(x,t)$	shift variant spatio-temporal filter
$\hat{G}(\xi,\omega)$	the spatio-temporal spectrum of w

3.2 Constant Velocity Motion

First, let us consider the simplest motion, constant velocity motion. In this case, the image at t can be represented by

$$f(x;t) = f_0(x + v_0(t_0 - t)), \tag{2}$$

where v_0 is the velocity of the pattern. Its spatio-temporal spectrum is

$$\begin{aligned} \hat{F}(\xi,\omega) &= \int \exp(\imath\omega t)dt \int f_0(x + v_0(t_0 - t)) \exp(\imath\xi x)dx \\ &= \int F_0(\xi) \exp(\imath\xi v_0(t - t_0)) \exp(\imath\omega t))dt \\ &= 2\pi F_0(\xi) \exp(-\imath\xi v_0 t_0)\delta(v_0\xi + \omega), \end{aligned} \tag{3}$$

where δ is Dirac's delta function and we used the equality

$$\int \exp(\imath uv)dv = 2\pi\delta(u).$$

Equation 3 clarifies a very important fact: *the spectrum $\hat{F}$ can be separated from the replicas even though the spatial spectrum $F_0(\xi)$ ranges beyond the Nyquist frequency.* Figure 2 illustrates this situation. The replicas can be filtered out as shown in the figure if velocity v_0 is known. Fortunately, the velocity can be easily calculated from animation data in graphics applications. Thus, an ideal anti-aliasing filter in this case looks like[1]

$$\hat{G}_v(\xi,\omega) = 2\pi\delta(v_0\xi + \omega). \tag{4}$$

The linear filtering in the Fourier domain $\hat{G}_v\hat{F}_s$ is equivalent to convolution in real time-space, that is,

$$\int\int f_s(x,t)\delta((x_0 - x) - (t_0 - t)v_0)dxdt. \tag{5}$$

This motivates us to study more general cases.

[1] Strictly speaking, the filter $\hat{G}_v$ involves a convergence problem because infinite animation sequences are assumed here. This will be solved in the next section.

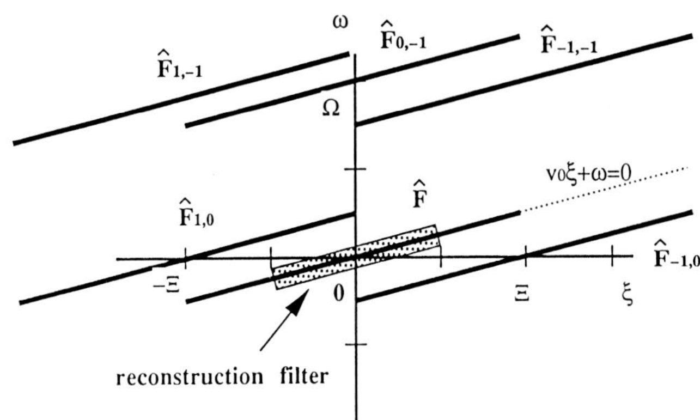

Figure 2: Spatio-temporal spectrum of constant velocity motion.

3.3 General Motion

Let us consider general motion. When the image point x_0 at t_0 moves to x_1 at t_1, we denote the motion by

$$x_1 = \chi(t_1; x_0, t_0). \tag{6}$$

For example, the flow χ_v for constant motion is:

$$\chi_v(t; x_0, t_0) = x_0 + v(t - t_0).$$

Note that the reciprocity generally holds from the definition

$$x = \chi(t; \chi(t_0; x, t), t_0).$$

To avoid convergence problems, a finite animation sequence should be considered. With the flow χ, the sequence can be described as:

$$f(x,t) = \begin{cases} f_0(\chi(t_0; x, t)) & \text{if } t \in [-T/2, T/2] \\ 0 & \text{otherwise,} \end{cases}$$

where T is the length of the animation. The sampled image sequence are represented by

$$\begin{aligned} f_s(x,t) &= f(x,t)\sum_{k,l} \delta(x - 2\pi k/\Xi)\delta(t - 2\pi l/\Omega), \\ \hat{F}_s(\xi,\omega) &= \sum_{n,m} \int_{-T/2}^{T/2} dt \int_{-\infty}^{\infty} f_0(\chi(t_0; x, t)) \\ &\quad \exp(\imath(\xi + n\Xi)x + \imath(\omega + m\Omega)t)dx \\ &= \sum_{n,m} \hat{F}_{n,m}. \end{aligned}$$

Next, let us consider the anti-aliasing filter g. Filtering for constant motion, Eq. 5, can be rewritten as

$$\int\int f_s(x,t)\delta(x_0 - \chi_v(t_0; x, t))dxdt.$$

By analogy, we set our filter kernel g as

$$\begin{aligned} g(x,t) &= (1/T)w(x_0 - \chi(t_0; x, t))(\partial\chi/\partial x)_{t_0,t} \\ &= (1/T)w(x_0 - \chi(t_0; x, t))D_\chi(t_0; x, t) \end{aligned} \tag{7}$$

for space-variant filtering at (x_0, t_0):

$$h(x_0, t_0) = \int\int f_s(x,t)g(x,t)dxdt. \quad (8)$$

Here, $w(x)$ represents some appropriate anti-aliasing filter, such as a sinc-function, Gauss function, box function, and so on. The factor $1/T$ is the normalization constant, and $D_\chi = (\partial\chi/\partial x)$ compensates for image magnification variation due to spatially non-uniform motion.

Now, we prove that the filtering defined by Eq. 8 becomes an ideal anti-aliasing filter in the limit that $T \to \infty$. From the Parseval Identity, Eq. 8 can be rewritten as

$$\begin{aligned} h(x_0, t_0) &= (1/2\pi)^2 \int\int \hat{F}_s(\xi,\omega)\hat{G}^*(\xi,\omega)d\xi d\omega \\ &= (1/2\pi)^2 \sum_{n,m} \int\int \hat{F}_{n,m}(\xi,\omega)\hat{G}^*(\xi,\omega)d\xi d\omega \\ &= \sum_{n,m} h_{n,m}, \end{aligned}$$

where $\hat{G}^*$ denotes the complex conjugate of $\hat{G}$. The function $\hat{G}$ is the spatio-temporal spectrum of g, calculated by

$$\begin{aligned} \hat{G}(\xi,\omega) &= (1/T)\int\int w(x_0 - \chi(t_0; x, t))(\partial\chi/\partial x) \\ &\quad \exp(\imath(\xi x + \omega t))dtdx \\ &= (1/T)\int\int w(x_0 - u) \\ &\quad \exp(\imath\chi(t; u, t_0)\xi)\exp(\imath\omega t)dudt, \end{aligned}$$

where $u = \chi(t_0; x, t)$. Then, the integral $h_{n,m}$ can be evaluated as

$$\begin{aligned} h_{n,m} &= 1/(2\pi)^2(1/T)\int_{-T/2}^{T/2} \exp(\imath(\omega + m\Omega)t_1)dt_1 \\ &\quad \int f_0(\chi(t_0; x_1, t_1))\exp(\imath(\xi + n\Xi)x_1)dx_1 \\ &\quad \int\int w(x_0 - u)\exp(-\imath\chi(t_2; u, t_0)\xi) \\ &\quad \exp(-\imath\omega t_2)dudt_2 \\ &\quad \int d\xi \int d\omega \\ &= (1/T)\int_{-T/2}^{T/2} \exp(\imath m\Omega t_1)dt_1 \\ &\quad \int f_0(\chi(t_0; x_1, t_1))\exp(\imath n\Xi x_1)dx_1 \\ &\quad \int\int w(x_0 - u)\delta(t_1 - t_2)\delta(x_1 - \chi(t_2; u, t_0))dudt_2 \\ &= \int w(x_0 - u)f_0(u)du \\ &\quad \int_{-T/2}^{T/2} \exp(\imath n\Xi\chi(t_1; u, t_0)\exp(\imath m\Omega t_1)dt_1/T, \end{aligned}$$

where we used the reciprocity $\chi(t_0; \chi(t_1; u, t_0), t_1) = u$. Consequently,

$$\lim_{T\to\infty} h_{n,m} = \int w(x_0 - u)f_0(u)du(\lim_{T\to\infty} K_n(m\Omega; u)/T),$$

where $K_n(\omega; u)$ is the Fourier transform of the function k_n,

$$k_n(t; u) = \exp(\imath n\Xi\chi(t; u, t_0)).$$

Obviously,

$$h_{0,0} = \int w(x_0 - u)f_0(u)du.$$

On the other hand, when K_n is not singular at $\omega = m\Omega$, the aliasing pattern tends to 0, as

$$\lim_{T\to\infty} h_{n,m} = 0.$$

This completes the proof.

Note that $K_n(m\Omega, u)$ can be singular when, for example, motion is periodic with a frequency of $(m\Omega/n)$, or constant motion with a velocity of $(m\Omega/n\Xi)$.

3.4 Discrete Filtering

The filtering Eq. 8 can also be represented in a discrete form. By setting $\Xi = 2\pi$ and $\Omega = 2\pi$ (1 sample/pixel/frame sampling), we have

$$\begin{aligned} h(x_0, t_0) &= \int\int f_s(x; t)g(x,t)dxdt \\ &= (1/T)\int_{-T/2}^{T/2} dt \int_{-X/2}^{X/2} f(x; t)g(x,t) \\ &\quad \sum_{k,l} \delta(x - k)\delta(t - l)dtdx \\ &= (1/T)\sum_{k=-X/2}^{X/2}\sum_{l=-T/2}^{T/2} f(k; l)w(x_0 - \chi(t_0; k, l)) \\ &\quad D_\chi(t_0; k, l) \end{aligned} \quad (9)$$

for T-frame image sequences at the X pixel image resolution. Since Eq. 9 is a finite weighted sum of the sampled images, it can be directly computed.

The magnification factor $D_\chi = (\partial\chi/\partial x)$ compensates for image distortion due to non-uniformity of motion flow. For spatially uniform motion (more generally, incompressible flow), $D_\chi \equiv 1$. Furthermore, since $D_\chi(t_0; t, x) \to 1$ as $t \to t_0$, we can assume

$$D_\chi \simeq 1,$$

when the filter size T is small. If non-uniformity is not negligible, we have to evaluate D_χ point by point. Analytic formulae for D_χ are given in the Appendix.

For practical implementation, we slightly modify the filtering equation Eq. 9. By assuming local uniformity of motion flows, we have

$$h(x_0, t_0) = (1/T)\sum_{k,l} f(k; l)w(\chi(l; x_0, t_0) - k), \quad (10)$$

where we used the uniformity $x - y = \chi(t; x, t') - \chi(t; y, t')$. The advantage of Eq. 10 over Eq. 9 is that only one flow $\chi(l; x_0, t_0)$ should be traced for (x_0, t_0) rather than all flows $\chi(t_0; l, k)$.

The normalization factor $(1/T)$ relies on

$$\lim_{T\to\infty}(1/T)\sum_{l=-T/2}^{T/2}\sum_{k} w(\chi(l;x_0,t_0)-k)=1,$$

and would cause a normalization problem for finite T. Thus, it is better to adopt explicit normalization such as

$$h(x_0,t_0)=\sum_{k,l} f(k;l)w(\chi(l;x_0,t_0)-k)/\sum_{k,l} w(\chi(l;x_0,t_0)-k). \tag{11}$$

4 Algorithm

This section shows a simple algorithm for applying the anti-aliasing filter. When only one velocity field occupies the image, the only problem is to calculate the flow $\chi(t;x_0,t_0)$. However, when more than two velocity fields overlap, the filter should be separately applied because the theories rely on the uniqueness of the field. This happens when the projections of differently moving objects overlap (Figure 3).

Thus, the keys to the implementation are how to evaluate the motion flow χ and how to separate fields of different velocity. To deal with multiple flows, we adopt the filtering equation Eq. 11, assuming local uniformity of flows.

Data From animation models, we receive animation data for the sequence, such as transformation of objects and camera parameters. From the rendering process, RGB values, z-values, and object-id values are provided for each pixel at each frame, for example, in the form of G-buffers [SAITO]. Here, the object-id's are only used to identify object motion, and can be omitted for walk-through scenes. Let us denote these values for the pixel (k_x,k_y) at the frame l by rgb$[k_x][k_y][l]$,z$[k_x][k_y][l]$, and id$[k_x][k_y][l]$, respectively.

As the work space to capture multiple flows, we have a list structure of rgb, z, and α for each pixel, denoted by rgb_{flow}[ix][iy], $z_{flow}[ix][iy]$, and $\alpha_{flow}[ix][iy]$.

Pixel Tracing We now treat two-dimensional images. Let us denote two-dimensional vectors and their x,y-components by using the arrow and suffix notation, such as $\vec{k}=(k_x,k_y)$.

The motion flow, $\vec{\chi}(l;\vec{k}_0,l_0)=(\chi_x,\chi_y)$, corresponding to the sample point $\vec{k}_0=(k_{0x},k_{0y})$ at $t=l_0$, can be easily calculated from the animation information, the object-id, A, and the z-value (Figure 3). Let the transformation from the object coordinate of Object A to the screen space at t be $T_A(t)$. Then, the corresponding object point $p_A=(x_A,y_A,z_A,w_A)$ is given by

$$p_A=(k_{0x},k_{0y},z[k_{0x}][k_{0y}][l_0],1)T_A^{-1}(l_0).$$

At $t=l$, the object point p_A is projected by $T_A(l)$, and thus, the flow $\vec{\chi}$ and the corresponding depth $\zeta(l;\vec{k}_0,l_0)$ can be calculated as

$$\begin{aligned}\vec{\chi}(l;\vec{k}_0,l_0) &= (x/w,y/w)\\ \zeta(l;\vec{k}_0,l_0) &= z/w.\\ (x,y,z,w) &= p_AT_A(l_0)\\ &= (k_{0x},k_{0y},z[k_{0x}][k_{0y}][l_0],1)\\ &\quad T_A^{-1}(l_0)T_A(l)\end{aligned} \tag{12}$$

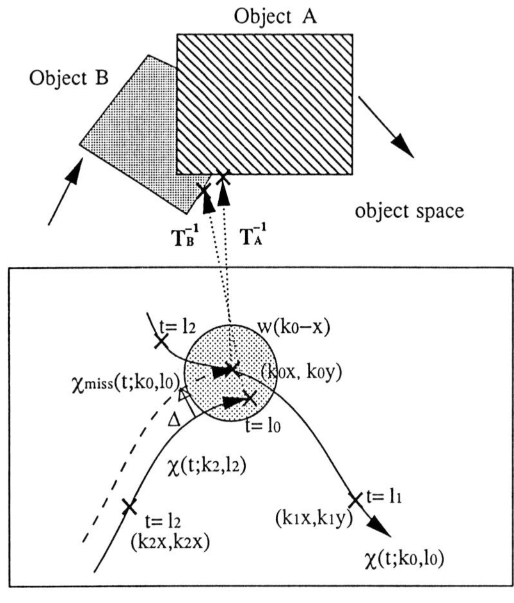

Figure 3: Pixel-tracing.

When the sample point misses an object, the filtering can be applied in the following way. In the example in the Figure 3, Object B fails to hit the sample point at $\vec{k}_0,t=l_0$, but pixel tracing from $\vec{k}_2=(k_{2x},k_{2y}),t=l_2$, reveals that Object B should exist in the reconstruction area of $\vec{k}_0,t=l_0$ because the traced point $\chi(l_0;\vec{k}_2,l_2)$ lies in the area. Therefore, we trace the flow for $\vec{k}_0$ by

$$\vec{\chi}_{miss}(l;\vec{k}_0,l_0)=\vec{\chi}(l;\vec{k}_2,l_2)+\Delta, \tag{13}$$

where

$$\Delta=\vec{k}_0-\vec{\chi}(l_0;\vec{k}_2,l_2).$$

Separation and Summation To separate different velocity fields, we adopt a simple rule, that is, *when the difference between two flows is smaller than some threshold, we regard them as the same flow.*

This can be described as follows. If both of the inequalities,

$$\|\vec{k}_0-\vec{\chi}(l_0;\vec{k}_1,l_1)\|<d_{th}, \tag{14}$$

and

$$\|\vec{k}_1-\vec{\chi}(l_1;\vec{k}_0,l_0)\|<d_{th}, \tag{15}$$

hold, the two sampled data are judged to belong to the same flow. Here, $\|\cdot\|$ denotes some norm on the image plane. The threshold d_{th} can be determined, for example, according to the diameter of the support of the filter kernel $w(\vec{x})$.

In the example in Figure 3, Inequality 15 is not true, so the two samples are processed as different flows. Note that the projection points of the same object do not necessarily belong to the same flow because of perspective.

With this criteria function, same_flow(), which returns 1 when two samples are judged as being in the same flow and 0 otherwise, the actual filtering for each velocity flow becomes

$$\begin{aligned}\mathrm{rgb}_{flow} &= \sum_{l}\sum_{\vec{k}} \mathrm{same\_flow}(\vec{k}, l; \vec{k}_0, l_0) w(\vec{\chi}(l; \vec{k}_0, l_0) - \vec{k}) \\ &\quad \mathrm{rgb}[k_x][k_y][l] / \sum \mathrm{same\_flow}() w() \\ \alpha_{flow} &= \sum \mathrm{same\_flow}() w() / \sum w(), \\ z_{flow} &= \min(z_{flow}, \zeta(l; \vec{k}_0, l_0)) \qquad (16)\end{aligned}$$

Here, α represents the 'coverage' of this flow. Note that the summation with $\vec{k}$ can be calculated only in a neighborhood of the flow $\vec{\chi}$ when the filter $w(\vec{x})$ is compactly supported.

At each pixel, we store the calculated RGB values, α-values, and z-values for all flows as a list, like the A-buffer structure [CARPENTER]. After the filtering, we sort the list with respect to the z-values at each pixel, and the final RGB values are determined by simple α-blending in the order of the sorted list, from near to far,

$$\mathrm{rgb}_{final} = \alpha_{flow1}\mathrm{rgb}_{flow1} + (1 - \alpha_{flow1})\alpha_{flow2}\mathrm{rgb}_{flow2} + \ldots \qquad (17)$$

Procedure The procedure for filtering the frame l_0 can be summarized in the following way.

1) For each sample, $\vec{k}_0$, at frame $l = l_0$, do the following for all frames l within the filter.
   i) Calculate $\vec{\chi}(l; \vec{k}_0, l_0)$ according to Eq. 12.
   ii) Calculate the weighted sum according to Eq. 16.
2) For $l \neq l_0$ within the filter, do the following for all the samples, $\vec{k}$.
   i) Calculate the flow $\vec{\chi}(l_0; \vec{k}, l)$ according to Eq. 12.
   ii) For all samples $\vec{k}_0{}'$ at l_0 such that $w(\vec{k}_0' - \vec{\chi}(l_0; \vec{k}, l)) \neq 0$, do the following.
      a) If $\vec{k}, l$ belongs to any flow listed for $\vec{k}_0', l_0$, skip b) and c).
      b) Calculate the flow $\vec{\chi}_{miss}(l'; \vec{k}_0', l_0)$ according to Eq. 13, and calculate the weighted sum according to Eq. 16.
      c) Append the result to the list of $\vec{k}_0', l_0$.
3) For each pixel at l_0, sort the resulting list with respect to the z-values and apply alpha-blending according to Eq. 17.

As this filter involves a pixel tracing process, we call it the *pixel-tracing filter*.

5 Experiments and Discussion

The first experiment shows the influence of filter size, T. The test pattern is an almost horizontal (1 degree from the horizon) thin rectangle with the width of 1/8 pixel, constantly moving in the vertical direction at a speed of $0.22 = 11/50$ pixel/frame. Note that $\lim_{T\to\infty}(h_{50,11}/T) \neq 0$.

Figures 4-a, -b, and -c show the original image, and the results of applying filters of various sizes. As the filter kernel $w(x)$, we used the box function with one pixel area. Figures 4-d and -e show the analytic solution and the root-mean-square error of the filtered results with respect to the filter size. As shown in the figure, effective anti-aliasing was achieved with a filter size 128. The remaining error comes from the replica $\hat{F}_{50,11}$.

The second experiment shows an example of non-uniformly accelerated motion. The test pattern is rotating radial thin rectangles. As shown in Figure 5, aliasing was mostly removed with the 32-frame filter.

The final experiment shows application to a more practical image sequence taken from a walk-through scene in 'Také Tera.' In the sequence, only the camera moves and everything else is fixed in space. The original images were synthesized by using the GL library on the IRIS workstations at a resolution of 256 × 256. The scene consists of about 4M polygons. Figure 6 demonstrates the efficiency of the algorithm, where the severe aliasing artifacts seen in the original image were largely removed. The filter size was 16 frames.

The execution time is about 30 CPU seconds per frame on an IRIS Crimson R4000-50 at 256 × 256 resolution. The computation cost is directly proportional to $n_x \times n_y \times n_t$, where $n_x \times n_y$ is the image resolution, and n_t is the filter size. Considering that frame-by-frame recording onto a VCR takes about thirty seconds per frame, this powerful anti-aliasing is almost free! Furthermore, as the filtering is simple image processing with pixel-level independence, it might be possible to design parallel hardware to execute it in real-time, which would be attractive for visual simulators and virtual reality applications.

Future work includes application to reflected/refracted images, and coupling with stochastic sampling techniques. The algorithm relies on transformation between the screen space and the object space. Although conventional ray tracers cannot provide the transformation, the beam tracing/pencil tracing approach [HECKBERT,SHINYA] can calculate it in the form of system matrices and thus may be applicable to the filtering.

Since stochastic sampling techniques are powerful tools for anti-aliasing, it is an attractive idea to combine the two approaches. If we jitter the sample point of each pixel at each frame, the pixel-tracing filter acts exactly as a purely spatial filter for objects that are steady on the image plane. This means that spatial stochastic super-sampling can be performed by the pixel-tracing filter with only one point per pixel per frame sampling. This could also reduce the problems with constant velocity motion in the case of $n\Xi v_0 = m\Omega$, which we observed in Figure 4.

6 Conclusion

A new type of efficient anti-aliasing filter, the pixel-tracing filter, was proposed for animation sequences. The filter sums sub-pixel information using the correlation among images calculated from animation information. Theoretical studies prove the ability of the filter, and experimental results demonstrate the efficiency.

The algorithm is simple image processing implemented as post-filtering. The computational complexity is of constant order with regard to the complexity of scenes (e.g., number of polygons). With the pixel-tracing filter, effective anti-aliasing can be completed for animation sequences with a very modest computational cost.

Acknowledgments

The author would like to thank the Siggraph reviewers, whose comments greatly contributed to improving the theoretical part. He also wishes to thank Takahiko Kamae, Rikuo Takano, and Kazuyoshi Tateishi for their administrative support and encouragement, Atsushi Kajiyama for his technical support, and Toki Takahashi, Taka Saito, and Toshi Tanaka for helpful discussion.

References

[CARPENTER] Loren Carpenter, 'The A-buffer, An Antialiased Hidden Surface Method,' Computer Graphics **18**, No.3, pp.103-108, 1984.

[CATMULL84] Edwin Catmull, 'An Analytic Visible Surface Algorithm for Independent Pixel Processing,' Computer Graphics **18**, No.3, pp.109-115, 1984.

[COOK84] R. L. Cook, T. Porter, L. Carpenter, 'Distributed Ray Tracing,' Computer Graphics **18**, No.3, pp.137-145, 1984.

[COOK86] R. L. Cook, 'Stochastic Sampling in Computer Graphics,' ACM Trans. Graphics, **5**, No.1, pp.51-57, 1986.

[DIPPE] M. A. Dippé, 'Anti-aliasing through Stochastic Sampling,' Computer Graphics **19**, No.3, pp.69-78, 1985.

[FOLEY] James D. Foley, Andies van Dam, Steven K. Feiner, John F. Hughes, 'Computer Graphics Principal and Practice,' Addison-Wesley, 1990.

[GRANT] Charles W. Grant, 'Integrated Analytic Spatial and Temporal Anti-Aliasing for Polyhedra in 4-Space,' Computer Graphics **19**, No.3, pp.79-84, 1985.

[HAEBERLI] P. Haeberli, K. Akeley, 'The Accumulation Buffer: Hardware Support for High-Quality Rendering,' Computer Graphics, **24**, No.4, pp.309-318, 1990.

[HECKBERT] P. S. Heckbert, P. Hanrahan, 'Beam Tracing Polygonal Objects,' Computer Graphics, **18**, No.3, pp.119-128, 1984.

[LEE] Mark E. Lee, Richard A. Redner, and Samuel P. Uselton, 'Statistically Optimized Sampling for Distributed Ray Tracing,' Computer Graphics **19**, No.3, pp.61-67, 1985.

[MITCHELL] D. Mitchell, 'Spectrally Optimal Sampling for Distributed Ray Tracing,' Computer Graphics **25**, No.4, pp.157-164, 1991.

[NETRA] A. N. Netravali and B. G. Haskell, 'Digital Pictures - Representation and Compression,' Prenum Press, 1988.

[SAITO] Takafumi Saito and Toki Takahashi, 'Comprehensible Rendering of 3-D Shapes,' Computer Graphics **24**, No.4, pp.197-206, 1990.

[SHINYA] M. Shinya, T. Takahashi, and S. Naito, 'Principles and Applications of Pencil Tracing,' Computer Graphics, **21**, No.4, pp. 45-54, 1987.

Appendix: Calculation of D_χ

Here, we derive D_χ in Eq. 9 for two-dimensional images. We assume motion flows $\vec{\chi}(t; x_0, y_0, t_0)$ represented by Eq. 12. In the two-dimensional case, D_χ becomes the Jacobian of $\vec{\chi}$,

$$\begin{aligned} D_\chi &= \begin{vmatrix} (\partial\chi_x/\partial x_0)_{y0} & (\partial\chi_x/\partial y_0)_{x0} \\ (\partial\chi_y/\partial x_0)_{y0} & (\partial\chi_y/\partial y_0)_{x0} \end{vmatrix} \\ &= (\partial\chi_x/\partial x_0)_{y0}(\partial\chi_y/\partial y_0)_{x0} \\ &\quad -(\partial\chi_x/\partial y_0)_{x0}(\partial\chi_y/\partial x_0)_{y0}. \end{aligned}$$

By setting the translation matrix

$$T_A^{-1}(t_0)T_A(t) = \{\tau_{ij}\},$$

the partial deviation $(\partial\chi_x/\partial x_0)_{y0}$, etc., can be calculated as

$$\begin{aligned} (\partial\chi_x/\partial x_0)_{y0} &= (1/w)(\partial x/\partial x_0)_{y0} - (x/w^2)(\partial w/\partial x_0)_{y0} \\ &= (1/w)(\tau_{11} - (n_x/n_z)\tau_{31}) - (x/w^2) \\ &\quad (\tau_{14} - (n_x/n_z)\tau_{34}), \end{aligned}$$

where $\vec{n} = (n_x, n_y, n_z)$ is the normal vector of the object surface at p_A, and we used

$$\begin{aligned} (\partial x/\partial x_0)_{y0} &= (\partial x/\partial x_0)_{y0,z0} + (\partial z_0/\partial x_0)_{y0}(\partial x/\partial z_0)_{x0,y0} \\ &= \tau_{11} - (n_x/n_z)\tau_{31}, \end{aligned}$$

and so on.

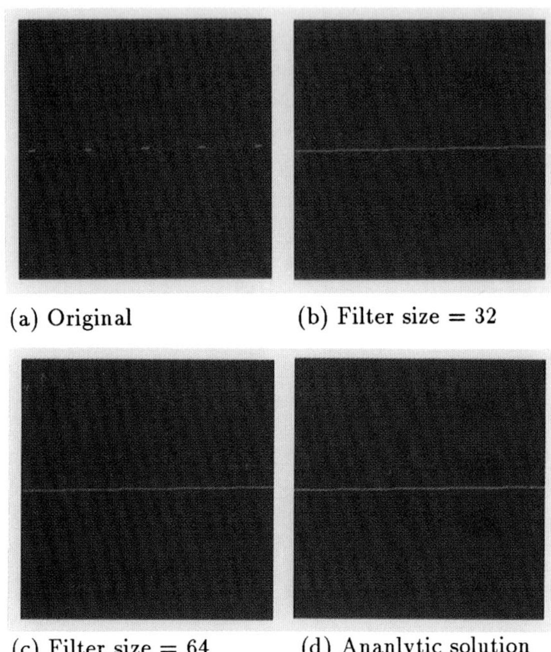

(a) Original (b) Filter size = 32

(c) Filter size = 64 (d) Ananlytic solution

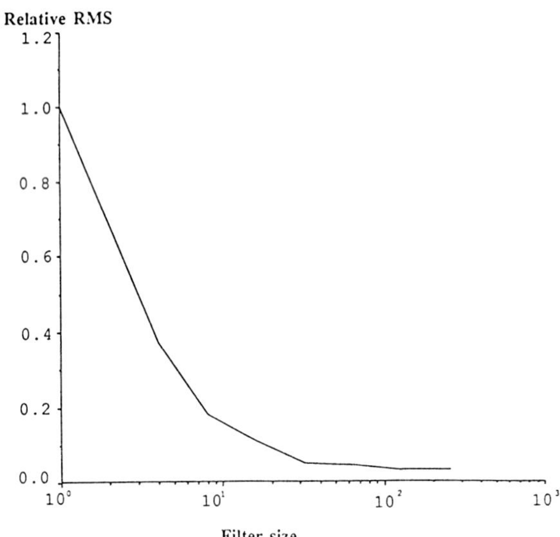

(e) Relative root-mean-square error

Figure 4: Thin rectangle.

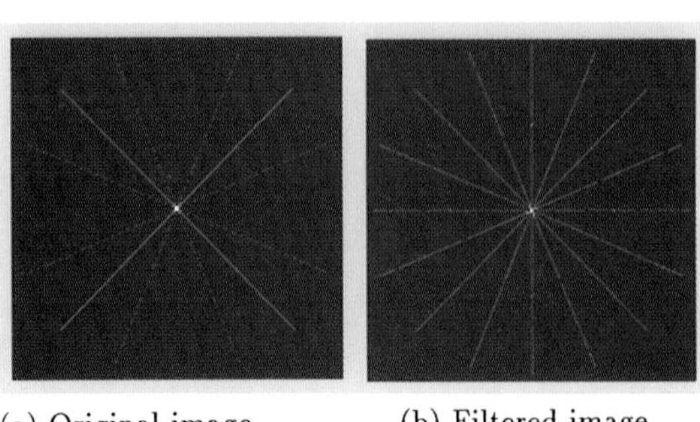

(a) Original image (b) Filtered image

Figure 5: Rotating thin rectangles.

(a) Original image

(b) Filtered image

Figure 6: Také Tera(Bamboo Temple).

Motion Compensated Compression of Computer Animation Frames *

Brian K. Guenter † Hee Cheol Yun, and Russell M. Mersereau ‡

Abstract

This paper presents a new lossless compression algorithm for computer animation image sequences. The algorithm uses transformation information available in the animation script and floating point depth and object number information stored at each pixel to perform highly accurate motion prediction with very low computation. The geometric data, i.e., the depth and object number, is very efficiently compressed using motion prediction and a new technique called direction coding, typically to 1 to 2 bits per pixel. The geometric data is also useful in z-buffer image compositing and this new compression algorithm offers a very low storage overhead method for saving the information needed for z-buffer image compositing. The overall compression ratio of the new algorithm, including the geometric data overhead, is compared to conventional spatial linear prediction compression and is shown to be consistently better, by a factor of 1.4 or more, even with large frame-to-frame motion.

CR Categories: I.4.2[compression(coding)]exact coding.
Additional keywords: compression,computer animation,computer graphics, motion prediction

1 Introduction

With the increasing popularity and falling cost of computer animation comes a new problem: storing the enormous data files which even short computer animation sequences require. Five minutes of NTSC resolution computer animation takes up approximately 8.5 gigabytes of storage; film resolution takes many times more. This amount of data cannot be economically stored on line in high speed secondary storage devices. Animation image files are typically stored off-line on removable media.

An alternative to using off-line storage is to compress the image data and store it on-line. This is very desirable for sequence editing and image manipulation, for example. For high image quality only lossless compression is acceptable; images can then be exactly reconstructed from their compressed representation. Errors do not accumulate if images are combined or manipulated and run through the compression decompression cycle several times.

Much more information is available to a compression algorithm for computer animation than is the case for live action video. However, surprisingly little work has been done on exploiting the information in a computer animation script to improve image compression efficiency. Previous work such as that described in [1] and [5] is actually image based compression although the application is to computer animation.

The lossless compression algorithm for computer animation to be described in this paper combines elements of both motion prediction and spatial linear prediction compression techniques, using each when most appropriate. The new compression algorithm uses transformation information in the animation script to perform essentially perfect image space motion prediction with very low computation. This is a major advantage of the new algorithm because motion prediction with subpixel accuracy based only the information present in the image sequence is computationally expensive [6][3]. Poor quality motion prediction increases the motion prediction error which reduces the maximum achievable compression ratio.

One of the most effective lossless image compression techniques is DPCM followed by entropy coding [4][8]. For typical live action video sequences the best compression achievable using this method is usually less than 2 to 1 [7]. The best computer generated images are nearly indistinguishable from real images so we can expect that good synthetic images will not compress any better than live action video.

For scenes with fairly rapid camera and object motion the compression ratio we have achieved with our new motion prediction compression is approximately 1.5 times that of spatial linear prediction compression techniques - about 3 to 1 compression with the new technique as opposed to 2 to 1 compression with DPCM. As camera and object motion decrease the compression ratio of the new technique steadily increases while spatial prediction compression remains constant at roughly 2 to 1.

Extra geometric information, the object number and the depth at each pixel, is stored in each frame to perform motion prediction. The geometric information is compressed very efficiently in our new algorithm, typically to 1 or 2 bits per pixel. For z-buffer compositing applications [2] this is another advantage of the new algorithm, because the depth information needed for z-buffer compositing is stored in very little space.

We assume the animation script contains a homogeneous matrix transformation for every object in every frame. The matrix transforms the object from the model space coordinate frame into the screen space coordinate frame. The transformation matrices are stored in an auxiliary file along with the compressed image data and constitute part of the overhead of the new compression algorithm. This limits the current implementation to rigid body motion but this is not an intrinsic limitation of the algorithm. Non-rigid body motion can be accommodated by storing appropriate transformation information, such as free form deformation

*This work was supported by the National Science Foundation under grant MIP-9205853

†Computer Animation Laboratory, GVU center, College of Computing, Georgia Institute of Technology, Atlanta GA 30332, E-mail: brian.guenter@cc.gatech.edu

‡Digital Signal Processing Labratory, School of Electrical Engineering, Georgia Institute of Technology, Atlanta GA 30332, E-mail: yun@eedsp.gatech.edu, rmm@eedsp.gatech.edu

 ACM-0-89791-601-8/93/008/0297 $01.50

mesh points for example [9], in the animation script.

The current implementation assumes that objects are represented as polygonal surfaces. Algorithms exist for converting many different surface representations to approximating polygonal surfaces. Many commercial image synthesis programs perform this conversion internally so the limitation to a polygonal representation is not unduly restrictive.

The geometric data has special properties we exploit to improve compression. As a consequence the coder is split into two parts: a geometrical data coder and a color data coder. General notation used throughout the paper is presented in Section 2.

Section 3 of the paper presents block diagrams of the algorithm. Section 4 describes the geometrical data coding algorithm. Section 5 describes the color data coding algorithm. Animation test results are presented in section 6 and conclusions and suggestions for further research are presented in section 7.

2 Notations and Data structure

In this paper the frame number, which is used to identify the specific frame, is expressed as a superscript. A subscript represents the object number when it is expressed as a single value and the spatial location when it is expressed as a pair of values. If the subscripts are omitted, that symbol represents the whole set of the corresponding data for that frame.

The data structure of a frame is divided into two parts. The first part is the set of 4×4 homogeneous matrices for all the objects $\{ T_j^i, j = 0..N_o - 1 \}$ by which the point in the model object space is transformed to the screen space. The other part is the 2-dimensional array of the data $P_{m,n}^i, m = 0..N_x - 1, n = 0..N_y - 1$, where N_o represents the number of objects and N_x and N_y represent the number of pixels in each direction. Each pixel datum $P_{m,n}^i$ is composed of the object number $N_{m,n}^i$, depth $Z_{m,n}^i$ and colors $C_{m,n}^i$ of the pixel at the spatial location (m, n). For example, the point in the i-th frame $(m, n, Z_{m,n}^i)^T$ is transformed to the point $(x^j, y^j, z^j)^T$ in the *j-th* frame as follows:

$$T_k^j (T_k^i)^{-1} \begin{pmatrix} m \\ n \\ Z_{m,n}^i \\ 1 \end{pmatrix} = \alpha \begin{pmatrix} x^j \\ y^j \\ z^j \\ 1 \end{pmatrix} \quad (1)$$

where $k = N_{m,n}^i$.

As mentioned above, the symbols without the subscripts represent the whole set of data for the frame. For example T^i stands for the set of matrices and N^i, Z^i, C^i represent the whole two dimensional array, also called a field, containing the object number, depth and color values of the *i-th* frame, respectively. The object number N^i and the depth Z^i are collectively called the geometrical data field. The color field C^i represents the R,G,B color fields, but sometimes can be used for one specific color field.

The object number and color values are represented as integers, but the depth is a real number. In our implementation, each of the RGB color values is usually represented by 8 bits/pixel (256 levels), and the depth is double precision floating point. Since the compression efficiency of the geometrical data is highly dependent on the accuracy of the calculation, the double precision representation is preferred. The required number of bits for the object number depends on the total number of objects.

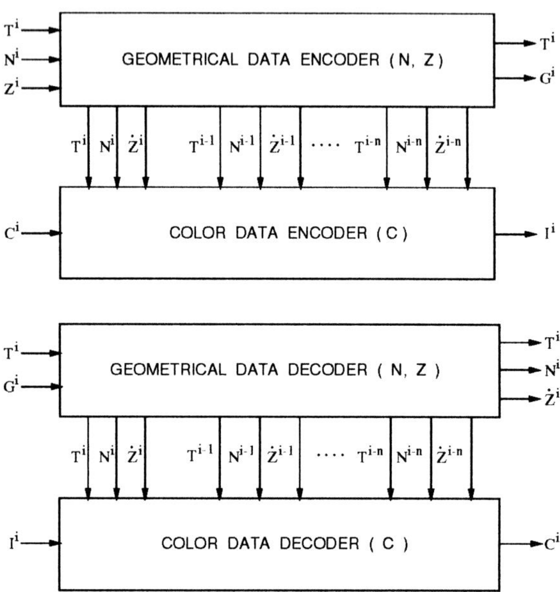

Figure 1: *n-th* Order Frame Encoder and Decoder

3 System Block diagrams

The heart of the coding scheme uses a linear predictive coding algorithm (DPCM) [4]. Since there exists substantial correlation between successive frames in computer animation as well as in real-life video, good compression gain can be achieved by these predictive schemes. Since both the object number and depth fields are needed to compute the motion trajectory of each pixel and these are encoded together into one data stream G^i, the whole system is divided into a geometrical data coding block for N^i, Z^i and a color data coding block for C^i as shown in Figs 1.

The object number N^i and color data C^i are coded losslessly, but the depth Z^i is allowed to contain error within a specified limit to achieve a high compression gain, because Z^i requires a relatively larger number of bits (64 bits/pixel for a double precision representation) than N^i, C^i.

The DPCM system requires storage for several frames determined by the order of the predictor. The geometrical data coding block stores the object number fields N^i and the depth fields $\dot{Z}^i$ of previous frames. Since only the decoded values are available for the depth field in the decoder, the geometrical data encoder uses the decoded depth field $\dot{Z}^i$ instead of the original depth field Z^i for correct reconstruction from the encoded data. The stored geometrical data $N^i, \dot{Z}^i$ are provided to the color data coding block to predict the color data in other frames by motion prediction.

4 Geometrical Data Coding

Figs 2 show the block diagrams of the encoder and decoder for geometrical data. The principle behind the geometrical data coding is that the geometrical data of the current frame is predicted from several previous frames which are compared to the current original frame pixel-by-pixel. Each pixel $P_{m,n}^i$ is classified as matched if $N_{m,n}^i$, $Z_{m,n}^i$ of the current frame are the same as $\tilde{N}_{m,n}^i$, $\tilde{Z}_{m,n}^i$ of the predicted frame, and unmatched otherwise. Since the object number and depth for the matched pixels can be recovered from the

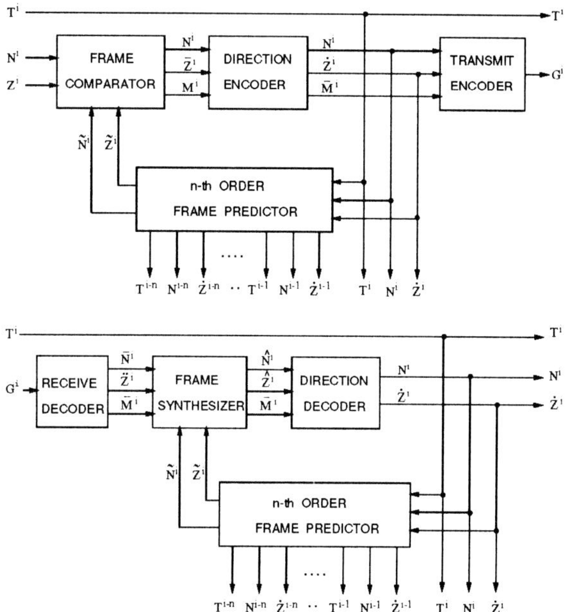

Figure 2: Geometrical Data Encoder and Decoder

predicted frame in the decoder, the only information that needs to be transmitted are the matching status field M^i which records whether or not each pixel is matched, and the complete geometrical data for the unmatched pixels. Unmatched pixels occur mainly in recently uncovered regions which cannot be predicted from previous frames, or from highly curved regions that are difficult to predict.

For the unmatched regions the geometrical data can be coded effectively by exploiting the spatial correlations between pixels, because pixels which belong to the same planar polygon satisfy the same plane equation. An algorithm called direction coding is proposed and described later. With direction coding, the unmatched pixels are classified into direction matched pixels and totally unmatched pixels. This matching information replaces $M^i_{m,n}$ at the unmatched pixel and this modified matching status field is $\bar{M}^i$. After the direction coding, since the majority of the frame is matched, the entropy of $\bar{M}^i$ is very small. Thus $\bar{M}^i$ can be compressed effectively by entropy coding or run-length coding and the original geometrical data $N^i_{m,n}$, $Z^i_{m,n}$ are transmitted in uncompressed form only for the totally unmatched pixels.

At the receive decoder, the matching status field $\bar{M}^i_{m,n}$, and the geometrical data $N^i_{m,n}$,$Z^i_{m,n}$ for totally unmatched pixels are obtained. For the matched pixels which can be identified by the $\bar{M}^i$, the object number $N^i_{m,n}$ and the depth $\tilde{Z}^i_{m,n}$ are copied from the predicted frame. Then for the unmatched pixels the $N^i_{m,n}$, $\acute{Z}^i_{m,n}$ are recovered by the direction decoder and the complete recovered frame data is fed into the frame predictor for the next frame prediction.

4.1 Frame Predictor

The set of four pixels $P^i_{m,n}$, $P^i_{m,n+1}$, $P^i_{m+1,n+1}$, $P^i_{m+1,n}$ is defined as a pixel square $S^i_{m,n}$. Each pixel square can be classified into one of three categories. The first is the plane pixel square where all four corner pixels come from the same planar polygon and make a planar square. The second is the adjacent polygon pixel square where four pixels are from the two adjacent polygons that share an edge that intersects the pixel square. The third is a non-adjacent polygon pixel square where the polygon boundary is across the pixel square but the polygons do not share an edge. These three cases are illustrated in Fig. 3.

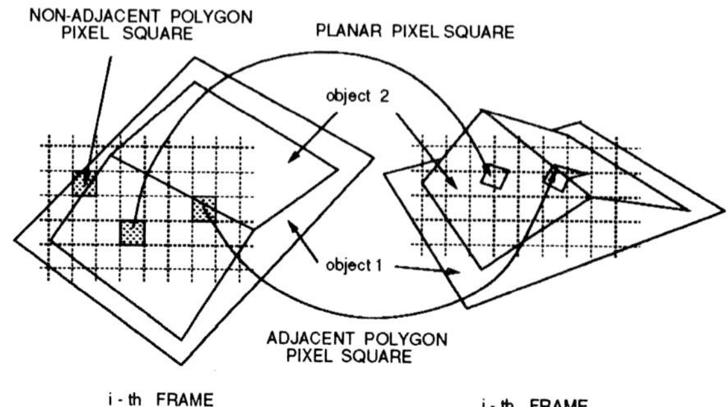

Figure 3: Transform of Pixel Squares between Frames

The planar pixel square can be easily transformed by Eq. 1 and rendered into other frames. For the adjacent polygon pixel square, if the plane equations of the two polygons can be obtained by exploiting the neighboring pixel squares, then the pixel square can be partitioned into two polygons and each polygon can be transformed and rendered onto other frames in the same way. There is not enough information to make correct partitions for the non-adjacent polygon pixel squares, then these cannot be used to predict other frames. The pixel square $S^i_{m,n}$ can be defined as a planar pixel square if the four pixels satisfy the following plane conditions.

$$N^i_{m,n} = N^i_{m,n+1} = N^i_{m+1,n+1} = N^i_{m+1,n} \tag{2}$$

$$|Z^i_{m,n} + Z^i_{m+1,n+1} - Z^i_{m,n+1} - Z^i_{m+1,n}| < \epsilon \tag{3}$$

In Eq. 3 the inequality is used to deal with the error due to the limited precision of computation and the small number ϵ is determined as the allowable error for the depth of the pixels which are from the same planar polygon.

In some cases, the above two conditions are not enough to determine whether the pixel square is planar or not. For example, the pixels lying across the boundary of two separate polygons which are parallel to each other might satisfy these two conditions. There are several ways of reducing the possibility of an incorrect classification of a planar pixel square. One way is to add the following conditions, which test the relations between the depths of the surrounding pixels. If the following plane conditions are satisfied with regard to at least one corner of the pixel square, $S^i_{m,n}$ can be considered to be a plane pixel square.

$$|2Z^i_{l,k} - Z^i_{l-1,k} - Z^i_{l+1,k}| < \epsilon$$

$$|2Z^i_{l,k} - Z^i_{l,k-1} - Z^i_{l,k+1}| < \epsilon \tag{4}$$

$$\text{for } l = m, m+1 \text{ and } k = n, n+1.$$

For the non-planar pixel square which does not satisfy the above plane conditions, if some two pixel squares around it are planar and if the intersection of those two planes are found to be across the pixel square by solving the plane equations of those two planes, then this pixel square is an adjacent polygon pixel square that can be divided into two polygons and transformed into other frames. One way to find the two plane pixel squares is to test the above plane conditions for each pair of pixel squares which are on the opposite sides of the current pixel square.

The geometrical data for most of a frame can be computed by transforming all the planar and adjacent polygon pixel squares of the previous frame into the current frame and rendering the transformed polygons on the frame buffer of geometrical data using the z-buffer algorithm.

Since the current frame does not change much from the previous frame, the transformed polygon of one pixel square is small and covers only a few pixels. Under this assumption, there are several effective techniques for geometrical data rendering. One simple method is to find the bounding box of the transformed pixel square and test whether each pixel point inside the bounding box is inside the polygon or not. For each inside pixel point, the depth of that point can be computed from the plane equation of the transformed polygon for the z-buffer rendering process. The back-face removal step might be applied before rendering.

There is one special case where the viewpoint and object are not moving. In this case the transform matrices of the current and previous frames are the same and the whole transform matrix $T_k^j(T_k^i)^{-1}$ will be the identity matrix in Eq. 1. For these pixels, the above complicated steps are not necessary and the only thing to do is simply to apply the depth of the previous frame to the z-buffer algorithm at the same pixel location. All these pixels are classified as matched pixels.

Due to occlusion some parts of the current frame may not be predictable from the previous frame. The percentage of predictable pixels can be increased by using higher order prediction. In the n-th order case, the previous n frames are transformed and rendered on the same frame buffers of object number and depth.

The frame predictor used in both the encoder and decoder have identical frame buffers for a object number and depth for higher order prediction. The encoder and decoder should store the same frame data in both predictors so that the predicted frames in both blocks will be the same.

4.2 Frame Comparator

The frame comparator compares the input frame data to the predicted frame data on a pixel-by-pixel basis and records the result in the matching status field M^i. If a pixel $P^i_{m,n}$ of the current frame and $\tilde{P}^i_{m,n}$ of the predicted frame satisfy the following conditions, then the pixel is considered to be predictable from the previous frames and said to be a matched pixel.

$$N^i_{m,n} = \tilde{N}^i_{m,n} \quad (5)$$

$$|Z^i_{m,n} - \tilde{Z}^i_{m,n}| < \epsilon \quad (6)$$

In Eq. 6, an inequality is used for the same reason as in Eq. 3. If a pixel $P^i_{m,n}$ is found to be matched, $M^i_{m,n}$ is set to 1 and otherwise set to 0. Because of the similarity between the adjacent frames, most of M^i will be 1. For matched pixels, the depth $Z^i_{m,n}$ of the input frame is replaced by the predicted depth $\tilde{Z}^i_{m,n}$ to guarantee the consistency of data between the encoder and decoder, because only $\tilde{Z}^i_{m,n}$ will be available in the decoder. By Eq. 6 the accuracy of the new depth $\tilde{Z}^i_{m,n}$ is guaranteed to be within ϵ. This modified depth field is $\bar{Z}^i$ and will be given to the direction coder along with N^i and M^i.

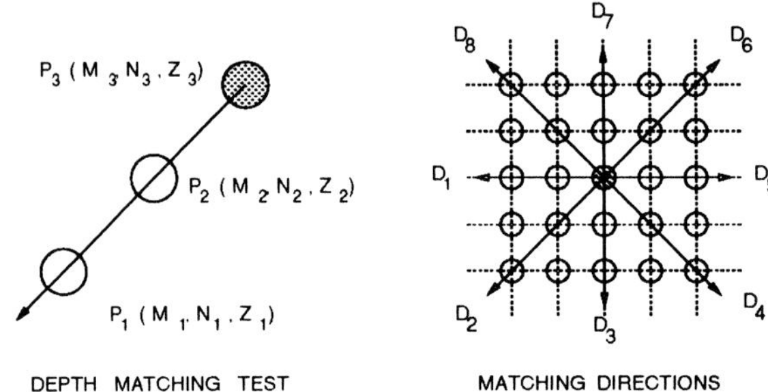

Figure 4: Determination of Direction Matching

4.3 Direction Encoder

Unmatched regions are usually from recently uncovered regions or highly curved regions that cannot be predicted. Since the pixels in those regions might come from some plane polygons or might be on the extension of a plane from a surrounding matched regions, a spatial prediction technique exploiting the plane relationship between neighboring pixels can be used to code these pixels. One such method is to find the matching direction in which two neighbor pixels lying on a straight line match the object number and depth of the current pixel and record the direction value by overwriting the $M^i_{m,n}$ which was originally zero. Since only the reconstructed data are available in the decoder, those two pixels should be pixels that have been already coded. Therefore it should be checked whether the matching status values of those two pixels is still zero. The matching conditions for a direction at P_3 in Fig. 4 are described as follows :

$$M_1 \neq 0 \text{ and } M_2 \neq 0 \quad (7)$$

$$N_1 = N_2 = N_3 \quad (8)$$

$$|Z_3 - \acute{Z}_3| < \epsilon \quad (9)$$

where $\acute{Z}_3$ is the spatially predicted depth of the pixel P_3 in the specified direction as in Eq. 10.

$$\acute{Z}_3 = 2Z_2 - Z_1 \quad (10)$$

These conditions are tested for eight directions from direction D_1 to D_8 as in Fig. 4. The first matched direction becomes the matching direction of the pixel and the corresponding direction value, which is defined as $D_i = i + 1$ in Fig. 4, is assigned to $M^i_{m,n}$ which was originally zero. The depth of the current pixel is replaced by the predicted value in the matched direction as in Eq. 10 for consistency of the data in the encoder and decoder. If there is no matching direction, the number 10 is assigned, corresponding to a totally unmatched pixel. After direction coding, the frame data will be:

$$\bar{M}^i_{m,n} = \begin{cases} 1 & \text{matched} \\ 2..9 & \text{direction matched} \\ 10 & \text{totally unmatched} \end{cases} \quad (11)$$

$$\acute{Z}^i_{m,n} = \begin{cases} \tilde{Z}^i_{m,n} & \text{matched} \\ \acute{Z}^i_{m,n} & \text{direction matched} \\ Z^i_{m,n} & \text{totally unmatched} \end{cases} \quad (12)$$

N^i remains unchanged because the object number is losslessly coded.

Fig. 5 shows an example of direction coding where the region inside the polygon is originally unmatched. The encoding is performed from left to right and from bottom to top

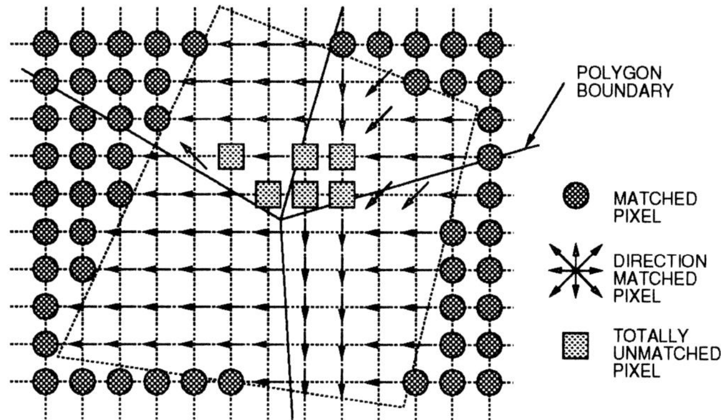

Figure 5: Example of Direction Encoding. The unmatched region inside the dashed polygon is coded by direction coding. Coding is performed from left to right and from bottom to top.

and the arrows represent the direction of matching. This illustrates that the number of totally unmatched pixels is very small and the matching directions are mostly 2 because direction 2 is the first test direction in Fig. 4. Since the geometrical data for the matched and direction matched pixels are predictable, the data to be transmitted are the matching status field $\bar{M}^i$ which has very low entropy and the $\{N^i_{m,n}, Z^i_{m,n}\}$'s for a few totally unmatched pixels.

4.4 Frame Synthesizer

Since the matched pixels can be identified from the matching status field $\bar{M}^i$ decoded in the receive decoder, the frame synthesizer can recover the geometrical data for all the matched pixels by copying the data from the predicted frame. Then the geometrical data $\hat{N}^i_{m,n}$, $\hat{Z}^i_{m,n}$ for the matched pixels and totally unmatched pixels are correctly recovered whereas those for direction matched pixels remain undetermined:

$$\hat{N}^i_{m,n} = \begin{cases} \bar{N}^i_{m,n} = N^i_{m,n} & \text{if } \bar{M}^i_{m,n} = 10 \\ \bar{N}^i_{m,n} = N^i_{m,n} & \text{if } \bar{M}^i_{m,n} = 1 \\ \text{undetermined} & \text{if } \bar{M}^i_{m,n} = 2..9 \end{cases} \quad (13)$$

$$\hat{Z}^i_{m,n} = \begin{cases} \ddot{Z}^i_{m,n} = Z^i_{m,n} & \text{if } \bar{M}^i_{m,n} = 10 \\ \tilde{Z}^i_{m,n} & \text{if } \bar{M}^i_{m,n} = 1 \\ \text{undetermined} & \text{if } \bar{M}^i_{m,n} = 2..9 \end{cases} \quad (14)$$

4.5 Direction Decoder

For the direction matched pixels, the object number $N^i_{m,n}$ is recovered by copying the object number of the pixel which is located in the matching direction and the depth $\dot{Z}^i_{m,n}$ becomes the predicted value $\acute{Z}^i_{m,n}$ from the two pixels located in the matching direction as in Eq. 10. $N^i_{m,n}$ are recovered correctly for all the pixels and the depth field $\dot{Z}^i$ is the same as $\dot{Z}^i$ in Eq. 12. The accuracies of $\tilde{Z}^i_{m,n}$ for the matched pixel and $\acute{Z}^i_{m,n}$ for the direction matched pixel are guaranteed by Eq. 6 and Eq. 9, respectively. These decoded data are fed into the predictor and are the same for both the encoder and decoder to make the same predictions as in Fig. 2.

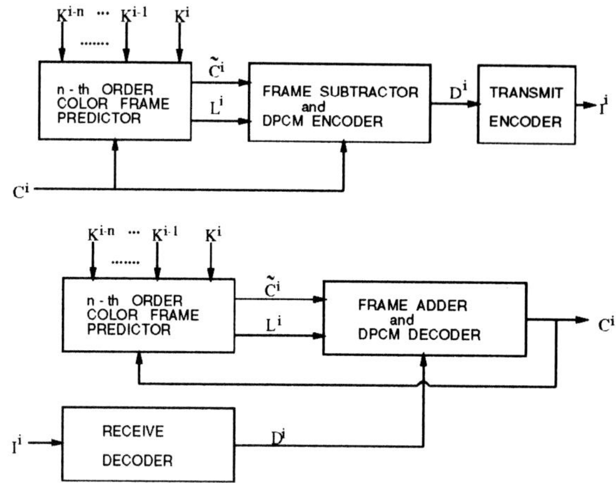

Figure 6: Color Data Encoder and Decoder, where $K^i = (T^i N^i \dot{Z}^i)$

5 Color Data Coding

Since the (T, N, Z)'s from the geometrical data coding block can be used to compute the locations of a current frame pixel on the previous frames and the previous color data frames are stored, the color of the pixel can be predicted by estimating the color at the transformed locations in the previous frames. The error image between the original and the predicted frame, also called the residual image R^i, has a relatively low entropy compared to the original. The pixels are classified into two classes, matched and unmatched pixels, based on whether the locations in the old frames are traceable or not. Since this residual image still has some spatial correlation, spatial linear prediction coding (DPCM) can be applied to reduce the entropy. This DPCM coded residual image is called a differential residual D^i and entropy coding using Huffman coding or arithmetic coding, can compress the differential residual losslessly. In decoder after the residual R^i is recovered by DPCM decoding, the original color data $C^i_{m,n}$ is obtained as the sum of the predicted value $\tilde{C}^i_{m,n}$ and the residual $R^i_{m,n}$ for the matched pixel. The color $C^i_{m,n}$ of the unmatched pixel is the same as residual $R^i_{m,n}$.

5.1 Color Frame Predictor

A pixel of one frame can be mapped to another frame by the transformation in Eq. 1 and if the transformed point satisfies the following condition, it is considered to be the same point as the current pixel and the pixel is said to be matched. If the pixel $P^i_{m,n}$ is transformed into the j-th frame and the transformed point is inside the pixel square $S^j_{p,q}$, the matching condition is as follows:

$$Z^j_{min} \le Z^j_{trans} \le Z^j_{max} \quad (15)$$

where the Z^j_{trans} is the depth of the transformed point and Z^j_{min} , Z^j_{max} are the minimum and maximum depth of the four corner pixels of $S^j_{p,q}$, respectively. Since several previous frames of geometrical and color data are available to deal with the occlusion problem, the transformed point in the nearest frame which satisfies the above condition is used to predict the color data of the current pixel.

L^i records the matching status values for color data which are zeros for the unmatched and ones for the matched pixels. Since generally the transformed point is not the pixel point, an interpolation is necessary for the computation of the color.

5.2 Subtractor and DPCM Encoder

Colors of matched regions in the residual R^i are residual values generated by sutracting the predicticed colors from the original colors whereas the colors in the unmatched regions remain unchanged as follows:

$$R^i_{m,n} = \begin{cases} C^i_{m,n} & \text{if } L^i_{m,n} = 0 \\ C^i_{m,n} - \tilde{C}^i_{m,n} & \text{if } L^i_{m,n} = 1 \end{cases} \quad (16)$$

Unmatched regions are mostly from recently uncovered regions and the entropy of such unmatched regions can be reduced by spatial linear predictive coding (DPCM). The residual image in the matched region has low entropy caused by changes of illumination, by the movement of objects, viewpoints or light sources between frames. Since this kind of error has relatively slow spatial variation, DPCM can be effectively applied also to the matched regions of the residual image.

These two steps, frame subtraction and DPCM, can be implemented with a combined operation as in Fig. 6. Since the matched and unmatched regions have different kind of data as explained above, each region should be coded independently. Usually 2-D DPCM uses three left and lower neighboring pixels $\acute{C}_{p,q}$ to predict the current pixel $C^i_{m,n}$. If the current pixel is an unmatched pixel, $\acute{C}^i_{p,q}$ should be the original color $C^i_{p,q}$. If the current pixel is a matched pixel, $\acute{C}^i_{p,q}$ should be the residual value. Since the residual value is not available for an unmatched pixel, the $\acute{C}^i_{p,q}$ is set to zero when $L^i_{p,q} = 0$ as follows:

$$\acute{C}^i_{p,q} = \begin{cases} C^i_{p,q} & \text{if } L^i_{m,n} = 0 \\ L^i_{p,q}(C^i_{p,q} - \tilde{C}^i_{p,q}) & \text{if } L^i_{m,n} = 1 \end{cases} \quad (17)$$

The spatially predicted value $\dot{C}^i_{m,n}$ is the integer part of a linear combination of those as follows:

$$\dot{C}^i_{m,n} = \text{int}(\alpha \acute{C}^i_{m-1,n} + \beta \acute{C}^i_{m-1,n-1} + \gamma \acute{C}^i_{m,n-1}) \quad (18)$$

In this paper, the prediction coefficients α, β, γ are selected to be 0.75,-0.5,0.75 respectively.

Then the differential residual image D^i is obtained by subtracting the spatially predicted value $\dot{C}^i_{m,n}$ from the residual value as follows:

$$D^i_{m,n} = \begin{cases} C^i_{m,n} - \dot{C}^i_{m,n} & \text{if } L^i_{m,n} = 0 \\ C^i_{m,n} - \tilde{C}^i_{m,n} - \dot{C}^i_{m,n} & \text{if } L^i_{m,n} = 1 \end{cases} \quad (19)$$

The differential residual D^i, which has very small entropy, can be compressed losslessly by an entropy coding technique.

5.3 Adder and DPCM decoder

The $L^i_{m,n}$ and $\tilde{C}^i_{m,n}$ in the predictor of the decoder are the same as those in the encoder. The original color field C^i is recovered by the combined step of DPCM decoding and frame addition as follows:

$$C^i_{m,n} = \begin{cases} D^i_{m,n} + \dot{C}^i_{m,n} & \text{if } L^i_{m,n} = 0 \\ D^i_{m,n} + \tilde{C}^i_{m,n} + \dot{C}^i_{m,n} & \text{if } L^i_{m,n} = 1 \end{cases} \quad (20)$$

where the spatial prediction $\dot{C}^i$ is the same as in the encoder. The recovered color C^i is fed back to the predictor for the prediction of the next frames.

6 Test Results

31 animation frames were generated to test the proposed compression algorithm. Each frame is composed of 7 objects and various kinds of textures were mapped by solid texture mapping. Through the whole 31 frames the ball bounces back and forth between the two wood blocks. In the first 11 frames the viewpoint does not change and in the next 10 frames the view point moves approximately 5 degrees/frame. During the last 10 frames zooming is performed. Plate 2,3, and 4 show the frames for above three cases.

In the case of Plate 2, since most of the objects are not moving and the view point is fixed, all regions except the rolling ball are matched regions. Pixel points in the current frame are transformed exactly to the same pixel points of other frames, then there are no errors due to bilinear color interpolation and since even the colors on the edges of stationary objects are predictable, the residual will have extremely small entropy which results in very high compression gain.

Plate 3 is a more general case in which both an object and the viewpoint are moving.There are mainly three kinds of residual errors. First, the recently uncovered regions are the major error regions which can be compressed only by DPCM. Second, in matched regions the changes in illuminations on the object surfaces causes residual errors. Usually illumination changes are due to the changes of specular reflection which varies with the movement of the view point or the object itself. Generally these errors change slowly and can be lowered by DPCM. Third, since the object boundaries are often unmatched regions which do not satisfy Eq. 15, the residual errors are large there. And even in the case where the pixels on the object boundary are matched, relatively large errors due to the color interpolation occur because the color data of these pixels were generated by antialiasing. In Plate 4, since with zooming there are no recently uncovered regions and the spatial frequency is decreasing, the entropy of the residual signal will be smaller than that in Plate 3.

The second order compression algorithm was implemented and tested on this test sequence. Fig. 7 shows the entropies of the original pictures and the differential residual images by 2-D DPCM and motion prediction algorithm. Table 1 illustrates the entropies of several frames. Plates 5 and 6 show the differential residual images of the RED component by linear predictive coding (DPCM) and the new motion prediction, respectively. As explained above, the major errors in Plate 6 are on recently uncovered regions and along the object boundaries which are often unmatched regions. The biggest differences between DPCM and motion prediction occurred on the wood texture which has relatively higher spatial frequency than any other regions. In these high spatial frequency regions, motion prediction shows much higher performance than spatial linear predictive coding. Through the whole 31 frames, the entropy of the original frame is around 20.7 bits/pixel. In the first 11 frames where the viewpoint is fixed, only about 1 bits/pixel is required for the motion prediction technique, except for the first frame which cannot be motion predicted and is coded only by DPCM. This contrasts with DPCM which needs around 11.4 bits/pixel. The necessary bits/pixel for the next 10 frames in which both the viewpoint and object are moving is around 8.3 bits/pixel which is about 3 bits/pixel gain over DPCM.

	frame 5	frame 15	frame 25
$N_{ORIGINAL}$	20.88	20.78	20.58
N_{DPCM}	11.35	11.23	10.59
N_{GEOM}	0.32	1.06	0.93
N_{RGB}	0.67	7.20	6.19
N_{MOTION}	0.99	8.26	7.12

Table 1: Entropies of original image and residuals by DPCM and Motion Prediction (unit : bits/pixel)

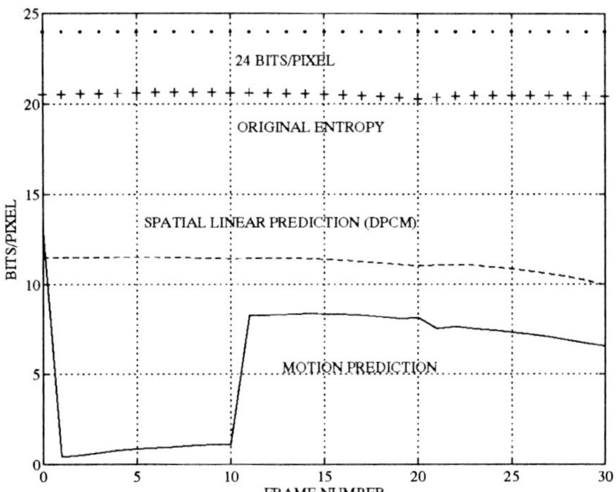

Figure 7: Entropies of the Bouncing Ball Sequence. The data for motion prediction are the sum of compressed geometrical data and entropy of residual.

In the next 10 frames, all entropies are decreasing with zooming as expected above, but the motion prediction algorithm still outperforms DPCM by about 3.5 bits/pixel.

7 Conclusion

The motion prediction compression algorithm for computer animation image sequences presented here consistently outperforms spatial linear prediction. This is true even though the new algorithm encodes double precision depth and integer object number information for a total of 96 bits/pixel including RGB data while the spatial compression algorithm does not. The depth and object number information are useful in their own right for performing z-buffer image compositing. The compression ratio achieved by the new algorithm was 1.4 times or more greater than that achieved with spatial linear prediction even for scenes with rapid changes in camera view point and substantial changes in object occlusion relationships. The overall compression ratio achieved with the new algorithm for image sequences with significant object and viewpoint motion was approximately 3 to 1.

There is still scope for improvement in the algorithm. We have noticed significant remaining correlation in the residual images. Long strings of zero residual values are punctuated by short bursts of plus and minus one residual values. Additionally the geometric overhead can be significantly reduced by storing the polygonal surface data and re-rendering it with the z- buffer algorithm, a process which should be no more time consuming than re-rendering pixel squares as in the current implementation. This makes the auxiliary data file more complex but for animation sequences more than a few seconds long the geometric data overhead should drop to .1 bit/pixel or less. We are currently implementing this extension.

The current implementation of the algorithm is limited to objects represented as polygonal surfaces. As discussed in the introduction this is not an undue restriction since efficient algorithms exist for approximating many different surface types with polygonal surfaces. However it would be an interesting research project to extend the geometric coder to other surface types so that an exact, rather than an approximating polygonal, surface representation could be used. This extension would require modifying both the motion prediction stage and the direction coding stage to compute surface equations directly from the depth information stored in the image.

8 Acknowledgments

The authors acknowledge help from Ragnar Jonsson, Stephen A. Martucci, Wayne Wooten and Lonnie D. Harvel.

References

[1] Denber, Michael J. and Turner, Paul M. A Differential Compiler for Computer Animation. Proceedings of SIGGRAPH '86 (Dallas, Taxas, August 18–22,1986). In *Computer Graphics* 20,4 (August 1986), 21–27.

[2] Duff, Tom. Compositing 3-D Rendered Images. Proceedings of SIGGRAPH '85 (San Francisco, California, July 22–26,1985). In *Computer Graphics* 19, 3(July 1985), 41–44.

[3] Jain, Anil K. *Fundamentals of Digital Image Processing.* Prentice-Hall, Englewood Cliffs, New Jersey, 1989.

[4] Jayant, Nuggehally S. and Noll, Peter. *Digital Coding of Waveforms.* Prentice-Hall, Englewood Cliffs, New Jersey, 1984.

[5] Jones, Stephen C. and Moorhead II, Robert J. Hardware-specific Image Compression Techniques for the Animation of CFD data. Proceedings of SPIE - International Society for Optical Engineering, 1668 (San Jose, California, February 10–11,1992), 141–146.

[6] Lim, Jae S. *Two-Dimensional Signal and Image Processing.*, Prentice-Hall, Englewood Cliffs, New Jersey, 1990.

[7] Martucci, Stephen A. Reversible Compression of HDTV Images Using Median Adaptive Prediction and Arithmetic Coding. Proceedings of IEEE ISCAS, 2(New Orleans, Louisiana, May 1–3,1990),1310–1313.

[8] Melnychuck, Paul W. and Rabbani, Majid. Survey of Lossless Image Coding Techniques. Proceedings of SPIE - International Society for Optical Engineering, 1075 (Los Angeles, California, January 17–20, 1989), 92–100.

[9] Sederberg, Thomas W. and Parry, Scott R. Free-Form Deformation of Solid Geometric Models. Proceedings of SIGGRAPH '86 (Dallas, Taxas,August 18–22,1986). In *Computer Graphics* 20,4 (August 1986), 151–160.

[10] Witten, Ian H., Neal, Radford M., and Cleary, John G. Arithmetic Coding for Data Compression. In *Communications of the ACM* 30,6 (June 1987), 520–540.

Plate 2: Frame 0,9

Plate 1: Frame 5 of the test sequence

Plate 3: Frame 10,19

Plate 4: Frame 20,29

Plate 5: The differential image of frame 5 by DPCM (512×512).

Space Diffusion: An Improved Parallel Halftoning Technique Using Space-Filling Curves

Yuefeng Zhang and Robert. E. Webber
Computer Science Department
The University of Western Ontario
London, Ontario, Canada N6A 5B7

ABSTRACT

Dot diffusion has been proposed as a way of combining the strengths of ordered dithering and error diffusion to create a parallelizable halftoning technique. However, dot diffusion pays a price in image quality in order to achieve parallelizability. Space-filling curves have been used to improve error diffusion. We show that by combining dot diffusion with a space-filling curve traversal technique, a parallelizable halftoning technique results that does not pay a cost in image quality. This new technique we call *space diffusion*.

KEYWORDS: Space-filling curves, dot diffusion, error diffusion, ordered dithering, digital halftoning, parallel algorithms.

1 INTRODUCTION

1.1 OVERVIEW

To print a gray scale image on a binary (e.g., black and white) device such as a laser printer, the gray image has to be transformed into a binary image. The process of doing this while not significantly altering the appearance of the image is called digital halftoning. Although grey-scale display devices are becoming cheaper and cheaper, there seems to consistently be a trade-off between the spatial resolution of display devices and the range of usable intensities at each spatial location. Thus it is reasonable to expect that for quite some time into the future, there will continue to be situations where the digital halftoning process will be necessary.

As the spatial resolution of display devices increases, the parallelizability of digital halftoning algorithms will play a greater role in the evaluation of the usefulness of a particular method in the design of an effective display system. Many digital halftoning methods have been proposed in the literature. The ones we will consider in this paper are: ordered dithering, error diffusion, dot diffusion, error diffusion along space-filling curves, and error diffusion along space-filling curves combined with patterning. Other methods may be found elsewhere [3, 5, 7]. We will propose a new method, called space diffusion, which combines the best features of these methods while remaining parallelizable.

In the following subsection, the above mentioned previously known halftoning methods are presented in more detail. After that, the space diffusion method is presented in Section 2. Then, Section 3 contains a discussion of experimental results aimed at evaluating the performance of this method. Final remarks are contained in Section 4.

For convenience, in the following discussion, we assume that the gray image and its corresponding binary image have the same size.

1.2 BACKGROUND

Of the previously known halftoning methods, ordered dithering [3] is one of the more widely used digital halftoning techniques. It is based on the idea of mapping grey values to black and white by comparing them to a threshold value that varies across the image. Suitable patterns of thresholds map regions of similar grey values into corresponding patterns of black and white values. Because the thresholds are independent of the image values and the mapping for each image value is independent of all the other image values, the method is very easily parallelized. The major drawback of this method is that it tends to produce regular patterning in large uniform regions as shown later in Section 3 where experimental results are presented.

This drawback is avoided in Floyd and Steinberg's error diffusion technique [2]. The error diffusion method is based on using a single threshold that is the same across the whole image. Instead of ignoring the difference between the actual value and the result of the thresholding (as ordered dithering does), error diffusion takes this difference and passes it on to neighboring nodes. This process is performed left-to-right row-by-row, so the error is spread (diffused) over the values in front and below the value currently being processed. This method is inherently non-parallel as it is based on a very specific order of processing of the individual grey values.

The error diffusion technique usually produces images that are much sharper than the images produced by the ordered dither methods. One difficulty with this method is that it sometimes generates features that do not appear in the original image. These features are the result of the distribution of error values across the image and hence do not occur in ordered dithering where the error values are not distributed at all.

Knuth [6] presents a new technique, called dot diffusion, that inherits the main advantages of ordered dithering and error diffusion techniques. At the same time, it avoids some of the difficulties with these two methods. The strategy of dot diffusion is to replicate a fixed matrix over the image. This assignment of matrix values to image locations divides the pixels of the image into classes that map to the same matrix value. Then, a technique similar to error diffusion is used to halftone these classes simultaneously. Specifically, the following matrix

$$\begin{pmatrix} 34 & 48 & 40 & 32 & 29 & 15 & 23 & 31 \\ 42 & 58 & 56 & 53 & 21 & 5 & 7 & 10 \\ 50 & 62 & 61 & 45 & 13 & 1 & 2 & 18 \\ 38 & 46 & 54 & 37 & 25 & 17 & 9 & 26 \\ 28 & 14 & 22 & 30 & 35 & 49 & 41 & 33 \\ 20 & 4 & 6 & 11 & 43 & 59 & 57 & 52 \\ 12 & 0 & 3 & 19 & 51 & 63 & 60 & 44 \\ 24 & 16 & 8 & 27 & 39 & 47 & 55 & 36 \end{pmatrix}$$

is usually used to classify the pixels of the image into 64 classes according to ($x\ mod\ 8$, $y\ mod\ 8$), where (x, y) is the location of a pixel.

Starting with the pixels that map to the index value 0, at each stage, the thresholded value of pixels in the lowest numbered unprocessed class is computed and the resulting error difference is distributed to the remaining neighboring pixels that are in unprocessed classes with higher matrix numbers. As with error diffusion, the threshold used is the same at each location.

This method is related to error diffusion in that it also distributes the error term that correspond to the difference between the original grey value and the resulting thresholded binary value. It is related to ordered dithering in that ordered dithering is also generally implemented by way of a replicated matrix that establishes a positional bias in location of black and white values in the image. This matrix replication structure causes bother ordered dithering and dot diffusion to suffer from the problem of having regular patterning occur in large regions of uniform intensity as illustrated in Section 3. Fixing this problem with dot diffusion is one of the main aspects of this paper.

Recently [1, 8, 9, 10, 11], it has been observed that error diffusion itself can be improved by replacing the left-to-right row-by-row order of processing of pixels by an order patterned after the discrete version of space filling curves. Two commonly used curves are Peano curves [1] and Hilbert curves [8]. Our method is based on Hilbert curves and they are discussed in more detail in Section 2.

The main idea of the halftoning techniques that are based on space-filling curves is to use the space-filling curves to establish the order in which the pixels of the image are visited. Error terms are then distributed along this path in a manner similar to error diffusion.

One problem with using traditional space-filling curves for traversal patterns is that they fit best on square images that have widths that are powers of two. However, two approaches exist in the literature to addressing this problem for halftoning algorithms. One approach is based on a generalization of Peano curves called Murray polygons [1]. Another approach exists based on decomposing rectangles into smaller rectangles from one of a few standard sizes [11].

However, these methods have two other drawbacks. One is that, like traditional error diffusion, they are inherently serial (as the algorithm is driven by a particular serial traversal of the pixels). The other is that they do not handle long narrow features in images as well as either dot diffusion or error diffusion do. On the other hand, this method does handle large uniform regions in images better than dot diffusion or ordered dithering. These aspects of the method are illustrated in Section 3.

A further refinement of the space-filling traversal method is to use small standard patterns to replace segments of the halftoned image [8]. This can be used to compensate for some problems common to laser printing involving interaction between neighboring 'dots' on a page of paper. This method was also investigated in Section 3. Its main drawback is that it blurs the image.

In this paper, we propose a parallel mechanism for the halftoning techniques using space-filling curves. Specifically, discrete Hilbert curves are used to subdivide the image into regions. Other space-filling curves could be used as well. A strategy similar to dot diffusion is used to halftone the resulting regions simultaneously. This method avoids the difficulties with both the dot diffusion and the above space-filling curve halftoning techniques.

2 SPACE DIFFUSION

In our method, the gray image is subdivided into small regions along a space-filling curve. Then, the order of pixels along the segment that traverses a given region is used to assign the pixels of that region to their appropriate classes. Finally, a strategy similar to the dot diffusion technique is used to halftone these classes of pixels simultaneously.

Figure 1a shows a discrete Hilbert curve covering an 8×8 square region. Such curves can be easily generated to cover any $2^n \times 2^n$ region. The particular curve in Figure 1a defines a traversal ordering of the 8×8 image as shown in Figure 1b. This ordering is derived by labeling the pixel at one end of the curve by 0 and then incrementally labelling each of the remaining pixels as one moves along the curve until the last pixel is reached which is labeled 63.

This image can be subdivided into 4×4 regions by replacing each label by its value mod16 (4×4) as shown in Figure 1c. In general, we could break any $2^n \times 2^n$ image up into $2^m \times 2^m$ regions by first labeling each pixel of the region by its Hilbert curve ordering and then reducing these labels $\pmod{2^{2m}}$. Within each of these regions, the pixels are assigned classes whose numbers are integer values from 0 to 2^{2m}. These class assignments can then be used as the basis of a dot diffusion process. However, it differs from the traditional dot diffusion setup in that the matrices are not all oriented in the same manner. Figure 1d shows what the class assignments might be if we had attempted to replicate the initial 4×4 matrix of Figure 1c, rather than allowing the Hilbert curve to re-orient each of the matrices.

The class assignments shown in Figure 1d can be viewed as the basis of a standard dot diffusion process using a slightly different base matrix. Indeed, if we were breaking an image into 8×8 regions, then we would end up with matrices similar to that of Figure 1b. If we compare that matrix of class assignments to those in the matrix given for dot diffusion in Section 1, we see that matrix defined by the space filling curve does not.distribute the classes as well as the matrix given in the original presentation of the dot diffusion method [6]. However, the defects of this matrix are

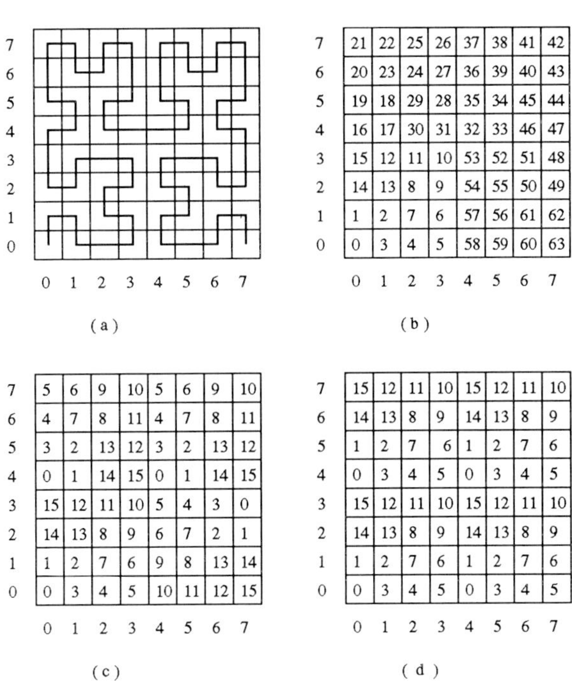

Figure 1: A 8x8 Hilbert polygon and its corresponding subdivisions.

more than compensated for by the result of constantly re-orienting it along a space-filling path as illustrated by the experimental results in Section 3. It is worthwhile noting that determining a good matrix when the orientation of the matrix is kept constantly the same was a particularly difficult aspect of the development of the original dot diffusion method.

The method based on this restructuring of the matrix orientations we call *space diffusion*. Although the example in Figure 1 presents the method in terms of square matrices being re-oriented, unlike dot diffusion, there is no need to break the image up into square regions. We can make the class assignments by reducing the original Hilbert labels by mod k for any value of k rather than restricting ourselves to values of k that are squares of powers of 2. However, in using these odd shaped decompositions, we haven't observed any significant differences in image quality from when we used squares of powers of two as the basis for class assignments.

The details of error distribution are exactly the same as those presented in Knuth's paper [6]. As with dot diffusion, the error distribution process is inherently parallel since information does not pass between pixels in different regions.

3 EXPERIMENTAL RESULTS

By combining space filling traversals with diffusion of the error term, we hope to gain the sharper detail characteristic of methods such as error diffusion and dot diffusion while taken advantage of other space filling methods' superior handling of large uniform regions (i.e., areas lacking sharp details).

Figure 2: Space diffusion method on enhanced image of boat scene

However, to know if this goal is actually accomplished, it is necessary to evaluate the method on actual grey images.

Figures 2 through 13 show a good image for comparing the various methods in that these figures combine both finely detailed regions with large uniform regions. The scene of these figures is a couple of boats in front of a light house. The rigging of the boats provides the fine detail and the hull of the boat provides the main example of a large uniform region although the sky is also of interest in this regard. The image is 256×256. Traditional edge enhancement has been applied to the original image since that improves the results of all methods in Figures 2 through 7. Figures 8 through 13 illustrate the results on the un-enhanced version of the same images. In the un-enhanced images, most of the fine detail is lost by all methods.

Figures 2 through 7 illustrate each of the 6 digital halftoning techniques described in this paper. Figure 2 was done using the space diffusion method described in Section 2 where the number of distinct classes assigned was 36. The significant fine detail to observe occurs in two places: 1) the rigging to the immediate right of the lighthouse (which is itself midway down the left-hand side of the image) and 2) the curved rigging immediately above the cabin of the boat on the right-hand side of the image.

Figure 3 was done using dot diffusion. Figure 4 was done using error diffusion. Both of these images preserve this fine detail. However, Figure 5, which was done using the traditional space filling curve, can be seen to have lost the sharpness of the details in these areas. Figure 6 was done using the pattern based version of the space filling method and shows significant loss of fine detail. Figure 7 was done by ordered dithering and seems to have a similar loss of fine detail to the traditional space filling method.

Looking at the large uniform areas in each of these images, we observe that the ships hull in the dot diffusion im-

Figure 3: Dot diffusion method on enhanced image of boat scene

Figure 5: Space-filling curve method using run summation on enhanced image of boat scene

Figure 4: Error diffusion method on enhanced image of boat scene

Figure 6: Space-filling curve method using patterns of up to 8 pixels on enhanced image of boat scene

Figure 7: Ordered dithering method using 8x8 patterns on enhanced image of boat scene

Figure 9: Dot diffusion method on un-enhanced image of boat scene

Figure 8: Space diffusion method on un-enhanced image of boat scene

Figure 10: Error diffusion method on un-enhanced image of boat scene

Figure 11: Space-filling curve method using run summation on un-enhanced image of boat scene

Figure 13: Ordered dithering method using 8x8 patterns on un-enhanced image of boat scene

Figure 12: Space-filling curve method using patterns of up to 8 pixels on un-enhanced image of boat scene

age and in the ordered dither image show significant regular patterning. In the error diffusion method, there appears to be a fairly regular grain to the patterning underlying the sky portion of the image. This patterning is not evident in the space diffusion image. This kind of regular patterning is more evident in pictures with larger more uniform regions. Figure 14 shows such an image.

Figure 14 presents the same six methods as used to create the images of Figure 2 through 7, but this time the underlying grey image is a simple rectangle with a constantly increasing intensity moving from right to left. The top image was produced using space diffusion. The image immediately below it is the result of dot diffusion and the regular patterning is quite evident. Below that is an image produced by error diffusion. As one moves across this image, one encounters many grey regions where there is a regular bias in the patterning. Below the error diffusion image is the traditional space-filling curve method. On this image it produces very much the same result as the space diffusion method. Below the space-filling image is an image produced by ordered dithering that produces strikingly regular patterning artifacts. The bottom image was produced using the patterning version of the space-filling method. These small patterns produce very regular patterning at some of the grey intensity values (for example, near the middle of the rectangle).

In summary, experimental results indicate that the space diffusion method is similar in quality to both the error diffusion method and the traditional space-filling curve method. However, each of these methods as a slight weakness in comparison to the space diffusion method (the error diffusion method is worse on large uniform regions and the space-filling method is worse on fine detail). In addition to this, both of these methods are inherently serial whereas the space diffusion method is easily parallelizable.

Figure 14: From top to bottom, the binary images are produced by: (1) space diffusion, (2) dot diffusion, (3) error diffusion, (4) space-filling curve method using run summation, (5) ordered dithering with 8×8 patterns, and (6) space-filling curve method using patterns of up to 8 pixels.

4 CONCLUSION

In this paper, we presented a new digital halftoning technique that subdivides the image into regions by subdividing a space-filling curve over the image into segments. The pixels of the image are then divided into classes by using coordinate translations on these segments. A strategy similar to dot diffusion is used to halftone these classes of pixels simultaneously.

So far, all the published halftoning techniques based on space-filling curves are sequential. This paper provides a parallel mechanism for these methods. The traditional dot diffusion method uses a fixed square matrix to divide the pixels of the image into classes. Our method, however, allows various subdivisions of the image by dividing the space-filling curve over the image into segments in different ways or using different space-filling curves. In this sense, our method may serve as a generalization of the traditional dot diffusion method.

In comparing various halftoning methods, the key problems appear to be loss of fine detail (or image sharpness) on the one hand and regular patterning in large uniform regions on the other hand. The space diffusion method appears to be better than other known methods in both these measures although the difference is not always large.

In general, we believe that space diffusion is a significantly better way of parallelizing error diffusion than is the dot diffusion method.

References

[1] Cole, A. J. Halftoning Without Dither or Edge Enhancement. *The Visual Computer* 7 (1991), 232 – 246.

[2] Floyd, R. W. and Steinberg, L. An Adaptive Algorithm for Spatial Greyscale. *Proceedings of the S. I. D.* 17, 2 (Second Quarter 1976), 75 – 77.

[3] Jarvis, J. F., Judice, C. N., and Ninke, W. H. A Survey of Techniques for the Display of Continuous Tone Pictures on Bilevel Displays. *Computer Graphics and Image Processing* 5 (1976), 13 – 17.

[4] Judice, C. N., Jarvis, J. F. and Ninke, W. H. Using Ordered Dither to Display Continuous Tone Pictures on an AC Plasma Panel. *Proceeding of the S.I.D.* 15, 4 (Fourth Quarter, 1974), 161 – 169.

[5] Knowlton, K. and Harmon, L. Computer-Produced Grey Scales. *Computer Graphics and Image Processing* 1 (1972), 1 – 20.

[6] Knuth, D. E. Digital Halftones by Dot Diffusion. *ACM Transactions on Graphics* 6, 4 (October 1987), 245 – 273.

[7] Ulichney, R. *Digital Halftoning.* The MIT Press, Cambridge, Massachusetts, 1988.

[8] Velho, L. and de M. Gomes, J. Digital Halftoning with Space Filling Curves. Proceedings of SIGGRAPH '91 (Las Vegas, 28 July-2 August 1991). In *Computer Graphics* 25, 4 (July 1991), 81 – 90.

[9] Witten, I. H. and Neal, M. Using Peano Curves for Bilevel Display of Continuous Tone Images. *IEEE Computer Graphics and Applications* (May 1982), 47 – 52.

[10] Witten, I. H. and Wyvill, B. On the Generation and Use of Space-filling Curves. *Software Practice and Experience* 13 (1983), 519 – 525.

[11] Wyvill, G. and McNaughton, C. Three Plus Five Makes Eight: A Simplified Approach to Halftoning. *Scientific Visualization of Physical Phenomena* (Boston, 1991), Springer-Verlag, New York, 379 – 392.

An Implicit Formulation for Precise Contact Modeling between Flexible Solids

Marie-Paule Gascuel*
iMAGIS, LIENS, CNRS URA 1327
Ecole Normale Supérieure, 45 rue d'Ulm
75005 Paris, France

Abstract

This paper presents an implicit deformable model, based on isosurfaces of potential fields generated by skeletons, that provides elegant and unified formulations for both geometric parameters such as shape or deformation and physical properties such as rigidity. The model is especially designed to improve collision and contact processing for non-rigid objects. In particular, it generates and maintains exact contact surfaces during interactions.

Keywords: animation, simulation, deformation, implicit surface, collision detection, collision response.

1 Introduction

Dynamic animation systems based on simplified physical laws have drawn a lot of attention during the past few years. One of the reasons why they seem so attractive is their ability to respond automatically to collisions. Nevertheless, contrary to rigid solid animation where complete analytical solutions have been found [1], modeling interactions between deformable objects still remains a challenge. In particular, none of the models proposed up to now generates an exact contact surface between interacting flexible solids.

This paper presents a new, continuous model for deformable material based on an implicit formulation which unifies the description of geometry and of physical properties of solids. Well adapted to the simulation of local deformations, the model is especially designed to improve collision and contact processing for non-rigid objects. In addition to an efficient collision detection mechanism, it generates and maintains exact contact surfaces during interactions. These surfaces are then used for the calculation of reaction forces.

Compact, efficient, easy to implement and to control, our implicit deformable model would be a particularly convenient tool in character animation where locally deformable flesh must be simulated.

*From september: iMAGIS, IMAG, BP53X 3841 Grenoble Cedex.

1.1 Previous approaches

Flexible models in Computer Graphics result from either nodal approaches (which include finite elements [6], finite differences [12, 13], and systems using elementary masses [8, 7]) or global approaches [10, 14]. The latter optimize the animation by approximating deformations by particular classes of global transformations. Well adapted to the animation of homogeneous blocks of elastic material, they would not, however, be convenient to use when simulating a material subject to local deformations (a sponge for instance), or when modeling non homogeneous complex objects like those used in character animation (typically, deformable coating over rigid skeletons).

Collisions between flexible objects are a complex phenomenon. In particular, they are not instantaneous and do not conserve energy. Among the solutions used to cope with this problem in Computer Graphics, penalty methods [9] are probably the most widely spread. They don't generate any contact surface between interacting flexible solids but use instead the amount of local interpenetration to find a force that pushes the objects apart. A different solution consists in using the relative stiffnesses of solids to find correct deformed shapes in contact situations. Here, response is computed by integrating deformation forces within the contact areas. But combined with a deformable model based on spline surfaces controlled by discrete spring systems [5], this method does not generate exact contact surfaces. A third approach [2] extends the analytical interaction processing used for rigid solids [1] to a global deformable model [14]. Contact surfaces are approximated by discrete sets of contact points which, as the authors emphasize, is somewhat unsatisfactory.

In all these methods, the lack of a contact surface between interacting flexible solids generates local interpenetration and imperfectly deformed shapes. The extent of these artifacts is exacerbated by the lasting quality of soft collisions, and forbids any correct evaluation of reaction forces.

1.2 Overview

This paper presents a new deformable model which improves interaction processing for flexible solids. Our main point is the use of isopotential implicit surfaces generated by "skeletons" to model the objects. Developed up to now as a tool for free form modeling [4, 3], this formalism has not been used as a way to model physical properties[1]. It leads to a concise formulation for both geometric parameters, such as shape and deformation, and physical properties, such as rigidity and elastic behavior. The deformable model is continuous and provides easy modeling of local deformations.

The associated method for collision detection and response is an improved version of [5]. The inside/outside functions associated with implicit solids greatly reduces the computational cost of collision detection. The model generates and maintains exact contact surfaces between interacting objects. Opposite compression forces are respectively applied to the solids along contact surfaces, so a correct integration of response forces can be calculated.

Section 2 describes the implicit deformable model, and explains how to design both homogeneous and non-homogeneous flexible solids. The processing of interactions is detailed in Section 3, including the particular cases of multiple collisions and of interactions with rigid solids. Section 4 discusses implementation. Section 5 focuses on the possibilities for future research opened by our method.

2 Implicit Deformable Solids

Our aim is to simulate damped material where deformations due to collisions remain local. Rather than considering the general Lagrange equations of motion for non-rigid objects (as in [12]), we use the same approximation as in [13, 5]: the mass distribution of solids is considered to be constant, so motion is calculated using rigid body equations which lead to a more efficiently computed animation. More precisely, deformable solids are split into two layers:

- A rigid component which obeys the rigid body equations of motion. Its mass distribution corresponds to the object's rest shape.
- A deformable layer at rest relative to the rigid layer.

This section presents a new model for the deformable layer based on implicitly defined isopotential surfaces generated by skeletons. We first review the definition of these surfaces.

2.1 Implicit surfaces

Implicit surfaces such as "distance surfaces" [4] and "convolution surfaces" [3] allow the free form design of shapes through the manipulation of "skeletons" that generate potential fields. Very simple to define and to control, they constitute a good alternative to traditional implicit surfaces defined by analytical equations. An implicit surface S generated by a set of skeletons $S_i (i = 1..n)$ with associated "field functions" f_i is defined by:

$$S = \{P \in \Re^3 \ / \ f(P) = 1\} \quad \text{where} \quad f(P) = \sum_{i=1}^{n} f_i(P)$$

[1]Flexible solids have been described by superquadrics [10, 11], another kind of implicit surface. Contrary to the approach developed here, the choice of an implicit geometric description of objects was not closely related to the way physical properties were modeled.

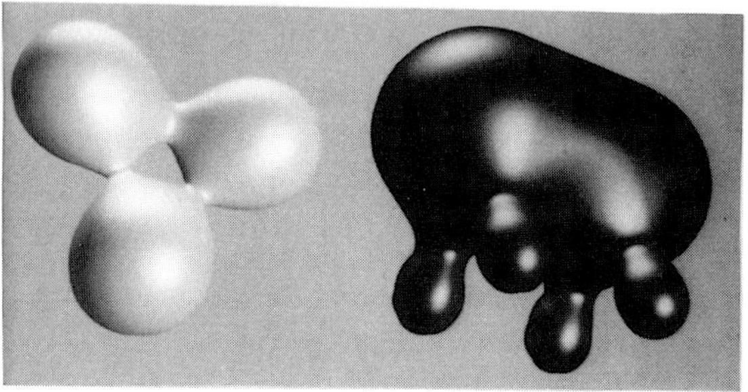

Figure 1: Isopotential objects generated by skeletons.

This surface surrounds the solid defined by $f(P) \geq 1$, which can have several disconnected components. Normal vectors are directed along the field's gradient.

The skeletons S_i can be any geometric primitive admitting a well defined distance function, such as: points, curves, parametric surfaces, or volumes. The field functions f_i are monotonically decreasing functions of the distance to the associated skeleton [4]. For convolution surfaces [3], they are given by integrals of exponential contributions from each point of the skeleton. In order to optimize the computations, these functions usually have a restricted scope of influence. Examples of isopotential surfaces are shown in Figure 1.

An implicit surface can easily be deformed by introducing a deformation term g in its implicit representation e.g. $f(P) + g(P) = 1$. In the remainder of this paper, only this type of deformations are considered.

2.2 Defining elastic material with potential fields

The method is based on the following observation: the set of points P satisfying $f(P) = 1$ (where f is the field function) is sufficient to define a surface. This set of points being fixed, the variation of f around the isosurface can be used to model physical properties. The next section explains how to express stiffness with field functions in a way which yields a very simple correspondence between applied forces and resulting deformations.

Correspondence between forces and deformations

A deformable model is defined by a correspondence between forces and deformations. In computer graphics, this correspondence has been given by both linear [13, 6, 14] and non-linear [12] elasticity. In non-linear models, the stiffness k is not only a function of the point P you consider, but may also depend on its current location inside the solid. The applied force during a displacement of P from $X_0 = (x_0, y_0, z_0)$ to $X(P) = (x(P), y(P), z(P))$ is:

$$R(P) = \int_{X_0}^{X(P)} k_P(Y)\, dY \qquad (1)$$

To improve generality, implicit deformable solids should be capable of exhibiting both linear and non-linear behaviors.

In practice, the correspondence between forces and deformations will be used during the collision process, to integrate the reaction forces colinear to normal vectors along contact surfaces between solids. For this application, defining solids with exact elastic properties at each point P along the principal deformation direction (or "radial direction") defined by the normal vector $N(P)$ is sufficient.

To express exact non-linear elasticity in radial directions, we let $dR(Y)$ be a small radial force and dY the resulting small radial displacement. From equation (1) they must satisfy: $k_P(Y)dY = dR(Y)$. If we express deformations by variations in the field function, it yields:

$$df(Y) = Grad(f,Y).dY = Grad(f,Y).\frac{dR(Y)}{k_P(Y)} \quad (2)$$

As said previously, we want to use the way the field function varies inside the implicit solid to express physical properties. Let us directly model stiffness with the field's gradient:

$$\forall Y \quad Grad(f,Y) = -k_P(Y)\, N(Y) \quad (3)$$

This choice simplifies equation (2) which yields:

$$\int_{X_0}^{X(P)} df(Y) = -\int_{X_0}^{X(P)} (N(P).dR(Y)) = -N(P).R(P) \quad (4)$$

where the normal vector $N(P)$ remains constant during radial deformations. Let $g(P) = f(X(P)) - f(X_0)$ be the deformation field term associated at equilibrium with the radial force R. Here, the correspondence formula (4) becomes:

$$g(P) = -N(P).R(P) \quad (5)$$

We use equation (5) to define the general correspondence between deformations and forces characterizing implicit deformable solids. Used with a field function satisfying (3), this correspondence gives exact elastic properties in radial directions, but it associates no deformation at all with forces lying in the local tangent plane. Again, this is not a problem since the formula will only be used for computing the radial component of compression forces due to collisions.

Modeling stiffness with field functions

Let S be an object defined by a single skeleton and P_S a point of this skeleton. The field function along the segment between P_S and the closest point of the surface can be expressed as a function $f(r)$ of the distance $r(P) = d(P, P_S)$. From equation (3), the local stiffness at point P satisfies:
$k(P)\, N(P) = -f'(r(P))\ Grad(r,P)$.
But $Grad(r,P) = (P - P_S)/||P - P_S|| = N(P)$, so:

$$k(P) = -f'(r(P))$$

The resulting geometric representation of stiffness (the opposite of the field function's slope) facilitates the control of the simulated material. The user does not need to be a specialist in mathematical physics to easily design linear and non-linear elastic models as those of Figure 2. The field functions currently implemented are given in Appendix A.

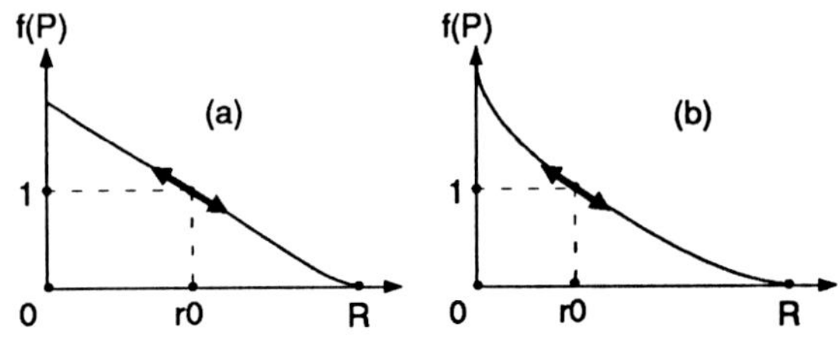

Figure 2: Examples of field functions.
(a) Linear elasticity: stiffness is constant during deformations.
(b) Non-linear elasticity: stiffness increases during compressions.

Homogeneity of the solids

When an object is generated by several skeletons, different field functions f_i can be associated with each one allowing non-homogeneous objects to be readily designed. The object behaves according to the local stiffness k_i in a zone influenced by a single skeleton. Otherwise, stiffness contributions from different skeletons blend together:

$$k(P)N(P) = -Grad(f,P) = -\sum Grad(f_i,P)$$

When "distance surfaces" are used, summing stiffness contributions in blending areas can be a problem. The stiffness may pass by a local extremum while varying between values associated with different skeletons. This problem corresponds to the bulge (or the narrowing) in shape which can appear when two fields superimpose [3]. Indeed, there is no reason why $||\sum_{j=1}^{n} Grad(f_j,P)||$ should take intermediate values between the k_i. In particular, homogeneous objects are not easy to model with distance surfaces. Giving the same field function to all the skeletons is far from sufficient.

"Convolution surfaces", for which field functions f_i are integrals of field contributions from each point of the associated skeleton, solve this problem. With this model, if the same field functions are used for several neighboring skeletons there is no bulge in shape nor in the stiffness function, so complex homogeneous objects can be designed. More generally, stiffness smoothly assumes intermediate values in areas influenced by multiple skeletons as does the field's gradient.

2.3 Animation of implicit deformable solids

Implicit deformable solids are especially suitable for a precise modeling of interactions. While penalty methods directly use the degree of interpenetration between objects to evaluate response forces, our model completely suppresses interpenetrations by introducing an intermediate "contact modeling" step between the detection and the response to collisions. The general animation algorithm is the following: At each time step,

1. Integrate the equations of motion for the rigid components of the solids by taking external forces F and torques T into account:

$$\sum F = mA$$
$$\sum T = I\dot{\Omega} + \Omega \wedge I\Omega$$

where I is the matrix of inertia of a solid computed from its rest shape. A represents linear acceleration and $\dot{\Omega}$ angular acceleration.

2. Displace flexible components from their rest shapes.
3. Treat interactions between objects:
   (a) Detect interpenetrations.
   (b) Model contact by deforming each solid in order to generate contact surfaces.
   (c) Integrate reaction and friction forces. Add them to the set of external actions to be applied to the rigid components at the next time step.
4. Display the objects with their new deformed shapes.

This algorithm is used with an adaptive time step. As with penalty methods, overly deep interpenetrations generate overly large response forces (resulting, in the modeling contact phase, in excessive deformation of the objects). When this situation is detected, the system recomputes the objects positions using a smaller time interval.

The next section details the three steps of the interaction processing module and studies extensions to multiple collisions and to interactions with rigid implicit solids.

3 Interactions between Implicit Solids

3.1 Interpenetration detection

We use axis-parallel bounding boxes to quickly cull most non-intersecting cases. Afterwards, we benefit from the implicit representation of the objects, as in [10]. For each pair of solids, sample points associated with one of them are tested against the inside/outside function of the other. This is done, of course, only for the sample points located inside the second solid's bounding box. As the list of solids interacting together is the only information needed for the modeling contact step, detection is stopped for a given pair of solids as soon as an interpenetration point is found.

The method used for computing sample points at each time step is detailed in Section 4. As will be shown, the detection process can be optimized by starting detection in the neighborhood of points (if any) that most penetrated the other object during the last time step.

3.2 Modeling contact

Once detected, an interpenetration must be suppressed by deforming each object according to the set of interacting solids. Deforming objects involves generating contact surfaces as well as modeling the transverse propagation of deformations (see Figure 3). Rather than simulating local interactions inside the objects, the system directly computes deformed shapes at equilibrium using a model for damped propagation. Deformations outside a given "propagation area", an offset of the interpenetration zone, are ignored.

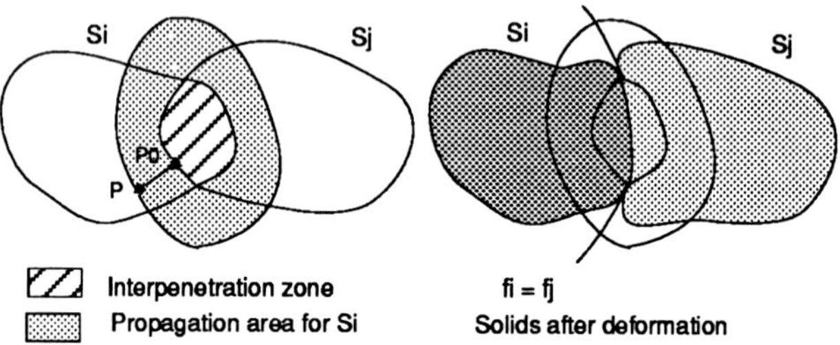

Figure 3: Modeling contact consists in applying different deformation fields in the interpenetration zone and in the "propagation area" associated with each solid (view in cross section).

Interpenetration areas: Generating contact surfaces

In addition to being a very natural model to express physical properties, the implicit surface formalism is also convenient for generating exact contact surfaces. See Figure 4.

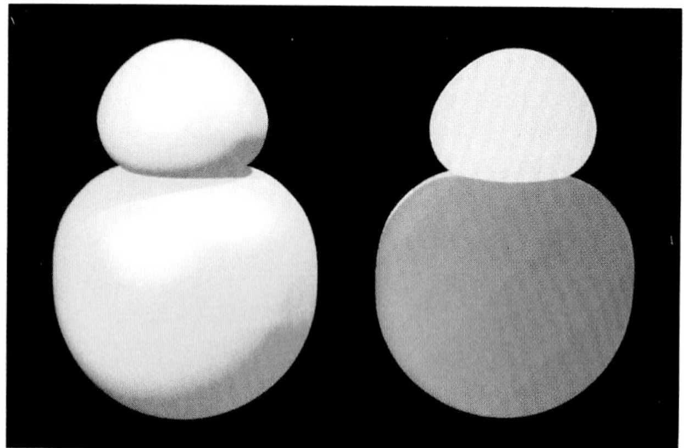

Figure 4: (left) Contact between two colliding objects.
(right) View in cross section showing the exact contact modeling.

Suppose that two objects S_i and S_j interact locally. We are looking for new terms g_{ji} and g_{ij} to add to their respective field functions f_i and f_j in the interpenetration zone (g_{ji} represents the action of object j on object i). After deformation, the objects will be defined in this area by:

$$f_i(P) + g_{ji}(P) = 1 \tag{6}$$

$$f_j(P) + g_{ij}(P) = 1 \tag{7}$$

The deformation fields g_{ji} and g_{ij} must be negative (they model local compression of the objects) and locally generate a contact surface, thus equations (6) and (7) must have common solutions. In order to give the new contact surface exactly the same border as the interpenetration area, deformation fields must satisfy $g_{ij}(P) = g_{ji}(P) = 0$ in points P where $f_i(P) = f_j(P) = 1$. Moreover, the contact surface generated must fit with the local rigidities of colliding objects. So opposite forces must be applied by the two compressed objects on each point of this surface. Adding extra skeletons to generate deformation field terms would be inconvenient; Indeed, we prefer to directly use S_j's skeleton to deform S_i and vice versa. Consequently, the deformation field terms of an interpenetration area are defined by:

$$g_{ji}(P) = 1 - f_j(P)$$
$$g_{ij}(P) = 1 - f_i(P)$$

With this choice, all the properties needed are verified: deformation field terms are negative in the interpenetration zone, and generate a contact surface defined by:

$$f_i(P) = f_j(P) \quad (8)$$

Let $P \in S_i$ be a point of the contact surface, $N_i(P)$ be S_i's unit normal vector, and $N_j(P) = -N_i(P)$.
Let $R_i(P) = ||R_i(P)||N_i(P)$ be the radial force applied by S_j at P. The correspondence (5) between forces and deformations yields : $g_{ji}(P) = -R_i(P).N_i(P) = -||R_i(P)||$, so: $R_i(P) = -g_{ji}(P)N_i(P)$. From equation (8), opposite forces are then applied by the objects along the contact surface:

$$R_i(P) = (1 - f_j(P))\ N_j(P) = (1 - f_i(P))\ N_j(P) = -R_i(P)$$

Deformations in "propagation areas"

We want to optimize the contact modeling process by directly computing deformed shapes in contact positions rather than simulating local interactions inside the flexible material. Designing a purely geometric layer is justified here: only deformations along contact surfaces will be used for computing response forces. The use of geometric propagation will not affect the motion at all. Moreover, we wish to model damped material where deformations outside given "propagation areas" can be neglected. Providing the user with a set of intuitive parameters, such as the thickness of the propagation areas around interpenetration zones or the way deformations are attenuated, offers a simple and efficient control of the simulated material.

More precisely, the user controls S_i's propagation field term $p_{ji}(P)$ (due to the collision with S_j) through two additional parameters in S_i's description:

- A thickness value w_i giving the size of the offset were deformations propagate around an interpenetration zone. Deformations will be neglected outside this area.
- An "attenuation value" α_i giving the ratio between the maximal value desired for p_{ji} and the current maximal compression term in the interpenetration area.

Because of the parameter α_i, the size of the bulge due to propagation of deformations will first increase during a collision, while the solid is progressively compressed, and then decrease back to zero when the colliding objects move off.

The propagation field p_{ji} must be positive within the propagation area in order to model a local expansion of the solid, compensating for the compression due to collision. To preserve the shape's first order continuity[2] p_{ji} and its derivative must become zero at the exterior limit of the propagation area, and have the same value and gradient vector as the contact term g_{ji} in the border of the interpenetration zone. Let P be a point within the propagation area, and P_0 the closest point of S_j in S_j's gradient direction (see Figure 3). To satisfy the conditions just listed, we define p_{ji} along the line (P_0, P) by:

$$p_{ji}(P) = a_{k,a0,w_i}(d(P, P_0))$$

where $k = ||Grad(f_j, P_0)||$, a_0 is the maximal propagation value equal to α_i times the maximal compression field value, and $a_{k,a0,w}(x)$ is the piecewise polynomial function shown in Figure 5. An exact formula is given in Appendix B.

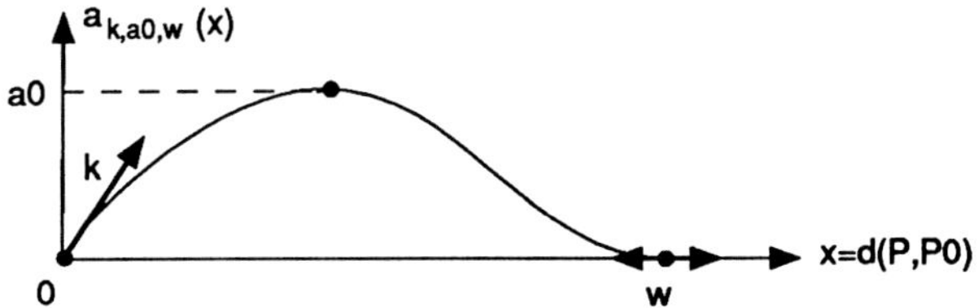

Figure 5: Attenuation function defining the propagation field.

With this choice, all the conditions on p_{ji} can be verified. Let us prove that $Grad(p_{ji}, P_0) = Grad(g_{ji}, P_0)$.

$$Grad(p_{ji}, P) = a'_{k,a0,w_i}(d(P, P_0))\ N_0$$

With the value of $a_{k,a0,w_i}$'s derivative in zero, we obtain:

$$Grad(p_{j,i}, P_0) = -Grad(f_j, P_0) = Grad(g_{ji}, P_0)$$

Expansion of the objects in propagation areas must not produce new interpenetrations. To best avoid this situation, we insure that each deformed object does not cross the median surfaces of equation $f_i(P) = f_j(P)$ (see Figure 3). In other words, $p_{j,i}(P)$ must be less than or equal to $1 - f_j(P)$ throughout the propagation area. If the problem does occur, the system truncates the propagation term and issues a warning that a smaller value should be chosen for α_i.

3.3 Computation of response forces

Radial reaction forces

The reaction forces directed along normal vectors are given by the correspondence (5) between forces and deformations. They are are numerically integrated along contact surfaces (this process is detailed in Section 4). Because of our choice for the contact surface, the principle that opposite reactions occur on two colliding objects is verified.

Friction and damping forces

To model both tangential friction in contact areas and damping due to the progressive compression of the solids, we include a friction coefficient λ_i in the description of each object. When a collision occurs, the friction and damping force F_i at a point P of the contact surface between S_i and S_j is expressed by:

$$F_i(P) = \lambda_i \lambda_j (V_j(P) - V_i(P)) \quad (9)$$

[2]The method would be easy to extend to higher order continuity by considering constraints over higher order derivatives, and by using more complex attenuation functions.

where $V_i(P)$ (respectively $V_j(P)$) is the speed of P, a point on the surface of the solid S_i (respectively S_j). Like radial reaction forces, friction forces are numerically integrated along contact surfaces.

Figure 6 shows the action of response forces during a few steps of an animation.

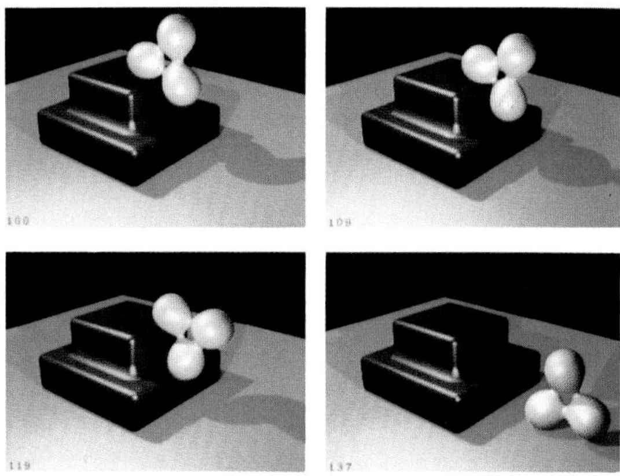

Figure 6: Flexible clover falling on a quite rigid staircase.

From collisions to lasting contacts

The deformed shapes generated during the contact modeling step can be conveniently used for lasting contacts and equilibrium states, because opposite forces are applied to each side of a contact surface. In Equation (9), F_i's tangential component represents friction due to the different tangential speeds of the solids at a contact point, while the normal component models the loss of energy due to the progressive deformation of the solids. The energy consumed over time enables colliding objects to settle into lasting contact situations, and then into resting stable states without unwanted oscillations. Figure 7 is an example of equilibrium state between four solids.

Figure 7: An equilibrium state between a rigid floor, a flexible vaulting horse, and two soft balls.

3.4 Multiple interactions

An important benefit of our model is that, in multiple interaction situations such as in Figure 7, the resulting shapes and reaction forces are *completely independent* of the order in which objects, or pairs of objects, are considered.

When an object interacts with several others, its compression field term (which produces the contact forces) is defined as a sum of terms due to the different collisions. No propagation term must be added in an interpenetration zone with another object, so, in practice, we always use a procedural method to compute field values. To evaluate the field generated by a deformed object S_0 at a given point P:

1. Compute the initial field value $f_0(P)$.
2. For each object S_i interacting with S_0, if P lies inside S_i, add the contact deformation term $1 - f_i(P)$.
3. If P was not lying inside any of the S_i, compute and sum all non-zero propagation terms at P. Truncate this sum if needed (as explained at the end of Section 3.2) before adding it to the field value.

If an intersection area is detected between more than two solids as in Figure 8, several negative compression terms are simultaneously added in this area. This leaves a small space between the solids, whose shapes remain C^1 continuous (generating multiple contact points would produce singularities).

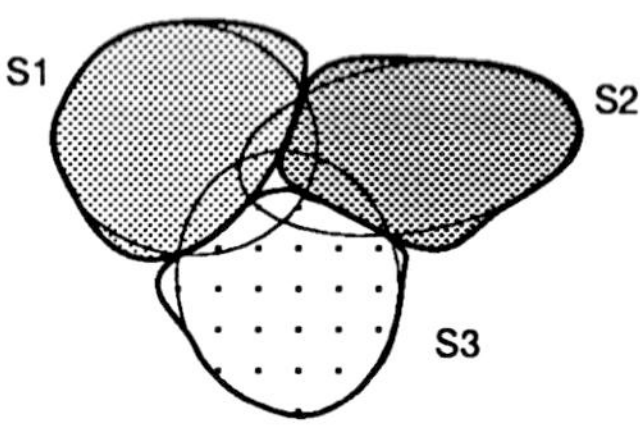

Figure 8: Deformation of 3 intersecting solids (cross sections).

3.5 Interactions with rigid implicit solids

Another important issue for our model is its ability to simulate interactions between flexible and rigid objects[3], like the vaulting horse and the floor in Figure 7.

Suppose an interpenetration has been detected between a rigid solid S_j and a flexible object S_i. The deformation field term applied to S_i in the contact area must make S_i exactly fit S_j's shape; i.e., the solutions of $f_i(P)+g_{ji}(P) = 1$ must be points satisfying $f_j(P) = 1$. Moreover, the deformation field term must be negative in the interpenetration zone given by $f_i(P) \geq 1, f_i(P) \geq 1$. Then, we define $g_{ji}(P)$ by:

$$g_{ji}(P) = (1 - f_j(P)) + (1 - f_i(P))$$

The usual formula is used for the attenuation function in S_i's propagation area. Simply, S_j's gradient vector (used to

[3] Analytical solutions such as those developed in [1] should be used for interactions between pairs of rigid objects.

define the slope of the attenuation function) is now replaced by $-(Grad(f_i + f_j, P_0))$ so that the bulge will exactly fit S_j's normal vectors at the border of the contact surface. When this is done, response forces corresponding to S_i's deformation are integrated along the contact surface, and opposite forces are applied to the rigid solid S_j according to the principle that opposite reactions occur on two colliding objects.

4 Implementation

Our modeling and animation system for implicit deformable solids is implemented in C++ on an SGI Indigo workstation. The current implementation uses distance surfaces which provide us with analytical expressions of normal vectors.

4.1 Optimizing the animation process

One of the main problems raised by implicit isosurfaces is the search for efficient ways to discretize objects. The animation process uses discretizations three times by animation step: for collision detection, for integrating response forces, and for displaying objects. Despite recent improvements in adaptive octree techniques, spatial partitioning polygonizations remain quite expensive. Using this type of algorithm at each time step would prevent any interactive computation and display of the animation.

Fortunately, the solids only deform locally during animations and return to their rest shapes. Their topology never changes (otherwise, our hybrid model with its invariant matrix of inertia would be invalid). Consequently, the objects need not be completely re-sampled at each time step.

Before an animation is calculated, sample points and the associated normal vectors are precomputed form the object's rest shape, and stored relative to the local coordinate system. Then, at each animation step:

- The sample points are positioned according to the current position and orientation of the solid's rigid component.
- They are used to detect collisions. To benefit from temporal coherence, tests for interpenetration are first performed in the neighborhood of points P_j which penetrated most deeply into the other object at the previous time step[4].
- Finally, the sample points in deformed areas are recomputed, before display, by using a linear search algorithm along the undeformed normal direction. The use of this direction insures that the points will come back to their initial positions after any deformation.

  To improve in efficiency, response forces in contact areas are integrated during this process. If a point is located in an interpenetration zone, the field function computes the deformation term, which is equal to the local reaction force. As soon as a point of the contact surface is found, this force (plus the friction force term), multiplied by the area of an elementary surface ds, is added to the sum of external actions applied to the object. In the current implementation, ds is approximated by an average value computed from the size of the discretization voxels.

[4] We use a continuation method for sampling, so starting detection a few points before P_j in the list of sample points is sufficient.

4.2 Rendering

The implicit formalism provides us with exact high level descriptions of deformed solids, even if only a few sample points are used during the computations. During animations, we directly save the parameters needed to compute the deformed field functions defining the objects (including stiffness, scope of influence, attenuation parameters, and the current list of colliding objects). To give an idea of required disc space, the file describing the implicit objects of Figure 7 take less than 1 Kbyte, while the storage of the associated sample points with their normal vectors and the list of triangles takes more than 1200 Kbyte.

Once the objects are stored, any method could be used for rendering, including computing polygonizations with an arbitrary precision. We currently use direct ray-tracing on implicit surfaces, implemented as an extension to the public domain renderer *Rayshade* (by C. Kolb). If a ray intersects an implicit solid's bounding box, we first look for a seed point along the ray which is located inside the solid. If we find one, an intersection point is computed by binary search. Testing if a point is inside or outside is done by evaluating the solid's potential field. Normal vectors at the intersection points are analytically computed from the field gradient.

5 Conclusion

This paper presents a novel way to model deformable solids. The implicit formalism provides a compact and unified formulation for both geometric and physical properties, and enables to keep a continuous high level representation of the objects. The model offers simple and quite general control of the simulated material. One can experiment with field function curves to adjust stiffness variations when objects are compressed, or with different ways to propagate deformations due to collisions. All the parameters are easy to understand, even for a non-specialist.

Well adapted to local deformations, the system is especially designed for a precise modeling of interactions. It generates exact contact surfaces between solids which facilitates a precise evaluation of reaction forces. The model applies to sudden collisions, lasting contacts, and equilibrium situations. It gives an elegant solution to the multiple collision problem, producing new deformed shapes and response forces which are independent of the order in which collisions are detected. The model can be generalized to treat interactions between flexible and rigid objects.

During animations, discretized representations of the objects are displayed at interactive rates, while a compact storage of their implicit description is performed. This description, which still defines curved contact surfaces, is used for producing subsequent, high-quality images.

Future work

Implementing convolution surfaces [3] would facilitate the design of complex objects composed of homogeneous materials. To improve generality, these surfaces should be extended to non-exponential potential fields.

At present, deformed shapes only depend on the set of external forces currently applied to the solids, so deformations disappear as soon as there is no longer contact between objects. Modeling visco-elastic or elasto-plastic behaviors in addition to pure elasticity would be a good extension. Moreover, some objects of the real world conserve their volume during deformations while others are partially compressible. Modeling the propagation of deformations according to a compressibility parameter would provide easier control.

The implicit deformable model opens new directions for future research, particularly within the area of human simulation. Modeling complex objects such as deformable flesh covering rigid skeletons could not be done with previous global deformation techniques (the skeleton must not be deformed, nor the flesh on the opposite side of the skeleton). Nodal approaches can be used, but they demand complicated databases [6] and involve an expensive numerical simulation of deformations propagating in damped material. Our ability to model local deformations while preserving a compact continuous representation of objects, even when they are non-homogeneous, would be helpful. Moreover, the precise contact modeling presented here should allow human models to interact with the simulated world.

Acknowledgements

Many thanks to Jean-Dominique Gascuel for his constant support during this research and for implementing direct ray-tracing on implicit surfaces. Thanks to Philippe Limantour, Christophe Vedel, Frédéric Asensio and Julien Signes for interesting early discussions, and to François Sillion, Alain Chesnais, Dave Forsey, Phil Brock and Jules Bloomenthal for re-reading this paper.

References

[1] David Baraff. Dynamic simulation of non-penetrating rigid bodies. *PHD Thesis*, Cornell University, May 1992.

[2] David Baraff and Andrew Witkin. Dynamic simulation of non-penetrating flexible bodies. *Computer Graphics*, 26(2):303–308, July 1992. Proceedings of SIGGRAPH'92 (Chicago, Illinois, July 1992).

[3] Jules Bloomenthal and Ken Shoemake. Convolution surfaces. *Computer Graphics*, 25(4):251–256, July 1991. Proceedings of SIGGRAPH'91 (Las Vegas, Nevada, July 1991).

[4] Jules Bloomenthal and Brian Wyvill. Interactive techniques for implicit modeling. *Computer Graphics*, 24(2):109–116, March 1990.

[5] Marie-Paule Gascuel, Anne Verroust, and Claude Puech. A modeling system for complex deformable bodies suited to animation and collision processing. *Journal of Visualization and Computer Animation*, 2(3), August 1991. A shorter version of this paper appeared in *Graphics Interface'91*.

[6] Jean-Paul Gourret, Nadia Magnenat Thalmann, and Daniel Thalmann. Simulation of object and human skin deformations in a grasping task. *Computer Graphics*, 23(3):21–29, July 1989. Proceedings of SIGGRAPH'89 (Boston, MA, July 1989).

[7] Annie Luciani, Stéphane Jimenez, Olivier Raoult, Claude Cadoz, and Jean-Loup Florens. An unified view of multitude behaviour, flexibility, plasticity, and fractures: balls, bubbles and agglomerates. In *IFIP WG 5.10 Working Conference*, Tokyo, Japan, April 1991.

[8] Gavin Miller. The motion dynamics of snakes and worms. *Computer Graphics*, 22(4):169–177, August 1988. Proceedings of SIGGRAPH'88 (Atlanta, August 1988).

[9] Matthew Moore and Jane Wilhelms. Collision detection and response for computer animation. *Computer Graphics*, 22(4):289–298, August 1988. Proceedings of SIGGRAPH'88 (Atlanta, August 1988).

[10] Alex Pentland and John Williams. Good vibrations: Modal dynamics for graphics and animation. *Computer Graphics*, 23(3):215–222, July 1989. Proceedings of SIGGRAPH'89 (Boston, MA, July 1989).

[11] Demetri Terzopoulos and Dimitri Metaxas. Dynamic 3-D models with local and global deformations : deformable super quadrics. *IEEE Transactions on Pattern Analysis and Machine Intelligence*, PAMI-13(7):703–714, July 1991.

[12] Demetri Terzopoulos, John Platt, Alan Barr, and Kurt Fleischer. Elastically deformable models. *Computer Graphics*, 21(4):205–214, July 1987. Proceedings of SIGGRAPH'87 (Anaheim, California, July 1987).

[13] Demetri Terzopoulos and Andrew Witkin. Physically based model with rigid and deformable components. *IEEE Computer Graphics and Applications*, pages 41–51, December 1988.

[14] Andrew Witkin and William Welch. Fast animation and control for non-rigid structures. *Computer Graphics*, 24(4):243–252, August 1990. Proceedings of SIGGRAPH'90 (Dallas, Texas, August 1990).

Appendix A. Equation for the field functions

Field functions currently implemented are parameterized by a scope of influence R, a thickness value r_0, and a stiffness value k:

$$\begin{aligned} f_i(P) &= ar^2 + br + c && \text{if } r \in [0, r_0] \\ f_i(P) &= (r-R)^2(dr+e) && \text{if } r \in [r_0, R] \\ f_i(P) &= 0 && \text{elsewhere} \end{aligned}$$

$d = -(k(r_0 - R)+2)/(r_0 - R)^3$, $e = (kr_0(r_0 - R)+3r_0 - R)/(r_0 - R)^3$.

If linear elasticity is chosen, $a = 0$, $b = -k$ and $c = kr_0 + 1$. If non-linear elasticity is selected, we use $a = k/(2r_0)$, $b = -2k$, $c = 3kr_0/2 + 1$ (of course any other stiffness variation inside the object would be easy to implement).

Appendix B. Equation for the attenuation function

The equation we use for the attenuation function is:

$$\begin{aligned} a_{k,a0,w}(r) &= cr^3 + dr^2 + kr && \text{if } r \in [0, w/2] \\ a_{k,a0,w}(r) &= \frac{4a0 + (x-w)^2(4x-w)}{w^3} && \text{if } r \in [w/2, w] \end{aligned}$$

Where $c = 4(wk - 4a0)/w^3$ and $d = 4(3a0 - wk)/w^2$.

Interval Methods for Multi-Point Collisions between Time-Dependent Curved Surfaces

John M. Snyder, Adam R. Woodbury,
Kurt Fleischer, Bena Currin, Alan H. Barr
California Institute of Technology
Pasadena, CA 91125

Abstract

We present an efficient and robust algorithm for finding points of collision between time-dependent parametric and implicit surfaces. The algorithm detects simultaneous collisions at multiple points of contact. When the regions of contact form curves or surfaces, it returns a finite set of points uniformly distributed over each contact region.

Collisions can be computed for a very general class of surfaces: those for which inclusion functions can be constructed. Included in this set are the familiar kinds of surfaces and time behaviors encountered in computer graphics.

We use a new interval approach for constrained minimization to detect collisions, and a tangency condition to reduce the dimensionality of the search space. These approaches make interval methods practical for multi-point collisions between complex surfaces. An interval Newton method based on the solution of the interval linear equation is used to speed convergence to the collision time and location. This method is more efficient than the Krawczyk–Moore iteration used previously in computer graphics.

CR Categories: I.3.5 [Computer Graphics]: Computational Geometry and Object Modeling; G.4 [Mathematical Software]: Reliability and Robustness

General Terms: collision detection, parametric surface, constrained minimization, interval analysis

Additional Key Words: inclusion function, interval Newton method, interval linear equation

1 Introduction

Detecting geometric collisions between curved, time-dependent (moving and deforming) objects is an important and difficult problem in computer graphics. This paper discusses a practical and robust algorithm for detecting collisions between objects represented as parametric or implicit surfaces. We ignore the problem of computing the physical response to collisions; much of this topic is treated in other work [BARA90,META92]. Instead, we concentrate on the purely geometric problem of computing a solution set

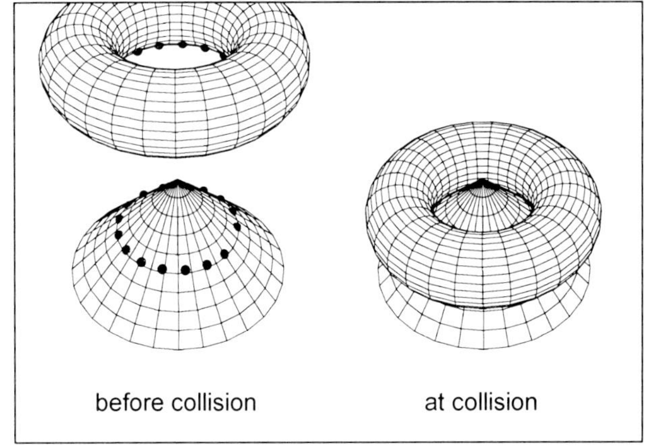

Figure 1: Problem Statement: Given a collection of time-dependent curved surfaces, find a set of collision points representing the contact regions. In this example, the dots show the points detected by the collision algorithm when a torus moves down over a cone, contacting it in a circle.

of points where a set of time-dependent surfaces first contact (Figure 1).

Previous work on geometric collision detection is fairly extensive, both in computer graphics and in other fields such as CAD/CAM and robotics. Detection of collisions between polyhedral objects was studied in [MOOR88]. Baraff [BARA90] presented a method of computing collisions between parametric or implicit surfaces by computing extremal points using non-linear equation solvers. Sclaroff and Pentland [SCLA91] present a method for detecting collisions between implicit surfaces by "plugging" vertices of a polyhedral approximation of one surface into the inside-outside function of the other. Von Herzen, et. al., [VONH90] presented an algorithm for detecting collisions of parametric surfaces using Lipschitz bounds. Duff [DUFF92] used interval methods to compute collisions between boolean combinations of implicit surfaces.

To make collision detection practical, much of the previous work traded off accuracy and robustness for efficiency, or limited the kinds of shapes that could be handled. Polyhedral methods such as in [MOOR88], although fairly efficient, are not well suited to surfaces that deform in time. Exploiting coherence for rolling or sliding contact of polyhedral objects is difficult, and use of a fixed sampling mesh can cause severe approximation errors. Polyhedral methods also require many numerically difficult special cases which led [MOOR88] and [SCLA91] to neglect cases where "tunneling" may occur either between polygon edges or between small implicit surfaces passing entirely through a large polygon.

Baraff [BARA90] chose to limit objects to the union of con-

 ACM-0-89791-601-8/93/008/0321 $01.50

```
take one or more steps in the ODE solver
compute collisions in the resulting time interval
if a collision occurs (at time t*) in the interval
      compute a collision response
      reset ODE solver to t = t*
endif
```

Figure 2: Computational Model for Collision Detection and Response

vex polyhedra and strictly convex closed surfaces. This restriction simplified his collision detection algorithm and allowed tracking of single contact points between curved objects. He did not treat non-convex surfaces (such as saddle shapes) and manifolds with boundary (such as half a sphere). We solve the problem for a more general class of surfaces with many points of contact, as shown in Figure 1.

As noted in [VONH90], methods which depend solely on point-wise evaluations, including the above methods, cannot guarantee accurate collision detection. To solve this problem, Von Herzen bounded the output of functions over a region using a Lipschitz bound. Duff [DUFF92] used interval analysis to produce tighter bounds than Von Herzen's Lipschitz bound. Both of these methods used binary subdivision to search for collisions; we speed up the approach significantly by combining binary subdivision with an interval Newton method.

The technique we describe offers several fundamental improvements over previous techniques:

1. The most novel aspect of our technique is the ability to detect simultaneous collisions (multiple contacts at the same time), *even when the collisions occur at a higher dimensional manifold of contact, rather than at a set of isolated points.* In this case, the algorithm samples the region of contact with a finite, uniformly-distributed set of points. The spatial sampling density is a parameter to the algorithm. To our knowledge, no previous algorithm handles this situation.
2. Our technique works for both rigid and deforming objects, and for implicit or parametric objects.
3. Our technique is practical for computer graphics applications, and has been used in animations involving hundreds of objects.
4. Our technique includes a method (tangency constraints) to reduce the dimensionality of the space of possible solution points, as shown in Figure 3, dramatically speeding up the method. The tangency constraints also provide a square system of equations for the interval Newton method, helping us detect isolated point collisions.
5. Our technique uses a test for uniqueness of roots of a system of equations in a region. This test can be verified in many cases, allowing the algorithm to terminate without further subdivision around collision points.
6. Our technique can be used both to compute collisions between formerly disjoint bodies which come into contact, or to compute additional points of contact between bodies as they roll or slide over each other (see Section 1.1).

1.1 Fitting Collision Detection into a Larger System

Figure 2 shows how collision detection fits into a larger program for computing physical simulations of dynamic systems. The system is composed of three parts: the ODE (ordinary differential equation) solver module, the collision detection module, and the collision response computation module. The ODE solver computes the motions of objects over time, using equations governing the dynamic behavior of bodies, and produces a functional representation of the motion.[1] Motion is computed without considering collisions, so that the results are only valid until the next collision occurs. The collision detection module takes the functional representation produced by the ODE solver and computes when and where the first collision occurs in the given time interval. If a collision occurs, a collision response is computed, which may discontinuously change the state of the system of bodies. The ODE solver continues forward in time from this computed collision time, discarding any state after it.

Two modes of operation are required in collision detection:

1. compute any collisions for bodies that are initially not in contact
2. compute *additional* collisions for bodies that are already in continuous (rolling or sliding) contact

The algorithm described in this paper handles both situations. For greatest efficiency and modularity, we advocate handling coherence in the ODE solver. By coherence, we mean the tracking of contact points between bodies rolling or sliding over each other. In these situations, collision detection is required only to compute new points of contact not already tracked by the ODE solver (mode 2 above). The solver must therefore inform the collision detection module of the motion of the contact points it is tracking, so that these points may be excluded from consideration (see Eq. 7). The collision detection module must also compute the initial points of contact when the simulation is begun or when continuous contact begins between bodies (mode 1 above).

1.2 Overview

The mathematics of the collision detection problem is treated in Section 2. Sections 3, 4, and 5 discuss the constrained minimization algorithm, an interval Newton enhancement, and termination criteria, respectively. Section 6 presents a simple culling test which discards non-colliding surface pairs and tightens a bound on the collision time. The full collision algorithm, combining constrained minimization, the culling test, and other tools from computational geometry, is presented in Section 7. Our technique, like all interval methods, requires inclusion functions, whose construction is summarized in Section 8. Finally, results and conclusions are described in Sections 9 and 10. Appendix A extends our approach to surfaces that are piecewise smooth by adding conditions for face, edge, and vertex interactions (see Figure 11). Appendix B describes the construction of inclusion functions for Chebyshev polynomials.

2 The Collision Problem

The equations that specify that two surfaces collide may be divided into two parts: a *contact* constraint, that specifies that the two surfaces intersect, and a *tangency* constraint, that specifies that the two surfaces are tangent at their point of intersection. The tangency constraint reduces the dimensionality of the space of possible collision points, as shown in Figure 3. It also allows faster convergence (using interval Newton, which we will describe in Section 4)

[1] In our rigid body simulations, the solver produces a time-varying quaternion and translation vector. Each component of the quaternion and vector is represented using univariate Chebyshev polynomials.

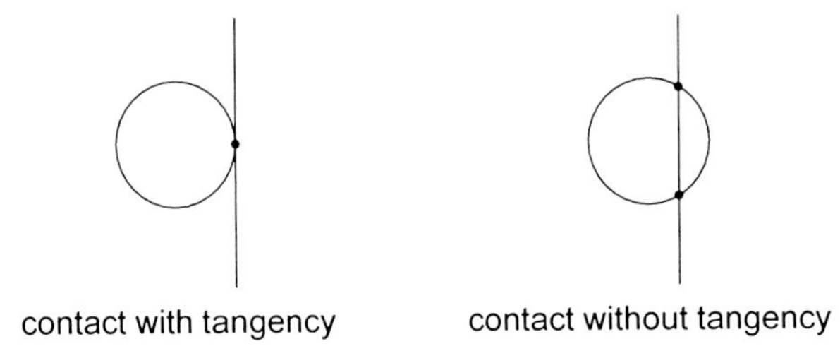

Figure 3: Reducing the Dimensionality of the Space of Collision Points Using the Tangency Condition: The intersection of two bodies (like a sphere moving to the right with a stationary plane) typically forms a whole 2D manifold of contact through time. With the tangency constraint, the solution space is often reduced to one or a few points by eliminating cases like that shown on the right. Reducing the solution space to an isolated space-time point is one of the ideas that makes this method practical.

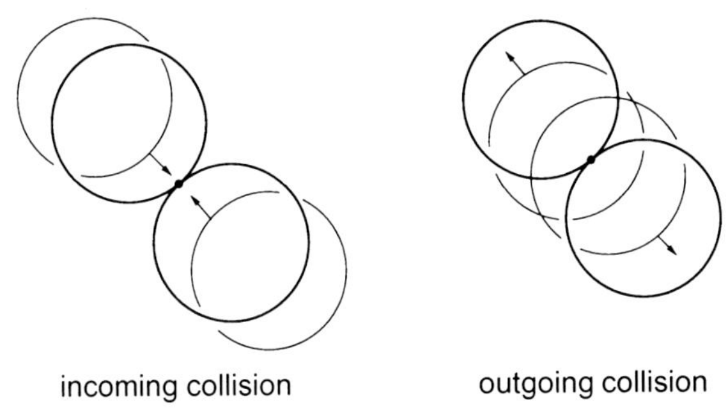

Figure 4: Incoming and Outgoing Collisions: The unbroken circles represent bodies later in time. A dot represents the collision point; the arrows represent the direction of movement.

and robust testing of isolated collisions (using an interval solution uniqueness test described in Section 5).

We also distinguish between *incoming* collisions, in which the surfaces collide by moving closer to each other, and *outgoing* collisions, in which the surfaces are interpenetrating and become tangent as they move apart. These situations are compared in Figure 4. The distinction is necessary in the simulation of dynamic systems where each surface encloses a solid. Eliminating outgoing collisions allows the simulator to ignore collisions which were previously detected; i.e., collisions between surfaces already in contact which are moving away as a *response* to the collision.

2.1 Parametric Surfaces

Let two deforming parametric surfaces be represented by the twice-differentiable mappings $S_1(u_1, v_1, t)$ and $S_2(u_2, v_2, t)$, where $S_i\colon \mathbf{R}^3 \rightarrow \mathbf{R}^3$. At a particular instant of time, each of the surfaces is formed by the image of S_i over a rectangle in (u_i, v_i) space.[2] In this section, we consider the case of collisions between solids each bounded by a single, smooth, closed parametric surface. Appendix A generalizes the discussion to parametric surfaces which are only piecewise smooth.

Contact Constraint The contact constraint merely states that the two surfaces intersect (i.e., the vector difference of the two surfaces is the zero vector):

$$S_1(u_1, v_1, t) - S_2(u_2, v_2, t) = 0. \qquad (1)$$

Tangency Constraint The tangency constraint implies that the instantaneous normal vectors on the two surfaces at their point of contact are anti-parallel. Stated another way, the (u, v) tangent vectors on one surface must be perpendicular to the instantaneous normal vector on the other surface. We thus have the following system of two equations[3]

$$\begin{pmatrix} \frac{\partial S_1}{\partial u_1}(u_1, v_1, t) \cdot N_2(u_2, v_2, t) \\ \frac{\partial S_1}{\partial v_1}(u_1, v_1, t) \cdot N_2(u_2, v_2, t) \end{pmatrix} = 0 \qquad (2)$$

where N_1 and N_2 are the outward normal vectors to the surfaces S_1 and S_2, respectively, given by

$$N_i(u_i, v_i, t) \equiv \frac{\partial S_i}{\partial u_i}(u_i, v_i, t) \times \frac{\partial S_i}{\partial v_i}(u_i, v_i, t) \quad \text{for } i = 1, 2.$$

The algorithms that follow here assume that N_1 and N_2 are nowhere 0; that is, surfaces have a nonvanishing normal vector everywhere and for all relevant time.[4] The whole collision equality constraint is given by a nonlinear system of 5 equations in 5 variables, three from Eq. 1 and two from Eq. 2.

Incoming Constraint The incoming collision condition states that the relative velocity of the collision point must face the same way as the surface normal (the two vectors must form an acute angle),[5] and the two normals must face in opposite directions (forming an obtuse angle). This condition yields two inequality constraints:

$$\begin{aligned} &\left(\frac{\partial S_1}{\partial t}(u_1, v_1, t) - \frac{\partial S_2}{\partial t}(u_2, v_2, t)\right) \cdot N_1(u_1, v_1, t) \geq 0 \\ &\text{and} \quad -N_1(u_1, v_1, t) \cdot N_2(u_2, v_2, t) \geq 0. \end{aligned} \qquad (3)$$

2.1.1 Example: Rigid Parametric Surfaces

The above constraints may be applied to the special case of rigid parametric surfaces. In this case, we have two time-independent surfaces $s_1(u_1, v_1)$ and $s_2(u_1, v_1)$. The time-varying version of these surfaces is given by

$$S_i(u_i, v_i, t) \equiv R_i(t) s_i(u_1, v_1) + T_i(t) \quad \text{for } i = 1, 2$$

where $R_i(t)$ is a time-varying rotation matrix and $T_i(t)$ is a time-varying translation vector, specifying the trajectory of surface i's coordinate origin.

Contact Constraint The contact constraint may be expressed as

$$R_1(t) s_1(u_1, v_1) + T_1(t) - R_2(t) s_2(u_2, v_2) - T_2(t) = 0.$$

[2] Using a rectangular domain for parametric surfaces does not limit the kinds of surfaces that can be collided. Parametric surfaces defined on non-rectangular domains can be handled by mapping a rectangle into the required non-rectangular domain before mapping onto the surface [SNYD92b].

[3] A similar, though functionally dependent, constraint may be derived by switching S_1 and S_2.

[4] If the calculated normal vector becomes zero, such as at the poles of a parametric sphere, the tangency constraint becomes trivially true. The algorithm will therefore rely on the contact constraint to detect a collision in this case.

[5] We assume here that the surfaces are parameterized so that the normals N_1 and N_2 face outward.

Tangency Constraint Let $n_1(u_1, v_1)$ and $n_2(u_2, v_2)$ be the time-independent normals of the surfaces s_1 and s_2, given by

$$n_i(u_i, v_i) \equiv \frac{\partial s_i}{\partial u_i}(u_i, v_i) \times \frac{\partial s_i}{\partial v_i}(u_i, v_i).$$

The time-varying surface normals can therefore be expressed as

$$N_i(u_i, v_i, t) \equiv R_i(t)\, n_i(u_i, v_i)$$

since $R_i(t)$ is a rotation matrix. The tangency constraint is then given by

$$\begin{pmatrix} (R_1(t)\, \frac{\partial s_1}{\partial u_1}(u_1, v_1)) \cdot N_2(u_2, v_2, t) \\ (R_1(t)\, \frac{\partial s_1}{\partial u_2}(u_1, v_1)) \cdot N_2(u_2, v_2, t) \end{pmatrix} = 0.$$

Incoming Constraint The incoming constraint is given by

$$\left[\dot{R}_1(t) s_1(u_1, v_1) + \dot{T}_1(t) - \dot{R}_2(t) s_2(u_2, v_2) - \dot{T}_2(t)\right] \cdot N_1(u_1, v_1, t) \geq 0$$

$$\text{and} \quad -N_1(u_1, v_1, t) \cdot N_2(u_2, v_2, t) \geq 0$$

where $\dot{R}_i$ and $\dot{T}_i$ are the time derivatives of the rotation matrix and translation vector of the two surfaces.

2.2 Implicit Surfaces

Let two time-varying implicit surfaces be represented using the scalar functions $F_1(x, y, z, t)$ and $F_2(x, y, z, t)$. Points on each surface are defined as the zero-sets of these functions.

Contact Constraint The contact constraint is the system of two equations

$$\begin{pmatrix} F_1(x, y, z, t) \\ F_2(x, y, z, t) \end{pmatrix} = 0. \tag{4}$$

Tangency Constraint Let the function $\nabla F_i(x, y, z, t)$ be the spatial gradient of the implicit functions (i.e., with respect to x, y, and z). The tangency constraint is then given by

$$\nabla F_1(x, y, z, t) \times \nabla F_2(x, y, z, t) = 0. \tag{5}$$

This constraint, although a system of three equations, contains only two functionally dependent equations. The entire collision equality constraint for implicit surfaces is thus given by a system of five (four functionally independent) equations in the four variables x, y, z, and t (Eqs. 4 and 5).[6]

Incoming Constraint The incoming constraint is given by

$$-\frac{\partial F_1}{\partial t}(x, y, z, t)\, \|\nabla F_2(x, y, z, t)\| - \frac{\partial F_2}{\partial t}(x, y, z, t)\, \|\nabla F_1(x, y, z, t)\| \geq 0 \tag{6}$$

$$\text{and} \quad -\nabla F_1(x, y, z, t) \cdot \nabla F_2(x, y, z, t) \geq 0.$$

[6]We note that detecting collisions between implicit and parametric surfaces is a simpler problem than colliding pairs of parametric or implicit surfaces. By substituting the output of the parametric surface as the input (x, y, z) of the implicit surface, a system in 3 variables, (u, v, t), results, where u and v are the parametric surface coordinates.

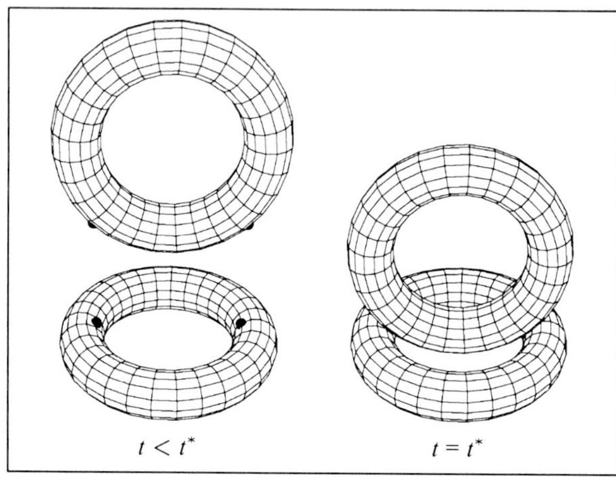

Figure 5: Simultaneous Collisions — The tori collide at two isolated points.

We also note that CSG operations on implicit surfaces, as in [DUFF92], can be handled very efficiently using our techniques. Assume the surface F_1 is represented as the boolean subtraction of two simple implicit surfaces $F_a(x, y, z, t)$ and $F_b(x, y, z, t)$. The first equation in the contact constraint (Eq. 4) then becomes

$$(F_a = 0 \text{ and } F_b \geq 0) \text{ or } (F_b = 0 \text{ and } F_a \leq 0)$$

assuming implicit surface functions are positive outside the surface they represent. Similar restricted equality constraints can be derived for the tangency constraint.

Constraints for rigid motion of implicit surfaces are easily derived by applying the above general equations to the rigidly moving implicit surface

$$F(x, y, z, t) \equiv f(w) \text{ where } w \equiv R^T(t)((x, y, z)^T - T(t))$$

where $f: \mathbf{R}^3 \rightarrow \mathbf{R}$ is the implicit equation of the time-independent surface, $R^T(t)$ is the transpose of the time-varying rotation matrix, and $T(t)$ is the time-varying translation vector.

2.3 Collision As a Constrained Minimization Problem

The final collision constraint may be described as an equality constraint involving a function C (for the contact and tangency constraints) and a logical composition of inequality constraints involving a function D (for the incoming constraint). For collisions between parametric surfaces, C and D are vector functions of (u_1, v_1, u_2, v_2, t) (equations 1–3); for implicit surfaces they are functions of (x, y, z, t) (equations 4–6). We are interested only in the minimum t collision, since our representation for the time behavior of the surfaces may be invalid after this time.

The desired collision time for parametric surfaces, t^*, can therefore be expressed using the constrained minimization problem

$$\underset{(u_1, v_1, u_2, v_2, t) \in X_0}{\text{minimum}} \left\{ t \;\middle|\; \begin{matrix} C(u_1, v_1, u_2, v_2, t) = 0 & \text{and} \\ D(u_1, v_1, u_2, v_2, t) \geq 0 & \end{matrix} \right\}.$$

A similar statement results for detection of collisions between implicit surfaces. We would like to compute t^* or detect that the constraint is satisfied nowhere in the parameter space X_0.

We also need the location of the collision and the surface normal vectors there. There may be multiple points of contact at the time of collision, which we call *simultaneous* collisions, as shown in Figure 5. The points of contact may be a finite number of *isolated points* as in Figure 5, or they may form a curve or surface, called the *contact manifold*. For example, if the falling torus from Figure 5 were in the same orientation as the stationary one at the bottom, the collision points would form a circle.

To detect simultaneous collisions, we need to detect minimum t solutions which are simultaneous or simultaneous within some tolerance ϵ. Mathematically, we require the set of *collision points* $(u_1^*, v_1^*, u_2^*, v_2^*)$ such that

$$C(u_1^*, v_1^*, u_2^*, v_2^*, t^*) = 0 \text{ and } D(u_1^*, v_1^*, u_2^*, v_2^*, t^*) \geq 0.$$

For a given collision point, the location of the collision, p^*, is

$$p^* \equiv S_1(u_1^*, v_1^*, t^*) \equiv S_2(u_2^*, v_2^*, t^*).$$

The normal vectors at the collision may be defined similarly by evaluating N_1 and N_2 at the collision point.

To compute a collision among a set of N time-varying parametric surfaces $S_i(u_i, v_i, t)$, we first use simple culling procedures to exclude pairs of surfaces which can't collide. Section 3.2 will discuss a method of solving these sets of constrained minimization problems which can compute simultaneous collisions and which does not spend undue computation on collisions which occur after t^*. It returns the collision points when these occur at a finite set of isolated points, or a finite subset of the collision points uniformly distributed over the contact manifold.

3 Interval Tools for Computing Collisions

We now turn to a discussion of the interval tools necessary to solve the sets of constrained minimization problems that arise in collisions.

3.1 Review of Interval Analysis

An *interval*, $A = [a, b]$, is a closed subset of $\mathbf{R}$ defined as

$$[a, b] \equiv \{x \mid a \leq x \leq b,\ x, a, b \in \mathbf{R}\}.$$

The lower and upper bounds of an interval are written as

$$\begin{aligned} \mathsf{lb}[a, b] &\equiv a \\ \mathsf{ub}[a, b] &\equiv b. \end{aligned}$$

A *vector-valued interval of dimension n*, $A = (A_1, A_2, \ldots, A_n)$, is a subset of $\mathbf{R}^n$ defined as

$$A \equiv \{x \mid x_i \in A_i, i = 1, 2, \ldots, n\}$$

where each A_i is an interval. An interval A_i that is a component of a vector-valued interval is called a *coordinate interval of A*.

The *width* of an interval, written $\mathsf{w}([a, b])$, is defined by

$$\mathsf{w}([a, b]) \equiv b - a.$$

The *midpoint* of an interval, written $\mathsf{mid}([a, b])$, is defined by

$$\mathsf{mid}([a, b]) \equiv \frac{a + b}{2}.$$

Similarly, the width and midpoint of a vector-valued interval of dimension n, A, are defined as

$$\begin{aligned} \mathsf{w}(A) &= \max_{i=1}^{n} \mathsf{w}(A_i) \\ \mathsf{mid}(A) &= (\mathsf{mid}(A_1), \mathsf{mid}(A_2), \ldots, \mathsf{mid}(A_n)). \end{aligned}$$

Hereafter, we will use the term interval to refer to both intervals and vector-valued intervals; the distinction will be clear from the context.

An *inclusion function* for a function f, written $\Box f$, produces an interval bound on the output of f over an interval representing its input domain. Mathematically, for all intervals X in the domain of f, if a point x is in the input interval X then $f(x)$ is contained in the output interval $\Box f(X)$; i.e.,

$$x \in X \Rightarrow f(x) \in \Box f(X) \quad \text{for all } x \in X.$$

Much more information about inclusion functions and their properties can be found in the literature (see, for example, [MOOR79, ALEF83,RATS88]). Section 8 and the Appendices discuss ways to create inclusion functions given the functions they are to bound.

3.2 Constrained Minimization Algorithm

The constrained minimization problem involves finding the global minimizers[7] of an objective function $f\colon \mathbf{R}^n \rightarrow \mathbf{R}$ for all points that satisfy a constraint function $F\colon \mathbf{R}^n \rightarrow \{0, 1\}$.

For the case of computing collisions between parametric surfaces, we have the following variables, objective function, and constraint function:

$$\begin{aligned} x &\equiv (u_1, v_1, u_2, v_2, t) \\ f(x) &\equiv t \\ F(x) &\equiv (C(u_1, v_1, u_2, v_2, t) = 0) \text{ and} \\ &\quad\ (D(u_1, v_1, u_2, v_2, t) \geq 0) \end{aligned}$$

A region in the minimization algorithm is a 5D interval vector of the form

$$\begin{aligned} X &\equiv (U_1, V_1, U_2, V_2, T) \\ &\equiv \left([u_1^l, u_1^u], [v_1^l, v_1^u], [u_2^l, u_2^u], [v_2^l, v_2^u], [t^l, t^u]\right) \end{aligned}$$

where the superscripts l and u denote lower and upper bounds. The relevant inclusion functions are[8]

$$\begin{aligned} \Box f(X) &\equiv [t^l, t^u] \\ \Box F(X) &\equiv \begin{cases} [0, 1], & \text{if } \mathsf{lb}\,\Box C(X) \leq 0,\ \mathsf{ub}\,\Box C(X) \geq 0, \\ & \quad \text{and } \mathsf{ub}\,\Box D(X) \geq 0 \\ [0, 0], & \text{otherwise} \end{cases} \end{aligned}$$

where $\Box C$ is an inclusion function for the collision equality constraint C, and $\Box D$ is an inclusion function for the incoming inequality constraint D.

The algorithm in Figure 6 finds solutions to the constrained minimization problem in a specified region X_0. The algorithm uses a priority queue to order regions based on the upper bound of the objective function. Regions bounding the set of global minimizers

[7] The global minimizers are the domain points at which the global minimum of the objective function is achieved, subject to the constraints.

[8] The terminology $\mathsf{lb}\,\Box C(X) \leq 0$ denotes that $\mathsf{lb}\,\Box C_i(x) \leq 0$ for *each* component interval i of $\Box C(X)$ (and similarly for upper bounds).

```
Minimize(□f,□F,A,X_0,□d,ε,δ)
place initial region X_0 on priority queue L
initialize f's upper bound u ← +∞
initialize solution set S ← ∅
initialize singular solution set S̄ ← ∅
while L is nonempty
    get next region Y from L
    if lb □f(Y) > u + ε discard Y
    else if lb □f(Y) > u − ε and
            there exists S_i ∈ S̄ such that ||□d(Y) − □d(S_i)|| < δ
            then discard Y
    else if Y satisfies acceptance criteria A then
            add Y to solution list S
            if Y doesn't contain a unique feasible point
                add Y to S̄
            endif
            u ← min(u, ub □f(Y))
            delete from S and S̄ all S_i ∋ lb □f(S_i) > u + ε
    else
            subdivide Y into regions Y_1 and Y_2
            for Y_i ∈ {Y_1, Y_2}
                evaluate □F on Y_i
                if □F(Y_i) = [0, 0] discard Y_i
                evaluate □f on Y_i
                if lb □f(Y_i) > u + ε discard Y_i
                insert Y_i into L according to ub □f(Y_i)
            endfor
    endif
endwhile
```

Figure 6: Global Constrained Minimization Algorithm: This algorithm finds the global minimizers of an objective function f, with constraints F, acceptance criteria A, initial region X_0, solution distance mapping function d, simultaneity threshold ϵ, and solution separation distance δ.

are subdivided until they are rejected or satisfy the acceptance criteria, A, and are accepted as solutions. It halts with an empty list of solutions if there are no solutions to the constraint function in X_0, or a list of regions, S, representing the set of global minimizers of the constrained minimization problem.

The variable u is a progressively refined least upper bound for the global minimum of the objective function. If we were only looking for a single collision point, we could halt the algorithm immediately after finding the first solution. To find collisions at multiple points of contact, the algorithm must be continued until the priority queue is empty. The variable u helps to prune the search after finding the first solutions.

Selecting Finite Sets of Points from Contact Manifolds The parameters ϵ, δ, and $\Box d$ allow the algorithm to select a finite set of regions distributed "uniformly" within the set of global minimizers, when this set is not finite. The parameter ϵ is the *simultaneity threshold*, which specifies how close the value of the objective function must be for two points to be considered global minimizers. For collisions, ϵ specifies how close in time two events must be in order to be considered simultaneous. The parameter δ is the *solution separation distance*, which specifies how far apart two accepted regions must be to be accepted as separate solutions. The parameter $\Box d$ is an inclusion function for the mapping which takes points in parameter space to points in whatever space we desire distances to be compared. We call the function d the *solution distance mapping function*.

As the algorithm progresses, it maintains two solution lists, S and $\bar{S}$. S contains all accepted regions. We call $\bar{S}$ the *singular solution set*. The elements of S not in $\bar{S}$ are regions in which the existence of a unique feasible point has been verified. The statements

if lb $\Box f(Y) > u - \epsilon$ and there exists $S_i \in \bar{S}$
such that $||\Box d(Y) - \Box d(S_i)|| < \delta$
then discard Y

check that the region Y is not too close to regions already accumulated onto $\bar{S}$. Note that the test lb $\Box f(Y) > u - \epsilon$ is critical to ensure that Y doesn't have an objective function value small enough to invalidate all the currently accepted regions.[9]

We use two lists, S and $\bar{S}$, so that in the case that the global minimizers form a finite set of points, the algorithm can find all such points without discarding some based on distance to those already found. The algorithm is therefore able to resolve multiple isolated collisions that happen in a small area, regardless of the value of δ.[10]

Ordering Based on Upper Bounds Constrained minimization algorithms that have appeared before [RATS88,SNYD92c] order regions based on the *lower bound* of the objective function. We use the upper bound to make tractable computing solutions on a contact manifold.

At any time, the union of all regions on the priority queue forms a bound on the set of global minimizers of the constrained minimization problem. As the algorithm progresses, regions are subdivided or rejected, so that the regions which remain on the priority queue become a tighter bound on this set. Because of the inclusion monotonicity property of inclusion functions,[11] as regions on the queue shrink, the computed lower bound on the objective function tends to increase and the upper bound tends to decrease.

Assume the set of global minimizers forms a continuous manifold rather than a finite collection of isolated points, as shown Figure 1. If the priority queue is ordered using lower bounds, when a given region is subdivided, its children will generally have larger lower bounds for the objective function, and will be placed in the priority queue behind less highly subdivided regions. A breadth first traversal tends to result, with less highly subdivided regions examined first. If we have a whole manifold of global minimizers and stringent acceptance criteria, we will have to compute a huge number of tiny regions bounding the entire solution manifold before even the first region is accepted as a solution.

By ordering based on the upper bound, more highly subdivided regions tend to be examined first because they tend to have smaller upper bounds. We quickly get to a region which is small enough to satisfy the acceptance criteria. This allows our upper bound u to be updated. It also allows regions to be accumulated onto our singular list $\bar{S}$. Regions that are too close to any member of $\bar{S}$ can then be eliminated, making it possible to find a distribution of points on the contact manifold without undue computation.

Acceptance Criteria The constraint inclusion function, $\Box F(X)$, because it contains an equality constraint, returns either [0, 0] (i.e.,

[9] If a region can possibly have a feasible point with a value of f less than ϵ from the value of f in regions on $\bar{S}$, we should not reject it just because it is close with respect to the function d to these regions. The algorithm might then discard a global minimizer because of its closeness to regions which are possibly far from the global minimizer, in terms of bounds on the objective function.

[10] One problem with this technique is that if the collisions happened at a contact manifold *and* a finite number of additional isolated points, the algorithm may discard some of the isolated points because of the closeness criterion. We consider this problem minor since the set of global minimizers is infinite and the algorithm must chose a subset anyway.

[11] An inclusion function, $\Box f$, is inclusion monotonic if $Y \subset X \Rightarrow \Box f(Y) \subset \Box f(X)$. In practice, the standard ways of constructing inclusion functions generate inclusion monotonic inclusion functions.

the constraint is satisfied nowhere in X) or $[0, 1]$ (i.e., the constraint *may* be satisfied in X). We must resort to other means to determine if the constraint is *actually* satisfied. Section 5 discusses conditions which guarantee that a region contains a unique solution to the equality constraints. These conditions can therefore be used as acceptance criteria in the algorithm, which we call the *isolated point acceptance criteria*. They also allow the upper bound u to be updated via

$$u \leftarrow \min(u, \text{ub}\,\Box f(Y))$$

since Y is guaranteed to contain a feasible point.

The algorithm also makes use of *emergency acceptance criteria* which do not guarantee a unique solution but are guaranteed to be satisfied for regions of small enough size.[12] The simplest such criterion is $\text{w}(X) < \epsilon$; a better one is $\text{w}(\Box S(X)) < \epsilon$ where $\Box S$ is the parametric mapping of one of the colliding surfaces. Regions which are accepted via the emergency acceptance criteria are inserted both onto the list of solutions, S, and the singular solutions, $\overline{S}$.

Subdivision The simplest method of subdividing candidate intervals in the minimization algorithm is bisection, in which two intervals are created by subdividing one of the input dimensions at its midpoint. Many methods can be used to select which dimension to subdivide. For example, we can simply pick the dimension of greatest width. A better alternative is to scale the parametric width by some measure of its importance to the problem we are solving. For each variable in the collision problem x_i, and a given candidate region X, we have used a scaling value s_i defined by

$$s_i \equiv \sum_{j=1}^{m} \max(|\,\text{lb}\,\Box\frac{\partial f_j}{\partial x_i}(X)|, |\,\text{ub}\,\Box\frac{\partial f_j}{\partial x_i}(X)|).$$

Here, f refers to the equality constraints (contact and tangency) of the collision problem. We then pick a dimension to subdivide, i, such that the scaled width $s_i\ \text{w}(X_i)$ is largest.

Given a candidate interval, techniques also exist which allow us to compute a smaller interval which can possibly contain feasible points of the constraint. These methods and how they can be added to our simple minimization algorithm are discussed in Section 4. Even more sophisticated subdivision methods exist, such as Hansen's method which involves accumulating gaps inside candidate intervals by using infinite interval division (see [RATS88] for a full description).

Multiple Element Constrained Minimization The algorithm can easily be modified to accept an array of sets of minimization parameters $(\Box f, \Box F, A, X_0)_i$. This allows simultaneous solution of sets of problems from different pairs of surfaces, or different tangency situations for the same pair of piecewise parametric surfaces. As a result, computation is not wasted on collisions which happen after the first collision, $t > t^*$. We call this modified constrained minimization algorithm the *multiple element constrained minimization algorithm*.

Sets of minimization subproblems may be implemented by associating the array index of the appropriate minimization subproblem with each region inserted onto the priority queue, and using the appropriate indexed inclusion functions and acceptance criteria when processing the region.

[12] Although we cannot guarantee a region X contains a solution, we can guarantee that it is arbitrarily close, in the sense that $\text{w}(\Box C(X)) < \epsilon$ where $\Box C$ is an inclusion function for the collision equality constraint function C.

Avoiding Detection of Tracked Points We can add additional inequality constraints to the constraint function F in order to avoid detecting collisions which occur at contact points already being tracked. If p is such a tracked point on a surface $S(u, v, t)$, the ODE solver computes a trajectory for $p = S(\tilde{u}(t), \tilde{v}(t), t)$. We then discard all global minimizers to the constrained minimization problem which satisfy

$$||S(u, v, t) - S(\tilde{u}(t), \tilde{v}(t), t)|| < \lambda, \tag{7}$$

where λ is a constant chosen by the user. The functions $\tilde{u}$ and $\tilde{v}$ have known representations, as computed by the solver. A natural interval extension of this constraint involving an inclusion function for S is then included in the constraint inclusion $\Box F$. An additional constraint is added for each tracked point.

4 Interval Newton Methods

In order to more quickly refine our intervals towards the solutions of the collision equality constraint $C = 0$, we make use of an interval Newton method. Interval Newton methods are applicable to the general problem of finding zeroes of a differentiable function $f\colon \mathbf{R}^n \rightarrow \mathbf{R}^m$ in an interval $X \subset \mathbf{R}^n$. They allow us to find an interval bound on the set

$$X^* = \{x \in X \mid f(x) = 0\}$$

Let $Z(X)$ be such a bound (i.e., $X^* \subset Z(X)$). We can reduce the size of our candidate region X by[13]

$$X' = X \bigcap Z(X)$$

In particular, $Z(X) \bigcap X = \emptyset$ implies that X contains no solutions. We call the operator $Z(X)$ the *interval Newton operator*.

Since X can only decrease in size after it is intersected with $Z(X)$, this procedure can be applied iteratively to produce smaller and smaller regions, as in

$$X_{i+1} = (X_i \bigcap Z(X_i))$$

Note however that a smaller region is not *necessarily* produced. Interval Newton methods should therefore be combined with bisection. When interval Newton iteration is effective at reducing the size of X its use is continued. Otherwise, bisection subdivision is performed.

The following sections present three methods for computing $Z(X)$:

- use of the Krawczyk-Moore form (Section 4.1)
- use of the interval inverse (Section 4.2.1)
- use of matrix iteration (Section 4.2.2)

In each case, we modify the constrained minimization algorithm from Figure 6 by replacing the subdivide step with the code shown in Figure 7.

4.1 Fixed Point Methods: the Krawczyk–Moore Form

The familiar (point-wise) Newton's method is used to converge on the solution to a system of equations $f(x) = 0$ where $f\colon \mathbf{R}^n \rightarrow \mathbf{R}^n$.

[13] $A \bigcap B$ denotes the interval formed by the intersection of the intervals A and B.

```
Newton(Y)
compute interval Newton step on Y
if step succeeds then
    Y' ← Y ∩ Z(Y)
    if Y' = ∅, discard Y
        (proceed with next region)
    else if Y' is sufficiently smaller than Y, insert Y' into L
        (proceed with next region)
    else subdivide Y'
        (continue with Y replaced by Y')
else subdivide Y
        (continue with Y)
```

Figure 7: Interval Newton Modification to the Constrained Minimization Algorithm: The above algorithm replaces the subdivide step in the algorithm of Figure 6.

The method starts with an initial "guess" at a solution x_0 and iterates via

$$x_{i+1} = p(x_i)$$

where

$$p(x) = x - Yf(x).$$

Y is a nonsingular $n \times n$ matrix which in straightforward Newton's method is the inverse of the Jacobian matrix of f at x, i.e.

$$Y \equiv J^{-1}(x)$$

Under certain conditions, this iterative procedure converges to a fixed point x^*. If convergence is achieved, then the fixed point x^* is a solution since

$$p(x^*) = x^* \iff f(x^*) = 0$$

because Y is nonsingular.

An interval analog of this method may be developed. Let X be an interval in $\mathbf{R}^n$ in which zeroes of f are sought. We require a bound on X^*. But

$$\begin{aligned} X^* &\equiv \{x \in X \mid f(x) = 0\} \\ &= \{x \in X \mid p(x) = x\} \subset (\Box p(X) \bigcap X) \end{aligned}$$

where $\Box p(X)$ is an inclusion function for the Newton operator $p(x)$.

The Krawczyk–Moore form, $K(X, c, Y)$, provides the necessary inclusion function for the Newton operator $p(x)$. It is simply a mean value form for p (see [SNYD92c] for a discussion of the mean value form) given by

$$K(X, c, Y) \equiv c - Yf(c) + (I - Y\Box J(X))(X - c)$$

where I is the $n \times n$ identity matrix, $\Box J(X)$ is an inclusion function for the Jacobian of f evaluated on X, and c is any point in X. Note that the vector addition and subtraction and the matrix/vector multiplication operations used in K must be computed using interval arithmetic.

We therefore have

$$X^* \subset (X \bigcap K(X, c, Y))$$

for any $c \in X$ and nonsingular matrix Y. Thus, $K(X, c, Y)$ can be used as an interval Newton operator. Fairly good results can be achieved with $c = \text{mid}(X)$ and $Y = J^{-1}(c)$ [TOTH85,MITC92].

In our research, we have found a different method to be superior, described in the next section.

4.2 Linear Interval Equation Methods

A second method for finding an interval bound on X^* involves solving the interval analog of a linear equation.

Let the coordinates of x be $x_1, x_2, \ldots, x_n$. By the Mean Value Theorem, given a $c \in X$, for each $x \in X$, there exist n points, $\xi_1, \xi_2, \ldots, \xi_n$ such that

$$f(x) = f(c) + J(\xi_1, \ldots, \xi_n)(x - c),$$

where the jacobian matrix J is given by

$$J_{ij}(\xi_1, \xi_2, \ldots, \xi_n) = \frac{\partial f_i}{\partial x_j}(\xi_i)$$

and where each $\xi_i \in X$. Let $\Box J$ be an inclusion function for the Jacobian matrix of f, i.e.,

$$\Box J(X) \equiv \left\{ J \mid J_{ij} \in \Box \frac{\partial f_i}{\partial x_j}(X) \right\}$$

If x is a zero of f, then there exists $J \in \Box J(X)$ such that

$$f(x) = 0 = f(c) + J(x - c).$$

Therefore, if $Q(X)$ is the set of solutions

$$Q(X) \equiv \{x \mid f(c) + J(x - c) = 0 \text{ for some } J \in \Box J(X)\},$$

then $Q(X)$ contains all zeroes of f in X.

To compute an interval bound, Z, on $Q(X)$, let $y = x - c$, and let Z' be an interval bound on the set

$$\{y \mid Jy = -f(c) \text{ for some } J \in \Box J(X)\}.$$

Then the interval Z defined using interval addition as

$$Z \equiv Z' + [c, c],$$

is an interval bound on $Q(X)$. Thus, computing the interval Newton bound Z can be accomplished by solving an interval linear equation of the form

$$Mx = b$$

where $M \equiv \Box J(X)$ is an $n \times n$ interval matrix, and $b \equiv -f(c)$ is an interval vector.[14] Stated another way, we require a bound on the set

$$Q(M, b) \equiv \{x \mid \exists \mathcal{M} \in M, \beta \in b \text{ such that } \mathcal{M}x = \beta\}.$$

The next two sections discuss two methods for solving these interval linear equations.

4.2.1 Solving the Interval Linear Equation with the Interval Inverse

One method to bound the set of solutions to the interval linear equation involves computing the interval inverse. We seek a bound on $Q(M, b)$: the set of solutions, x, for $Mx = b$. If M is an $n \times n$ interval matrix, an interval that bounds $Q(M, b)$ is

$$Z \equiv M^{-1}b$$

[14] In this case, the interval b has a lower bound equal to its upper bounds in each coordinate (called a *point* interval), neglecting inaccuracies in the computation of f.

where M^{-1} is the *interval inverse* of the interval matrix. Assuming M contains no singular matrices, the interval inverse is an interval bound on the set

$$\{m^{-1} \mid m \in M\}$$

A simple way of computing the interval inverse is to use the interval analog of LU decomposition. That is, we take the LU decomposition algorithm [PRES86, pages 31–38] and replace all arithmetic operations with their corresponding interval arithmetic counterparts (see [MOOR79] for a discussion of interval arithmetic). If at any point in the iteration we attempt to divide by an interval which contains zero, then we cannot compute the interval inverse, and the interval Newton step fails (but see the next section for a way to reduce the size of candidate regions without using the interval inverse). After enough iterations of the constrained minimization algorithm, and assuming the conditions discussed in Section 5 hold, candidate regions are usually small enough to make this technique effective.

4.2.2 Solving the Interval Linear Equation with Matrix Iteration

Another method to bound the set of solutions to the interval linear equation involves matrix iteration. The algorithm we present here requires an initial bound on the set of solutions; that is it finds a bound on the set $Q(M, b) \bigcap X$ where X is a given interval. The algorithm is therefore effective at reducing the size of a candidate interval in which solutions to an equality constraint are sought, but cannot be used to verify solution existence using the theorems in Section 5.[15]

Figure 8 contains the code for Linear_Solve, which finds bounds on the solution to the linear interval equation. Linear_Solve is based on the observation that the i-th equation of the linear system $Mx = b$:

$$M_{i1}x_1 + M_{i2}x_2 + \cdots + M_{in}x_n = b_i$$

implies, for each j such that $M_{ij} \neq 0$, that

$$x_j = \frac{b_i - \sum_{k \neq j} M_{ik}x_k}{M_{ij}}.$$

The interval analog of this equation may therefore be used for each interval matrix entry, M_{ij}, which does not contain 0 to find a bound on one of the variables x_j. This bound is intersected with the old bound on x_j yielding an interval which is possibly smaller but no larger than it was. Reducing the size of one interval may then further reduce the sizes of others as the iteration proceeds. Note that the algorithm does not halt when an interval element of M contains 0; it just proceeds to the next element which excludes 0.

An important property of Linear_Solve is that it can be applied to a nonsquare linear equation,[16] and is therefore useful in the "overconstrained" equality constraint for implicit surfaces, and the vertex-to-edge and vertex-to-vertex tangency situations of piecewise parametric surfaces (see Appendix A). Linear_Solve can be applied in many situations where LU decomposition fails because of the singularity of the interval Jacobian matrix. Even when the Jacobian matrix is singular *at the solution point*, Linear_Solve is usually effective at reducing the widths of some of the input variables. These features are critical in making the singular situations described in Section 5 computationally tractable.[17]

[15] This is because, unlike the technique presented in Sections 4.2.1, this technique does not bound $Q(M, b)$ directly, but instead bounds $Q(M, b) \bigcap X$.

[16] That is, the number of equations, m, is unequal to the number of variables, n.

```
Linear_Solve(M,b,x)
repeat
    loop through rows of M (i = 1, 2, . . . , m)
        loop through columns of M (j = 1, 2, . . . , n)
            if 0 ∉ M_ij then
                x'_j ← (b_i − Σ_{k≠j} M_ik x_k)/M_ij
                x_j ← x'_j ∩ x_j
                if x_j = ∅ return no solution
            endif
        endloop
    endloop
while there is sufficient improvement in x
```

Figure 8: Interval Linear Equation Solution Algorithm: This algorithm computes the interval Newton step (first statement of the algorithm in Figure 6).

The "sufficient improvement" condition mentioned in the algorithm can be implemented as

$$\mathrm{w}(x^{i+1}) \leq \alpha\, \mathrm{w}(x^i)$$

where a typical value of the improvement factor, α, is 0.9. Here x^i denotes the interval bound computed after i iterations of the repeat loop. Specifying a maximum number of repeat iterations also limits the amount of computation.

5 Termination Criteria

Two theorems in interval analysis specify conditions under which a square system of equations contains a unique solution in a region.[18]

Theorem 1 (Krawczyk–Moore Existence) If $K(X, c, Y) \subset X$, $K(X, c, Y) \neq \emptyset$, and $\|I - Y\Box J(X)\| < 1$, then there is a unique root in X, and pointwise Newton's method will converge to it.

Theorem 2 (Linear Interval Equation Existence) If $Q(X) \subset X$ and $Q(X) \neq \emptyset$, then there is a unique root in X.

The conditions implied by these theorems thus lead to acceptance criteria, A, for the constrained minimization algorithm. Implementation of Theorem 1's conditions is clear from the discussion in Section 4.1. To verify the conditions of Theorem 2, we use the interval inverse method discussed in Section 4.2.1. We have been able to verify solution uniqueness much earlier (i.e., in larger regions) using Theorem 2's test.

We note the conditions for Theorems 1 and 2 can only be verified when the determinant of the Jacobian of the equality constraint function, C, is nonzero in some neighborhood of the solution. For collision detection, the Jacobian determinant is zero at a solution to the contact and tangency constraints in the following situations:

- the contacting surfaces become tangent but never interpenetrate. They can even stay tangent for an interval of time.

[17] We prefer the method of matrix iteration described here to a faster method (the interval analog of Gauss-Seidel iteration) which involves solving only for the diagonal matrix elements after a preconditioning step (see [RATS88]). This method requires a square system of equations, and will fail when the Jacobian matrix is singular at the solution. Interval computations in the preconditioning step also have the effect of increasing the size of the solution set $Q(M, b)$ even before any iteration takes place.

[18] See [TOTH85] for a proof sketch and references for Theorem 1, [SNYD92b] for a proof of Theorem 2.

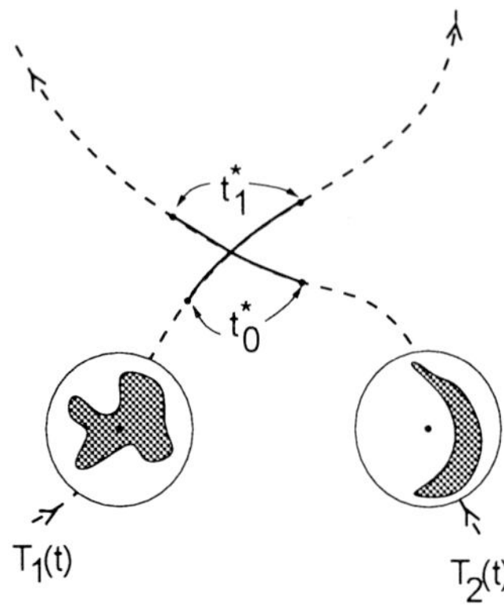

Figure 9: Bounding Sphere Collision Time Bound

- the surfaces contact instantaneously on a curve or higher-dimensional region.
- both — the surfaces contact at an infinite set of points through an interval of time.

In these cases, we can not verify that a unique solution exists and must resort to heuristic criteria (the "emergency" criteria of the constrained minimization algorithm). That is, we consider surfaces to have collided when a bound on C is sufficiently small in a region.[19]

If a solution is on the boundary of a candidate region, we note that the conditions of either theorem will be difficult to verify since the set result (e.g., $Q(X)$) will always slightly spill out of the original region X. To solve this problem, we should slightly increase the region examined for acceptance, X, via

$$X' \equiv c + (X - c)(1 + \gamma)$$

where γ is a small constant (like .1). We then can perform the test on this bigger region X'. Then, even if the solution is on the boundary of X, the theorem conditions will eventually be satisfied if the Jacobian of C is nonsingular in a neighborhood of the solution.

6 A Simple Bound for the Time of Collision

We can save time in the collision algorithm by using a fast algorithm to reduce the time interval over which collisions are searched. This time bound may also tell us, with a minimum of computation, if the two surfaces fail to intersect, obviating the need for further computation. The test presented here uses 1D minimization (only over time) rather than minimization over the 4 or 5 dimensional space required to solve the full problem.

As shown in Figure 9, we compute two bounding spheres around each of our parametric surfaces. In the case of rigid motion, this may be computed beforehand as a preprocessing step. We specify two points for each parametric surface O_1 and O_2 about which to compute a bounding sphere. These points should be chosen to minimize the size of the resulting bound; using the center of mass of the surface is a good choice. The bounding radii are:

$$R_1 \equiv \max_{(u_1, v_1)} \|s_1(u_1, v_1) - O_1\|$$

$$R_2 \equiv \max_{(u_2, v_2)} \|s_2(u_2, v_2) - O_2\|.$$

[19]This implies, because of the contact constraint, that the surfaces come within a specified constant.

Note that these bounding radii can be computed using a 2D unconstrained minimization problem, for which the algorithm of Section 3.2 is suitable.

Using the constrained minimization algorithm, this time on a simple 1D problem, we then find a bound on the time of collision via

$$t_0^* \equiv \operatorname*{minimum}_{t \in [t_0, t_1]} \{ \; t \mid \|T_1(t) + O_1 - T_2(t) - O_2\| \leq R_1 + R_2 \}$$

$$t_1^* \equiv -\operatorname*{minimum}_{t \in [t_0, t_1]} \{ -t \mid \|T_1(t) + O_1 - T_2(t) - O_2\| \leq R_1 + R_2 \}.$$

We can then replace the $[t_0, t_1]$ interval in the full collision minimization problem for that pair of surfaces with $[t_0^*, t_1^*]$, or cull the pair of surfaces if no solutions to the 1D problem are found.

7 The Full Collision Algorithm

The complete algorithm for detecting collisions can now be described. The following discussion pertains to a set of parametric surfaces; a similar algorithm can be developed for the case of implicit surfaces or parametric/implicit combinations. We are given a set of solids defined by a parametric boundary representation, and a time interval in which to detect collisions, $[t_0, t_1]$. The following steps summarize the final algorithm:

1. Detect pairs of objects which can possibly collide. For this step, we bound each time-varying surface by evaluating an inclusion function for its time-varying mapping over $[t_0, t_1]$. More precisely, a bounding box through time on the surface $S(u, v, t)$ is given by

   $$\square S([0, 1], [0, 1], [t_0, t_1])$$

   assuming S is evaluated on the unit square.[20] We can then test whether any of the resulting bounding boxes intersect using highly efficient algorithms from computational geometry [SIX82]. All pairs of bounding boxes which do intersect must be processed further; the rest are culled.

2. For rigid bodies, additional object pairs can be culled using the bounding sphere test of Section 6. A variant of this test can also be used for deformable surfaces.

3. If any pairs of objects remain to be processed, we must invoke the full constrained minimization algorithm. Here, we distinguish between "free" objects and objects already in continuous contact, whose contact points are being tracked with the ODE solver. For objects already in continuous contact, additional constraints are added (Section 3.2) to prevent re-detection of the tracked points. All such problems are placed on the initial priority queue of the multiple element constrained minimization algorithm.

4. We use local methods, such as Newton's method, to converge to the actual collision point in each solution region which contains an isolated collision (i.e., for which the interval existence and uniqueness test of Section 5 succeeded). We arbitrarily choose the midpoint as the collision point for the rest of the solution regions (termed singular solutions in Section 3).

[20]Note that for rigid surfaces we can cache a bounding box on the time-independent rigid surface and compute only a bound over time on the resulting rotated and translated bounding box.

8 Implementing Inclusion Functions

The collision detection algorithm depends on inclusion functions for the time-varying surfaces and their various derivatives. Note that the equality constraint for the parametric surface case (Equation 2) involves derivatives of the time-varying surface mappings $S_i(u_i, v_i, t)$. The interval Newton method then requires an additional derivative of the equality constraint with respect to each of the independent variables. Interval analysis provides the necessary theory for constructing inclusion functions for these functions.

For simple polynomial surfaces (e.g., bicubic patches or algebraic surfaces) interval arithmetic suffices to provide an inclusion function for the time-independent surface. Toth [TOTH85] has presented efficient inclusion functions for Bezier surfaces. Mitchell and Hanrahan have proposed a simple stack-based representation of surfaces which allows generation of inclusion functions for the surface and its derivatives [MITC92]. Inclusion functions for more complicated surfaces and their derivatives can also be constructed. We have used the system described in [SNYD92a,SNYD92b], which automates the construction of inclusion functions (and inclusion functions for the derivatives) of any functions formed by the composition of a quite powerful set of symbolic operators.

For physical simulations, the ODE solver computes a representation of the time behavior of the surfaces. The solver may directly compute a continuous representation or it may be later reconstructed by point sampling the solver's results, typically producing a polynomial. Appendix B discusses a method to bound Chebyshev polynomials.

9 Results

We have successfully tested this method on a series of collision detection examples, including both rigidly moving and deforming objects. For example, Figure 12 shows the results of a difficult collision detection run in which the contact manifold forms a series of disjoint 2D regions. A collection of 59 points was generated in the contact region with a simultaneity threshold of 0.001 and solution separation distance of 0.04, using 28704 iterations and 88.81 CPU seconds.[21] While the running time may seem large, the problem itself is sufficiently difficult that its running time exceeded our threshold of 8 CPU hours without the use of *every* new technique presented in this paper: adding the tangency constraint (rather than using the contact constraint alone), sorting by upper bound in the constrained minimization algorithm (rather than by lower bound), and using Linear_Solve for the interval Newton step (rather than the Krawczyk–Moore operator). Figure 1, 5, and 12–16 show the results of the algorithm for several different time-varying shapes.

The table in Figure 10 compares running times for a second example involving two rotating and translating bumpy parametric surfaces which collide at an isolated point. Several solution methods are compared: LEQN (interval Newton using the linear equation solution techniques of Section 4.2), KM (interval Newton using the Krawczyk–Moore operator), NIN (without interval Newton), and NTAN (without the tangency condition). Since the collision occurs at an isolated point, both the LEQ and KM methods were able to accept a single solution region by verifying the solution existence and uniqueness test. The other methods required an accuracy parameter for acceptance; we used the simple criterion $\mathrm{w}(X) < \gamma$.

Running Times		
Example	Iterations	CPU (secs)
LEQN	6331	32.67
KM	10087	148.28
NIN,γ=1e-3	17395	8.58
NIN,γ=1e-4	29921	15.46
NIN,γ=1e-5	40127	21.52
NIN,γ=1e-6	48187	23.25
NIN,NTAN,γ=1e-3	52307	14.59
NIN,NTAN,γ=1e-4	587711	169.87
NIN,NTAN,γ=1e-5	3822605	1207.46

Figure 10: Table of Results for Various Methods: see Section 9

Because we used a prototype system to gather the data, we emphasize the importance of iteration count data over CPU time. Our system requires the traversal of a complicated data structure for each inclusion function evaluation which overwhelms the floating point computation actually needed in the function. The interval Newton methods are sensitive to this bias, since their implementation required many symbolic operators. We believe the iteration counts shown here to be a reasonable measure of expected running time, if the inclusion functions are hand-coded for the surfaces of interest.

10 Conclusions

We have presented a robust interval algorithm that can detect collisions between complex curved surfaces. The algorithm handles a greater range of situations than previous algorithms. It detects both isolated collision points and collision points on contact manifolds. It can avoid detection of points close to a set of tracked points with specified trajectories. It efficiently handles detection of simultaneous collisions between sets of moving objects. The technique is practical for simulations involving large numbers of moving and deforming objects (see Figures 15 and 16).

We draw several conclusions from our experimental results. First, interval methods, such as [VONH90] and [DUFF92], which do not make use of the interval Newton method or the tangency condition soon become impractical as we increase the accuracy parameter (refer to the NIN,NTAN lines of the table in Figure 10). Interval Newton iteration combined with the tangency condition (especially using the interval linear equation approach) is very effective at reducing computation. Second, our method can solve the difficult problem of detecting collision points on a contact manifold. We have found the methods described here to be indispensable, including the idea of the tangency constraint, the constrained minimization algorithm discussed in Section 3, and the interval linear equation approach to interval Newton iteration.

We note that many areas for improvement remain. Sorting by lower bound of the objective function rather than by upper bound is more efficient for isolated point collisions. We have noted an efficiency gain of a factor of from 1 to 10 in using the lower bound for such cases. On the other hand, sorting by lower bound is completely impractical for detecting collisions on a contact manifold. If we know the nature of the collision solution set a priori, we can choose the appropriate method. Alternatively, combining the two approaches, perhaps by "racing" them in parallel on the same problem, may decrease the average running time. We are studying several ways to increase efficiency that involve more optimally

[21] The term *iteration* refers to an evaluation of the inclusion functions $\Box f$ and $\Box F$ (objective function and constraint function) in the constrained minimization algorithm. All CPU times are measured on a HP 9000 Series 750 computer.

choosing the next dimension to subdivide, and determining a subdivision location other than the midpoint.

Acknowledgments

We wish to thank Mark Montague and Allen Corcorran for their production help. Thanks also go to the Siggraph reviewers for their careful reading, suggestions, and bug fixes. This work was supported in part by grants from Apple, DEC, Hewlett Packard, and IBM. Additional support was provided by NSF (ASC-89-20219), as part of the NSF/DARPA STC for Computer Graphics and Scientific Visualization. All opinions, findings, conclusions, or recommendations expressed in this document are those of the author and do not necessarily reflect the views of the sponsoring agencies.

References

[ALEF83] Alefeld, G., and J. Herzberger, *Introduction to Interval Computations*, Academic Press, New York, 1983.

[BARA89] Baraff, David, "Analytical Methods for Dynamic Simulation of Non-penetrating Rigid Bodies," Computer Graphics, 23(3), pp. 223-232, July 1989.

[BARA90] Baraff, David, "Curved Surfaces and Coherence for Non-penetrating Rigid Body Simulation," Computer Graphics, 24(4), pp. 19-28, August 1990.

[BARA91] Baraff, David, "Coping with Friction for Non-penetrating Rigid Body Simulation," Computer Graphics, 25(4), pp. 31-39, July 1991.

[BARA92] Baraff, David, and A. Witkin, "Dynamic Simulation of Non-penetrating Flexible Bodies," Computer Graphics, 26(2), pp. 303-308, July 1992.

[DUFF92] Duff, Tom, "Interval Arithmetic and Recursive Subdivision for Implicit Functions and Constructive Solid Geometry," Computer Graphics, 26(2), July 1992, pp. 131-138.

[META92] Metaxas, Dimitri, and D. Terzopoulos, "Dynamic Deformation of Solid Primitives with Constraints," Computer Graphics, 26(2), pp. 309-312, July 1992.

[MITC92] Mitchell, Don, and P. Hanrahan, "Illumination from Curved Reflectors," Computer Graphics, 26(2), July 1992, pp. 283-291.

[MOOR66] Moore, R.E., *Interval Analysis*, Prentice Hall, Englewood Cliffs, New Jersey, 1966.

[MOOR79] Moore, R.E., *Methods and Applications of Interval Analysis*, SIAM, Philadelphia.

[MOOR80] Moore, R.E., "New Results on Nonlinear Systems," in *Interval Mathematics 1980*, Karl Nickel, ed., Academic Press, New York, 1980, pp. 165-180.

[MOOR88] Moore, M. and Wilhelms, J., "Collision Detection and Response for Computer Animation," Computer Graphics, 22(4), pp. 289-298, August 1988.

[PRES86] Press, W. H., B. P. Flannery, S. A. Teukolsky, and W. T. Vetterling, *Numerical Recipes*, Cambridge University Press, Cambridge, England, 1986.

[RATS88] Ratschek, H. and J. Rokne, *New Computer Methods for Global Optimization*, Ellis Horwood Limited, Chichester, England, 1988.

[SCLA91] Sclaroff, Stan, and A. Pentland, "Generalized Implicit Functions for Computer Graphics," Computer Graphics, 25(4), pp. 247-250, July 1991.

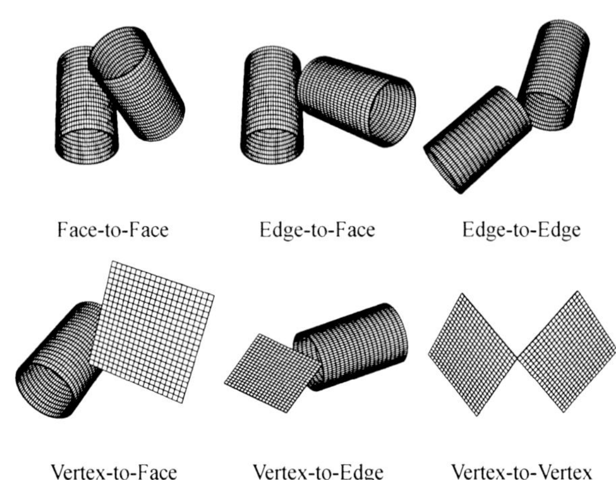

Figure 11: Types of Collision Tangency

[SIX82] Six, H.W., and D. Wood, "Counting and Reporting Intersections of *d*-Ranges," IEEE Transactions on Computers, C-31(3), March 1982, pp. 181-187.

[SNYD92a] Snyder, John, and J. Kajiya, "Generative Modeling: A Symbolic System for Geometric Modeling," Computer Graphics, 26(2), pp. 369-378, July 1992.

[SNYD92b] Snyder, John, *Generative Modeling for Computer Graphics and CAD: Symbolic Shape Design Using Interval Analysis*, Academic Press, Cambridge, MA, July 1992.

[SNYD92c] Snyder, John, "Interval Analysis for Computer Graphics," Computer Graphics, 26(2), pp. 121-130, July 1992.

[TOTH85] Toth, Daniel L., "On Ray Tracing Parametric Surfaces," Computer Graphics, 19(3), July 1985, pp. 171-179.

[VONH90] Von Herzen, B., A.H. Barr, and H.R. Zatz, "Geometric Collisions for Time-Dependent Parametric Surfaces," Computer Graphics, 24(4), August 1990, pp. 39-48.

A Collision Constraints for Piecewise Parametric Surfaces

A piecewise surface is composed of a set of smooth *faces*, a set of *edges* where these faces meet, and a set of *vertices* or points where edges meet. Edges form the 1D boundaries over which the surface is not smooth; vertices are the 0D boundaries between smooth edge curves. A data structure containing the faces, edges, and vertices of a solid is called its *boundary representation*. For example, the boundary representation of a cylindrical solid contains three faces: one cylinder and two circular endcaps, two edges where the cylinder and endcap meet, but no vertices.

To detect collisions between two piecewise surfaces, we must search for collisions between each pair of faces, between edges and faces, between vertices and faces, etc. The constraints governing collisions are different in each of these cases, which we call *tangency situations*. There are 6 types of tangency conditions in a collision between piecewise surfaces as shown in Figure 11. Constraints for the face-to-face tangency situation are identical to the constraints discussed in Section 2.1. The following paragraphs discuss the other tangency situations.

We must combine all the constrained minimization problems for the various possible types of tangency situations. For example, if the surfaces are a pair of cylindrical solids, we obtain 25 separate constrained minimization subproblems: 9 face-to-face problem, 12 edge-to-face problems, and 4 edge-to-edge problems. Two tori require only a single face-to-face problem. Each problem is then solved simultaneously using the multiple element constrained minimization algorithm.

Edge-to-Face For the *edge-to-face* case, we have an edge curve, $C(s,t)$, which forms a boundary of a surface, $S_a(u_a, v_a, t)$, and another surface, $S(u, v, t)$. The edge curve is typically formed by evaluating a parametric surface S_a at a specific value for either the u or v parameter, e.g.

$$C(s,t) \equiv S_a(s, v^{\text{fixed}}, t)$$

where v^{fixed} is a constant set at one of the extremes of the v interval over which S_a is evaluated. The contact constraint for edge-to-face collisions is

$$C(s,t) - S(u,v,t) = 0 \tag{8}$$

and the tangency constraint by

$$\frac{\partial C}{\partial s}(s,t) \cdot N(u,v,t) = 0 \tag{9}$$

where N is the time-varying normal to the surface S. The edge-to-face equality constraint can be represented a system of 4 equations in 4 variables.

To define the incoming collision condition, we need to define what "outwardness" means on an edge curve. Assuming all surfaces form the valid boundaries of a closed solid, the edge curve $C(s,t)$ is shared between two surfaces S_a and S_b. We can therefore define two "outward" directions, given by the outward pointing normals to the shared surfaces S_a and S_b. For example, these outward directions may be defined as

$$\begin{aligned} C^{\text{outward-1}}(s,t) &\equiv N_a(s, v^{\text{fixed}}, t) \\ C^{\text{outward-2}}(s,t) &\equiv N_b(u^{\text{fixed}}, s, t) \end{aligned}$$

where N_a and N_b are the outward normal vectors of the respective surfaces.

The incoming constraint forces the relative velocity between the surface and the edge curve to be in the same direction (using a dot product test) as the surface's normal. The surface's normal must also face away from at least one of the edge curve's outward directions. The incoming constraint is:

$$\begin{aligned} &(\frac{\partial S}{\partial t}(u,v,t) - \frac{\partial C}{\partial t}(s,t)) \cdot N(u,v,t) \geq 0 \quad \text{and} \\ &\Big(-N(u,v,t) \cdot C^{\text{outward-1}}(s,t) \geq 0 \quad \text{or} \\ &-N(u,v,t) \cdot C^{\text{outward-2}}(s,t) \geq 0\Big). \end{aligned} \tag{10}$$

Edge-to-Edge The *edge-to-edge* case involves two edge curves, $C_1(s_1, t)$ and $C_2(s_2, t)$. For this case, just a contact constraint is sufficient, given by the following system of three equations in three variables:

$$C_1(s_1, t) - C_2(s_2, t) = 0. \tag{11}$$

To define the incoming collision condition, we define two outward directions for each edge curve, as in the previous discussion for the edge-to-face case. The relative velocity between the edge curves must face in the same direction as at least one of the first curve's outward directions:

$$\begin{aligned} &(\frac{\partial C_1}{\partial t}(s_1,t) - \frac{\partial C_2}{\partial t}(s_2,t)) \cdot C_1^{\text{outward-1}}(s_1,t) \geq 0 \quad \text{or} \\ &(\frac{\partial C_1}{\partial t}(s_1,t) - \frac{\partial C_2}{\partial t}(s_2,t)) \cdot C_1^{\text{outward-2}}(s_1,t) \geq 0 \end{aligned} \tag{12}$$

Also, at least one of the outward directions on one curve must face away from one of the outward directions of the other curve. A logical combination of 6 inequalities is the result.

Vertex-to-Face, Vertex-to-Edge, Vertex-to-Vertex The *vertex-to-face* case involves a vertex $P(t)$ and a surface $S(u, v, t)$. As in the edge-to-edge case, a contact constraint is sufficient, of the form

$$P(t) - S(u,v,t) = 0. \tag{13}$$

where the point P is formed by evaluating a surface at a fixed point in its (u, v) parameter space, e.g.

$$P(t) \equiv S_a(u^{\text{fixed}}, v^{\text{fixed}}, t)$$

A system of three equations in three unknowns results. Similarly, a system of three equations in two unknowns results for the vertex-to-edge case, and a system of three equations in a single unknown for the vertex-to-vertex case.

The incoming collision condition can be derived by defining a number of outward directions for the colliding vertex, corresponding to the normal vector of each surface containing that vertex. The normal to the surface S must face away from at least one of these outward directions, as in the edge-to-face case. The relative velocity between the surface and the vertex must face in the same direction as the surface's normal, via

$$(\frac{\partial S}{\partial t}(u,v,t) - \frac{\partial P}{\partial t}(t)) \cdot N(u,v,t) \geq 0.$$

Similar systems of inequalities can be derived for situations where a vertex collides with an edge or another vertex.

B Inclusion Functions for Chebyshev Polynomials

Chebyshev polynomials are a good basis for a continuous representation of time behavior. They allow simple control of approximation error, and can be differentiated using a simple method to produce a Chebyshev representation of the derivative (see [PRES86, pages 158–165] for a discussion of the advantages of Chebyshev polynomials, their properties, and algorithms for their manipulation). The basis functions for a Chebyshev polynomials are

$$T_n(x) \equiv \cos(n \arccos(x))$$

which expand to a series of polynomials of the form

$$\begin{aligned} T_0(x) &= 1 \\ T_1(x) &= x \\ T_2(x) &= 2x^2 - 1 \\ &\vdots \\ T_{n+1}(x) &= 2xT_n(x) - T_{n-1}(x) \quad n \geq 1 \end{aligned}$$

The function $T_n(x)$ has $n+1$ extrema with values of ± 1 at the locations

$$x_i \equiv \cos(\frac{\pi i}{n}) \quad i = 0, 1, \ldots, n$$

The i-th extremum of the basis function T_n is either a minimum or maximum according to the rules

$$T_n(x_i) = \begin{cases} -1, & \text{if } (i+n) \equiv 1 \bmod 2 \\ +1, & \text{if } (i+n) \equiv 0 \bmod 2 \end{cases}$$

A Chebyshev approximation of order N is given by specifying N coefficients $c_i, i = 0, 1, \ldots, N-1$, which determine the polynomial

$$C(x) = \sum_{i=1}^{N-1} c_i T_i(x) + \frac{c_0}{2}$$

Given the order of the Chebyshev approximation function $C(x)$, N, we can easily compute an inclusion function for $C(x)$. Let the interval over which we are to bound $C(x)$ be given by $X = [x_0, x_1]$. As a preprocessing step, we first tabulate the locations of the extrema of the basis functions, up to some maximum order. (Note that the results can then be used for any approximating polynomial.) For each Chebyshev basis function, $T_i(x)$, $i = 0, 1, \ldots, N-1$, we first evaluate $T_i(x_0)$ and $T_i(x_1)$. We then determine whether any extrema of $T_i(x)$ occur in $[x_0, x_1]$ using the tabulated locations of the extrema. A lower bound on the basis function over $[x_0, x_1]$, b_i^0 is

$$b_i^0 \equiv \begin{cases} \min(T_i(x_0), T_i(x_1), -1), & \text{if min of } T_i(x) \in [x_0, x_1] \\ \min(T_i(x_0), T_i(x_1)), & \text{otherwise.} \end{cases}$$

Similarly, an upper bound is

$$b_i^1 \equiv \begin{cases} \max(T_i(x_0), T_i(x_1), 1), & \text{if max of } T_i(x) \in [x_0, x_1] \\ \max(T_i(x_0), T_i(x_1)), & \text{otherwise.} \end{cases}$$

The final inclusion function is then

$$\Box C(X) \equiv \sum_{i=1}^{N-1} c_i [b_i^0, b_i^1] + \frac{c_0}{2}$$

where operations are computed with interval arithmetic.

Scenes from test animations: In the following figure pairs, the upper image is the scene immediately before the collision, while the bottom image is the scene at the collision time. Points of contact are shown as white dots, which are uniformly distributed over regions where there are line and surface contacts. At the time of collision, surfaces become transparent to make the dots visible.

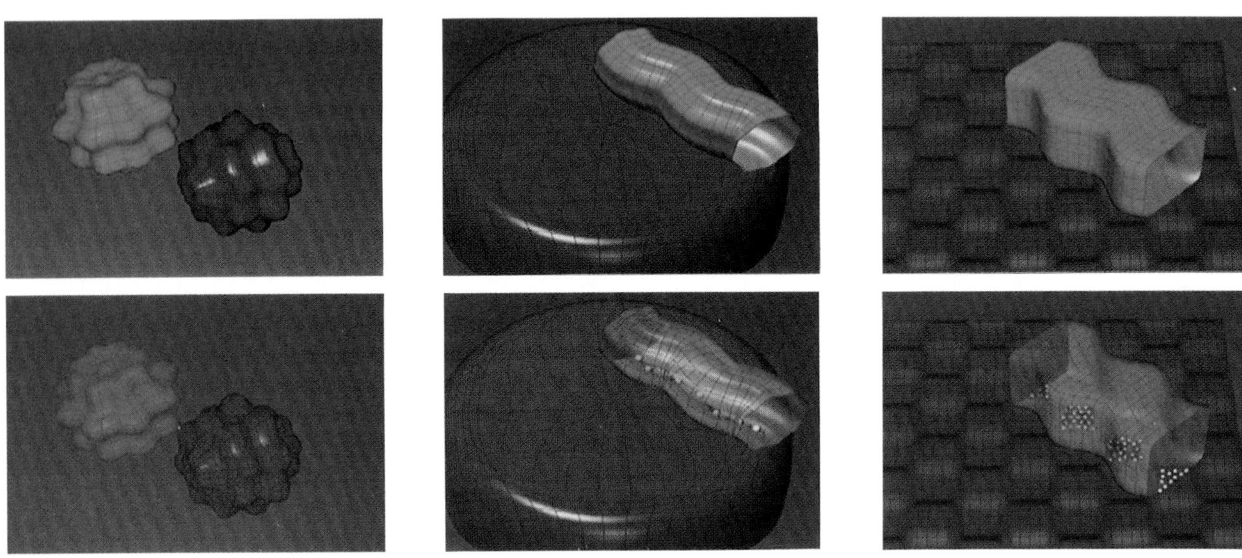

Figure 12: Two bumpy objects collide at one point.

Figure 13: A time-varying tube contacts a cushion along a curve.

Figure 14: A wavy object contacts a raised checkerboard floor in several flat patches.

Scenes from "Fruit Tracing": This animation shows the results of collision detection for a more complicated setting involving hundreds of colliding objects. In this animation, moving parametric surfaces representing fruit are collided with a static lobster shape, defined as an implicit surface. (Lobster data generated by David Laidlaw, Matthew Avalos, Caltech, and Jose Jimenez, Huntington MRI Center.)

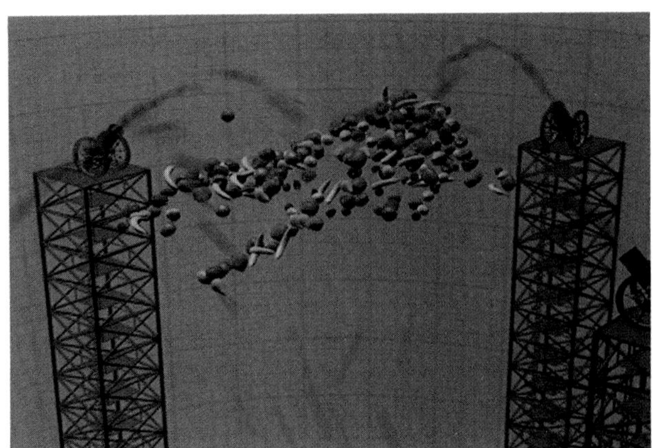

Figure 15: Colliding dynamic fruits.

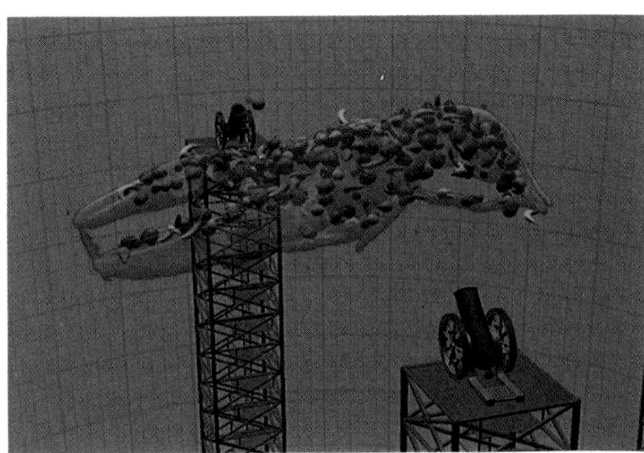

Figure 16: Scene showing lobster shape.

Sensor-Actuator Networks

Michiel van de Panne
*Eugene Fiume**

Department of Electrical Engineering and *Computer Science
University of Toronto†
Toronto, Canada, M5S 1A4

Abstract

Sensor-actuator networks (SANs) are a new approach for the physically-based animation of objects. The user supplies the configuration of a mechanical system that has been augmented with simple sensors and actuators. It is then possible to automatically discover many possible modes of locomotion for the given object. The SANs providing the control for these modes of locomotion are simple in structure and produce robust control. A SAN consists of a small non-linear network of weighted connections between sensors and actuators. A stochastic procedure for finding and then improving suitable SANs is given. Ten different creatures controlled by this method are presented.

CR Categories: G.3 [Probability and Statistics]: Probabilistic Algorithms; I.2.6 [Artificial Intelligence]: Learning, Robotics; I.3.7 [Computer Graphics]: Three-Dimensional Graphics and Realism - animation; I.6.3 [Simulation and Modeling] - Applications.

1.0 Introduction

Many recent investigations have involved the use of physical simulations for creating life-like animations of creatures. The problem is less one of simulation than it is of control: how should the muscles in the creature act to make it move in a desired way? Once known, the forces and torques produced by the muscles can be used as input to a physical simulation to obtain the resulting motion.

Broadly speaking, there exist two approaches to this problem. The first is to apply the laws of physics as constraints on the motion of the various parts of the creature while at the same time optimizing a given goal function. This goal function may be something like "get from point A to point B in the fastest way". An initial guess at the possible trajectory of the creature is iteratively refined until a trajectory is produced that both satisfies the physics constraints and optimizes the goal function.

The second approach is to synthesize a controller. A controller makes control decisions based upon sensory information presently available and does not explicitly calculate a trajectory. A controller thus makes use of feedback to perform its task. Our solutions, called sensor-actuator networks (SANs) are in the form of controllers. There are two main novel features of SAN controllers. First, they are entirely sensor-based. Control solutions are usually cast into a form where sensory information is processed to produce an estimate of the system state. For mechanical systems, the state is the tuple of values sufficient to specify the position and velocity of every point on the object. SANs have no notion of the state of the system as conventionally defined. Second, the stochastic synthesis procedures used to create SANs are unique and powerful tools.

† Email: van@dgp.utoronto.ca, elf@dgp.utoronto.ca

The financial assistance of the Natural Sciences and Engineering Research Council of Canada, and of the Information Technology Research Centre of Ontario, is gratefully acknowledged.

A principal advantage of our method is that it requires less knowledge to use than other physically-based animation systems. The user provides the construction of a creature and can then ask the question "how would it move?" Our method can then yield several controllers providing feasible modes of locomotion (there is no *guarantee* that a suitable controller will be found). We have been surprised with many of the modes of locomotion discovered. Even the simplest objects are capable of a large repertoire of interesting motions. Many of the controllers generated using our method can take advantage of phenomena such as surface friction or collision impact, which can be simulated but are hard to incorporate in many optimization methods. Figure 1 shows modes of locomotion discovered for 4 different creatures.

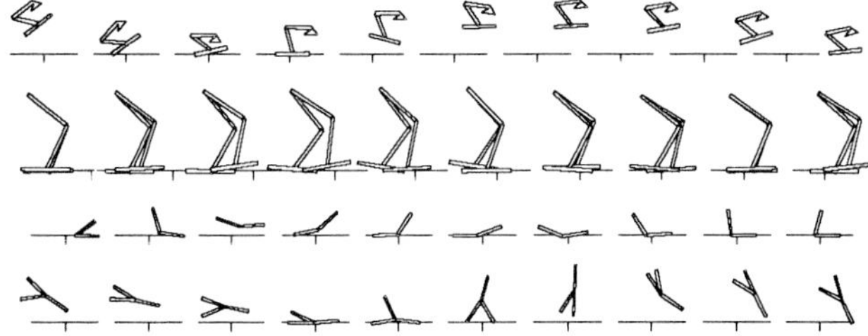

FIGURE 1. Some modes of locomotion using SANs

A sensor-actuator network is a non-linear network of weighted connections between a small number of binary sensors and the actuators (the muscles of our creatures). The network has internal delays, thereby giving it dynamic properties. In this paper we provide a method for determining the parameters associated with SANs in order to obtain instances of a desired behaviour. We show that SANs can be used to control a variety of interesting creatures.

The next section relates our work to important previous work. Section 3 discusses how to construct a creature. Section 4 presents the architecture of SANs. Section 5 gives the algorithms for synthesizing and fine-tuning SANs. Section 6 presents a variety of results, and section 7 concludes.

© 1993 ACM-0-89791-601-8/93/008/0335 $01.50

2.0 Background

Developing control solutions for arbitrary dynamical systems is a difficult problem. Consequently, control solutions are usually specific to a constrained class of control problems. We briefly consider various classes of control problems applicable to animation and their solution techniques.

Linear systems are often the simplest to control. A linear system can be written in the form $\dot{x} = Ax + b$ where x is the state vector. Brotman and Netravali[5] applied linear control theory to the animation of some linear systems. Unfortunately, most interesting systems are very non-linear.

We shall define *smooth* systems as being those that are not necessarily linear, but whose state variables are C^0 continuous over time. This implies positions and velocities are C^1 and C^0 continuous, respectively. This notably excludes mechanical systems that undergo collisions, which instantaneously lose velocity. Smooth systems have states that follow a continuous trajectory through state-space. The solution to smooth control problems typically involves iteratively refining a state trajectory[6][17][24] or performing dynamic programming[8][22]). Solutions to smooth problems are often useful for animation. The take-off and aerial trajectories of many jumping motions fall within this class.

Statically stable systems are those that can be effectively controlled through kinematic means. This means that the motion of a creature can be halted in mid-action and then resumed without it falling over or otherwise collapsing. These can often be controlled by a cyclic motion passing through the body or legs. Realistic animations of snakes and worms[14] and a cockroach[13] have been performed using suitable controllers.

Specialized controllers have been constructed for many systems through careful analysis and simplification of the motions involved. Examples of interesting specialized controllers for walking, hopping, swinging, and juggling are given in [9][18][20][21]. The work in *Making Them Move*[1] presents a variety of specific solutions to control problems in animation.

We shall deal with a class of control problems in which the systems are non-linear, non-smooth, and not statically stable. A large number of crawling, jumping, hopping, flipping, and walking creatures fall in this category. Our sensor-actuator networks (SANs) prove to be particularly adept at controlling creatures in this class. It is difficult to try to perform an optimization that incorporates discontinuities. It should be noted, however, that it is not difficult to simulate many systems of this class.We shall use this to our advantage by performing repeated trials to determine a suitable controller. This means that a minimal knowledge of the physics of the mechanical system is required. We carry out our trials using physical simulations, although they could equally well be carried out directly on the real objects in principle.

Our work has similarities with the work of Wilhelms and Skinner[23] and Braitenberg[3]. Both discuss controllers constructed using weighted connections between sensors and actuators (or *effectors*), possibly through intermediate nodes of some kind. Braitenberg presents a series of thought experiments showing that such networks are capable of producing complex and seemingly intelligent behaviour. Wilhelms and Skinner allow the user to interactively construct the mapping between sensors and actuators. Their creature consists of a rigid body that can propel itself in three dimensions using a jet. Several different kinds of nodes are suggested for use in the connection network. Examples of attraction and avoidance behaviours can be constructed using their approach. Our work will show that SANs, which are similar networks, can be *automatically* synthesized and can be used to control a large variety of physically realizable creatures. Furthermore, we show it is only necessary to consider *one* kind of network node.

Our synthesis technique embodies a *generate-and-test* philosophy that can also be found in some other recent work. Ngo and Marks[16] use it to achieve similar goals to ours. Maes and Brooks[11] learn to coordinate leg motions for an insect robot. Sims uses the same notion to produce striking images[19]. A discussion of search-based control methodology is given in [15].

McGeer's work on passive walking[12] illustrates the phenomenon of mechanical systems reaching and maintaining stable limit cycles. Such *attractors* or limit cycles have also been studied in neural networks and have been conjectured as being the basis for behavioural action in nervous systems. In our work, the dynamical system consisting of the SAN and the creature has a propensity for such limit cycles, in which case it results in periodic motions, some of which are the useful gaits we are looking for.

SANs are similar in topology to many artificial neural networks (ANNs), but are different in several respects. Non-recurrent ANNs have no internal delays and thus provide a static input-output mapping. Furthermore, the synthesis method we employ does not use derivative-based learning methods.

SANs are loosely related to Brooks' work[4] on subsumption architectures for the control of mobile robots. The subsumption architecture is used to implement control at various levels in a control hierarchy. Beer presents a model of an insect nervous system that produces interesting behaviour[2].

3.0 Constructing a Creature

The details of our method are best described through the use of an example. We shall use the *bounder* creature, shown in Figure 2. The bounder consists of 5 links, has 4 angular actuators, and 8 binary sensors. SANs take the binary sensor values as inputs and produce a set of desired angles or lengths as outputs. These desired values are used by proportional-derivative (PD) controllers to determine the internal torques or forces to apply. A PD controller is functionally equivalent to a spring and damper between the desired position and current position of a link. We shall now discuss each of the components of a creature in more detail and then discuss our simulator.

3.1 Mechanical Configuration

The user begins by specifying the desired mechanical configuration for the creature. All our creatures are built of rigid links and have planar dynamics, most of them operating in a vertical plane (i.e., under the influence of gravity). This is a limitation of our current implementation rather than the technique in general. As we shall

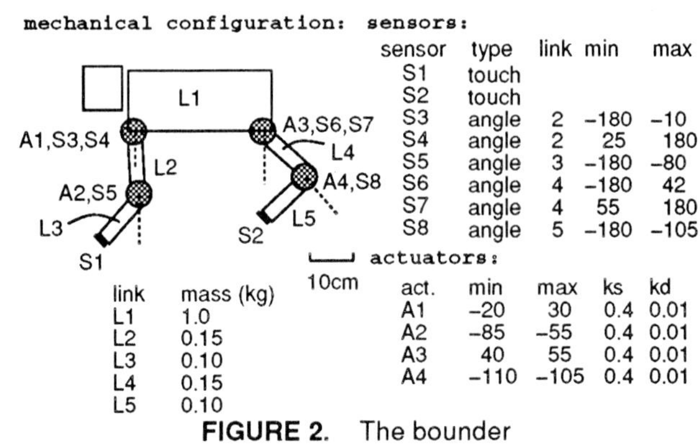

sensor	type	link	min	max
S1	touch			
S2	touch			
S3	angle	2	−180	−10
S4	angle	2	25	180
S5	angle	3	−180	−80
S6	angle	4	−180	42
S7	angle	4	55	180
S8	angle	5	−180	−105

act.	min	max	ks	kd
A1	−20	30	0.4	0.01
A2	−85	−55	0.4	0.01
A3	40	55	0.4	0.01
A4	−110	−105	0.4	0.01

link	mass (kg)
L1	1.0
L2	0.15
L3	0.10
L4	0.15
L5	0.10

FIGURE 2. The bounder

soon see, planar creatures can have a very large repertoire of interesting behaviours. Specifying the physical structure of the creature requires specifying the mass, moment of inertia, and shape of each link, as well as how they are connected with joints.

3.2 Sensors

All sensors for our creatures are binary. If a sensor is 'on,' it produces a value of 1; otherwise it produces a 0. We currently use the four kinds of sensors shown in Figure 3. Touch sensors (e.g., S1 and S2 for the bounder) turn on when in contact with the ground and otherwise remain off. Angle sensors (e.g., S3-S8) determine if the angle of a limb is within the fixed range determined by the minimum and maximum angle specified for the sensor. This angle is measured relative to the link it is attached to, and the zero position is indicated with a dashed line in the creature diagrams. Eye sensors turn on if the *follow point* is in their cone of view. The follow point is a point to which some of our creatures will be attracted. One can thus control these creatures by dragging the follow point in front of them along a desired path. The cone of view for an eye is defined by a minimum and maximum angle. The zero-degree reference for eyes is shown in the creature diagrams with a dashed line. Length sensors are similar to angle sensors, but measure linear distances.

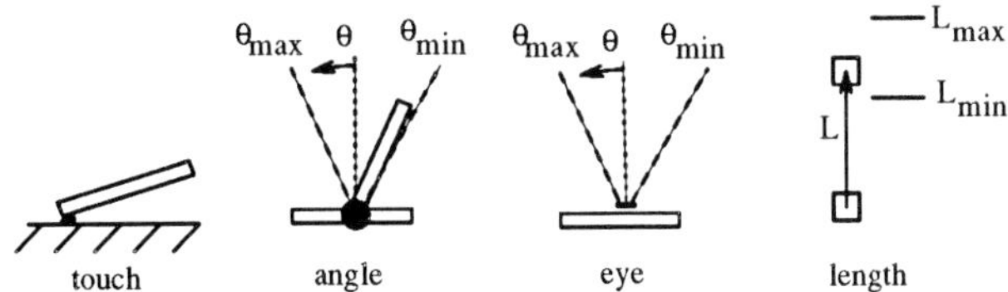

FIGURE 3. Sensor types

Sensors are added to a creature after the mechanical configuration has been designed. It is necessary to use some intuition and creativity in deciding what sensors will be useful to a creature. Touch sensors are useful for points expected to be in contact with the ground. Angle sensors are useful for detecting when a limb has reached the end of its swing. Eye sensors are necessary to be able to track a follow point. Length sensors are useful in the control of linear actuators. The total number of sensors should also be considered. Too many or too few sensors can introduce problems for the network synthesis technique to be outlined shortly.

3.3 Actuators

We shall use two kind of actuators in our creatures: *linear* and *angular*. These are shown in Figure 4. Specifying an angular actuator requires specifying the joint concerned, the upper and lower limits that the desired angle can take (measured in degrees in our creature diagrams), and specifying the *strength* of the actuator.

The strength of an actuator is determined by the constants k_s and k_d associated with the PD controller for the joint. An angular actuator generates an internal joint torque $T = k_s(\theta_d - \theta) - k_d\dot{\theta}$, while a linear actuator generates a force $F = k_s(l_d - l) - k_d\dot{l}$. For many motions, choosing $k_d/k_s = 0.10$ provides suitable energetic motions with some damping. The value of k_s can often be chosen by doing a simple calculation. For example, a 10 degree deflection of limb L5 of the bounder should give a large enough force to support half the body weight when the leg is bent. A simple calculation will produce $k_s = 0.4$ Nm/deg, which is used for all the actuators in the bounder. No hard joint limits are provided by the actuators, although they can of course be implemented in the simulaton if desired.

Length actuators are similar to angular actuators, except that they exert linear forces between a pair of points. Besides the two points, the minimum and maximum desired length allowable for

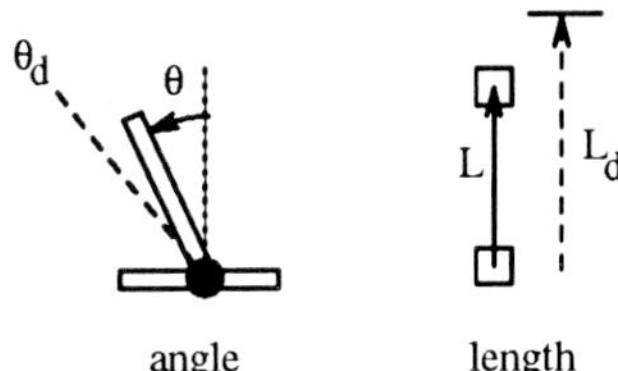

FIGURE 4. Actuator types

the actuator must be specified, as well as its strength. As with the angular actuators, the strength of the actuator is determined by its k_s and k_d constants.

3.4 Dynamics Simulation

Generating and using SANs requires only the capability to simulate the dynamics of a system. It is, however, beneficial to have a fast dynamics simulator, as our method for generating suitable SANs requires many simulation trials.

We make use of a dynamics compiler that uses the mechanical configuration information to generate a 'C' procedure which solves the equations of motion for a single time step. The procedure generates and solves a set of linear equations Ax = b, where x is the set of unknown accelerations. The elements in A and b are functions of the system state, the physical parameters of the system, the internal torques, and external forces. A recursive Newton-Euler formulation is used. This is $O(n^3)$ in the number of links and is quite suitable for $n < 10$.

The creatures are treated as free bodies in space. The external forces applied by the ground are calculated using stiff spring and dampers. We favour this approach as being simpler and more flexible than the alternative choice of reformulating the equations of motion upon impact of a link with the ground. The coefficient of friction of the ground can be set to a desired value. Other physical phenomena such as wind and water forces are easily added in as external forces. For example, for our fish creature, we calculate the water force for each link as $F = k\int(v \bullet N)\,dA$, where $v \bullet N$ defines the component of the velocity in the direction of the surface normal and A is the surface area of the link.

4.0 Sensor-Actuator Networks

SANs provide control by connecting sensors to actuators through a network of weighted connections. We will discuss in the next section the important question of how to determine the weight values. This section describes the structure and operation of SANs

A simplified example of a SAN is shown in Figure 5. The network consists of nodes and unidirectional weighted connections. The weights of the connections can take on values in a fixed range. In our implementation we choose integer values in the range [-2,2]. As shown, there are three kinds of nodes: sensor nodes, hidden nodes, and actuator nodes. The sensor nodes are fully connected to all hidden nodes and actuator nodes. All hidden nodes and actuator nodes are fully interconnected. The number of hidden nodes is usually chosen to be approximately equal to the number of sensor nodes. For example, the SANs for the bounder have 8 sensor nodes, 8 hidden nodes, and 4 actuator nodes.

Sensor nodes take on the values of their associated sensors. The hidden and actuator nodes function as shown in Figure 6. A node sums the weighted inputs and outputs a '1' if the sum is positive. This is a function similar to those performed in neural networks. It is important, however, for the controller to be a dynamical system on its own. This is effected by having a time delay associated with the operation of each node. This delay is implemented with the integrator and the following hysteresis function. The constants k_1

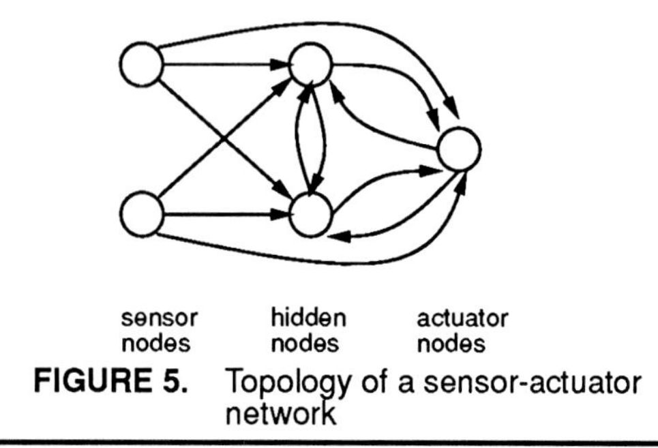

FIGURE 5. Topology of a sensor-actuator network

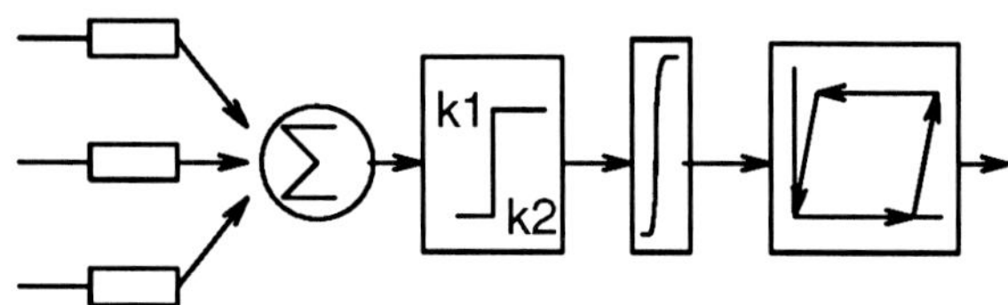

FIGURE 6. Function of a SAN node

```
sum = 0
for (each input i)
        sum = sum + input[i]*weight[i]
if (sum>0) then
        istate = istate + k1*dt
else
        istate = istate + k2*dt
if (istate>1.0) then istate = 1.0
if (istate<0.0) then istate = 0.0
if (output==1 and istate==0.0) then output=0
if (output==0 and istate==1.0) then output=1
```

FIGURE 7. Code corresponding to node function

and k_2 provide control over the time delay for a node to turn on and off, respectively. A hysteresis function is used instead of a simple threshold function to prevent the node output from chattering when some sensors make only momentary contact.

Actuator nodes make direct use of the result of the summing operation at a node to determine the desired angle or length of the actuator. The sum is first bounded to lie in a fixed range and is then linearly mapped to the length or angle range of the actuator. We bound the sum to the range [-2,2] in our implementation.

The function of a node is both simple to program and to build directly in hardware. The code implementing the functionality of a node is shown in Figure 7. The variable 'istate' is the internal state of a node associated with the integrator. We initialize istate to zero for all nodes at the start of a simulation. A hardware implementation would require three resistors, a capacitor, and three opamps per node.

The constants k_1 and k_2 should be chosen in relation to the expected duration of a periodic locomotion cycle for the creature. Thus the node delays for an elephant should be much larger than those for a mouse. The delays are given by $T_{on} = 1/k_1$ and $T_{off} = -1/k_2$ (note: $k_2 < 0$). Typically, good results can be obtained with $T_{on} = T_{off} = 0.25 \times T_c$, where T_c is the expected duration of one locomotion cycle. The delays used for all of our examples fall in the range of 0.07-0.15s. Because of the delays and the internal interconnectivity, the SAN has dynamic properties of its own that are important for generating useful control networks. We view the motions that the SANs produce as being the result of two interacting dynamical systems, that of the SAN and that of the creature itself. One can also think of SANs as being similar in function to the oscillators hypothesized to exist in some animals[13]. When the node delays were removed and the node functions were made more linear in several experiments, it most frequently resulted in a creature that rested in an immobile state after some initial motion. It is perhaps no coincidence that these are exactly the features that make the SANs operate as interesting oscillators by themselves.

5.0 Network Synthesis

We have now defined the construction of creatures and the structure of SANs, but we still need a method to obtain the weight values in the SAN. These will ultimately determine a creature's behaviour. Before outlining our solution, let us briefly consider another possible approach. Consider a top-down method whereby we assume we know the type of motion or desired gait and must now determine the details to generate it. Such an approach has several problems. First, it is often difficult to come up with the desired gait, especially if the creature has no counterpart in nature. Many of our creatures are capable of modes of locomotion that we never could have conceived of beforehand. Second, motion in the desired way might be physically impossible for the creature. We wish to restrict our search to strictly those solutions that are physically feasible. Lastly, the non-linear nature of the creature and its sensing devices makes any such top-down synthesis a very difficult task.

The top-down approach tries to determine a controller given a desired behaviour. The bottom-up approach that we shall take repeatedly generates and evaluates controllers (through simulations) until one or several are found that have desirable behaviours. We thereby exploit the fact that the simulation function is much less expensive than the top-down synthesis function. We have found that the SAN architecture defines a controller space that is highly populated with useful controllers.

Our network synthesis procedure consists of two phases. Phase 1 involves random SAN generation and evaluation. Phase 2 takes the best SAN controllers found in phase 1 and improves upon them. These two phases together define a coarse-to-fine strategy in searching for suitable controllers.

5.1 The Evaluation Metric

An evaluation metric is required for being able to determine the quality of a motion generated by any given SAN. For most of our creatures, this is simply the distance travelled in a fixed amount of time: $f_{eval} = |x(t_{final})|$. The creatures that travel the furthest are usually the ones that have an interesting mode of locomotion. We do usually not care whether the creature moves to the right or the left because both can yield interesting motions. The evaluation metric can be further qualified to be the distance travelled without falling over. For such events we set the evaluation metric to zero. To obtain a controller with energetic hops, the average height of the creature can be incorporated into the evaluation metric: $f_{eval} = \int_0^{t_{final}} (\dot{x} + ky^2)\, dt$. For creatures that should make use of their eye sensors to track a follow-point, the evaluation metric is: $f_{eval} = \int_0^{t_{final}} (v \bullet F)\, dt$, where v is the velocity of the creature and F the unit vector pointing towards the follow point. This metric is a simple measure of how well pursuit is maintained.

5.2 Phase 1: Random Generation and Evaluation

A controller is generated at random by choosing all of its weights at random. This is roughly equivalent to randomly selecting the reactions to be associated with each sensor. A randomly generated

SAN is then evaluated by simulating the behaviour of the creature with the SAN controller and calculating the evaluation metric.

The random search performed by phase 1 is used to discover different possible modes of locomotion for a creature. For this process to be an effective synthesis method, however, we must have some reasonable expectation of finding desirable controllers. At first glance, this does not seem a likely proposition. The space being randomly sampled is very large. For our bounder example it contains 5^{240} possible samples: each of the 240 weights can take any of 5 values. Furthermore, there is no guarantee that any point in this space corresponds to a useful controller.

It is our hypothesis that within the large search space there are many pockets containing useful weight combinations. While the SAN architecture clearly imposes a structure on the solutions, it is not obvious how to search this space. We have found that our dart-throwing strategy is successful a small but significant proportion of the time. The distribution of controllers ranked according to the evaluation metric is a sharply decreasing function with a long tail. Typically 1-5% of the random SANs result in useful motions. This has limitations; as creatures get more complex (6 or more links), fewer candidate motions are aesthetically pleasing.

5.3 Phase 2: Fine Tuning

A second fine-tuning phase may be applied to improve the controllers obtained as a result of the first phase. The fine-tuning phase makes small adjustments to some of the parameters of the SAN and the creature to improve its performance. The weights chosen in the previous step are not among the parameters to be adjusted, however. Because of the non-linear operation of the nodes in the SAN, small changes in the weights often result in either no change at all or a very large change in the dynamics of the system.

The parameters we shall adjust in the fine-tuning phase are those associated with the sensors and the actuators, as well as the delays for the hidden nodes. This list of parameters is shown in Figure 8. We wish to retain the same fundamental mode of locomotion but *evolve* the values of some of the parameters to obtain an improved gait. There are 4 parameters to adjust for each actuator, 2 for each network node, and 2 for each sensor. For our bounder, this results in a total of 44 adjustable parameters.

k1	delay in SAN node for turning on
k2	delay in SAN node for turning off
Amin	minimum desired angle or length for actuator
Amax	maximum desired angle or length for actuator
ks	spring constant for actuator
kd	damper constant for actuator
Smin	lower bound of sensing range for sensor
Smax	upper bound of sensing range for sensor

FIGURE 8. Adjustable parameters for SAN fine-tuning

The approach taken in phase 2 is to make small positive or negative perturbations to randomly chosen parameters. Evaluations are then performed to see if a given change improves the result. We consider two different approaches for performing and evaluating the parameter changes. These are stochastic gradient ascent (SGA) and simulated annealing (SA). These two approaches are distinguished in that one searches for a local optimum, while the second searches for a global optimum.

The structure of the SGA algorithm is shown in Figure 9. The simulated annealing algorithm used is equivalent to that described in [7] and [10]. The simulated annealing algorithm accepts some parameter changes that result in worse performance in order to be able to escape local minima (or maxima in our case). Both algorithms begin with the nominal parameter values assigned when the sensors and actuators were first designed.

```
for (1000 trials)
        randomly choose a parameter to vary
        perturb the parameter value by +delta or -delta
        evaluate the new creature by simulation
        if (creature improved) then
                keep change
        else
                reject change
```

FIGURE 9. Pseudocode for stochastic gradient ascent

A simulated annealing run of 1000 trials was usually sufficient to produce good results. The annealing schedule consisted of 65 evaluations at each annealing temperature, with the next 'temperature' being 0.75 times the previous one. In some cases SGA produced better results than SA for the same number of evaluations. For other cases the reverse was true. We expect that simulated annealing would find better solutions given many evaluations and a suitable annealing schedule, while stochastic gradient ascent quickly finds a reasonable local maximum.

6.0 Results

SANs appear to be capable of serving as useful controllers for almost any relatively simple creature. We have successfully experimented with a total of 10 creatures. These creatures are listed in Table 1, and some of their mechanical configurations are given in the Appendix. The creatures are drawn in the vertical plane and make use of the ground to propel themselves forward, with the exception of the fish. The fish makes use of the reaction forces of water to propel itself forward. The crawler consists of four point masses placed in a rectangular configuration. These masses experience less friction sliding forward than backwards. The crawler uses this property to be able to move forward.

Most of the creature designs are the original and only attempts at designing the creature. There remains, however, a certain measure of intuition involved in determining what sensors and actuators might be useful to the creature. The angle ranges of the sensors and actuators for both the bounder and luxo were varied in several experiments before settling on the given choices, which seem to be capable of yielding a broad range of interesting gaits. The forces and torques produced by the SAN controllers are usually not smooth because of the presence of impacts and the use of binary sensors.

TABLE 1. The experimental creatures

creature	links	sensors	actuators	hidden nodes	speed cm/sec
crawler	4	8	2	10	11
fish	4	6	2	5	19
bounder	5	8	4	8	115
luxo	3	6	2	6	79
cart	2	6	1	5	23
walker	6	11	5	6	101
twolink	2	6	1	5	12
threelink	3	8	2	7	33
fourlink	4	11	3	8	55
star	3	8	2	7	9

An evaluation of 200 random controllers (phase 1) finds useful controllers for each of the creatures, although a wider variety of gaits can be obtained by evaluating more. We retain the top 10 results automatically for examination by the user. For most creatures we use the distance moved in 6 seconds as an evaluation metric. A 30 second evaluation is used for the crawler and the fish in order to be able to test their tracking ability. An evaluation of 200 controllers thus requires 1200 seconds of simulation for most creatures. This can take from 1 hour for the cart creature to 6 hours for the walker creature (on a Sun SPARC IPC).

The crawler and the fish were designed to perform tracking. Their purpose in life is to always swim or crawl towards the follow point. They perceive this follow point only through their binary eye sensors. The joint connecting link L4 to L3 in the fish has a passive angular spring and damper. This joint and link L4 serve as the caudal fin of the fish, a necessary feature for efficient swimming. The crawler and the fish are creatures that form a dynamical system with their SANs that is capable of tracking an object successfully. They can do so with binary eyes and have never been given any information on how to move forward, turn, or associate eye information with turning. Figure 10 shows an example of the pursuit motion of the fish.

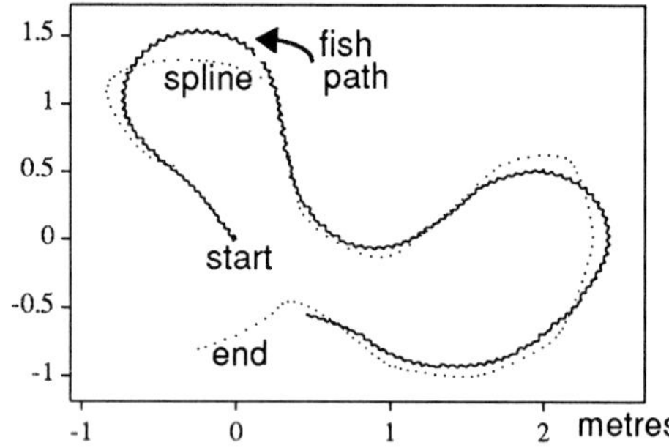

FIGURE 10. The fish chasing a point being dragged along a spline curve.

6.1 Variety of Solutions

The most novel modes of locomotion were discovered for very simple creatures, such as those having only two or three links. The cart creature, shown in Figure 11, is perhaps the best example. The creature derives its name from 'cartwheel' because it was originally designed with the hope it could move by performing cartwheels. Performing cartwheels is indeed one of the physically-feasible modes of locomotion discovered. The creature is also capable of four other unique and valid gaits, however. All 5 modes are shown in Figure 12. These modes were found in a run of 1000 controller evaluations. Several modes looked promising, but were unable to fully sustain periodic locomotion initially. These motions were easily fixed to yield proper periodic locomotion using the fine-tuning phase as described in the previous section.

A simple two-link chain is also capable of remarkable motions. It is important to note that one of the links is heavier than the other, which is necessary to avoid some situations where the chain is unable to locomote because of its symmetry. One SAN moves the creature forward using a flapping motion that lifts the joint vertex upwards and forwards in small hops. Another performs repeated 'jumps' onto its back. Yet another manages to get the links into a position such that it can do a big aerial jump. It 'falls' upon landing, but manages to get up to perform another jump, forming a repetitive motion.

More complex figures such as the bounder and the walker produce gaits more familiar to us. The bounder has gaits moving in small hops, big hops, shuffling, and others which are difficult to describe succinctly. The walker moves by performing shuffles, hops, and taking alternating steps. For many objects, the gaits

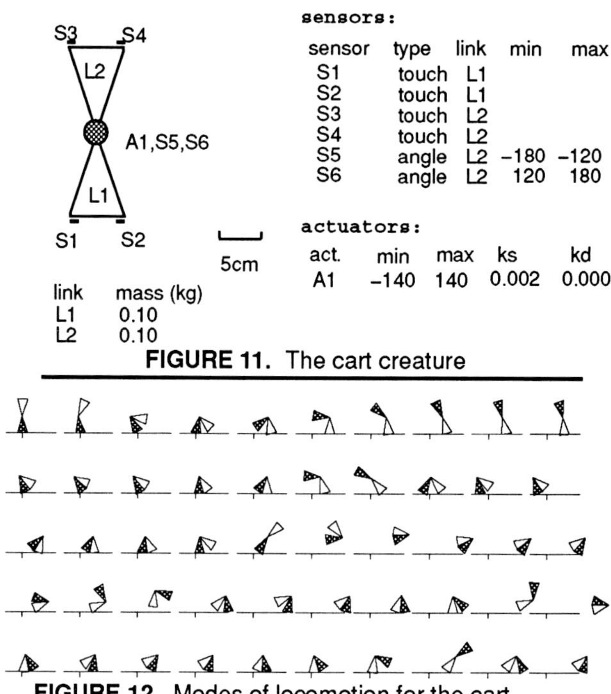

FIGURE 11. The cart creature

FIGURE 12. Modes of locomotion for the cart

produced are dependent upon the coefficient of friction. This is particularly the case for the three-link and four-link chain creatures.

Many of the solutions not ranking among the best in terms of the evaluation metric can also be interesting. Some creatures fall over but can still succeed in moving forward while on their back. Others move a bit and then become fixed, apart from a repeated twitching motion of leg. This is also the case for creatures that fall over into a state from which they cannot get up. These often repetitively twitch their legs in a style reminiscent of an upside-down insect.

There are limits to the complexity of motion that can be expected to emerge by evaluating randomly-generated controllers. It would be futile, for example, to expect to use our method directly to find a SAN to control a reasonable model of a human body in performing a high-jump. As we will discuss shortly, however, we believe that more complex controllers might be achievable through an evolutionary approach.

6.2 Robustness of Solutions

SANs are also an interesting control structure because they can provide robust control. Figure 13 shows a bounder moving over rough terrain using a SAN that was chosen for its performance over flat terrain. A measure of robustness could be included in the search procedure of phase 1 by performing all the evaluations over terrain of the desired roughness. We believe the robustness is a property related to the inherent simplicity of SAN controllers.

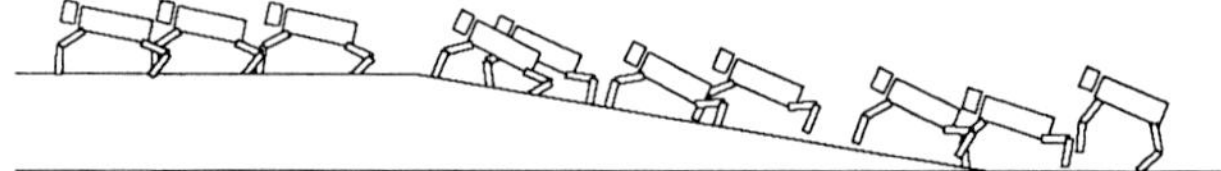

FIGURE 13. The bounder creature climbing a hill

The robustness has limits because the creatures as presently constructed have no means of detecting the upcoming terrain. As such, they are functioning in a manner equivalent to a person walking over rough terrain in the dark. When moving over rough terrain, the same mode of locomotion is usually maintained, with the variations in terrain causing the timing of events to be changed slightly. The gaits are not as robust once they have been fine-tuned. The situation is analogous to running blindly as opposed to walking blindly. Motions optimized for speed are usually less stable.

6.3 Evolution

The second phase of the network synthesis involves making small changes to some parameters of the sensors, actuators, and delays in the SAN. One could also consider including small changes to the actual physical parameters of the system in order to improve its motion. These parameters could include the link lengths, masses, and points of attachment. Such changes are akin to an artificial kind of evolution. For adherance to the constraints of biological systems, the values of these parameters should be interrelated. For example, a stronger spring constant in the actuator, corresponding to a stronger 'muscle', should increase the mass of the appropriate link. Similarly, a larger link should also have an increased mass.

The evolutionary principle could also perhaps be applied to the synthesis of controllers for more complex systems. It is unlikely that random search will stumble upon the best mode of locomotion for a complex articulated figure, such as a good model of a horse. We feel that this is not a large shortcoming of our method because nature herself does not directly arrive at suitable controllers for such creatures. The skeleton, musculature, and control for a horse are the result of a long series of evolutionary changes. We believe it might be possible to arrive at complex controllers by first beginning with the control of simpler figures, such as those that have fewer joints or that have more stable locomotion.

7.0 Conclusions

We have presented a new method that automatically searches for interesting and physically-feasible modes of locomotion for arbitrarily-designed creatures. The solutions are in the form of simple controllers that use binary sensors as input and produce actuator forces and torques as output. Sensor-actuator networks are a compact representation of the complex and varied gaits that they produce. A typical controller has 240 weights that can take on 5 values, and can thus be represented in 70 bytes.

There are several advantages to using SANs. Using the method requires no knowledge of the underlying equations of motion. The user can rapidly construct a new creature and have the method 'discover' several ways it can locomote. It is easy to generate controllers that take advantage of more complex physical phenomena. As an example, the coefficient of friction can have a profound impact on the choice of the best gait. SANs can control mechanical systems that do not always have smooth motion. The user can influence the motion through the specification of the evaluation metric and evaluation terrain in order to achieve the desired speed, energy, height, and robustness of the control. The ability to fine-tune the sensors, actuators, and delays in the SAN means the creature designer need not choose the optimal design parameters to begin with.

SANs have some disadvantages from the point of view of an animator. They do not at present provide the user with as much control over the resulting motion as keyframing or physics-as-constraints methods. Furthermore, there is no guarantee that any useful solution will be found. SANs in their current incarnation do not work very well for systems dominated by linear or smooth dynamics. The synthesis method also fails to find the best modes of locomotion for complex creatures. Our method always results in physically-realizable motions, something that can be an advantage or a restriction in animation.

We believe there are many possible future directions for this work. Many experiments can be carried out using other types of architectures, sensors, and actuators. The fine-tuning phase could be used to determine how to insert passive elastic elements in the system to reduce the amount of expended energy for a given mode of locomotion. The use of SANs as the bottom level of a control hierarchy needs to be investigated. More understanding and analysis of the dynamical systems formed by the SANs and the creatures is needed.

Appendix

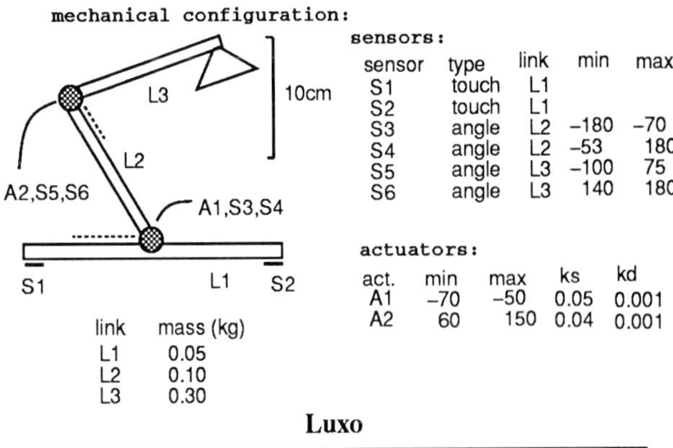

sensors:

sensor	type	link	min	max
S1	touch	L1		
S2	touch	L1		
S3	angle	L2	-180	-70
S4	angle	L2	-53	180
S5	angle	L3	-100	75
S6	angle	L3	140	180

actuators:

act.	min	max	ks	kd
A1	-70	-50	0.05	0.001
A2	60	150	0.04	0.001

link	mass (kg)
L1	0.05
L2	0.10
L3	0.30

Luxo

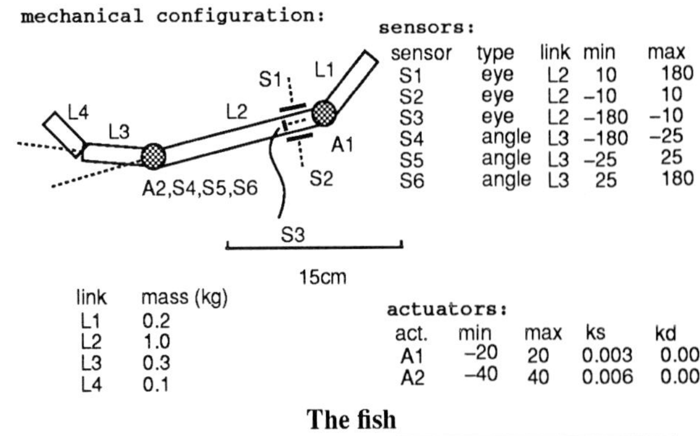

sensors:

sensor	type	link	min	max
S1	eye	L2	10	180
S2	eye	L2	-10	10
S3	eye	L2	-180	-10
S4	angle	L3	-180	-25
S5	angle	L3	-25	25
S6	angle	L3	25	180

link	mass (kg)
L1	0.2
L2	1.0
L3	0.3
L4	0.1

actuators:

act.	min	max	ks	kd
A1	-20	20	0.003	0.001
A2	-40	40	0.006	0.001

The fish

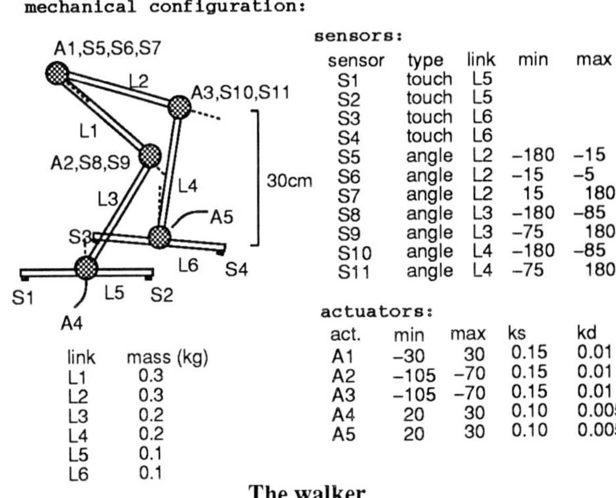

sensors:

sensor	type	link	min	max
S1	touch	L5		
S2	touch	L5		
S3	touch	L6		
S4	touch	L6		
S5	angle	L2	-180	-15
S6	angle	L2	-15	-5
S7	angle	L2	15	180
S8	angle	L3	-180	-85
S9	angle	L3	-75	180
S10	angle	L4	-180	-85
S11	angle	L4	-75	180

actuators:

act.	min	max	ks	kd
A1	-30	30	0.15	0.01
A2	-105	-70	0.15	0.01
A3	-105	-70	0.15	0.01
A4	20	30	0.10	[illegible]
A5	20	30	0.10	[illegible]

link	mass (kg)
L1	0.3
L2	0.3
L3	0.2
L4	0.2
L5	0.1
L6	0.1

The walker

References

[1] N. Badler, B. Barsky, and D. Zeltzer (Eds). *Making Them Move*. Morgan Kaufmann, 1991.

[2] R. Beer. *Intelligence as Adaptive Behavior*. Academic Press, 1990.

[3] V. Braitenberg. *Vehicles: experiments in synthetic psychology*. MIT Press, 1984.

[4] R. A. Brooks. A Robust Layered Control System for a Mobile Robot. *IEEE Journal of Robotics and Automation*, 2, 1 (March 1986), 14-23.

[5] L. S. Brotman and A. N. Netravali. Motion Interpolation by Optimal Control. Proceedings of SIGGRAPH '88. In *ACM Computer Graphics*, 22, 4 (August 1988), 309-315.

[6] M. F. Cohen. Interactive Spacetime Control for Animation. Proceedings of SIGGRAPH '92. In *ACM Computer Graphics*, 26, 2 (July 1992), 293-302.

[7] E. Fiume and M. Ouellette. On distributed, probabilistic algorithms for computer graphics. *Proceedings of Graphics Interface '89*, 211-218, 1989.

[8] M. Girard. Constrained Optimization of Articulated Animal Movement in Computer Animation. In *Making Them Move*, Morgan Kaufmann, 1991, 209-232.

[9] J. K. Hodgins, P. K. Sweeney, and D. G. Lawrence. Generating Natural-looking Motion for Computer Animation. *Proc. of Graphics Interface '92*, 265-272.

[10] S. Kirkpatrick, C. D. Gelatt, and M. P. Vecchi. Optimization by simulated annealing. *Science*, 220,13 (May 1983), 671-680.

[11] P. Maes, R. Brooks. Learning to Coordinate Behaviors. *Proc. of AAAI '90*, 1990, 796-802.

[12] T. McGeer. Passive Walking with Knees. *Proceedings of the IEEE International Conference on Robotics and Automoation*, 1640-1645, 1990.

[13] M. McKenna and D. Zeltzer. Dynamic Simulation of Autonomous Legged Locomotion. Proceedings of SIGGRAPH '90. In *ACM Computer Graphics*, 24, 4 (August 1990), 29-38.

[14] G. S. P. Miller. The Motion Dynamics of Snakes and Worms. Proceedings of SIGGRAPH '88. In *ACM Computer Graphics*, 22, 4 (August 1988), 169-178.

[15] W.-Y. Ng. Perspectives on Search-Based Computer-Aided Control System Design. *IEEE Control Systems Magazine*, 13, 2 (April 1993), 65-72.

[16] J. T. Ngo and J. Marks. Spacetime Constraints Revisited. Proceedings of SIGGRAPH '93. In *ACM Computer Graphics*, 27 (August 1993).

[17] M. G. Pandy, F. E. Zajac, E. Sim, and W. S. Levine. An Optimal Control Model for Maximum-Height Human Jumping. *J. Biomechanics*, 23, 12, 1185-1198, 1990.

[18] M. H. Raibert and J. K. Hodgins. Animation of Dynamic Legged Locomotion. Proceedings of SIGGRAPH '91. In *ACM Computer Graphics*, 25, 4 (July 1991), 349-358.

[19] K. Sims. Artificial Evolution for Computer Graphics. Proceedings of SIGGRAPH '91. In *ACM Computer Graphics*, 25, 4 (July 1991), 319-328.

[20] A. J. Stewart and J. F. Cremer. Beyond Keyframing: An Algorithmic Approach to Animation. *Proceedings of Graphics Interface '92*, 273-281, 1992.

[21] M. van de Panne, E. Fiume, and Z. G. Vranesic. A Controller for the Dynamic Walk of a Biped Across Variable Terrain. *Proceedings of the 31st IEEE Conference on Decision and Control*, 1992.

[22] M. van de Panne, E. Fiume, and Z. G. Vranesic. Reusable Motion Synthesis Using State-Space Controller. Proceedings of SIGGRAPH '90. In *ACM Computer Graphics*, 24, 4 (August 1990), 225-234.

[23] J. Wilhelms and R. Skinner. An Interactive Approach to Behavioral Control. *Proceedings of Graphics Interface '89*, 1-8, 1989.

[24] A. Witkin and M. Kass. Spacetime Constraints. Proceedings of SIGGRAPH '88. In *ACM Computer Graphics*, 22, 4 (August 1988), 159-168.

FIGURE 14. Bounders on the run

FIGURE 15. Walking on campus

Spacetime Constraints Revisited

J. Thomas Ngo
Graduate Biophysics Program
*Harvard University**

Joe Marks
Cambridge Research Lab
Digital Equipment Corporation†

Abstract

The Spacetime Constraints (SC) paradigm, whereby the animator specifies what an animated figure should do but not how to do it, is a very appealing approach to animation. However, the algorithms available for realizing the SC approach are limited. Current techniques are local in nature: they all use some kind of perturbational analysis to refine an initial trajectory. We propose a global search algorithm that is capable of generating multiple novel trajectories for SC problems from scratch. The key elements of our search strategy are a method for encoding trajectories as behaviors, and a genetic search algorithm for choosing behavior parameters that is currently implemented on a massively parallel computer. We describe the algorithm and show computed solutions to SC problems for 2D articulated figures.

CR Categories: I.2.6 [**Artificial Intelligence**]: Learning—*parameter learning*. I.2.6 [**Artificial Intelligence**]: Problem Solving, Control Methods and Search—*heuristic methods*. I.3.7 [**Computer Graphics**]: Three-Dimensional Graphics and Realism—*animation*. I.6.3 [**Simulation and Modeling**]: Applications.

Additional Key Words: Genetic algorithms, evolutionary computation, massive parallelism.

1 Introduction

The Spacetime Constraints (SC) formulation was proposed in 1988 by Witkin and Kass as a powerful paradigm for indirectly controlling the physically realistic motion of articulated figures ("creatures") for animation purposes [17]. The essence of the SC approach is to have the animator specify what the animated creature should do, and the computer determine how the creature should do it. Specifically, the animator defines:

- the physical structure of the creature;
- the actuators that control the creature's internal configuration; and
- criteria for evaluating the creature's motion.

*Present address: Interval Research Corporation, 1801-C Page Mill Road, Palo Alto, CA 94304. Email: ngo@interval.com.

†One Kendall Square, Building 700, Cambridge, MA 02139. Email: marks@crl.dec.com.

The computer is left with the task of computing a physically realistic trajectory for the creature that is optimal according to the animator-supplied criteria.

The computer's role in this paradigm is quite challenging.[1] Finding globally optimal solutions to SC problems is hard for two main reasons [13]:

- Multimodality—even when the problem is suitably discretized, there are an exponential number of possible trajectories that a creature can follow, many of which may be locally optimal or near optimal.
- Search-space discontinuities—a small change in the behavior of a creature's actuators can lead to a large change in its trajectory.

Current algorithmic techniques for SC problems sidestep the difficulties of global optimization entirely by settling for some form of local optimization: typically an initial trajectory is perturbed in some way until it is locally optimal [2, 17, 3]. In this paper we propose a global search algorithm that fulfills a complementary need by generating multiple near-optimal trajectories for SC problems from scratch. The key elements of our search strategy are a method for encoding trajectories as sets of stimulus-response behavior rules [14, 16, 13], and a genetic algorithm (GA) [10, 8, 5] for choosing behavior parameters that is currently implemented on a massively parallel SIMD computer.

2 Algorithm

Our algorithm can be described in summary as follows:

- A dynamics module (§2.1) simulates a physically correct virtual environment in which the effects of creature behaviors may be tested by trial and error.
- A behavior module (§2.2) generates such behaviors using a parameterized algorithm that is based on the concepts of stimulus and response [14].
- A search module (§2.3) uses a genetic algorithm to choose values for the stimulus and response parameters that will generate near-optimal behaviors according to the evaluation criteria for the given SC problem.

[1]This is not to suggest that the animator's role has been trivialized completely—far from it! Specifying appropriate evaluation criteria for a creature's motion is a challenging problem, as is the task of reducing a complex animation problem to a concatenated sequence of related SC problems [3].

2.1 Physical simulator

Like Hahn's [9], our physical simulator employs forward *dynamics*, but treats an articulated figure as an autonomously deforming object without internal degrees of freedom. The deformations are produced *kinematically* by the creature's stimulus-response control algorithm (§2.2). The principal advantage of this approach is dramatically reduced CPU cost.[2] We find that in practice there is little sacrifice in terms of physical realism even though torques about the joints are never computed explicitly. If torque limits were to be important for a particular application, a penalty for excessive torques could be added to the evaluation criteria; the torques can be computed using inverse dynamics [11]. However, we have found that simply limiting the rate at which a creature's internal degrees of freedom can accelerate—something that can be specified trivially in our behavior-based representation—is enough to produce visually reasonable behavior.

Friction is taken to be static when one joint is in contact with the floor, and slippage is proportional to contact force when two joints touch. Collision and contact forces are treated essentially[3] as in Baraff [1]. We specialized Baraff's elegant treatment to two dimensions, then extended it to accommodate autonomous deformations. For a rigid polygon in 2D interacting with a flat 1D floor, the contact-force computation is much simpler than in the 3D case, because the number of contact points is limited to two. The extension to accommodate autonomous deformations is straightforward as well. The key to Baraff's technique is that the relative normal acceleration ($\ddot{\chi}_i$) for a given contact point i turns out to be a linear function of the vector of normal contact forces ($\vec{f}$). The relation remains linear after adding a contribution to $\ddot{\chi}_i$ that takes into account the creature's deformation, so the procedure for satisfying the "non-penetration" and "non-stickiness" constraints ($\ddot{\chi}_i \geq 0$ and $f_i \geq 0$) remains essentially unchanged.

2.2 Stimulus-response representation

Trial behaviors to be tested in the simulator (§2.1) are generated by the stimulus-response (SR) control algorithm. This algorithm neither learns nor plans; rather, it causes the creature to execute instinctive reflexes triggered by conditions sensed in its virtual environment. The conditions are called *stimulus functions* and the reflexes are called *responses*; and their parameters remain fixed for the duration of a trial behavior. The search module (§2.3) finds values for both the stimulus parameters and the response parameters essentially by trial and error. The use of these SR parameters in lieu of a more conventional time series of configurations or forces may be the most important factor in the success of our approach to SC problems.

A *response* is a prescription for changing the creature's shape smoothly. It consists of a time constant and a complete set of target values for the creature's internal angles. Applying the response for one time step means iterating through one time step of the critically damped equation of motion

$$\tau^2 \ddot{\theta}_i + 2\tau \dot{\theta}_i + (\theta_i - \theta_i^0) = 0$$

for each of the internal angles, where τ is the time constant, θ_i^0 is the target value of the internal angle, and θ_i is its actual value. The effect of this equation of motion is to cause the real shape of the creature, given by $\{\theta_1, \theta_2, \ldots, \theta_N\}$, to approach the target shape $\{\theta_1^0, \theta_2^0, \ldots, \theta_N^0\}$ smoothly, even when the target shape changes abruptly due to a switch from one response to another.

To define a stimulus function we must introduce the concept of a sense variable. A *sense variable* is some real-valued function of the physical environment. Our standard list includes:

- proprioceptive senses—each joint angle;
- tactile senses—the force exerted by each rod endpoint on the floor (and *vice versa*);
- kinesthetic sense—the vertical velocity of the center of mass; and
- position sense—the vertical position of the center of mass relative to the floor.

A *stimulus function* is a scalar function defined over sense space. If the sense variables are $\{v_1, v_2, \ldots, v_V\}$, then the expression that we use for a stimulus function is:

$$W \left\{ 1 - \max_{j=1}^{V} \left[\lambda_j (v_j - v_j^0)\right]^2 \right\},$$

where the v_j^0 and λ_j are parameters determined by the search module (§2.3), the weight W is:

$$W = \sum_{j=1}^{V} \log \left(\frac{\lambda_j}{\lambda_j^{\min}} \right),$$

and $\lambda_j^{\min}$ is the predetermined smallest permissible value of λ_j (§2.3). (In practice all of these constants are normalized so that the sense variables v_j fall between 0 and 1.) The locus of points in sense space for which the stimulus-function expression is positive—its *sensitive region*—is a hyper-rectangle with dimensions $\{2/\lambda_1, 2/\lambda_2, \ldots, 2/\lambda_V\}$ centered at $\{v_1^0, v_2^0, \ldots, v_V^0\}$.

The set of SR parameters for a creature consists of an array of SR pairs (10 pairs in all the tests we have run to date). In the following pseudocode, which describes how an SR array is used to generate behavior, the state variables are the creature's physical state and a pointer to the active response:

Initialize creature state from SC problem description
Activate response 0
for t = 1 **to** T
    Determine deformation for time t from active response
    Simulate resulting *dynamics* for time t
    Measure sense variables from the environment
    Identify highest-valued stimulus function
    Activate corresponding response if stimulus positive
end for

The final step may or may not change which response is active; a change is made only if the highest-valued stimulus function is positive. Thus, a response is typically active for several consecutive time steps and produces coherent motion.

[2] Physical simulation is the CPU-intensive portion of our approach.

[3] A modification was necessitated by the SIMD architecture of our machine, because of which we implemented a fixed-timestep integrator with analytic recomputation after a mid-timeslice collision, rather than a more accurate variable-timestep integrator with instantaneous handling of the impulsive forces that arise from collisions.

2.3 Genetic algorithm

In §2.1 and §2.2 we described what a creature would do given a structural specification, initial conditions, and values for its stimulus and response parameters. In §3 we will supply examples of how the resulting behaviors might be evaluated quantitatively. Taken together, these ingredients define a scalar function of the SR parameters. It remains to show how to find near-optimal values of this function.

Our search procedure is a parallel genetic algorithm (GA) written in C* on a Thinking Machines CM-2 with 4096 processors. In a GA, a population of candidate solutions is subjected to a procedure that simulates biological evolution. Each candidate solution—each *genome*, in GA parlance—has some probability of being mutated, recombining with another genome, and dying, based on its value. In our implementation, each processor is responsible for evaluating one genome per generation. Our GA is described below in pseudocode:

```
do parallel
    Randomize genome
end do
for generation = 1 to number_of_generations
    do parallel
        Evaluate genome
        Select mate from another processor
        Cross genome with mate
        Mutate genome
    end do
end for
```

In this section we shall explain the component operations of this genetic algorithm: *Randomize*, *Select mate*, *Cross*, and *Mutate*. Although these operations have worked without modification for all of the test cases shown here and elsewhere [13], they should not be considered optimal.

Symbol	Description	Lo	Hi	Distribution
τ	Time constant	$2\Delta t$	$\frac{1}{4}T$	Logarithmic
θ_i^0	Target angles	$\theta_i^{\min}$	$\theta_i^{\max}$	Uniform
v_j^0	Stimulus centers	-0.5	1.5	Uniform
$2/\lambda_j$	Stimulus extents	0.4	4	Logarithmic

Table 1: The parameters that comprise one SR pair in the genome, their typical ranges, and their probability distributions in the initial random population. The timestep size and total simulation time are Δt and T, respectively; and the quantities $\theta_i^{\min}$ and $\theta_i^{\max}$ are lower and upper bounds on the joint angles taken from the structural specification of the creature.

Randomization Values for all of the parameters in the genome are chosen at random in the initial population, with the probability distributions given in Table 1. We then employ a form of hill-climbing to enrich the initial gene pool: after evaluating this initial population, we mutate and re-evaluate each solution four times, and on each processor choose the best out of five. Because of our highly specialized mutation operator (see below), this has the effect of producing a fairly non-random population that is skewed in favor of multi-step behaviors.

Figure 1: Visualization of a GA population. The display consists of 64×64 pixels, each one corresponding to a processor in the CM-2. Each pixel is colored according to the value of the solution stored at the corresponding processor: the colors range from dark blue for the worst solutions to bright yellow for the best ones. In this mature population two relatively homogeneous regions ("colonies") have emerged from a background of mediocre solutions; the corner areas form one region on the toroidal grid.

Mate selection This is the only step in the algorithm that requires interprocessor communication, and it is also the only stage at which better solutions are given an advantage. In the simplest GA's, mating between any two individuals is possible. To prolong the diversity of the population—this helps cope with multimodality—it is common practice to impose a geographic distribution on the population and to permit only local mating. In our implementation, the processors are laid out on an imaginary 64×64 toroidal grid; this scheme is especially easy to achieve on the CM-2. To choose a mate, each processor performs a random walk of (typically) 10 steps on the grid, and identifies the best solution encountered. If the best solution encountered is itself, it does not mate. (Thus, a solution that is best in its neighborhood is protected from crossover and mutation; this is a form of *elitism* [7].) Otherwise, it fetches a copy of the selected mate's genome in preparation for crossover.

This local mating scheme causes good "genes" (solution fragments) to diffuse slowly through the population, leading to the formation of "colonies" of similar solutions. Figure 1 depicts a population that arose in one of our experiments. As a colony spreads, more processors are put to work on variations of the supe-

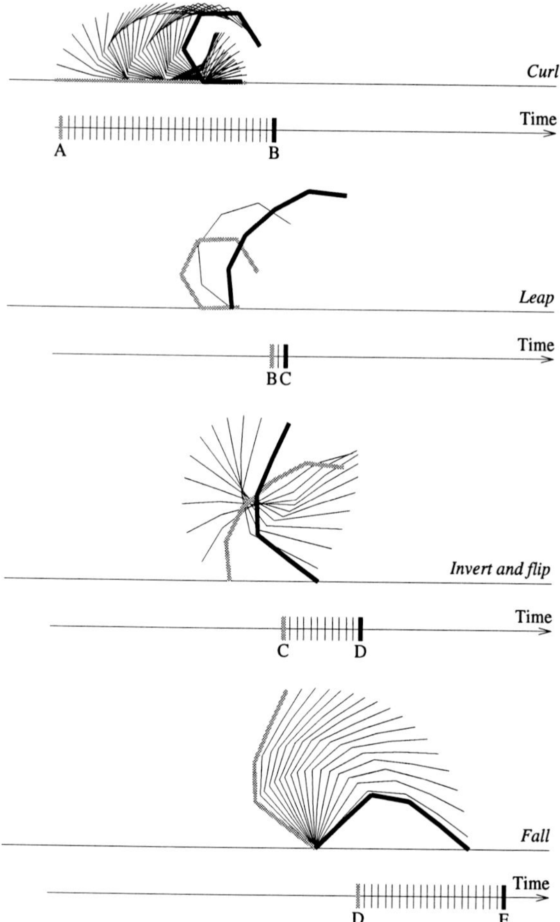

Figure 2: Five-Rod Fred moves to the right by curling and leaping. Since his initial configuration is symmetric, his curling action must be asymmetric in order to generate net rightward motion. Momentum is essential in permitting a forward leap. Inversion in the air is necessary to delay landing long enough to fall forward instead of backward. **Note:** In this and subsequent figures we have arbitrarily broken the motion into easily perceived phases. This is only for presentation purposes, and is not indicative of any aspect of the algorithm. Ticks along the horizontal time axis show which time slices are drawn, and in what linestyles. The first, intervening, and last frames in each phase are drawn with thick grey, thin black, and thick black lines, respectively. An italicized phrase at the lower right of each figure describes the corresponding action.

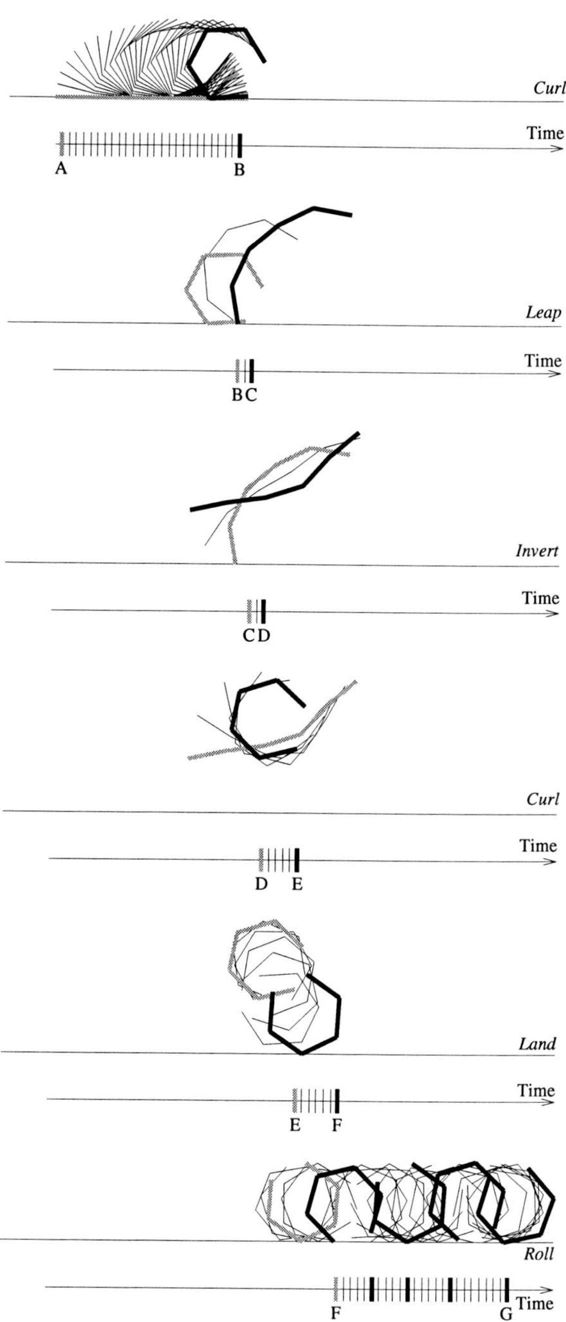

Figure 3: Fred rolls on landing. Because his curled configuration is a hexagon and not a circle, Fred bounces as he rolls.

rior solution that spawned the colony. But because the spreading is not instantaneous, suboptimal solutions still get some processing time. When one colony dominates (a typical outcome when genetic algorithms of this type are left to run indefinitely), the population is said to have converged.

Crossover The crossover operators used in the GA as it was originally described [10] are based on a relatively literal interpretation of the biological metaphor: the bit representations of the parameters in the genomes are placed end-to-end in linear fashion, and crossover operations call for snipping two genomes at analogous locations along the bit string, and swapping one pair of ends.

In the SR representation, a linear layout would not be very meaningful, and we know in advance that certain groups of parameters should migrate together between genomes. Therefore our crossover operator is tailored to treat the genome in a more structured fashion. Given the probabilities that we use, a hybrid might be constructed from two genomes (of ten SR pairs each) as follows: six intact SR pairs are taken from the mate and two from

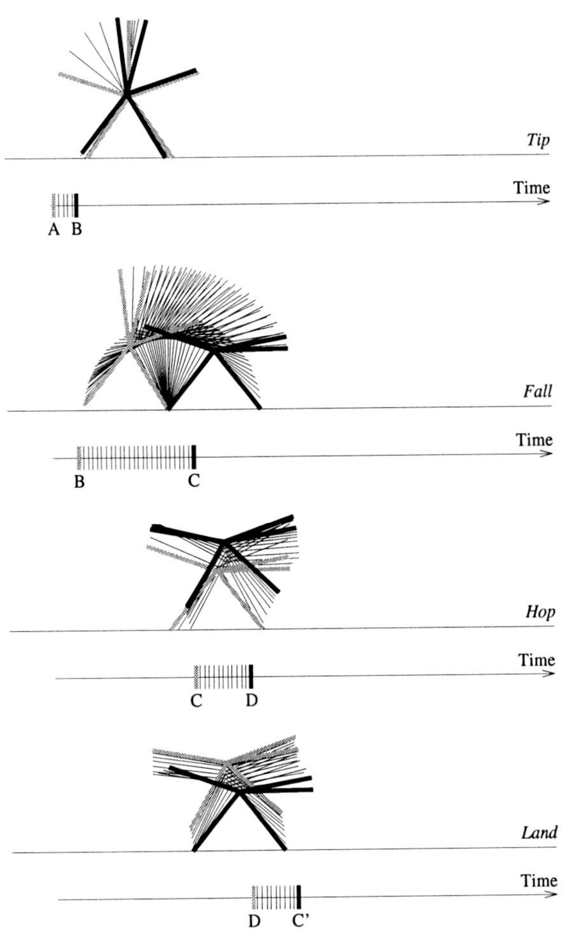

Figure 4: Mr. Star-Man canters on two side limbs. The C–D–C' sequence is repeated cyclically. Were Mr. Star-Man to have human-like strength and structure he would not be able to walk this way for very long, since his arm would get tired. This is one situation in which penalties for excessive torques might influence the range of behaviors discovered.

the original genome; one new SR pair is constructed by taking a stimulus and a response from each parent, respectively; and one new SR pair is constructed by uniform crossover [15], *i.e.*, each number in the SR data structure is copied at random from one or the other parent. The precise probabilities that we use in performing the crossover are not critical; we have not tried to optimize them because the values we use currently are probably irrelevant for future implementations of our general approach (§4). The key point is that the crossover operation must be tailored to the problem to get good performance.

Mutation Our mutation operator [13] is also tailored specifically for the SR representation. One SR pair is subjected to *creep* [5]; *i.e.*, each of the parameters in that SR pair is changed by a small amount. Another SR pair is randomized from scratch, with one stipulation that turns out to be quite important in coping with a large number of sense variables: that at least one corner of the sensitive region (§2.2) of the newly generated stimulus function

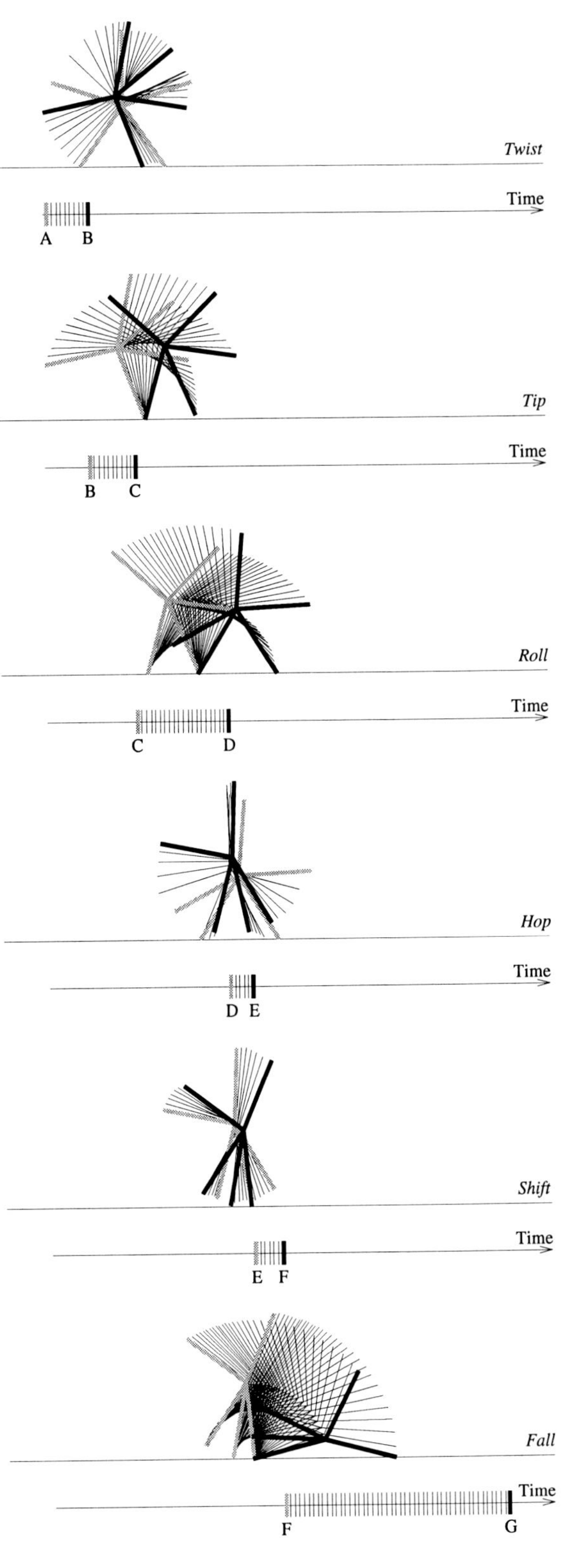

Figure 5: Mr. Star-Man begins to cartwheel, but when his time is nearly up, he falls to the finish line. The subtle posture shifts in A–B and E–F are critical to the motion.

be guaranteed to coincide with the original sense-space trajectory.

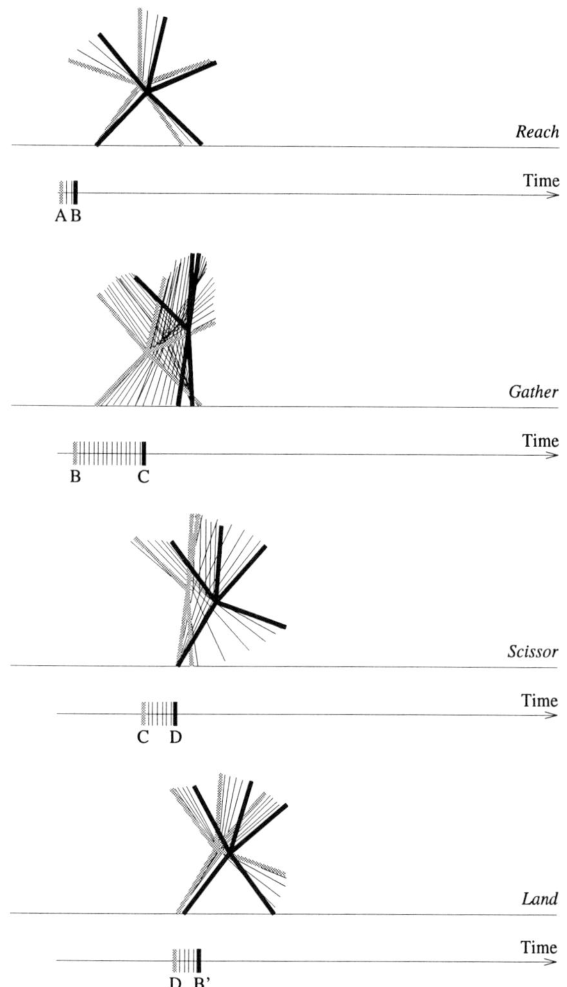

Figure 6: Mr. Star-Man shuffles. The B–C–D–B' sequence is repeated cyclically. Star-Man's stride length is limited by how long his right "foot" can stay off the ground during the step marked *Scissor*. His "arm" helps prolong this step by swinging down, offsetting the upward momentum contribution by his "leg."

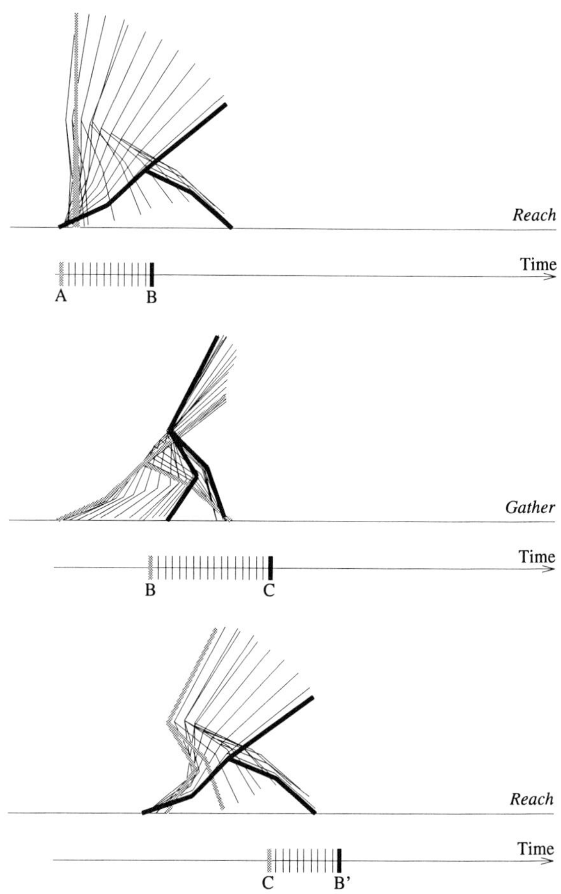

Figure 7: Beryl Biped skips. The B–C–B' sequence is repeated cyclically. Skipping differs from walking; the foot that starts out in the back never moves to the front. Balance is less of an issue in this type of skipping than in walking because intermediate postures are statically stable. However, this skipping is evidently not as fast as walking can be.

Without this restriction, freshly generated stimulus functions tend either to dominate the trajectory or not to modify it at all.

3 Results

In an earlier suite of tests involving unbranched articulated figures [13], we showed that the algorithm could cope with two-point boundary conditions as well as one-point boundary conditions with "athletic" evaluation functions (jump height and walking distance). The present test suite is a further exploration of the "walking" problem that involves bigger, more complex articulated figures, most of which are branched.

We present results for three selected runs. In the first two cases, the evaluation function was proportional to the net horizontal distance covered by the creature's center of mass in the given time. The farther the creature's center of mass moved to the right, the better the trajectory—regardless of how the movement was accomplished. In the third case, the evaluation function had to be modified slightly to obtain the desired behavior. In each case, approximately 30 to 60 minutes of elapsed time on the CM-2 was required to compute each solution shown.[4]

The first problem involves Five-Rod Fred, a creature comprised of five equal-length rods, linked consecutively. The middle rods are of equal mass, but the terminal rods are five times heavier. Each joint allows its pair of connected rods to be at most 30° from collinear. We constructed this creature in the expectation that it would behave like an inchworm. To our surprise, 64 generations of evolution produced the solution depicted in Figure 2. After 100 generations, this behavior was improved by the addition of a rolling phase at the end of the motion (Figure 3).

Fred's final behavior is generated by just five of the ten available SR pairs, which is not unusual for the behaviors described here. Ini-

[4] The quoted times are for 5 rods, 50 time steps, and 100 generations.

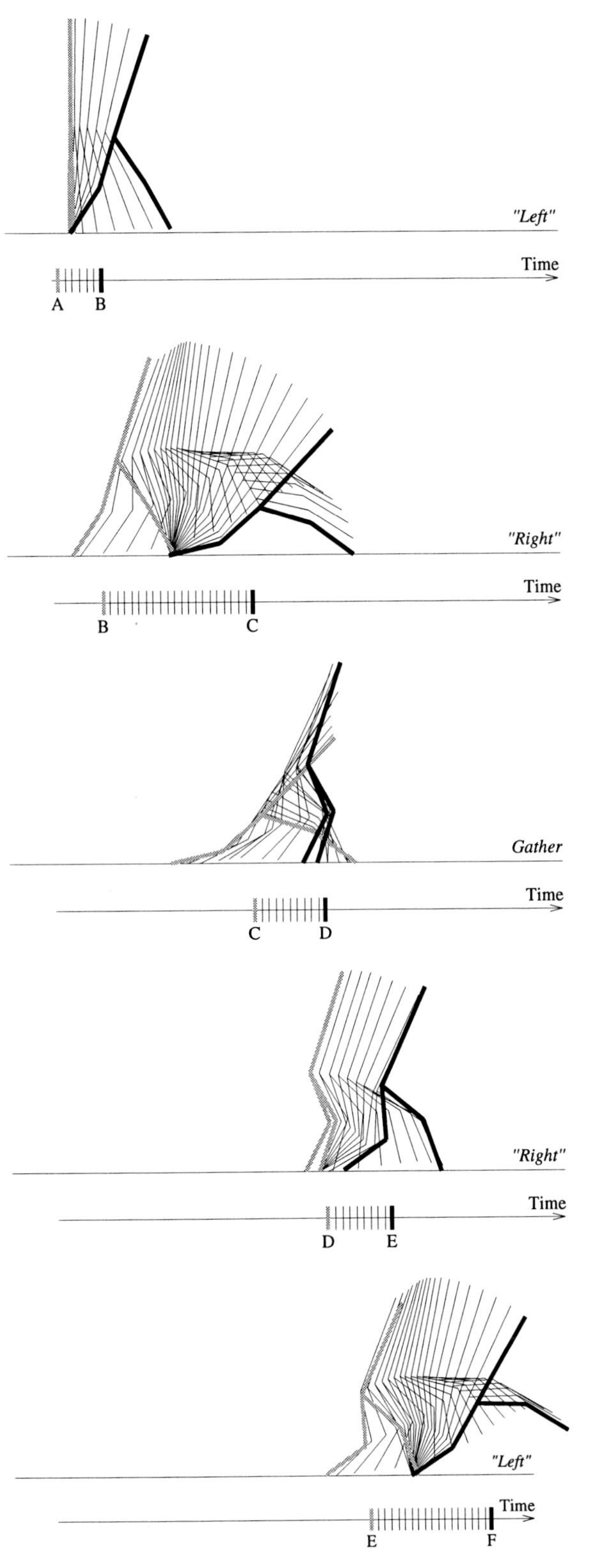

Figure 8: Beryl walks, but one step (C–D–E) is really a skip. The GA/SR combination frequently produces hybrid gaits of this type.

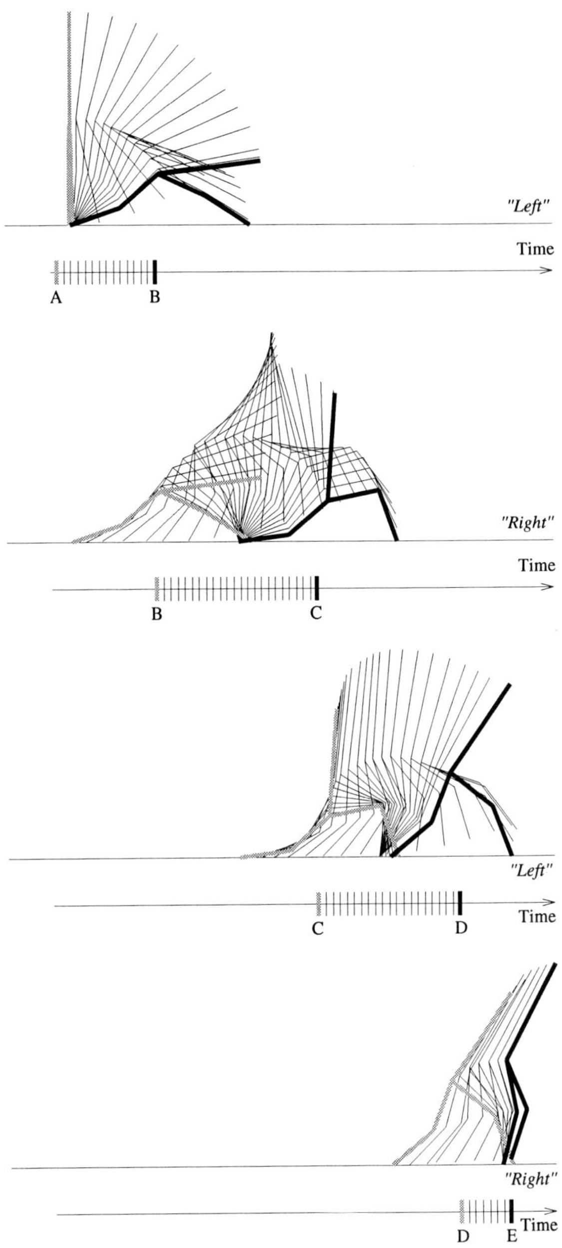

Figure 9: Beryl walks. How to modify the evaluation function to reward grace as well as distance remains an open question.

tially, two SR pairs produce the asymmetric curling motion shown in the first panel of Figure 3. Two more SR pairs produce the leaping motion. Finally, a single SR pair causes Fred to adopt an inversely curled configuration for the remainder of the trajectory.

Mr. Star-Man is another five-rod creature, but one with a different, branched topology. All of his rods are of equal length and mass. Joint-angle ranges are defined with respect to Star-Man's "torso": each "limb" rod is confined to one of the quadrants defined relative to his top "torso" rod. The trajectory in Figure 4 depicts a behavior that evolved after 20 generations: Star-Man tips over on his side, and then employs a sideways cantering motion. This motion is cyclic; the hop-land sequence (C–D–C') is repeated several times. By generation 37 a new behavior had evolved—the start of a cartwheel maneuver followed by a fall to the right (Figure 5). The best behavior after 94 generations was yet a third strategy that involved sideways shuffling (Figure 6).

Beryl Biped is a headless 2D humanoid with a rigid torso, jointed legs, point feet, and rod masses of human proportion. Despite her limitations, Beryl learns human-like locomotion. To elicit these behaviors, we had to change the evaluation function. When center-of-mass translation was used as the measure of progress, Beryl adopted the short-term strategy of plunging headlong into the ground (not shown). When the reference point was changed from the center of mass to the midpoint between her two feet, she still tried falling forward, but in 100 generations she discovered the more tactically sound gaits depicted in Figures 7–9. Thus, like any optimization procedure, the genetic algorithm will fail to find good optima if the evaluation function is sufficiently "deceptive," but simple changes to the evaluation function can often restore acceptable behavior.

4 Conclusions and future work

We have presented an effective algorithm for 2D SC problems involving articulated figures. The trajectories computed by our algorithm differ qualitatively from those that would be produced by existing local-search techniques: they are complex, varied, multi-staged, and sometimes far from obvious. Our work differs from previous global-search and learning approaches to articulated-figure motion control [6, 4, 12] in its adherence to physical law, the nature of the articulated figures being considered, and the generality of the problem statement, respectively.

Developing an algorithm of this type requires numerous decisions regarding the design of mutation and crossover operators and the assignment of parameter values. It is difficult to be sure that one has chosen optimally, since doing so is itself a combinatorial search problem! However, few of the choices are critical. In this paper and elsewhere [13] we have described what we believe are the important choices to get right.

Our current work is directed towards gaining a better understanding of how the algorithm works and making more use of its present capabilities. In particular we are investigating other stimulus-response representations, ways in which a user can influence the GA interactively, alternative search algorithms, and editing techniques whereby composite trajectories can be formed by splicing together precomputed behaviors. In the future, we hope to extend our techniques to work with 3D articulated figures.

5 Acknowledgments

We thank Tom Cheatham for use of the CM-2 at Harvard. Carter Cornwall, Dave Davis, Steven Salzberg, Stuart Shieber, and the members of the Harvard Animation Group, the MIT Leg Lab, and the Cambridge Seminar on Natural and Artificial Computation all provided useful advice and suggestions. Adam Ginsburg wrote support software for the project. JTN is grateful for a Graduate Fellowship from the Fannie and John Hertz Foundation. This work was supported in part by an NSF grant to Martin Karplus.

References

[1] D. Baraff. Coping with friction for non-penetrating rigid body simulation. *Computer Graphics*, 25(4):31–40, July 1991.

[2] L. S. Brotman and A. N. Netravali. Motion interpolation by optimal control. *Computer Graphics*, 22(4):309–315, August 1988.

[3] M. F. Cohen. Interactive spacetime control for animation. *Computer Graphics*, 26(2):293–302, July 1992.

[4] Y. Davidor. A genetic algorithm applied to robot trajectory generation. In L. Davis, editor, *Handbook of Genetic Algorithms*, chapter 12, pages 144–165. Van Nostrand Reinhold, New York, 1991.

[5] L. Davis. *Handbook of Genetic Algorithms*. Van Nostrand Reinhold, New York, 1991.

[6] H. de Garis. Genetic programming: Building artificial nervous systems using genetically programmed neural network modules. In *Proceedings of the Seventh International Conference on Machine Learning*, pages 132–139, Austin, Texas, June 1990.

[7] K. A. De Jong. *An Analysis of the Behavior of a Class of Genetic Algorithms*. PhD thesis, University of Michigan, 1975.

[8] D. E. Goldberg. *Genetic Algorithms in Search, Optimization, and Machine Learning*. Addison-Wesley, Reading, Massachusetts, 1988.

[9] J. K. Hahn. Realistic animation of rigid bodies. *Computer Graphics*, 22(4):299–308, August 1988.

[10] J. H. Holland. *Adaptation in Natural and Artificial Systems*. University of Michigan Press, 1975.

[11] J. Luh, M. Walker, and R. Paul. On-line computational scheme for mechanical manipulators. *Trans. ASME, J. Dynamic Systems, Measurement, and Control*, 102:69–76, 1980.

[12] P. Maes and R. A. Brooks. Learning to coordinate behaviors. In *Proceedings of the Eighth National Conference on Artificial Intelligence*, pages 796–802, Menlo Park, California, 1990. American Association for Artificial Intelligence.

[13] J. T. Ngo and J. Marks. Physically realistic trajectory planning in animation: A stimulus-response approach. Technical Report TR-21-92, Center for Research in Computing Technology, Harvard University, October 1992.

[14] B. F. Skinner. *The Behavior of Organisms; An Experimental Analysis*. The Century Psychology Series. D. Appleton-Century, New York, London, 1938.

[15] G. Syswerda. Uniform crossover in genetic algorithms. *Proceedings of the Third International Conference on Genetic Algorithms*, pages 2–9, 1989.

[16] J. Wilhelms and R. Skinner. A "notion" for interactive behavioral animation control. *IEEE Computer Graphics and Applications*, 10(3):14–22, May 1990.

[17] A. Witkin and M. Kass. Spacetime constraints. *Computer Graphics*, 22(4):159–168, August 1988.

Animation of Plant Development

Przemyslaw Prusinkiewicz
Department of Computer Science
University of Calgary
Calgary, Alberta, Canada T2N 1N4

Mark S. Hammel
Department of Computer Science
University of Calgary
Calgary, Alberta, Canada T2N 1N4

Eric Mjolsness
Department of Computer Science
Yale University
New Haven, CT 06520-2158

ABSTRACT

This paper introduces a combined discrete/continuous model of plant development that integrates L-system-style productions and differential equations. The model is suitable for animating simulated developmental processes in a manner resembling time-lapse photography. The proposed technique is illustrated using several developmental models, including the flowering plants *Campanula rapunculoides, Lychnis coronaria*, and *Hieracium umbellatum*.

CR categories: F.4.2 **[Mathematical Logic and Formal Languages]**: Grammars and Other Rewriting Systems: *Parallel rewriting systems*, I.3.7 **[Computer Graphics]**: Three-Dimensional Graphics and Realism: *Animation*, I.6.3 **[Simulation and Modeling]**: Applications, J.3 **[Life and Medical Sciences]**: Biology

Keywords: animation through simulation, realistic image synthesis, modeling of plants, combined discrete/continuous simulation, L-system, piecewise-continuous differential equation.

1 INTRODUCTION

Time-lapse photography reveals the enormous visual appeal of developing plants, related to the extensive changes in topology and geometry during growth. Consequently, the animation of plant development represents an attractive and challenging problem for computer graphics. Its solution may enable us to retrace the growth of organs hidden from view by protective cell layers or tissues, illustrate processes that do not produce direct visual effects, and expose aspects of development obscured in nature by concurrent phenomena, such as the extensive daily motions of leaves and flowers. Depending on the application, different degrees of realism may be sought, ranging from diagrammatic representations of developmental mechanisms to photorealistic recreations of nature's beauty.

Known techniques for simulating plant development, such as L-systems [16, 27, 28, 31], their variants proposed by Aono and Kunii [1], and the AMAP software [4, 10], operate in discrete time, which means that the state of the model is known only at fixed time intervals. This creates several problems if a smooth animation of development is sought [27, Chapter 6]:

- Although, in principle, the time interval can be arbitrarily small, once it has been chosen it becomes a part of the model and cannot be easily changed. From the viewpoint of computer animation, it is preferable to specify this interval as an easy to control parameter, decoupled from the underlying model.
- The continuity criteria responsible for the smooth progression of shapes during animation can be specified more easily in the continuous time domain.
- It is conceptually elegant to separate the model of development, defined in continuous time, from its observation, taking place in discrete intervals.

Smooth animations of plant development have been created by Miller (a growing coniferous tree [19]), Sims (artificially evolved plant-like structures [30]), and Prusinkiewicz *et. al.* (a growing herbaceous plant *Lychnis coronaria* [24]), but the underlying techniques have not been documented in the literature. Greene proposed a model of branching structures [12] suitable for animating accretive growth [11], but this model does not capture the non-accretive developmental processes observed in real plants.

This paper introduces a mathematical framework for modeling plants and simulating their development in a manner suitable for animation. The key concept is the integration of discrete and continuous aspects of model behavior into a single formalism, called *differential L-systems* (dL-systems), where L-system-style productions express qualitative changes to the model (for example, the initiation of a new branch), and differential equations capture continuous processes, such as the gradual elongation of internodes.

The proposed integration of continuous and discrete aspects of development into a single model has several predecessors.

Barzel [2] introduced *piecewise-continuous ordinary differential equations (PODEs)* as a framework for modeling processes described by differential equations with occasionally occurring discontinuities. PODEs lack a formal generative mechanism for specifying changes to system configuration resulting from discrete events, and therefore cannot be directly applied to simulate the development of organisms consisting of hundreds or thousands of modules.

Fleischer and Barr [7] addressed this limitation in a model of morphogenesis consisting of cells developing in a continuous medium.

© 1993 ACM-0-89791-601-8/93/008/0351 $01.50

The configuration of the system is determined implicitly by its geometry. For example, in a simulated neural network, a synapse is formed when a growing dendrite of one cell reaches another cell.

Mjolsness *et. al.* [21] pursued an alternative approach in a *connectionist model of development.* Differential equations describe the continuous aspects of cell behavior during interphase (time between cell divisions), while productions inspired by L-systems specify changes to the system configuration resulting from cell division and death. The connectionist model makes it possible to consider networks with arbitrary topology (not limited to branching structures), but requires productions that operate globally on the entire set of cells constituting the model. This puts a practical limit on the number of components in the system.

Fracchia *et. al.* [9] (see also [27, Chapter 7]) animated the development of cellular layers using a physically-based model in which differential equations simulate cell growth during the interphase, and productions of a *map L-system* capture cell divisions. The productions operate locally on individual cells, making it possible to simulate the development of arbitrarily large layers using a finite number of rules. Unfortunately, this technique does not seem to extend beyond the modeling of cellular layers.

Timed L-systems [27, Chapter 6] were introduced specifically as a formal framework for constructing models of branching structures developing in continuous time. They operate under the assumption that no information exchange between coexisting modules takes place. This is a severe limitation, as interactions between the modules are known to play an important role in the development of many plant species [14, 27, 28]. A practical application of timed L-systems to animation is described by Noser *et. al.* [22].

The model of development proposed in this paper combines elements of PODEs, the connectionist model, and L-systems. The necessary background in L-systems is presented in Section 2. Sections 3 and 4 introduce the definition of differential L-systems and illustrate it using two simple examples. Section 5 applies combined discrete/continuous simulation techniques to evaluate dL-systems over time. Section 6 focuses on growth functions, which characterize continuous aspects of model development. Application of differential L-systems to the animation of the development of higher plants is presented in Section 7, using the models of a compound leaf and three herbaceous plants as examples. A summary of the results and a list of open problems conclude the paper.

2 L-SYSTEMS

An extensive exposition of L-systems applied to the modeling of plants is given in [27]. Below we summarize the main features of L-systems pertinent to the present paper.

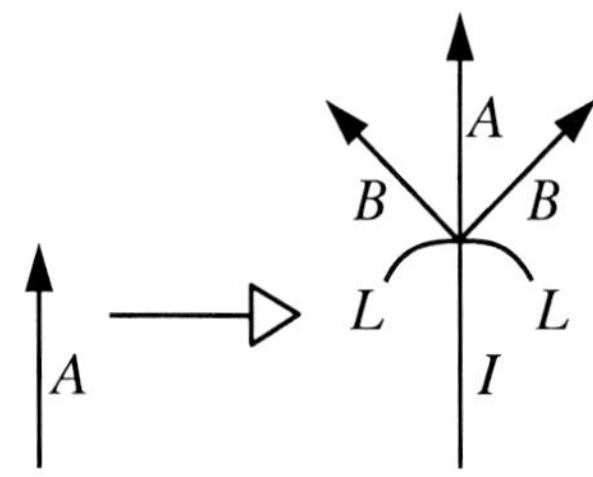

Figure 1: Example of a typical L-system production

We view a plant as a linear or branching structure composed of repeated units called *modules*. An L-system describes the development of this structure in terms of *rewriting rules* or *productions*, each of which replaces the *predecessor* module by zero, one, or more *successor* modules. For example, the production in Figure 1 replaces apex A by a structure consisting of a new apex A, an internode I, and two lateral apices B supported by leaves L.

In general, productions can be *context free* and depend only on the replaced module, or *context-sensitive* and depend also on the neighborhood of this module. A *developmental sequence* is generated by repeatedly applying productions to the consecutively obtained structures. In each step, productions are applied in parallel to all parts of the structure obtained so far.

The original formalism of L-systems [16] has a threefold discrete character [17]: the modeled structure is a finite collection of modules, each of these modules is in one of a finite number of states, and the development is simulated in discrete derivation steps. An extension called *parametric L-systems* [25, 27] increases the expressive power of L-systems by introducing a continuous characterization of the module states. Each module is represented by an identifier denoting the module *type* (one or more symbols starting with a letter) and a *state vector* of zero, one, or more numerical *parameters*. For instance, $M = A(5, 9.5)$ denotes a module M of type A with two parameters $w_1 = 5$ and $w_2 = 9.5$, forming the vector $\mathbf{w} = (5, 9.5)$. The interpretation of parameters depends on the semantics of the module definition, and may vary from one module type to another. For example, parameters may quantify the shape of the module, its age, and the concentration of substances contained within it.

Figure 2: Turtle interpretation of a sample string

In the formalism of L-systems, modeled structures are represented as *strings* of modules. Branching structures are captured using *bracketed* strings, with the matching pairs of brackets [and] delimiting branches. We visualize these structures using a *turtle interpretation* of strings [23, 28], extended to strings of modules with parameters in [13, 25, 27]. A predefined interpretation is assigned to a set of reserved modules. Some of them represent physical parts of the modeled plant, for example a leaf or an internode, while others represent local properties, such as the magnitude of a branching angle. Reserved modules frequently used in this paper are listed below:

$F(x)$	line segment of length x,
$+(\alpha), -(\alpha)$	orientation change of the following line by $\pm\alpha$ degrees with respect to the preceding line,
$@X(s)$	a predefined surface X scaled by the factor s.

The interpretation of a string of modules proceeds by scanning it from left to right and considering the reserved modules as commands that maneuver a LOGO-style turtle. For example, Figure 2 shows the turtle interpretation of a sample string:

$$F(1)[+(45)@L(0.75)]F(0.8)[-(30)@L(0.5)]F(0.6)@K(1),$$

where symbols $@L$ and $@K$ denote predefined surfaces depicting a leaf and a flower.

3 DEFINITION OF dL-SYSTEMS

Differential L-systems extend parametric L-systems by introducing continuous time flow in place of a sequence of discrete derivation steps. As long as the parameters $\mathbf{w}$ of a module $A(\mathbf{w})$ remain in the *domain of legal values* $\mathcal{D}_A$, the module develops in a continuous way. Once the parameter values reach the boundary $\mathcal{C}_A$ of the domain $\mathcal{D}_A$, a production replaces module $A(\mathbf{w})$ by its descendants in a discrete event. The form of this production may depend on which segment $\mathcal{C}_{A_k}$ of the boundary of $\mathcal{D}_A$ has been crossed.

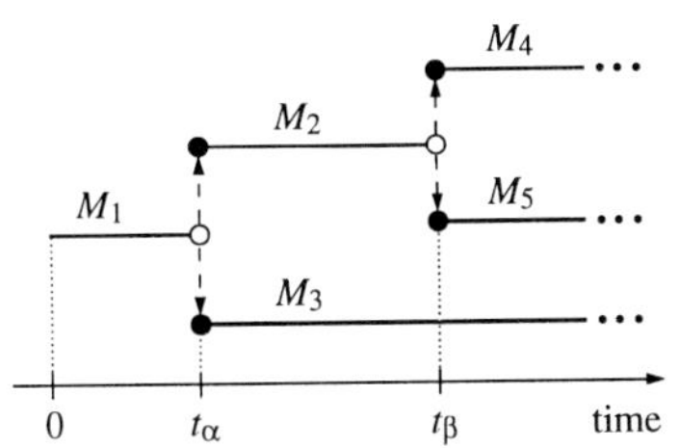

Figure 3: Fragment of the lineage tree of a hypothetical modular structure

For example, module M_2 in Figure 3 is created at time t_α as one of two descendants of the initial module M_1. It develops in the interval $[t_\alpha, t_\beta)$, and ceases to exist at time t_β, giving rise to two new modules M_4 and M_5. The instant t_β is the time at which parameters of M_2 reach the boundary of its domain of legal states $\mathcal{D}$. A hypothetical trajectory of module M_2 in its parameter space is depicted in Figure 4.

In order to formalize the above description, let us assume that the modeled structure consists of a sequence of modules (an extension to branching structures is straightforward if a proper definition of context is used [27, 28]). The state of the structure at time t is represented as a string:

$$\mu = A_1(\mathbf{w}_1)A_2(\mathbf{w}_2)\cdots A_n(\mathbf{w}_n).$$

The module $A_{i-1}(\mathbf{w}_{i-1})$ immediately preceding a given module $A_i(\mathbf{w}_i)$ in the string μ is called the *left neighbor* or *left context* of $A_i(\mathbf{w}_i)$, and the module $A_{i+1}(\mathbf{w}_{i+1})$ immediately following $A_i(\mathbf{w}_i)$ is called its *right neighbor* or *right context.* When it is inconvenient to list the indices, we use the symbols $<$, $>$, and/or subscripts l, r to specify the context of $A(\mathbf{w})$, as in the expression:

$$A_l(\mathbf{w}_l) < A(\mathbf{w}) > A_r(\mathbf{w}_r).$$

The continuous behavior of $A(\mathbf{w})$ is described by an *ordinary differential equation* that determines the rate of change $d\mathbf{w}/dt$ of parameters $\mathbf{w}$ as a function of the current value of these parameters and those of the module's neighbors:

$$\frac{d\mathbf{w}}{dt} = f_A(\mathbf{w}_l, \mathbf{w}, \mathbf{w}_r).$$

The above equation applies as long as the parameters $\mathbf{w}$ are in the domain $\mathcal{D}_A$ characteristic to the module type A. We assume that $\mathcal{D}_A$ is an open set, and specify its boundary $\mathcal{C}_A$ as the union of a finite number $m \geq 1$ of nonintersecting segments $\mathcal{C}_{A_k}$, $k = 1, 2, \ldots, m$. The time t_β at which the trajectory of module $A(\mathbf{w})$ reaches a segment $\mathcal{C}_{A_k}$ of the boundary of $\mathcal{D}_A$ satisfies the expression:

$$\lim_{t \to t_\beta^-} \mathbf{w}(t) \in \mathcal{C}_{A_k}.$$

The replacement of module $A(\mathbf{w})$ by its descendants at time t_β is described by a *production*:

$$p_{A_k} : A_l(\mathbf{w}_l) < A(\mathbf{w}) > A_r(\mathbf{w}_r) \longrightarrow$$
$$B_{k,1}(\mathbf{w}_{k,1})B_{k,2}(\mathbf{w}_{k,2})\cdots B_{k,m_k}(\mathbf{w}_{k,m_k}).$$

The module $A(\mathbf{w})$ is called the *strict predecessor* and the sequence of modules $B_{k,1}(\mathbf{w}_{k,1})B_{k,2}(\mathbf{w}_{k,2})\cdots B_{k,m_k}(\mathbf{w}_{k,m_k})$ is called the *successor* of this production. The index k emphasizes that different productions can be associated with individual segments $\mathcal{C}_{A_k}$ of the boundary $\mathcal{C}_A$. The initial value of parameters assigned to a module $B_{k,j}(\mathbf{w}_{k,j})$ upon its creation is determined by a function $h_{A_{k,j}}$ which takes as its arguments the values of the parameters $\mathbf{w}_l$, $\mathbf{w}$, and $\mathbf{w}_r$ at the time immediately preceding production application:

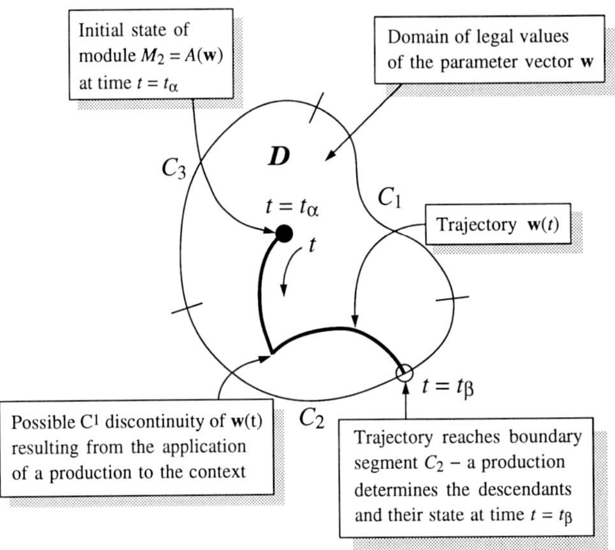

Figure 4: A hypothetical trajectory of module M_2 in its parameter space

$$\mathbf{w}_{k,j} = \lim_{t \to t_\beta^-} h_{A_{k,j}}(\mathbf{w}_l(t), \mathbf{w}(t), \mathbf{w}_r(t)).$$

The vector $\mathbf{w}_{k,j}$ must belong to the domain $\mathcal{D}_{B_{k,j}}$. (A stronger condition is needed to insure that the number of productions applied in any finite interval $[t, t + \Delta t]$ will be finite.)

In summary, a differential L-system is defined by the initial string of modules μ_0 and the specification of each module type under consideration. The specification of a module type A consists of four components:

$$< \mathcal{D}_A, \mathcal{C}_A, f_A, P_A >,$$

where:

- the open set $\mathcal{D}_A$ is the domain of legal parameter values of modules of type A,
- the set $\mathcal{C}_A = \mathcal{C}_{A_1} \cup \ldots \cup \mathcal{C}_{A_m}$ is the boundary of $\mathcal{D}_A$, consisting of nonintersecting segments $\mathcal{C}_{A_1}, \ldots, \mathcal{C}_{A_m}$,
- the function f_A specifies a system of differential equations that describe the continuous behavior of modules of type A in their domain of legal parameter values $\mathcal{D}_A$,
- the set of productions $P_A = \{p_{A_1}, \ldots, p_{A_m}\}$ captures the discrete behavior of modules of type A.

A production $p_{A_k} \in P_A$ is applied when the parameters of a module M of type A reach segment $\mathcal{C}_{A_k}$ of the boundary $\mathcal{C}_A$. At this time module M disappears, and zero, one, or more descendant modules are created. The functions $h_{A_{k,j}}$ embedded in productions p_{A_k} determine the initial values of parameters in the successor modules.

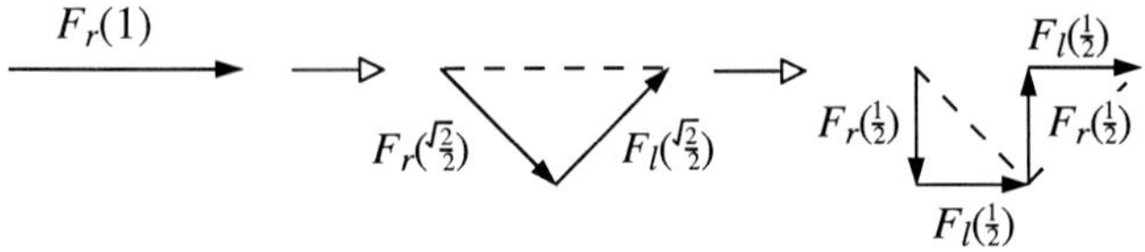

Figure 5: Initial steps in the construction of a dragon curve

4 EXAMPLES OF dL-SYSTEMS

We will illustrate the notion of a dL-system using two sample models suitable for animating the development of the *dragon curve* and the filamentous alga *Anabaena catenula.*

4.1 A dL-system model of the dragon curve

In the discrete case, consecutive iterations of the *dragon curve* (described, for example, in [27, Chapter 1]) can be obtained by the following parametric L-system:

$$\begin{aligned} \omega &: \ --F_r(1) \\ p_1 &: \ F_r(s) \rightarrow -F_r(s\tfrac{\sqrt{2}}{2}) + +F_l(s\tfrac{\sqrt{2}}{2}) - \\ p_2 &: \ F_l(s) \rightarrow +F_r(s\tfrac{\sqrt{2}}{2}) - -F_l(s\tfrac{\sqrt{2}}{2}) + \end{aligned}$$

Assuming that symbols $+$ and $-$ represent turns of $\pm 45°$, this L-system encodes a Koch construction [18, Chapter 6] that repeatedly substitutes sides of an isosceles right-angled triangle for its hypotenuse (Figure 5). Subscripts l and r indicate that the triangle is formed respectively on the left or right side of the oriented predecessor segment. A corresponding dL-system that generates the dragon curve through the continuous progression of shapes indicated in Figure 6 is given below:

initial string: $--F_r(1,1)$
$F_r(x,s)$:
  if $x < s$ **solve** $\frac{dx}{dt} = \frac{s}{T}, \frac{ds}{dt} = 0$
  if $x = s$ **produce** $-F_r(0, s\frac{\sqrt{2}}{2}) + F_h(s,s) + F_l(0, s\frac{\sqrt{2}}{2}) -$
$F_l(x,s)$:
  if $x < s$ **solve** $\frac{dx}{dt} = \frac{s}{T}, \frac{ds}{dt} = 0$
  if $x = s$ **produce** $+F_r(0, s\frac{\sqrt{2}}{2}) - F_h(s,s) - F_l(0, s\frac{\sqrt{2}}{2}) +$
$F_h(x,s)$:
  if $x > 0$ **solve** $\frac{dx}{dt} = -\frac{s}{T}, \frac{ds}{dt} = 0$
  if $x = 0$ **produce** ε

The operation of this model starts with the replacement of the initial module $F_r(1,1)$ with the string:

$$-F_r(0, \frac{\sqrt{2}}{2}) + F_h(1,1) + F_l(0, \frac{\sqrt{2}}{2}) -,$$

which has the same turtle interpretation: a line segment of unit length [1]. Next, the horizontal line segment represented by module F_h decreases in length with the speed $\frac{dx}{dt} = -\frac{1}{T}$, while the diagonal segments represented by modules F_r and F_l elongate with the speed $\frac{dx}{dt} = \frac{\sqrt{2}}{2}\frac{1}{T}$. The constant T determines the lifetime of the modules: after time T, the module F_h reaches zero length and is removed from the string (replaced by the empty string ε), while both modules F_r and F_l reach their maximum length of $\frac{\sqrt{2}}{2}$ and are replaced by their respective successors. These successors subsequently follow the same developmental pattern.

It is not accidental that the predecessor and the successor of the productions for $F_r(x,s)$ and $F_l(x,s)$ have identical geometric interpretations. Since productions are assumed to be applied instantaneously, any change of the model's geometry introduced by a production would appear as a discontinuity in the animation. In general, correctly specified productions satisfy *continuity criteria* [27, Chapter 6], which means that they conserve physical entities such as shape, mass, and velocity of modules.

4.2 A dL-system model of *Anabaena catenula*

The continuously developing dragon curve has been captured by a context-free dL-system, in which all productions and equations depend only on the strict predecessor module. A simple example of a context-sensitive model inspired by the development of the blue-green alga *Anabaena catenula* [3, 20, 27] is given below.

Anabaena forms a nonbranching filament consisting of two classes of cells: *vegetative cells* and *heterocysts*. A vegetative cell usually divides into two descendant vegetative cells. However, in some cases a vegetative cell differentiates into a heterocyst. The spacing between heterocysts is relatively constant, in spite of the continuing growth of the filament. Mathematical models explain this phenomenon using a biologically motivated hypothesis that the distribution of heterocysts is regulated by nitrogen compounds produced by the heterocysts, diffusing from cell to cell along the filament, and decaying in the vegetative cells. If the compound concentration in a vegetative cell falls below a specific level, this cell differentiates into a heterocyst (additional factors are captured by more sophisticated models). A model operating in continuous time according to this description can be captured by the following dL-system:

initial string: $F_h(x_{max}, c_{max})F_v(x_{max}, c_{max})F_h(x_{max}, c_{max})$
$F(x_l, c_l) < F_v(x,c) > F(x_r, c_r)$:
  if $x < x_{max}$ & $c > c_{min}$
    solve $\frac{dx}{dt} = rx, \frac{dc}{dt} = D \cdot (c_l + c_r - 2c) - \mu c$
  if $x = x_{max}$ & $c > c_{min}$
    produce $F_v(kx_{max}, c)F_v((1-k)x_{max}, c)$
  if $c = c_{min}$
    produce $F_h(x,c)$
$F_h(x,c)$:
    solve $\frac{dx}{dt} = r_x(x_{max} - x), \frac{dc}{dt} = r_c(c_{max} - c)$

Vegetative cells F_v and heterocysts F_h are characterized by their length x and concentration of nitrogen compounds c. The differential equations for the vegetative cell F_v indicate that while the cell length x is below the maximum value x_{max} and the compound concentration c is above the threshold c_{min}, the cell elongates exponentially according to the equation $\frac{dx}{dt} = rx$, and the compound concentration changes according to the equation:

$$\frac{dc}{dt} = D \cdot (c_l + c_r - 2c) - \mu c.$$

The first term in this equation describes diffusion of the compounds through the cell walls. Following *Fick's law* [5, page 404], the

[1]The turtle interprets the first parameter as the segment length, and ignores the second parameter.

Figure 6: Development of the dragon curve simulated using a dL-system, recorded in time intervals $\Delta t = \frac{1}{8}T$. Top left: Superimposed stages $0-8$, top right: stages $8-16$, bottom row: stages $16-24$ and $24-32$.

rate of diffusion is proportional to the differences of compound concentrations, $c_r - c$ and $c_l - c$, between the neighbor cells and the cell under consideration. The term μc describes exponential decay of the compounds in the cell.

In addition to the differential equations, two productions describe the behavior of a vegetative cell. If the cell reaches maximum length x_{max} while the concentration c is still above the threshold c_{min}, the cell divides into two vegetative cells of length kx_{max} and $(1-k)x_{max}$, with the compound concentration c inherited from their parent cell. Otherwise, if the concentration c drops down to the threshold c_{min}, the cell differentiates into a heterocyst. Both productions satisfy the continuity criteria by conserving total cell length and concentration of nitrogen compounds.

The last line of the model specifies the behavior of the heterocysts. Their length and compound concentration converge exponentially to the limit values of x_{max} and c_{max}. The heterocysts do not undergo any further transformations.

Simulation results obtained using the above model are shown in Figure 7. The cells in the filament are represented as horizontal line segments with the colors indicating the concentration of nitrogen compounds. Consecutive developmental stages are drawn one under another. An approximately equal spacing between the heterocysts (shown in white) is maintained for any horizontal section, as postulated during model formulation.

Note that for incorrectly chosen constants in the model, the spacing between heterocysts may be distorted; for example, groups of adjacent vegetative cells may almost simultaneously differentiate into heterocysts.

5 EVALUATION OF dL-SYSTEMS

Although Figures 6 and 7 were obtained using dL-systems, we have not yet discussed the techniques needed to *evaluate* them. This term denotes the calculation of the sequence of strings $\mu(0) = \mu_0$, $\mu(\Delta t) = \mu_1$, ..., $\mu(n\Delta t) = \mu_n$ representing the states of the modeled structure at the desired intervals Δt. We address the problem of dL-system evaluation in the framework of the combined discrete/continuous paradigm for system simulation introduced by Fahrland [6] and presented in a tutorial manner by Kreutzer [15].

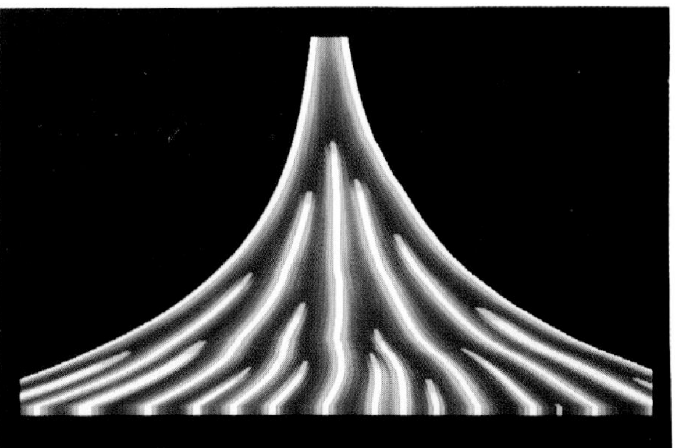

Figure 7: Diagrammatic representation of the development of *Anabaena catenula*, simulated using a dL-system with the constants set to the following values: $x_{max} = 1$, $c_{max} = 255$, $c_{min} = 5$, $D = \mu = 0.03$, $r = 1.01$, $k = 0.37$, $r_x = 0.1$, $r_c = 0.15$. The development was recorded from $t_{min} = 200$ to $t_{max} = 575$ at the intervals $\Delta t = 1$. Developmental stages are shown as horizontal lines with the colors indicating the concentration c of nitrogen compounds. Dark brown represents c_{min}; white represents c_{max}.

According to this paradigm, the evaluation can be viewed as a *dynamic process* governed by a *scheduler*: a part of the simulation program that monitors the state of the model, advances time, and dispatches the activities to be performed. In the absence of discrete events (productions), the scheduler repeatedly advances time by the *time slice* Δt. During each slice, the differential equations associated with the modules are integrated numerically (using an integration technique appropriate for the equations in hand), thus advancing the state of the structure from $\mu(t)$ to $\mu(t+\Delta t)$. If the scheduler detects that a discrete event should occur (i.e., a production should be applied) at time t' within the interval $[t, t+\Delta t)$, this interval is divided into two subintervals $[t, t')$ and $[t', t+\Delta t)$. The differential equations are integrated in the interval $[t, t')$ and yield parameter values for the production application at time t'. The production determines the initial values for the differential equations associated with the newly created modules; these equations are integrated in the remaining interval $[t', t+\Delta t)$. Each of the intervals $[t, t')$ and $[t', t+\Delta t)$ is subdivided further if more discrete events occur during $[t, t+\Delta t)$.

Plant structures generated using dL-systems may consist of large numbers (thousands) of modules. If many modules are replaced at different times t' during the interval $[t, t+\Delta t)$, the global advancement of time may require an excessive subdivision of this interval, leading to a slow evaluation of the model. This problem can be solved by detecting and processing events the interval $[t, t+\Delta t)$ individually for each module. The increase of simulation speed is obtained at the expense of accuracy, since the state of the context of a module replaced at time $t' \in (t, t+\Delta t)$ must be approximated, for example, by its state at time t. No accuracy is lost in the context-free case.

In the above description we assumed that the scheduler is capable of detecting each instant t' at which a discrete event occurs. If the differential equations are sufficiently simple, we can solve them analytically and determine time t' explicitly. In general, we need numerical techniques for special event location in piecewise-continuous ordinary differential equations, as described by Shampine *et. al.* [29], and Barzel [2, Appendix C].

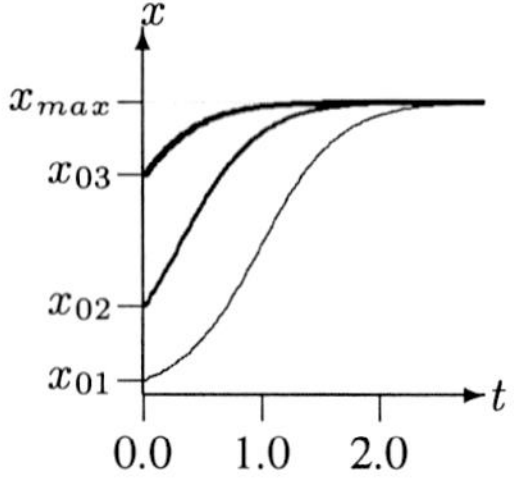

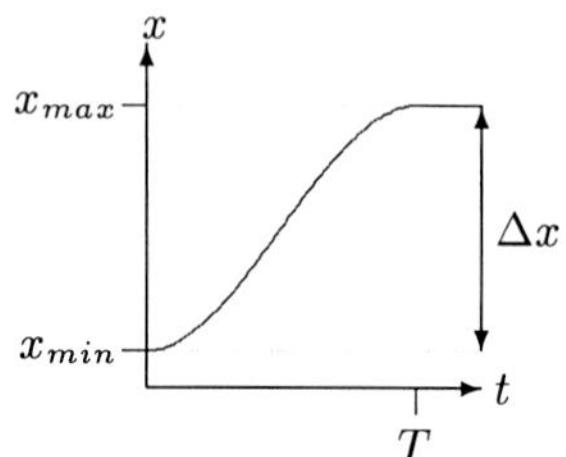

Figure 8: Examples of sigmoidal growth functions. a) A family of logistic functions plotted using $r = 3.0$ for different initial values x_0. b) A cubic function $G_{\Delta x,T}$.

6 GROWTH FUNCTIONS

Growth functions describe continuous processes such as the expansion of individual cells, elongation of internodes, and gradual increase of branching angles over time. For example, the differential equations included in the dL-system for the dragon curve (Section 4.1) describe linear elongation of segments F_r and F_l, and linear decrease in length of segments F_h. The dL-system model of *Anabaena* (Section 4.2) assumes exponential elongation of cells.

In higher plants, the growth functions are often of *sigmoidal* (S-shaped) type, which means that they initially increase in value slowly, then accelerate, and eventually level off at or near the maximum value. A popular example of a sigmoidal function is Velhurst's *logistic* function (c.f. [5, page 212]), defined by the equation:

$$\frac{dx}{dt} = r\left(1 - \frac{x}{x_{max}}\right)x$$

with a properly chosen initial value x_0 (Figure 8a). Specifically, x_0 must be greater than zero, which means that neither the initial length nor the initial growth rate of a module described by the logistic function will be equal to zero. In order to obtain a continuous progression of forms, it is often convenient to use a growth function that has zero growth rates at both ends of an interval T within which its value increases from x_{min} (possibly zero) to x_{max}. These requirements can be satisfied, for example, by a *cubic* function of time. Using the Hermite form of curve specification [8, page 484], we obtain:

$$x(t) = -2\frac{\Delta x}{T^3}t^3 + 3\frac{\Delta x}{T^2}t^2 + x_{min},$$

where $\Delta x = x_{max} - x_{min}$ and $t \in [0, T]$. The equivalent differential equation is:

$$\frac{dx}{dt} = -6\frac{\Delta x}{T^3}t^2 + 6\frac{\Delta x}{T^2}t = 6\frac{\Delta x}{T^2}\left(1 - \frac{t}{T}\right)t$$

with the initial condition $x_0 = x_{min}$. In order to extend this curve to infinity (Figure 8b), we define:

$$\frac{dx}{dt} = G_{\Delta x,T}(t) = \begin{cases} 6\frac{\Delta x}{T^2}\left(1 - \frac{t}{T}\right)t & \text{for } t \in [0, T] \\ 0 & \text{for } t \in (T, +\infty). \end{cases}$$

Although the explicit dependence of the function G on time is questionable from the biological point of view (a plant module does not have a means for measuring time directly), parametric cubic functions constitute a well understood computer graphics tool [8, Chapter 11.2] and can be conveniently used to approximate the observed changes of parameter values over time.

Figure 9: Development of a compound leaf simulated using a dL-system. Parameter values are: $n_0 = 4$, $x_0 = 1.0$, $x_{th} = 2.0$, $k = 0.5$, $r_a = 2.0$, $x_{amax} = 3.0$, $r_i = 1.0$, $x_{imax} = 3.0$, $s_0 = 0.05$, $r_s = 2.0$, $s_{max} = 6.0$, $\alpha_0 = 2.0$, $r_\alpha = 1.0$, $\alpha_{max} = 60.0$, and $\Delta t = 0.01$. The stages shown represent frames 50, 215, 300, 400, 500, 600, and 900 of an animated sequence.

7 MODELING OF HIGHER PLANTS

In this section we present sample applications of dL-systems to the animation of the development of higher plants.

7.1 Pinnate Leaf

A pinnate leaf provides a simple example of a *monopodial* branching structure. *Monopodial* branching occurs when the apex of the main axis produces a succession of *nodes* bearing *organs* — leaves or flowers — which are separated by *internodes*. In the case of pinnate leaves with the leaflets occurring in pairs (termed *opposite* arrangement), the essence of this process can be captured by the L-system production [27, page 71]:

$$F_a \longrightarrow F_i[+@L][-@L]F_a,$$

where F_a denotes the apex, F_i — an internode, and $@L$ — a leaflet. The dL-system model given below extends this L-system with growth functions that control the expansion of all components and gradually increase branching angles over time.

initial string: $F_a(x_0, n_0)$
$F_a(x, n)$:
  if $x < x_{th}$
    solve $\frac{dx}{dt} = r_a\left(1 - \frac{x}{x_{amax}}\right)x,\ \frac{dn}{dt} = 0$
  if $x = x_{th}$ & $n > 0$
    produce $F_i(kx)[+(\alpha_0)@L(s_0)][-(\alpha_0)@L(s_0)]$
      $F_a((1-k)x, n-1)$
  if $x = x_{th}$ & $n = 0$
    produce $F_i(x)@L(s_0)$
$F_i(x)$: **solve** $\frac{dx}{dt} = r_i\left(1 - \frac{x}{x_{imax}}\right)x$
$L(s)$: **solve** $\frac{ds}{dt} = r_s\left(1 - \frac{s}{s_{max}}\right)s$
$\pm(\alpha)$: **solve** $\frac{d\alpha}{dt} = r_\alpha\left(1 - \frac{\alpha}{\alpha_{max}}\right)\alpha$

The apex F_a has two parameters x and n which indicate its current length and the remaining number of internodes to be produced. The apex elongates according to the logistic function with parameters r (controlling growth rate) and x_{amax} (controlling the asymptotic apex length). Upon reaching the threshold length x_{th}, the apex produces a pair of leaflets $@L$ and subdivides into an internode F_i of length kx and a shorter apex of length $(1-k)x$. Once the predefined number n_0 of leaf pairs have been created, the apex

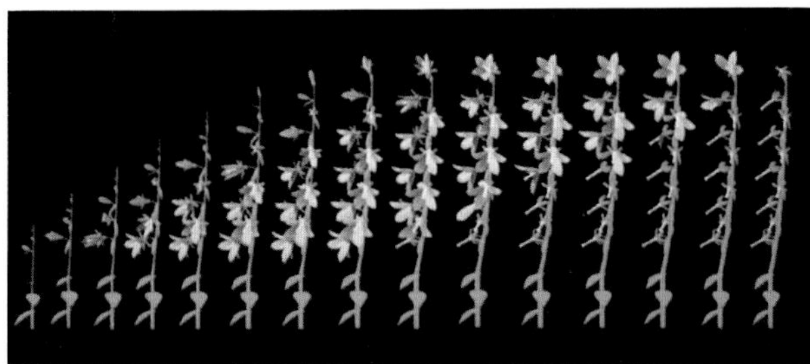

Figure 10: Development of the herbaceous plant *Campanula rapunculoides*. The snapshots show every 25th frame of a computer animation, starting with frame 175.

transforms itself into an internode and produces the terminal leaflet. The length of internodes, the size of leaflets, and the magnitude of the branching angles increase according to the logistic functions. Snapshots of the leaf development simulated by the above model are shown in Figure 9.

7.2 *Campanula rapunculoides*

The inflorescence of *Campanula rapunculoides* (creeping bellflower) has a monopodial branching structure similar to that of a pinnate leaf; consequently, it is modeled by a similar dL-system:

initial string: $F_a(x_0, n_0)$
$F_a(x, n)$:
  if $x < x_{th}$
    solve $\frac{dx}{dt} = v$, $\frac{dn}{dt} = 0$
  if $x = x_{th}$ & $n > 0$
    produce $F_i(kx)[+(\alpha_0)@K]F_a((1-k)x, n-1)$
  if $x = x_{th}$ & $n = 0$
    produce $F_i(x)@K$
$F_i(x)$: **solve** $\frac{dx}{dt} = G_{\Delta x, T_1}(t)$
$+(\alpha)$: **solve** $\frac{d\alpha}{dt} = G_{\Delta\alpha, T_2}(t)$

The apex is assumed to grow at a constant speed. Cubic growth functions describe the elongation of internodes and the gradual increase of branching angles. The combination of the linear growth of the apex with the cubic growth of the internodes results in first-order continuity of the entire plant height (except when apex F_a is transformed into internode F_i and terminal flower $@K$).

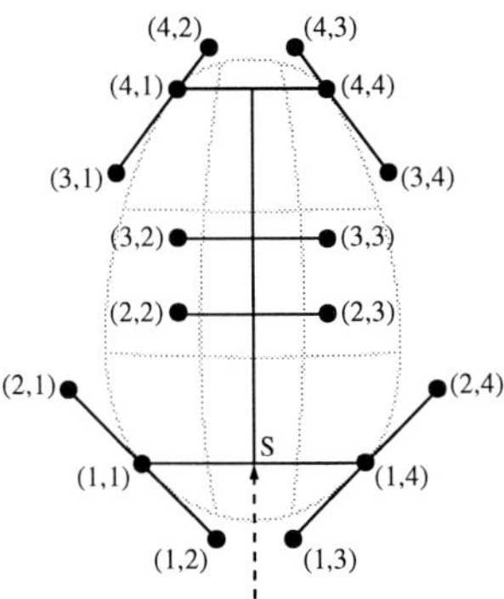

Figure 11: A Bézier patch defined by a branching structure

Figure 10 presents a sequence of snapshots from an animation of *Campanula*'s development. It was obtained using the above dL-system augmented with rules that govern the development of flowers $@K$ from a bud to an open flower to a fruit. The petals and sepals have been modeled as Bézier patches, specified by control points placed at the ends of simple branching structures (Figure 11). Each structure is attached to the remainder of the model at point S. The lengths of the line segments and the magnitudes of the branching angles have been controlled by cubic growth functions, yielding the developmental sequence shown in Figure 12. When the flower transforms into a fruit, productions instantaneously remove the petals from the model (it is assumed that the time over which a petal falls off is negligible compared to the time slice used for the animation of development). Manipulation of Bézier patches using L-systems has been described in detail by Hanan [13].

Figure 12: Development of a single flower of *Campanula rapunculoides*

7.3 *Lychnis coronaria*

The inflorescence of *Lychnis coronaria* (rose campion) is an example of a sympodial branching structure, characterized by large branches that carry the main thrust of development. As presented in [27, page 82] and [28], the apex of the main axis turns into a flower shortly after the initiation of a pair of lateral branches. Their apices turn into flowers as well, and second-order branches take over. The lateral branches originating at a common node develop at the same rate, but the development of one side is delayed with respect to the other. This process repeats recursively, as indicated by the following L-system:

$$\begin{array}{lll} \omega : & A_7 & \\ p_1 : & A_7 \longrightarrow F[A_0][A_4]F@K & \\ p_2 : & A_i \longrightarrow A_{i+1} & 0 \le i < 7 \end{array}$$

Production p_1 shows that, at their creation time, the lateral apices have different states A_0 and A_4. Consequently, the first apex requires eight derivation steps to produce flower $@K$ and initiate a new pair of branches, while the second requires only four steps.

A corresponding dL-system using cubic growth functions to describe the elongation of internodes F is given below:

initial string: $A(\tau_{max})$
$A(\tau)$:
  if $\tau < \tau_{max}$ **solve** $\frac{d\tau}{dt} = 1$
  if $\tau = \tau_{max}$ **produce** $F(0)[A(0)][A\left(\frac{\tau_{max}}{2}\right)]F(0)@K$
$F(x)$: **solve** $\frac{dx}{dt} = G_{\Delta x, T}(t)$

For simplicity, we have omitted leaves and symbols controlling the relative orientation of branches in space. The operation of the model

Figure 13: Development of *Lychnis coronaria*. The snapshots show every 25th frame of a computer animation, starting with frame 150.

is governed by apices A characterized by their age τ and assumed to have negligible size. Upon reaching the maximum age τ_{max}, an apex splits into two internodes F, creates two lateral apices A with different initial age values 0 and $\frac{\tau_{max}}{2}$, and initiates flower $@K$. In order to satisfy continuity criteria, the initial length of internodes is assumed to be zero.

Figure 13 shows selected snapshots from an animation of the development of *Lychnis* obtained using an extension of this dL-system. As in *Campanula*, the individual flowers have been modeled using Bézier patches controlled by the dL-system.

7.4 *Hieracium umbellatum*

The compound leaf and the inflorescences of *Campanula* and *Lychnis* have been captured by context-free dL-systems, assuming no flow of information between coexisting modules. Janssen and Lindenmayer [14] (see also [27, Chapter 3] and [28]) showed that context-free models are too weak to capture the whole spectrum of developmental sequences in plants. For example, the *basipetal* flowering sequence observed in many compound inflorescences requires the use of one or more signals that propagate through the developing structure and control the opening of buds. Such a sequence is characterized by the first flower opening at the top of the main axis and the flowering zone progressing downward towards the base of the plant.

Figure 14: A model of *Hieracium umbellatum*.

Figure 14 shows a synthetic image of *Hieracium umbellatum*, a sample composite plant with a basipetal flowering sequence. Following *model I* postulated by Janssen and Lindenmayer, we assume that the opening of buds is controlled by a *hormone* generated at some point of time near the base of the plant and transported towards the apices. The hormone propagates faster in the main axis than in the lateral branches. As a result, it first reaches the bud of the main axis, then those of the lateral branches in the basipetal sequence. The growth of the main axis and of the lateral branches stops when the hormone attains their respective terminal buds. In addition, the hormone penetrating a node stops the development of a leaf originating at this node. Snapshots from a diagrammatic animated developmental sequence illustrating this process are shown in Figure 15.

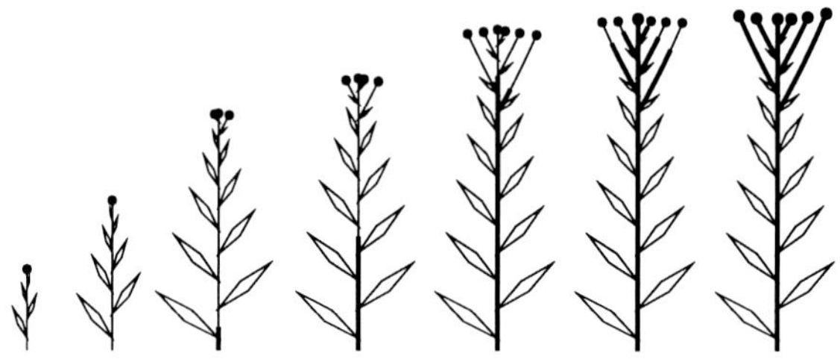

Figure 15: Development of *Hieracium umbellatum*. The stages shown represent frames 170, 265, 360, 400, 470, 496, and 520 of an animated sequence.

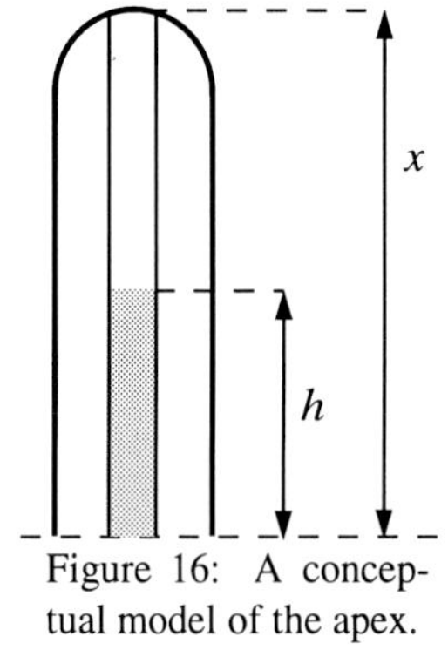

Figure 16: A conceptual model of the apex.

The complete listing of the dL-system capturing the development of *Hieracium* is too long to be included in this paper, but a specification of the activities of the main apex provides a good illustration of the context-sensitive control mechanism involved. We conceptualize this apex as a growing and periodically dividing tube of length x, which may be penetrated by the hormone to a height $h \leq x$ (Figure 16). The apex can assume three states: F_{a0} (not yet reached by the hormone), F_{a1} (being penetrated by the hormone), and F_{a2} (completely filled with the hormone). The apical behavior is captured by the following rules:

$F_l(x_l, h_l) < F_{a0}(x)$:
  if $x_l > h_l \ \& \ x < x_{th}$
    solve $\frac{dx}{dt} = G(x)$
  if $x = x_{th}$
    produce $F_{i0}(kx)[F_{a0}(0)]F_{a0}((1-k)x)$
  if $x_l = h_l \ \& \ x < x_{th}$
    produce $F_{a1}(x, 0)$
$F_{a1}(x, h)$:
  if $x > h \ \& \ x < x_{th}$
    solve $\frac{dx}{dt} = G(x), \ \ \frac{dh}{dt} = v$
  if $kx > h \ \& \ x = x_{th}$
    produce $F_{i1}(kx, h)[F_{a0}(0)]F_{a0}((1-k)x)$
  if $x > h \geq kx \ \& \ x = x_{th}$
    produce $F_{i2}(kx, kx)F_{a1}((1-k)x, h - kx)$
  if $x = h$
    produce $F_{a2}(x, x)$

The first three rules model the apex without the hormone. If the preceding internode F_l is not yet completely penetrated by the hormone ($x_l > h_l$) and the length x of the apex is below the threshold value x_{th}, the apex elongates according to the growth function $G(x)$. Upon reaching the threshold length ($x = x_{th}$), the apex F_{a0} subdivides, producing an internode F_{i0} and a lateral apex F_{a0}. Finally, once the hormone penetrates the entire internode F_l (as indicated by the condition $x_l = h_l$), it flows into the apex, which then changes its state to F_{a1}.

Figure 17: Development of a single flower head of *Hieracium umbellatum*

The continuous rule for F_{a1} describes the growth of the apex with rate $G(x)$ and the propagation of the hormone with constant speed v. The next two productions capture the alternate cases of the apex subdivision, with the hormone level h below or above the level kx at which the new internode splits from the apex. The last production is applied when the hormone reaches the tip of the apex, and changes its state to the flowering state F_{a2}.

The complete model of *Hieracium umbellatum* contains additional rules that describe the elongation of internodes, the propagation of the hormone within and between the internodes, and the development of flower heads. The heads undergo the sequence of transformations illustrated in Figure 17. The bracts (green parts of the flower head) have been represented using Bézier patches controlled by the dL-system, while the petals have been formed as extending chains of filled rectangles, with the angles between consecutive rectangles controlled by cubic growth functions. This technique allowed us to represent each petal with a relatively modest number of polygons (10).

8 CONCLUSIONS

We have introduced differential L-systems as a combined discrete/continuous model suitable for computer simulation and animation of plant development. Continuous aspects of module behavior are described by ordinary differential equations, and discontinuous qualitative changes are captured by productions. The link between L-systems and dL-systems makes it possible to use existing discrete developmental models as a starting point for constructing dL-systems suitable for animation.

Differential L-systems have a wide spectrum of prospective applications, ranging from modest projects, such as the diagrammatic animation of developmental mechanisms employed by plants, to ambitious ones, such as the realistic animation of the growth of extinct plants. On the conceptual level, dL-systems expand piecewise-continuous differential equations with a formal specification of discrete changes to system configuration. The resulting formalism makes it possible to model developing branching structures with a theoretically unlimited number of modules. From a different perspective, dL-systems can be considered as the continuous-time extension of parametric L-systems.

The following problems still require solutions:

- **Combined differential-algebraic specification of continuous processes.** In some cases it is convenient to describe continuous aspects of model behavior using explicit functions of time instead of differential equations. For example, the expression of the cubic growth function using the differential equation presented in Section 6 is somewhat artificial. In order to accommodate explicit function specifications, the definition of dL-systems should be extended to comprehend differential-algebraic equations.

- **Incorporation of stochastic rules.** Differential L-systems have been formulated in deterministic terms. Stochastic rules should be incorporated to capture the specimen-to-specimen variations in modeled plants, as has been done for L-systems.

- **Development of the simulation software.** The simulations discussed in this paper were carried out using a programming language based on parametric L-systems [13, 26]. In this environment, the user must explicitly specify the formulae for numerically solving the differential equations included in the models (the forward Euler method was used in all cases). From the user's perspective, it would be preferable to incorporate a differential equation solver into the simulator, and specify the models directly in terms of dL-systems.

- **Improved realism of dL-system models.** We have not addressed many practical problems related to the construction of realistic models, such as the avoidance of intersections between modules, the improved modeling of growing plant organs (petals, leaves, and fruits), and the simulation of wilting.

The simulation and visualization of natural phenomena has the intriguing charm of blurring the line dividing the synthesis of images from the re-creation of nature. The animation of plant development adds a new phenomenon to this (un)real world.

Acknowledgements

We would like to thank Jim Hanan for his essential work on the plant modeling software *cpfg* used in the simulations, and for valuable references and comments. At different points in time, Gavin Miller, Karl Sims and Alvy Ray Smith revealed to us the techniques used in their developmental animations. M. Raju and C. C. Chinnappa explained the details of the development of *Lychnis coronaria* and *Hieracium umbellatum*. We also gained many insights from illuminating discussions with Bill Remphrey, John Reinitz, Stan Letovsky, and Keith Ferguson. This research was sponsored by an operating grant and a graduate scholarship from the Natural Sciences and Engineering Research Council of Canada, and a grant from the U.S. Air Force Office of Scientific Research.

References

[1] M. Aono and T. L. Kunii. Botanical tree image generation. *IEEE Computer Graphics and Applications*, 4(5):10–34, 1984.

[2] R. Barzel. *Physically-based modeling for computer graphics — a structured approach.* Academic Press, Boston, 1992.

[3] C. G. de Koster and A. Lindenmayer. Discrete and continuous models for heterocyst differentiation in growing filaments of blue-green bacteria. *Acta Biotheoretica*, 36:249–273, 1987.

[4] P. de Reffye, C. Edelin, J. Françon, M. Jaeger, and C. Puech. Plant models faithful to botanical structure and development. Proceedings of SIGGRAPH '88 (Atlanta, Georgia, August 1–5, 1988), in *Computer Graphics* 22, 4 (August 1988), pages 151–158, ACM SIGGRAPH, New York, 1988.

[5] L. Edelstein-Keshet. *Mathematical models in biology*. Random House, New York, 1988.

[6] D. A. Fahrland. Combined discrete event – continuous systems simulation. *Simulation*, 14(2):61–72, 1970.

[7] K. W. Fleischer and A. H. Barr. A simulation testbed for the study of multicellular development: Multiple mechanisms of morphogenesis. To appear in *Artificial Life III*, Addison-Wesley, Redwood City, 1993.

[8] J. D. Foley, A. van Dam, S. Feiner, and J. Hughes. *Computer graphics: Principles and practice*. Addison-Wesley, Reading, 1990.

[9] F. D. Fracchia, P. Prusinkiewicz, and M. J. M. de Boer. Animation of the development of multicellular structures. In N. Magnenat-Thalmann and D. Thalmann, editors, *Computer Animation '90*, pages 3–18, Tokyo, 1990. Springer-Verlag.

[10] J. Françon. Sur la modélisation de l'architecture et du développement des végétaux. In C. Edelin, editor, *L'Arbre. Biologie et Développement*. Naturalia Monspeliensia, 1991. No hors série.

[11] N. Greene. Organic architecture. SIGGRAPH Video Review 38, segment 16, ACM SIGGRAPH, New York, 1988.

[12] N. Greene. Voxel space automata: Modeling with stochastic growth processes in voxel space. Proceedings of SIGGRAPH '89 (Boston, Mass., July 31–August 4, 1989), in *Computer Graphics* 23, 4 (August 1989), pages 175–184, ACM SIGGRAPH, New York, 1989.

[13] J. S. Hanan. *Parametric L-systems and their application to the modelling and visualization of plants*. PhD thesis, University of Regina, June 1992.

[14] J. M. Janssen and A. Lindenmayer. Models for the control of branch positions and flowering sequences of capitula in *Mycelis muralis* (L.) Dumont (Compositae). *New Phytologist*, 105:191–220, 1987.

[15] W. Kreutzer. *System simulation: Programming styles and languages*. Addison-Wesley, Sydney, 1986.

[16] A. Lindenmayer. Mathematical models for cellular interaction in development, Parts I and II. *Journal of Theoretical Biology*, 18:280–315, 1968.

[17] A. Lindenmayer and H. Jürgensen. Grammars of development: Discrete-state models for growth, differentiation and gene expression in modular organisms. In G. Rozenberg and A. Salomaa, editors, *Lindenmayer systems: Impacts on theoretical computer science, computer graphics, and developmental biology*, pages 3–21. Springer-Verlag, Berlin, 1992.

[18] B. B. Mandelbrot. *The fractal geometry of nature*. W. H. Freeman, San Francisco, 1982.

[19] G. S. P. Miller. Natural phenomena: My first tree. Siggraph 1988 Film and Video Show.

[20] G. J. Mitchison and M. Wilcox. Rules governing cell division in *Anabaena*. *Nature*, 239:110–111, 1972.

[21] E. Mjolsness, D. H. Sharp, and J. Reinitz. A connectionist model of development. *Journal of Theoretical Biology*, 152(4):429–454, 1991.

[22] H. Noser, D. Thalmann, and R. Turner. Animation based on the interaction of L-systems with vector force fields. In T. L. Kunii, editor, *Visual computing – integrating computer graphics with computer vision*, pages 747–761. Springer-Verlag, Tokyo, 1992.

[23] P. Prusinkiewicz. Graphical applications of L-systems. In *Proceedings of Graphics Interface '86 — Vision Interface '86*, pages 247–253, 1986.

[24] P. Prusinkiewicz, M. Hammel, and J. Hanan. Lychnis coronaria. QuickTime movie included in the Virtual Museum CD-ROM, Apple Computer, Cupertino, 1992.

[25] P. Prusinkiewicz and J. Hanan. Visualization of botanical structures and processes using parametric L-systems. In D. Thalmann, editor, *Scientific Visualization and Graphics Simulation*, pages 183–201. J. Wiley & Sons, Chichester, 1990.

[26] P. Prusinkiewicz and J. Hanan. L-systems: From formalism to programming languages. In G. Rozenberg and A. Salomaa, editors, *Lindenmayer systems: Impacts on theoretical computer science, computer graphics, and developmental biology*, pages 193–211. Springer-Verlag, Berlin, 1992.

[27] P. Prusinkiewicz and A. Lindenmayer. *The algorithmic beauty of plants*. Springer-Verlag, New York, 1990. With J. S. Hanan, F. D. Fracchia, D. R. Fowler, M. J. M. de Boer, and L. Mercer.

[28] P. Prusinkiewicz, A. Lindenmayer, and J. Hanan. Developmental models of herbaceous plants for computer imagery purposes. Proceedings of SIGGRAPH '88 (Atlanta, Georgia, August 1–5, 1988), in *Computer Graphics* 22, 4 (August 1988), pages 141–150, ACM SIGGRAPH, New York, 1988.

[29] L. F. Shampine, I. Gladwell, and R. W. Brankin. Reliable solution of special event location problems for ODEs. *ACM Transactions on Mathematical Software*, 17, No. 1:11–25, March 1991.

[30] K. Sims. Panspermia. SIGGRAPH Video Review, ACM SIGGRAPH, New York, 1990.

[31] A. R. Smith. Plants, fractals, and formal languages. Proceedings of SIGGRAPH '84 (Minneapolis, Minnesota, July 22–27, 1984) in *Computer Graphics*, 18, 3 (July 1984), pages 1–10, ACM SIGGRAPH, New York, 1984.

Modeling Soil: Realtime Dynamic Models for Soil Slippage and Manipulation

Xin Li and J. Michael Moshell

Institute for Simulation and Training
University of Central Florida

ABSTRACT

A physically based model of an object is a mathematical representation of its behavior, which incorporates principles of Newtonian physics. Dynamic soil models are required in animations and realtime interactive simulations in which changes of natural terrain are involved. Analytic methods, based on soil properties and Newtonian physics, are presented in the paper to model soil slippage and soil manipulations. These methods can be used to calculate the evolution of a given soil configuration under the constraint of volume conservation and to simulate excavating activities such as digging, cutting, piling, carrying or dumping soil. Numerical algorithms with linear time and space complexities are also developed to meet the requirement of realtime computer simulation.

CR Categories: I.3.7 [Computer Graphics]: Graphics and Realism; I.6.3 [Simulation and Modeling]: applications.
Additional Keywords: physically based modeling, real-time simulation, soil dynamics, slippage, soil manipulation.

1. INTRODUCTION

Physically-based modeling is a growing area of computer graphics research. A good deal of work has been done toward physically based models of objects such as rigid and nonrigid bodies, hydraulic surfaces or natural terrain. However, soil models that are both physically realistic and computationally efficient in realtime simulations have not been developed. Recently, substantial interest in dynamic soil models has been expressed by some developers of realtime simulations of Dynamic Terrain systems. Such systems provide the capability, within a realtime graphical simulation, of reconstructing landscape architecture or rearranging the terrain surface. These systems essentially involve allowing the simulation's user to conduct excavating activities in the terrain database at any freely chosen location. These activities may include digging ditches, piling up dirt, cutting the soil mass from the ground, carrying it for a distance, and dumping it at another location. To these deformations, the soil mass must behave in realistic manners under external stimuli.

Moshell and Li developed a visually plausible kinematic soil model [10]. In their work, a bulldozer blade serves as a local force function used to change the heights of the terrain. Excess terrain volume which is "scaped off" by the moving blade is added to the moving berm in front of the blade. The berm is then smoothed by a bidirectional Cardinal spline algorithm. The demonstration of the model appears realistic and runs in realtime. The simulation, however, is kinematic. No forces are computed. The soil does not slump when the bulldozer leaves. The volume of given soil is not conserved.

Burg and Moshell focussed on the problem of piling up soil such that the soil spills down from the mounds in a realistic-looking way [3]. In their approach, the terrain is modeled by a 2-d grid of altitude posts. Constraint equations are defined to describe relationships among altitude posts and their neighbors. An iterative relaxation algorithm, suggested in [11], is used to simulate the falling soil. The constraints enforce an averaging or "smoothing" of each altitude post with its neighbors. The algorithm is volume-preserving under certain conditions. The model is purely kinematic. The physical properties of different types of soil are not modeled.

Our research work is focused on dynamic models of soil slippage and soil manipulations. For the slippage model, we determine if a given soil configuration is in static equilibrium, calculate forces which drive a portion of the soil to slide if the configuration is not stable, and meanwhile preserve the volume conservation. For the soil manipulation models, we investigate interactions between soil and excavating machines, implement a bulldozer model and a scooploader model. These models are based on analytic methods and Newtonian physics. The computational times of the corresponding algorithms are fast enough to meet the requirement of realtime graphical simulations. For clarity, this paper mainly focuses on the 2-d case. Extensions to 3-d have been completed and are briefly discussed.

2. PRELIMINARIES

The discussion of soil models needs some understanding of soil properties. In this section, we introduce some concepts which are borrowed directly from civil engineering. Interested readers are referred to [2], [4], [5] and [7] for more details.

The *shear strength* of the soil is the resistance per unit area to deformation by continuous shear displacement of soil particles along surfaces of rupture. It may be attributed to three basic components: 1) frictional resistance to sliding among soil particles; 2) cohesion and adhesion among soil particles; and 3) interlocking of solid particles to resist deformation. (Cohesion is molecular attraction among like particles. Adhesion is a molecular attraction among unlike particles.)

The *shear stress*, on the other hand, is the force per unit area experienced by a slope, which pushes the mass to move along the failure plane. The combined effects of gravity and water are the primary influences on the shear stress. It may also be influenced by some natural phenomena such as chemical actions, earthquakes, or wind.

The shear *strength force* and *stress force*, denoted by s and τ respectively, are defined as the shear strength and stress multiplied by the total area. The measure of s and τ can be determined from the *Mohr-Coulomb theory* indicated in [5]:

12424 Research Parkway, Suite 300, Orlando, Florida.
Phone: (407) 658-5073, email: lix@ist.ucf.edu

This work is sponsored by the U.S. Army Simulation, Training and Instrumentation Command (STRICOM). All opinions are, however, solely due to the authors.

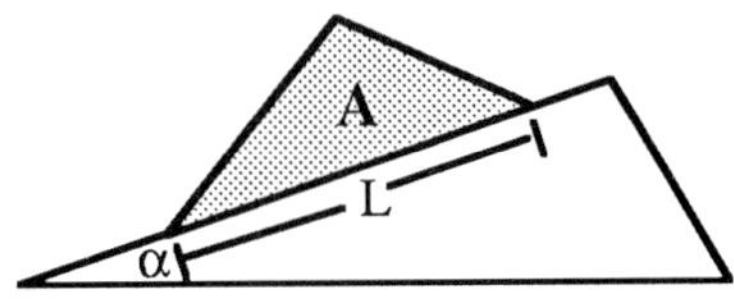

Fig. 1: The Failure Plane

(2.1) $s = c\,L + W\cos(\alpha)\tan(\phi)$

(2.2) $\tau = W\sin(\alpha)$

where L is the length of the failure plane, α is the degree of natural slope, and $W=\gamma A$ is the weight of soil above the failure plane (see Fig. 1). c, ϕ and γ describe properties of the soil, where c indicates the cohesion, ϕ is the angle of internal friction (i.e. it is a measure of the friction among soil particles) and γ is the unit weight. Some typical parameters and their units are listed in the table below [1]:

SOIL TYPE	c (t/m)	ϕ (degree)	γ (t/m^2)
dry sand	0	26-33	1.9-2.0
Sandy loam	0-2.0	14-26	1.8-2.0
Loam	0.5-5.0	10-28	1.8-2.1

Soil is a very complex material. It may be influenced by changes in the moisture content, pore pressures, structural disturbance, fluctuation in the ground water table, underground water movements, stress history, time, chemical action or environmental conditions. Predicting the changes of complex configurations is either intractable or highly costly. However, for many interactive applications, speed and realistic appearance are more important than accuracy. Hence in this paper, we assume that only homogeneous and isotropic soil will be processed. Conditions such as seepage, pore pressure, existence of tension cracks and deformation resulting from permanent atomic dislocation will not be considered.

3. STATIC EQUILIBRIUM AND RESTORING FORCE

In this section, we develop methods to determine whether or not a given configuration is stable, calculate the critical angle above which sliding occurs, and quantify the force which pushes the soil mass moving along the failure plane.

3.1 STABILITY

The stability of a given soil configuration is determined by the *factor of safety*, denoted by F, of a potential failure surface. From the Mohr-Coulomb theory, F is defined as a ratio between the strength force and the stress force [5]:

$$\text{(3.1)}\quad F = \frac{s}{\tau} = \frac{c\,L + W\cos(\alpha)\tan(\phi)}{W\sin(\alpha)}$$

When F is greater than 1, the configuration is said to be in a state of equilibrium. Otherwise, failure is imminent. To analyze the factor of safety, we divide the given soil mass into n slices with equal width Δx:

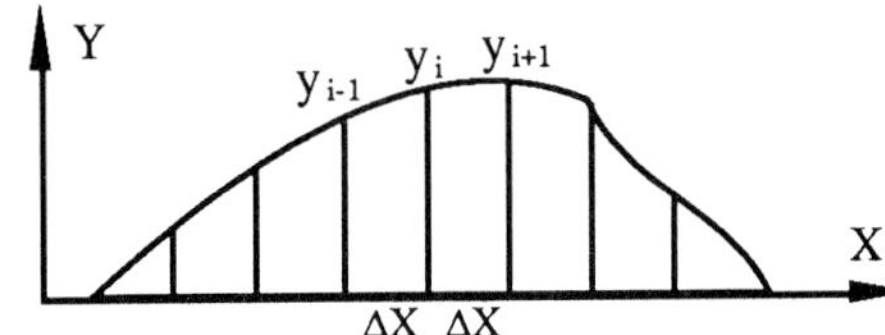

Fig. 2: Dividing the given mass into small slices

The calculation of the factor of safety of each slice can be done individually. The following free body diagram shows forces applied on slice i:

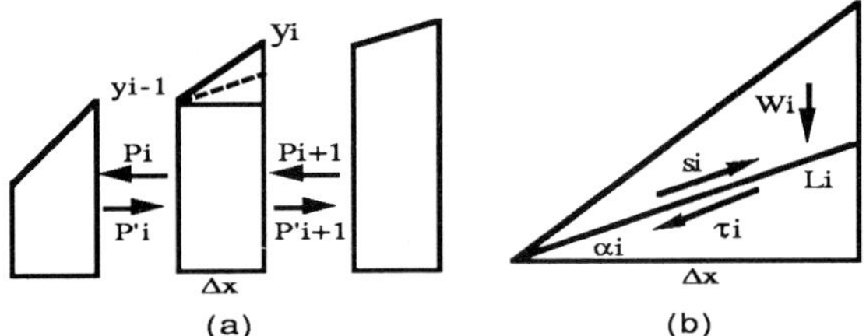

Fig. 3: Free body diagram for slice i

In (a), the P's are forces exerted between slices. They are pairwise equal and in opposite directions and thus can be cancelled. At any time t, therefore, sliding can only happen in the top triangle area of a slice. (b) shows forces acting on this area, where strength and stress forces are given by (2.1) and (2.2) with L, W and α replaced by L_i, W_i and α_i respectively.

To determine if there exists a failure angle α_i (so that the soil mass above it will slide) and calculate the net force exerted on the failure plane if α_i does exist, we start from (3.1). Note that L_i and W_i can be expressed in terms of α_i. Replacing L_i and W_i in (3.1) with functions of α_i, we obtain

$$\text{(3.2)}\quad F(\alpha_i) = \frac{2c+\gamma\tan(\phi)[h\cos(\alpha_i)-\Delta x\sin(\alpha_i)]\cos(\alpha_i)}{\gamma(h\cos(\alpha_i)-\Delta x\sin(\alpha_i))\sin(\alpha_i)}$$

where $h=y_i-y_{i-1}$ is the height of the triangle in Fig. 3-(b). For any angle $\alpha_i>\tan^{-1}(h/\Delta x)$, function $F(\alpha_i)$ makes no physical sense. In the range of $[0, \tan^{-1}(h/\Delta x)]$, $F(\alpha_i)$ reaches its minimum when the first derivative of $F(\alpha_i)$, with respect to α_i, is equal to 0. That is

$$\text{(3.3)}\quad \frac{dF}{d\alpha} = \frac{1}{\tau^2}\,[A\cos(2\alpha_i) + B\sin(2\alpha_i) + C] = 0$$

where

$$A = \frac{\gamma^2}{2}\tan(\phi)(\Delta x^2-h^2)-2\gamma ch,$$

$$B = \gamma^2 h\Delta x\tan(\phi)+2\gamma c\Delta x, \text{ and}$$

$$C = -\frac{\gamma^2}{2}\tan(\phi)(\Delta x^2+h^2).$$

Solving (3.3) gives us four angles (see [9]). We can choose the one which satisfies $0\le\alpha_i\le\tan^{-1}(h/\Delta x)$ in (3.2) to calculate the factor of safety F. The given configuration is statically stable if F>1. Otherwise sliding is inevitable.

3.2 CRITICAL SLOPE ANGLE

Suppose that we have F<1 for a given configuration. In the range of $[0, \tan^{-1}(h/\Delta x)]$ there are at most two angles, say β_1 and β_2, such that $F(\beta_1)=F(\beta_2)=1$. The angle $\beta_0=\min(\beta_1, \beta_2)$ is said to be the *critical-slope angle* of the configuration. Above this angle impending slip occurs. β_1 and β_2 can be obtained by solving the equation (3.4) for α:

$$\text{(3.4)}\quad F(\alpha) = \frac{2c+\gamma\tan(\phi)[h\cos(\alpha)-\Delta x\sin(\alpha)]\cos(\alpha)}{\gamma[h\cos(\alpha)-\Delta x\sin(\alpha)]\sin(\alpha)} = 1$$

where all symbols are as explained earlier. The solution to (3.4) is derived in [9].

3.3 RESTORING FORCE

Let a configuration be given in Fig.4-(a) with β_0 as the critical-slope angle. The force that pushes the mass in the triangle along the edge gh_0 can be computed as follows. First the line segment h_0h_n is divided into n small segments with equal length Δh. Fig 4-(b) shows the free body diagram of the i-th dovetail indicated by the shaded area in (a).

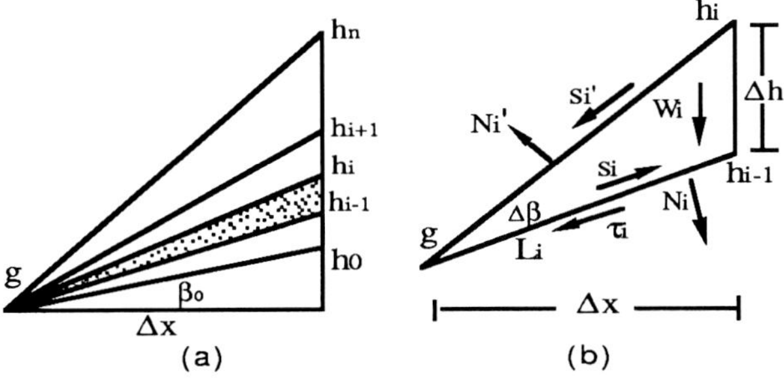

Fig. 4: Analyzing the restoring force

Let's analyze forces exerted on the dovetail. The weight W_i can be decomposed into two forces, namely N_i and τ_i, which are normal and parallel to the edge L_i respectively. s_i is the strength force resisting the sliding motion, s_i' the opponent force generated by strength force s_{i+1}, and N_i' the force supporting the dovetail above it. The net force f_i applied on dovetail-i is therefore given by a vectorial summation:

$$(3.5) \quad f_i = N_i + \tau_i + s_i + s_i' + N_i'$$

The total net force f acting on the whole triangle area is the summation of f_i's, $1 \le i \le n$, i.e.

$$(3.6) \quad f = \sum_{i=1}^{n}(N_i+\tau_i+s_i+s_i'+N_i') = \sum_{i=2}^{n}\tau_i$$

since $\tau_1 = s_1$ (due to $F(\beta_0)=1$), $N_n'=0$, $s_n'=0$, $N_i' = N_{i+1}$ and $s_i' = -s_{i+1}$ for $1 \le i \le n-1$. Based on (3.6) and Fig.4, [9] gives a derivation of (3.7) by letting Δh tend to zero.

$$(3.7) \quad f = \frac{\gamma \Delta x^2}{4} \, Ln\left(\frac{h_n^2+\Delta x^2}{h_0^2+\Delta x^2}\right)\cos(\beta_0) + \frac{\gamma \Delta x}{2}\left(h_n - h_0 - \Delta x(\beta_n-\beta_0)\right)\sin(\beta_0)$$

where $\beta_n = \tan^{-1}(h_n/\Delta x)$ and $\beta_0 = \tan^{-1}(h_0/\Delta x)$. (3.7) can be used to quantify the total force on the top triangle area of each slice.

4. VOLUME CONSERVATION

The approach used in this section is strongly related to [8]. Recall that, in the previous discussion, a given configuration is divided into n slices. The i-th slice, $1 \le i \le n$, can be conveniently thought of as a container holding an amount of soil whose quantity is given by $(y_i+y_{i-1})\Delta x/2$.

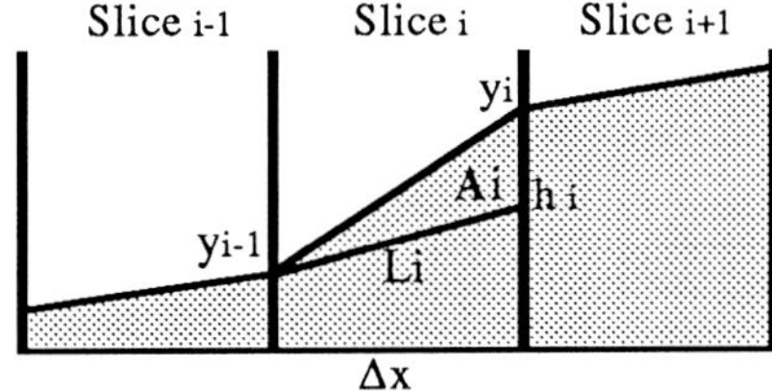

Fig. 5: Considering slices as containers

Let us consider a small change, denoted by ΔW_i, of the mass W_i in slice_i. Since $W_i = (y_i+y_{i-1})\gamma\Delta x/2$, we have

$$(4.1) \quad \Delta W_i = (y_i+\Delta y_i+y_{i-1}+\Delta y_{i-1})\gamma\Delta x/2 - (y_i+y_{i-1})\gamma\Delta x/2 = (\Delta y_i+\Delta y_{i-1})\gamma\Delta x/2$$

On the other hand, let us assume that there is a force f_i exerted on the triangle area A_i at the top of slice_i, which is parallel to the edge L_i. Due to f_i, A_i tends to move along the direction of f_i at a velocity v_i. The rate of the "flow" of mass of A_i through slice i can be computed by $\gamma A_i v_i/\Delta x$. Thus, the "mass throughput" of slice_i can be quantified by $\gamma A_i v_i \Delta t/\Delta x$, where Δt is a unit of time. Similarly, the mass throughput of slice_{i+1} is given by $\gamma A_{i+1} v_{i+1} \Delta t/\Delta x$.

From the principle of volume conservation, the change of soil quantity in slice_i is the amount of soil which goes out, minus the amount of soil which goes in. It can be expressed by

$$(4.2) \quad \Delta W_i = \frac{\gamma A_i}{\Delta x} v_i \Delta t - \frac{\gamma A_{i+1}}{\Delta x v_{i+1}} \Delta t$$

where $A_i = (y_i - h_i)\Delta x/2$. Putting (4.1) and (4.2) together and rearranging it, we have

$$(4.3) \quad \frac{\Delta y_i}{\Delta t} + \frac{\Delta y_{i-1}}{\Delta t} = \frac{1}{\Delta x}[(y_i-h_i))v_i - (y_{i+1}-h_{i+1}))v_{i+1}]$$

Now let Δt tend to 0. It follows that

$$(4.4) \quad \frac{dy_i}{dt} + \frac{dy_{i-1}}{dt} = \frac{1}{\Delta x}[(y_i-h_i))v_i - (y_{i+1}-h_{i+1}))v_{i+1}]$$

Recall that (3.7) gives us a formula to compute force f_i. From Newton's second law, we have

$$(4.5) \quad f_i = \gamma A_i \frac{dv_i}{dt} = \frac{\gamma \Delta x}{2}(y_i-h_i)\frac{dv_i}{dt}$$

Rearranging, we obtain both

$$(4.6) \quad \frac{dv_i}{dt} = \frac{2f_i}{\gamma\Delta x(y_i-h_i)}, \text{ and}$$

$$(4.7) \quad v_i = \frac{2}{\gamma\Delta x}\int \frac{f_i}{y_i-h_i}dt$$

Now we take the second derivative of (4.4) with respect to t and plug (4.6) and (4.7) into the resulting formula. That yields

$$(4.8) \quad \frac{d^2y_i}{dt^2} + \frac{d^2y_{i-1}}{dt^2} = \frac{2}{\gamma\Delta x}\left[\frac{dy_i-dh_i}{dt}\int\frac{f_i}{y_i-h_i}dt + f_i - \frac{dy_{i+1}-dh_{i+1}}{dt}\int\frac{f_{i+1}}{y_{i+1}-h_{i+1}}dt + f_{i+1}\right]$$

Note that we can denote h_i and f_i as functions of y_{i-1} and y_i, i.e. $h_i = h(y_{i-1}, y_i)$ and $f_i = f(y_{i-1}, y_i)$, since they can be determined based only on y_{i-1} and y_i if Δx and other soil properties are fixed. Hence, (4.8) is an equation with three variables, namely y_{i-1}, y_i, y_{i+1}. Let us suppose that we have divided the given configuration into n slices. Now we end up with n+1 unknowns, y_0, y_1, ..., y_n, and n+1 ordinary differential equations involving y_i's, their time derivatives and integrals. Solving these equations, we will obtain the solution for the soil behavior which satisfies both the soil dynamics and the volume conservation.

5. NUMERICAL SOLUTION

In this section we linearize equations (4.8) for both purposes of simplification and discretization. we start from (4.4). Assume that, at any instance of time t_m, velocity v_i of the mass on the top of slice$_i$ is represented by $v_i(t_m)$, the value of y_i is represented by $y_i(t_m)$, the rate of the change of y_i is represented by $y_i'(t_m)=dy_i(t_m)/dt$. Then, at the very next time instance t_{m+1}, the force $f_i=f_i(y_{i-1}(t_m), y_i(t_m))$ can be computed by (3.7) according to the value of y_{i-1} and y_i from the previous step. If the Euler integration algorithm is used, the velocity v_i at the time t_{m+1} can be computed by

$$(5.1) \qquad v_i(t_{m+1}) = v_i(t_m) + \frac{f_i(y_{i-1}(t_m), y_i(t_m))}{W_i}\Delta t$$

where Δt is the integration step size. Similarly $v_{i+1}(t_{m+1})$ is calculated. It follows that, from (4.5), we have

$$(5.2) \qquad y_i'(t_{m+1}) + y_{i-1}'(t_{m+1}) = \frac{1}{\Delta x}\left[(y_i(t_m)-h(y_{i-1}(t_m),y_i(t_m)))v_i(t_{m+1}) - (y_{i+1}(t_m)-h(y_i(t_m),y_{i+1}(t_m)))v_{i+1}(t_{m+1})\right]$$

Since at the time instance t_{m+1}, all items on the right hand side are knowns, either from the previous step of the simulation or from the calculations of $v_i(t_{m+1})$ and $v_{i+1}(t_{m+1})$, we may treat it as a constant, namely C_i. We now have n+1 equations in the following format:

$$(5.3) \qquad \begin{aligned} & y_0'(t_{m+1}) = C_0 \\ & y_1'(t_{m+1}) + y_0'(t_{m+1}) = C_1 \\ & \ldots\ldots \\ & y_n'(t_{m+1}) + y_{n-1}'(t_{m+1}) = C_n \end{aligned}$$

Solving (5.3) for $y_i'(t_{m+1})$, i=0, 1, ... n, we will be able to use the Euler method again to determine the new values for each y_i:

$$(5.4) \qquad y_i(t_{m+1}) = y_i(t_m) + y_i'(t_{m+1})\Delta t$$

Algorithm 1 describes the procedure of the numerical solution, in which each step of the algorithm takes linear time to execute. Thus the time complexity of the algorithm is O(n) where n is the number of elevation posts in a given configuration. The space required to store forces, velocities and heights of posts is also proportional to n.

Algorithm 1.

At any time t_{m+1} of simulation, do the following:

1) *for each post y_i, calculate its mass velocity $v_i(t_{m+1})$ by using (5.1);*
2) *for y_i, compute the right hand side of (5.2);*
3) *use forward substitution to solve equations (5.3) for $y_i'(t_{m+1})$, i=0, 1, ... n;*
4) *use Euler integration to determine new value for each $y_i(t_{m+1})$.*

6. EXTENSION TO 3-D

In going to 3-d soil dynamics, we use some essential concepts and results from the discussion on 2-d. First, a given soil configuration is partitioned into small prisms. The values of elevation posts (i.e. vertices) of each prism are evolved by an approximation procedure as follows.

Consider, in Fig. 6, the post z(i,j) chosen arbitrarily:

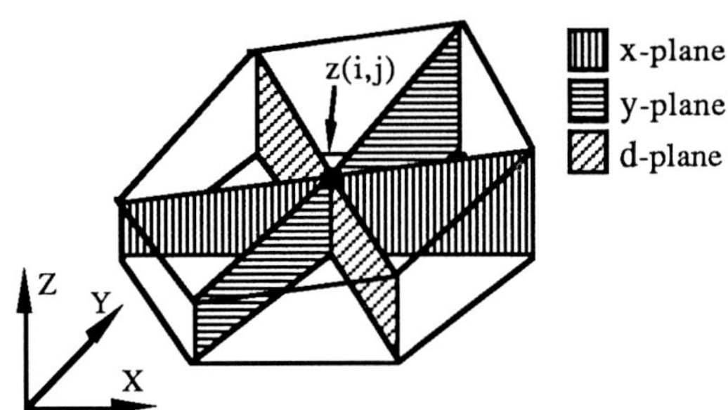

Fig. 6: An approximation of the 3-d configuration

z(i, j) is surrounded by six prisms. At any time instance t, those prisms are the only ones that affect the height of z(i,j). The effect caused by those prisms can be approximated by considering forces exerted on three planes, namely the x-plane, y-plane and d-plane. They are indicated by different types of shaded areas in Fig. 6. Thus the 3-d problem is reduced to a 2-d problem. The finer the partitioning is, the smaller the base triangles of prisms are, and the more accurate the approximation will be.

Let's assume that, at any time t_m, the height of post z(i,j) is represented by $z_{ij}(t_m)$, and the rate of change of z(i,j) is represented by $z_{ij}'(t_m)$. Since $z_{ij}'(t_m)$ is affected by forces from 3 planes, it can be expressed as a summation of three terms:

$$(6.1) \quad z_{ij}'(t_m) = zx_{ij}'(t_m) + zy_{ij}'(t_m) + zd_{ij}'(t_m)$$

where $zx_{ij}'(t_m)$, $zy_{ij}'(t_m)$ and $zd_{ij}'(t_m)$, are rates of changes of $z_{ij}'(t_m)$ caused by forces exerted on the x-plane, y-plane and d-plane respectively.

During a simulation, each time slice Δt is divided into two substeps $\Delta t1$ and $\Delta t2$. In $\Delta t1$, we first use (3.7) to compute forces exerted on three different planes. Then $zx_{ij}'(t_{m+1})$, $zy_{ij}'(t_{m+1})$ and $zd_{ij}'(t_{m+1})$ can be obtained by solving equations (5.3). In step $\Delta t2$, Euler integration is used to determine new values for each $z_{ij}(t_{m+1})$:

$$(6.2) \quad z_{ij}(t_{m+1}) = z_{ij}(t_m) + [zx_{ij}'(t_m) + zy_{ij}'(t_m) + zd_{ij}'(t_m)]\Delta t$$

For $\Delta t1$ and $\Delta t2$ of each iteration in the simulation, we split our 2-d computational problem into 3 terms: x-plane scan, y-plane scan and d-plane scan. Each scan has two phases corresponding to two time substeps. A scan on any plane involves calculations of forces exerted on that plane, rates of changes of z(i, j) caused by the forces, new height of each post, etc. Computations for each scan in a time substep are independent of scans on the other planes in the same substep, and therefore can be performed either sequentially or in parallel. It is important to notice that, in the same time substep, scans in different orders (x-scan then y-scan then d-scan, or y-scan then x-scan then d-scan, etc.) will have the same effect. The reasons are discussed in [9].

The 3-d algorithm can be briefly described as follows: Each iteration of simulation is divided into two phases. Steps (1)-(3) of Algorithm 1 are performed first for each scan. Then step (4) is applied for each scan to calculate new values of posts. Both time and space complexity of the 3-d algorithm remain linear in the number of posts.

7. INTERACTION BETWEEN SOIL AND BLADE

In this section, we analyze the interaction between the soil mass and a bulldozer's blade. Let's assume that the height of the blade is H. The shape of the blade can be modeled by an arc of a circle centered at the location $<x_c,y_c>$ with radius R. We divide the arc into n segments, each of which has length $R\Delta\beta$. Furthermore, the soil mass in front of the blade is also partitioned into n slices by horizontal lines at each joint point of two arc segments as shown in Fig. 7.

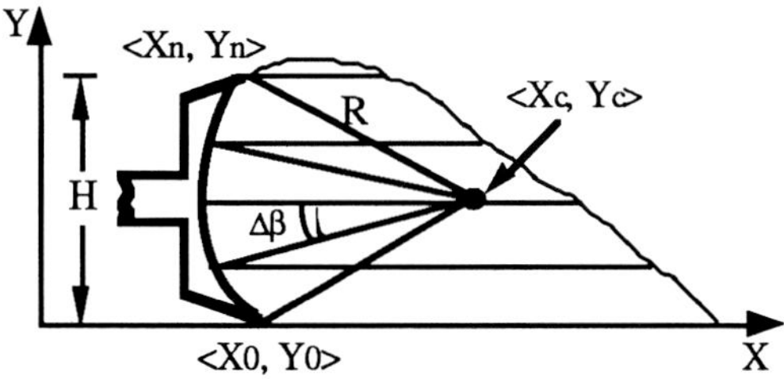

Fig. 7: Dividing the blade and soil mass

To calculate the force resisting cutting, we arbitrarily pick the i-th slice from the partitioning. The arc segment can be approximated by a line segment from point $<x_i,y_i>$ to point $<x_{i+1}, y_{i+1}>$. Note that the length of the line segment, denoted by ΔL, approaches the length of the arc when $\Delta\beta$ approaches 0. The idea is explained in Fig. 8:

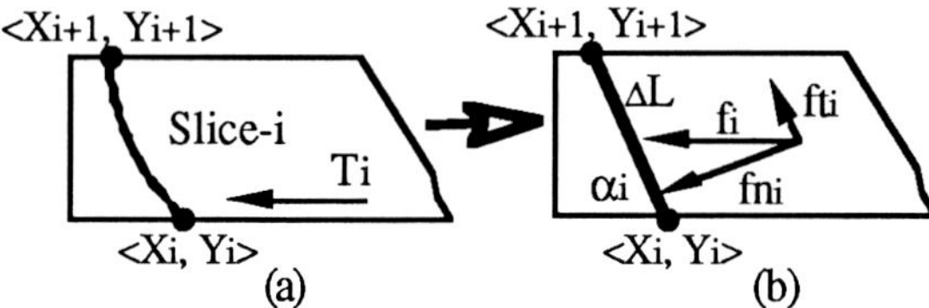

Fig. 8: Free body diagram for i-th slice

If the cutting part of the bulldozer pushes the soil mass with enough force, the equilibrium will be destroyed. At this moment, the resistance parallel to blade motion at the point $<x_i,y_i>$ can be calculated by the formula [1]:

$$(7.1) \qquad T_i = Ae^{2\alpha_i+B}[\gamma(H + y_0 - y_i) + c\cot(\phi)]\tan(\phi)$$

where T_i is the localized shear stress and α_i is the magnitude of the angle of inclination of ΔL to the horizon. The remaining symbols are as explained earlier. All angles are given in radians. Constants A and B are only related to ϕ and δ (δ is the angle of external friction), of the given soil:

$$(7.2) \qquad A = \frac{\sin(\delta)\,[\,\cos(\delta) + \sqrt{\sin^2(\phi) - \sin^2(\delta)}\,]}{1 - \sin(\phi)}$$

$$(7.3) \qquad B = \delta + \sin^{-1}\left(\frac{\sin(\delta)}{\sin(\phi)}\right) - \pi$$

Due to different cutting depths (given by $H+y_0-y_i$) and different inclination angles α_i, the magnitudes of T_i vary. The resistance force exerted on ΔL can be computed by $f_i = T_i\,\Delta L$. As shown in Fig. 8-(b), f_i can be further decomposed into two components, one normal to ΔL and another parallel to ΔL. The normal force is cancelled by the opposite force contributed by ΔL. The parallel force has the following property: In the upper portion of the blade, it has a smaller magnitude and points in the negative y-direction. In the lower portion, it has a larger magnitude and points in the positive y-direction. Let fy_i be the y component of the parallel force. It can be computed by:

$$(7.4) \qquad fy_i = (C_1 - C_2y_i)\, e^{2\alpha_i}\sin(\alpha_i)\cos(\alpha_i)\,\Delta L$$

where $C_1=Ae^B[\gamma(H+y_0)\tan(\phi)+ c]$ and $C_2 =Ae^B\gamma\tan(\phi)$.

Now we calculate the summation of all fy_i's, represented by F^y, which gives us the total force pushing the soil mass in front of the blade upwards.

$$(7.5) \qquad F^y = \frac{1}{2}\sum_{i=1}^{n} (C_1 - C_2y_i)\, e^{2\alpha_i}\sin(2\alpha_i)\,\Delta L$$

To get an accurate solution, we let $\Delta\alpha$ approach 0. In this case we have the following equations [9]:

$$(7.6) \qquad \alpha_i = \alpha_0 + i\,\Delta\alpha$$

$$(7.7) \qquad \lim_{\Delta\alpha\to 0} \Delta L = R\,\Delta\alpha$$

$$(7.8) \qquad \lim_{\Delta\alpha\to 0} y_i = y_c - R\cos(\alpha_0 + i\,\Delta\alpha)$$

Replacing α_i, ΔL and y_i in (7.5) by right hand sides of above equations and making $\Delta\alpha$ infinitesimal, we obtain:

$$(7.9) \qquad F^y = \frac{R}{2}\int_{\alpha_0}^{\alpha_n} [C_1-C_2y_c+C_2R\cos(\alpha)]\, e^{2\alpha}\sin(2\alpha)\, d\alpha$$

To simulate cases in which the blade are not fully loaded, we fix the lower bound angle of the definite integral and keep the upper bound angle changing from α_0 to α_n. That will give us the following figure:

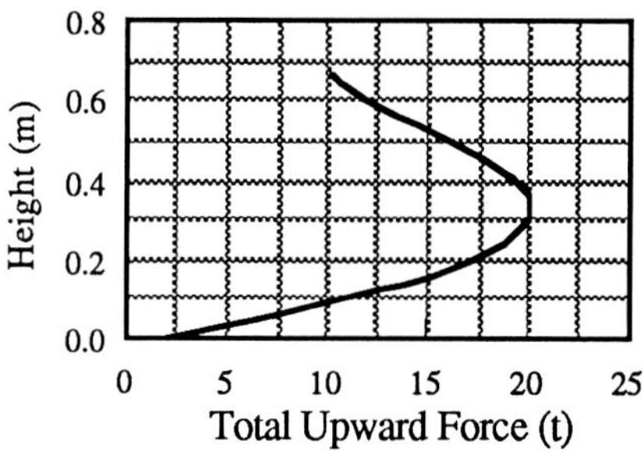

Fig. 9: Total upward force along the blade

In Fig 9, the vertical axis indicates y coordinates of points up to which the soil is loaded and the horizontal axis gives F^y under the given configuration. The data is recorded with α_0=1.22, R=100cm, c=1.9, δ=0.5, ϕ=0.54 and γ=2.0 (angles are measured in radius). For example, if the soil is loaded up to the middle point of the height of the blade, i.e. y=36.0 cm, the curve shows that at this point the total upward force reaches its maximum (about 20 metric tons).

The analysis shows that the total force is always positive. That is, the soil mass being cut always moves upward along the blade. This phenomenon is also observed experimentally [1]. The sequence of events occurring during the process of interaction between the cutting blade and the excavated soil before the blade can be described by 3 steps. 1) the soil chip being cut from the main soil mass moves upward along the blade because of resistance to the soil. 2) the soil chip is broken up into individual lumps on the upper part of the blade. 3) These lumps move downward toward the soil layers being further cut and from the soil prism which is being dragged. This phenomenon is depicted by Fig. 10:

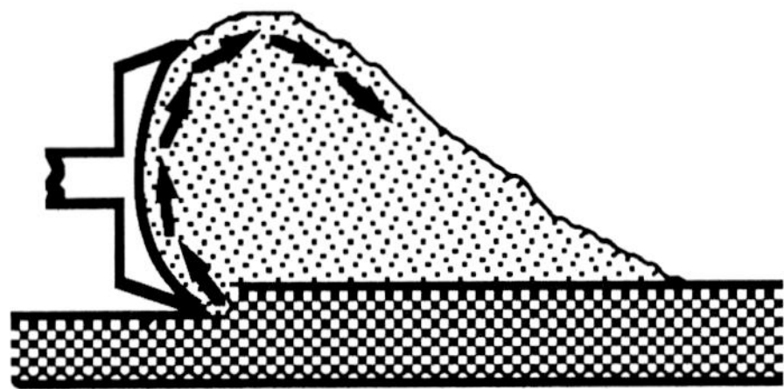

Fig. 10: Pattern of soil movement ahead of the blade

8. SOIL IN A BUCKET

In this section, we present a graphical model of a scooploader. For clarity, we assume that only buckets which can be represented by convex polygons will be processed. Again we first divide the soil configuration and the bucket into n slices with equal width Δx. This is shown in Fig 11, where the thick line segments indicate the bucket:

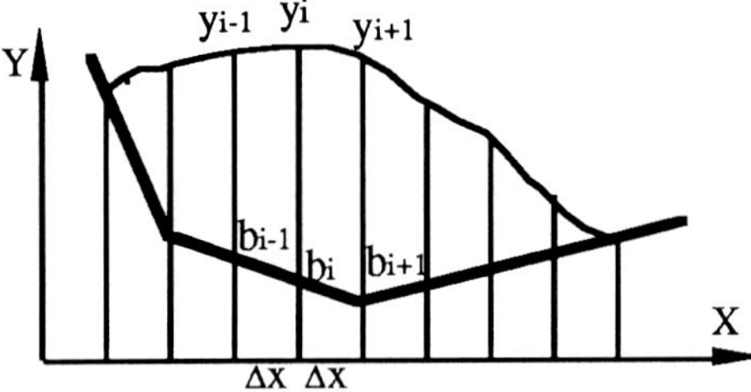

Fig. 11: Dividing the soil mass in a bucket

The motion of the soil mass in the bucket is a combination of two movements: 1) the movement of a portion of the given soil mass along a potential failure plane on the top; and 2) the whole mass along the bucket surface. We will refer to these motions as *local movement* and *global movement* respectively. In general, a local movement is caused by an unstable configuration of the given soil, while a global movement is due to the shear stress experienced by a surface of the soil mass in contact with the bucket. This can be seen more clearly through the free body diagram of slice-i arbitrarily picked from the partitioning (see Fig. 12), where f_i is the force driving a local movement along the failure plane denoted by line segment $<y_{i-1}, h_i>$. This force can be quantified by (3.7).

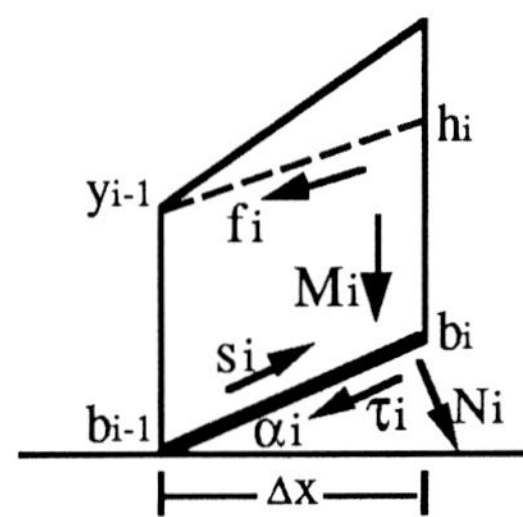

Fig. 12: Analyzing forces of slice-i

Let's now consider the global movement. The driving force, denoted by G, can be calculated by analyzing the free body diagram of each free body. As shown in Fig. 12, the weight M_i of slice-i can be decomposed into two elements: the shear stress force τ_i and the normal stress force N_i. N_i is canceled by the opposite force provided by the bucket surface $<b_{i-1}, b_i>$. τ_i is the force which pushes the mass to move along the bucket surface. The shear strength force s_i, on the other hand, resists the shear displacement of soil particles along the bucket surface. These forces can be determined from the Mohr-Coulomb theory as indicated by [5]:

(8.1) $\tau_i = M_i \sin(\alpha_i)$

(8.2) $s_i = cL_i + M_i \cos(\alpha_i) \tan(\delta)$

where c is the coefficient of cohesion, δ is the angle of external friction, L_i is the length of the line segment from b_{i-1} to b_i, M_i is the weight of slice-i, and α_i is the angle between the bucket surface and the horizontal. δ indicates a measure of the friction between soil and the surface of the bucket. It is given in radians. For loamy clay and sand, the typical values of δ are 18 and 30 respectively [1]. The units of these symbols are as explained earlier.

For equilibrium consideration, we use a method similar to the one described in [6]. The stress force τ and the strength force s can be expressed by vectorial summations:

(8.3) $\tau = \sum_{i=1}^{n} \tau_i = \sum_{i=1}^{n} M_i \sin(\alpha_i) <\cos(\alpha_i), \sin(\alpha_i)>$

(8.4) $s = \sum_{i=1}^{n} s_i = \sum_{i=1}^{n} M_i \cos(\alpha_i) \tan(\delta) <\cos(\alpha_i), \sin(\alpha_i)>$

Note that the term cL_i is dropped from(8.4), since the cohesion coefficient c describes molecular attraction among like particles and is zero between soil and a bucket surface. Thus, the safety factor F_s can be defined as

(8.5) $$F_s = \frac{|s|}{|\tau|}$$

When F_s is less than one, sliding of the whole mass along the bucket surface is inevitable. In this case, the total driving force G of the global movement can be computed by

(8.6) $$G = \begin{cases} \tau - s, & \text{if } \tau > 0 \\ \tau + s, & \text{otherwise} \end{cases}$$

In order to simulate the movement of soil mass in a bucket, we decompose G to smaller components which are parallel to the bucket surface. These component forces are distributed to slices so that the dynamics of soil can be considered individually for each slice. After carefully analyzing the behavior of the soil mass, we know that the following constraints must be satisfied:

1) The summation of component forces should equal G;
2) All slices should have the same x-acceleration.

The first constraint is obvious. The second one should be always true simply because: 1) a bucket always has a convex shape; and 2) some slices would fall apart and tension cracks or deformation would occur if the x components of their accelerations are different.

Let $G^x = G\cos(\alpha)$ and $G^y = G\sin(\alpha)$ be the x and y components of G respectively, where α is the angle between the vector G and the horizontal. Let g_i be a component force of G, which is experienced by the bucket surface of i-th slice. From the constraints we have

(8.7) $G \cos(\alpha) = \sum_{i=1}^{n} g_i \cos(\alpha_i)$

(8.8) $G \sin(\alpha) = \sum_{i=1}^{n} g_i \sin(\alpha_i)$

(8.9) $$\frac{g_1}{M_1} \cos(\alpha_1) = \frac{g_2}{M_2} \cos(\alpha_2) = \cdots = \frac{g_n}{M_n} \cos(\alpha_n)$$

(8.7)~(8.9) give us n+1 equations with n+1 unknowns, namely $g_1, g_2, \ldots g_n$ and α. Other variables can be computed according to the geometry of the given configuration. Solving the equations we obtain

$$(8.10) \quad g_i = \frac{M_i \cos(\alpha)}{M \cos(\alpha_i)} G, \qquad \text{for } i = 1, 2, \ldots, n.$$

where $\alpha = \tan^{-1}(\frac{1}{M} \sum_{i=1}^{n} M_i \tan(\alpha_i))$.

Having f_i and g_i computed, we model the soil dynamics in a bucket by using Algorithm 1 to evaluate simultaneous equations in (5.3). In order to do so, we simply replace f_i by f_i+g_i when calculating the rate of changes of each post at the time t_{m+1}. The rest of the algorithm remains unchanged.

9. IMPLEMENTATIONS

9.1 IMPLEMENTATION OF A BULLDOZER

Recall that the terrain surface is represented by a regular tessellation model. An array, namely z, of size m×n is used to store the height of elevation posts. An element z(i,j) in the array represents the elevation at the location <i,j>.

As mentioned in section 7, an excavating process of a bulldozer can be separated into three phases. These actions can be simulated by an algorithm with three corresponding stages: digging, piling and soil slipping. First, the algorithm keeps track of the motion of the blade. If the altitude value of the bottom of the blade is denoted by b(i,j) at the location <i,j>, then any elevation post z(i,j) passed through by b(i,j) are forced to have the same value. This procedure will create a ditch along the path of the bulldozer on the terrain surface.

The second stage models the upward movement of the soil along the blade. Let P be a set of soil prisms which have been passed through by the blade in the last time step. Let $z_p(i,j)$, $z_q(i,j)$ and $z_r(i,j)$ be surrounding posts of a prism p(i,j). The amount of soil contributed by prisms in P to the soil chip moving upwards can be computed by:

$$(9.1) \quad V = \frac{\Delta x \Delta y}{6} \sum_{p(i,j) \in P} \Delta V(i,j)$$

where

$$\Delta V(i,j) = z_p(i,j)+z_q(i,j)+z_r(i,j) - b_p(i,j)-b_q(i,j)-b_r(i,j)$$

Finally, in the third stage the amount of soil computed by (9.1) is put in front of the blade. Since the height that the soil is lifted upward along the blade and the speed in which the soil chips are broken into individual lumps depend on the cohesion property of the given soil, the procedure can be simulated by spreading the soil to a chunk shown below:

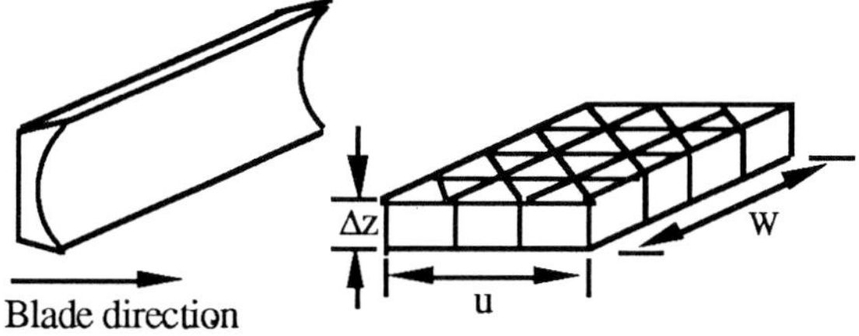

Fig. 13: Dimensions of soil chunk

The dimensions of the soil chunk are determined according to the following equation:

$$(9.2) \quad \Delta z = \kappa\,(1+c)$$
$$u = \frac{V}{w\,\kappa\,(1+c)}$$

where V is the total volume calculated by (9.1), w the width of the blade, c the cohesion coefficient, and κ a constant which determines how far forward the soil chip moves during one time step. In the implementation, κ is chosen experimentally to make the simulation looks more realistic.

After all this is done, Δz is added to the elevations of corresponding posts, and the slippage model introduced in previous sections is used to simulate the free flow motion of broken lumps of soil. It should be mentioned that the soil being brought to the top of the berm arrives continuously in the real world. However, with a discrete time simulation process, the chunk is a reasonable representation of the amount and location of the soil that would really arrive during one time step. The slippage model smoothly integrates this chunk into the berm, resulting in a realistic appearance.

Another important phenomena associated with physical properties of soil is swelling, which is due to a number of reasons: 1) the affinity of the soil for water; 2) the base exchange behavior and electrical repulsion; and 3) the expansion of entrapped air within the soil mass [4]. The model simulating the expansion of excavated soil is also discussed and implemented in [9].

9.2 IMPLEMENTATION OF A BUCKET

In implementing a 3-d bucket, we first divide it into m×n cross sections in a way such that they are parallel to either the x-z plane or the y-z plane. We refer to these sections as x-sections and y-sections respectively. The result of the division is shown in Fig. 14, where an x-section and a y-section are emphasized by two shaded polygons.

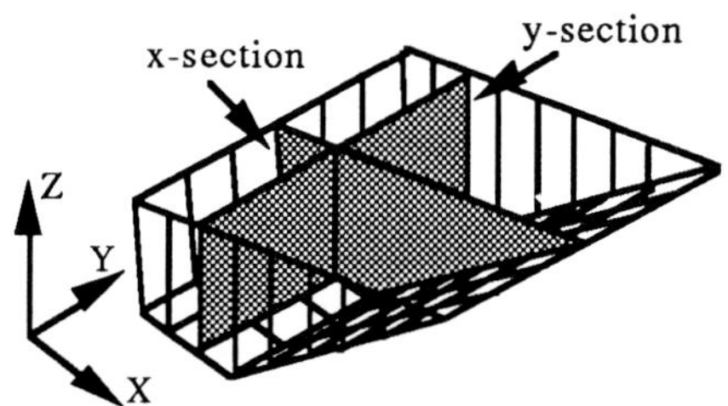

Fig. 14: Dividing a bucket into sections

Therefore, the 3-d soil dynamics in a bucket is reduced to m×n 2-d cases. For each individual cross section, we further partition a 2-d soil configuration into soil slices (see Fig. 11.). The soil dynamics of each slice is handled by means of the technique introduced in section 8.

A simulation procedure can be described as follows: Each iteration of a simulation can be accomplished by two steps. The first step computes forces for each soil slice of every bucket section according to (5.3) and (8.10). The second step uses the Euler integration method to determine new values for each elevation post (see Algorithm 1). These posts are intersections of x-sections and y-sections.

The cutting and loading activities of a scooploader can be modeled by a method similar to the one presented in section 7. The discussion, therefore, is omitted.

10. CONCLUSION AND FUTURE WORK

Experimental realtime models of a bulldozer and a scooploader have been implemented in the c programming language. Both time and space costs of algorithms are linear in the size of the bulldozer's blade, the size of the bucket and the resolution of the ground mesh. The simulations were done on a Silicon Graphics 4D/240 GTX computer. When using 4 processors, two bulldozers run at 6-8 frames/second. The scooploader model uses 2 processors, running at 10-15 frames per second. The number of elevation posts to model the ground for both models is 90×90. The simulations look very realistic.

Future research work may include soil compressibility and moisture content. The compression of soil layers is due to deformation and relocation of soil particles and expulsion of air or water from the void spaces [6]. Fundamental principles for estimating settlements of soil under superimposed loading should be explored so it can be used to provide vehicle tracks or conduct trafficability studies. The moisture content of the soil affects its unit weight and cohesion and results in different behaviors. Those properties should be incorporated into analytical models to provide more realistic simulations.

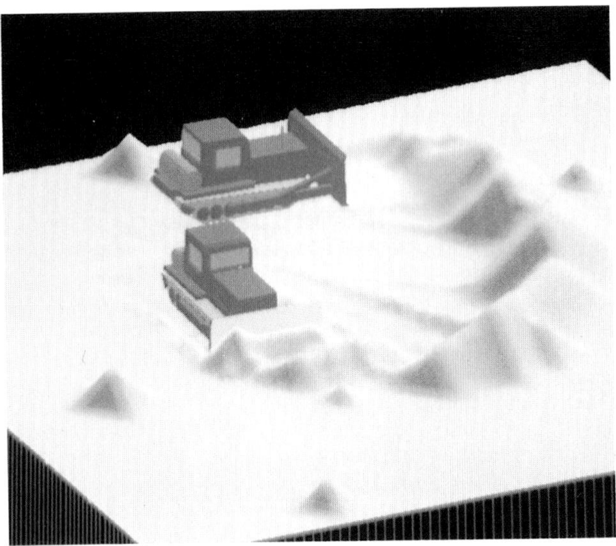

Fig. 15: Two bulldozers are at a work scene

Fig. 16: A scooploader is loading

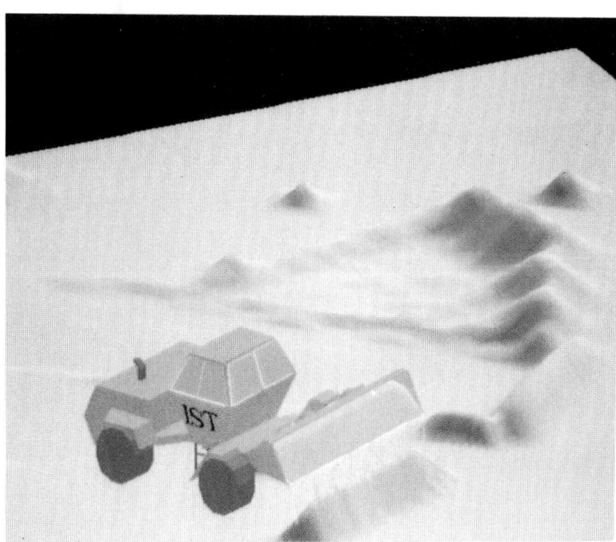

Fig. 17: A scooploader is dumping

ACKNOWLEDGMENTS

The authors are very grateful to Dr. Charles E. Hughes and Clay Johnson for revising the paper; to Lance Marrou and Jinxiong Chen for their support.

REFERENCES

1. Balovnev, V.I. *New Methods for Calculating Resistance to Cutting of Soil.* Translated from Russian, Published for the U.S. Department of Agriculture and the National Science Foundation. Washington, D.C., 1983.
2. Bromhead, E. N. *The Stability of Slopes.* Surrey University Press, 1986.
3. Burg, Jeniffer, Moshell, J. Michael, et al., Behavioural Representation in Virtual Reality. *Proceedings of Behavioral Representation Symposium.* Institute for Simulation and Training. Orlando, FL, 1991.
4. Cernica, J. N., *Geotechnical Engineering.* Holt, Rinehart & winston, 1982.
5. Chowdhury, R. N., *Slope Analysis.* Elsevier North-Holland Inc., 1978.
6. Das, Braja M. *Principles of Geotechnical Engineering.* Second Edition, PWS-KENT Publishing Company, 1990.
7. Huang, Y. H., *Stability Analysis of Earth Slopes.* Van Nostrand Reinhold Co., 1983.
8. Kass, Michael and Miller, Gavin. Rapid, Stable Fluid Dynamics for Computer Graphics. Proceedings of SIGGRAPH '90 (Dallas, Texas, August 6-10, 1990). In *Computer Graphics* 24, 4(August 1992).
9. Li, Xin. Physically-Based Soil Models of Dynamic Terrain in Virtual Environments. *Technical Report.* CS-TR-92-26, University of Central Florida. Nov. 1992.
10. Moshell, J. Michael. Li, Xin. et al. Nap-of-Earth Flight and the Realtime Simulation of Dynamic Terrain. *Proceedings of International Society for Optical Engineering.* Apr. 1990.
11. Winston, P. H., *Artificial Intelligence.* Addison-Wesley, pp.75-78, 1984.

Turbulent Wind Fields for Gaseous Phenomena

Jos Stam
Eugene Fiume[0]

Department of Computer Science
University of Toronto
10 King's College Circle
Toronto, Canada, M5S 1A4

Abstract

The realistic depiction of smoke, steam, mist and water reacting to a turbulent field such as wind is an attractive and challenging problem. Its solution requires interlocking models for turbulent fields, gaseous flow, and realistic illumination. We present a model for turbulent wind flow having a deterministic component to specify large-scale behaviour, and a stochastic component to model turbulent small-scale behaviour. The small-scale component is generated using space-time Fourier synthesis. Turbulent wind fields can be superposed interactively to create subtle behaviour. An advection-diffusion model is used to animate particle-based gaseous phenomena embedded in a wind field, and we derive an efficient physically-based illumination model for rendering the system. Because the number of particles can be quite large, we present a clustering algorithm for efficient animation and rendering.

CR Categories and Subject Descriptors: I.3.7 [**Computer Graphics**]: Three-Dimensional Graphics and Realism; I.3.3 [**Computer Graphics**]: Picture/Image Generation; G.3 [**Probability and Statistics**]: Probabilistic algorithms.

Additional keywords and phrases: turbulent flow, stochastic modelling, Kolmogorov energy spectrum and cascade, transport model of illumination, Fourier synthesis, advection-diffusion, gaseous phenomena.

1 Introduction

We have come to appreciate the central role that irregularity plays in modelling the shape of natural objects. The analogue for wind and fluids is *turbulence*, and its effects are no less essential to the realistic portrayal of gaseous natural phenomena: curling wisps of smoke, mist blowing across a field, car exhaust, an aerosol spray, steam rising from a coffee mug, clouds forming and moving across the sky, the fall of leaves, a swirl of dust in a room, a hurricane. These effects are caused by the interaction of objects with a wind velocity field. Modelling the effect of wind requires that we model both the wind field and this interaction. Both Sims [14] and Wejchert and Haumann [17] model a wind field as the superposition of deterministic fields. Modelling a visually convincing turbulent wind field this way is painstaking. The greatest success in this direction was the particle-based "Blowing in the Wind" animation by Reeves and Blau [10].

Stochastic modelling is a natural alternative strategy. In [13], Shinya and Fournier describe an approach developed independently of ours but which has some similarities. They employ stochastic processes and Fourier synthesis to derive a wind field in spatiotemporal frequency domain, and invert the result to get a periodic space-time wind field. We employ the same paradigm, but our model and application are quite different. Although both wind models can be applied to a wide range of phenomena, and [13] demonstrates this very well, their main concern is with coupling the wind model to macroscopic physical models of rigid or deformable objects, whereas we are mostly concerned with microscopic interaction with gaseous and fluid phenomena. Consequently, our model of turbulence is dissimilar: Shinya and Fournier assume a constant deterministic temporal evolution (Taylor Hypothesis), while for us temporal evolution is also a stochastic process. Our wind model also differs in that an animator has direct control over deterministic and stochastic components of a field.

In this paper, turbulent wind fields are modelled as stochastic processes. The model is empirically plausible[5]. A wind field is generated from large-scale motion and from the statistical characteristics of the small turbulent motion, both freely chosen by an animator. This is analogous to modelling rough terrain by providing the global shape as given by a set of height samples, and the desired roughness of the terrain [2]. The large scale of the wind field will be modelled using simple wind field primitives [14, 17]. The small scale of the wind field will be modelled as a three-dimensional random vector field varying over space and time. This field is generated using inverse an FFT method[16] that we have generalized to a vector field. The resulting wind field has two desirable properties. First, it is periodic and is thus defined for any point in space-time. Second, it is generated on a discrete lattice and can be interactively calculated using four-linear interpolation.

Gases have been modelled in several ways. Ebert models a gas as a solid texture. With some trial-and-error (and in our experience, significant human effort), realistic animations were obtained[1]. Sakas models a gas as a 3-D random density field, generating it using spectral synthe-

[0]The financial support of the Natural Sciences and Engineering Research Council of Canada and of the Information Technology Research Centre of Ontario is gratefully acknowledged. The helpful suggestions of the referees are greatly appreciated.

© 1993 ACM-0-89791-601-8/93/008/0369 $01.50

sis [12]. While spectral synthesis is useful in generating turbulent wind fields, it is not ideal for directly generating density fields: visual artifacts appear due to the periodicity of the field and the entire density field must be computed at once. The temporal evolution of the density field is limited to simple translations. Both of the above models are computationally expensive to visualize, and hence interactive modelling is not feasible. Using physically-based turbulence to animate density fields is mathematically nontrivial, but we shall show that this can be done efficiently.

We model gases as density distributions of particles. The evolution of a density distribution within our wind field is described by an advection-diffusion equation. We efficiently solve this equation by modelling the gas as a "fuzzy blobby" with time varying parameters. A fast ray-tracing algorithm is used, based on a front to back single-scattering illumination model, to render such a density distribution.

2 A Multiple-Scale Wind Field Model

Physically, wind fields are the result of the variations of the velocity $\mathbf{u}(\mathbf{x},t)$ and the pressure $p(\mathbf{x},t)$ of a fluid (including air) over space and time. These variations are caused by various forces: external forces $\mathbf{F}$ applied to the fluid, non-linear interactions between different modes of the velocity field and viscous dissipation at a rate ν. By summing these forces and equating them to the acceleration of the fluid we obtain the Navier-Stokes equations:

$$\frac{\partial \mathbf{u}}{\partial t} = -(\mathbf{u}\cdot\nabla)\mathbf{u} - \frac{1}{\rho_f}\nabla p + \nu\nabla^2\mathbf{u} + \mathbf{F}, \qquad (1)$$

where ρ_f is the density of the fluid. If the velocities of the fluid are much smaller than the speed of sound, we can assume that the fluid is incompressible [5], i.e.,

$$\nabla\cdot\mathbf{u} = 0. \qquad (2)$$

When proper initial conditions and boundary conditions are specified, Eqs. 1 and 2 are sufficient to solve for the velocity field and the pressure of the fluid for any time instant.

The above equations could be used to animate realistic wind fields. One would first specify the physical properties of the fluid that make up the model, including an initial velocity field and boundary conditions. One would then control the fluid motion by applying external forces. Realistic wind fields would be obtained by solving the Navier-Stokes equations as needed. This is entirely akin to the control problem for articulated figures, and it shares the same difficulties. First, a desired effect is hard to achieve by "programming" it using only external forces. Second, the non-linearities present in the Navier-Stokes equations make them hard to solve numerically, especially in the presence of turbulence (low viscosity). Linearizing the equations can improve stability and efficiency, which has been done by Kass and Miller to model the surface of water [4]. This results in highly viscous fluids that do not exhibit turbulence.

We shall model a turbulent wind field by separating it into a large-scale component $\mathbf{u}_l$ and a small scale component $\mathbf{u}_s$. The large-scale term is composed of simple wind fields, resulting in very viscous fluids. The small-scale term is a random field. We shall make a useful but physically implausible assumption that the components are independent, that is, that large scales do not affect the small scales and vice-versa. Hence we will write

$$\mathbf{u}(\mathbf{x},t) = \mathbf{u}_l(\mathbf{x},t) + \mathbf{u}_s(\mathbf{x},t). \qquad (3)$$

This assumption permits the real-time simulation and independent control of both large-scale and small-scale effects. The results, as we shall see, are quite convincing. We shall further discuss this assumption in our conclusions.

3 Small Scale Modelling

3.1 Random Vector Fields

In this section we will denote the small scale component $\mathbf{u}_s$ simply by $\mathbf{u}$. It is defined as a random space-time vector field, a function that assigns a random velocity to each point $(\mathbf{x},t)$ in space-time [15]. We shall invoke the standard Gaussian assumption [7]: that the random vector field is entirely determined by its second-order moments. These moments are obtained by statistically averaging (denoted by $\langle\ \rangle$) components of the evolving random velocity field. We will assume that the mean values of each component $\mu_i(\mathbf{x},t) = \langle u_i(\mathbf{x},t)\rangle$ $(i=1,2,3)$ of $\mathbf{u}$ are constant and equal to zero. The *cross-correlation* between different components of the velocity field at two different points in space-time $(\mathbf{x},t)$ and $(\mathbf{x}',t')$ are given by the functions

$$\Gamma_{ij}(\mathbf{x},t;\mathbf{x}',t') = \frac{\langle u_i(\mathbf{x},t)u_j(\mathbf{x}',t')\rangle}{\langle \mathbf{u}^2\rangle}, \quad i,j=1,2,3. \qquad (4)$$

Where $\langle\mathbf{u}^2\rangle = \langle u_1^2+u_2^2+u_3^2\rangle$ denotes the variance of the velocity field and physically is equal to twice the kinetic energy of the field. We will assume that the velocity field is *homogeneous* in space and *stationary* in time, which means that the cross-correlation only depends on the difference $\mathbf{r} = \mathbf{x}'-\mathbf{x}$ between the two points and the difference $\tau = t'-t$ between the two times: $\Gamma_{ij}(\mathbf{x},t;\mathbf{x}',t') = \Gamma_{ij}(\mathbf{r},\tau)$.

Homogeneous velocity fields have a corresponding representation in spatial-frequency domain via a spatial Fourier transform. Intuitively this transformation can be thought of as a decomposition of the velocity field into "eddies" of different sizes: large eddies correspond to small spatial frequencies and conversely for small eddies. The stationarity of the velocity field allows it to be represented in frequency domain by a temporal Fourier transform. We will denote spatial frequencies by $\mathbf{k} = (k_1,k_2,k_3)$ and temporal frequencies by ω.[1] We represent the velocity field in frequency domain via the usual Fourier transform:

$$\hat{\mathbf{u}}(\mathbf{k},\omega) = \int\int \mathbf{u}(\mathbf{x},t)\exp(-i\mathbf{k}\cdot\mathbf{x} - i\omega t)\,d\mathbf{x}dt. \qquad (5)$$

Writing the transform in this manner facilitates its separation into spatial and temporal frequency components. The Fourier-domain equivalent of the cross-correlation functions are the cross-spectral density functions:

$$\Phi_{ij}(\mathbf{k},\omega) = \langle \hat{u}_i^*(\mathbf{k},\omega)\hat{u}_j(\mathbf{k},\omega)\rangle, \quad i,j=1,2,3, \qquad (6)$$

where the "$*$" denotes the complex conjugation. Conveniently for us, the cross-spectral density functions and the cross-correlation functions are Fourier-transform pairs [15].

Finally, we assume that the velocity field is spatially *isotropic*, meaning that the cross-correlation functions are invariant under rotations. Thus the cross-correlation functions only depend on the distance $r = \|\mathbf{r}\|$ between two points. Isotropy and incompressibility (Eq. 2) imply that the cross-spectral density functions are of the form [5]

$$\Phi_{ij}(\mathbf{k},\omega) = \frac{E(k,\omega)}{4\pi k^4}(k^2\delta_{ij} - k_ik_j), \quad i,j=1,2,3, \qquad (7)$$

[1] In the turbulence literature, the term *wave number* is often used instead of *spatial frequency*. We will use *spatial frequency*, which is more common in computer graphics, but we shall denote spatial frequencies by $\mathbf{k}$, reserving the letter ω for temporal frequencies.

where δ_{ij} is the *Kronecker delta*, k is the length of the spatial frequency $\mathbf{k}$ and E is a positive function called the *energy spectrum function*. Its physical interpretation is that it gives the contribution of all spatial frequencies of length k and frequency ω to the total kinetic energy of the velocity field:

$$\frac{1}{2}\langle \mathbf{u}^2 \rangle = \int_0^\infty \int_{-\infty}^\infty E(k,\omega)\, d\omega\, dk. \quad (8)$$

3.2 The Energy Spectrum Function

Eq. 7 states that the structure of a velocity field (via its cross-spectral density functions) is entirely determined by its energy spectrum function. In other words, an animator can control the qualities of turbulent motion by specifying the shape of the energy spectrum. This function can be arbitrary as long as the integral of Eq. 8 exists. In the turbulence literature one can find a wide variety of different energy spectra for various phenomena. These models are either determined from experimental data or obtained from simplifying assumptions about the fluid. The best-known example of the latter for turbulence that has reached a steady-state (i.e., $\int_{-\infty}^{\infty} E(k,\omega)\, d\omega \rightarrow E(k)$) is the *Kolmogorov energy spectrum* [5]:

$$E_K(k) = \begin{cases} 0 & \text{if } k < k_{\text{inertial}} \\ 1.5\, \epsilon^{3/2}\, k^{-5/2} & \text{otherwise} \end{cases} \quad (9)$$

This spectrum results from an *energy cascade*, where energy introduced at frequency k_{inertial} is propagated to higher frequencies at a constant rate ϵ. Instead of invoking Taylor's Hypothesis [13] we model the temporal frequency dependence of the energy spectrum function $E(k,\omega)$ by multiplying the Kolmogorov energy spectrum $E_K(k)$ by a temporal spread function $G_k(\omega)$ subject to:

$$\int_{-\infty}^{\infty} E(k,\omega)\, d\omega = E_K(k) \int_{-\infty}^{\infty} G_k(\omega)\, d\omega = E_K(k). \quad (10)$$

This guarantees conservation of kinetic energy (cf. Eq. 8). Furthermore, we want the small eddies to be less correlated in time than the large eddies. Spatially, this means that small eddies spin, ebb and flow more quickly than large eddies; this behaviour can be observed when watching a water stream or smoke rising from a cigarette. We can achieve this behaviour by setting G_k to a Gaussian with a standard deviation proportional to k:

$$G_k(\omega) = \frac{1}{\sqrt{2\pi}\, k\sigma} \exp\left(-\frac{\omega^2}{2k^2\sigma^2}\right). \quad (11)$$

Indeed, for large eddies (as $k \rightarrow 0$), G_k is a spike at the origin, corresponding to the spectral distribution of a highly-correlated signal; for small eddies (as $k \rightarrow \infty$) the spectral density becomes constant, denoting an uncorrelated signal.

3.3 Generating the Small Scale Component

We now describe an algorithm to generate a random velocity field having specified cross-spectral density functions Φ_{ij}. The algorithm is a generalization of Voss's inverse FFT method[16]. The idea is to filter an uncorrelated white noise velocity field in the Fourier domain, and then to take an inverse Fourier transform to obtain the desired random velocity field. The challenge is thus to find the right filter such that the resulting velocity field has the desired statistics.

We first compute the velocity field in the frequency domain for discrete spatial frequencies (i,j,k) and temporal frequencies l.[2] Let us assume that the discretization is uniform and that there are N samples per dimension. Then the discrete Fourier transform (DFT) of the velocity field $\hat{\mathbf{u}}_{i,j,k,l}$ is defined on a discrete lattice of size $3N^4$. To ensure that the resulting space-time velocity field is real valued, the elements of the DFT must satisfy the following symmetries: $\hat{\mathbf{u}}_{i,j,k,l} = \hat{\mathbf{u}}^*_{N-i,N-j,N-k,N-l}$, where the indices are taken modulo N, i.e., $N - 0 = 0$[9]. In the special case when the indices on both sides of the equality are identical (e.g., $\hat{\mathbf{u}}_{N/2,0,N/2,N/2}$) we have to set the imaginary parts of $\hat{\mathbf{u}}_{i,j,k,l}$ to zero. The following algorithm generates a DFT with the required properties.

for i,j,k,l in $\{0,\ldots,N/2\}$ do
  compute $\hat{\mathbf{u}}_{i,j,k,l}$, $\hat{\mathbf{u}}_{N-i,j,k,l}$, $\hat{\mathbf{u}}_{i,N-j,k,l}$, $\hat{\mathbf{u}}_{i,j,N-k,l}$,
    $\hat{\mathbf{u}}_{i,j,k,N-l}$, $\hat{\mathbf{u}}_{N-i,N-j,k,l}$, $\hat{\mathbf{u}}_{N-i,j,N-k,l}$, $\hat{\mathbf{u}}_{N-i,j,k,N-l}$
  $\hat{\mathbf{u}}_{N-i,N-j,N-k,N-l} = \hat{\mathbf{u}}^*_{i,j,k,l}$
  $\hat{\mathbf{u}}_{i,N-j,N-k,N-l} = \hat{\mathbf{u}}^*_{N-i,j,k,l}$
  $\hat{\mathbf{u}}_{N-i,j,N-k,N-l} = \hat{\mathbf{u}}^*_{i,N-j,k,l}$
  $\hat{\mathbf{u}}_{N-i,N-j,k,N-l} = \hat{\mathbf{u}}^*_{i,j,N-k,l}$
  $\hat{\mathbf{u}}_{N-i,N-j,N-k,l} = \hat{\mathbf{u}}^*_{i,j,k,N-l}$
  $\hat{\mathbf{u}}_{i,j,N-k,N-l} = \hat{\mathbf{u}}^*_{N-i,N-j,k,l}$
  $\hat{\mathbf{u}}_{i,N-j,k,N-l} = \hat{\mathbf{u}}^*_{N-i,j,N-k,l}$
  $\hat{\mathbf{u}}_{i,N-j,N-k,l} = \hat{\mathbf{u}}^*_{N-i,j,k,N-l}$
end for

for i,j,k,l in $\{0,N/2\}$ do
  set imaginary parts of $\hat{\mathbf{u}}_{i,j,k,l}$ to zero
end for

To compute each element $\hat{\mathbf{u}}_{a,b,c,d}$ in the first loop, three independent complex random variables $X_m = r_m e^{2\pi i\theta_m}$ $(m = 1,2,3)$ are generated with normally distributed gaussian random amplitudes r_m and with uniformly distributed random phases θ_m. The components of that element are then calculated as

$$\begin{aligned}
(\hat{u}_1)_{a,b,c,d} &= \hat{h}_{11}((i,j,k),l)X_1, \\
(\hat{u}_2)_{a,b,c,d} &= \hat{h}_{21}((i,j,k),l)X_1 + \hat{h}_{22}((i,j,k),l)X_2, \\
(\hat{u}_3)_{a,b,c,d} &= \hat{h}_{31}((i,j,k),l)X_1 + \hat{h}_{32}((i,j,k),l)X_2 + \\
&\quad \hat{h}_{33}((i,j,k),l)X_3.
\end{aligned}$$

The functions $\hat{h}_{mn}$ are derived from the cross-spectral density functions as shown in Appendix A (Eq. 21). The velocity field is then obtained by taking three inverse DFT's:

$$\begin{aligned}
u_1 &= \text{invFFT4D}(\hat{u}_1) \\
u_2 &= \text{invFFT4D}(\hat{u}_2) \\
u_3 &= \text{invFFT4D}(\hat{u}_3).
\end{aligned}$$

The resulting velocity field is defined on a discrete lattice and is periodic in space and time. Thus even a small lattice defines a field everywhere in space-time. The spacing of this grid determines the smallest scale of the turbulence.

4 Animation of Gaseous Phenomena

Physically a gas is composed of many particles. We could therefore animate a gas by moving its particles about the wind field, but this would require a vast set of particles. We shall instead consider the *density* $\rho(\mathbf{x},t)$ of particles at space-time point $(\mathbf{x},t)$. Assuming that the particles have no effect on the wind field, the evolution of the density distribution is given by an *advection-diffusion* (A-D) equation

[2] The choice of i,j,k here as indices should not be confused with their different use above.

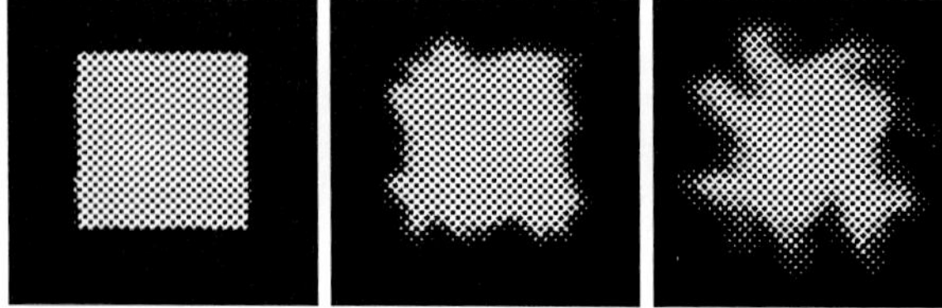

Figure 1: Evolution of a density distribution

[5] to which we have added a dissipation term:

$$\frac{\partial \rho}{\partial t} = -\mathbf{u}\nabla\rho + \kappa\nabla^2\rho - \alpha\rho. \qquad (12)$$

The first term on the right hand side is the advection term that accounts for the effects of the wind field on the density. The second term accounts for molecular diffusion at rate κ. This term can also be used to model turbulent diffusion from scales smaller than the smallest scale of the modelled turbulence. The third term accounts for dissipation of density at rate α. Since the velocity $\mathbf{u}$ is given, the equation is linear in ρ and can be solved by finite differences. The density distribution is then resolved on a finite grid and can be rendered using an efficient voxel-based volume renderer [1, 6]. Figure 1 depicts the evolution of an initially square distribution evolving under the influence of a two-dimensional wind field calculated using a standard PDE solver [9]. Computations for four-dimensional wind fields become rapidly prohibitive both in computation time and memory. To obtain tractable animations we propose an alternative strategy. We shall assume that the density distribution is a weighted sum of a simple distribution f:

$$\rho(\mathbf{x},t) = \sum_{i=1}^{n} m_i(t) f(\|\mathbf{x}-\mathbf{x}_i(t)\|, t-t_i) = \sum_{i=1}^{n} \rho_i(\mathbf{x},t). \quad (13)$$

In other words the density distribution is a "fuzzy blobby" with time-dependent field function f, where $\mathbf{x}_i(t)$ is the centre of mass, t_i is the time at which the "blob" ρ_i is created and $m_i(t)$ is its mass. If we suppose that f is a gaussian distribution with a standard deviation σ_0 much smaller than the smallest scale of the turbulent wind field, the wind field can be assumed to be constant on each blob. The advection term therefore only moves the blob, but does not deform its shape. The movement of the blob is hence given by integrating its centre of mass over the wind field:

$$\mathbf{x}_i(t) = \mathbf{x}_i(t_i) + \int_{t_i}^{t} \mathbf{u}(\mathbf{x}_i(s), s)\, ds, \qquad i = 1, \cdots, n. \quad (14)$$

The deformation of the shape of the blob is given by the diffusion term. Here we note that the diffusion at rate κ after time $t - t_i$ of a gaussian with variance σ_0^2 is equivalent to convolving a gaussian of variance $\kappa(t - t_i)$ with a gaussian of variance σ_0^2 (cf. [18]). Gaussians are closed under convolution, and the resulting gaussian has variance $\sigma_i^2(t) = \sigma_0^2 + \kappa(t - t_i)$:

$$f(r, t - t_i) = \frac{1}{(2\pi)^{\frac{3}{2}}\sigma_i^3(t)} \exp\left(-\frac{r^2}{2\sigma_i^2(t)}\right). \qquad (15)$$

Thus f diffuses outward with variance $\sigma_i^2(t)$ that increases with t. The normalization factor $(2\pi)^{\frac{3}{2}}\sigma_i^3(t)$ guarantees that the mass of the blob is invariant under diffusion. Once the variance of a blob becomes comparable to the smallest scale of the turbulent wind field we can replace it by smaller blobs and distribute the mass equally among them. The effect of the dissipation term is an exponential decay of the masses over time:

$$m_i(t) = m_0 \exp\left(-\alpha(t - t_i)\right). \qquad (16)$$

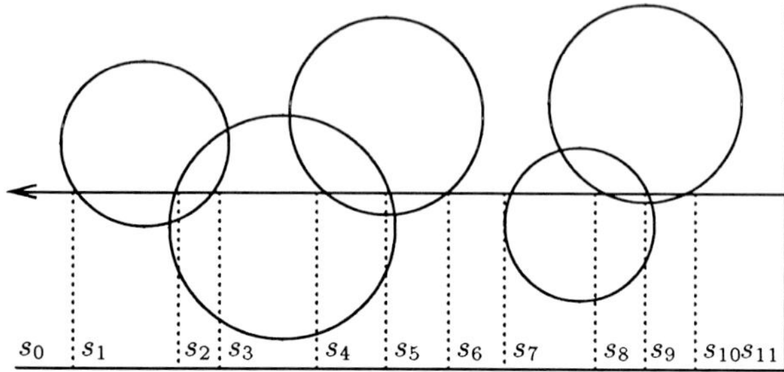

Figure 2: Subdivision of ray into intervals

5 Efficient Rendering of Gas

In conventional ray-tracing, light-object interactions are only computed at object boundaries. Hence light travelling along a ray is only modified at its endpoints. In the presence of a participating medium, the light carried by a ray can be attenuated and increased: attenuation is caused by light absorbed and scattered away by the gas; an increase may arise from light scattered in the direction of the ray from other directions and by self-emission of the gas. These effects can be included into a standard ray-tracer, by modifying the intensity value returned along any ray in the ray-tree. For each such ray we first determine which blobs have domains intersecting the ray (in practice we truncate the domain of each gaussian). For each such blob we store in a sorted list the parameter value s both for the entry and exit points of the ray. This subdivides the ray into N disjoint intervals $I_i = [s_i, s_{i+1}]$ $(i = 0, \cdots, N-1)$ as illustrated in Figure 2, with $s_0 = 0$ being the origin of the ray and the s_i being points of ray/blob intersections.

Once the ordered list of blobs intersecting the ray is calculated, the intensity of light C reaching the origin of the ray is computed by shading the list from front to back [6]:

$\tau_{total} = 1$
$C = 0$
for $i = 1$ to $N - 2$ do
 $C = C + \tau_{total}(1 - \tau_i)C_i$
 $\tau_{total} = \tau_{total}\tau_i$
end for
$C = C + \tau_{total}C_N$,

Here, τ_i is the transparency of the density distribution on interval I_i, and C_i is the intensity of light emitted on that interval by the density distribution. These values are defined in Appendix B, in which we also derive the illumination model. C_N is the intensity returned by the standard ray-tracer. In case the ray is cast to determine a shadow, only τ_{total} has to be returned.

The transparency along an interval I_i due to a single blob is a function only of the distance of the ray to the centre of the blob and the endpoints s_i and s_{i+1} of the interval as shown in Figure 3. The exact relationship and an efficient way to compute them is given in Appendix B. The transparency τ_i of the interval is then computed by

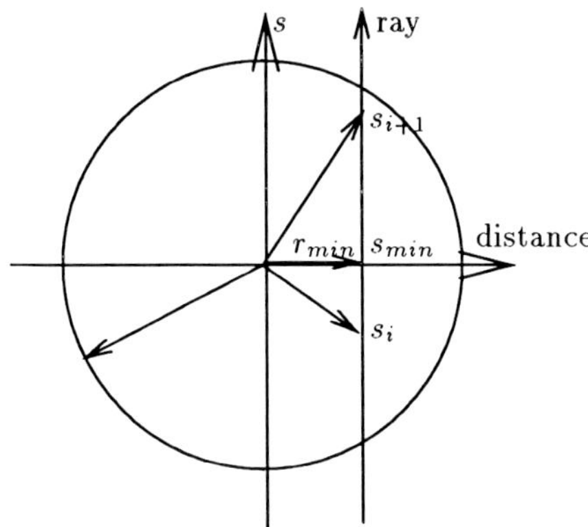

Figure 3: Calculation of transparencies τ_i

combining the transparency values calculated for each blob that intersects the ray along that interval.

Instead of testing separately for an intersection of the ray with each blob, we traverse a tree data structure of bounding spheres. The tree is constructed prior to rendering a frame as follows. First all the blobs are put in a linked list. The tree is then constructed by the following algorithm:

```
while list has at least two elements do
    for each blob b in the list do
        search for blob b' closest to b
        remove b' from list
        create new blob b'' which bounds b and b'
        set b and b' to children of b''
        replace b by b'' in list
    end for
end while
```

There are some obvious optimizations that can be made to this brute-force algorithm, such as non-binary blob groupings and the use of a k-d tree to accelerate the search, but the cost of ray tracing overwhelms even brute-force preprocessing cost. On average, the use of the tree data structure has reduced rendering times by an order of magnitude. The tree can be thought of as a multi-scale representation of the density distribution and hence could be used to render the distribution at different levels of detail.

6 Interactive Field Modelling/Results

In our implementation, modelling wind fields and their effects consists of several steps. First the energy spectrum for the spatial component of the small-scale turbulence is specified by providing numerical values for the rate ϵ and the inertial frequency k_{inertial} of the Kolmogorov energy cascade. The standard deviation σ for the temporal component of the energy spectrum is also specified. The overall energy spectrum (cf. Section 3.2) is the product of the temporal and spatial (Kolmogorov) energy spectra. A 4-D vector field is then generated (cf. Section 3.3) which can be placed in a library (although its computation is swift).

We have developed an interactive animation system in which an animator can design a complex wind field and visualize its effect on a gas density. Complex wind fields are formed by the superposition of small-scale turbulence with large-scale fields such as directional, spherical, and exponentially decaying fields. The user is also able to change the grid spacing of the small scale independently in each component of space and time, allowing the specification of non-homogeneous fields. This also permits the same prototypical small-scale field to be given different behaviours in different contexts (which is precisely what has been for the images shown below).

Our animation system also simulates the effect of a wind field on a gas. A specific gaseous phenomenon is specified as a particle system characterized by the following values: the region over which blobs of particles are born, their birth rate, and the initial standard deviation and the initial mass of each blob. During a simulation, the system introduces blobs at the given rate, animates their motion by advection, modifies the standard deviations by diffusion and the masses by dissipation, as described in Section 4. Additionally, particles can be given illumination parameters such as a colour. In this modelling step the centre of each blob is depicted (with intensity modulated by parameters such as duration), but positions and other data can be piped into a high-quality renderer for image synthesis. About 6,000 particles can be animated in real time on an SGI Indigo.

The parameters needed for rendering include (Appendix B): the extinction coefficient κ_t, which describes the decay of light in inverse proportion to distance; the albedo $\Omega \in [0,1]$, which defines the proportion of light scattered at a given point; the phase function p, giving the spherical distribution of scattered light; and self-emission Q, which is the amount of light emitted by a blob at a given position. The illumination computation for gas densities at a resolution of 640×480 typically requires from one to ten minutes, although 1-2 hour computations are possible when rendering scenes of high optical complexity.

For the images presented below, we have assumed that the phase function is constant and we have ignored shadows cast onto the density distribution for all but one image sequence. In all simulations the same statistical parameters were used for the small scale component: $\epsilon = 1$, $k_{\text{inertial}} = 4$ and $\sigma = 1$.

Steam from a mug: One global directional wind field was used to model the rising of the steam due to thermals. The particles were generated uniformly on a disk.

Psychedelic steam: Three trails of smoke of different colours were combined. As for the steam we used a directional wind field, this time tilted in the direction of the teapot spout. Particles were again generated on small disks.

Cigarette smoke: Two smoke trails originating from the tip of a cigarette are derived from the similar small-scale turbulence as the steam with a directional heat source.

Interaction of a sphere with smoke: This simulation shows how objects can interact with our wind field model. Instead of testing for collision of particles with the objects, we define a repulsion field around each object. We modelled the repulsion force by a radial potential field. The sphere is moved along a path given by a spline curve. Note that this image sequence depicts self-shadowing.

Three-dimensional morphing: The cylindrical range data of two human heads was converted into two sets of blobs and input to the animation system. The scene was illuminated by setting the self-illumination parameter (Q in Eq. 24) of each blob to the illumination given by the range data. The albedo was set to zero and dissipation was set to a large value to allow rapid dissolution of each set of blobs (with one run in reverse).

7 Conclusions and Extensions

We have presented a new model for the visual simulation of gaseous phenomena in turbulent wind fields. Our model provides an animator with control over both the large-scale motion and the statistical features of the small-scale turbulence. This model has been successfully applied to the animation of gaseous phenomena. Our model, however, can be applied to many other phenomena resulting from the interactions of objects with a wind field. For example, the wind field model can be included in any existing physically-based animation system. Our model can in fact generate a random vector field of any dimension, not only three-dimensional vector fields with a four dimensional domain. The derivation of the algorithm can be adapted in a straightforward manner. Our fast rendering algorithm can be used to visualize sparsely sampled data. The rendering of the heads in the morphing animation is a good example. Also our animation system could be used to visualize wind fields calculated by direct numerical simulation for fluid dynamics applications.

There are many other extensions to our model that we will explore in future research. We have assumed that the large scale motions of the wind do not modify the small turbulent scale. This is implausible. One possible solution is to warp the domain of the turbulent scale according to the large scales. We would require the use of a global deformation algorithm. Also it is possible to use a physical model for the large scales. A numerical technique in computational fluid dynamics known as *Large Eddie Simulation (LES)* solves the Navier-Stokes equations on a coarse grid using a statistical model for the small scales [11]. However, a physical simulation might not be relevant in computer graphics when a specific behaviour is intended.

A Inverse FFT Method Derivation

A white noise velocity field has cross-spectral density functions defined by:[3]

$$\Phi^w_{kl}(\mathbf{k},\omega) = \langle \hat{w}^*_k(\mathbf{k},\omega)\hat{w}_l(\mathbf{k},\omega)\rangle = \delta_{kl}. \qquad (17)$$

A random field with cross-spectral density functions Φ_{ij} can be obtained by *cross-convolving* this white noise with a set of deterministic kernels h_{kl}:

$$u_k(\mathbf{x},t) = \sum_{l=1}^{3}\int_{\mathbf{R}^3}\int_{-\infty}^{\infty} h_{kl}(\mathbf{x}-\mathbf{y},t-s)w_l(\mathbf{y},s)\,ds\,d\mathbf{y}, \quad (18)$$

which in the Fourier domain becomes

$$\hat{u}_k(\mathbf{k},\omega) = \sum_{l=1}^{3}\hat{h}_{kl}(\mathbf{k},\omega)\hat{w}_l(\mathbf{k},\omega). \qquad (19)$$

We obtain an equation for the transformed kernels $\hat{h}_{kl}$ in terms of the cross-spectral density functions Φ_{ij} by inserting the expressions for the Fourier velocity components $\hat{u}_i$ and $\hat{u}_j$ given by Eq. 19 into the definition of the cross-spectral density function Φ_{ij} (see Eq. 6).

$$\begin{aligned}\Phi_{ij}(\mathbf{k},\omega) &= \langle \hat{u}^*_i(\mathbf{k},\omega)\hat{u}_j(\mathbf{k},\omega)\rangle \\ &= \sum_{k=1}^{3}\sum_{l=1}^{3}\hat{h}^*_{ik}(\mathbf{k},\omega)\hat{h}_{jk}(\mathbf{k},\omega)\Phi^w_{kl}(\mathbf{k},\omega) \\ &= \sum_{n=1}^{3}\hat{h}^*_{in}(\mathbf{k},\omega)\hat{h}_{jn}(\mathbf{k},\omega). \qquad (20)\end{aligned}$$

We thus have 9 equations for the 9 kernels $\hat{h}_{kl}$ in terms of the cross-spectral density functions. Because of the symmetry of the cross-spectral density functions ($\Phi_{ij} = \Phi_{ji}$), only 6 of these kernels are independent and three kernels can be chosen arbitrarily. If we set $\hat{h}_{12} = \hat{h}_{13} = \hat{h}_{23} = 0$, then the system of equations given by Eq. 20 becomes diagonal and can easily be solved as follows.

$$\begin{aligned}\hat{h}_{11} &= \sqrt{\Phi_{11}}, \quad \hat{h}_{21} = \frac{\Phi_{21}}{\hat{h}_{11}}, \quad \hat{h}_{31} = \frac{\Phi_{31}}{\hat{h}_{11}} \\ \hat{h}_{22} &= \sqrt{\Phi_{22}-\hat{h}^2_{21}}, \quad \hat{h}_{32} = \frac{\Phi_{32}-\hat{h}_{31}\hat{h}_{21}}{\hat{h}_{22}} \\ \hat{h}_{33} &= \sqrt{\Phi_{33}-\hat{h}^2_{31}-\hat{h}^2_{32}}. \qquad (21)\end{aligned}$$

B Illumination Model

Consider a ray $\mathbf{x}_s = O + sD$, with origin O and direction D. Let C_N be the intensity of light reaching O along the ray from point $\mathbf{x}_b$ in the absence of a density distribution (i.e., given by a conventional ray-tracer). If we ignore multiple scattering effects, then the illumination C_0 reaching point O along the ray for each visible wavelength λ is [3]

$$C^\lambda_0 = \int_0^b \tau^\lambda(0,s)\rho(\mathbf{x}_s)\kappa^\lambda_t C^\lambda(\mathbf{x}_s)\,ds, \qquad (22)$$

where

$$\begin{aligned}\tau^\lambda(s',s'') &= \exp\left(-\kappa^\lambda_t\int_{s'}^{s''}\rho(\mathbf{x}_s)\,ds\right), \qquad (23)\\ C^\lambda(\mathbf{x}_s) &= \Omega^\lambda L^\lambda(\mathbf{x}_s) + (1-\Omega^\lambda)Q^\lambda(\mathbf{x}_s), \qquad (24)\end{aligned}$$

and κ_t is the *extinction coefficient*, and Ω is the *albedo*. The term $L(\mathbf{x}_s)$ is the contribution due to N_l light sources:

$$L^\lambda(\mathbf{x}_s) = \sum_{k=1}^{N_l} p^\lambda(cos\theta_k(\mathbf{x}_s))S_k(\mathbf{x}_s)L^\lambda_k, \qquad (25)$$

where p is the phase function characterizing the scattering properties of the density distribution, the θ_k are the angles between the ray and the vectors pointing to the light sources, S_k determines if the light source is in shadow and L_k is the colour of the light source. The term $Q^\lambda(\mathbf{x}_s)$ accounts for self-emission and can be used to approximate the effects of multiple scattering. If we assume that $C^\lambda(\mathbf{x}_s) = C^\lambda_i$ is constant on each interval I_i, which is reasonable in the case of many small blobs, then Eq. 22 becomes

$$\begin{aligned}C^\lambda_0 &= \sum_{i=0}^{N-1} C^\lambda_i \int_{s_i}^{s_{i+1}} \tau^\lambda(0,s)\rho(\mathbf{x}_s)\kappa^\lambda_t\,ds \\ &= \sum_{i=0}^{N-1} C^\lambda_i\left(\tau^\lambda(0,s_i) - \tau^\lambda(0,s_{i+1})\right). \qquad (26)\end{aligned}$$

If we define $\tau^\lambda_i = \tau^\lambda(s_i, s_{i+1})$ as the transparency along interval I_i then the equation becomes

$$C^\lambda_0 = \sum_{i=0}^{N-1}\left(\prod_{j=0}^{i-1}\tau^\lambda_j\right)C^\lambda_i\left(1-\tau^\lambda_i\right). \qquad (27)$$

We now show how the integral occurring in the calculations of the transparencies τ^λ_i can be computed efficiently. Let us assume that the blobs $\rho_{j_1},\cdots,\rho_{j_{n_i}}$ intersect the ray on interval I_i. The transparency on interval I_i is then

$$\tau^\lambda_i = \exp\left(-\kappa^\lambda_t\sum_{k=1}^{n_i}\int_{s_i}^{s_{i+1}}\rho_{j_k}(\mathbf{x}_s)\,ds\right). \qquad (28)$$

[3] All subscripted indices in this appendix take on the values $1,2,3$.

As we render for a particular frame in time we define $\sigma_j^2 = \sigma_0^2 + \kappa(t - t_j)$ and $m_j = m_j(t)$. Using these definitions, each integral in Eq. 28 can be written as [8]:

$$\int_{s_i}^{s_{i+1}} \rho_j(\mathbf{x}_s)\,ds = \frac{m_j}{(2\pi)^{\frac{3}{2}}\sigma_j^3}\int_{s_i}^{s_{i+1}} \exp\left(-\frac{r_{min}^2 + (s - s_{min})^2}{2\sigma_j^2}\right) ds$$

$$= \frac{m_j}{(2\pi)^{\frac{3}{2}}\sigma_j^2}\exp\left(-\frac{r_{min}^2}{2\sigma_j^2}\right)\left(T\left(\frac{s_{i+1} - s_{min}}{\sigma_j}\right) - T\left(\frac{s_i - s_{min}}{\sigma_j}\right)\right).$$

The first equality results from the geometry of Figure 3. The function T is the following integral:

$$T(s) = \int_0^s \exp\left(-\frac{u^2}{2}\right) du, \qquad (29)$$

and can be precomputed and stored in a table for efficiency.

References

[1] D. S. Ebert and R. E. Parent. "Rendering and Animation of Gaseous Phenomena by Combining Fast Volume and Scanline A-buffer Techniques". *ACM Computer Graphics (SIGGRAPH '90)*, 24(4):357–366, August 1990.

[2] A. F. Fournier, D. Fussell, and L. Carpenter. "Computer Rendering of Stochastic Models". *Communications of the ACM*, 25(6):371–384, June 1982.

[3] A. Ishimaru. *VOLUME 1. Wave Propagation and Scattering in Random Media. Single Scattering and Transport Theory.* Academic Press, New York, 1978.

[4] M. Kass and G. Miller. "Rapid, Stable Fluid Dynamics for Computer Graphics". *ACM Computer Graphics (SIGGRAPH '90)*, 24(4):49–57, August 1990.

[5] M. Lesieur. *Turbulence in Fluids: Stochastic and Numerical Modelling.* Kluwer Academic Publisher, Dordrecht, The Netherlands, 1990.

[6] M. Levoy. "Efficient Ray Tracing of Volume Data". *ACM Transactions on Computer Graphics*, 9(3):245–261, July 1990.

[7] J. P. Lewis. "Generalized Stochastic Subdivision". *ACM Transaction on Graphics*, 6(3):167–190, July 1987.

[8] N. Max, R. Crawfis, and D. Williams. "Visualizing Wind Velocities by Advecting Cloud Textures". In *Proceedings of Visualization '92*, pages 179–183, Los Alamitos CA, October 1992. IEEE CS Press.

[9] W. H. Press, B. P. Flannery, S. A. Teukolsky, and W. T. Vetterling. *Numerical Recipes in C. The Art of Scientific Computing.* Cambridge University Press, Cambridge, 1988.

[10] W. T. Reeves and R. Blau. "Approximate and Probabilistic Algorithms for Shading and Rendering Structured Particle Systems". *ACM Computer Graphics (SIGGRAPH '85)*, 19(3):313–322, July 1985.

[11] R. S. Rogallo and P. Moin. "Numerical Simulation of Turbulent Flows". *Annual Review of Fluid Mechanics*, 16:99–137, 1984.

[12] G. Sakas. "Modeling and Animating Turbulent Gaseous Phenomena Using Spectral Synthesis". *The Visual Computer*, 9:200–212, 1993.

[13] M. Shinya and A. Fournier. "Stochastic Motion - Motion Under the Influence of Wind". In *Proceedings of Eurographics '92*, pages 119–128, September 1992.

[14] K. Sims. "Particle Animation and Rendering Using Data Parallel Computation". *ACM Computer Graphics (SIGGRAPH '90)*, 24(4):405–413, August 1990.

[15] E. Vanmarcke. *Random Fields.* MIT Press, Cambridge, Massachussetts, 1983.

[16] R. P. Voss. "Fractal Forgeries". In R. A. Earnshaw, editor, *Fundamental Algorithms for Computer Graphics.* Springer-Verlag, 1985.

[17] J. Wejchert and D. Haumann. "Animation Aerodynamics". *ACM Computer Graphics (SIGGRAPH '91)*, 25(4):19–22, July 1991.

[18] A. Witkin and M. Kass. "Reaction-Diffusion Textures". *ACM Computer Graphics (SIGGRAPH '91)*, 25(4):299–308, July 1991.

Sphere interacting with a gas (note the shadowing)

A strange brew

The lonely cigarette

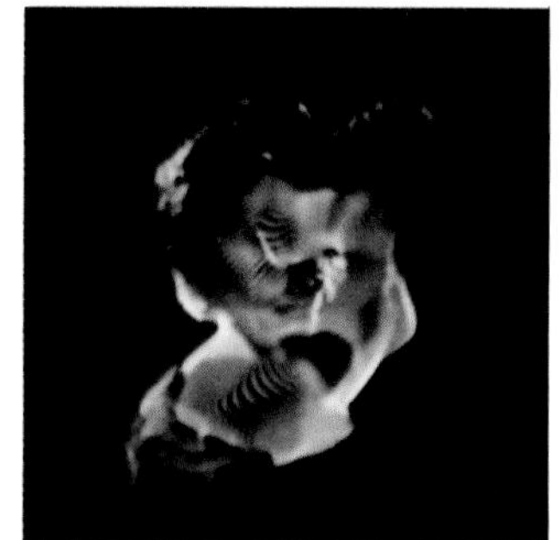

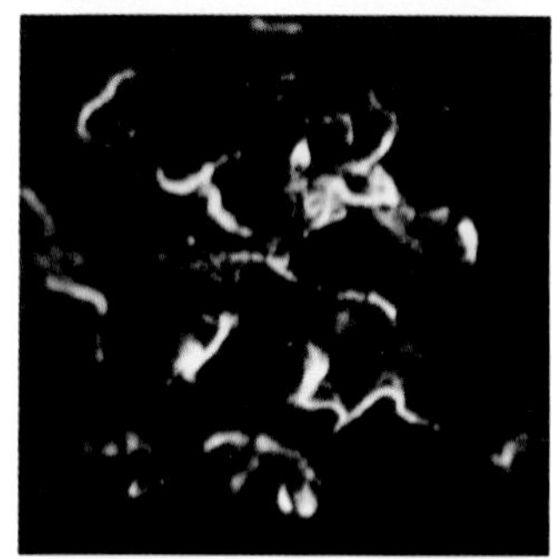

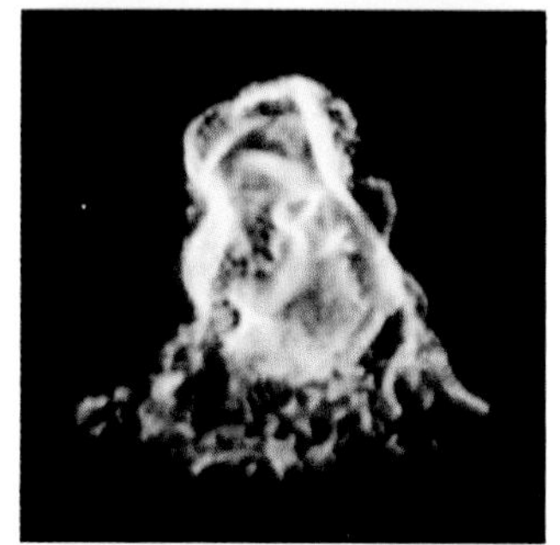

From David to Heidi

Real Virtuality: StereoLithography — Rapid Prototyping in 3-D

Chair:
Jack Bresenham, Winthrop University

Panelists:
Paul Jacobs, 3D Systems Inc.
Lewis Sadler, University of Illinois at Chicago
Peter Stucki, University of Zurich

Realistic Virtuality

Solid reality from virtual abstractions is now possible in mere minutes. Innovations in laser generation of 3-D objects offer rapid prototyping from computer synthesized graphics or scanned images to real solids in just a few hours or less. Photopolymers and thermoplastics offer new expectations for CAD, visualization, manufacturing, and medicine. Panelists from industry and academe will discuss current state-of-the art and expectations for the future of instant 3-D copies using new technologies such as StereoLithography, laser sintering, and fused deposition.

Panel Background

Real virtuality, in contrast to virtual reality, takes abstract images from computer synthesis and quickly turns them into actual 3-D objects as reality. This 'glimpse ahead' panel addresses use of StereoLithography, laser sintering and fused deposition as techniques for rapid prototyping. Engineering, manufacturing, medical, and artistic uses of this new technology offer significant growth potential as we enter the 21st century.

This panel brings together three leaders in innovative use and leading edge research for stereolithographic rapid prototyping. All of the panelists have been active in this new field of instant prototyping using laser-induced polymerization of photocurable resins. They will discuss industrial applications, biomedical usages, university research, associated software, and their views of what future challenges are likely in this rapidly developing technology.

Panel Goals and Issues

A glimpse ahead is the objective of this panel. Laser generated 3-D embodiments of virtual objects synthesized in CAD can be created as real physical objects in not much more time than was taken for 2-D computer plots a couple of decades ago. Panelists will discuss successful commercial applications and on-going research in which they're involved. They'll also address anticipated areas of activity such as data exchange standards, chemical & mechanical properties expectations, productivity enhancement and software paradigms.

The panel will first present views of 'real virtuality' or rapid prototyping together with illustrations of their work. To conclude the session they'll answer questions from attendees. If you've never seen laser generated 3-D parts nor held a computer fabricated polymer knee joint or gear box, the panelists will introduce you to this rapid prototyping in 3-D. If you're already quite knowledgeable and working in the area, the panel will share their research areas with you and expect you to comment and to question and to share your experiences of your own research and applications of StereoLithography.

Paul Jacobs

Currently over 370 StereoLithography Systems have been installed at major corporations, universities, government agencies and service bureaus in 25 countries on five continents. Dramatic cost and time savings have been achieved through the ability to rapidly proceed from the idea for an object to the object itself. The ability to hold a real object in your hands, to look at it from different directions, and to take advantage of the human brain's extraordinary pattern recognition capability has been one of the earliest benefits of this exciting new technology. We have referred to these capabilities for the early detection of design errors under the general headings of Visualization and Verification. The great majority of Rapid Prototyping and Manufacturing (RP&M) systems in current use have been justified on the basis of improved design visualization and verification.

However, during the past year we at 3D Systems have become aware of numerous applications of StereoLithography for design Iteration and Optimization. Substantial improvements in part accuracy, comparable to CNC machining, coupled with the proven ability to generate such objects very rapidly, at low cost and with greatly improved reliability, has now made it possible for designers and engineers to produce three, four or even five interactions within a few weeks. The result: improved product designs with fewer errors, available quickly, at lower cost.

Finally, we are now moving into an incredibly exciting era in which RP&M will enable the designer or engineer to achieve prototype and or limited run manufacturing Fabrication in final, end use, materials. With the release of the new QuickCast™ build style by 3D Systems, numerous users have already generated CAD models of a wide range of objects of varying complexity, produced a QuickCast quasi-hollow pattern of the object, and then, working directly with specific foundries, received precision shell investment castings of these objects in aluminum, stainless steel, beryllium cooper, titanium, silicon bronze, and incomel. The ability to generate functional prototypes, without the need for tooling, can save many months and tens to hundreds of thousands of dollars per component. Aggressively pursued, RP&M has the potential to significantly enhance industrial productivity.

Lewis Sadler

Rapid prototyping technology offers many advantages to biomedical applications that were previously unavailable. The ability to model complex, compound geometries is essential in the fabrication of maxillofacial prosthetics, facial implants, selected somato prostheses as well as anatomical models and simulators that have been developed to assist in surgical planning. Clinical experience has proven the efficacy of rapid prototyping technology as a new tool in the armamentarium of the surgeon in the restoration of facial cosmesis. The unusual educational mix of communication media (all of which are becoming digital) and the basic biological sciences (anatomy, pathology, physiology, histology, embryology, and genetics) and over twenty years of practical experience in communication problems for researchers and basic scientists have provided me with the necessary background to serve as liaison between groups of biomedical scientists and engineers. My experience is that these two groups have no common background, no shared language or customs and act very much as separate nations, unable to communicate effectively with each other. BVL's success in this new technology area relates to the establishment of a multidisciplinary team in both the biomedical sciences and in engineering.

Peter Stucki

While a minimal set of algorithms and data structures have evolved for laser generation of 3D copies, further research and experimentation is necessary to achieve a good set of standard formats, algorithms, and tools. Abstract languages, formats for CT, PET and MRI scans, and specialized CAD/CAM software tools for rapid 3D object prototyping with StereoLithography, laser sintering and fused deposition are active research areas. Shrinkage compensation, cross-industry data exchange, and device characterizations are also fruitful areas for future advances. My multi-media laboratory at the University of Zurich has been involved for the past three years in the subject topic and I look forward to sharing our outlook. Of special interest are:

Chemistry for StereoLithography and Rapid Prototyping: The process of photopolymerization, e.g. the process of linking small molecules into larger molecules comprised of many monomer and oligomer units is key and will be shown as animated scientific visualization. For StereoLithography, radical and cationic processes of multifunctional monomers and oligomers resulting in cross linked polymers are of prime interest. Topics for discussion: building properties, mechanical characteristics.

Informatics for StereoLithography and Rapid Prototyping: 3D interactive computer graphics and natural image processing as well as their underlying algorithms, procedures and software tools represent the back-bone for StereoLithography and Rapid Prototyping object reconstruction. A systematic approach to classify processing options available includes the procedures of interactive and automated object design as well as procedures of interactive and automated object analysis. Data exchange standards such as the SLA and SLC formats are key in making StereoLithography and Rapid Prototyping applications platform independent. Yet, data volumes are enormous and very often represent the critical upper bound of what can be handled with ease in a given workstation environment. Topics for discussion: algorithmic efficiency, automatic and semi- automatic procedures, standards, hardware platforms, networks, application programming paradigms.

Post-Processing of StereoLithography and Rapid Prototyping Models: Topics for discussion: silicon casts, epoxy cast, metal cast, quick casting.

StereoLithography and Rapid Prototyping for CIM Applications: Topics for discussion: responding to fast changes, reducing time- to-market, total product modeling, prototyping and test quality control, pre-production marketing.

Jack Bresenham

In the late 1950's and early 1960's, research and use of numerical tool control was a hot 'computer' topic and leading edge graphics application. APT is a cooperative research & joint development effort I recall as having significant impact. Today laser generation of instant, or rapid prototype 3-D objects is a comparable new technology. It can allow blind persons to more easily 'view' mathematical functions, doctors to model individualized joints or restorations, and car manufacturers to model engine blocks without prohibitive cost and time delays that made typical tooling set-up for multiple models impractical. Our panelists each have well established reputations of long standing in other areas of computer graphics, imaging and visualization. For the past several years each has devoted significant research effort to advance the state of the art in laser generation of 3-D objects for rapid prototyping. I believe you'll find their insights into what I sometimes call instant 3-D hardcopy to be truly a glimpse ahead into what Dr. Stucki often calls real virtuality.

REFERENCES

Fuchs, W.A. and O. Trentz, StereoLithography for Medicine, International Workshop on StereoLithography in Medicine, April 1-2, 1993, University of Zurich, Zurich, Switzerland.

Hunziker, M., Chemistry for StereoLithography, International Workshop on StereoLithography in Medicine, April 1-2, 1993, University of Zurich, Zurich, Switzerland.

Jacobs, P., *Rapid Prototyping & Manufacturing: Fundamentals of StereoLithography*, SME, Dearborn, MI, 1992, (434 pages).

Marsh, J.L. and M.V. Vannier, Surface imaging from computerized tomographic scans, *Surgery*, 94, pp. 159-165, 1983.

Proceedings of the Second International Conference on Rapid Prototyping, University of Dayton, Dayton, Ohio, June 23-26, 1991.

Proceeding of the Third International Conference on Rapid Prototyping, University of Dayton, Dayton, Ohio, June 7-10, 1992.

Proceedings of the First European Conference on Rapid Prototyping, University of Nottingham, Nottingham, England, July 6-7, 1992.

Proceeding of the SME Rapid Prototyping & Manufacturing Conference, SME, Schaumberg, Illinois, September 29-30, 1992.

3D Hardkopien als Alternative zur 3D Visualisierung am Bildschrim, *Informatik Forschung and Entwicklung* 1992 (7), pp.121-125, Springer Verlag, 1992.

Visual Thinkers in an Age of Computer Visualization: Problems and Possibilities

Chair:
Kenneth R. O'Connell, University of Oregon, Eugene

Panelists:
Vincent Argiro, Vital Images
John Andrew Berton, Jr., Industrial Light & Magic
Craig Hickman, University of Oregon, Eugene
Thomas G. West, Author of *In the Mind's Eye*

We think that the same mind's eye that can justly survey and appraise and prescribe beforehand the values of a truly great picture in one all-embracing regard, in one flash of simultaneous and homogeneous comprehension, would also ... be able to pronounce with sureness upon any other high activity of the human intellect.

—Winston Churchill, *Painting As A Pastime*, 1932

It is now becoming increasingly clear that new technologies and techniques currently being developed in computer graphics, scientific visualization and medical imaging could have important implications in the larger society—in time having a profound effect on education and work at all levels. As visualization hardware and software become more sophisticated and are used more widely, there is a need to focus on differing abilities among individual users. Some are very good at processing visual material, while others find it an area of great difficulty.

For centuries, most of education and many occupations have been largely dominated by verbal approaches to knowledge and understanding. If current trends continue, it seems likely that there will be a gradual but dramatic reversal in many spheres, as powerful visualization techniques are used to find solutions to complex problems that are well beyond the limits of traditional modes of verbal and mathematical analysis. In many fields, visual approaches have been relatively unfashionable and under-used for about a century. Yet visual approaches have been major factors in the most creative and original work of a number of important historical physicists, chemists, mathematicians, inventors, engineers and others.

A dramatic revival of long-neglected visual approaches is already underway in several fields. Mathematicians are rediscovering the power and effectiveness of visual approaches that were long considered unacceptable. Calculus professors, with higher-powered graphic computers and well-designed software, are discovering ways to move rapidly to high level work, even with unexceptional students. Critics of engineering education in recent decades lament the excessive prestige of highly mathematical analysis and design while the "art" and "feel" and high visual content of previous design approaches have been denigrated—leading sometimes to major design failures. The revival of visual approaches is now increasingly apparent at the forefront of many fields. However, the high value of these approaches is nowhere more apparent than in the new fields that have been emerging in the last decade or so—chaos, fractals, system dynamics, complexity.

The continued spread of increasingly powerful and inexpensive graphic hardware and software (together with simulation and interactive media) can be expected to only further accelerate these trends—making it possible for many people to use methods and approaches that previously only a small number of extremely gifted people could apply through their own mental models alone.

Gradually, it is being recognized in some professions (such as engineering, medicine, architecture and scientific research) that those with high visual and spatial talents may have moderate or severe difficulties with certain verbal or numerical material—and that professional training programs that do not (formerly or informally) acknowledge this pattern may serve to eliminate some of the most talented (and ultimately most creative and productive) individuals.

Certain psychologists consider visual-spatial abilities a distinct form of intelligence, like logical or verbal intelligence, while certain neurologists suggest that there may sometimes be an inverse relationship between visual-spatial abilities and conventional verbal and academic abilities. Thus, there is a growing awareness that some very highly gifted visual thinkers may be expected to show a pattern of traits consistent with dyslexia or learning disabilities—having significant difficulties with reading, writing, composition, counting, speaking, memory or attention.

The late Harvard neurologist Norman Geschwind was interested in the apparently paradoxical pattern of high visual talents with verbal difficulties. He observed that "it has become increasingly clear in recent years that dyslexics themselves are frequently endowed with high talents in many areas. ... I need only point out the names of Thomas Edison and Albert Einstein to make it clear that dyslexics do not merely succeed in making a marginal adjustment in some instances, but that they rank high among those who have created the very fabric of our modern world." He suggested "that this is no accident." Rather, "there have been in recent years an increasing number of studies that have pointed out that many dyslexics have superior talents in certain areas of non-verbal skill, such as art, architecture, engineering, and athletics." He argued that the early formation of the brain may explain these patterns and should help us not to be surprised at those who have such mixed abilities.

It is possible, therefore, that conditions are being reversed in a way that will be especially favorable to some strong visual thinkers, many of whom may have had significant difficulties in conventional academic settings. With the further development of these technologies, we may see the development of a new visual language and striking new opportunities for creative, visual thinking persons. Increasingly, we may see them forming bridges between the arts, their traditional stronghold, and the scientific and technical fields that have been closed to many of them. We are used to hearing of scientists, computer programmers and mathematicians who are also talented musicians. Possibly in the future we may see the solution of complex problems in molecular biology, statistics, financial markets, neuroanatomy, materials development and higher mathematics coming from people who are sculptors, graphic artists, craftsmen, film makers and designers of computer graphic visualizations. Different kinds of tools and different kinds of problems may demand different talents and favor different kinds of brains.

As part of the panel, an "overview" presentation will be provided to describe relevant recent neurological and psychological research, to provide brief examples of historical and contemporary visual thinkers and to suggest the possible social, economic, educational and cultural implications of shifting from a predominantly verbal culture to one that is increasingly focused on visual approaches to learning, knowledge and experience. Subsequently, panelists will give presentations referring to their own work in computer graphics—generally representing perspectives related to scientific visualization, education and entertainment. The panelists will discuss and debate the extent to which they agree or disagree with the views put forth by other panelists and issues raised by the audience.

Vincent Argiro

In our need to comprehend space, volume visualization becomes an interdisciplinary adventure. Cells are 3D space-filling objects. Human brains are 3D space-filling objects. The bedrock under the Gulf of Mexico is an enormous 3D space-filling object. In each case we are curious, even desperate to know what lies inside these spaces. We want to see freely inside, with the mere intention to do so, like the Superman of our childhood with his X-ray vision.

We are a long way yet from fully actualizing this vision. But recent strides in digital imaging and computer graphics hardware and software suggest that this goal is becoming less remote. Moreover, in our own adventures with scientists, physicians and engineers, we find striking parallels in the specific visualization, analysis, modeling and communication tools these professionals require. To peer into and comprehend these regions of space, whether microscopic or macroscopic, living or inanimate, common approaches prevail over unique requirements.

This indeed suggests that digital imaging and volume visualization may be creating a fundamentally new visual language for communicating insights into the natural and artificial worlds. My presentation will make this case, illustrated with actual instances of overlap, osmosis and cross-pollination among investigations into cellular, neural, and geologic space.

John Andrew Berton, Jr.

Cinema is a medium where ideas are routinely communicated through primarily visual means. Films and videos are created by strong visual thinkers and viewers' interpretations of these works are based largely on visual information. This is especially true of visual effects work, where images must carry important content with little verbal assistance.

At Industrial Light and Magic, artists and technicians work with film directors and visual effects supervisors to bring important and demanding visual concepts to the screen. The techniques required to achieve these visual effects are often highly technical and, in many cases, based on logical systems, such as computers and computer graphics programs. The results of these techniques are judged in the visual realm, creating a unique opportunity to observe the translation of visual ideas into the verbal/technical realm and back again. Case studies of recent feature film projects at ILM indicate possible solutions to problems faced by visual thinkers in a verbal/technical arena. Topics of discussion include evaluations of how visual thinkers use existing images to describe their vision for images yet to be created and how ILM builds and uses interactive computer graphics tools to help visual thinkers communicate their ideas and create compelling visual effects.

Craig Hickman

While media attention centers on high-end scientific visualization and virtual reality as the epitome of what the computer can offer to visual thinking, a quieter but equally significant revolution is occurring on the desktop. Users are now expecting everyday software to display data in a visually satisfying way, and when they are confused using the software they are less apt to blame their confusion on their own ignorance rather they assume the fault lies with bad software design. The visual logic of software must be as well thought out as the logic of the data structures and software design teams will have greater need for "visual thinkers."

My own software "Kid Pix" attempts to provide a rich visual experience. It approaches this in two ways. First the user interface is as straightforward and as "self defining" as possible. Users are not expected to read a manual to get started and are invited to learn the program by exploration. Second, "Kid Pix" is full of randomness, visual surprises, and visual jokes. Even though these two approaches seem at odds, they support each other.

Thomas G. West

For some 400 or 500 years we have had our schools teaching basically the skills of a Medieval clerk—reading, writing, counting and memorizing texts. But with the deepening influence of computers of all kinds, it now seems that we might be on the verge of a really new era when we will be required to cultivate broadly a very different set of skills—the skills of a Renaissance thinker such as Leonardo da Vinci, recombining the arts and the sciences to create elegant and integrated solutions to urgent and complex problems.

As part of this change, in the not-too-distant future, past ideas of desirable traits could be transformed. In time, machines will be the best clerks. Consequently, in place of the qualities desired in a well-trained clerk, we might, instead, find preferable: a propensity to learn directly through experience (or simulated experience) rather than primarily from books and lectures; a facility with visual content and modes of analysis instead of mainly verbal (or symbolic or numerical) fluency; the more integrated perspective of the global generalist rather than the increasingly narrow specialist; a habit of innovation through making connections among many diverse fields; habit of continuous and life-long learning in many different areas of study (perhaps with occasional but transient specialization); an ability to rapidly progress through many stages of research and development and design using imagination and mental models along with 3D computer-aided design.

Leonardo da Vinci's emphasis on imitating nature and analysis through visualization may come to serve us as well as it served him—providing results well in advance of those who follow other more conventional approaches. Accordingly, in the near future, it seems that we might be in a position to come full circle, using the most sophisticated technologies and techniques to draw on the most elementary approaches and capacities—to simulate reality rather than describe it in words or numbers. To learn, once again, by doing rather than by reading. To learn, once again, by seeing and experimenting rather than by following memorized algorithms. Sometimes the oldest pathways can be the best guides into unfamiliar territory.

References

Brown, D., H. Porta and J.J. Uhl, "Calculus and Mathematica," in *The Laboratory Approach to Teaching Calculus*, L. Carl Leinbach et al, (eds.), Mathematical Association of America, 1991.

Ferguson, Eugene S., *Engineering and the Mind's Eye*, MIT Press, 1992.

Gardner, Howard, *Frames of Mind: The Theory of Multiple Intelligences*, Basic Books, 1983.

Geschwind, Norman, and Albert M. Galaburda, *Cerebral Laterialization: Biological Mechanisms, Associations and Pathology*, MIT Press, 1987.

Jolls, Kenneth R. and Daniel C. Coy, "The Art of Thermodynamics," *IRIS Universe*, No. 12, spring, 1990.

Jolls, Kenneth R.,"Understanding Thermodynamics through Interactive Computer Graphics," *Chemical Engineering Progress*, February 1989.

Kaufmann, William J., and Larry L. Smarr, *Supercomputing and the Transformation of Science*, Scientific American Library, 1993.

Ritchie-Calder, Peter R., *Leonardo & the Age of the Eye*, Simon and Schuster, 1970.

Satori, Giuseppe, and M. Mitchell Leonaop, *Complexity: The Emerging Science at the Edge of Order and Chaos*, Simon & Schuster, 1992.

West, Thomas G., "A Return to Visual Thinking," *Computer Graphics World*, November 1992.

West, Thomas G., *In the Mind's Eye: Visual Thinkers, Gifted People with Learning Difficulties, Computer Images and the Ironies of Creativity*, Prometheus Books, 1991.

Zimmerman, Walter, and Steve Cunningham (eds), *Visualization in Teaching and Learning Mathematics*, Mathematical Association of America, 1991.

Updating Computer Animation: An Interdisciplinary Approach

Chair:
Jane Veeder, San Francisco State University

Panelists:
Charlie Gunn, Technisches Universitat Berlin
Scott Liedtka, Forensic Technologies International
William Moritz, California Institute of the Arts
Tina Price, Walt Disney Pictures

Computer animation currently enjoys a wide range of applications from children's entertainment to disaster simulation, esoteric mathematics to personal fine art statements. In order to develop useful technology and train future professionals, we need to update our model of "Animation" and "Animator" into a pluralistic model that encompasses these and other applications. This panel will articulate and compare the conceptual framework, design gestalt, relation of design to content, and development process used by the very different animation application areas of entertainment, scientific and engineering visualization, and fine art as well as explore the connection between current forms and historical animation. Lively discussion will highlight points of commonality and contrast, reveal how these fields view each other and what each can learn from the other.

Panel Overview

With the zoetrope and other accessible contraptions, we began the transition from the era of the static media image to that of the dynamic. Motion film and video accelerated this transition and now digital technology is blurring the traditional differences between film and video, the optical and the synthetic image, science and art. For some, "Animation" is synonymous with "Cartoon." For others, it means "Dynamic Simulation.. Do we need new terminology? First, we need updated information: What is the mental model of animation and viewer? How will the needs of the application area drive the development of hardware and software? How does the use of computers impact the design and production process? What are the design constraints? How are design and production roles defined? What backgrounds do these animators have and what new skills must they learn? Who are valuable collaborators? How are "Time," "Space," and "Story" dealt with in each of these application areas? How do these animations relate to historical animation and other forms of contemporary representation? How can technical and media arts education better prepare people to work in these areas?

As animation joins writing as a basic skill for the communication of complex information, we must articulate the combined knowledge and experience of traditional and emerging practitioners. As computer animation, much like computer graphics, becomes a ubiquitous, enhancing technology, we must inform the development of that technology with our design experience and diverse creative goals.

Charlie Gunn

Mathematical animation represents a "return of the repressed": in its best moments, it reaches behind the symbolic artifacts preserved in textbooks to reveal the ding-an-sich of mathematical activity. In this presentation I'll make a case study of the mathematical animation, "Not Knot," tracing the decisions made to convert "equations" into "pixels." I suggest that the conversion is closer to archeology than discovery: behind the equations stands the original human imagination which in many ways is closer to a picture than to an equation. Part of the historical mission of scientific visualization is to reclaim the original form of much scientific creativity, which is intuitive, plastic, dynamic.

Animation is a key ingredient in this revelation by showing the mathematical universe to be alive with metamorphosis and movement. Attempting to open a window onto this universe using standard animation systems is often frustrating. I'll examine how the modeling, animation, and rendering requirements of "Not Knot" could not be met by existing monolithic systems. How can this situation be improved? I propose some guidelines for the design of open and flexible animation systems that have "room to grow" as new directions of mathematical exploration are pursued. Results obtained would have application to wider realms of animation practice. As an example, there are several places in "Not Knot" where transitions to infinity occur. Through integrating such limiting processes into animation technique we can begin to understand and represent qualitative metamorphosis, a key feature of much interesting animation. Such a system would also improve the aesthetic component of mathematical animation by simplifying collaboration with artist/ designers. Going in the other direction, it would also be of interest to artists working in the non-representational animation tradition of Fischinger, Whitney, and Cuba.

Scott Liedtka

At FTI, we produce for the courtroom computer animations that recreate accidents or explain technical processes. In either case, we attempt to teach technical concepts to lay people who must use them to make serious decisions. In doing so, we design our animations to draw attention to important events and to the relationship between different events. We often study an event by changing its timing, speeding it up or slowing it down, using repetition, or even reversing it. Also, our animations are often shown out of order as well because presenters using a bar coded laserdisc have random access to the animation segments we produce. Forensic animation has a special and legal relationship to reality. For instance, most of our motion is based upon recorded real world data, witness testimony, or established dynamics formulas. Camera views may be that of an eye witness or just an unglamorous close-up of a part in the process of failing. Although the technical aspects of our work are significant, it is also important to keep our audience's attention. Traditional animation techniques and timing as well as good design are crucial to keeping our audience watching and learning but we must not cross over into the kind of graphical fictions so successful in the entertainment domain. Our staff, a combination of mechanical engineers with computer artists and media specialists, reflects this balancing act.

Tina Price

In an era of dramatic change and expansion in animation, it is useful to try to define terms and take a new look at convention. I want to look at the long-used design philosophies of full character animation and discuss the difference between character animation and just moving things around. Using the Magic Carpet in "Aladdin" as an example, I'll show and discuss why character animation is so tied to human input and why character animation techniques are effective whether you're using a pencil, a potato or a computer. Just as the application of computers to character animation is changing the complexion of our development process so is "Computer Animation" being transformed by the application of character animation. In order to articulate our current situation, it is useful to identify some aesthetic parallels between the growth and development of early, hand-drawn animation and early computer animation.

Contemporary character animation filmmaking integrates images generated by a variety of techniques and technologies including hand drawn work. Using examples from Walt Disney's Feature Animation Department of computer animation elements from 1986-1993 I will discuss how computers have fit into our traditional animation work flow and, in turn, how they have changed how we view, develop, and produce animation. Some animation work roles have changed dramatically with the introduction of computers, with several traditionally separate roles collapsed into the single role of "Computer Animator."

Computer animation products have recently begun to actively integrate character animation principles and techniques. What direction can animation hardware and software take to support character animation more fully? And how can character animation training change to adjust to the expanding role of computers?

Jane Veeder

Education Fine Arts Animation: Like many others, I moved without benefit or burden of traditional animation training into computer animation as an extension of analog dynamic media (e.g. video, video synthesis) as small digital computers with graphics capabilities appeared in the late 1970's, offshoots of the booming videogame industry. As a fine artist, I have a central interest in digital technology as an inherently dynamic art medium [italics], not merely one of many animation "tools." In addition, much art theory surrounding the fine artist derives from the impact of computers and telecommunications on human culture. Thus I would work with other computer-based media before I would work with non-electronic animation techniques. In the same vein, I appropriate into my work formal conventions and modes of representation from other areas of computer graphics/animation. My design and development process is an interactive, evolutionary one whose open endedness reflects the nature of the medium. Through this method I decided what to do in large part, no simply to do what I have decided. This self-consciousness about the process of interacting with the medium and incorporating that, formally and conceptually, into the artwork is a habit of fine artists. This motivates us to try to interpret the medium to contemporary culture rather than retell old stories in a cost effective or more visually compelling manner.

Animation Education: In all areas of contemporary life boundaries between disciplines are eroding, driven primarily by technological opportunity. Common digital workspaces are arising between the traditional arts disciplines and between the arts and sciences. Fine arts or independent animation may seem a tiny island in a sea of commercial production and engineering/scientific visualization but it is here that most future computer animators are being trained. Soon, animation education everywhere will entail training in both physical and digital media and a merging of vocabularies, techniques, and wisdom. Even more computer and physical science majors will take our courses and more art students will get computer science degree minors. Inspired by the example of a few, early interdisciplinary graduate programs and incorporating new opportunities such as multimedia and virtual reality, we can articulate a new curriculum that embraces a wide range of creative and vocational potential and encourages students to prototype interdisciplinary collaborations.

William Moritz

Since computers are merely tools, "Computer Animation" is not separate from animation produced by other means, so it must be evaluated comparatively. The pin-screen of Claire Parker and Alexander Alexeieff contained 500,000 articulate light-points — quite like pixels — and their 1933 "Night on Bald Mountain" uses them for astonishing transformations of human forms; similarly PDI's morphing for Michael Jackson's "Black or White" video makes brilliant use of transformations to reinforce a social message, while the banal use of morphing in ads for soda pop and autos seems futile. John Lasseter's "Luxo, Jr." is an excellent character animation, even using the limitations of his programs (the rather glossy plastic/ metallic surfaces) as part of the characters. Larry Cuba's "TWO SPACE" is an outstanding abstract animation, with a conceptual framework of positive and negative space that gives it a metaphysical resonance: inclusion/exclusion, matter/anti-matter, being and nothingness and creation out of nothingness. "Not Knot" is fine scientific educational animation in that it teaches not only spatial geometry but also our perceptual experience of it and how we learn about our world through seeing.

Summary

Animation is a field whose knowledge base and diversity of application is expanding rapidly. In order to develop useful tools and train successful students, we need to know more about how various application areas are using animation, how animation is impacting the applications, and what new problems, concepts, and opportunities for creativity are emerging. With this panel, we do not hope to close the discussion with definitive answers to all attendant questions, but rather to open it wide.

Recommended Reading

John Berger, *Ways of Seeing*, Penguin Books, 1988

John Canemaker, Ed., *Storytelling in Animation*, American Film Institute, 1988

Andrew Glassner, *3D Computer Graphics: A Guide for Artists and Designers*, Design Press, 1989

Donald Graham, *Composing Pictures, Still and Moving*, Van Nostrand Reinhold, 1983

Roger Noake, *Animation*, MacDonald, 1988

Frank Thomas and Ollie Johnston, *Too Funny for Words*, Abbeville Press, 1987

Edward R. Tufte, *Envisioning Information*, Graphics Press, 1990

Robert Russett and Cecille Starr, *Experimental Cinema*, DeCapo Press, 1988

Jack Soloman, *The Signs of Our Times*, Harper & Row, 1988

Brian Wallis, Ed., *Art After Modernism: Rethinking Representation*, Godine, 1988

Harold Whitaker and John Halas, *Timing for Animation*, Focal Press Ltd, 1981

John Whitney, *Digital Harmony*, Byte Books, 1980

Facilitating Learning with Computer Graphics and Multimedia

Chair
G. Scott Owen, Georgia State University

Panelists
Robert V. Blystone, Trinity University
Valerie A. Miller, Georgia State University
Barbara Mones-Hattal, George Mason University
Jacki Morie, University of Central Florida

Abstract
With the recent advent of inexpensive yet powerful computers, the use of high quality graphics and multimedia systems to facilitate learning is rapidly increasing. This panel will review leading-edge work by focusing on several areas, including computer science, mathematics, biology, and art and design. Each panelist will describe how they currently use computer graphics and/or multimedia and give their view of future applications. Emphasis will be placed on how using these techniques fosters interdisciplinary collaboration both for creating learning environments and for working in these career areas.

Panel Overview
It is becoming increasingly evident that a highly educated and/or skilled work force is necessary for a successful economy, thus the need for more effective means of education/training is extremely important. Recent developments in technology have created the possibility of a paradigm shift in the delivery of information. Such a paradigm shift requires a change in the way we define and understand information exchange, resulting in more effective means of communication. One way in which this change may be effected provides for the possibility of interaction and integration of traditional disciplines to maximize the potential of these emerging technologies.

The objective of this panel is to investigate how this paradigm shift is being implemented in several areas of learning. While the focus is on academic areas of learning, the lessons learned and principles developed will also apply to industrial training and continuing education.

Robert V. Blystone: Computer Graphics in Undergraduate Biology
Biological microscopy is a visual discipline; however, when traditionally used in support of undergraduate learning, microscopy is descriptive, of limited sample size, and two dimensional. By coupling computer graphics with biological microscopy, these limitations can be overcome. At Trinity University, microscope intensive courses such as histology and embryology have been dramatically enhanced through this union of computer graphics and microscopy.

The application of graphics can expand two dimensional microscope images into three and four dimensional data sets. Two approaches have been commonly employed in our lab to develop digital scientific visualizations. The first approach utilizes images of intact structures such as embryos or blood cells. These images are collected under conditions of different age or treatment and then morphed to create visualizations of change through time. As an example, the white blood cell known as a neutrophil demonstrates significant changes in its nuclear shape during its week long existence in the circulation. By collecting images of different aged neutrophils and then morphing these images, a "virtual" time lapse movie can be created to represent the aging process. The second approach requires the image capture of sequential (serial) images (sections) of histological elements. These serial sections can be digitally "glued" back together and projected into three dimensional space. Projections taken at different times can be morphed to show change in three dimensions. As an example, projected serial sections through the developing pituitary of a chick embryo of one age can be morphed with a different aged embryo and, as a consequence, the pituitary can be made to grow in space through time. Animations of these types allow for discussions and inquiry-based activities never before possible in the lab and well as the lecture.

Biology students are generally unskilled in the use of computer graphics; thus, lab exercises had to be carefully organized to lead the students into the transparent use of computer graphics so as not to take time away from the biology subject material. As students request to do undergraduate research utilizing this technology, they must agree to tutor students new to the technology. Further, as students developed quality animations and image analysis procedures, the results could be saved and incorporated into the next semester's class.

Valerie A. Miller: Computer Graphics in Undergraduate Mathematics
The use of graphical images has been traditional in teaching lower level mathematics. However, when a student enters a mathematics class beyond the calculus level the use of images disappears, except for the occasional graph theorist's graph or the plotting of a function. This is rapidly changing, as the use of computer graphics and multimedia in teaching and learning mathematics is a mode of instruction that is becoming an accepted technique in the classroom. With the advent of inexpensive graphing calculators and various software packages that assist in the visualization of 2- and 3-dimensional mathematical concepts, mathematics instruction is beginning to examine avenues of learning other than endless rote calculations.

As an example of mathematical visualization in numerical analysis, we present ways in which this may be used to aid the instruction of iterative techniques for solving the problem $f(x) = 0$. Fractal images are generated based upon the number of iterations needed for convergence for various functions via various methods. These images are then presented simultaneously so that the important aspects of each of these methods, such as the order of convergence and cost per iteration, can be more easily illustrated, compared and, hence, more thoroughly understood. The concept of one method being "more expensive" than another is one that is not easily understood by students and the ability to inspect these "costs" visually is very appealing.

Fractal images that are generated based upon the basins of attraction of a function are also presented as means of illustrating how an iterative method can converge to an unwanted solution. As there are many possible criteria for terminating an iterative process, two different criteria are used to illustrate the subtle effects of a stopping criterion to the student.

Barbara Mones-Hattal: Using Computer Graphics to Teach Art Concepts

Currently, in the art and design area, computer graphics and computer imaging are taught as separate course of study in many schools. At these schools, software tools are used primarily to investigate potential computer applications in 2D and 3D design, animation, and interactive design. The available software tools are designed for the artist to create end-products such as illustrations, design for print, and all forms of animation. To a degree, tool and medium aspects of the technology are very difficult to isolate. However, using these same tools, one can de-emphasize the end-product and more fully explore the design process. It is this process of exploration that underscores the potential of computer graphics and multimedia for facilitated learning.

In this panel session, an overview of projects in the fine and applied arts, from intermediate to advanced level, will be presented. These projects focus on the enhancement of the learning process by utilizing computer graphics or multimedia tools (including paint and draw software, modeling and animation software, stereo display, and virtual reality tools). In some cases, mixing computer skills with other real world objects is included. The acquisition of computer graphics skills is less important in these cases as the purpose is to learn to communicate sensory information effectively and expressively. Important questions involving the potential to use the technologies to pose questions to the participant/viewer about the relationship of physical realities to simulate realities will be discussed.

Computer Graphics and multimedia options have provided many profoundly more efficient ways to learn about basic concepts such as color theories and applications, spatial relationships, and mixed media design. Some new additions to the repertoire of tools available are emerging as the inter-relationship of dimensional design forces us to separate our tools into paint (2D), modeling (3D), or moving images (4D), and encourages us to think of developing our works in new and innovative ways.

Learning both fundamental and sophisticated skills is important as both are required of the artist/designer. But some combination of these skills will enhance the capabilities of the non-artists, or any participant in a collaborative or interdisciplinary research team who wishes to work with artists. As more and more computer graphics and multimedia professionals seek to integrate their skills in order to develop and deliver better products, more effective ways to create and enhance learning environments are needed.

Jacquelyn Ford Morie: Using Computer Graphics to Teach Computer Graphics Concepts to Art Students

It is well known that students learn most effectively with hands on experience that reinforces concepts presented by an instructor through assigned reading or lectures. In computer graphics students can read extensively about a particular technique or algorithm, and still not fully understand it. Providing students with hands on exercises can cause an immediate and intuitive understanding of a complex graphic concept.

Computer Science students studying computer graphics have long been expected to have a "hands on" understanding of graphics algorithms in the context of writing the code to implement them. While this does provide a very thorough and complete understanding of the mechanics of how a given procedure works internally, the overhead of writing code is not the only method to cultivate understanding of graphics concepts. In addition, it may not be the most effective way for a student to understand the rich possibilities inherent in a given graphics technique. For example, writing an L-systems piece of code, while challenging, does little to uncover the wealth and variety of forms it is possible to make with such a system. An interactive program that allows a student to play with making many fern-like objects through L-system rules can, in an hour's time, provide a different and valuable intuitive grasp of the concepts behind the process.

This type of learning is also accessible to a greater range of students. This is especially true for visually oriented students, such as the computer animation students (in both art and film programs) that I have been teaching for the last five years. It is sometimes difficult to get them to read research articles or popular magazine articles about various computer graphics techniques. Give these same students an interactive demo on a computer and it is difficult to get them to go home.

Many such programs are available commercially or through public domain sources. Silicon Graphics provides a series of "Button Fly" demos which illustrate some concepts such as B-splines, environment mapping, ray tracing, and radiosity. There are many interactive fractal generating programs on the market. In conjunction with videos, such as those available from computer graphics suppliers, such as the SIGGRAPH Video Review, these can be valuable tools for understanding. In addition, advanced computer science students can provide interactive instructional programs and tools in the context of a summer class or independent study. These can then be tested and used by students of all disciplines studying computer graphics concepts.

Some very interesting results of using computer graphics to teach Computer Graphics concepts include the following:

- Visually-oriented students get "hooked." Since many of these same students are very "process-oriented" (e.g. they have a keen interest in following through a project from mechanics to the final creation), they become very curious about the process behind computer graphics. Some even enroll in UNIX and computer programming classes. If it is seen to be a means to their specific ends, they will spend the effort to become knowledgeable about all aspect of the process.
- Computer Science students see a greater picture and spend the extra time and effort to make their demo or program "better" than the interactive demo they have been exposed to, increasing the amount of learning they derive from the exercise.

G. Scott Owen: Computer Graphics and Multimedia in Computer Science

While computer graphics has been somewhat used to teach computer graphics, it has not been much used in the rest of the computer science curriculum. This is beginning to change as more instructors are beginning to develop and use graphics software to illustrate different concepts. Graphics programs are used in courses to illustrate such concepts as graphs or tree structures. Algorithm animation has been used at a few select places on workstations but is now becoming available on PC-class machines. Another use of graphics is in programming assignments for introductory classes. Multimedia has just begun to be used and I will discuss one system, HyperGraph, which is used to teach computer graphics. HyperGraph runs on PCs and consists of text, images, animations, and video. HyperGraph is being developed by both artists and computer scientists and the ultimate goal is for it to be used by both types of students for learning aspects of computer graphics.

Panel Summary

The examples given in this panel session of using computer graphics and multimedia for learning should help others who are thinking of incorporating these techniques into their own teaching. Lessons learned can also be incorporated into industrial training systems.

Visualizing Environmental Data Sets

Chair
Theresa Marie Rhyne, Martin Marietta/U.S. EPA Scientific Visualization Center

Panelists:
Kevin J. Hussey, Jet Propulsion Laboratory
Jim McLeod, San Diego Supercomputing Center
Brian Orland, University of Illinois/Landscape Arch.
Mike Stephens, Computer Sciences Corp./U.S. Army Corp of Engineers
Lloyd A. Treinish, IBM T. J. Watson Research Center

This panel session focuses on issues pertaining to visualizing environmental sciences data sets. Here the term "multi-dimensional" refers to the simultaneous display of data sets associated with air quality, water quality and subsurface contaminated soil regions. Issues associated with facilitating collaborative environmental visualization efforts among various research centers are presented. These include high speed networking, data base management, visualization toolkits, and heterogeneous computing platform concerns.

Visualization researchers dealing with the display of environmental sciences data sets present their different viewpoints on controversial issues. Panelists highlight and contrast projects associated with the U.S. Environmental Protection Agency, the U.S. Forestry Service, the Jet Propulsion Laboratory, Scripps Institute of Oceanography, National Aeronautics and Space Administration, U.S. Army Corps of Engineers, IBM T.J. Watson Research Center, University of Illinois, and other government, university, and industry centers working with environmental data sets.

The controversial issues include:

- Visualization of Multi Model data: issues associated with validity of data and approaches to data consolidation for a single visualization are discussed.
- Toolkit Applicability: Each panelists has their own unique viewpoint on how and when toolkits should be used for environmental research projects.
- Renaissance Teams (yes or no??): Some of panelists are at visualization centers which continue to advocate collaborative efforts among researchers, programmers, and artists for environmental visualization projects. Other panelists are involved with efforts focused on developing tools for the direct use by environmental researchers with minimal involvement of Renaissance Teams.
- Research versus Policy Making: Visualization for research efforts versus visualization for regulatory and policy making efforts can yield different end products and toolkit requirements.
- Data Format Standards: Multi dimensional environmental visualization involves the merger of data from multiple sources. This points toward the controversial issue of whether a standard data format for environmental research models which supports heterogeneous computing should be required.
- Data Management: The management of terabyte and gigabyte data sets is one of the critical challenges to environmental research and visualization.

Multi-dimensional data visualizations not only require management of data from satellites but also the maintenance of historical geological data sets.

Theresa Marie Rhyne

The U.S. EPA Scientific Visualization Center serves the U.S. Environmental Protection Agency's community of researchers throughout the United States and collaborates on interagency and university research projects. Within EPA, there are a wide range of interests. The Visualization Center has depicted pollutant transport and deposition in regional domains of the United States, total global ozone distribution, fluid flow around buildings, sedimentation in large bodies of water, subsurface contaminated soil regions, and the molecular chemistry of carcinogens.

Visualization toolkits are used by researchers to examine their data, and intensive 3-day workshop sessions are designed to handle environmental researchers' desires for training in the use of these toolkits. High speed networking concerns and the development of visualization tools to support heterogeneous computing platforms across the Agency are explored using the U.S. EPA's National Environmental Supercomputing Center, located in Bay City, Michigan. Collaborations on multi-dimensional environmental visualizations that display the co-registration of air quality, water quality, and subsurface soil data sets are underway. Issues associated with visualization technology transfer to State and local government environmental protection agencies are being examined.

Jim McLeod

Faced with ever increasing environmental data collection rates (soon approaching terabytes of information a day), the ability to disseminate and analyze these data sets at comparable rates is crucial to the success of future global studies. Visualization plays a vital role. However, visualization should not overshadow the ultimate goal of scientific discovery and global understanding. To this end, visualization should hold equal weight with traditional scientific analysis techniques until its value as a research tool can be measured and evaluated. At the Advanced Scientific Visualization Laboratory in the San Diego Supercomputer Center, we provide a multi-level visualization support service. By utilizing visualization toolkits, at one level, to obtain analytical imagery quickly, researchers and members of our visualization staff (collectively referred to as "Envelope Teams") can determine the feasibility and merit of these visual studies before proceeding to a higher level of custom visualization.

Although this collaborative approach has been tried in the past, it has rarely succeeded scientifically. These visualization efforts have failed to recognize past experiences and techniques to which scientists are accustomed. Therefore, to achieve a smooth migration to new visual analysis methods through the use of computer graphics, visualization tools must involve traditional representation techniques (plots, graphs, and numerical analysis) as well as object rendering. Only after getting these types of tools in the hands of the researchers and maintaining a dialogue to improve the usefulness of these applications will tough visualization issues involving database management and co-registration of data be resolved properly. This communication process will rely heavily on advances being made in high speed networking, which will play an important role in the promising future of environmental visualization.

Kevin J. Hussey

The Jet Propulsion Laboratory's (JPL's) Digital Image Animation Laboratory (DIAL) and the associated Visualization and Earth Science and Applications (VESA) Group have produced a number of notable environmental visualizations over the past 12 years. Visualization topics have encompassed submarine geology in the Monterey Bay to the Ozone "hole" over Antarctica. Scientific data resolutions ranged from one Angstrom to 345 miles. During the course of producing these visualizations several lessons were learned, difficult issues raised and new technology developed. Examples are highlighted below.

A Lesson: No matter how good, flexible, extensible, comprehensive, powerful or expensive your visualization system (hardware and software) is, it will not perform what the scientist wants. You will have to modify some code to make it happen.

An Issue: Remember the book "How To Lie With Statistics" by D. Huff? If you can lie with statistics then just imagine what you could do with Data Visualization! Sometimes very realistic looking visualizations may be "seeing" things that are not supported by the data. Should we do something about this?

Some Technology: Incorporating technology developed and lessons learned, members of the VESA and Image Analysis Systems (IAS) group at JPL are developing Surveyor, a three-dimensional data visualization system which runs in a heterogeneous distributed computing environment. Surveyor is used by scientists and simulators to analyze and animate a three-dimensional "world". The world consists of a variety of three-dimensional data, such as satellite imagery combined with topography information. In addition to rendering of data, Surveyor can retrieve the original data values for selected areas in a three-dimensional rendered scene. This capability is used as a user interface for the analysis of scientific data, such as geological data bases from desktop computers or across a network to allow use of more powerful machines. Surveyor is utilized as the graphical user interface (GUI) for the Caltech/JPL portion of the Casa Gigabit Network Testbed.

Lloyd A. Treinish

Areas of great interest in the environmental sciences today focus on large-scale data processing and analysis of remotely sensed and in situ data from many instruments and the supercomputer-based simulation of dynamic phenomena. Often these studies involve the integration of the observations with simulations for the creation of empirical models, using the acquired data as input. The structure of these data may be point or sparse, uniformly or irregularly meshed, in rectilinear or curvilinear coordinates, and will consist of many parameters. Visualization is key in understanding these data sets.

Effective visual examination also requires advances in data management. There is no consensus today about solutions to problems involving: addressing inconsistencies and irregularities associated with observational data, maintenance of a connection between image representations of the data and the data themselves, integration of observational data with output from computer models, and scalability to potentially very large size (i.e., greater than one terabyte). One aspect of the data management problem is the ability to uniformly support data of disparate structure, preserve the fidelity of the data (e.g., by noting missing data and original grid resolution), and provide the ability to define coordinate systems onto which different data may be registered in space and time. For visualization tools, data management is important in matching a class of data models to the structure of scientific data and determining how such data is used (e.g., qualitative three-dimensional displays AND precise, analysis and quantitative presentations). In work with disparate data, there is a need to support correlative data analysis providing a common basis for the examination of different data sets in the same way at the same time and providing multiple ways to study the same or different data.

Brian Orland

The author directs a research program in environmental visualization and perception. Research ranges from modeling fishing and ski resort choices, to scenic and policy impacts of forest insect damage. Evaluations are based on calibrated visualizations of forest conditions. Few participants are expert in all scientific areas represented in a forest ecological system. Thus, visualizations must not assume ability to deal with visual abstractions of particular scientific data. Focus is on more realistic visual images than typically found in scientific visualization. A second concern is that a forest scientist, manager, or interested citizen should do more than just respond to pre-planned situations. Our user makes modifications to the visualization and obtains immediate feedback on the implications for data or models.

Software development supports this research and addresses a number of inadequacies in current natural resource scientific visualizations:

(1) Realistic, "concrete," representations of biological models and data support interpretation and evaluation by non- specialists while retaining their validity as data representations.

(2) Data entries and model parameters are manipulated via the visualization and the database is continually updated. Users can participate in forest operations, modify scientific assumptions by direct mouse-click operations, and continually monitor their progress through data summary tables.

(3) Visualizations are truly interactive. Advances in time, changes in viewpoint, and model parameters are viewed immediately — the design criterion is a maximum 3 second delay for display update.

Current work will extend visualizations from thousands of trees to millions of trees, and will distribute model computing to faster machines — such as NCSA's CM5 Connection Machine.

Mike Stephens

The scientific visualization center (SVC) at the U.S. Army Corp of Engineers'' Waterways Experiment Station (WES) assists research engineers and scientists in the six major labs which comprise WES. Since environmental research involves a large number of highly coupled, interdependent processes, these efforts are spread throughout the Hydraulics Lab, Coastal Engineering Research Center, Information Technology Lab, and Environment Lab. The SVC advocates a technology transfer approach. Project researchers and their staffs are exposed to visualization alternatives and then determine appropriate methodologies for displaying their own data sets. The SVC has been active in environmental studies from simple conceptual animations of how a newly designed dredge head will reduce the number of turtles adversely effected during dredging operations to complex interactions of ground water flows on sub- surface contaminants from leaking storage tanks.

Several environmental projects involve not only teams from different WES labs, but also include other research agencies. A project on the management of the United States' largest estuary, the Chesapeake Bay, has research teams from WES hydraulics and environment labs as well as the U.S. EPA and several universities. Perhaps it is the highly interdependent nature of environmental processes that make them particularly challenging to visualization teams to offer solutions which aid researchers to further their understanding. The Chesapeake Bay effort has used visualization in almost every aspect of the project. Techniques for evaluating and editing finite element meshes used in computing hydrodynamics models of the bay were developed. The results from these hydrodynamics models were visualized. Once the models were validated from physical measurements they were used in turn by the water quality group which is concerned with the viability of the bay and the effects that different management strategies have on the bay and the long term results of these newly proposed strategies. This involved the examination of 22 interrelated parameters.

How to Lie and Confuse with Visualization

Chair
Nahum D. Gershon, The MITRE Corporation

Panelists:
James M. Coggins, University of North Carolina at Chapel Hill
Paul R. Edholm, The University Hospital of Linkoping, Sweden
Al Globus,Computer Sciences Corporation at NASA Ames Research Center
Vilayanur S. Ramachandran, University of California at San Diego,

Abstract:
As in other fields such as statistics and cartography, it is also possible to misrepresent data in visualization. Most of the time, people do it unintentionally and it goes unnoticed. But traps await the unwary. The Panel "How to Lie and Confuse with Visualization" will discuss this issue and educate the visualization and computer graphics community about these potential traps. Topics to be discussed in this panel include the use of color, interpolation, smoothing, boundaries, and shading. The panel and the audience will also debate whether there are ways to judge the degree of "lying" in visualization, and how to prevent inadvertent misrepresentations from happening. The panel and the audience will come up with recommendations for "dos" and "don'ts" for the process of creating faithful visualizations. During the discussions and the debates, the panelists and the audience will present many examples of data misrepresentations taken from science, medicine, and art.

Other points include the question if lying with visualization is evil or good and necessary and appropriate in many situations. How much is lying with visualization application-dependent ? Does visual perception have problems or is it very efficient? This point may affect the mechanisms underlying the perception of misrepresentation of visualized data.

The audience and the public have been encouraged to submit samples of slides and video material illustrating visualization "lies." In addition, contributors could bring their samples directly to the session.

Nahum Gershon— "How to Lie and Confuse with Visualization"
Inappropriate use of color could reduce the effectiveness of the results of the visualization process. Color scales without sufficient contrasting regions in the range of values where the data is varying could mask these data variations from the final display. Data structures with shapes familiar to our perceptual system could also create false impressions of the data. For example, if a structure in the data appears as to occlude another it could be perceived as having a higher value than its surrounding area. Colors such as light green and blue are usually perceived as background colors in everyday life. In data visual representation, these background colors could be perceived as representing lower values especially if these regions are large. Crowded color scales, on the other hand, could give too much detail, preventing effective perception of the general trends.

Interpolation (the process used to enlarge the display of small spatial data sets and to eliminate the appearance of the visual annoyance of large pixels) could create the false impression of high spatial resolution. Smoothing (the operation used to eliminate random noise in the data) could make small details disappear.

James M. Coggins —"Lying Toward the Truth"
The challenge of the visualization specialist is to cleverly communicate the truth. Truth can be very, very complicated. Revealing the truth a layer at a time is a reasonable strategy for managing the complexity of the whole truth. Half-truths or even outright fabrications are appropriate and necessary mechanisms for sneaking up on the truth.

Visualization provides new ways to present half-truths that advance understanding toward the whole truth. However, when we begin to rely on the half-truths as if they were the whole truth, crucial aspects of the intended communication can be lost. Hard-edged surfaces of discrete objects make beautiful visualizations but hide the often arbitrary criteria used to form the surfaces. The essential uncertainty in the existence or location of boundaries is masked. Naive interpretations of such visualizations may yield faulty decisions.

Mechanisms for visualizing uncertainty are required to communicate error bars on the measurements that are visualized. Whether the hard-edged visualization is adequate is a question for the application domain client, not for the visualization specialist nor for the visualization system. The visualization system must provide the client with error bars: a sense of when to believe the beautiful, hard-edged rendering and when to disregard or disbelieve it. Examples of how error bars can be visualized will be illustrated. Discussion of other alternatives will be solicited.

Paul R. Edholm —"How the Visual System Interprets Images"
The task of the visual system is to give to the conscious mind a mental representation of the relevant features of the external world. From the flat two-dimensional (2-D) images on the retina, the visual system reconstructs the external three-dimensional (3-D) scene. This is in theory impossible because there are so many 3-D scenes which could yield the same 2-D image. So, the visual system has to try to select the right solution from all the possible solutions. This solution is then presented to our conscious mind as the external world. The mechanisms in the intuitive and unconscious interpretation system of the visual system are in their most part unknown. We only know that they are very complex and highly sophisticated. They probably constitute the most complex structure in the world. But when we see, we are not aware of this. We experience (the illusion) that what we see is a direct perception of the external world. In reality, what we see is a very sophisticated guesswork of the interpretation system.

Boundaries: The boundaries are the most important structures in the interpretation of a picture. Thus, the visual system is more or less developed as a boundary detector and it is a poor judge of density values in a picture. I will discuss lateral inhibition, Mach bands, and illusions caused by lateral inhibition. I will also describe the perception

of boundaries and various kinds of boundaries. Boundaries in "natural" images (produced on the retina by real scenes) and images of other kinds (produced on the retina by different artificial means) will be discussed. This will include illusory contours, statistical boundaries, boundaries in X-rays, edge boundaries, boundaries produced by curved interfaces, lamellar boundaries, and illusions caused by curved interfaces combined with lamellas.
Reconstruction of 3-D Scenes from 2-D Images: The clues used by the visual system to reconstruct three-dimensional scenes from two-dimensional images, impossible figures, and 3-D illusions will be discussed.

Al Globus —"Thirteen Ways to Say Nothing with Scientific Visualization"

Scientific visualization should be used to produce beautiful images. Those not properly initiated into the mysteries of visualization research often fail to appreciate the artistic qualities our pictures. For example, scientists will frequently use visualization to needlessly understand their data. I will describe a number of effective techniques to confound such pernicious activity. The audience and the panel will be solicited for additional techniques. The 13 ways are:

1. Never Include a Color Legend
2. Avoid Annotation
3. Never Mention Error Characteristics
4. When in Doubt, Smoothe
5. Avoid Provide Performance Data
6. Quietly Use Stop-Frame Video Techniques

Faithful adherence to the rest of the rules will help avoid tedious debugging of software that already produces pretty pictures.

7. Never Learn Anything About the Data or Scientific Discipline
8. Never Compare Your Results with Other Visualization Techniques
9. Avoid Visualization Systems
10. Never Cite References for the Data
11. Claim Generality but Show Results from a Single Data Set
12. Use Viewing Angle to Hide Blemishes
13. 'This is easily extended to 3-D'

Vilayanur S. Ramachandran—"What Could be Learned from Perception?"

Computers have provided us with new ways of creating visual images from abstract and non- abstract data. Reaching out to the fields of visual physiology, psychophysics, and cognitive psychology could not only explain why human vision is so efficient, but also how to create better images and what could be the limitations of particular representations. The relevance of the knowledge acquired from perception research to the process of creating faithful visualizations will be described. Examples are the areas of stereopsis, perception of transparency, derivation of shape from shading and illusory contours, and color. In particular, I will discuss and illustrate the possible trap of locating the light source in the "wrong" location in simulating shading. I will then specify the situations where the perception of shape from shading could be affected by the location of the light source.

Afterword

Data could be misrepresented in visualization quite effortlessly and inadvertently. The main culprits are perception's complex and intricate nature and the varied experiences of each human being that could make a picture mean different things to different people. Becoming aware of how to lie and confuse with visualization could teach us how to prevent it from happening or at least how to reduce its occurrences.

References

D. Bailey, "Twelve Ways to Fool the Masses When Giving Performance Results on Parallel Computers," *Supercomputer Review*, Aug. 1991, pp. 54-55.

J. M. Coggins, "Computer-Aided Object Definitions from Digital Images," *Proceedings* of Joint U.S.-Scandinavian Symposium on Future Directions of Computer-Aided Radiotherapy, Radiation Research Program, Division of Cancer Treatment, National Cancer Institute, pp. 79-97.

P. Edholm, "Boundaries in the Radiographic Image. I. General Principles for Perception of Boundaries and Their Application to the Image." *Acta Radiol.* 22, 457 (1981).

P. Edholm, "Boundaries in the Radiographic Image. II. Principles for the Representation of the Object as Boundary Circuits in the Image." *Acta Radiol.* 23, 161 (1982).

N. D. Gershon, "Enhanced Visualization of Multi-Dimensional Structures. Applications in Positron Emission Tomography and Climate Data", *Proceedings* of Visualization '91, pp. 188- 192, IEEE Computer Society Press, Washington, DC (1991).

N. D. Gershon, "How to Lie and Confuse with Visualization," *IEEE Computer Graphics and Applications*, pp. 102-103, January 1993.

A. Globus, "13 Ways to Say Nothing with Scientific Visualization," Report RNR- 92-006 NAS, Applied Research Branch MS T045-1, NASA Ames Research Center Moffett Field, CA 94035-1000.

S. M. Pizer, J. M. Coggins and C. A. Burbeck, "Formation of Image Objects in Human Vision," *Computer-Aided Radiology* (invited paper in *Proceedings* of 1991 Conference on Computer- Aided Radiology), Springer-Verlag, Berlin, 1991, pp. 535-542.

V. S. Ramachandran, "Perception of Shape from Shading," *Scientific American*, 269, 76-83 (1988).

V. S. Ramachandran, "Visual Perception in Humans and Machines," in *AI and the Eye*, A. Blake, and T. Troscianko, (eds), pp. 21-77, John Wiley & Sons, New York (1990).

The Applications of Evolutionary and Biological Processes to Computer Art and Animation

Panel Organizer: William Latham, IBM UK Scientific Centre
Chair: George Joblove, Industrial Light & Magic

Panel Members:
William Latham. IBM UK Scientific Centre
Karl Sims. Thinking Machines Corp.
Stephen Todd. IBM UK Scientific Centre
Michael Tolson. Xaos Inc.

Abstract
The panel will discuss new techniques for evolving art designs which are based on "Evolution and Biological processes" from the natural world. In particular techniques such a mutation, breeding and selection, marriage, and rules for artificial life animations are discussed. In addition to addressing the advantages and disadvantages of using these techniques, the panel will also discuss their effectiveness as construction and user interface tools for the artist making images, designs and animations.

Background
In general "artistic" computer graphics involves detailed analytical knowledge to specify a design or animation. Often a designer when setting up a geometric structure realizes the huge possible number of variations that can be produced by changing the parameters. Invariably these variations are not explored, even though a variation may be better than the analytically specified design. The reason for this is the vastness of parameter space and time taken to explore it.

Computer Evolutionary techniques allow a more systematic and intuitive exploration of parameter and structure space which allows the user to evolve artistic designs and animations through a method of random mutation, breeding and selection. This allows not just rapid sampling of possible variations but allows a directional and purposeful exploration of variations. This exploration often uncovers possibilities which are beyond the artists'/designers' powers of human visualization, and are arguably beyond their imagination.

These techniques are based on the evolutionary and biological processes in the natural world. They have a major advantages in terms of user interface as they allow the user to interact in a "non-analytic" way intuitively with the computer, so that highly complex models can be evolved. The use of these techniques creates a new style of user interface where the role of the artist can be separated in two: First as "creator" of the Evolutionary system and then as "selector."

This exploits techniques such as simulated annealing, steepest ascent and Monte Carlo optimization. Genetic algorithms borrow from the biological models of genotype (encoding the form), phenotype (expression of coded form), Mutation and sexual reproduction, and selection for simulating evolution. The most exciting effects have been created when these evolutionary techniques have been merged with their own "home grown" growth systems such as Latham and Todd's "Form Grow" or Sim's "Growing Equations." The resulting films are very organic and portray virtual computer worlds operating under alternative evolutionary systems. As the cinema and Virtual Reality's insatiable appetite for the extraordinary increases, these techniques currently being used by a few key experimenters will find their way into the popular domain.

Panel Goal and Issues
The purpose of the panel is to propose the new use of evolutionary and biological concepts as methods for making art and animations and show the unique effects that can be achieved, and try and define their advantages and differences compared to other techniques for artistic design.

The panel will identify the differences in techniques between the work Sims, Latham and Todd and Tolson. Specific techniques such as "structure mutation," "equation mutation," and "automatic offspring selection" will be discussed. Mike Tolson will contrast these techniques with his work with growing brushed patterns using evolution genetic fitness algorithms which use no human user selection.

Having laid down the technical overview, the following types of questions will try to be answered:

* In creating alternative evolutions is this just another manifestation of man's innate desire to create new life as a "pseudo god," or is it a parody of man's manipulation of the natural world through modern technology?
* What is the role of the artist: to be both the "creator" of the system and be the "selector." If these roles are done to by two people who then is the author of the artwork?
* Mutation techniques use randomness, does this make them difficult to use with exact control? or is it possible to mix mutation with analytical techniques?
* In building menu options such as "kill," "breed," or "marry" and applying them to artificial life that often to appear to have a life of their own, does this raise any morality questions?
* What are the future possibilities of these techniques in scientific visualization?
* Latham proposes an Evolution Virtual Reality where the artist would become a "gardener" in an accelerated evolutionary world growing and breeding "giant virtual pumpkins" in "living sculpture gardens," a kind of modern day "Garden of Earthly Delights" (Hieronymous Bosch). What other applications of these techniques in VR could exist in the future.
* Genetic Algorithms have been around for 15 years, is Evolutionary Art just a novel application? What is new?
* When the artist subjectively selects mutations for breeding what criteria are they using? If this can be defined would it not be possible to write a piece of software that could replace the artist?
* Can one label the products of computer evolution art? And if one does, surely then the products of nature should be labeled "art" also in that they also went through an evolutionary process. As Computer Art and Animation become more natural do they become less artistic as the human element becomes less apparent.

William Latham
William Latham will focus on the artistic side of the work and discuss the user interface of Mutator program and outline it's successes and weaknesses as a method for making art.

Latham describes using the Mutator program to be a little like being a gardener breeding, selecting, pruning and marrying forms. The evolved forms look like strange organic sculptural fruits. In the

Mutator program, unlike the natural world, the "natural selection" process is replaced with "aesthetic selection controlled by the artist," so that the process of making art is an explorative evolution steered by the results of aesthetic choices. The evolutionary process helps the artist navigate in an infinite multi-dimensional parameter and structure space to find artistic forms.

Latham argues that when using the "mutator" program the computer ceases to be like a tool but is more like a creative partner where the artist is continually surprised by the results which are automatically produced. This close interaction between artist and machine produces unexpected and strange results.

Recent work has involved inventing "Life Cycle" rules to create organic animations showing chains of living, breeding and dead mutations gradually forming vast colonial formations.

Latham will discuss the problems of setting up "artificial animations" and in particular the "Life Cycle" rules. He will also identify some of the artistic issues in the work such as randomness, the balance of power between artist and machine, displaying the artworks in the gallery world and its position in 20th Century Modern art.

Stephen Todd

Stephen Todd will discuss the program Mutator as a user interface tool. Mutator is a tool to assist a user in a search of a multidimensional parameter space. The computer makes moves in space and displays the results of these moves, and the user selects the results that are liked.

Mutator can be looked at as a computer implementation of the process of natural selection, with the mutation process performed by the computer and the selection by the user. Alternatively, it can be looked at as an optimization process, with the cost function provided by the user.

Mutator gives the user a variety of ways to control the movement in parameter space.

- The simplest is random mutation of the parameters.
- The simple random search can be directed by judging some of the available choices as 'good' or 'bad.' These judgments set up a direction of movement, similar to the use of hill climbing in optimization.
- Finally, preferred objects can be 'married' to create new objects that use a mixture of the parameters of the parents.

The augmentation of random mutation by judgment and marriage considerably enhances the speed and effectiveness of Mutator in reaching interesting areas of the search space.

The primary advantage of Mutator is that it permits the user to search using *subjective* decisions. This contrasts with more conventional user interface tools, which make it easier for the user to carry out *analytic* decisions.

Todd will discuss the potential for Mutator as an interface in other applications such as scientific visualization, economic modeling and the generation of 'identikit' pictures by witnesses.

Karl Sims

Karl Sims will present several applications of interactive evolution. The evolutionary mechanisms of variation and selection are used to "evolve" equations used by various procedural models for computer graphics and animation. The following examples will be briefly discussed and results from each will be shown:

- Procedurally generated pictures and textures
- 3D objects defined by parametric equations
- Dynamical systems described by differential equations.

Each uses hierarchical lisp expressions as "genotypes" to define arbitrary equations which are evaluated to create resulting "phenotypes." The equations and their corresponding phenotypes can be mutated, mated, and interactively selected to search "hyperspaces" of possible results. A comparison between evolving values of parameter sets and evolving arbitrary length equations will be made.

"Genetic cross dissolves" can be used to create smooth interpolations between evolved entities. Their use in creating the animation "Primordial Dance" will be described.

It is proposed that these methods have potential as powerful tools for exploring procedural models and achieving flexible complexity with a minimum of user input and knowledge of details. Complex equations can be efficiently found that might not be easily designed or even understood by humans alone.

Mike Tolson

Michael Tolson will talk about his recent work evolutionary and biological techniques: He is creating "eco systems" of many simple "animals" which are visualized by brush strokes. Their behaviors are controlled by neural networks (their "brains") which are a part of the genotype and can be evolved. The animals use up energy by moving and can gain energy by performing appropriately, for example moving towards a light. They can interact with their environment in various ways and can achieve "biological" effects such as phototropism and reaction-diffusion like systems. He is not using interactive selection, but instead the more traditional genetic algorithm approach with defined fitness functions. He is however, more interested in creating "art" than in the scientific details of the process.

Summary Statement

The aim of the panel is to give an overview by leading exponents, contextulise their work, to provoke discussion and be provoked.

References

Evolutionary Art and Computers. Stephen Todd and William Latham. Academic Press. ISBN 0-12-437185-X.

"Interactive Evolution of Dynamical Systems," *Proceedings* of the First European Conference on Artificial Life, Paris, Dec. 11-13, 1991, K.Sims.

The Blindwatchmaker. Richard Dawkins. Longmans Scientific and Technical.

Computer Sculpture Design and Animation." S.Todd, W.Latham,P.Hughes. *The Journal of Visualisation and Computer Animation*. Vol 2. 1991. 98-1. Wiley.

"Mutator, A Subjective Interface for Evolution of Computer Sculptures." IBM UKSC Report. No.248. W.Latham and S.Todd.

"Evolution by Aesthetics." M.Haggerty. *IEEE Computer Graphics and Applications*. March 1991..

"Surreal Art or Artificial Life," *Proceedings* of the First European Conference on Artificial Life, Paris, Dec. 11-13, 1991, S.Todd and W.Latham.

"Artificial Evolution for Computer Graphics," *Computer Graphics*, Vol.25, No.4, July 1991, pp.319-328, K.Sims.

Genetic Algorithm - in Search, Optimisation and Machine Learning. D.Goldberg. Addison Wesley. 1989.

Adaption in Natural and Artificial Systems. J.Holland. University of Michegan Press 1975.

Urban Tech-Gap: How the Museum/University Liaisons Propose to Create a Learning Ladder for Visual Literacy

Chair: Richard Navin, Brooklyn College, City University of New York

Panelists:
Lynn Holden, Carnegie Mellon University
Edward Wagner, The Franklin Institute Science Museum
Robert Carlson, Director, Tech 2000: Gallery of Interactive Multimedia
Michael McGetrick, Brooklyn College

Summary
Universities and public education are putting the creative means of professional multimedia production into their own hands. Science and industry museums engaging media as producers now offer serious instructional visualizations through creative hands-on components drawing visitors into active participation. The distance is closing between museums' high-calibre productions and educational usage through open electronic toolboxes in the individual classroom. Yet a severe dislocation exists between the producing centers and the decay in their immediate environment — the inner city.

Collaboration bridges strengths and resources from two methodologically different environments. This panel seeks to place a bridge between the differences of these two professional worlds and develop a ladder for visual literacy as a common domain.

Issues Under Discussionn

- The finest science and industry museums exist in midst of the worst financially-blighted urban centers the most abandoned urban school districts. Are minority-dominated, overcrowded classrooms unable to come to grips with, or understand in a rudimentary fashion, rapidly advancing technology linguistics — particularly when their computer labs are crippled or virtually non-existent? Tax-levied education faces increasing draconian budgets for three to five year. How can tools and multiculturalism be integrated with the means at hand?
- What curriculum bridges can be created in advance of exhibitions? What social components should determine their final form? Between usage and exhibit production values, can a more sensitive awareness enter "opening the architecture" and creating tools that bridge the discontinuity between high-level productions finished in a museum "Hollywood" setting and real learning? What is needed are forms that transmute content through "the language of the street" — forms understood by the average (and deprived) urban public school classroom and those students snarled in its chaos.
- Why are most high-quality, master computer centers distanced (safely) from the largest inner city school districts? Should high-tech be physically downloaded into some form for urban equilibration following the marketing of GI Joe, comics, pop-up books, music or rap oriented materials? This is such an untried avenue that we cannot even begin to believe we approach "separate but equal" social segregation.
- Downloading: High production values in themselves induce passivity (i.e. the "Carl Sagan" approach gives us very high, but passive values on the edu-tainment meter). Few projects of meaningful application are developed in the argot of the children watching. Nothing induces vocational interest or offers access to a science career in a designated spot within the viewer's interactive participation and behavior modeling. Should productions including some staffing role that incorporates "human tools" drawn directly from the disenfranchised and underprivileged where we deem to do good?
- Do exhibition, production-value approaches too easily adopt a TV cultural fast-food pace and too speedily send viewers on their way?

At the museum level, sheer numbers of viewers and the fifteen minute message are determined by large attendance traffic necessities. At the schools, amateurism often mars the connectivity of video, hypertext, and programming, detouring the expectations of visually astute and sophisticated youths. Educators and museum program designers on this panel offer real links between visitor/learners and serious instruction. Written materials can support strong visuals and supply stick to the ribs knowledge in the wake of video flash. The dialogue between panelists contrasts the style and formatting problems of exhibiting and instructing and offers a "how to" on establishing usage between museum educational institutions and visually attractive teaching modules, while still downloading qualified and deep instruction without losing the sweep and verve of highly attractive visualization.

Lynn Holden: The great pressing need is how to link and move forward the existing elements of the multimedia matrix. The human, hardware and software components all exist, but they are dislocated and without adequate resources and financial support from government, industry and local communities/institutions.

If there is not a concerted effort, cooperatively between universities, non-profit institutions and industries to set high quality standards in new applications and products, the near-term ramifications will be disastrous for us as professionals, for our organizations and for out culture!

We must create and support an effective, functional network for developers and creative individuals working on new multimedia and interdisciplinary project, and facilitate completing and making visible actual examples which address short and long term issues.

Ed Wagner: The Cutting Edge Gallery presents new technologies and products to a wide range and intellects. As gallery coordinator I procure these devices and have to quickly learn how to operate them and understand the technology, then present this information to the visitor. The challenge is to take complex scientific information and translate it into a form that is comprehensible to the lay person. The Gallery, like other areas within the Franklin Institute, transfers this knowledge to wide range of visitors while in an informal setting.

Richard Navin: One clearly sees across the audiences of all national conferences a lack of color... minorities are no where to be bound in a significant population as makers of multimedia except as strategically marketed talking head so news shows and sit-coms. City University of New York is woefully behind in adapting the media-designing computer to its constituency — the representation student population. In some small but significant way Image and Communications Projects now place students in design roles with government-aligned agencies. Our next step from the advantaged position of a new Media Center created by a new administration is to begin electronic publishing. We have reasonable found self esteem. We now need to advance into an articulate electronic venacular.

Virtual Reality and Computer Graphics Programming

Chair:
Bob C. Liang, IBM T. J. Watson Research Lab

Panelists:
William Bricken, University of Washington
Peter Cornwell, Division, Inc.
Bryan Lewis, IBM T. J. Watson Research Lab
Ken Pimental, Sense8 Corporation
Michael J. Zyda, Naval Postgraduate School

Virtual Reality provides a multi-sensor 3D human machine interface. VR applications requires system software interface to various input/output devices, e.g. tracker, glove, head mount display, sound, speech recognition, etc., and a programming environment for building and interacting with the virtual world.

We are addressing software issues of Virtual Reality related to computer graphics: the building of the virtual world, and the management of its underlying data structure; the communication software issues in building a cooperative virtual world environment; and the issues in programming the interaction in the virtual world.

Michael J. Zyda: The Software Required for the Computer Generation of Virtual Environments

The first phase of virtual world development has focused on the novel hardware (3D input and 3D output) and the "cool" graphics demo. The second phase of virtual world development will be to focus in on the more significant part of the problem, the software bed underlying "real" applications. The focus of this talk is on the software required to support large scale, networked, multi-party virtual environments. We discuss navigation (virtual camera view point control and its coupling to real-time, hidden surface elimination), interaction (software for constructing a dialogue from the inputs read from our devices and for applying that dialogue to display changes), communication (software for passing changes in the world model to other players on the network, and software for allowing the entry of previously undescribed players into the system), autonomy (software for playing autonomous agents in our virtual world against interactive players), scripting (software for recording, playing back and multi-tracking previous play against live or autonomous players, with autonomy provided for departures from the recorded script), and hypermedia integration (software for integrating hypermedia data-audio, compressed video, with embedded links —into our geometrically described virtual world). All of this software serves as the base for the fully detailed, fully interactive, seamless environment of the third phase of virtual world development.

William Bricken: Virtual Reality is Not a Simulation of Physical Reality

One of the weakest aspects of current software tools for VR is that designers are bringing the assumptive baggage of the world of mass into the digital world, undermining the essential qualities of the virtual. Information is not mass; meaning is *constructed* in the cognitive domain. Psychology is the Physics of VR. In building virtual worlds, we are continually discovering that they are strongly counter-intuitive, that our training as physical beings obstructs our use of the imaginary realm.

The greatest design challenge for VR tools is mediating between physical sensation and cognitive construction. VR software must directly resolve the mind-body duality which plagues both Western philosophy and computer languages. VR calls for a philosophy of *immaterial realism*. VR doesn't matter, it informs.

I will briefly describe a new generation of software tools which emphasize virtual rather than physical modeling concepts. VR tools are situated, pluralistic, synesthetic, paradoxical, and most importantly, autonomous. Their programming techniques include behavioral specification (entity-based models), inconsistency maintenance (imaginary booleans), possibility calculi (set functions), relaxation (satisfying solutions), experiential mathematics (spatial computation), participatory programming (inclusive local parallelism) and emergence (realtime non-linear dynamics).

Peter J. Cornwell

Division Inc. is a VR systems company which has supplied hardware, software and integrated systems products to application developers and end users worldwide for over three years.

Research and commercial applications of VR in the fields of pharmaceutical engineering and marketing, landscape architecture, industrial furnishing and lighting will be described and the evolution of installed hardware and software briefly reviewed.

The important trends arising from these installations will then be identified with particular emphasis on:

1. protection of investment in applications development through portability across a range of different vendor and performance hardware configurations.
2. interfacing VR facilities with existing computer systems and software

Finally, current and proposed developments to address the evolving VR marketplace will be covered.

Bryan Lewis : Software Architecture

Virtual Reality applications are difficult to build, involving multiple simultaneous input and output devices, complex graphics, and dynamic simulations, all of which have to cooperate in real time. If a simulation expert wishes to imbed a complex simulation or model into a virtual environment, one approach is to add functionality one call at a time to the existing simulation code. This appears to be the easy way to get started. But simulations are already quite complex, and adding code for multiple devices and multiple machines can become unwieldy. The problem is made worse by the fact that simulation experts generally do not have the time or inclination to learn a book full of user interface calls.

A better approach is a "minimally invasive" software architecture that allows the simulation to be connected to the rest of the world without surgery. Such an architecture hides the complexities of connecting the simulation to other modules on other machines. This provides the foundation for a useful tool kit; to that must be added a kit of ready-to-reuse modules (for various devices and interaction techniques), and graphical tools to assist in building the world.

Kenneth Pimentel : 3D Graphics programming simplification
I would discuss how the process of interacting and creating a 3D simulation can be drastically simplified by using an object-oriented graphics programming language. I will also mention how this approach provides the utmost in flexibility which is critical in an emerging field. No one knows the "right way" to do things. Experimentation, rapid prototyping, and flexibility are key.

I will contrast the benefits and trade-offs of a graphic oriented interface versus a programming interface for the creation of virtual worlds.

I will bring a video tape showing various types of simulations created using WorldToolKIt. This will show the audience the diversity of applications already created.

Ubiquitous Computing and Augmented Reality

Chair:
Rich Gold, Xerox PARC

Panelists:
Bill Buxton, University of Toronto & Xerox PARC
Steve Feiner, Columbia University
Chris Schmandt, M.I.T. Media Labs
Pierre Wellner, Cambridge University & EuroPARC
Mark Weiser, Xerox PARC

" The door refused to open. It said, 'Five cents, please.' He searched his pockets. No more coins; nothing. "I'll pay you tomorrow,' he told the door. Again he tried the knob. Again it remained locked tight. 'What I pay you,' he informed it, 'is in the nature of a gratuity; I don't have to pay you.' 'I think otherwise,' the door said. 'Look in the purchase contract you signed when you bought this conapt.' "

-Philip K. Dick, from "Ubik"

Panel Background
Ubiquitous Computing is a radical alternative to the desktop and virtual reality models of computing. It turns these models inside out: instead of using computers to simulate or replace our common physical space, computers are embedded invisibly and directly into the real world. Everyday objects and our normal activities become the I/O to this highly sensuous and reactive environment. Objects are aware of and can respond to the location, state and activities of other objects in the world, both animate and inanimate. The implications are important: computing should be part of our everyday existence rather than isolated (and isolating) on a desktop; of equal importance, computer-based systems can take advantage of, and be compatible with, the rich environments in which we live. The poverty of the workstation, with its limited display, array of keys and single, simple pointing device (bad for the eyes, bad for the back, bad for the marriage) becomes clear when designers try to integrate it into our complex social and physical environments.

Panel Goals
The July 1993 issue of the Communications of the A.C.M., co-edited by Pierre Wellner, Wendy Mackay and Rich Gold, explores the research fields collectively known as Augmented Environments. This panel brings together five visionaries within this field to look at its implications and future. Each member is an expert within a different domain including ubiquitous video, projected reality, augmented reality, ubiquitous audio and infrastructure. Combined, these areas create a powerful new way of interacting and living within a computational environment. After a brief overview, each panel member will present a perspective on their own work in the field. Following these presentations panel members will have an opportunity to discuss the over-arching features of ubiquitous computing and answer questions from the audience.

Bill Buxton
Work in UbiComp has been paralleled by work in Video "Mediaspaces." Our position is that in such Mediaspaces, it is just as inappropriate to channel all of one's video interactions through a single camera/monitor pair; as it is to channel all of one's computational activity through a single keyboard, mouse and display. This leads us to the notion of Ubiquitous Video, which parallels that of Ubiquitous Computing.

When UbiComp and UbiVid converge, all of the transducers used for human-human interaction are candidates for human-computer interaction. Hence, for example, your computer can "see" you using the same camera that you use for videoconferencing, and it can hear you using the same microphone that you use for teleconferencing. These are not just changes in the source of input, however. They imply important changes in the nature of information available. Traditional human-computer dialogues have focused on foreground "conversational" interaction. Much of what will emerge from this Ubiquitous Media environment is much more similar to remote sensing. What is provided is background information about the context in which conversational interactions take place. It is this bimodal foreground/background interaction which we will pursue in our presentation.

Steve Feiner
Virtual reality systems use 3D graphics and other media to replace much or all of the user's interaction with the real world. In contrast, augmented reality systems supplement the user's view of the real world. By adding to, rather than replacing, what we experience, an

augmented reality can annotate the real world with additional information, such as descriptions of interesting features or instructions for performing physical tasks. For this supplementary material to be as effective as possible, we believe that it should not be created in advance, but should rather be designed on the fly using knowledge-based techniques that take into account the specific information to be communicated and the state of the world and user.

To test our ideas, we have been building an experimental, knowledge-based, augmented reality system that uses a see-through head-mounted display to overlay a complementary virtual world on the user's view of the real world. In a simple equipment maintenance domain that we have developed, the virtual world includes 3D representations of actual physical objects and virtual metaobjects such as arrows, textual callouts, and leader lines. A knowledge-based graphics component designs the overlaid information as it is presented. The design is based on a description of the information to be communicated and on data from sensors that track the position and orientation of the user and selected objects.

Chris Schmandt

Communication is what needs to be ubiquitous. "Computing" is what will provide the backbone to allow transparent mobility, and, perhaps more important, filter or control access so we do not get overwhelmed with all the stuff that comes down the pipes at us. Communication is even more about voice than it is about text and/or graphics. Ubiquitous computing has to handle voice! Voice interfaces may let me wander around my office and interact with computers through a window larger than that provided by a 19 inch display. Voice is how my environment will communicate with me as I move through it in the course of a work day. Voice is what will let us miniaturize devices below the sizes of buttons and displays.

The pocket phone provides a highly mobile computer terminal with today's technology. Telephone access to email, voicemail, my calendar and my rolodex, as well as various online information services, has already begun to change the way my group works. Wireless digital telephone networks using low powered pocket transceivers are inevitable. Although these are usually touted as "Personal" Communication Networks, telephone service providers have never understood that personalization requires dynamic decisions about how to route communication, and cannot be expressed as static routing tables in a telephone switch. Here's where the "computing" comes in — deciding which calls (or which email for that matter) will make it through my filters to ring the phone in my pocket.

Mark Weiser

A technological response to the challenge of making life better is to radically reconceive the computer around people's natural activity. Two key points are: people live in an environmental surround, using space, muscle memory, 3-D body surround; and that people live through their practices and tacit knowledge so that the most powerful things are those that are effectively invisible in use. How can we make everyday computing conform better to these principles of human effectiveness?

Our approach: Activate the world. Provide hundreds of wireless computing devices per person per office, of all scales (from 1" displays to wall sized). We call it: "ubiquitous computing" — and it means the end of the personal computer. These things in the office, every place you are, are not workstations or PC's. You just grab anything that is nearby, and use it. Your information and state follows you; the hundreds of devices in your office or meeting room adjust to support you.

Pierre Wellner

What is the best way to interact with computers in our future offices? We could make workstations so powerful and so versatile that they integrate all our office activities in one place. Or, we could make virtual offices that could free us from all the constraints of the real world. Both of these approaches aim to eliminate the use of traditional tools such as paper and pencil, but my position is that we should do the opposite. Instead of *replacing* paper, pens, pencils, erasers, desks and lamps, we should keep them and use computers to augment their capabilities.

Let's take paper, for example. Screen-based documents have not (and will not) replace paper completely because, despite its limitations, paper is portable, cheap, universally accepted, high resolution, tactile and familiar. Like with many traditional tools, we hardly think about the skills we use to manipulate paper because they are embedded so deeply into our minds and bodies. A lot of effort goes into making electronic documents more like paper, but the approach I propose is to start with the paper, and augment it to behave more like electronic documents. With a projected display and video cameras that track fingertips and tools, we can create spaces in which everyday objects gain electronic properties without losing their familiar physical properties. I will briefly discuss work to date on a system that does this: the DigitalDesk. I will also show some future envisionment videos that illustrate more ideas for how we could augment (instead of replace) paper, pencils, erasers, desks and other parts of the traditional office.

References

Books and Articles

deBord, Guy, "Society of the Spectacle", *Black & Red* 1983

Polanyi, Michael, *The Tacit Dimension*, Doubleday & Company, Inc 1966.

Communications of the ACM, Special Issue on Augmented Environments, July 1993

Wellner, P., Interacting with Paper on the DigitalDesk. *Communications of the ACM*, July 1993.

Stifelman, Lisa J., Barry Arons, Chris Schmandt, and Eric A. Hulteen, VoiceNotes: A Speech Interface for a Hand-Held Voice Notetake, *Proceedings* of INTERCHI '93, ACM April 1993

Weiser, Mark, "The Computer for the 21st Century," *Scientific American*, Sept. 1991

Bajura, M., H. Fuchs, and R. Ohbuchi, Merging Virtual Objects with the Real World: Seeing Ultrasound Imagery within the Patient. *Computer Graphics* (Proc. SIGGRAPH '92) 26(2):203-210, July, 1992.

Feiner, S. and A. Shamash, Hybrid User Interfaces: Breeding Virtually Bigger Interfaces for Physically Smaller Computers. *Proc.* UIST '91 (ACM Symp. on User Interface Software and Technology), Hilton Head, SC, November 11-13, 1991, 9-17.

Feiner, S., B. MacIntyre, and D. Seligmann, Annotating the Real World with Knowledge-Based Graphics on a See-Through Head-Mounted Display, In *Proc.* Graphics Interface '92, pages 78-85. Vancouver, Canada, May 11-15, 1992.

Feiner, S., B. MacIntyre, and D. Seligmann, Knowledge-Based Augmented Reality, *Communications of the ACM*, 36(7), July 1993.

Magazines

Electronic House, published bi-monthly by Electronic House Inc.

Merging 3-D Graphics and Imaging - Applications and Issues

Chair
William R. Pickering, Silicon Graphics Computer Systems

Panelists:
Paul Douglas,Earthwatch Communications
Kevin Hussey, Jet Propulsion Laboratory
Michael Natkin, Industrial Light and Magic

There are many applications that require both image processing and 3D graphics techniques. The panelists present application specifics and demonstrations of how image processing and 3D graphics are used together, and why these applications cannot be solved without the use of both disciplines.

Panel Background

Computer graphics and image processing were once two very distinct disciplines, with different hardware, software, and users. Now they are becoming increasingly intertwined. Applications are being developed that use both 3D graphics and imaging techniques for a broad spectrum of uses, including realistic scene simulations, interesting visual effects, and improved analysis and understanding of complex information. What should graphics users learn from their imaging counterparts, and vice versa? This panel brings together people from both disciplines who have been developing a variety of applications that merge graphics and imaging technologies. They will illustrate both the benefits and current limitations.

Panel Goals and Issues

Many applications require the use of real-world data most often obtained from sensors in the form of images. To view the data in the three dimensional space that it was obtained from, 3D graphics techniques are often used. How is image data transformed into a 3D view? The solution has been approached from both the image processing and 3D graphics disciplines.

Image processing technology is used to take real-world image data and process it into an image that highlights desired features. The final image can then be used in conjunction with 3D graphics techniques to render a 3D scene.

How are images used in conjunction with 3D graphics techniques to create more realistic views? What image processing techniques are used to enhance the image before rendering? How can images be utilized as sources for 3D models? How can 3D graphics techniques be used to view the image data?

The panel will offer discussion and demonstrations of how image processing and 3D graphics are jointly used to create 3D scenes from 2D images. Questions from the attendees will be answered during the concluding portion of the session.

Kevin Hussey

Kevin will describe the image processing techniques necessary for texture map preparation in the context of a complex scientific visualization entitled "Monterey: The Bay". The visualization simulates a flight through the Monterey Bay environment (above and below the ocean surface) using seven different geophysical data sets. Data from a numerical model of ocean currents were interpolated into sufficient time intervals for a smooth animation. Sets of polygonal "ribbons" were created to visualize the current flow. These ribbons were then rendered, anti-aliased and composited into a perspective ray-cast scene comprised of 3 additional image data sets.

Paul Douglas

Paul will describe a weather graphics system that he has developed and uses to provide visuals for his nightly weather broadcasts. The system transforms flat, 2-D pixel imagery of clouds and radar data into 3-D geometry allowing the viewer to view weather from multiple perspectives. The system merges images, ingested from live weather feeds including geostationary weather satellites over the Pacific, Europe and North America., with a full GIS system containing data from all over the world, to create a 3-D model. Weather phenomena is supplemented with imagery from SPOT, Landsat or aerial photography for enhanced realism.

Michael Natkin

Successful special effects depend on the seamless integration of computer generated objects with live action environments on film. Two-dimensional image techniques are a critical component of Industrial Light and Magic's production process. Michael will describe the use of painting, digital compositing, color balancing and edge quality adjustment, wire removal, image warping (morphing), texture projection, and 3D painting in movies such as *Terminator 2* and *Jurassic Park.* He will also discuss the future of special effects image processing, design of software for special effects production, and system hardware and software performance requirements.

Nan-o-sex and Virtual Seduction

Co-chairs:
Joan I. Staveley, Artist/Educator
David Steiling, Ringling School of Art and Design

Panelists:
Paul Brown, Mississippi State University
Michael Heim, Philosopher/Author
Jill Hunt, Angel Studios
Chitra Shriram, Xaos Inc. and The Ohio State University

Goals and Principle Issues

Among the principal issues the panel should address are:

1) Is virtual space really interactive or merely voyeuristic?
2) What are some of the alternatives to classic male erotica that might unfold within the possibilities of virtual space?
3) Who will be constructing the space? Who will be the audience? Who will be the target market?
4) Who/what are the real subjects and objects in virtual eroticism? How are the subject and objects constructed?
5) Is virtual reality a challenge or an aid to the development of better understanding and relations between the genders?
6) Is Cartesian coordinate space "neutral" or is it, like language, male-constructed?

The purpose of the discourse is not to add to cross-gender recriminations or to arrive at satisfactory conclusions, but to start a discussion based on the inevitability that eroticism is one of the first uses to which virtual reality is being put.

Panel Background

This panel is organized to apply some of the techniques and positions of recent criticism to virtual reality and computer graphics. The panel is committed to doing this in a manner that would avoid much of the jargon that can make such discussions hard to follow. The panel also wishes to avoid moral judgments on the subject being discussed in favor of allowing a plurality of voices to be heard on this controversial topic. Among the positions that will inform the discussion are those of feminism, deconstruction, Marxism, and a number of other post-modern critical attitudes. Among the assumptions of the panel is that, like it or not, virtual reality eroticism is going to be with us, and is in fact avidly anticipated.

Paul Brown

Some have proposed that we can expect virtual realities that are as 'fine grained' as physical reality by the year 2000. At this point our whole appreciation of "the natural world" may well break down. Instead of a defined reality, with myriad imaginary worlds, we will have a continuum of potential realities where the 'real' reality will have lost any particular significance. Our model is the renaissance period when the planet Earth changed from the center of the universe to an undistinguished speck in an unremarkable galaxy in an inconceivably vast and growing universe. The sexual implications of this breakdown of reality are tantalizing. The likely result is a tight symbiosis which will include humankind and their machines—virtual sex will be existentially 'real sex' where mutual human activity will be only one manifestation, distinguished perhaps only by the amount of mess it makes. Researchers report that women prefer linguistic eroticism while men prefer visual (Iconic) forms. The new eroticism with its immersive, symbiotic qualities may well bridge the gender gap. A lot will depend on who controls it. If it is developed within the traditional male hierarchical power structure it could become yet another form of constraint; however, the networks that will enable this evolution have an intrinsic matriarchal hetrachical quality. The growing number of technical conferences which have responded to the need for critical discussion of human/gender oriented issues is evidence of a move towards a more humanistic mode of enquirey.

Michael Heim

Primitive VR has become a screen on which we project our fantasies, both collectively and individually. Soon, the entertainment industry will sell gender-based sex fantasies for virtually safe sex. But the hazards of teledildonics will trap sex in the same voyeuristic cage that imprisoned painting, the novel, and cinema. Computer-generated realities have sprung from a deep erotic drive to see, hear, touch, and be touched by a perfect, knowable world. The thrill of speed, the elan of flight, and the freedom of a liquid self have attracted humans for centuries. Plug this Eros into electronics, and you think you can have it both ways, keep a distance while at the same time put yourself on the line. Beyond gender voyeurism moves a freely active and self-aware body that revels in the flow of internal energy without genital fixation. VR could eventually become a tool for training and sharing this body of spiral energy. Rather than a corpse dangling in frustration while trying to 'have it both ways,' the old erotic body may learn to move and love in entirely new ways.

Jill Hunt

Currently VR, in terms of eroticism, is purely voyeuristic. In the future, VR gender-independent interactive spaces could be used a creative outlet to help bridge the gap between the sexes, particularly in the workplace, creating a more direct method of communication and information exchange. By developing gender-independent spaces we might also risk repressing gender awareness altogether; therefore we must also develop gender-dependent experiences and exchanges in order to further our awareness of ourselves and the opposite sex. There is room for more variety of expression than is currently predominant in our male dominated society, although it will take time to develop and educate people on the benefits of this exposure. Repression is imbedded in our society and directly related to gender discrimination and sexuality. The current and confused view of repression causes many problems that I feel can be work out in VR.

Chitra Shriram

Battles for power, money and ideology rage about the still largely anticipated phenomena of virtual reality. An ancient myth comes to mind. Gods and Demons had once grown so powerful that neither could gain and advantage of the other. Each side strove to prevail by drinking the nectar of immortality that flowed deep in the ocean depths, so Gods and demons together began to churn the ocean. Incredible gifts spewed forth and both nectar and poison rose to the surface of the water, inviting consumption. The god Shiva drank the poison, arresting the evil in his throat. He saved the world from destruction. The God Vishnu, disguised as an enchantress, lured away the demons so that the Gods could create good with the life-giving nectar.

We barely know what poisons or nectars we court. The very notion of looking to ancient spiritual disciplines to inform us on how and what we could do with our latest scientific and technological feats is likely to sound ludicrous—tolerated only in the convenient name of 'multiculturalism.' But the very absurdity of the exercise is warranted by an urgent need to widen the base of value systems which nourish this new manifestation of our psychic and technological desire and energy.

References

Benedikt, Michael (ed). *Cyberspace: First Steps*. MA: The MIT Press, 1992.

Bodychello, *Heavenly Bodies*, Multimedia Publication 1993.

Bonobo Production, *Digital Dancing*, Multimedia Publication 1993.

Brand, Steward, *The Media Lab - Inventing the Future at MIT*, Viking/Penguin, 1987.

Bright, Susie. *Susie Bright's Sexual Reality: A Virtual Sex World Reader*. USA: Cleis Press, Inc., 1992.

Bright, Susie; Blank, Joani. *Herotica: A Collection of Women's Erotic Fiction*. New York: Penguin Group, 1992

Brown, Paul. "Metamedia and Cyberspace - Advanced Computers and the Future of Art," in Hayward, Philip (ed.), *Culture Technology and Creativity in the Late Twentieth Century*. Arts Council of Great Britain and John Lebby Press, London, 1990. See also Paul Brown, "Beyond Art," in Clifford Pickover (ed.), *Visions of the Future*, To appear 1992.

Brown, Paul. "Communion and Cargo Cults," Proceedings of the Second International Symposium on Electronic Arts - SISEA, Groningen, The Netherlands 1990.

Brown, Paul. "The Convergence of Reality and Illusion," Proceedings Hi-Vision 92, Tokyo, 1992.

Brown, Paul. "Reality versus Illusion," Visual Proceedings SIGGRAPH 92, Chicago, July 1992.

Brown, Paul. "Symbiosis, Semiosis and Communication Technology - The Ethics and Aesthetics of Computer Human Interaction." To appear.

Dorsey, Candas Jane, *Machine Sex and Other Stories*, Women's Press, London 1988.

Faludi, Susan. *Backlash: The Undeclared War on American Women*. New York: An Anchor Book, Doubleday, 1991.

Foster, Hal (ed). *The Anti-Aesthetic: Essays on Postmodern Culture*. WA: Bay Press, 1983.

Gibson, William. The Cyperpunk Trilogy - *Neuromancer*, Gollancz London 1984; *Count Zero*, Gollancz London 1986; *Mona Lisa Overdrive*, Gollancz London 1988.

Handhardt, John (ed). *Video Culture: A Critical Investigation*. New York: Visual Studies Workshop, 1986.

Heim, Michael. *The Metaphysics of Virtual Reality*, with a foreword by Myron Krueger, Oxford University Press, 1993.

Heim, Michael. *Electric Language: A Philosophical Study of Word Processing*, Yale Univesity Press, 1989 Yale paperback, c1987.

Heim, Michael. "The Computer as Component: Heidegger and McLuhan," *Philosophy and Literature*, Johns Hopkins University Press, October 1992.

Heim, Michael. "Cybersage Does Tai Chi," in the anthology *Falling in Love with Wisdom: On Becoming a Philosopher*, David Karnos and Robert Shoemaker (eds.), Oxford University Press, 1993.

Heim, Michael. "The Erotic Ontology of Cyberspace," in *Cyberspace: First Steps*, edited by Michael Benedikt, MIT Press 1991. An early version of the paper was a talk at the First Conference on Cyberspace held at the University of Texas in Austin, May 4-5, 1990.

Heim, Michael. "The Metaphysics of Virtual Reality," *Multimedia Review*, Issue Three ("New Paradigms"), published by Meckler Publishing. This essay also appears in the Meckler reprint of Issue Two ("Virtual Reality") and was the basis for a talk on the program "Virtual Reality: Theory, Practice, and Promise" in San Francisco, December 10, 1990.

Hershman, Lynn. *Deep Contact - the Incomplete Sexual Fantasy Disk*, CD-ROM 1990.

Laurel, Brenda. "On Finger Flying & Other Faulty Notions," in Linda Jacobson (ed.), *CyberArts*, Miller Freeman 1992.

Laurel, Brenda. *Computers as Theatre*. Addison-Wesley Publishing Company, 1991.

Mulvey, Laura. "Visual Pleasure and Narrative Cinema," in the anthology *The Sexual Subject: A Screen Reader in Sexuality*, edited by *Screen*, Routledge 1992.

Mondo 2000, California: Published by Fun City Megamedia.

Nelson, Ted, *Computer Lib/Dream Machines*, republished in a revised and updated edition by Tempus/Microsoft in 1987.

Reactor Software, *Virtual Valerie*, Multimedia Publication, 1993.

Rheingold, Howard. *Virtual Reality*. New York: Simon & Schuster Inc., Copyright 1991 Howard Rheingold.

Rucker, Rudy, "R U Sirius and Queen Mu, A Users Guide to the New Edge," *Mondo 2000*, 1992.

Singer, Linda. *Erotic Welfare: Sexual Theory and Politics in the Age of Epidemic*, Routledge, Ny, London 1993.

Stefanac, Susanne. "Sex and the New Media," *New Media Magazine*, Vol. 3 No. 4, April 1993, pp. 38-45.

Wired, California: Published by Louis Rossetto.

Critical Art/Interactive Art/Virtual Art: Rethinking Computer Art

Chair:
Timothy Druckrey, International Center of Photography

Panelists:
Regina Cornwell, Independent art critic
Kit Galloway, Electronic Cafe International
Sherrie Rabinowitz, Electronic Cafe International
Simon Penny, Univerisity of Florida
Richard Wright, University of London Polytechnic

Richard Wright:
This essay explores how scientific knowledge is diffused into society through the medium of scientific visualization, taking the late eighties phenomena of *Chaos Culture* as an example.

Beginning with Peitgen and Richter's initial popularization of fractals in their *Frontiers of Chaos* exhibition and catalogue, we study readings of Chaos Theory and Fractals from the scientific to cultural critiques like Vivian Sobchack's article in [Art Forum,] and popular media forms in youth magazines and 'style' culture. This provides us with an overview of many interpretations of this science from the cynical to the mystical and how it captured the public's imagination.

Donna Haraway's study of how to contest scientific knowledge or stories for the creation of public meanings in relevant here to the extent that it shows a way in which we can critique the cultural impact these scientific concepts on the basis of their scientific credentials directly. A difference here is that the situation is complicated by the mediation of the Chaos story by imagery and media. This has many arguable effects such as obscuring the scientific background or conversely making it more 'accessible,' and by creating a conflict between critical scientific readings of scientific discourses through imagery and aesthetic readings of them. The latter problem is most pressing in the context of scientifically related graphics that are presented in the context of Art. We conclude that a deeper level of cultural readings of scientific visualization are needed, especially in the context of art, readings that address scientific discourse more thoroughly and attend to how it now operates through imagery to take effect socially and politically.

Kit Galloway & Sherrie Rabinowitz:
If you look at the aesthetic quality of the communication and you're true to your art form and your art logic, then you very naturally put one foot in front of the other and get to these places. The art logic marches you right out the art institutions into life. From "Defining The Image as Place: A Conversation With Kit Galloway, Sherrie Rabinowitz & Gene Youngblood," High Performance Magazine #37, 1987.

If the arts are to take a role in shaping and humanizing emerging technological environments, individuals and arts constituencies must begin to image at the much larger scale of creativity.

We must begin to create at the same scale as we can destroy, or else art, and more dangerously the human spirit and imagination, will be rendered decorative and impotent.

If the boundaries between art and life dissolve, it will be the result of artists migrating towards a new order of artmaking, abandoning the conventional standards and practices and becoming 'new practitioners' or systems integrators, who produce situations, contexts, and permanent environments or utilities. The 'new practitioners' can begin the process of healing and aesthetic wound that has disfigured the business of Art, and continue the aesthetic quest in more relevant directions.

New creative activities must emerge such as multi-media creative solutions networks, not simply computer networks for Artists, but rather multi-media telecommunications networks with agendas that can engage multi-disciplinary constituencies. This will require the development of new skills and the cultivation of new relationships between the participants. The movement is towards the control of a meaningful context, creating environments not just to support art, but that create the possibility for new scales of creativity across all disciplines and boundaries.

The dark side of the "new world information order" suggests that a new scale aesthetics be created. It will take several years from the time this work begins for creative solutions networks of appropriate number, scale, velocity, and dexterity to evolve to maturity. Consider: co-creating non-imperialistic, multi-cultural or domestic agendas for community or global scale aesthetic endeavors. Consider: the continuous re-invention of non-hierarchical telecom networks that will allow people to bypass cultural gatekeepers and power brokers. We must accept these kinds of challenges and recognize what can be gained by solving them.

All of this implies that there is a new way to be in the world. That the counterforce to the scale of destruction is the scale of communication, and that our legacy or epitaph will be determined in many ways by our ability to creatively employ informal, multi-media, multi-cultural, conversational, telecommunications and information technologies.

Tim Druckrey:
If images are to become increasingly experiential, then a theory of representation must be evolved to account for the effects of a new form of transaction with art. The issues raised by the convergence of technology and creativity are crucial. Interactive art will require a complex reassessment of the relationship linking experience and discourse. At the core of this fundamental shift in the development of both communications and art is the ability of the digital media to encompass text, still and moving images, feedback systems, sound, animation and simulation. How the effects of this integrated model of creative production is joining with the development of content is an essential component in the development of interactive art.

For some time the definition of interactivity has been something of a rote signifier of hands-on activity. Yet the relationship between behavior and the concept of interaction are not so easily resolved. Interactive technologies need to be linked with both cogent content and flexible form. However, a simplified concept of the interactive cannot suffice to fructify this complex and dynamic field.

Interactive media is now wildly touted as the creative medium for this decade. What is not articulated in this equation is the demand made on both producer and recipient of this panacea. The equipment and resources necessary for this media too easily limit both its accessibility and its audience. Whether multimedia will reach it intended audience or not is hinged on a market that should stabilize enough for users to invest in it. Unfortunately, too much multimedia reaches the market as either prepackaged or as marginal.

Art that demands more than visual attention will refocus criticism on the issues of experience. Because interactive works begin to pose the problem of the breakdown not the meaning but of a certain concept of order grounded in ideas of unity and form, they propose an alternative unity. Non-linear principles of organization, in fact, are the signifier of a culture accustomed to fragmentation and montage. Information in this environment comes as an array rather than as a sequence. Deciphering the array — or even producing the array — is a challenge that must be accompanied by considered conceptual and theoretical practices. Lingering narrative concepts, simplistic montage, and furtive use of digitized video and television cannot substitute for expressive order. Intention must become reciprocal. While this endangers the authorial position of the producer, it simultaneously must account for an audience willing to investigate the space of electronic expression.

Regina Cornwell:
Art made with the computer means the end of the unique object as it has been traditionally conceived of and cherished in the art world. Fine art museums exist to collect, preserve and exhibit unique objects. As institutions they flourish on concepts such as originality, the individuality of the artist, genius, the trace of the artist's hand. An entire language exists to support such thinking and concepts.

What place do objects such as interactive computer installations and flat wall pieces, made with a computer, have in the fine arts museum now? But more importantly, what place will they and museums gives us? What might the future hold for art made with the computer? Film and photography are mechanical forms from the nineteenth century. One can find lessons in both their histories within the fine arts museum, yet cinema as an art form suggests more challenging issues which seem closer to art made with the computer than does the area of traditional photography.

Art and the computer exist in distinctly separate worlds, each with its own vocabulary, sensibility, culture, and economics. What can and will bridge the gaps between these two worlds in order to open up dialogue and new possibilities?

Simon Penny:
Simon will serve as a respondent to the panel.

Digital Illusion: Theme Park Visualization

Chair:
Clark Dodsworth, Rising Star Graphics, Ltd.

Panelists:
Kevin Biles, KBD Innovative Arts
Richard Edlund, Boss Film Studios
Michael Harris, NCR/AT&T Human Interface Technology Center
Phil Hettema, MCA Recreation Services
Mario Kamberg, MCA Recreation Services
Brenda Laurel, Interval Research Corporation
Sherry McKenna, Rhythm & Hues
Allen Yamashita, Entertainment Design Production Group

Panel Background

As entertainment delivery systems become digital, a major venue for large interactive visual databases will be theme parks and LBE (location-based entertainment) facilities. What new expressions in the existing set of theme park experiences can digital imaging and sensing provide? The present state-of-the-art might be non-interactive attractions using 70mm films, often showing CG integrated with live action. Some of this imaging is seamless hyperreality; some is grounded in the fantasy worlds of traditional cell animation. These experiential installations are typically unique, expensive, and exciting in ways not previously possible. As cost decline for hi-res real-time rendering, actual audience participation and interaction will be incorporated in attraction scenarios that are, by their very design, user interfaces. Such recreational interfaces are at one end of a scale which extends to handheld videogame platforms at the other. There will eventually be systems with multiuser telecommunications between the two. Panelists will show footage form their attractions in the parks around the world and discuss issues of creative development, system design, visualization tools, cost per park attendee per hour, interactivity, licensed properties, appropriate technology, the search for better illusions, and the art of telling a good story.

Michael Harris

Location Based entertainments (LBE) reflect the cutting edge of our industry, where convincing sensory illusions and natural interactivity can translate directly into fascination and profit.

We focus on 70mm, simulation, full motion HDTV, networking, cyberspace, virtual reality.... But these are all adjectives. Will players embrace this high-end media stuff? Pay for it? Enough to convince owners and operators to invest in it? The key issue is likely to be: what will players do with it all? What will the *nouns* be?

At the beginning of the era of truly capable technologies ("we've got the gear"), we have a unique opportunity to discover/create new frameworks, scenarios, situations, Which disciplines will become crucial? What will actually work? Can we develop new worlds, play in them, and thus learn to prosper in them as they become reality?

Richard Edlund

Thrillrides encompass many techniques - models, motion control photography, animation, live photography, etc. - and ideally culminate in the digital realm. Still, a good story/concept is the key to success and creative attention to preparing an audience for the experience is a must.

Allen Yamashita

Our preoccupation with technology, digital or otherwise, continues to be fundamentally uninteresting to me. I didn't become a filmmaker because I was interested in cameras and lenses, but because this technology accommodated stories of a form and style which, say, writing or dancing did not. I've been making simulator attractions because people are interested in stories which are also experiences. What kind of stories will we be telling tomorrow? They will determine the methodology and therefore, the technology I'll be involved with.

Kevin Biles

Theme park guests expect an experience that is out of the ordinary and something they cannot see, do or experience elsewhere; an experience that puts them in another time, place or world.

CGI has evolved to the degree that it now fits affordably on the palette of techniques we bring to bear in creating theme park experiences. We are less likely to avoid CG imaging because of its former "computer" look, or its cost.

Since it can now easily blend with live action, we are turning to this medium (usually in conjunction with other media) to tell stories and create unique experiences. CGI is becoming a freeing rather than limiting medium. We can keep our focus on audience satisfaction rather than technical limitations of the medium.

Phil Hettema

The "true" theme park experience (which is continually being redefined) requires us to create new applications and interfaces for digital media.

The notion of an all "simulator" or "V.R." theme park is a myth, but digital technology will provide a new level of amazing experiences. Before that can happen, we need to understand the group dynamics which are fundamental to the "themed" experience, and issues of interactive capacity, group interface, and large format display must all be addressed with great creativity.

Brenda Laurel

Brenda Laurel will address issues of interactive collaborative recreation and virtual reality from her unique perspective.

Sherry McKenna

"I want something totally unique—something that's never been done before and, by the way, I want to know how much it's going to cost and how long it's going to take by tomorrow!"

Clients haven't changed but the medium has.

Mario Kamberg

The climate was once dominated by Brut Force and Proprietary Technologies. But now, with the new medium we are back to what film making is all about... creative challenges. Everything in the ride is determined by the stylistic approach of its artisans as the computer is now the slave.

Today's challenges are creative ones, not who's got the most CPU's or a user friendly interface. Particle systems are in everyone's palette... and do you know anyone who can't do a morph?

Now is the time to understand the sinergy of film design and the physical experience. The role of the ride film director/designer becomes more crucial than ever.

We are back in the saddle again: our imaginations are our biggest challenge.

Man vs. Mouse

Chair: Jonathan Luskin

Panelists:
Terri Hansford, MA, PT, CHT, Hand Therapy of San Francisco
Robert E. Markison, M.D, SACS, San Francisco Hand Specialists
Joan Stigliani, Author of *The Computer Users' Guide to Health and Vitality*

Abstract
The purpose of the panel is to raise awareness about Repetitive Strain Injuries (RSI).

RSI, also known as Cumulative Trauma Disorder or overuse syndrome, consists of many different injuries: carpal tunnel syndrome, tendinitis, tynosynovitis, thoracic outlet syndrome, lateral epicondilitis, etc. In 1992, 185,000 office and factory workers suffered RSI. These injuries are now responsible for 1/2 of all occupational illnesses. The panel will describe RSI, other computer related health risks, and how to avoid them. An injured worker, a leading hand surgeon, a physical therapist, and the author of The Computer User' Guide to Health and Vitality, will focus on positive things we can do to improve our health and happiness as computer users.

Topics will include: awareness of the problem, why the "sudden epidemic," form and function of the upper limbs, proper use of limbs, blood circulation, stress, hardware and software ergonomics, and responsibilities of workers, companies, computer manufacturers and government.

The panel will also discuss better computer interfaces for the future, improved work station design, physical therapy and treatment of RSI. There will be an ample questions and answer period allowing for a broad discussion of RSI and other related computer health issues such as eye strain, electromagnetic radiation, and the like.

Multimedia and Interactivity in the Antipodes

Chair:
Lynne Roberts-Goodwin, University of New South Wales

Panelists:
Chris Caines, University of Wollongong
Paula Dawson, University of New South Wales
Adam Lucas, University of New South Wales
Cameron McDonald-Stuart, Apple Australia

Artists, educators and researchers address the development of interactive art and multimedia in Australia, and its relation to similar issues overseas. The panelists present multimedia and interactive artwork from Australia and other countries, discussing issues of availability of these technologies to indigenous peoples, evolving human relationships with interactive multimedia and the role of these new media in cultural, educational and institutional development.

Panel Background

In Australia, interactive art using multimedia technologies is a relatively recent phenomenon. This situation can be attributed to complex cultural, curatorial, aesthetic and technological factors. However, artists, funding bureaucrats, gallery directors and curators in Australia are now beginning to appreciate the importance of interactivity and multimedia, firstly as constituting new formal strategies for critically addressing traditional boundaries between the observer and the artwork, and secondly, as useful tools for opening computing and communications technology to a wider public.

This panel addresses emerging developments in the field of interactivity and multimedia in Australia, mapping out some of the more salient cultural, theoretical and technological factors shaping the current interactive discourse in this country and related patterns and practices in other countries.

The five panelists come from a variety of backgrounds, including art, cultural theory, education and technological development. Each of them has an idiosyncratic perspective on multimedia and interactivity, but a common feature is their commitment to broadening the availability and mode of operation of these new technologies.

Panel Goals and Issues

A fundamentally appealing aspect of interactivity is how the user can navigate the artwork's space of audio-visual information, thereby personally transforming it. The number of permutations in the technological and syntactic means of conveying this information appears to be only limited by the human imagination, so it is perhaps natural that artists have become attracted to these new media with their potential for an expansion of notions of art as merely "object." For an artist working with interactive multimedia, the viewer can become a participant or even co-creator in the artwork and the artwork can become a process of ongoing creativity with a de-centred and de-stratified site of authorship. Communication, participation and creative expansion can all fall together in this process. Enlightenment notions of an individual artistic "genius" are undermined and collectivized. To paraphrase Joseph Beuys, "Anyone can become an artist" by participating in creative dialogues, whether it be with interactive artworks or through electronic networks.

Issues pertaining to the critical reception, funding and production of interactive art and multimedia technologies will be highlighted by the relevant panelists. The emphasis will be placed on issues which are not only specifically relevant to the Australian "Antipodes" at present, but also those which address the common perceptions and reception in global terms of interactivity and multimedia in an arts and cultural context. The presentations will include discussions of artistic and educational uses of CD Rom interactives, electronic networks, and multimedia computing, as well as theories of perception and the use of interactive multimedia by indigenous peoples in Australia and North America.

Chris Caines
The panelist will present his own CD Rom Interactive artwork, titled "The History of Luminous Motion," which is based on a 1992 video artwork dealing with issues of the utopian parallels in the exploration of landscape in technology. The CD will be presented as an example of multimedia interactive art. Through this presentation, the panelist will discuss the ways in which video art and electronic music have been absorbed into interactive multimedia technology, with particular reference to the operation of sound in interactive CD Rom presentations.

The panelist will also give a brief overview of production methodologies relating to the amalgamation of video and interactive multimedia; how this amalgamation transforms language but at the same time creates barriers to artistic expression, and how some artists have made breakthroughs in the artistic potentials of interactive CD Rom.

The panelist will conclude by describing his artistic practice in terms of "the alchemy of converting the linear video work into the fluid interactive rhizomatic CD ROM."

Paula Dawson
This paper will discuss the ways in which multi-dimensional media within contemporary visual arts practice constructs human beings as viewers, respondents or participants. A particular focus will be how the development of 3 Dimensional Spatial Imaging Technology has been shaped through research into patterns of observation (perception theory). Through this development, the relevant properties of humans have become isolated and defined in the extreme. As a result, the means of exchange of stimulus and the precise amount of information needed to generate an image or an environment has become quantifiable.

If we think of how "non-interactive" Renaissance painting constructs the human observer as little more than an "eyeball on a stick," are we in fact less or more? This precision, in relation of the human to the perceived image, speaks primarily of the physiological, sensory connection, whereas the emotional and psychological terrain of virtual interactivity has yet to be defined.

Adam Lucas
The panelist will argue that since the Australian Bicentennial in 1988, the white population's slowly dawning recognition of the continued ill-treatment of the Aboriginal people of this country is finally starting to generate a broad-based cultural dialogue between black and white Australians. New interactive and multimedia technologies have already made a significant contribution to this cultural dialogue.

"Multimedia is Multicultural" is a catch phrase currently being used by computer companies to promote their latest offerings. However, if multiculturalism is to become a reality, rather than just rhetoric, the dominant Western culture must assimilate and come to terms with the knowledge and histories of indigenous peoples throughout the world. This process must involve the active participation of indigenous people in their representations and education of themselves, rather than a continuation of colonialism with members of the dominant culture speaking for and on behalf of the "Other."

Collaborative work between artists and educators from European, non-European and indigenous backgrounds will be discussed as a possible strategy for encouraging this process, with particular reference to projects being undertaken in this area in Canada, the United States and Australia. Issues related to the perception of multimedia/interactive art and the manner in which marginalized groups are integrating new electronic media into their art and cultural practices will be cited, and examples of artwork shown.

Cameron McDonald-Stuart
This paper will present a philosophical, historical and current cultural overview of "Media Integration" in the local and global context of academic and artistic ventures and presentations. Through this overview, the panelist will present and highlight particular examples of New Media Integration in multimedia technologies, citing examples, case studies of projects, research and development and artistic applications of interactivity. The panelist will present and report on the positive and negative aspects of projects and their subsequent outcomes, demonstrating the existence of certain "developmental barriers" that exist in the delivery of the artifacts or products, regardless of their final context and placement. It will be emphasized that definite criteria must be in place at the project's inception in order to fulfill fundamental paradigms of cultural reading. These criteria are skill sets and relevant media issues. The paper and presentation will also cover basic computing and its perceived image in the mass media, in addition to addressing the uses of computing technology in the delivery of education.

Lynne Roberts-Goodwin
The chair will introduce the panel by delivering a short paper encompassing the topics to be discussed by the various panelists, in order to provide a cohesive map of issues and perspectives, including: historical perspectives; cultural considerations; educational paradigms; artistic pursuits; technology transfers and relationships of interactive technologies to present forms of everyday information retrieval i.e. books, video, film, audio-tape, etc.

The chair will also briefly discuss the ways in which people respond to interactive multimedia and assimilate them into their experience through the viewing of artworks, soundworks, performances and broadcast media. This notion of "reception values," which resides with the viewer/respondent, can be paradoxical and problematic due to the nature of the medium and its placement in the gallery, museum, shopping mall, library, expo, etc. The reception/response is obviously dependent on the cultural conditioning of the viewer/respondent, their geographical location and their preconceptions of that technology's potentials. The intention of introducing these issues is to cite the locations at which interactive multimedia is critically assessed, ranging from entertainment, education, artistic production and historical and cultural development.

References

Adilkno, "The artist and his media," *Mediamatic*, Vol. 5 # 1&2, pp 27 - 30.

Ballard, J.G., "The Voices of Time," *The Garden of Time*, pp115 - 123, Phoenix , Great Britain 1992.

Berndt, Catherine H. & Ronald M., *The Speaking Land: Myth and Story in Aboriginal Australia*, Penguin, 1989.

Cassirer, Ernst, *The Individual and the Cosmos in Renaissance Philosophy*. Trans. Fritz C.A. Koelln and James P. Petlegrove. Princeton: Princton University Press, 1972.

Crary, Johnathan, "Techniques of the Observer," *On Vision and Modernity in the Nineteenth Century*. October Book, MIT Press, Cambrige, Massachusetts, London, England.

Deleuse, Gilles, "Cinema; The Movement Image," Trans. Hugh Tomlinson and Barbara Habberjam. Minneapolis: Univ. of Minnesota Press.

Grassmuck, Volker, "Art X Technology," *Mediamatic* , Vol. 5 # 1 & 2.

Hedlund, Patric, "Virtual Reality Warriors: Native American Culture in Cyberspace," *High Performance*, Spring 1992, pp. 31-35.

Morgan, M. J., *Molyneux's Question: Vision, Touch and the Philosophy of Perception*, Cambridge Univ. Press, 1977.

Nicholson, Shirley (ed.), *Shamanism: An Expanded View of Reality*, Theosophical Publishing House, 1987.

Turnbull, Clive, *Black War*, Penguin, 1967.

The Integrative Use of Computer Graphics in a Medical University

Chair:
Dave Warner, Loma Linda University School of Medicine

Panelists:
A. Douglas Will, Loma Linda University School of Medicine
Jodi Reed, Loma Linda University School of Medicine

The problems in medicine addressed at the Loma Linda University Medical School are problems common to the field of medicine in general. Solutions applied at Loma Linda generalize to the field of medicine, both in study and practice of medicine.

The goal of this panel is two fold. The first goal is to establish a bridge between the computer graphics community and the medical community. The second goal is to demonstrate by example how the integrative use of computer graphics and advanced human computer interface techniques are transforming both the study and practice of medicine. The field of medicine has both the need and the resources to provide the computer graphics industry with new market areas which will aid in the streamlining of the global healthcare system. Examples include innovative applications of educational multimedia, computer graphic visualization of medical data and clinical applications of virtual reality interface technology.

The field of medicine is one of few areas of human endeavor which penetrates almost all aspects of the human experience. Recent developments in human computer interface technology hold great potential in dramatically changing the face of modern medicine.

This panel will present real applications that utilize recently developed computer graphics and interface technologies to assist in the endeavor to continue to enhance health care.

Dave Warner: Clinical applications of advanced interface technologies

Normal people are naturally enabled. They are born with the capacity to interact with the world and willfully manipulate their environments. Disabled people have lost the capacity for such interaction and manipulation through either trauma or disease. Advanced human-computer interface technology that has been developed as natural user interfaces for interaction with virtual reality has immediate application in re-enabling the disabled persons. While virtual reality promises to solve many problems in the future, the immediate application of these advanced interfaces can improve the lives of millions today. At the Loma Linda University Medical Center, we have had many successes in utilizing these technologies. The utility of these devices has already been demonstrated as augmentative communication devices, as environmental controllers, as therapeutic tools in rehabilitation and as tools for quantitative assessment for diagnostic evaluation. Patients who have lost the ability to communicate verbally have successfully used an instrumented glove configured in a gesture to speech mode. Spinal cord injury, stroke and traumatic brain injury patients have virtual reality technology to manipulate virtual objects and practice specific skilled motor tasks. Quadriplegics have used physiological input devices to move objects on the screen with only their eyes and to play virtual instruments merely by contracting face and neck muscles. These are just a few examples of immediate uses for this promising technology that can profoundly improve the quality of life of real people today.

The study and the practice of medicine are intrinsically linked. As information technology becomes more and more relied on in the practice of medicine, so must the study of medicine be adjusted to help prepare the emerging medical professionals for the changes that they are most likely to encounter. This "adjusted" study of medicine must not only modify behavior, but must go beyond and intrinsically change the thinking of the modern health care professional. The integration of computer interaction as a fundamental skill required for the modern healthcare professional will herald a new paradigm for medicine. Technology has only recently reached a result/effort ratio which will propel the medical industry into the 21st century.

A. Douglas Will: Computer graphics and interactive multimedia in the practice of medicine

Today, scientific, economic, technological, social, political and legal forces are converging to form a powerful stimulus for change in health care. The collision of those forces will have an effect that will be as far reaching as the advent of powered flight and as important in its economic and social impact as both World Wars. In 1991, health care jumped a full percentage point, the sharpest one-year increase in three decades. If today's rate of growth continues, health care is projected to reach $16 trillion dollars by 2030, or one-third of the nation's economic output. At the same time 37 million Americans are living today without health insurance coverage.

Health care is a service industry that is intensely dependent on information. Physicians are knowledge workers. Physicians drive most health care costs through the power of their pens. The best way to influence physician behavior and directly impact cost is to provide them with contextually sensitive information in time to impact decisions and improve outcomes. To be successful today, physicians must abandon 19th century industrial aged technologies that they continue to use for maintaining patient's medical records and adopt information tools that place contextually sensitive information at their finger tips.

Knowledge is the unseen phantom driving health care costs. Keeping up with the constant infusion of new knowledge has become intractable. The explosion of knowledge has led to ever increasing specialization resulting in highly inefficient and fractionated care. New tools are needed to acquire knowledge, to access knowledge, and to use knowledge. Three dimensional visualization of anatomic structures must be joined by multidimensional presentation of complex semantic relationships. Animation of molecular processes must replace intellectually opaque verbal descriptions. Perceptualization tools must be developed to enable the knowledge worker to encounter knowledge.

The human computer interface requirements of a real world health care application are demanding. Ease of use and very high performance are coupled to the economic requirement of low cost. Once the fundamental tools have been created to provide the compelling reason for physicians to widely adopt the computerized medical record, new vistas of opportunity will emerge for imaginative visualization of the elaborate "worlds within worlds" of medical knowledge.

Jodi Reed: Issues in the application of advanced educational technologies in medicine

The knowledge explosion of the information age is especially apparent in medicine. Most medical educators have responded by adding content to curriculum. Unfortunately, neither student brain size nor the number of years of medical school has grown. Students respond to this information buildup by studying what they think will help them pass multiple choice exams, resulting in a great deal of frustration, both for students and faculty. Some medical schools have addressed this issue by cutting back content and focusing on process. Problem-based learning, for example, begins a learning session with a clinically-oriented case rather than a barrage of facts. Students are responsible for their learning and are more likely to retain what they've learned when it is learned in context and is learner-directed.

Clinical education, usually the 3rd and 4th years of medical school, is also plagued by the information explosion. Clinicians have turned to increased specialization in response, but medical schools are charged with providing a generalist experience, especially since there is a shortage of lower-paid primary care physicians. Clinical education is often characterized by disorganization and inconsistency, both between and within clerkships. Yet most medical educators would attest that there is an identifiable core of knowledge, skills, and values that should guide curriculum and assessment. How can these issues be addressed?

Systems thinking can help us identify issues and organize solutions, cognitive science can help us create more efficient and meaningful learning situations, and computer science can serve as a tool for both. Intelligent use of computer graphics takes advantage of all three.

This presentation will demonstrate ways we have used computer graphics to address pressing issues in medical education. Obviously, computer graphics alone cannot resolve the administrative organizational challenges, but graphics can be used to increase the efficiency of learning.

Cognitive science has shown us that human working memory can only handle about 7 items at a time. Unless we process these items in some way, they will be forgotten. Much of the utility of good computer courseware lies in its tendency to reduce the load on a learner's working memory. It does this via learner control of pace and detail, reduced time for information access and comparisons, and rich, dynamic, integrated information representation.

We have also learned from cognitive science that facts isolated from meaningful context are easily forgotten. Recent efforts have directed courseware toward case-based simulations that provide meaningful situations and activities for the learner. Timely feedback improves the learner's diagnostic reasoning skills. Use of computer graphics links visual representation with experience, a powerful combination.

Certainly, the future holds increased use of simulation, including use of physiologically-based feedback systems to enhance fidelity and increase the scope of assessment. We are now beginning to use simulation to assess diagnostic and problem-solving skills. Perhaps we will some day use technology to assess a student doctor's communication ability as well.

For more information please contact
Dave Warner
Loma Linda University Medical Center
Loma Linda Ca. 92354
Voice 909-799-6190
Fax 909-799-6180
eMail davew@well.sf.ca.us

Cumulative Index (SIGGRAPH '84 - SIGGRAPH '93)

Stephen Noel Spencer
The Advanced Computing Center for the Arts and Design
The Ohio State University
1224 Kinnear Road
Columbus, OH 43212

Author/Title Index

[1] G. ABRAM, L. WESTOVER, AND T. WHITTED. Efficient alias-free rendering using bit-masks and look-up tables. In *Computer Graphics (SIGGRAPH '85 Proceedings)* (July 1985), B. A. Barsky, Ed., vol. 19, 53–59.

[2] G. D. ABRAM AND T. WHITTED. Building block shaders. In *Computer Graphics (SIGGRAPH '90 Proceedings)* (Aug. 1990), F. Baskett, Ed., vol. 24, 283–288.

[3] K. AKELEY. RealityEngine graphics. In *Computer Graphics (SIGGRAPH '93 Proceedings)* (Aug. 1993), J. T. Kajiya, Ed., vol. 27, 109–116.

[4] K. AKELEY AND T. JERMOLUK. High-performance polygon rendering. In *Computer Graphics (SIGGRAPH '88 Proceedings)* (Aug. 1988), J. Dill, Ed., vol. 22, 239–246.

[5] J. AMANATIDES. Ray tracing with cones. In *Computer Graphics (SIGGRAPH '84 Proceedings)* (July 1984), H. Christiansen, Ed., vol. 18, 129–135.

[6] J. AMANATIDES AND D. P. MITCHELL. Antialiasing of interlaced video animation. In *Computer Graphics (SIGGRAPH '90 Proceedings)* (Aug. 1990), F. Baskett, Ed., vol. 24, 77–85.

[7] P. AMBURN, E. GRANT, AND T. WHITTED. Managing geometric complexity with enhanced procedural models. In *Computer Graphics (SIGGRAPH '86 Proceedings)* (Aug. 1986), D. C. Evans and R. J. Athay, Eds., vol. 20, 189–195.

[8] S. ANSALDI, L. DE FLORIANI, AND B. FALCIDIENO. Geometric modeling of solid objects by using a face adjacency graph representation. In *Computer Graphics (SIGGRAPH '85 Proceedings)* (July 1985), B. A. Barsky, Ed., vol. 19, 131–139.

[9] B. APGAR, B. BERSACK, AND A. MAMMEN. A display system for the Stellar graphics supercomputer model GS1000. In *Computer Graphics (SIGGRAPH '88 Proceedings)* (Aug. 1988), J. Dill, Ed., vol. 22, 255–262.

[10] J. ARVO AND D. B. KIRK. Fast ray tracing by ray classification. In *Computer Graphics (SIGGRAPH '87 Proceedings)* (July 1987), M. C. Stone, Ed., vol. 21, 55–64.

[11] J. ARVO AND D. B. KIRK. Particle transport and image synthesis. In *Computer Graphics (SIGGRAPH '90 Proceedings)* (Aug. 1990), F. Baskett, Ed., vol. 24, 63–66.

[12] L. AUPPERLE AND P. HANRAHAN. A hierarchical illumination algorithm for surfaces with glossy reflection. In *Computer Graphics (SIGGRAPH '93 Proceedings)* (Aug. 1993), J. T. Kajiya, Ed., vol. 27, 155–162.

[13] G. AVRAHAMI, K. P. BROOKS, AND M. H. BROWN. A two-view approach to constructing user interfaces. In *Computer Graphics (SIGGRAPH '89 Proceedings)* (July 1989), J. Lane, Ed., vol. 23, 137–146.

[14] C. L. BAJAJ AND I. IHM. Smoothing polyhedra using implicit algebraic splines. In *Computer Graphics (SIGGRAPH '92 Proceedings)* (July 1992), E. E. Catmull, Ed., vol. 26, 79–88.

[15] M. BAJURA, H. FUCHS, AND R. OHBUCHI. Merging virtual objects with the real world: Seeing ultrasound imagery within the patient. In *Computer Graphics (SIGGRAPH '92 Proceedings)* (July 1992), E. E. Catmull, Ed., vol. 26, 203–210.

[16] D. BARAFF. Analytical methods for dynamic simulation of non-penetrating rigid bodies. In *Computer Graphics (SIGGRAPH '89 Proceedings)* (July 1989), J. Lane, Ed., vol. 23, 223–232.

[17] D. BARAFF. Curved surfaces and coherence for non-penetrating rigid body simulation. In *Computer Graphics (SIGGRAPH '90 Proceedings)* (Aug. 1990), F. Baskett, Ed., vol. 24, 19–28.

[18] D. BARAFF. Coping with friction for non-penetrating rigid body simulation. In *Computer Graphics (SIGGRAPH '91 Proceedings)* (July 1991), T. W. Sederberg, Ed., vol. 25, 31–40.

[19] D. BARAFF AND A. WITKIN. Dynamic simulation of non-penetrating flexible bodies. In *Computer Graphics (SIGGRAPH '92 Proceedings)* (July 1992), E. E. Catmull, Ed., vol. 26, 303–308.

[20] A. C. BARKANS. High speed high quality antialiased vector generation. In *Computer Graphics (SIGGRAPH '90 Proceedings)* (Aug. 1990), F. Baskett, Ed., vol. 24, 319–326.

[21] M. F. BARNSLEY, A. JACQUIN, F. MALASSENET, L. REUTER, AND A. D. SLOAN. Harnessing chaos for image synthesis. In *Computer Graphics (SIGGRAPH '88 Proceedings)* (Aug. 1988), J. Dill, Ed., vol. 22, 131–140.

[22] A. H. BARR. Global and local deformations of solid primitives. In *Computer Graphics (SIGGRAPH '84 Proceedings)* (July 1984), H. Christiansen, Ed., vol. 18, 21–30.

[23] A. H. BARR. Ray tracing deformed surfaces. In *Computer Graphics (SIGGRAPH '86 Proceedings)* (Aug. 1986), D. C. Evans and R. J. Athay, Eds., vol. 20, 287–296.

[24] A. H. BARR, B. CURRIN, S. GABRIEL, AND J. F. HUGHES. Smooth interpolation of orientations with angular velocity constraints using quaternions. In *Computer Graphics (SIGGRAPH '92 Proceedings)* (July 1992), E. E. Catmull, Ed., vol. 26, 313–320.

[25] P. J. BARRY AND R. N. GOLDMAN. A recursive evaluation algorithm for a class of Catmull-Rom splines. In *Computer Graphics (SIGGRAPH '88 Proceedings)* (Aug. 1988), J. Dill, Ed., vol. 22, 199–204.

[26] R. H. BARTELS AND R. T. HARDOCK. Curve-to-curve associations in spline-based inbetweening and sweeping. In *Computer Graphics (SIGGRAPH '89 Proceedings)* (July 1989), J. Lane, Ed., vol. 23, 167–174.

[27] R. BARZEL AND A. H. BARR. A modeling system based on dynamic constraints. In *Computer Graphics (SIGGRAPH '88 Proceedings)* (Aug. 1988), J. Dill, Ed., vol. 22, 179–188.

[28] D. R. BAUM, S. MANN, K. P. SMITH, AND J. M. WINGET. Making radiosity usable: Automatic preprocessing and meshing techniques for the generation of accurate radiosity solutions. In *Computer Graphics (SIGGRAPH '91 Proceedings)* (July 1991), T. W. Sederberg, Ed., vol. 25, 51–60.

[29] D. R. BAUM, H. E. RUSHMEIER, AND J. M. WINGET. Improving radiosity solutions through the use of analytically determined form-factors. In *Computer Graphics (SIGGRAPH '89 Proceedings)* (July 1989), J. Lane, Ed., vol. 23, 325–334.

[30] B. G. BECKER AND N. L. MAX. Smooth transitions between bump rendering algorithms. In *Computer Graphics (SIGGRAPH '93 Proceedings)* (Aug. 1993), J. T. Kajiya, Ed., vol. 27, 183–190.

[31] T. BEIER AND S. NEELY. Feature-based image metamorphosis. In *Computer Graphics (SIGGRAPH '92 Proceedings)* (July 1992), E. E. Catmull, Ed., vol. 26, 35–42.

[32] C. BENNIS, J.-M. VÉZIEN, G. IGLÉSIAS, AND A. GAGALOWICZ. Piecewise surface flattening for non-distorted texture mapping. In *Computer Graphics*

(SIGGRAPH '91 Proceedings) (July 1991), T. W. Sederberg, Ed., vol. 25, 237–246.

[33] L. D. BERGMAN, H. FUCHS, E. GRANT, AND S. SPACH. Image rendering by adaptive refinement. In *Computer Graphics (SIGGRAPH '86 Proceedings)* (Aug. 1986), D. C. Evans and R. J. Athay, Eds., vol. 20, 29–37.

[34] L. D. BERGMAN, J. S. RICHARDSON, D. C. RICHARDSON, AND F. P. BROOKS JR. VIEW – an exploratory molecular visualization system with user-definable interaction sequences. In *Computer Graphics (SIGGRAPH '93 Proceedings)* (Aug. 1993), J. T. Kajiya, Ed., vol. 27, 117–126.

[35] E. A. BIER AND M. C. STONE. Snap-dragging. In *Computer Graphics (SIGGRAPH '86 Proceedings)* (Aug. 1986), D. C. Evans and R. J. Athay, Eds., vol. 20, 233–240.

[36] E. A. BIER, M. C. STONE, K. PIER, W. BUXTON, AND T. DEROSE. Toolglass and Magic Lenses: The see-through interface. In *Computer Graphics (SIGGRAPH '93 Proceedings)* (Aug. 1993), J. T. Kajiya, Ed., vol. 27, 73–80.

[37] G. BISHOP AND D. M. WEIMER. Fast Phong shading. In *Computer Graphics (SIGGRAPH '86 Proceedings)* (Aug. 1986), D. C. Evans and R. J. Athay, Eds., vol. 20, 103–106.

[38] J. BLOOMENTHAL. Modeling the mighty maple. In *Computer Graphics (SIGGRAPH '85 Proceedings)* (July 1985), B. A. Barsky, Ed., vol. 19, 305–311.

[39] J. BLOOMENTHAL AND K. SHOEMAKE. Convolution surfaces. In *Computer Graphics (SIGGRAPH '91 Proceedings)* (July 1991), T. W. Sederberg, Ed., vol. 25, 251–256.

[40] C. F. BORGES. Trichromatic approximation for computer graphics illumination models. In *Computer Graphics (SIGGRAPH '91 Proceedings)* (July 1991), T. W. Sederberg, Ed., vol. 25, 101–104.

[41] C. BOUVILLE. Bounding ellipsoids for ray-fractal intersection. In *Computer Graphics (SIGGRAPH '85 Proceedings)* (July 1985), B. A. Barsky, Ed., vol. 19, 45–52.

[42] F. P. BROOKS JR., M. OUH-YOUNG, J. J. BATTER, AND P. J. KILPATRICK. Project GROPE — Haptic displays for scientific visualization. In *Computer Graphics (SIGGRAPH '90 Proceedings)* (Aug. 1990), F. Baskett, Ed., vol. 24, 177–185.

[43] L. S. BROTMAN AND A. N. NETRAVALI. Motion interpolation by optimal control. In *Computer Graphics (SIGGRAPH '88 Proceedings)* (Aug. 1988), J. Dill, Ed., vol. 22, 309–315.

[44] M. H. BROWN AND R. SEDGWICK. A system for algorithm animation. In *Computer Graphics (SIGGRAPH '84 Proceedings)* (July 1984), H. Christiansen, Ed., vol. 18, 177–186.

[45] A. BRUDERLIN AND T. W. CALVERT. Goal-directed, dynamic animation of human walking. In *Computer Graphics (SIGGRAPH '89 Proceedings)* (July 1989), J. Lane, Ed., vol. 23, 233–242.

[46] C. BUCKALEW AND D. FUSSELL. Illumination networks: Fast realistic rendering with general reflectance functions. In *Computer Graphics (SIGGRAPH '89 Proceedings)* (July 1989), J. Lane, Ed., vol. 23, 89–98.

[47] W. BUXTON, R. HILL, AND P. ROWLEY. Issues and techniques in touch-sensitive tablet input. In *Computer Graphics (SIGGRAPH '85 Proceedings)* (July 1985), B. A. Barsky, Ed., vol. 19, 215–224.

[48] B. CABRAL AND L. C. LEEDOM. Imaging vector fields using line integral convolution. In *Computer Graphics (SIGGRAPH '93 Proceedings)* (Aug. 1993), J. T. Kajiya, Ed., vol. 27, 263–272.

[49] B. CABRAL, N. MAX, AND R. SPRINGMEYER. Bidirectional reflection functions from surface bump maps. In *Computer Graphics (SIGGRAPH '87 Proceedings)* (July 1987), M. C. Stone, Ed., vol. 21, 273–281.

[50] G. CAMBELL, T. A. DEFANTI, J. FREDERIKSEN, S. A. JOYCE, L. A. LESKE, J. A. LINDBERG, AND D. J. SANDIN. Two bit/pixel full color encoding. In *Computer Graphics (SIGGRAPH '86 Proceedings)* (Aug. 1986), D. C. Evans and R. J. Athay, Eds., vol. 20, 215–223.

[51] A. T. CAMPBELL III AND D. S. FUSSELL. Adaptive mesh generation for global diffuse illumination. In *Computer Graphics (SIGGRAPH '90 Proceedings)* (Aug. 1990), F. Baskett, Ed., vol. 24, 155–164.

[52] L. CARDELLI AND R. PIKE. Squeak: A language for communicating with mice. In *Computer Graphics (SIGGRAPH '85 Proceedings)* (July 1985), B. A. Barsky, Ed., vol. 19, 199–204.

[53] M. CARIGNAN, Y. YANG, N. M. THALMANN, AND D. THALMANN. Dressing animated synthetic actors with complex deformable clothes. In *Computer Graphics (SIGGRAPH '92 Proceedings)* (July 1992), E. E. Catmull, Ed., vol. 26, 99–104.

[54] L. CARPENTER. The A-buffer, an antialiased hidden surface method. In *Computer Graphics (SIGGRAPH '84 Proceedings)* (July 1984), H. Christiansen, Ed., vol. 18, 103–108.

[55] E. CATMULL. An analytic visible surface algorithm for independent pixel processing. In *Computer Graphics (SIGGRAPH '84 Proceedings)* (July 1984), H. Christiansen, Ed., vol. 18, 109–115.

[56] G. CELNIKER AND D. GOSSARD. Deformable curve and surface finite elements for free-form shape design. In *Computer Graphics (SIGGRAPH '91 Proceedings)* (July 1991), T. W. Sederberg, Ed., vol. 25, 257–266.

[57] J. E. CHADWICK, D. R. HAUMANN, AND R. E. PARENT. Layered construction for deformable animated characters. In *Computer Graphics (SIGGRAPH '89 Proceedings)* (July 1989), J. Lane, Ed., vol. 23, 243–252.

[58] S.-L. CHANG, M. SHANTZ, AND R. ROCCHETTI. Rendering cubic curves and surfaces with integer adaptive forward differencing. In *Computer Graphics (SIGGRAPH '89 Proceedings)* (July 1989), J. Lane, Ed., vol. 23, 157–166.

[59] D. T. CHEN AND D. ZELTZER. Pump it up: Computer animation of a biomechanically based model of muscle using the finite element method. In *Computer Graphics (SIGGRAPH '92 Proceedings)* (July 1992), E. E. Catmull, Ed., vol. 26, 89–98.

[60] H. CHEN AND E.-H. WU. An efficient radiosity solution for bump texture generation. In *Computer Graphics (SIGGRAPH '90 Proceedings)* (Aug. 1990), F. Baskett, Ed., vol. 24, 125–134.

[61] M. CHEN, S. J. MOUNTFORD, AND A. SELLEN. A study in interactive 3-D rotation using 2-D control devices. In *Computer Graphics (SIGGRAPH '88 Proceedings)* (Aug. 1988), J. Dill, Ed., vol. 22, 121–129.

[62] S. E. CHEN. Incremental radiosity: An extension of progressive radiosity to an interactive image synthesis system. In *Computer Graphics (SIGGRAPH '90 Proceedings)* (Aug. 1990), F. Baskett, Ed., vol. 24, 135–144.

[63] S. E. CHEN, H. E. RUSHMEIER, G. MILLER, AND D. TURNER. A progressive multi-pass method for global illumination. In *Computer Graphics (SIGGRAPH '91 Proceedings)* (July 1991), T. W. Sederberg, Ed., vol. 25, 165–174.

[64] S. E. CHEN AND L. WILLIAMS. View interpolation for image synthesis. In *Computer Graphics (SIGGRAPH '93 Proceedings)* (Aug. 1993), J. T. Kajiya, Ed., vol. 27, 279–288.

[65] N. CHIN AND S. FEINER. Near real-time shadow generation using BSP trees. In *Computer Graphics (SIGGRAPH '89 Proceedings)* (July 1989), J. Lane, Ed., vol. 23, 99–106.

[66] J. CLARK. A TeleComputer. In *Computer Graphics (SIGGRAPH '92 Proceedings)* (July 1992), E. E. Catmull, Ed., vol. 26, 19–23.

[67] M. F. COHEN. Interactive spacetime control for animation. In *Computer Graphics (SIGGRAPH '92 Proceedings)* (July 1992), E. E. Catmull, Ed., vol. 26, 293–302.

[68] M. F. COHEN, S. E. CHEN, J. R. WALLACE, AND D. P. GREENBERG. A progressive refinement approach to fast radiosity image generation. In *Computer Graphics (SIGGRAPH '88 Proceedings)* (Aug. 1988), J. Dill, Ed., vol. 22, 75–84.

[69] M. F. COHEN AND D. P. GREENBERG. The Hemi-Cube: A radiosity solution for complex environments. In *Computer Graphics (SIGGRAPH '85 Proceedings)* (Aug. 1985), B. A. Barsky, Ed., vol. 19, 31–40.

[70] R. L. COOK. Shade trees. In *Computer Graphics (SIGGRAPH '84 Proceedings)* (July 1984), H. Christiansen, Ed., vol. 18, 223–231.

[71] R. L. COOK, L. CARPENTER, AND E. CATMULL. The Reyes image rendering architecture. In *Computer Graphics (SIGGRAPH '87 Proceedings)* (July 1987), M. C. Stone, Ed., 95–102.

[72] R. L. COOK, T. PORTER, AND L. CARPENTER. Distributed ray tracing. In *Computer Graphics (SIGGRAPH '84 Proceedings)* (July 1984), H. Christiansen, Ed., vol. 18, 137–145.

[73] S. COQUILLART. Extended free-form deformation: A sculpturing tool for 3D geometric modeling. In *Computer Graphics (SIGGRAPH '90 Proceedings)* (Aug. 1990), F. Baskett, Ed., vol. 24, 187–196.

[74] S. COQUILLART AND P. JANCÉNE. Animated free-form deformation: An interactive animation technique. In *Computer Graphics (SIGGRAPH '91 Proceedings)* (July 1991), T. W. Sederberg, Ed., vol. 25, 23–26.

[75] S. M. COURTER AND J. A. BREWER III. Automated conversion of curvilinear wire-frame models to surface boundary models; A topological approach. In *Computer Graphics (SIGGRAPH '86 Proceedings)* (Aug. 1986), D. C. Evans and R. J. Athay, Eds., vol. 20, 171–178.

[76] G. A. CROCKER. Invisibility coherence for faster scan-line hidden surface algorithms. In *Computer Graphics (SIGGRAPH '84 Proceedings)* (July 1984), H. Christiansen, Ed., vol. 18, 95–102.

[77] G. A. CROCKER AND W. F. REINKE. Boundary evaluation of non-convex primitives to produce parametric trimmed surfaces. In *Computer Graphics (SIGGRAPH '87 Proceedings)* (July 1987), M. C. Stone, Ed., vol. 21, 129–136.

[78] F. C. CROW. Summed-area tables for texture mapping. In *Computer Graphics (SIGGRAPH '84 Proceedings)* (July 1984), H. Christiansen, Ed., vol. 18, 207–212.

[79] C. CRUZ-NEIRA, D. J. SANDIN, AND T. A. DEFANTI. Surround-screen projection-based virtual reality: The design and implementation of the CAVE. In *Computer*

Graphics (SIGGRAPH '93 Proceedings) (Aug. 1993), J. T. Kajiya, Ed., vol. 27, 135–142.

[80] P. DE REFFYE, C. EDELIN, J. FRANCON, M. JAEGER, AND C. PUECH. Plant models faithful to botanical structure and development. In *Computer Graphics (SIGGRAPH '88 Proceedings)* (Aug. 1988), J. Dill, Ed., vol. 22, 151–158.

[81] M. F. DEERING. High resolution virtual reality. In *Computer Graphics (SIGGRAPH '92 Proceedings)* (July 1992), E. E. Catmull, Ed., vol. 26, 195–202.

[82] M. F. DEERING AND S. R. NELSON. Leo: A system for cost-effective 3D shaded graphics. In *Computer Graphics (SIGGRAPH '93 Proceedings)* (Aug. 1993), J. T. Kajiya, Ed., vol. 27, 101–108.

[83] M. F. DEERING, S. WINNER, B. SCHEDIWY, C. DUFFY, AND N. HUNT. The triangle processor and normal vector shader: A VLSI system for high performance graphics. In *Computer Graphics (SIGGRAPH '88 Proceedings)* (Aug. 1988), J. Dill, Ed., vol. 22, 21–30.

[84] S. DEMKO, L. HODGES, AND B. NAYLOR. Construction of fractal objects with iterated function systems. In *Computer Graphics (SIGGRAPH '85 Proceedings)* (July 1985), B. A. Barsky, Ed., vol. 19, 271–278.

[85] M. J. DENBER AND P. M. TURNER. A differential compiler for computer animation. In *Computer Graphics (SIGGRAPH '86 Proceedings)* (Aug. 1986), D. C. Evans and R. J. Athay, Eds., vol. 20, 21–27.

[86] R. DEYO, J. A. BIGGS, AND P. DOENGES. Getting graphics in gear: Graphics and dynamics in driving simulation. In *Computer Graphics (SIGGRAPH '88 Proceedings)* (Aug. 1988), J. Dill, Ed., vol. 22, 317–326.

[87] M. A. Z. DIPPÉ AND J. SWENSEN. An adaptive subdivision algorithm and parallel architecture for realistic image synthesis. In *Computer Graphics (SIGGRAPH '84 Proceedings)* (July 1984), H. Christiansen, Ed., vol. 18, 149–158.

[88] M. A. Z. DIPPÉ AND E. H. WOLD. Antialiasing through stochastic sampling. In *Computer Graphics (SIGGRAPH '85 Proceedings)* (July 1985), B. A. Barsky, Ed., vol. 19, 69–78.

[89] D. DOBKIN, L. GUIBAS, J. HERSHBERGER, AND J. SNOEYINK. An efficient algorithm for finding the CSG representation of a simple polygon. In *Computer Graphics (SIGGRAPH '88 Proceedings)* (Aug. 1988), J. Dill, Ed., vol. 22, 31–40.

[90] J. O. DORSEY, F. X. SILLION, AND D. P. GREENBERG. Design and simulation of opera lighting and projection effects. In *Computer Graphics (SIGGRAPH '91 Proceedings)* (July 1991), T. W. Sederberg, Ed., vol. 25, 41–50.

[91] R. A. DREBIN, L. CARPENTER, AND P. HANRAHAN. Volume rendering. In *Computer Graphics (SIGGRAPH '88 Proceedings)* (Aug. 1988), J. Dill, Ed., vol. 22, 65–74.

[92] T. DUFF. Compositing 3-D rendered images. In *Computer Graphics (SIGGRAPH '85 Proceedings)* (July 1985), B. A. Barsky, Ed., vol. 19, 41–44.

[93] T. DUFF. Interval arithmetic and recursive subdivision for implicit functions and constructive solid geometry. In *Computer Graphics (SIGGRAPH '92 Proceedings)* (July 1992), E. E. Catmull, Ed., vol. 26, 131–138.

[94] D. S. EBERT AND R. E. PARENT. Rendering and animation of gaseous phenomena by combining fast volume and scanline A-buffer techniques. In *Computer Graphics (SIGGRAPH '90 Proceedings)* (Aug. 1990), F. Baskett, Ed., vol. 24, 357–366.

[95] G. ELBER AND E. COHEN. Hidden curve removal for free form surfaces. In *Computer Graphics (SIGGRAPH '90 Proceedings)* (Aug. 1990), F. Baskett, Ed., vol. 24, 95–104.

[96] H. FERGUSON, A. ROCKWOOD, AND J. COX. Topological design of sculptured surfaces. In *Computer Graphics (SIGGRAPH '92 Proceedings)* (July 1992), E. E. Catmull, Ed., vol. 26, 149–156.

[97] K. P. FISHKIN AND B. A. BARSKY. A family of new algorithms for soft filling. In *Computer Graphics (SIGGRAPH '84 Proceedings)* (July 1984), H. Christiansen, Ed., vol. 18, 235–244.

[98] D. R. FORSEY AND R. H. BARTELS. Hierarchical B-spline refinement. In *Computer Graphics (SIGGRAPH '88 Proceedings)* (Aug. 1988), J. Dill, Ed., vol. 22, 205–212.

[99] A. FOURNIER AND E. FIUME. Constant-time filtering with space-variant kernels. In *Computer Graphics (SIGGRAPH '88 Proceedings)* (Aug. 1988), J. Dill, Ed., vol. 22, 229–238.

[100] A. FOURNIER AND W. T. REEVES. A simple model of ocean waves. In *Computer Graphics (SIGGRAPH '86 Proceedings)* (Aug. 1986), D. C. Evans and R. J. Athay, Eds., vol. 20, 75–84.

[101] D. R. FOWLER, H. MEINHARDT, AND P. PRUSINKIEWICZ. Modeling seashells. In *Computer Graphics (SIGGRAPH '92 Proceedings)* (July 1992), E. E. Catmull, Ed., vol. 26, 379–388.

[102] D. R. FOWLER, P. PRUSINKIEWICZ, AND J. BATTJES. A collision-based model of spiral phyllotaxis. In *Computer Graphics (SIGGRAPH '92 Proceedings)* (July 1992), E. E. Catmull, Ed., vol. 26, 361–368.

[103] W. R. FRANKLIN AND M. S. KANKANHALLI. Parallel object-space hidden surface removal. In *Computer Graphics (SIGGRAPH '90 Proceedings)* (Aug. 1990), F. Baskett, Ed., vol. 24, 87–94.

[104] W. T. FREEMAN, E. H. ADELSON, AND D. J. HEEGER. Motion without movement. In *Computer Graphics (SIGGRAPH '91 Proceedings)* (July 1991), T. W. Sederberg, Ed., vol. 25, 27–30.

[105] M. FRIEDELL. Automatic synthesis of graphical object descriptions. In *Computer Graphics (SIGGRAPH '84 Proceedings)* (July 1984), H. Christiansen, Ed., vol. 18, 53–62.

[106] H. FUCHS, J. GOLDFEATHER, J. P. HULTQUIST, S. SPACH, J. D. AUSTIN, F. P. BROOKS, JR., J. G. EYLES, AND J. POULTON. Fast spheres, shadows, textures, transparencies, and image enhancements in Pixel-Planes. In *Computer Graphics (SIGGRAPH '85 Proceedings)* (July 1985), B. A. Barsky, Ed., vol. 19, 111–120.

[107] H. FUCHS, J. POULTON, J. EYLES, T. GREER, J. GOLDFEATHER, D. ELLSWORTH, S. MOLNAR, G. TURK, B. TEBBS, AND L. ISRAEL. Pixel-Planes 5: A heterogeneous multiprocessor graphics system using processor-enhanced memories. In *Computer Graphics (SIGGRAPH '89 Proceedings)* (July 1989), J. Lane, Ed., vol. 23, 79–88.

[108] T. A. FUNKHOUSER AND C. H. SÉQUIN. Adaptive display algorithm for interactive frame rates during visualization of complex virtual environments. In *Computer Graphics (SIGGRAPH '93 Proceedings)* (Aug. 1993), J. T. Kajiya, Ed., vol. 27, 247–254.

[109] R. S. GALLAGHER AND J. C. NAGTEGAAL. An efficient 3D visualization technique for finite element models and other coarse volumes. In *Computer Graphics (SIGGRAPH '89 Proceedings)* (July 1989), J. Lane, Ed., vol. 23, 185–194.

[110] T. A. GALYEAN AND J. F. HUGHES. Sculpting: An interactive volumetric modeling technique. In *Computer Graphics (SIGGRAPH '91 Proceedings)* (July 1991), T. W. Sederberg, Ed., vol. 25, 267–274.

[111] M. GANGNET, J.-C. HERVÉ, T. PUDET, AND J.-M. VAN THONG. Incremental computation of planar maps. In *Computer Graphics (SIGGRAPH '89 Proceedings)* (July 1989), J. Lane, Ed., vol. 23, 345–354.

[112] G. Y. GARDNER. Simulation of natural scenes using textured quadric surfaces. In *Computer Graphics (SIGGRAPH '84 Proceedings)* (July 1984), H. Christiansen, Ed., vol. 18, 11–20.

[113] G. Y. GARDNER. Visual simulation of clouds. In *Computer Graphics (SIGGRAPH '85 Proceedings)* (July 1985), B. A. Barsky, Ed., vol. 19, 297–303.

[114] M. GASCUEL. An implicit formulation for precise contact modeling between flexible solids. In *Computer Graphics (SIGGRAPH '93 Proceedings)* (Aug. 1993), J. T. Kajiya, Ed., vol. 27, 313–320.

[115] N. GHARACHORLOO, S. GUPTA, E. HOKENEK, P. BALASUBRAMANIAN, B. BOGHOLTZ, C. MATHIEU, AND C. ZOULAS. Subnanosecond pixel rendering with million transistor chips. In *Computer Graphics (SIGGRAPH '88 Proceedings)* (Aug. 1988), J. Dill, Ed., vol. 22, 41–49.

[116] N. GHARACHORLOO, S. GUPTA, R. F. SPROULL, AND I. E. SUTHERLAND. A characterization of ten rasterization techniques. In *Computer Graphics (SIGGRAPH '89 Proceedings)* (July 1989), J. Lane, Ed., vol. 23, 355–368.

[117] M. GIRARD AND A. A. MACIEJEWSKI. Computational modeling for the computer animation of legged figures. In *Computer Graphics (SIGGRAPH '85 Proceedings)* (July 1985), B. A. Barsky, Ed., vol. 19, 263–270.

[118] A. GLASSNER. Adaptive precision in texture mapping. In *Computer Graphics (SIGGRAPH '86 Proceedings)* (Aug. 1986), D. C. Evans and R. J. Athay, Eds., vol. 20, 297–306.

[119] M. GLEICHER AND A. WITKIN. Through-the-lens camera control. In *Computer Graphics (SIGGRAPH '92 Proceedings)* (July 1992), E. E. Catmull, Ed., vol. 26, 331–340.

[120] J. GOLDFEATHER, J. P. M. HULTQUIST, AND H. FUCHS. Fast constructive-solid geometry display in the Pixel-Powers graphics system. In *Computer Graphics (SIGGRAPH '86 Proceedings)* (Aug. 1986), D. C. Evans and R. J. Athay, Eds., vol. 20, 107–116.

[121] C. M. GORAL, K. E. TORRANCE, D. P. GREENBERG, AND B. BATTAILE. Modeling the interaction of light between diffuse surfaces. In *Computer Graphics (SIGGRAPH '84 Proceedings)* (July 1984), H. Christiansen, Ed., vol. 18, 213–222.

[122] S. J. GORTLER, P. SCHRÖDER, M. F. COHEN, AND P. HANRAHAN. Wavelet radiosity. In *Computer Graphics (SIGGRAPH '93 Proceedings)* (Aug. 1993), J. T. Kajiya, Ed., vol. 27, 221–230.

[123] S. GOTTSCHALK AND J. F. HUGHES. Autocalibration for virtual environments tracking hardware. In *Computer Graphics (SIGGRAPH '93 Proceedings)* (Aug. 1993), J. T. Kajiya, Ed., vol. 27, 65–72.

[124] J.-P. GOURRET, N. M. THALMANN, AND D. THALMANN. Simulation of object and human skin deformations in a grasping task. In *Computer Graphics (SIGGRAPH '89 Proceedings)* (July 1989), J. Lane, Ed., vol. 23, 21–30.

[125] C. W. GRANT. Integrated analytic spatial and temporal anti-aliasing for polyhedra in 4-space. In *Computer Graphics (SIGGRAPH '85 Proceedings)* (July 1985), B. A. Barsky, Ed., vol. 19, 79–84.

[126] M. GREEN. The University Of Alberta User Interface Management System. In *Computer Graphics (SIGGRAPH '85 Proceedings)* (July 1985), B. A. Barsky, Ed., vol. 19, 205–214.

[127] N. GREENE. Voxel space automata: Modeling with stochastic growth processes in voxel space. In *Computer Graphics (SIGGRAPH '89 Proceedings)* (July 1989), J. Lane, Ed., vol. 23, 175–184.

[128] N. GREENE, M. KASS, AND G. MILLER. Hierarchical Z-buffer visibility. In *Computer Graphics (SIGGRAPH '93 Proceedings)* (Aug. 1993), J. T. Kajiya, Ed., vol. 27, 231–238.

[129] R. GREENE. The drawing prism: A versatile graphic input device. In *Computer Graphics (SIGGRAPH '85 Proceedings)* (July 1985), B. A. Barsky, Ed., vol. 19, 103–110.

[130] B. K. GUENTER, H. C. YUN, AND R. M. MERSEREAU. Motion compensated compression of computer animation frames. In *Computer Graphics (SIGGRAPH '93 Proceedings)* (Aug. 1993), J. T. Kajiya, Ed., vol. 27, 297–304.

[131] C. GUNN. Discrete groups and visualization of three-dimensional manifolds. In *Computer Graphics (SIGGRAPH '93 Proceedings)* (Aug. 1993), J. T. Kajiya, Ed., vol. 27, 255–262.

[132] P. E. HAEBERLI. ConMan: A visual programming language for interactive graphics. In *Computer Graphics (SIGGRAPH '88 Proceedings)* (Aug. 1988), J. Dill, Ed., vol. 22, 103–111.

[133] P. E. HAEBERLI. Paint by numbers: Abstract image representations. In *Computer Graphics (SIGGRAPH '90 Proceedings)* (Aug. 1990), F. Baskett, Ed., vol. 24, 207–214.

[134] P. E. HAEBERLI AND K. AKELEY. The accumulation buffer: Hardware support for high-quality rendering. In *Computer Graphics (SIGGRAPH '90 Proceedings)* (Aug. 1990), F. Baskett, Ed., vol. 24, 309–318.

[135] J. K. HAHN. Realistic animation of rigid bodies. In *Computer Graphics (SIGGRAPH '88 Proceedings)* (Aug. 1988), J. Dill, Ed., vol. 22, 299–308.

[136] M. HALSTEAD, M. KASS, AND T. DEROSE. Efficient, fair interpolation using Catmull-Clark surfaces. In *Computer Graphics (SIGGRAPH '93 Proceedings)* (Aug. 1993), J. T. Kajiya, Ed., vol. 27, 35–44.

[137] P. HANRAHAN AND P. E. HAEBERLI. Direct WYSIWYG painting and texturing on 3D shapes. In *Computer Graphics (SIGGRAPH '90 Proceedings)* (Aug. 1990), F. Baskett, Ed., vol. 24, 215–223.

[138] P. HANRAHAN AND W. KRUEGER. Reflection from layered surfaces due to subsurface scattering. In *Computer Graphics (SIGGRAPH '93 Proceedings)* (Aug. 1993), J. T. Kajiya, Ed., vol. 27, 165–174.

[139] P. HANRAHAN AND J. LAWSON. A language for shading and lighting calculations. In *Computer Graphics (SIGGRAPH '90 Proceedings)* (Aug. 1990), F. Baskett, Ed., vol. 24, 289–298.

[140] P. HANRAHAN, D. SALZMAN, AND L. AUPPERLE. A rapid hierarchical radiosity algorithm. In *Computer Graphics (SIGGRAPH '91 Proceedings)* (July 1991), T. W. Sederberg, Ed., vol. 25, 197–206.

[141] C. B. HARRELL AND F. FOULADI. Graphics rendering architecture for a high performance desktop workstation. In *Computer Graphics (SIGGRAPH '93 Proceedings)* (Aug. 1993), J. T. Kajiya, Ed., vol. 27, 93–100.

[142] J. C. HART AND T. A. DEFANTI. Efficient anti-aliased rendering of 3D linear fractals. In *Computer Graphics (SIGGRAPH '91 Proceedings)* (July 1991), T. W. Sederberg, Ed., vol. 25, 91–100.

[143] J. C. HART, D. J. SANDIN, AND L. H. KAUFFMAN. Ray tracing deterministic 3-D fractals. In *Computer Graphics (SIGGRAPH '89 Proceedings)* (July 1989), J. Lane, Ed., vol. 23, 289–296.

[144] X. D. HE, P. O. HEYNEN, R. L. PHILLIPS, K. E. TORRANCE, D. H. SALESIN, AND D. P. GREENBERG. A fast and accurate light reflection model. In *Computer Graphics (SIGGRAPH '92 Proceedings)* (July 1992), E. E. Catmull, Ed., vol. 26, 253–254.

[145] X. D. HE, K. E. TORRANCE, F. X. SILLION, AND D. P. GREENBERG. A comprehensive physical model for light reflection. In *Computer Graphics (SIGGRAPH '91 Proceedings)* (July 1991), T. W. Sederberg, Ed., vol. 25, 175–186.

[146] P. S. HECKBERT. Filtering by repeated integration. In *Computer Graphics (SIGGRAPH '86 Proceedings)* (Aug. 1986), D. C. Evans and R. J. Athay, Eds., vol. 20, 315–321.

[147] P. S. HECKBERT. Ray tracing Jell-O brand gelatin. In *Computer Graphics (SIGGRAPH '87 Proceedings)* (July 1987), M. C. Stone, Ed., vol. 21, 73–74.

[148] P. S. HECKBERT. Adaptive radiosity textures for bidirectional ray tracing. In *Computer Graphics (SIGGRAPH '90 Proceedings)* (Aug. 1990), F. Baskett, Ed., vol. 24, 145–154.

[149] P. S. HECKBERT AND P. HANRAHAN. Beam tracing polygonal objects. In *Computer Graphics (SIGGRAPH '84 Proceedings)* (July 1984), H. Christiansen, Ed., vol. 18, 119–127.

[150] R. D. HERSCH. Character generation under grid constraints. In *Computer Graphics (SIGGRAPH '87 Proceedings)* (July 1987), M. C. Stone, Ed., vol. 21, 243–252.

[151] R. D. HERSCH AND C. BÉTRISEY. Model-based matching and hinting of fonts. In *Computer Graphics (SIGGRAPH '91 Proceedings)* (July 1991), T. W. Sederberg, Ed., vol. 25, 71–80.

[152] H. HOPPE, T. DEROSE, T. DUCHAMP, J. MCDONALD, AND W. STUETZLE. Surface reconstruction from unorganized points. In *Computer Graphics (SIGGRAPH '92 Proceedings)* (July 1992), E. E. Catmull, Ed., vol. 26, 71–78.

[153] H. HOPPE, T. DEROSE, T. DUCHAMP, J. MCDONALD, AND W. STUETZLE. Mesh optimization. In *Computer Graphics (SIGGRAPH '93 Proceedings)* (Aug. 1993), J. T. Kajiya, Ed., vol. 27, 19–26.

[154] W. M. HSU, J. F. HUGHES, AND H. KAUFMAN. Direct manipulation of free-form deformations. In *Computer Graphics (SIGGRAPH '92 Proceedings)* (July 1992), E. E. Catmull, Ed., vol. 26, 177–184.

[155] J. F. HUGHES. Scheduled Fourier volume morphing. In *Computer Graphics (SIGGRAPH '92 Proceedings)* (July 1992), E. E. Catmull, Ed., vol. 26, 43–46.

[156] K. ICHI ANJYO, Y. USAMI, AND T. KURIHARA. A simple method for extracting the natural beauty of hair. In *Computer Graphics (SIGGRAPH '92 Proceedings)* (July 1992), E. E. Catmull, Ed., vol. 26, 111–120.

[157] D. S. IMMEL, M. F. COHEN, AND D. P. GREENBERG. A radiosity method for non-diffuse environments. In *Computer Graphics (SIGGRAPH '86 Proceedings)* (Aug. 1986), D. C. Evans and R. J. Athay, Eds., vol. 20, 133–142.

[158] P. M. ISAACS AND M. F. COHEN. Controlling dynamic simulation with kinematic constraints, behavior functions and inverse dynamics. In *Computer Graphics (SIGGRAPH '87 Proceedings)* (July 1987), M. C. Stone, Ed., vol. 21, 215–224.

[159] H. IWATA. Artificial reality with force-feedback: Development of desktop virtual space with compact master manipulator. In *Computer Graphics (SIGGRAPH '90 Proceedings)* (Aug. 1990), F. Baskett, Ed., vol. 24, 165–170.

[160] B. JOE. Discrete beta-splines. In *Computer Graphics (SIGGRAPH '87 Proceedings)* (July 1987), M. C. Stone, Ed., vol. 21, 137–144.

[161] K. I. JOY AND M. N. BHETANABHOTLA. Ray tracing parametric surface patches utilizing numerical techniques and ray coherence. In *Computer Graphics (SIGGRAPH '86 Proceedings)* (Aug. 1986), D. C. Evans and R. J. Athay, Eds., vol. 20, 279–285.

[162] J. T. KAJIYA. Anisotropic reflection models. In *Computer Graphics (SIGGRAPH '85 Proceedings)* (July 1985), B. A. Barsky, Ed., vol. 19, 15–21.

[163] J. T. KAJIYA. The rendering equation. In *Computer Graphics (SIGGRAPH '86 Proceedings)* (Aug. 1986), D. C. Evans and R. J. Athay, Eds., vol. 20, 143–150.

[164] J. T. KAJIYA AND T. L. KAY. Rendering fur with three dimensional textures. In *Computer Graphics (SIGGRAPH '89 Proceedings)* (July 1989), J. Lane, Ed., vol. 23, 271–280.

[165] J. T. KAJIYA AND B. P. VON HERZEN. Ray tracing volume densities. In *Computer Graphics (SIGGRAPH '84 Proceedings)* (July 1984), H. Christiansen, Ed., vol. 18, 165–174.

[166] D. KALRA AND A. H. BARR. Guaranteed ray intersections with implicit surfaces. In *Computer Graphics (SIGGRAPH '89 Proceedings)* (July 1989), J. Lane, Ed., vol. 23, 297–306.

[167] K. KANEDA, F. KATO, E. NAKAMAE, T. NISHITA, H. TANAKA, AND T. NOGUCHI. Three dimensional terrain modeling and display for environmental assessment. In *Computer Graphics (SIGGRAPH '89 Proceedings)* (July 1989), J. Lane, Ed., vol. 23, 207–214.

[168] M. KASS. CONDOR: Constraint-based dataflow. In *Computer Graphics (SIGGRAPH '92 Proceedings)* (July 1992), E. E. Catmull, Ed., vol. 26, 321–330.

[169] M. KASS AND G. MILLER. Rapid, stable fluid dynamics for computer graphics. In *Computer Graphics (SIGGRAPH '90 Proceedings)* (Aug. 1990), F. Baskett, Ed., vol. 24, 49–57.

[170] A. KAUFMAN. Efficient algorithms for 3D scan-conversion of parametric curves, surfaces, and volumes. In *Computer Graphics (SIGGRAPH '87 Proceedings)* (July 1987), M. C. Stone, Ed., vol. 21, 171–179.

[171] J. K. KAWAI, J. S. PAINTER, AND M. F. COHEN. Radioptimization – goal-based rendering. In *Computer Graphics (SIGGRAPH '93 Proceedings)* (Aug. 1993), J. T. Kajiya, Ed., vol. 27, 147–154.

[172] T. L. KAY AND J. T. KAJIYA. Ray tracing complex scenes. In *Computer Graphics (SIGGRAPH '86 Proceedings)* (Aug. 1986), D. C. Evans and R. J. Athay, Eds., vol. 20, 269–278.

[173] A. D. KELLEY, M. C. MALIN, AND G. M. NIELSON. Terrain simulation using a model of stream erosion. In *Computer Graphics (SIGGRAPH '88 Proceedings)* (Aug. 1988), J. Dill, Ed., vol. 22, 263–268.

[174] M. KELLEY, S. WINNER, AND K. GOULD. A scalable hardware render accelerator using a modified scanline algorithm. In *Computer Graphics (SIGGRAPH '92 Proceedings)* (July 1992), E. E. Catmull, Ed., vol. 26, 241–248.

[175] J. R. KENT, W. E. CARLSON, AND R. E. PARENT. Shape transformation for polyhedral objects. In *Computer Graphics (SIGGRAPH '92 Proceedings)* (July 1992), E. E. Catmull, Ed., vol. 26, 47–54.

[176] D. B. KIRK AND J. ARVO. Unbiased sampling techniques for image synthesis. In *Computer Graphics (SIGGRAPH '91 Proceedings)* (July 1991), T. W. Sederberg, Ed., vol. 25, 153–156.

[177] D. B. KIRK AND A. H. BARR. Implementing rotation matrix constraints in analog VLSI. In *Computer Graphics (SIGGRAPH '93 Proceedings)* (Aug. 1993), J. T. Kajiya, Ed., vol. 27, 45–52.

[178] D. B. KIRK AND D. VOORHIES. The rendering architecture of the DN10000VS. In *Computer Graphics (SIGGRAPH '90 Proceedings)* (Aug. 1990), F. Baskett, Ed., vol. 24, 299–307.

[179] R. V. KLASSEN AND K. BHARAT. Correcting for short-range spatial nonlinearities of CRT-based output devices. In *Computer Graphics (SIGGRAPH '93 Proceedings)* (Aug. 1993), J. T. Kajiya, Ed., vol. 27, 53–56.

[180] D. H. U. KOCHANEK AND R. H. BARTELS. Interpolating splines with local tension, continuity, and bias control. In *Computer Graphics (SIGGRAPH '84 Proceedings)* (July 1984), H. Christiansen, Ed., vol. 18, 33–41.

[181] W. KRUEGER. Intensity fluctuations and natural texturing. In *Computer Graphics (SIGGRAPH '88 Proceedings)* (Aug. 1988), J. Dill, Ed., vol. 22, 213–220.

[182] D. KURLANDER AND E. A. BIER. Graphical search and replace. In *Computer Graphics (SIGGRAPH '88 Proceedings)* (Aug. 1988), J. Dill, Ed., vol. 22, 113–120.

[183] D. H. LAIDLAW, W. B. TRUMBORE, AND J. F. HUGHES. Constructive solid geometry for polyhedral objects. In *Computer Graphics (SIGGRAPH '86 Proceedings)* (Aug. 1986), D. C. Evans and R. J. Athay, Eds., vol. 20, 161–170.

[184] J. LASSETER. Principles of traditional animation applied to 3D computer animation. In *Computer Graphics (SIGGRAPH '87 Proceedings)* (July 1987), M. C. Stone, Ed., vol. 21, 35–44.

[185] D. LAUR AND P. HANRAHAN. Hierarchical splatting: A progressive refinement algorithm for volume rendering. In *Computer Graphics (SIGGRAPH '91 Proceedings)* (July 1991), T. W. Sederberg, Ed., vol. 25, 285–288.

[186] M. E. LEE, R. A. REDNER, AND S. P. USELTON. Statistically optimized sampling for distributed ray tracing. In *Computer Graphics (SIGGRAPH '85 Proceedings)* (July 1985), B. A. Barsky, Ed., vol. 19, 61–67.

[187] P. LEE, S. WEI, J. ZHAO, AND N. I. BADLER. Strength guided motion. In *Computer Graphics (SIGGRAPH '90 Proceedings)* (Aug. 1990), F. Baskett, Ed., vol. 24, 253–262.

[188] J. LENGYEL, M. REICHERT, B. R. DONALD, AND D. P. GREENBERG. Real-time robot motion planning using rasterizing computer graphics hardware. In *Computer Graphics (SIGGRAPH '90 Proceedings)* (Aug. 1990), F. Baskett, Ed., vol. 24, 327–335.

[189] A. LEVINTHAL AND T. PORTER. Chap — A SIMD graphics processor. In *Computer Graphics (SIGGRAPH '84 Proceedings)* (July 1984), H. Christiansen, Ed., vol. 18, 77–82.

[190] J.-P. LEWIS. Texture synthesis for digital painting. In *Computer Graphics (SIGGRAPH '84 Proceedings)* (July 1984), H. Christiansen, Ed., vol. 18, 245–252.

[191] J.-P. LEWIS. Algorithms for solid noise synthesis. In *Computer Graphics (SIGGRAPH '89 Proceedings)* (July 1989), J. Lane, Ed., vol. 23, 263–270.

[192] X. LI AND J. M. MOSHELL. Modeling soil: Realtime dynamic models for soil slippage and manipulation. In *Computer Graphics (SIGGRAPH '93 Proceedings)* (Aug. 1993), J. T. Kajiya, Ed., vol. 27, 361–368.

[193] H. LIEBERMAN. There's more to menu systems than meets the screen. In *Computer Graphics (SIGGRAPH '85 Proceedings)* (July 1985), B. A. Barsky, Ed., vol. 19, 181–189.

[194] S.-L. LIEN, M. SHANTZ, AND V. PRATT. Adaptive forward differencing for rendering curves and surfaces. In *Computer Graphics (SIGGRAPH '87 Proceedings)* (July 1987), M. C. Stone, Ed., vol. 21, 111–118.

[195] B. J. LINDBLOOM. Accurate color reproduction for computer graphics applications. In *Computer Graphics (SIGGRAPH '89 Proceedings)* (July 1989), J. Lane, Ed., vol. 23, 117–126.

[196] D. LISCHINSKI, F. TAMPIERI, AND D. P. GREENBERG. Combining hierarchical radiosity and discontinuity meshing. In *Computer Graphics (SIGGRAPH '93 Proceedings)* (Aug. 1993), J. T. Kajiya, Ed., vol. 27, 199–208.

[197] R. J. LITTLEFIELD. Priority windows: A device independent, vector oriented approach. In *Computer Graphics (SIGGRAPH '84 Proceedings)* (July 1984), H. Christiansen, Ed., vol. 18, 187–193.

[198] P. C. LITWINOWICZ. Inkwell: A $2\frac{1}{2}$-D animation system. In *Computer Graphics (SIGGRAPH '91 Proceedings)* (July 1991), T. W. Sederberg, Ed., vol. 25, 113–122.

[199] C. LOOP AND T. DEROSE. Generalized B-spline surfaces of arbitrary topology. In *Computer Graphics (SIGGRAPH '90 Proceedings)* (Aug. 1990), F. Baskett, Ed., vol. 24, 347–356.

[200] W. E. LORENSEN AND H. E. CLINE. Marching cubes: A high resolution 3D surface construction algorithm. In *Computer Graphics (SIGGRAPH '87 Proceedings)* (July 1987), M. C. Stone, Ed., vol. 21, 163–169.

[201] J. D. MACKINLAY, S. K. CARD, AND G. G. ROBERTSON. Rapid controlled movement through a virtual 3D workspace. In *Computer Graphics (SIGGRAPH '90 Proceedings)* (Aug. 1990), F. Baskett, Ed., vol. 24, 171–176.

[202] J. MAILLOT, H. YAHIA, AND A. VERROUST. Interactive texture mapping. In *Computer Graphics (SIGGRAPH '93 Proceedings)* (Aug. 1993), J. T. Kajiya, Ed., vol. 27, 27–34.

[203] D. L. MAULSBY, I. H. WITTEN, AND K. A. KITTLITZ. Metamouse: Specifying graphical procedures by example. In *Computer Graphics (SIGGRAPH '89 Proceedings)* (July 1989), J. Lane, Ed., vol. 23, 127–136.

[204] N. L. MAX. Atmospheric illumination and shadows. In *Computer Graphics (SIGGRAPH '86 Proceedings)* (Aug. 1986), D. C. Evans and R. J. Athay, Eds., vol. 20, 117–124.

[205] N. L. MAX. Cone-spheres. In *Computer Graphics (SIGGRAPH '90 Proceedings)* (Aug. 1990), F. Baskett, Ed., vol. 24, 59–62.

[206] N. L. MAX AND D. M. LERNER. A two-and-a-half-D motion-blur algorithm. In *Computer Graphics (SIGGRAPH '85 Proceedings)* (July 1985), B. A. Barsky, Ed., vol. 19, 85–93.

[207] M. MCKENNA AND D. ZELTZER. Dynamic simulation of autonomous legged locomotion. In *Computer Graphics (SIGGRAPH '90 Proceedings)* (Aug. 1990), F. Baskett, Ed., vol. 24, 29–38.

[208] D. METAXAS AND D. TERZOPOULOS. Dynamic deformation of solid primitives with constraints. In *Computer Graphics (SIGGRAPH '92 Proceedings)* (July 1992), E. E. Catmull, Ed., vol. 26, 309–312.

[209] A. E. MIDDLEDITCH AND K. H. SEARS. Blend surfaces for set theoretic volume modeling systems. In *Computer Graphics (SIGGRAPH '85 Proceedings)* (July 1985), B. A. Barsky, Ed., vol. 19, 161–170.

[210] G. S. P. MILLER. The definition and rendering of terrain maps. In *Computer Graphics (SIGGRAPH '86 Proceedings)* (Aug. 1986), D. C. Evans and R. J. Athay, Eds., vol. 20, 39–48.

[211] G. S. P. MILLER. The motion dynamics of snakes and worms. In *Computer Graphics (SIGGRAPH '88 Proceedings)* (Aug. 1988), J. Dill, Ed., vol. 22, 169–178.

[212] J. V. MILLER, D. E. BREEN, W. E. LORENSEN, R. M. O'BARA, AND M. J. WOZNY. Geometrically deformed models: A method for extracting closed geometric models from volume data. In *Computer Graphics (SIGGRAPH '91 Proceedings)* (July 1991), T. W. Sederberg, Ed., vol. 25, 217–226.

[213] M. R. MINSKY. Manipulating simulated objects with real-world gestures using a force and position sensitive screen. In *Computer Graphics (SIGGRAPH '84 Proceedings)* (July 1984), H. Christiansen, Ed., vol. 18, 195–203.

[214] D. P. MITCHELL. Generating antialiased images at low sampling densities. In *Computer Graphics (SIGGRAPH '87 Proceedings)* (July 1987), M. C. Stone, Ed., vol. 21, 65–72.

[215] D. P. MITCHELL. Spectrally optimal sampling for distributed ray tracing. In *Computer Graphics (SIGGRAPH '91 Proceedings)* (July 1991), T. W. Sederberg, Ed., vol. 25, 157–164.

[216] D. P. MITCHELL AND P. HANRAHAN. Illumination from curved reflectors. In *Computer Graphics (SIGGRAPH '92 Proceedings)* (July 1992), E. E. Catmull, Ed., vol. 26, 283–291.

[217] D. P. MITCHELL AND A. N. NETRAVALI. Reconstruction filters in computer graphics. In *Computer Graphics (SIGGRAPH '88 Proceedings)* (Aug. 1988), J. Dill, Ed., vol. 22, 221–228.

[218] K. MIYATA. A method of generating stone wall patterns. In *Computer Graphics (SIGGRAPH '90 Proceedings)* (Aug. 1990), F. Baskett, Ed., vol. 24, 387–394.

[219] S. MOLNAR, J. EYLES, AND J. POULTON. PixelFlow: High-speed rendering using image composition. In *Computer Graphics (SIGGRAPH '92 Proceedings)* (July 1992), E. E. Catmull, Ed., vol. 26, 231–240.

[220] M. MOORE AND J. WILHELMS. Collision detection and response for computer animation. In *Computer Graphics (SIGGRAPH '88 Proceedings)* (Aug. 1988), J. Dill, Ed., vol. 22, 289–298.

[221] H. P. MORETON AND C. H. SÉQUIN. Functional optimization for fair surface design. In *Computer Graphics (SIGGRAPH '92 Proceedings)* (July 1992), E. E. Catmull, Ed., vol. 26, 167–176.

[222] K. MULMULEY. An efficient algorithm for hidden surface removal. In *Computer Graphics (SIGGRAPH '89 Proceedings)* (July 1989), J. Lane, Ed., vol. 23, 379–388.

[223] S. MURAKI. Volumetric shape description of range data using "blobby model". In *Computer Graphics (SIGGRAPH '91 Proceedings)* (July 1991), T. W. Sederberg, Ed., vol. 25, 227–235.

[224] F. K. MUSGRAVE, C. E. KOLB, AND R. S. MACE. The synthesis and rendering of eroded fractal terrains. In *Computer Graphics (SIGGRAPH '89 Proceedings)* (July 1989), J. Lane, Ed., vol. 23, 41–50.

[225] B. A. MYERS AND W. BUXTON. Creating highly-interactive and graphical user interfaces by demonstration. In *Computer Graphics (SIGGRAPH '86 Proceedings)* (Aug. 1986), D. C. Evans and R. J. Athay, Eds., vol. 20, 249–258.

[226] T. NADAS AND A. FOURNIER. GRAPE: An environment to build display processes. In *Computer Graphics (SIGGRAPH '87 Proceedings)* (July 1987), M. C. Stone, Ed., vol. 21, 75–84.

[227] A. NAIMAN AND A. FOURNIER. Rectangular convolution for fast filtering of characters. In *Computer Graphics (SIGGRAPH '87 Proceedings)* (July 1987), M. C. Stone, Ed., vol. 21, 233–242.

[228] E. NAKAMAE, K. HARADA, T. ISHIZAKI, AND T. NISHITA. A montage method: The overlaying of the computer generated images onto a background photograph. In *Computer Graphics (SIGGRAPH '86 Proceedings)* (Aug. 1986), D. C. Evans and R. J. Athay, Eds., vol. 20, 207–214.

[229] E. NAKAMAE, K. KANEDA, T. OKAMOTO, AND T. NISHITA. A lighting model aiming at drive simulators. In *Computer Graphics (SIGGRAPH '90 Proceedings)* (Aug. 1990), F. Baskett, Ed., vol. 24, 395–404.

[230] B. NAYLOR, J. AMANATIDES, AND W. THIBAULT. Merging BSP trees yields polyhedral set operations. In *Computer Graphics (SIGGRAPH '90 Proceedings)* (Aug. 1990), F. Baskett, Ed., vol. 24, 115–124.

[231] G. NELSON. Juno, A constraint-based graphics system. In *Computer Graphics (SIGGRAPH '85 Proceedings)* (July 1985), B. A. Barsky, Ed., vol. 19, 235–243.

[232] R. C. NELSON AND H. SAMET. A consistent hierarchical representation for vector data. In *Computer Graphics (SIGGRAPH '86 Proceedings)* (Aug. 1986), D. C. Evans and R. J. Athay, Eds., vol. 20, 197–206.

[233] J. T. NGO AND J. MARKS. Spacetime constraints revisited. In *Computer Graphics (SIGGRAPH '93 Proceedings)* (Aug. 1993), J. T. Kajiya, Ed., vol. 27, 343–350.

[234] T. M. NICHOLL, D. T. LEE, AND R. A. NICHOLL. An efficient new algorithm for 2-D line clipping: Its development and analysis. In *Computer Graphics (SIGGRAPH '87 Proceedings)* (July 1987), M. C. Stone, Ed., vol. 21, 253–262.

[235] H. NIIMI, Y. IMAI, M. MURAKAMI, S. TOMITA, AND H. HAGIWARA. A parallel processor system for three-dimensional color graphics. In *Computer Graphics (SIGGRAPH '84 Proceedings)* (July 1984), H. Christiansen, Ed., vol. 18, 67–76.

[236] T. NISHITA, Y. MIYAWAKI, AND E. NAKAMAE. A shading model for atmospheric scattering considering luminous intensity distribution of light sources. In *Computer Graphics (SIGGRAPH '87 Proceedings)* (July 1987), M. C. Stone, Ed., vol. 21, 303–310.

[237] T. NISHITA AND E. NAKAMAE. Continuous tone representation of three-dimensional objects taking account of shadows and interreflection. In *Computer Graphics (SIGGRAPH '85 Proceedings)* (July 1985), B. A. Barsky, Ed., vol. 19, 23–30.

[238] T. NISHITA AND E. NAKAMAE. Continuous tone representation of three-dimensional objects illuminated by sky light. In *Computer Graphics (SIGGRAPH '86 Proceedings)* (Aug. 1986), D. C. Evans and R. J. Athay, Eds., vol. 20, 125–132.

[239] T. NISHITA, T. W. SEDERBERG, AND M. KAKIMOTO. Ray tracing trimmed rational surface patches. In *Computer Graphics (SIGGRAPH '90 Proceedings)* (Aug. 1990), F. Baskett, Ed., vol. 24, 337–345.

[240] T. NISHITA, T. SIRAI, K. TADAMURA, AND E. NAKAMAE. Display of the earth taking into account atmospheric scattering. In *Computer Graphics (SIGGRAPH '93 Proceedings)* (Aug. 1993), J. T. Kajiya, Ed., vol. 27, 175–182.

[241] M. OKA, K. TSUTSUI, A. OHBA, Y. KURAUCHI, AND T. TAGO. Real-time manipulation of texture-mapped surfaces. In *Computer Graphics (SIGGRAPH '87 Proceedings)* (July 1987), M. C. Stone, Ed., vol. 21, 181–188.

[242] H. OKABE, H. IMAOKA, T. TOMIHA, AND H. NIWAYA. Three dimensional apparel CAD system. In *Computer Graphics (SIGGRAPH '92 Proceedings)* (July 1992), E. E. Catmull, Ed., vol. 26, 105–110.

[243] P. E. OPPENHEIMER. Real time design and animation of fractal plants and trees. In *Computer Graphics (SIGGRAPH '86 Proceedings)* (Aug. 1986), D. C. Evans and R. J. Athay, Eds., vol. 20, 55–64.

[244] J. PAINTER AND K. SLOAN. Antialiased ray tracing by adaptive progressive refinement. In *Computer Graphics (SIGGRAPH '89 Proceedings)* (July 1989), J. Lane, Ed., vol. 23, 281–288.

[245] T. V. PAPATHOMAS, J. A. SCHIAVONE, AND B. JULESZ. Applications of computer graphics to the visualization of meteorological data. In *Computer Graphics (SIGGRAPH '88 Proceedings)* (Aug. 1988), J. Dill, Ed., vol. 22, 327–334.

[246] T. PAVLIDIS AND C. J. VAN WYK. An automatic beautifier for drawings and illustrations. In *Computer Graphics (SIGGRAPH '85 Proceedings)* (July 1985), B. A. Barsky, Ed., vol. 19, 225–234.

[247] D. R. PEACHEY. Solid texturing of complex surfaces. In *Computer Graphics (SIGGRAPH '85 Proceedings)* (July 1985), B. A. Barsky, Ed., vol. 19, 279–286.

[248] D. R. PEACHEY. Modeling waves and surf. In *Computer Graphics (SIGGRAPH '86 Proceedings)* (Aug. 1986), D. C. Evans and R. J. Athay, Eds., vol. 20, 65–74.

[249] M. S. PEERCY. Linear color representations for full spectral rendering. In *Computer Graphics (SIGGRAPH '93 Proceedings)* (Aug. 1993), J. T. Kajiya, Ed., vol. 27, 191–198.

[250] A. PENTLAND AND J. WILLIAMS. Good vibrations: Modal dynamics for graphics and animation. In *Computer Graphics (SIGGRAPH '89 Proceedings)* (July 1989), J. Lane, Ed., vol. 23, 215–222.

[251] K. PERLIN. An image synthesizer. In *Computer Graphics (SIGGRAPH '85 Proceedings)* (July 1985), B. A. Barsky, Ed., vol. 19, 287–296.

[252] K. PERLIN AND D. FOX. Pad: An alternative approach to the computer interface. In *Computer Graphics (SIGGRAPH '93 Proceedings)* (Aug. 1993), J. T. Kajiya, Ed., vol. 27, 57–64.

[253] K. PERLIN AND E. M. HOFFERT. Hypertexture. In *Computer Graphics (SIGGRAPH '89 Proceedings)* (July 1989), J. Lane, Ed., vol. 23, 253–262.

[254] C. B. PHILLIPS AND N. I. BADLER. Interactive behaviors for bipedal articulated figures. In *Computer Graphics (SIGGRAPH '91 Proceedings)* (July 1991), T. W. Sederberg, Ed., vol. 25, 359–362.

[255] J. PINEDA. A parallel algorithm for polygon rasterization. In *Computer Graphics (SIGGRAPH '88 Proceedings)* (Aug. 1988), J. Dill, Ed., vol. 22, 17–20.

[256] T. S. PIPER AND A. FOURNIER. A hardware stochastic interpolator for raster displays. In *Computer Graphics (SIGGRAPH '84 Proceedings)* (July 1984), H. Christiansen, Ed., vol. 18, 83–92.

[257] J. C. PLATT AND A. H. BARR. Constraint methods for flexible models. In *Computer Graphics (SIGGRAPH '88 Proceedings)* (Aug. 1988), J. Dill, Ed., vol. 22, 279–288.

[258] T. PORTER AND T. DUFF. Compositing digital images. In *Computer Graphics (SIGGRAPH '84 Proceedings)* (July 1984), H. Christiansen, Ed., vol. 18, 253–259.

[259] M. POTMESIL AND E. M. HOFFERT. FRAMES: Software tools for modeling, rendering and animation of 3D scenes. In *Computer Graphics (SIGGRAPH '87 Proceedings)* (July 1987), M. C. Stone, Ed., vol. 21, 85–93.

[260] M. POTMESIL AND E. M. HOFFERT. The Pixel Machine: A parallel image computer. In *Computer Graphics (SIGGRAPH '89 Proceedings)* (July 1989), J. Lane, Ed., vol. 23, 69–78.

[261] P. POULIN AND A. FOURNIER. A model for anisotropic reflection. In *Computer Graphics (SIGGRAPH '90 Proceedings)* (Aug. 1990), F. Baskett, Ed., vol. 24, 273–282.

[262] V. PRATT. Techniques for conic splines. In *Computer Graphics (SIGGRAPH '85 Proceedings)* (July 1985), B. A. Barsky, Ed., vol. 19, 151–159.

[263] V. PRATT. Direct least-squares fitting of algebraic surfaces. In *Computer Graphics (SIGGRAPH '87 Proceedings)* (July 1987), M. C. Stone, Ed., vol. 21, 145–152.

[264] P. PRUSINKIEWICZ, M. S. HAMMEL, AND E. MJOLSNESS. Animation of plant development. In *Computer Graphics (SIGGRAPH '93 Proceedings)* (Aug. 1993), J. T. Kajiya, Ed., vol. 27, 351–360.

[265] P. PRUSINKIEWICZ, A. LINDENMAYER, AND J. HANAN. Developmental models of herbaceous plants for computer imagery purposes. In *Computer Graphics (SIGGRAPH '88 Proceedings)* (Aug. 1988), J. Dill, Ed., vol. 22, 141–150.

[266] M. H. RAIBERT AND J. K. HODGINS. Animation of dynamic legged locomotion. In *Computer Graphics (SIGGRAPH '91 Proceedings)* (July 1991), T. W. Sederberg, Ed., vol. 25, 349–358.

[267] W. T. REEVES AND R. BLAU. Approximate and probabilistic algorithms for shading and rendering structured particle systems. In *Computer Graphics (SIGGRAPH '85 Proceedings)* (July 1985), B. A. Barsky, Ed., vol. 19, 313–322.

[268] W. T. REEVES, D. H. SALESIN, AND R. L. COOK. Rendering antialiased shadows with depth maps. In *Computer Graphics (SIGGRAPH '87 Proceedings)* (July 1987), M. C. Stone, Ed., vol. 21, 283–291.

[269] C. W. REYNOLDS. Flocks, herds, and schools: A distributed behavioral model. In *Computer Graphics (SIGGRAPH '87 Proceedings)* (July 1987), M. C. Stone, Ed., vol. 21, 25–34.

[270] D. RHODEN AND C. WILCOX. Hardware acceleration for window systems. In *Computer Graphics (SIGGRAPH '89 Proceedings)* (July 1989), J. Lane, Ed., vol. 23, 61–67.

[271] H. RIJPKEMA AND M. GIRARD. Computer animation of knowledge-based human grasping. In *Computer Graphics (SIGGRAPH '91 Proceedings)* (July 1991), T. W. Sederberg, Ed., vol. 25, 339–348.

[272] A. ROCKWOOD, K. HEATON, AND T. DAVIS. Real-time rendering of trimmed surfaces. In *Computer Graphics (SIGGRAPH '89 Proceedings)* (July 1989), J. Lane, Ed., vol. 23, 107–116.

[273] J. ROSSIGNAC, A. MEGAHED, AND B.-O. SCHNEIDER. Interactive inspection of solids: Cross-sections and interferences. In *Computer Graphics (SIGGRAPH '92 Proceedings)* (July 1992), E. E. Catmull, Ed., vol. 26, 353–360.

[274] D. RUBINE. Specifying gestures by example. In *Computer Graphics (SIGGRAPH '91 Proceedings)* (July 1991), T. W. Sederberg, Ed., vol. 25, 329–337.

[275] H. E. RUSHMEIER AND K. E. TORRANCE. The zonal method for calculating light intensities in the presence of a participating medium. In *Computer Graphics (SIGGRAPH '87 Proceedings)* (July 1987), M. C. Stone, Ed., vol. 21, 293–302.

[276] P. SABELLA. A rendering algorithm for visualizing 3D scalar fields. In *Computer Graphics (SIGGRAPH '88 Proceedings)* (Aug. 1988), J. Dill, Ed., vol. 22, 51–58.

[277] T. SAITO AND T. TAKAHASHI. Comprehensible rendering of 3-D shapes. In *Computer Graphics (SIGGRAPH '90 Proceedings)* (Aug. 1990), F. Baskett, Ed., vol. 24, 197–206.

[278] T. SAITO AND T. TAKAHASHI. NC machining with G-buffer method. In *Computer Graphics (SIGGRAPH '91 Proceedings)* (July 1991), T. W. Sederberg, Ed., vol. 25, 207–216.

[279] D. SALESIN AND J. STOLFI. Rendering CSG models with a ZZ-buffer. In *Computer Graphics (SIGGRAPH '90 Proceedings)* (Aug. 1990), F. Baskett, Ed., vol. 24, 67–76.

[280] H. SAMET AND M. TAMMINEN. Bintrees, CSG trees, and time. In *Computer Graphics (SIGGRAPH '85 Proceedings)* (July 1985), B. A. Barsky, Ed., vol. 19, 121–130.

[281] H. SATO, M. ISHII, K. SATO, M. IKESAKA, H. ISHIHATA, M. KAKIMOTO, K. HIROTA, AND K. INOUE. Fast image generation of constructive solid geometry using a cellular array processor. In *Computer Graphics (SIGGRAPH '85 Proceedings)* (July 1985), B. A. Barsky, Ed., vol. 19, 95–102.

[282] A. SCHILLING. A new simple and efficient anti-aliasing with subpixel masks. In *Computer Graphics (SIGGRAPH '91 Proceedings)* (July 1991), T. W. Sederberg, Ed., vol. 25, 133–141.

[283] A. SCHILLING AND W. STRASSER. EXACT: Algorithm and hardware architecture for an improved A-buffer. In *Computer Graphics (SIGGRAPH '93 Proceedings)* (Aug. 1993), J. T. Kajiya, Ed., vol. 27, 85–92.

[284] F. J. M. SCHMITT, B. A. BARSKY, AND W. HUI DU. An adaptive subdivision method for surface-fitting from sampled data. In *Computer Graphics (SIGGRAPH '86 Proceedings)* (Aug. 1986), D. C. Evans and R. J. Athay, Eds., vol. 20, 179–188.

[285] C. SCHOENEMAN, J. DORSEY, B. SMITS, J. ARVO, AND D. P. GREENBERG. Painting with light. In *Computer Graphics (SIGGRAPH '93 Proceedings)* (Aug. 1993), J. T. Kajiya, Ed., vol. 27, 143–146.

[286] P. SCHRÖDER AND P. HANRAHAN. On the form factor between two polygons. In *Computer Graphics (SIGGRAPH '93 Proceedings)* (Aug. 1993), J. T. Kajiya, Ed., vol. 27, 163–164.

[287] W. J. SCHROEDER, J. A. ZARGE, AND W. E. LORENSEN. Decimation of triangle meshes. In *Computer Graphics (SIGGRAPH '92 Proceedings)* (July 1992), E. E. Catmull, Ed., vol. 26, 65–70.

[288] S. SCLAROFF AND A. PENTLAND. Generalized implicit functions for computer graphics. In *Computer Graphics (SIGGRAPH '91 Proceedings)* (July 1991), T. W. Sederberg, Ed., vol. 25, 247–250.

[289] T. W. SEDERBERG AND D. C. ANDERSON. Ray tracing of Steiner patches. In *Computer Graphics (SIGGRAPH '84 Proceedings)* (July 1984), H. Christiansen, Ed., vol. 18, 159–164.

[290] T. W. SEDERBERG, P. GAO, G. WANG, AND H. MU. 2D shape blending: An intrinsic solution to the vertex path problem. In *Computer Graphics (SIGGRAPH '93 Proceedings)* (Aug. 1993), J. T. Kajiya, Ed., vol. 27, 15–18.

[291] T. W. SEDERBERG AND E. GREENWOOD. A physically based approach to 2D shape blending. In *Computer Graphics (SIGGRAPH '92 Proceedings)* (July 1992), E. E. Catmull, Ed., vol. 26, 25–34.

[292] T. W. SEDERBERG AND S. R. PARRY. Free-form deformation of solid geometric models. In *Computer Graphics (SIGGRAPH '86 Proceedings)* (Aug. 1986), D. C. Evans and R. J. Athay, Eds., vol. 20, 151–160.

[293] T. W. SEDERBERG AND A. K. ZUNDEL. Scan line display of algebraic surfaces. In *Computer Graphics (SIGGRAPH '89 Proceedings)* (July 1989), J. Lane, Ed., vol. 23, 147–156.

[294] M. SEGAL. Using tolerances to guarantee valid polyhedral modeling results. In *Computer Graphics (SIGGRAPH '90 Proceedings)* (Aug. 1990), F. Baskett, Ed., vol. 24, 105–114.

[295] M. SEGAL, C. KOROBKIN, R. VAN WIDENFELT, J. FORAN, AND P. E. HAEBERLI. Fast shadows and lighting effects using texture mapping. In *Computer Graphics (SIGGRAPH '92 Proceedings)* (July 1992), E. E. Catmull, Ed., vol. 26, 249–252.

[296] D. D. SELIGMANN AND S. FEINER. Automated generation of intent-based 3D illustrations. In *Computer Graphics (SIGGRAPH '91 Proceedings)* (July 1991), T. W. Sederberg, Ed., vol. 25, 123–132.

[297] C. H. SÉQUIN AND E. K. SMYRL. Parameterized ray tracing. In *Computer Graphics (SIGGRAPH '89 Proceedings)* (July 1989), J. Lane, Ed., vol. 23, 307–314.

[298] M. SHANTZ AND S.-L. CHANG. Rendering trimmed NURBS with adaptive forward differencing. In *Computer Graphics (SIGGRAPH '88 Proceedings)* (Aug. 1988), J. Dill, Ed., vol. 22, 189–198.

[299] M. SHANTZ AND S.-L. LIEN. Shading bicubic patches. In *Computer Graphics (SIGGRAPH '87 Proceedings)* (July 1987), M. C. Stone, Ed., vol. 21, 189–196.

[300] M.-Z. SHAO, Q.-S. PENG, AND Y.-D. LIANG. A new radiosity approach by procedural refinements for realistic image synthesis. In *Computer Graphics (SIGGRAPH '88 Proceedings)* (Aug. 1988), J. Dill, Ed., vol. 22, 93–101.

[301] M. SHINYA. Spatial anti-aliasing for animation sequences with spatio-temporal filtering. In *Computer Graphics (SIGGRAPH '93 Proceedings)* (Aug. 1993), J. T. Kajiya, Ed., vol. 27, 289–296.

[302] M. SHINYA, T. TAKAHASHI, AND S. NAITO. Principles and applications of pencil tracing. In *Computer Graphics (SIGGRAPH '87 Proceedings)* (July 1987), M. C. Stone, Ed., vol. 21, 45–54.

[303] K. SHOEMAKE. Animating rotation with quaternion curves. In *Computer Graphics (SIGGRAPH '85 Proceedings)* (July 1985), B. A. Barsky, Ed., vol. 19, 245–254.

[304] J. L. SIBERT, W. D. HURLEY, AND T. W. BLESER. An object-oriented user interface management system. In *Computer Graphics (SIGGRAPH '86 Proceedings)* (Aug. 1986), D. C. Evans and R. J. Athay, Eds., vol. 20, 259–268.

[305] F. X. SILLION, J. R. ARVO, S. H. WESTIN, AND D. P. GREENBERG. A global illumination solution for general reflectance distributions. In *Computer Graphics (SIGGRAPH '91 Proceedings)* (July 1991), T. W. Sederberg, Ed., vol. 25, 187–196.

[306] F. X. SILLION AND C. PUECH. A general two-pass method integrating specular and diffuse reflection. In *Computer Graphics (SIGGRAPH '89 Proceedings)* (July 1989), J. Lane, Ed., vol. 23, 335–344.

[307] K. SIMS. Particle animation and rendering using data parallel computation. In *Computer Graphics (SIGGRAPH '90 Proceedings)* (Aug. 1990), F. Baskett, Ed., vol. 24, 405–413.

[308] K. SIMS. Artificial evolution for computer graphics. In *Computer Graphics (SIGGRAPH '91 Proceedings)* (July 1991), T. W. Sederberg, Ed., vol. 25, 319–328.

[309] A. R. SMITH. Plants, fractals and formal languages. In *Computer Graphics (SIGGRAPH '84 Proceedings)* (July 1984), H. Christiansen, Ed., vol. 18, 1–10.

[310] A. R. SMITH. Planar 2-pass texture mapping and warping. In *Computer Graphics (SIGGRAPH '87 Proceedings)* (July 1987), M. C. Stone, Ed., vol. 21, 263–272.

[311] B. E. SMITS, J. R. ARVO, AND D. H. SALESIN. An importance-driven radiosity algorithm. In *Computer Graphics (SIGGRAPH '92 Proceedings)* (July 1992), E. E. Catmull, Ed., vol. 26, 273–282.

[312] S. S. SNIBBE, K. P. HERNDON, D. C. ROBBINS, D. B. CONNER, AND A. VAN DAM. Using deformations to explore 3D widget design. In *Computer Graphics (SIGGRAPH '92 Proceedings)* (July 1992), E. E. Catmull, Ed., vol. 26, 351–352.

[313] J. M. SNYDER. Interval analysis for computer graphics. In *Computer Graphics (SIGGRAPH '92 Proceedings)* (July 1992), E. E. Catmull, Ed., vol. 26, 121–130.

[314] J. M. SNYDER AND A. H. BARR. Ray tracing complex models containing surface tessellations. In *Computer Graphics (SIGGRAPH '87 Proceedings)* (July 1987), M. C. Stone, Ed., vol. 21, 119–128.

[315] J. M. SNYDER AND J. T. KAJIYA. Generative modeling: A symbolic system for geometric modeling. In *Computer Graphics (SIGGRAPH '92 Proceedings)* (July 1992), E. E. Catmull, Ed., vol. 26, 369–378.

[316] J. M. SNYDER, A. R. WOODBURY, K. FLEISCHER, B. CURRIN, AND A. H. BARR. Interval method for multi-point collision between time-dependent curved surfaces. In *Computer Graphics (SIGGRAPH '93 Proceedings)* (Aug. 1993), J. T. Kajiya, Ed., vol. 27, 321–334.

[317] S. SPENCER. Cumulative index (SIGGRAPH '84 - SIGGRAPH '93). In *Computer Graphics (SIGGRAPH '93 Proceedings)* (Aug. 1993), J. T. Kajiya, Ed., vol. 27, 405–418.

[318] J. STAM AND E. FIUME. Turbulent wind fields for gaseous phenomena. In *Computer Graphics (SIGGRAPH '93 Proceedings)* (Aug. 1993), J. T. Kajiya, Ed., vol. 27, 369–376.

[319] S. N. STEKETEE AND N. I. BADLER. Parametric keyframe interpolation incorporating kinetic adjustment and phasing control. In *Computer Graphics (SIGGRAPH '85 Proceedings)* (July 1985), B. A. Barsky, Ed., vol. 19, 255–262.

[320] A. STETTNER AND D. P. GREENBERG. Computer graphics visualization for acoustic simulation. In *Computer Graphics (SIGGRAPH '89 Proceedings)* (July 1989), J. Lane, Ed., vol. 23, 195–206.

[321] C. STOLL. GKS for imaging. In *Computer Graphics (SIGGRAPH '84 Proceedings)* (July 1984), H. Christiansen, Ed., vol. 18, 271–274.

[322] S. STRASSMANN. Hairy brushes. In *Computer Graphics (SIGGRAPH '86 Proceedings)* (Aug. 1986), D. C. Evans and R. J. Athay, Eds., vol. 20, 225–232.

[323] P. S. STRAUSS AND R. CAREY. An object-oriented 3D graphics toolkit. In *Computer Graphics (SIGGRAPH '92 Proceedings)* (July 1992), E. E. Catmull, Ed., vol. 26, 341–349.

[324] M. C. SURLES. An algorithm with linear complexity for interactive, physically-based modeling of large proteins. In *Computer Graphics (SIGGRAPH '92 Proceedings)* (July 1992), E. E. Catmull, Ed., vol. 26, 221–230.

[325] R. W. SWANSON AND L. J. THAYER. A fast shaded-polygon renderer. In *Computer Graphics (SIGGRAPH '86 Proceedings)* (Aug. 1986), D. C. Evans and R. J. Athay, Eds., vol. 20, 95–101.

[326] R. SZELISKI AND D. TERZOPOULOS. From splines to fractals. In *Computer Graphics (SIGGRAPH '89 Proceedings)* (July 1989), J. Lane, Ed., vol. 23, 51–60.

[327] R. SZELISKI AND D. TONNESEN. Surface modeling with oriented particle systems. In *Computer Graphics (SIGGRAPH '92 Proceedings)* (July 1992), E. E. Catmull, Ed., vol. 26, 185–194.

[328] A. TAKAGI, H. TAKAOKA, T. OSHIMA, AND Y. OGATA. Accurate rendering technique based on colorimetric conception. In *Computer Graphics (SIGGRAPH '90 Proceedings)* (Aug. 1990), F. Baskett, Ed., vol. 24, 263–272.

[329] T. TAKALA AND J. HAHN. Sound rendering. In *Computer Graphics (SIGGRAPH '92 Proceedings)* (July 1992), E. E. Catmull, Ed., vol. 26, 211–220.

[330] M. TAMMINEN AND H. SAMET. Efficient octree conversion by connectivity labeling. In *Computer Graphics (SIGGRAPH '84 Proceedings)* (July 1984), H. Christiansen, Ed., vol. 18, 43–51.

[331] P. P. TANNER, S. A. MACKAY, D. A. STEWART, AND M. WEIN. A multitasking switchboard approach to user interface management. In *Computer Graphics (SIGGRAPH '86 Proceedings)* (Aug. 1986), D. C. Evans and R. J. Athay, Eds., vol. 20, 241–248.

[332] R. M. TAYLOR II, W. ROBINETT, V. L. CHI, F. P. BROOKS JR., W. V. WRIGHT, R. S. WILLIAMS, AND E. J. SNYDER. The Nanomanipulator: A virtual reality interface for a scanning tunnelling microscope. In *Computer Graphics (SIGGRAPH '93 Proceedings)* (Aug. 1993), J. T. Kajiya, Ed., vol. 27, 127–134.

[333] S. J. TELLER. Computing the antipenumbra of an area light source. In *Computer Graphics (SIGGRAPH '92 Proceedings)* (July 1992), E. E. Catmull, Ed., vol. 26, 139–148.

[334] S. J. TELLER AND P. HANRAHAN. Global visibility algorithms for illumination computations. In *Computer Graphics (SIGGRAPH '93 Proceedings)* (Aug. 1993), J. T. Kajiya, Ed., vol. 27, 239–246.

[335] S. J. TELLER AND C. H. SÉQUIN. Visibility preprocessing for interactive walkthroughs. In *Computer Graphics (SIGGRAPH '91 Proceedings)* (July 1991), T. W. Sederberg, Ed., vol. 25, 61–69.

[336] D. TERZOPOULOS AND K. FLEISCHER. Modeling inelastic deformation: Viscoelasticity, plasticity, fracture. In *Computer Graphics (SIGGRAPH '88 Proceedings)* (Aug. 1988), J. Dill, Ed., vol. 22, 269–278.

[337] D. TERZOPOULOS, J. PLATT, A. BARR, AND K. FLEISCHER. Elastically deformable models. In *Computer Graphics (SIGGRAPH '87 Proceedings)* (July 1987), M. C. Stone, Ed., vol. 21, 205–214.

[338] W. C. THIBAULT AND B. F. NAYLOR. Set operations on polyhedra using binary space partitioning trees. In *Computer Graphics (SIGGRAPH '87 Proceedings)* (July 1987), M. C. Stone, Ed., vol. 21, 153–162.

[339] D. E. THOMPSON, W. L. BUFORD, L. M. MYERS, D. J. GIURINTANO, AND J. A. BREWER III. A hand biomechanics workstation. In *Computer Graphics (SIGGRAPH '88 Proceedings)* (Aug. 1988), J. Dill, Ed., vol. 22, 335–343.

[340] J. G. TORBORG. A parallel processor architecture for graphics arithmetic operations. In *Computer Graphics (SIGGRAPH '87 Proceedings)* (July 1987), M. C. Stone, Ed., vol. 21, 197–204.

[341] D. L. TOTH. On ray tracing parametric surfaces. In *Computer Graphics (SIGGRAPH '85 Proceedings)* (July 1985), B. A. Barsky, Ed., vol. 19, 171–179.

[342] T. TOTSUKA AND M. LEVOY. Frequency domain volume rendering. In *Computer Graphics (SIGGRAPH '93 Proceedings)* (Aug. 1993), J. T. Kajiya, Ed., vol. 27, 271–278.

[343] R. TROUTMAN AND N. L. MAX. Radiosity algorithms using higher order finite elements. In *Computer Graphics (SIGGRAPH '93 Proceedings)* (Aug. 1993), J. T. Kajiya, Ed., vol. 27, 209–212.

[344] G. TURK. Generating textures for arbitrary surfaces using reaction-diffusion. In *Computer Graphics (SIGGRAPH '91 Proceedings)* (July 1991), T. W. Sederberg, Ed., vol. 25, 289–298.

[345] G. TURK. Re-tiling polygonal surfaces. In *Computer Graphics (SIGGRAPH '92 Proceedings)* (July 1992), E. E. Catmull, Ed., vol. 26, 55–64.

[346] K. TURKOWSKI. Anti-aliasing in topological color spaces. In *Computer Graphics (SIGGRAPH '86 Proceedings)* (Aug. 1986), D. C. Evans and R. J. Athay, Eds., vol. 20, 307–314.

[347] J. U. TURNER. A programmer's interface to graphics dynamics. In *Computer Graphics (SIGGRAPH '84 Proceedings)* (July 1984), H. Christiansen, Ed., vol. 18, 263–270.

[348] C. UPSON AND M. KEELER. VBUFFER: Visible volume rendering. In *Computer Graphics (SIGGRAPH '88 Proceedings)* (Aug. 1988), J. Dill, Ed., vol. 22, 59–64.

[349] M. VAN DE PANNE AND E. FIUME. Sensor-actuator networks. In *Computer Graphics (SIGGRAPH '93 Proceedings)* (Aug. 1993), J. T. Kajiya, Ed., vol. 27, 335–342.

[350] M. VAN DE PANNE, E. FIUME, AND Z. VRANESIC. Reusable motion synthesis using state-space controllers. In *Computer Graphics (SIGGRAPH '90 Proceedings)* (Aug. 1990), F. Baskett, Ed., vol. 24, 225–234.

[351] T. VAN HOOK. Real-time shaded NC milling display. In *Computer Graphics (SIGGRAPH '86 Proceedings)* (Aug. 1986), D. C. Evans and R. J. Athay, Eds., vol. 20, 15–20.

[352] J. J. VAN WIJK. Spot noise-texture synthesis for data visualization. In *Computer Graphics (SIGGRAPH '91 Proceedings)* (July 1991), T. W. Sederberg, Ed., vol. 25, 309–318.

[353] L. VELHO AND J. D. GOMES. Digital halftoning with space filling curves. In *Computer Graphics (SIGGRAPH '91 Proceedings)* (July 1991), T. W. Sederberg, Ed., vol. 25, 81–90.

[354] X. G. VIENNOT, G. EYROLLES, N. JANEY, AND D. ARQUÉS. Combinatorial analysis of ramified patterns and computer imagery of trees. In *Computer Graphics (SIGGRAPH '89 Proceedings)* (July 1989), J. Lane, Ed., vol. 23, 31–40.

[355] B. VON HERZEN AND A. H. BARR. Accurate triangulations of deformed, intersecting surfaces. In *Computer Graphics (SIGGRAPH '87 Proceedings)* (July 1987), M. C. Stone, Ed., vol. 21, 103–110.

[356] B. VON HERZEN, A. H. BARR, AND H. R. ZATZ. Geometric collisions for time-dependent parametric surfaces. In *Computer Graphics (SIGGRAPH '90 Proceedings)* (Aug. 1990), F. Baskett, Ed., vol. 24, 39–48.

[357] D. VOORHIES, D. B. KIRK, AND O. LATHROP. Virtual graphics. In *Computer Graphics (SIGGRAPH '88 Proceedings)* (Aug. 1988), J. Dill, Ed., vol. 22, 247–253.

[358] C. N. WAGGONER, C. TUCKER, AND C. J. NELSON. NOVA*GKS, a distributed implementation of the Graphical Kernel System. In *Computer Graphics (SIGGRAPH '84 Proceedings)* (July 1984), H. Christiansen, Ed., vol. 18, 275–282.

[359] J. R. WALLACE, M. F. COHEN, AND D. P. GREENBERG. A two-pass solution to the rendering equation: A synthesis of ray tracing and radiosity methods. In *Computer Graphics (SIGGRAPH '87 Proceedings)* (July 1987), M. C. Stone, Ed., vol. 21, 311–320.

[360] J. R. WALLACE, K. A. ELMQUIST, AND E. A. HAINES. A ray tracing algorithm for progressive radiosity. In *Computer Graphics (SIGGRAPH '89 Proceedings)* (July 1989), J. Lane, Ed., vol. 23, 315–324.

[361] G. J. WARD. Measuring and modeling anisotropic reflection. In *Computer Graphics (SIGGRAPH '92 Proceedings)* (July 1992), E. E. Catmull, Ed., vol. 26, 265–272.

[362] G. J. WARD, F. M. RUBINSTEIN, AND R. D. CLEAR. A ray tracing solution for diffuse interreflection. In *Computer Graphics (SIGGRAPH '88 Proceedings)* (Aug. 1988), J. Dill, Ed., vol. 22, 85–92.

[363] K. WATERS. A muscle model for animating three-dimensional facial expression. In *Computer Graphics (SIGGRAPH '87 Proceedings)* (July 1987), M. C. Stone, Ed., vol. 21, 17–24.

[364] M. WATT. Light-water interaction using backward beam tracing. In *Computer Graphics (SIGGRAPH '90 Proceedings)* (Aug. 1990), F. Baskett, Ed., vol. 24, 377–385.

[365] J. WEIL. The synthesis of cloth objects. In *Computer Graphics (SIGGRAPH '86 Proceedings)* (Aug. 1986), D. C. Evans and R. J. Athay, Eds., vol. 20, 49–54.

[366] J. WEJCHERT AND D. HAUMANN. Animation aerodynamics. In *Computer Graphics (SIGGRAPH '91 Proceedings)* (July 1991), T. W. Sederberg, Ed., vol. 25, 19–22.

[367] W. WELCH AND A. WITKIN. Variational surface modeling. In *Computer Graphics (SIGGRAPH '92 Proceedings)* (July 1992), E. E. Catmull, Ed., vol. 26, 157–166.

[368] S. H. WESTIN, J. R. ARVO, AND K. E. TORRANCE. Predicting reflectance functions from complex surfaces. In *Computer Graphics (SIGGRAPH '92 Proceedings)* (July 1992), E. E. Catmull, Ed., vol. 26, 255–264.

[369] L. WESTOVER. Footprint evaluation for volume rendering. In *Computer Graphics (SIGGRAPH '90 Proceedings)* (Aug. 1990), F. Baskett, Ed., vol. 24, 367–376.

[370] J. WILHELMS AND A. VAN GELDER. A coherent projection approach for direct volume rendering. In *Computer Graphics (SIGGRAPH '91 Proceedings)* (July 1991), T. W. Sederberg, Ed., vol. 25, 275–284.

[371] L. WILLIAMS. Performance-driven facial animation. In *Computer Graphics (SIGGRAPH '90 Proceedings)* (Aug. 1990), F. Baskett, Ed., vol. 24, 235–242.

[372] A. WITKIN, K. FLEISCHER, AND A. BARR. Energy constraints on parameterized models. In *Computer Graphics (SIGGRAPH '87 Proceedings)* (July 1987), M. C. Stone, Ed., vol. 21, 225–232.

[373] A. WITKIN AND M. KASS. Spacetime constraints. In *Computer Graphics (SIGGRAPH '88 Proceedings)* (Aug. 1988), J. Dill, Ed., vol. 22, 159–168.

[374] A. WITKIN AND M. KASS. Reaction-diffusion textures. In *Computer Graphics (SIGGRAPH '91 Proceedings)* (July 1991), T. W. Sederberg, Ed., vol. 25, 299–308.

[375] A. WITKIN AND W. WELCH. Fast animation and control of nonrigid structures. In *Computer Graphics (SIGGRAPH '90 Proceedings)* (Aug. 1990), F. Baskett, Ed., vol. 24, 243–252.

[376] G. WOLBERG AND T. E. BOULT. Separable image warping with spatial lookup tables. In *Computer Graphics (SIGGRAPH '89 Proceedings)* (July 1989), J. Lane, Ed., vol. 23, 369–378.

[377] X. WU. An efficient anti-aliasing technique. In *Computer Graphics (SIGGRAPH '91 Proceedings)* (July 1991), T. W. Sederberg, Ed., vol. 25, 143–152.

[378] L. YAEGER, C. UPSON, AND R. MYERS. Combining physical and visual simulation — creation of the planet Jupiter for the film "2010". In *Computer Graphics (SIGGRAPH '86 Proceedings)* (Aug. 1986), D. C. Evans and R. J. Athay, Eds., vol. 20, 85–93.

[379] F. YAMAGUCHI. A unified approach to interference problems using a triangle processor. In *Computer Graphics (SIGGRAPH '85 Proceedings)* (July 1985), B. A. Barsky, Ed., vol. 19, 141–149.

[380] H. R. ZATZ. Galerkin radiosity: A higher order solution method for global illumination. In *Computer Graphics (SIGGRAPH '93 Proceedings)* (Aug. 1993), J. T. Kajiya, Ed., vol. 27, 213–220.

[381] R. C. ZELEZNIK, D. B. CONNER, M. M. WLOKA, D. G. ALIAGA, N. T. HUANG, P. M. HUBBARD, B. KNEP, H. KAUFMAN, J. F. HUGHES, AND A. VAN DAM. An object-oriented framework for the integration of interactive animation techniques. In *Computer Graphics (SIGGRAPH '91 Proceedings)* (July 1991), T. W. Sederberg, Ed., vol. 25, 105–112.

[382] R. C. ZELEZNIK, K. P. HERNDON, D. C. ROBBINS, N. HUANG, T. MEYER, N. PARKER, AND J. F. HUGHES. An interactive 3D toolkit for constructing 3D widgets. In *Computer Graphics (SIGGRAPH '93 Proceedings)* (Aug. 1993), J. T. Kajiya, Ed., vol. 27, 81–84.

[383] Y. ZHANG AND R. E. WEBBER. Space diffusion: An improved parallel halftoning technique using space-filling curves. In *Computer Graphics (SIGGRAPH '93 Proceedings)* (Aug. 1993), J. T. Kajiya, Ed., vol. 27, 305–312.

Author Index

Conference Committee

CONFERENCE CO-CHAIRS

Bob Judd
(Los Alamos National Laboratory)
Mark Resch
(Luna Imaging, Inc.)

CONFERENCE COMMITTEE CHAIRS

Molly Morgan-Kuhns, *Conference Coordinator*
Jim Kajiya, *Papers*
(Caltech)
Donna Cox, *Panels*
(NCSA)
Rich Ehlers, *Courses*
(Evans and Sutherland)
Jamie Thompson, *Electronic Theater*
(TIVOLI Systems, Inc.)
Simon Penny, *Machine Culture*
(University of Florida)
Alyce Kaprow, *Designing Technology*
(The New Studio)
Enrique Godreau, *Tomorrow's Realities*
(Aldus Corporation)
J. J. Garcia-Luna, *Multimedia 93 Conference Chair*
(SRI International)
P. Venkat Rangan, *Multimedia 93 Program Chair*
(University of California at San Diego)
Peter Pathe, *Electronic Publishing*
(Microsoft Corporation)
Jackie Wollner, *Exhibits*
(Independent)
Carolyn Williams, *Marketing*
(Kubota Pacific Computer, Inc.)
Coco Conn, *SIGKids*
(Homer & Associates)
John E. French, Jr., *Operations Chair*
(GeoQuest Systems)
Lyn Bartram, *Student Volunteer Operationss*
(Simon Fraser University)
Phil Getto, *Special Interest Group Operations*
(Rasna Corp.)
Jeff Jortner, *Registration Operations*
(Sandia National Laboratories)
Jim Kuhns, *Materials Operations*
(City of San Diego)
Mark Leon, *Speaker Materials Operations*
(Forward Edge Technologies)
Jeff Mayer, *Environmental Design Operations*
(CRSS Architects)
Dave Nadeau, *Computer Operations*
(San Diego Supercomputer Center)
John Michael Pierobon, *International Operations*
(Silicon Graphics)
Roger Wilson, *Child Care Operations*
(Rhythm & Hues)

CONFERENCE PLANNING COMMITTEE

Mike Bailey (San Diego Supercomputing Center)
Maxine D. Brown (University of Illinois at Chicago)
Carol Byram (Sony Computer Peripherals Co.)
Patti Harrison (SIGGRAPH 94 coordinator)
Brian Herzog (SunSoft, Inc.)
Bob Judd (Los Alamos National Laboratory)
Peter Meechan (Wavefront Technologies, Inc.)
Molly Morgan-Kuhns (SIGGRAPH 93 coordinator)
Adele Newton (Consultant)
Mark Resch (Luna Imaging, Inc.)
Dino Schweitzer (U.S. Air Force Academy)
Steve Van Frank (independent)

PAPERS COMMITTEE

James T. Kajiya (California Institute of Technology)
Brian Barsky (University of California, Berkeley)
Forest Baskett (Silicon Graphics Computer Systems)
Ingrid Carlbom (Digital Equipment Corporation)
Ed Catmull (Pixar)
Frank Crow (Apple Computer, Inc.)
Tony DeRose (University of Washington)
Andrew Glassner (Xerox PARC)
Paul Heckbert (Carnegie Mellon University)
Christoph Hoffmann (Purdue University)
John F. Hughes (Brown University)
Michael Kass (Apple Computer, Inc.)
Mike Keeler (Silicon Graphics Computer Systems)
Marc Levoy (Stanford University)
Jock Mackinlay (Xerox PARC)
Nelson Max (Lawrence Livermore National Laboratory)
Don P. Mitchell (AT&T Bell Labs)
Bruce Naylor (AT&T Bell Labs)
Tomoyuki Nishita (Fukuyama University)
Darwyn Peachey (Pixar)
Marc H. Raibert (Massachusetts Institute of Technology)
David F. Rogers (U.S. Naval Academy)
Jarek Rossignac (IBM Research)
Tom Sederberg (Brigham Young University)
Francois Sillion (École Normale Supèrieure)
Ken Torrance (Cornell University)
Andries van Dam (Brown University)

PANELS COMMITTEE

Donna Cox (National Center for Supercomputing Applications/University of Illinois)
Mark Bajuk (University of Illinois)
Mike Keeler (Silicon Graphics Computer Systems)
Bruce McCormick (Texas A&M University)
Mike McNeill (National Center for Supercomputing Applications/University of Illinois)
Barbara Mones-Hattal (George Mason University)
Jon Steinhart (Consultant)
Pierre Van Cleve (Art Cellar Exchange)
Jim Winget (Silicon Graphics Computer Systems)

COURSE JURY

Rich Ehlers (Evans & Sutherland)
Michael Bailey (San Diego Supercomputer Center)
Jeffrey J. McConnell (Canisius College)
Alan Norton (IBM T.J. Watson Research Center)
Scott Senften (Shell Development Company)
Harry Smith (University of North Carolina)
Lauretta Jones (IBM T.J. Watson Research Center)

COURSE COMMITTEE

Michael Bailey (San Diego Supercomputer Center)
Ed Council (Timberfield Systems)
Michel Denber (Xerox Corporation)
Nan Schaller (Rochester Institute of Technology)
Scott Senften (Shell Development Company)

SIGKIDS COMMITTEE

Coco Conn (Homer & Associates)
Laura London (Autodesk, Inc.)
Ellen McWhirter (Texas A&M University)
Katie Poole (Walt Disney Imagineering)
Robert Price (Hoffer Elementary School, Yucaipa, CA)
Judy Sachter (IBM)
Diane Schwartz (Northwestern University)

COMPUTER OPERATIONS COMMITTEE

David R. Nadeau (San Diego Supercomputer Center)
Thomas E. Hutton (San Diego Supercomputer Center)
John L. Moreland (San Diego Supercomputer Center)

INTERNATIONAL COMMITTEE

John Michael Pierobon (Silicon Graphics)
Marsha Anderson
Bernard M. Dresner
Masa Inakage (The Media Studio)
Lars Kjelldahl (Royal Institute of Technology, Sweden)
Martin Malamud (Imagica)
Peter Meechan (Wavefront Technologies)
Maria Grazia Mattei (Mediatech/IBTS)
Nan C. Schaller (Rochester Institute of Technology)
Roberto Scopigno (CNUCE - Consiglio Nazionale delle Ricerche)
Piero Scotti (Silicon Graphics S. p. A.)
Marcelo Knorich Zuffo (Universidade de Sao Paulo - LSI)

TECHNICAL SLIDE SET JURY

Rosalee Nerheim-Wolfe (DePaul University)
Mike Bailey (San Diego Supercomuter Center)
Steve Cunningham (California State University Stanislaus)
Jim Kajiya (Caltech)

PROCEEDINGS PRODUCTION

Steve Cunningham, Production Editor (California State University Stanislaus)
Maureen Stone, Color Consultant (Xerox PARC)

FUNDAMENTALS SEMINAR

Wayne E. Carlson, Chair (The Ohio State University)
Mike Bailey (San Diego Supercomputer Center)
Judith R. Brown (The University of Iowa)

PAPERS REVIEWERS

Salim Abi-Ezzi
Debra Adams
Kurt Akeley
Mark Altman
John Amanatides
George Philip Amburn
Jennifer Anderson
Tony Apodaca
Jim Arvo
Clara Asmail
Bob Bacon
Norman Badler
Sig Badt
Ezekial Bahar
Ruzena Bajcsy
Tom Banchoff
David Baraff
Al Barr
Richard H. Bartels
Ronen Barzel
Carl Bass
Michael Bauer
Barry Becker
Thad Beier
Ian Bell
Mark Benzel
Matthew Berkemeier
Fausto Bernardini
Cliff Beshers
Eric Bier
Avi Bleiweiss
Jim Blinn
Jules Bloomenthal
Bruce Blumberg
Paul Borrel
Mark Brown
Robert Brown
Freddy Bruckstein
Steve Bryson
John Buchanan
Richard Buckius
Martin Buehler
Derrick Burns
David Busath
Brian Cabral
Tom Calvert
A.T. Campbell
Lee Campbell
John Canny
Stuart K. Card
Rikk Carey
Wayne Carlson
Loren Carpenter
Robert Cess
Sheue-Ling Chang
Eric Chen
Richard Chuang
Beth Cobb
Elaine Cohen
Michael F. Cohen
William Cohen
Brook Conner
Michael Connolly
Perry Cook
Rob Cook
Nancy Cornelius
C. Adam Crane
Roger Crawfis
Jim Cremer
Jill Crisman
Steve Cunningham
Tom Davis
Jonas de M. Gomes
Michael Deering
Gary Demos
John Dill
Bruce Donald
Laura Downs
Bob Drebin
Tom Duff
Craig Dunwoody
Scott Dyer
David S. Ebert
Stephen Ellis
Nick England
Michael Erdman
Steve Feiner
Scott Fisher
Ken Fishkin
Eugene Fiume
James D. Foley
James Foran
David Forsey
Farhad Fouladi
Alain Fournier
Charles Francois
William Randolph Franklin
Henry Fuchs
Kikuo Fujimura
Thomas Funkhouser
Don Fussell
Andre Gagalowicz
Tinsley Galyean
Dan Garcia
Itay Gat
Larry Gelberg
Ron Gentile
Mike Gleicher
Andrew Golding
Ronald N. Goldman
Michael T. Goodrich
Ilya Gorelick
Suresh Goyal
Mark Green
Ned Greene
Cindy Grimm
Mark Grossman
Stanley Guan
Leo Guibas
Charlie Gunn
Stefan Haas
Paul Haeberli
Tom Hahn
Eric Haines
Roy Hall
Mark Halstead
Patrick M. Hanrahan
Chuck Hansen
Paul Hansen
Chandlee Harrell
John Hart
Dave Haumann
Xiao Dong He
Jeff Heisserman
James Helman
Ken Herndon
David Hill
Lewis Hitchner
John Hobby
Jessica Hodgins
Andrey Hodulev
Richard Holloway
Nicolas Holzschuch
Robert Howe

PAPERS REVIEWERS (Continued)

John Howell
William Hsu
Philip Hubbard
Scott Hudson
Jeff Hultquist
Insung Ihm
Frederik W. Jansen
David Jevans
Leo Joskowicz
Avi Kak
Michael Kallay
Deven Kalra
Kazufumi Kaneda
Dina Karon
Dan Kartch
J.K. Kearney
Michael Kelley
Pradeep Khosla
David Kirk
Victor Klassen
Gundrun Klinker
Brian Knep
Huseyin Kocak
Jeff Koechling
Craig Kolb
Gary Kopec
Carl Korobkin
Myron Kruger
William Kubitz
Steven D. Kugelmass
Toshiyasu Kunii
David Laidlaw
Jean-Claude Latombe
Mark Lee
Ralph Levien
Bryan Lewis
John Lewis
Peter Link
Mark Linton
Richard Lipes
James Lipscomb
Peter Litwinowicz
Chris Long
Charles Loop
Bill Lorensen
Bradley J. Lucier
Wayne Lytle
Takahashi Maekawa
Nadia Magnenat-Thalman
Dinesh Manocha
Joe Marks
Ralph Martin
Larisa Matejic
Robert Mazaika
David F. McAllister
Mike McKenna
David McKeown
Tom McMahon
Barbara Meier
Jai Prakash Menon
Phil Mercurio
Russell Mesereau
Dimitris Metaxas
Gary Meyer
Tom Meyer
James Michener
Gavin Miller
Joseph Mitchell
Steven Molnar
Peter Monta
John Montrym
John Morse
David Moulton
David Mount
Ernst Mucke
Heinrich Muller
Sesh Murthy
F. Ken Musgrave
Karol Myszkowski
Michael Nagy
Eihachiro Nakamae
Sundar Narasimhan
Shawn Neely
Ulrich Neumann
Derek Ney
Tom Ngo
Jason Nieh
Greg Nielson
Kevin Novins
T. J. O'Donnell
Larry O'Gorman
Dan R. Olsen
Art Olson
David Orton
Eben Ostby
G. Scott Owen
Jerry Owens
Dinesh Pai
Jamie Painter
Alberto Paoluzzi
Thrasyvoulos N. Pappas
Fred Parke
Nicholas M. Patrikalakis
Richard R. Patterson
Randy Pausch
Joseph Pegna
Catherine Pelachaud
Qunsheng Peng
Joe Pentland
Sandy Pentland
Ken Perlin
Bernard Peroche
Jorg Peters
Steve Pieper
Michael Pique
Catherine Plaisant
Robert Playter
Andres Polit
Luis Porcelli
Tom Porter
Michael Potmesil
Helmut Pottmann
Pierre Poulin
Vaughan Pratt
Przemyslaw Prusinkiewicz
Sarah Rajala
Ramana Rao
Ari Rappaport
Craig Reynolds
Jim Rhyne
Dan Rice
Robert Ringrose
Richard Robb
George Robertson
Philip Robertson
Warren Robinett
Alyn Rockwood
John Rohlf
Robert Rose
Joseph M. Rosen
Holly Rushmeier
Robert Safranek

PAPERS REVIEWERS (Continued)

Takafumi Saito
Georgios Sakas
David Salesin
Eric Saund
Rick Sayre
Bengt-Olaf Schnieder
Peter Schroeder
Larry Schumaker
Jack Schwartz
Mark Segal
Michael Seibert
H.P. Seidel
Adrian Sfarti
Min-Zhi Shao
Vadim Shapiro
Rajeev Sharma
Miko Shinya
Peter Shirley
Ken Shoemake
John Sibert
Maryann Simmons
Eero Simoncelli
Karl Sims
Mel Slater
Kenneth Sloan
Philipp Slussallek
Theodore Smith
John Snyder
Ajay Sreekanth
George Stiny
Maureen Stone
Steve Strassman
Paul Strauss
Carol Strohecker
K.R. Subramanian
Shankar Subramanian
Kokichi Sugihara
Richard Szeliski
Masashi Takagi
Tokiichiro Takahashi
Roberto Tamassia
Toshimitsu Tanaka
John Tang
Gabriel Taubin
Seth Teller
Dimitri Terzopoulos
Greg Thaggard
Carlo Tomasi
Alan Tuchman
Greg Turk
Rolf Van Widenfelt
Jarke van Wijk
Mark VandeWettering
George Vanecek
Michael Vannier
Christophe Vedal
Luis Velho
Pamela Vermeer
Alan Vermuelen
Anne Verroust
Guy Vezina
Marie-Luce Viaud
John Vlissides
Douglas Voorhies
Christopher Walker
John Wallace
Greg Walsh
Gregory J. Ward
Colin Ware
Joe Warren
Kevin Weiler
Marceli Wein
Will Welch
Stephen H. Westin
Lee Westover
Turner Whitted
Dave Wiemer
Bud Wildin
Jane Wilhelms
Lance Williams
Peter Williams
Andy Witkin
Larry Wolff
Christopher Wren
Brian Wyvill
Geoff Wyvill
Hussein Yahia
Zijiang Yang
Harold Zatz
Robert Zeleznik
Dave Zeltzer

COURSES REVIEWERS

Tony Apodaca
Michael Bailey
Daniel Bergeron
Richard Becker
Teresa Bleser
Ed Council
Janet Chin
Steve Cunningham
Wayne Carlson
Michel Denber
Edward Farrell
Andrew Glassner
Brenda Hash
Eric Haines
John C. Hart
Lou Harrison
Mark Henderson
Lauretta Jones
Alyce Kaprow
David Kramlich
Lorene Lavora
Olin Lathrop
Tony Longson
Jeffrey J. McConnell
Frank Bliss
Maureen Nappi
Scott Nelson
Alan Norton
Egondu Onyejekwe
Jeffrey Persch
Tina Price
Jim Rhyne
Sylvie J. Rueff
Harry F. Smith
Jon Steinhart
Matt Schemenaur
Ming-Jen Shyu
Scott D. Senften
Bret Verde
Annette Weintraub
Brian Wyvill
Bruce Wands
Lee Westover
Michael Wollman

PROFESSIONAL SUPPORT

ACM SIGGRAPH Conference Coordinators

Molly Morgan-Kuhns, SIGGRAPH 93
Debbie Buuck, Deputy Conference Coordinator, SIGGRAPH 93
Patti Harrison, SIGGRAPH 94

ACM SIGGRAPH Program Director

Lois Blankstein
Donna Goldsmith, *ACM SIGGRAPH Coordinator*

Administrative Assistants

MK Haley, papers
Terri Haines, panels
Wendi DeHoop, courses

Audio/Visual Support

AVW Audio Visual, Inc.
Ed Goodman
Gary Clark
Jim Costigan

Conference Accounting

Smith, Bucklin and Associates
Ruth Kerns
Roger Albert
Natalie Patton

Conference Management

Smith, Bucklin and Associates
Cindy Stark
Peggy Sloyan
Maureen Baumann
Jackie Groszek

Conference Travel Agency

ATI Travel Management, Inc.
Laurie Shapiro
Renee Peavler
Susan Neal

Service Contractor

Andrews-Bartlett Exposition Services
John Patronski
John Loveless
Bob Borsz

Exhibition Management

Hall-Erickson, Inc.
Pete Erickson
Barbara Voss
Mike Weil

Graphic Design

Mo Viele

Graphic Design/Editing

Ann Redelfs

Copy Coordinator

Smith, Bucklin and Associates
Leona Caffey

Communications

Pacific Visions Communications
Val Marmillion
Elizabeth Bailey
Jaclyn McKendree

Organization Development Consultant

Jeanette Overgard

Exhibitors

5D Solutions Ltd.
ABEKAS
Academic Press, Inc.
Accom, Inc.
Addison-Wesley Publishing Company
Adobe Systems Inc.
Advance Reproductions Corporation
Advanced Digital Imaging
Advanced Imaging
Advanced Technology Center
Advanced Visual Systems Inc.
Agfa Division
AK Peters, Ltd.
Alias Research Inc.
Alpha Systems Lab, Inc.
American Showcase, Inc.
AmPro Corporation
Andromeda Systems Inc.
aniMedia
Anjon & Associates
Apple Computer, Inc.
Apunix
Ascension Technology Corporation
ASDG, Incorporated
Association for Computing Machinery (ACM)
Aurora Systems
Autodesk
autodessys Inc.
AVC Presentations
AV Video
Aztek, Inc.
Barco, Inc.
Bit 3 Computer Corporation
Byron Preiss Multimedia Company, Inc.
Byte by Byte Corporation
Canon U.S.A., Inc.
CELCO
Center for Creative Imaging
Chromatek Inc.
CIRAD/Lab. de Modelisation
Color Publishing
Computer Artist
Computer Design, Inc.
Computer Expressions
Computer Graphics World
Computer Pictures
Computers in Physics
Core Software Technology
Covid, Inc.
CrystalGraphics, Inc.
Cyberware
Cymbolic Sciences International
Data Translation
Diaquest, Inc.
Digital Arts
Digital Equipment Corporation
Dimension International
Discreet Logic Inc.
Division Inc.
Du Pont Pixel Systems
Dynamic Graphics, Inc.
Eastman Kodak Company, Motion Analysis Systems Div.
Electric Image, Inc.
ElectroGIG USA Inc.
Electronic Publishing
Engineering Animation, Inc.
ENHANCE Memory Products, Inc.
Eurographics
Evans & Sutherland Design Systems Division
Evans & Sutherland Industrial Products Group
Extron Electronics
Fairchild Defense
FARO Technologies Inc.
Focus Graphics Inc.
Folsom Research, Inc.
FOR.A Corporation of America
Fractal Design Corporation
Fraunhofer Computer Graphics Research Group (USA)
FSI (F and S, Inc.)
Global Intermedia
Gossett Graphics
Grass Valley Group
GW Hannaway & Associates, Inc.
Helios Systems
Herstal Automation Ltd.
Hewlett-Packard Company
High Color, Imagetech Publications
Hotronic, Inc.
Hyperspeed Technologies, Inc.
IBM Corporation
IBM-Technology Products
IEEE Computer Society
Imagina-INA
Impediment Incorporated
Information International Inc.
Inline, Inc.
Integrix, Inc.
Intelligent Resources Integrated Systems
International Communications Industries Association
International Design Magazine
IRIS Graphics, Inc.
Ithaca Software
JVC Professional Products Company
Kingston Technology Corporation
Knowledge Industry Publications/Montage Publishing Inc.
KOZMO Ltd.
Kubota Pacific Computer
Kurta Corporation
Lasergraphics, Inc.
LAZERUS
Legacy Systems International, Inc.
Lightwave Communications, Inc.
Lyon Lamb Video Animation Systems, Inc.
Management Graphics, Inc.
Marco International, Inc.
Mathematica Inc.
Maximum Strategy, Inc.
Meckler Publishing/CD ROM World
Megatek Corporation
Minicomputer Exchange, Inc.

Minolta Corporation
MIT Press
Mitsubishi - Professional Electronics Division
Mondo 2000
Monitor/Media Age
Moonlight Computer Products
Morgan Kaufmann Publishers
NASA Tech Briefs
National Computer Graphics Association
Network Computing Devices
Nippon Computer Graphics Association
Numerical Algorithms Group, Inc.
OpenVision Technologies, Inc.
Optigraphics
O'Reilly & Associates, Inc.
Oxberry
Pacific Data Group
Panasonic Communications & Systems, OA Group
Parallax Graphics, Inc.
Parallax Software Inc.
Parity Systems
Philips Semiconductors
Photometrics, Ltd.
Photron Limited
Pioneer New Media Technologies, Inc.
Pixar
Pixel Vision
Polhemus
Portable Graphics, Inc.
Post Magazine/Testa Communications
PRE-
Prentice Hall
Preston Publications/IMAGEBase
PRIOR Data Sciences Product Sales Inc.
Programs Plus & Video
Proxima Corporation
Psychic Lab, Inc.
Quarterdeck Office Systems
R-Squared
Rainbow Technologies, Inc.
Raster Graphics Inc.
Raytheon Company, Submarine Signal Division
Resolution
RFX Inc.
RGB Spectrum
Roche Image Analysis Systems, Inc.
Ron Scott Inc.
Santos Technology Inc.
Sanyo Fisher (USA) Corporation
School of Communication Arts
Science Accessories Corporation
Scientific Computing & Automation
Seiko Instruments USA, Inc.
Sense 8 Corporation
Sharp Electronics Corporation
Shooting Star Technology
Side Effects Software Inc.
Sierra Video Systems, Inc.
SIGGRAPH 94
SIGGRAPH Education Committee
SIGGRAPH Local Groups
SIGGRAPH Video Review
Sigma Electronics, Inc.
Silicon Graphics Computer Systems
Sixty Eight Thousand, Inc.
Society of Motion Picture & Television Engineers
SOFTIMAGE Inc.
Software Security, Inc.
Software Systems
Sony Corporation
Specular International
Springer-Verlag New York, Inc.
StereoGraphics Corporation
Sun Microsystems, Inc.
Superflou Inc.
Syndesis Corporation
Tamron Industries, Inc.
Tatung Science and Technology, Inc.
Techexport, Inc.
Tech Images International
Tech-Source Inc.
Tektronix, Inc.
TELOS: The Electronic Library of Science
Template Graphics Software, Inc.
Texas Memory Systems, Inc.
Thomson Digital Image
Truevision Inc.
Uniras, Inc.
UNIX Review
UNIXWorld Magazine
Vertigo Technology Inc.
VIC Hi-Tech Corporation
Video Graphic Technologies
Video Systems Magazine
Videomedia, Inc.
Viewpoint Animation Engineering
Visionetics International Corporation
Vision Quest
Visual Information Development Inc. (VIDI)
Visual Numerics
Visual Software
The Vivid Group
VRontier Worlds of Stoughton, Inc.
Wacom Technology Corporation
Waite Group Press
Wasatch Computer Technology, Inc.
Wavefront Technologies, Inc.
John Wiley & Sons, Inc.
Winsted Corporation
Wired USA
Xaos Tools Inc.
Yamashita Engineering Manufacture Inc.
Yarc Systems Corporation
Zeh Graphics Systems, Inc.
Zen Over Zero

Index

(Pages marked with * contain panel summaries)

Cover Image Credits

Front cover

"Flowers"
Copyright © 1993 Regents of the University of California
An image of flowers is filtered by a Line Integral Convolution (LIC). The original image was created by pixel replicating a 256 x 256 image to 1024 x 1024. The vector field for the LIC operation was created by taking the gradient of bandlimited noise and rotating each of the gradient vectors 90 degrees. A ramp filter was used in the LIC to simulate brush strokes.

The separations for the front cover image were created through the same digital process used for the recent ACM/Transactions on Graphics special issue on color. The original TIFF file was converted to a device independent color representation and then mapped to a set of printable colors that match, as best as possible, the appearance as the original monitor image. This process provides better color fidelity and more image detail than printing and rescanning the picture. See the introduction to the October 1992 issue of TOG for more information about the process.
Reference: *"Imaging Vector Fields Using Line Integral Convolution,"* Brian Cabral and Leith (Casey) Leedom, p. 266

Title image

"Room with Books"
Copyright © 1993, Program of Computer Graphics, Cornell University
An architectural interior rendered using a combination of hierarchical radiosity and discontinuity meshing. The interior was modeled by Matt Hyatt and rendered by Dani Lischinski and Filippo Tampieri.
Reference: *"Combining Hierarchical Radiosity and Discontinuity Meshing,"* Dani Lischinski, Filippo Tampieri, Donald P. Greenberg, p 207

Back cover, top left

"Traffic Jam to Point Reyes"
Copyright © 1993, Scott R. Nelson and Michael F. Deering, Sun Microsystems Computer Corporation
Inspired by Rob Cook's 1983 image "Road to Point Reyes," this image was rendered on a SPARCstation 10 ZX as a single scene using hardware lighting and Z-buffer. Eight-pass stochastic sampling was used to antialias the scene, which contains more than 2.3 million triangles. Models are courtesy of Viewpoint Animation Engineering.
Reference: *"Leo: A System for Cost Effective 3D Shaded Graphics,"* Michael F. Deering, Scott R. Nelson, p. 108

Back cover, top right

"Interior of a Temple"
Coypright © 1992, 1993 Harold R. Zatz and Cornell University
This image was computed in parallel on an Apollo DN10000, five HP 9000/720's, and five DECstation 3000's. It shows the interior of a temple composed of 607 parametrically defined surfaces. Using the Galerkin method, radiosity values were determined as polynomial functions over these surfaces, eliminating any need for meshing or tessellation. The image was ray-traced directly from the radiosity solution, without interpolation.
Reference: *"Galerkin Radiosity: A Higher Order Solution Method for Global Illumination,"* Harold R. Zatz, p. 220

Back cover, middle left

"Development of *Hieracium umbellatum*"
Copyright © 1992, Przemyslaw Prusinkiewicz, Mark Hammel, and Eric Mjolsness
The head of *Hieracium umbellatum* undergoes a sequence of transformations during its development from a bud to a flower to a fruit. The figure combines selected frames from an animation of this process. The model has been expressed using the formalism of differential Lindenmayer systems. The image was created on a Silicon Graphics 4D/310 workstation.
Reference: *"Animation of Plant Development,"* Przemyslaw Prusinkiewicz, Mark S. Hammell, Eric Mjolsness, p. 359

Back cover, middle right

"Hyperbolic Space"
Copyright © 1993, The Geometry Center, University of Minnesota
Modeling and rendering by Charlie Gunn using Mathematica™ and Renderman™
This image shows a tessellation of hyperbolic space by regular right-angled dodecahedron. It arises in the investigation of the geometry of the complement of the three linked circles known as the Borromean rings and is featured in the mathematical animation "Not Knot."
Reference: *"Discrete Groups and Visualization of Three-Dimensional Manifolds,"* Charlie Gunn, p. 261

Back cover, bottom left

"The Earth taking into Account Atmosphere"
Copyright © 1993, Fukuyama University and Hiroshima Prefectural University
Artists: Tomoyuki Nishita, Takao Sirai, Katsumi Tadamura, Eihachiro Nakamae
This image was created on an IRIS Indigo Elan using software by the authors. The intention of the image is application to space flight simulators and the simulation of surveys of the earth; displaying the earth including the surface of the sea viewed from outer space taking into account particles (air molecules and aerosols) in the atmosphere and water molecules in the sea.
Reference: *"Display of The Earth Taking into Account Atmospheric Scattering,"* Tomoyuki Nishita, Takao Sirai, Katsumi Tadamura, Eichahiro Nakamae, p. 181

Back cover, bottom right

"Surface of Ion-Bombarded Graphite"
Copyright © 1992, The University of North Carolina at Chapel Hill
Created by Russell M. Taylor II and R. Stanley Williams with custom software on the Pixel-Planes 5
Shaded STM image of ion-bombarded graphite sample. This image shows tip scratches on the lower left part of the sample and ripples in the upper right corner caused by sheets of graphite pushing up out of the surface. The surface is colored according to height, with redder areas at higher elevations.
Reference: *"The Nanomanipulator: A Virtual-Reality Interface for a Scanning Tunneling Microscope,"* Russell M. Taylor II, Warren Robinett, Vernon L. Chi, Frederick P. Brooks Jr., William V. Wright, R. Stanley Williams, Eric J. Snyder, p. 132

Notes

Notes

Notes

Local Groups Currently Operating/Forming

LocalGroupChairs@siggraph.org

California
Bay Area
Bay_Area_SIGGRAPH_Chapter
@siggraph.org

Los Angeles
Coco Conn
2207 Willetta Avenue
Los Angeles, CA 90068
(213) 962-1662
Los_Angeles_SIGGRAPH_
Chapter@siggraph.org

San Diego
Mike Amron
2334 Galahad Road
San Diego, CA 92123
(619) 277-5699

Colorado
Denver/Boulder
Denver/Boulder
ACM SIGGRAPH
P.O. Box 440785
Aurora, CO 80041
(303) 696-6863
Denver/Boulder_SIGGRAPH_
Chapter@siggraph.org

Florida
Miami
Bob Corti
(305) 621-5266

North Central Florida
Millard Pate
Micron / Green
1240 N. W. 21st Avenue
Gainesville, FL 32609
(904) 376-1529
(904) 376-0466 FAX
Florida_SIGGRAPH_Chapter
@siggraph.org

Orlando
Lynn Finch
P.O. Box 2208
Winter Park, FL 32790-2208
(407) 672-3654 (voicemail)
(407) 859-3269 (bulletin board)
Orlando_SIGGRAPH_Chapter
@siggraph.org

Tampa Bay
Rob Rothfarb
P.O. Box 6402
Clearwater, FL 34618-6402
(813) 797-5770
Tampa_Bay_SIGGRAPH_Chapter
@siggraph.org

Georgia
Atlanta
Anita Critz
P.O. Box 250382
Atlanta, GA 30325
(404) 785-2911
(404) 436-6097 FAX, ATTN:
Anita Critz

Illinois
Chicago
Chicago ACM SIGGRAPH
P.O. Box 578365
Chicago, IL 60657-8365
(708) 387-2149
(708) 387-2159 FAX
Chicago_SIGGRAPH_
Chapter@siggraph.org

Massachusetts
New England
New England ACM SIGGRAPH
P.O. Box 194
Bedford, MA 01730
(508) 881-6467
New_England_SIGGRAPH_
Chapter@siggraph.org

Minnesota
Minneapolis/St. Paul
Mark Feyereisen
16650 Marystown Road
Shakopee, MN 53379
(612) 445-2492 (H)
(612) 893-0077 FAX, ATTN:
Mark Feyereisen

New Jersey
Princeton
Ron Lussen
P.O. Box 1324
Princeton, NJ 08524
(609) 734-3176
(609) 734-2259 FAX
Princeton_SIGGRAPH_Chapter
@siggraph.org

New Mexico
Rio Grande
Ray Elliott
P.O. Box 8352
Albuquerque, NM 87198
(505) 667-1449
(505) 575-6442 FAX
Rio_Grande_SIGGRAPH_Chapter
@siggraph.org

New York
New York City
Tim Binkley
School of Visual Arts
209 E. 23rd St.
New York, NY 10010
(212) 645-0852
New_York_SIGGRAPH_Chapter
@siggraph.org

Rochester
Karla Kuzawinski
Xerox Business Products
800 Phillips Road
Webster, NY 14580

North Carolina
Research Triangle
Tom Palmer
North Carolina Supercomputer
Center
3021 Cornwallis Road
Research Triangle Park, NC
27709
(919) 248-1117 (W)
(919) 248-1101 FAX
tom_palmer@siggraph.org

Texas
Dallas
Dallas ACM SIGGRAPH
P.O. Box 800691
Dallas, TX 75380-0691
Dallas_Area_SIGGRAPH_
Chapter@siggraph.org

Houston
Jim Maida
(713) 483-1113
(713) 488-3755
Houston_Area_SIGGRAPH_
Chapter@siggraph.org

Washington
Richland
Don Jones
djones@carbun.pnl.gov

Washington, D.C.
Washington, D.C.
Paul Lipsky
P.O. Box 32244
Washington, D.C. 20007
(703) 532-3917
Washington_DC_SIGGRAPH_
Chapter@siggraph.org

Argentina
Buenos Aires
Alejandro Delgado
(305) 882-0861 (c/o Miami, FL)

Brazil
San Paulo
Sergio Martinelli
Digital Group
Rua Bairi 294
05059 San Paulo, SP1 Brazil

Bulgaria
Sofia
Stoyan Maleshkov
Technical Univ. of Sofia
Dept. of Prog. & Computer Appl.
1756 Sofia, Bulgaria

Canada
Calgary
Paul Smith
(403) 253-6129

Montreal
Kaveh Kardan
(514) 842-6172

Toronto
Michael McCool
(416) 978-6619 (W)
Toronto_SIGGRAPH_Chapter
@siggraph.org

Vancouver
Brian D. McMillan
P.O. Box 33986 Postal Station D
Vancouver, B.C. V6J 4L7
Canada
(604) 822-2466 (W)
(604) 224-1119 (H)
(604) 822-3808 FAX
Vancouver_BC_SIGGRAPH_
Chapter@siggraph.org

England
London
Greg Moore
27 Sinclair House
Sandwish Street
London, WC1H 9PT
44 (81) 368-1299 X7475
London_SIGGRAPH_Chapter
@ siggraph.org

France
Paris
Alain Chesnais
#2 Rue Henre Matisse
59300 Aulnoy-les-Valenciennes
France
33 27-30-18-10
33 27-42-52-00 FAX
Paris_SIGGRAPH_Chapter
@siggraph.org

Korea
Seoul
Yomi Choi
Hanmuc Systems
4th UIC B/D 543 Shinsa-Dong
Kang Nam-Ku, Seoul, Korea
822 516-0637
822 516-3305 FAX

Mexico
Mexico City
Yahebet Olegnowicz
Mexico D.F. Sierra Gorda 465
Loma Chapultepec 11010
Mexico
(525) 540-4130

Portugal
Lisbon
Harold Santo
CMEST-IST
Av Rovisco Pais
1096 Lisboa Codex
Lisbon, Portugal

Spain
Madrid
Felix Berges Munoz
Postdata
c/ Breton de los Herreros
35 3 Izqda.
Madrid, 28003 Spain
ruy@asterix.fi.upm.es

U.S.S.R.
Moscow
Yuri Bayakovski
Keldysh Institute of Appl. Maths
Miusskaya Sq., 4
Moscow, 125047 Russia
095 250-7817
Moscow_SIGGRAPH_
Chapter@siggraph.org

Local Groups Steering Committee
lgsc@siggraph.org

For more information about local groups
localgroupinfo@siggraph.org